Business Planning: Financing the Start-Up Business and Venture Capital Financing

ASPEN CASEBOOK SERIES

BUSINESS PLANNING: FINANCING THE START-UP BUSINESS AND VENTURE CAPITAL FINANCING

Second Edition

THERESE H. MAYNARD
William G. Coskran Professor of Law
Loyola Law School, Los Angeles

DANA M. WARREN
Patrick J. McDonough Director,
Business Law Practicum and
Clinical Professor of Law
Loyola Law School, Los Angeles

Wolters Kluwer
Law & Business

Published by Wolters Kluwer Law & Business in New York.

Wolters Kluwer Law & Business serves customers worldwide with CCH, Aspen Publishers, and Kluwer Law International products. (www.wolterskluwerlb.com)

To contact Customer Service, e-mail customer.service@wolterskluwer.com, call 1-800-234-1660, fax 1-800-901-9075, or mail correspondence to:

Wolters Kluwer Law & Business
Attn: Order Department
PO Box 990
Frederick, MD 21705

Printed in the United States of America.

2 3 4 5 6 7 8 9 0

ISBN 978-1-4548-3768-8 (Casebound)

ISBN 978-1-4548-4799-1 (Loose-Leaf)

Library of Congress Cataloging-in-Publication Data

Maynard, Therese H., author.
   Business planning : financing the start-up business and venture capital financing / Therese H. Maynard, William G. Coskran Professor of Law Loyola Law School, Los Angeles; Dana M. Warren, Patrick J. McDonough Director, Business Law Practicum and Clinical Professor of Law Loyola Law School, Los Angeles. — Second Edition.
       pages cm. — (Aspen casebook series)
   Includes bibliographical references and index.
   ISBN 978-1-4548-3768-8 (casebound : alk. paper)
   1. Business enterprises — Law and legislation — United States. 2. New business enterprises — Law and legislation — United States. 3. Business enterprises — Finance — Law and legislation — United States. 4. Securities — United States. 5. Venture capital — Law and legislation — United States. 6. Corporation law — United States. 7. Commercial law — United States. I. Warren, Dana M., author. II. Title.

KF1355.M26 2014
346.73'065 — dc23
                                                                        2014010672

About Wolters Kluwer Law & Business

Wolters Kluwer Law & Business is a leading global provider of intelligent information and digital solutions for legal and business professionals in key specialty areas, and respected educational resources for professors and law students. Wolters Kluwer Law & Business connects legal and business professionals as well as those in the education market with timely, specialized authoritative content and information-enabled solutions to support success through productivity, accuracy and mobility.

Serving customers worldwide, Wolters Kluwer Law & Business products include those under the Aspen Publishers, CCH, Kluwer Law International, Loislaw, ftwilliam.com and MediRegs family of products.

CCH products have been a trusted resource since 1913, and are highly regarded resources for legal, securities, antitrust and trade regulation, government contracting, banking, pension, payroll, employment and labor, and healthcare reimbursement and compliance professionals.

Aspen Publishers products provide essential information to attorneys, business professionals and law students. Written by preeminent authorities, the product line offers analytical and practical information in a range of specialty practice areas from securities law and intellectual property to mergers and acquisitions and pension/benefits. Aspen's trusted legal education resources provide professors and students with high-quality, up-to-date and effective resources for successful instruction and study in all areas of the law.

Kluwer Law International products provide the global business community with reliable international legal information in English. Legal practitioners, corporate counsel and business executives around the world rely on Kluwer Law journals, looseleafs, books, and electronic products for comprehensive information in many areas of international legal practice.

Loislaw is a comprehensive online legal research product providing legal content to law firm practitioners of various specializations. Loislaw provides attorneys with the ability to quickly and efficiently find the necessary legal information they need, when and where they need it, by facilitating access to primary law as well as state-specific law, records, forms and treatises.

ftwilliam.com offers employee benefits professionals the highest quality plan documents (retirement, welfare and non-qualified) and government forms (5500/PBGC, 1099 and IRS) software at highly competitive prices.

MediRegs products provide integrated health care compliance content and software solutions for professionals in healthcare, higher education and life sciences, including professionals in accounting, law and consulting.

Wolters Kluwer Law & Business, a division of Wolters Kluwer, is headquartered in New York. Wolters Kluwer is a market-leading global information services company focused on professionals.

For Philip, with love.
— TM

To my wife, Linnea McPherson Warren, my partner in all endeavors.
If these words do not succinctly and clearly express my love, appreciation,
and wonder at her willingness and desire to tirelessly rework
and improve every sentence I wrote for this book, it is simply
because this is the only part she didn't see first.
— DW

SUMMARY OF CONTENTS

CONTENTS

6 EQUITY-BASED COMPENSATION: STOCK OPTIONS, INCENTIVE COMPENSATION, AND RELATED FOUNDER ISSUES — 327

PREFACE

The second edition of this casebook continues to be inspired by the legions of law school graduates who sought to practice law as first year corporate law associates, but who had no idea what it is that corporate lawyers *actually do*. We wrote this casebook for these students in order to bridge the gap between law school and practice as a transactional lawyer, much in the same way that the well-established Trial Advocacy course offered at our law school (as well as at most law schools today) prepares our graduates to "hit the ground running" as first-year litigation associates.

However, this casebook does not bear any resemblance to the traditional form of law school casebook typically used in upper-division law school courses. Indeed, in helping us finalize our manuscript for publication, one of our research assistants pointed out that our casebook does not include very many cases at all! This was done deliberately because our goal was to write a casebook that would educate law students as to what is expected of them as a first-year corporate law associate — whether they practice as a transactional lawyer on Wall Street or Main Street.

In order to expose law students to the expectations of senior lawyers supervising the work of first year corporate law associates, this casebook adopts a simulated deal format that is designed to teach law students exactly what it is that transactional lawyers *actually do* in the context of planning a capital rising transaction. While transactional lawyers represent business clients in a wide variety of transactions, this casebook focuses on one type of business transaction that occurs on a daily basis out there in the real world: organizing and financing a new business. Since literally hundreds of thousands of new businesses are formed annually in this country, this type of transaction is likely to be a regular part of the professional life of those law students who plan to practice law in a transactional setting.

By using a simulated deal format, our casebook integrates (i) the teaching of new substantive knowledge about financing a start-up business venture with (ii) the development of the skills that are required for today's law student to be prepared "to hit the ground running" in a transactional practice. In this way, law students will gain a real world perspective on the life cycle of a deal, as well as exposure to the kind of problems that typically arise over the course of a deal and frequently jeopardize its successful completion. In addition, use of the simulated deal format provides law students with a meaningful opportunity to identify and reflect on the ethical considerations that face the modern transactional lawyer, a particularly important concern in our post-Enron world.

This book is organized in a straightforward way. Chapter 1 introduces the client, a new technology business that is seeking start-up funding. The primary focus of the materials in this chapter is to describe the role of the lawyer and the lawyer's relationship with the client in connection with representing an entrepreneurial business of any size — ranging from a small family-owned business to a large high-tech, start-up business. The remaining chapters of our casebook are organized in a manner that tracks the evolution of our client's capital raising transaction. Thus, Chapters 2 and 3 discuss the issues that typically arise when entrepreneurs consider entering into a strategic joint venture with a larger well-established business that will contribute the necessary capital to launch the new business venture. The remaining chapters analyze the issues that typically arise in the course of planning and consummating a venture capital financing transaction.

We have tried to organize the casebook so as to present the relevant topics in a sequence that has later materials building on earlier chapters. By this sequencing and by including a fair amount of explanatory material, our casebook is organized on the fundamental precept that the law student who takes this course is curious about this subject, but has limited familiarity with the business world in general and with the life cycle of a venture capital financing transaction in particular. By introducing the topics traditionally covered in a course on Business Planning in terms that are accessible to the uninitiated law student, we hope to stimulate the law student's curiosity in this subject and to demystify what is often an intimidating and overwhelmingly jargon-laden body of law. Accordingly, the objective is to treat the topics covered in each chapter in a comprehensive, understandable and yet intellectually challenging manner that combines both the theoretical and practical aspects of the subject matter area. In this way, our casebook combines theory and practice in order to prepare law students for the types of projects and challenges that they will confront in the first year of a transactional law practice. In addition, by using a simulated deal format, we hope to instill in the law student a sense of the inherent dynamics and fluidity of a capital raising transaction, thus allowing the law student to become an effective junior member of a law firm that represents start-up businesses.

To that end, this book includes a lengthy appendix that consists of many different types of documents that are typically prepared as part of a financing transaction. These documents are an integral part of the book, as the chapters make specific references to these agreements and ask students to review these agreements in order to give advice to clients, in a manner similar to what real-world corporate lawyers must do in advising their business clients. Thus, it is hoped that the text will stimulate class discussion of *both* the business and legal considerations involved in planning a capital raising transaction and at the same time provide law students with the opportunity to engage in practical problem-solving skills of the type required to be an effective transactional lawyer.

We hope that you enjoy teaching out of our casebook as much as we do. We would be delighted to hear from you with any criticisms or suggestions. With any luck, we hope to publish a third edition of this casebook in a few years and we will do our best to make the next edition better for both students and their professors.

January 2014
Therese H. Maynard
Dana M. Warren
Loyola Law School, Los Angeles, California

ACKNOWLEDGMENTS AND EDITORIAL NOTE

In our editing of the cases, articles and other materials included in the second edition of this casebook, we have omitted most footnotes and case and statutory citations without indication. As to the footnotes that remain, the footnote numbers appear as they do in the original text, with no renumbering to take account of footnotes that we deleted. In addition, the formatting of headings does not necessarily correspond to the text of the original, since we made every effort for consistency of format within our casebook.

We are indebted to many persons for providing the impetus and encouragement to pursue this unusual and innovative casebook. This project never would have been conceived without many generations of law students (taught by Therese Maynard) and young corporate law associates (who sought guidance from Dana Warren), all of whom impressed on us the need to develop a course that would facilitate the young lawyer's ability to understand the life cycle of a typical capital raising transaction for a new business. We owe a debt of gratitude to those many law students who suffered through various drafts of both editions of this casebook as we experimented with our innovative approach to teaching the traditional Business Planning course. We are both eternally grateful for your patience, understanding, and feedback. This project is truly the better for having the benefit of your suggestions and guidance. In particular, we wish to extend a special word of gratitude to our colleague, Professor William Fischer of the University of Richmond School of Law, who was brave enough to teach his Business Planning course using our materials while our casebook was still in draft form. We are grateful to Bill for his thoughtful and insightful comments.

This book was inspired not only by our students, but also by the many fine business lawyers who gave us the benefit of their sage counsel as we sought to develop a casebook that would prepare law students to be ready to "hit the ground running" as young corporate lawyers in a transactional practice. We are particularly grateful for the insightful comments and generous contributions of Josh Armstrong, Mark Bonenfant, Randy Churchill, Molly Coleman, Jeff DuRocher, Scott Miller, and Bob Schroeder. In addition, we appreciate the thoughtful review and comments from serial entrepreneur Mark Goodstein and accounting guru Don Rudkin. Further, Linnea Warren sat through the entire course several times, which led to invaluable advice based on how it all looked from the other side of the lectern. She also devoted uncounted hours to editing and re-editing the drafts.

We also wish to express our deep appreciation to our former students, Katherine Duncan, Arif Sikora, Margaret Karakashian, and Sean Montgomery who have provided invaluable research and editorial assistance in connection with preparing the first and second editions of our casebook.

Finally, we wish to thank our administrative assistants, Ruth Busch and Thelma Wong Terre, for going above and beyond over the past few years in the preparation of both the first and second editions of our casebook. We are also grateful to Darren Kelly, Lynn Churchill, and Lisa Connery, and likely many others unknown to us, at Aspen Publishers who helped make this casebook into a reality.

We appreciate the permission of the following publishers, authors, and periodicals to reprint excerpts from their publications:

ABA Model Rules of Professional Conduct, 2013. Copyright ©2013 by the American Bar Association. Reprinted with permission. Copies of ABA Model Rules of Professional Conduct, 2013 Edition are available from Service Center, American Bar Association, 321 North Clark Street, Chicago, IL 60654, 1-800-285-2221. This information or any or portion thereof may not be copies or disseminated in any form or by any means or stored in an electronic database or retrieval system without the express written consent of the American Bar Association.

ABA Model Rules of Professional Conduct, 2002. Copyright ©2002 by the American Bar Association. Reprinted with permission. Copies of ABA Model Rules of Professional Conduct, 2013 Edition are available from Service Center, American Bar Association, 321 North Clark Street, Chicago, IL 60654, 1-800-285-2221. This information or any or portion thereof may not be copies or disseminated in any form or by any means or stored in an electronic database or retrieval system without the express written consent of the American Bar Association.

Adamson, Louise, Yusef Alexandrine and Remsen Kinne, *Profit and Purpose: Two New Types of California Corporations that Promote Social as well as Financial Benefits*, K & L Gates LLP, Corporate Alert (April 3, 2012). Reprinted with permission.

Barker, William W., *Outside Bucks: A Practical Guide to Raising Capital for a Business*, 9 Bus. L. Today 6 (July/August 2000). ©2000 by the American Bar Association. Reprinted with permission. All rights reserved. This information or any or portion thereof may not be copies or disseminated in any form or by any means or stored in an electronic database or retrieval system without the express written consent of the American Bar Association.

Beck, Joel *"We're Not Lawyers or Accountants, and Won't Give you Advice." Where's the Value in That? (Or, Why You Shouldn't Do Legal Work For Yourself Online)*, The Beck Law Firm, LLC Blog (July 29, 2013), *available at* http://www.bdlawblog.com/2013/07/. Reprinted with permission.

Bendremer, Fredric J., *Those Delaware LLCs – Another Look: How They Could Work for You*, 10 Bus. L. Today 43 (May/June 2001). ©2001 by the American Bar Association. Reprinted with permission. All rights reserved. This information or any or portion thereof may not be copies or disseminated in any form or by any means or stored in an electronic database or retrieval system without the express written consent of the American Bar Association.

Bronstein, Felix J., *The Lawyer as Director of the Corporate Client in the Wake of Sarbanes-Oxley*, 23 Journal of Law & Commerce 53 (2004). Reprinted with permission.

Burwell, Robert, and Howard Miller, *When a Non-Binding Term Sheet Becomes Binding*, Mintz, Levin, Cohn, Ferris, Glovsky and Popeo, PC, Law Firm Memo (July 8, 2013). Reprinted with permission.

Cahill, Gordon & Reindel, LLP, *SEC Amends Rules 144 and 145 to Shorten the Holding Period Requirement for Affiliates and Non-affiliates*, Firm Memoranda, (December 13, 2007). Reprinted with permission.

Chandler, Stephanie L., *A Practical Guide to Raising Capital*, Jackson, Walker, LLP, Law Firm Memo (2004-2014). Reprinted with permission.

The Corporation Secretary's Blog, *Our Delaware Franchise Tax is WHAT ?!?*, (posted on July 22, 2013) *available at* http://thecorpsecblog.com/2013/07/22/our-delaware-franchise-tax-is-what. Reprinted with permission.

Cox, James D. & Thomas Lee Hazen, Corporations (2d ed. 2003). Reprinted by permission of Wolters Kluwer.

Davis, Polk & Wardwell LLP, *Private Offering Reform: Analysis and Implications*, Law Firm Memo (July 29, 2013). Reprinted with permission.

Fenwick & West, LLP, *Guide to Starting A Corporation*, Law Firm Memo (2013). Reprinted with permission.

Fershee, Joshua P., *LLCs And Corporations: A Fork in the Road in Delaware?*, 1 Harv. Bus. L. Online 82 (2011), *available at* http://www.hblr.org/?p = 1181. Reprinted with permission.

Fromm, Jeffrey A., Whitney Holmes and Joel Acevedo, *"Benefit Corporations" to be Allowed in Delaware Starting August 1, 2013*, Dorsey & Whitney LLP, Attorney Articles (July 17, 2013). Reprinted with permission.

Frutos, Alex and Kristina M. Campbell, *SEC Adopts New Net Worth Standard for Accredited Investors*, Jackson Walker LLP, Corporate and Securities E-Alert (January 9, 2012). Reprinted with permission.

Gartenberg, Edward, *A Review of Fiduciary Duties in California and Delaware Corporations*, State Bar of California, Business Law News, Oct. 2006. Reprinted with permission.

Gazur, Wayne M., *The Limited Liability Company Experiment: Unlimited Flexibility, Uncertain Role*, 58 Law & Contemp. Probs. 135 (Spring 1995). Reprinted with permission of author. All rights reserved.

Gosfield, Gregory, *It's a Question of What's Binding: A Look at Letters of Intent*, 13 Bus. L. Today 55, (July/August 2004). ©2004 by the American Bar Association. Reprinted with permission. All rights reserved. This information or any or portion thereof may not be copies or disseminated in any form or by any means or stored in an electronic database or retrieval system without the express written consent of the American Bar Association.

Herr, Mitchell E. & Stephen P. Warren, *Lawyer Liability: Why the SEC Should Clarify Policy on Its Actions Against Attorneys for Advising Clients*, 21 Corp. Couns. Weekly (BNA) 200 (June 28, 2006). Reproduced with permission from BNA's Corporate

Counsel Weekly, 21 CCW 200 (June 28, 2013). Copyright ©2013 by the Bureau of National Affairs, Inc. (800-372-1033) http://www.bna.com.

Hofstrand, Don, *What Is an Entrepreneur?*, *available at* http://www.extension.iastate.edu/agdm/wholefarm/html/c5-07.html, (Jan. 2006). Reprinted with permission.

Jacob, Valerie Ford, Stuart H. Gelfond, Michael A. Levitt & David A. Kanarek, *Key Considerations in Drafting a Registration Rights Agreement from the Company's Perspective*, 41 Rev. Sec. & Comm. Reg. 113 (May 21, 2008). Reprinted with permission.

Keller, Stanley, *Securities Enforcement: Searching Google for Meaning: Equity Compensation Pitfalls and a Changed Climate for Lawyer Responsibility*, 19 Insights 2 (August 2005). Reprinted by permission of Wolters Kluwer.

Kim, Young J. & Jeffrey L. Braker, *Taking Stock in Your Client: Strengthening the Client Relationship and Avoiding Pitfalls*, Bus. L. News 1 (Issue 1, 2008). Reprinted with permission.

Kleinberger, Daniel S., *Two Decades of "Alternative Entities": From Tax Rationalization Through Alphabet Soup to Contract as Diety*, 14 Fordham Journal of Corporate and Financial Law 445 (2009). Reprinted with permission.

Kleinberger, Daniel, Agency, Partnerships, and LLCs: Examples & Explanations (4th ed. 2012). Reprinted by permission of Wolters Kluwer.

Korn, Brian, *The Trouble With Crowdfunding*, Pepper Hamilton LLP, Corporate and Securities Law Alert (April 17, 2013). Reprinted with permission.

Kubicki, Joshua, *The Thin Line Between Legal & Business Advice*, Joshua P. Kubicki, Business Design for Legal Matters Blog (June 7, 2010), *available at* http://www.joshuakubicki.com/blog/legaltransformationblog.com/2010/thin-line-between-legal-businessadvice.html. Reprinted with permission.

LaRose, Stephen and Kathleen Burns, *"But I Thought We were Just Negotiating" — Are the Good Faith Provisions in a Term Sheet Enforceable Upon the Parties?*, Nixon Peabody, LLP, Law Firm Memo (July 24, 2013). Reprinted with permission.

Litov, Lubomir P., Simone M. Sepe, and Charles K. Whitehead, *Lawyers and Fools: Lawyer-Directors in Public Corporations*, 102 The Georgetown Law Journal 413 (2014). Reprinted with permission.

Maynard, Therese, *Ethics for Business Lawyers Representing Start-Up Companies*, 11 Wake Forest J. Bus. & Intell. Prop. L. 401 (2011). Reprinted with permission.

Miller, Sandra K., *What Buy-Out Rights, Fiduciary Duties, and Dissolution Remedies Should Apply in the Case of the Minority Owner of a Limited Liability Company?*, 38 Harv. J. on Legis. 413 (2001).

Palmiter, Alan R., Securities Regulation: Examples & Explanations (5th ed. 2011). Reprinted by permission of Wolters Kluwer.

Palmiter, Alan R., Corporations: Examples & Explanations (7th ed. 2012). Reprinted by permission of Wolters Kluwer.

Peters, Philip, *The California Corporation: Legal Aspects of Organization and Operation*, vol. 31 Corporate Practice Series (3rd ed. 2003). Excerpted from *Corporate Practice*

Series, *"The California Corporation: Legal Aspects of Organization and Operation,"* Portfolio No. 31-3rd, pp. A-19 & A-20 (Apr. 2011). Copyright ©2011 by the Bureau of National Affairs, Inc. (800-372-1033). http://www.bna.com. Reprinted with permission.

Reiser, Dana Brakman, *The Next Big Thing: Flexible-Purpose Corporations*, Brooklyn Law School Research Paper No. 311 (Oct. 2012). Reprinted with permission.

Robins, Martin B., *Recipe for an Overdue Change: Why Corporate Lawyers Sometimes Need to Give Business Advice*, 12 Bus. L. Today 6 (July/August, 2003). ©2003 by the American Bar Association. Reprinted with permission. All rights reserved. This information or any or portion thereof may not be copies or disseminated in any form or by any means or stored in an electronic database or retrieval system without the express written consent of the American Bar Association.

Rutledge, Thomas E., *State Law & State Taxation Corner: Going to Delaware(?)*, Journal of Passthrough Entities (July-Aug. 2013), at 45. This excerpt is reprinted with the publisher's permission from the Journal of Passthrough Entities, a bi-monthly journal published by CCH, a part of Wolters Kluwer. Copying or distribution without the publisher's permission is prohibited.

Schwartz, Andrew A., *Keep It Light, Chairman White: SEC Rulemaking Under the CROWDFUND Act*, 66 Vand. L. Rev. 43 (2013). Reprinted with permission.

Smith, Gregory C., *Start-up and Emerging Companies*. Reprinted with permission from the "ISSUE DATE" edition of the "PUBLICATION" © 2013 ALM Media Properties, LLC. All rights reserved. Further duplication without permission is prohibited. ALMReprints.com - 877-257-3382 - reprints@alm.com.

Stafford, Blake, *2009 Update: Raising the Initial Funding for High Technology Companies in the San Francisco Bay Area*, Fenwick & West LLP, Law Firm Memo (2009). Reprinted with permission.

Steele, Myron T., *Freedom of Contract and Default Contractual Duties in Delaware Limited Partnerships and Limited Liability Companies*, 46 Am. Bus. L.J. 221 (John Wiley & Sons Ltd, 2009). Reprinted with permission.

Sullivan & Cromwell LLP, *General Solicitation and Investor Protection in Private Offerings*, Law Firm Memo (July 15, 2013). Copyright © Sullivan & Cromwell LLP 2013. Reprinted with permission. (www.sullcrom.com)

Wry, Charles A., Jr., *Choosing the Proper Form of Organization for a New Business Venture*, Morse, Barnes-Brown, Pendleton, PC, Law Firm Memo (2011). Reprinted with permission.

CHAPTER 1

INTRODUCTION TO BUSINESS PLANNING

Imagine yourself, a newly licensed lawyer, pursuing a career as a transactional lawyer. It is your first day at work as a first-year associate with a corporate law firm that specializes in representing start-up businesses. Before you had even a moment to enjoy your new office, the senior partner comes into your office to ask you to help her prepare to meet a new client the next day. After describing the client and the nature of the financing transaction that the client proposes to enter into, the senior lawyer presents you with a document and then tells you, "Look over this agreement and let me know first thing in the morning what issues I should be worried about when I meet with the client tomorrow."

This is a fairly typical assignment to be delegated to a first-year corporate law associate. If you are like many first-year associates, however, your initial reaction may be one of utter panic, followed closely by bewilderment as to *exactly* what the senior lawyer expects you to *do* when you review the agreement that she has just left on your desk. Moreover, if your law school is like most across the country, you may be thinking, "Nothing that I learned in law school prepared me for this kind of legal work! What am I going to *do* now?"

This casebook has been deliberately constructed to give you a practical, hands-on learning experience that will leave you well prepared to tackle this kind of assignment. We hope that, rather than experiencing the typical wave of panic, you will feel confident that you have the substantive knowledge, the critical thinking skills, and some experience to immediately engage with the problem. Moreover, you will be familiar with the expectations of the senior lawyers who will be supervising your work so that you will be in a position to understand both the needs of the client and the senior lawyer who is relying on you to help her diligently represent this new start-up business. In other words, this casebook is designed to prepare law students to be ready "to hit the ground running" as transactional lawyers.

To accomplish this teaching objective, this casebook departs from the traditional law school casebook by adopting a "simulated deal" format to the study of the subject matter covered in the traditional Business Planning course. Over the years, it has been our experience that use of a "simulated deal" format provides law students with the opportunity to bring their understanding of relevant legal materials to bear upon the problems that typically arise in the course of completing a particular business financing transaction. In this way, the law student develops some feel for the process of exercising judgment and reaching a decision in order to advise the client regarding the best way to structure a particular transaction. By participating in a simulated deal, law students will learn the necessary skills to engage in a financing transaction, regardless of the size of the transaction (e.g., whether it is a $10,000 or a $100 million deal) or the types of parties involved (e.g., a large venture capital firm, a small business, or a major Web 2.0 start-up business).

In addition, the use of a simulated deal format exposes law students to the real world expectations of experienced senior lawyers who will be evaluating the work product of a first-year associate working in the corporate law department of a law firm — whether on Wall Street or Main Street. Finally, we have found that the simulated deal format provides the law student with a more realistic view of the lawyer's work as a corporate lawyer practicing in a transactional setting, thereby providing the student with a meaningful opportunity to bridge the gap between law school and practice as a transactional lawyer.

A. What Is "Business Planning"?

Business Planning is an essential process for most, if not all, businesses. It begins with the very inception of a business idea. Many business ideas never reach beyond this stage for numerous reasons: lack of marketability, funding, entrepreneurial energy, etc. However, those ideas formed by entrepreneurs with the necessary gumption to forge ahead must *plan* out their business. In planning the business, an entrepreneur must figure out what type of company will be created (e.g., corporation, limited liability company (LLC), partnership), generate a business plan, locate financing, contemplate how the idea will develop and grow into a successful business, etc. As the idea evolves into a viable business model, its needs will change, perhaps to include venture capital financing, a capital restructuring, or maybe even an initial public offering (IPO) or acquisition by a larger company. During this entire process, from idea to exit, the entrepreneur will need legal assistance to help them on this journey.

This casebook is designed to familiarize you both with the business planning and the lifecycle involved in a typical financing transaction for a start-up business and the transactional lawyer's role in that process. Since business planning, in this context, covers such a broad range of issues, it requires the corporate associate to have a broad range of knowledge of fundamental corporate law issues. Over the years, the description for a typical Business Planning course has emphasized the "inter-disciplinary" (or "cross-disciplinary") nature of this upper-division course. In other words, the traditional Business Planning course required law students to synthesize the substantive knowledge that they had acquired from previous courses in order to analyze problems and make recommendations to business clients regarding the best way to structure a particular business transaction. This integration of multiple bodies of substantive legal expertise led many law schools to impose certain prerequisites, most often introductory courses on Corporations or Business Associations, Securities Regulation, and Federal Income Taxation.

Accordingly, the focus of the doctrinal materials contained in the traditional Business Planning casebook reflects that the students would need to *expand* their basic understanding of corporate, tax, and securities materials beyond the core principles that students are exposed to as part of these introductory courses.

This casebook carries forward certain attributes of this pedagogical approach to teaching Business Planning. By compiling the necessary background material in the subsequent chapters of this casebook, students are provided with a road map that will help them identify and analyze the relevant legal and business issues that typically arise in connection with planning a capital-raising transaction for a start-up business. This approach allows the law student to concentrate on *synthesizing* the various areas of substantive legal knowledge in order to formulate a sound and well-reasoned recommendation in the context of planning and structuring a particular financing transaction. In the process, students also will learn *new* substantive legal doctrines that are typically not covered in other courses in the traditional law school curriculum.

As such, students will be asked to go beyond the material covered in the core prerequisite for this course, and also will be exposed to new materials regarding capital-raising transactions, including the use of venture capital financing, a topic that is often the subject of a freestanding, upper-division course in many law schools today. However, we deliberately eschew any emphasis on tax issues. This was very much a conscious choice on our part, born out of our conviction that this approach best reflects the real world of practice. Rather than ask law students to master the minutiae of tax law, we prefer the more realistic approach that identifies tax issues, without trying to offer the breadth of materials (as part of our casebook) that are necessary in order to resolve *all* relevant tax issues that may potentially arise as part of planning a capital-raising transaction. We believe that this approach best comports with the real-world practice of modern corporate lawyers, who, in our collective experience, issue-spot on tax questions, but consult with a knowledgeable tax practitioner for definitive advice in the course of structuring a particular business transaction.

The organizational approach we adopt in our casebook also reflects our view that the modern corporate lawyer serving as a transaction planner really is something of "a jack of all trades." This observation is based on the fact that the modern corporate lawyer giving advice on the best way to structure a particular capital-raising transaction usually must have a foundational knowledge of intellectual property, employee benefits, executive compensation, and tax matters, as well as a thorough mastery of agency, partnership, LLC, general corporate, contract, and federal securities law. (The breadth of issues that typically confront the lawyer as the planner of a capital-raising transaction is reflected in the table of contents for this casebook.) Reflecting the view that the modern corporate lawyer is "a jack of all trades," the only prerequisite for this class is the basic, introductory course, Business Associations or Corporations, which is offered at all law schools. Thus, the topics to be covered in each chapter of the casebook assume that students will have completed a Corporations course. Accordingly, the materials included in the various chapters of the casebook provide ample coverage of all the relevant topics so that students will be able to master the doctrinal material needed to analyze the issues that surface in the course of the simulated deal without the need to do any additional research on their own.

As part of our simulated deal format, you will assume the role of counsel to a start-up business seeking capital and will be required to handle a series of increasingly complex matters typical in the representation of an early stage business. By using a simulated deal format, you will be expected to analyze *both* the legal and the business considerations that must be taken into account in planning the structure, and negotiating the terms, of a typical capital-raising transaction involving venture capital investors. In the process, you will gain a meaningful sense for the role of the lawyer in the deal-making process, including the ethical dilemmas that are common — and unique — to the practice of law in a transactional (rather than litigation) setting.

This casebook will integrate (i) the acquisition of new substantive knowledge about financing a start-up business (including the use of venture capital) with (ii) the development of the skills that are required for you to hit the ground running as a first-year associate in a transactional practice. Thus, our focus was to design a curricular approach that meets two objectives: first, the materials in the casebook must teach students to *think* like a transactional lawyer; and second, the materials must teach students to *perform* as a deal lawyer.

In addition, the reading materials in connection with several of the chapters (as well as many of the *Homework Assignments* contained in Appendix A) will often ask you to review relevant documents. For administrative convenience, all of these documents are collected in one place — Appendix B. Through the use of the materials contained in Appendices A and B, you will be exposed to the type of projects that junior corporate associates typically are asked to complete, such as reviewing documents, comparing documents to term sheets, and drafting documents such as articles of incorporation or LLC operating agreements. By the end of the semester, you will have completed a "deal," and, in the process, you will have synthesized the learning of new substantive doctrinal material with the development of the skills that you need when you graduate and start practicing as a transactional lawyer.

Although this casebook adopts a practical approach to teaching Business Planning, the materials in this casebook also challenge law students to think about the role of corporate lawyers in the business community at large. We ask you to consider the ethical issues as they arise at various points in completing this particular financing transaction. Although we deliberately eschew a strictly theoretical approach to the materials that make up our casebook, at the same time we ask you to consider the role of corporate lawyers in the modern world of business transactions. As made clear in the materials contained in the various chapters of this casebook, we firmly believe that corporate lawyers have an opportunity to be a strong voice and an important influence as the American business community reflects upon the wave of recent corporate scandals. The format that we have adopted in this casebook is designed to encourage you to contemplate important public policy questions that are peculiar to the lawyer serving as a transaction planner: *Why* structure a particular deal in this particular way? Is this the *best way* to structure a particular deal from a larger public policy perspective? The classroom setting encourages discussion of these important questions — a luxury that is often not allowed for the busy practitioner laboring under the considerable pressures of the modern practice of law. In this way, we also hope to make the intellectual richness of practice as a transactional lawyer come alive for the law student.

B. Meet Our New Clients

The transaction that is the focus of this casebook is based on the deal files of practicing lawyers in the real world. In this way, the deal is authentic in that it is representative of the type of capital-raising transactions that lawyers are routinely asked to complete on behalf of their business clients. In addition, the *Homework Assignments* emphasize the drafting and analytical skills necessary to be successful as an entry-level associate in a transactional practice. We have prepared the materials in our casebook on the assumption that the professor will assume the role of the senior, experienced corporate lawyer who relies on the students — serving in the role of junior associates working under the partner's supervision — for assistance in completing this capital-raising transaction.

The memo (set forth below) introduces the law student to a new, capital-seeking client with whom the senior partner recently met. As we progress through the various *Homework Assignments* in Appendix A, new information, circumstances, and objectives will be presented as the client moves ahead and its financing goals evolve. It bears emphasizing that this is typical of the life cycle of business transactions in the real world of practice. As reflected in the memo below, the facts and circumstance surrounding this new client matter are inherently fluid. This fluidity — both as to the source of funding and as to the form of business entity to be used — is fairly typical in connection with taking on a new client who proposes to start up a new business. As a pedagogical matter, this fluidity also allows us to engage in a more fulsome discussion of the factors involved in the choice of entity decision (the use of the LLC, often to be formed with a strategic partner), and gives us the freedom to consider the different financing alternatives that are typically available to a new business (including the possibility of obtaining funding from a venture capitalist). By addressing the range of options typically available to finance a new business, the materials in this casebook are designed to be relevant, enlightening, and helpful in preparing law students for practice as entry-level corporate lawyers — and that is true whether they expect to be doing the more complex transactions at a big firm on Wall Street (or in Silicon Valley), or to be representing local entrepreneurs at a small law firm on Main Street.

To: Associate
From: Partner
Re: New Software Business

I met yesterday with two recent graduates of the California Institute of Technology who are forming a new software business, which they have tentatively called "SoftCo." Maynard & Warren, LLP, has been retained in connection with the formation of the business and to serve as its primary outside counsel, and I would like you to be SoftCo's main contact person at the firm. As SoftCo has not yet been formed, one of the first issues we will have to address will be entity selection.

SoftCo's founders have developed platform-agnostic operating system utilities software that reportedly could revitalize the personal computer industry. It allows mobile device users to create a seamless, encrypted link to their desktop computer. The users can access data and operate programs housed on their desktop, as well as move files in either direction.

The founders, Joan Smith and Michael Jones, developed part of the software while students and post-doctoral fellows at Caltech in a program seeking to develop secure, remotely accessible personal networks. The students called it "Hey, Goo(gle), I Got My Own Cloud." Since finishing at Caltech, Joan and Michael have been working on the software at Joan's home.

Joan and Michael are still in the development phase with their software and envision that if they go it alone—that is, not seek financial support from investors—it will take them another 12 to 18 months to get the software ready for initial testing by customers (which is referred to as "beta testing") and then an additional 18 to 24 months to beta-test the elements of the product and make necessary fixes and improvements. Alternatively, they estimate that if they take in approximately $500,000 from investors, they can cut in half the time to get to the beta-testing phase. Further, if they can obtain several million dollars more, they can cut in half the time to get through beta testing and to have the product ready to market.

Joan and Michael told me they believe that, if they choose to pursue it, the initial $500,000 could be raised from family and friends, but that the several million dollars will need to be raised from professional venture capitalists or a strategic partner.

Based on conversations Joan and Michael have already had, they believe the $500,000 could come from a group of seven investors: (a) Joan's parents; (b) Michael's parents; (c) Michael's family doctor; (d) Joan's elderly aunt; and (e) Joan's pastor from her church (who, according to Joan, says he just "inherited a bundle"). Joan and Michael report that they, as well as all of these potential investors, are concerned about exposing their personal assets through their involvement with the business. In addition, several of the potential investors asked about being able to take tax deductions based on SoftCo's expected early losses.

Joan and Michael made it clear that they are nervous about the decision of taking on friends and family investors. If they do it, they want to be scrupulously fair, but they also want to be sure that there is no issue about their ability to be in charge of the management of SoftCo.

In addition, and what prompted their call to our firm, Joan and Michael have been contacted by Big Bad Software, Inc. (BadSoft), which, as you know, dominates the personal computer operating system software market. They said that BadSoft was feeling them out regarding a joint venture to provide the funding to finish the development of SoftCo's technology, complete the products, and then to market and distribute the products. As you probably know, part of BadSoft's growth has come through making investments in new technologies, including through funding joint venture relationships. Joan and Michael are interested and have scheduled a preliminary meeting with BadSoft next week. More details should become clear then.

As to Maynard & Warren's role, in addition to our entity selection analysis, we need to be prepared for the first steps on that potential joint venture transaction.

I will be in touch with you later regarding the matters that arise in serving this new relationship. Thank you for your help!

As the materials in the next section make abundantly clear, starting a new business can mean many things. It can mean starting a law firm, starting a landscaping business, arranging a joint venture between two large, established Fortune 500 businesses, or even the purchase of an ailing business out of bankruptcy and helping to recapitalize and restructure the bankrupt business. This casebook does not propose to cover all of these various possible scenarios. Instead, we will focus on the types of financing transactions that are typically used by start-up businesses. However, it bears mentioning that many of the business considerations and legal issues that we will study in the remaining chapters are equally relevant to *all* of the different types of financing transactions described above and are not limited to the two types of financing transactions that we will cover in this casebook, namely the investment in a new business (such as SoftCo) by a strategic investor through a joint venture and the use of outside professional venture capital investor(s) to fund the business operations of a start-up firm, such as our new client. As you go through the remaining materials in this casebook, you will be asked to consider how to address the business and legal issues raised by these materials in the context of representing our new client, SoftCo, and its founders, Joan and Michael.

C. What Is an Entrepreneur?

Our new clients, Joan and Michael, describe themselves as "entrepreneurs," which leads to the obvious question: *What is an entrepreneur?* Credit for coining the word *"entrepreneur"* is generally given to Jean-Baptiste Say, a nineteenth-century French economist and businessman. In his *Treatise on Political Economy*, he described an entrepreneur as "one who undertakes an enterprise, especially a contractor, acting as intermediatory between capital and labour."[1] The word derives from the French *"entre"* (to enter) and *"prendre"* (to take). In general terms, an entrepreneur is an individual who takes financial risks by undertaking (i.e., entering into) a new business venture; thus, the term is often synonymous with *founder*. More commonly today, in business school terms, the term *entrepreneur* is used to describe someone who creates value by offering a new product or service, or by carving out a niche in the market that may not currently exist. So, generally speaking, entrepreneurs will identify a market opportunity and then exploit it by organizing the resources necessary to affect an outcome that changes existing interactions within a particular sector of an industry, or perhaps even the entire industry.

While much has been written about entrepreneurs, one author has pared it down to the following classic — and simple — definition that also explains why the process of entrepreneurship:

> . . . is so hard. . . . Here it is: *Entrepreneurship is the pursuit of opportunity without regard to resources currently controlled.* [This definition] was conceived [some] 37 years ago by [a Harvard Business School professor,] Howard Stevenson. [More recently, Professor] Stevenson [talked] about his classic definition. . . . Back in 1983 [when he first articulated his definition, Professor Stevenson observed that] people tended to define entrepreneurship almost as a personality disorder, a kind of risk addiction. "But that didn't fit the entrepreneurs I knew," he said. "I never met an entrepreneur who got up in the morning saying 'What's the most risk in today's economy, and how can

---

1. As quoted in TIM HINDLE, GUIDE TO MANAGEMENT AND GURUS 77 (2008).

I get some? Most entrepreneurs I know are looking to lay risk off — on investors, partners, lenders, and anyone else.'" As for personality, he said, "The entrepreneurs I know are all different types. They're as likely to be wallflowers as to be the wild man of Borneo. . . . They see an opportunity and don't feel constrained from pursuing it because they lack resources . . . [Entrepreneurs] are *used* to making do without resources."

The perception of opportunity in the absence of resources helps explain much of what differentiates entrepreneurial leadership from that of corporate administrators: The emphasis on team rather than hierarchy, fast decisions rather than deliberation, and equity rather than cash compensation.

Eric Schurenberg, *What's an Entrepreneur? The Best Answer Ever*, INC. MAGAZINE (Jan. 9, 2012), *available at* http://www.inc.com/eric-schurenberg/the-best-definition -of-entrepreneurship.html.

At least one prominent theorist has viewed the entrepreneur as an innovator and has popularized the use of the phrase "creative destruction" to describe the role of the entrepreneur in changing "business norms."[2] Many observers point to Apple, Inc. as an example of entrepreneurship that launched "a Schumpeterian 'gale' of creation destruction" within the computer industry.[3] As a practical matter, very few new businesses have the potential to launch such a "gale of creation-destruction" sufficient to revolutionize an entire industry — or even rearrange world economic order — in the way that modern giants such as Wal-Mart, Microsoft, and eBay have done or are now doing. It is much more likely that an entrepreneur will launch a new business that will effect incremental change within an existing market.

Given that it has been reported that "[m]ore than a thousand new businesses are born every hour of every working day in the United States,"[4] it is clear that entrepreneurs are an important part of the U.S. economy. These new businesses "create a very large proportion of [the] innovative products and services that transform the way we work and live, such as personal computers, software, the Internet, biotechnology drugs, and overnight package deliveries."[5]

While our new client, SoftCo, is a technology-based start-up business, entrepreneurship is not limited to Silicon Valley–based, high-tech start-ups. Entrepreneurship extends to all industries that comprise the U.S. (indeed, the global) economy, such as gourmet ice cream, fast-food restaurants, and drug packaging, to name but a few. Indeed, the well-known, high-profile "serial entrepreneur," Wayne Huizenga, launched new businesses in several, completely unrelated industries, starting with Waste Management (garbage disposal); then Blockbuster (video sales); then still later AutoNation

---

2. *See* JOSEPH SCHUMPETER, CAPITALISM, SOCIALISM AND DEMOCRACY. In this book, first published in 1942, Schumpeter popularized the term "creative destruction," a term he used to describe the process of transformation that accompanies radical innovations introduced by entrepreneurs.

3. WILLIAM D. BYGRAVE & ANDREW ZACHARAKIS, THE PORTABLE MBA IN ENTREPRENEURSHIP 2 (John Wiley & Sons, 3d ed. 2004).

4. *Id.* at 1.

5. *Id.*

(automobile sales), not to mention that along the way, he was the original owner of the Florida Marlins.[6]

Another, more recent example of "creative destruction" is Jeff Bezos, the well-known founder and CEO of Amazon, Inc. In naming Bezos as "Business Person of the Year" in 2012, *Fortune* magazine described him as the "ultimate disrupter," noting that he "has upended the book industry and displaced electronics merchants. . . . He is willing to take risks and lose money, yet investors have embraced him. . . ." Adam Lashinsky, *Amazon's Jeff Bezos: The Ultimate Disrupter*, FORTUNE (Nov. 16, 2012), *available at* http://management.fortune.cnn.com/2012/11/16/jeff-bezos-amazon/.

Query: Why do you suppose investors "embrace" an entrepreneur such as Jeff Bezos, even if not all of his ideas are profitable? In August 2013, Jeff Bezos took the newspaper world by surprise when he agreed to purchase the storied newspaper, the *Washington Post*, from the Graham family, which had owned the newspaper since 1933. *See* Peter Whoviskey, *For Jeff Bezos, A New Frontier*, THE WASHINGTON POST (Aug. 10, 2013), *available at* http://articles.washingtonpost.com/2013-08-10/business/41267449_1_jeff -bezos-washington-post-co-life-expectancy. With this latest foray into journalism, the world waits to see if Jeff Bezos (who will personally own the newspaper organization*) will unleash the same force of creative destruction that led Amazon.com to "upend the book industry." In other words, can Jeff Bezos do for newspaper publishing what he did for the book industry? Only time will tell.

This casebook does not propose to *teach* entrepreneurship, although it bears mentioning that a recent study found that over 60 percent of colleges and universities offer at least one course on entrepreneurship.[7] Instead, the focus of this casebook is on the *role of the lawyer* in the process of organizing and financing a new business to be launched by an entrepreneur. Having said that, it bears emphasizing that, to be effective as a transaction planner, the deal lawyer must have some basic understanding of the *entrepreneurial process*. This section briefly describes the functions, activities, and actions generally associated with an entrepreneur perceiving an opportunity and creating a new business to pursue this opportunity.[8]

---

6. There are many notable examples of entrepreneurs who start new businesses that become wildly successful, leaving the entrepreneur a very wealthy person. However, rather than retire and rest on their laurels (and personal wealth), the "serial entrepreneur" goes off and does it all over again. According to the *Wall Street Journal*,

> Call them serial-preneurs. While some entrepreneurs struggle their whole lives to bring one idea or product to market, there's another breed: those who do it once, twice or three times more, disproving the notion of beginner's luck. In some cases, the brands and people are household names, such as Steve Jobs with Apple, Pixar, and NeXT. But the ranks are also populated with lesser-known entrepreneurs who fly under the radar, hitting one start-up home run after another.

Gwendolyn Bounds, Kelly K. Spors, & Raymund Flandez, *The Secrets of Serial Success: How Some Entrepreneurs Manage to Score Big Again and Again and . . .*, WALL ST. J., Aug. 20, 2007, at R1.

* Amazon will have no role in the purchase of the *Washington Post* news organization.

7. *See* BYGRAVE & ZACHARAKIS, *supra* note 3, at 2 (citing to statistics published by the Kaufman Foundation). For those interested in entrepreneurship more generally, the Ewing Marion Kaufman Foundation, *available at* http://www.kaufman.org/, is an excellent resource.

8. For those law students who are interested in a more in-depth examination of the *entrepreneurial process*, we strongly recommend THE PORTABLE MBA IN ENTREPRENEURSHIP, *supra* note 3, which is self-described as providing "complete coverage of what leading business schools teach about entrepreneurship."

The Entrepreneurial Process.   Here, we are referring to the personal, sociological, and environmental factors that typically guide the founder in making the decision to launch a new business enterprise. While there are many descriptions of this decision-making process, the following general description offers a succinct summary of this process.

Ideas for new businesses can come from a wide variety of sources. New businesses can be the direct outgrowth of an existing business. Or, the idea for a new business may grow out of the brainstorming of a few individuals sitting around a kitchen table. No matter where the idea for a new business originates, the idea has to be translated into a viable business concept. This process usually entails defining why the new business idea has merit. On the one hand, the new business idea may involve developing a new product to fill an unmet need in the marketplace. On the other hand, the new business idea may involve producing a product that is either better or cheaper than that of an existing competitor. In either case, the new business idea is viable only if it can be shown that people (i.e., customers) are willing to pay for the product (or service) that is reflected in the new business idea.

To move the new business idea to a viable business model usually involves some form of investigation to assess the validity and merits of the new idea. Depending on the nature of the business idea, investigation usually involves some form of feasibility study (or marketing study) or perhaps retaining consultants to help evaluate various aspects of the proposed new business model. At some point, however, the entrepreneur must make the "go/no-go" decision. That is to say, at some point in this business development process, the decision must be made whether the new idea is sufficiently viable to proceed with creating a new business; or alternatively, the project must be abandoned because the business idea is just not viable.

Business Plan.   Once the decision is made to proceed with creating a new business, the next step typically involves preparing a *business plan*, which is an outline (or a blueprint) as to how the new business will be created. If a feasibility study was done as part of the investigative process, then such a study will often provide much of the information needed to draft the business plan. Issues that are typically addressed in even the simplest of business plans include the following:

- **Organizing a legal entity to operate the new business**
  - What form of business entity is to be used?
  - Has the business entity been created?
  - What will be the governance structure for the new business entity?
- **Identifying the potential market and method for accessing this market**
  - How will the business make money?
  - Why will the business make money?
  - If the new business is to produce a product, what are its attributes?
  - If there is an existing competitor, how does the new product differ from those of the competitor?
  - Who are the prospective customers for the new product or service?

- **Raising financing to launch the new business**
  - What are the available sources of financing?
  - How much equity ownership are the founders willing to give up in order to obtain the necessary financing?
  - How will the business attract the necessary investors?
  - If the business plan requires it, are the necessary credit sources in place?
- **Hiring management or other staff to run the business operations**
  - Who will manage the company once the business is up and running?
  - *Note:* It is important that the qualifications and experience of the management team are described with sufficient specificity to convince the reader that they will be successful in managing this new business.
- **Identifying the facility (or facilities) where the new business is to operate**
  - Is there an advantage to being in a certain location?
  - Are there environmental concerns with respect to operating in a certain facility?
- **Business strategy** — Any good business plan should address the following key strategic planning questions:
  - Where are we now?
  - Where do we want to be?
  - How do we get there?
- **Financial information** — This section should include the projected revenues, costs, and returns for the proposed new business.
  - This section should take all of the information provided above and convert this information into a financial projection or outcome.
  - This section is scrutinized carefully by most prospective investors. Therefore, the value and persuasiveness of the numbers in this section depend heavily on how accurately it represents the economic assumptions that were made in the previous sections of the plan. Very often, entrepreneurs will present projections that are based on a worst-case scenario at one end of the spectrum and a best-case scenario at the other end of the spectrum.
- **Executive summary** — This section is a self-contained summary that makes a compelling case for why the new business venture will be successful. While the executive summary is customarily placed at the beginning of the business plan, it is usually the last section to be drafted as a practical matter.

At this point, it bears emphasizing that the preparation of a compelling business plan generally constitutes the essential foundation for the successful launch of a new business of any size or scope. Indeed, the most important way that the entrepreneur convinces *any* prospective investor (of any size or sophistication) to invest in his or her "new idea" is to prepare a compelling business plan. While lawyers typically are not involved in the actual writing of a business plan, it is important for lawyers to have some sense of this process in order for the lawyer to effectively represent the participants in the new, start-up business — and that is true regardless of whether the lawyer is representing the founders or the prospective investors. The information that is typically contained in a business plan directed toward venture capital investors and the process typically involved in creating a business plan and preparing a company for venture capital investment is described in more detail as part of the materials in Chapter 8.

Personal Attributes of an Entrepreneur.   Much also has been written about the character traits of the successful entrepreneur. While there is no definitive list of the personality traits required to be a successful entrepreneur, the characteristics of an entrepreneur generally include spontaneous creativity, the willingness to make decisions in the absence of solid, verifiable data, and the drive and willingness to take risks in order to create something new. The following article offers one perspective on this topic.

Don Hofstrand
What Is an Entrepreneur?
Ag Decisionmaker File C5-07 (Jan. 2006), Iowa State University Extension*

Much has been written about entrepreneurs. Some of it portrays entrepreneurs as almost mythical characters who obtain their skills from a unique genetic combination. However, research tells us that entrepreneurship can be learned. The information below provides some characteristics and skills you may want to acquire to improve your entrepreneurial ability.

[Generally speaking, in] the context of a value-added business, an entrepreneur is someone who identifies a market opportunity for [new] commodities and products and creates a business organization to pursue the opportunity.

To help you understand entrepreneurs, here are four characteristics of successful entrepreneurs.

Characteristics of Successful Entrepreneurs

1. Successful entrepreneurs are able to identify potential business opportunities better than most people. They focus on opportunities — not problems — and try to learn from failure.

2. Successful entrepreneurs are action-oriented. This comes from a sense of urgency. They have a high need for achievement, which motivates them to turn their ideas into action.

3. Successful entrepreneurs have a detailed knowledge of the key factors needed for success and have the physical stamina needed to put their lives into their work.

4. Successful entrepreneurs seek outside help to supplement their skills, knowledge and ability. Through their enthusiasm they are able to attract key investors, partners, creditors and employees.

---

* *Available at* http://www.extension.iastate.edu/agdm/wholefarm/html/C5-07.html.

Risk Takers

It is commonly believed that entrepreneurs are risk-takers. However, the evidence suggests that they are risk-averse just like you and me. Successful entrepreneurs attempt to minimize their risk exposure whenever appropriate. They do this by carefully assessing the risk/reward relationship of their actions. Risk is assumed only when the opportunity for reward is sufficiently large enough to warrant the risk.

Sense of Limits

At a very early age, from our parents, friends and teachers, we begin developing a sense of limits. These are limits of what we can and cannot do and what we can and cannot accomplish. It is manifest in many ways such as "we're not good enough, not smart enough, or not capable enough." This sense of limits is based on emotions rather than logic.

Entrepreneurs either don't have this sense of limits or fight against it. All things are possible. Removing the sense of limits unleashes the creativity and innovative juices that are needed for successful entrepreneurship.

Locus of Control

Entrepreneurs tend to have a strong internal locus of control. Locus of control is a concept defining whether a person believes he/she is in control of his/her future or someone else is in control of it. For example, we all know people who believe they have no control over their lives. They believe that what happens to them is dictated by outside forces. People who feel they are victims of outside forces have an external locus of control — "it's not my fault this happened to me." By contrast, entrepreneurs have a very strong internal locus of control. They believe their future is determined by the choices they make.

Control of Their Future

Entrepreneurs want to be self-directed. They want to be in control of their activities. This is linked to the "locus of control" discussion above. Entrepreneurs often don't fit well in traditional employment positions. They don't want to be told what to do. Entrepreneurs know what they want to do and how to do it.

Creators

Entrepreneurs like to create things. A business entrepreneur likes to create businesses and organizations. Often the more unique the business the better entrepreneurs like it. They like the challenge of coming up with new solutions.

Entrepreneurs may not be the best managers. After the organization is built they may lose interest or not have the skills needed to manage the business. Just because they are good at creating a business doesn't mean they will be good at running a business.

The Ten D's of an Entrepreneur[2]

Below are ten D's that help define an entrepreneur. If you want to be an entrepreneur, you will need to possess many of these behaviors. As you read over the list, compare yourself to these behaviors. How do you stack up? What do you need to change?

1. **Dream**. Entrepreneurs have a vision of what the future could be like for them and their businesses. And, more importantly, they have the ability to implement their dreams.
2. **Decisiveness**. They don't procrastinate. They make decisions swiftly. Their swiftness is a key factor in their success.
3. **Doers**. Once they decide on a course of action, they implement it as quickly as possible.
4. **Determination**. They implement their ventures with total commitment. They seldom give up, even when confronted by obstacles that seem insurmountable.
5. **Dedication**. They are totally dedicated to their business, sometimes at considerable cost to their relationships with their friends and families. They work tirelessly. Twelve-hour days and seven-day work weeks are not uncommon when an entrepreneur is striving to get a business off the ground.
6. **Devotion**. Entrepreneurs love what they do. It is that love that sustains them when the going gets tough. And it is love of their product or service that makes them so effective at selling it.
7. **Details**. It is said that the devil resides in the details. That is never more true than in starting and growing a business. The entrepreneur must be on top of the critical details.
8. **Destiny**. They want to be in charge of their own destiny rather than dependent on an employer.
9. **Dollars**. Getting rich is not the prime motivator of entrepreneurs. Money is more a measure of their success. They assume that if they are successful they will be rewarded.
10. **Distribute**. Entrepreneurs distribute the ownership of their businesses with key employees who are critical to the success of the business.

NOTES AND QUESTIONS

1. *Management Conflicts.* As a general rule, entrepreneurs are highly independent, which (as we shall see in the materials in later chapters of this casebook) often can cause problems when their business ventures succeed. At the outset, the entrepreneur is usually able to personally manage most (if not all) aspects of the new business. But this is usually not sustainable once the business has grown beyond a certain size. Management conflicts will often arise in those situations where the entrepreneur fails to realize that running a large, stable business is very different from running a small, growing business. This type of management conflict is very

---

2. Bygraves, William D. and Andrew Zacharakis, THE PORTABLE MBA IN ENTREPRENEURSHIP, John Wiley & Sons, (3d. ed. 2004), page 6.

often resolved by the entrepreneur leaving — either voluntarily or involuntarily — and often starting a new business venture. Indeed, according to one study, "Four out of five entrepreneurs . . . are forced to step down from the CEO's post." Noam Wasserman, *The Founder's Dilemma*, 86 HARV. BUS. REV. 103 (Feb. 2008). To offer but one high-profile example, consider the case of Apple Computer, where one of the founders, Steve Wozniak, left to pursue other interests, while the other founder, Steve Jobs, was ultimately forced out, to be replaced with a more experienced CEO from a much larger company (although Steve Jobs did return many years later to resume leadership of the company). In later chapters of this casebook, we study the types of management conflicts that are likely to surface as a start-up business grows and matures into a larger business with a very different set of management concerns, and we examine various ways to resolve these conflicts.

2. ***Will the New Business Succeed?*** For those lawyers who represent entrepreneurs, it bears emphasizing that entrepreneurship is often difficult and quite risky, resulting (not surprisingly) in many new ventures failing. Statistics show that upwards of 75 percent of all new businesses fail within the first year and upwards of 90 percent are out of business by the end of the second year. *See* WILLIAM D. BYGRAVE & ANDREW ZACHARAKIS, THE PORTABLE MBA IN ENTREPRENEURSHIP 10 (John Wiley & Sons, 3d ed. 2004); *see also* Paul Gompers et al., *Performance Persistence in Entrepreneurship and Venture Capital*, 96 JOURNAL OF FINANCIAL ECONOMICS 18 (2010) ("[F]irst time entrepreneurs have only an 18% chance of succeeding. . . ."). The reasons for the high mortality rate are numerous and varied, including lack of commitment and perseverance on the part of the entrepreneur who started the business; employee problems; lack of funding and/or difficulty in obtaining sufficient financial resources; family problems related to the time and energy required to launch a new business; and finally, managerial incompetence that leads to difficulty in executing the business plan to achieve success with the new product or service.

Potential investors in the entrepreneur's new start-up business are also well acquainted with these statistics. Hence, it pays for the entrepreneur to evaluate the prospects of the proposed new business venture from the perspective of a potential investor, such as a bank or a venture capitalist. Professional investors, including venture capitalists, know that the success of a new business generally depends on three crucial components: the opportunity, the entrepreneur (including the management team), and the resources needed to start and grow the business. We have already described the strong entrepreneurial and management skills necessary to launch a new business. The remaining materials in this section explore the other two components in more detail: the opportunity and the resources.

3. ***The Opportunity.*** The founders of SoftCo, Joan and Michael, believe that they have developed "a fantastic new approach to operating system software" that will "revolutionize" the industry. But as any professional investor worth his or her salt will tell you — ideas are a dime a dozen. What is important is not the idea by itself. Instead, what separates merely another "new idea" from the field of "new ideas" that are regularly pitched to prospective investors is evidence that the entrepreneur can develop the idea, implement it, and build a successful business based on this new idea. Naturally, these questions lead to a discussion of the all-important topic: developing a business plan that will persuade prospective investors that the

entrepreneur's new idea really does present the potential for a successful business opportunity.

4. ***When Does an "Idea" Become an "Opportunity"?*** One time-honored maxim — at least from the perspective of the professional investor — is that the crucial components for entrepreneurial success are a superb entrepreneur (backed by a solid management team) and an excellent market opportunity. The preceding materials described the process of preparing a solid business plan that allows the entrepreneur to communicate his or her idea to the prospective investor. The next step on the entrepreneur's journey is to convince the would-be investor that the entrepreneur's new idea constitutes a high-potential opportunity. The criteria to be used by the prospective investor to decide whether to finance the new start-up business, while overlapping, will vary somewhat depending on the business objectives and the profile of the prospective investor. Thus, the criteria used by a bank in deciding whether to make a loan to launch a new business will typically be different than the criteria used by the venture capitalist in deciding whether to finance a start-up business. The nature of these criteria — and the inherent differences — is explored in more detail in Chapter 8.

5. ***Resources Necessary to Start a New Business.*** As part of the process of preparing a business plan, the entrepreneur must determine the amount of capital that the business needs to get started. This determination turns on an accurate assessment of the minimum set of essential resources required to open the business and to make it grow. Assuming a thoughtful and thorough business plan is in place, the entrepreneur should be able to determine — either on his or her own or with the assistance of a professional advisor — how much start-up capital is required to get the business to a point where it will generate a positive cash flow.[9]

As we discuss in more detail in Chapter 8, there are essentially two types of start-up capital: debt and equity. The key difference is that with debt, the founders do not have to give up any ownership interest in the business, although they do have to pay interest and will be required to pay back the borrowed funds to the investor. In the case of equity, the founder must be prepared to give up some portion of the ownership of the business to the investor in exchange for the necessary capital to launch the new business.

As a practical matter, most entrepreneurs do not have much flexibility in their choice of financing. The vast majority of small businesses are financed by the entrepreneurs leveraging their own savings and labor, such as taking out a home equity loan to fund the new business. More often than not, the entrepreneur will also work in the business financed by his or her own personal savings, building what is popularly referred to as *sweat equity*, i.e., an ownership interest in the business that is earned in lieu of wages. Very often, additional capital to grow the business will later be obtained from a wealthy investor — sometimes referred to as an *angel investor* — who invests some

---

9. To keep this in perspective, the founders of Digital Equipment Corporation (DEC) started the company with only $70,000 and used this start-up capital to grow the business so that, at its peak, DEC ranked in the top 25 of Fortune 500 companies. What is the moral of this story? Not every new business requires multimillion-dollar funding to get started — not even a high-tech start-up such as DEC.

personal funds in exchange for an equity interest in the business, which usually occurs when the business reaches the stage where it is actually selling goods and/or services. At this point, the business may also be able to obtain a bank line of credit secured by its inventory and/or accounts receivable. If the business is growing quickly in a large market, the business may be able to raise financing from venture capital investors. Further expansion of the business may then come in the form of a public offering of the company's stock (known as an IPO — initial public offering).

The truth of the matter, however, is that the vast majority of new businesses will never qualify for an IPO, for reasons that will become clear as we go through the remaining materials in this casebook. Nevertheless, all of these new businesses need to find some source of equity capital. In many cases, after they have exhausted their personal savings (the *Go-It-Alone* approach to financing the new business), entrepreneurs will very often seek financing from family, friends, and business acquaintances (the *Friends and Family* alternative). And, of the hundreds of thousands of new businesses that are launched every year, some will be able to obtain the necessary funding from venture capitalists. However, in the case of *all* of these different possible financing scenarios, it bears emphasizing that entrepreneurs "often find themselves with *all* of their personal net worth tied up in the same business that provides *all* their income. That is 'double jeopardy,' because if their business fails, entrepreneurs lose *both* their savings and their means of support"[10] for themselves and their families.

In the remaining chapters, we will analyze the issues and challenges that typically face the lawyer in planning a capital-raising transaction in all three of these very common real-world financing alternatives, which we will refer to in shorthand form as the *Go-It-Alone* option; the *Friends and Family* financing; and the *Venture Capital* deal. For a brief introduction to the range of issues that the lawyer typically encounters in the process of completing a capital-raising transaction for a new business, consider the following two excerpts, both of which were prepared by experienced corporate lawyers:

Stephanie L. Chandler
A Practical Guide to Raising Capital

Jackson Walker L.L.P., Law Firm Memo (2004-2014)*

Without sufficient capital even a well-run business with great potential may fail. The financing of a start-up company tends to follow a predictable pattern, with money being raised from the same types of investors over and over and over. A typical equity investment cycle for a start-up company might be: issuance of founders' shares, sales to "friends and family," sales to a mixed bag of accredited and nonaccredited investors, venture capital financing ("VC") and initial public offering [IPO] or acquisition.

* * *

---

10. Bygrave & Zacharakis, *supra* note 3, at 22 (emphasis added).
* *Available at* http://images.jw.com/com/publications/1256.pdf.

Most start-ups begin by creating a business plan that they can use when approaching investors. The business plan tells the story of the company. A business plan must convey credibility and accuracy, while at the same time generating excitement and enthusiasm. It should also be professional, realistic and concise.

Early-stage investors typically invest in a "concept" and do not require detail, but a business plan [for a start-up company] typically includes a description of [at least the following]:

- market;
- business, products or services, properties, etc.;
- capitalization and securities being sold;
- management and principal shareholders;
- material risks;
- selected financial data and financial statements; and
- some type of discussion and analysis of the financial situation and operations of the company.

Statements of facts should be supported as fact and statements of opinion or belief must have a reasonable basis. When it comes to discussing risks and uncertainties, do not hide the ball from investors for to do so will impair your credibility. . . .

* * *

The parties to an equity investment have divergent interests to consider. [The founders generally will] want to minimize the dilution [to be suffered] as a result of funding [the new] business. [Founders usually] also want to maintain sufficient control over and avoid unnecessary restraints on the direction of [their new] business, transfer of [their] shares, and [their] own economic interests. . . . Investors[, however,] have their own agenda. Aside from wanting the "upside" appreciation of owning equity, investors are most interested in anti-dilution protections and having an exit strategy [i.e., an IPO or sale of the business in an acquisition transaction]. They also would like to avoid "downside" risks and avoid windfalls at their expense to noncash contributors.

In the negotiation process, investors may seek a variety of concessions, such as restrictions on payment of dividends. Concessions that may be inappropriate in early rounds with angel investors may become more relevant in later rounds with venture capital financings. Similarly, concessions that might interfere with subsequent larger VC financings should be avoided. Ultimately, the deal points will depend on [the founders'] leverage . . . and, often on how badly and [how] quickly [the founders] need the money.

Raising capital is one of the most important activities that emerging companies engage in. To be successful, it requires planning, good counseling and common sense. As you can see, many of the legal requirements are complex and interrelated. However, there are things [that founders] can do to benefit [their] cause and to move the process along. . . .

Blake Stafford
2009 Update: Raising the Initial Funding for High-Technology Companies in the San Francisco Bay Area

Fenwick & West LLP (2009) *

Introduction

This is a brief summary of the process for raising initial funding . . . for high technology companies. [This article is intended] to help entrepreneurs seeking initial funding understand the alternatives, identify potential funding sources and, most importantly, understand the practical realities of raising initial funding. . . .

Although a number of business forms exist (e.g., limited liability companies, limited partnerships, general partnerships, S-Corps), we assume that your high technology enterprise will be formed as a C-Corp. The C-Corp form is almost always selected for many good reasons. [These reasons are to be explored in more detail as part of the materials in Chapters 5 and 8 of this casebook.] Nonetheless, under some particular circumstances, one of the other forms may be chosen. Again, the following discussion assumes that you [the entrepreneur] will form a C-Corp.

Although we touch upon initial funding from the entrepreneur and "friends and family," the primary focus of the following discussion is how you can maximize your probability of obtaining initial funding from institutional angels [i.e., angel investors] and/or VCs [i.e., venture capitalists]. Both of these groups are sophisticated investors that insist upon thoroughly vetting your company. We want to prepare you to achieve success in this vetting process by getting the attention of institutional angels and VCs and by performing well when you are "on stage."

Seed Capital Financings

Seed capital is primarily available from the entrepreneur, "friends and family," an institutional angel investor and/or a prospective customer. Seed capital financing is needed to form the C-Corp, clear its name, create its by-laws and other corporate documents, create a stock option plan and complete other preliminary matters as well as to satisfy the validation requirements for a VC financing. "Friends and family" investors invest basically because they trust the entrepreneur, and thus the polished materials (discussed below) you will prepare to attempt to get the attention of institutional angels and VCs often are not required. Many institutional angels approach these initial financings much like a VC and want the validation required by a VC. . . .

Seed financing usually comes in the form of the purchase of common stock, preferred stock or notes convertible into common or preferred stock. Selling common stock often is not useful for the seed financing because of the dilutive effect.

* * *

---

* *Available at* http://www.fenwick.com/FenwickDocuments/Legal%20Resource%20Guide.pdf.

Defining the Business and Communicating its Value

Preparing and refining an . . . executive summary [of the business plan] and power point presentation for institutional angels and/or VCs to fully understand the business, its value proposition and the execution steps is a critical part of the initial fund raising process.

* * *

Forming the Team

Your team can be assembled from friends and other business contacts. . . . In most cases, the technical founder must be from and have credibility in the business space of the company. . . . Investors don't invest in technology; they invest in companies with a product that the market wants that generates scalable revenues. Defining and refining product requirements is a continuous task.

Meeting Angels and VCs

. . . The best route to an institutional angel or a VC is through an introduction from someone they know such as a lawyer, accountant or another institutional angel or VC. . . . This approach usually results in the institutional angel or VC reading at least [a portion of] the executive summary.

* * *

Use of Finders

You may be approached by a "finder" who offers to help you raise money through introductions to prospective investors. Do a reference check on the finder's track record. If the finder is asking for a "success fee" then the finder needs to be a registered broker dealer under federal and state securities laws. Institutional angels and VCs will not look kindly upon the use of a finder who has a claim to cash from the proceeds of the investment. Introductions to institutional angels and VCs can usually be arranged without the use of a finder.

* * *

Basic Legal Issues

Federal and state securities laws [to be covered in Chapter 4 of this casebook] need to be complied with in selling securities to investors. Investors have, in effect, a money-back guarantee from the company and possibly its officers if you do not comply. Borrowing money from persons not in the business of making loans is a security under these laws. You should seek investment only from accredited investors or a tight circle of friends and family.

Due diligence by both professional angels and VCs includes a hard look at intellectual property ownership. An initial focus will be the relationship of the technical founders to their prior employers' technology. In California, even if the technical founder has not used any of his prior employer's resources, trade secrets or other property, the prior employer may have a claim to any inventions that relate to the prior employer's business or actual or demonstrably anticipated research or development [for reasons that are described in detail in Chapter 7 of this casebook]. In today's financing environment, there is much tension on this issue because entrepreneurs are reluctant to give up their jobs without funding. This means there may be a "hot" departure of the technical founder from the old employer and a "hot" start at the new company without any cooling off period or, even worse, an overlap of the technical founder working for both companies at the same time. Some entrepreneurs underestimate this risk since their perception is that many . . . companies have been started in the past by entrepreneurs who leave a company and start a company in the same [geographic location]. Trying to delay a departure until funding is imminent is very risky and may in fact materially reduce the probability of funding. Investors will not want to buy into a lawsuit.

NOTES AND QUESTIONS

1. What is dilution?
2. Why do founders generally seek "to minimize the dilution to be suffered"?
3. *Documenting the Deal.* The foregoing articles allude to negotiations and documents that are typically prepared as part of a financing transaction for a start-up business. We examine in more detail the nature of this deal-making process (and its documentation) as we study the steps typically involved in the life cycle of a capital-raising transaction for a start-up business.
4. *The Parlance of Deal Lawyers*. The Chandler article makes reference to terminology (and issues) about which experienced transactional lawyers are quite knowledgeable. This terminology, which may not be familiar to you, includes concepts such as "accredited investors" under the federal securities laws, the investigative process known commonly as "due diligence," and the term "convertible notes." However, over the course of the remaining chapters, we will flesh out the meaning of all of these terms and concepts and also describe their legal significance within the scope of a capital-raising transaction. These last two articles serve to introduce the parlance and perspective of deal lawyers, which are likely new (and perhaps confusing) terrain, but which will become quite familiar and understandable by the end of this course on Business Planning.

D. Thinking Like a "Deal Lawyer" vs. Thinking Like a "Business Litigator"

Notwithstanding the business-oriented materials that comprise most of the last section of this chapter, it bears emphasizing that this casebook is *not* a business-oriented text that examines the business-related steps involved in starting up a new business enterprise. Rather, this casebook focuses on the *role of the lawyer* who is retained by the entrepreneur for legal assistance in organizing and launching a new business enterprise/venture. This approach emphasizes the role of the lawyer as *transaction planner* — a very different professional perspective than the business lawyer serving as litigation counsel. To be most effective as a transaction planner, the lawyer must understand the client's business objectives — in order to plan the financing transaction to preserve maximum flexibility for the new business in the future. That is, so that the business will be well positioned to take advantage of future opportunities.

In the last section, we described the essential traits of entrepreneurs who propose to start a new business. While it is important for the business lawyer to understand the essential attributes of entrepreneurs in order to provide effective legal representation, it is equally important that the business lawyer explore the principal motivating force of the founders/entrepreneurs in establishing their new business venture. In other words, it is important that the lawyer retained by a new business enterprise understand what the *real goals* of the founders are. These goals can potentially encompass a broad range, including the following:

- Do the founders plan to take the company public?
- Do the founders plan to sell the business within a specific (or target) time frame (say, five years)?
- Do the founders plan to merge the new business with another company and continue to operate the business, sharing management control with managers of the acquiring company?
- Do the founders plan to form a joint venture with a larger company, perhaps a competitor in the industry?
- Do the founders intend to run a privately owned company as a "cash cow"?

While these questions may seem to pose business-related issues, experienced counsel understand that the answers to these questions will have a dramatic impact on the nature of the legal advice and ultimately will help the lawyer steer the new business in a direction that will enable it to achieve the desired business objectives. From the lawyer's perspective, the issues that are of the highest priority for counsel to address in the context of representing a start-up business will be dictated in large part by the goals of the owner-managers. This idea has been expressed by experienced corporate lawyers as follows:

Lee R. Petillon & Robert Joe Hull
REPRESENTING START-UP COMPANIES

§2.1 (2006)

2.1 Goals of the Founders

For example, many legal, financial, and business decisions would be made in a certain way if the goal [of the owner-managers] were to go public within three years, as compared with staying private indefinitely. . . . On the other hand, if the founders' goal is to be acquired by a large company, perhaps a strong research and development effort or expanding market share is more important than building up earnings per share.

* * *

At the outset, the founders, owners and managers are usually the same persons. However, as outside passive investors such as angel investors or venture capitalists invest in the company, there may be differing views as to the proper direction of the company. Thus, if the founders are looking to go public and continue to operate [the business] independently, whereas the major outside investors are planning for the company to be acquired, the lawyer should ensure that the investors are fully informed in the investors' disclosure document as to the true goals of management, so as to avoid misleading the outside investors.

Unless the lawyer takes the time to understand the short-term and long-term objectives of the founders/owners/managers, he or she will at best be rendering legal advice in a vacuum, and at worst may, by commission or omission, lead his or her client down the wrong path, with adverse legal and business consequences.

The lawyer may be hesitant to request his or her clients to take valuable time to formulate and review the basic direction of the company and the founders. Most founders, however, recognize that the lawyer who is interested in better understanding their business is trying to be a more perceptive, knowledgeable, and effective counsel, and will accordingly take the time to orient the lawyer to the details of the company's business.

Another recent article (also written by an experienced corporate lawyer) describes ten mistakes commonly made by lawyers representing start-up companies. The author contends that all of these common mistakes are easy for counsel to avoid. We will analyze all of these potential pitfalls in the remaining chapters of this casebook, so we have provided (in brackets) a cross-reference to the relevant chapters where we consider the following common legal mistakes:

- **Mistake No. 1**: Not properly licensing technology patented by others [*see* Chapter 7]
- **Mistake No. 2**: Incautiously hiring former employees of a competitor [*see* Chapters 5 and 7]
- **Mistake No. 3**: Not conducting a timely trademark search [*see* Chapter 7]
- **Mistake No. 4**: Not properly maintaining organizational records [*see* Chapter 5]
- **Mistake No. 5**: Selling securities to nonaccredited investors [*see* Chapter 4]
- **Mistake No. 6**: [Failing to make a timely] Section 83(b) election [*see* Chapter 6]
- **Mistake No. 7**: Not adopting an appropriate employee stock option plan [*see* Chapter 6]
- **Mistake No. 8**: Failing to institute a trade secret protection program [*see* Chapter 7]
- **Mistake No. 9**: Failing to obtain good title to intellectual property [*see* Chapter 7]
- **Mistake No. 10**: Creating a "cheap stock" problem [*see* Chapters 4 and 6]

James J. Greenberger, *Top Ten Legal Mistakes of Early Stage Tech Companies*, 10 Bus. L. Today 3 (Jan.-Feb. 2001).

Since the goals and objectives of a new business are evolving constantly, it is wise for counsel to meet regularly with his or her clients to learn about recent developments affecting the company's business. The founders will usually appreciate the lawyer's desire to keep abreast of the company's opportunities and risks, and this type of ongoing dialogue will also allow the lawyer to be more effective in his or her representation of the business over time.

E. Ethical Obligations of "Deal Lawyers"

This section explores the ethical issues and challenges that corporate lawyers must address on a recurring basis. The first set of materials examines the vitally important threshold issue that arises in connection with establishing the lawyer-client relationship for a new business enterprise: *Who is the client?* As we shall see, this seemingly simple question can become quite complicated when meeting with founders (such as Joan and Michael) who plan to form a new business (such as SoftCo) and raise capital from others in order to finance their new business. The remaining materials in this chapter concern other business-related issues that routinely confront transactional lawyers in the process of organizing a new business, especially one that plans to operate as a corporation. These issues include whether it is proper for the transactional lawyer (i) to accept stock in the company (i.e., an ownership interest in the new business) in lieu of fees for the lawyer's legal services; and (ii) to serve as a member of the board of directors of the new corporation.

1. Who Is the Client? Multiple Party Representation

Selected Provisions — ABA's Model Rules of Professional Conduct (2004)*

Rule 1.7 Conflict of Interest: Current Clients

(a) Except as provided in paragraph (b), a lawyer shall not represent a client if the representation involves a concurrent conflict of interest. A concurrent conflict of interest exists if:

(1) the representation of one client will be directly adverse to another client; or

(2) there is a significant risk that the representation of one or more clients will be materially limited by the lawyer's responsibilities to another client, a former client or a third person or by a personal interest of the lawyer.

(b) Notwithstanding the existence of a concurrent conflict of interest under paragraph (a), a lawyer may represent a client if:

(1) the lawyer reasonably believes that the lawyer will be able to provide competent and diligent representation to each affected client;

---

* In 2002, the American Bar Association amended its Model Rules of Professional Conduct to reflect the recommendations of the so-called "Ethics 2000" commission, which was officially known as the Commission on the Evaluation of the Model Rules of Professional Conduct [and which was chaired by Norm Veasey, former chief justice of the Delaware Supreme Court]. Among the various changes that were implemented in 2002, the ABA amended Rules 1.7 and 1.8 and deleted former 2.2, entitled "Intermediary," [the text of which is reproduced *infra* at pg. 29].

(2) the representation is not prohibited by law;

(3) the representation does not involve the assertion of a claim by one client against another client represented by the lawyer in the same litigation or other proceeding before a tribunal; and

(4) each affected client gives informed consent, confirmed in writing.

Comment

Identifying Conflicts of Interest: Material Limitation

[8] Even where there is no direct adverseness, a conflict of interest exists if there is a significant risk that a lawyer's ability to consider, recommend or carry out an appropriate course of action for the client will be materially limited as a result of the lawyer's other responsibilities or interests. For example, a lawyer asked to represent several individuals seeking to form a joint venture is likely to be materially limited in the lawyer's ability to recommend or advocate all possible positions that each might take because of the lawyer's duty of loyalty to the others. The conflict in effect forecloses alternatives that would otherwise be available to the client. The mere possibility of subsequent harm does not itself require disclosure and consent. The critical questions are the likelihood that a difference in interests will eventuate and, if it does, whether it will materially interfere with the lawyer's independent professional judgment in considering alternatives or foreclose courses of action that reasonably should be pursued on behalf of the client.

* * *

Nonlitigation Conflicts

* * *

[28] Whether a conflict is consentable depends on the circumstances. For example, a lawyer may not represent multiple parties to a negotiation whose interests are fundamentally antagonistic to each other, but common representation is permissible where the clients are generally aligned in interest even though there is some difference in interest among them. Thus, a lawyer may seek to establish or adjust a relationship between clients on an amicable and mutually advantageous basis; for example, in helping to organize a business in which two or more clients are entrepreneurs, working out the financial reorganization of an enterprise in which two or more clients have an interest or arranging a property distribution in settlement of an estate. The lawyer seeks to resolve potentially adverse interests by developing the parties' mutual interests. Otherwise, each party might have to obtain separate representation, with the possibility of incurring additional cost, complication or even litigation. Given these and other relevant factors, the clients may prefer that the lawyer act for all of them.

Special Considerations in Common Representation

[29] In considering whether to represent multiple clients in the same matter, a lawyer should be mindful that if the common representation fails because the potentially adverse interests cannot be reconciled, the result can be additional cost, embarrassment and recrimination. Ordinarily, the lawyer will be forced to withdraw from representing all of the clients if the common representation fails. In some situations, the risk of failure is so great that multiple representation is plainly impossible. For example, a lawyer cannot undertake common representation of clients where contentious litigation or negotiations between them are imminent or contemplated. Moreover, because the lawyer is required to be impartial between commonly represented clients, representation of multiple clients is improper when it is unlikely that impartiality can be maintained. Generally, if the relationship between the parties has already assumed antagonism, the possibility that the clients' interests can be adequately served by common representation is not very good. Other relevant factors are whether the lawyer subsequently will represent both parties on a continuing basis and whether the situation involves creating or terminating a relationship between the parties.

* * *

[31] As to the duty of confidentiality, continued common representation will almost certainly be inadequate if one client asks the lawyer not to disclose to the other client information relevant to the common representation. This is so because the lawyer has an equal duty of loyalty to each client, and each client has the right to be informed of anything bearing on the representation that might affect that client's interests and the right to expect that the lawyer will use that information to that client's benefit. See Rule 1.4. The lawyer should, at the outset of the common representation and as part of the process of obtaining each client's informed consent, advise each client that information will be shared and that the lawyer will have to withdraw if one client decides that some matter material to the representation should be kept from the other. In limited circumstances, it may be appropriate for the lawyer to proceed with the representation when the clients have agreed, after being properly informed, that the lawyer will keep certain information confidential. For example, the lawyer may reasonably conclude that failure to disclose one client's trade secrets to another client will not adversely affect representation involving a joint venture between the clients and agree to keep that information confidential with the informed consent of both clients.

[32] When seeking to establish or adjust a relationship between clients, the lawyer should make clear that the lawyer's role is not that of partisanship normally expected in other circumstances and, thus, that the clients may be required to assume greater responsibility for decisions than when each client is separately represented. Any limitations on the scope of the representation

made necessary as a result of the common representation should be fully explained to the clients at the outset of the representation. See Rule 1.2(c).

[33] Subject to the above limitations, each client in the common representation has the right to loyal and diligent representation and the protection of Rule 1.9 concerning the obligations to a former client. The client also has the right to discharge the lawyer as stated in Rule 1.16.

* * *

Rule 1.8 Conflict Of Interest: Current Clients: Specific Rules

(a) A lawyer shall not enter into a business transaction with a client or knowingly acquire an ownership, possessory, security, or other pecuniary interest adverse to a client unless:

(1) the transaction and terms on which the lawyer acquires the interest are fair and reasonable to the client and are fully disclosed and transmitted in writing in a manner that can be reasonably understood by the client;

(2) the client is advised in writing of the desirability of seeking and is given a reasonable opportunity to seek the advice of independent legal counsel on the transaction; and

(3) the client gives informed consent, in a writing signed by the client, to the essential terms of the transaction and the lawyer's role in the transaction, including whether the lawyer is representing the client in the transaction.

* * *

Rule 1.13 Organization as Client

(a) A lawyer employed or retained by an organization represents the organization acting through its duly authorized constituents.

(b) If a lawyer for an organization knows that an officer, employee or other person associated with the organization is engaged in action, intends to act or refuses to act in a matter related to the representation that is a violation of a legal obligation to the organization, or a violation of law that reasonably might be imputed to the organization, and that is likely to result in substantial injury to the organization, then the lawyer shall proceed as is reasonably necessary in the best interest of the organization. Unless the lawyer reasonably believes that it is not necessary in the best interest of the organization to do so, the lawyer shall refer the matter to higher authority in the organization, including, if warranted by the circumstances to the highest authority that can act on behalf of the organization as determined by applicable law.

(c) Except as provided in paragraph (d), if

(1) despite the lawyer's efforts in accordance with paragraph (b) the highest authority that can act on behalf of the organization insists upon or fails to address in a timely and appropriate manner an action, or a refusal to act, that is clearly a violation of law, and

(2) the lawyer reasonably believes that the violation is reasonably certain to result in substantial injury to the organization,

then the lawyer may reveal information relating to the representation whether or not Rule 1.6 permits such disclosure, but only if and to the extent the lawyer reasonably believes necessary to prevent substantial injury to the organization.

(d) Paragraph (c) shall not apply with respect to information relating to a lawyer's representation of an organization to investigate an alleged violation of law, or to defend the organization or an officer, employee or other constituent associated with the organization against a claim arising out of an alleged violation of law.

(e) A lawyer who reasonably believes that he or she has been discharged because of the lawyer's actions taken pursuant to paragraphs (b) or (c), or who withdraws under circumstances that require or permit the lawyer to take action under either of those paragraphs, shall proceed as the lawyer reasonably believes necessary to assure that the organization's highest authority is informed of the lawyer's discharge or withdrawal.

(f) In dealing with an organization's directors, officers, employees, members, shareholders or other constituents, a lawyer shall explain the identity of the client when the lawyer knows or reasonably should know that the organization's interests are adverse to those of the constituents with whom the lawyer is dealing.

(g) A lawyer representing an organization may also represent any of its directors, officers, employees, members, shareholders or other constituents, subject to the provisions of Rule 1.7. If the organization's consent to the dual representation is required by Rule 1.7, the consent shall be given by an appropriate official of the organization other than the individual who is to be represented, or by the shareholders.

Comment

The Entity as the Client

[1] An organizational client is a legal entity, but it cannot act except through its officers, directors, employees, shareholders and other constituents. . . . The duties defined in this Comment apply equally to unincorporated associations. "Other constituents" as used in this Comment means the positions equivalent to officers, directors, employees, and shareholders held by persons acting for organizational clients that are not corporations.

* * *

[3] When constituents of the organization make decisions for it, the decisions ordinarily must be accepted by the lawyer even if their utility or prudence is doubtful. Decisions concerning policy and operations, including ones entailing serious risk, are not as such in the lawyer's province. Paragraph (b) makes clear, however, that when the lawyer knows that the organization is likely to be substantially injured by action of an officer or other constituent that violates a legal obligation to the organization or is in violation of law that might be imputed to the organization, the lawyer must proceed as is reasonably necessary in the best interest of the organization. As defined in Rule 1.0(f), knowledge can be inferred from circumstances, and a lawyer cannot ignore the obvious.

* * *

[5] Paragraph (b) also makes clear that when it is reasonably necessary to enable the organization to address the matter in a timely and appropriate manner, the lawyer must refer the matter to higher authority, including, if warranted by the

circumstances, the highest authority that can act on behalf of the organization under applicable law. The organization's highest authority to whom a matter may be referred ordinarily will be the board of directors or similar governing body. However, applicable law may prescribe that under certain conditions the highest authority reposes elsewhere, for example, in the independent directors of a corporation.

* * *

Rule 2.2 Intermediary [pre-2002 Model Rules]

(a) A lawyer may act as intermediary between clients if:

(1) the lawyer consults with each client concerning the implications of the common representation, including the advantages and risks involved, and the effect on the attorney-client privileges, and obtains each client's consent to the common representation;

(2) the lawyer reasonably believes that the matter can be resolved on terms compatible with the clients' best interests, that each client will be able to make adequately informed decisions in the matter and that there is little risk of material prejudice to the interests of any of the clients if the contemplated resolution is unsuccessful; and

(3) the lawyer reasonably believes that the common representation can be undertaken impartially and without improper effect on other responsibilities the lawyer has to any of the clients.

(b) While acting as intermediary, the lawyer shall consult with each client concerning the decisions to be made and the considerations relevant in making them, so that each client can make adequately informed decisions.

(c) A lawyer shall withdraw as intermediary if any of the clients so requests, or if any of the conditions stated in paragraph (a) is no longer satisfied. Upon withdrawal, the lawyer shall not continue to represent any of the claims in the matter that was the subject of the intermediation.

NOTES AND QUESTIONS

1. With entrepreneurs such as Joan and Michael, who are seeking legal advice in connection with their decision to start a new business such as SoftCo, who is the client?

2. What information would you want to know as part of your decision to take on a new business as a client in your law firm? Would this decision be influenced by whether you think that the new business is going to be successful? For these purposes, how do you define "success"? How do the entrepreneurs define "success"? Is their definition of success relevant to your decision whether to take on the new business as a client?

3. *Conflicts Check*. As a threshold matter, every lawyer must undertake a "conflicts check" to determine whether the lawyer can take on a new business client consistent with the lawyer's professional responsibilities. Most law firms today have procedures in place to expedite this process of "checking for conflicts," and young lawyers must be sure to familiarize themselves with the policies and procedures to be followed by

their law firm. As part of this process of taking on a new business as a client, the lawyer confronts the important threshold question — *who is the client?* For example, in the context of Joan and Michael's decision to form a new business, SoftCo, what would you have to do to complete an appropriate "conflicts check" before taking on this new client matter?

4. *What Is a "Conflict"?* The corporate lawyer needs to be sensitive to the wide variety of situations that may give rise to a (potential) conflict of interest. Very often, in the context of the business lawyer practicing in a transactional setting, the ABA Rules, generally speaking, provide little guidance on this threshold issue, unlike in the litigation context. To illustrate this point, consider the following (not uncommon) situation: Assume that you have been asked to represent a company whose CEO serves on the board of directors of another company that you represent. Do you see any problems?

5. *The "Three C's."* In deciding whether to take on a new business as a client, practicing lawyers often refer to the "Three C's" — *Competence, Capacity*, and (absence of) *Conflicts*. The preceding materials described the analysis that the lawyer typically undertakes to determine whether the engagement puts the lawyer into a conflict (or potential conflict) position. In addition, the lawyer will also have to consider whether the lawyer has sufficient expertise to do the legal work required by this engagement (Competence) and whether the lawyer has the resources to meet the client's expectations (particularly with respect to deadlines) and needs (Capacity). In connection with the facts of the next case, you may want to ask whether there was adequate consideration of the "Three C's" on the lawyer's part.

The next case also highlights the importance of the transactional lawyer clearly establishing *who* the client is (i.e., clearly establishing the identity of the interests that the lawyer represents). In addition, as a matter of professional responsibility in connection with representing a corporation, it is incumbent on the lawyer to clearly communicate this information to the company and its individual board members in order to eliminate any possibility of a misunderstanding. The following case reflects the potential consequences of failing to clearly communicate this information to all relevant parties.

Waggoner v. Snow, Becker, Kroll, Klaris, & Krauss

991 F.2d 1501 (9th Cir. 1993)

SNEED, Circuit Judge:

I. Facts and Prior Proceedings

Thomas Waggoner is a cofounder of STAAR Surgical Company (Staar), a publicly held company incorporated in California in 1982. Until 1989, he was also its Chief Executive Officer and a member of its Board of Directors (Board). Waggoner hired defendant Elliot Lutzker as counsel for Staar in 1984.[2] In April of 1986, Lutzker supervised Staar's reincorporation to Delaware.

From 1982 to 1986, Staar was principally engaged in the manufacture and sale of a patented soft intraocular lens (IOL) used in treating cataracts. In 1986 Staar expanded into other markets. In July 1987, however, finding the company short of capital, Staar negotiated a line of credit from the Bank of New York (BONY), secured primarily by accounts receivable and inventory. By September of 1987, BONY determined that Staar was under-collateralized and over-advanced on its credit line by almost $2 million. BONY threatened to discontinue the credit line and initiate foreclosure proceedings unless Staar's officers would personally guarantee the outstanding loans.

On December 13, 1987, the Staar Board convened to discuss the company's options. During the course of that meeting, Waggoner declared that he was willing to guarantee $3.5 million of BONY debt and $2.8 million of other debt in exchange for voting control of Staar for as long as his personal guarantees were outstanding. Lutzker was at the meeting and reminded everyone there that he was present only in his capacity as counsel for Staar.

On December 16, 1987, BONY informed Waggoner that he had only three days in which to provide the Bank with a written personal guarantee of the overdrawn line of credit. Staar's directors convened an emergency telephone meeting on December 17, 1987. At that meeting, Waggoner explained Staar's financial straits to the directors and advised them that he was the only person who could afford to guarantee personally Staar's debt. The Board then adopted a resolution transferring 100 shares of Class A Preferred Stock to Waggoner in exchange for his guarantee. One of those shares was to be convertible into 2 million shares of common stock after January 16, 1988, if Waggoner's guarantees were still outstanding.

Following that meeting, at the Board's direction, Lutzker drew up the Shareholders Agreement and the Certificate of Designation, the papers necessary to transfer voting control of the company to Waggoner. Waggoner had the documents reviewed by Staar's California patent counsel, Frank Frisenda, and on December 24, 1987, Waggoner personally guaranteed Staar's debt and pledged his Staar stock to BONY. Although Staar's directors tried to obtain financing in order to replace Waggoner's guarantees in the month that followed, they were not successful. Consequently, on January 19, 1988, after consulting with Lutzker, Waggoner converted one of his Preferred shares in exchange for 2 million shares of common stock.

Staar's financial trouble continued throughout 1988 and early 1989. Finally, in the summer of 1989, Staar considered the possibility of a merger with Vision Technologies, Inc. (VTI). VTI submitted a written proposal to Staar regarding a potential merger on June 29, 1989. On July 22, 1989, another company, by the name of Chiron, submitted a bid to acquire Staar's IOL business. On August 8, 1989, the Board, including Waggoner, adopted a resolution that Staar would attempt

---

2. At the time, Lutzker was a lawyer with the New York–based firm of Bachner, Tally, Polevoy, Misher, & Brinberg (Bachner Tally). In 1985, Lutzker left Bachner Tally in order to become a partner at Snow, Becker, Kroll, Klaris, & Krauss, P.C. (Snow Becker), another New York–based firm. Nevertheless, Lutzker retained his position as Staar's counsel. Lutzker and Staar apparently never signed a written retainer agreement.

in good faith to complete a merger with VTI. The Board sent Chiron written notice terminating negotiations on August 9, 1989. In spite of the Board's resolution, however, Waggoner continued negotiations with Chiron. On August 10, 1989, one of Staar's directors unexpectedly discovered Waggoner in a secret meeting with Chiron agents at Staar's offices.

The Board convened an emergency meeting without Waggoner the next day. The Board found that Waggoner had violated his fiduciary duties to Staar and voted to remove Waggoner from his positions as president, CEO, and director of Staar. In response, Waggoner called Lutzker to ascertain if his preferred stock empowered him to remove the other directors from the Board and create a new Board. Lutzker informed Waggoner that he knew of nothing to hinder Waggoner from using his voting power in that manner. Thus, after voting to remove the other directors from the Board, Waggoner named a new Board consisting of himself, his wife, and one vacancy. Waggoner sent his written consent regarding the removal of the other directors to Lutzker, who informed the other Board members what had transpired.

The Board members sought relief in court, filing two suits in Delaware. As a result of the ensuing litigation, Waggoner lost his position in and control over Staar. He also lost ownership of the common stock which he had allegedly derived from the convertible preferred stock.[3]

On August 23, 1990, Waggoner filed this diversity action for legal malpractice against Lutzker and Snow Becker. Waggoner alleged that the defendants breached their duty of care because Lutzker: negligently failed to include the power to fix voting rights among the Board of Directors' powers when Staar was reincorporated in Delaware; failed to advise Waggoner that the Board did not have the power to fix voting rights; and knew or should have known that the Board lacked that power. Waggoner further alleged that Lutzker was aware that Waggoner would rely on his advice, that Waggoner did in fact rely on that advice, and that Waggoner suffered damage as a result. On September 12, 1991, the district court granted summary judgment for the defendants.

This diversity action requires exploration of the limits of liability for alleged malpractice under the laws of either New York or California by an attorney whose advice was relied on by both a corporation and one of its officers. Because the relevant transactions had contacts in both New York and California, it is necessary to determine the proper law to fix the limits of the attorney's liability.

The district court resolved these issues by finding that the defendants showed as a matter of law that: (1) there was no direct attorney-client relationship between Lutzker and Waggoner during the instances when Waggoner asserts he detrimentally relied on Lutzker's advice; (2) California's choice of law test required the district court to apply New York law to the action before it; and (3) New York law required the court to dismiss

---

3. The Delaware Supreme Court found that the Board's transfer of preferred stock endowed with voting rights was invalid on the ground that it was ultra vires, or beyond the Board's powers, because Staar's Certificate of Incorporation did not expressly allow the Board to create a class of preferred stock with voting rights. The Delaware Supreme Court further found that Waggoner's attempt to convert one of his preferred shares into common stock was invalid. See Waggoner v. Laster, 581 A.2d 1127 (Del. 1990); STAAR Surgical Co. v. Waggoner, 588 A.2d 1130 (Del. 1991).

Waggoner's case because there was no privity between Lutzker and Waggoner. Waggoner timely appealed.

* * *

III. Discussion

A. Attorney-Client Relationship

Waggoner first contends that Lutzker and Snow Becker are liable to him for Lutzker's negligence because Lutzker was acting as Waggoner's attorney during the preferred stock transaction.[4] New York and California treat the formation of an attorney-client relationship similarly. An attorney-client relationship is formed when an attorney renders advice directly to a client who has consulted him seeking legal counsel. A formal contract is not necessary to show that an attorney-client relationship has been formed. The court may look to the intent and conduct of the parties to determine whether the relationship was actually formed.

To support his allegation that Lutzker acted as his counsel during the preferred stock transaction, Waggoner emphasizes that: (1) Lutzker informed him by telephone between the December 13th and December 17th meetings in 1987 that Delaware law did not prevent Staar from transferring preferred stock with a conversion feature to Waggoner; (2) the Board approved of the transaction only after Lutzker represented to all the Board members, including Waggoner, that the Board was authorized to issue super majority voting stock in exchange for Waggoner's guarantees; (3) Lutzker sent Waggoner the documents regarding the voting stock exchange for review and advised Waggoner that they complied with all the necessary laws and regulations; (4) Lutzker reassured Waggoner that the voting rights were valid in January 1988 and in the summer of 1988; (5) Lutzker assured Waggoner that he could exercise his voting rights should the need arise, and advised him on the procedure involved; and (6) Lutzker did not advise him to seek outside counsel until the summer of 1989. While Lutzker does not contest that he spoke with Waggoner on these occasions, Lutzker contends that any advice he rendered to Waggoner was only in his role as corporate counsel for Staar.

Despite Waggoner's allegations, the intent and conduct of the parties supports the district court's finding that Waggoner and Lutzker were not in an attorney-client relationship. As noted above, it is undisputed that Lutzker informed everyone at the Board meeting on December 13, 1987, including Waggoner, that Lutzker was only present as counsel for Staar and that he did not represent Waggoner. Waggoner's claim is further undermined by his own repeated references to Lutzker as corporate counsel and to Rick

---

4. Waggoner initially contends that he and Lutzker had an on-going attorney-client relationship based on several instances in which he sought and received legal counsel from Lutzker on personal matters. As the district court properly pointed out, however, the issue here is whether Lutzker and Waggoner had an attorney-client relationship during the transactions giving rise to this malpractice suit: Lutzker's drafting and filing of the documents reincorporating Staar from California to Delaware, and Lutzker's drafting of the documents ostensibly transferring preferred stock to Waggoner in exchange for his personal guarantees. We need only focus on the transaction involving preferred stock, because all parties concede Lutzker was acting solely on behalf of Staar at the time Staar was reincorporated.

Love as his personal counsel. Before the Delaware court, Waggoner specifically stated that Lutzker was "not empowered to negotiate" for him and did not negotiate on his behalf regarding the merger discussions with VTI. He described Lutzker as "corporate counsel" at his September 11, 1989 deposition in preparation for proceedings in the Delaware court and at trial before that court. On September 13, 1989, in an attempt to clarify the situation, an attorney asked Waggoner: "So when you say 'your attorney' you are talking about Mr. Love?" Waggoner responded: "Mr. Love is my attorney, Mr. Lutzker is not." Finally, Waggoner's counsel at the Delaware trial made a point of establishing that Lutzker was Staar's corporate counsel in response to allegations by the other directors that Lutzker had not acted appropriately on behalf of the Board. He pointed out that: Lutzker had been described as corporate counsel by virtually all the directors; the directors sought his counsel about filing a bankruptcy petition; and Lutzker prepared the minutes of Board meetings even after Waggoner purportedly removed them as directors. Thus, the district court did not err by granting summary judgment for defendants on the issue of whether an attorney-client relationship existed between Waggoner and Lutzker.

B. Choice of Law

Waggoner argues, alternatively, that the district court erred by granting summary judgment for defendants because there is a genuine issue regarding Lutzker's liability to Waggoner as a third party. Although the district court conceded that Waggoner would be able to pursue a claim for liability in California, the district court found that New York law applied and that the defendants were entitled to summary judgment under New York law. Thus, before we reach the issue of whether New York law precludes liability in this case, we must determine whether the district court erred in its analysis of the choice of law issue.

* * *

In the instant case, there is a clear conflict between the laws of California and New York: California allows a third party to recover from an attorney in situations where New York generally precludes it. Under California law, attorneys may be liable to a third party where the third party "was an intended beneficiary of the attorney's services, or where it was reasonably foreseeable that negligent service or advice to or on behalf of the client could cause harm to others." Fox v. Pollack, 181 Cal. App. 3d 954, 960, 226 Cal. Rptr. 532, 535 (1986).

Under New York law, by contrast, attorneys are not liable to a party for economic injury arising from negligent misrepresentation unless there was privity between the injured party and the attorney, or unless there was "a relationship so close as to approach that of privity." Prudential Ins. Co. v. Dewey, Ballantine, Bushby, Palmer, & Wood, 80 N.Y.2d 377, 590 N.Y.S.2d 831, 833, 605 N.E.2d 318 (1992). The New York courts have recognized a limited number of situations where an attorney can be held liable by a non-client. In the absence of privity, or a relationship approximating privity, an attorney is not liable to a third party for actions taken in furtherance of his role as counsel.

Once a court has established the existence of a true conflict between states, the court must apply the law of the state whose interest would be more impaired if its law were not applied. This analysis does not require the court to balance which state has the "better" social policy on the issue in question. Rather, the comparative impairment analysis "attempts to determine the relative commitment of the respective states to the laws involved" by considering such factors as "the history and current status of the states' laws" and "the function and purpose of those laws." The court may also look to the reasonable expectations of the parties as to which state law would govern a dispute between them.

California's policy demonstrates a commitment to ensuring that lawyers who have not perpetrated fraud may be held liable by a third party for negligence if it was reasonably foreseeable that the third party would rely on the attorney's advice, or if the third party was an intended beneficiary of that advice.

The policy behind New York's privity rule, on the other hand, is to ensure that attorneys will "be free to advise their clients without fear that [they] will be personally liable to third persons if the advice [they] have given to their clients later proves erroneous."

* * *

We conclude that New York would suffer more if the court did not apply New York law to this case. Committed though California may be to its policy holding lawyers liable to third parties where it was foreseeable that the party would rely on the attorney's advice, California's ties to this lawsuit are weak. California's only ties to the suit are Waggoner, who was a California resident at the time of these events, and Staar, which was incorporated in California before it was reincorporated in Delaware, and whose principal place of business apparently remained in California. The residence of the parties is not the determining factor in a choice of law analysis. The mere fact that California laws are more favorable to Waggoner's claim also cannot make California law controlling.

New York's interest in this litigation is significant because of its numerous contacts with the events giving rise to the litigation. In fact, the wealth of transactions and events which occurred in New York demonstrate that the reasonable expectations of the parties can only have been that New York law would apply to a dispute between them. Lutzker has been a New York resident since 1976. He has been licensed to practice law in New York since 1979, and he is a partner in a New York law firm. He has never been licensed to practice law in California. In addition, it was Staar which originally retained the New York firm of Bachner Tally for its corporate counsel and which decided to retain Lutzker as its corporate counsel when he left Bachner Tally to become a partner at Snow Becker. Neither Bachner Tally nor Snow Becker have ever had offices outside of New York. Moreover, almost all of the transactions relevant to this litigation took place in New York: Lutzker prepared the Certificate of Incorporation, reincorporating Staar in Delaware, in New York; the December 13, 1987 meeting of Staar's Board was held at Snow Becker's offices in New York; Lutzker prepared the Shareholders Agreement and the Certificate of Designation in New York; and each time Waggoner contacted Lutzker regarding these and other transactions, it was at Lutzker's office in New York.

New York has a clear interest in seeing that an attorney practicing in its jurisdiction, sought out by a foreign corporation and presiding over transactions brokered in New York, is covered by New York's policy that there must be a relationship at least approaching privity before an attorney can be held liable for his advice. Thus, the district court did not err by finding that New York law should apply to Waggoner's action.

C. Summary Judgment

We must next determine whether the district court erred by granting summary judgment for the defendants. As noted above, New York law, with few exceptions, requires privity before a lawyer can be held liable by a party not his client in the absence of fraud, collusion, or a malicious or tortious act. "The fact that an attorney represents a corporation does not thereby make that attorney counsel to the individual officers and directors thereof." Stratton Group v. Sprayregen, 466 F.Supp. 1180, 1184 n.3 (S.D.N.Y. 1979). On the contrary, attorneys are specifically required by the New York Code of Professional Responsibility, Ethical Consideration 5-18, to act in the interests of the entity they represent, rather than on behalf of the officers of that entity.

Unless the attorney for a corporation or partnership affirmatively assumes a duty toward an officer or partner, the lawyer is not liable to a partner or director who relied on his advice. In the instant case, Lutzker's duty as counsel for Staar lay with the corporation, not with its officers and directors individually. In addition, the record reveals no sign that Lutzker affirmatively adopted Waggoner as a client during the transfer of preferred stock. Thus, the district court did not err by granting summary judgment for the defendants.

IV. Conclusion

The district court did not err by granting summary judgment for defendants because the record does not support Waggoner's assertion that Lutzker was his personal attorney. Further, the district court did not err by applying New York law to Waggoner's case pursuant to California's choice of law analysis. Finally, the district court did not err by granting summary judgment for the defendants because Waggoner did not present a triable issue of fact regarding whether Lutzker is liable to Waggoner as a third party. Thus, the defendants are entitled to summary judgment as a matter of law.

AFFIRMED.

NOTES AND QUESTIONS

1. Do you think the court reached the right result in the *Waggoner* case? Do you agree with the court's conclusion as to whether the facts of this case demonstrate that an attorney-client relationship existed between Waggoner and Lutzker?
2. As a matter of professional responsibility, do you think that Lutzker acted properly?
3. Based on the court's reasoning in *Waggoner*, consider the following facts: A duly licensed New York corporate lawyer represents a Delaware company that resides in California. Do you see any (potential) problems — either legal or practical — with this arrangement?
4. For purposes of this question, assume that a shareholder of a publicly traded company calls company counsel and asks this lawyer what voting rights his shares have. How should this lawyer respond? Is this a question that the lawyer can answer, consistent with the lawyer's claim that he represents the company?

5. *Lawyer's Expertise.* As we noted at the outset of this chapter, lawyers who serve their clients as transaction planners are often called upon to serve as something akin to a jack-of-all-trades. In other words, to adequately address the range of business and legal issues that are likely to arise in the course of planning a capital-raising transaction for a new business, the lawyer often needs to draw on a number of areas of special expertise, including tax and securities regulation. This leads to the rather obvious question: *Can the general business lawyer be competent in all aspects of substantive law that may be relevant to planning that particular transaction?* This leads to a closely related question: *When must (should?) the lawyer bring in specialists?*

6. *Client Recruitment.* How do lawyers find new clients, such as the start-up business that Joan and Michael propose to launch? On the other hand, how do entrepreneurs (such as Joan and Michael) go about finding legal counsel (such as Maynard & Warren LLP) to help them get their new business off the ground?

7. As a first-year transactional lawyer, would you be willing to take on the representation of the founders, Joan and Michael, in connection with the formation of their new business SoftCo, on your own and without a more experienced lawyer supervising your legal work?

8. *ABA Rule 1.1.* In addition to exposing the lawyer to potential civil liability, the lawyer also runs the risk of professional discipline should the lawyer undertake the representation of a start-up business without adequate expertise in the subject matter of business planning for a capital-raising transaction. In this regard, consider the implications of ABA Rule 1.1, which provides:

ABA's Model Rules of Professional Conduct (2004)

Rule 1.1 Competence

A lawyer shall provide competent representation to a client. Competent representation requires the legal knowledge, skill, thoroughness, and preparation reasonably necessary for the representation.

Comment

Legal Knowledge and Skill

[1] In determining whether a lawyer employs the requisite knowledge and skill in a particular matter, relevant factors include the relative complexity and specialized nature of the matter, the lawyer's general experience, the lawyer's training and experience in the field in question, the preparation and study the lawyer is able to give the matter, and whether it is feasible to refer the matter to, or associate or consult with, a lawyer of established competence in the field in question. In many instances, the required proficiency is that of a general practitioner. Expertise in a particular field of law may be required in some circumstances.

[2] A lawyer need not necessarily have special training or prior experience to handle legal problems of a type with which the lawyer is unfamiliar. . . . A lawyer can provide adequate representation in a wholly novel field through necessary study. Competent representation can also be provided through the association of a lawyer of established competence in the field in question.

* * *

[4] A lawyer may accept representation where the requisite level of competence can be achieved by reasonable preparation.

2. *Business Advice vs. Legal Advice*

The following article addresses the time-honored question of *why* entrepreneurs seek the advice of lawyers. Apart from the apparent need for the lawyer's services as part of the formation of a separate business entity (which will serve as the vehicle for carrying on the activities of the new business venture), is there any other role for the transactional lawyer to play in connection with taking on a new business as a client?

Martin B. Robins
Recipe for an Overdue Change: Why Corporate Lawyers Sometimes Need to Give Business Advice

12 BUSINESS LAW TODAY 46 (July/Aug. 2003)

Business lawyers as business advisers? Could be. Read on.

The recent series of corporate implosions should cause every business lawyer to wonder what counsel could have done to prevent these disasters. Many observers, in and outside of the profession, wonder the same thing.

While it will take years for the courts and regulators to sort out exactly what happened in these corporate debacles, I suggest that a big part of the problem is the written and unwritten constraint taught to most aspiring business lawyers concerning the need to defer to their clients' business decisions. See, for example, the Model Rules of Professional Conduct, Sec. 1.2(a): "A lawyer shall abide by a client's decisions concerning the objectives of representation. . . ." From law school through the associate and junior partner ranks, business transactional lawyers are taught the traditional paradigm that their job is to advise clients as to available options and legal implications and work diligently to implement the client's decision from among the options.

The product of the present approach has been noted in the pages of this magazine: "In this dramatic context, what has been the role of lawyers? Has our profession been battling misconduct, and taking heroic steps to protect companies and their investors? For the most part, our profession has not distinguished itself." Murphy, "Enron, Ethics and Lessons for Lawyers," *Bus. Law Today*, Jan./Feb. 2003 at 11.

The author's thesis is that we must revisit this premise in order to make meaningful the current admonitions to public company counsel in Section 307 of the Sarbanes-Oxley Act (the act) and related regulations, to protest illegal acts of corporate management. SEC Release 2003-13 announcing the release of regulations under the act, Jan. 23, 2003, "SEC Adopts Lawyer Conduct Rule under Sarbanes-Oxley Act," at the SEC Web site, www.sec.gov (the "Implementing Release") summarizes the objective:

> The rules adopted today by the commission will require an attorney to report evidence of a material violation, determined according to an objective standard, "up the ladder" within the issuer . . . [ultimately to] the full board of directors. . . .

See also Cramton, "Enron and the Corporate Lawyer: A Primer on Legal and Ethical Issues," 58 *Bus. Law.* 143, 179 (2002).

It is submitted that in the transactional context, a potential legal violation must in most cases be analyzed in the context of an economic transaction. Disclosure violations and fiduciary violations almost invariably involve a misrepresentation or diversion of economic consequences.

Accordingly, counsel must be made responsible for understanding the economic basics of their client's business, industry and the financial marketplace as well as being responsible for a minimal critique as to whether a given major action is at least minimally viable in such context. Protest as to a legal violation will often require advice as to economic flaws in a proposed transaction or policy.

This article suggests a *new* requirement to govern the manner in which a lawyer advises their client. Pending any change in formal requirements, lawyers engaged at an entity level are urged to take a broad view of their roles and speak up to their direct contacts whenever they see something that appears questionable, whether or not the matter is clearly legal in nature.

Of course, they must in all events heed the language of the act to pursue "up the ladder" evidence of legal violations. Frequently, an objective perspective from counsel not directly involved in the matter will be sufficient to dissuade clients from disastrous paths that they have lost the ability to identify. Counsel choosing to act in this way should communicate their intention to their client, preferably at the inception of the representation in order to minimize any disruption from counsel's acting in a "nontraditional" way.

The traditional approach may have worked well during the early and middle parts of the last century in the midst of a goods-based economy where it was frequently possible to easily distinguish business and legal issues. Where people and companies usually made their livings by producing and selling things to each other and financial markets consisted essentially of common stock and long term bonds, intellectual property and financial engineering were much less important than they are today.

Opportunities for financial maneuvering by operating companies, let alone businesses based solely on financial maneuvering, were of little significance, meaning that in most cases, legal concerns did not directly affect business viability and it was often possible to identify "pure" business issues not warranting legal review.

Today, however, things are different. With so many businesses based on intellectual capital, as opposed to plant and equipment, and so many businesses tied directly to the financial markets and the exotic strategies they now permit, it is often impossible to readily distinguish "legal" and "business" issues.

Yet, in the face of so much change, we still see lawyers seeking to limit their advice to legal matters when it is clear that such matters could not be meaningfully distinguished from business matters and that the client's fundamental approach to its business was seriously flawed and leading it toward disaster. A headline in the *Wall Street Journal* of May 10, 2002, is illustrative: "Lawyers for Enron Faulted Its Deals, Didn't Force Issue."

* * *

Based on my own training and observations of numerous other transactional lawyers, I believe that in the majority of cases, well-meaning lawyers felt powerless to challenge their clients' "business decisions" despite the fact that it was clear that client management was either personally interested in the specific decision or policy or had become so close to the situation that they could no longer analyze it objectively — making a third-party critique that much more important.

Our complex economy and financial markets and the critical "gatekeeper" role of lawyers vis-à-vis those markets (See "Understanding Enron: "It's About the Gatekeepers, Stupid," John C. Coffee, 57 *Bus. Law.* 1403 (2002)) demand that we banish this arcane distinction and require lawyers to use their objective perspective to advise their clients of significant reservations as to the prudence or propriety of the clients' business practices.

Both client expectations and the public interest in these troubled times demand that those who are capable of heading off catastrophic losses be charged with the responsibility for making reasonable efforts to do so, as opposed to using their narrow specialty to rationalize looking the other way. When counsel sees their client headed for disaster, they should be required to speak up, whether or not the disaster is strictly "legal" in nature.

Are lawyers equipped to do so? From my observations, it appears that a business lawyer who has practiced at least 10 years or so will pick up enough of a feel for what makes economic sense and what doesn't, to make their comments meaningful at a high level. Senior-level lawyers by definition possess the talent and training to advise intelligently on *all* legal aspects of a given matter. Frequently, lawyers will have addressed a given situation enough times to develop a good idea of an intelligent business solution, in contrast to a client, who may not have prior experience with the particular matter.

It is suggested that if a lawyer does not develop or has not yet developed some feel for the business ramifications of major client actions, he or she should not be functioning in a senior capacity. The effort is not to constitute the business bar as some sort of *uber*-board-of-directors or management committee sitting in judgment on day-to-day matters.

The goal simply is to keep them alert for fundamental problems that imperil the future of the enterprise or its investors. That would include, among other things, major accounting irregularities that should be palpably evident without formal accounting training — such as drastic changes in accounting policy, financial statements that are not readily understandable and transactions producing material financial-statement benefit to the organization or its management without a discernible business purpose.

To the author, existing standards and commentary dealing with organizational-level violations fall short of the mark by defining the problem in strictly legal terms. Murphy argues persuasively for a "beefing up" of the compliance function but implicitly defines compliance in terms of existing legal authority. Similarly, Sarbanes-Oxley and the related regulations condition the lawyer's obligation to do anything on a breach of statutory or common securities or fiduciary law.

By encouraging such a narrow view, the authorities make it likely that lawyers will fail to note the existence of many situations requiring their vigilance. Without counsel being required to address the business rationale for a given action, simply admonishing them to report legal violations is likely to be of limited practical value.

NOTES AND QUESTIONS

1. Can business and legal issues be separated? What do you think?
2. In the preceding article, the author maintains that, as a matter of professional responsibility, lawyers who see "their client headed for disaster . . . , should be

required to speak up, whether or not the disaster is strictly 'legal' in nature." Do you agree that we should hold lawyers to such a standard?

3. Should lawyers be charged with shouldering both legal issues and business issues? What are the malpractice implications if lawyers are held to such a standard?

4. What do you see as your role in connection with representing the founders, Joan and Michael, in connection with their new business, SoftCo? In considering this question, the following observations may be helpful:

> Reading the most recent *Inc.* magazine (June 2010 edition) I glanced over the *Street Smarts* section. For those of you not familiar with this section it is where veteran entrepreneur, Norm Brodsky, answers questions submitted by various businesses and entrepreneurs. Most of the time it focuses on such primal entrepreneurial issues as how to compete better in a local market or the best strategy for running operations. In the latest version however, there was a question submitted by a lawyer (hopefully this lawyer and I are not the only two lawyers who read this magazine). The gentleman asked how entrepreneurs can get the most benefit and the best value from their [lawyers].
>
> Before I read Norm's answer I reread the question again and focused on "benefit" and "value." In most businesses and professions the definitions of these two words are well established and known. In the law, however, it appears we are in a time where these two concepts are being debated and fleshed out. Certainly the traditional services of a lawyer are well understood and arguably therefore so are the accompanying benefits and values. We know the benefit of having a will drawn up and its value both in terms of cost in the immediate term and in the long term by having clarity over disposition of property. In the corporate sense we know the benefit of having our lawyers review potential transactions for liabilities or outline a proactive sexual harassment training/avoidance program. The value represents both the cost of the legal services and the prospective avoidance of future legal liability.
>
> What happens though when a business faces an issue that touches both upon a legal issue as well as a business issue? After reaching this point in thinking I returned to the article to read Norm's answer. In short, Norm states quite clearly and emphatically that lawyers should stick to giving legal advice and not business advice. He goes on further to state that business advice when given by a lawyer is almost always bad advice. The point — there is no benefit or value to seeking business advice from a lawyer. This is fairly damning language about the legal profession by a well-regarded businessperson so I took Norm's point seriously and not as a cynical pot shot at lawyers (considering he is one himself).
>
> So can lawyers ever give sound and useful business advice? Or better yet, where is the line drawn between legal advice and business advice? Is it not foreseeable, if not unavoidable, to have a scenario where a legal question directly informs a business decision or strategy? Or vice versa?
>
> To use a medical analogy; when a person goes to their doctor should they only listen to "medical" advice? How can one determine what is medical advice versus other types of advice, such as lifestyle advice? When a doctor says to a patient "you should exercise more often" — is that medical or lifestyle advice? Thus in the business context when a lawyer says to the entrepreneur that they should be protecting their assets, is this legal advice or business advice or is it both?

A lawyer is in many ways like a doctor — they have seen many different patients/ clients with similar problems and therefore have a perspective that the individual may not possess. There is value in this experience — though it may not directly apply to every situation. How one evaluates and considers advice is the key. Just because advice is given does not mean that it should be followed. It is worth remembering that lawyers dispensing legal advice may not always be 100% correct but that should not make their advice of no benefit or value. In fact getting a lawyer to proclaim that their legal advice is 100% accurate may be a Herculean task. Nevertheless their advice is considered valuable.

I do agree with Mr. Brodsky when he states that most lawyers, by training and habit, think differently than business people. I do not agree, however, that therefore their business advice should be avoided. As always it comes down to the individual lawyer — some may be great with business while many if not most may not be (despite what they think). Certainly the profession can and should move towards a more business capable mindset. . . .

So while Mr. Brodsky's advice should be respected, it is somewhat shallow in that it does not recognize that the two types of advice are not so neatly decoupled and isolated from one another. In fact, as many businesses come to recognize, the challenges that are most perplexing and worrisome are the ones in which business and legal concerns collide. In these situations I would argue it unwise to forgo any type of advice — that said it should all be weighed and evaluated. In the end, though, most businesses, especially entrepreneurs have to rely on something even more innate yet powerful — [their] own street smarts.

Joshua Kubicki, *The Thin Line Between Legal & Business Advice*, JOSHUA P. KUBICKI, BUSINESS DESIGN FOR LEGAL MATTERS BLOG (June 7, 2010), *available at* http://www .joshuakubicki.com/blog/legaltransformationblog.com/2010/thin-line-between-legal -businessadvice.html.

5. ***SEC's Professional Responsibility Rules***. The Robins article (excerpted above) refers to the professional responsibility rules that were promulgated by the SEC pursuant to the legislative mandate set forth by Congress as part of the Sarbanes-Oxley Act of 2002. We examine the scope of the SEC's rules in Chapter 4, as part of our discussion of the federal securities laws, and revisit this article to examine the author's suggestions for revising the ABA's rules. This article also raises an important perspective on the role of the lawyer as a transaction planner, a topic that we revisit in the remaining chapters of this casebook, as the issue surfaces in connection with the various stages that are part of the life cycle of a financing transaction.

6. ***Lawyers "Breaking the Deal."*** In thinking about the role of the lawyer in completing a business transaction, such as the capital-raising transaction that is the focus of this casebook, consider the following observations penned by well-known corporate law scholars:

> One of the interesting and significant aspects of the process of drafting [business agreements] has to do with the concern often expressed by experienced lawyers that their efforts might "spoil the deal." One of the most important functions of the [transactional] lawyer is to look beyond the days of heady optimism and mutual

good will that [generally] characterize the initiation of a business venture. . . . [Thus, in drafting business agreements, the lawyer must anticipate that, as the business grows, the needs of the parties will change, as well as the nature of the business problems to be encountered over time. This means that it is quite foreseeable that the parties to the agreement will confront issues of business strategy and the like on which they cannot agree. It is at this point — when these issues and problems later surface — that the rules set forth in the relevant agreement become vitally important. However, as every experienced corporate lawyer well knows, at the time that the agreement was originally being prepared,] [t]here are choices about how these rules should be drafted and many lawyers consider that they should explain those choices to their clients. But this gets tricky, for if the [parties] start worrying too much about the problems that might arise [in the future] and become excessively concerned about the difficulty of solving them, they may become overly anxious and walk away from a [business] venture that would have been good for them. . . .

* * *

Some lawyers think it is their responsibility not only to try to raise all the significant issues with which their clients may be confronted in the future but also to be sure that the clients understand those issues. Others will tend to pay less attention to such matters, fearing, as suggested, that it is too easy for the parties, because of their unfamiliarity with the law, or with business, to exaggerate the significance of the problems and, consequently, to forgo a business opportunity that the lawyer thinks they ought not to forgo. This kind of lawyer may express the idea by saying that he did not want to "spoil the deal." Other lawyers will tend more often to think that if raising issues and pointing to problems kills a deal then it deserves to die. Obviously there are no formulas to tell the lawyer how to act with respect to this basic issue of client-handling strategy. No two deals, no two sets of clients, and no two lawyers are alike. There is no widely agreed upon "correct" approach.

WILLIAM A. KLEIN, JOHN C. COFFEE, AND FRANK PARTNOY, BUSINESS ORGANIZATION AND FINANCE 66-67 (11th ed. 2010). *Query:* What do you think is the proper role for the lawyer to adopt in connection with drafting business agreements on behalf of the lawyer's clients? What do you think is the proper role for you in connection with representing the founders, Joan and Michael, in connection with the launch of their new business, SoftCo?

7. *What Is the Role of the Lawyer?* For another closely related perspective on the role of the lawyer practicing in a transactional setting, consider the following observations by another well-known commentator:

> What do business lawyers *really* do? . . .

* * *

> Clients have their own, often quite uncharitable, view of what business lawyers do. In an extreme version, business lawyers are perceived as evil sorcerers who use their special skills and professional magic to relieve clients of their possessions. Kurt Vonnegut makes the point in an amusing way. A law student is told by his favorite professor that, to get ahead in the practice of law, "a lawyer should be

looking for situations where large amounts of money are about to change hands."* . . .

Clients frequently advance other more charitable but still negative views of the business lawyer that also should be familiar to most practitioners. Business lawyers are seen at best as a transaction cost, part of a system of wealth redistribution from clients to lawyers; legal fees represent a tax on business transactions to provide an income maintenance program for lawyers. At worst, lawyers are seen as deal killers whose continual raising of obstacles, without commensurate effort at finding solutions, ultimately causes transactions to collapse under their own weight. . . .

Lawyers, to be sure, do not share these harsh evaluations of their role. . . .

Ronald J. Gilson, *Value Creation by Business Lawyers: Legal Skills and Asset Pricing*, 94 YALE L. J. 239, 241-242 (1984) (emphasis in original). *Query*: What do you think? Is the role of the corporate lawyer to serve as a "transaction cost engineer"?

3. Lawyers That Invest in Their Clients

The practice of transactional law is itself a business. As a transactional lawyer, you will charge a fee for your legal services, and the client will be expected to pay these fees. However, this business model is itself fraught with ethical dilemmas that are just an inherent part of practicing law. As a threshold matter, you will not be paid if your client does not have the financial resources to pay its bills, including your invoice for services rendered. How do you determine whether founders (such as Joan and Michael) will be able to pay for your legal services? Is this something that you should take into account in deciding whether to take on a new client?

A closely related question is whether it is appropriate for the lawyer to take an ownership interest in the new business (i.e., stock in a new corporation) in lieu of paying fees for the lawyer's services. New start-up businesses frequently will ask the lawyer to accept this arrangement for the very practical reason that it conserves the cash resources of the new business and thereby allows these financial resources to be devoted to the more pressing matter of getting the business operations up and running. However, from the lawyer's perspective, this client request raises a host of practical and ethical concerns that are explored in the materials below. The following article provides general background on these compensation arrangements and highlights the range of business, legal, ethical, and practical issues inherent in such arrangements.

Young J. Kim & Jeffrey L. Braker
Taking Stock in Your Client: Strengthening the Client Relationship and Avoiding Pitfalls

BUS. L. NEWS 1 *(Issue 1, 2008)*

Beginning in the 1990's, led by Silicon Valley firms and fueled by the rising stock market, attorneys started investing in their clients in a strategic way. These firms used

---

* K. VONNGEGUT, GOD BLESS YOU, MR. ROSEWATER 17-18 (1965).

equity investment not only as a means of getting their fees paid (and, in some cases, of achieving considerable wealth), but also to help drive their relationship with their clients and demonstrate that they were not just attorneys, but key business partners. While this practice lulled during the stock market decline, it is again becoming relevant, with the strong market and the emergence of Web 2.0 and other companies showing explosive growth. Taking stock in a client, if done in conformity with the California Rules of Professional Conduct and best corporate practices, has the potential to strengthen an attorney's bond with the client and can be perceived as a vote of confidence in the client's business prospects.[1] There is anecdotal evidence that attorneys who accommodate their clients by forgoing or deferring legal fees build loyal followings by their clients. Indeed, for start up clients with limited cash resources but a promising future, granting equity compensation in lieu of or as a supplement to cash legal fees may be a significant or sometimes the only way to access quality legal representation.[2]

Types of Investments

An attorney may acquire stock in a client by purchasing shares either directly through the attorney's firm or through the firm's investment vehicle.[3] He may purchase stock at the initial formation of the client or at various subsequent stages during the life of the company, such as during the venture capital or private equity round, during the IPO, or after the client becomes a mature public company. The types of investments range from plain vanilla common stock to preferred stock, debt, or any other form of securities.

The attorney may also acquire the client stock as part of the attorney's compensation for performing legal services to the client. These types of alternate billing arrangements take many forms, but include the following:

- The attorney receives warrants[4] to purchase common stock in addition to her regular fees or in exchange for agreeing to discount her regular fees for some period of time. Warrants are typically fully vested and have set terms ranging from three to ten years. The warrant may have a "net exercise" provision,

---

1. For the purposes of this article, we assume the client is a C corporation, which is the most common scenario likely to be faced by an attorney considering investing in a client. Many of the points raised in this article will be applicable to an investment in non-corporate entities, such as limited liability companies and partnerships, but a specific discussion of an investment in different entities is beyond the scope of this article.

2. There are a myriad of distinct issues raised in connection with the issuance of stock or stock options to in-house lawyers, but these are outside the scope of this article.

3. The focus of this article is the direct relationship between the client and an individual attorney. Many potentially complex partnership, fiduciary, tax, and related issues are raised in situations where a law firm invests in a client. Those issues are also beyond the scope of this article.

4. A warrant, much like a stock option, gives the holder the right to purchase a specified number of shares of stock for a price set at the time of issuance of the warrant. The key terms to be agreed upon are the number of shares the warrant is exercisable into, the exercise price, the term of the warrant and the vesting features, if any. While options granted to employees are typically subject to some period of vesting, a warrant issued to an attorney may be fully vested at issuance. A warrant expires after a specified period, following which the holder cannot exercise his right to purchase the underlying shares. [In Chapter 6, we describe the use of warrants in more detail, as part of our discussion of issues related to the use of equity based compensation. — EDS.]

permitting the holder to exercise the warrant without using any cash and also allowing the holder to "tack" the holding period of the warrant onto that of the underlying shares for purposes of the Rule 144 holding period.

- The client issues shares of its stock to the attorney in lieu of payment of cash fees. The issuance may be at the outset of the engagement or in exchange for fees already incurred. In some instances, the client may have the right to buy back the stock under certain conditions, such as if the attorney ceases working with the client within a certain period.

- The attorney agrees to defer billing until the client receives its first round of financing, in return for which the attorney receives stock or warrants. The stock or warrants may be for common stock at the founder price or preferred stock issued in the first round of financing.

Before investing in a client or entering into an equity billing arrangement, the attorney should undertake a careful analysis of the client, its management, and its business prospects to determine whether the client is a suitable candidate.[5]

Professional Responsibility and Ethical Considerations

A prerequisite for investing in a client is the attorney's strict compliance with the California Rules of Professional Conduct and a careful examination of whether an investment would be consistent with the attorney's fiduciary duties and role as a disinterested and trusted advisor to the client. Under Rule 3-300 of the California Rules of Professional Conduct, an attorney may not invest in a client unless the following conditions are met:

- The investment and its terms must be fair and reasonable to the client;
- The terms of the investment must be fully disclosed in writing to the client in a manner that can be reasonably understood by the client;
- The client is advised in writing that the client may seek the advice of independent counsel of the client's choice and the client is given a reasonable opportunity to do so; and
- The client consents in writing to the terms of the investment.

In general, the attorney has the burden of proof of showing that the terms of the investment are fair and reasonable[8] and courts have subjected transactions between an attorney and client to strict scrutiny to ensure fairness. Determining whether a particular investment is fair and reasonable is fact intensive, however, and must necessarily be undertaken on a case by case basis. Moreover, in certain instances, courts have held that rule 3-300 applies to transactions between an attorney and a former client.

The penalties for not complying with the requirements set forth in rule 3-300 are severe. In addition to being subject to discipline by the state bar, courts have invalidated transactions in which the attorney failed to strictly adhere to the rule. In *Passante v.*

---

5. For example, a closely held company with no realistic prospects of a liquidity event such as an acquisition or public offering may not be a suitable candidate for investment or equity billing.

8. *Beery v. State Bar* (1987) 43 Cal. 3d 802, 812-13 (citing *Felton v. Le Breton* (1891) 92 Cal. 457, 469).

McWilliam, the Court of Appeal ordered an attorney to forfeit $32 million of client stock for failing to advise the client in writing that it had the right to seek the advice of independent counsel, among other reasons.[11] Notably, the client does not have to suffer any actual harm in order for an attorney to be subject to discipline for violating rule 3-300.

In order to comply with this rule and its fiduciary obligations generally, the attorney should prepare a written stock purchase agreement or warrant documenting the transaction, and a separate letter or engagement agreement clearly describing the material terms of the investment and advising the client to seek the advice of independent counsel.[13] The client should be given a reasonable period of time to consider the agreement and an opportunity to review it with independent counsel before signing it. An attorney's law partner or associate is not considered to be independent counsel.

The attorney should also disclose to the client the extent to which she believes her exercise of independent judgment with respect to the client may be affected by her equity investment and should clearly enumerate all of the actual and potential conflicts that might reasonably arise from her investment. Bar opinions have, as a general rule, recognized that the interests of an attorney who holds stock in a client are aligned with the company's because both seek to increase the company's value for the shareholders. For example, some grants of stock (or stock options) are either contingent upon, or in some ways measured based on, the financing to be achieved by the client. In such cases, the attorney will need to be attentive to the possibility that his interest in such financing (such as perhaps the attorney's personal interest in "getting the deal done" and receiving the stock) may cloud his ability to render independent professional advice to make the requisite disclosure in connection with an investment transaction. It would be prudent for the attorney to describe in his conflicts letter to be signed by his client the various scenarios in which his rendering of legal advice might be construed as less than completely objective and impartial as a result of his holding the stock.

Taking stock in a client clearly raises ethical issues of fairness and conflict of interest, among others, but the issue facing an attorney is whether those issues are materially heightened by holding stock in a client as opposed to issues that arise in the normal course of an attorney's representation. For example, an attorney may risk alienating his other clients if the attorney's investment is in a competitor of his other clients. For the most part, an attorney will have to judge each situation on a case by case basis with a view to complying with his fiduciary obligations to exercise his best independent professional judgment on the client's behalf.

In addition, if the investment is made in lieu of fees or in exchange for discounted fees, the attorney will have to comply with rule 4-200 of the California Rules of Professional Conduct which prohibits illegal or unconscionable fees. Rule 4-200 sets out a non-exclusive list of relevant factors for determining whether a fee is reasonable although the determination of whether a fee is unconscionable is based on all of the facts

---

11. *Passante v. McWilliam* (1997) 53 Cal. App. 4th 1240.

13. The California Supreme Court in *Rose v. State Bar* (1989) 49 Cal.3d 646, has made clear that merely telling the client that it *could* seek the advice of independent counsel is insufficient; the attorney must affirmatively advise the client to do so. *Id.* at p. 663.

and circumstances existing at the time the investment is made.[18] Among the additional factors to be considered in the case of equity billing are (a) the present and anticipated future liquidity of the client's stock; (b) the present and anticipated value of the stock given the business risk associated with the client's business; (c) whether the stock is subject to restrictions; and (d) the amount of stock given and whether it gives the attorney voting control.[19] The determination of whether the equity fee is reasonable should be made at the time of the investment, including the uncertainty at such time that the client will receive funding or other milestone or will even survive. In setting a reasonable fee, attorneys should be careful not to inadvertently set the valuation of the client prior to an equity round, as doing so may place the client at a disadvantage in negotiating the valuation and other terms with the next round of investors.

* * *

Corporate Law Considerations

The attorney needs to ensure that the issuance of the client stock, like any other client issuance of securities, adheres to all corporate governance formalities. The issuance of the client stock must be duly authorized by the company's board of directors and should be memorialized in a written document, such as a stock purchase or subscription agreement.[22] Board authorization should be reasonably contemporaneous with the agreement between the parties to avoid any backdating or other timing issues. With some exceptions, the issuance of stock in consideration for services may be made only for services actually rendered, and not for future services.[23] Hence, the attorney must be careful in the written agreement to make clear that the grant of the client stock will be issued in consideration for services already rendered. He also has to ensure that adequate consideration exists at the time the agreement is entered into, for instance by reciting that the stock grant is being made in consideration for continuing legal services.[24] If the agreement to grant stock is solely for future services, then such actual grant may not be effective (or the shares deemed fully paid) until such services are actually performed.

---

18. Rule 4-200(B).

19. Ethics Advisory Opinion Comm., Utah State Bar, Op. 98-13 (1998) (citing Model Rules of Prof'l Conduct Rule 1.5).

22. *See* [Cal.] Corp. Code, §409.

23. *Id.* [*But see* MBCA §6.21(b), which allows future services (i.e., contracts to work in future) to serve as valid consideration in connection with the issuance of shares — EDS.]

24. An attorney should ensure that adequate consideration for the issuance of stock exists at the time the agreement between the client and attorney is concluded, for example, by agreeing to issue the stock after the attorney has begun providing services or in consideration for the attorney's engagement itself. If the client agrees, after the fact, to grant stock to the attorney for services already provided, then a court may invalidate the grant for lack of adequate consideration. *See Passante v. McWilliam, supra,* 53 Cal. App. 4th at pp. 1247-48 ("past consideration cannot support a contract") and *Chaganti v. 12 Phone International, Inc.* (N.D. Cal. July 23, 2007) 2007 WL 2122654.

Securities Law Considerations

Because the attorney presumably has access to significant knowledge of the client's business and other information and owes a fiduciary obligation to the client, the attorney must be vigilant in complying with both the federal and California securities laws in connection with the purchase and sale of the client stock. Unless the issuance of the stock is registered or qualified under both federal and California laws, the attorney will need to ensure that the issuance transaction falls under one of the exemptions. Such exempt transaction will almost always be required for taking stock in a company that is not publicly held. Moreover, the attorney will need to again comply with both federal and state securities laws if he wishes to resell his stock. If the client is a publicly traded company or is undertaking an IPO, then the following are some of the additional considerations the attorney will need to comply with:

- Federal securities laws make it unlawful to engage in insider trading or fail to disclose material facts or make false or misleading statements in connection with the purchase or sale of any security.[28] Because the attorney quite often has access to material nonpublic information regarding the client as a result of his legal representation, the attorney must exercise extra care in the purchase or sale of the client securities to avoid violating insider trading and anti-fraud provisions of federal and state securities laws. The client may have insider trading policies for its employees and services providers, including its attorneys, mandating black out periods during which the attorney may not trade in stock of the client.
- In a public offering of securities, the federal regulations governing the registration statement for such offering may require the lawyers representing the corporate issuer and the underwriter to disclose their stock ownership in the corporate issuer.[30]
- If the attorney's ownership stake in the client causes him to actively participate in the affairs and decisions of the client, then there is the potential risk that the attorney may be deemed to be a "controlling person" of the client under the federal securities laws, which may subject the attorney to joint and several liability to the same extent as the client.[31]
- Similar to any other shareholder of the client, federal securities regulations require certain filings for directors, officers, and significant shareholders.[32]

Professional Liability Insurance Considerations

Some professional liability insurance carriers may deny coverage for any losses sustained by an attorney where the attorney has any ownership interest in a client, or

---

28. *See* 17 C.F.R. 240.10b-5 and 17 C.F.R. 240.10b-5-1(b).

30. The registration statement may be required to provide a brief statement of the interest of any counsel for the registrant, underwriters or selling security holders, if the counsel is to receive a "substantial interest" in the issuer in connection with the offering. An interest is not considered to be a "substantial interest" if the fair market value does not exceed $50,000. (*See* 17 C.F.R. 229.509.)

31. *See* 15 U.S.C. §77o (Section 15 of the Securities Act) and 15 U.S.C. §78t (Section 20 of the Securities Exchange Act of 1934, as amended (the "Exchange Act")).

32. *See* Forms 3, 4, and 5 under the Exchange Act. *See* 17 C.F.R. 240.16a-2, 17 C.F.R. 249.103 through 17 C.F.R. 249.105. *See also* Schedule 13D and 13G under the Exchange Act. *See* 17 C.F.R. 240. 13d-1.

an interest beyond a specified maximum percentage.[33] An attorney should carefully review his professional liability insurance policy before taking stock in a client to ensure that doing so would not adversely affect his coverage. Moreover, an attorney's violation of rule 3-300 may itself be sufficient to conclusively establish her liability for legal malpractice.[34]

Tax Considerations

An attorney should be mindful that receiving stock may have substantial tax consequences depending on how the billing arrangement is structured.[35]

* * *

Valuation of the Client Stock

How many shares of the client stock, and at what price, can the attorney purchase? The prohibition on unconscionable legal fees, the conflicts inherent in entering into a transaction in which both the client and the attorney have an interest, the corporate prohibition on issuing stock for future services, as well as potential tax consequences to the attorney, often make structuring the stock for fees arrangement a tricky exercise. Excessive stock being granted at the initial engagement of the attorney and before any substantial services have been rendered may be subject to challenge for being unconscionable or being tantamount to stock for future services. Moreover, the purchase price of the client stock substantially below the price at which the client has issued its stock to other investors may be subject to a similar scrutiny. Such risks can be even more pronounced if the amount of stock based compensation is determined by certain measurements such as percentage ownership of a client or a percentage of future financing amount. Again, a written agreement detailing the terms of any issuance is imperative to protect the interests of both the client and the attorney.

Conclusion

When accomplished with the appropriate degree of caution and attention to the canons of the legal profession, taking stock in a client may strengthen the bonds of the attorney-client relationship and provide access to potentially lucrative investment opportunities. Because the attorney will inevitably be expected by the client to understand the pitfalls such an arrangement entails, however, it is incumbent upon the attorney to correctly navigate the various regulatory and ethical pitfalls.

---

33. Halman, *Noncoverage for Client Investment* (June 2002) California Lawyer.

34. *See Clearstream Communs., Inc. v. Murray* (E.D. Cal. Jan. 13, 2003) U.S. Dist. Lexis 27101.

35. A detailed discussion of the tax consequences of investing in a client is beyond the scope of this article. For a comprehensive discussion of this topic, *see* Banoff, "*1, 61, 83, Pay Me with Your E-qui-ty*": *Tax Problems Facing Service Firms (and Their Partners) Who Receive Stock or Options in Lieu of Cash Fees* (2001) 79 Taxes 3. Furthermore, the tax consequences for partnerships of the receipt of equity and warrants can be expected to be very different from those described in this article.

1. The authors of the preceding article focused primarily on California law concerning the professional responsibility rules that apply in the context of a lawyer taking stock in a client in lieu of fees. However, this issue is by no means peculiar to California. The practice of taking stock in lieu of fees is widespread and the issues that the authors have identified in connection with this practice are issues that must be addressed as a matter of local law no matter in which state the lawyer practices.

2. It bears mentioning that many of the issues raised in the preceding article are analyzed in more detail in the remaining chapters of this casebook. Most notably, we discuss the implications of the SEC's new professional responsibility rules as part of our discussion of the federal securities laws in Chapter 4, and we analyze the compensation-related issues in Chapter 6.

3. What criteria do (should?) lawyers use in making the decision whether to accept stock in lieu of fees? For example, what criteria would you want to consider in deciding whether to accept stock in Joan and Michael's new business, SoftCo, in lieu of cash payment of the legal fees to be incurred in connection with organizing this new business? Would your decision be influenced by whether Joan and Michael plan to seek financing from friends and family, or alternatively, from professional investors such as venture capitalists? If so, why? In thinking about this decision, you may want to consider the differing viewpoints summarized in the following article.

The decision whether to take stock in a client company as compensation (either in whole or in part) for performing legal services on behalf of a new corporate client is often referred to as an "equity billing arrangement." Entrepreneurs, such as Joan and Michael, who have a promising idea for a new high-tech product, eventually will seek the advice of counsel to help them set up a new corporation that will develop and sell their new idea for the "Next Big Thing." In the case of lawyers who agree to represent start-up businesses, such as SoftCo, the entrepreneurs very often will explain that they do not have the cash resources to pay the lawyer's legal fees. In such a case, the lawyer often will be asked to accept an "equity billing arrangement" in lieu of cash compensation. When faced with such a request, how should the lawyer respond? The following essay explores the ethical and business issues that face the lawyer when presented with a request from a start-up business to accept an "equity billing arrangement."

Therese Maynard
Ethics for Business Lawyers Representing Start-Up Companies
11 Wake Forest J. Bus. & Intell. Prop. L. 401 (2011)

Starting in the 1990s, it became an increasingly common practice for lawyers, particularly Silicon Valley lawyers, to take an equity investment in the business ventures of their new clients.[1] While the practice lulled somewhat in the aftermath of the burst of the dot-com bubble, it is becoming relevant again as the market for stocks of high-tech companies[2] has rebounded in the wake of recovery from the recent Great Recession. . . .

It had long been the view of the legal community that such equity investments present conflicts of interest between lawyers and their business clients, which would then trigger certain requirements under the relevant rules of professional responsibility.[3] While it is widely regarded today that the lawyer's equity investment in the new client can be structured in a manner that is in compliance with the lawyer's professional responsibility requirements, this Essay asks the more profound (and perhaps more provocative) question, namely: Do these equity investments, particularly investments in growth-oriented companies that compete for venture capital financing, in fact present a conflict of interest between the lawyer and the new client corporation?

This Essay explores the ethical issues as well as the general business considerations that arise in connection with the practice of taking stock in lieu of payment of legal fees in cash, which is otherwise the customary billing practice for legal services. As described in more detail below, many academics and experienced venture capital lawyers believe that taking stock in a client presents significant potential to strengthen the lawyer's relationship with the client. At the other end of the spectrum, there are others within the legal community (both academics and practicing lawyers) who just as strongly believe that these equity investment arrangements significantly undermine time-honored ideals that have long guided the legal profession in determining how lawyers

---

1. In 1999, the well-known Silicon Valley law firm Wilson Sonsini Goodrich & Rosati ("Wilson Sonsini") took stock as part of its compensation for legal services rendered in connection with the initial public offering ("IPO") transactions of thirty-three of the fifty-three companies that the firm represented in IPO transactions that year. To illustrate just how lucrative these arrangements can be for law firms (and their owners), it has been reported that Wilson Sonsini's holdings in twenty-four of those fifty-three companies were valued in excess of $1 million *each* at the close of the first day of trading. Debra Baker, *Who Wants to Be a Millionaire?* 86 A.B.A. J. 36, 37 (2000); *see also* Robert C. Kahrl & Anthony Jacono, *"Rush to Riches": The Rules of Ethics and Greed Control in the Dot.com World*, 2 MINN. INTELL. PROP. REV. 51, 54 n.1 (2001); Peter D. Zeughauser, *The New Math: Associate Pay Raises Will Have a Domino Effect on the Entire Legal Industry. Clients Will Build In-House Empires, and Many Firms Will Collapse*, 23 LEGAL TIMES, no. 18, May 1, 2000, at 46 ("Wilson Sonsini Goodrich & Rosati's investment partnership took in $88 million in first-day gains on its top three IPOs last year; the average Wilson Sonsini partner owns a $2 million share in the investment partnership."); and Sharon Mary Mathew, Comment, *Stock-Based Compensation for Legal Services: Resurrecting the Ethical Dilemma*, 42 SANTA CLARA L. REV. 1227, 1229-30 (2002). This investment practice is not limited to Wilson Sonsini. Indeed, Wilson Sonsini's cross-town rival, Cooley LLP (then named Cooley Godward LLP), also reportedly made lavish returns on its equity investments in law firm clients. *See* Baker at 37; *see generally* Donald C. Langevoort, *When Lawyers and Law Firms Invest in Their Corporate Clients' Stock*, 80 WASH. U. L.Q. 569 (2010).

2. For purposes of this Essay, I assume that the new business client is to be organized as a corporation, which is the most common scenario likely to be faced by an attorney considering investing in an emerging growth business that will be competing for professional venture capital financing. Although many of the points that I will describe in this Essay will be applicable to an equity investment in a non-corporate business entity, such as a limited liability company or a partnership, any specific discussion of an investment in these other forms of business entities is beyond the scope of this Essay.

3. For purposes of this Essay, I will rely on the ABA's Model Rules of Professional Conduct to provide the relevant guidelines for the lawyer to determine whether the proposed equity investment in the new client corporation is undertaken in a manner that is consistent with the lawyer's professional responsibilities to the new client. *See generally* MODEL RULES OF PROF'L CONDUCT ("Model Rules").

should go about fulfilling their ethical and fiduciary obligations to their business clients. This Essay [first discusses the professional responsibility concerns associated with equity billing arrangements] and then proceeds to describe the [traditional views within the legal community as to the] advantages and disadvantages of these fee arrangements. . . .

* * *

III. Professional Responsibility and Ethical Considerations

The very essence of the attorney-client relationship rests on the long-standing, fundamental premise that the client depends on the lawyer to provide sound legal advice and independent judgment that is not tainted by concerns regarding the lawyer's personal financial well-being.[9] As a result, the long-standing practice of lawyers has been to avoid taking stock in their corporate clients in lieu of fees.[10] In fact, until quite recently, even Silicon Valley law firms avoided making equity investments in their clients. One rather high-profile example of such traditional reticence to take stock in law firm clients in lieu of fees was recounted by Bill Fenwick, one of the founders of the well-known Palo Alto, California, law firm of Fenwick & West, who turned down shares in Apple Computer's IPO:

> [W]e incorporated Apple Computer and represented them exclusively for a number of years. At one point, at a very young point in their development, they wanted us to take $50,000 off of our fees in stock. And, quite frankly, I had come from the East

---

9. The history of billing practices within the legal profession has been succinctly described as follows:

> In early Rome, legal advocates contributed their services free of charge and laws were passed against the peddling of legal services for monetary gain. Even after Emperor Claudius issued a decree allowing for the payment of legal fees up to a maximum amount, an attorney did not have a right to collect those fees if the client declined to pay. Although attorneys' fees in the United States are definitely a matter of course and both blessed and prescribed by law, attorneys, especially attorneys at large law firms, are still loath to discuss the matter of fees with clients. Although most lawyers have new clients sign representation agreements, lawyers prefer not to focus on fee matters when counseling clients, much like a physician treats a patient in an examination room without any mention of the cost of the office visit. Because of the desire to be part of a profession, not a vocation, many attorneys in this century have avoided talking about fees until the end of a representation and then simply have sent a bill for "legal services rendered."
>
> In the latter half of [the twentieth] century, hourly billing became the convention among most U.S. attorneys. The practice has been an integral part of life at traditional law firms where leveraged young associates, hoping to one day be partners, used to toil for the benefit of current partners on work steadily and loyally provided by long-term clients.

Christine Hurt, *Counselor, Gatekeeper, Shareholder, Thief: Why Attorneys Who Invest in Their Clients in a Post-Enron World Are "Selling Out," Not "Buying In,"* 64 OHIO ST. L. J. 897, 902 (2003).

10. *See* John C. Coffee, Jr., *The Lawyer as Gatekeeper: Legal Ethics, Professional Independence, and the New Compensation*, COLUM. L. SCH. REP., Spring 2000, at 44 ("For the thirty-odd years that I have practiced law, New York firms have resisted stock as payment for legal services, viewing the practice as suspect at best."), *quoted in* John S. Dzienkowski & Robert J. Peroni, *The Decline in Lawyer Independence: Lawyer Equity Investments in Clients*, 81 TEX. L. REV. 405, 408 n. 10 (2002). It bears mentioning that the same ethical issues arise regardless of whether the ownership interest is acquired directly by the individual lawyer, or alternatively, by the lawyer's firm, or (in taking advantage of an investment opportunity offered to the lawyer) by an investment partnership controlled by the individual lawyer or by members of the lawyer's firm.

and . . . there are a host of problems you've got to deal with if you're going to do that. Well, that $50,000 that they wanted us to take in stock was worth $12 million when they went public, so that is a pretty humbling experience.[11]

This long-standing perspective on equity billing arrangements began to erode in the 1990s and quickly became the subject of numerous lawyer requests for guidance from their bar ethics committees as to the propriety of such fee arrangements.[12] Ultimately, in 2000, the American Bar Association ("ABA") issued its guidance under ABA Rule 1.8 (the ABA's general rule on conflicts of interest with respect to current clients) concerning equity billing arrangements.[14] Without a doubt, those who object to the use of equity billing arrangements largely base their objections on the ethical implications of these fee arrangements.

The ABA's 2000 Ethics Opinion emphasized that, at the very minimum, the lawyer considering taking stock in lieu of fees must ensure that the lawyer's investment in the client complies with the requirements of the relevant professional responsibility rules. Under the terms of ABA Rule 1.8 (as interpreted in the ABA's 2000 Ethics Opinion), the following conditions must be satisfied:

1. The investment and its terms must be *fair and reasonable* to the client;
2. The terms of the investment must be *fully disclosed in writing* to the client in a manner that can be reasonably understood by the client;
3. The client must be advised in writing that the client may seek the *advice of independent counsel* of the client's choice and the client must be given a reasonable opportunity to do so; and
4. The client gives *informed consent in a signed writing* to the essential terms of the investment and the lawyer's role in the investment transaction.

In the Comments to Rule 1.8, the ABA explained the basis for the Rule's requirements by observing that a "lawyer's legal skill and training, together with the relationship of trust and confidence between lawyer and client, create the possibility of overreaching when the lawyer participates in a business, property, or financial transaction with a

---

11. Bill Fenwick, *Remarks at the American Lawyer Media Roundtable: Building a Technology Law Practice: Let's Make This Equitable — How Flexible Must Firms Be on Pricing?* (Aug. 1999), at WL 8/1999 Recorder SF S5, *quoted in* Dzienkowski & Peroni, *supra* note 10, at 413 n. 24. For a more detailed description of equity billing arrangements used by many high-profile Silicon Valley law firms, *see* Kevin Miller, *Lawyers as Venture Capitalists: An Economic Analysis of Law Firms That Invest in Their Clients*, 13 HARV. J.L. & TECH. 435 (2000).

12. *See* Barbara S. Gillers, *Law Firm as Investor: Ethical and Other Considerations*, 1259 Pract. L. Inst./ Corp. 457 (2001) (collecting cites to the views of various bar ethics committees); *see also* Dzienkowski & Peroni, *supra* note 10, at 461-77.

14. *See, e.g.*, ABA Comm. on Ethics & Prof'l Responsibility, Formal Op. 00-418 (2000) [hereinafter 2000 Ethics Opinion]. In its 2000 Ethics Opinion, the ABA observed in a footnote that it was "aware that sometimes the lawyer will ask the corporation to issue her a percentage of the shares initially issued to the founders as a condition to the lawyer agreeing to become counsel to the new enterprise." *Id.* at n. 16. While the ABA declined to opine as to the "ethical propriety of the practice," other bar association ethics committees strongly discourage such practice. *See, e.g.*, *Taking Stock in Your Client as Legal Fees or as an Investment*, 2000 N.H. Bar Ass'n Ethics Comm. Op. 2 [hereinafter NHBA 2000 Ethics Opinion]. This Essay does not address the situation where the lawyer *insists* that the client issue stock in the new corporation to the lawyer as a condition to representing the new business as its lawyer.

client." Because of this possibility for overreaching, the courts, as a general rule, will strictly scrutinize the terms of transactions between lawyers and their clients to ensure fairness, with the lawyer usually carrying the burden to demonstrate that the terms of the lawyer's investment in the client is "fair and reasonable" to the client.

Accordingly, under ABA Rule 1.8, there are two main ethical issues that the lawyer must resolve at the outset of a business relationship in connection with a proposed equity billing arrangement. The first is whether the size of the fee is fair and reasonable:

> Given the variability of future outcomes at the time when the parties agree on a fee arrangement, no simple rules [as to the size of the lawyer's fee] are practical. Hence, the question largely becomes one of informed written consent by the client, which, at the very least, imposes upon the lawyer a duty of candor. When the client is less sophisticated, many of the bar opinions . . . require the lawyer to urge the client to seek separate legal representation about the fee arrangement. . . .

* * *

> The [second] main requirement [that must be satisfied pursuant to Rule 1.8] for representation under an [equity billing] arrangement is that the lawyer must reasonably believe that the fee arrangement will not adversely affect the exercise of his professional judgment.[15]

With respect to the first requirement under ABA Rule 1.8, whether the fee is reasonable to the client, there arises the issue of hindsight bias. That is to say, even though ABA Rule 1.8 requires that the fairness and reasonableness of the transaction between the lawyer and client be assessed *ex ante* — at the time the parties entered into the arrangement and based on the information available to the parties at that time — judges will often take into account the actual large payout to the lawyer *without* also taking into account the extremely low probability of its occurrence.[16] . . .

* * *

To minimize the risk that a fee paid in stock will appear unreasonable if the business should ultimately succeed (and become wildly successful . . .), the ABA's 2000 Ethics Opinion recommends that the lawyer:

> [E]stablish a reasonable fee for her services based on the factors enumerated under Rule 1.5(a) and then accept stock that at the time of the transaction is worth the reasonable fee. Of course, the stock should, if feasible, be valued at the amount per share that cash investors, knowledgeable about its value, have agreed to pay for their stock about the same time.[19]

---

15. Langevoort, *supra* note 1, at 571. *See also* Poonam Puri, *Taking Stock of Taking Stock*, 87 CORNELL L. REV. 99, 127 (2001) ("While lawyers who engage in equity billing may expose themselves to discipline by their self-regulatory bodies, the reality is that professional discipline in the context of fee arrangements is very rare, particularly where competent business clients are involved.").

16. *See* Puri, *supra* note 15, at 138.

19. 2000 Ethics Opinion, *supra* note 14, at 4 (citation omitted); *Taking Stock in Your Client As Legal Fees or an Investment*, New Hampshire Bar Association (Jan. 19, 2001), http://www.nhbar.org/publications/archives/display-news-issue.asp?id = 82.

This recommendation leads to the rather obvious question — *What if the stock cannot be valued?* In that case, the ABA suggests that the lawyer agree to take a percentage of the stock to be issued by the corporate client and that:

> [T]he percentage of stock agreed upon should reflect the value, as perceived by the client and the lawyer at the time of the transaction, that the legal services will contribute to the potential success of the enterprise. The value of the stock received by the lawyer will, like a contingent fee permitted under Rule 1.5(c), depend upon the success of the undertaking.[20]

While the ABA and other commentators have analogized equity billing arrangements to the well-established lawyer billing practice of relying on contingency fee arrangements in the litigation context,[21] at least one bar association ethics committee has questioned this proposition:

> The ABA accepted without question the proposition that taking stock was like a contingent fee. The Committee is not so sure. A contingent fee in a civil case depends in large measure on the efforts of the lawyer, whereas the value of stock usually depends on the client's efforts and other factors little influenced by the lawyer's work, unless as part of her representation she is to find sources of financing or otherwise contribute directly to the client's financial success.[22]

At the same time, however, equity billing arrangements *do* resemble contingent fee arrangements in that the problems inherent in assessing the reasonableness of an equity-based fee are very similar to the problems in evaluating a contingency fee arrangement.[23] In other words, in the case of both contingency fee and equity billing arrangements, the lawyer stands to collect nothing or to collect a windfall. Today, courts regularly uphold contingency fee arrangements (particularly in connection with personal injury litigation) even though the personal injury lawyer may collect a fee that, with the benefit of hindsight, seems unreasonable.[25]

The ABA's 2000 Ethics Opinion also emphasized that Rule 1.8(a) requires that the transaction and its terms must be *fully disclosed in writing* to the client.[26] According to the ABA, this requires the lawyer to do the following:

1. to *explain* so the client can understand the transaction, its terms, and its potential effects on the lawyer client relationship;
2. to *describe* the scope of the services to be performed for receipt of the stock, including whether the lawyer may retain the stock if she is terminated before all the services are performed;
3. to *inform* the client that, following receipt of the stock, matters could arise that would create a conflict between the lawyer's exercise of independent professional judgment and her desire to protect the value of her stock; and

---

20. 2000 Ethics Opinion, *supra* note 14, at 5.
21. *See, e.g.,* Puri, *supra* note 15, at 125, 130-31.
22. NHBA 2000 Ethics Opinion, *supra* note 14, at n.3.
23. *See* Hurt, *supra* note 9, at 914.
25. *Id.* at 943.
26. 2000 Ethics Opinion, *supra* note 14, at 5-6.

4. to *advise* the client that, as a consequence of such a conflict, she might have to withdraw as counsel, or, at the very least, to recommend that another lawyer advise the client on the matter giving rise to the conflict.

As a threshold matter, however, some commentators have questioned the effectiveness of requiring that the client be advised — in writing — that the client may seek the advice of independent counsel, at least as applied to the situation where the new corporation proposes to enter into an equity billing arrangement with the lawyer of the client's choice.[28] These commentators point out that, in order for the new company to take advantage of the ABA's recommendation and get *independent legal advice* as to the wisdom of the proposed equity billing arrangement with the *first lawyer*, the cash-starved, newly formed company now must be advised to retain the services of yet another lawyer in order to get a *second opinion*. Presumably, the newly formed company cannot afford to pay for the second lawyer's legal services in cash. Most likely, then, the start-up company will have to offer this *second lawyer* stock in exchange for his or her services in rendering an opinion as to the wisdom of entering into an equity billing arrangement with the *first lawyer*. Of course, this will necessitate that the *second lawyer* advise the newly formed start-up company as to the need to seek a *third opinion* before this lawyer can accept stock in lieu of fees, thereby creating this inevitable "domino effect" in order to satisfy the requirements of ABA Rule 1.8.[31]

This "domino effect" ultimately leads many observers to conclude that the practice of requiring the lawyer to obtain *written consent* from the client may not be as meaningful as the ABA's Rules seem to anticipate because the practical reality of the situation is that the typical high-tech start-up business usually has *no* viable option other than to give the required consent.[32] So, if the new client cannot pay in cash and can only pay for legal services in stock, then it would seem that written consent will be easy to obtain from the client but may not serve the purposes intended by the ABA's rules.

Furthermore, some commentators (and practicing lawyers) have questioned whether strict compliance with the requirements of Rule 1.8 is sufficient to show that the lawyer's investment in the new corporate client is made on terms that are *entirely consistent* with the lawyer's ethical and fiduciary obligations to the client.[33] On the other hand, other observers take the position that "the interests of an attorney who holds stock in a [corporate] client are *aligned* with the company's because both seek to increase the company's value for the shareholders."[34] However, is this always the case? For example, very often the issuance of stock to the lawyer will be contingent on the client obtaining necessary financing.

In such cases, the attorney will need to be attentive to the possibility that *his [personal financial] interest* in such financing (such as perhaps the attorney's personal interest in

---

28. *See* Puri, *supra* note 15, at 138-39.

31. *Id.* (referring to "domino effect").

32. *See* Puri, *supra* note 15, at 139 ("The reality is that many technology start-up clients are financially constrained from obtaining independent legal advice.").

33. *See* Dzienkowski & Peroni, *supra* note 10, at 414-15.

34. Kim & Braker, *supra* note 6, at 23 (emphasis added).

"getting the deal done" and receiving the stock) may cloud his ability to render *independent professional advice* [as to] the requisite disclosure in connection with an investment transaction. It would be prudent for the attorney to describe in his conflicts letter to be signed by his client the various scenarios in which his rendering of legal advice might be construed as less than completely objective and impartial as a result of his holding the stock.[35]

With respect to the extensive disclosure that the ABA Ethics Opinion recommends that the lawyer provide to the client *prior* to entering into any equity billing arrangement, some commentators questioned the effectiveness of such disclosure. For example, just how realistic is it to expect that the lawyer will be able to anticipate (and thus disclose to the prospective client) *all* or even *most* of the scenarios where the lawyer's ability to give independent legal advice *may* be compromised as a result of the lawyer taking stock in the client? Even if it were possible to anticipate (and thus disclose) all such potential situations where the lawyer's independence may be compromised, there still remains the question of whether such disclosure would be sufficient to mitigate the potential adverse consequences of the lawyer's investment so as to fully satisfy the lawyer's ethical responsibilities to his or her client. In the words of one leading criticism of equity billing arrangements:

> [T]he current practice of allowing [equity billing arrangements] continues to severely undercut many time-honored ideals of the legal profession. How can lawyers exercise independent professional judgment and offer unbiased legal advice to their clients if they have an ownership interest at stake in the venture? How can lawyers fulfill their function as gatekeepers of the securities laws if their personal equity interests in the venture will be injured by disclosure of negative information concerning the client? How can a client exercise its right to discharge a law firm, with or without cause, if that law firm has an investment in the client?[37]

On the other hand, the practical reality for many high-tech, start-up businesses, often with limited cash resources but promising business prospects, is that the only way for these new businesses to access quality legal representation is through an equity billing arrangement that calls for the lawyer to accept stock in the new corporate client in lieu of (or as a supplement to) payment of legal fees in cash.[38] Moreover, some lawyers claim that this billing practice:

> has the potential to strengthen an attorney's bond with the client and can be perceived [by the new client] as a vote of confidence in the client's business prospects. [In addition, there] is anecdotal evidence that attorneys who accommodate their clients by forgoing or deferring legal fees build loyal followings by their clients.[39]

What if the lawyer is skeptical as to the viability of the new client's business prospects? These kinds of reservations on the lawyer's part lead us back to the question that was raised earlier in this Essay, namely: if the lawyer thinks so little of the entrepreneur's

---

35. *Id.* (emphasis added).
37. [Dzienkowski & Peroni, *supra* note 10, at 414-15.]
38. *See generally* Puri, *supra* note 15.
39. *See* Kim & Braker, *supra* note 6, at 42-43.

proposed business venture, then how can the lawyer take the entrepreneur's money to perform what the lawyer believes is ultimately likely to be fruitless legal work? Does the lawyer owe the prospective client an obligation to disclose his skepticism before taking on the new business as a client? Alternatively, will the client benefit from the lawyer's investment, especially if the entrepreneur does not have the cash resources to pay for the lawyer's services? The next section describes the advantages and disadvantages to the new client and the lawyer that flow from a decision to enter into an equity billing arrangement.

IV. Advantages and Disadvantages of Investing in Clients

* * *

The advantage of equity billing arrangements most often proffered by those who support this practice is that these arrangements provide:

> [B]enefits to cash-starved clients by providing them with a way to pay for, and thus to gain access to, premium legal representation otherwise beyond their financial reach. In addition, by associating themselves with prestigious law firms, cash-starved clients effectively rent their firms' reputation and benefit from their firms' business contacts and acumen.[40]

While this is the most frequently cited advantage to equity billing arrangements from the client's perspective, there are a couple of other advantages that are also put forth by proponents of this alternative billing practice:

> Start-up clients undergo a constant search for funding and the lawyer as investor presents an option with low transaction costs. In addition, the lawyer who has a stake in the company may be more likely to share the benefit of his business networking with the client. By involving the lawyer in the company, the client gains a business partner, in addition to a provider of legal services. . . . This arrangement greatly benefits the start-up clients.[41]

Therefore, through equity billing arrangements, "the role of the high-tech lawyer often includes being a matchmaker between the client and potential investors or business advisors."[42]

From the client's perspective, the biggest disadvantage to an equity billing arrangement is that the lawyer's personal financial interests will impair his or her exercise of independent professional legal judgment in contravention of the lawyer's ethical and fiduciary obligations, as more fully described in the preceding section of this Essay. There is also the related concern that the "savvy lawyer [will use] his legal knowledge

---

40. Puri, *supra* note 15, at 103.
41. McAlpine, *supra* note 4, at 596.
42. *Id.* at 575. It bears mentioning, however, that many practicing lawyers believe that the ethical and fiduciary nature of the attorney-client relationship obligates the lawyer to "share the benefit of his [or her] business network" with the lawyer's client, regardless of whether the client pays the lawyer's fees in cash or stock. If one believes that lawyers' professional and ethical responsibilities to their business clients include this "matchmaking function," then this eliminates this factor as an advantage to equity billing arrangements.

to take advantage of his unsophisticated client."[43] For many commentators, the professional responsibility rules described in the preceding section provide sufficient constraints to ensure adequate protection of the clients' interests.

Notwithstanding these potential ethics concerns, many entrepreneurs also view the equity billing arrangement as making "good business sense."[44] According to this perspective, the new client sees the outside lawyer who invests in the entrepreneur's new business as having the same motivations as the client: to bring the company's goals to fruition. So, in a typical high-tech start-up scenario [such as the situation presented by SoftCo and its founders, Joan and Michael], the entrepreneur who contacts the lawyer is indeed the one who started the company and is often the sole owner of the new company. Alternatively, the only other investors at this point generally are "friends and family" of the entrepreneur. In this situation, it would seem that one could assume that the entrepreneur's goals are in fact aligned with the company's goals. From this perspective, having an attorney as an investor in the new company does seem to *align* the attorney's goals with the goals of both the entrepreneur and the company. Indeed, the lawyer's investment may be viewed by the entrepreneur as a vote of confidence in the entrepreneur's new business and may also have the added advantage of signaling to the new client that the attorney is a team player. In fact, these were among the arguments made by many of the Silicon Valley law firms who originally pioneered these equity billing arrangements.

Another way in which lawyers argue that equity billing arrangements *align* the interests of the lawyer and the client is with respect to the lawyer's billing practices.[47] From the client's perspective, having the lawyer take stock in the company alleviates some of the criticisms that many clients have with respect to the lawyers' traditional practice of billing by the hour. Generally speaking, many clients believe that a lawyer who bills by the hour would prefer that legal work for a client fill the lawyer's calendar for a longer time, and thus result in a larger bill for legal services. If the client enters into an equity billing arrangement with the lawyer, the client often perceives that this arrangement will operate to motivate the lawyer to work more efficiently. Since "the [lawyer's] piece of the pie may be worth more as the company is valued more, so the [lawyer] has the same incentive as the client to ensure that the quality of the [legal] services performed . . . is sufficiently high."[50] Moreover, since the lawyer's fee is "fixed," the client does not need to worry that the legal fee is growing excessively large (as it might if the lawyer were to bill hourly).

However, this purported "alignment of interests" of the client and the lawyer must be critically examined by asking two important questions: (1) "Who is the client?"; and (2) "What are the client's true goals?"

According to ethical rules, the corporate attorney's client is the corporation.[52] The client is not the [entrepreneur who hired] the attorney, . . . [nor is it] the current

---

43. *Id.* at 553.
44. *See* Hurt, *supra* note 9, at 912-13.
47. *Id.* at 931.
50. *Id.*
52. *See* MODEL RULES OF PROF'L CONDUCT R. 1.13 (2007).

or future shareholders of the corporation. This concept becomes especially troublesome when considered in the context of a start-up company. At the point at which the attorney is contacted, the [entrepreneur] on the phone and the entity he or she represents seem to be one and the same. . . . [The entrepreneur] is the sole shareholder, the president, and one of the directors. The other officers and directors are [usually] family members [of the entrepreneur]. In the beginning, the goals of [the new company and the entrepreneur] seem to be perfectly aligned. [The entrepreneur] wants her new attorney to be interdependent, not independent; she wants the attorney to be economically and emotionally invested in what [the entrepreneur] sees as her project.[53]

At the same time, however, the entrepreneur wants to obtain venture capital financing in order to launch the company's new business.

[So] at some point, the venture capitalists will give the project seed money and become investors. They [will generally] negotiate for slots as members of the board of directors. [Generally speaking, at some point, the entrepreneur's] short-term goals [for] the company [will] become inconsistent with the company's long-term goals. In addition, [the entrepreneur] and other early [friends and family] investors may have goals that are inconsistent with [the venture capital] investors. [All of this growing tension leads to the ultimate conundrum for the lawyer as an investor in the new company:] [w]ith whose goals will the attorney [now] be aligned?[54]

Obviously, this "conundrum" is going to place a significant — if not impossible — strain on the lawyer's ability to effectively represent his or her client — the corporation. At this point, the question becomes: can the lawyer exercise *independent professional judgment* and offer *unbiased* legal advice to his or her client — the corporation — notwithstanding his *personal financial interest* in the corporation? As any experienced venture capital lawyer will attest, these tensions between entrepreneurs and their venture capital investors inevitably will arise at some point during the course of the company's life cycle, and thus the lawyer who enters into an equity billing arrangement almost certainly will find himself or herself confronting this troublesome conundrum at some point during the course of the attorney-client relationship.[55]

Faced with this inevitable conundrum, many lawyers who decide to enter into equity billing arrangements will follow the practice of taking a small percentage interest in the new company, which they plan to hold as a long-term investment, and the size of the equity stake that these lawyers acquire in the new corporate client is not significant in the context of the lawyer's entire portfolio. While this practice may have the benefit of mitigating the lawyer's conflict of interest with the client when the inevitable conundrum arises, it bears emphasizing that the client's stated goal of "aligning the interests" of the new company with its new lawyer will probably not be achieved in any meaningful sense under the terms of this type of equity billing arrangement.[56]

Shifting focus, what are the benefits to *lawyers* who enter into equity billing arrangements with their corporate clients? First, and perhaps most importantly, lawyers "accept

---

53. Hurt, *supra* note 9, at 931-32.
54. *Id.*
55. *See* Dzienkowski & Peroni, *supra* note 10, at 528-35.
56. *Id.* at 533.

stock in technology start-ups because they recognize the moneymaking potential in the arrangement."[57] Another benefit to the equity billing arrangement is that it offers the lawyer "an opportunity to forge longer-term relationships with clients" because lawyers "hope that after their initial representation, clients will use them for subsequent corporate work and transactions," if for no other reason than it would be "costly [for the client] to change law firms."[58]

In addition, many lawyers (and their law firms) "view equity billing [arrangements] as a way to improve associate and partner satisfaction and, in particular, to deal with the high turnover rate of associates."[59] Especially at the height of the dot-com bubble, another reason given by law firms (especially Silicon Valley law firms) for entering into equity billing arrangements was that it was necessary for the law firm to create investment opportunities in order for the law firm to compete effectively in an environment where junior associates, as well as law firm partners, could easily go to work for start-up clients and receive lucrative stock option packages.[60] These lawyers were "quick to point out that other advisors to the corporation, such as investment bankers, routinely take equity in clients."[61] Indeed, very "often the entire investment bank[er]'s fee will be contingent on the closing of the transaction."[62] The obvious response to this justification is that it has *nothing* to do with whether the equity billing arrangement promotes the clients' best interests, nor does it have any bearing on the ethical and fiduciary responsibilities of lawyers as a profession. I have long told my law students that the analogy to investment bankers is fundamentally misplaced because investment bankers, unlike lawyers, do *not* owe fiduciary duties and ethical obligations to their clients.

These advantages to law firms need to be balanced against the disadvantages associated with equity billing arrangements. First and foremost is the financial risk of taking stock in lieu of payment of legal fees. Start-up businesses have a notoriously high rate of business failure which means that, if the business fails, "not only does the law firm fail to make a profit, but it will have provided free legal work."[63] In addition, there is a reputational risk to the lawyer. Some commentators have argued that lawyers who routinely represent start-up businesses (and invest in these new companies) run the risk of being perceived as too closely affiliated with their clients and thus "could be placing their own reputations on the line. However, it would appear that [lawyers and their] law firms

---

57. Puri, *supra* note 15, at 110 (noting many lawyers are likely "motivated by greed"); McAlpine, *supra* note 4, at 551 (In addition to the substantial profit that can be made if the new company is successful, some lawyers may also be "motivated" to take stock in lieu of fees because they know that the lawyer "will negotiate the financing with the venture capitalists, [and therefore] can make sure the terms of the stock purchase are favorable to [the lawyer and] his firm for the initial [shares] and for investment in later financings. As corporate counsel, [the lawyer] can also advise the client in a manner that protects his shareholder interests and his lucrative return."). To the extent that this is the motivation for the lawyer to enter into an equity billing arrangement with a new client, this almost certainly seems to run afoul of the ethical considerations imposed on lawyers pursuant to the requirements of ABA Rule 1.8, as discussed in the prior section of this Essay.

58. Puri, *supra* note 15, at 110-11.

59. *Id.* at 111; *see also* McAlpine, *supra* note 4, at 581-82.

60. *See* McAlpine, *supra* note 4, at 581-82.

61. Hurt, *supra* note 9, at 950.

62. *Id.*

63. Puri, *supra* note 15, at 113.

could minimize this reputational risk by engaging in greater scrutiny of the client's business plan and management team" before taking on the new business as a client.[64]

All of this leads me to the final and very personal concern that I want to raise regarding equity billing arrangements — and this concern goes to the very heart of why I decided to become a corporate lawyer. As I repeatedly emphasize to my students, I truly believe that the lawyer is the "conscience of the boardroom," and that is true regardless of whether the company is a small start-up business or a large publicly-traded corporation. To be able to meet professional obligations as a lawyer, I believe it is vitally important that the lawyer always maintain his or her independence. In the aftermath of the recent financial scandals, I believe it is more important than ever for lawyers to maintain their independence, and thus it is more important than ever for the legal profession to examine just how closely connected lawyers should be to their corporate clients. This has been made all the more important in the wake of the Great Recession as the general public has begun to question the activities of lawyers (as well as other professionals such as auditors[65] and financial analysts) that have been perceived as being too close to their corporate clients. The legal profession must decide what is the proper role of a corporate attorney. Since I decided to go to law school because I truly believe that the law is a noble profession — a profession that requires its members to have the courage to be the conscience of the boardroom and thereby promote good corporate governance practices — any activity that calls into question the independence of the lawyer in the practice of his or her profession needs to be examined very seriously in order to protect the future of the legal profession as a "noble calling."[66]

QUESTIONS

1. Now that you have read about the varying perspectives on the issue of equity billing arrangements, have you changed your mind about whether you would be willing to take stock in Joan and Michael's new business in lieu of cash payment of your fees?

2. For purposes of this problem, let's assume that SoftCo is a publicly traded company and is not your client. A business acquaintance of yours, who is also serving as the Chief Financial Officer of SoftCo, describes recent positive developments to you over lunch, all of which is information that has been publicly disclosed by SoftCo. After doing further research on your own, you purchase SoftCo stock for a total investment of $100,000. A few months later, the board of SoftCo approaches you and asks you to represent SoftCo as legal counsel.

---

64. *Id.* at 115.

65. For an interesting analysis of the difficulties that ensnared the accounting profession in the 1990s when they expanded their business model to include an ever-expanding array of consulting services, *see* Hurt, *supra* note 9, at 950-53; *see also* Comments of Karl Groskaufmanis, *Corporate Citizenship: A Conversation Among the Law, Business, and Academia*, 84 Marq. L. Rev. 723, 754-58 (2001).

66. Hurt, *supra* note 9, at 929 ("Independence of the attorney is critical to the [lawyer's] gatekeeping function."); *see also* Dzienkowski & Peroni, *supra* note 10, at 479-84.

   a. Would you take on SoftCo as a client?
   b. If you decide to represent SoftCo, would you sell your investment in SoftCo?
   c. If you decide to keep your investment in SoftCo and also represent SoftCo, would you increase your investment in SoftCo?
   d. How would you deal with potentially damaging information about SoftCo?
   e. Would your answer (or analysis) of any of the preceding questions change if we assume that you are a partner in a well-known, reputable Silicon Valley law firm that is known for representing start-up companies?

4. Lawyers That Serve as Directors of Their Clients

Very often, the founders will ask the lawyer for the new corporation to serve as a member of the new company's board of directors. This raises a separate set of ethical concerns, the nature of which is examined in the materials below. As you read through this section, you should be prepared to answer the question — "Would you be willing to serve on the board of directors of SoftCo, assuming that the founders, Joan and Michael, decide to incorporate their new business and ask you to serve as a board member?" In thinking about this question and in reflecting on the viewpoints expressed in the following materials, you may want to consider the advantages and disadvantages of this practice, both from the perspective of you as outside counsel to the new business as well as from the perspective of SoftCo and its Founders.

The following article offers a fairly typical description of the traditional perspective as to the relative advantages and disadvantages of lawyers serving on their clients' boards of directors.

Felix J. Bronstein
The Lawyer as Director of the Corporate Client in the Wake of Sarbanes-Oxley

23 JOURNAL OF LAW & COMMERCE 53 (2004)

The phenomenon of lawyers serving on their clients' boards of directors has been around for many years, as has the debate on its ethical implications.[1] This practice has both a number of advantages and disadvantages, from the point of view of lawyers and clients, as well as from a societal point of view. The bar and the courts have both spoken on this issue, as have numerous commentators. Most bar associations and courts have taken either a neutral or even a somewhat negative position on the issue, though a per se prohibition on such dual service has not been established. . . .[2]

---

1. American lawyers have been serving on the boards of their clients since at least the 1860s. *See* John F. X. Peloso & Irwin H. Warren, *The Lawyer-Director, Implications for Independence,* 1998 ABA SECTION ON LITIGATION REPORT OF THE TASK FORCE ON THE INDEPENDENT LAWYER 14. The issue has been publicly debated since at least the 1970s. *See* RONALD D. ROTUNDA, PROFESSIONAL RESPONSIBILITY: A STUDENT'S GUIDE §8-6.11 n. 100 (2002).

2. This paper does not specifically deal with the related issue of lawyers' equity investments in their clients' companies. For a discussion of this issue *see generally* John S. Dzienkowski & Robert J. Peroni,

A. The Advantages

There are numerous benefits involved in a lawyer serving on a client's board of directors. The lawyer-director's dual service benefits his client as well as his law firm "by cementing a long-term relationship and ensuring that legal advice is both consistent and readily available."[4] The law firm will be better informed about the various aspects of the client's business[5] and the lawyer will command greater respect, attention, and consideration as a board member.[6] The lawyer-director is familiar with the issues facing the board and management. He can "provide greater guidance at initial stages of a transaction or potential problem,"[7] thus potentially resolving early what could later have become a significant and costly legal problem. This makes the lawyer-director more efficient, effective, and valuable to his client. Such an arrangement will be beneficial both in terms of money[9] and prestige for the lawyer-director and his law firm.

Indeed, corporations often ask their lawyers to serve on their boards because of the many benefits to them.[11] Such dual service is quite common in corporate America.[12] The lawyer will "bring unique and valuable perspectives that other directors may not have and that corporations . . . may not otherwise be able to obtain,"[13] because of his analytical skills and legal background. In fact, lawyers make some of the best directors.[14] "[T]he other board members will have greater trust and comfort in [the lawyer-director's] legal advice . . . because of [his or her] increased risk of personal liability."[15]

Society in general also benefits from such dual service. Dual service is very effective in helping "women and minority lawyers to 'crack the glass ceiling' [by] obtain[ing] clients . . . and . . . gain[ing] prominence and respect in the profession."[16] Under federal securities laws, the courts will treat lawyer-directors as insiders, "ratcheting up . . . due diligence, [and thus] reduc[ing] the frequency and scale of misleading statements in the

---

The Decline in Lawyer Independence: Lawyer Equity Investments in Clients, 81 Tex. L. Rev. 405 (2002); Donald C. Langevoort, *When Lawyers and Law Firms Invest in Their Corporate Clients' Stock*, 80 Wash U. L.Q. 569 (2002); Poonam Puri, *Taking Stock of Taking Stock*, 87 Cornell L. Rev. 99 (2001). . . .

4. Geoffrey C. Hazard, Jr. & W. William Hodes, The Law of Lawyering §11.17 (3d ed. 2001 & Supp. 2003). *See generally* William Freivogel, *Board Positions, in* Freivogel on Conflicts, available at http://www.freivogelonconflicts.com/new_page_29.htm.

5. *See* Robert P. Cummins & Megyn M. Kelly, *The Conflicting Roles of Lawyer as Director*, 23 Litig. 48, 48 (1996).

6. *See* Micalyn S. Harris & Karen L. Valihura, *Outside Counsel as Director: The Pros and Potential Pitfalls of Dual Service*, 53 Bus. Law. 479, 483 (1998).

7. James H. Cheek, III & Howard H. Lamar, III, *Lawyers as Directors of Clients: Conflicts of Interest, Potential Liability and Other Pitfalls*, 712 PLI/Corp. 461, 464 (1990).

9. *See* Bethany Smith, *Sitting on Vs. Sitting in on Your Client's Board of Directors*, 15 Geo. J. Legal Ethics 597, 604 (2002).

11. *See* [Craig C. Albert, *The Lawyer-Director: An Oxymoron?*, 9 Geo. J. Legal Ethics 413, 419 (1996)].

12. *See* Patrick W. Straub, Note, *ABA Task Force Misses the Mark: Attorneys Should Not Be Discouraged From Serving on Their Corporate Clients' Board of Directors*, 25 Del. J. Corp. L. 261 n. 4 (2000).

13. Peloso & Warren, *supra* note 1, at 2.

14. *See* Robert H. Mundhelm, *Should Code of Professional Responsibility Forbid Lawyers to Serve on Boards of Corporations for Which They Act as Counsel*, 33 Bus. Law. 1507, 1515 (1978) (remarks of Kenneth J. Bialkin).

15. Straub, *supra* note 12, at 263-64.

16. Peloso & Warren, *supra* note 1, at 3.

registration statements."[17] This means that "the protection afforded investors by [S]ection 11 [of the Securities Act of 1933 ("1933 Act")] [will be] greatly heightened."[19] Under the often used Section 10(b) of the 1934 Securities Exchange Act ("1934 Act"), investors will be afforded greater protection because of the lawyer-director's dual service.[21]

B. The Disadvantages

Dual service by a lawyer-director may create situations where a conflict of interest is likely to arise, compromising the individual's "ability to fulfill properly his . . . responsibility in either or both roles."[22] Directors owe a fiduciary duty to the corporation, which encompasses such duties as the duty of care and the duty of loyalty,[23] with a primary goal being the maximization of profit.[24] On the other hand, "the lawyer's ethical responsibility is to provide competent, professional legal advice for the [client]."[25] There are numerous situations in which there could be a conflict of interest for the lawyer-director, including issues related to legal fees and litigation brought against the board of directors.

Attorney-client privilege[26] can be destroyed because of the dual service of the lawyer-director. Most courts have no problem quickly denying the privilege or finding that it was waived, because the client carries the burden to prove each element of this evidentiary privilege.[27]

Courts hold lawyer-directors to a higher standard of care than either directors or lawyers individually, because of their dual service.[28] Indeed, "[n]ot only does a lawyer-director face an enhanced risk of individual liability, but [his] law firm may be held vicariously liable for [his] actions" as well.[29] Professional liability insurance for

---

17. James D. Cox, *The Paradoxical Corporate and Securities Law Implications of Counsel Serving on the Client's Board*, 80 WASH. U. L.Q. 541, 560 (2002).

19. Cox, *supra* note 17, at 559.

21. *See* Cox, *supra* note 17, at 562.

22. Peloso & Warren, *supra* note 1, at 36-37.

23. *See* FRANKLIN A. GEVURTZ, CORPORATION LAW §4.0 (2000). . . .

24. *See* Peloso & Warren, *supra* note 1, at 37.

25. *Id. See also* MODEL RULES OF PROF'L CONDUCT R. 1.1 (2002); RESTATEMENT (THIRD) OF LAW GOVERNING LAWYERS: A LAWYER'S DUTIES TO A CLIENT — IN GENERAL §16 (2002).

26. *See, e.g.*, 8 JOHN HENRY WIGMORE, EVIDENCE IN TRIALS AT COMMON LAW §§2285, 2290-95 (John. T. McNaughton rev., Little, Brown, and Co. 1969 & Supp. 2003). The general principles of the privilege are "(1) [w]here legal advice of any kind is sought (2) from a professional legal adviser in his capacity as such, (3) the communications relating to that purpose, (4) made in confidence (5) by the client, (6) are at his instance permanently protected (7) from disclosure by himself or by the legal adviser, (8) except the protection [may] be waived." *Id.* §2292.

27. *See* Federal Sav. & Loan Ins. Corp. v. Fielding, 343 F. Supp. 537, 546 (D. Nev. 1972) (holding that in the case of a lawyer-director, the privilege is not available because "[w]hen the attorney and the client get in bed together as business partners, their relationship is a business relationship, not a professional one, and their confidences are business confidences unprotected by [the attorney-client] privilege") for perhaps the furthest that a court has gone. *See also* Deutsch v. Cogan, 580 A.2d 100, 108 (Del. Ch. 1990) ("Where a fiduciary has conflicting interests [as a lawyer-director], to allow the [attorney]-client privilege to block access to the information . . . might allow the perpetration of frauds.").

28. *See* Peloso & Warren, *supra* note 1, at 54-52.

29. *Id.* at 56.

professional legal services usually covers only attorneys serving in their capacity as attorneys, and "Directors and Officers Insurance" ("D&O Insurance") usually covers only directors and officers acting in their capacity as directors and officers. Thus, "[e]ven where [a lawyer]-director is covered by both types of insurance, coverage conceivably could be denied under both [policies]."[30]

The lawyer-director's law firm may also be deemed to owe a fiduciary duty to persons to whom it would not otherwise owe a duty, such as the minority shareholders of a corporation the law firm represents and on whose board one of its lawyers serves.[31] [Moreover], the lawyer-director also potentially faces increased liability under Section 11 of the 1933 Act and Section 10(b) of the 1934 Act because of the "higher standard of care that is required by an ordinarily prudent . . . lawyer-director."[33] Lawyer-directors also face an increased risk of liability under Section 20 of the 1934 Act.

C. [Traditional Resolution of These Competing Considerations]

There is no ethics rule or law that prohibits dual service. Neither the Canons of Professional Ethics, promulgated in 1908, nor the Model Code of Professional Responsibility, adopted in 1969, specifically address the issue of lawyer-directors.[35] Both contain general rules about lawyer's duties, conflicts of interest, independence, and representation of corporate entities. However, the Model Rules of Professional Conduct promulgated in 1983, specifically address the issue of lawyer-directors. A comment[37] to the general rule on conflicts of interest[38] discusses the various situations in which a conflict may arise for a lawyer-director because of his dual service. It concludes by stating that "[i]f there is material risk that the dual role will compromise the lawyer's independence of professional judgment, the lawyer should not serve as a director."[39] After adopting many changes recommended by the Ethics 2000 Commission, the latest version of the Model Rules contains a modified version of this comment. The new comment is identical to the old, but, in addition, calls on the lawyer-director to advise the other directors of the potential conflicts and loss of privilege and of the possibility of recusal as director or the law firm's withdrawal from representation.[40] The new comment also states that "[i]f there is material risk that the dual role will compromise the lawyer's independence of professional judgment, the lawyer should not serve as a director or *should cease to act as the corporation's lawyer when conflicts of interest arise.*"[41]

---

30. Albert, *supra* note 2, at 455.

31. *See* Harris & Valihura, *supra* note 6, at 496-99.

33. Harris & Valihura, *supra* note 6, at 501.

35. *See* Peloso & Warren, *supra* note 1, at 21-23.

37. "The Comment accompanying each Rule explains and illustrates the meaning and purpose of the Rule. . . ." The Comments are intended as guides to interpretation, but the text of each Rule is authoritative. MODEL RULES OF PROF'L CONDUCT: SCOPE [21] (2001). This version of the ethics rules promulgated by the ABA is the basis for the rules of lawyer conduct adopted by the majority of jurisdictions in this country. *See* COMPENDIUM OF PROF'L RESPONSIBILITY RULES AND STANDARDS 555 (ABA 2001).

38. MODEL RULES OF PROF'L CONDUCT R. 1.7 cmt. [14] (2001).

39. *Id.*

40. MODEL RULES OF PROF'L CONDUCT R. 1.7 cmt. [35] (2002).

41. *Id.* (emphasis added).

The Restatement of the Law Governing Lawyers, published in its final form in 2000, takes a more sympathetic view of lawyer-directors. A comment to Section 135 of the Restatement (Third) of Law Governing Lawyers states that a conflict can arise in a lawyer-director's dual service, but that "[s]imultaneous service . . . is not forbidden."[42] In fact, the comment goes on to state:

> The requirement that a lawyer for an organization serve the interests of the entity . . . is generally consistent with the duties of a director or officer. However, when the obligations or personal interests as director are materially adverse to those of the lawyer as corporate counsel, the lawyer may not continue to serve as corporate counsel without the informed consent of the corporate client.[43]

In 1995, the American Bar Association ("ABA") Section on Litigation commissioned the Task Force on the Independent Lawyer, which issued its report in 1998.[44] The Task Force Report concluded that while dual service by lawyer-directors "presents difficult issues for [all the parties involved] . . . , it is not appropriate to . . . bar [such dual] practice."[45] However, "because of the pitfalls that may arise from [such] practice," this highly critical report recommended that dual service "should be discouraged in most cases."[46] Fortunately for the report's critics, at approximately the same time, the ABA issued an "even milder"[47] formal ethics opinion that did not specifically discourage such service.[48] The Opinion recognized that clients will continue to ask their lawyers to serve as directors and that it is ethical for the lawyers to comply. It called upon lawyer-directors "to be sensitive to [such] issues" as conflicts of interest, independent professional judgment, and potential loss of privilege, and recommended a number of steps that a lawyer should take before, and in the course of, such dual service.[50]

A number of state and local bar and ethics authorities have issued opinions on the matter. In 1988, the New York State Bar Association, citing the ethics opinions of seven other jurisdictions, concluded that lawyers can serve as directors on their corporate clients' boards, as long as they fulfill their ethical obligations and disclose the potential problems to the client.[51] Later that same year, the Association of the Bar of the City of New York issued a somewhat stricter opinion.[52]

---

42. RESTATEMENT (THIRD) OF LAW GOVERNING LAWYERS §135 cmt. [d] (2002).

43. *Id.*

44. *See* Peloso & Warren, *supra* note 1, at 1-9.

45. *Id.* at 63.

46. *Id.* at 63-64. "The . . . Report refused to recommend a complete ban on the practice mainly because the legal community would not likely support such a prohibition." Straub, *supra* note 12, at 261 n.3.

47. Cox, *supra* note 17 at 542. n. 3.

48. ABA Comm. on Ethics and Prof'l Responsibility, Formal Op. 98-410 (1998) (Lawyer Serving as Director of Client Corporation).

50. *Id.*

51. N.Y. St. Bar Ass'n Comm. on Prof'l Ethics, Op. 589 (1988).

52. The Ass'n of the Bar of the City of N.Y. Comm. on Prof'l and Judicial Ethics, Formal Op. 1988-95 n. 3 (1988) (Lawyers should decline the representation in dual service situations "where there is a material risk that the lawyer's own interests will adversely affect the representation [even] if the client consents after full disclosure.").

The Restatement position, coupled with following advice along the lines of that given in the ABA Opinion, is the better view. First of all, an absolute prohibition on dual service is not justified by any of the concerns and possible pitfalls of such service, and would, in any case, be over-inclusive.[53] Rules already in existence — ethical, corporate, and securities — address any potential problems and abuses. If a lawyer fully discloses the potential consequences of dual service after being asked to serve on the board of a client, and the client fully consents, and if the lawyer-director abstains from participating in self-interested transactions,[55] there should be no reason to prohibit such a practice. Dual service offers a number of benefits to all the parties involved, as well as to others. Indeed, many good lawyers make "damn good businessmen; and to deprive the business community of the opportunity to use those people's services in both roles . . . would be a terrible mistake."[57] Contrary to the fear that there will be pressure on the lawyer-director to not fully exercise his independent profession judgment, "because of a lawyer's experience in handling such pressures in other circumstances, [he or she] is more able and more skilled at resisting those pressures and expressing unpopular views that require a board's attention and consideration."[58]

Moreover, a ban on dual service by lawyer-directors would be a major shock not only to the legal world, but also to the business world.[59] Indeed, even some proponents of prohibition realized long ago that, because of the widespread practice of dual service, a ban would at the very least be impractical and burdensome. A complete ban also would be inconsistent with the other ethical rules, in that the only blanket bans called for by the ethical rules involve situations that by definition produce conflicts of interest, not those which may merely have the potential to produce such conflicts.[61]

═══════════════════

Query: Do you think the advantages of lawyers serving on their clients' boards of directors outweigh the disadvantages?

The following article offers a more modern perspective on the ongoing debate as to whether lawyers should serve as directors of publicly traded corporations. As you read through the following excerpt, consider whether the observations made by these authors influence your decision whether to serve as a director of a privately held start-up company, such as your new client, SoftCo.

---

53. *See* Albert, *supra* note [11], at 472-74.

55. Namely, the lawyer-director should abstain from voting on legal fees and other matters related to his law firm. *See* Cox, *supra* note 17, at 543 n. 6.

57. Mundheim, *supra* note 14, at 1516 (remarks of an unidentified speaker).

58. Harris & Valihura, *supra* note 6, at 491.

59. As one judge has noted, "the personnel of a great many, if not most, American corporations would have to be reconstituted" if a ban were to be implemented. Gries Sports Enter., Inc. v. Cleveland Browns Football Co., 496 N.E.2d 959, 982 (Ohio 1986) (Wright, J., dissenting).

61. *See* Straub, note 12, at 273 n. 75.

Lubomir P. Litov, Simone M. Sepe, and Charles K. Whitehead
Lawyers and Fools: Lawyer-Directors in Public Corporations

102 The Georgetown Law Journal 413 (2014)

For over a half-century, the legal profession has debated whether lawyers should be directors of public corporations.[1] The accepted wisdom has been that lawyers should steer clear of public company boards. A lawyer-director[3] is less able to objectively assess board actions in which she participates, and if she is outside counsel, she also is less able to monitor and manage the executives who pay her legal fees. Those costs are significant and outweigh the benefits she brings to the board — her ability to spot issues,[6] provide a perspective on decisions that non-lawyers may hot have,[7] and assist in navigating legal and regulatory problems as they arise.[8] In short a lawyer who represents herself — by acting as both a lawyer and a director — has a fool for a client.

This Article explains why the accepted wisdom is outdated . . . The costs of being a lawyer-director can still be significant, but the balance has now shifted in its favor — reflecting a lawyer-director's ability to assist the board in managing the significant rise in litigation and regulation affecting businesses and changes in CEO compensation that occur when a lawyer is on the board. In fact, based on an average of 10,000 or more observations from 2000 to 2009, we find a statistically and economically significant increase in firm value . . . of non-financial companies that have a lawyer on the board.[13] A lawyer-director increases firm value by 9.5 percent, and when the lawyer is also a company executive, [the increase in firm value rises to] 10.2 percent. The result has been an almost doubling in the percentage of public companies with lawyer-directors from 2000 to 2009.[15]

---

1. *See* John F. X. Peloso, et al., *The Lawyer-Director: Implications for Independence*, Report of the Task Force on the Independent Lawyer, 1998 A.B.A. Sec. Litig. Rep. 17-35 (1998) (describing the history of ethical concerns over a lawyer serving as a director of a corporate client) [hereinafter ABA Task Force Report].

3. In this Article, the term "lawyer-director" refers to a director of a public corporation with a legal degree, regardless of whether she is practicing as a lawyer or as outside counsel to the firm at the time she is on the board.

6. *See* Report and Recommendations of the Comm. on Lawyer Bus. Ethics of the ABA Section of Bus. Law, *The Lawyer as Director of a Client*, 57 Bus. Law. 387, 388 (2001) (offering guidance on whether and how a lawyer should become a director) [hereinafter ABA Report and Recommendations]; Craig C. Albert, *The Lawyer-Director: An Oxymoron?* 9 Geo. J. Legal Ethics 413, 417-18 (1996).

7. *See* ABA Task Force Report, *supra* note 1, at 2.

8. *See* Harold M. Williams, *Corporate Accountability and the Lawyer's Role*, 34 Bus. Law. 7, 10 (1978) (describing the view that lawyer-directors have "special knowledge of litigation and other matters of vital significance to directors"); Robert H. Mundheim, *Should Code of Professional Responsibility Forbid Lawyers to Serve on Boards of Corporations For Which They Act as Counsel?*, 33 Bus. Law. 1507, 1508, 1511 (1978) (noting the importance of an "appropriate relationship" between counsel and a board that represents public shareholders); Micalyn S. Harris & Karen L. Valihura, *Outside Counsel as Director: The Pros and Potential Pitfalls of Dual Service*, 53 Bus. Law. 479, 482-83 (1998).

13. The empirical findings described in this Article are based on data that exclude financial institutions.

15. The percentage of public companies with lawyer-directors was 24.5 percent in 2000, up to 47.5 percent in 2005, and 43.9 percent in 2009. *See infra* Figure 1 and note 107 and accompanying text.

This Article is the first to analyze the rise in lawyer-directors. It makes a variety of other empirical contributions — each of which is statistically significant and large in magnitude — in addition to explaining this important shift in board composition.

We begin by explaining why the number of lawyer-directors has grown.[16] Only recently have studies examined the effect on board composition of the environment in which a firm operates. We add to those studies by showing that businesses with intangible assets, such as patents,[18] value lawyer-directors who can assist in protecting those assets. Firms that are more likely to be involved in litigation also benefit from having a lawyer on the board. In addition, we identify the greater likelihood of having a lawyer-director as a business becomes more complex.

Next, we describe the impact of lawyer-directors on corporate monitoring and incentives. We consider the decline in CEO risk-taking incentives that occurs with a lawyer-director. In addition, we analyze changes in board structure (such as whether the CEO is also board chairman) and takeover protections (such as the addition of a poison pill or classified board) that can insulate the board and CEO from shareholder oversight. We also consider the effect of lawyer-directors on board integrity, using as a proxy the substantial decline in stock option backdating litigation when a lawyer is on the board. Our results are consistent with lawyer-directors providing meaningful oversight over senior managers, similar to recent changes in board composition and director-officer relationships described by others.[25] In addition, diversity among directors can improve the quality of a board's decisions, partly by bringing a depth of perspective that may not be present if the board is comprised of only like-minded people.[26]

Finally, we describe the benefits of having a lawyer-director. Our intuition is that a lawyer's training and experience, and the judgment that comes with it, can add value to a board's decisionmaking and promote more informed monitoring, as well as assist in managing litigation and regulatory costs.[27] A lawyer-director brings a special perspective based on her experience with the law and legal issues, and an appreciation of doing

---

16. Based on our sample, the number of lawyer-directors was 340 (in 1,393 firms) in 2000 and 541 (in 1,237 firms) in 2009, with a high of 642 (in 1,357 firms) in 2007. The average number of independent directors in public companies also grew over the last thirty years. *See* Sanjai Bhgat & Bernard Black, *The Non-Correlation Between Board Independence and Long-Term Firm Performance*, 27 J. CORP. L. 231, 232 (2002).

18. Intellectual property rights have become an increasingly important source of cash and non-cash value for corporations. *See* MARSHALL PHELPS & DAVID KLINE, BURNING THE SHIPS: INTELLECTUAL PROPERTY AND THE TRANSFORMATION OF MICROSOFT 89-95 (2009) (describing Microsoft's ability to leverage intellectual property into value-producing assets); *see also* Bronwyn H. Hall, *Exploring the Patent Explosion, in* ESSAYS IN HONOR OF EDWIN MANSFIELD: THE ECONOMICS OF R&D, INNOVATION, AND TECHNOLOGICAL CHANGE 195, 197 (Albert N. Link & F. M. Scherer eds., 2005). . . .

25. The recent changes in board composition have been described in Marcel Kahan & Edward Rock, *Embattled CEOs*, 88 TEX. L. REV. 987, 1044 (2010). Among other characteristics, Professors Kahan and Rock indicate that outside directors are more likely to enjoy a less collegial relationship with insiders, have occasional need to be confrontational, and deal more often with shareholders. *See id.* Directors who may be well-qualified for the position, they suggest, include "retired CEOs and other retired high-level executives, bankers, accountants, consultant, or investment professionals." *Id.* To that list, we would also add lawyers.

26. *See* Mathias Dewatripont & Jean Tirole, *Advocates*, 107 J. POL. ECON. 1, 4, 29-30 (1999) (providing a formal discussion of the use of advocacy systems within various organizational contexts); . . .

27. *See* Constance E. Bagley, *Winning Legally: The Value of Legal Astuteness*, 33 ACAD. MGMT. REV. 378, 381-82 (2008).

things "by the book" that likely comes with that experience.[28] In fact, we find that financial stability is likely to increase as a result of a lawyer-director's influence on decisions regarding litigation and CEO compensation. Although lawyer-directors may favor a board structure and takeover defenses that can reduce shareholder welfare, the potential decline is balanced by the benefits of lawyer-directors, such as the valuable advice they can provide. As noted earlier, the result is an increase in firm value by 9.5 percent, and for inside lawyer-directors, the increase rises further to 10.2 percent.

Could those results be replicated by a lawyer who advises the board, rather than joins it? We think not. A lawyer-director is more likely than outside counsel to attend board meetings and have access to information needed to properly advise the board.[34] She may also become aware of new information at an earlier stage, enabling her to flag concerns as they arise.[35] In particular, she can assist her colleagues to better understand legal and regulatory problems and, as necessary, act as a bridge between the board and outside advisors to resolve them.[36] Directors and managers are also more inclined to follow the advice of a colleague who shares equal responsibility for its outcome.[37] That may be particularly true of lawyer-directors in light of the higher standards to which the courts have held them.

QUESTIONS

1. Would you be willing to serve as a director of Joan and Michael's new business, SoftCo, assuming that SoftCo is organized as a corporation? Would your answer vary if SoftCo were a publicly traded corporation?
2. How would your decision whether to serve as member of SoftCo's board of directors affect your personal and legal relationship with the company's founders, Joan and Michael?
3. How do you think your relationship with the client will be impacted by virtue of becoming a board member? Indeed, who is the client that you represent as a lawyer?
4. How do you think that your relationship with other members of your law firm might be affected if you should become a member of SoftCo's board of directors?
5. What are the advantages to becoming a member of SoftCo's board of directors? What are the disadvantages? Do the advantages outweigh the disadvantages?

---

28. *See id.*

34. *See* Conference, *Should Code of Professional Responsibility Forbid Lawyers to Serve on Boards of Corporations for Which they Act as Counsel?*, 33 Bus. Law. 1511, 1514 (1978); Harris & Valihura, *supra* note 8, at 482-83 (describing how a lawyer-director is able to counsel the board before outside legal advice becomes necessary).

35. *See* Harris & Valihura, *supra* note 8, at 482-83.

36. *See* Bagley, *supra* note 27, at 381, 383.

37. *See* Albert, *supra* note 6, at 417-18 (discussing the board's potential reluctance to follow the advice of outside counsel who does not share the same responsibility).

PROBLEMS

1. For purposes of this problem, let's assume that you are a successful partner at a well-known, reputable law firm in Silicon Valley and that the vast majority of your clients consist of start-up companies. One of your clients is SoftCo, a newly formed corporation. SoftCo prefers to pay your fees by giving you stock options in SoftCo in lieu of cash.
   a. Would you agree to take stock options in SoftCo in lieu of cash? Do you see any potential conflicts?
   b. Assume that SoftCo pays you part cash and part stock options in SoftCo. Would that change your answer?
   c. What if most of your clients, like SoftCo, made similar stock option offers to you — would you accept stock options in some, all, or none of these clients? Would you accept restricted stock? What factors would influence your decision?

2. Let's assume that you accepted SoftCo's offer and took stock options in SoftCo amounting to $25,000, and that your stake was worth less than 1 percent of SoftCo at the time that you received these stock options. Let's further assume that, five years later, you are representing SoftCo in connection with its IPO of its common stock, and now your stock options are worth approximately $5 million.
   a. Do you see any conflicts? At what point did those conflicts, if any, arise?
   b. Let's further assume that, prior to exercising your stock options, you discover information about SoftCo that could be potentially damaging, and that you are serving as a member of SoftCo's board of directors in addition to continuing in your role as SoftCo's counsel. How should you respond to these developments?

CHAPTER 2

CHOICE OF BUSINESS ENTITY

In the last chapter, we were introduced to our new client, SoftCo, and its founders, Joan and Michael. As the lawyer for this start-up business, one of the first decisions that you and your new client must make is: What form of entity should be used to organize this new business? In practice, many lawyers will have an easy answer: *Use a limited liability company (LLC) or a corporation* (usually a C corporation, for reasons to be elaborated on later in this chapter). The problem with this answer is *not* that it is inherently wrong, but rather that this answer is *not always* the right answer. At the other end of the spectrum, another answer frequently given to this question by many practicing lawyers is: *Whatever the client wants.* While this answer is right in the sense that the business lawyer should effect the client's desires, this answer overlooks the fundamental role of the lawyer as transaction planner.

In Chapter 1, we learned that one of the most important services that the corporate lawyer can offer a start-up business is to help the client make decisions that maximize the new business's flexibility to take advantage of future opportunities. For this reason, if none other, both of the answers to the "choice of entity" question described above are flawed, in that these answers fail to appreciate the lawyer's *counseling function* in advising the new client regarding the most appropriate form of business entity. So, for example, if the lawyer routinely gives the same advice — "Form an LLC" — this answer fails to appreciate the potential for disadvantageous consequences that may flow from choosing the wrong form of business entity — consequences that may not become apparent for many years, but which (in many situations) could have been anticipated (and addressed) upon formation of the new business. In a similar vein, in the case of the lawyer who routinely responds, "Whatever the client wants," this answer suffers from the failure to appreciate that the client's desires (in many situations) may not be in the client's best interests. As many practicing lawyers can attest, clients will often develop rather eccentric views about the type of business entity they desire, views that are often based on what their friends have advised or other business acquaintances may have recommended. In this case, it is incumbent on the lawyer to make sure that the client understands the potential consequences of the client's choice of entity decision, in order for the transactional lawyer to fulfill the lawyer's professional responsibilities as outlined in the preceding chapter.

But all of this leads to the rather obvious question: How should the lawyer reach the decision regarding the most appropriate form of business entity to recommend to a start-up business? That question is the focus of the materials contained in this chapter, which begins by providing a thumbnail sketch of the different types of business entities that are generally available in most states today. This discussion provides a brief overview of the essential characteristics of the sole proprietorship, the general partnership, the limited partnership, the corporation, and the LLC. The remaining materials in this chapter will describe the essential factors that are generally included as part of the lawyer's analytical process in deciding on the most appropriate form of entity to recommend to a new business. As we shall see, this decision-making process is not an exact science; rather, it involves consideration (and balancing) of a number of different factors, while at the same time being sensitive to the consequences of alternative options that are available to the new business.

A. Overview of Key Attributes of Different Forms of Business Entities

This overview will be brief on the assumption that much (if not all) of this material is covered at length as part of the introductory course, Business Associations, offered at most law schools today. This discussion takes a historical perspective, starting with the oldest form of business organization known to the law — the sole proprietorship — and concluding with a recent (and, by all accounts, very popular) development in the law of business entities — the LLC. The very last part of this section provides a brief summary of the newest form of business entity to emerge in the (continuing) development of forms of business entities: the public benefit corporation. By taking this chronological approach, we hope to impart a sense of the historical pattern involved in the evolution of business entities.

1. Sole Proprietorship

The sole proprietorship is the oldest of the business entities that we consider in this chapter, dating itself back to the very origins of mankind's entrepreneurial spirit. In essence, the individual conducts the business — and owns all of the assets of the business — in his or her own name. As a direct result, the individual is directly and personally liable for all of the debts and other obligations of the business. Thus, the sole (or individual) proprietorship does not involve the use of any separate legal entity since the law does not make any distinction between the property owned by the sole proprietor for business use versus personal use, nor does it distinguish between the income earned by the new business and the sole proprietor's other potential sources of income.

Very often, practitioners refer to the sole proprietorship as the "default choice." This means that the individual who "goes it alone" (i.e., starts up a new business alone and without doing anything else) has probably formed a sole proprietorship. As counterin-tuitive as it may seem, the prospect of personal liability does not mean that the sole proprietorship is *never* going to be the best choice of entity for a new business. As we shall see in the remaining materials in this chapter, the ease of formation and operation often make this form of business organization the superior choice for many new small businesses, particularly where the owner/entrepreneur plans to work full time managing the business.

QUESTIONS

1. Is this form of business entity available in the case of our new client, SoftCo?
2. How will the income generated by the new business operated as a sole proprietorship be taxed for federal income tax purposes?

---

2. *The (General) Partnership*

As a general rule, when practicing lawyers (and usually their clients, too) refer to a partnership, they are referring to what is properly known in the law as a *general partnership* — to distinguish it from a limited partnership or a limited liability partnership (LLP), each of which will be discussed later in this section. If the sole proprietorship is the oldest form of business entity, then the partnership cannot be far behind because it is the oldest form of "cooperative [business] activity."[1] Thus, this form of business entity is modernly defined as "an association of two or more persons to carry on as co-owners a business for profit."[2] As this definition implies, no particular legal formalities are required to organize a business as a partnership.[3]

Since partnerships date back to the earliest days of commercial (entrepreneurial) activity, there is a long history of common law development of partnership law dating back to the medieval courts in England. In this country, by the early 20th century, the common law development of partnership law gave way to codification as a matter of state law in the form of partnership statutes. The Uniform Partnership Act (UPA) was first promulgated as a uniform law in 1914 and subsequently was substantially revised by the National Conference of Commissioners on Uniform State Laws (NCCUSL) in 1994. That statute then went through several important amendments and finally emerged in 1997 as the current Uniform Partnership Act. As a technical matter, both statutes are referred to in the literature by the acronym "UPA," generally by adopting the convention to refer to earlier statute as UPA (1914) and the later revision as UPA (1997). However, to

---

1. *See* I ALAN R. BROMBERG & LARRY E. RIBSTEIN, BROMBERG AND RIBSTEIN ON PARTNERSHIP §1.02(a) at 1:19 (1996).

2. UPA §6(i); RUPA §202(a).

3. Nor, for that matter, are any particular (legal) formalities required to create the sole proprietorship — hence the reference to the sole proprietorship as the default entity. In the case of partnerships, however, this means that two or more persons can form a general partnership without even knowing it. These situations are often referred to in the law as "inadvertent partnerships," a topic discussed in more detail later in this section.

make things simpler, many lawyers and commentators refer to the 1997 revision as the Revised Uniform Partnership Act, or more affectionately known as "RUPA," and the 1914 enactment as the "UPA." This casebook follows that convention. The vast majority of states today have adopted some form of RUPA, while the remaining states (other than Louisiana) largely continue to follow the UPA.[4]

Prior to the adoption of the UPA, partnerships were governed by judicial case law, which varied widely from state to state. While the enactment of the UPA helped to eliminate some of the confusion regarding partnership law, considerable uncertainty remained with respect to the rules governing general partnerships. Indeed, many provisions of the UPA are ambiguous or vague and offer little practical guidance with respect to the operation of the partnership. One of the primary goals of the NCCUSL in amending the 1914 statute was to reduce the ambiguity inherent in various provisions of the original statute. Notwithstanding this laudable goal, RUPA has itself created new uncertainties in those states where it has been adopted. Moreover, the case law governing partnerships continues to be conflicting and often confusing.

Even though the following language was written in 1914, the prefatory note to the UPA continues to reflect a fairly accurate assessment of the current state of partnership law:

> There is probably no other subject connected with our business law in which a greater number of instances can be found where, in matters of almost daily occurrence, the law is uncertain. This uncertainty is due, not only to conflict between the decisions of different states, but more to the general lack of consistency in legal theory. In several of the sections [of the UPA] . . . there exists an almost hopeless confusion of theory and practice, making the actual administration of the law difficult and often inequitable.

In general, RUPA carried forward the basic rules of the UPA. But RUPA also introduced several major reforms in order to update the default provisions of the UPA, most notably in the following areas:

- RUPA treats the existence of the partnership as an entity separate and apart from the individual partners, so that the withdrawal of an individual partner generally does not end the partnership.
- While retaining the concept of "dissolution," RUPA introduces the concept of "dissociation," which, as we shall see, results in greater stability of the partnership form upon the withdrawal or death of an individual partner.
- RUPA modifies the nature and scope of fiduciary duties owed by the individual partners to each other and to the partnership, replacing what had been generally regarded as a fairly high standard with more limited duties of loyalty and care.
- RUPA introduces certain reforms with regard to the contribution and transfer of partnership property by allowing the partnership to file a "statement of authority" relating to acts of a partner in general, and the authority of a partner to transact real property, in particular.

---

4. Daniel Kleinberger, Agency, Partnerships, and LLCs: Examples & Explanations at pp. 230-231 (4th ed. 2012).

The nature of these reforms under RUPA is described in more detail in section B of this chapter.

Perhaps the most important characteristic of the partnership is that the individual partners will be held personally liable for the debts of the partnership. However, RUPA does not allow a creditor of the partnership to collect from the assets of an individual partner unless the creditor has been unsuccessful in satisfying the creditor's judgment against the assets of the partnership.

The other key, defining characteristic of the partnership is its informality. As we have previously observed, inadvertent partnerships continue to arise because there are no specific, legal formalities that must be followed in order to create the general partnership under either RUPA or the UPA. However, as a practical matter, it is customary (and certainly good practice) for the individual partners to enter into a written partnership agreement that defines the rights and obligations of the parties. In the absence of a partnership agreement that provides otherwise, the default rules of RUPA (or the UPA, as the case may be) will govern to determine the scope of the parties' rights and obligations. Since no specific form of agreement is required under the terms of either RUPA or the UPA, partnership agreements can be as simple as a 1-page document or can run to 100 pages or more of densely printed text.

As such, the modern form of general partnership statute typically extends broad freedom of contract to the parties that provide the partners with great flexibility to customize the terms of their business arrangement in order to meet the needs of the individual partners and their new business. While there is no legal requirement mandating the parties to prepare a written partnership agreement, most practicing lawyers recommend that their clients incur the cost (and delay) associated with preparing a comprehensive, well-drafted agreement for primarily three reasons.

First, and probably most important, to the extent that the partners desire to modify the default rule of either RUPA or the UPA, a partnership agreement is necessary because otherwise the terms of these statutes will apply. Second, to the extent that the individual partners wish to define certain matters with greater specificity or detail than is otherwise provided under RUPA or the UPA, these provisions must be set forth in the partnership agreement in order to be effective. So, for example, it is not uncommon to find that a comprehensive, well-drafted partnership agreement will include provisions covering voting rights of the partners, distributions to the partners, and buy-sell agreements, all of which are matters not addressed under the UPA and only covered in the most general of terms under RUPA. Finally, the third reason most commonly given to encourage clients to enter into a written partnership agreement is that the preparation of such an agreement will customarily decrease the likelihood of disagreement (or even litigation) regarding the terms of the partnership. To offer but one example, there are legions of cases that stem fundamentally from differences regarding control of the business or the proper division of profits from the business, matters which should be carefully and thoroughly addressed in the partnership agreement.

An obvious drawback to the partnership form of doing business (at least from the perspective of the individual partners) is the unlimited personal liability imposed on each of the partners for the business debts of the partnership. Today, though, most states have adopted statutes to address this concern. These statutes establish a new form of business entity known as the *limited liability partnership (LLP)*. Generally speaking, LLPs are general partnerships that have made an election to be treated as an LLP by filing the requisite forms with the secretary of state's office. The effect of becoming an LLP is to shield all partners from personal liability on partnership debts, although the individual partners remain personally liable for their own actions as partners. In addition, the assets of the partnership and its business continue to be available to satisfy all of the claims of the partnership's creditors, whether in contract or tort. So, for example, a lawyer who is a partner in a law firm that has elected to be treated as an LLP will be liable to clients for his or her own malpractice, as will the assets of the partnership. If, however, the assets of the malpracticing partner and the assets of the partnership are not sufficient to make the client whole, the effect of making the election to be an LLP is to shield the other partners from any personal liability on this debt of the law firm partnership. As originally conceived, LLP statutes were designed to protect partners of professional general partnerships, particularly lawyers and accountants, from personal liability for malpractice committed by *other* partners in the partnership. The first such statute was adopted in 1991 in Texas, with other states soon following, including Delaware. Today, most LLP statutes extend the limited liability protection to partnerships engaged in all types of businesses, not just professional partnerships. Moreover, many states' LLP statutes extend the liability protection to include contractual obligations of the partnership as well as tort liability. Under this type of LLP statute, the limited liability protection offered to general partners more closely approximates the shield of limited liability offered to shareholders of a corporation, which is described in more detail later in this chapter. In light of their relatively recent development, there are many open questions under these LLP statutes, including the scope of the individual partner's protection against vicarious liability on partnership debts.

QUESTIONS

1. What is the law in your state — RUPA or the UPA?
2. Have Joan and Michael formed an "inadvertent partnership"?

3. The Limited Partnership

Like the general partnership, the limited partnership dates back to medieval times and developed as part of the common law of merchants. In the United States, the law of limited partnerships evolved in a manner similar to that of general partnerships with the first uniform act — the Uniform Limited Partnership Act (ULPA) — promulgated in 1916. This statute was substantially revised in 1976 and again in 1985, with the first revision generally referred to as the Revised Uniform Limited Partnership Act (RULPA) and the second revision generally referred to as RULPA with the 1985 Amendments

(RULPA (1985)). Today, "most states have in effect some version" of either RULPA or RULPA (1985).[5]

A limited partnership consists of at least one limited partner and at least one general partner. The key distinguishing feature of the limited partnership is the limited liability of the limited partners for the debts of the limited partnership's business. Generally speaking, a limited partner is an investor whose personal liability for partnership obligations is limited to the amount of his or her or its contribution to the limited partnership. Historically, in exchange for this limited liability protection, the general rule was that the limited partners may not participate in managing the business affairs of the limited partnership. If they did take part in control of the business, such participation would strip them of their limited liability.[6]

As mentioned above, the general rule is that every limited partnership must have at least one general partner, who by statute bears unlimited liability for the debts of the limited partnership's business and who bears all responsibility for managing the business affairs of the limited partnership. However, a corporation or an LLC may serve as the sole general partner. Alternatively, several states, including Texas, Pennsylvania, and Florida, have adopted statutes permitting limited liability limited partnerships (LLLPs)–which shield even the general partner's personal assets from liability on the debts of the limited partnership's business.

For federal income tax purposes, general partners in a limited partnership receive essentially the same treatment as in a general partnership, since both are "pass-through" entities (a concept described in more detail later in this chapter). Limited partners, however, are treated differently because they are subject to the "passive activity" limitations of I.R.C. §469, a provision that was adopted by Congress as part of the Tax Reform Act of 1986. While tax considerations that influence the choice of entity decisions are described more generally in section C of this chapter, at this point suffice it to say that the practical impact of §469 is that it often prevents limited partners from receiving the benefit of the tax losses generated by the limited partnership's business. Notwithstanding the practical impact of I.R.C. §469, limited partnerships are often used to attract income-seeking investors who wish to limit their personal liability and do not wish to actively participate in managing the business. At this point, it bears emphasizing that prospective investors are often attracted to the limited partnership because this form of business entity eliminates the "double taxation burden" associated with "C corporations," a topic discussed in more detail later in this chapter.

In the past, as described in more detail in section C of this chapter, the Internal Revenue Service (IRS) has sought to tax certain limited partnerships as corporations, thereby eliminating many of the tax incentives of investing in a limited partnership.[7] Today, however, the IRS treats business entities, including limited partnerships, as partnerships if they meet the requirements of the so-called check-the-box regulations,

---

5. *Id.* at 457.
6. *See* ULPA §7; RULPA §303(a) (1976); RULPA §303(a) (1985).
7. The primary tax incentive to organizing the business as a partnership (either general or limited) is to obtain "pass-through" treatment, which is described in section C of this chapter. If the business entity is taxed as a "regular C corporation," then the tax incentives of investing in a limited partnership are eliminated.

provided, however, that the partnership is not a "publicly traded limited partnership" under I.R.C. §7704. The developments that led Congress to enact §7704 have been described by one knowledgeable commentator as follows:

> During the 1980s, the publicly traded limited partnership emerged as a capital financing tool primarily in the real estate and natural resources industries, but its use also expanded into other areas. The principal difference between the traditional limited partnership and the publicly traded limited partnership ["PTLP"] is that limited partnership interests in the latter are readily tradable. Thus, before enactment of I.R.C. §7704, the PTLP provided the tax treatment and liability protection of traditional limited partnerships and the liquidity of publicly held corporations.
>
> Because of congressional concern that PTLPs would proliferate and thus erode the corporate tax base, the Revenue Act of 1987 added §7704 to the I.R.C. Under this provision, PTLPs are generally treated as C corporations for federal income tax purposes and PTLP profits are thus subject to double taxation. . . .
>
> . . . Because PTLPs . . . will be treated as C corporations, it seems unlikely that the PTLP form will be very useful. . . .

Bruce P. Ely & Christopher R. Grissom, *Choice of Entity: Legal Considerations of Selection*, 50 Corporate Practice Series A-10 to A-11 (4th ed. 2001).

As was mentioned earlier, under the ULPA, limited partners who "took part in control of the business" risked losing their shield of limited liability. Because of the possibility for draconian consequences, one of the major reforms introduced by the RULPA was to clarify the scope of management participation permitted by limited partners in the partnership's business without losing their shield of limited liability protection.

However, we need not dwell on the nature of these reforms because, as a practical matter, the limited partnership is less commonly used as a result of the development of the LLC — the limited liability company. As described later in this chapter, the evolution of the LLC provided transaction planners with the key combination of limited liability protection for all investors in the new business along with "pass-through" treatment of the new business for federal income tax purposes. As a result of this "revolution" in business entity law, the limited partnership, which historically had often been the preferred choice of entity, has largely been replaced with a more flexible and effective way of accomplishing essentially the same result.

Although it seemed to many commentators that the days of the limited partnership were numbered, the drafters of the uniform laws (the NCCUSL) came to the rescue and revitalized this form of business entity for the twenty-first century. The new act, the Uniform Limited Partnership Act (2001) (more popularly known as "Re-RULPA"), attempts to carve out a small but rather clearly defined niche for the limited partnership. Re-RULPA has been adopted in a handful of states, and its goal is described in the prefatory note to Re-RULPA as follows:

> The new Act has been drafted for a world in which limited liability partnerships and limited liability companies can meet many of the needs formerly met by limited partnerships. This Act therefore targets two types of enterprises that seem largely beyond the scope of LLPs [limited liability partnerships] and LLCs: (i) sophisticated, manager-entrenched commercial deals whose participants commit for the long term, and

(ii) estate planning arrangements (family limited partnerships). This Act accordingly assumes that, more often than not, people utilizing it will want:

- Strong centralized management, strongly entrenched, and
- Passive investors with little control over or right to exit the entity.

The Act's rules, and particularly its default rules, have been designed to reflect these assumptions.

Uniform Limited Partnership Act (2001), *available at* http://www.uniformlaws.org/shared/docs/limited%20partnership/ulpa_final_2001rev.pdf.

4. *The Corporation*

The modern corporation originated in England approximately 500 years ago, where (perhaps somewhat oddly enough) it was primarily used to organize ventures of great public importance, such as universities. In this country, the corporation first developed in the early nineteenth century, and each corporation was created by a specific legislative act, "as distinguished from a general law allowing any persons to organize themselves . . . [as] a corporation by complying with prescribed conditions." JAMES D. COX & THOMAS LEE HAZEN, CORPORATIONS 31 (2d ed. 2003). These same noted scholars describe this legislative process and the subsequent evolution of modern corporation statutes as follows:

> . . . To incorporate by special act, a private bill had to be introduced in the state leg-islature, be considered by the legislative committees, pass both houses, and be signed by the governor. . . .
>
> With the increasing pressures of industrialization, legislatures found themselves deluged with requests for legislation bestowing corporate status. The early reliance on special legislative acts to confer corporate status on individual entities proved not only inefficient but also was rife with the opportunity for favoritism and corruption. Ultimately, states adopted constitutional provisions declaring that, with specified excep-tions, the legislature should not pass any special act creating a corporation. These constitutional provisions permitted corporations to be formed only by compliance with general incorporation laws. General incorporation legislation has now developed to the extent that almost any legitimate enterprise can be conducted in corporate form upon compliance with simple statutory formalities. . . .
>
> The first American general incorporation act — that is, an act allowing any persons to incorporate by compliance with the terms of the statute, apparently was a statute passed in 1811 in the State of New York. . . .
>
> Soon after New York's pioneer enactment, other states passed acts authorizing the incorporation of manufacturing companies. The more modern general corporation acts were expansive. They covered almost every kind of lawful business. The trend toward use of general acts permitting incorporation by signing and filing articles of incorpora-tion began immediately after 1835. With the arrival of general incorporation laws, in contrast to incorporation by special act, businessmen could with certainty and efficiency gain the benefits of corporate status for their businesses.
>
> * * *
>
> In 1896, New Jersey enacted what may be regarded as the first permissive modern incorporation act — that is, a statute that conferred broad powers on corporations,

empowered promoters of corporations to set up almost any kind of corporate structure they desired, granted broad powers to corporate directors and managers, and provided great protection against liability for corporate directors and managers. . . .

In 1913, however, reform-minded then-governor Woodrow Wilson caused New Jersey to amend its more permissive provisions. Delaware, which had borrowed most of its corporation law from New Jersey, seized the opportunity to assume leadership in providing and keeping up-to-date a body of permissive corporate laws. . . . Still other states have liberalized their statutes to encourage their local businesses to "stay at home" by incorporating locally rather than organizing in Delaware, New Jersey, or some other permissive jurisdiction.

It can thus be said that, by the end of the nineteenth century, the states had loosened the bonds that once hobbled the corporation's formation and operation. . . .

It is safe to say that the liberalization trend that began toward the end of the nineteenth century continued throughout the twentieth century so that today all states have broadly permissive enabling corporation statutes with very little evidence in any state statute of regulatory or paternalistic provisions. . . . Legislatures, especially since the 1960s, have consistently embraced the philosophy of allowing corporations, within the broad framework of local law, to tailor their governance structure to accommodate their own special needs and relationships.

* * *

The Model Business Corporation Act first appeared in completed form in 1950 [and was promulgated by the Section on Business Law of the American Bar Association (ABA)]. The Model Act continued the liberalizing trend that originated in New Jersey and Delaware and for a long time has been universally viewed as "'enabling,' 'permissive,' and 'liberal' as distinguished from 'regulatory' and 'paternalistic.'" [HARRY G. HENN, HANDBOOK ON THE LAW OF CORPORATIONS AND OTHER BUSINESS ENTERPRISES, 22 n.40 (2d ed. 1970).] From time to time, other states have competed for the lead in this type of liberalization (which at times has been referred to as "the race to the bottom" although others view it as a "race to the top"). The Delaware legislature, however, continues to be the leader in originating permissive corporate legislation. Delaware's continued popularity among public corporations is documented by the fact that nearly 90 percent of public corporations that change their corporate domicile choose to reincorporate in Delaware. The Model Act was intended not to become a uniform corporation law but rather to serve as a drafting guide for the states. Eventually the Model Act became the pattern for large parts of the corporation statutes in most states (notable exceptions being California, Delaware, and New York). The [ABA] revises the Model Act from time to time, and typically a number of states amend their corporation statutes to adopt the latest revisions.

The first complete revision of the Model Act appears in the Revised Model Business Corporation Act (1984) [MBCA]. The Revised Model Act incorporates many simplifying and innovative provisions that the states had experimented with over the years. In addition, the Revised Model Act has through subsequent revisions continued the liberalizing trend that started in Delaware.

Most states, in addition to a general business corporation act, have more specialized general chartering acts governing the formation and regulation of corporations in special fields of business such as banking, building and loan associations, insurance, railroads, and public utilities. Similarly, virtually all states now have a separate act for professional corporations.

Corporation laws [typically] deal with such matters as the following: the content of the articles of incorporation; the rights of shareholders; the powers and liabilities of directors; rules governing shareholders' meetings and directors' meetings; restrictions on corporate finance, such as limitations on the withdrawal of funds by way of dividends and share purchases; the keeping and inspection of corporate records; and authorization of organic changes, such as charter amendments, sale of all corporate assets, merger and consolidation, and dissolution and winding up. . . .

COX & HAZEN, *supra*, at pp. 31-35. The mechanics of forming a corporation under these modern statutes is the focus of the materials in Chapter 5, where we revisit the "race of the lax" that was described in the preceding excerpt, most notably focusing on the relative advantages (and disadvantages) of organizing a new corporation under the corporation codes of either Delaware or California.

It bears emphasizing that the MBCA serves as a "model" act rather than a "uniform" act. As such, the MBCA does not stress uniformity, and therefore, it is constantly being amended by the ABA. So while the MBCA forms the basis for the corporation statutes enacted in over 30 states, it is not exactly the same in all of these jurisdictions. In adopting the MBCA, the local state legislature may have made changes to the MBCA, and the law of a particular state may not reflect all of the modern updates that the ABA has made to the MBCA.

This leads to a brief mention of the modern importance of the "internal affairs doctrine." As we have just seen, corporations are inherently creatures of state law. The internal affairs doctrine is a choice of law principle that specifies that the law of the state of incorporation governs matters involving the "internal affairs" of the corporation — that is, the relationships among the corporation's shareholders, directors, officers and agents — even if the company's business operations are located in a state other than the company's state of incorporation. The ramifications of this choice of law principle are explored in more detail in Chapter 5, as part of our discussion of the decision regarding which state to incorporate in, assuming the transaction planner has settled on the corporation as the preferred choice of entity.

Recall from your introductory course on Business Associations that the key, defining characteristic of the corporation is its shield of limited liability. That is to say, the shareholders, regardless whether they hold common or preferred shares, are generally "limited" to losing their initial investment and otherwise have no personal liability for the debts of the corporation. However, this shield of limited liability is not completely bulletproof:

> It follows that any business planner is well versed in the general black-letter-law proposition that shareholders of a corporation enjoy limited liability. However, such generalities are over-broad and may wane when applied to specific situations; this is especially true in the context of the closely-held concern.
>
> To begin with, as a practical matter a shareholder's potential liability will go further. When a small incorporated concern decides to raise funds by borrowing, prudent creditors will require the major shareholders to personally guarantee corporate obligations. Similarly, third parties contracting with the corporation will often require performance bonds or individual guarantees by the shareholders. Accordingly, at least until the enterprise becomes well established and sufficiently stable in the eyes of outsiders, limited liability will be limited in application to insulating the shareholders against tort judgments.
>
> In addition to the demands of the market place, there are various judicially created doctrines that may be applied to extinguish the shareholders' limited liability.

> Application of these doctrines [most notably, the doctrine of piercing the corporate veil] can work extreme harshness since the lack of predictability of result makes this an extremely difficult risk to anticipate and guard against.

Thomas Lee Hazen, *The Decision to Incorporate*, 58 Neb. L. Rev. 627, 630-631 (1979).

Another important distinction between the corporate and partnership forms of business entities relates to management of the business affairs. In the corporation, directors are charged with managing the company's business affairs. These directors are elected by the shareholders and, in turn, the directors appoint the corporate officers over whom the shareholders have no direct control. Although the shareholders are owners of the corporation, they exert very little control over the business affairs of the corporation. In contrast, the individual partners, as co-owners in a general partnership, retain managerial control over the partnership's business affairs.

As described in more detail later in this chapter, for federal income tax purposes, the Internal Revenue Code (the Code) makes a fundamental distinction between businesses that are treated as "pass-through" entities and those that are treated as separate taxpayers. The Code divides business entities into two general categories: C corporations, which are separate taxpaying entities; and "pass-through" entities, which are further divided into S corporations and partnership-type entities that are subject to Subchapter K of the Code. This leads to the imposition of a "double taxation burden" on those corporations that are treated as separate taxpayers. The nature of this double taxation burden and its ramifications for the business and its owners are explored in section C of this chapter. At this point in our discussion of the different forms of business entities, the federal income tax distinction between C corporations and pass-through entities is important because of its important role in the evolution of the LLC.

5. *The Limited Liability Company*

The story of the creation of the LLC is described at greater length in Chapter 3, along with a detailed examination of the mechanics involved in creating and operating a new business as an LLC. It bears emphasizing that, as a lawyer, understanding the evolution of the LLC is important for at least two reasons. First, as a matter of your professional development as a lawyer, the story of the creation of the LLC reflects how lawyers add value to their clients' business activity when they "think outside the box" and create innovative solutions for recurring problems in the commercial world. "The explanation behind the LLC's birth boils down to innovative professionals creating solutions when the current legal system fails to meet client needs." Susan Pace Hamill, *The Origins Behind the Limited Liability Company*, 59 Ohio St. L.J. 1459, 1463 (1998). Second, the evolution of the LLC reflects that, as a business lawyer, you will be a lifelong learner since nothing about the law is static, and thus, it is inevitable that the tools available to solve your clients' business problems will change over the years.

The LLC is a hybrid form of business entity in that it combines the pass-through attributes of partnerships for federal income tax purposes with the corporate characteristic of limited liability. Before the advent of the LLC, limited liability was generally available only to shareholders and limited partners. Historically, as passive investors, however, these owners had very little, if any, role in the management of the business on pain of losing the protections afforded by the shield of limited liability.

The key defining characteristic of the LLC is that it combines three important attributes that many new, start-up businesses seek: limited liability, the ability to participate in business management, and favorable income tax treatment. With the development of the LLC, all of these attributes can now be found in a single entity.

So how is it that the LLC allows a new business to achieve all three desired attributes within a single form of business organization? Although the LLC statutes are not uniform across all 50 states (as we shall see in the next chapter), they are similar with respect to certain basic attributes. All LLC statutes provide for limited liability of the members (i.e., the owners of the LLC), similar to the shield of limited liability extended to shareholders (i.e., the owners of the corporation). With respect to managing the LLC's business affairs, the LLC statutes offer great flexibility in that the LLC is permitted to have almost any assortment of attributes that the founders desire. The members can decide to manage the business themselves (which is referred to as a "member-managed" LLC), or the members may delegate this authority to managers who may or may not be members of the LLC (which is referred to as a "manager-managed" LLC). Thus, the LLC can have the corporate-like attributes of centralized management, free transferability of interests, and unlimited life, all of which are described in more detail later in this chapter. On the other hand, the LLC can have the partnership-like attributes of equal management rights in every owner, no transferability of interests, and automatic dissolution upon the request of any owner. Or, alternatively, the LLC can have whichever combination of these attributes that the founders may desire. (The mechanics of implementing this flexibility under today's LLC statutes are discussed in Chapter 3.)

Given the extraordinary flexibility of the LLC, you may logically wonder why any other form of business entity would ever be used today. However, the truth of the matter is that corporations and partnerships continue to be used for many small business start-ups. There are a number of reasons that corporations and partnerships have proven to be so durable. Probably the most important reason is that transaction planners (i.e., business lawyers) are generally risk averse, although indeed their clients (i.e., the entrepreneurs) are usually not nearly so risk averse. This observation leads to a general truism that no lawyer worth his or her salt wants to run the risk of *legal* uncertainty if it can be avoided. And, at the risk of stating the obvious, the LLC is still a relatively new form of business entity. As a practical consequence, this means that the common law surrounding LLCs has not begun to develop the depth and robustness that exists in most states with respect to corporations and partnerships, and this is particularly true of Delaware law with respect to publicly traded corporations (see Chapter 5). Moreover, partnership law remains a necessary alternative in that it continues to provide a set of default rules for those entrepreneurs who do not consult a lawyer, but instead simply go into business for themselves. And, finally, good business lawyers continue to need corporation law, even for the new, start-up business regardless of its size because they and their clients often desire the clear answers that modern corporation statutes (and settled case law interpreting these statutes) provide for many of the recurring issues that the transaction planner must address, such as the extent of limited liability, the nature of fiduciary duties, the scope of duties owed to creditors, and the status of investments as securities, to name just a few of the recurring issues facing the transaction planner.

QUESTIONS

1. How does the LLC improve on the common attributes of a corporation? On the limited partnership? In other words, which of the three attributes that many start-up businesses seek can be achieved by organizing the new business as a corporation? Does the limited partnership allow the founders to achieve any of these three objectives?

2. Prior to the development of the LLC, what were the business entities (or combination of business entities) that were available to business lawyers to help their clients achieve these three objectives? Generally speaking, the goal was to select a form of business entity and then "bend the rules" as far as possible to achieve all three objectives. Can you give some examples of how the default rules for partnerships and corporations could be "bent" to achieve all three of these attributes within a single form of business entity? (*Hint*: You may want to revisit this question after you finish reading the remaining materials in this chapter since some of these possibilities anticipate later material, particularly with respect to federal income tax law.) In this regard, you may want to consider the following possibilities, and analyze the respective advantages and disadvantages of each alternative:

   a. Incorporate and make an S corporation election — any drawbacks?
   b. Use a limited partnership and, by appropriate provisions in the agreement, extend basic management rights to limited partners — any drawbacks?
   c. Use a limited partnership with a corporate general partner — any drawbacks?
   d. Incorporate and allow investors to serve as officers and directors of the new corporation and then "zero out" the income to avoid (or at least minimize) the incidence of double taxation — any drawbacks?
   e. Use a general partnership and then attempt to contractually limit partner's liability — any drawbacks?

Notwithstanding the apparent rationality of the current arrangement, the proliferation of business entities has led some commentators to question the continued rationality of the current legal rules in the future. Without question, the LLC is on the rise, and in many states, has eclipsed the corporation as the preferred choice of entity for new businesses. Moreover, as time passes, judicial precedent will become more stable, yielding greater certainty and predictability to the use of the LLC. This has led some commentators to question the wisdom of continuing with the current arrangement. In other words, is it time for "entity rationalization"? That is the topic taken up by the author of the following article:

Richard A. Booth
Form and Function in Business Organizations

58 Bus. Law 1433 (2003)

Lawyers and academics who deal with the law of business organizations on a regular basis tend to minimize the differences between partnerships, corporations, and other forms of business organization. It is possible — perhaps even quite easy — to set up a corporation that works like a partnership or a partnership that works like a corporation. Some of us even question whether the law matters in this realm other than in connection with taxes — [and now] it may not matter much there. The question that naturally arises is why not get rid of this ever expanding alphabet soup of corporations, partnerships, limited partnerships, LLCs, LLPs, and LLLPs, and replace it with a unified system? In other words, is it not time for entity rationalization?

Why do people choose the business forms that they do? And why do they modify some default rules but not others? Presumably, one would want to know the answer before tinkering too much with the existing forms as they have evolved over the years . . .

QUESTIONS

---

1. Do you think there is a need for "entity rationalization"? You may want to reconsider this fundamental public policy question after reading the materials in Chapters 3 and 5, where we explain the default rules of LLCs and corporations in more detail.
2. Should the goal of entity rationalization mean more choice for entrepreneurs (and their lawyers) or should it mean a general movement toward fewer business entities? In thinking about the need for entity rationalization going forward, there is yet another development in the law of business entities that needs to be taken into account — the newest form of business entity that is known as the "public benefit corporation." This recent development is described in the next section.

---

6. *Public Benefit Corporations*

The newest entrant into the field of business entities is popularly known as the "public benefit corporation," a form of business entity intended to address the particular needs of social entrepreneurship. This section first describes the concept of social enterprise and then broadly describes legislation enacted by several states to accommodate the recent interest in — and proliferation of — social enterprises, with a particular focus on recently enacted statutes in Delaware and California.

a. What Is "Social Entrepreneurship"?

At the outset, it is necessary to distinguish "social enterprise" from "non-profit" legal entities:

> A non-profit entity is chartered under state law, and the organizing documents must include a statement of specific charitable purpose if filed as a public benefit non-profit corporation. Once incorporated as a state non-profit entity, the organization can then seek federal tax exempt status from the Internal Revenue Service (IRS). The IRS categorizes entities into exempt categories, of which the ones most analogous to benefit corporations are: Treas. Reg. §1.501(c)(3) public benefit organizations, private foundations, and private operating foundations.
>
> * * *
>
> Contrary to popular misconception, non-profit legal entities actually *can* earn profits.[1] They simply cannot distribute those profits to officers or employees. Rather, non-profit entities are required to dedicate their funds and activities "exclusively" to providing public benefits by serving one or more exempt purposes.[2] If a non-profit organization conducts activities unrelated to its exempt purpose, with an aim simply to generate revenue, those activities will be subject to taxation pursuant to the unrelated business income tax.[3] And if those unrelated activities constitute a "substantial nonexempt purpose," they will result in revocation of the organization's tax-exempt status. Thus, while it is possible for non-profit legal entities to generate revenue, doing so may in fact risk the organization's exempt status, profits may [then] be subject to the same tax rules as normal for-profit entities, and at any rate such profits cannot inure to stockholders, officers, employees, or other private individuals. Additional defining characteristics of non-profit legal entities include strict governance and accountability standards, which impose annual filing requirements in order for the organization to keep its tax exempt status once acquired from the state and/or the IRS.

Dirk Sampselle, *Social Enterprise: Choice of Legal Entity* (March 22, 2012), *available at* http://ssrn.com/abstract = 2234882.

So, what is "social enterprise?"

Over the past few years, jurisdictions across the country have enacted specialized organizational forms to house social enterprises. Social enterprises are entities dedicated to a blended mission of earning profits for owners and promoting social good. They are neither typical businesses, concentrated on the bottom line of profit, nor traditional [not-for-profit] charities, geared toward achieving some mission of good for society. Their founders instead see value in blending both goals. They believe their social enterprises will be superior to traditional businesses by considering and internalizing the social costs they produce.[2] They believe social enterprises more efficiently produce social goods than traditional charities by applying business methods to this important

---

1. *E.g.*, Aid to Artisans, Inc., v. Comm'r, 71 T.C. 202, 211 (1978).
2. Rev. Rul. 72-369, 1972-2 C.B. 245.
3. IRS Pub. 598, Tax on Unrelated Business Income of Exempt Organizations (Rev. March 2010).
2. *See, e.g.*, Julie Battilana, Matthew Lee, John Walker, & Cheryl Dorsey, *In Search of the Hybrid Ideal*, 10 Stan. Soc. Innov. Rev. 51, 52 (Summer 2012) (describing the desire of social entrepreneurs to exploit the positive externalities of linking social value and revenue creation).

work.[3] Yet, these social entrepreneurs worry traditional organizational forms designed for either businesses or charities will constrain their ability to achieve the gains they see in blended mission enterprises.[4] Legislatures have obviously been convinced. Since 2008, lawmakers in nearly one third of U.S. jurisdictions have enacted enabling legislation providing one or more specialized forms designed to house social enterprises.

Dana Brakman Reiser, *The Next Big Thing: Flexible Purpose Corporations*, Brooklyn Law School Research Paper No. 311 (Oct. 24, 2012), *available at* http://papers.ssrn.com/sol3/papers.cfm?abstract_id = 2166474.

b. Development of "Social Enterprise" Legislation

To date, legislative action has primarily concentrated on three specialized forms of business entities that are specifically designed to accommodate the particular needs of social enterprises: the low-profit limited liability company (L3C), the benefit corporation (sometimes referred to as the *public benefit corporation* or *B Corporation*),* and the flexible purpose corporation (FPC). The following article provides a broad overview of these most recent entrants to the growing proliferation of "business entities":

Dana Brakman Reiser
The Next Big Thing: Flexible-Purpose Corporations

Brooklyn Law School Research Paper No. 311 (Oct. 24, 2012)**

The flexible purpose corporation became available under the California Corporate Flexibility Act of 2011 (the "FPC statute").[6] It joined its (only slightly) older colleagues: the low-profit limited liability company (L3C) inaugurated by Vermont in 2008[7] and the

---

3. *See, e.g.*, Kyle Westaway, *New Legal Structures for "Social Entrepreneurs,"* WALL ST. JOURNAL ONLINE, Dec. 12, 2011 ("Social entrepreneurs believe a business can be part of the solution to some of the world's greatest challenges."); Dan Palotta, UNCHARITABLE 2008 (arguing that greater social good would be gained by allowing charities to follow a range of practices typically identified with for-profit enterprises).

4. *See, [e.g.,]* Heerad Sabeti, *The For-Benefit Enterprise*, HARVARD BUSINESS REVIEW, Nov. 2011 (lamenting that "socially-minded entrepreneurs end up shoehorning their vision into one structure or the other and accepting burdensome trade-offs in the process"); [and] Thomas Kelley, *Law and Choice of Entity on the Social Enterprise Frontier*, 84 TUL. L. REV. 337, 363-64 (2009).

I am sympathetic to the view that corporate law would not prevent adopters of a standard for-profit corporation from pursuing both businesses and non-business goals. *See, e.g.*, LYNN STOUT, THE SHAREHOLDER VALUE MYTH, 25-31 (2012); Einer Elhauge, *Sacrificing Corporate Profits in the Public Interest*, 80 N.Y.U. L. REV. 733, 738-47 (2005). This, however, clearly is not the perception from which social enterprise form creators and enthusiasts are working.

* *See* http://americansforcommunitydevelopment.org/laws.html (listing 9 states and a Native American tribe with L3C statutes as of fall 2013) and http://benefitcorp.net/state-by-state-legislative-status (listing 20 states with benefit corporation statutes, four of which also have L3C legislation on the books as of fall 2013).

** *Available at* http://papers.ssrn.com/sol3/papers.cfm?abstract_id = 2166474.

6. Cal. Sen. Bill 201 (2011) (approved by Governor Oct. 9, 2011).

7. VT. STAT. ANN. tit. 11 §3001(207); *see also* Vermont Secretary of State, Low-Profit Limited Liability Company, available at http://www.sec.state.vt.us/corps/dobiz/llc/llc_l3c.htm ("A low-profit LLC is a new type of company, called an 'L3C.' Vermont is the first state to enact this new type of company.")

[public] benefit corporation first adopted by Maryland in 2010.[8] Since their initial adoption, these forms have each been adopted by several other jurisdictions, and proposed in still others.[9] These later adoptions are not identical to the originals, though sufficient overlap exists to examine the L3C and benefit corporation as archetypes. Shortly after California adopted its FPC statute, Washington approved legislation enabling a Social Purpose Corporation form, which shares some, though by no means all, of the elements of the FPC.[10] Other state legislatures have considered new forms sharing features with the FPC,[11] and other countries have implemented yet further models.[12] To situate the FPC form in context, without overwhelming the reader with details on too many jurisdiction-specific enactments, this [paper] will discuss the major features of the L3C and [flexible or public] benefit corporation in brief.

The low-profit limited liability company operates like a standard limited liability company (LLC) with only a handful of deviations. All of these changes address the specialized purposes adopting entities must pursue. Specifically, L3Cs must "significantly further the accomplishment of one or more charitable or educational purposes within the meaning of" the Internal Revenue Code sections defining charitable contributions[13] and "no significant purpose of the company is the production of income or property."[14]

That said, an L3C that actually produces significant income or capital appreciation will not be disqualified from this statutes [sic] by virtue of those facts alone.[15] Other than these adaptations of the L3C's purposes, the statutes typically subject them to ordinary for-profit LLC law. Their governance structures are highly flexible, subject to private ordering by an operating agreement. In contrast to the [flexible or public] benefit corporation and FPC [flexible purpose corporation to be described below], L3Cs have no special disclosure obligations, no expressly modified fiduciary duties,[16] and no

---

8. Md. Code Ann., Corps. & Ass'ns §§5-6C-01 to -08 (2011).

9. For current listings of L3C and benefit corporation enabling legislation enactments, see http://americansforcommunitydevelopment.org/laws.html and http://wwwbenefitcorp.net/state-by-state-legislative-status respectively. See also Bishop, Carter G., Fifty State Series: L3C & B Corporation Legislation Table (July 10, 2012). *Suffolk University Law School Research Paper No. 10-11.* Available at SSRN: http//ssrn.com/abstract=1561783 or http://dx.doi.org/10.2139/ssrn.1561783 (analyzing the contents of legislation); Murray, J. Haskell, Benefit Corporations: State Statute Comparison Chart (December 27, 2011). Available at SSRN: http://ssrn/com/abstract=1988556 or http://dx.koi.org/10.2139/ssrn.1988556 (analyzing the contents of benefit corporation statutes).

10. Washington SHB 2239 (2012).

11. See Indiana Sen. Bill 62 (2012) (withdrawn); Minnesota H.F. No. 697 (2011) (stuck in committee).

12. *See, e.g.,* Dana Brakman Reiser, 85 CHI.-KENT L. REV. 619, 630-36 (2010) (discussing the UK's community interest company (CIC)); Matthew F. Doering, *Note, Fostering Social Enterprise; A Historical and International Analysis,* 20 DUKE J. COMP. & INT'L L. 291, 306-16 (2010) (describing the CIC and the Belgian Societe a Finalite Sociale).

13. Vt. Stat. Ann. tit. 11 §3001(27)(A).

14. Vt. Stat. Ann. tit. 11 §3001(27)(B).

15. Vt. Stat. Ann. tit. 11 §3001(27)(B). In addition, L3C's may not be formed to "accomplish [one] or more political or legislative purposes," again as defined by the tax code. Vt. Stat. Ann. tit. 11§3001(27)(C).

16. Some commentators argue adapted duties for L3C fiduciaries are created by statutory implication. *See e.g.,* John Tyler, *Negating the Legal Problem of Having "Two Masters": A Framework for L3C Fiduciary Duties and Accountability,* 35 VT. L. REV. 117, 141 (2010); J. Haskell Murray & Edward I. Hwang, *Purpose with Profit: Governance, Enforcement, Capital-Raising and Capital-Locking in Low-Profit Limited Liability Companies,* 66 U. MIAMI L. REV. 601, 639-40 (2011). Others, including myself, argue that L3C statutes

limitations on change of status. In fact, an L3C ceases to exist as such, and transforms immediately into an ordinary LLC, if at any time it no longer meets the special purpose requirements.[17] This transformation occurs by operation of law. The entity need not file any documents indicating the change, managers and members have no official input, and no regulator is involved.[18]

When compared to the L3C, the statutory framework establishing the [flexible or public] benefit corporation is both more extensive and more rigid. This is due, in part, to the fact that benefit corporations borrow the for-profit corporate form as a starting point. The signature innovation of the benefit corporation form, however, is its reliance upon "third-party standards."[19] These standards play a powerful role, as benefit corporations must: (1) frame their required public benefit purposes with reference to them, and (2) issue reports to shareholders and the public evaluating their achievements according to them. Benefit corporation statutes differ in the level of detail at which they define the content of such standards. For example, California's statute defines a third party standard as "a comprehensive assessment of the impact of the business and the business's operations upon" a broad range of stakeholder groups identified by the statute.[20] In contrast, Maryland's legislation requires only a generic "standard for defining, reporting, and addressing best practices in corporate social and environmental performance."[21] All [flexible or public] benefit corporation statutes demand that third-party standards be developed by transparent, independent entities.[22]

Benefit corporation statutes also make several important revisions to standard for-profit corporate governance arrangements. Benefit corporation directors must consider a very broad range of non-shareholder stakeholder interests when taking [sic] decisions.[23] Benefit corporations must report to shareholders and the public on their pursuit and achievement of their public benefit purposes.[24] With this information in hand, benefit

---

impose no such prioritization and leave fiduciary obligations dangerously uncertain. *See* Dana Brakman Reiser, *Blended Enterprise and the Dual Mission Dilemma*, 35 VT. L. REV. 105, 109-11 (2010); Dana Brakman Reiser, *Governing And Financing Blended Enterprise*, 85 CHI.-KENT L. REV. 619, 623-30 (2010); Dana Brakman Rieser, *Theorizing Forms for Social Enterprise*, at pp. 18-19 (forthcoming EMORY L.J. 2012).

17. *See* Vt. Stat. Ann. tit. 11 §3001(27)(D).

18. A more detailed account and critique of the L3C form can be found in Brakman Reiser, 85 CHI.-KENT L. REV. *supra* note __, at 620-30.

19. *See* Dana Brakman Reiser, *Benefit Corporations — A Sustainable Form of Organization?*, 46 WAKE FOREST L. REV. 591, 592, 600-03 (2011); Murray AU draft at 21; Callison AU draft at 6-7, 10-11.

20. CAL. CORP. CODE §14601(g). References in this article will cite legislation as adopted by various jurisdictions as an example, rather than the model statute drafted by proponents. This model statute can be consulted at: http://benefitcorp.org/storage/Model_Legislation.pdf. A thorough description and evaluation of the benefit corporation form can be found in Dana Brakman Reiser, *Benefit Corporations — A Sustainable Form of Organization?*, 46 WAKE FOREST L. REV. 591 (2011).

21. MD. CODE ANN., CORPS. & ASS'NS §5-6C-01(e).

22. *See, e.g.*, MD. CODE ANN., CORPS & ASS'NS §5-6C-01(e); N.J. STAT. ANN. §14A:18-1 (West 2011); VA. CODE ANN. §13.1-782 (2011).

23. *See, e.g.*, MD. CODE ANN., CORPS. & ASS'NS §5-6C-07 (LexisNexis 2011); VT. STAT. ANN. tit. 11A, §21.09 (2011).

24. *See, e.g.*, VA. CODE ANN. §113.1-791 (2011); HAW REV. STAT. §420D-11.

corporation shareholders can sue fiduciaries to hold them to their expanded duties, sometimes using new enforcement actions created under the statutes.[25] Shareholders also must approve adoption or abandonment of benefit corporation status by a super-majority vote.[26]

The L3C and the [flexible or public]-benefit corporation represent poles on a spectrum of flexibility. On the one hand, the L3C allows almost complete contractual freedom to order a social enterprise as founders might desire. The statutory scheme imposes no new obligations on fiduciaries and no disclosure requirements. It is a status that may be taken on and thrown off with ease, merely by changing the purposes the entity pursues. On the other hand, the benefit corporation provides a comprehensive set of off-the-rack governance arrangements, many of which cannot be varied by adopters. It enlists the assistance of third-party standard setters to assess the public benefit bona fides of adopting entities. It also varies fiduciary duties, creates reporting obligations, and empowers shareholders with voting and litigation rights. [On the other hand, California's legislation enacting the flexible purpose corporation (FPC)] sits somewhere between these two poles, offering significant flexibility and discretion for founders and directors, but paired with expansive rights, powers and protections for shareholder investors.

Query: Would you recommend that Joan and Michael organize their new business as an L3C? As a flexible (or public) benefit corporation? The preceding article referred to the "flexible purpose corporation," a new form of business that is (as of this writing in fall 2013) unique to California. The next section describes this new form of business entity in more detail.

c. California's Social Enterprise Legislation

Effective January 2012, California law permits businesses to organize under two new forms of corporate entities: the Benefit Corporation[1] and the Flexible Purpose Corporation.[2] The following article provides general background regarding these two new forms of business organization that are now available to social entrepreneurs as a matter of California business law.

---

25. *See, e.g.,* N.J. STAT. ANN. §14A:18-10 (West 2011); LA. REV. STAT. §1825(2012).

26. *See, e.g.,* N.Y. BUS. CORP. L. §1705; S.C. Code tit. 33, ch. 38 §§220-230.

1. The Benefit Corporation was created by California Assembly Bill 361, which adds Part 13 to Division 3 of Title 1 of the California Corporations Code (http://www.leginfo.ca.gov/pub/11-12/bill/asm/ab_0351 -0400/ab_361_bill_20111009_chaptered.pdf). Codified at California Corporations Code, Section 14600 *et seq.*

2. The Flexible Purpose Corporation was created by California Senate Bill 201, which adds Division 1.5 to Title 1 of the California Corporations Code and amends other related sections of the Code (http:// www.leginfo.ca.gov/pub/11-12/bill/sen/sb_0201-0250/sb_201_bill_2011109_chaptered.pdf). Codified at California Corporations Code, Section 2500 *et seq.*

Louise Adamson, Yusef Alexandrine, and Remsen Kinne
*Profit and Purpose: Two New Types of California Corporations
that Promote Social as well as Financial Benefits*

K & L Gates LLP, Corporate Alert (April 3, 2012)*

. . . These [two] new corporate forms facilitate companies' efforts to advance social welfare and environmental sustainability objectives while creating profits and value for their shareholders.

The primary purposes of traditional for-profit corporations are to promote long-term value growth and maximize shareholder profit. Other purposes, such as social benefit, should not conflict with these primary goals. Although some for-profit corporations are currently able to devote resources to advancing social benefit goals, these efforts must be balanced with the corporate directors' mandate of maximizing growth and profit.

Corporate directors who prioritize social benefit objectives to the detriment of profitability or value optimization risk being sued for breaching their fiduciary duty to the shareholders. Conversely, non-profit corporations have flexibility to pursue social welfare goals, but are prohibited from earning profit for shareholders. . . .

[California's new] Benefit Corporations and Flexible Purpose Corporations are hybrids between for-profit and non-profit corporate forms that permit corporations to pursue profits as well as social benefit goals. The new corporate structures:

- Require directors to consider not only shareholders' interests, but also the interests of stakeholders such as employees, suppliers, customers and community (which includes environmental concerns); and
- Create transparency and accountability in the implementation of social benefit goals by requiring the company to publish an annual report which provides an assessment of the successes, failures and hurdles to be overcome in achieving those goals.

California is the first state to adopt the Flexible Purpose Corporation form. It is among a growing number of states that have adopted the Benefit Corporation form. . . .

These corporate forms are new and have not yet been widely adopted. It is uncertain how they will be construed in states that have not yet adopted similar statutes. As more states adopt similar statutes, this should facilitate planning to organize a company using one of these forms.

* * *

III. Benefit Corporations

A. Overview

A Benefit Corporation must pursue social welfare objectives and must meet more transparency requirements than those required of traditional for-profit corporations.

---

* *Available at* http://klgates.com/profit-and-purpose-two-new-types-of-california-corporations-that-promote-social-as-well-as-financial-benefits-04-03-2012/.

Benefit Corporations are generally well suited for use by private companies that are focused on social and environmental goals and that are able to avail themselves of socially responsible capital funding sources.

A Benefit Corporation must be formed for the broad purpose of creating a "general public benefit," which is defined as "a material positive impact on society and the environment, taken as a whole" as assessed against a third party standard. In addition, the corporation may elect to also identify one or more specific public benefits for society or the environment, including:

- Providing low-income or underserved individuals or communities with beneficial products or services.
- Promoting economic opportunity for individuals or communities beyond the creation of jobs in the ordinary course of business.
- Preserving the environment.
- Improving human health.
- Promoting the arts, sciences, or advancement of knowledge.
- Increasing the flow of capital to entities with a public benefit purpose.
- Accomplishing any other particular benefit for society or the environment.

* * *

E. Potential Advantages

Benefit Corporations offer a number of benefits over traditional for-profit and non-profit corporations:

Protection from Liability. Directors owe no fiduciary duties to beneficiaries of the Benefit Corporation's general or specific public benefit purposes arising solely from such persons' status as actual or intended beneficiaries of a public benefit.

Third Party Standards. Accountability associated with assessment and reporting of general and specific public benefit goals to third party standards allows a Benefit Corporation to substantiate social and environmental performance, thereby differentiating itself from "greenwashing" competitors that make unsubstantiated claims to be operating responsibly.

Shareholder Protection. A Benefit Corporation protects mission-focused investors by requiring directors in board decision-making to consider a specific set of considerations and requiring a two-thirds majority vote to approve any conversion, merger, or change in specific benefit purpose.

IV. Flexible Purpose Corporations

A. Overview

A Flexible Purpose Corporation permits the pursuit of profit in addition to one or more specific purposes, which may be broad (e.g., reducing GHG [greenhouse gas] emissions) or narrow (e.g., providing an after school music program) in scope. The statute seeks to protect directors who perform their duties according to relevant statutory provisions from liability for any alleged breach of their fiduciary duties.

A Flexible Purpose Corporation is required to adopt one or more of the following "special purposes":

- Charitable or public purpose activities that a non-profit public Benefit Corporation is authorized to carry out, or
- Purposes aimed at promoting positive short-term or long-term benefits (or minimizing adverse short-term or long-term impacts) upon the company's stakeholders including employees, suppliers, customers, and creditors specifically, the community and society in general, or the environment.

The special purpose or purposes must be set forth in the corporate Articles filed with the Secretary of State as well as share certificates, which must also state that the company is a Flexible Purpose Corporation. The Articles may also specify the duration of the company's existence and can limit or restrict the business of the company so long as those limitations are aligned with the stated special purpose.

* * *

E. Potential Advantages

Flexible Purpose Corporations offer a number of benefits over traditional for-profit and non-profit corporations:

Protection from Liability. Directors owe no fiduciary duties to beneficiaries of the Flexible Purpose Corporation's public benefit purposes arising solely from such persons' status as actual or intended beneficiaries of a public benefit.

Special Purpose MD&A. Accountability associated with reporting of public benefit objectives, planning and material actions taken in the prior year provides shareholders of a Flexible Purpose Corporation with the means to evaluate the effectiveness of the company in pursuing its public benefit objectives. Mandatory public availability of the special purpose MD&A provides increased public oversight.

Shareholder Protection. A Flexible Purpose Corporation protects mission-focused investors by providing them with recourse against the company for failure to pursue its public benefit goals, requiring a two-thirds majority vote to approve any material changes in the company's special purpose or to convert to a traditional for-profit corporation and requiring a unanimous vote to convert the company to a non-profit corporation.

V. Contrasting Benefit Corporations and Flexible Purpose Corporations

There are two key differences between the Benefit Corporation and the Flexible Purpose Corporation:

- The Flexible Purpose Corporation allows its directors to adopt a broad mandate of making a profit while also seeking to improve the social welfare in one or more specific ways, whereas Benefit Corporation directors are required to consider the effect of each decision on a list of potential beneficiaries in the context of a general public benefit. Thus, Flexible Purpose Corporations offer more flexibility with regard to determining the purpose(s) of the company and provide directors with a high level of discretion in how they balance and prioritize both traditional economic and special purpose goals

- A Benefit Corporation must issue an annual benefit report that must be prepared subject to a third party standard. Flexible Purpose Corporations are required to issue an MD&A that is very similar to the benefit report, but which is not subject to assessment in accordance with any third party standard.

It should be noted that Benefit Corporations are recognized in a handful of states, while Flexible Purpose Corporations exist only in California.

Flexible Purpose Corporations are closer in nature to traditional for-profit corporations due to their clear profit motive and deference to shareholder oversight. On the other hand, Benefit Corporations are closer in nature to non-profit corporations because, though they are entitled to make a profit, they are required to create a public benefit and must use a third party standard to evaluate the progress of the company towards achieving its goal. The decision of which corporate form to adopt should take into account the specific circumstances and goals of a given company.

Query: If Joan and Michael have a social enterprise goal, would you recommend that Joan and Michael take advantage of either of these two new California statutes in deciding what form of business entity to use to organize their new business, SoftCo? In a privately held corporation with a small number of owners, could you achieve the owners' social enterprise goals *without* using one of these new specialized forms of business entities?

d. Delaware's New "Benefit Corporation" Statute

Not to be left behind, Delaware joined the social entrepreneurship movement in July 2013, when the state legislature enacted its own version of a (public) benefit corporation statute. The following article provides a broad overview of this new legislation, together with a summary of some of the considerations to be taken into account in deciding whether to organize a new business as a public benefit corporation under Delaware law:

Jeffrey A. Fromm, Whitney Holmes, and Joel Acevedo
"Benefit Corporations" to be Allowed in Delaware Starting August 1, 2013

Dorsey & Whitney LLP, Attorney Articles (July 17, 2013)*

Many of today's entrepreneurs, executives, and investors want to develop businesses that have a positive social impact without sacrificing their profit motive. . . . Enter the "benefit corporation" (or "B-corp") — pursuant to legislation [recently] signed by Delaware Governor Markell . . . as of August 1[, 2013,] Delaware will be the nineteenth U.S. state to establish a statutory framework for a type of corporation that balances specific public benefit purposes with the interests of stockholders. Delaware's joining

---

* *Available at* http://www.dorsey.com/eu_csl_benefit_corp_allowed_delaware/.

the B-corp movement is likely to be a watershed event that unleashes a torrent of corporations pursuing dual or triple purposes.

The Legal Framework

Public Benefit Purpose

B-corps will be governed by new Subchapter XV (Sections 361-368) of the Delaware General Corporation Law (the "DGCL"). Section 362 defines a public benefit corporation ("P.B.C.") as *"a for-profit corporation . . . that is intended to produce a public benefit or public benefits and to operate in a responsible and sustainable manner."* That same section defines a public benefit as *"a positive effect (or reduction of negative effects) on one or more categories of persons, entities, communities or interests* (other than stockholders in their capacities as stockholders) including, but not limited to, effects of an *artistic, charitable, cultural, economic, educational, environmental, literary, medical, religious, scientific or technological nature."*

Modified Fiduciary Duties

Once a P.B.C. is formed, under Section 365(a) of the DGCL, the directors of the P.B.C. not only may, but must, manage its business and affairs *"in a manner that balances the pecuniary interests of the stockholders, the best interests of those materially affected by the corporation's conduct, and the specific public benefit or public benefits* identified in its certificate of incorporation."

While directors have to take into account a broader set of interests, according to Section 365(b) of the DGCL, no duty to the broader stakeholders (other than stockholders) is created, and directors will be deemed to satisfy their fiduciary duties if their decisions are "informed and disinterested and not such that no person of ordinary, sound judgment would approve."

P.B.C. [must be included] in the Corporate Name

To indicate that a benefit corporation is different than a traditional corporation, benefit corporations in Delaware must use the designator "P.B.C." (or certain equivalents) in their names instead of the traditional "Inc." or "Corp."

Stockholder Approval; Appraisal Rights

It will be easy to form a new P.B.C. in Delaware, simply by adopting the P.B.C. form and specifying the public benefit purpose in the certificate of incorporation. For existing corporations, however, converting to a P.B.C. will require the evaluation of multiple factors (including contractual arrangements) and approval from stockholders holding 90% of the shares of each class of stock. Moreover, when a traditional Delaware corporation converts to a P.B.C., any stockholder who voted against that conversion will be entitled to appraisal rights for its shares.

Socially Minded Companies Should Consider Converting to a P.B.C.

The P.B.C. movement started a few years ago and, now that Delaware is on board, will gain steam quickly. Hundreds of companies have obtained formal benefit corporation status (or its equivalent) in the states that already allow it. Hundreds of companies have also obtained third party certification, assessing their performance against "rigorous standards of social and environmental performance, accountability, and transparency" from organizations such as the non-profit B Lab. There is still time to be a pioneer and leader in this movement, though. In fact, we anticipate that dozens of companies will be in Delaware on August 1, to register on "day 1" as B-corps in a ceremonial event with the Governor of Delaware. . . .

Companies should consider many factors in deciding whether to convert to a P.B.C. There is no "one right answer," nor is there "one size fits all" in terms of the public benefit purpose that should be specified. Some factors to consider include (among many others) the following:

Opportunities include:

- Broad latitude for directors to balance public benefit purposes with stockholder interests, with relatively low risk of liability.
- Potentially enhanced public perception among consumers who value socially minded businesses.
- Potentially greater access to capital from institutions and individuals that support socially minded businesses.

Risks include:

- Potentially lower profitability and enterprise value due to diffusion of focus and resources.
- Higher costs associated with pursuing the public benefit purpose and periodic reporting to stockholders about success in promoting the public purpose.
- Uncertain legal framework due to the recent emergence of P.B.C.'s and the lack of case law on various legal issues that may emerge.
- Potentially reduced access to capital from institutions and individuals that prefer sole focus on profitability.

QUESTIONS

1. Do you agree with the authors' suggestion (in the preceding article) that the new benefit corporation legislation in Delaware will unleash "a torrent of corporations pursuing dual or triple purposes"?
2. In light of the "risks" and "opportunities" associated with organizing a new business as a benefit corporation (that were described in the preceding materials), do you see any potential problems in recommending use of this new form of business entity to entrepreneurs who seek your advice as to the proper choice of business entity for their new start-up business?

3. In thinking about the need for "entity rationalization" that was raised in the materials in the preceding section of this chapter, does the recent emergence of the benefit corporation movement further influence your perspective on this topic?

B. Non-Tax Considerations That Influence the Choice of Entity Decision

While many practitioners perceive the "choice of entity" decision as primarily (if not exclusively) a tax-driven analysis, it is important to remember that there are many non-tax factors that must be taken into account in making the ultimate decision. With the proliferation of different forms of business entity, the rules of the game, so to speak, have changed in recent years. Thus, some factors that were once deemed vitally important (e.g., continuity of existence) have diminished in importance, while new issues have surfaced that now must be factored into the analysis (e.g., extraterritorial recognition of choice of entity decision). In most, if not all, situations, the analytical process requires lawyers and their clients to anticipate (and perhaps even handicap the likelihood of) events that may happen down the road once the new business is up and running. Consequently, in the case of most start-up businesses, there is a need to consider and project earnings, losses, capital expansion needs, the use of debt, the possibility of bringing on new owners/investors, potential exit strategies, estate planning needs of the owners, and the possibility that the business may be sold, among other things. Given the multitude of things that may be implicated, it should be readily apparent that the decision making process is not an exact science that yields a single, perfect answer for each start-up business. Instead, the lawyer must help the client weigh and consider a number of factors, while also being sensitive to the consequences that result from the other available options. The complexity of this challenge is the focus of the following materials. In this section, we consider the non-tax factors that influence the analysis involved in making the choice of entity decision. In the next section, we briefly consider the key tax considerations that impact the choice of entity decision.

Given the range of business entities available today, it should be clear that there is no uniform "right" choice. Rather, this decision must be guided by a careful review of the details, strategies, and goals of the new business. The materials in Chapter 1 emphasized the need for the business lawyer to be fully informed on these matters to be effective as a transaction planner. The choice of entity decision will depend heavily on these business needs and goals of the new client. The lawyer, as transaction planner, must be able to guide the client through the basic similarities and differences between each form of business entity. More often than not, practicing lawyers use the following criteria for this comparative analysis:

- Costs of formation and operation;
- Liability for business debts (personal liability vs. limited liability);
- Management and control (i.e., agency and authority issues);
- Continuity of existence (i.e., term of existence);

- Allocations of profits and losses and payments to owners;
- Flexibility in raising capital;
- Fiduciary duties and relationships; and
- Transferability of ownership interests.

Before we examine each of these criteria in more detail, it bears reemphasizing that the form of business entity that will ultimately be most advantageous depends on the objectives of the new business. Thus, rather than consider each of these criteria in the abstract, we examine the analytical process typically undertaken by the lawyer in assessing the importance of (and in balancing) these criteria within the context of a particular client situation. In the last chapter, we were introduced to the founders, Joan and Michael, who propose to launch a new software business, SoftCo. From our discussion in Chapter 1, we know that a new business typically entertains three potential sources of start-up financing, which we briefly identified as the *Go-It-Alone* option, the *Friends and Family* alternative, and finally, the use of *Venture Capital* funding. As part of our consideration of the founders' decision regarding choice of entity, let us expand on the first two of these possible sources of start-up financing, so that we can engage in a more fulsome discussion of each of the eight factors listed above. In other words, we can engage in a more nuanced assessment of the most appropriate form of business entity in light of the concerns of the *participants* (founders as well as prospective investors) in addition to the *needs* (financial and otherwise) of the new business. The third alternative, Venture Capital funding, is considered in more detail in Chapter 8.

1) **Go-It-Alone**. Under this alternative, Joan and Michael plan to finance their new business out of their own pockets, presumably by using their own personal savings; or by taking on debt using their credit cards, personal loans, or perhaps obtaining a home-equity line of credit in order to provide the funds necessary to finance the launch of their new business. As another option, they may envision that the new business will be self-funding from the start — that is, they may plan to grow the business organically using the profits from the business to finance the continued development of the new business. Alternatively, they may have the proceeds from the sale of a prior business that they are willing to commit to financing this new start-up business (reminiscent of our discussion in Chapter 1 of "serial entrepreneurs"). While this Go-It-Alone option is attractive because it allows Joan and Michael to continue as the sole owners of the business (an idea that has some appeal to these founders), at the same time they and their spouses are worried about exposing their entire net worth to the creditors of their new business.

2) **Friends and Family**. Under this alternative, Joan and Michael seek funding for their new software business from friends and family and do not go to a strategic partner or to professional venture capital investors. After obtaining their initial capital needs (which they believe will be approximately $500,000), their intent is to operate their new business on a self-funding basis. They have advised that so far they have approached seven prospective investors, consisting of Michael's family doctor; Joan's parents and Michael's parents; Joan's elderly aunt; and Joan's pastor from her church (who recently inherited a "bundle of money"). Joan and Michael have also advised that none of these potential investors — including Joan and Michael themselves — want any personal liability on the debts to be incurred on behalf of the

new business. In addition, it is very important to Joan and Michael that they maintain managerial control over the business operations of the new enterprise. Finally, for federal income tax purposes, it is very important to several of the prospective investors that the business be taxed on a pass-through basis.

As you review the remaining materials in this chapter, consider how to evaluate the eight criteria that are typically used by the transaction planner in selecting an appropriate form of business entity in the context of these two financing scenarios under consideration for SoftCo. In particular, you should consider where your analysis of these factors varies depending on which financing alternative the founders ultimately decide to pursue. In addition, you should be sensitive to other factors that may loom in the context of a particular financing possibility, even if it is not included on the foregoing list. It is important for the transaction planner to remember that start-up businesses vary infinitely and thus the foregoing list of eight factors is by no means exhaustive. However, the list set forth above does provide a helpful starting point in analyzing the issues that SoftCo and its founders face in selecting the most appropriate form of business entity.

1. Costs of Formation and Operation

On one level, the general partnership is probably the simplest and least expensive business entity to organize because the existence of a partnership does not depend on the existence — or the public filing — of any particular document. Rather, as described earlier in this chapter, the partnership depends on the existence of an association of two or more persons carrying on, as co-owners, a business for profit. UPA §6(1); and RUPA §202. As a result, no written partnership agreement is required and thus no significant (legal) expense is incurred in organizing a new business as a partnership. As a practical matter, however, individual investors typically wish to have their business relationship governed by a written partnership agreement rather than rely on the default rules of the relevant partnership statute. In the event that the partners agree to prepare a written agreement, the costs associated with forming a partnership, of necessity, increase and generally vary according to the complexity of the parties' business arrangement. Because of the broad freedom of contract afforded by modern partnership statutes, it is usually the case that "standard forms" of partnership agreement are less likely to be useful. This means that the time and expense involved in preparing a partnership agreement can be significant; in some cases, the cost of organizing a general partnership will be higher than the cost of forming a corporation.

While formation of general partnerships may often result in higher legal fees than is typically required to organize a corporation, partnerships generally have significantly lower maintenance expenses than corporations since they are not generally required to pay taxes (although they must file returns with the IRS); they do not have to make regular public filings; nor are they required to document actions taken by the partnership with as much specificity as is required of corporations. By contrast, with respect to the maintenance of a corporation once it is validly organized, the corporation is subject to what can often be substantial expenses, in terms of payment of franchise taxes and other expenses incurred in connection with documenting actions taken on behalf of the corporation.

With respect to the operation of the partnership, the basic governing document in most partnerships is the partnership agreement (whether oral, or more preferably, written), which is in essence a private contract. Today, most states' partnership statutes generally impose minimal restrictions, thus affording the parties broad freedom of contract to operate the partnership in whatever manner the agreement provides. RUPA provides the default rules regarding those aspects of partnership management that are not addressed in the agreement or in those (relatively infrequent) situations where there is no partnership agreement.

Since the general partnership is the residual form of business entity that exists if no other form of business entity is validly organized, then a general partnership may be created as a result of pre-formation business activities. So, for example, before seeking the advice of a lawyer, very often the founders of a new business (such as Joan and Michael) will begin operating their new business prior to doing the paperwork and otherwise complying with the formalities required to create a particular form of business entity (such as a corporation or an LLC). In these cases, the parties may be deemed to have formed a partnership by operation of law, or what is often referred to as an "inadvertent partnership." Generally speaking, this "transitory partnership" is never formally documented and is often largely ignored by the founders. Many practicing lawyers, however, recommend that the parties prepare some form of "conveyance document" that operates to transfer to the newly formed business entity all rights that may have been created during this preformation period in which the parties undertook business activities as an "inadvertent partnership." *Query*: If Joan and Michael formed an inadvertent partnership, what would you advise them to do?

With respect to the formation of an LLC, most states require that "articles of organization" (or some other similarly titled document) be filed in the state of formation, usually to be filed with the office of the Secretary of State. The precise information required to be included in this public filing varies from state to state, but generally speaking minimal information is required. Most states require that LLCs enter into operating agreements, which may be oral or written. For reasons that are described in more detail in Chapter 3, the operating agreement governs the "internal affairs" of the LLC. Thus, the operating agreement in many ways resembles a partnership agreement and typically covers many of the same issues that are addressed in the bylaws of a corporation. Although the LLC statutes in most states do not specify the contents of an operating agreement — nor do they require that the agreement be publicly filed — it is customary for the operating agreement to address basic principles of management; to specify the allocation of profits and losses; and to describe the rights and obligations of the owners of the LLC, which are generally referred to as the "members." As we will describe in more detail in the next chapter, most states' LLC statutes provide default rules that are effective when the parties have not provided otherwise in their operating agreement.

The cost associated with forming an LLC typically varies with the parties' circumstances and their state of organization. At one extreme, if the parties simply decide to file articles of organization and enter into an oral operating agreement, then they usually only have to pay filing fees, which in most states is not a substantial amount. However, if the parties decide to enter into a fairly detailed written operating agreement (usually recommended by practicing lawyers), then the costs of preparing such an agreement could become significant for reasons that are described at length in Chapter 3. The costs of maintaining the new business as an LLC generally should not be as high as if the business had decided to incorporate. However, certain states — most notably, California and New York — do impose annual franchise taxes on LLCs.[8]

In contrast to the general partnership, strict compliance with the relevant statutory formalities is required to organize a valid new business as a limited partnership. These formalities are set forth in the ULPA or the RULPA, a variation of which has been adopted in virtually every state except Louisiana. In almost all jurisdictions, a limited partnership cannot be formed unless a "certificate of limited partnership" is executed and filed with the appropriate state office, which is usually the secretary of state's office. The required contents of this certificate are set forth in the applicable statute, but typically, under RULPA, the certificate must include the following five items of information:

- The name of the limited partnership (which must include the words "limited partnership" or the initials "L.P.");
- The address of the office and the name and address of the agent for service of process;
- The name and address of each partner;
- The latest date on which the limited partnership is to dissolve; and
- Any other matters that the parties decide to include in the certificate.

See, e.g., 6 Del. Code §17-201. By contrast, the ULPA requires that the certificate include a much more exhaustive list of information, including the names of the limited partners and key economic terms. By requiring this level of specificity, not surprisingly, the facts described in the certificates are soon outdated and thus require frequent amendments. Under RULPA, it is generally permissible to file the agreement of limited partnership in lieu of the required certificate; however, as a practical matter, few partnerships elect to do so because that would mean public disclosure of the deal terms of the parties' agreement, not to mention the administrative hassle of filing what is usually a very substantial document.

While we describe the process of forming a corporation in more detail in Chapter 5, it is important to mention certain basic requirements as part of our choice of entity discussion. It is well established that corporations are creatures of state law and thus must comply with the formal requirements of the state where the new business plans to incorporate. While these requirements vary slightly by jurisdiction, the basic requirements include:

- Filing written articles of incorporation;
- Adopting written by-laws;
- Electing a board and appointing officers; and
- Holding an organization meeting of the shareholders, and then of the directors.

---

8. For example, under sections 17941 and 23153 of California's Revenue and Tax Code, LLCs are subject to an $800 minimum annual franchise tax, plus an additional fee. In addition, California LLCs must pay an annual graduated fee based on their income. In the past, this fee has ranged from $500 to $4,500. *See* Cal. Rev. & Tax Code §17942.

See, e.g., MBCA §§2.01-2.07. For reasons that we describe in detail in Chapter 5, the most important aspect of modern articles generally is the statement of authorized capital. Ownership of the corporation is evidenced by corporate stock. A corporation may issue various types of stock for the purpose of allocating control over the management of the company's business affairs or to vary the nature of the shareholders'/owners' potential risks and returns on their investment. The range and complexity of the most frequently used classes of shares — common and preferred — are described later in this section as part of the discussion of the allocation of profits.

QUESTIONS

1. With respect to the first factor — costs of formation and operation — which form of business entity is most appropriate for Joan and Michael's new business, SoftCo?
2. Does your answer vary depending on which of the financing alternatives Joan and Michael decide to pursue?

2. *Liability for Business Debts — Limited Liability vs. Personal Liability*

The key defining characteristic of the corporation is its "shield of limited liability," which operates to protect shareholders from personal liability on the debts of the business. Thus, generally speaking, the personal liability of shareholders for the debts of the new business will be limited to the amount they have invested in the corporation. This is often given as the most important reason for choosing the corporate form over the partnership form. In the case of general partnerships, the individual partners are subject to unlimited personal liability for all of the obligations of the business, whether in tort or contract. RUPA §§305-306. Thus, under RUPA, individual partners have unlimited personal liability for those partnership obligations incurred after the date of the partner's admission into the partnership. RUPA §306(b). However, RUPA §307 did clarify that a judgment creditor of the partnership may recover from individual partners *only after* failing to recover on the creditor's judgment out of the assets of the partnership, or what is popularly referred to as the "exhaustion rule." Although a partner's personal liability cannot be limited by a provision in the partnership agreement, a partner may have a right of contribution from the other partners if such a provision is contained in the partnership agreement or is granted as a matter of state law.

In the case of a limited partnership, the general partners (which may be a corporation or an LLC) are subject to unlimited liability for the debts of the limited partnership's business. RULPA (1985) §403(b). However, the liability of the limited partners is limited to the amount of their capital contributions, so long as they do not take part in the management and control of the business of the limited partnership, in which case they may lose their limited liability status.

Finally, in the case of the LLC, members of the LLC generally are not personally liable for the debts or business obligations of the LLC. In contrast to the requirements of limited partnerships, no member of an LLC must be designated as a "general partner" subject to unlimited liability for the business debts of the LLC. Moreover, unlike limited partners, members of an LLC may freely participate in the management and control of the business of the LLC without jeopardizing their limited liability status.

Notwithstanding the shield of limited liability that is provided by both the LLC and the corporation, the fact of the matter is that the personal liability of both LLC members and corporate shareholders can very often be extended beyond the amount of their original investment in the business entity. While the corporation is generally regarded as a legal entity separate and distinct from its shareholders, the courts can decide to disregard this shield of limited liability by relying on an equitable doctrine known as "piercing the corporate veil."

In deciding whether to "pierce the corporate veil," the courts generally weigh a variety of factors, and no one factor is outcome determinative. While a detailed discussion of this doctrine is beyond the scope of this casebook, as a general rule, three factors are typically given the greatest weight by most courts: failure to observe corporate formalities; domination and control over a corporation by a controlling shareholder (i.e., "alter ego" allegations); and undercapitalization of the corporation. *See generally* JAMES D. COX & THOMAS LEE HAZEN, CORPORATIONS 103-10 (2d ed. 2003).

In the case of the LLC, some state LLC statutes, either directly or by implication, authorize actions analogous to a claim of "piercing the corporate veil," in which case LLC members may likewise be stripped of their "shield of limited liability." *See, e.g.,* Cal. Corp. Code §17703.04(b). The lack of case law interpreting these LLC statutes leaves considerable uncertainty as to whether, and under what circumstances, courts are going to be willing to disregard the LLC's "shield of limited liability" to hold LLC members personally liable for business debts of the LLC.

Both corporate shareholders and LLC members can also be exposed to personal liability beyond their investment in the business entity even in cases where there is no possibility for a claim based on "piercing the corporate veil." Very often, in the case of a new start-up business, third parties contracting with the corporation (or LLC) will require personal guarantees from the shareholders (or LLC members) as a means of assuring performance, given that the business has no established history (or may be thinly capitalized).

QUESTIONS

1. With respect to the second factor — liability for business debts — which form of business entity is most appropriate for Joan and Michael's new business, SoftCo?
2. Does analysis of this factor vary depending on which of the financing alternatives (described above) that Joan and Michael should decide to pursue?

---

3. Management and Control

Each of the different forms of business entities offers a different fundamental approach to management and control of the business affairs of the new enterprise.

In the case of the corporation, modern statutes clearly prescribe a very centralized and hierarchical management structure. The shareholders generally elect the board of directors who "manage the business affairs of the corporation." In turn, the board of directors appoints the officers of the corporation who handle the day-to-day business affairs of the corporation under the direction of the board of directors. The acts of the corporation's officers and employees (i.e., its agents) acting within the scope of their employment generally constitute acts of the corporation and thus are binding on the corporation. The authority delegated to the company's officers to act on behalf of the corporation is generally found in either a resolution that has been duly adopted by the company's board of directors; a provision in the company bylaws; or, on occasion, by a provision contained in the relevant state's corporation statute. The centralized management structure of the modern corporation is referred to by many commentators as the "corporate norm." While the board is charged with managing the business affairs of the corporation, certain types of major, organic, fundamental changes (such as mergers and amendments to the company's articles of incorporation) require shareholder approval in addition to the requisite board approval.

In contrast to the corporation, management of a partnership is generally decentralized. Under both the UPA and RUPA, all partners are deemed co-owners of the partnership business, even if their capital contributions (or their share of the business' profit and losses) are unequal. UPA §6(1); and RUPA §401. By statute, each partner has an equal right to participate in managing the partnership's business affairs. However, the partnership agreement may modify this default rule, by providing that actual management and control is vested in one or more partners. And, unless the partnership agreement provides otherwise, no partner is entitled to compensation for services rendered in managing the partnership business, with a limited exception for services rendered in connection with winding up the business affairs of the partnership as part of its dissolution. UPA §18; and RUPA §401.

Since there is no management or control structure specifically prescribed by either the UPA or RUPA, an infinite variety of management arrangements is available, and thus, the partnership can be tailored to meet the specific needs of individual partners and/or the partnership's business. Clearly, the partnership agreement should specify the terms of the management structured desired by the parties. So, for example, the partnership agreement may provide that management is centralized in a committee, or is vested in one (or more) managing partners selected by the individual partners. Likewise, voting arrangements among the partners may be allocated in any manner that the parties agree (for example, according to partners' capital contributions or seniority). It should be clear that the partnership form of doing business offers much greater flexibility than does the more rigid and hierarchical structure of the modern corporation.

As a result of the broad freedom of contract offered to the parties under the terms of both the UPA and RUPA, the management structure of the partnership can be molded to more closely resemble that of some other form of business entity. So, for example, if the parties' agreement vests decision making authority in a single individual, the control structure of the partnership begins to resemble that of a sole proprietorship. On the other hand, if the partnership agreement delegates exclusive authority to a committee of partners, the partnership's control structure begins to resemble the centralized management structure of the corporation. Because of this flexibility, the partnership form has traditionally been used for a wide range of businesses — both large and small. However, where the business involves many owners, the partnership form is generally less desirable than either the corporation or the limited partnership, primarily because of an inherent attribute of the partnership known as the "mutual general agency of partners."

Under both the UPA and RUPA, partners are generally deemed mutual agents of the partnership. UPA §9(1); and RUPA §301. Under this principle, the act of every partner within the scope of his or her apparent authority binds the partnership. Even in those cases where the partnership agreement specifically limits the authority of a partner to act on behalf of the partnership, the partner's actions nonetheless may bind the partnership if the third parties with whom the partner is dealing have no knowledge of the partner's lack of authority.[9] Furthermore, by virtue of taking actions that constitute a breach of the partnership agreement (which results in the partner being liable to his/her/its remaining partners), the partnership will nonetheless remain legally bound to the third party.

Under general principles of agency law, any general partner may, on behalf of the partnership, execute instruments, borrow money, transfer or purchase property, and hire (or fire) employees. The broad grant of authority vested in each individual partner stands in stark contrast to the more limited authority that is typically delegated to officers of a corporation.

With respect to this mutual general agency principle, RUPA §303 authorizes a mechanism to clarify the scope of a partner's authority to act on behalf of the partnership. This section permits the partnership to file a "statement of partnership authority" with the office of the Secretary of State. These filed statements may, among other things, expressly grant (or limit) the authority of some or all of the partners. Similarly, a partner named in a statement filed pursuant to RUPA §303 may file a statement denying authority or status as a partner. RUPA §304.

With respect to the limited partnership, managerial control over the business is vested in the general partner or partners, who in turn have all the rights and powers of a partner in a general partnership. ULPA §9(1); and RULPA (1985) §403(a). Since, as we have previously observed, the limited partners risk subjecting themselves to personal liability if they should participate in the management of the limited partnership's business, the management structure of the limited partnership tends to be centralized in the hands of the general partner or partners. However, the safe harbor provisions introduced in RULPA (1985) §303(b) mitigate the otherwise general passivity of limited partner status by giving limited partners greater latitude in management of the limited partnership. In addition, RULPA (1985) imposes record keeping and reporting requirements on limited partnerships that are analogous to those governing corporations, including the right of limited partners to inspect such records.

The LLC management structure is generally established under the terms of the operating agreement. As such, the LLC may operate under a wide variety of management structures that can be centralized or decentralized depending on the needs of the parties or of the business to be operated by the LLC. As we describe in more detail in Chapter 3, the members may choose to share responsibility for managing the LLC

---

9. *See* UPA §9(1); under the reforms introduced by RUPA §301(1), alternatively, the third party must receive notification that the partner lacked authority.

equally among themselves, in which case the LLC more closely resembles the general partnership. This situation is typically referred to as a "member-managed" LLC.

On the other hand, the operating agreement may provide that the members elect one or more managers, who need not be members of the LLC. This situation is generally referred to as a "manager-managed" LLC. In contrast to the centralized management structure that is prescribed by modern corporations codes, the broad freedom of contract offered by most LLC statutes allows the parties to draft operating agreements that establish groups of members and managers with different rights and responsibilities and may allocate voting rights among managers and members in a multitude of ways. As a result of this broad freedom of contract, the control structure of the LLC can be as decentralized as that of the general partnership; or alternatively, the LLC operating agreement can establish a control structure that more closely resembles the hierarchical management structure of the corporation. The practical and legal ramifications of the broad freedom of contract offered by most LLC statutes are explored at length in the next chapter.

QUESTIONS

1. With respect to the third factor — management and control — which form of business entity is most appropriate for Joan and Michael's new business, SoftCo?
2. Does your analysis of this factor vary depending on which of the financing alternatives described above that Joan and Michael should decide to pursue?

4. Continuity of Existence

An essential attribute of the corporate form of doing business is that corporations exist separate and apart from their owners, the shareholders. Thus, the modern corporation generally has perpetual existence unless its articles of incorporation provide otherwise. As a result, the death (or withdrawal) of a shareholder, or a change in its management, generally speaking, has no impact on the continued existence of the corporation.

In contrast to a corporation, the general partnership does not have perpetual existence. Although both the UPA and RUPA provide for *dissolution* of a partnership in certain situations, RUPA introduced the concept of *dissociation* of a partner on the occurrence of specified events. RUPA §601. As noted in the following excerpt, the UPA and RUPA take very different approaches to the continued existence of the partnership:

> Dissolution of a partnership [under the UPA] will occur at the end of the stated term [as] set forth in the partnership agreement and is also generally triggered by the death, retirement, withdrawal, expulsion, incapacity or bankruptcy of any partner.[84] Grounds

---

84. U.P.A. §§31, 32 (1914).

for dissolution by court decree are also specified in the U.P.A.[85] Each partner has the power to dissolve the partnership by express will at any time.[86] However, unless the partnership agreement permits dissolution by express will, such action would constitute a breach of the partnership agreement and could subject the partner causing the dissolution to liability for damages and possibly to a reduced valuation of the partner's interest in the partnership.[87] In addition, the other partners are allowed to continue to operate the business by themselves or with new partners rather than having to wind up the partnership affairs.[88]

Dissolution does not terminate the partnership. The partnership continues to exist after dissolution in order to allow the "winding up" of partnership affairs. Winding up is the process of concluding all pre-existing partnership matters. It involves the application of the assets of the partnership to [satisfy] partnership obligations and the distribution of any remaining assets to the partners. . . .

Continuation of the partnership business without liquidation of its affairs is possible if appropriate provisions are included in the partnership agreement which prevent the partnership from dissolving when certain events occur that would otherwise trigger a dissolution. However, the power of any partner under the U.P.A. to cause a dissolution of the entity at any time gives the partnership an underlying fragility that limited partnerships and corporations do not have.

In response to this frailty, the R.U.P.A. allows a partner to dissociate from a continuing partnership without causing dissolution in situations which result in dissolution of the partnership under the U.P.A.[92] A partner may dissociate at any time, but if the dissociation is wrongful[93] the partner is liable for any damages caused to the partnership or other partners.[94] After dissociation, the dissociated partner's rights and duties relative to the partnership cease, except for a duty of loyalty and care with respect to events occurring before the partner's dissociation.[95] Following dissociation, a continuing partnership must cause the dissociated partner's interest to be purchased.[96] A dissociated partner may file a "Statement of Dissociation" with the Secretary of State to limit the partner's authority to bind the partnership and liability for partnership obligations.[97] Thus, the R.U.P.A.'s dissolution provisions

---

85. U.P.A. §32 (1914).

86. U.P.A. §31(1)(b) (1914).

87. U.P.A. §38(2) (1914).

88. U.P.A. §§37, 38(2)(b) (1914).

92. R.U.P.A. §601 (1994). The events which will cause a partner's dissociation under R.U.P.A. include: (1) withdrawal of a partner, (2) an event agreed upon in the partnership agreement, (3) expulsion of a partner pursuant to partnership agreement or unanimous vote in certain circumstances, (4) expulsion of a partner by judicial decree because of wrongful acts, (5) the partner becoming a debtor in bankruptcy, (6) death or incapacity of a partner, (7) distribution of a partnership trust, and (8) the termination of a partner who is not an individual, partnership, corporation, trust, or estate.

93. R.U.P.A. §602 (1994). Under the R.U.P.A., dissociation is wrongful if (1) it breaches the partnership agreement, (2) it prematurely violates a partnership for definite term, (3) the partner is judicially expelled, (4) the partner becomes a debtor in bankruptcy, or (5) or if the partner is not an individual and willfully dissolves or terminates.

94. R.U.P.A. §602(c) (1994). A partner's liability for wrongful dissociation is in addition to the other obligations which the partner owes the partnership.

95. R.U.P.A. §603 (1994).

96. R.U.P.A. §701 (1994). The R.U.P.A.'s default rules on the buy-out price require valuation of the partnership assets on the dissociation day as if the partnerships were being wound up. If the dissociation was wrongful, the partnership's damages will be deducted from the dissociated partner's buy-out share.

97. R.U.P.A. §704 (1994). *See also* R.U.P.A. §§702, 703 (1994) for dissociated partner's power to bind and liability to partnership.

embrace the continued existence of partnerships and may reduce the number of unintended dissolutions occurring under the U.P.A. Nevertheless, as under the U.P.A., the R.U.P.A. provides for the dissolution of a partnership following specific events which are determined in part by whether the partnership is at will or for a definite term or undertaking.[98]

GREGORY C. SMITH, START-UP AND EMERGING COMPANIES §1.06[10] at 1-37–1-38 (1997).

With regard to the limited partnership, its continuity of existence is not interrupted by either the death or withdrawal of the limited partner. However, as a general rule, the withdrawal, death, or incapacity of the general partner will result in dissolution in the absence of an appropriate provision in the limited partnership agreement. Thus, it is safe to say that the limited partnership more nearly resembles the general partnership and does not have continuity of existence to the same extent as a corporation.

Unlike corporations, the LLC cannot exist perpetually, as a general rule. Indeed, many states' LLC statutes provide for the dissolution of an LLC after a specified period of time unless all of the remaining members agree to carry on the business.

QUESTIONS

1. With respect to the fourth factor — continuity of existence — which form of business entity is most appropriate for Joan and Michael's new business, SoftCo?
2. Does your analysis of this factor vary depending on which of the financing alternatives described above that Joan and Michael should decide to pursue?

5. *Allocation of Profits and Losses and Payments to Owners*

Traditionally, the general partnership has been viewed as an aggregation of its individual members. Today, though, while the modern partnership statutes generally treat the partnership as a separate entity, it is still the case that each individual partner has a capital account. And, as a general rule, the very heart of the partnership agreement is the partner's capital account. The partners' initial contributions (and any additional contributions) are credited to his (or her or its) capital account, as well as the individual partner's allocative share of the income and profits generated by the partnership's business activity. In a similar manner, any distributions made by the partnership to the individual partner are debited to his (or her or its) capital account, as are the individual partner's allocative share of the partnership's deductions and losses.

Typically, the partnership agreement will specify the contributions to the partnership that each individual partner has agreed to make. The contribution can be made in lump sum at the time of admission of the individual partner to the partnership, or the contribution can be made over a period of time. The partnership form of business entity allows the parties great flexibility regarding the form of contribution, which can be cash, property (tangible or intangible), or services (past or future). RUPA §101(11).

---

98. R.U.P.A. §801 (1994).

The partnership agreement typically specifies the form and the amount of each individual partner's contribution — that is to say, the dollar amount of cash and the agreed-upon value of any non-cash consideration (i.e., property and/or services). The partnership agreement typically includes provisions about the timing and procedures to be followed for making contributions in the future. The partnership agreement should provide procedures and/or remedies to address the possibility that an individual partner may fail to make the required contribution, including the delivery of future services, in a timely manner.

Unlike corporate law, there is no concept of "par value" as a matter of partnership law, so there is no required minimum contribution and no prohibition on the use of future services and/or promissory notes. In fact, under most states' partnership statutes, no contribution of any kind or amount is required in order for an individual to be admitted to the partnership and recognized as such as a matter of law.

The partnership agreement should also describe how the individual partners share in the profits and losses of the partnership's business activities. The extraordinary flexibility of modern partnership law with respect to the partners' capital accounts is a great advantage, but at the same time is also the source of frequent complexity in drafting this aspect of the partnership agreement. In the absence of any provisions to the contrary in the partnership agreement, the statutory default rule is that the individual partners will share equally in the partnership's profits. And, in the absence of any provision to the contrary in the parties' partnership agreement, the partners share in the partnership's losses to the same extent that they share in its profits. As a practical matter, this means that allocations of the partnership's profits (and losses) need not correspond to the amount of capital contributed by an individual partner. So, for example, an early stage investor in a start-up business, or a service provider, may be allocated a larger share of the profits than the amount of capital (i.e., cash contributions) that the partner has made.

Likewise, profits and losses need not be shared by an individual partner in the same proportion. Moreover, the sharing ratios may shift over the life of the partnership. So, for example, an early stage investor may be allocated more of the partnership losses in the early years of the business than the service provider, but share equally in the profits of the partnership's business. Or the early stage investor might receive a fixed return on the partner's capital contribution during the development stage of the new business. Then, once certain defined milestones have been achieved, this partner is allocated a percentage of profits until the partner has received two times his (or her or its) money back, and then receives a smaller percentage of profits thereafter.

As you can readily see, the extraordinary flexibility and broad freedom of contract offered under modern partnership statutes means that the variations are potentially endless and presumably limited only by the partner's imagination. Obviously, this can present significant drafting issues for the lawyer serving as the transaction planner for this new start-up business, particularly as the complexity of the parties' allocations of profits and losses increases. It is vitally important, however, that all partners clearly understand how the agreed-upon sharing ratios will work as a practical business matter.

All contributions made by the partners, as well as allocations of profits and losses to the individual partners, should be run through the partners' capital accounts. The same is true of distributions. The partnership agreement will typically provide for the timing and the amounts of distributions to be made by the partnership to the individual partners. This is particularly important in light of the "pass-through" nature of the general partnership for purpose of federal income taxes, the nature of which is described in the next section of this chapter. At this point, suffice it to say that a well-crafted partnership agreement will generally require certain minimum distributions to be made by the partnership to its partners. The amount of such distributions is generally fixed to enable the individual partners to pay their respective tax liabilities on their allocative share of the partnership's profits. The partnership agreement may also include provisions for additional distributions of profits to be made in the discretion of the managing partner (or of some committee of partners). In addition, the agreement may provide that distributions to certain partners are given priority over distributions to other partners. Finally, it should come as no surprise that most partnership statutes today include provisions that limit distribution to partners in order to protect the interests of the partnership's creditors. As a general rule, a partnership will be prohibited from making any distributions to its partners if, after giving effect to the distribution, the partnership's liabilities will exceed its assets.

At the other end of the spectrum lies the modern corporation code, which typically offers less flexibility than the modern partnership with respect to capital contributions and the allocation of profits and losses from the new business. Many founders (as well as employees of the new business once it is up and running) desire to pay for their shares with non-cash consideration, most notably by providing future services for the corporation. Historically, many state statutes did not consider future services or promissory notes as permissible forms of consideration for the issuance of shares. California continues to follow this traditional view and provides that future services are not valid consideration; on the other hand, promissory notes can constitute valid consideration, but only if they are adequately secured by collateral other than the shares acquired or if they are received in connection with certain stock purchase (or stock option) plans. Cal. Corp. Code §409(a)(1). Delaware, however, amended its statute in 2004 to eliminate these traditional restrictions. Thus, today in Delaware, the board of directors determines the adequacy of consideration, including consideration such as future services and promissory notes. Del. §152.

Generally speaking, the most important aspect of modern articles of incorporation is the statement of authorized capital (also known as the "statement of capital structure"). As mentioned earlier in this chapter, each state has its own requirements for the articles of incorporation. Every state, however, requires at a minimum that the articles contain the aggregate number of shares that the corporation may validly issue, the par value (if any) of these shares, and the class or classes into which these shares are to be divided. In Chapter 5, we discuss the process of forming a corporation, including the required contents of the articles of incorporation (or certificate of incorporation as the charter document is known in Delaware). In the event that more than one class of stock is to be issued by the corporation, the articles must describe the rights, preferences, and privileges of each class (or series) of shares that the corporation is authorized to issue. This offers the new corporation some flexibility to create a capital structure that meets the current and anticipated financing needs of the new business. The nature of these rights, preferences, and privileges can become quite complex, for reasons that are discussed at length in Chapter 9, where we examine the typical attributes of preferred shares that are issued as part of a typical venture capital financing transaction. Consequently, the discussion that follows highlights a few basic considerations regarding share issuance and distributions (i.e., payments) to shareholders that are particularly relevant in the context of the choice of entity decision that faces the founders of any new business.

While the initial statement of authorized capital can later be changed by an appropriate amendment to the company's articles, it is generally true that the founders can avoid significant expense and delay by adopting a capital structure that accommodates their anticipated financing needs, which (as we saw in Chapter 1) are generally described in the business plan. Consequently, the articles should authorize a number of shares sufficient to cover not only the shares to be issued to the founders, but also the number of shares to be issued to prospective employees and investors. For reasons to be developed in later chapters, investors in a start-up business — including venture capitalists — typically receive preferred shares. While it is important to anticipate the issuance of preferred stock to prospective investors in drafting the articles of incorporation for the new business, it is not advisable to fix the precise terms of the preferred stock because most sophisticated investors will negotiate their own set of rights, preferences, and privileges. So, in order to provide maximum flexibility in connection with future financing transactions, the founders may wish to consider authorizing what are popularly referred to as "blank check" preferred shares, which empower the board to determine — at some future date and without obtaining shareholder approval — the specific rights, preferences, and privileges of each specific series of preferred stock to be issued. However, before the issuance of any such shares of "blank check" preferred stock, a certificate must be filed with the secretary of state's office specifying the terms of the series to be issued, so that such shares will be validly authorized and issued. It is axiomatic that each share will have the same rights, preferences, and privileges as every other share issued within the same series.

By way of summary with respect to the flexibility offered by the modern corporation in financing a start-up business, one commentator has offered the following observations:

> From the viewpoint of financing, the corporate entity easily accommodates a wide variety of forms of capitalization tailored to the requirements of the business. For example, it may be desirable in organizing the entity to give priority on liquidation or payment of dividends to a particular class of equity investors. Or it may be desirable for estate planning purposes to fix the existing value of the ownership of the business in an older generation, giving any future increases in the value of shares to a younger generation. Or it may be desirable to have public stockholders own a class of securities with different voting or other rights from those of "founding" shareholders. Or it may be desirable to permit certain employees to have the right to share in future increases in the value of the business without risking capital at the beginning. The corporate form can readily accommodate a wide range of capital structures, using such well-established financing vehicles as common or preferred stock, stock options, warrants, subordinated debt, and convertible securities. For many entrepreneurs, the flexibility afforded by the capital structure of the corporate form represents a very substantial advantage over other business entities.

SMITH, *supra*, at §1.08[11] at 1-64.

In the case of organizing new businesses as limited partnerships, they are typically characterized by the same flexibility as general partnerships. Thus, as a general rule, modern limited partnership statutes permit contributions made by a limited partner to consist of any tangible or intangible benefit to the limited partnership, including property of any kind, future services, and promissory notes. As is the case with general partnerships, the heart of the limited partnership agreement is the partner's capital account (both limited and general). As is the case with the general partnership, the limited partnership agreement plays a vitally important role in the allocation of profits and losses, as well as in the timing and amounts of distributions to be made by the limited partnership to its limited partners.

Finally, with respect to LLCs, modern statutes extend essentially the same broad freedom of contract that characterizes the partnership form of doing business. Thus, the contribution of a member of an LLC may consist of any tangible or intangible benefit to the LLC or other property of any kind or nature, including promissory notes and contracts for services to be performed in the future. The LLC's operating agreement usually contains provisions regarding the members' capital accounts, as well as provisions regarding the allocation of profits and losses, similar to those found in a partnership agreement. Likewise, distributions made by an LLC to its members generally would be made in the manner set forth in the LLC's operating agreement. Unless otherwise provided in the operating agreement, the default rule of most states' LLC statutes provides that allocations of profits and losses and distributions are made on the basis of the agreed-upon value of the (capital) contributions made by each member. Generally speaking, a member is not entitled to receive a distribution from an LLC (prior to its winding up in liquidation) unless such distributions are required by the terms of the LLC's operating agreement. *See, e.g.*, ULLCA (1996) §405 and §404(c).

QUESTIONS

1. With respect to this factor — establishing the capital structure of a new business — which form of business entity is most appropriate for Joan and Michael's new business, SoftCo?
2. Does your answer vary depending on which of the financing alternatives Joan and Michael should decide to pursue?

6. *Flexibility in Raising New Capital*

Most experienced lawyers believe that raising capital for a start-up business organized as a general partnership can be challenging. For reasons described at greater length in subsequent chapters, a big part of this challenge derives from the need to recruit key employees for the start-up business to grow and become profitable. As we will see in Chapter 6, successful recruitment and retention frequently requires the use of equity incentives. Equity-based incentive compensation can be extremely complex in the partnership context, unlike the corporate form of doing business. The very heart of the corporate equity incentive structure — such as stock options, stock purchase plans, and employee stock ownership plans — involves tools that are not readily available in the partnership context (for reasons explained in Chapter 6).

Another factor that makes use of the general partnership more challenging in terms of raising capital for the start-up business is that many emerging companies are driven by the investors' need for a "liquidity event." The liquidity events seen most often in the corporate world are the public offering (i.e., more popularly referred to as "going public"), the asset sale, and the acquisition. The partnership entity poses special challenges in the case of each of these liquidity events.

The limited partnership is designed to raise capital that will then be put to use by an experienced and knowledgeable general partner. The separation between management and investors furthers that purpose. Limited partnerships historically were used regularly for financing projects, such as real estate development. At the end of the project, the limited partnership (it hoped) would sell its then-appreciated real estate asset and liquidate, paying out the increased value to its limited partner investors. With the growth in the use of the LLC, limited partnerships are now most commonly used as investment entities. Most venture capital funds and many private equity funds are organized as limited partnerships. These entities, like a real estate development project, are expected to have a limited life. While liquidation is efficient at the end of a project (or after all committed investment funds have been invested), it does not foster continuity of the business entity because liquidation requires the death of the current entity and the formation of a new entity for the next project.

For many practicing lawyers, the corporate form is regarded as an attractive business entity because it readily accommodates a wide range of capital structures, both upon formation and as the business matures into a much larger, more stable business entity. On the other hand, just as many experienced practitioners believe that the LLC suffers from the same drawbacks as the partnership form in this regard.

QUESTIONS

1. With respect to this factor — flexibility in raising capital — which form of business entity is most appropriate for Joan and Michael's new business, SoftCo?
2. Does your recommendation change depending on which of the financing scenarios that Joan and Michael decide to pursue?

---

7. *Fiduciary Duties*

As a direct outgrowth of the mutual general agency principle that applies to general partnerships and of the partners' unlimited personal liability for the debts of the business, partners owe fiduciary duties to each other and to the partnership with respect to all matters affecting the partnership. The nature of this fiduciary relationship originated in case law and the scope of this fiduciary obligation has since been further refined by modern partnership statutes.

Early case law established that general partners must act with undivided loyalty, complete good faith, fairness, and honesty in their dealings with each other. Perhaps the most famous statement of this traditional view of partners' fiduciary duty obligations was articulated by Justice Benjamin Cardozo:

> Joint adventurers, like copartners, owe to one another, while the enterprise continues, the duty of the finest loyalty. Many forms of conduct permissible in a workaday world for those acting at arm's length, are forbidden to those bound by fiduciary ties. A trustee is held to something stricter than the morals of the market place. Not honesty alone, but the punctilio of an honor the most sensitive, is then the standard of behavior. As to this there has developed a tradition that is unbending and inveterate. . . . Only thus has the level of conduct for fiduciaries been kept at a level higher than that trodden by the crowd.

Meinhard v. Salmon, 164 N.E. 545, 546 (1928).

Under UPA §21(1), every partner is required to account to the partnership for any benefit and hold as trustee for the partnership any profits derived without the consent of the other partners from any transaction connected with the formation, conduct, or liquidation of the partnership business, or from any use by the partner of any partnership property. In cases where a transaction is claimed to involve a breach of fiduciary duty, the burden is generally on the partner to prove that his, her, or its conduct conformed to the high standards required of partners as fiduciaries, and therefore, the transaction did not involve a breach of fiduciary duty.

While the UPA only briefly addresses the scope of partners' fiduciary duties, RUPA clarified these duties by expanding the statute's definition of the duty of loyalty and introducing a provision that addresses the partner's duty of care and the obligation of good faith and fair dealing. RUPA §404 (1997). Under RUPA, a partner's duty of loyalty requires him (or her or it) to account to the partnership for any benefit derived from the partnership business, to forbear from representing an adverse party to the partnership during the winding up of partnership business, and to refrain from directly competing with the partnership before the partnership's dissolution. RUPA §404(b) (1997). Under RUPA §404(c), a partner's duty of care requires him to abstain from "engaging in grossly negligent or reckless conduct, intentional misconduct, or knowing violation of the law." Finally, a partner is required by RUPA §404(d) to "discharge the duties to the partnership and the other partners . . . with the obligation of good faith and fair dealing," although under §404(e), a partner does not violate this duty "merely because the partner's conduct furthers the partner's own interest." Under RUPA §103(b)(3)(i), the partnership agreement may not eliminate the duty of loyalty but may "identify specific types or categories of activities that do not violate the duty of loyalty, if not manifestly unreasonable." Similarly, the partnership agreement may not "unreasonably reduce the duty of care" required of partners nor "eliminate the obligation of good faith and fair dealing . . . [but may] . . . prescribe the standards by which the performance of the obligation is to be measured, if . . . not manifestly unreasonable." RUPA §§103(b)(4)-(b)(5) (1997). Given the dearth of case law interpreting these statutory provisions, it is difficult to ascertain definitive standards regarding the ability of a partnership agreement to vary the statutory duties of loyalty and care and the obligation of good faith.

It is well established that a corporation's directors and officers owe fiduciary duties of care and loyalty to the corporation and its shareholders. Generally speaking, the scope of these fiduciary duty obligations are established by case law, with Delaware's judiciary assuming a preeminent role in this important area. However, as you will see when we elaborate on this topic in Chapter 5, several states (most notably California) have attempted to codify a general statement of these fiduciary duty obligations. In addition, most states (including both Delaware and California) authorize the company's certificate (or articles) of incorporation to include a provision that exculpates the director from personal liability, in the form of money damages, for certain breaches of the director's fiduciary duty obligations. It bears emphasizing that these fiduciary obligations are imposed on officers and directors regardless of whether the corporation is publicly or privately held.

As a general rule, shareholders do not owe fiduciary duties to one another. However, with increasing frequency in recent years, courts have shown a willingness to impose fiduciary duties on "controlling shareholders," generally obligating the shareholders in control of a corporation to act fairly towards minority shareholders. As a general rule, this means that controlling shareholders, as a result of their position of influence over the corporation, will be required to demonstrate that they have acted fairly toward the interests of other shareholders. The precise scope of this fiduciary duty obligation varies considerably and local case law must be consulted to determine the standards that are imposed on controlling shareholders.

With respect to the limited partnership, the same basic principles concerning the fiduciary duty obligations of general partners in a general partnership apply to govern the fiduciary duty obligations that general partners owe to the limited partnership and its limited partners. Accordingly, a general partner owes the limited partnership and its limited partners the duties of good faith, loyalty, and due care. The limited partnership agreement often attempts to modify these fiduciary duty obligations by articulating an alternative contractual standard that governs the scope of the general partner's duties to the limited partnership. It is also customary to include in the limited partnership agreement a provision that describes the scope of permissible outside activities in which the general partner may properly engage. By including these provisions in the limited partnership agreement, the objective, generally speaking, is to put boundaries on the scope of the general partner's fiduciary duty obligations to the limited partnership. Finally, the general rule is that limited partners, as passive owners, do not owe fiduciary duties to each other.

There is wide divergence among the states regarding the scope of fiduciary duties required of LLC members and their managers. We describe this range of standards in more detail in Chapter 3. At this point, as part of our choice of entity discussion, suffice it to say that many states' LLC statutes require LLC managers — whether they are members or not — to carry out their duties in good faith, keeping in mind the best interests of the LLC and exercising that degree of care that an ordinarily prudent person in a similar position would exercise under similar circumstances. *See* Daniel Kleinberger, Agency, Partnerships, and LLCs: Examples & Explanations at pp. 569-574 (4th ed. 2012).

1. With respect to this factor — fiduciary duties of managers and owners — which form of business entity is most appropriate for Joan and Michael's new business, SoftCo?
2. Does your recommendation change depending on which of the financing scenarios that Joan and Michael should decide to pursue?

8. *Transferability of Ownership Interests*

As a matter of partnership law, the traditional rule, expressed in UPA §18(g), is that "no person can become a member of the partnership without the consent of all the partners." This default rule derives from the inherently consensual nature of the partnership relationship. Thus, the right to participate in the management of the partnership's business is not assignable and will be granted to a new member only with the express consent of all other partners unless the partnership agreement provides otherwise. However, a partner's financial interest in the partnership (generally defined as the individual partner's allocative share of profits and surplus) may be assigned. UPA §27 and RUPA §503. In the case of an assignment of an individual partner's interest in the partnership, the assignee will generally receive the partner's allocative share of profits and of partnership assets on dissolution, although the assignee may not take part in the management of the partnership's business affairs and generally is not entitled to access to information regarding the partnership and its business (unless, of course, the partnership agreement provides to the contrary).

With limited partnerships, the general rule under both the ULPA and RULPA (1985) is that the financial interest of an individual limited partner may be assigned. ULPA §19; and RULPA §702. However, like general partnerships, an assignee of a limited partner can be substituted in as a full limited partner only with the consent of all the partners or as provided under the terms of the limited partnership agreement. Thus, as a practical matter, an assignee of a limited partner acquires only the right to receive the limited partner's allocative share of profits and of the assets of the limited partnership on dissolution, but has no right to vote as a limited partner nor to inspect the books and records of the limited partnership. ULPA §19(3); and RULPA (1985) §702.

Similarly, in the case of the LLC, a member's interest may be transferred, but typically the transferee will receive only the economic rights of the member. For the transferee to become a full member of the LLC, the general rule is that the members of the LLC must give their unanimous written consent to such transfer unless the LLC's operating agreement provides otherwise. *See, e.g.,* ULLCA (1996) §§501-503 and §404(c). Thus, the default rule for the LLC is similar to partnership law and unlike the rights of shareholders of a corporation.

In stark contrast to partnership and LLC law, the general rule is that shares of stock in a corporation are freely transferable. However, reasonable restrictions may be imposed on such transfers to third parties by appropriate provisions in the company's articles of incorporation or its bylaws or by the terms of a separate contract. As mentioned earlier in this chapter, controlling shareholders of a corporation, by virtue of their position of influence, may be subject to restrictions on the transferability of their shares as a matter of judicial decisions imposing fiduciary obligations on these shareholders. The nature of these limitations is explored in later chapters of this casebook.

However, as a practical matter, shares of a closely held corporation are often difficult to transfer since there is very little market for these shares. Moreover, for reasons explored in Chapter 5, shareholders in a closely held corporation are often quite interested in limiting the transferability of shares in their company since they usually do not want ownership to be transferred to unrelated third parties. On formation of a new business, an important task for the lawyer (as a transaction planner) and for the founders (as a business matter) is to determine how to deal with this issue. In Chapter 5, we look at the devices that are generally available to limit the free transferability of shares in a closely held enterprise. For purposes of this discussion, suffice it to say that courts today are generally willing to enforce a restraint on the transferability of shares so long as the terms of the restriction are not unreasonable.

With regard to shares of a publicly traded corporation, these are among the most freely transferable of all ownership interests. As we see in Chapter 4, however, the sale of all securities — including the shares of both privately and publicly held corporations — are subject to both federal and state securities regulation. In addition, the federal securities laws, most notably, the Securities Exchange Act of 1934, carefully regulate the trading of shares of publicly traded corporations.

QUESTIONS

1. With respect to this factor — the transferability of ownership interests — which form of business entity is most appropriate for Joan and Michael's new business, SoftCo?
2. Does your recommendation change depending on which financing scenario Joan and Michael should decide to pursue?

C. Tax Considerations That Influence the Choice of Entity Decision

This casebook deliberately eschews any effort to provide a comprehensive analysis of tax issues, preferring a more realistic approach that identifies potential tax issues that typically arise when forming a start-up business. By no means comprehensive, the following materials provide general background regarding the relevant tax issues that typically arise in the context of the founders' "choice of entity" decision. Of course, any definitive resolution of these tax-related issues requires consultation with a knowledgeable tax practitioner.

Daniel S. Kleinberger
Two Decades of "Alternative Entities": From Tax Rationalization Through Alphabet Soup to Contract as Deity

14 FORDHAM JOURNAL OF CORPORATE AND FINANCIAL LAW 445 (2009)

Although unincorporated business organizations involve much more than tax concerns, it is impossible to understand their development in the law without understanding key elements of the U.S. tax system as applied to the income of business organizations. That system distinguishes fundamentally between the taxation of organizations classified as partnerships, on the one hand, and the taxation of organizations classified as corporations, on the other. In most situations, partnership tax status is preferable because corporate shareholders face "double taxation" on any dividends they receive. An ordinary "C corporation" is a taxable entity; it pays corporate income tax on any profits it earns. Dividends to shareholders are therefore made in "after-tax" dollars. Nonetheless, dividends are also taxable as received by the shareholders. Thus, the profits [distributed as] corporate dividends are taxed twice.

Partners do not suffer double taxation because a partnership is not a taxable entity. For income tax purposes, partnerships are "pass through" structures: the entities' profits (whether distributed or not) are allocated and taxable directly to the partners. Partnership losses also "pass through" and can serve as deductions on each partner's own tax return. In contrast, the losses of an ordinary corporation stay with the entity and are useful only if the entity later enjoys a profit. In 1988, the advantages of partnership tax status were diminished by "owner liability" — i.e., to be taxed as a partnership, an entity had to include at least one owner (almost always a "general partner") who was automatically liable for all debts of the entity. The driving force behind the development and spread of the limited liability company . . . has thus been the desire to solve this "tax-shield conundrum" — i.e., to create an entity that, as a matter of tax law, is classified as a partnership with each owner treated as a partner, but whose owners are shielded by state law from automatic personal liability.

Before the advent of the LLC, entrepreneurs could achieve partnership tax status and limit liability exposure by using an ordinary limited partnership with a corporate general partner. Alternatively, entrepreneurs could use an S corporation to obtain a full liability shield while achieving some of the advantages of partnership tax status or try to "zero out" the profits of a C corporation. None of these approaches, however, was fully satisfactory[, for reasons that are described below].

1. Ordinary Limited Partnerships with a Corporate General Partner

Under the traditional approach, typically a corporation would be formed for the sole purpose of serving as the general partner of the limited partnership. However, this approach had a number of disadvantages. The structure was complex and involved a significant risk of "piercing" for the corporate general partner (unless that corporation had assets of its own, thereby diverting capital from use in the limited partnership's business). The structure also raised tax classification issues, unless the corporate general partner had assets of its own. Furthermore, difficult questions of fiduciary duty arose, pertaining to the officers of the corporate general partner. As a formal matter, those officers owed duties to the corporation, but as a practical matter they were managing and typically controlling the limited partnership. . . .

2. S Corporations

An S corporation provides a full corporate liability shield with some of the benefits of pass-through tax status. Like a partnership, an S corporation generally pays no tax on its earnings; its profits and losses are passed through and taxed directly to its shareholders. S corporations, however, face significant constraints which do not apply to partnerships, including: (i) ownership restrictions, both in terms of the number and character of owners (i.e., excluding most institutional and foreign investors); (ii) the "one class of stock" requirement, which restricts the type of debt the corporation may issue, hampers efforts to gradually shift control of family-owned businesses, and generally makes passive investment very difficult to structure; and (iii) preclusions of a long list of business types and structures.

3. C Corporations and "Zeroing Out"

A corporation that cannot — or chooses not to — elect S status can try to avoid double taxation by "zeroing out." To "zero out," the C corporation makes ostensibly deductible payments to shareholder-employees, thereby reducing or eliminating corporate profits. Such payments can be made in a number of ways, the simplest being [payment of] salaries and bonuses.

This approach is not risk-free, however. The Internal Revenue Service may view the payments as disguised dividends, especially where: (i) the payments are excessive compared with the value of the services rendered to the corporation, (ii) the payments are proportional to the shareholders equity interests, or (iii) capital is a material income-producing factor for the business and the corporation is not paying reasonable dividends. Even when successful, zeroing out techniques provide none of the other advantages of pass-through tax status.

=====

Charles A. Wry, Jr.
Choosing the Proper Form
of Organization for a New Business Venture
Morse, Barnes-Brown, Pendleton, PC, Law Firm Memo (2011)*

Founders of a new business generally realize early on that they need to conduct the business through some kind of legal entity to limit their personal liabilities for the debts and obligations the business generates. Often, the three entity types from which the founders must choose are the "C" corporation, the "S" corporation and the limited liability company (or "LLC"). While all three entity types insulate the founders from personal liability, the differences among the three types for tax purposes are substantial. A C corporation, on the one hand, reports and pays tax on its income separately from its owners. The income or loss of an S corporation or LLC, on the other hand, generally is

---

* *Available at* http://www.mbbp.com/resources/business/entity.html.

reported by the owners on their personal returns. The choice, therefore, is often tax-driven and requires an analysis of how the founders expect to profit from the business.

I. The C Corporation

a. ***Some Basics***. A C corporation reports and pays taxes on its income. Because any income (including gain from an asset sale) that a C corporation distributes to its shareholders is taxable again in the hands of the shareholders, distributed income of a C corporation can be subject to tax at higher effective rates than those applicable to the distributed income of an S corporation or LLC.[1] The losses of a C corporation are also reported by the corporation rather than by its shareholders. With limited exceptions, owners report any losses of their investments as capital losses only when they dispose of their shares. Individuals may use capital losses to offset only capital gains and small amounts of ordinary income (and may carry unused capital losses forward but not back).

b. ***Factors Favoring the C Corporation***. While the potential for double taxation is a serious concern, a number of factors may favor the C corporation. Those factors include the following:

- Venture capital funds often prefer to invest in C corporations. The funds may not make equity investments in S corporations because the funds are partnerships.[2] Equity investments in LLCs can cause tax problems for the funds' tax-exempt and foreign partners.
- Equity based compensation arrangements are simplest with C corporations. C corporations (and S corporations, but not LLCs) may grant tax favored "incentive stock options" (or "ISOs").[3]
- Only shares of stock in C corporations may be "qualified small business stock." If certain requirements are satisfied, and subject to certain limitations, an individual

---

1. Currently, a C corporation (that is not a "qualified personal service corporation") is taxed federally at a rate of 34% on its taxable income greater than $75,000 (35% on its taxable income greater than $10,000,000). At least through 2010, a U.S. individual is subject to a maximum federal tax rate of (i) 35% on his or her ordinary income, (ii) with certain exceptions, 15% on his or her long-term capital gains, and (iii) 15% on his or her dividends from domestic C corporations. Thus, $100 of income earned by a C corporation leaves only $56.10 for the shareholders if the corporation pays $34 of tax on the income and the shareholders pay $9.90 of tax on the $66 remaining for distribution to them after the corporation has paid its tax (a 43.9% effective federal rate on the $100 of corporate earnings). After 2010, dividends are scheduled to be taxable at ordinary rates again, and the 15% individual long-term capital gain rate is scheduled to be increased to 20%. The absence of any preferential federal rates applicable to long-term capital gains of C corporations can exacerbate the double taxation of distributed long-term capital gains of C corporations. Income that is paid out to the owners in a way that is deductible for the corporation (e.g., as reasonable compensation) is not subject to double taxation but is taxable to the recipient at ordinary compensation rates (and, in addition, is subject to employment or self-employment tax).

2. In addition, the funds usually want to purchase preferred stock which an S corporation may not offer. See the discussion of S corporation qualification requirements below.

3. In practice, it can be difficult to provide corporate equity incentives that permit the participants to both avoid tax (or an obligation to pay the then fair market value of their stock) upon receiving their stock and report the benefits of their arrangements at long-term capital gain rates when they dispose of their stock. Although equity compensation arrangements with LLCs can be complicated, an LLC's ability to issue "profits interest" based on liquidation value presents the possibility of minimizing up-front tax costs of awards while preserving the timing and character advantages generally associated with restricted stock awards.

may (i) exclude a portion of his or her gain on the sale of qualified small business stock held for more than five years or (ii) roll his or her gain on a sale of qualified small business stock held for more than six months into another qualified small business.[4] Special look-through rules apply to stock held by partnerships. Stock issued while a corporation is an S corporation generally may not be qualified small business stock even if the corporation becomes a C corporation.

- [If certain requirements are satisfied, the] shareholders of a C corporation (or an S corporation, but not an LLC) may exchange their stock for stock of a corporate acquiror without tax (other than on any cash or other non-stock property they receive) if the exchange is part of a transaction that qualifies as a "reorganization" for tax purposes. Instead, the shareholders defer the reporting of their gains until they dispose of their stock in the acquiror.
- At any time that C corporate tax rates are lower than individual rates, reinvested income of a C corporation may be taxed at a lower effective rate than reinvested income of an S corporation or LLC.
- The use of a C corporation prevents the owners from having to file tax returns in all the states and other jurisdictions in which the business has a tax presence.

c. *When a C Corporation Makes Sense*. Founders should consider the C corporation if they intend to grow their business for a public offering or sale by (i) obtaining venture capital financing and (ii) motivating employees and consultants with equity. The primary risk to forming the business as a C corporation is the potential for double taxation if the business becomes a "cash cow" or if an acquiror wants to buy the assets of the business in a taxable transaction. Sometimes, founders of a business with this type of plan want to take a "wait and see" approach to preserve their ability (i) to sell assets without double tax and at individual capital gain rates and (ii) to report early stage losses (subject to applicable "passive activity loss," "at risk" and other limitations) on their personal returns. The "wait and see" approach is generally better served by using an LLC as the interim entity. . . .

II. The S Corporation

a. *Some Basics*. The income and, subject to certain limitations, losses of an S corporation are reported by the corporation's shareholders in proportion to their shareholdings. Thus, the use of an S corporation usually avoids the double taxation of

---

4. Historically (at least from 2001 to February of 2009), the maximum excludible portion was 50%, and the non-excluded portion was generally taxed at a 28% rate. In addition, a portion of any excluded gain has historically been a preference item under the alternative minimum tax. Given the rate at which the unexcluded portion was taxed, the qualified small business stock provision lost much of its luster in 2003 when the maximum rate generally applicable to long-term capital gains from stock sales was reduced to to 15%. The benefits of the provision have been enhanced, at least on a temporary basis, by recent legislation. The American Recovery and Reinvestment Tax Act of 2009 breathed some new life into the provision by increasing the maximum excludible portion to 75% for qualified small business stock acquired after February 17, 2009 (and, as enacted, before January 1, 2011). For qualified small business stock purchased after September 27, 2010 and before January 1, 2012, the Tax Relief, Unemployment Insurance Reauthorization and Job Creation Act of 2010 increased the maximum excludible portion to 100% and exempted excluded gain from the alternative minimum tax.

distributed earnings characteristic of the C corporation.[5] Distributions of "tax-paid" S corporation income are not subject to further taxation in the hands of the shareholders. Unfortunately, due to qualification requirements, the S corporation is not always available as an option. Among the more onerous qualification requirements are that the corporation (i) have only a single class of stock (differences solely in voting rights are permissible) and (ii) have 100 or fewer shareholders (all of whom must be U.S. resident individuals, estates or certain types of trusts, qualified retirement plan trusts or charitable organizations).[6]

b. *Factors Favoring the S Corporation.* Often, founders must first decide between a C corporation, on the one hand, and an S corporation or an LLC on the other (that is, between a taxable entity and a non-taxable, or "pass-through," entity). Then, once the founders have ruled out the C corporation (usually because they suspect that their returns may take the form of periodic distributions of operating income or a distribution of the proceeds of a sale of the assets of the business), they must decide between the S corporation and the LLC. Among the factors that may favor the S corporation over the LLC are the following:

- S corporations may be more versatile than LLCs in terms of exit strategy. Like shareholders of a C corporation (but not the owners of an LLC), shareholders of an S corporation may exchange their stock for stock of a corporate acquiror without tax (other than on any cash or other non-stock property they receive) if the exchange is part of a transaction that qualifies as a "reorganization" for tax purposes. In addition, it may be easier for the owners of an S corporation than for the owners of an LLC to report their exit gains as capital gains rather than ordinary income by structuring their exit as a stock (as opposed to asset) sale.

- Although equity incentive arrangements are more complicated with S corporations than with C corporations, they are simpler with S corporations than with LLCs. Like C corporations, S corporations may grant ISOs.

- If a participating owner of an S corporation receives reasonable wage payments from the S corporation as well as S corporation distributions, only the wage payments are subject to employment tax. A participating owner of an LLC, on the other hand, may be subject to self-employment tax on his or her entire share of the LLC's business income.[7]

---

5. Special rules apply to an S corporation that has assets acquired, or earnings and profits accumulated, while it or any corporation it acquired in a tax-free exchange was a C corporation. Since the focus of this memorandum is on structuring a new business venture, those special rules are not discussed. It should also be noted that S corporations may be subject to state income tax. For example, Massachusetts taxes S corporations with annual gross receipts exceeding a certain threshold amount.

6. For purposes of the 100 shareholder limitation, spouses are, and members of a family may be, treated as one shareholder.

7. While the amount of income subject to the social security component of the employment or self-employment tax is subject to a cap, the cap does not apply to a 2.9% Medicare component. The employment tax advantages of the S corporation may be the subject of future legislation.

- S corporations may be eligible for local property tax exemptions that are not available to LLCs. These exemptions can be particularly important if the business will have significant amounts of inventory, machinery or other personal property.

c. *When an S Corporation Makes Sense*. Founders should consider the S corporation if they want a simple arrangement that will avoid double taxation while (i) preserving their ability to sell the business for stock of an acquiror on a non-taxable basis, (ii) maintaining their ability to motivate employees and consultants by granting ISOs and (iii) minimizing employment taxes.

III. The LLC

a. *Some Basics*. Unless an LLC elects to be treated as a C corporation, it is treated as a partnership (or, if it has only a single owner, as a sole proprietorship) for tax purposes. Because the income and, subject to certain limitations, losses of an LLC are reported by the LLC's owners (referred to as "members") in accordance with their agreement, the LLC also avoids the double taxation issues presented by a C corporation. While an LLC is far more flexible than an S corporation in many respects, the added flexibility often comes at the price of added complexity.[8]

b. *Factors Favoring the LLC*. Among the factors that may favor the LLC over the S corporation are the following:

- An LLC is not subject to the S corporation qualification requirements. In particular, an LLC may have multiple classes of owners (with different economic rights and preferences), and may include entities and foreigners among its owners.
- With certain exceptions, an LLC may distribute appreciated assets without triggering gain. Assets may therefore pass in and out of an LLC more freely than with an S corporation. For this reason, the LLC is the type of entity that is most easily converted to another type if circumstances change. The conversion of a C corporation or S corporation to an LLC generally triggers tax on any appreciation in the value of the corporation's assets.
- To avoid tax on a contribution of appreciated property to an S corporation (or C corporation) for stock, the person making the contribution must, among other things, own (either individually or together with other persons making contemporaneous contributions of cash or property) at least 80% of the outstanding stock of the corporation as of the time immediately after the contribution is made. No such "control" requirement applies to contributions of appreciated property to LLCs. As a result, adding new owners for property contributions can be simpler for LLCs than for S corporations.
- If the owners of an LLC exchange their LLC interests for shares of stock in a conversion of the LLC to a C corporation, the shares of stock issued to the owners

---

8. There may, though, be situations where the LLC is simpler than the S corporation. For example, an LLC with a single owner generally need not even file separate tax returns.

are not precluded from being qualified small business stock by reason of the prior existence of the LLC. If all the other requirements for qualified small business stock treatment are satisfied, the owners have merely postponed the beginning of their holding periods until they receive their shares of stock.

- The owners of an LLC may include their shares of the LLC's borrowings in their tax bases in their interests in the LLC, even if they are not personally liable for the borrowings. The inclusion of borrowings in basis enables the owners to withdraw borrowing proceeds from the LLC on a tax-free basis and (subject to applicable "passive activity loss," "at risk" and other limitations) report greater amounts of loss.
- If an LLC makes a special tax election, a person who acquires an interest in the LLC by purchase or inheritance may "write up" his or her share of the LLC's basis in its assets to his or her initial basis in his or her interest in the LLC (thereby enabling him or her to report less income or greater deductions with respect to the assets). The same election permits the LLC to "write up" its tax basis in its assets when an owner's interest is redeemed by the LLC at a gain.

c. **When an LLC Makes Sense**. Founders should consider the LLC if they want to avoid the double taxation of distributed corporate earnings (or any taxation on in-kind distributions) while preserving their ability to issue interests of multiple classes (providing holders with different economic rights and preferences) or to owners who could not qualify as S corporation shareholders. The LLC is also the best choice when the founders want to use a pass-through entity on an interim basis without precluding the ultimate treatment of their interests in the business as qualified small business stock. The LLC may also be better suited than the C corporation or the S corporation to activities involving investments in assets such as real estate or securities.

IV. Conclusion

In conclusion, a C corporation may be the best choice if the founders intend to reap their profits by selling their shares after growing the business using venture capital financing and equity incentives to personnel. If the founders anticipate reaping their profits in the form of distributions of income from the business (including gain from an exit structured as an asset sale), however, they should consider using an S corporation or an LLC.

The following chart dramatically illustrates the impact of the double taxation burden described in the preceding materials, which is widely considered to be one of the principal disadvantages of organizing a start-up business as a C corporation.

Effective Tax Rate on an Asset Sale: C Corporation Compared to LLC

The chart assumes that: (1) the individual owners invest $200; (2) the entity incurs $200 of expenses, which are deductible in year of sale against sale proceeds; (3) the entity does not realize any taxable operating income; (4) the entity sells assets, which consist solely of goodwill, for $1,000; and (5) all gain recognized by the owners is treated as long-term capital gain.

		C Corp	LLC
Asset sale price		$1000.00	$1000.00
Federal Corporate Tax Calculation:			
Asset sale proceeds	$1000.00		
Less: expenses	(200.00)		
Taxable gain	$800.00		
Times: Federal corporate tax rate	x 35%*		
Federal corporate taxes due		(280.00)	—
Proceeds distributable to owners		$720.00	$1000.00
Owner Tax Calculation:			
Proceeds received from C Corp/LLC		$720.00	$1000.00
Less: cost basis of investment		(200.00)	—
Less: flow-through losses		—	(200.00)
Capital gain		520.00	800.00
Times: Federal individual capital gains tax rate		x 20%*	x 20%*
Federal individual capital gains tax		$104.00	$ 160.00
Proceeds distributable to owners		$720.00	$1000.00
Less: Federal individual capital gains tax		(104.00)	(160.00)
Net after-tax proceeds		$616.00	$840.00
SUMMARY			
Gross Proceeds		$1000.00	$1000.00
Less: Initial investment		(200.00)	(200.00)
Net proceeds		$800.00	$800.00
Less: entity-level tax		(280.00)	—
Less: owner-level tax		(104.00)	(160.00)
Net after-tax gain		$416.00	$640.00
Effective tax rate		48%	20%

* Under federal income tax law, tax rates are graduated and generally vary from year to year. In addition, deductions, credits and exclusions can change the effective tax rate applicable in particular circumstances. The rates used in this chart are examples consistent with historical levels and are not intended to reflect the specific rates in effect at a particular time.

As another example of the impact of the double taxation burden, consider the following situations, which describe the tax consequences of a distribution of the business' profits to the owners of the firm depending on whether the business is organized as a partnership or a corporation:

Daniel Kleinberger
AGENCY, PARTNERSHIPS, AND LLCS: EXAMPLES & EXPLANATIONS
(4th ed. 2012) at pp. 492-493

(i) **Example:** In its most recent taxable year, Fencing, Inc., a C Corporation, made a profit of $100,000 and would like to distribute all of its profits to its shareholders. Assuming a corporate income tax rate of 25 percent, an individual tax rate of 20 percent, and that Athos, Porthos, and Aramis each own the same number of shares of stock (and therefore share dividends equally), the calculations and results are:

Taxable Corporate Profit	100,000
Less Corporate Income Tax	(25,000)
Available for Distribution	75,000
Dividend to Each Shareholder	25,000
Less Individual Income Tax	(5,000)
Net to Each Shareholder	20,000
The Federal Government's "take" (corp. $25,000; ind. 3 x $5,000)	**40,000**
"After tax" net to the shareholders	**60,000**

(ii) **Example:** Same facts, except that Athos, Porthos, and Aramis have formed a partnership. The calculations and results are:

Profit	100,000
No Partnership Income Tax	(0)
Available for Distribution	100,000
Distribution to Each Partner	33,333[*]
Less Individual Income Tax	(6,667)[*]
Net to Each Partner	26,666
The Federal Government's "take" (ind. 3 x $6,667)	20,001
"After tax" Net to Partners	79,998[**]

Comparison of Examples

	Corporation	Partnership
Federal Government's "take"	$40,000	$20,001
Owners' "after tax" net	$60,000	$79,998

* Rounded, for simplicity's sake.

** One dollar is unaccounted for, due to rounding

QUESTIONS

1. How do the tax consequences influence your advice regarding the most appropriate form of business entity for SoftCo? Does your recommendation vary depending on which financing alternative the founders, Joan and Michael, decide to pursue — that is, whether they decide to *Go-It-Alone* or to seek financing from *Friends and Family*?
2. In considering your recommendation for SoftCo, how do the tax consequences rank in relation to the earlier discussion of non-tax considerations in section B of this chapter? How does the funding choice that Joan and Michael decide to pursue affect your relative ranking of tax vs. non-tax considerations?

CHAPTER 3

OVERVIEW OF *LLC* LAW

In the previous two chapters, we have learned that the founders of SoftCo, Joan and Michael, face a number of different possibilities in terms of financing their new business. For purposes of this chapter, Joan and Michael are evaluating three different possible funding sources: (i) they could decide to *Go-It-Alone*; (ii) they could decide to obtain the necessary funding from *Friends and Family*; or finally, (iii) they could decide to pursue a strategic joint venture relationship with BadSoft, with Bad-Soft providing the necessary funding to develop the business model that Joan and Michael set forth in the business plan they prepared for SoftCo. As we move to our new topic — an examination of LLC law — it bears emphasizing that these three financing alternatives are not unique to these founders. As a practical matter, the financing of any new business follows a predictable pattern that usually involves some variation of the three funding sources currently under consideration by the founders of SoftCo.

Although still relatively new to the legal landscape of business entities, the limited liability company (LLC) has proven to be tremendously popular with entrepreneurs and their lawyers. Indeed, the flexibility offered by the LLC makes this form of business entity an attractive choice for SoftCo regardless of the financing alternative that the founders (Joan and Michael) should decide to pursue. The characteristics of the LLC that make it such a popular form to organize a new start-up business (such as SoftCo) are the focus of this chapter.

In section A, we consider why the LLC was developed and trace the evolution of LLC statutes over the past 35 years, ever since Wyoming became the first state to enact such a statute. In section B, we examine the process of organizing a new business as an LLC, and in section C we take up the all-important topic of preparing an Operating Agreement with a particular focus on managerial rights within the context of an LLC. The last set of materials in this chapter focuses on one of the most controversial issues currently surrounding the LLC: What is the proper scope of fiduciary duties within the LLC framework?

A. Development of LLC

In this section, we consider the origins of the LLC in the United States (which date back to the mid-1970s) and provide a brief overview of its evolution since then. The materials in this section provide necessary background that will be useful for considering the issues that are the focus of the remaining materials in this chapter. Most notably, the materials in this section highlight the public policy considerations that are part of our analysis of the proper scope of fiduciary duties in the context of the LLC, including the issue of whether those duties can be contractually limited (or even eliminated altogether).

Daniel S. Kleinberger

Two Decades of "Alternative Entities": From Tax Rationalization Through Alphabet Soup to Contract as Deity

14 FORDHAM JOURNAL OF CORPORATE FINANCIAL LAW 445 (2009)

C. Invention and Development of the Modern (U.S.) LLC[35]

1. Wyoming Starts a Revolution

Wyoming started the LLC revolution by taking seriously the Internal Revenue Service's (IRS) "Kintner" Regulations on tax classification. Before January 1, 1997, the Kintner Regulations stated the rules for classifying unincorporated business organizations [that were therefore entitled to "pass-through" tax treatment and thus could avoid the "double taxation" burden of the ordinary "C corporation"], and the rules were biased toward finding partnership status. The regulations identified six key corporate characteristics — among them limited liability, continuity of life, free transferability of ownership interests, and centralized management — and classified an unincorporated organization as a corporation only if the organization had more corporate characteristics than non-corporate characteristics. Thus, although limited liability may seem to be the hallmark corporate characteristic, the Kintner Regulations contained no "super" factor. Each characteristic was equally significant.

* * *

. . . The driving force behind the development . . . of the LLC [was the desire to solve] the "tax-shield conundrum" — [in other words,] to create an entity that, as a matter of tax law, is classified as a partnership with each owner treated as a partner but whose owners are shielded by state law from automatic personal liability [that otherwise would be imposed on a partner in a business organized as a general partnership under state law].

---

35. The name "limited liability company" appears in the jurisprudence of other nations, but that fact is a mere linguistic coincidence. "[E]xcept perhaps as to name, foreign LLCs are not antecedents to U.S. LLCs." CARTER G. BISHOP & DANIEL S. KLEINBERGER, LIMITED LIABILITY COMPANIES: TAX AND BUSINESS LAW ¶ 1.01[4][a] (Warren Gorham & Lamont/RIA 1994 & Supp. 2007-2) [hereinafter BISHOP & KLEINBERGER, LIMITED LIABILITY COMPANIES]. . . .

* * *

In 1977, the Wyoming legislature sought to exploit [the] "equal significance" aspect of the Kintner Regulations in order to resolve the "tax-shield conundrum." The Wyoming LLC Act[39] provided for a new form of business organization with a full, corporate-like liability shield but partnership-like characteristics [with respect] to entity management, continuity of life, and transferability of ownership interests. Like a general partnership, a Wyoming LLC was managed by its owners. Like a limited partnership, it risked dissolution if one of its owners ceased to be an owner. As with any partnership, Wyoming LLC ownership interests were not freely transferable; absent a contrary agreement, an LLC member had the right to transfer only the economic aspect of the ownership interest. If the Kintner Regulations meant what they said, then a Wyoming LLC would be accorded partnership tax status.

2. IRS Response to Wyoming: Common Characteristics of Early LLCs

The IRS took over ten years to acknowledge the consequences of its own tax classification regulations. [In 1988,] Revenue Procedure 88-76 classified a Wyoming LLC as a partnership,[43] causing legislatures around the country to consider seriously the LLC phenomenon. For the most part, Wyoming's early emulators were faithful copiers, imposing through their LLC statutes the same basic structure as ordained in the Wyoming statute.[44] The one major innovation was to establish an alternative governance template for manager-management (modeled on the limited partnership structure), while continuing to set the "default mode" as member-management.[45]

Fidelity to the Wyoming model gave the earliest LLCs some common characteristics — at least to the extent that they followed the default blueprint of their respective LLC statutes. An LLC that left in place the statutory "default" rules was managed by its members in their capacity as members and was threatened with dissolution each time a member dissociated. Members had the right to freely transfer the economic rights associated with membership, but could [not] [sic] transfer their membership interest (or any management rights associated with membership) without the consent of all the other members. These characteristics meant respectively that the LLC: lacked centralized management (like a general partnership); lacked continuity of life (like a limited partnership with respect to the dissociation of any general partner); and lacked free transferability of interests (like both a general and limited partnership).

In two senses, therefore, the LLC was a hybrid entity. First, it combined the liability shield of a corporation with the federal tax classification of a partnership. Second, it housed a partnership-like capital structure and governance rules within a corporate liability shield.

---

39. Wyoming Limited Liability Company Act, Wyo. Stat. Ann. §§17-15-107(a)(viii)-(ix), 17-15-113, 17-15-122 (1977).

43. Rev. Rul. 88-76, 1988-2 C.B. 360.

44. Robert J. Tribeck, *Cracking the Doctrinal Wall*, 5 Widener J. Pub. L. 89, 102-103 (1995) (describing the trend by the different states in adopting the Wyoming LLC model exactly in the beginning).

45. *See* Susan Price Hamill, *The Limited Liability Company: A Possible Choice for Doing Business?* 41 Fla. L. Rev. 721, 733 (1989).

3. Increasing Flexibility of Form: IRS Bias Toward Manager-Managed LLCs

This characteristic picture began to lose focus in 1989 as the IRS began to loosen its approach to tax classification. In a series of public and private rulings, the IRS allowed for increasing flexibility of form, especially as to the continuity of life characteristic. This characteristic had done much to keep a "family resemblance" among LLCs because, until 1989, every LLC "blessed" by the IRS had lacked that characteristic. Beginning in 1989, however, the IRS began to accept both: (i) a shrinking of the categories of member dissociation that threatened dissolution, and (ii) a decrease in the quantum of member consent necessary to avoid dissolution following member dissociation. As a result, LLC organizers had a greater variety of structures from which to choose.

At the same time, however, the IRS's pronouncements on continuity of life and free transferability of interests were conducing toward a new characteristic LLC structure. Beginning with Private Letter Ruling 9210019, the IRS revealed a bias toward manager-managed LLCs. In contrast to a member-managed LLC, a manager-managed LLC could achieve partnership tax status while enjoying significant protection from business disruption and considerable control over member exit rights. Thus, in both official and unofficial ways, the IRS suggested that, for purposes of tax classification, LLCs were properly analogized to limited partnerships rather than to general partnerships.

In 1994, the IRS issued Revenue Procedure 95-10 and made its earlier suggestion a matter of policy.[55] Revenue Procedure 95-10 purported to provide guidelines for LLCs seeking advance assurance of partnership tax status under the Kintner Regulations. In reality, however, these guidelines provided a series of safe harbors that rested heavily on the limited partnership analogy.

4. "Check-the-Box" and the End to Family Resemblance

Revenue Procedure 95-10 might well have pushed LLCs into the limited partnership mold if the IRS had not subsequently decided to do away with the Kintner Regulations entirely. Effective January 1, 1997, the Treasury Department adopted a "check-the-box" tax classification regime under which, in general, a business organization organized under a corporate or joint stock statute is taxed as a corporation. Any other business organization formed under the law of a U.S. jurisdiction — is taxed as a partnership if it has two or more owners, or is disregarded for income tax purposes if it has one owner — unless it elects to be taxed as a corporation by "checking the box."[56]

"Check-the-box" severed the connection between tax classification and organizational structure, inviting entrepreneurs (and their attorneys) to specially tailor the structure of an LLC as each "deal" might require. "Check-the-box" also resulted in widespread changes to LLC statutes, as states moved quickly to take advantage of the newly permitted flexibility. These changes included: (i) eliminating the requirement

---

55. Rev. Proc. 95-10, 1995-1 C.B. 501.

56. Simplification of Entity Classification Rules, 60 Fed. Reg. 66,584 (Dec. 18, 1996) (to be codified at 26 C.F.R. pt. 301); . . .

that an LLC have at least two members (like a general or limited partnership) and authorizing one-member LLCs; (ii) authorizing operating agreements in one-member LLCs; (iii) allowing LLCs to have perpetual existence; (iv) changing the default rule on member dissociation to make dissociation more difficult, either by depriving members of the power to dissociate, or by freezing in the economic interest of dissociated members; and (v) changing the default rule on the relationship between member dissociation and entity dissolution, either by providing that member dissociation does not even threaten dissolution, or by changing the quantum of consent necessary to avoid dissolution following a member's dissociation.[57]

* * *

E. The Current Landscape

1. Dominance of LLCs

As of 2007, in the U.S. world of non-publicly traded entities, unincorporated business organizations predominate over corporations, and limited liability companies dominate the world of unincorporated business organizations.

* * *

Ironically, as the limited liability company has increased in prominence, LLC law has become increasingly subject to corporate concepts and legal doctrines. Some have criticized this influence as "conceptual miscegenation" — a "corpufuscation" foreign to "the practice, philosophy and law of partnerships" that engendered the LLC.[66]

At least in some respects, however, the extrapolation from corporate to LLC law is proper and even inevitable. For example, the doctrine of piercing the veil originated in the corporate sphere but depends on two more general concepts: limited liability for an organizations' owner and a legal identity for the organization separate from the legal identities of its owners. These twin concepts apply as much to limited liability companies as they do to corporations; it would be neither efficient nor logical to re-invent the wheel.

Another major area of overlap concerns the rights of minority owners. Over the past fifty years, the U.S. law of close corporations has evolved to recognize that dangers of "oppression" or "unfairly prejudicial" conduct exist when: (i) a minority shareholder is subject to the will of the majority shareholder, and (ii) market limitations or stock transfer restrictions combine to effect a "lock in" preventing the minority shareholder from "voting with his feet."

Comparable dangers exist within limited liability companies, where transfer restrictions are built into LLC statutes and [today] most LLCs, like corporations, have

---

57. States did not, however, change the default rules on transferability of ownership interests. *See* BISHOP & KLEINBERGER, LIMITED LIABILITY COMPANIES, *supra* note 35, ¶¶ 1.08, 8.06[1][a].

66. *See* Daniel S. Kleinberger, *The Closely Held Business Through the Entity-Aggregate Prism*, 40 WAKE FOREST L. REV. 827, 868-75 (2005) [hereinafter Kleinberger, *The Closely Held Business*]; Daniel S. Kleinberger, *Progress Report on the Revised Uniform Limited Liability Company Act ("ULLCA II") and the Issue of "Corpufuscation*,*"* XXIII PUBOGRAM 7 (March 2006) (Committee on Partnerships and Unincorporated Business Organizations of the ABA Business Law Section), *available at* http://abanet.org/buslaw/committees/CL590000/newsletter/20060320000000.pdf.

perpetual existence. Predictably, courts have begun to analogize LLCs to close corporations and provide remedies for oppression.

* * *

In the preceding article, Professor Kleinberger noted that the "partnership-like" characteristics of the early generation of LLC statutes had morphed over time, as LLC law was "increasingly subject to corporate concepts and legal doctrines." This same phenomenon has been observed by others with respect to the drafting of LLC statutes over time:

Wayne M. Gazur
The Limited Liability Company Experiment: Unlimited Flexibility, Uncertain Role

58 LAW & CONTEMP. PROBS. 135 (Spring 1995)*

I. Introduction

From the standpoint of form, most states' LLC laws utilize, in varying degrees, provisions clearly of partnership origin. In part, this resemblance probably reflects a judgment that the business relationships for which the LLC is particularly suited will resemble the model of the partnership or closely held corporation[2] that otherwise would have been the choice of the parties.[3] In other cases, language was simply borrowed to facilitate the drafting process; it had been used in the other contexts, and apparently there was no principled objection to its use in the LLC statutes.[4]

. . . Because the availability of federal partnership income taxation treatment has been the driving force in the rise of the LLC, the partnership flavor is more decisively dictated by the inclusion of provisions that serve to support classification of the entity as a "partnership" for federal income tax purposes. In that regard, the common LLC statutory requirements of multiple members, the potential dissolution upon events occurring with regard to members, and the limited transferability of ownership interests all play roles in securing the desired partnership income tax classification.

Apart from those similarities, the relationship of the LLC to the partnership and other organizational forms promises to be even more profound, while uncertain. . . .

---

* Reprinted with permission of author.

2. There are a number of definitions of the general term "closely held corporation." A workable definition would look to a relatively small number of shareholders, with a substantial portion of their personal wealth invested in the corporation, intimate involvement in its management, and restricted membership in the corporation.

3. *See, e.g.,* Scott R. Anderson, *The Illinois Limited Liability Company: A Flexible Alternative for Business,* 25 LOY. U. CHI. L.J. 55, 103-04 (1993) ("LLCs, particularly member-managed LLCs, are likely to be closely held. . . ."). . . .

4. In interpreting the results of such transplantation activities, judges will face the difficult task of determining whether established interpretations of the provisions in their corporate or partnership context should also apply under the unique circumstances of the LLC. [This means that] fiduciary duties will probably be developed by analogy to partnership or corporate rules. . . .

Because of the LLC's superiority in offering both limited liability to participants and federal partnership income tax treatment, it may render obsolete at least the general partnership, limited partnership, and S corporation. At this stage of LLC development, this is not a revelation, but it does potentially diminish the overall significance of "partnership law,"[9] except as a default regime principally impacting those who are unaware of its application to their situation, those for whom the LLC is unavailable, or those for whom limited liability is not important.[11]

* * *

If the ever-increasing popularity of the LLC does ultimately diminish the importance of the other forms of business organization, the emergence of the LLC will not represent simplification. The LLC's future will be marked by legislative, judicial, regulatory, and practitioner experimentation with the new entity, revisiting issues already settled in other contexts. The law relating to the long-standing forms of business organization will not be irrelevant, because LLC law will develop through a heavy emphasis on analogy. . . . In that regard, the Uniform Limited Liability Company Act (the "ULLCA") recently adopted by the National Conference of Commissioners on Uniform State Laws [NCCUSL], while very flexible and contractarian overall, incorporates as a nonwaivable core many of the controversial fiduciary duty aspects of the Revised Uniform Partnership Act ("RUPA"). In contrast, several LLC statutes[18] do not include such limitations.

. . . [T]he open-ended[,] flexible quality of much LLC legislation [has quite predictably generated much uncertainty]. A common solution for [such] uncertainty is a uniform statute, and the ULLCA is being offered in this regard. Much of the uniformity will be provided only with respect to the default provisions, inasmuch as the ULLCA itself is crafted in a flexible manner in which the agreement of the parties controls. The certainty provided by the ULLCA could therefore be illusory when the parties depart from the default rules. On the other hand, as noted above, the ULLCA imposes a nonwaivable core of fiduciary obligations, while some of the existing LLC statutes do not follow this approach. I conclude that, for most users of the LLC, this difference will not be of enough significance to create preferences among LLC statutes and competition among states catering to demand based on such preferences. If that proves accurate, some degree of uniformity, although not necessarily along the lines of the ULLCA, will develop. . . .

---

9. Formal partnership law as such would decline in importance, but the "LLC law" that would rise would probably incorporate substantive concepts of partnership law due to the similarities shared by the relations.

11. If the parties appreciate the consequences of their actions, but nevertheless prize the simplicity of a handshake deal over the limited liability of the LLC, partnership law, with decades of judicial development and practitioner experience, offers guidance as to matters for which there is no agreement. Although the implementation of RUPA may upset that predictability, the partnership still provides more certainty in the absence of extensive written agreement. Although analogies might be made to comparable provisions in partnership or corporate law for guidance, the LLC is an untested commodity. If, however, limited liability is important to the participants, then the LLC will clearly be preferred, assuming that it is available.

18. The Arkansas and Delaware LLC acts are highly flexible in this regard.

NOTES AND QUESTIONS

1. The preceding article asserts that the "emergence of the LLC will not represent simplification." Do you agree? Indeed, most of the materials in this chapter reflect on the uncertainty (and ensuing controversy) surrounding LLCs as courts, regulators, legislators, and practitioners grapple with the myriad issues raised by this new form of business entity. You may want to reconsider this issue as you read through the remainder of this chapter.

2. The two preceding articles refer to the "hybrid" nature of the LLC, something that we first encountered in our discussion of the recent development of the LLC in Chapter 2. The public policy implications of the LLC's hybrid nature are explored in greater detail in this chapter, most notably in connection with our analysis of the scope of fiduciary duties in the LLC context and the variety of default rules with respect to these duties, further reflecting on the "open-ended flexible quality of much LLC legislation."

3. Do you agree with the author's prediction in the preceding article that the development of the LLC has "render[ed] obsolete . . . the general partnership, limited partnership, and S corporation"? With respect to the obsolescence of partnership law, consider the results where the facts show that the owners signed an LLC operating agreement, commenced business operations holding the business out as an LLC, but never filed the certificate of formation as required by the relevant LLC statute in order to validly create an LLC.

4. As was referred to in both of the preceding articles, the NCCUSL adopted the ULLCA in 1996. By then, however, 47 states had already adopted some form of LLC statute. Consequently, the ULLCA came too late for most states to use as a starting point in drafting their LLC statutes. Even more important, the ULLCA was largely designed by the NCCUSL to have the LLC substantially resemble general partnership. By contrast, the original Delaware LLC statute was based on that state's limited partnership statute, which made Delaware's LLC statute look more like a corporation. (We will examine Delaware's LLC statute in more detail later in this chapter.) Reflecting the further evolution of LLC law, the NCCUSL adopted the Revised Uniform Limited Liability Company Act (RULLCA) in 2006. The prefatory note to the RULLCA states:

> Eighteen years have passed since the IRS issued its gate-opening Revenue Ruling 88-76, declaring that a Wyoming LLC would be taxed as a partnership despite the entity's corporate-like liability shield. More than eight years have passed since the IRS opened the gate still further with the "check the box" regulations. It is [now] an opportune moment to identify the best elements of the first "generation" LLC statutes and to infuse these elements into a new, "second generation" uniform act.

The RULLCA "reflects the strong trend toward entity permanence and corporate-like dissolution rules, [but] it also contains provisions that are more likely to be attractive to closely held entities . . . Time will tell whether the RULLCA will gain widespread acceptance." CHARLES R. T. O'KELLEY AND ROBERT B. THOMPSON, CORPORATIONS AND OTHER BUSINESS ASSOCIATIONS: CASES AND MATERIALS (6th ed. 2010) at pg. 545. As of this writing (fall 2013), several states, including California, have adopted the RULLCA*; the California version of the RULLCA became effective on January 1, 2014. We will examine the California LLC statue in more detail later in this chapter.

5. Despite the broad array of LLC statutes and the resulting variety of their state-specific provisions, it is safe to say that today, virtually every LLC:

    *   is organized under a state statute other than a corporation statute, which allows the LLC to exist as a legal person and provides rules (many of them "default" rules) for structuring, governing, and operating the entity;
    *   comes into existence through the filing of a specified public document (under most statutes called "articles of organization") with a specified state agency [which very often is the secretary of state's office];
    *   exists as a legal entity, separate from its owners; and
    *   has a full, corporate-like shield to protect its owners against automatic, vicarious liability for the debts of the enterprise.

DANIEL S. KLEINBERGER, AGENCY, PARTNERSHIPS, AND LLCS: EXAMPLES & EXPLANATIONS at pg. 499 (4th ed. 2012). In addition, in almost every LLC, there will be an agreement among the members of the LLC that sets forth the "LLC's governance structure and provides its key operating rules. This agreement is analogous to a partnership agreement and most LLC statutes call it the 'operating agreement.' LLC governance structure runs the gamut . . . Most state LLC statutes[, however,] dichotomize governance between 'member-managed' LLCs and 'manager-managed' LLCs. Governance in a member-managed LLC resembles governance in a general partnership. Governance in a manager-managed LLC resembles governance in a limited partnership." *Id.*, at pp. 500-501. It bears noting, though, that some LLC operating agreements provide for "corporate-style governance . . . and [that] two state LLC statutes [Minnesota and North Dakota] provide that arrangement as the default structure." *Id. See* Minn. Stat. §322B.60; N.D. Cent. Code §10-32-67.

The origins of the LLC clearly reflect the hybrid nature of this new form of business entity. In creating the LLC, it is clear that the states' LLC statutes sought to pair the corporation's shield of limited liability with the benefits of pass-through tax treatment of partnerships. As the law of LLCs continues to evolve, this often has left courts and counsel grappling with the fundamental question of how to fit the LLC within the context of legal doctrines, rules, and general principles of law and equity that were developed before the birth of the LLC.

More specifically,

In a children's book published in 1946, Ben Ross Berenberg described an imaginary amalgam called the churkendoose — "part chicken, turkey, duck, and goose." In 1977, Wyoming invented a business law churkendoose: the limited liability company — part

---

* As of fall 2013, nine states (including California) have enacted the RULLCA. *See* http://www.uniformlaws.org/act.aspx?title = limited+liability+company+(revised).

corporation, part general partnership, part limited partnership. That churkendoose has revolutionized the law of business organizations, becoming the vehicle of choice for tens of thousands of ventures every month and causing the IRS to radically overhaul its approach to taxing business entities.

These developments have given courts and counsel much to learn. . . . More problematic is how these new forms of business organization fit with [existing] legal doctrines, rules and contracts [, all of which were] developed before the new forms saw the light of day.

With limited liability companies, the problem is gaps — that is, statutes, regulations, and even private agreements that by their terms apply to specified business entities but do not mention LLCs. The problem is most likely to occur under statutes and rules that regulate business activity, and most often a "gap" will raise questions of coverage.

Daniel S. Kleinberger, *Sorting Through the Soup: How Do LLCs, LLPs, and LLLPs Fit Within the Regulations and Legal Doctrines?* 13 Bus. L. Today (Nov./Dec. 2003).

When faced with this LLC "gap," the courts are required to make "new entity common law" in the words of one noted jurist. *See* Jack B. Jacobs, *Entity Rationalization: A Judge's Perspective*, 58 Bus. Law 1043, 1044-1043 (2003). This leads to the obvious question: how should the courts go about the process of addressing "fundamental issues that in the conventional world of corporate law [or, alternatively, in the well-established world of partnership law] had long been settled — and then deciding those issues afresh through the lens of new entity law grounded on" a new set of rules, such as the unchartered world of LLC statutes. *Id.* at 1044. How to address this judicial conundrum posed by the recent explosive growth of LLCs (and the resulting LLC "gap") is the focus of the following article.

Joshua P. Fershee
LLCs and Corporations: A Fork in the Road in Delaware?

1 Harv. Bus. L. Online 82 (2011)*

The limited liability company (LLC) has evolved from a little used entity option to become the leading business entity of choice. The primary impetus for this change was an Internal Revenue Service (IRS) determination in 1988 that permitted pass-through tax status for a Wyoming LLC. Then, in 1997, the IRS passed its check-the-box regulations permitting LLCs (and other non-corporate entities) to simply opt-in to the benefits of partnership tax treatment. These two rulings have been viewed as having "had a profound, unprecedented, and perhaps unpredictable impact on the future development of unincorporated business organizations."[4] Since that time, some scholars argued that the LLC should be treated as a third, and separate, entity unto itself with its own developing body of law.[5] Nonetheless, many courts have applied corporate law to LLCs

---

* *Available at* http://www.hblr.org/?p = 1181.

4. [Carter G. Bishop, *Through the Looking Glass*, 42 Suffolk L. Rev. 459, 460 (2009).]

5. *See, e.g.,* Larry E. Ribstein, *Litigating in LLCs*, 64 Bus. Lawyer 739, 741 (2009) ("[T]his Article demonstrates the dangers of failing to analyze carefully the special functions of the LLC form and forcing structures from other business associations on the LLC business entity.").

with seemingly little appreciation of the differences between LLCs and corporations.[6] That may be about to change.

Some legal scholars and practicing attorneys were highly skeptical of LLCs because, unlike partnerships and corporations, LLCs lacked a significant body of well-developed, LLC-specific law. This has changed over time, and there seem to be some indications that a body of LLC law is developing.[8] Still, LLCs are often viewed as "hybrid" entities,[9] and as such, LLCs will be treated like a partnership in some settings and like a corporation in others. Of course, the other option is to treat LLCs as truly an entity unto themselves, but courts have a tendency to choose to fill in empty segments of LLC law with either partnership law or the law of corporations, rather than crafting an LLC-specific set of rules.

Among some legal scholars, one of the more controversial areas in LLC law has been courts' treatment of plaintiffs' requests to "pierce the veil" of LLCs.[12] Veil piercing occurs when a court disregards the veil of limited liability granted to equity holders of an entity, which is traditionally a corporation. Plaintiffs seek this option when the limited liability entity lacks resources to pay a debt, but the equity holder or holders have the resources to cover some or all of the debt. Thus, the plaintiff would be unable to collect on the debt because the shareholder is not liable for the debts of the corporation unless the veil is pierced.

The veil-piercing concept has long been a part of corporate law, and many states added the concept to their state's LLC law. Minnesota and North Dakota, for example, specifically incorporate the state's corporate veil piercing laws.[17] Wyoming, the state that originated the LLC in the United States in 1977, did not put veil-piercing language in the original statute, but the state's court nonetheless incorporated veil-piercing principles.[18]

Some scholars have taken an adamant view that courts should not read the veil-piercing concept into LLC law where the underlying statute does not address the issue

---

6. *See, id.* at 739 ("Not surprisingly, legislators and courts frequently apply rules from existing business entities. Unfortunately, they sometimes apply the wrong analogies.").

8. Peter J. Walsh, Jr. & Dominick T. Gattuso, *Delaware LLCs: The Wave of the Future and Advising Your Clients About What to Expect*, Bus. Law Today, Sept.-Oct. 2009, at 11 (stating that some recent Delaware judicial opinions "reflect a concerted effort by Delaware's courts, legislators, and practitioners to develop a body of law for LLCs with the depth, breadth, and stability that are hallmarks of the state's corporate law.").

9. Anderson v. Wilder, No. E2003-00460-COA-R3-CV, 2003 WL 22768666, at *4 (Tenn. Ct. App. Nov. 21, 2003) (stating that the LLC is a "relatively new form of business entity, a hybrid" that has some of the benefits of partnerships and some of the benefits of a corporation); Larry E. Ribstein, *Are Partners Fiduciaries?* 2005 U. Ill. L. Rev. 209, 248 (2005) (citing the same).

12. *Compare* Stephen M. Bainbridge, *Abolishing LLC Veil Piercing*, 2005 U. Ill. L. Rev. 77, 77-78 (2005) *with* Geoffrey Christopher Rapp, *Preserving LLC Veil Piercing: A Response to Bainbridge*, 31 Iowa J. Corp. L. 1063, 1064-65 (2006). Professor Rapp explains: "Veil piercing has been one of the most hotly debated concepts in business law. Unlike many concepts in American corporate law, there are strong, even moralistic arguments on both sides of the veil piercing debate, and thus it has become a lightning rod for academic dispute." Rapp, *supra* at 1065 (footnote omitted).

17. Minn. Stat. §322B.303(2) (2003) ("The case law that states the conditions and circumstances under which the corporate veil of a corporation may be pierced under Minnesota law also applies to limited liability companies."); N.D. Cent. Code §10-32-29(3) ("The case law that states the conditions and circumstances under which the corporate veil of a corporation may be pierced under North Dakota law also applies to limited liability companies."). [*See also* California RULLCA §17703.04(b).]

18. *See* Kaycee Land & Livestock v. Flahive, 46 P.3d 323, 326-27 (Wyo. 2002).

and have argued against including veil piercing as an option for LLCs.[19] Despite this opposition, most (if not all) courts faced with the question of whether to allow piercing of an LLC veil where the statute is silent have done so.[20]

Similarly, some courts have applied other corporate law rules to LLCs, such as granting standing for creditors of an insolvent LLC to sue the LLC derivatively, as if the LLC were a corporation.[21] Thus, the law of LLCs seemed to be developing as a true hybrid law of partnership and corporate law, without a clearly stated rationale for how or why that should be the case.[22] . . .

*   *   *

Where legislatures have decided that distinctly corporate concepts should apply to LLCs — such as allowing piercing the veil or derivative lawsuits — those wishes (obviously) should be honored by the courts. And where state LLC laws are silent, the court should carefully consider the legislative context and history, as well as the policy implications of the possible answers to the questions presented. Courts should put forth cogent reasons for their decisions, rather than blindly applying corporate law principles in what are seemingly analogous situations between LLCs and corporations.[45]

The members of an LLC chose the LLC as their entity, and they should enjoy both the benefits and burdens of that choice.[46] Where courts refuse to acknowledge the distinct nature of LLCs, the promoters' choice of entity is, at least in part, ignored. . . . Hopefully future courts, and thus the law of LLCs, will [respect the LLC as a form of business entity, as well as the legislature's choice of language in the LLC statute].

NOTES AND QUESTIONS

1. The following excerpt is from an article penned by Justice Jack Jacobs, a well-known member of the Delaware judiciary, who offers some insight into the hybrid nature of the LLC and the inherent temptation to analogize to established precedent of either partnership or corporate law in order to resolve issues that arise in the LLC context:

---

19. *See, e.g.,* Bainbridge, *supra* note 12, at 79 ("[O]ther than in those jurisdictions whose statute commands courts to do so, courts have erred by importing the corporate veil piercing doctrine into LLC law.").

20. *See* Rapp, *supra* note 12, at 1065.

21. *See* Ribstein, *supra* note 5, at 739.

22. *Cf. Id.* at 755 ("A generation after the LLC's birth, it is time to start analyzing the LLC as a distinct business entity and to stop dressing it in hand-me-down clothes.").

45. *See* [Bainbridge, *supra* note 12, at 79] (stating that courts are often applying the veil piercing doctrine to LLCs "in a way that can only be described as unthinking"); Ribstein, *supra* note 5, at 747-55 (explaining that courts are often wrong to assume that corporate law remedies are often not the best or appropriate alternative for LLCs).

46. *Cf.* eBay Domestic Holdings, Inc. v. Newmark, No. 3705, 2010 WL 3516473, at *23 (Del. Ch. Sept. 9, 2010) ("Having chosen a for-profit corporate form, the craigslist directors are bound by the fiduciary duties and standards that accompany that form.").

I begin by describing the judge's problem, . . . [with respect to the increasing] volume of litigation that [the new forms of alternative business entities have] spawned in such a short time. . . . [I]n an alternative entity governance case, courts must in effect "start all over again," by engaging in a predicate analysis of what principles — contract law, fiduciary law, or some combination of both — will be the source of law for deciding the substantive issue for the entity in question. This exercise often [becomes] problematic in specific cases, because the various alternative entity statutes reflect underlying policies different from those that drive the Delaware corporate statute.

In corporation law, the function of fiduciary precepts is to protect investors in circumstances where management appears to be overreaching, and where the corporate statute and the charter and by-laws do not address the propriety of man-agement's conduct. In those cases, fiduciary principles become the default rule. This factual paradigm is not unique to corporations, however. The need to protect investors in a business where the power relationship between management and investors is unequal, cuts across all entity forms. Wherever there is a separation of management and control, the agency problem persists, regardless of entity form. That problem does not vanish because a state legislature decrees that for a particular kind of entity, internal governance will be fixed by contract. . . .

[The experience of the Delaware courts] in this area has required us as judges to reinvent "rules of the road," that is, the choice of doctrine for each alternative entity and for each particular case that arises in a specific alternative entity context. That amounts to a lot of reinventing. From our perspective, it would certainly be desirable if that common law process of reinvention could be avoided by cementing the appropriate choice of doctrine rules into legislative form. That would relieve courts of having to develop a choice of [law] doctrine for each entity form and for each specific case arising within that form. The question is whether that is feasible, . . .

Jack B. Jacobs, *Entity Rationalization: A Judge's Perspective*, 58 Bus. Law. 1043, 1044-1045, and 1050 (2003). *Query*: Do you think it is feasible for the legislature to adopt clear choice of doctrine principles, as recommended in the preceding excerpt? What are the arguments for and against a uniform scheme of application? What does this suggest about the role of the judiciary in the future development of the law of alternative business entities?

2. In the excerpt in the preceding note, Justice Jacobs refers to the "agency problem" that is inherent in any form of business entity involving the "separation of manage-ment and control" over the income-producing assets of the business. What is the nature of this "agency cost problem"? Is it relevant in the context of entrepreneurs (such as Joan and Michael) forming a new business (such as SoftCo)?

3. With the advent of the LLC, it is clear that a "revolution has occurred in the world of business organization law. Rising from near obscurity in the 1990s, the LLC has now taken its place as the 'king-of-the-hill' among business entities, utterly dominating its closest rivals. As the research reported in this article indicates, the number of new LLCs formed in America in 2007 now outpaces the number of new corporations formed by a margin of nearly two to one." Rodney D. Chrisman, *LLCs Are the New King of the Hill*, 15 Ford. J. of Corp. & Fin. L. 459, 459-460 (2010).

4. On occasion, creditors of an LLC have tried to reach the personal assets of LLC members when the business is unable to satisfy the creditors' claims. These attempts to hold LLC members personally liable reflect another example of the "churken-doose" issues that arise in connection with the continuing evolution of LLC law. In many instances, the courts have borrowed from corporate law doctrines, and thus they have expressed a willingness to "pierce the veil" of an LLC, much as they would "pierce the veil" of a corporation. *See generally* J. William Callison, *Rationalizing Limited Liability and Veil Piercing*, 58 Bus. Law. 1063 (2003); *Litchfield Asset Mgmt. Corp. v. Howell*, 799 A.2d 298 (Conn. Ct. App. 2002). However, section 17703.04(b) of California's LLC statute specifically provides that the failure to hold meetings of the LLC members is *not* sufficient by itself to "pierce the veil" of limited liability. But, in the corporate context, this failure often does lead the courts to "pierce the corporate veil." *Query*: Should the corporate law doctrine of "piercing the veil" of limited liability extend to *any* form of limited liability business entity, such as the LLC? What do you think is the appropriate default rule in this context?

B. Formation of an LLC

Nowhere is the extraordinary flexibility of the LLC more dramatically showcased than in connection with the preparation of the Operating Agreement. In this section, we explore the practical (and public policy) consequences that flow from the broad freedom of contract that characterizes most LLC statutes today.

Fredric J. Bendremer
Those Delaware LLCs — Another Look: How They Could Work for You

10 Bus. L. Today 43 (May/June 2001)

Could the limited liability company be the way of the future?

In recent years, business lawyers have been making unprecedented use of the limited liability company (LLC) form of business organization. Delaware, because of its business-friendly disposition, well-developed body of corporate law, business savvy courts, and attentive legislature, is often considered the jurisdiction of choice for forming LLCs.

[This article] provides an overview of the Delaware Limited Liability Company Act, 6 Del. C. §18-101, *et seq.* (the act), the nature of an LLC organized under the act, as well as the essential legal principles governing Delaware LLCs.

The LLCs' operating agreement also governs many LLC matters. The act emphasizes principles of freedom of contract and the enforceability of operating agreements. An LLC's members thus have broad latitude in structuring the LLC, providing for its operation, and defining their relationships in the operating agreement. As a result, the operating agreement may modify or supplement many provisions of the act.

* * *

LLCs are relatively new in the United States and constitute something of a hybrid between a partnership and a corporation. One of the major advantages of LLCs is that they offer the same pass-through income tax characteristics as a partnership while providing limited liability similar to that of a corporation, but without the burdens and rigidity of a corporate organization. LLCs have existed for many years in other countries, particularly in Europe and Latin America.

* * *

The Delaware act, which was one such piece of [LLC] legislation, went into effect in 1992. . . .

An LLC is formed on the filing of a certificate of formation with the Delaware Secretary of State, or any later time specified in the certificate. The LLC constitutes a separate legal entity and will continue as such until its certificate is canceled. The act requires the maintenance of a registered office and registered agent for service of process. Only limited information must appear in the certificate of formation, namely, the LLC's name, the address of the registered office and the name and address of the LLC's registered agent. Neither the operating agreement nor the identity of the members and managers need be made a public record. The LLC's members may include additional information at their election. The name of the LLC must include "Limited Liability Company" or the abbreviation "L.L.C." or "LLC." Another entity may also convert to a Delaware LLC.

The LLC may carry on any lawful business, purpose or activity, whether or not for profit, except for insurance or banking. An LLC has the powers and privileges conferred under the act and its operating agreement, and so-called incidental powers, including those necessary or convenient to the conduct of its business. Except as provided in the agreement, members or managers may transact business with the LLC on the same basis as third parties, subject to other applicable law, and may be indemnified by the LLC.

The only filing that Delaware requires on a periodic basis, from the standpoint of continuing legal existence, is an annual tax statement. That statement, which is essentially a coupon that the Delaware Secretary of State's office forwards to the LLC's registered agent, must be returned with $100 in annual franchise tax by June 1 of each year. Of course, Delaware and other jurisdictions may require additional filings on other matters.

Significantly, the act does not prescribe the familiar "formalities" usually associated with corporations. There are no specific requirements along the lines of annual shareholder meetings, periodic meetings of directors, regular corporate resolutions or votes, and the like. By design, the LLC thus can be streamlined from a formalities standpoint and have a more informal management process.

Unlike a number of jurisdictions, the act requires that the LLC maintain certain records, including information on the status of the business and financial condition of the LLC, tax returns, members and managers, cash on hand and contributions, as well as agreements to make future contributions, among other things. In general, members must have reasonable access to the books and records of the LLC. Some exceptions exist, such as with respect to trade secrets and other confidential business information. An LLC may maintain its records in other than written form if conversion to written form is possible within a reasonable time.

Notwithstanding these requirements, it would still be prudent for an LLC to maintain sufficient records for members to determine their share of profits and losses and their rights on dissociation. Also, federal and state taxing authorities require the maintenance of certain records.

One of the principal characteristics of an LLC is limited liability for members and managers. In that respect, LLCs are similar to corporations. All things being equal, members and managers should bear no liability for the debts and obligations of the LLC, and the risk to holders of equity interests should be limited to their investment. Unlike a corporation, however, members may participate in the management of the LLC without enhancing their risk of personal liability.

The act specifically states that except as otherwise provided, the "debts, obligations and liabilities of a limited liability company, whether arising in contract, tort or otherwise, shall be solely the debts, obligations and liabilities" of the LLC, and no member or manager shall be "obligated personally for any such debt, obligation or liability . . . solely by reason of being a member or acting as a manager" of the LLC. Act §18-303(a). According to the operating agreement or another agreement, however, members or managers may agree to be obligated personally for the LLC's obligations.

The protections against personal liability conferred by the act are not necessarily absolute. Although the absence of corporate-type formalities may reduce the burdens of LLC maintenance, a court could still conceivably apply the doctrine of piercing the corporate veil if it finds a failure to follow the procedural or substantive provisions of the act or the operating agreement.

* * *

The operating agreement is the LLC's central organizational document. It combines the materials that would ordinarily appear in a corporation's certificate of incorporation or charter, and the corporation's bylaws. The operating agreement may also contain provisions that would ordinarily appear in a shareholder's agreement as well as various other corporate documents. The act does not mandate a written agreement but recognizes that one will usually exist. A Delaware LLC need not have more than one member.

Among the many matters that the operating agreement might address are:

- formation;
- purpose;
- term;
- principal office;
- management;
- capitalization;
- profits, losses and distributions:
- books and records;
- liability of managers and members, exculpation and indemnification;
- rights and limitations of members;
- transfers and assignments;
- changes to managers; and
- dissolution and winding up.

Given the flexibility of the Delaware act, members have the opportunity to address all matters of particular business or legal concern. In addition, the members may in many cases include their own provisions regarding matters covered by the act, and in essence "opt out" of provisions of the act that would otherwise apply.

Members of an LLC are analogous to shareholders in a corporation, partners in a general partnership and limited partners in a limited partnership — albeit with a number of critical distinctions. Once admitted to membership, subject to the operating agreement, members generally hold an LLC interest that represents the member's share of the profits and losses of an LLC and the right to receive distributions of its assets. Any person or entity may be a member of an LLC, but not all members need hold an LLC interest. In general, the agreement will set out the procedures for admitting new members. Unless otherwise provided, the consent of all members is generally required.

The act states that the operating agreement may establish "classes or groups of members having such relative rights, powers and duties" as the agreement may provide. Act §18-302(a). In addition, the agreement may provide for the future creation of additional classes or groups, as well as the taking of an action, including the amendment of the agreement, without a vote. Further, the agreement may provide for the absence of any voting rights for any member or class or group of members.

According to the operating agreement, specified members or classes or groups may vote separately or in virtually any combination, with votes calculated on a per capita, number, financial interest, class, group or any other basis. The agreement may contain provisions addressing the time, place, or purpose of a meeting, notice and waiver of notice, action by consent without a meeting, establishment of the record date, quorum requirements, voting in person or by proxy or any other related matter.

An action of the members may be taken by written consent without a meeting, prior notice and without a vote so long as it is signed by the members having at least the minimum number of votes that would be necessary to authorize the action at a meeting with all eligible members voting. Subject to the operating agreement, voting may be in person or by proxy. The act provides that a person ceases to be a member of an LLC, unless provided otherwise in the agreement or with the consent of all members, on various voluntary or involuntary events of insolvency or bankruptcy, exceeding in certain cases time that may be specified.

Unless otherwise provided in the operating agreement, the act states that management of an LLC shall be vested in members in proportion to the then current percentage or other interest of members in the profits of the LLC owned by all members, with the decision of members owning more than 50 percent controlling. Consequently, members may have complete management authority. Unless otherwise provided in the agreement, each of the members and the managers, if any, has the right to bind the LLC.

While the act provides that the operating agreement will generally govern voting matters, the following specific matters require a vote by members or managers, or both, in the absence of controlling provisions in the agreement:

- mergers;
- transfer or domestication;
- termination of a series;
- conversion;

- admission of a nonassignee as a member;
- termination of membership following bankruptcy of a member;
- compromise of the obligation of a member to make a contribution;
- participation in the business and affairs of the LLC by an assignee;
- full membership for an assignee;
- dissolution; and
- appointment of a person or entity to wind up the affairs of the LLC.

The act states that if the operating agreement provides "for the management, in whole or in part, of a limited liability company by a manager, the management of the limited liability company, to the extent so provided, shall be vested in the manager." Act §18-402. The act also states that the manager shall hold the offices and have the responsibilities accorded to the manager set forth in the agreement. Managers may make their own contributions to an LLC and share in the LLC's profits, losses and distributions.

With respect to managers, the act contains provisions very similar to those concerning members in terms of the permissibility of creating classes or groups with different rights, powers and duties, as well as the future creation of additional classes or groups. The provisions respecting voting and the basis on which votes are calculated track those pertaining to members. Procedures for voting, including notice, waiver, action by consent without a meeting, voting by proxy and the like, are similar as well.

As for any potential liability for managers and members acting in a managerial capacity, the act provides exculpatory provisions for good faith reliance on the records of the LLC and information obtained from the LLC's other managers, members and other related parties, as well as from any other person, as to matters the member or manager reasonably believes are within the other person's professional or expert competence.

Unless the operating agreement provides otherwise, members and managers may delegate their respective rights and powers to "manage and control the business and affairs" of the LLC Act §18-407. That delegation may be directed to agents, officers and employees of a member or manager or the LLC, and may be embodied in management or other agreements. Unless otherwise provided in the agreement, delegation will not affect the status of the member or manager of the LLC.

The nature and extent of any fiduciary duties of members or managers or other persons is not specifically set out in the act and is thus not entirely clear. The act does state, however, "[t]o the extent that, at law or in equity, a member or manager or other person has duties (including fiduciary duties) and liabilities relating thereto" to an LLC or to another member or manager or certain other persons, none shall be liable for good faith reliance on the provisions of the operating agreement. Act §18-1101(c). In addition, the act states that those duties and liabilities may be expanded or restricted by the agreement.

In keeping with the principle of flexibility embodied in the act, an LLC may have multiple series of members, managers or LLC interests, having "separate rights, powers or duties with respect to specified property or obligations of the limited liability company or profits and losses associated with specified property or obligations." Act §18-215(a). Further, a series may have a "separate business purpose or investment objective."

When the operating agreement creates one or more series, and the LLC satisfies certain record keeping, accounting and notice requirements, and the agreement so provides, then the "debts, liabilities and obligations incurred, contracted for or otherwise existing with respect to a particular series shall be enforceable against the assets of such series only." Act §18-215(b).

In addition, unless otherwise provided in the agreement, the debts of the LLC or another series may not be enforced against the assets of the series. Therefore, an LLC with a separate series is analogous to two corporations in the same corporate family, with the attendant limitation on the availability of each entity's assets to satisfy the obligations of the other.

The act also permits the creation of classes or groups associated with a given series, with varying powers, rights and duties, including voting. Unless the operating agreement provides otherwise, management of a series will be conducted by members associated with the series, with members owning more than a 50 percent interest in the profits controlling. Alternatively, a manager may manage the series.

Members' contributions may take the form of cash, property, services or a promissory note or other undertaking. If a member fails to make the required contribution, the act authorizes a number of remedies, depending on the provisions of the operating agreement and the type of contribution at issue. Those remedies may include, among other things, requiring payment of cash in lieu of promised services, elimination or reduction of a membership interest, forced sale, subordination or forfeiture.

The operating agreement controls the allocation of profits and losses among members, and among classes and groups of members. If profits and losses are not specifically allocated in the agreement, they shall be "allocated on the basis of the agreed value (as stated in the records of the limited liability company) of the contributions made by each member." Act §18-503. Similarly, distribution rights with respect to cash or other assets will be allocated in accordance with the agreement. In the absence of an express allocation, the agreed value of members' contributions will control. The act provides that an LLC shall not make a distribution if, after giving effect to the distribution, all liabilities of the LLC exceed the fair value of the LLC's assets.

The operating agreement may provide for "interim distributions" — those distributions available prior to a member's resignation and before dissolution and winding up. On resigning, a member has the right to receive any distribution to which the member is entitled under the agreement. In addition, if not otherwise provided, the member shall receive within a reasonable time the fair value of the member's interest based on the member's right to share in distributions. The form of distribution to which a member is entitled is generally cash. Under some circumstances, however, a member can be compelled to accept a distribution in kind if consistent with the members percentage interest.

With regard to resignation, the operating agreement may deny a manager the right to resign. The manager may nevertheless resign, subject to damages for breach of the agreement, which damages may be subject to offset against any distributions due the manager. Members may not resign except in accordance with the agreement. Unless the agreement provides otherwise, and notwithstanding any applicable law to the contrary, a member may not resign prior to dissolution and winding up.

An LLC interest is personal property and the holder has no interest in specific property of the LLC. Holders of LLC interests may assign the interests to third parties unless prohibited by the agreement. An assignment generally pertains only to the economic entitlements of the membership interest and does not otherwise confer rights of membership, including any rights to participate in management. If a member assigns the entirety of the member's interests, the assignor-member's interest will generally terminate. The LLC interest may be certificated.

The LLC may acquire, by purchase, redemption or otherwise, outstanding LLC interests held by members or managers. Unless otherwise specified in the operating agreement, the acquired interests will be deemed canceled. Assignees who become members will succeed to certain obligations of the assignor-member, which may include obligations to make contributions to the LLC. The assignor-member, in turn, will remain liable for certain obligations.

An LLC is dissolved and its affairs must be wound up:

- at the time specified in the operating agreement, if any;
- on the events specified in the agreement, if any;
- unless otherwise provided in the agreement, on a vote or written consent of two-thirds of the members, or each class or group of members, in each case based on the percentage or other interest in the profits of the LLC;
- when there are no members, under certain circumstances and after the expiration of certain time periods; and
- on the entry of a judicial decree. Act §18-801(a).

Absent any contrary provision in the operating agreement, the LLC will have perpetual existence. The death, retirement, resignation, expulsion, bankruptcy or dissolution of any member or any other event that terminates the membership of any member will not cause the dissolution of the LLC.

The driving force behind the passage of many LLC statutes was an IRS ruling in 1988 that provided qualifying LLCs with the same pass-through income tax status as a partnership. That status had already existed with respect to S corporations. Essentially, qualifying LLCs under the IRS ruling were not subject to taxation as a separate entity. Instead, the benefits and burdens of the profits, losses, gains, deductions and credits pertaining to the LLC, as allocated under the operating agreement, would be taxable at the level of the LLCs membership interests.

Notwithstanding the IRS ruling, however, some uncertainty continued to exist as to the availability of pass-through income tax status for LLCs. The IRS maintained in its ruling that an LLC could qualify for classification as a partnership only if it possessed no more than two of the following four characteristics usually associated with corporations:

- limited liability for corporate debts;
- free transferability of corporate ownership interests;
- centralized management; and
- continuity of life.

The IRS subsequently issued its so-called "check-the-box" regulations, which provided that effective Jan. 1, 1997, an LLC will be treated as a partnership for tax purposes unless it elects otherwise. The uncertainty that followed the IRS ruling has thus abated to a large degree and LLCs have proliferated.

While a qualifying S corporation has pass-through status, restrictions continue in terms of the number of permitted shareholders, the different types and residencies of shareholders and classes of stock, among other things. Also, S corporations are subject to limitations on filing consolidated tax returns and a number of other matters.

LLCs have far fewer restrictions. Moreover, LLCs have the additional flexibility of making disproportionate allocations and distributions. I.R.C. §704. Members may also receive appreciated property from the LLC and exchange appreciated property for membership interests without recognizing gain or loss. I.R.C. §731(b), §721. Under the act, a Delaware LLC will be treated as a partnership for state tax purposes unless classified otherwise for federal income tax purposes.

Note that with few exceptions, such as certain investment companies, an LLC that becomes a public company will be deemed a publicly traded partnership and thus a C corporation for tax purposes. I.R.C. §7704. Conversion to corporate form prior to an initial public offering is thus the norm. It so happens, as well, that the securities markets still favor corporations over LLCs because of the relative maturity of corporate law over the law of LLCs.

LLCs are now accepted as being in the mainstream of business law. Indeed, they are being used in a wide variety of circumstances. Those uses range from special-purpose vehicles and bankruptcy-remote entities in sophisticated financial transactions to more ordinary business ventures, such as small businesses operating through single-member LLCs. LLCs, and in particular Delaware LLCs, are adaptable organizations that give their members maximum freedom to structure the LLC in the manner that suits their business objectives.

Commentators and lawyers alike have taken the view that LLCs are largely creatures of contract, and the Delaware act explicitly supports the notion of a substantial contractual element to LLCs. On one level, the act may be viewed as a piece of enabling legislation of sorts — enabling private parties to form a statutorily authorized entity within the general parameters of the act but with the specific structure and characteristics of the organization left to the parties themselves. Given that the act has been in existence only since 1992, however, there are relatively few cases of precedential import.

Whether the legal rights and standards applicable to LLCs thus will be derived from contract law, corporate law, partnership law or some combination or other law, or will be unique in all respects to LLCs, is not entirely clear. Even assuming that only contract law governs a particular matter, one should keep in mind that courts may well recognize legal rights and impose legal standards even when the contract itself does not purport, at least on its face, to create those rights or establish those standards.

Consequently, until ample precedent exists, the law will remain uncertain with regard to a number of critical issues, including the nature and extent of fiduciary duties and the applicability of the doctrine of piercing the corporate veil.

The LLC offers great flexibility in structuring the organization and defining the rights, powers and duties of members, managers and other relevant parties. Significantly, the LLC can provide limited liability in a manner similar to that of a corporation. The LLC form of organization also provides considerable latitude in allocating profits, losses, gains, deductions and credits, and qualifies for the same pass-through income tax status as a partnership.

1. As noted in the preceding article, although LLCs are now quite popular, they have been in existence for a relatively brief period of time and thus "there are relatively few cases of precedential import." This chapter does contain a few LLC cases from Delaware and other jurisdictions. These cases provide insight into the issues that lawyers (and their business clients) must grapple with in deciding to organize a new business as an LLC, and then negotiating (and drafting) the terms of the Operating Agreement (or its equivalent under the LLC statutes of other states).

2. It bears emphasizing that the Delaware LLC statute is amended regularly by the legislature, in order to update its statutory provisions. While the Delaware LLC statute has been amended several times since the preceding article was originally published, the essence of this article's broad description of Delaware's LLC statute remains current. However, as to any specific provision of Delaware's LLC statute, the transaction planner is *always* well advised to consult the most recent version of such provisions under the relevant state's LLC statute (Delaware or otherwise) before giving any advice to the lawyer's business clients.

3. How does the Certificate of Formation compare to the Certificate (or Articles) of Incorporation as to the scope of information required to be part of this public filing?

4. Must an Operating Agreement be in place in order to establish the existence of a validly organized LLC? Does the Operating Agreement have to be in writing?

5. What is the corporate analog to the LLC's Operating Agreement?

6. Based on the observations made by the experienced practitioner who wrote the preceding article, what features of the LLC have caused it to become such a popular entity choice — especially as compared to the traditional C or S corporation — in such a short period of time?

7. This article reflects the broad freedom of contract afforded by modern LLC statutes, including Delaware's. While maximizing the flexibility of the organizers of a new LLC to customize the LLC to meet the particular needs of the business and its owners, this flexibility is not without a price. Broad freedom of contract, in essence, means that each LLC Operating Agreement must be created out of whole cloth. The resulting complexity (and potential for ambiguity) is explored in more detail in the next section.

C. Preparation of LLC Operating Agreement: Analysis of Management Rights

In this section, we examine the issues that counsel typically must consider in preparing the Operating Agreement of a new business that the founders have decided to organize as an LLC. The discussion that follows emphasizes several important themes, including the broad freedom of contract offered by modern LLC statutes, particularly Delaware's statute; whether the LLC is to be member-managed or manager-managed, which relates directly to whether the founders seek a decentralized or centralized management structure for their new business; and finally, what the relationship is between the provisions that are included in the Operating Agreement and the default rules set forth under the relevant LLC statute.

As you read through this section, you should reflect on the relative importance of these themes in the context of organizing SoftCo as an LLC. In particular, does your view as to the importance of these issues vary depending on whether Joan and Michael decide to pursue the necessary financing to launch SoftCo from *Friends and Family*, or alternatively, whether they decide to *Go-It-Alone* and self-finance their new business? Does your analysis change in the context of an LLC for the proposed Big Bad Software (BadSoft) transaction?

Elf Atochem North America, Inc. v. Jaffari

727 A.2d 286 (Del. 1999)

VEASEY, Chief Justice:

* * *

This is a case of first impression before this Court involving the Delaware Limited Liability Company Act (the "Act"). The limited liability company ("LLC") is a relatively new entity that has emerged in recent years as an attractive vehicle to facilitate business relationships and transactions. The wording and architecture of the Act is somewhat complicated, but it is designed to achieve what is seemingly a simple concept — to permit persons or entities ("members") to join together in an environment of private ordering to form and operate the enterprise under an LLC agreement with tax benefits akin to a partnership and limited liability akin to the corporate form.

This is a purported derivative suit brought on behalf of a Delaware LLC calling into question whether: (1) the LLC, which did not itself execute the LLC agreement in this case ("the Agreement") defining its governance and operation, is nevertheless bound by the Agreement; and (2) contractual provisions directing that all disputes be resolved exclusively by arbitration or court proceedings in California are valid under the Act. Resolution of these issues requires us to examine the applicability and scope of certain provisions of the Act in light of the Agreement.

We hold that: (1) the Agreement is binding on the LLC as well as the members; and (2) since the Act does not prohibit the members of an LLC from vesting exclusive subject matter jurisdiction in arbitration proceedings (or court enforcement of arbitration) in California to resolve disputes, the contractual forum selection provisions must govern.

Accordingly, we affirm the judgment of the Court of Chancery dismissing the action brought in that court on the ground that the Agreement validly predetermined the fora in which disputes would be resolved, thus stripping the Court of Chancery of subject matter jurisdiction.

Facts

Plaintiff below-appellant Elf Atochem North America, Inc., a Pennsylvania Corporation ("Elf"), manufactures and distributes solvent-based maskants to the aerospace and aviation industries throughout the world. Defendant below-appellee Cyrus A. Jaffari is the president of Malek, Inc., a California Corporation. Jaffari had developed an innovative, environmentally-friendly alternative to the solvent-based maskants that presently dominate the market.

For decades, the aerospace and aviation industries have used solvent-based maskants in the chemical milling process. Recently, however, the Environmental Protection Agency ("EPA") classified solvent-based maskants as hazardous chemicals and air contaminants. To avoid conflict with EPA regulations, Elf considered developing or distributing a maskant less harmful to the environment.

In the mid-nineties, Elf approached Jaffari and proposed investing in his product and assisting in its marketing. Jaffari found the proposal attractive since his company, Malek, Inc., possessed limited resources and little international sales expertise. Elf and Jaffari agreed to undertake a joint venture that was to be carried out using a limited liability company as the vehicle.

On October 29, 1996, Malek, Inc. caused to be filed a Certificate of Formation with the Delaware Secretary of State, thus forming Malek LLC, a Delaware limited liability company under the Act. The certificate of formation is a relatively brief and formal document that is the first statutory step in creating the LLC as a separate legal entity. The certificate does not contain a comprehensive agreement among the parties, and the statute contemplates that the certificate of formation is to be complemented by the terms of the Agreement.

Next, Elf, Jaffari and Malek, Inc. entered into a series of agreements providing for the governance and operation of the joint venture. Of particular importance to this litigation, Elf, Malek, Inc., and Jaffari entered into the Agreement, a comprehensive and integrated document of 38 single-spaced pages setting forth detailed provisions for the governance of Malek LLC, which is not itself a signatory to the Agreement. Elf and Malek LLC entered into an Exclusive Distributorship Agreement in which Elf would be the exclusive, worldwide distributor for Malek LLC. The Agreement provides that Jaffari will be the manager of Malek LLC. Jaffari and Malek LLC entered into an employment agreement providing for Jaffari's employment as chief executive officer of Malek LLC.

The Agreement is the operative document for purposes of this Opinion, however. Under the Agreement, Elf contributed $1 million in exchange for a 30 percent interest in Malek LLC. Malek, Inc. contributed its rights to the water-based maskant in exchange for a 70 percent interest in Malek LLC.

The Agreement contains an arbitration clause covering all disputes. The clause, Section 13.8, provides that "any controversy or dispute arising out of this Agreement, the interpretation of any of the provisions hereof, or the action or inaction of any Member or Manager hereunder shall be submitted to arbitration in San Francisco, California. . . ." Section 13.8 further provides: "No action . . . based upon any claim arising out of or related to this Agreement shall be instituted in any court by any Member except (a) an action to compel arbitration . . . or (b) an action to enforce an award obtained in an arbitration proceeding. . . ." The Agreement also contains a forum selection clause, Section 13.7, providing that all members consent to: "exclusive jurisdiction of the state and federal courts sitting in California in any action on a claim arising out of, under or in connection with this Agreement or the transactions contemplated by this Agreement, provided such claim is not required to be arbitrated pursuant to Section 13.8"; and personal jurisdiction in California. The Distribution Agreement contains no forum selection or arbitration clause.

Elf's Suit in the Court of Chancery

On April 27, 1998, Elf sued Jaffari and Malek LLC, individually and derivatively on behalf of Malek LLC, in the Delaware Court of Chancery, seeking equitable remedies. Among other claims, Elf alleged that Jaffari breached his fiduciary duty to Malek LLC, pushed Malek LLC to the brink of insolvency by withdrawing funds for personal use, interfered with business opportunities, failed to make disclosures to Elf, and threatened to make poor quality maskant and to violate environmental regulations. Elf also alleged breach of contract, tortious interference with prospective business relations, and (solely as to Jaffari) fraud.

The Court of Chancery granted defendants' motion to dismiss based on lack of subject matter jurisdiction. The court held that Elf's claims arose under the Agreement, or the transactions contemplated by the agreement, and were directly related to Jaffari's actions as manager of Malek LLC. Therefore, the court found that the Agreement governed the question of jurisdiction and that only a court of law or arbitrator in California is empowered to decide these claims. Elf now appeals the order of the Court of Chancery dismissing the complaint.

* * *

General Summary of Background of the Act

* * *

Limited partnerships date back to the 19th Century. They became an important and popular vehicle with the adoption of the Uniform Limited Partnership Act in 1916. Sixty years later, in 1976, the National Conference of Commissioners on Uniform State Laws approved and recommended to the states a Revised Uniform Limited Partnership Act ("RULPA"), many provisions of which were modeled after the innovative 1973 Delaware Limited Partnership (LP) Act. Difficulties with the workability of the 1976 RULPA prompted the Commissioners to amend RULPA in 1985.

* * *

The Delaware [LLC] Act was adopted in October 1992. The Act is codified in Chapter 18 of Title 6 of the Delaware Code. To date, the Act has been amended six times with a view to modernization. The LLC is an attractive form of business entity because it combines corporate-type limited liability with partnership-type flexibility and tax advantages. The Act can be characterized as a "flexible statute" because it generally permits members to engage in private ordering with substantial freedom of contract to govern their relationship, provided they do not contravene any mandatory provisions of the Act. Indeed, the LLC has been characterized as the "best of both worlds."

The Delaware Act has been modeled on the popular Delaware LP Act. In fact, its architecture and much of its wording is almost identical to that of the Delaware LP Act. Under the Act, a member of an LLC is treated much like a limited partner under the LP Act. The policy of freedom of contract underlies both the Act and the LP Act.

In August 1994, nearly two years after the enactment of the Delaware LLC Act, the Uniform Law Commissioners promulgated the Uniform Limited Liability Company Act (ULLCA).[21] To coordinate with later developments in federal tax guidelines regarding manager-managed LLCS, the Commissioners adopted minor changes in 1995. The Commissioners further amended the ULLCA in 1996. Despite its purpose to promote uniformity and consistency, the ULLCA has not been widely popular. In fact, only seven jurisdictions have adopted the ULLCA since its creation in 1994. . . .

Policy of the Delaware Act

The basic approach of the Delaware Act is to provide members with broad discretion in drafting the Agreement and to furnish default provisions when the members' agreement is silent. The Act is replete with fundamental provisions made subject to modification in the Agreement (e.g., "unless otherwise provided in a limited liability company agreement. . . .").

Although business planners may find comfort in working with the Act in structuring transactions and relationships, it is a somewhat awkward document for this Court to construe and apply in this case. To understand the overall structure and thrust of the Act, one must wade through provisions that are prolix, sometimes oddly organized, and do not always flow evenly. Be that as it may as a problem in mastering the Act as a whole, one returns to the narrow and discrete issues presented in this case.

Freedom of Contract

Section 18-1101(b) of the Act, like the essentially identical Section 17-1101(c) of the LP Act, provides that "[i]t is the policy of [the Act] to give the maximum effect to the principle of freedom of contract and to the enforceability of limited liability company agreements." Accordingly, the following observation relating to limited partnerships applies as well to limited liability companies:

> The Act's basic approach is to permit partners to have the broadest possible discretion in drafting their partnership agreements and to furnish answers only in situations where the partners have not expressly made provisions in their partnership agreement. Truly, the partnership agreement is the cornerstone of a Delaware limited partnership, and effectively constitutes the entire agreement among the partners with respect to the admission of partners to, and the creation, operation and termination of, the limited partnership. Once partners exercise their contractual freedom in their partnership agreement, the partners have a great deal of certainty that their partnership agreement will be enforced in accordance with its terms.[27]

---

21. Jennifer J. Johnson, *Limited Liability for Lawyers: General Partners Need Not Apply*, 51 Bus. Law. 85, n.69 (1995).

27. Martin I. Lubaroff & Paul Altman, Delaware Limited Partnerships §1.2 (1999) (footnote omitted). In their article on Delaware limited liability companies, Lubaroff and Altman use virtually identical language in describing the basic approach of the LLC Act. Clearly, both the LP Act and the LLC Act are uniform in their commitment to "maximum flexibility." *See* Lubaroff & Altman, *supra* note 14, at §20.4.

In general, the commentators observe that only where the agreement is inconsistent with mandatory statutory provisions will the members' agreement be invalidated. Such statutory provisions are likely to be those intended to protect third parties, not necessarily the contracting members. As a framework for decision, we apply that principle to the issues before us, without expressing any views more broadly.

* * *

Malek LLC's Failure to Sign the Agreement Does Not Affect the Members' Agreement Governing Dispute Resolution

Elf argues that because Malek LLC, on whose behalf Elf allegedly brings these claims, is not a party to the Agreement, the derivative claims it brought on behalf of Malek LLC are not governed by the arbitration and forum selection clauses of the Agreement.

Elf argues that Malek LLC came into existence on October 29, 1996, when the parties filed its Certificate of Formation with the Delaware Secretary of State. The parties did not sign the Agreement until November 4, 1996. Elf contends that Malek LLC existed as an LLC as of October 29, 1996, but never agreed to the Agreement because it did not sign it. Because Malek LLC never expressly assented to the arbitration and forum selection clauses within the Agreement, Elf argues it can sue derivatively on behalf of Malek LLC pursuant to 6 Del. C. §18-1001.[35]

We are not persuaded by this argument. Section 18-101(7) defines the limited liability company agreement as "any agreement, written or oral, of the member or members as to the affairs of a limited liability company and the conduct of its business." Here, Malek, Inc. and Elf, the members of Malek LLC, executed the Agreement to carry out the affairs and business of Malek LLC and to provide for arbitration and forum selection.

Notwithstanding Malek LLC's failure to sign the Agreement, Elf's claims are subject to the arbitration and forum selection clauses of the Agreement. The Act is a statute designed to permit members maximum flexibility in entering into an agreement to govern their relationship. It is the members who are the real parties in interest. The LLC is simply their joint business vehicle. This is the contemplation of the statute in prescribing the outlines of a limited liability company agreement.

Classification by Elf of Its Claims as Derivative Is Irrelevant

Elf argues that the Court of Chancery erred in failing to classify its claims against Malek LLC as derivative. Elf contends that, had the court properly characterized its claims as derivative instead of direct, the arbitration and forum selection clauses would not have applied to bar adjudication in Delaware.

---

35. 6 Del. C. §18-1001 provides: "Right to bring action. A member may bring an action in the Court of Chancery in the right of a limited liability company to recover a judgment in its favor if managers or members with authority to do so have refused to bring the action or if an effort to cause those managers or members to bring the action is not likely to succeed."

In the corporate context, "the derivative form of action permits an individual share-holder to bring 'suit to enforce a corporate cause of action against officers, directors and third parties.'" The derivative suit is a corporate concept grafted onto the limited liability company form. The Act expressly allows for a derivative suit, providing that "a member . . . may bring an action in the Court of Chancery in the right of a limited liability company to recover a judgment in its favor if managers or members with authority to do so have refused to bring the action or if an effort to cause those managers or members to bring the action is not likely to succeed." Notwithstanding the Agreement to the contrary, Elf argues that Section 18-1001 permits the assertion of derivative claims of Malek LLC against Malek LLC's manager, Jaffari.

Although Elf correctly points out that Delaware law allows for derivative suits against management of an LLC, Elf contracted away its right to bring such an action in Delaware and agreed instead to dispute resolution in California. That is, Section 13.8 of the Agreement specifically provides that the parties (i.e., Elf) agree to institute "[n]o action at law or in equity based upon any claim arising out of or related to this Agreement" except an action to compel arbitration or to enforce an arbitration award.[42] Furthermore, under Section 13.7 of the Agreement, each member (i.e., Elf) "consent[ed] to the exclusive jurisdiction of the state and federal courts sitting in California in any action on a claim arising out of, under or in connection with this Agreement or the transactions contemplated by this Agreement."

Sections 13.7 and 13.8 of the Agreement do not distinguish between direct and derivative claims. They simply state that the members may not initiate any claims outside of California. Elf initiated this action in the Court of Chancery in contravention of its own contractual agreement. As a result, the Court of Chancery correctly held that all claims, whether derivative or direct, arose under, out of or in connection with the Agreement, and thus are covered by the arbitration and forum selection clauses.

This prohibition is so broad that it is dispositive of Elf's claims (counts IV, V and VI of the amended complaint) that purport to be under the Distributorship Agreement that has no choice of forum provision. Notwithstanding the fact that the Distributorship Agreement is a separate document, in reality these counts are all subsumed under the rubric of the Agreement's forum selection clause for any claim "arising out of" and those that are "in connection with" the Agreement or transactions "contemplated by" or "related to" that Agreement under Sections 13.7 and 13.8. We agree with the Court of Chancery's decision that:

---

42. Agreement, §13.8 (emphasis added). In its entirety, §13.8 provides:

Disputed Matters. Except as otherwise provided in this Agreement, any controversy or dispute arising out of this Agreement, the interpretation of any of the provisions hereof, or the action or inaction of any Member or Manager hereunder shall be submitted to arbitration in San Francisco, California before the American Arbitration Association under the commercial arbitration rules then obtaining of said Association. Any award or decision obtained from any such arbitration proceeding shall be final and binding on the parties, and judgment upon any award thus obtained may be entered in any court having jurisdiction thereof. No action at law or in equity based upon any claim arising out of or related to this Agreement shall be instituted in any court by any Member except (a) an action to compel arbitration pursuant to this Section 13.8 or (b) an action to enforce an award obtained in an arbitration proceeding in accordance with this Section 13.8.

plaintiffs' claims arise under the LLC Agreement or the transactions contemplated by the Agreement, and are directly related to Jaffari's "action or inaction" in connection with his role as the manager of Malek. Plainly, all of plaintiff's claims revolve around Jaffari's conduct (or misconduct) as Malek's manager. Virtually all the remedies that plaintiff seeks bear directly on Jaffari's duties and obligations under the LLC Agreement. Plaintiff's complaint that "Jaffari . . . has totally disregarded his obligations under the LLC Agreement" also lends support to my conclusion.

The Court of Chancery was correct in holding that Elf's claims bear directly on Jaffari's duties and obligations under the Agreement. Thus, we decline to disturb its holding.

The Argument that Chancery Has "Special" Jurisdiction for Derivative Claims Must Fail

Elf claims that 6 Del. C. §§18-110(a), 18-111 and 18-1001 vest the Court of Chancery with subject matter jurisdiction over this dispute. According to Elf, the Act grants the Court of Chancery subject matter jurisdiction over its claims for breach of fiduciary duty and removal of Jaffari, even though the parties contracted to arbitrate all such claims in California. In effect, Elf argues that the Act affords the Court of Chancery "special" jurisdiction to adjudicate its claims, notwithstanding a clear contractual agreement to the contrary.

Again, we are not persuaded by Elf's argument. Elf is correct that 6 Del. C. §§18-110(a) and 18-111 vest jurisdiction with the Court of Chancery in actions involving removal of managers and interpreting, applying or enforcing LLC agreements respectively. As noted above, Section 18-1001 provides that a party may bring derivative actions in the Court of Chancery. Such a grant of jurisdiction may have been constitutionally necessary if the claims do not fall within the traditional equity jurisdiction. Nevertheless, for the purpose of designating a more convenient forum, we find no reason why the members cannot alter the default jurisdictional provisions of the statute and contract away their right to file suit in Delaware.

For example, Elf argues that Section 18-110(a), which grants the Court of Chancery jurisdiction to hear claims involving the election or removal of a manager of an LLC, applies to the case at bar because Elf is seeking removal of Jaffari. While Elf is correct on the substance of Section 18-110(a), Elf is unable to convince this Court that the parties may not contract to avoid the applicability of Section 18-110(a). We hold that, because the policy of the Act is to give the maximum effect to the principle of freedom of contract and to the enforceability of LLC agreements, the parties may contract to avoid the applicability of Sections 18-110(a), 18-111, and 18-1001. Here, the parties contracted as clearly as practicable when they relegated to California in Section 13.7 "any" dispute "arising out of, under or in connection with [the] Agreement or the transactions contemplated by [the] Agreement. . . ." Likewise, in Section 13.8: [n]o action at law or in equity based upon any claim arising out of or related to [the] Agreement may be brought, except in California, and then only to enforce arbitration in California.

Our conclusion is bolstered by the fact that Delaware recognizes a strong public policy in favor of arbitration. Normally, doubts on the issue of whether a particular issue is arbitrable will be resolved in favor of arbitration. In the case at bar, we do not believe there is any doubt of the parties' intention to agree to arbitrate all disputed matters in California. If we were to hold otherwise, arbitration clauses in existing LLC agreements could be rendered meaningless. By resorting to the alleged "special" jurisdiction of the Court of Chancery, future plaintiffs could avoid their own arbitration agreements simply by couching their claims as derivative. Such a result could adversely affect many arbitration agreements already in existence in Delaware.

* * *

Conclusion

We affirm the judgment of the Court of Chancery dismissing Elf Atochem's amended complaint for lack of subject matter jurisdiction.

NOTES AND QUESTIONS

1. The holding of *Elf Atochem* has now been codified by the Delaware legislature, which amended the language of Delaware §18-101(7) to provide that an LLC "is not required to execute its [LLC] agreement. A [LLC] is bound by its [LLC] agreement whether or not the [LLC] executes the [LLC] agreement."
2. Why would the parties include the provision quoted by the court in footnote 42 of its opinion as part of their LLC Operating Agreement?
3. Do you agree with the court's construction of the LLC Operating Agreement in its disposition of Elf's claims arising under the Distributorship Agreement?
4. What do you think of the broad freedom of contract afforded by the Delaware LLC statute? From a public policy perspective, what are the advantages or disadvantages to this approach to business entity law?
5. As noted in *Elf Atochem*, Delaware, like New York, created its LLC statute essentially by modifying its limited partnership statute (which was largely based on RULPA). Other states, such as California, originally developed their LLC statutes by amalgamating their corporation statute with selected provisions of their limited partnership statute. But California has since shifted course and adopted the RULLCA, which became effective on January 1, 2014. *Query*: Should these differences in legislative origins of the LLC statute impact the court's analysis of the statute's provisions?

Taghipour v. Jerez

52 P.3d 1252 (Utah 2002)

RUSSON, Justice:

On a writ of certiorari, Namvar Taghipour, Danesh Rahemi, and Jerez, Taghipour and Associates, LLC, seek review of the decision of the court of appeals affirming the trial court's dismissal of their causes of action against Mount Olympus Financial, L.C. ("Mt. Olympus"). We affirm.

Background

Namvar Taghipour, Danesh Rahemi, and Edgar Jerez ("Jerez") formed a limited liability company known as Jerez, Taghipour and Associates, LLC (the "LLC"), on August 30, 1994, to purchase and develop a particular parcel of real estate pursuant to a joint venture agreement. The LLC's articles of organization designated Jerez as the LLC's manager. In addition, the operating agreement between the members of the LLC provided: "No loans may be contracted on behalf of the [LLC] . . . unless authorized by a resolution of the [m]embers."

On August 31, 1994, the LLC acquired the intended real estate. Then, on January 10, 1997, Jerez, unbeknownst to the LLC's other members or managers, entered into a loan agreement on behalf of the LLC with Mt. Olympus. According to the agreement, Mt. Olympus lent the LLC $25,000 and, as security for the loan, Jerez executed and delivered a trust deed that conveyed the LLC's real estate property to a trustee with the power to sell the property in the event of default. Mt. Olympus then dispensed $20,000 to Jerez and retained the $5,000 balance to cover various fees. In making the loan, Mt. Olympus did not investigate Jerez's authority to effectuate the loan agreement beyond determining that Jerez was the manager of the LLC.

After Mt. Olympus dispersed the funds pursuant to the agreement, Jerez apparently misappropriated and absconded with the $20,000. Jerez never remitted a payment on the loan, and because the other members of the LLC were unaware of the loan, no loan payments were ever made by anyone, and consequently, the LLC defaulted. Therefore, Mt. Olympus foreclosed on the LLC's property. The members of the LLC, other than Jerez, were never notified of the default or pending foreclosure sale.

On June 18, 1999, Namvar Taghipour, Danesh Rahemi, and the LLC (collectively, "Taghipour") filed suit against Mt. Olympus and Jerez. Taghipour asserted three claims against Mt. Olympus: (1) declaratory judgment that the loan agreement and subsequent foreclosure on the LLC's property were invalid because Jerez lacked the authority to bind the LLC under the operating agreement, (2) negligence in failing to conduct proper due diligence in determining whether Jerez had the authority to enter into the loan agreement, and (3) partition of the various interests in the property at issue. In response, Mt. Olympus moved to dismiss all three claims, asserting that pursuant to Utah Code section 48-2b-127(2), the loan agreement documents are valid and binding on the LLC since they were signed by the LLC's manager. This section provides:

> Instruments and documents providing for the acquisition, mortgage, or disposition of property of the limited liability company shall be valid and binding upon the limited liability company if they are executed by one or more managers of a limited liability company having a manager or managers or if they are executed by one or more members of a limited liability company in which management has been retained by the members.

The trial court granted Mt. Olympus' motion and dismissed Taghipour's claims against Mt. Olympus, ruling that under the above section, "instruments and documents providing for the mortgage of property of a limited liability company are valid and binding on the limited liability company if they are executed by the manager," that the complaint alleges that Jerez is the manager of the LLC, and that therefore the loan documents Jerez executed are valid and binding on the LLC.

Taghipour appealed to the Utah Court of Appeals. Taghipour argued that the trial court's interpretation of section 48-2b-127(2) was in error, inasmuch as it failed to read it in conjunction with Utah Code section 48-2b-125(2)(b), which provides that a manager's authority to bind a limited liability company can be limited by the operating agreement. That section provides in relevant part:

> If the management of the limited liability company is vested in a manager or managers, any manager has authority to bind the limited liability company, unless otherwise provided in the articles of organization or operating agreement.

The Utah Court of Appeals affirmed the trial court, concluding that the plain language of section 48-2b-127(2) provided no limitation on a manager's authority to execute certain documents and bind a limited liability company, and specifically stated such documents shall be valid and binding upon the limited liability company if executed by one or more managers. Further, the court of appeals concluded that this specific statute prevailed over the general statute, section 48-2b-125(2)(b), and that the loan documents executed by Jerez were therefore binding upon the LLC in this case. It also held that Mt. Olympus did all that it was required to do under section 48-2b-127(2) and that Taghipour waived the right to appeal the dismissal of the partition claim by failing to object to the dismissal of that claim. Taghipour petitioned this court for certiorari, which we granted.

Taghipour asks this court to reverse the court of appeals, arguing that (1) sections 48-2b-125(2)(b) and 48-2b-127(2) should be read in harmony to require that managers "be properly authorized to bind the limited liability company in all situations," and therefore Jerez lacked authority to bind the LLC under the operating agreement, and (2) a commercial lender has a due diligence obligation to determine the authority of a manager of a limited liability company before that manager can encumber the assets of the company, which Mt. Olympus failed to do by neglecting to determine whether Jerez had the authority to bind the LLC. In reply, Mt. Olympus contends that under Utah Code section 48-2b-127(2), Mt. Olympus could properly rely on Jerez's execution of the loan agreement as the manager of the LLC without further inquiry.

* * *

Analysis

The issue in this case is whether the loan agreement documents executed by Jerez, as manager of the LLC, are valid and binding on the LLC under section 48-2b-127(2) of the Utah Limited Liability Company Act (the "Act"), as the statute existed at the time Jerez executed the loan agreement or whether the documents were not binding on the LLC because, consistent with section 48-2b-125(2)(b) of the Act, the operating agreement effectively denied Jerez the necessary authority to bind the LLC where the agreement provides: "No loans may be contracted on behalf of the [LLC] . . . unless authorized by a resolution of the [m]embers." Taghipour reasons that this operating agreement provision precludes Jerez from executing a loan without a resolution of the members since under section 48-2b-125(2)(b) of the Act a manager cannot bind a limited liability company if the articles of organization or operating agreement does not afford the manager the authority to do so.

I. Competing Statutory Provisions

To determine whether the loan agreement in this case is valid and binding on the LLC, it must first be determined whether this case is governed by section 48-2b-127(2), which makes certain kinds of documents binding on a limited liability company when executed by a manager, or section 48-2b-125(2)(b), which provides that a manager's authority to bind a limited liability company can be limited or eliminated by an operating agreement.

When two statutory provisions purport to cover the same subject, the legislature's intent must be considered in determining which provision applies. To determine that intent, our rules of statutory construction provide that "when two statutory provisions conflict in their operation, the provision more specific in application governs over the more general provision." Hall v. State Dep't of Corr., 2001 UT 34, P 15, 24 P.3d 958. . . .

In this case, the Utah Court of Appeals, affirming the trial court, concluded that section 48-2b-127(2) was more specific than section 48-2b-125(2)(b), and therefore took precedence over it. However, Taghipour contends that in determining which of the two provisions is more specific, the more restrictive clause is more specific because it is more limiting and "would require authority in all situations." Accordingly, Taghipour contends that section 48-2b-125(2)(b) is the more restrictive, and consequently, the more specific, provision.

The question of which statute the legislature intended to apply in this case is determined by looking to the plain language of the statutes that purport to cover the same subject. Section 48-2b-125(2)(b) provides in relevant part:

> If the management of the limited liability company is vested in a manager or managers, any manager has authority to bind the limited liability company, unless otherwise provided in the articles of organization or operating agreement.

Utah Code Ann. §48-2b-125(2)(b) (1998). In contrast, section 48-2b-127(2) provides:

> Instruments and documents providing for the acquisition, mortgage, or disposition of property of the limited liability company shall be valid and binding upon the limited liability company if they are executed by one or more managers of a limited liability company having a manager or managers or if they are executed by one or more members of a limited liability company in which management has been retained by the members.

Section 48-2b-127(2) is the more specific statute because it applies only to documents explicitly enumerated in the statute, i.e., the section expressly addresses "[i]nstruments and documents" that provide "for the acquisition, mortgage, or disposition of property of the limited liability company." . . . Thus, this section is tailored precisely to address the documents and instruments Jerez executed, e.g., the trust deed and trust deed note. For example, a trust deed is similar to a mortgage in that it secures an obligation relating to real property, and a trust deed "is a conveyance" of title to real property, which is a disposition of property as contemplated by the statutory provision. Conversely, section 48-2b-125(2)(b) is more general because it addresses *every* situation in which a manager can bind a limited liability company.

Further, a statute is more specific according to the content of the statute, not according to how restrictive the statute is in application. Indeed, a specific statute may be either more or less restrictive than the statute more general in application, depending upon the intent of the legislature in enacting a more specific statute.

Moreover, if we were to hold that section 48-2b-125(2)(b) is the more specific provision, we would essentially render section 48-2b-127(2) "superfluous and inoperative," because section 48-2b-127(2) would simply restate section 48-2b-125(2)(b) and would therefore be subsumed by section 48-2b-125(2)(b). Accordingly, the court of appeals correctly concluded that section 48-2b-127(2) is more specific, and therefore, the applicable statute in this case.

II. Valid and Binding Loan Agreement Documents

Section 48-2b-127(2) must be applied to the facts of this case to determine whether the documents are valid and bind the LLC. At the time relevant to this case, section 48-2b-127(2), the statute applicable to the issue in this case, provided:

> Instruments and documents providing for the acquisition, *mortgage*, or disposition *of property of the limited liability company shall be valid and binding upon the limited liability company if they are executed by one or more managers* of a limited liability company having a manager or managers or if they are executed by one or more members of a limited liability company in which management has been retained by the members.

Utah Code Ann. §48-2b-127(2) (1998) (emphasis added). According to this section, the documents are binding if they are covered by the statute and if executed by a manager. There are no other requirements for such documents to be binding on a limited liability company.

In this case, as Taghipour acknowledges in the complaint and Taghipour's brief on appeal, Jerez was designated as the LLC's manager in the articles of organization. Jerez, acting in his capacity as manager, executed loan agreement documents, e.g., the trust deed and trust deed note, on behalf of the LLC that are specifically covered by the above statute. As such, these documents are valid and binding on the LLC under section 48-2b-127(2). Therefore, the court of appeals correctly concluded that the LLC was bound by the loan agreement and, consequently, that Mt. Olympus was not liable to Taghipour for Jerez's actions.

Conclusion

The court of appeals correctly determined that section 48-2b-127(2) (1998) governs this case, that under this statutory section the loan agreement is valid and binding on the LLC, and that Mt. Olympus did all that was required by statute. Therefore, the court of appeals correctly affirmed the trial court's dismissal of Taghipour's claims against Mt. Olympus. Accordingly, we affirm.

1. In a concurring opinion filed in the decision of the Utah Court of Appeals, Judge Orme said:

    > I concur in the court's opinion. In so doing, I must note that I find the policy reflected in sections 48-2b-125(2)(b) and 48-2b-127(2) to be quite curious. If, as in this case, there are restrictions in a limited liability company's organic documents on its managers' ability to unilaterally bind the company, those restrictions will be effective across the range of mundane and comparatively insignificant contracts purportedly entered into by the company, but the restrictions will be ineffective in the case of the company's most important contracts. Thus, if the articles of organization or operating agreement provide that the managers will enter into no contract without the approval of the company's members, as memorialized in an appropriate resolution, the company can escape an unauthorized contract for janitorial services, coffee supplies, or photocopying, but is stuck with the sale of its property for less than fair value or a loan on unfavorable terms. Surely, this is at odds with the expectations of the business community. A manager or officer typically can bind the company to comparatively unimportant contracts, but, as is provided in the Operating Agreement in this case, needs member or board approval to borrow against company assets. Financial institutions known this and are able to protect themselves by insisting on seeing articles of incorporation, bylaws, and board resolutions — or the limited liability company equivalents — as part of the mortgage loan process. A cursory review of such documents in this case would have disclosed that Jerez lacked the authority to bind the company to the proposed loan agreement.
    >
    >   In short, I suspect that the strange result in this case is not so much the product of carefully weighed policy considerations as it is the product of a legislative oversight or lapse of some kind. That being said, I readily agree that the language of both statutory sections is clear and unambiguous and that it is not the prerogative of the courts to rewrite legislation. If the laws which dictate the result in this case need to be fixed, the repairs must come via legislative amendment rather than judicial pronouncement.

    26 P.3d 885, 889 (Utah Ct. App. 2001). *Query*: As a public policy matter, what would prompt the state legislature to separate out the execution of instruments and documents relating to real property and subject these to a different standard than all other instruments and documents? Or, is this simply a matter of "legislative oversight or lapse of some kind"?
2. What result under the RULLCA? [*Hint*: See RULLCA §301]
3. What result under the Delaware LLC statute? Under the California LLC statute?
4. What could Taghipour and Rahemi have done to protect themselves against this outcome?
5. Do LLCs have "officers" in addition to (or instead of) "managers"? What is the legal significance of either choice?

PROBLEM

In the context of our client, SoftCo (whose founders, Joan and Michael, are seeking financing for their start-up business), would you recommend that the business be manager-managed or member-managed? Does your analysis of this issue depend on whether SoftCo will obtain the necessary start-up funds from: (i) *Friends and Family*; or alternatively, (ii) *Go-It-Alone* and finance the business themselves out of their personal savings?

D. Fiduciary Duties in the Context of LLCs

The remaining two topics in this chapter address, first, the scope of fiduciary duties within the context of the LLC, and second, the remedies that are/should be available as a matter of law in the event that the minority interest in the LLC is treated unfairly. At some level, these topics are intertwined. As you read through the remaining materials in this chapter, you should consider in what way these two topics are related, and further, what is the appropriate default rule in each context. Or, to frame the question in slightly different terms, should the law impose a mandatory default rule with respect to fiduciary duties? Alternatively, should we allow the parties broad freedom of contract — which, as we have seen in the preceding materials, is perhaps the key defining characteristic of the LLC, at least as a matter of Delaware LLC law — in this context as well?

Daniel S. Kleinberger
Two Decades of "Alternative Entities": From Tax Rationalization Through Alphabet Soup to Contract as Deity

15 FORDHAM J. CORP. AND FIN. L. 445 (2009)

F. Contract as Deity and the Death of Cardozo

It has been hornbook law for centuries that a partnership inherently and inescapably involves fiduciary duties among the partners.[80] Until quite recently, fiduciary duty has been the unquestioned lodestar of partnership law in the United States. Justice Cardozo's pronouncement in *Meinhard v. Salmon* was once unquestionably emblematic:

> Many forms of conduct permissible in a workaday world for those acting at arm's length, are forbidden to those bound by fiduciary ties. A trustee is held to something stricter than the morals of the marketplace. Not honesty alone, but the punctilio of an honor the most

---

80. JOSEPH STORY, COMMENTARIES ON THE LAW OF PARTNERSHIP §§172, 174-81 (William S. Hein & Co., Inc. 1980) (1841) ("The necessity of entire good faith, and of the absence of fraud on the part of partners towards each other, is inculcated by Cicero in terms of deep import and sound morality.") [hereinafter STORY, COMMENTARIES ON THE LAW OF PARTNERSHIP]. Sections 174 through 181 catalogue various aspects of what Story terms "good faith" and what in modern parlance is called "the duty of loyalty." . . .

sensitive, is then the standard of behavior. As to this there has developed a tradition that is unbending and inveterate.

Uncompromising rigidity has been the attitude of courts of equity when petitioned to undermine the rule of undivided loyalty by the "disintegrating erosion" of particular exceptions. Only thus has the level of conduct for fiduciaries been dept at a level higher than that trodden by the crowd.[81]

Cardozo's seminal view was questioned in the early 1990s during a Uniform Laws[82] project to revise the then-80-year-old general Uniform Partnership Act ("UPA").[83] The revision process fueled a debate over whether the partnership agreement should have the power to annul fiduciary duties. So-called "contractarians" argued that fiduciary duties were merely default rules, completely subject to revision — or even elimination — by agreement.[84] Traditionalists defended fiduciary duty as a core value not only for society generally but also within business enterprises.[85] Eventually, in 2007, the Revised Uniform Partnership Act ("Re-UPA") sided with tradition, while nonetheless making clear that the partnership agreement has great powers to regulate the partners' relation *inter se*.[86]

The advent of limited liability companies created a forum to renew the contractarian-fiduciary duty debate. From its very inception, the Delaware LLC Act has proclaimed: "It is the policy of this chapter to give the maximum effect to the principle of freedom of contract and to the enforceability of limited liability company agreements."[87] . . .

. . . However, *dicta* in some decisions of the Delaware Chancery Court suggested that the power to restrict might encompass the power to eliminate fiduciary duties entirely.[90] In 2002, in *Gotham Partners, L.P. v. Hallwood Realty Partners, L.P.*, the Delaware Supreme Court engaged in some "counter-*dicta*" and announced that the power to restrict did *not* include the power to eliminate.

---

81. 249 N.Y. 458, 464 (N.Y. 1928).

82. The Nat'l Conference of Comm'rs on Unif. State Laws Homepage, http://www.nccusl.org/Update (last visited Jan. 16, 2009).

83. The Nat'l Conference of Comm'rs on Unif. State Laws, Uniform Partnership Act (1994), *available at* http://www.nccusl.org/Update/uniformact_summaries/uniformacts-s-upa1994.asp (last visited Jan. 16, 2009).

84. Michael Haynes, Comment, *Partners Owe to One Another a Duty of the Finest Loyalty . . . Or Do They? An Analysis of the Extent to Which Partners May Limit Their Duty of Loyalty to One Another*, 37 Tex. Tech. L. Rev. 433, 449 (2005); Mark J. Lowenstein, *Fiduciary Duties and Unincorporated Business Entities: In Defense of the "Manifestly Unreasonable" Standard*, 41 Tulsa L. Rev. 411, 414 (2006); Larry E. Ribstein, *Are Partners Fiduciaries?*, 2005 U. Ill. L. Rev. 209, 236 (2005).

85. J. William Callison, *"The Law Does Not Perfectly Comprehend . . . ": The Inadequacy of the Gross Negligence Duty of Care Standard in Unincorporated Business Organizations*, 94 Ky. L.J. 451, 485 (2005); Sandra K. Miller, *The Role of the Court in Balancing Contractual Freedom with the Need for Mandatory Constraints on Opportunistic and Abusive Conduct in the LLC*, 152 U. Pa. L. Rev. 1609, 1621 (2004).

86. Revised Uniform Partnership Act §103 (2007).

87. Del. Code Ann. Tit.6 §18-1101(c) (1992).

90. *See, e.g., Sonet v. Timber Co., L.P.*, 722 A.2d 319, 323 (Del. Ch. 1998) ("[c]onsidering §17-1101(d) of the Delaware Revised Uniform Limited Partnership Act's apparently broad license to enhance, reform, or even eliminate fiduciary duty protections"); *Gotham Partners, L.P. v. Hallwood Realty Partners, L.P.*, No. CIV. A. 15754, 2000 WL 1476663, at *13 (Del. Ch. Sept. 27, 2000) (stating that section 17-1101(d)(2) "expressly authorizes the elimination, modification, or enhancement of . . . fiduciary duties in the written agreement governing the limited partnership"), *aff'd* in part, *rev'd* in part and remanded, 817 a.2d 160 (Del. 2002).

But the Delaware legislature soon overruled the Delaware Supreme Court. Statutory amendments enacted in 2004 expressly provided that an LLC agreement may eliminate fiduciary duties.[92] Now, the American Bar Association's Committee on Limited Liability Companies, Partnerships and Unincorporated Business Entities is considering whether a "model" LLC act should follow the Delaware approach.[94]

The ABA model act is in its early phases and the more or less ad hoc group of attorneys who make up the drafting subcommittee includes both individuals strongly opposed to the "eliminate" approach and individuals who favor the approach.[95] Meanwhile, the chief justice of the Delaware Supreme Court has embraced the "eliminate" approach as being the proper course for the law of unincorporated business organizations. In a law review article published in 2007, Chief Justice Myron Steele stated that "Delaware courts need to be mindful of the distinction between status relationships and contractual relationships."[96] In addition, he urged that we:

> [C]ome to grips with the reality that the contractual relationship between parties to limited partnership and limited liability company agreements should be the analytical focus for resolving governance disputes — not the status relationship of the parties. When the parties specify duties and liabilities in their agreement, the courts should resist the temptation to superimpose upon those contractual duties common law fiduciary duty principles. . . . [97]

Chief Justice Steele criticized the *Gotham Partners* decision for its "singular focus on status relationships" and for "treating the parties to all limited partnership or limited liability company agreements as having a dependency relationship (e.g., a trustee to beneficiary or agent to principal), rather than a contractual relationship. . . ."[98] Moreover, Chief Justice Steele disparaged the *Gotham Partners* court for "its nostalgia for the familiar, and inability to escape the lure of the common law" and for importing into the pristine world of contractual relationships status-related fiduciary duties "analogized from the law of corporate governance."[100]

Chief Justice Steele's remarks illustrate the contractarian's "sleight of hand" with regard to fiduciary duty. While for some purposes the limited liability company is seen as

---

92. DEL. CODE ANN. Tit. 6 §18-1101(c) (2004). [As amended, the statute now reads as follows:] To the extent that, at law or in equity, a member or manager or other person has duties (including fiduciary duties) to a limited liability company or to another member or manager or to another person that is a party to or is otherwise bound by a limited liability company agreement, the member's manager's or other person's duties may be expanded, restricted, or eliminated by provisions in the limited liability company agreement, provided that the limited liability company agreement may not eliminate the implied contractual covenant of good faith and fair dealing.

94. Prototype Limited Liability Co. Act §402 (1992) (defining duties as avoiding "gross negligence or willful misconduct").

95. American Bar Association, Section of Business Law: Partnerships and Unincorporated Business Organizations: Model Limited Liability Company Act, *available* at www.abanet.org/buslaw/committees/CL590005pub/materials.shtml. The disposition of the committee members as to contractual elimination of fiduciary duties is asserted by the author and is not official.

96. Myron T. Steele, *Judicial Scrutiny of Fiduciary Duties in Delaware Limited Partnerships and Limited Liability Companies*, 32 DEL. J. CORP. L. 1, 9 (2007).

97. *Id.* at 25.

98. *Id.* at 13.

100. *Id.* At 25.

a form of partnership,[101] that connection (and the historical antecedents) disappear when fiduciary duty is at issue. In that context, the LLC is characterized as purely a creature of contract. Moreover, to further "re-frame" the debate, the lodestar role for fiduciary duty is linked to corporate, rather than partnership law.

But *Meinhard v. Salmon* was not a corporate case. Rather, it involved joint adventurers (essentially partners for a particular undertaking) arguing over a lacuna in their agreement. Moreover, "status relationship" and "contract" are not dichotomous concepts. Status relationships often arise by or in connection with a contract, and the creative tension between agreement and fiduciary duty within closely held businesses dates back at least to the formation of the United States and most likely before.[102] In the twentieth century, the law of corporations approached close corporations as "incorporated partnerships" in order to establish shareholder-to-shareholder fiduciary duties and to validate shareholder contracts displacing the standard corporate governance structure.[103]

=====

The preceding article summarizes the general principles that form the essential foundation of fiduciary law as part of the well-established law of partnerships. This background provides the starting point for the remaining materials in this chapter, which focus on the scope of fiduciary duties in the context of an LLC.

The tension described in the preceding article has given rise to two varying perspectives as to the proper default rule regarding fiduciary obligations in the LLC context and whether those duties can be modified, or perhaps even eliminated altogether. In California, for example, fiduciary duty obligations are established by Section 17704.09 of the state's LLC statute, and these duties *cannot* be eliminated completely — although the scope of these obligations can be modified by appropriate provisions in the LLC Operating Agreement. Reflecting a somewhat more traditionalist view of fiduciary duties, Section 17704.09 of California's LLC statute establishes that managers of the LLC (whether members or not) owe the duties of care, loyalty, good faith, and fair dealing to the LLC and its members. In Section 17701.10(c)(4), the California LLC statute provides that an LLC operating agreement may not "eliminate the duty of care, the duty of loyalty, or any other fiduciary duty," although Section 17701.10(c)(14) does permit the LLC Operating Agreement to set forth the "types of conduct or activities that do not violate the duty of loyalty, if not manifestly unreasonable." Similarly, Section 17701.10(c)(15) provides that a manager's duty of care may be "reasonably" reduced (or, to quote the statute's language, the LLC Operating Agreement may not "unreasonably reduce the duty of care" prescribed in Section 17704.09(c)). Finally, the LLC Operating Agreement may not eliminate the obligation of good faith

---

101. Bishop & Kleinberger, Limited Liability Companies, *supra* note 35, ¶¶ 5.04[2][d][i], 8.06[1].

102. *See* Story, Commentaries on the Law of Partnership, *supra* note 80, §169-215.

103. *See* Margaret M. Blair & Lynn A. Stout, *A Team Production Theory of Corporate Law*, 85 Va. L. Rev. 247, 302 (1999); Kleinberger, *Why Not Good Faith? supra* note 68, at 1152-53; Daniel S. Kleinberger & Imanta Bergmanis, *Direct vs. Derivative, or "What's a Lawsuit Between Friends in an 'Unincorporated Partnership?'"*, 22 Wm. Mitchell L. Rev. 1203, 1268 (1996); Douglas K. Moll, *Shareholder Oppression v. Employment at Will in the Close Corporation: The Investment Model Solution*, 1999 U. Ill. L. Rev. 517, 528-29 (1999); Model Business Corporation Act §7.32 (2003) (demonstrating that most state corporate laws now directly authorize shareholder control agreements).

and fair dealing set forth in Section 17704.09(d), although the Operating Agreement "may prescribe the standards by which the performance of [this] obligation is to be measured," so long as "the standards are not manifestly unreasonable."

In an interesting twist with respect to limitations on the scope of managers' fiduciary duties, Section 17701.10(e) of the California LLC statute requires that any such modifications "must be included in the *written* operating agreement with the *informed consent* of the members" (emphasis added). The term *informed consent* is not defined in the statute, although Section 17701.10(e) goes on to provide that assenting to the operating agreement pursuant to Section 17701.11(b) "shall *not* constitute informed consent." (emphasis added). *Query*: How should lawyers advise their business clients with respect to satisfying this "informed consent" requirement?

Unlike California, Delaware's LLC statute does not provide this type of foundational basis with respect to *mandatory* fiduciary duties that *cannot* be waived as part of the LLC's operating agreement. This, of course, leads to the obvious question of what happens in the situation where the operating agreement for a Delaware LLC is *silent* with respect to fiduciary duty obligations. Analysis of this question is complicated further by the contractarian approach of Delaware's LLC statute (and case law), which affords broad freedom of contract in drafting the provisions of an operating agreement for a Delaware LLC — even to the extent of permitting fiduciary duties to be *completely eliminated*, although the LLC agreement may not eliminate the implied contractual covenant of good faith and fair dealing. *See* Section 18-1101(c) of Delaware's LLC statute.

With respect to the treatment of fiduciary duties as a matter of Delaware LLC law, calendar year 2012 proved to be a watershed year. In January 2012, Chancellor Leo Strine handed down his opinion in *Auriga Capital Corp. v. Gatz Properties, LLC*, 40 A.3d 839, 865 (Del. Ch. 2012). In this opinion (following a trial on the merits in this case), Chancellor Strine concluded that the default rule under Delaware law is that *equitable* fiduciary duties exist on the part of a manager of a Delaware LLC. Specifically, Chancellor Strine held that the manager of the LLC (who also happened to be the holder of a majority interest in the LLC) failed to act as a responsible fiduciary would act and thus breached the equitable (and contractual) fiduciary duty that the manager owed to the minority members of the LLC. In December 2012, on appeal, the Delaware Supreme Court agreed that the manager of the LLC breached the fiduciary duty that was owed to the minority members of the LLC based on *contractual* grounds and *not* based on equitable principles of fiduciary duty law.

While affirming the judgment entered by the trial court, the Delaware Supreme Court was explicit in its criticism of Chancellor Strine's conclusion that Delaware's LLC statute imposes fiduciary duties on LLC managers (whether the LLC is member-managed or manager-managed) as the relevant default rule. The reasoning of the Delaware Supreme Court, emphasizing the broad freedom of contract that the court views to be the very essence of the Delaware LLC, stands in stark contrast to the approach taken by the trial court, where Chancellor Strine emphasized the application of fiduciary duties that have long been grounded in fundamental principles of equity jurisprudence. As such, these two opinions, both from esteemed Delaware jurists, reflect the fundamental tension — and continuing controversy — regarding how to define the proper default rule regarding the scope of fiduciary duties in the LLC context, as well as the scope of contractual freedom to limit (or even eliminate) those statutorily-imposed default duties (if any). As such, the difference in perspective on these issues, as reflected in these two Delaware opinions, is simply the most recent chapter in a controversy that has been raging since the inception of the LLC.

This section starts by examining the Delaware Supreme Court's views on these issues, as set forth in its December 2012 opinion, which is then followed by an excerpt from Chancellor Strine's opinion in the same case. The excerpt included from the trial court's decision focuses exclusively on Chancellor Strine's ruling on the issue of Delaware's default rule regarding the scope of fiduciary duties of managers in an LLC. As you read through these next two opinions (which offer very different perspectives), consider what you think the relevant default rule should be from a public policy perspective.

Gatz Properties, LLC, v. Auriga Capital Corporation

59 A.3d 1206 (Del. 2012)

Before STEELE, Chief Justice, HOLLAND, BERGER, JACOBS and RIDGELY, Justices, constituting the Court en Banc.

PER CURIAM:

In resolving this dispute between the controlling member-manager and the minority investors of a Delaware Limited Liability Company ("LLC"), we interpret the LLC's governing instrument (the "LLC Agreement") as a contract that adopts the equitable standard of entire fairness in a conflict of interest transaction between the LLC and its manager. We hold that the manager violated that contracted-for fiduciary duty by refusing to negotiate with a third-party bidder and then, by causing the company to be sold to himself at an unfair price in a flawed auction that the manager himself engineered. For that breach of duty the manager is liable. Because the manager acted in bad faith and made willful misrepresentations, the LLC Agreement does not afford him exculpation. We **AFFIRM** the damages award solely on contractual grounds. We also **AFFIRM** the court's award of attorneys' fees.

I. Factual and Procedural History

In 1997, Gatz Properties, LLC and Auriga Capital Corp., together with other minority investors,[1] formed Peconic Bay, LLC, a Delaware limited liability company ("Peconic Bay"). That entity was formed to hold a long-term lease and to develop a golf course on property located on Long Island that the Gatz family had owned since the 1950s.

The instrument that governed Peconic Bay was the Amended and Restated Limited Liability Company Agreement (the "LLC Agreement"). The Gatz family and their affiliates controlled over 85% of the Class A membership interests, and over 52% of the Class B membership interests of Peconic Bay. The LLC Agreement requires that

---

1. William Carr manages Auriga Capital. This Opinion sometimes refers to all of the minority members of Peconic Bay, LLC (including Auriga Capital) as "Auriga."

95% of all cash distributions first be made to the Class B members until they recoup their investment. Thereafter, the cash distributions are to be made to all members pro rata.

The LLC Agreement designated Gatz Properties as manager [of the Peconic Bay LLC]. Gatz Properties [, turn in,]was managed and controlled by William Gatz ("Gatz"), . . . The LLC Agreement precluded the manager from making certain major decisions without the prior approval of 66 2/3% of the Class A and 51% of the Class B membership interests. The Gatz family owned the requisite percentages of those membership interests. As a consequence, the family had a [controlling] power over any decision to (among other things) sell Peconic Bay, to enter into a long-term sublease with a golf course operator, or permit Peconic Bay to operate the course itself.

Beginning January 1, 1998, Gatz Properties leased the family property to Peconic Bay under a Ground Lease that ran for an initial 40-year term, with an option to renew for two ten-year extensions. The Ground Lease limited the property's use to a high-end, daily fee, public golf course. The LLC Agreement contemplated that a third party would operate the golf course. (Peconic Bay could not operate the golf course itself without majority membership interest approval.) To finance the golf course construction, Peconic Bay borrowed approximately $6 million, evidenced by a Note secured by the property. The LLC Agreement contemplated that Gatz Properties, as manager, would collect rent from the third-party golf course operator, make the required payments on the Note, and then distribute the remaining cash as the LLC Agreement provided.

On March 31, 1998, Peconic Bay entered into a sublease (the "Sublease") with American Golf Corp., a national golf course operator. The Sublease ran for a term of 35 years, but granted American Golf an early termination right after the tenth year of operation. Under the Sublease, American Golf would pay rent to Peconic Bay, starting at $700,000 per year and increasing annually by $100,000, until leveling out to $1 million per year in 2003. American Golf would also pay additional rent amounting to 5% of the revenue from its golf course operations. Under the Ground Lease between Gatz Properties and Peconic Bay, the revenue-based portion of the rent would "pass through" directly to Gatz Properties.

The golf course's operations were never profitable. Both sides characterized American Golf as a "demoralized operator" that neglected maintenance items to the extent that the poor condition of the course adversely affected revenue. By at least 2005, Gatz knew that American Golf would elect to terminate the Sublease in 2010. Anticipating that, in 2007 Gatz commissioned an appraisal that valued the land with the golf course improvements at $10.1 million, but at a value 50% higher — $15 million — as vacant land available for development. By mid-2009, again in anticipation of the sublease's termination, Gatz Properties [as manager of the Peconic Bay LLC] had set aside almost $1.6 million in cash under Section 11 of the LLC Agreement, which authorized the manager to retain distributions reasonably necessary to meet present or future obligations.

In August 2007, Matthew Galvin, on behalf of RDC Golf Group, Inc. ("RDC"), contacted Gatz and expressed an interest in acquiring Peconic Bay's long-term lease. Galvin asked Gatz to permit RDC to conduct basic due diligence, and told Gatz that he was willing to enter into a confidentiality agreement. Gatz refused to provide the requested due diligence information, and moreover, criticized Galvin's gross revenue projections of $4 million as overly optimistic.

Nevertheless, Galvin submitted a nonbinding letter of intent to Gatz, offering to acquire the Peconic Bay Ground Lease and the Sublease, exclusive of other assets and liabilities, for $3.75 million. Gatz put the Galvin offer to a membership vote, knowing that the offer would be rejected not only because it would render Peconic Bay insolvent,[3] but also because the Gatz family intended to vote its controlling interest against the offer.

Galvin later submitted a second offer, this time for $4.15 million. Gatz put Galvin's second bid up for a membership vote, and the members unanimously rejected that offer as well. On November 12, 2007, Auriga Capital's William Carr suggested that Gatz should ask Galvin if he would agree to a deal at $6 million. Purportedly following up that suggestion, Gatz told Galvin on December 14, 2007, that "no further discussions would be fruitful unless RDC is willing to discuss a price *well north* of $6 million."[4] On December 29, 2007, Galvin responded that RDC "may have an interest north of $6 million," and asked Gatz to suggest a target range of values. Gatz refused to suggest a range. On January 4, 2008, Galvin wrote, "[W]e may be able to get more aggressive but that would probably open up a can of worms — for example, we could offer more money but would want to extend the lease term." Thereafter, Galvin asked Gatz to sit down with him and negotiate, but Gatz did not respond.

On January 22, 2008, Galvin proposed a "Forward Lease" whereby RDC would take over the Sublease from American Golf if American Golf exercised its 2010 early termination option. RDC would maintain the Sublease's noneconomic features, but would renegotiate the rent terms. Again, Gatz made no response. The reason is that Gatz himself wanted to acquire the Sublease and Peconic Bay's other assets.

The proof is that one week earlier, on January 14, 2008, Gatz had written to Peconic Bay's minority investors and offered to purchase their interests for a "cash price equal to the amount which would be distributed for those interests as if [Peconic Bay's] assets sold for a cash price of $5.6 million as of today." Gatz characterized his offer as equivalent to a sale price of over $6 million, by not having to pay certain related closing costs and prepayment penalties that would result if the buyer were a third party. The Gatz letter then informed the minority investors that "[n]egotiations with RDC have broken off with their best offer of $4.15 million being rejected. Offering a counter proposal of $6 million to RDC as Bill Carr suggested did not receive majority approval from the members." What Gatz did not tell the minority investors was that Galvin had expressed an interest in negotiating an offer "north of $6 million," and that Gatz had never responded. As his "bottom line," Gatz offered the minority members $734,131, conditioned on their unanimous acceptance.

All but one of the minority members rejected that offer. Gatz then changed strategy and hired Laurence Hirsh to appraise the property, but without giving Hirsh complete information. Gatz did not inform Hirsh of Galvin's $4.15 million offer, of Galvin's gross revenue projections of $4 million which implied a value of $6 to 8 million, or that American Golf was a "demoralized operator." As a result, Hirsh relied solely on American Golf's historical financials and data from comparable courses in the geographic area. On that basis Hirsh appraised Peconic Bay's leasehold, as of June 2008,

---

3. Peconic Bay's debt exceeded $5.4 million. Even accounting for the cash reserves, an offer of $3.75 million would leave Peconic Bay insolvent.

4. *Auriga Capital Corp. v. Gatz Props., LLC*, 40 A.3d 839, 865 (Del. Ch. 2012) (emphasis added) [*Auriga*].

at $2.8 million as a daily fee golf course, and at $3.9 million as a private golf course. Relying on Hirsh's appraisal as proof that Peconic Bay had no net positive value, Gatz then made a new offer to the minority members on August 7, 2008. This time Gatz offered to pay 25% of each member's capital account balance. In connection with that offer, Gatz also retained Blank Rome LLP as legal counsel. That firm advised the LLC's minority members that:

> Under the provisions of the [LLC Agreement], the majority members have the right to vote out the minority members, *so long as a fair price is paid for the interests of the minority members.* Given the existing debt which [Peconic Bay] is obligated to repay, as well as the value determined by [Hirsh], *that value is, at best, zero. Thus, the offer to the minority members to pay substantially more than zero to acquire the interest[s] of the minority members is more than fair. . . .*
>
> *If the minority members are not willing to negotiate a resolution of the value of their interests in [Peconic Bay], the majority will have no choice but to file an appropriate action with the Delaware Court of Chancery to establish such a price through the litigation process.*[5]

On December 8, 2008, Gatz formally proposed to sell Peconic Bay at auction and informed the minority members that Gatz Properties intended to bid. Exercising their majority voting power, the Gatz family and their affiliates approved Gatz's auction proposal. By this point, Peconic Bay had almost $1.4 million in cash reserves and debt service of about $520,000 per year.

Assisted by Blank Rome, Gatz next hired an auctioneer in February 2009. Although Gatz claimed to have considered three different auction firms, he hired Richard Maltz of Maltz Auctions, Inc. ("Maltz"). Maltz specialized in "debt related" sales and conducted the majority of its work in connection with bankruptcy court proceedings, but had never auctioned off a golf course. Gatz and Maltz entered into an agreement in late May 2009, whereby the golf course would be marketed for 90 days, after which the auction would take place on August 18, 2009. As actually carried out, the marketing effort consisted of small-print classified advertisements in general circulation newspapers and in a few magazines, online advertisements on websites, and direct mailings. At trial, Maltz was unable to produce documents or testimony evidencing the content of the direct mailings. The Court of Chancery found no credible evidence that any golf course brokers, managers, or operators had ever been contacted. The court also found that Gatz had not informed Maltz about the RDC bids or suggested that Maltz contact Galvin.[6]

Due diligence materials, which the trial court described as "less than optimal," were made available to potential bidders on or about July 16, 2009, for a $350 fee. In mid-July 2009, Maltz set the auction terms, which were as follows: "Peconic Bay would be sold as-is, where-is, and with all faults, without any representations or warranties"; the winning bidder must repay the debt in full or assume the debt with the consent of the bank lender; and Gatz "reserved the right to cancel the auction at any time before

---

5. *Id.* at 869 (emphasis added).
6. Although Galvin did eventually learn of the auction, he decided not to bid, in part because of the auction terms.

bidding." Maltz did not contact a bank to propose that prepackaged financing be offered to qualified bidders.

In 2009, Auriga brought a Court of Chancery action against Gatz. Auriga then moved to enjoin the Auction* from taking place, but the court denied the injunction motion. Thereafter, Gatz reengaged appraiser Hirsh to opine on the advisability of proceeding with the auction. Hirsh opined that an auction would be quick and efficient, but he did not express any view on the fairness of the auction terms or of the pre-auction marketing process.

On August 18, 2009, the day of the auction, Maltz informed Gatz that he (Gatz) would be the only bidder. Gatz then proceeded to bid and then to purchase Peconic Bay for $50,000 cash plus assumption of the LLC's debt. The minority members collectively received $20,985. Maltz received $80,000 for his services. At trial Gatz admitted that "had there been another bidder at the Auction, he 'might have bid higher' than $50,000."

In 2010, Auriga and the remaining LLC minority members brought this Court of Chancery action for money damages. After a trial, the court ruled in favor of Auriga, holding that Gatz had breached "both his contractual and fiduciary duties" to Peconic Bay's minority members. The court awarded damages of $776,515 calculated as of January 1, 2008, plus prejudgment interest at the statutory rate, compounded monthly. The court also awarded the minority members one half of their requested attorneys' fees and costs. This appeal by Gatz followed.

* * *

III. ANALYSIS

A. Did Gatz Owe Fiduciary Duties to the Other Members of Peconic Bay?

The pivotal legal issue presented on this appeal is whether Gatz owed contractually-agreed-to fiduciary duties to Peconic Bay and its minority investors. Resolving that issue requires us to interpret Section 15 of the LLC Agreement, which both sides agree is controlling. Section 15 pertinently provides that:

> Neither the Manager nor any other Member shall be entitled to cause the Company to enter into any amendment of any of the Initial Affiliate Agreements which would increase the amounts paid by the Company pursuant thereto, or enter into any additional agreements with affiliates on terms and conditions which are less favorable to the Company than the terms and conditions of similar agreements which could then be entered into with arms-length third parties, without the consent of a majority of the non-affiliated Members (such majority to be deemed to be the holders of 66–2/3% of all Interests which are not held by affiliates of the person or entity that would be a party to the proposed agreement).

---

* Although not expressly defined as part of the Supreme Court's decision, the term "Auction" was defined by Chancellor Strine as part of the statement of facts in his trial court opinion, which is then referenced by Delaware Supreme Court in its opinion. *See Auriga*, at 40 A.3d at 847; and *see* 59 A.3d at 1211-12, fn. 9.

The Court of Chancery determined that Section 15 imposed fiduciary duties in transactions between the LLC and affiliated persons. We agree. To impose fiduciary standards of conduct as a contractual matter, there is no requirement in Delaware that an LLC agreement use magic words, such as "entire fairness" or "fiduciary duties." Indeed, Section 15 nowhere expressly uses either of those terms. Even so, we construe its operative language[18] as an explicit contractual assumption by the contracting parties of an obligation subjecting the manager and other members to obtain a fair price for the LLC in transactions between the LLC and affiliated persons. Viewed functionally, the quoted language is the contractual equivalent of the entire fairness equitable standard of conduct and judicial review.[19]

We conclude that Section 15 of the LLC Agreement, by its plain language, contractually adopts the fiduciary duty standard of entire fairness, and the "fair price" obligation which inheres in that standard. Section 15 imposes that standard in cases where an LLC manager causes the LLC to engage in a conflicted transaction with an affiliate without the approval of a majority of the minority members. There having been no majority-of-the-minority approving vote in this case, the burden of establishing the fairness of the transaction fell upon Gatz. That burden Gatz could easily have avoided. If (counterfactually) Gatz had conditioned the transaction upon the approval of an informed majority of the nonaffiliated members, the sale of Peconic Bay would not have been subject to, or reviewed under, the contracted-for entire fairness standard.[20]

Gatz's admissions in the pleadings and during his cross examination at trial confirm our contractual interpretation. In his Answer to Auriga's First Amended Complaint, Gatz admitted four times that he owed "certain fiduciary duties."[21] In his Opening Pretrial Brief, Gatz argued that he had "fully complied with [his] fiduciary duties, the LLC Agreement and the implied covenant." In his Answering Pretrial Brief, Gatz stated in a footnote that "[t]o be absolutely clear, [Gatz is] not arguing that the LLC Agreement waives all fiduciary duties."

---

18. The operative language of Section 15 is "on terms and conditions which are less favorable to the Company than the terms and conditions of similar agreements which could then be entered into with arms-length third parties, without the consent of a majority of the non-affiliated Members."

19. We previously have reached a similar result in the partnership context. *See Gotham Partners [L.P. v. Hallwood Recenty Partners, L.P.,* 817 A.2d 160, 171 (Del. 2002)]. In *Gotham,* we affirmed the Court of Chancery's finding, which the parties did not contest, that the Partnership Agreement imposed entire fairness obligations. Section 7.05 of that Agreement permitted self-dealing transactions, "provided that the terms of any such transaction are substantially equivalent to terms obtainable by the Partnership from a comparable unaffiliated third party," reflecting the fair price prong [of the entire fairness test as established under Delaware case law]. Section 7.10, which required an independent audit committee to review and approve the self-dealing transactions, reflected the fair dealing prong. *Id.* The LLC Agreement language employed in this case is substantially identical. Section 15 explicitly mandates a fair price analysis, but offers as a safe harbor a majority-of-the-minority vote. We interpret that contractual obligation here, as we did in *Gotham,* as the contracted-for functional equivalent of entire fairness.

20. That result contrasts with the outcome that it would obtain in the traditional corporate law setting, where an informed majority-of-the-minority shareholder vote operates to shift the burden of proof on the issue of fairness. *Kahn v. Lynch Commc'n Sys., Inc.,* 638 A.2d 1110, 1117 (Del. 1994).

21. App. to Ans. Br. B 44 ("Admitted only that Gatz Properties is Manager of PBG and owes certain fiduciary duties as a result thereof."); *id.* at B 45 ("Admitted that Gatz is the manager and an equity holder of Gatz Properties. It is also admitted that Gatz Properties is Manager of PBG and owes certain fiduciary duties as a result thereof."); *id.* at B 46 ("Admitted that Gatz Properties is [the] Manager of PBG and owes certain fiduciary duties as a result thereof."); *id.* ("Admitted that Gatz Properties knew it owed fiduciary duties.").

Equally if not more illuminating is Gatz's trial testimony during cross examination. When asked, "Would you agree Gatz Properties owed fiduciary duties to the members of Peconic Bay?", Gatz answered unequivocally "Yes." When asked, "And you understood that you personally had a fiduciary duty to all members of Peconic Bay[,] right?", Gatz again answered unequivocally "Yes." When asked, "So, in that capacity [as Peconic Bay's manager], you understood that you had a fiduciary duty to all the members of Peconic Bay?", Gatz again answered "Yes."

We therefore uphold the Court of Chancery's determination that Gatz breached his contractually adopted fiduciary duties to the minority members of Peconic Bay. Although the trial court reached that conclusion after first having determined that Delaware's LLC statute imposed "default" fiduciary duties — a conclusion that we address elsewhere in this Opinion — we affirm the court's holding that Gatz was subject to fiduciary duties and that he breached them. We do that exclusively on contractual grounds, however.

Entire fairness review normally encompasses two prongs, fair dealing and fair price.[27] "However, the test for fairness is not a bifurcated one as between fair dealing and price. All aspects of the issue must be examined as a whole since the question is one of entire fairness."[28] In this case, given the language of Section 15, which speaks only in terms of fair price, the Court of Chancery formally applied only the fair price prong. But, in doing so[,] that court also properly considered the "fairness" of how Gatz dealt with the minority "because the extent to which the process leading to the self-dealing either replicated or deviated from the behavior one would expect in an arms-length deal bears importantly on the price determination."[29] The court further held that "in order to take cover under the contractual safe harbor of Section 15, Gatz bears the burden to show that he paid a fair price to acquire Peconic Bay."[30] We agree.

The trial judge found facts, solidly grounded in the record, that firmly support his conclusion that Gatz breached his contracted-for duty to the LLC's minority members. Regarding price, the court found that "Peconic Bay was worth more than what Gatz paid."[31] Gatz argued, but failed to convince the court, that "the Property had no positive value. . . ." The court did not regard the absence of competing bids at the auction as persuasive evidence that the price Gatz paid to cash out the minority members was fair.[33] As the court found, "even as of the date of the Auction, the fundamentals of Peconic Bay

---

27. *Weinberger v. UOP, Inc.*, 457 A.2d 701, 711 (Del. 1983). Fair dealing "embraces questions of when the transaction was timed, how it was initiated, structured, negotiated, disclosed to the directors, and how the approvals of the directors and the stockholders were obtained." *Id.* Fair price "relates to the economic and financial considerations of the proposed" transaction. *Id.*

28. *Id.*

29. *Auriga Capital Corp. v. Gatz Props., LLC*, 40 A.3d 839, 857 (Del. Ch. 2012) (citing *Flight Options Int'l, Inc. v. Flight Options, LLC*, 2005 WL 2335353, at *7 n. 32 (Del. Ch. Sept. 20, 2005)). Indeed, this Court has recognized that a fair process generally leads to a fair price. *See Americas Mining Corp. v. Theriault*, 51 A.3d 1213, 1244 (Del. 2012).

30. *Auriga*, 40 A.3d at 857–58.

31. *Auriga*, 40 A.3d at 875.

33. "The fact that Carr would not stake his credibility with investors on the line by funding a full purchase of Peconic Bay after having had the investors he procured receive no return of capital for ten years is not one that can be given much weight." *Id.* "Furthermore, the fact that Galvin of RDC did not bid was understandable based on the unfair Auction rules and the prior treatment he had received at Gatz's hands." *Id.*

were such as to make [the court] conclude that an offer above the debt would have been economically justifiable." The Court of Chancery also properly relied on Auriga's expert witness's discounted cash flow analysis, which valued Peconic Bay at approximately $8.9 million.

The court also found as fact that had "Gatz dealt with Galvin with integrity in 2007, it seems probable that Peconic Bay could have been sold in a way that generated to the Minority Members a full return of their invested capital ($725,000) plus a 10% aggregate return ($72,500)." In reaching that result, the court relied on the fact that Gatz had rebuffed Galvin's interest in discussing a deal "well north of $6 million." The court also found persuasive Galvin's explanation of why, under the circumstances, an over $6 million price was justifiable.

As for fair dealing, the Court of Chancery did not "view the Auction process as generating a price indicative of what Peconic Bay would fetch in a true arms-length negotiation."[39] Indeed, the court found, the Auction was a "sham," "the culmination of Gatz's bad faith efforts to squeeze out the Minority Members." The court concluded that "[b]y failing for years to cause Peconic Bay to explore its market alternatives, Gatz manufactured a situation of distress to allow himself to purchase Peconic Bay at a fire sale price at a distress sale."

These conclusions flow persuasively from the evidence of record. Gatz's decision to auction off Peconic Bay as a distressed property — as opposed to engaging a broker experienced in the golf course industry to sell the company or its prime assets in an orderly way — was wholly unnecessary. Peconic Bay's cash reserves would have afforded Gatz ample time to structure a sale of the property consistent with his contracted-for fiduciary obligation. The court found that "even in the context of an auction approach, the indifference and unprofessionalism of the marketing effort [was] patent." That finding rested on, among other things: (i) the absence of any direct outreach to industry players, (ii) the fact that Gatz failed to inform Maltz of RDC's expressions of interest, (iii) the rushed time frame of the marketing, and (iv) the auction terms themselves. The Court of Chancery properly concluded "that the Auction was not a process that anyone acting with minimal competency and in good faith would have used to obtain fair value for Peconic Bay."

We are satisfied that Gatz failed to carry his burden of proving that he discharged his contracted-for entire fairness obligation. Accordingly, we affirm that court's determination of liability solely on contractual grounds.

B. Does Section 16 of the LLC Agreement Exculpate Gatz?

Although the trial court's adjudication subjects Gatz to liability under Section 15 of the LLC Agreement, another provision, Section 16, permits both exculpation and indemnification of Peconic Bay's manager in specified circumstances. Gatz, however, did not cause those circumstances to come about. Having failed to satisfy the criteria of

---

39. *Id.* at 874–75 (citing *Flight Options Int'l, Inc. v. Flight Options, LLC*, 2005 WL 2335353, at *8 (Del.Ch. Sept. 20, 2005); *Neal v. Ala. By–Prods. Corp.*, 1990 WL 109243, at *11 (Del.Ch. Aug. 1, 1990), *aff'd*, 588 A.2d 255 (Del. 1991)).

Section 16, Gatz was not eligible for exculpation or indemnification, and the Court of Chancery properly so held.

Section 16 of the LLC Agreement pertinently provides:

No Covered Person [defined to include, among others, the members, manager, and officers and the employees] shall be liable to the Company, [or] any other Covered Person or any other person or entity who has an interest in the Company for any loss, damage or claim incurred by reason of any act or omission performed or omitted by such Covered Person in good faith in connection with the formation of the Company or on behalf of the Company and in a manner reasonably believed to be within the scope of the authority conferred on such Covered Person by this Agreement, except that a Covered Person shall be liable for any such loss, damage or claim incurred by reason of such Covered Person's gross negligence, willful misconduct or willful misrepresentation.[47]

Gatz was not entitled to exculpation because the Court of Chancery properly found that he had acted in bad faith and had made willful misrepresentations in the course of breaching his contracted-for fiduciary duty. Consequently, Section 16 of the LLC Agreement provides no safe harbor. We highlight the most egregious instances below.

This Court and the Court of Chancery have defined "bad faith" in the corporate fiduciary duty of loyalty context as (among other things) a failure "to act in the face of a known duty to act," which demonstrates a "conscious disregard" of one's duties.[48] Here, the Court of Chancery made factual findings, rooted solidly in the record, that firmly support its conclusion that in breaching his contractual fiduciary obligation, Gatz acted in bad faith. The court found that "Gatz knew, by at latest 2005, that American Golf was very likely to terminate the Sublease in 2010,"[49] and that there was no "credible evidence suggesting that Gatz engaged in a serious or thoughtful effort to look for a replacement operator." The court described Gatz's actions as "consistent with those of someone who was hoping that that [sic] Peconic Bay would simply revert back to his family's ownership once Peconic Bay's primary source of revenue ran dry, without regard for the interests of the Minority Members." As the record establishes, in 2007, Gatz refused to provide basic due diligence to RDC, a credible buyer. Gatz also criticized RDC's financial projections as being too optimistic, and refused in any way to engage with RDC even though Gatz knew that American Golf was likely to terminate the lease payments in 2010.

Likewise, the factual findings support the court's conclusion that Gatz conducted the Auction in bad faith. Gatz decided to pursue an auction process on distressed sale terms, rather than a broker-led process based on a fully developed analysis of strategic alternatives. That conduct was particularly egregious, because Peconic Bay's cash cushion would have allowed the LLC to continue "to pay the bills for three years" while searching for a buyer. No less egregious was Gatz's failure to tell the auctioneer about RDC's recent interest in acquiring Peconic Bay and Galvin's willingness to pay "north of $6 million." We agree with the trial court that "the Auction was not a process

---

47. [*Auriga*, 40 A.3d] at 858. The indemnification provisions are identical for our purposes.
48. *Stone ex rel. AmSouth Bancorporation v. Ritter*, 911 A.2d 362, 370 (Del. 2006) (citing *In re Walt Disney Co. Derivative Litig.*, 906 A.2d 27, 67 (Del. 2006)).
49. *Auriga*, 40 A.3d at 861.

anyone acting with minimal competency and in good faith would have used to obtain fair value for Peconic Bay."

Further, that court correctly found that Gatz's offer to Peconic Bay's minority members in 2008 "contained incomplete and misleading information about the RDC negotiations."[58] Gatz "intentionally [misled] the Minority Members when accurate information concerning third-party offers would have been material to their decision whether to accept Gatz's own offer . . .":

> Specifically, Gatz failed to inform the Minority Members that Galvin had told Gatz that RDC "may have an interest north of $6 million," and that [Galvin] "may be able to get more aggressive" than his last bid of $4.15 million. Gatz also failed to inform the Minority Members that Gatz never followed up on Galvin's invitations to negotiate or that RDC had bid without any benefit of due diligence. Rather, Gatz conveyed the misleading impression that RDC — a reputable third-party buyer — was only willing to pay $4.15 million for Peconic Bay's assets so that Gatz's own offer would appear more attractive.[60]

Those findings support the court's determination that Gatz acted in bad faith and made willful misrepresentations. We therefore uphold the trial court's finding that Section 16 of the LLC Agreement does not immunize Gatz from liability for his conduct.

C. Unnecessary Construction of LLC Statute to Provide Default Fiduciary Duties

At this point, we pause to comment on one issue that the trial court should not have reached or decided. We refer to the court's pronouncement that the Delaware Limited Liability Company Act imposes "default" fiduciary duties upon LLC managers and controllers unless the parties to the LLC Agreement contract that such duties shall not apply. Where, as here, the dispute over whether fiduciary standards apply could be decided solely by reference to the LLC Agreement, it was improvident and unnecessary for the trial court to reach out and decide, *sua sponte*, the default fiduciary duty issue as a matter of statutory construction. The trial court did so despite expressly acknowledging that the existence of fiduciary duties under the LLC Agreement was "no longer contested by the parties."[61] For the reasons next discussed, that court's statutory pronouncements must be regarded as dictum without any precedential value.

First, the Peconic Bay LLC Agreement explicitly and specifically addressed the "fiduciary duty issue" in Section 15, which controls this dispute. Second, no litigant asked the Court of Chancery or this Court to decide the default fiduciary duty issue as a matter of statutory law. In these circumstances we decline to express any view regarding whether default fiduciary duties apply as a matter of statutory construction. The Court of Chancery likewise should have so refrained.

---

58. *Id.* at 868.
60. *Id.*
61. *Auriga*, 40 A.3d at 856, n. 67.

Third, the trial court's stated reason for venturing into statutory territory creates additional cause for concern. The trial court opinion identifies "two issues that would arise if the equitable background explicitly contained in the statute were to be judicially excised now."[63] The opinion suggests that "a judicial eradication of the explicit equity overlay in the LLC Act could tend to erode our state's credibility with investors in Delaware entities."[64] Such statements might be interpreted to suggest (hubristically) that once the Court of Chancery has decided an issue, and because practitioners rely on that court's decisions, this Court should not judicially "excise" the Court of Chancery's statutory interpretation, even if incorrect.[65] That was the interpretation gleaned by Auriga's counsel. During oral argument before this Court, counsel understood the trial court opinion to mean that "because the Court of Chancery has repeatedly decided an issue one way, . . . and practitioners have accepted it, that this Court, when it finally gets its hands on the issue, somehow ought to be constrained because people have been conforming their conduct to" comply with the Court of Chancery's decisions. It is axiomatic, and we recognize, that once a trial judge decides an issue, other trial judges on that court are entitled to rely on that decision as *stare decisis*, Needless to say, as an appellate tribunal and the court of last resort in this State, we are not so constrained.

Fourth, the merits of the issue whether the LLC statute does — or does not — impose default fiduciary duties is one about which reasonable minds could differ. Indeed, reasonable minds arguably could conclude that the statute — which begins with the phrase, "[t]o *the extent that*, at law or in equity, a member or manager or other person has duties (including fiduciary duties)"[69] — is consciously ambiguous. That possibility suggests that the "organs of the Bar" (to use the trial court's phrase) may be well advised to consider urging the General Assembly to resolve any statutory ambiguity on this issue.

Fifth, and finally, the court's excursus on this issue strayed beyond the proper purview and function of a judicial opinion. "Delaware law requires that a justiciable controversy exist before a court can adjudicate properly a dispute brought before it."[71] We remind Delaware judges that the obligation to write judicial opinions on the issues presented is not a license to use those opinions as a platform from which to propagate their individual world views on issues not presented.[72] A judge's duty is to resolve the issues that the parties present in a clear and concise manner. To the extent Delaware judges wish to stray beyond those issues and, without making any definitive pronouncements, ruminate on what the proper direction of Delaware law should be, there are appropriate platforms, such as law review articles, the classroom, continuing legal education presentations, and keynote speeches. That said, we next turn to the issue of damages.

---

63. *Id.* at 853.

64. *Id.* at 854.

65. *Id.* at 853–56.

69. 6 *Del. C.* §18–1101(c) (emphasis added).

71. *Crescent/Mach 1 Partners L.P. v. Dr Pepper Bottling Co. of Texas*, 962 A.2d 205, 208 (Del. 2008) (quoting *Warren v. Moore*, 1994 WL 374333, at *2 (Del.Ch. July 6, 1994)).

72. *See Americas Mining Corp. v. Theriault*, 51 A.3d 1213, 1263 (Del. 2012) (Berger, J., concurring and dissenting) (arguing that "the trial court did not apply" the law, but rather "its own world views on incentives, bankers' compensation, and envy").

D. Damages

Having found that the defendants had breached a contracted-for fiduciary duty arising from equity, and that the LLC Agreement did not dictate otherwise, the Court of Chancery awarded equitable damages as a remedy.[74] Damages awards are reviewed under an abuse of discretion standard. As earlier stated, we do "not substitute our own notions of what is right for those of the trial judge if that judgment was based upon conscience and reason, as opposed to capriciousness or arbitrariness."

Conscience and reason appropriately circumscribed the trial court's award of damages in this case. The law requires the trial judge to weigh the evidence, including the credibility of live witness testimony. The trial judge very clearly detailed his reasons, based on facts of record, for "not reach[ing] the same conclusion [as] Gatz . . . about whether he should suffer a damages award."[78] Gatz failed to convince the Court of Chancery "that the Property had no positive value." That court found that, "even as of the date of the Auction, the fundamentals of Peconic Bay were such as to make [the court] conclude that an offer above the debt would have been economically justifiable." The court relied in part upon Auriga's damages expert, who presented a discounted cash flow analysis that valued Peconic Bay at $8.9 million as of the Auction date. That analysis, although optimistic, was found reasonable.

The trial court determined that if Gatz had engaged with Galvin in 2007, as Gatz's contracted-for entire fairness duty required, Peconic Bay could probably have been sold at a price that returned to the minority investors both their initial capital ($725,000) plus a 10% aggregate return ($72,500). The court found Galvin's testimony sufficiently credible to support a "fair price" above $6 million. Auriga's damages expert's report also supports that finding. As the trial court aptly noted, although Gatz "had no duty to sell his interests," he did not have "a free license to mismanage Peconic Bay so as to deliver it to himself for an unfair price."

The Court of Chancery arrived at a damage award of $776,515, which represented a full return of the minority members' capital contributions plus a 10% aggregate return, less the $20,985 the minority members received at the Auction. That award is slightly less than the amount a sale in 2007 for $6.5 million would have yielded. The court noted that

---

74. This case echoes our ruling in *Gotham Partners, L.P. v. Hallwood Realty Partners, L.P.*:

> The Partnership Agreement provides for contractual fiduciary duties of entire fairness. Although the contract could have limited the damage remedy for breach of these duties to contract damages, it did not do so. The Court of Chancery is not precluded from awarding equitable relief as provided by the entire fairness standard where, as here, the general partner breached its contractually created fiduciary duty to meet the entire fairness standard and the partnership agreement is silent regarding damages. The Court of Chancery in this case may award equitable relief as provided by the entire fairness standard and is not limited to contract damages for two reasons: (1) this case involves a breach of the duty of loyalty and such a breach permits broad, discretionary, and equitable remedies; and (2) courts will not construe a contract as taking away other forms of appropriate relief, including equitable relief, unless the contract explicitly provides for an exclusive remedy.

817 A.2d 160, 175 (Del. 2002).
  78. *Auriga*, 40 A.3d at 876.

its damages award was modest and that "the record could support a higher one." The damages award was based on conscience and reason, and we uphold it.

E. Attorneys' Fees

Gatz's final claim of error attacks the trial court's award of attorneys' fees. We review an award of attorneys' fees for abuse of discretion. The Court of Chancery, under its equitable powers, has latitude to shift attorneys' fees, and properly did so here. Although this case involved a legal dispute over a contractual provision of an LLC Agreement, even at law a court has inherent authority to shift fees where necessary to control the court's own process.[88]

"Under the American Rule, absent express statutory language to the contrary, each party is normally obliged to pay only his or her own attorneys' fees."[89] The American Rule applies in Delaware. Our courts have, however, recognized bad faith litigation conduct as a valid exception to that rule.[91] "Although there is no single definition of bad faith conduct, courts have found bad faith where parties have unnecessarily prolonged or delayed litigation, falsified records, or knowingly asserted frivolous claims."[92]

In this case, the Court of Chancery made specific findings that detailed Gatz's bad faith conduct throughout the course of the trial. Even so, the court awarded plaintiffs only one-half of their reasonable attorneys' fees and costs because of Auriga's own "less than ideal" litigation efforts.[93] The record amply supports that result. Particularly troubling are the findings that Gatz's counsel left "Gatz himself the primary role of collecting responsive documents," and that Gatz "delete[d] relevant documents while litigation was either pending or highly likely."[94] In addition, "Gatz and his counsel simply splattered the record with a series of legally and factually implausible assertions."[95] The court did not abuse its discretion in awarding attorneys' fees. We affirm that award.

IV. CONCLUSION

For the foregoing reasons, the judgment of the Court of Chancery is AFFIRMED.

---

88. *Dover Historical Soc'y, Inc. v. City of Dover Planning Comm'n,* 902 A.2d 1084, 1090 n. 14 (Del. 2006) ("[I]n this case the appellants' request for attorneys' fees under the bad faith exception to the American Rule would require the Superior Court to exercise its inherent equitable authority to control its own process.") (internal quotations omitted).

89. *Johnston v. Arbitrium (Cayman Is.) Handels AG,* 720 A.2d 542, 545 (Del. 1998) (citing John F. Vargo, *The American Rule on Attorney Fee Allocation: The Injured Person's Access to Justice,* 42 Am. U.L. Rev. 1567 (1993)).

91. *Johnston,* 720 A.2d at 546.

92. *Id.*

93. *Auriga Capital Corp. v. Gatz Props., LLC,* 40 A.3d 839, 881–82 (Del. Ch. 2012).

94. *Id.* at 881.

95. *Id.*

1. Assume that the Operating Agreement expressly provided that the LLC members owed each other *no* fiduciary duties. Would the Delaware Supreme Court's analysis or result be different on the facts of the *Gatz Properties* case? On these facts, would the analysis or result be different if the LLC were organized under California's LLC statute?

2. Assume that the Operating Agreement was *silent* with respect to the scope of members' fiduciary duties. Would the Delaware Supreme Court's analysis or result be different on the facts of the *Gatz Properties* case? On these facts, would the analysis or result be different if the LLC were organized under California's LLC law?

3. What result would you reach on the facts of the *Gatz Properties* case if the business had been organized as a corporation? As a partnership under RUPA?

4. Do you agree with the Supreme Court's observation (in footnote 29) that a "fair process" generally leads to "fair price"? Why is that relevant to the Court's analysis of whether Gatz has breached fiduciary duties that he owes to the minority interest in the LLC?

5. With respect to the Supreme Court's decision to affirm the trial court's award of attorney fees, does the attorney conduct described in this case meet the relevant standards of professional responsibility (i.e., ethics rules)? Should the courts be in the business of enforcing standards of professionalism by shifting payment of attorneys' fees? In deciding that the trial court possessed the (inherent) "equitable powers" to shift attorneys' fees, do you think that the Delaware Supreme Court is acting consistent with its reasoning in the *Gatz* opinion regarding a court's (inherent) equitable powers as to fiduciary duty obligations?

6. With respect to the language quoted by the court from Section 15 of the LLC Agreement, do you agree with the Delaware Supreme Court's interpretation of this contractual language as reflecting "the contractual equivalent of the entire fairness equitable standard of conduct and judicial review"? Do you think that this is the result intended by the parties when they included Section 15 in their LLC Agreement?

7. How would the Delaware Supreme Court have ruled in this case if the facts showed that Gatz Properties had *not* successfully purchased the property at the auction? Since the court's reasoning depends heavily on this factual posture, what conclusion would the court have reached in the absence of a self-dealing transaction whereby Gatz Properties buys the property owned by the LLC? In other words, do you think the Delaware Supreme Court would still reach the conclusion that Gatz Properties had breached its fiduciary duties as manager of the LLC if Gatz Properties had *not* successfully purchased the real estate — especially since Section 15 of the Peconic Bay LLC Agreement speaks only in terms of "self-dealing transactions" as requiring that the LLC receive a "fair price"? Alternatively, would these facts still result in a breach of fiduciary duty by Gatz Properties (under the reasoning of the Delaware Supreme Court's opinion) — given the treatment of the minority interest in the time period leading up to the ultimate auction of the property — even if Gatz Properties did *not* ultimately purchase the real property?

8. Delaware's LLC Statute does allow for the express disavowal of all fiduciary duties, but the LLC Agreements may *not* eliminate the contractual duty of good faith and fair dealing. Although this issue was not addressed by the Delaware Supreme Court, do you think the facts of the *Gatz Properties* case give rise to a breach of the contractual duty of good faith and fair dealing?

In Part III.C. of its opinion, the Delaware Supreme Court rebuked the Chancery Court for reaching out to decide issues that were not presented by the facts of the *Gatz Properties* case — namely, whether "the traditional fiduciary duties of loyalty and care apply *by default* as to managers and members of a" Delaware LLC. (emphasis added) In his opinion, Chancellor Strine first summarized the factual basis for plaintiffs' causes of action. As he framed it, Chancellor Strine was asked to rule on allegations that Gatz breached fiduciary duties that were owed to minority members of the LLC by engaging in conduct that was designed to "squeeze out" the minority interest:

> . . . Specifically, the Minority Members claim that Gatz breached the fiduciary duties and contractual duties owed to Peconic Bay's Minority Members by engaging in a "protracted course of self-interested conduct conceived and implemented in bad faith" for the purpose of eliminating the Minority Members' interest. The Minority Members contend that Gatz was motivated to oust the Minority Members in order to realize the upside in value that would result from eliminating Peconic Bay's long-term leasehold interest in the Property. . . . What's more, the Minority Members continue, Gatz used the leverage obtained from his own bad faith breaches of loyalty to make coercive buy-out offers to the Minority Members, and finally to acquire Peconic Bay through a sham auction process at an unfairly low price.
>
> For his part, Gatz maintains that he acted reasonably and in good faith throughout the entirety of events described by the Minority Members. . . . Although by the end of the trial, Gatz admitted that he and his family were never interested in selling their membership interests, he seeks to use that fact as a defensive bulwark, contending that he and his family were entitled to vote their economic interest against selling Peconic Bay to a third-party buyer and to choke off the LLC's pursuit of any other strategic options. Throughout much of the litigation, Gatz took the view that he either owed no fiduciary duties at all; that if these duties existed, they allowed him to engage in a self-dealing transaction subject only to a hands-off business judgment rule review, and that even if a more intensive review applied, Gatz ran a thorough, professional auction upon credible independent advice, thus satisfying any fairness burden. . . . Finally, Gatz says, even if his actions did constitute a breach of his fiduciary duties, his actions were supposedly taken in good faith and with due care, and thus he cannot be held liable due to the terms of the exculpation clause of the LLC Agreement.

Auriga Capital Corp. v. Gatz Properties, LLC, 40 A. 3d 839, 848-849 (Del. Ch. 2012). After noting that the Delaware LLC statute did not speak directly to the issues raised in the plaintiffs' complaint, Chancellor Strine proceeded to analyze the law that applied to plaintiffs' claims as follows:

Auriga Capital Corp. v. Gatz Properties LLC

40 A. 3d 839, 849-859 (Del. Ch. 2012)

STRINE, Chancellor.

* * *

1. Default Fiduciary Duties Do Exist in the LLC Context

The Delaware LLC Act does not plainly state that the traditional fiduciary duties of loyalty and care apply by default to managers or members of a [LLC]. In that respect, of course, the LLC Act is not different than the [Delaware General Corporation Law (DGCL)], which does not do that either. . . . But our Supreme Court [has emphasized that the provisions of the DGCL are] to be read in concert with equitable fiduciary duties . . . , stating famously that "inequitable action does not become legally permissible simply because it is legally possible."

The LLC Act is more explicit than the DGCL in making the equitable overlay mandatory. Specifically, §18-1104 of the LLC Act provides that "[i]n any case not provided for in this chapter, *the rules of law and equity . . . shall govern.*"[33] In this way, the LLC Act provides for a construct similar to that which is used in the corporate context. But unlike in the corporate context, the rules of equity apply in the LLC context *by statutory mandate*, creating an even stronger justification for application of fiduciary duties grounded in equity to managers of LLCs to the extent that such duties have not been altered or eliminated under the relevant LLC agreement.[34]

It seems obvious that, under traditional principles of equity, a manager of an LLC would qualify as a fiduciary of that LLC and its members. Under Delaware law, "[a] fiduciary relationship is a situation where one person reposes special trust in and reliance on the judgment of another or where a special duty exists on the part of one person to protect the interests of another."[35] Corporate directors, general partners, and trustees are

---

33. 6 *Del. C.* §18-1104 (emphasis added).

34. Section 18-1101(c) of the LLC Act provides: *"To the extent that, at law or in equity, a member or manager or other person has duties (including fiduciary duties) to a limited liability company or to another member or manager or to another person that is a party to or is otherwise bound by [an LLC] agreement, the member's or manager's or other person's duties may be expanded or restricted or eliminated by provisions in the [LLC] agreement;* provided, that the [LLC] agreement may not eliminate the implied covenant of good faith and fair dealing." 6 *Del. C.* §18-1101(c) (emphasis added). Although §18-1101(c) allows parties to an LLC agreement to contract out of owing fiduciary duties to one another, the fact that these duties can be contractually avoided suggests that they exist by default in the first place. When read together, the most logical reading of §18-1104 and §18-1101(c) that results is that if, *i.e.,* "to the extent that," equity would traditionally make a manager or member a fiduciary owing fiduciary duties, then that manager or member *is* a fiduciary, subject to the express right of the parties to contract out of those duties. By contrast, if a member or manager would not be considered a fiduciary owing circumstantially-relevant duties under traditional equitable principles, then the member or manager is immune from fiduciary liability, not because of the statute, but because equity itself would not consider the member or manager to have case-relevant fiduciary duties. The "to the extent that" language makes clear that the statute does not itself impose some broader scope of fiduciary coverage than traditional principles of equity.

35. *Metro Ambulance, Inc. v. E. Med. Billing, Inc.,* 1995 WL 409015, at *2 (Del.Ch. July 5, 1995) (citing *Cheese Shop Int'l, Inc. v. Steele,* 303 A.2d 689, 690 (Del.Ch.1973), *rev'd on other grounds,* 311 A.2d

analogous examples of those who Delaware law has determined owe a "special duty." Equity distinguishes fiduciary relationships from straightforward commercial arrangements where there is no expectation that one party will act in the interests of the other.

The manager of an LLC — which is in plain words a limited liability "company" having many of the features of a corporation — easily fits the definition of a fiduciary. The manager of an LLC has more than an arms-length, contractual relationship with the members of the LLC.[38] Rather, the manager is vested with discretionary power to manage the business of the LLC.[39]

Thus, because the LLC Act provides for principles of equity to apply, because LLC managers are clearly fiduciaries, and because fiduciaries owe the fiduciary duties of loyalty and care, the LLC Act starts with the default that managers of LLCs owe enforceable fiduciary duties.

This reading of the LLC Act is confirmed by the Act's own history. Before 2004, §18–1101(c) of the LLC Act provided that fiduciary duties, to the extent they existed, could only be "expanded or restricted" by the LLC agreement.[40] Following our Supreme Court's holding in *Gotham Partners*,[41] which questioned whether default fiduciary duties could be fully eliminated in the limited partnership context when faced with similar statutory language and also affirmed our law's commitment to protecting investors who have not explicitly agreed to waive their fiduciaries' duties and therefore expect their fiduciaries to act in accordance with their interests, the General Assembly amended not only the Delaware Revised Limited Uniform Partnership Act ("DRULPA"),[43] but also the LLC Act to permit the "eliminat[ion]" of default fiduciary duties in an LLC agreement.[44] At the same time, the General Assembly added a provision to the LLC Act (the current §18-1101(e)) that permits full contractual exculpation for breaches of fiduciary and contractual duties, except for the implied contractual covenant of good faith and fair dealing.[45]

If the equity backdrop I just discussed did not apply to LLCs, then the 2004 "Elimination Amendment" would have been logically done differently. Why is this so? Because the Amendment would have instead said something like: "The managers, members, and other persons of the LLC shall owe no duties of any kind to the LLC and its

---

870 (Del.1973)); *see also Lank v. Steiner*, 213 A.2d 848, 852 (Del.Ch.1965), *aff'd*, 224 A.2d 242 (Del.1966); *In re USACafes, L.P. Litig.*, 600 A.2d 43, 48 (Del.Ch.1991).

38. *See Grace v. Morgan*, 2004 WL 26858, at *2 (Del.Super. Jan. 6, 2004) (concluding that the manager of an LLC "had more than an arms-length, commercial relationship" with the LLC's member when that member "placed a very particular and special trust in [the manager] in her position as [manager] to find and hire a competent architectural and engineering firm, to contribute meaningfully to the project plans, to oversee the planning and construction, and to ensure that goals as well as codes and specifications were met."). . . .

39. *See* 6 *Del. C.* §18-402. In this regard, managers of an LLC bear resemblance to directors of a corporation, who are charged with managing "the business and affairs" of the corporation. 8 *Del. C.* §141(a).

40. 6 *Del. C.* §18-1101(c) (2003).

41. *Gotham Partners, L.P. v. Hallwood Realty Partners, L.P.*, 817 A.2d 160 (Del.2002).

43. 74 Del. Laws ch. 265, §15 (2004).

44. 74 Del. Laws ch. 275, §13 (2004).

45. *Id.* §14; *see also id.* at ch. 265, §16 (amending DRULPA in same way).

members except as set forth in this statute and the LLC agreement."[46] Instead, the Amendment only made clear that an LLC agreement could, if the parties so chose, "eliminat[e]" default duties altogether, thus according full weight to the statutory policy in favor of giving "maximum effect to the principle of freedom of contract and to the enforceability of [LLC] agreements."[47] The General Assembly left in place the explicit equitable default in §18-1104 of the Act. Moreover, why would the General Assembly amend the LLC Act to provide for the elimination of (and the exculpation for) "something" if there were no "something" to eliminate (or exculpate) in the first place? The fact that the legislature enacted these liability-limiting measures against the backdrop of case law holding that default fiduciary duties did apply in the LLC context, and seemed to have accepted the central thrust of those decisions to be correct, provides further weight to the position that default fiduciary duties do apply in the LLC context to the extent they are not contractually altered.

Thus, our cases have to date come to the following place based on the statute. The statute incorporates equitable principles. Those principles view the manager of an LLC as a fiduciary and subject the manager as a default principle to the core fiduciary duties of loyalty and care. But, the statute allows the parties to an LLC agreement to entirely supplant those default principles or to modify them in part.[50] Where the parties have clearly supplanted default principles in full, we give effect to the parties' contract choice. Where the parties have clearly supplanted default principles in part, we give effect to their contract choice. But, where the core default fiduciary duties have not been supplanted by contract, they exist as the LLC statute itself contemplates.[53]

There are two issues that would arise if the equitable background explicitly contained in the statute were to be judicially excised now. The first is that those who crafted LLC agreements in reliance on equitable defaults that supply a predictable structure for assessing whether a business fiduciary has met his obligations to the entity and its investors will have their expectations disrupted. The equitable context in which the contract's specific terms were to be read will be eradicated, rendering the resulting terms shapeless and more uncertain. The fact that the implied covenant of good faith and fair dealing would remain extant would do little to cure this loss.

The common law fiduciary duties that were developed to address those who manage business entities were, as the implied covenant, an equitable gap-filler. If, rather than well thought out fiduciary duty principles, the implied covenant is to be used as the sole

---

46. An agreement containing a provision with this language was analyzed in *Fisk Ventures, LLC v. Segal*, 2008 WL 1961156 (Del.Ch. May 7, 2008), and the court found it to waive all fiduciary duties except those that were contractually provided for. *Id.* at *9 (where the provision stated: "No Member shall have any duty to any Member of the Company except as expressly set forth herein or in other written agreements. . . .").

47. 6 *Del. C.* §18-1101(b).

50. 6 *Del. C.* §18-1101(c); . . .

53. From my experience as a trial judge, I note that few LLC agreements contain an express, general provision that states what fiduciary duties are owed in the first instance. Rather, the agreements assume that such fiduciary duties are owed, and then they proceed to cut back on liability for breaches of those duties through exculpation provisions or through provisions that displace the traditional duties in favor of a contractual standard addressing specific types of transactions or conduct. *See, e.g., Kelly*, 2010 WL 629850, at *11-12; *Related Westpac*, 2010 WL 2929708, at *2.

default principle of equity, then the risk is that the certainty of contract law itself will be undermined. The implied covenant has rightly been narrowly interpreted by our Supreme Court to apply only "when the express terms of the contract indicate that the parties would have agreed to the obligation had they negotiated the issue."[54] The implied covenant is to be used "cautious[ly]" and does not apply to situations that could be anticipated, which is a real problem in the business context, because fiduciary duty review typically addresses actions that are anticipated and permissible under the express terms of the contract, but where there is a potential for managerial abuse. For these reasons, the implied covenant is not a tool that is designed to provide a framework to govern the discretionary actions of business managers acting under a broad enabling framework like a barebones LLC agreement. In fact, if the implied covenant were used in that manner, the room for subjective judicial oversight could be expanded in an inefficient way. The default principles that apply in the fiduciary duty context of business entities are carefully tailored to avoid judicial second-guessing. A generalized "fairness" inquiry under the guise of an "implied covenant" review is an invitation to, at best, reinvent what already exists in another less candid guise,[59] or worse, to inject unpredictability into both entity and contract law, by untethering judicial review from the well-understood frameworks that traditionally apply in those domains.[60]

The second problem is a related one, which is that a judicial eradication of the explicit equity overlay in the LLC Act could tend to erode our state's credibility with investors in Delaware entities. To have told the investing public that the law of equity would apply if the LLC statute did not speak to the question at issue, and to have managers of LLCs easily qualify as fiduciaries under traditional and settled principles of equity law in Delaware, and then to say that LLC agreements could "expan[d] or restric[t] or eliminat[e]" these fiduciary duties, would lead any reasonable investor to

---

54. *Nemec v. Shrader*, 991 A.2d 1120, 1127 n. 20 (Del.2010) (citing *Fitzgerald v. Cantor*, 1998 WL 842316, at *1 (Del.Ch. Nov. 10, 1998)); *see also Katz v. Oak Indus. Inc.*, 508 A.2d 873, 880 (Del.Ch.1986) (stating that the legal test for implying contractual obligations is whether it is "clear from what was expressly agreed upon that the parties who negotiated the express terms of the contract would have agreed to proscribe the act later complained of as a breach of the implied covenant of good faith — had they thought to negotiate with respect to that matter.").

59. If, to put it in implied covenant terms, the expectation that an LLC manager will act loyally and with due care is "so fundamental that it is clear that the [parties] [would] not feel a need to negotiate about [it]," *Allied Capital*, 910 A.2d at 1032-33, isn't that another way of saying that the parties expected that the manager could only take contractually permissible (*i.e.*, legal) action if he acted in compliance with his fiduciary duties, *i.e.*, equitably? If we imply these equity duties in the guise of the contractual implied covenant, are we adding clarity or simply confusing things? I believe it would be the latter.

60. In Vice Chancellor Noble's well-reasoned decision in *Gerber v. Enterprise Products Holdings, LLC*, he explains convincingly why the concepts in the contractual term, the "implied covenant of good faith and fair dealing," do not have the same meaning as when the terms *good faith* or *fair dealing* are used in defining the duty of loyalty owed by a corporate fiduciary. 2012 WL 34442, at *11 n. 46 (Del.Ch. Jan. 6, 2012); *see also id.* at *13 n. 58. To broaden the carefully constrained, albeit still important, contractual covenant to act as an equitable constraint on the broad managerial authority that an LLC agreement might vest in the manager would involve a transformation of its role that would seem to have little benefit (as it would involve judges reinventing an equitable overlay in the guise of contract rather than using one that has been carefully shaped by generations of experience) but great cost (as it would risk reducing the predictability of contract law by changing settled principles and entity law, by constraining the exercise of legal, *i.e.*, contractual and statutory, action by managers not to understood principles of equity, but by a novel deployment of an implied covenant).

conclude the following: the managers of the Delaware LLC in which I am investing owe me the fiduciary duties of loyalty and care except to the extent the agreement "expand[s]," "restrict[s]," or "eliminate[s]" these duties.[61] That expectation has been reinforced by our Supreme Court in decisions like *William Penn Partnership v. Saliba*, where it stated that "[t]he parties here agree that managers of a Delaware [LLC] owe traditional fiduciary duties of loyalty and care to the members of the LLC, unless the parties expressly modify or eliminate those duties in an operating agreement;"[62] in a consistent line of decisions by this court affirming similar principles;[63] in the reasoning of *Gotham Partners* in the analogous limited partnership context;[64] and culminating with legislative reinforcement in the 2004 Elimination Amendment inspired by *Gotham Partners* that allowed LLC agreements to eliminate fiduciary duties altogether. Reasonable investors in Delaware LLCs would, one senses, understand even more clearly after the Elimination Amendment that they were protected by fiduciary duty review unless the LLC agreement provided to the contrary, because they would of course think that there would have been no need for our General Assembly to pass a statute authorizing the elimination of something that did not exist at all.

Reasonable minds can debate whether it would be wise for the General Assembly to create a business entity in which the managers owe the investors no duties at all except as set forth in the statute and the governing agreement. Perhaps it would be, perhaps it would not. That is a policy judgment for the General Assembly. What seems certain is that the General Assembly, and the organs of the Bar who propose alteration of the statutes to them, know how to draft a clear statute to that effect and have yet to do so. The current LLC Act is quite different and promises investors that equity will provide the important default protections it always has, absent a contractual choice to tailor or eliminate that protection. Changing that promise is a job for the General Assembly, not this court.

With that statement of the law in mind, let us turn to the relevant terms of Peconic Bay's LLC Agreement.

2. The Relevant Provisions of the LLC Agreement

I note at the outset that the Peconic Bay LLC Agreement contains no general provision stating that the only duties owed by the manager to the LLC and its investors are set forth in the Agreement itself. Thus, before taking into account the existence of an exculpatory provision, the LLC Agreement does not displace the traditional fiduciary duties of loyalty and care owed to the Company and its members by Gatz Properties and by Gatz, in his capacity as the manager of Gatz Properties. And although LLC agreements may displace fiduciary duties altogether or tailor their application, by substituting

---

61. 6 *Del. C.* §18-1101(c).

62. *William Penn P'ship v. Saliba*, 13 A.3d 749, 756 (Del.2011) (citing *Bay Ctr. Apartments Owner, LLC v. Emery Bay PKI, LLC*, 2009 WL 1124451, at *8 (Del.Ch. Apr. 20, 2009)).

63. *See Phillips v. Hove*, 2011 WL 4404034, at *24 (Del.Ch. Sept. 22, 2011); *In re Atlas Energy Res., LLC*, 2010 WL 4273122, at *6-7 (Del.Ch. Oct. 28, 2010); *Kelly v. Blum*, 2010 WL 629850, at *10 (Del.Ch. Feb. 24, 2010); *Bay Ctr. Apartments*, 2009 WL 1124451, at *8; *Metro Commc'n Corp. BVI v. Advanced Mobilecomm Techs. Inc.*, 854 A.2d 121, 153 (Del.Ch.2004); *VGS, Inc. v. Castiel*, 2000 WL 1277372, at *4-5 (Del.Ch. Aug. 31, 2000), *aff'd*, 781 A.2d 696 (Del.2001).

64. *Gotham Partners, L.P. v. Hallwood Realty Partners, L.P.*, 817 A.2d 160, 168, 170 (Del.2002).

a different form of review, here §15 of the LLC Agreement contains a clause reaffirming that a form akin to entire fairness review will apply to "Agreements with Affiliates," a group which includes Gatz Properties, that are not approved by a majority of the unaffiliated members' vote. In relevant part, §15 provides:

> 15. *Neither the Manager nor any other Member shall be entitled to cause the Company to enter . . . into any additional agreements with affiliates on terms and conditions which are less favorable to the Company than the terms and conditions of similar agreements which could be entered into with arms-length third parties, without the consent of a majority of the non-affiliated Members* (such majority to be deemed to be the holders of 66–2/3% of all Interests which are not held by affiliates of the person or entity that would be a party to the proposed agreement).

This court has interpreted similar contractual language supplying an "arm's length terms and conditions" standard for reviewing self-dealing transactions, and has read it as imposing the equivalent of the substantive aspect of entire fairness review, commonly referred to as the "fair price" prong. This interpretation is confirmed by the defendants' own understanding of §15 as requiring that Gatz pay a "fair price" to the Minority Members if Gatz were to acquire Peconic Bay, as reflected by a letter sent from Gatz's counsel to the Minority Members.

* * *

. . . [I]n order to take advantage of the contractual safe harbor of §15, Gatz bears the burden to show that he paid a fair price to acquire Peconic Bay, a conclusion that must be supported by a showing that he performed, in good faith, a responsible examination of what a third-party buyer would pay for the Company. . . . [The record, however,] convinces me that Gatz has failed to meet the terms of this proviso.

* * *

I now analyze the Minority Members' claim that Gatz breached his fiduciary and contractual duties as the Manager of Peconic Bay. Specifically, I conclude that Gatz breached his fiduciary duties of loyalty and care, and the fair price requirement of §15. . . .

NOTES AND QUESTIONS

1. In *Feeley v. NHAOCG, LLC*, 62 A.3d 649, 661, 663 (Del. Ch. 2012), a case decided shortly before the Delaware Supreme Court handed down its opinion in *Auriga*, Vice-Chancellor Laster relied extensively on Chancellor Strine's reasoning in his opinion in the *Auriga* case to conclude that "the language and the drafting history of [Delaware] section 18-1101(c) support the existence of default fiduciary duties." In reaching this conclusion, Vice-Chancellor Laster agreed with Chancellor Strine that "the long line of Court of Chancery precedents . . . provide persuasive reasons to apply fiduciary duties by default to the manager of a Delaware LLC," thereby allowing default fiduciary duties to play a "critical role . . . as an 'equitable gap-filler' in the context of an LLC Operating Agreement."

2. Assume that the Operating Agreement expressly provided that the LLC members owed each other *no* fiduciary duties. Based on the reasoning set forth above, what result would Chancellor Strine reach on the facts of the *Gatz Properties* case?

3. Assume that the Operating Agreement was *silent* with respect to the scope of members' fiduciary duties. Based on the reasoning set forth above, what result would Chancellor Strine reach on the facts of the *Gatz Properties* case?

4. In analyzing the facts of the *Gatz Properties* case, Chancellor Strine starts off by referring to the language of §18-1104 of Delaware's LLC statute, a provision that was not even mentioned by the Delaware Supreme Court. What do you think of this difference in judicial approach to statutory construction?

5. *The Legislative Response to the* Gatz *Controversy.* Needless to say, the Delaware Supreme Court's decision in *Gatz Properties* "surprised many corporate lawyers when [the court] declared that whether the Delaware LLC [statute] imposes fiduciary duties on LLC managers is an open question." This decision took many by surprise because prior to *Gatz Properties*, "most Delaware lawyers believed that Delaware LLC managers were subject to fiduciary duties, absent contrary provisions in the LLC agreement." While affirming the judgment of the court of Chancery, the Supreme Court "did so by relying only on the LLC agreement's contractual provisions for fiduciary duties" and went on to "rebuke[] the Court of Chancery for unnecessary expounding on the Statute's interpretation." In addition, the Supreme Court invited the Delaware Legislature to take action "to resolve any statutory ambiguity" on the question of whether fiduciary duties apply to LLC managers. *See Gatz Properties supra*, 59 A.3d at 1218. And, perhaps not surprisingly, the Delaware General Assembly did take up the issue. In an amendment to Section 18-1104 of Delaware's LLC Statute that became effective on August 1, 2013, the Delaware General Assembly added 11 words to the language of this statute so that this statutory provision as revised now reads as follows (with the new language appearing in italics):

> In any case not provided for in the chapter, the rules of law and equity including *the rules of law and equity relating to fiduciary duties and* the law merchant, shall govern.

The legislative synopsis to the proposed amendment reads as follows:

> Section 8. The amendment to Section 18-1104 confirms that in some circumstances fiduciary duties not explicitly provided for the limited liability company agreement apply. For example, a manager of a manager-managed limited liability company would ordinarily have fiduciary duties even in the absence of a provision in the limited liability company agreement establishing such duties. Section 18-1101(c) continues to provide that such duties may be expanded, restricted or eliminated by the limited liability company agreement.

In commenting on this legislative development, one experienced corporate lawyer has observed that:

> This is an intriguingly short insert to the statute. In one sense it says nothing, because the current language — "the rules of law and equity" — would normally be read to mean all the rules of law and equity. If the rules of law and equity include the rules relating to fiduciary duties, then why the insertion?
> Sometimes lawyers will use a phrase in contracts — "including, for the avoidance of doubt" — as a way of clarifying the purpose of an "including" clause.

>   That thinking may be behind the proposed revision, *i.e.*, it may be intended to
>   eliminate any doubt whether fiduciary duties are included in the statute's reference
>   to "the rules of law and equity."
>
>   Chancery's opinion in *Auriga Capital* characterized fiduciary duties as being in
>   equity, and the proposed amendment's emphasis on equitable rules can be viewed
>   as a nod to the Chancery Court analysis.

Doug Batey, *Uncertainty Over Delaware LLC Fiduciary Duties To Be Clarified*,
LLC LAW MONITOR BLOG (April 16, 2013), *available at* http://www.llclawmonitor
.com/2013/04/articles/fiduciary-duties/uncertainty-over-delaware-llc-fiduciaryduties
-to-be-clarified/. *Query*: Do you agree with this commentator that it would seem that
Chancellor Strine's views prevailed? Going forward, what are the implications of this
statutory amendment when drafting an LLC agreement?

6. ***Broad Freedom of Contract.*** While the Delaware Supreme Court clearly admon-
ished Chancellor Strine for "reaching out" to impose the traditional fiduciary duties
of care and loyalty on managers and members of Delaware LLCs as the "default
rule," the Supreme Court avoided addressing the (rather controversial) issue as to
scope of mandatory fiduciary duties in the LLC context. Elsewhere, though, Chief
Justice Steele has expressed his views rather emphatically, in speeches and law
review articles as well as in interviews. *See, e.g.*, Myron T. Steele, *Judicial Scrutiny
of Fiduciary Duties in Delaware Limited Partnerships and Limited Liability
Companies*, 32 DEL. J. CORP. L. 1 (2007); Myron T. Steele and J.W. Verrett, *Delaware's
Guidance: Ensuring Equity for the Modern Witenagemot*, 2 VA. L. & BUS. REV.
188 (2007), and this article formed the basis for Chief Justice Steele's *Keynote Address*
to the Business Law Section at the 2007 ABA Annual Meeting; Myron T. Steele,
The Moral Underpinnings of Delaware's Modern Corporate Fiduciary Duties,
26 NOTRE DAME J.L. ETHICS & PUB. POL'Y 3 (2012); and Francis Pileggi, *Interview
with Delaware Supreme Court Justice Myron Steele*, DELAWARE CORPORATE &
COMMERCIAL LITIGATION BLOG (December 28, 2009), *available at* http://www.delaware
litigation.com/2009/12/articles/commentary/interview-with-delaware-supreme-court
-chief-justice-myron-steele.pdf. In 2009, Chief Justice Steele addressed the issue of
"whether, given a clearly stated public policy of freedom of contract and maximization of enforceability of alternative entity agreements," as prevails in Delaware with
respect to LLC Operating Agreements, should fiduciary duty law "serve as the
default standard governing parties' internal agreements" or, alternatively, should
the implied contractual duty of good faith and fair dealing "supply the appropriate
default standard." Myron Steele, *Freedom of Contract and Default Contractual
Duties in Delaware Limited Partnerships and Limited Liability Companies*, 46 AM.
BUS. L.J. 221 (2009).

In sharp contrast to the perspective of Chancellor Strine on this issue, as expressed in
his trial court decision in the *Gatz Properties* case, Chief Justice Steele has asserted that
"economically and statutorily, . . . rationality [requires] a default *contractual* standard."
Id. at pg. 221 (emphasis added). In reaching this conclusion, Chief Justice Steele
reasoned as follows:

Myron T. Steele
Freedom of Contract and Default Contractual Duties in Delaware Limited Partnerships and Limited Liability Companies

46 AM. BUS. L.J. 221 (2009)

I. Introduction

Since its introduction, the Delaware Limited Liability Company Act (DLLCA) has been a powerful economic vehicle that, unlike its corporate counterpart, allows for ultimate contractual customization among its owners and management.[1] As evidence of the Delaware limited liability company's (LLC) prowess, the Delaware Secretary of State reports that nearly 112,000 new LLCs were formed in 2007, compared to just 43,000 new formations in 2001.[2] One reason for the success of the LLC is the carte blanche flexibility Delaware's legislature seemingly provided owners in crafting the LLC operating agreement, allowing the parties to contract between themselves. This flexibility made the LLC form ideal for those wanting to craft a highly specialized and customized vehicle, specifying the duties and benefits among owners and managers.[3]

Ronald Reagan famously said: "If it moves, tax it. If it keeps moving, regulate it. And if it stops moving, subsidize it."[4] Reagan's truism proved all too true for LLCs. The carte blanche some believed to be contemplated by the Delaware legislature gave way to judicially imposed mandatory and unwaivable fiduciary duties.[5]

In 2004, though, Delaware's legislature amended the LLC statute to clarify that, to the extent that default fiduciary duties[6] exist, as determined by Delaware courts, those duties can be entirely eliminated.[7] Today, Delaware courts are free to determine whether to apply default fiduciary duties at all.[8] It is clear from the language of the

---

1. The Delaware General Corporation Law (DGCL), DEL. CODE ANN. tit. 8, §§101(h)(7) & 122(17) (2009), provides substantially less freedom in contracting for fiduciary duties than the DLLCA, DEL. CODE ANN. tit. 6 §18-1101 (2009), and the Delaware Revised Uniform Limited Partnership Act (DRULPA), DEL. CODE ANN. tit. 6. §17-1101.

2. Over the same time period, the per annum number of new corporations has decreased.

3. Both DRULPA, DEL. CODE ANN. tit. 6, §17-1101, and DLLGA, DEL. CODE ANN. tit. 6, §18-1101, originally gave full effect to freedom of contract principles between the parties and, further, allowed for the modification of any judicially created fiduciary duties.

4. Remarks to State Chairpersons of the National White House Conference on Small Business (Aug. 15, 1986), *available at* http:// www.reagan.utexas.edu/archives/speeches/1986/081586e.htm.

5. *See Gotham Partners, L.P. v. Hallwood Realty Partners*, L.P., 817 A.2d 160, 167-68 (Del. 2002), *See also* Myron T. Steele, *Judicial Scrutiny of Fiduciary Duties in Delaware Limited Partnerships and Limited Liability Companies*, 32 DEL. J. CORP. L. 1 (2007) (holding "that, while a limited partnership agreement could provide for contractually created fiduciary duties substantially mirroring corporate common law fiduciary duties, a limited partnership agreement could not 'eliminate' the fiduciary duties or liabilities of a general partner.").

6. Throughout this article, when I refer to fiduciary duties, I refer to the corporate-like fiduciary duties of loyalty and care that have been applied to LPs and LLCs by Delaware courts. Fiduciary duty, in this article, does not refer to the implied contractual duty of good faith and fair dealing. Instead, I specifically identify when I do discuss that implied contractual duty. . . .

7. DEL. CODE ANN. tit. 6, §§17-1101(d) & 18-1101(c).

8. The statute provides that, "[t]o the extent that, at law or in equity, a member or manager or other person has duties (including fiduciary duties) to a limited liability company or to another member or manager or to another person that is a party to or is otherwise bound by a limited liability company agreement. . . ." *Id.* §18-1101(c). The legislature, here, did not provide for any default fiduciary duties.

LLC statute that Delaware's legislature wishes the courts to answer the policy question of whether default fiduciary duties exist in the first instance.

Even with this statutory permission — and perhaps mandate — to make the policy decision of whether to apply default fiduciary duties, Delaware courts have still commonly accepted default fiduciary duties, without engaging in a thorough policy analysis. Since the 2004 statutory amendment, one case, though, does question the long-held assumption that default fiduciary duties apply to LLCs.[10]

In this article, rather than embrace the commonly accepted puritanical default fiduciary duty norm, I analyze default fiduciary duties of LLCs from two different policy perspectives to determine whether courts should apply default fiduciary duties at all. First, I argue that default fiduciary duties violate the strong policy favoring freedom of contract enunciated by Delaware's legislature.[11] Considering Delaware's strong policy favoring freedom of contract, Delaware courts should analyze mutually bargained-for LLC agreements that define the parties' conduct without any application of default fiduciary duties, even if the parties have not specifically provided for the elimination of fiduciary duties. Where an operating agreement provides for a specific set of conduct, the court should not read any default fiduciary duties into the agreement because the parties' prescribed and proscribed conduct contains the entire agreement that the parties intend and expect. Courts should favor the contracting parties' ex ante calculation of costs and benefits of fiduciary duties, and courts should not, on their own, endeavor to reassess that (albeit perhaps now imprudent) decision ex post.

Second, I analyze the different economic rationales for and against default fiduciary duties, concluding that the costs of default fiduciary duties outweigh the minimal benefits that they provide. I contend we have no reason to assume that parties to an LLC agreement would have provided for fiduciary duties in the contract. As an elaboration on that point, I also argue that default fiduciary duties add significant contracting and litigation costs. When courts assume default fiduciary duties, parties bear the costs of those judicially created fiduciary duties. In the nebulous universe of default fiduciary duties,[12] speculating on whether the court will apply default fiduciary duties creates an inconsistency, making it more difficult for parties to effectively eliminate those default duties.

Moreover, the wholly Byzantine approach, whereby parties must define the duties and rights they intend to keep while simultaneously disclaiming other duties that the parties wish to exclude, adds unnecessary chaos into the parties' contract negotiations,

---

Instead, the legislature provided the court with the task of determining whether to apply any default fiduciary duties.

10. *Fisk Ventures, LLC v. Segal*, No. 3017-CC, 2008 Del. Ch. LEXIS 158, at *28 (Del. Ch. May 7, 2008) ("In the context of limited liability companies, which are creatures not of the state but of contract, those duties or obligations must be found in the LLC agreement or some other contract.").

11. *See, e.g.*, DEL. CODE ANN. tit. 6, §18-1101(b) ("It is the policy of this chapter to give the maximum effect to the principle of freedom of contract and to the enforceability of limited liability company agreements.").

12. *See, e.g.*, Robert Cooter & Bradley J. Freedman, *The Fiduciary Relationship: Its Economic Character and Legal Consequences*, 66 N.Y.U. L. REV. 1045, 1045 (1991) ("Fiduciary relationships have occupied a significant body of Anglo-American law and jurisprudence for over 250 years, yet the precise nature of the fiduciary relationship remains a source of confusion and dispute.").

thereby increasing their contracting costs. Instead, assuming a clean slate where the organic agreement crafts the rights and duties owed among and between members and managers gives the parties clear expectations about which duties will apply and clear expectations about the other parties' conduct.

Finally, from the prospect of potential litigation cost, without default duties, parties will focus their arguments specifically on the agreements they made, and not on default norms imposed on them by courts. To the extent that an answer to a party's contractual duty is not clear, parties will focus their litigation on contract interpretation rather than fiduciary duties, which will eliminate litigation on claims that the parties never intended to include in their agreements.

Before beginning my analysis of the issues I address in this article, I must first establish some relevant ground rules. This article specifically discusses the relationships among and between members, managers, and the LLC in an LLC and among partners, limited partners, and the limited partnership (LP) in LPs. Those relationships are governed by the relevant Delaware LP and LLC statutes,[13] which are in turn interpreted by Delaware courts. Because of the unique judicial system in Delaware, I do not imply that my analysis can or should be extended to other jurisdictions. Further, I assume that each partner, member, and manager had a bargained-for exchange when entering the relationship. By this I assume that the parties' organic agreement is not an agreement imposed on, for instance, a passive LLC member who simply purchased units in the LLC. Likewise, I assume that partners bargained for and received a benefit from the partnership agreement that they reached.

NOTES AND QUESTIONS

1. As a public policy matter, do you prefer the views expressed by Chancellor Strine or Chief Justice Steele? In other words, what should the courts do if the LLC Operating Agreement is silent with respect to fiduciary duties? Should the court impose fiduciary duties even though the relevant statute (such as the DLLCA) does not expressly provide for them?

2. In support of his claim that "from an economic policy perspective, default fiduciary duties should not be the norm, and instead Delaware courts should assume no default fiduciary duties apply," *id.* at 236, Chief Justice Steele asserts that

> it is important to note that sophisticated parties bargain for the obligations and duties provided in an LLC agreement. The choice of the LLC form was an intentional form, chosen by sophisticated parties because that form provides the contracting parties with the maximum ability to customize their relationship. Understanding this key difference between LLCs and corporations points us away from adopting default corporate-like fiduciary duties and, instead, applying only Delaware's default contractual duties. To understand this point, in the context of LLC contracting by sophisticated parties, we can assume that the parties' choice

---

13. DEL. CODE ANN. tit. 6, §§17-101 — 17-111 and 18-101 — 18-1109.

to *not* provide fiduciary duties is a conscious and deliberate choice — rather than a "rational gap."

Whether parties imprudently chose the LLC form, or whether it appears that ex post the parties ineffectively bargain for their rights and obligations,[62] should be of no moment for the court. The only time the court can intervene to add terms to the LLC contract is if the parties' intent can be implied from the agreement or other law fills in those terms.[63] In the alternative, a court may strike terms to an agreement if it finds some indicia of fraud, undue influence, or adhesion. Simply because, on occasion, parties may ineffectively bargain, ex ante, does not require the courts to swoop in as a protector for ill-advised contract makers.

Id. at pp. 237-238. *Query:* Are you persuaded by the claim that the "parties' choice" — at least where the parties are "sophisticated" — "to *not* provide [for] fiduciary duties [as part of the LLC Operating Agreement] is a conscious and deliberate choice?" If so, what factors would you consider relevant to determine whether the parties are "sophisticated"? Are you troubled by Chief Justice Steele's assertion that it "should be of no moment for the court" whether the "parties [have] imprudently chose[n]" to organize their business as an LLC or whether the parties have "ineffectively" bargained "for their rights and obligations"?

3. In expressing his views in the previous article, Chief Justice Steele assumed that the provisions in the LLC Operating Agreement were the product of "a bargained for exchange [when the parties entered the LLC] relationship" and were not part of "an agreement imposed on . . . a passive LLC member who simply purchased units in

---

62. In many situations, parties imprudently form contracts and Delaware courts do not meddle in the process to provide fiduciary duties to correct for ill-advised contract terms. For instance, imagine if Delaware courts, to the horror of negotiated acquisition lawyers, began applying fiduciary duty concepts to merger agreements between sellers and acquirers. Instead, Delaware courts loathe interpreting contracts using extrinsic evidence beyond the specific terms included in an agreement itself. *See United Rentals, Inc. v. RAM Holdings, Inc.*, 937 A.2d 810, 835 (Del. Ch. 2007) ("The Court must emphasize here that the introduction of extrinsic, parol evidence does not alter or deviate from Delaware's adherence to the objective theory of contracts. As I recently explained to counsel in this case, the private, subjective feelings of the negotiators are irrelevant and unhelpful to the Court's consideration of a contract's meaning, because the meaning of a properly formed contract must be shared or common. That is not to say, however, that a party's subjective understanding is never instructive. On the contrary, in cases where an examination of the extrinsic evidence does not lead to an obvious, objectively reasonable conclusion, the Court may apply the forthright negotiator principle. Under this principle, the Court considers the evidence of what one party subjectively 'believed the obligation to be coupled with evidence that the other party knew or should have known of such belief.'" (citations omitted).

63. The ability of a court to "add" terms to a contract is known as an "implied in fact" contract and is solely determined by the parties' intent. *See* RESTATEMENT (SECOND) OF CONTRACTS §204 (1981). . . . Terms may also be added by the default provisions of the applicable organic law governing the entity, for example, DLLCA or DRLUPA. Once terms are set in a contract, the contractual covenant of good faith and fair dealing *attaches to the performance and enforcement* of those terms. *See* RESTATE-MENT (SECOND) OF CONTRACTS §205 (1981) ("Every contract imposes upon each party a duty of good faith and fair dealing *in its performance and its enforcement.*" (emphasis added)). The contractual duty of good faith and fair dealing does not provide a method for courts to add terms to contracts. For an explanation that the implied covenant of good faith and fair dealing *cannot* provide the basis for "adding or implying" terms to a contract, *see* Ann F. Conaway. *The Multi-Facets of Good Faith in Delaware: A Mistake in the Duty of Good Faith and Fair Dealing; A Different Partnership Duty of Care: Agency Good Faith and Damages; Good Faith and Trust Law*, 10 DEL. L. REV. 89, 96-109 (2008).

the LLC." *Query:* Why do you suppose Chief Justice Steele assumed this factual premise as the starting point in his analysis that the default rule in Delaware should not impose the traditional fiduciary duties of loyalty and care on the LLC's members and managers?

4. As a public policy matter, given the broad freedom of contract offered by Delaware's LLC statute, what do you think should be the (relevant) default rule with respect to fiduciary duties in the context of LLCs?

PROBLEMS

In light of the analytical framework set forth above, what result would you reach (and be prepared to explain your analysis) based on the facts of the following hypotheticals:

1. A leading commentator in this area, Dean Donald Weidner has posited the following example:

    > [Consider] the example of a partnership agreement between Investor and Manager. The agreement provides that Investor will put up money to be managed by Manager, that Investor will have no information rights, no right to monitor Manager, and no right to any return of or on the investment unless and until Manager, in its sole discretion, if ever, provides. The agreement also provides that Manager can act on Manager's own behalf, taking from and competing with the partnership without limit, and that Investor has no right to seek judicial review of the behavior of Manager, unless Manager has violated the express language of the partnership agreement. In [addition], the agreement says Investor will remain a partner until Investor is dismissed by Manager and that, under no circumstances, will Manager be treated as a fiduciary of Investor.

    Donald J. Weidner, *RUPA and Fiduciary Duty: The Texture of Relationship*, 58 Law & Contemp. Probs. 81, 101 (Spring 1995).

    a) Assuming that the business had been organized as a partnership under RUPA, what conclusion would you reach as to the enforceability of this agreement?

    b) Assuming that the business had been organized as a Delaware LLC, what conclusion would you reach as to the enforceability of this agreement?

    c) Would you recommend including such a provision in the LLC agreement for SoftCo assuming that Joan and Michael decided to *Go-It-Alone?*

    d) Would your recommendation change assuming that Joan and Michael decided to obtain financing for their new business, SoftCo, from *Friends & Family?*

2. The following fact pattern, involving a family partnership, is based on the case of *Singer v. Singer*, 634 P.2d 766 (Okla. Ct. App. 1981). The partnership agreement in the *Singer* case provided in relevant part that:

    > Each partner shall be free to enter into business and other transactions for his or her own separate individual account, even though such business or other

transaction may be in conflict with and/or competition with the business of this partnership. Neither the partnership nor any individual member of this partnership shall be entitled to claim or receive any part of or interest in such transactions, it being the intention and agreement that any partner will be free to deal on his or her own account to the same extent and with the same force and effect as if he or she were not and never had been members of this partnership.

Id. at 768.

This family partnership, referred to by the court as "Josaline," was engaged in the oil production business. Prior to a meeting of the partners, a senior partner requested that Stanley, a young member of the family partnership, look into the possibility of purchasing a particular parcel of land that was known to contain valuable minerals. At the ensuing meeting, the partners briefly discussed the possibility of purchasing this parcel of land but decided to defer any action. After the meeting, Stanley and his sister Andrea, another young member of the family, formed a separate partnership and caused this partnership to purchase the land. Not surprisingly, when the other members of the family partnership learned of this land acquisition, they were quite upset and caused the partnership, Josaline, to bring an action against Stanley and Andrea that sought to have the land held in constructive trust for the benefit of Josaline.

(a) What result would you reach if this family partnership had been organized as an LLC under Delaware law?

(b) What result would you reach if this family partnership had been formed as a California LLC?

3. An LLC was formed to obtain a hockey franchise from the National Hockey League (NHL), with the proposed new team to play in Columbus, Ohio. The LLC proceeded to seek stadium financing in order to secure the NHL franchise. While these financing negotiations were pending, one of the LLC members stepped outside the LLC and began to negotiate individually with the NHL and the stadium financing source and subsequently presented the NHL with a fully-financed proposal. Ultimately, this individual was awarded the franchise by the NHL, and the remaining LLC members sued for breach of fiduciary duty. The LLC's Operating Agreement included the following provision:

> *Members May Compete.* Members shall not in any way be prohibited from or restricted in engaging or owning an interest in any other business venture of any nature, including any venture which might be competitive with the business of the Company.

Based on these facts:

(a) What result if the LLC were organized under Delaware law?

(b) What result if the LLC had been organized under California Law?

(c) Would these facts give rise to a breach of the contractual duty of good faith and fair dealing?

E. Oppression: Remedies for Dissension and Deadlock

Sandra K. Miller
What Buy-Out Rights, Fiduciary Duties, and Dissolution Remedies Should Apply in the Case of the Minority Owner of a Limited Liability Company?

*38 Harv. J. on Legis. 413 (2001)**

The elimination of rigid tax requirements for obtaining partnership tax treatment for unincorporated business entities has already begun to have a dramatic impact on the development of business entities. As a result of the Internal Revenue Service's adoption of so-called "Check-the-Box" regulations, partnership and limited liability company ("LLC") statutes need not defeat the "corporate" characteristic of continuity of life.[1] It is no longer necessary for partnership and LLC statutes to contain events that potentially dissolve the firm in order to gain favorable flow-through tax treatment as a partnership.[2]

Before the legislative ink on the early rounds of statutes dried,[3] a growing number of LLC statutes eliminated the LLC member's right to withdraw from the company prior to its dissolution and winding up, or otherwise eliminated the right to be paid the fair market value of the LLC interest upon withdrawal, unless otherwise provided in the agreement. Originally, most LLC statutes provided that the LLC member could withdraw and obtain the fair market value of his or her LLC interest, less damages caused by the withdrawal, unless the agreement provided to the contrary.[5] The new restrictions on the LLC member's withdrawal and distribution rights are designed to enhance the limited liability company as an estate and gift tax-planning vehicle. The driving force behind the reforms is to facilitate estate and gift tax valuation discounts for minority interests in family-owned limited liability companies. . . .

* * *

The Article emphasizes the continued importance of giving the LLC member a right to withdraw from the LLC and receive the fair market value of his or her interest in the absence of an agreement to the contrary in light of: (1) the illiquidity of an investment in a private firm; (2) the intended use of the LLC as a vehicle for the informal

---

* Reprinted with permission.

1. *See generally* Susan Pace Hamill, *The Limited Liability Company: A Catalyst Exposing the Corporate Integration Question*, 95 Mich. L. Rev. 393 (1996) (discussing the revision in the income tax regulations governing LLCs and its tax policy implications). . . .

2. *See* I.R.C. §7701 (2000); Treas. Reg. §301.7701-1(a) to -7(f) (2000) (setting forth tax classification rules that permit taxpayers to elect to be taxed as partnerships or corporations irrespective of whether the taxpayer possesses limited liability, continuity of life, or other characteristics traditionally associated with corporate status). . . .

3. *See* Carter G. Bishop, *Treatment of Members Upon Their Death and Withdrawal from a Limited Liability Company: The Case for a Uniform Paradigm*, 25 Stetson L. Rev. 255, 259 (1995) (discussing the "first generation bulletproof" LLC statutes that mandated compliance with formerly rigid tax classification regulations, and the later LLC statutes that permitted increased flexibility in drafting LLC agreements). . . .

5. Bishop, *supra* note 3, at 261 (indicating that in most respects the acts adopt the partnership rather than the corporate paradigm regarding the effect of a member dissociation on that member's right to be bought out by the company and to cause a liquidation). . . .

conduct of a wide variety of business ventures; (3) the potential lack of other built-in statutory protections against foul play and abusive behavior; and (4) the considerable uncertainties surrounding both the duty of loyalty and standard of care for members and managers, and the mechanisms for asserting a breach of such duties.

Many LLC statutes were drafted to avoid formalities in the conduct of business, and as a result may lack many of the statutory rules and requirements that protect minority owners in corporations. Not all LLC statutes provide for dissenters' rights in the case of certain mergers or acquisitions,[11] and relatively few provide an equitable remedy for a dissolution or buy-out in the event of certain illegal or fraudulent acts or other misconduct.[12] LLC statutes do not typically contain corporate-style notice provisions and other protections commonly contained in corporate statutes.[13] Without either the liquidity found in a general partnership or the protective remedies found in the corporation, a minority LLC owner without a strong bargaining position and a favorably negotiated operating agreement may be locked into a hybrid entity offering the worst, rather than the best, of the partnership and corporate worlds.

* * *

[Thus,] legislators should analyze whether the LLC statute contains mechanisms other than default buy-out rights that can protect minority LLC owners from fraudulent and other opportunistic misconduct by majority owners. Does the particular LLC statute articulate fiduciary duties or standards of care to guide members' conduct or establish non-waivable minimum standards for the duty of loyalty? Does the LLC statute provide remedies in the event of deadlock or dispute? What are the provisions concerning the potential ability to set salaries, amend the operating agreement, approve sales of assets, and vote upon mergers or the expulsion of members? Does the LLC statute provide a clearly defined process for pursuing grievances with the LLC or with other LLC

---

11. For a sample of statutes that do provide for dissenters' rights, *see* Cal. Corp. Code §§17600-17613 (West 1999) (providing for dissenters' rights with regard to certain reorganizations or mergers of LLCs); Fla. Stat. Ann. §608.4381(4)(d) (West 1999) (referring to offers required in connection with dissenters' rights); N.Y. Bus. Corp. Law §1005 (McKinney 1994) (providing for payments to dissenting members in the case of certain mergers or consolidations); Ohio Rev. Code Ann. §1705.40 (Anderson 1998) (outlining members' entitlement to relief as dissenting members). But *see* Del. Code Ann. tit. 6, §18-210 (1998) (providing that an LLC agreement or merger agreement may provide appraisal rights, but the statute fails to provide appraisal rights in the absence of such contracts).

12. For a sample of statutes that do provide equitable relief, *see* Ariz. Rev. Stat. Ann. §29-785 (West 2000) (providing for involuntary dissolution in certain cases involving deadlock, illegal or fraudulent conduct, or the wasting, misapplication, or diversion of substantial assets); Colo. Rev. Stat. Ann. §7-80-808 (West 1999) (providing for involuntary dissolution if the LLC exceeds or abuses its authority); Cal. Corp. Code §17351 (West 1999) (permitting dissolution when it is necessary for the protection of the rights and interests of the complaining members, in the event of deadlock or internal dissension, or where those in control have been guilty of or have knowingly countenanced persistent and pervasive fraud, mismanagement, or abuse of authority); Fla. Stat. Ann. §608.441 (West 1999) (authorizing a circuit court to dissolve an LLC if the managers or members are deadlocked, they are unable to break the deadlock, and irreparable injury will result or the LLC's assets are being misappropriated or wasted).

13. *See* Del. Code Ann. tit. 6, §18-302 (1998) (indicating that unless otherwise provided in the operating agreement, on any matter that is to be voted upon the members may take action without a meeting, without prior notice, and without a vote if consent in writing setting forth the action taken is signed by members having not less than the minimum number of votes that would be necessary to authorize the action).

members such as a suit for an accounting or other equitable remedy? This Article maintains that the elimination of default exit rights poses a threat to minority owners in states whose LLC statutes lack other features that are designed to protect minority owners against majority squeeze-outs and other majority misconduct.

The Article recommends that states re-visit their business entity statutes as a whole, consider how all of their business entity statutes interface, and in the process, carefully consider the Uniform Limited Liability Company Act ("ULLCA").[14] The ULLCA provides for at-will withdrawals for LLCs without a term, as well as restricted withdrawals for LLCs with a specific operating term. While the dichotomy between at-will and term LLCs may not be acceptable to those states determined to eliminate default exit rights, ULLCA contains several other protections that could be helpful in all states, especially where default exit rights have been eliminated. ULLCA's provisions restricting the ability to contractually reduce the duty of loyalty or the standard of care,[16] the process for authorizing extraordinary events such as changes in the operating agreement and mergers,[17] and the remedies in the case of internal dissension[18] serve as useful models.

In light of the intended use of the LLC as a vehicle for a wide variety of business ventures, the infancy of the case law interpreting the duty of loyalty and standard of care for members and managers, and the mechanisms for asserting a breach of these duties, this Article strongly advocates the enactment of at least two statutory protections for minority LLC owners: (1) a prohibition on contractual provisions that unreasonably restrict or reduce fiduciary duties and the standard of care; and (2) the right to seek a dissolution, or a buy-out in lieu of a dissolution, in the case of deadlock or where the managers or members in control of the company have engaged in specific types of misconduct delineated in the statute, *i.e.*, illegal, fraudulent, oppressive or unfairly prejudicial conduct. Such protections have been included in the ULLCA.[19]

Haley v. Talcott

864 A.2d 86 (Del. Ch. 2004)

STRINE, Vice Chancellor.

Plaintiff Matthew James Haley has moved for summary judgment of his claim seeking dissolution of Matt and Greg Real Estate, LLC ("the LLC"). Haley and

---

14. Unif. Ltd. Liab. Co. Act (1996).

16. *Id.* §§103, 409 (prohibiting the operating agreement from unreasonably reducing the duty of loyalty, standard of care, or access to information and records and providing for express fiduciary duties and a standard of care limited to refraining from grossly negligent or reckless conduct, intentional misconduct, or a knowing violation of law).

17. *Id.* §404(c) (requiring unanimous agreement for certain important events, including changes in the operating agreement, authorizations or ratifications of acts that would violate or modify the duty of loyalty, changes in the articles of organization, mergers, and the sale or other disposal of goodwill).

18. *Id.* §801 (providing for dissolution in the event of certain misconduct by managers or members in control).

19. *See id.* §103 (providing that the operating agreement may not unreasonably restrict the duty of loyalty or the duty of care); *id.* §801 (enumerating the occurrence of events upon which the LLC is dissolved, including where "the managers or members in control of the company have acted, are acting, or will act in a manner that is illegal, oppressive, fraudulent, or unfairly prejudicial to the petitioner").

defendant Gregory L. Talcott are the only members of the LLC, each owning a 50% interest in the LLC. Haley brings this action in reliance upon §18-802 of the Delaware Limited Liability Company Act which permits this court to "decree dissolution of a limited liability company whenever it is not reasonably practicable to carry on the business in conformity with a limited liability company agreement." The question before the court is whether dissolution of the LLC should be granted, as Haley requests, or whether, as Talcott contends, Haley is limited to the contractually-provided exit mechanism in the LLC Agreement.

Haley and Talcott have suffered, to put it mildly, a falling out. There is no rational doubt that they cannot continue to do business as 50% members of an LLC. But the path to separating their interests is complicated by a second company, Delaware Seafood, also known as the Redfin Seafood Grill ("Redfin Grill"), a restaurant that, at the risk of slightly oversimplifying, was owned by Talcott and, before the falling out, operated by Haley under an employment contract that gave him a 50% share in the profits. The LLC owns the land that the Redfin Grill occupies under an expired lease. The resolution of the current case and the ultimate fate of the LLC therefore critically affect the continued existence of a second business that one party owns and that the other bitterly contends, in other litigation pending before this court, wrongly terminated him.

The question before the court is essentially how the interests of the members of the LLC are to be separated. Haley asserts that summary judgment is appropriate because it is factually undisputed that it is not reasonably practicable for the LLC to carry on business in conformity with a limited liability company agreement (the "LLC Agreement") that calls for the LLC to be governed by its two members, when those members are in deadlock. Therefore, urges Haley, the LLC should be judicially dissolved immediately. Such an end will force the sale of the LLC's real property, which is likely worth, at current market value, far more than the mortgage that the LLC must pay off if it sells.

In response, Talcott stresses that the LLC Agreement provides an alternative exit mechanism that allows the LLC to continue to exist, and argues that Haley should therefore be relegated to this provision if he is unhappy with the stalemate. In other words, Talcott argues that it is reasonably practicable for the LLC to continue to carry on business in conformity with its LLC Agreement because the exit mechanism creates a fair alternative that permits Haley to get out, receiving the fair market value of his share of the property as determined in accordance with procedures in the LLC Agreement, while allowing the LLC to continue. Critically, the exit provision would allow Talcott to buy Haley out with no need for the LLC's asset (*i.e.*, the land) to be sold on the open market. The LLC could continue to exist and own the land (with its favorable mortgage arrangement) and Talcott, as owner of both entities, could continue to offer the Redfin Grill its favorable rent.

But the problem with Talcott's argument is that the exit mechanism is not a reasonable alternative. A principle attraction of the LLC form of entity is the statutory freedom granted to members to shape, by contract, their own approach to common business "relationship" problems. If an equitable alternative to continued deadlock had been specified in the LLC Agreement, arguably judicial dissolution under §18-802 might not be warranted. In this case, however, Talcott admits that the exit mechanism provides no method to relieve Haley of his obligation as a personal guarantor for the LLC's mortgage. Haley signed an agreement with the lender personally guaranteeing the entire mortgage of the LLC (as did Talcott) in order to secure the loan. Without relief from the guaranty, Haley would remain personally liable for the mortgage debt of the LLC, even after his exit. Because Haley would be left liable for the debt of an entity over which he had no further control, I find that the exit provision specified in the LLC Agreement and urged by Talcott is not sufficient to provide an adequate remedy to Haley under these circumstances.

With no reasonable exit mechanism, I find that Haley is entitled to exercise the only practical deadlock-breaking remedy available to him, and one that is also alluded to in the LLC Agreement,[2] the right to seek judicial dissolution. Haley argues, convincingly, that the analysis under §18-802 for an evenly-split, two-owner LLC ordinarily should parallel the analysis under 8 Del. C. §273, which enables this court to order the judicial dissolution of a joint venture corporation owned by deadlocked 50% owners. Because Haley has demonstrated an indisputable deadlock between the two 50% members of the LLC, and that deadlock precludes the LLC from functioning as provided for in the LLC Agreement, I also grant Haley's motion for summary judgment and order dissolution of Matt and Greg Real Estate, LLC.

* * *

IV. Conclusion

[On these facts,] I find that it is not reasonably practicable for the LLC to continue to carry on business in conformity with the LLC Agreement. The parties shall confer and, within four weeks, submit a plan for the dissolution of the LLC. The plan shall include a procedure to sell the Property owned by the LLC within a commercially reasonable time frame. Either party may, of course, bid on the Property.

IT IS SO ORDERED.

NOTES AND QUESTIONS

1. What do you think of the court's disposition in this case? Do you think that the court reached the correct result on the facts of this case? Do you think that the court ordered the proper remedy on the facts of this case? As a practical matter, is there any viable alternative other than the order that now-Chancellor Strine entered in this case?
2. It is fitting that we end this chapter on LLC law with yet another example of just how important it is for the transaction planner to understand the relevant default rules, and further, to understand the interplay between the default rule set forth in the

---

2. *See* LLC Agreement §17(1)(a)(iv) (providing that the company shall be dissolved "upon the occurrence of any event that the Delaware [Limited Liability Company] Act requires dissolution").

relevant LLC statute and the language used in the LLC Operating Agreement to be sure that the transaction planner is fully implementing the terms of the parties' business arrangement in a manner consistent with relevant law.

3. Based on the materials in this chapter, do you think that the Operating Agreement for SoftCo should include provisions that address the illiquid nature of LLC membership interests? Does your analysis of this issue change depending on which financing alternative that Joan and Michael should decide to pursue — *i.e.*, whether they decide to *Go-It-Alone*, seek funding from *Friends and Family*, or pursue a strategic joint venture with BadSoft? What is the role of the lawyer for the LLC in this context?

4. In the *Haley* case, the parties attempted to specify their "exit rights"; i.e., what was supposed to happen in the event that one of the owners/members sought to withdraw from the LLC. Does the decision in *Haley* indicate that the courts may be willing to intervene in order to address what may be (perceived as) incomplete drafting, notwithstanding the fact that the LLC (especially the Delaware LLC statute) is intended to give force and effect to the parties' broad freedom of contract? What do you think?

5. In the absence of planning, what should be the default rule for problems of dissension and deadlock in the context of an LLC?

6. Now that we have concluded our study of LLC law, have you changed your view about the appeal of the LLC in comparison to the other forms of business entities that are available?

7. What are the advantages and disadvantages for Joan and Michael in organizing SoftCo as an LLC? Are there hidden costs in organizing their new business as an LLC that are not associated with the other forms of business entities?

PROBLEM

Bain Property Management LLC was formed by Agatha, Bernice, and Caren for the purpose of acquiring, renovating, and managing a dilapidated apartment building in Manhattan. There was an understanding among the three founders that each would be actively involved in a different aspect of the business affairs of the LLC, and further, that there would be "constant communication" among the three founders. Their agreement provided that all three would be employed full time in the business, and that each intended to rely on this employment arrangement to provide their principal source of income. All three founders also were concerned with retaining ownership of the new business. To this end, Section 9 of their agreement specifically provided that, in the event of the death or disability of a member, or if a member should retire or cease to employed in the business for any reason, the LLC and/or the remaining members shall buy the LLC interest of the withdrawing member according to the terms of their agreement. Section 10 of the agreement provided that the purchase price of a buyback of an LLC interest would be set at its book value.

Five years later, Agatha and Bernie became dissatisfied with Caren's work performance. Consequently, Agatha and Bernie caused the LLC to terminate Caren's employment. Pursuant to the terms of their agreement, Agatha and Bernie gave Caren notice that each of them would purchase half of Caren's LLC interest at book value. Caren believes that her termination was arranged for the purpose of securing her interest in the business at an unfair price thereby depriving Caren of her salary, bonus, and future participation in the business on unfair terms. Caren has consulted you for advice regarding the remedies that she may have.

CHAPTER 4

SELECTED ISSUES UNDER THE FEDERAL SECURITIES LAWS

In this chapter, we examine various provisions of the federal securities laws that the lawyer must consider in the context of planning a capital-raising transaction. As a preliminary word of caution, this chapter presents only a cursory overview of the federal (and state) securities law provisions that must be considered as a threshold matter in planning any financing transaction for a start-up business. As was mentioned in Chapter 1, this overview is in no way intended to serve as a substitute for taking an introductory law school course on securities regulation, which is a vitally important body of knowledge for any lawyer working as a transaction planner.

Briefly summarized, this chapter focuses on certain aspects of the Securities Act of 1933 (the 1933 Act) and the Securities Exchange Act of 1934 (the 1934 Act). As we shall see, whenever a new business proposes to issue its own securities in order to obtain the necessary start-up capital, the issuer must comply with the registration requirements of the 1933 Act or find an exemption. With respect to the 1934 Act, issuers (and their lawyers) always must be mindful of the antifraud provisions of the federal securities laws (most notably Rule 10b-5) when planning and executing a financing transaction. This chapter ends with a discussion of the role of the lawyer in planning a capital-raising transaction in light of recent legislation that Congress enacted to address the spate of financial scandals that marked the first decade of the twenty-first century (and the ensuing Great Recession), with a particular emphasis on the professional responsibility rules that were promulgated by the Securities and Exchange Commission (SEC) pursuant to the legislative mandate set forth by Congress as part of the SOX reforms.[1] In addition to SOX, Congress enacted two other important pieces of legislation in the wake of the Great Recession: the Dodd-Frank Wall Street Reform and Consumer Protection Act, Pub. L. No. 111-203, 124 Stat. 1376 (2010) (more popularly known as

---

1. SOX is the acronym that is widely used among corporate lawyers to refer to the Sarbanes-Oxley Act of 2002, Pub. L. No. 107-204, 116 Stat. 745 (2002). This major piece of legislation is the direct outgrowth of Congress's investigation into Enron, WorldCom, and other corporate and accounting scandals of the early 2000s.

the "Dodd-Frank Act"); and the Jumpstart Our Business Startups Act, Pub. L. No. 112-106, 126 Stat. 306 (2012) (widely referred to as the "JOBS Act"). Where relevant, we will discuss certain aspects of the Dodd-Frank Act and the JOBS Act as part of our discussion of the provisions of the federal securities laws that are regularly implicated in the course of planning a capital-raising transaction for a new business such as Soft Co.

A. The Scope of the 1933 Act

We begin our discussion of the federal securities laws by presenting a broad overview of the basic framework of the 1933 Act. At the risk of oversimplifying the rules covered in an introductory law school course on securities regulation, all of the 1933 Act can be effectively summarized in the following sentence:

> Any time a corporation, regardless whether it is a large, publicly traded or a small, privately held company, proposes to use an instrumentality of interstate commerce in order to issue its stock (or any other securities such as convertible debentures), the corporation (as the issuer of the securities) *must* register the offering *or* find an exemption for the transaction.

Thus, in connection with any business seeking to raise start-up capital, if the business entity proposes to issue securities, then the financing transaction must comply with the requirements of the 1933 Act, regardless of the amount of capital to be raised. In deciding whether the 1933 Act applies, the crucial threshold question turns on whether the new business proposes to issue (i.e., sell) any of its securities as part of the financing transaction.

1. Definition of "Security"

If the new business entity issues a "security" as part of its capital-raising transactions, then it must either register or find an exemption for this distribution of its securities. Thus, the 1933 Act is "transaction oriented," meaning that the 1933 Act registers *transactions, not* the securities themselves. This is an important distinction. Since only the transaction in which the issuer sells the security to the investor is registered, any subsequent resale of the security is a *separate transaction*. As such, the *resale* either must be registered or an exemption must be available to the selling securityholder. This point will become important when we discuss the concept of *restricted securities* later in this chapter.

As a threshold matter, it bears emphasizing that *jurisdiction* under the 1933 Act depends on whether the new business proposes to use the instrumentalities of interstate commerce to engage in transactions to issue securities in order to raise capital. From the perspective of the transaction planner, the first issue to be analyzed is whether the issuer (i.e., the new business) proposes to sell "securities" as part of the financing transaction. The concept of a "security" is complex, however, so a few key points need to be emphasized in the context of a financing transaction for a start-up business.

First, Section 2(a)(1) of the 1933 Act broadly defines the term "security."[2] As such, if a new business decides to incorporate and sell stock to raise capital, the issuance of "shares" clearly falls within the statutory definition of a security. The use of debt, however, is a little bit trickier.[3] While the statutory definition of a "security" expressly includes "any note, stock, . . . bond, debenture, . . . [and] evidence of indebtedness," the courts have eschewed efforts to construe the statutory definition to literally include *all* notes, such as the mortgage debt owed by borrowers on their personal residences. Thus, over the years, the courts have developed a conceptually more nuanced framework in order to distinguish those "notes" that are "securities" from those that are not, culminating in the Supreme Court's 1990 decision in *Reves v. Ernst & Young*, 494 U.S. 56 (1990). According to the Supreme Court, if any new business, whether it be a corporation or a limited liability company (LLC) or some other form of business entity, proposes to use debt to raise capital, the 1933 Act will apply to that transaction *if* the debt instrument qualifies as a security under the analytical framework set forth in *Reves*. At the other end of the spectrum, if the new business is organized as a corporation and proposes to issue stock, those shares are quite clearly "securities" under the plain meaning of the statute, and thus, the requirements of the 1933 Act certainly will apply. However, with respect to investments in other forms of business entities, such as partnerships and LLCs, the analysis is more complicated.

Since equity (i.e., ownership) interests in partnerships (both general and limited) and LLCs are not specifically enumerated within the Section 2(a)(1) definition of a "security," the analysis of whether these interests constitute "securities" for purposes of the federal securities laws is more complicated. In the case of partnerships and LLCs, as a general rule, the federal courts must determine whether these interests qualify as "securities" under what is commonly referred to as the "*Howey* investment contract" analysis. Dating back to the early landmark Supreme Court decision in *SEC v. W. J. Howey Co.*, 328 U.S. 293 (1946), the courts generally employ a four-pronged analysis to determine whether unusual arrangements — that is, instruments that are not specifically enumerated within the statutory definition — may nonetheless constitute a "security" by virtue of being an "investment contract" as that term is used in Section 2(a)(i) of the 1933 Act.

---

2. The full text of the statutory definition of "security" reads as follows:

   (1) The term "security" means any note, stock, treasury stock, security future, security-based swap, bond, debenture, evidence of indebtedness, certificate of interest or participation in any profit-sharing agreement, collateral-trust certificate, preorganization certificate or subscription, transferable share, investment contract, voting-trust certificate, certificate of deposit for a security, fractional undivided interest in oil, gas, or other mineral rights, any put, call, straddle, option, or privilege on any security, certificate of deposit, or group or index of securities (including any interest therein or based on the value thereof), or any put, call, straddle, option, or privilege entered into on a national securities exchange relating to foreign currency, or, in general, any interest or instrument commonly known as a "security", or any certificate of interest or participation in, temporary or interim certificate for, receipt for, guarantee of, or warrant or right to subscribe to or purchase, any of the foregoing. . . .

   3. Recall from Chapter 1 that debt financing is frequently used by entrepreneurs to launch their new businesses. This topic is also explored in the context of venture capital financing in more detail in section C of Chapter 8.

Under the traditional *Howey* formulation of whether an instrument (or an investment arrangement taken as a whole) constitutes an "investment contract," the courts generally ask whether there has been (i) an investment of money, (ii) in a common enterprise, (iii) with the expectation of profits, (iv) to be derived solely from the efforts of others. Since LLC interests are not specifically listed in Section 2(a)(i), most courts have used the *Howey* investment contract analysis to determine whether a particular LLC investment constitutes a security. *Query*: What do you think? Does the LLC membership interest satisfy the judicially developed four-pronged definition of an "investment contract"? For that matter, what about a limited partnership interest — does it qualify as a security under the investment contract analysis? Does a general partnership interest qualify as a security? If you become a partner in a large mega-law firm (such as Skadden Arps or Latham & Watkins, both of which have literally hundreds of partners), does your general partnership interest qualify as a security (assuming that these law firms are organized as general partnerships)? Should any of these interests be treated as securities?

If the transaction planner determines that the financing transaction for a new business involves the issuance (or sale) of a "security," then the transaction must comply with the requirements of Section 5 of the 1933 Act. Generally speaking, the effect of Section 5 is to require registration of the offer and sale of the issuer's securities unless an exemption from registration is available. For start-up businesses, the process of registering the issuance transaction under the 1933 Act — and the burdens associated with becoming a publicly traded company that is subject to the periodic reporting requirements imposed by the 1934 Act — are usually too costly for the new business to undertake.[4] So, as a practical matter, the start-up business will usually seek an exemption from the Section 5 registration obligation in order to issue "securities" and obtain the capital necessary to launch the new business. The next section describes those exemptions most commonly relied on by start-up businesses.

PROBLEMS

1. Assume that Joan and Michael decide to *Go-It-Alone*. They form a California corporation and elect, for federal income tax purposes, to be an S corporation. As the only shareholders, they decide to enter into a shareholders' agreement in which they do away with the board of directors and agree that the two of them will co-manage the new business as equal owners. If they organize their new business in this manner, will the ownership interests that SoftCo issues to Joan and Michael constitute a "security" for purposes of the 1933 Act?

2. Assume that Joan and Michael decide to *Go-It-Alone* and invest all of their life savings in SoftCo, which is organized under the Revised Uniform Partnership Act (RUPA). Joan and Michael are the only partners. Since they plan to work full time on the development of the new software, Joan and Michael hire Marta to manage the finances and generally deal with operating the business on a day-to-

---

4. The nature of these burdens is explored in more detail at the end of section B in Chapter 8.

day basis. If they organize their new business in this manner, will the ownership interests that SoftCo issues to Joan and Michael constitute a "security" for purposes of the 1933 Act?

3. Assume that Joan and Michael decide to finance their new business using funds provided by their *Friends and Family*, which consist of the following seven investors: Michael's family doctor; Joan's parents and Michael's parents; Joan's elderly aunt; and Joan's pastor from her church (who recently inherited, in his words, a "bundle of money"). None of these potential investors — including Joan and Michael themselves — want any personal liability on the debts to be incurred on behalf of the new business. In addition, Joan and Michael want to maintain managerial control over the business operations of the new enterprise. If they decide to organize their new business as an LLC, will the membership interests that SoftCo issues to the investors constitute a "security" for purposes of the 1933 Act?

4. Assume that Paula and Pedro (who are both formerly practicing dentists) are the promoters of a new real estate investment opportunity. They plan to buy apartment buildings for investment, and they have decided to organize the new business as an LLC. Since Paula and Pedro have no experience as property managers, the LLC has entered into an agreement with a manager, GoodAcre Services, to develop, lease, and sell the apartment properties. Under the terms of this agreement, the LLC members retain the authority to approve the purchase of any new properties and to remove GoodAcre as manager. The funds to launch this new business are to be provided by 55 dentists, all of whom either Paula or Pedro met while they were practicing dentists. The investors will receive LLC membership interests in exchange for their capital contributions. If they organize their new business in this manner, will the membership interests that SoftCo issues to the investors constitute a "security" for purposes of the 1933 Act?

B. Overview of Exemptions from the Registration Requirement of the 1933 Act

While not an exhaustive list of all the exemptions potentially available to issuers in connection with their capital-raising transactions (regardless of whether the issuer is seeking capital to launch a new business or to expand an established business), the exemptions most commonly used by emerging growth companies are (i) a Section 4(a)(2) private placement; (ii) a Regulation D offering; (iii) a wholly intrastate offering under §3(a)(11) of the 1933 Act or the SEC's safe harbor thereunder, Rule 147; or (iv) a Regulation A offering. This section briefly describes each of these exemptions and also addresses the Rule 701 exemption that applies to equity incentive plans for employees. However, before we discuss the specific terms of these exemptions, some preliminary observations are in order.

Burden of Proof.   First, with respect to all of the exemptions that we analyze in this chapter, the general rule is that the issuer has the burden of demonstrating that the offering satisfies all of the terms and conditions of the particular exemption on which the issuer is relying. *See SEC v. Ralston Purina Co.*, 346 U.S. 119, 126 (1953). If the issuer fails to meet this burden, then the exemption is lost, which generally results in a

Section 5 violation for failure to register the offering. In this case, the issuer faces liability under Section 12(a)(1) for selling unregistered securities. While any detailed discussion of the elements of the Section 12(a)(1) express cause of action is beyond the scope of this casebook, it is worth noting that this statutory provision imposes *strict liability* on the issuer of unregistered securities in the absence of an exemption. As a practical matter, this means that the

> purchasers receive a "put" (an option to sell back their securities) if there is a §5 violation during an offering. . . . Once there is a violation of §5, later compliance does not retroactively cure the defect. . . . When securities are offered or sold in violation of §5, the purchaser may rescind the transaction and get his money back with interest or recover rescissionary damages if he has resold his stock.

ALAN PALMITER, SECURITIES REGULATION: EXAMPLES & EXPLANATIONS at pg. 243 (5th ed. 2011).

Integration.   The second observation to be made is that if an issuer seeks to make an offering under a transaction exemption, then the issuer must be sure that the entire offering meets all of the terms and conditions of that particular exemption. This is known among securities lawyers as the concept of *integration*. Under this "*integration principle*, an issuer cannot slice and dice an offering so that different parts fit separate exemptions, if the offering as a whole fits none." PALMITER, *supra*, at pg. 194 (emphasis in original). This principle extends across all of the exemptions that we discuss in this section and leads issuers (and their lawyers) to be careful in structuring an exempt offering so as to assure that the *entire offering* satisfies all of the requirements of the specific exemption. This raises the obvious question, how does the transaction planner determine when

> . . . multiple offers and sales constitute an integrated offering? The SEC has articulated a five-factor test that considers whether the multiple transactions (1) are part of single plan of financing, (2) involve the same class of security, (3) took place at about the same time, (4) involved the same consideration, and (5) were made for the same general purpose. See Securities Act Rel. No. 4552 (1962). In effect, the test asks whether there was *one financing*. See *In re Kunz*, Exchange Act Rel. No. 45290 (2002) (upholding NASD disciplinary sanctions arising from unregistered offerings of various notes with different maturities and secured by different assets, since all offerings [were] made "at about the same time" with the same general purpose to finance issuer's mortgage lending business).
>
> To alleviate uncertainty, many of the SEC exemptions contain a safe harbor integration test that focuses on the issuer's timing. Under the SEC safe harbor rules, sets of sales separated by six months are considered separate offerings and are not subject to integration. See Rule 502(a) (Regulation D); and Rule 147(b)(2) (intrastate offerings). In addition, the SEC permits an issuer to make a private placement under [Section 4(a)(2)] (which includes Rule 506 offerings) and then "subsequently" to initiate a public offering, without the two [financings] being integrated. Rule 152.

PALMITER, *supra*, at pp. 194-195 (emphasis in original).[5] With respect to the statutory private placement exemption available under Section 4(a)(2), it is important to note

---

5. It bears mentioning that in August 2007, the SEC proposed modifying Rule 502(a) to shorten the integration safe harbor from 6 months to 90 days. *See* SEC Release No. 33-8828 (Aug. 13, 2007) *available at*

that, as part of the JOBS Act, Congress renumbered the exemptions available under Section 4 to add a new Section 4(b), which sets forth a new exemption that permits "crowdfunding." We will discuss the crowdfunding provisions of the JOBS Act in more detail later in this chapter. With respect to the renumbering of the Section 4 exemptions, however, we have opted to change all references in the following text to any of the exemptions that are now contained in Section 4(a) to refer to the current statutory section, even if the original source referred to the now-superceded section number.

1. Wholly Intrastate Offerings: Section 3(a)(11) and Rule 147

Section 3(a)(11) exempts purely local in-state offerings from registration under Section 5. In essence, this exemption reflects the view that wholly intrastate offerings are adequately regulated by state securities laws. Thus, an offering that is exempt under Section 3(a)(11) will remain subject to state "blue sky laws,"[6] a topic briefly discussed at the end of this chapter. From the issuer's perspective, this exemption offers several advantages, including the following:

- No limitations on the number of purchasers
- No restrictions on the type of purchasers or their financial sophistication
- No dollar limit on the amount of money that can be raised
- No limit on how often this exemption can be used
- No prohibition on the use of general advertising or general solicitation as part of a purely local offering

Of course, the applicable state securities law may impose some or all of these requirements.

Despite these benefits, issuers usually do not rely on this exemption because the SEC and the courts have construed this exemption narrowly, leading to substantial uncertainty regarding what is required of issuers in order to perfect this exemption. For example, a single offer to a non-resident will destroy the exemption for all offers and sales that are part of the offering. In addition, the courts have required the issuer to conduct a "substantial" or "predominant" amount of business in the state in order for the issuer to qualify for the "purely local" offering exemption under Section 3(a)(11) exemption.

In an effort to provide greater clarity, the SEC has promulgated Rule 147 as a safe harbor rule that is designed to create bright-line standards that define the scope of "pure local offerings." The safe harbor of Rule 147 is not exclusive. Thus, an offering that fails to comply with the terms of Rule 147 can still be exempt under Section 3(a)(11).

---

www.sec.gov/rules/proposed/2007/33-8828.pdf. As of this writing (fall 2013), no action has been taken by the SEC to implement this proposal.

6. "Blue sky laws" is the common parlance used by transactional lawyers to refer to state securities laws. The term "blue sky laws" is derived from a well-known passage in a 1917 Supreme Court opinion where the Court observed that "[t]he name given to the law indicates the evil at which it is aimed; that is, [the sale of something that has no more substance than] so many feet of blue sky." *Hall v. Geiger-Jones Co.*, 242 U.S. 539, 550 (1917).

Section 3(a)(11) provides that the issuer must be "a person resident and doing business within" the state of the offering. According to the statute, a corporation is "resident" in its state of incorporation. With respect to the "doing business" requirement, the courts have generally held that an issuer is "doing business" in a state if its revenues, assets, principal office, and the use of the proceeds from the offering are principally devoted to in-state activities. *See* PALMITER, *supra*, at pg. 196. Rule 147 has provided some additional clarity in this area, primarily in two ways. First, Rule 147(c)(1) defines "residence" for purposes of non-corporate issuers as the state where the issuer is organized, or in the case of a partnership, the state where the partnership has its principal business. Second, Rule 147(c)(2) specifies quantitative guidelines for the "doing business" requirement, known popularly as the "triple 80% test." Under Rule 147, an issuer will be deemed to be "doing business" within a state if the issuer has its principal office in-state, *and* if 80 percent of its gross revenues, *and* 80 percent of its assets, *and* 80 percent of the proceeds of the offering are to be devoted to in-state activities.

Many experienced practitioners view the requirements of Rule 147 to be just as burdensome as complying with the requirements of Section 3(a)(11). Moreover, as with Section 3(a)(11), the failure to comply with all of the technical requirements of Rule 147 destroys the basis for the exemption for *all* offers and sales that are part of the transaction. Among practitioners, there is a general reluctance to rely on the rather fragile exemption of either Section 3(a)(11) or its safe harbor, Rule 147, except in the very narrowest of circumstances where it is relatively clear that the proposed offering is "purely local" based on the facts and circumstances surrounding the offering. *See* GREGORY C. SMITH, *Federal Securities Law Considerations of Raising Capital*, ch.4, vol. 1 START-UP & EMERGING COMPANIES at pp. 4-34 to 4-35 (Revised Edition).

2. Statutory Private Placements

"The most common exemption available in the start-up context is the private placement exemption available under Section [4(a)(2)] and Regulation D, promulgated under Sections 3(b) and [4(a)(2)]." SMITH, *supra* at §4.03[1] at pg. 4-7. In this section, we examine the statutory private placement available under Section 4(a)(2) of the 1933 Act (which was formerly numbered Section 4(2)), and the next section describes the terms of the exemptions available under Regulation D.

Section 4(a)(2) exempts "transactions with an issuer not involving a public offering." Although the statutory language seems deceptively simple on its face, in point of fact the body of case law interpreting this language is enormous, and unfortunately for us, often unclear and even in some cases contradictory. To address the uncertainty surrounding the scope of the Section 4(a)(2) exemption, the SEC adopted Regulation D in 1982, and in particular, Rule 506 was adopted as a safe harbor exemption for a private placement transaction. Because of the relative clarity of Regulation D in general and of Rule 506 in particular — at least as compared to the case law surrounding Section 4(a)(2) — it is safe to say that practitioners today prefer to rely on Rule 506 of Regulation D, and only rely on Section 4(a)(2) as a backup (or residual) exemption. First, we examine the case law approach to determining the availability of the Section 4(a)(2) exemption, and in the next section, we will examine Regulation D and the safe harbor of Rule 506. It bears noting that the terms of the Rule 506 safe harbor were heavily influenced by the courts' interpretation of the Section 4(a)(2) exemption.

We start with the seminal case interpreting Section 4(a)(2), *SEC v. Ralston Purina Co.*, 346 U.S. 119 (1953). In this case, the Supreme Court decided that the Section 4(a)(2) exemption was not available where the company offered securities to its employees, including its stock clerks and its bakers. The Supreme Court reasoned that these employees comprised a class of persons in need of the protections of the 1933 Act because they did not have access to the same kind of information that they would have received had the issuer prepared a registration statement in compliance with the requirements of Section 5 of the 1933 Act. The Supreme Court went on to hold that under Section 4(a)(2):

> The focus of inquiry should be on the need of the offerees for the protections afforded by registration. The employees here were not shown to have access to the kind of information which registration would disclose. The obvious opportunities for pressure and imposition make it advisable that they be entitled to compliance with §5. . . . The design of the statute is to protect investors by promoting full disclosure of information thought necessary to inform investment decisions. . . .

Id. at pp. 124-127. Since *Ralston Purina*, the lower courts have had numerous occasions to construe the scope of the Section 4(a)(2) exemption in light of the teachings of the Supreme Court's decision in that case.

While the principles that emerge from these cases are not crystal clear, it seems as though the courts, on a rather consistent basis, focus their analysis on the following factors:

(i) *The number of offerees and their "financial sophistication."* The requirement of "financial sophistication" has led to a rather substantial body of case law and academic commentary interpreting the (often conflicting) standards that the issuer must satisfy to demonstrate the "financial sophistication" of prospective investors.

(ii) *The information made available to the offerees.* Issuers will usually provide offerees information about the company and its proposed offering either by way of preparing a written disclosure document (generally referred to as a *private placement memorandum*, or *PPM*), or alternatively, by providing offerees with access to such information.

(iii) *The size of the offering.* Although the courts have never placed a finite number on how many offers can be made, issuers should be cautious in making a large number of offers. If the number is too large, this is a strong indicator of a public offering, rather than a "private transaction."

(iv) *The manner of the offering.* It is (relatively) clear that, pursuant to the Section 4(a)(2) exemption, the issuer cannot engage in any "general advertising or general solicitation." However, the limits of what conduct will constitute "general solicitation" are often unclear.

(v) *The limitations on resale of the securities originally sold in a statutory private placement.* This factor leads to the concept of "restricted securities," a topic which is discussed at length later in this chapter. At this point, suffice it to say that the issuer is generally required to take certain precautions against "impermissible resales" by the purchasers in a statutory private placement in order to perfect the Section 4(a)(2) exemption. The nature of these procedures will be described in more detail later in this chapter, as part of our discussion of the resale of "restricted securities" under Rule 144.

3. Regulation D

Today, the SEC safe harbor standard for Section 4(a)(2) is set forth as Rule 506 of Regulation D. Promulgated in 1982, Regulation D is composed of Rules 501 through 508. The substantive exemptions consist of Rules 504, 505, and 506. As discussed in the next paragraphs, the Rule 504 and 505 exemptions were promulgated by the SEC pursuant to the "small offering" exemption of Section 3(b) of the 1933 Act. One of the primary goals of Regulation D is to establish an integrated, consistent set of rules for application in the use of the statutory exemptions found in Sections 4(a)(2) and 3(b) of the 1933 Act. The Rule 506 safe harbor quantifies and further elaborates on the five factors (described above) that are used by the courts to define the terms of the Section 4(a)(2) exemption. While a detailed analysis of the terms and conditions of Regulation D is beyond the scope of this casebook, a few general observations are in order regarding the availability of the substantive exemptions found in Rules 504, 505, and 506 of Regulation D in connection with financing a start-up business.

Rule 504 Offerings.   The SEC promulgated Rule 504 pursuant to the small offering exemption found in Section 3(b) of the 1933 Act. Rule 504 exempts offerings of up to $1 million. The fact that the Rule 504 and 505 exemptions are both promulgated pursuant to Section 3(b) is important in that securities offered in a Rule 504 transaction are aggregated for purposes of the $1 million cap with other securities issued under Rule 504 or securities issued under the Rule 505 exemption during the 12 months before the start of and after the completion of the offering (i.e., a rolling 12-month period). On the other hand, there is no potential for aggregating securities sold in a Rule 506 offering with a Rule 504 (or Rule 505) offering because Rule 506 is promulgated pursuant to Section 4(a)(2) as opposed to Section 3(b). We describe the concept of aggregation in more detail later in this section.

In a Rule 504 offering, there is no limitation on the number of offerees or purchasers and there is no requirement that the issuer determine whether the purchaser is financially sophisticated. The issuer is not required to provide prospective purchasers with any information or written disclosure document in a Rule 504 offering, although the issuer must be mindful of the prospect of liability under Rule 10b-5, the broad antifraud provision promulgated under the 1934 Act. Consequently, for reasons explored in more detail later in this chapter, the issuer is generally well-advised to provide disclosure to the prospective investors about the issuer and its proposed offering. Generally speaking, securities issued in a Rule 504 offering are deemed to be restricted securities and thus will be subject to the resale limitations imposed by Rule 144, a topic which is addressed later in this chapter. Finally, Rule 504 prohibits general advertising and general solicitation. However, Rule 504 does permit the issuer to avoid the ban on general advertising provided that certain conditions are satisfied, which essentially require the issuer to register the offering at the state level in lieu of complying with the federal registration requirements. In these circumstances, the issuer is permitted to conduct, in essence, a "mini-public" offering of up to $1 million and the purchasers in such offerings will acquire freely transferable securities.

Rule 505 Offerings. Rule 505 was also promulgated pursuant to the small offering exemption of Section 3(b). As such, Rule 505 provides qualified issuers with an exemption for offerings of up to $5 million to (what the issuer reasonably believes is) not more than 35 non-accredited investors and an unlimited number of accredited investors; we describe the concept of an "accredited investor" later in this section. Since Rule 505 is promulgated pursuant to Section 3(b), the issuer may raise up to $5 million in any 12-month period, subject to certain "aggregation" principles discussed later in this section.

General advertising and general solicitation are prohibited in a Rule 505 offering, and securities issued in a Rule 505 offering are deemed restricted securities. However, Rule 505 does not require that unaccredited investors be financially sophisticated. If any sales are made to non-accredited investors, the issuer must provide disclosure of specified information that satisfies the detailed requirements of Rule 502(b) of Regulation D. Moreover, Rule 505 is not available to those issuers that have engaged in certain misconduct (or what is more popularly referred to as the "bad actor" disqualifiers).

Rule 506 offerings. In a Rule 506 offering, the issuer is permitted to raise an unlimited amount of capital from an unlimited number of accredited investors and up to 35 non-accredited investors. Rule 506 is promulgated pursuant to Section 4(a)(2); as such, there is no dollar limit to the aggregate amount of securities that may be offered and sold in a Rule 506 offering, unlike Rules 504 and 505. Moreover, there is no limit on the number of offerees in a Rule 506 exempt transaction, which represents a substantial advantage over the Section 4(a)(2) private placement.

However, consistent with Supreme Court precedent, Rule 506 does require the issuer to determine the financial sophistication of all non-accredited purchasers, unlike Rules 504 and 505. This means that, prior to sale, the issuer must "reasonably believe" that each non-accredited investor (either on his/her/its own or together with the purchaser representative) has such knowledge and experience in financial and business matters that he/she/it can evaluate the risks and merits of the proposed investment. Rule 506(b)(ii). If any sales are made to non-accredited investors, the issuer is required to provide them with disclosure of specified information about the issuer and its proposed offering as required under Rule 502(b), similar to the disclosure burden imposed by the terms of Rule 505. Finally, Rule 506 imposes a ban on "general advertising and general solicitation" and results in the issuance of "restricted securities."

Since Rule 506 is promulgated as a "safe harbor" to the Section 4(a)(2) exemption, compliance with Rule 506 may be viewed as an alternate method to perfecting a valid private placement. Perhaps the most significant advantage of Rule 506, though, is the preemption of state blue sky laws provided by Section 18(a) of the 1933 Act, a provision that Congress enacted as part of the National Securities Markets Improvement Act of 1996, widely known as "NSMIA." Broadly speaking, Section 18(a) prohibits state regulation of those securities offerings that involve a "covered security." For our purposes, Section 18(b)(4)(D) defines a "covered security" to include a transaction that is exempt from registration pursuant to rules that the SEC has promulgated pursuant to Section 4(a)(2), although the states may continue to impose certain filing obligations on issuers who conduct Rule 506 offerings. As a result, the issuer who conducts a Rule 506 offering may be required to file a copy of its Form D with the appropriate state regulators and pay the fees that would have been charged under the state regulatory scheme, although state regulators are otherwise preempted from regulating these offerings. (We describe the issuer's Form D filing obligation later in this section.)

Securities issued in a Rule 506 exempt offering are "covered securities" because Rule 506 was adopted by the SEC pursuant to Section 4(a)(2). By contrast, securities issued in a Rule 504 or 505 offering are not "covered securities" because they were promulgated under Section 3(b), and thus the states may continue to regulate these offerings. This gives the Rule 506 exemption a substantial advantage over the other Regulation D exemptions. For this reason, most seasoned practitioners prefer to rely on the Rule 506 exemption whenever possible. At the same time, however, the prudent practitioner seeks to establish compliance with multiple exemptions, if practically possible, so that the issuer has a fallback position if compliance with an expected exemption fails. As we saw earlier in this chapter, if the issuer has no valid exemption, it will face strict liability under §12(a)(1) of the 1933 Act, which in effect allows all purchasers in the failed offering to rescind the transaction and recover from the issuer the purchase price they paid for the securities.

Concept of "Accredited Investors." An important concept under both Rules 505 and 506 is the definition of "accredited investor." This definition is important because the limitation on the number of purchasers that are permitted excludes "accredited investors," and further, an offering made exclusively to "accredited investors" does not trigger the detailed disclosure requirements of Rule 502(b) of Regulation D. Rule 501(a) lists the types of persons and entities that qualify as "accredited investors." This definition includes officers and directors of the issuer, various types of institutional investors (such as banks, broker-dealers and investment companies, among others), as well as certain individuals who qualify as "fat cat" investors by virtue of satisfying an income or net worth standard set forth in Rule 501(a). The concept of an "accredited investor" is fundamentally grounded on the assumption that these investors can "fend for themselves" because the SEC deems these investors to have access to the information that would otherwise be provided in a registration statement, and further, they are deemed to be financially sophisticated investors for purposes of Rule 506.

Regulation D requires only that the issuer "reasonably believe" that a prospective investor falls within the Rule 501(a) definition of "accredited investor" at the time of sale. The determination of what constitutes "reasonable belief" obviously involves a factual inquiry, the scope of which will vary depending on the circumstances of a particular offering. Notably, the SEC has declined to provide specific guidance on this matter. As a general rule of thumb, most practitioners will require that the stock purchase agreement include the investor's representation that he/she/it qualifies as an "accredited investor," and also will usually require additional verification in support of this representation if the circumstances surrounding the offering suggest that this is appropriate. *Query*: As counsel for the issuer, what documentation would you require a venture capital firm to provide in support of its representation that it qualifies as an "accredited investor"?

Recent SEC Amendments to the Definition of "Accredited Investor." In 2010, Congress enacted the Dodd-Frank Act, which included a broad array of reform measures designed to address some of the causes of the meltdown in the financial markets and the ensuing Great Recession. As part of these reforms, Congress specifically instructed the SEC to revise the criteria used to qualify natural persons as "accredited investors" based on their net worth, as more fully described in the following excerpt:

Alex Frutos and Kristina M. Campbell
SEC Adopts New Net Worth Standard for Accredited Investors

Jackson Walker LLP, Corporate and Securities e-Alert
(Jan. 9, 2012)*

On December 21, 2011, the Securities and Exchange Commission ("SEC") amended its rules to exclude the value of a person's home for purposes of calculating net worth when determining whether an individual qualifies as an "accredited investor" in certain securities offerings exempt from registration under federal securities laws, including Regulation D private placement exemptions. [*See* SEC Rel. No. 33-9297 (Sept. 21, 2011).] This rule reflects the requirements of Section 413(a) of the Dodd-Frank Act and generally follows the Proposing Release issued by the SEC in January 2011 ("Proposing Release").

The "accredited investor" standards are used in determining whether certain exemptions from registration under the Securities Act of 1933 are available for private and other limited offerings. An individual may qualify as an "accredited investor" by having a net worth, alone or together with their spouse, of at least $1 million at the time of the sale of securities. The recent amendment by the SEC excludes the value of an individual's primary residence as an asset and the debt secured by the primary residence as a liability from the net worth calculation used to determine whether that individual is an "accredited investor." However, the individual must include the amount of indebtedness secured by his or her primary residence to the extent that the indebtedness exceeds the value of the primary residence. Of note, the "value" of a primary residence is not required to be based upon a third party opinion on valuation; all that is required is an estimate of fair market value ("FMV").

Unlike the Proposing Release, the new rules attempt to address manipulation in the calculation of net worth by eliminating the ability of individuals to artificially inflate net worth by borrowing against home equity shortly before participating in an exempt securities offering. Any increase in indebtedness of an individual secured by his or her primary residence in the 60 days preceding the purchase of securities in the exempt offering must be included in the net worth calculation, even if the estimated value of the primary residence exceeds the total amount of debt secured by the primary residence. In other words, the amended rules provide for a 60-day look-back provision solely to identify and include as a liability any increase in mortgage debt during the 60-day period, without including an offset for the value of the underlying property if it is the investor's primary residence, in the calculation of net worth.

---

* *Available at* http://images.jw.com/ealert/coporatesecurities/2012/0109sm.html.

For example, if an investor had $1,200,000 million in investment accounts, a house with a FMV of $500,000 with a mortgage of $600,000 and no additional assets or liabilities, they would qualify as an accredited investor under the amended Rules ($1,200,000 − ($600,000 − $500,000) = net worth of $1,100,000). However, an individual with $1,100,000 in investment accounts, a house with a FMV of $600,000 with a mortgage of $450,000 and no additional assets or liabilities, who borrowed $150,000 against the house thirty days prior to investment would not qualify under the amended rules ($1,100,000 − $150,000 = net worth of $950,000), as the equity in the home is not considered an asset under the new rules, but the new borrowing would be considered a liability.

Query: What do you think will be the impact of this change in the SEC's definition of "accredited investor"? At least one commentator has speculated that "thousands of informal investors — the providers of 'friends and family' backing to fledging companies — could be all but [eliminated from] the picture. And that's causing a lot of concern among prominent angel investors. According to the Angel Capital Association, about 225,000 people made angel investments in the past two years [referring to the time period of approximately 2008 to 2010]. By some estimates, at least half of these informal investors are friends, family, or former colleagues of the entrepreneurs seeking [start-up] funding. This pool [of potential investors] could be reduced by 50%, says Morgan, Lewis & Bockins LLP partner E. John Park." Olaf de Senerpont Domis, _Clipped Wings: By Changing the Definition of "Accredited Investor," the New Financial Reform Law Could Stifle Angel Investing_, THE DEAL at p. 19 (Dec. 2010).

General Advertising and General Solicitation. As a general proposition, Regulation D does not impose a numerical limit on the number of "offerees" who may participate in any of the offerings that are exempt under Regulation D. As a practical matter, however, there may be a limit on the permissible number of offerees by virtue of Rule 502(c), which prohibits any form of "general advertising" or "general solicitation" in connection with any Regulation D offering (with a limited exception under Rule 504 for "mini-public" offerings of up to $1 million, as mentioned earlier). This ban has proven to be quite controversial because Rule 502(c) not only lists certain activities that are specifically prohibited (i.e., newspaper ads, radio broadcasts) but also makes clear that these are not the only types of activities that may constitute a prohibited form of "general solicitation." Moreover, the SEC has cautioned issuers that even where the Regulation D offering is limited only to "accredited investors," if the offering involves a sufficiently large number of purchasers, it may result in a violation of the ban on "general solicitation" and thus destroy the basis for the issuer's exemption for the transaction.

In light of the continuing controversy, and in order to provide some guidance to the issuer community (and their lawyers), the SEC has issued a number of no-action letters that are designed to provide further clarification regarding the scope of activities that are permitted without running afoul of the Regulation D ban on general solicitation. _See, e.g., E. F. Hutton & Co._, 1985 SEC No-Act. LEXIS 2917; and _Bateman Eichler, Hill Richards, Inc._, 1985 SEC No-Act. LEXIS 2918.[7] However, the meaning of "general

---

7. Under the federal securities laws, "no-action letters" serve a very useful function. When lawyers face difficult issues in determining compliance with a provision of the federal securities laws, the lawyer can

solicitation" remains elusive and ultimately the existence of general solicitation will involve a fact-intensive inquiry that will turn on the facts and circumstances of a particular offering. It is worth noting that Regulation D's prohibition on general advertising is often quite problematic for small businesses, many of which are unable to take advantage of the line of SEC no-action letters referred to above because they do not have the services of financial advisors readily available to them. Consequently, small issuers will often find it quite difficult — if not impossible — to recruit investors to provide the capital necessary to launch their new business. Despite significant developments in communications technologies since the SEC first promulgated Regulation D in 1982, the SEC has steadfastly refused over the years to revise (much less eliminate) the prohibition on general solicitation that was made part of the original adoption of Rule 502(c).

The JOBS Act and Elimination of the Ban on "General Advertising." The SEC's unwillingness to relax the prohibition on the use of general solicitation and general advertising as part of a Regulation D offering finally met its match when Congress adopted legislation in April 2012 that directed the SEC to amend Rule 506 to permit general advertising to be used in connection with a new subcategory of Rule 506 offerings made exclusively to accredited investors — even though many experienced lawyers and commentators, along with the SEC, questioned the wisdom of eliminating this ban in light of some rather significant investor protection concerns.[8] This 2012 reform legislation and the SEC's rather tortured rule-making efforts to implement Congress's mandate are more fully described in the following excerpt:

General Solicitation and Investor Protection in Private Offerings

Sullivan & Cromwell LLP, Law Firm Memo (July 15, 2013) at pp. 2-3*

Existing Rule 506 of Regulation D provides an exemption from registration under the Securities Act for private placements by an issuer[1] where, among other things, "the issuer reasonably believes" that no more than 35 purchasers are not "accredited investors" and neither the issuer nor any person acting on its behalf makes offers or sales by "any

---

submit a letter to the SEC staff that, without naming the client, presents the relevant facts of the situation as a hypothetical. As part of this letter, the lawyer will submit his/her analysis of the issues presented under the federal securities laws based on the stated facts and will conclude the letter by setting forth the actions that the lawyer proposes to take to comply with the law. If the SEC agrees that the proposed compliance conduct is sufficient and appropriate as a matter of the federal securities laws, it will reply that, based on the information presented, the SEC staff will take "no action" should the proposed conduct be followed in exactly the manner described in the lawyer's letter. Alternatively, the SEC staff may reply that the proposed compliance is not adequate. These letters are published by the SEC and are regularly used by practitioners as informal guidance in similar or analogous fact situations.

8. The JOBS Act also addressed the use of crowdfunding as a potential source of funding for start-up businesses; this aspect of the JOBS Act is discussed later in this chapter.

* *Available at* http://www.sullcrom.com/files/Publication/58ce5441-4932-42cd-91e7-0fc5bf361beb/Presentation/PublicationAttachment/54ab1f0f-24be-431f-a6cf-15220ea4f96/SC_Publication_General_Solicitation_and_Investor_Protection_in_Private_Offerings.pdf

1. Rule 506 is available only for sales by an issuer, and not for resales by a financial intermediary or other party.

form of general solicitation or general advertising."[2] Section 201(a) of the Jumpstart Our Business Startups Act (the "JOBS Act"), enacted in April 2012, directs the SEC to amend Rule 506 . . . to eliminate [this] prohibition on general solicitation and general advertising[3] in transactions effected under [Rule 506], provided that all purchasers of the securities are accredited investors. . . .

In August 2012, the SEC proposed new Rule 506(c) that would permit issuers to use general solicitation to offer securities in reliance on Rule 506, provided that the securities are sold only to accredited investors and the issuer takes reasonable steps to verify that all purchasers are accredited investors. . . . Proposed Rule 506(c) did not mandate specific methods of verification.[4] The SEC received numerous comment letters relating to the proposed verification requirement, with many expressing the view that the new rule should mandate specific methods of verification or at least provide additional guidance on which methods would be sufficient. [On July 10, 2013, the SEC adopted amendments to Rule 506, specifically adding new subsection (c).*] The final amendments to [Rule 506] . . . are substantially similar to those [originally] proposed [by the SEC], including the verification requirement, except that the SEC included a non-exclusive, non-mandatory list of methods for verifying accredited investor status of natural persons that would be deemed to satisfy the verification requirement.

. . . [N]ew Rule 506(c) [as finally adopted by the SEC in July 2013] permits an issuer to offer and sell securities by means of general solicitation, provided that the following conditions are satisfied:

- All purchasers of the securities must be accredited investors, as defined in Rule 501(a) of Regulation D, at the time of the sale of the securities, either because they are within one of the enumerated categories of persons that qualify as accredited investors or because the issuer reasonably believes that they are.
- The issuer must take reasonable steps to verify that all purchasers of the securities are accredited investors.
- All terms and conditions of existing Rules 501 (definitions), 502(a) (integration restriction), and 502(d) (resale limitations) of Regulation D must be satisfied. Existing Rule 502(c), prohibiting general solicitation, would not apply.**

---

2. As noted below, the other general conditions in Rule 502 must also be met as applicable. Offerings under Rule 506, unlike those under Rule 504 or 505, are not limited by dollar amount. [It bears emphasizing that the exemption described in the accompanying text is still available to issuers, although it has now been renumbered Rule 506(b) as a result of the SEC's adoption of new Rule 506(c).]

3. In this memo, we refer to both general solicitation and general advertising as "general solicitation."

4. The SEC's proposing release is *available at* http://www.sec.gov/rules/proposed/2012/33-9354.pdf. See also our Client Memorandum "JOBS Act — 'General Solicitation' in Private Offerings: SEC Proposes Amendments to Rule 506 and Rule 144A to Remove the Prohibition," dated August 30, 2012, *available at* http://www.sullcrom.com/files/Publication/13f6b37a-a13c-4d39-b3dc-ff2fc0c573a7/Presentation/PublicationAttachment/86ec79df-2104-41fa-880e-65dd7367500e/SC_Publication_JOBS_Act_General_Solicitation_in_Private_offerings_2.pdf.

* The SEC's adopting release is available at http://www.sec.gov/rules/final/2013/33-9415.pdf (July 10, 2013).

** It bears emphasizing that the original substantive exemption of Rule 506, now contained in Rule 506(b), continues to be available to the issuer community, although the use of general advertising and general solicitation continues to be prohibited in connection with a Rule 506(b) offering.

With respect to the issuer's obligation to take steps to *verify* that purchasers in a Rule 506(c) offering qualify as "accredited investors," the following excerpt provides a useful summary of this new "reasonable verification" requirement:

> *Reasonable verification.* The determination of the reasonableness of the steps taken [by the issuer] to verify an accredited investor will be based on the particular facts and circumstances of the purchaser and the transaction. Factors that the issuer may consider include: (i) the nature of the purchaser and the type of accredited investor that the [purchaser] claims to be, (ii) the amount and type of information that the issuer has about the purchaser and (iii) the nature of the offering, such as the manner in which the purchaser was solicited to participate in the offering, and the terms of the offering, such as a minimum investment amount.
>
> The amendments include a non-exclusive list of methods that issuers may use to verify the accredited investor status of natural persons. None of these methods is mandatory. However, an issuer that uses one of the below methods will be deemed to have satisfied the "reasonable verification" requirement, so long as the issuer does not have knowledge that a particular person is not an accredited investor.
>
> - *On the basis of income.* To verify that a purchaser is an accredited investor on the basis of income, an issuer may review any IRS form (including Forms W-2, 1099, and 1040 and Schedule K-1 to Form 1065) that reports that the purchaser's income exceeded $200,000 (or that the purchaser had joint income of $300,000 with his or her spouse) for the two most recent years and obtain a written representation from the purchaser that he or she has a reasonable expectation of reaching the income level necessary to qualify as an accredited investor during the current year.
> - *On the basis of net worth.* To verify that a purchaser is an accredited investor on the basis of net worth, an issuer may review a number of financial documents for assets (including bank, brokerage, and other statements, certificates of deposits, tax assessments and independent appraisal reports) and for liabilities (a consumer report from a nationwide consumer reporting agency). The documents must be dated within the trailing three months. In addition, to satisfy this method, the issuer will need to obtain a written representation from the purchaser that all liabilities necessary to make a determination as to net worth have been disclosed.
> - *Third-party verification.* An issuer may also rely on a third party to verify accredited-investor status by receiving a written confirmation from a registered broker-dealer, a registered investment adviser, or a licensed attorney or certified public accountant in good standing to the effect that it, he, or she has within the prior three months taken reasonable steps to verify, and has determined, that the purchaser is an accredited investor. In this case, the implication is that the third party may (but need not) rely on any of the above verification methods.
> - *Existing investors.* If any person purchased an issuer's securities in a Rule 506 offering as an accredited investor prior to the effective date of the amendments and continues to hold those securities, then the issuer may verify accredited-investor status by obtaining a certification from that person at the time of sale that he or she qualifies as an accredited investor.
>
> Whether the issuer uses one of these non-exclusive methods or another method, it will be important for the issuer to establish procedures and maintain records that show the "reasonable verification" steps, since the burden will rest with the issuer to prove that this requirement was satisfied.

Private Offering Reform: Analysis and Implications, Davis Polk & Wardwell LLP, Law Firm Memo (July 29, 2013) at pp. 2-3 (*available at* http://davispolk.com/sites/default/files/07.29.13private%20offering%20reform.pdf). It is important to emphasize that this "reasonable verification" requirement is "separate and apart from the requirement that all sales be limited to accredited investors." *Id.* In other words, reliance on this new Rule 506(c) exemption requires that the issuer be able to satisfy this new "reasonable verification" requirement — "even if [it turns out that] *all* purchasers in the [Rule 506(c)] offering are accredited investors." *Id.* at p. 2 (emphasis added). However, if the issuer should decide to conduct a capital-raising transaction under Rule 506(b) — i.e., without resorting to the use of general advertising — then the issuer would *not* be required to satisfy this new "reasonable verification" requirement. Instead, the issuer "would need to comply with the current requirement [of Rule 506(b)] that [the issuer] have a reasonable belief, at the time of sale, that the purchasers are accredited investors." *Id. Query*: Would you recommend that SoftCo rely on the new Rule 506(c) exemption in connection with its efforts to obtain start-up financing? Does your recommendation depend on whether SoftCo plans to seek financing from *Friends and Family*, or alternatively, to seek *Venture Capital* funding?

Scope of Required Disclosure.   At the risk of stating the obvious, the time and expense involved in satisfying the detailed disclosure requirements of Rule 502(b) is significant and, for most start-up businesses, generally not cost-effective. Indeed, most offerings that involve venture capitalists are conducted pursuant to Rule 506 and are limited to accredited investors. This avoids preparation of a private placement memorandum (i.e., a PPM) that contains all of the information required by Rule 502(b), which obligates the issuer to provide prospective investors with the kind of information that is required to be set forth in the prospectus that is used in connection with either a Regulation A offering or a registered public offering. The general terms of this required disclosure are summarized in the following article. Even though venture capitalists generally prefer to avoid the costs and delay associated with preparing a detailed PPM in compliance with Rule 502(b), this does not mean that the issuer is "off the hook," so to speak, with respect to preparing some form of PPM (i.e., disclosure document) for distribution to prospective investors. The following excerpt describes other important reasons for preparing some form of disclosure document in connection with financing transactions for new businesses:

William W. Barker
Outside Bucks: A Practical Guide to Raising Capital for a Business

9 Bus. L. Today 6 (July/Aug. 2000)

Raising capital is as important to the business of your clients as a good business plan. . . .

The financing history of start-up companies follows a predictable pattern, with money being raised from the same types of investors over and over and over. The regulatory scheme contemplates that financings will start small and grow larger. A typical equity investment cycle for a start-up company might be: issuance of founders' shares, sales to "friends and family," sales to a mixed bag of accredited and nonaccredited investors, venture capital financing (VC) and initial public offering.

Of primary importance is the need to keep your client's financing activities private in nature, . . . [in order to avoid] SEC registration of the offering, which can be costly and time consuming. . . .

[In connection with a private offering, your] client will at some point probably need some type of offering document whether or not it is required under the securities laws. A private placement memorandum (PPM) gives investors the same general type of information that registration would provide, which would include a description of your:

- market;
- business, products or services, properties, etc.;
- material legal proceedings;
- capitalization and securities being sold;
- management and principal shareholders;
- material risks;
- selected financial data and financial statements; and
- some type of discussion and analysis of the financial statement and operations.

Most start-ups begin by approaching investors with a business plan, which is a scaled down version of a PPM. Both a PPM and a business plan tell the story of the company and document disclosures made to investors. Both must convey credibility and accuracy, while at the same time generating excitement and enthusiasm. Both should be thorough, professional and realistic. And both must be concise.

Early-stage investors typically invest in a "concept" and do not require detail. Statements of fact should be supported as fact, and statements of opinion or belief must have a reasonable basis. When it comes to discussing risks and uncertainties, do not hide the ball from investors for to do so will impair the credibility of you and your client. For liability reasons, it is best to let your client write his or her own plan with the aid of your comments.

A PPM is not required for every offering. For reasons discussed [earlier], a business plan would be sufficient to raise "seed capital" under Rule 504 of Regulation D but, for example, if more than $1 million is raised in a 12-month period, such that the limitations of Rule 504 are surpassed, a PPM would be required to offer securities to nonaccredited investors in reliance on Rule 505 or Rule 506 below. An offering to "all accredited" investors by comparison does not require a PPM. But, even if not required, delivering a PPM or at least a detailed business plan is probably advisable for liability and marketing reasons.

Remember that even exempt transactions are subject to the antifraud provisions of the federal securities laws [primarily Rule 10b-5 of the 1934 Act]. Advise your client that he or she and the company will be responsible for false or misleading statements, whether oral or written. The SEC enforces the federal securities laws through criminal, civil and administrative proceedings. Some enforcement proceedings are brought through private lawsuits.

Depending on the size of the offering and the nature of the purchasers, more or less documentation may be required. Typical [disclosure] documents [used] in a private financing [will often] include:

- *Term sheet* — contains the essential terms of the investment and business terms of the transaction, such as type of security, valuation/price, liquidation preference, conversion rights, registration rights, pre-emptive rights/rights of first refusal, voting rights, seats on the board of directors and dividends [and/or]
- *Business plan or PPM* — describes the business, products/services, and risks and may provide financial information

* * *

Although term sheets are not always used, using one will likely save you time and money in the long run because a term sheet helps the parties focus on key issues that need to be documented.

In addition to documenting the business terms, in all private placements each purchaser must:

- represent that he or she is acquiring the securities for his or her own account (investment) and not on behalf of others;
- acknowledge that the securities received have not been registered under the federal securities laws and therefore are "restricted securities"; and
- agree that he or she will not dispose of them in the absence of registration or an available exemption.

In offerings premised on access to or receipt of financial and other information about the issuer, the purchaser also represents that:

- he or she had access to or received this information (as the case may be), and
- that he or she (or his or her adviser) is sufficiently sophisticated to understand the information.

To enforce restrictions on resale (and protect your exemption), you will put restrictive legends on the stock certificates and give "stop transfer" instructions to your transfer agent.

Advise your client to document the manner of the offering. To document the private nature of the transaction, your client should keep a log of to whom offering documents are sent and how many are sent. Sequentially number each offering document and send them only to purchasers that qualify to buy securities in your offering. Restricting and tracking your offerings in this manner may help later to prove that you did not violate the requirement (applicable to all private offerings) not to solicit the sale of your securities generally or use general advertising. Require investors to fill out an "Investor Questionnaire" documenting their status (sophisticated, accredited, etc.)

* * *

Representations and warranties are very important. They lay out a framework to come to a mutual understanding of the company and the financing before an investment is made. To the extent that the understanding is violated, the representations and warranties will provide investors with a basis for recovery. Therefore, it is important to be complete and, if there are exceptions, note them in a schedule of exceptions.

A few of the basic representations and warranties typically requested by investors are:

- status of your client as a legal business entity;
- proper authorization of the transaction and issuance of shares;
- assurances that your client owns the necessary assets or technology to operate its business;
- disclosure of material contacts; and
- that there are no undisclosed material liabilities or litigation.

Of primary interest to your client are representations and warranties establishing proper corporate and board of director authorization of the transaction, receipt by the investor of information regarding the issuer, the factual basis for the exemption relied on, and investor's understanding that the shares he or she receives are "restricted securities" as well as the investor's intention to hold the securities until eligible for resale.

"Due diligence" is the investigation necessary to reasonably assure that the documentation is accurate and complete and that all necessary issues have been adequately considered. You and your client have an obligation to conduct due diligence.

How much due diligence is required depends, in part, on the size of the deal and the issues raised. In smaller offerings, savvy investors and counsel will want to keep the due-diligence process simple, keeping in mind that start-ups have fewer documents to look at that are relevant to investors. Basic due-diligence items are likely to include:

- Charter documents (articles, bylaws and any amendments);
- Board of director minutes, resolutions, etc.
- Prior financing documents including any registration-rights agreement;
- Agreements with affiliates (voting agreements, rights of first refusal, etc.);
- Material contracts (such as leases, contracts with certain customers or suppliers, etc.); and
- Stock option agreements and other agreements potentially involving issuance of additional shares.

QUESTIONS

---

1. What kind of securities compliance documentation would you recommend that Joan and Michael prepare in the event they decide to *Go-It-Alone*?
2. Would this recommendation change if Joan and Michael decide to obtain the necessary start-up capital from *Friends and Family* (i.e., the seven investors described earlier in this chapter)?

Integration vs. Aggregation.   As we have seen, Section 3(b) authorizes the SEC to adopt exemptions for small offerings; that is to say, the SEC is empowered to exempt offerings of securities where the "aggregate amount" of such an offering does not exceed $5 million. For our purposes, the most significant rules that the SEC has promulgated pursuant to this authority are Rules 504 and 505 of Regulation D, Rule 701, and Regulation A (the latter two exemptions are described later in this chapter). Since both Rules 504 and 505 cap the dollar amount that the issuer may raise in a 12-month period, this requires the transaction planner to undertake what is commonly referred to as an "aggregation" analysis. In order to determine the dollar amount that is available to the issuer under the terms of either the Rule 504 or the Rule 505 exemptions, this cap is calculated by "aggregating":

(i) the offering price of all securities sold pursuant to either the Rule 504 or 505 exemptions; *plus*

(ii) the offering price of all securities sold in the prior 12 months in reliance on any of the Section 3(b) exemptions — that is, the dollar amount of securities sold in reliance on Rule 504, Rule 505 or Regulation A; *plus*

(iii) the offering price of *all* securities sold over the previous 12 months in violation of Section 5 — which is to say that the dollar amount of *non-exempt* unregistered offerings (i.e., offerings for which no exemption is available) will count towards the cap.

For purposes of Rule 504, the aggregate offering amount (using this calculation method) cannot exceed $1 million, and in the case of Rule 505 exempt offerings, the dollar cap is $5 million. It is important to distinguish *aggregation* analysis from the *integration* principle that we introduced earlier in this chapter, for the reasons that are set forth in the following excerpt:

> Students (and securities lawyers) often confuse aggregation with integration. The two are distinct. *Aggregation* involves a simple calculation of whether the amount to be financed in a 12-month period exceeds the Rule 504 or 505 dollar limit. *Integration* involves treating different offers and sales as a single offering — treated together they may (or may not) satisfy the conditions of the relevant exemption. Integration can happen, for example, without there being an aggregation problem. Suppose a $1 million intrastate offering to 20 in-state purchasers in January is followed by a $2 million Rule 505 offering to 20 out-of-state purchasers in March. If integrated, the combined offering would not satisfy the intrastate exemption (because of the out-of-state purchasers) or the Rule 505 exemption (if the 40 purchasers were nonaccredited). But, even if we aggregate the January and March offerings, the $5 million cap of Rule 505 would not be exceeded.

PALMITER, *supra*, at pg. 204 (emphasis in original). One final point: Integration is generally applied with the benefit of hindsight, as we shall see when we review the materials later in this chapter regarding Google's initial public offering (IPO). As a practical matter, this means that application of the integration principle, with the benefit of hindsight, may result in a violation of Section 5, and thus give the purchasers in this "illegal offering" a remedy (i.e., they can get their money back) under the express private cause of action set forth in Section 12(a)(1), a remedy that might not otherwise be available if one or more of the offerings were viewed as separate, independent transactions. The moral of the story is that the lawyer, as the transaction planner, must be sensitive as to how the client's past and present offerings, as well as any plans for future sales of securities, relate to one another in order to avoid problems under the integration principle.

Form D Filing.   Rule 503(a) has long required that a notice be filed with the SEC on Form D within 15 days after the first sale in reliance on any of the Regulation D exemptions. In 2008, the SEC mandated that Form D filings be done electronically. *See* Securities Act Release No. 8876 (Dec. 19, 2007), No. 8891 (Feb. 6, 2008). The primary purpose of this Form D filing obligation is to allow the SEC to track usage of the Regulation D exemptions. Generally, though, the failure to file this form in a timely manner will not jeopardize the validity of the issuer's Regulation D exemption, although it may lead to other consequences. *See* Rule 507 of Regulation D. In addition, the failure of the issuer to comply with *all* of the terms and conditions of Regulation D does not mean that the issuer's exemption is automatically lost, so long as the issuer can demonstrate that its failure to satisfy Regulation D was "insignificant" in accordance with the requirements of Rule 508. And, as a final reminder, even where a particular offering fails to satisfy the safe harbor provisions of Regulation D, it is still possible that the offering may fit within another exemption, such as a statutory private placement under Section 4(a)(2) or the wholly intrastate offering exemption available under Section 3(a)(11), although the recent lift of the ban on general advertising does not extend to either of these exemptions.

In July 2013, when the SEC adopted Rule 506(c) to lift the ban on general solicitation in connection with certain offerings, the SEC also modified Form D to add a box for issuers to check if they use general solicitation in a Rule 506 offering. A new box titled "Rule 506(c)" will be added for issuers relying on the new exemption, and the existing box currently titled "Rule 506" will be renamed "Rule 506(b)." In amending Form D, the SEC noted that it expected that this additional information would help with its efforts to analyze issuers' use of general solicitation in future Rule 506 offerings. In addition to making this change in the Form D filing obligation, the SEC also proposed further amendments to Form D (and related rules under Regulation D) that are designed to address the SEC's ongoing concern that the use of general advertising could lead to an increase in fraudulent activity and, more specifically, could result in unlawful sales of securities to non-accredited investors. *See* Securities Act Release No. 33-9416 (July 10, 2013) ("Amendments to Regulation D, Form D and Rule 156 under the Securities Act").

Accordingly, the SEC has proposed changes in Form D that are intended to enhance the SEC's "ability to evaluate the development of market practices in Rule 506(c) offerings and the potential risks for investors that may result from the use of general solicitation in those offerings." Sullivan & Cromwell, *Law Firm Memo, supra*, at pg. 15. Among other things, the SEC proposes to amend Rule 503 of Regulation D "to require an issuer intending to engage in general solicitation for a Rule 506(c) offering to file an initial Form D at least 15 calendar days *in advance* of commencing any general solicitation and to disclose information required by various items [of existing Form D]. The issuer would also be required to amend [its advance Form D filing] within 15 calendar days after the first date of sale of securities [in the issuer's] offering, [in order] to provide the remaining information required by [the existing] Form D." *Id.*

(emphasis in original). Notably, several knowledgeable commentators have expressed concern that the SEC's proposed amendments will add a significant compliance burden that will undermine the legislative mandate of the JOBS Act, which was to promote the capital raising process for the issuer community. *See, e.g.,* Stanley Keller, *General Solicitation: What Congress Giveth, the SEC Proposes to Taketh Away,* 27 INSIGHTS 15 (Aug. 2013); Jay G. Baris, David M. Lynn, and Anna T. Pinedo, Morrisson & Forester, LLP, *Client Alert: Goldilocks, Porridge, and General Solicitation,* (July 10, 2013) *available at* http://blogs.law.harvard.edu/corpgov/2013/07/19/goldilocks-porridge -and-general-solicitation/.

As of this writing (in fall 2013), the SEC has not taken final action with respect to these proposed amendments. However, it is worth emphasizing that the SEC's proposed amendments to Rule 503 would operate to extend the revised Form D filing obligation to be a requirement of *all* Rule 506 offerings; i.e., the SEC's proposed revisions to the Form D filing requirements would apply to *both* Rule 506(b) offerings and the new Rule 506(c) offerings. In addition, the SEC's proposed amendments would impose sanctions if the issuer fails to satisfy the new Form D filing requirements as to *any* Rule 506 offering.

"Bad Actor" Disqualifications.   Section 926 of the Dodd-Frank Act instructed the SEC to adopt rules that would make the Rule 506 exemption unavailable for any securities offering in which certain "felons" or other "bad actors" are involved. On July 10, 2013, at the same time that the SEC lifted the ban on general solicitation in connection with certain Rule 506 offerings, the SEC also adopted rules to implement Section 926 of the Dodd-Frank Act. *See* Release No. 33-9414 (July 10, 2013). Section 926 provides a list of disqualifying events that include the following, among other things:

- A criminal conviction involving certain securities and financial matters
- A court injunction (either state or federal) or restraining order related to certain securities and financial matters
- Certain SEC disciplinary orders
- A U.S. Postal Service false representation order

The new provisions, enacted by the SEC as part of new Rule 506(d), generally track those events listed in Section 926 of the Dodd-Frank Act and, most notably, also track the "bad actor" disqualification provisions imposed on Rule 505 offerings. Those persons who are subject to the provisions of new Rule 506(d) are referred to as "covered persons" and include (among others) the issuer, as well as its directors and certain officers; 20% beneficial owners of the issuer; and promoters of the issuer. The SEC's new rule also includes an exemption from the "bad actor" disqualification in those circumstances where the issuer can establish that it did not know and could not have known (exercising reasonable care) that a "covered person" who was subject to a "disqualifying event" participated in the issuer's offering. *See generally* Bradley Berman, *Dodd-Frank Update: SEC Adopts Bad Actor Disqualifications for Private Placements Under Regulation D,* Morrison & Foerster LLP, Client Alert (July 15, 2013) (*available at* http://www.mofo.com/files/Uploads/Images/130715-Bad-Actor -Disqualifications.pdf). It is worth emphasizing that the SEC's new Rule 506(d) extends the "bad actor" disqualifications to *all* Rule 506 offerings i.e., to *both* Rule 506(b) and (c) offerings.

By way of general summary, the following chart reflects the key terms and conditions of the Regulation D exemptions:

	Rule 504	Rule 505	Rule 506[(b)]
Issuer qualification	No reporting companies, investment companies, "development stage companies"	No investment companies, [no] issuers [who are] disqualified under ["bad actor" provisions of] Regulation A	No [issuers who are disqualified under "bad actor" provisions of new Rule 506(d)]
Dollar ceiling	$1,000,000 (12 months)	$5,000,000 (12 months)	No limit
Number of investors	No limit	35 + unlimited AIs [Accredited Investors]	
Investor qualification	None	None	Non-AI purchaser must be sophisticated (alone or with rep)
Manner of offering	General solicitations [prohibited — unless] shares issued (1) in state(s) that require registration and disclosure doc, (2) in state(s) where purchasers receive disclosure doc, (3) exclusively to AIs	General solicitations prohibited	[General solicitations prohibited]
Resale limitations	[Restricted, except] . . . if issuance meets conditions for [use of] general solicitations (see above)	Restricted	[Restricted]
Info requirements	None (other than state law)	None, if all purchasers are AIs. If some purchasers are not AIs, issuers must furnish information (see [Rule 502(b)]).	
Notice of sale	Form [D] required (file [electronically] . . . with SEC [15 calendar] days after first sale)		

PALMITER, *supra*, at pg. 209.

4. Restricted Securities and Rule 144

a. What Are "Restricted Securities"?

We have previously observed that the 1933 Act registers *transactions*, not the securities that are issued in the course of a registered offering. Likewise, the exemptions set forth in Sections 3(b) and 4 of the 1933 Act (and the SEC's rules thereunder) focus on the nature of the *transaction*. Thus, securities that are issued as part of an exempt financing transaction do not themselves become exempt. As a practical matter, this means that each time a security is resold, the seller must find a transaction exemption in order to avoid the costs and burdens associated with the Section 5 registration obligation.

In the case of securities sold in a registered public offering, the resales of such securities are generally covered by the "market trading" exemption found in Section 4(a)(1) of the 1933 Act, which exempts any transaction by a person "other than an issuer, underwriter, or dealer." However, in the case of securities sold in an exempt offering, the application of the Section 4(a)(1) exemption becomes more problematic if the proposed resale involves "restricted securities." For reasons that are explored in more detail as part of the basic securities regulation course, "restricted securities" are securities that were originally acquired as part of a "non-public distribution" i.e., a private transaction, and as such, may not be resold into the public trading market without registering the securities under Section 5 or finding an exemption for the resale. For our purposes, "restricted securities" are securities that were originally acquired in a Section 4(a)(2) private placement or in a Regulation D offering where the exemption relied on imposes resale limitations. As a practical matter, this means issuers will usually "seek to restrict the transferability of privately placed securities, . . . Typically, the purchase agreement in a private placement will contain transfer restrictions (noted on the security certificates), and the issuer will instruct its transfer agent (often a bank that keeps records on shareholder ownership) not to record any transfer unless it is shown the resale is not subject to the Securities Act's registration requirements." PALMITER, *supra*, at pg. 192.

How do holders of restricted securities dispose of their holdings? More often than not, persons holding "restricted securities" will rely on the exemption found in Rule 144, which, in essence, is in the nature of a safe harbor for the Section 4(a)(1) market trading exemption under the 1933 Act. Alternatively, these purchasers may have bargained for registration rights, which typically require the issuer to register the securities for resale under certain circumstances. We discuss "registration rights" in more detail as part of Chapter 10. For now, though, we focus on Rule 144 (including recent revisions that were made by the SEC), the scope of which is set forth in the next section.

b. Rule 144 and Its Recent Amendments

SEC Amends Rules 144 and 145 to Shorten the Holding Period Requirement for Affiliates and Non-affiliates

Cahill Gordon and Reindel, LLP
Firm Memoranda (Dec. 13, 2007) *

On December 6, 2007, the Securities and Exchange Commission ("SEC") amended Rules 144 and 145 under the Securities Act of 1933 (the "Securities Act") to[, among other things,] shorten the holding period required for restricted securities of reporting companies under Rule 144, . . . [1] As the SEC noted in the proposing release, the revisions are intended to increase the liquidity of privately sold securities and reduce companies' cost of capital, while maintaining investor protections.[2] These amendments will be effective February 15, 2008, and will apply to securities acquired before or after that date. . . .

I. Rule 144 and the SEC's Amendments

A. Rule 144

Any person selling a security which is not exempt from the registration requirements of the Securities Act must register the sale or rely on an exemption for the transaction. [Section 4(a)(1)] of the Securities Act provides an exemption for any person other than an issuer, underwriter, or dealer. Rule 144 provides a non-exclusive safe harbor from the definition of "underwriter" [for sellers of "restricted securities"]. If a selling security holder satisfies all of Rule 144's conditions, the security holder is deemed not to be an "underwriter" and therefore the sale transaction is exempt [under the market trading exemption of Section 4(a)(1)] from the Securities Act's registration requirements. [By way of general background, the terms of Rule 144 generally permit resales of "restricted securities" if all of the following requirements are satisfied:

- adequate current public information about the issuer is available;
- the selling security holder must have held the securities for a minimum period of time ("holding period");
- the number of shares sold must not exceed certain thresholds ("volume limitations");
- the securities must be sold in a certain manner, for example, in a transaction using a broker ("manner of sale conditions"); and
- the selling security holder must file a Form 144 when required ("notice provision").]

---

* *Available at* http://www.cahill.com/publications/firm-memoranda/00130/_res/id = Attachments/index = 0/SEC%20Amends%20Rules%20144%20and%20145.pdf.

1. *See Revisions to Rules 144 and 145,* SEC Release No. 33-8869; File No. S7-11-07 (December 6, 2007), *available at* http://www.sec.gov/rules/final/2007/33-8869.pdf. (the "Adopting Release").

2. *See Revisions to Rule 144 and Rule 145 to Shorten Holding Period for Affiliates and Non-affiliates,* SEC Release No. 33-8813; File No. S7-11-07 (June 22, 2007), *available at* http://www.sec.gov/rules/proposed/2007/33-8813.pdf.

B. Adopted Amendments to Rule 144

The SEC [has] adopted several changes to Rule 144 that shorten the holding period and modify other provisions of the Rule which sellers desiring to avail themselves of the Rule 144 safe harbor must meet. The [SEC's amendments] include:

1. *Amending the holding period for restricted securities*

Rule 144 previously required persons owning restricted securities[3] to hold the securities for at least one year prior to any resale in reliance on the safe harbor afforded by the rule. The new rule:

- shortens the holding period from one year to six months for restricted securities of reporting issuers.[4]
- maintains the current one-year holding period for restricted securities of non-reporting issuers.

* * *

2. *Reducing the resale restrictions on non-affiliates*

Under the previous rules, non-affiliates[5] were required to (1) hold their restricted securities for one year, and (2) comply with all applicable conditions of Rule 144 when selling securities [that] they had held between one and two years. The SEC's amendments reduce the restrictions on non-affiliates [i.e., purchasers of securities in a private placement who are *not* officers, directors or significant shareholders of the issuer] in two [important] respects:

- After the six-month holding period but before one year, non-affiliates holding restricted securities in reporting companies may resell them freely, subject only to the Rule 144(c) requirement that current information regarding the issuer of the securities be publicly available. [In other words, the manner of sale conditions, volume limitations, and notice provisions of Rule 144 do not apply to the resale of restricted securities by non-affiliates.]
- After satisfying a twelve-month holding period, non-affiliates of [reporting] issuers can resell their restricted securities freely.*

---

3. "Restricted securities" is defined in Rule 144(a)(3) generally as "securities acquired directly or indirectly from an issuer, or from an affiliate of an issuer, in a transaction or chain of transactions not involving any public offering." [In other words, "restricted securities" are securities acquired from an issuer (or an affiliate of an issuer) in a private offering or other exempt offering described in Rule 144.]

4. A company is a reporting issuer provided [that] "[t]he issuer is, and has been for a period of at least 90 days immediately before the sale, subject to the reporting requirements of section 13 or 15(d) of the Exchange Act and has filed all required reports under section 13 or 15(d) of the Exchange Act, as applicable, during the 12 months preceding such sale (or for such shorter period that the issuer was required to file such reports), other than Form 8-K." Rule 144(c)(1).

5. An "affiliate" is defined in Rule 144 as "a person that . . . , controls, or is controlled by, or is under common control with, [the] issuer." Rule 144(a)(1).

* After satisfying a twelve-month holding period, non-affiliates of *non-reporting* issuers can resell their restricted securities freely, i.e., without regard to any of the requirements of Rule 144.

[With these changes, the SEC hopes to make it easier for issuers to sell restricted securities by allowing the securities to be sold more quickly and be subject to fewer restrictions on such resales. By increasing the liquidity of shares acquired in private offerings, the SEC also hopes to decrease the cost of raising capital for the issuer community.]

* * *

QUESTIONS

1. Of the exemptions that we have discussed thus far, what exemption(s) would you recommend that SoftCo rely on?
2. What are the practical implications for SoftCo and its investors of issuing restricted securities to raise the necessary start-up capital?

---

5. The Crowdfunding Exemption: New Section 4(a)(6)

In response to the dismal hiring market and persistently high unemployment rates, as well as the difficulties that new businesses were having in finding necessary capital in the wake of the Great Recession, Congress enacted the JOBS Act in spring 2012 as part of an ongoing effort to "jump-start" the economy. As part of the JOBS Act, Congress authorized the "crowdfunding" of securities, as more fully described in the following excerpt:

Andrew A. Schwartz
Keep It Light, Chairman White: SEC Rulemaking Under the CROWDFUND Act

66 VAND. L. REV. EN BANC 43, 44-46 (2013)

Title III of the JOBS Act, known as the CROWDFUND Act, authorizes the "crowdfunding" of securities, defined as raising capital online from many investors, each of whom contributes only a small amount.[1] The Act was signed into law in April 2012, and will go into effect once the Securities and Exchange Commission ("SEC") promulgates rules and regulations to govern the new marketplace for crowdfunded securities. This Essay offers friendly advice to the SEC as to how to exercise its rulemaking authority in a manner that will enable the Act to achieve its core goals.

The purpose of the CROWDFUND Act was described by President Barack Obama at the signing ceremony in April 2012:

---

1. *See generally* Andrew A. Schwartz, *Crowdfunding Securities*, 88 NOTRE DAME L. REV. 1457 (2013). Title III of the JOBS Act "may be cited as the 'Capital Raising Online While Deterring Fraud and Unethical Non-Disclosure Act of 2012' or the 'CROWDFUND Act.'" Jumpstart Our Business Startups Act §301, Pub. L. No. 11-106, 126 Stat. 306 (2012) (codified in scattered sections of 15 U.S.C.).

Right now, [start-ups and small businesses] can only turn to a limited group of investors — including banks and wealthy individuals — to get funding. Laws that are nearly eight decades old make it impossible for others to invest. But a lot has changed in 80 years, and it's time our laws did as well. Because of [the CROWDFUND Act], start-ups and small business[es] will now have access to a big, new pool of potential investors — namely, the American people. For the first time, ordinary Americans will be able to go online and invest in entrepreneurs that they believe in.[2]

In other words, the Act has two primary goals. First, the Act seeks to create an ultralow-cost method for startup companies, small businesses, farmers,[3] and others to raise up to $1 million per year from the "crowd" (*i.e.*, the public).[4] Second, it aims to democratize the market for speculative business investments by allowing investors of modest means to make investments that had previously been offered solely to wealthy, so-called "accredited" investors. The Act operates by adding a new exemption [Section 4(a)(6)] to the Securities Act's registration requirement for crowdfunded securities.

Securities crowdfunding holds great promise for entrepreneurs and public investors who will be able to connect without going through the cumbersome and expensive initial public offering ("IPO") process. A possible downside, however, is that unsophisticated retail investors may be defrauded by con artists posing as entrepreneurs. Charlatans could potentially crowdfund up to $1 million from unsuspecting folks across the country — and then disappear with the money.

Congress was highly attentive to the possibility of fraud in crowdfunding and included in the Act a private right of action for defrauded investors as well as preserved the power of the SEC and state regulators to bring enforcement actions against wrongdoers. Beyond these traditional techniques, however, Congress also included an innovative structural protection for investors, specifically a strict annual cap on the aggregate amount that a person may invest in any and all crowdfunded securities.[5]

For most people, this cap will be five percent of their annual income, up to $5,000 per year.[6] So, for a person with the median American income of about $50,000, her maximum annual investment would be $2,500 per year. Were she to invest the maximum and lose everything to a judgment-proof con artist, it would be unfortunate, but affordable.

This annual investment cap is designed to shield investors from losses of devastating magnitude. It is practically impossible to lose one's "life savings" in crowdfunding, no matter how unwise or unlucky one's choices may be. By contrast, an investor can lose her life savings — quickly, easily, and legally — by investing in the stock market, gambling at a casino, or playing the state lottery.

The CROWDFUND Act's investment cap differs from the usual type of regulation found in federal securities laws. The usual way that federal law tries to protect investors is

---

2. Barack Obama, U.S. President, Remarks at JOBS Act Bill Signing (April. 5, 2012), *available at* http://www.whitehouse.gov/the-press-office/2012/04/05/remarks-president-jobs-act-bill-signing.

3. *See* Andrew A. Schwartz, *Rural Crowdfunding*, 13 U.C. Davis Bus. L.J. (forthcoming 2013).

4. Jumpstart Our Business Startups Act §302, 15 U.S.C.A. §77d(a)(6)(A) (West Supp. 2012).

5. *Id.* §77d(a)(6)(B).

6. These limits are for those with incomes below $100,000. *Id.* §77d(a)(6)(B)(i). For wealthier individuals, the limits are slightly more liberal. *Id.* §77d(a)(6)(B)(ii).

by mandating extensive public disclosure, both at the IPO stage and regularly thereafter. And indeed, the Act includes a number of disclosure requirements — and invites the SEC to add more. But for the SEC to mandate a great deal of additional disclosure does not make sense in the crowdfunding context for two reasons.

First, experience in the IPO market has shown that mandatory disclosures can easily push the cost of a securities offering out of reach for offerings of modest size.[7] For the type of small offerings authorized by the Act (under $1 million), extensive disclosure is simply not an economically viable option. The only way that crowdfunding can work is if the process is exceedingly inexpensive.

Second, most crowdfunding investors are unlikely to read or take notice of required disclosures in any event. In the context of registered, publicly traded companies, professional securities analysts read and analyze the disclosures they make and then convey the information in plain English to investors. But crowdfunding companies will be far too small to warrant professional analysis, so investors will be on their own to read and understand any disclosures they make. Furthermore, ample experience with consumer contracting teaches that online disclosures (such as "terms of service" to which one must click "I agree") are ignored by almost everyone.[8]

For both of these reasons, the SEC should resist the temptation to follow its usual course and promulgate long lists of required disclosures for crowdfunded securities. The whole crowdfunding project depends on a very simple and inexpensive process for offering securities, so it is vital that the SEC not burden the CROWDFUND Act with any more rules and regulations than are absolutely necessary. In short, this Essay's advice to the SEC is to rely primarily on the existing statutory scheme, especially the annual investment cap, and add just a few additional rules and regulations, for that would be the best way to achieve the statutory goals of creating a low-cost method of raising business capital and democratizing the market for investing in startup companies.

What does all this mean for start-up companies such as SoftCo? This same author goes on to predict that the CROWDFUND Act will have two primary effects on securities laws and capital markets:

> First, it will liberate startup companies, small businesses and others to use peer networks and the Internet to obtain modest amounts of business capital at very low cost. Second, it will help democratize the market for financing speculative startup companies and allow investors of modest means to make investments that had previously been offered solely to wealthy, so-called "accredited" investors. . . .

---

7. *See, e.g.,* Stuart R. Cohn & Gregory C. Yadley, *Capital Offense: The SEC's Continuing Failure to Address Small Business Financial Concerns,* 4 N.Y.U. J.L. & Bus. 1, 10 (2007) (suggesting that an IPO only makes economic sense when raising $20 million or more).

8. Florencia Marotta-Wurgler, *Will Increased Disclosure Help? Evaluating the Recommendations of the ALI's "Principles of the Law of Software Contracts,"* 78 U. Chi. L. Rev. 165, 168 (2011) (empirical study showing that fewer than one percent of consumers read end user license agreements); *see also, e.g.,* Omri Ben-Shahar & Carl E. Schneider, *The Failure of Mandated Disclosure,* 159 U. Pa. L. Rev. 647, 651 (2011) ("Although mandated disclosure addresses a real problem and rests on a plausible assumption, it chronically fails to accomplish its purpose. Even where it seems to succeed, its costs in money, effort, and time generally swamp its benefits."). It is possible, however, that consumer-investors may be more interested in crowdfunding disclosures than they have been in contract disclosures.

[As to how securities crowdfunding will impact founders' ability to raise capital, the author goes on to] predict that crowdfunding issuers may prefer to sell debt securities, such as bonds, rather than equity (i.e., stock), to the public. Selling stock to strangers, even only a minority interest, can lead to serious distractions for company founders/management. Shareholders can bring derivative actions against founders in their personal capacity, demand [to inspect] books and records, and propose shareholder resolutions. Bondholders, by contrast, can do none of these things. So there is a good reason to expect that debt will become the security of choice for those that raise capital under the CROWDFUND Act.

Andrew Schwartz, *Crowdfunding Securities: Two Novel Predictions*, The CLS Blue Sky Blog (June 26, 2013), *available at* http://clsbluesky.law.columbia.edu/2013/06/26/crowdfunding-securities. In Chapter 8, we will discuss in more detail the advantages and disadvantages of using debt financing as a source of capital for a start-up business such as SoftCo.

For another, perhaps slightly more jaundiced view as to the likely impact of the crowd-funding provisions of the JOBS Act, consider the following excerpt, in which one experienced securities lawyer explains "why crowdfunding is not all that it's cracked up to be":

Brian Korn
The Trouble With Crowdfunding

Pepper Hamilton LLP, Corporate and Securities Law Alert (April 17, 2013) *

The SEC has not yet released crowdfunding rules for public comment [as of Fall 2013], but many folks aren't waiting for that. At last count there were nearly 200 public comment letters and staff meetings about the subject on record with the Securities and Exchange Commission. That's the highest of any provision of [the] JOBS Act.

Meanwhile, the LinkedIn group "CrowdSourcing and CrowdFunding" has over 19,000 members and is brimming with minute-by-minute activity, eclipsing the roughly 1,400 members of the "IPO" group. It is impressive that a concept barely in the investor lexicon two years ago has captured the imagination and attention of so many.

Unfortunately, crowdfunding perception does not align with crowdfunding reality. Crowdfunding will not be able to deliver the grassroots fundraising ease for which so many seem to be hoping. After reviewing the enthusiastic postings of entrepreneurs and discussing the concepts in detail with financial and venture industry insiders, many observers believe there is a fundamental disconnect between the promise of crowdfunding, and the system that the SEC will put in place exercising its authority under the JOBS Act. Put another way, the risks, burdens and limitations of crowdfunding render it almost completely useless. And since crowdfunding targets individual investors, maybe that's a good thing.

---

* *Available at* http://www.pepperlaw.com/publications_update.aspx?ArticleKey = 2615.

Social Media Meets Corporate Finance

The promise of social media has made it possible for unknown people and ideas to become viral sensations overnight without spending money on traditional media or promotion. We've all see the Facebook posting of some puppy or kitten video that has managed to garner over 1 million "Likes." We have become a society of direct engagement through social media, including Facebook, Twitter, Instagram, LinkedIn, Spotify, and Pinterest. In [April 2013], the staff of the SEC's Division of Corporation Finance endorsed social media as a bona fide corporate disclosure tool under certain conditions. But until the JOBS Act, social media could not be used as an effective capital-raising tool without violating [the federal] securities laws.

Crowdfunding Gains Political Traction

Crowdfunding began with the concept of small enterprises engaging in online capital-raising through social media and raising funds from people they did not previously know (and were not likely to meet). The notion that small individual investors could have the same access to early-stage investment as large venture capital funds, combined with the enhanced ability of start-up companies to raise money beyond their "friends and family" group was a compelling reason for Congress to add crowdfunding to the JOBS Act. Congress even cleverly fashioned Title III of the JOBS Act as the "Capital Raising Online While Deterring Fraud and Unethical Non-Disclosure Act of 2012."

Despite its detractors, including then-SEC Chairwoman Mary Schapiro, Title III added a new exemption [new Section 4(a)(6)] from the registration provisions of the Securities Act of 1933 for crowdfunding transactions. The JOBS Act was signed into law by President Obama on April 5, 2012, following a 73-26 Senate vote. Unlike some of the other provisions of the JOBS Act, before crowdfunding is lawful the SEC must proposed and finalize additional rules. [As of] December 31, 2012 [the congressional] deadline [for SEC rulemaking], no rules have been proposed. . . .

As a result of [the legislative process], crowdfunding emerged in the final version of the JOBS Act with a much heavier set of regulatory, legal and procedural burdens than what had been originally proposed. [Consequently,] these statutory requirements effectively weight it down to the point of making the crowdfunding exemption under the JOBS Act utterly useless. When compared to other forms of private placements, crowdfunding is not a feasible option. Here are ten reasons why:

1. Crowdfunding caps an amount an issuer can raise to $1 million in any 12-month period.
2. Shares issued in crowdfunding transactions are subject to a one-year restricted period.
3. Non-U.S. companies, public-reporting companies (other than "voluntary filers") and investment companies (mutual funds, for example) are not eligible to crowdfund.
4. Crowdfunding caps the amount a person can invest in all crowdfundings over a 12-month period at 10 percent of annual income or net worth (incomes of $100,000 or more) or the greater of $2,000 or 5 percent of annual income or net worth (incomes of less than $100,000).

5. Crowdfunding must be done through a registered broker-dealer or registered "funding portal." Broker-dealers and funding portals may not solicit investments, offer investment advice or compensate employees based on sales. Traditional investment banks have not yet registered for crowdfunding, leading to speculation that crowdfunding will be facilitated by lesser-known financial institutions with little or no retail investment track record.

6. Crowdfunding requires a disclosure document to be filed with the SEC at least 21 days prior to first sale, and requires scaled financial disclosure, including audited financial statements for raises of over $500,000.

7. Unlike Regulation D Rule 506 private placements to accredited investors following the JOBS Act, crowdfunding does not allow advertising except solely to direct investors to the appropriate broker/funding portal.

8. Annual reports and possibly more frequent reports (depending on SEC rulemaking) must be filed with the SEC by a company which completes a crowdfunding round.

9. Legal prospectus liability will apply to disclosures, with a "knowledge" exception for misstatements or omissions.

10. Extensive due diligence is required, including background checks on management and large stockholders.

Better Ways to Raise Money

Despite the sound and fury, the crowdfunding exemption will do little to help small start-ups raise capital. That's because it will not be economically feasible for most companies to comply with the filing and disclosure requirements; take on the risk of legal liability; and undertake annual reporting obligations to raise a maximum of $1 million in a 12-month period. A company might as easily consider filing for an IPO and raise enough to cover its offering costs. As demonstrated by the chart below, it is difficult to imagine why a company would opt for crowdfunding instead of other, less burdensome, forms of private placements — for example, a Regulation D Rule 506 raise or a Regulation A+ raise (another creation of the JOBS Act).

Feature	Crowdfunding	Regulation A+	Regulation D Rule 506
Maximum Amount Allowed to be Raised	$1 million per 12-month period	$50 million per 12-month period	Unlimited
Number of Investors	Unlimited but subject to maximum total raised	Unrestricted	Unlimited accredited investors; up to 35 non-accredited investors
Maximum Investment per Investor	Restricted by income/ net worth	Unrestricted	Unrestricted
Investor Disclosure	Required, must be filed with SEC	Required, must be filed with SEC	Not required if all accredited investors

Feature	Crowdfunding	Regulation A+	Regulation D Rule 506
Intermediary Required?	Yes - broker/dealer or funding portal	No	No
Subject to ongoing SEC reporting following raise?	Yes, at least annually, possibly more frequently	Yes; at least audited financials filed annually	No
Disclosure Liability?	Yes, full disclosure liability with a knowledge exception	Yes, full disclosure liability with a knowledge exception	Only anti-fraud liability
Is Resale of Shares Restricted?	Yes, for one year	No	Yes, for public companies most can sell under Rule 144 after six months
State Filing Required?	Possibly, depends on future rules by state	No, if securities sold are listed on a national securities exchange or if sold only to "qualified purchasers"	Yes
Advertising and General Solicitation	Not allowed	Allowed	Allowed if sales are made only to accredited investors [under new Rule 506(c)]
Can Public Companies, Foreign Issuers, Investment Companies and Exempt Investment Companies use this Exception?	No	Yes	Yes

The reason many firms may not be able to complete a traditional private placement is that they cannot find enough accredited investors. Many fear that crowdfunding will push the least desirable and riskiest investments that cannot attract mainstream investor support out to the retail investor base, essentially passing on the riskiest slice of investments to those who can least afford the risk.

Whether you're a company or an investor, don't try this without legal advice either. The myth of easy capital raising through crowdfunding has overtaken the social media start-up marketplace. Compliance with the crowdfunding rules is harder than it may look.

As was noted in the proceeding article, Congress imposed a deadline of December 31, 2012 for the SEC to implement the crowdfunding provisions of the JOBS Act. As of this writing (in fall 2013), the SEC has failed to adopt *final* rules with respect to the use of securities crowdfunding. On October 23, 2013, however, the SEC *proposed* rules to implement new Section 4(a)(6), the new crowdfunding exemption created by Congress. *See* Securities Act Release No. 33-9470 (Oct. 5, 2013) [78 Fed.Reg. 66427], *available at* http://www.sec.gov./rules/proposed/2013/33-9470.pdf. The SEC's proposing release is quite detailed (over 550 pages) and the proposed rules are subject to a 90-comment period that ends February 3, 2014.

Briefly summarized, the proposed rules provide an exemption from the registration requirements of the Securities Act, effectively expanding the use of crowdfunding from a primarily donation-based system to a capital investment system. Although many observers view the proposed rules as a welcome development for companies seeking to raise money online by offering equity to a wide range of individuals (including non-accredited investors), the proposed rules also impose many conditions to the availability of the exemption. As a general proposition, these conditions are intended to mitigate the potential for fraud in the sale of illiquid crowdfunding securities to retail investors. Accordingly, among other things, the proposed rules:

- set forth eligibility criteria for issuers who seek to rely on the exemption;
- place limits on the offering size and the amount that any investor can invest in crowdfunding offerings over a continuous 12-month period;
- regulate the financial intermediaries necessary to conduct crowdfunding transactions;
- require companies to provide detailed disclosures to the SEC; and
- restrict the advertising and transfer of securities issued pursuant to the crowdfunding exemption.

It bears emphasizing that issuers and intermediaries may not rely on the crowdfunding exemption until the SEC adopts final rules for such offerings. In addition to the uncertainty created by the considerable delay in the SEC's rulemaking process, there is also the further concern as to whether the SEC's crowdfunding rules (as ultimately adopted) will be compatible with state securities laws. With respect to the usefulness of the Section 4(a)(6) exemption as proposed by the SEC, at least one set of experienced corporate lawyers has observed:

> The extent to which issuers utilize the crowdfunding exemption is likely to be driven largely by issuers' determination as to whether the exemption's benefits outweigh its limitations, requirements, and potential liabilities, including costs and burdens arising from the statutory liability of intermediaries, which is similar to that of underwriters in a registered offering. In addition, the success of the exemption will depend in part on whether potential investors in these offerings are willing to make investments that may carry high risk in securities for which there will likely be severely limited liquidity.

Gibson, Dunn, & Crutcher, LLP, Law Firm Memo, *SEC Proposes Rules to Implement Crowdfunding Exemption: What Factors Will Affect Its Success?*, (Nov. 11, 2013),

available at http://www.gibsondunn.com/publications/pages/SEC-Proposes-Rules-to
-Implement-Crowdfunding-Exemption-What-Factors-Will-Affect-ITS-Success.aspx.

Query: Would you recommend that SoftCo raise the start-up capital that it needs through crowdfunding? How would you advise SoftCo's founders, Joan and Michael, as to the advantages and disadvantages of using crowdfunding as a source of necessary capital? Do you agree with Professor Schwartz's assertion that "crowdfunding holds great promise for entrepreneurs" seeking start-up financing? Or do you think that "crowdfunding is not all that it's cracked up to be"?

6. Regulation A (and New "Regulation A+")

Regulation A.   Section 3(b) of the 1933 Act is generally known as "the small offering exemption" because it authorizes the SEC to exempt from registration securities offerings in an amount less than $5 million. Pursuant to Section 3(b), the SEC has promulgated Regulation A, which exempts "mini-public" offerings not exceeding $5 million in any 12-month period. In order to rely on this exemption, the issuer must file a fairly detailed offering statement (called a "Form 1-A") with the SEC for its review and comment. Form 1-A consists of a notification, offering circular, and exhibits. Regulation A is available, however, only to nonreporting U.S. and Canadian issuers that are not subject to the "bad boy" disqualifying provisions discussed earlier as part of our examination of the Rule 505 exemption under Regulation D.

As a "mini-public" offering, Regulation A offerings share many characteristics with offerings that are registered under Section 5 of the 1933 Act. For example, the issuer must provide prospective purchasers with an offering circular that is similar in content to the detailed prospectus that an issuer must prepare as part of an IPO that is registered under the 1933 Act. Like registered offerings, the issuer (and its financial advisors) can offer the securities publicly (i.e., using general advertising and general solicitation) and the securities are not "restricted," (i.e., they are freely tradable in the secondary market after the offering is completed).

By way of a brief summary, the excerpt below describes the principal advantages of relying on Regulation A rather than undertaking a registered offering in compliance with the requirements of Section 5:

- The financial statements are simpler and do not need to be audited.
- There are no Exchange Act reporting obligations after the offering (unless the company has more than $10 million in total assets and more than 500 shareholders).
- Companies may choose among three formats to prepare the offering circular, one of which is a simplified question-and-answer document.
- [The issuer] may "test the waters" (make limited general solicitations) to determine if there is adequate interest in [its] securities before going through the expense of filing [the Form 1-A] and review with the SEC.

* * *

[If the issuer does] "test the waters," it can use general solicitation and advertising prior to filing an offering statement with the SEC. This allows [the issuer] the advantage of determining whether there is enough market interest in its securities before running up significant legal, accounting and other costs associated with filing an offering statement [i.e., Form 1-A]. The [issuer] may not, however, solicit or accept money until the SEC staff completes its review of the filed offering statement and [the issuer delivers the] prescribed offering materials to investors.

Regulation A offerings historically have not been popular with investors, probably because there are other exemptions [most importantly, Regulation D] that are easier to use. However, because general solicitations are permitted in a Regulation A offering and are not permitted under other exemptions, Regulation A offerings have become slightly more popular as a means to offer securities over the Internet.

Barker, *Outside Bucks, supra*, at pg. 10. *Query*: Would you recommend that SoftCo rely on Regulation A to raise the necessary capital to launch its new business?

New Exemption: "Regulation A+."   As part of the JOBS Act, Congress added Section 3(b)(2) to the 1933 Act. This new section, which has been dubbed "Regulation A+," authorizes the SEC to exempt offerings of up to $50 million during a 12-month period. This new exemption, which has been described by Professor Robert Thompson of Georgetown Law School as "Regulation A on steroids,"* was clearly designed to breathe some new life into the long-neglected Regulation A exemption. So it should come as no surprise that the terms of this new exemption substantially parallel the existing Regulation A regulatory framework, but with three notable differences:

1. The offering limits are raised from $5 million to $50 million.
2. Securities sold under the new exemption are "covered securities" and not subject to state regulation through registration or qualification if they are offered and sold on a national securities exchange or they are offered and sold only to qualified purchasers, as defined by the SEC.
3. The issuer must file with the SEC audited financial statements annually.

As of this writing (fall 2013), "it is unclear whether the SEC will use its authority under Section 3(b)(2) to replace the existing Regulation A with a new exemption offering a much higher offering limitation, or retain the existing Regulation A and create an entirely new exemption. In either case, the Section 3(b)(2) exemption likely will prove to be a popular exemption once the SEC defines its contours." JAMES D. COX, ROBERT W. HILLMAN, AND DONALD C. LANGEVOORT, SECURITIES REGULATION: CASES AND MATERIALS (7th ed. 2013) at pg. 323.

7. *Rule 701 and the Google IPO*

Rule 701 provides the issuer with an exemption for offers and sales of its securities that are made pursuant to written employee (and director and consultant)

---

* *See* JAMES D. COX, ROBERT W. HILLMAN, AND DONALD C. LANGEVOORT, SECURITIES REGULATION: CASES AND MATERIALS (7th ed. 2013), at pg. 323.

stock compensation plans. For many start-up companies, Rule 701 is an important exemption because it allows for the issuance of employee stock options to a broader group of employees than would otherwise be available under the Section 4(a)(2) private placement exemption or Regulation D. This exemption is available only to private companies that are not subject to the reporting requirements of the 1934 Act.

By way of general background, the SEC substantially revised Rule 701 in 1999 in order to enhance its availability, as described in more detail in the following excerpt:

> In 1999, the SEC used its . . . authority [under Section 28 of the 1933 Act] to revise the exemption available to nonreporting companies that offer employee stock compensation plans. Rule 701. The maximum value of securities that can be sold under these plans is now $1 million, 15 percent of the issuer's total assets or 15 percent of the outstanding securities of that class — whichever is greater. . . . If more than $5 million worth of securities are sold, the issuer must provide to each employee-purchaser specific disclosure that includes a summary of the compensation plan, risk factors, and financial statements [of the type used in a Regulation A] offering. [The revised rule does not include offers (as opposed to sales) within the price ceiling.] The rule can be used to give stock compensation to consultants and advisers.

PALMITER, *supra*, at pp. 201-202.

Of equal importance, securities that are offered and sold pursuant to Rule 701 are not to be integrated with any other offer or sale, regardless of whether these offers and sales are registered or exempt. As a practical matter, this means that options issued under Rule 701 will not be integrated with other issuers' financing transactions, such as an ongoing Regulation D offering.

It bears emphasizing that securities issued pursuant to Rule 701 are deemed "restricted securities," and thus may be resold only pursuant to a registration statement or an exemption (which usually will be Rule 144, the general terms of which were described above).

The difficulties that can arise if the financing transaction fails to comply strictly with all of the terms and conditions of the relevant exemption are nicely illustrated by Google's experience in preparing its initial public offering (IPO) in 2004, which is described in the next set of materials.

QUESTIONS

1. How is the Rule 701 exemption fundamentally different from the other exemptions that we have discussed in this chapter (e.g., Regulation D, §4(a)(2), etc.)?
2. In what way will the Rule 701 exemption be useful to Joan and Michael's new business?

In the Matter of Google, Inc. and David C. Drummond

Admin. Proc. File No. 3-11795, January 13, 2005

CEASE-AND-DESIST PROCEEDING PURSUANT TO SECTION
8A OF THE 1933 ACT
before the
SECURITIES AND EXCHANGE COMMISSION
Securities Act of 1933
Release No. 8523 / January 13, 2005

I.

The Securities and Exchange Commission ("Commission") deems it appropriate that cease-and-desist proceedings be, and hereby are, instituted pursuant to Section 8A of the Securities Act of 1933 ("Securities Act"), against respondents Google, Inc. ("Google") and David C. Drummond ("Drummond") (collectively "Respondents").

II.

In anticipation of the institution of these proceedings, Google and Drummond have submitted an Offer of Settlement ("Offer") which the Commission has determined to accept. Solely for the purpose of these proceedings and any other proceedings brought by or on behalf of the Commission, or to which the Commission is a party, and without admitting or denying the findings herein, except as to the Commission's jurisdiction over them and the subject matter of these proceedings, which are admitted, Respondents consent to the entry of this Order Instituting Cease-and-Desist Proceedings, Making Findings, and Imposing a Cease-and-Desist Order Pursuant to Section 8A of the Securities Act of 1933 ("Order"), as set forth below.

III.

On the basis of this Order and Respondents' Offer, the Commission finds that:

A. Summary

1. Google, a Silicon Valley search engine technology company, issued over $80 million worth of stock options to the company's employees and consultants from 2002 to 2004 without registering the offering and without providing financial information required to be disclosed under the federal securities laws. As a result, Google employees and other persons accepted Google securities as part of their compensation without certain detailed financial information about the company. By issuing the options without registering the offering and without the legally required disclosures, Google violated the securities registration provisions of Section 5 of the Securities Act. As described below, Google's General Counsel, David C. Drummond, caused Google to violate these provisions.

B. Respondents

2. Google, Inc. is a Delaware corporation with its principal executive offices located in Mountain View, California. Founded in 1998, Google is an Internet search engine technology provider. On April 29, 2004, Google filed a registration statement for an initial public offering of securities with the Commission, which became effective on August 19, 2004. The company's common stock is registered with the Commission pursuant to Section 12(g) of the Exchange Act, and is quoted on the NASDAQ Stock Market.

3. David C. Drummond, age 41, resides in San Jose, California. Drummond is Google's General Counsel, Vice President of Corporate Development and Secretary. He is an attorney licensed to practice law in the State of California.

C. Facts

Legal Background

4. Under Section 5 of the Securities Act of 1933, a company cannot offer or sell securities to the public without first registering the offering with the Commission or having a valid exemption from registration. Registration ensures that potential investors will have detailed information about the issuer's finances and business, and allows the Commission to review the company's disclosures.

5. Rule 701 promulgated under the Securities Act provides an exemption from registration for certain issuers offering and selling stock options (or other securities) to employees and consultants under compensatory benefit plans. However, Rule 701 requires (among other things) that any company issuing more than $5 million in stock options over a 12-month period provide detailed financial statements and other disclosures to the option recipients. The Rule allows privately-held companies to compensate their employees with securities without incurring the obligations of public registration and reporting, while ensuring that essential information is provided to employees.

Google's Failure to Comply with Rule 701

6. Since its inception, Google has granted stock options to its employees and consultants as a form of compensation. Under Google's stock option plans, Google's Board of Directors granted the company's employees and consultants options to buy a certain number of Google unregistered shares at an exercise price set by Google's Board. Although the stock options were not registered, Google relied on Rule 701 of the Securities Act to exempt those securities from the registration requirements of the federal securities laws.

7. In September 2002, Google became aware that its continued issuance of stock option grants might reach levels requiring financial disclosures under Rule 701. Google temporarily stopped issuing stock grants. In contrast to its chief competitors, Google was a private company, and did not have to report its financial results and other significant business information to the public in filings with the Commission. Google viewed the public disclosure of its detailed financial information as strategically disadvantageous, as

Drummond recognized, and the company was concerned that providing option recipients with the financial disclosures required by Rule 701 could result in the disclosure of this information to the public at large and, significantly, to Google's competitors.

8. By January 2003, Google was again considering granting stock options to its employees. Drummond learned that the stock option grants being considered for approval by Google's Board might cause Google to grant more than $5 million worth of options in a 12-month period and therefore would require Google to provide option recipients with financial disclosures under Rule 701. Drummond, in consultation with outside counsel and personnel in Google's legal department, determined that other exemptions for certain of the stock option grants permitted Google to issue the option grants without registering the securities or providing disclosures otherwise required by Rule 701. For example, Rule 506 of Regulation D of the Securities Act exempts from registration certain sales to "accredited investors" (including investors meeting a particular level of net worth or annual income). Drummond also considered the potential applicability of Section [4(a)(2)] of the Securities Act, an exemption from registration for certain private securities offerings. Finally, Drummond determined that, even if it were later determined that his analysis of the applicability of other registration exemptions was incorrect, Google could make an offer of rescission to the option holders.

9. Drummond concluded that a sufficient number of options had been issued to Google's employees and executives who were accredited investors under Rule 506 to avoid exceeding Rule 701's $5 million threshold, at least for the immediate future.

10. Drummond attended a January 2003 meeting of Google's Board of Directors and advised the Board to approve a new stock option plan for employee and consultant option grants going forward. Drummond also advised that the Board issue stock option grants pursuant to that new stock option plan, which grants were to become effective when the plan became effective in February. Drummond did not report to the Board that issuing the new option grants might cause Google to exceed the $5 million disclosure threshold of Rule 701, and that Google would be relying on other exemptions from the registration requirements.

11. At the January 2003 meeting, Google's Board approved the new stock option plan and the option grants pursuant to that plan, and the additional options became effective on February 7, 2003. Contrary to Drummond's expectations, the option grants resulted in Google exceeding Rule 701's $5 million disclosure threshold. Even excluding option grants arguably exempt from registration under Rule 506, the dollar value of options granted by Google over the prior 12-month period exceeded $5 million. Google, however, failed to provide the financial disclosures and other information mandated by Rule 701. Absent compliance with Rule 701, the options issued during this 12-month period were not exempt from registration, and Google's securities issuance violated the registration provisions of Section 5.

12. Between February and May 2003, Google continued to issue additional stock options to its employees. By unanimous written consent, Google's Board approved additional stock option grants on February 28, 2003, March 31, 2003, April 24, 2003, and May 9, 2003. As a result of these option grants, the value of securities issued by Google during a 12-month period was approximately $11 million, far in excess of the $5 million disclosure threshold of Rule 701, yet Google did not provide the legally

required disclosures to the option recipients. Throughout this period, Google failed to monitor its stock option grant levels, and failed to determine whether the company was in compliance with Rule 701.

13. In approximately June 2003, Drummond learned that Google probably had exceeded the $5 million disclosure threshold of Rule 701. Drummond further believed that there were not likely to be enough stock option recipients who qualified as accredited investors to render the securities exempt from registration, and thus the company could not avoid the disclosure obligations of Rule 701 by relying on Rule 506.

14. Drummond believed that Google's stock option grants might be exempt under Section [4(a)(2)] of the Securities Act, an exemption available for certain private placements of securities.

15. At a June 2003 meeting, Google's Board of Directors adopted two new stock option plans allowing for the issuance of additional options beginning in July 2003. Drummond discussed the need for the stock option plans, but he did not advise the Board that Google's option grants would exceed the $5 million disclosure threshold of Rule 701 or of the risk that other exemptions from registration may not apply. Based in part on Drummond's advice, Google issued additional options in the months following the Board approval exceeding the $5 million disclosure threshold.

16. Google's option grants did not qualify for exemption under Section [4(a)(2)]. Among other things, Google offered millions of dollars worth of stock options to all of its employees without considering the financial sophistication of each employee, and did not provide its employees with the information found in a registration statement.

17. For the twelve months ended December 31, 2003, Google issued approximately $49 million worth of stock options. Pursuant to the stock option plans adopted in June 2003, Google issued an additional $33 million worth of options in the first four months of 2004, prior to the company's filing of a registration statement for its initial public offering. None of these option grants were accompanied by the disclosures required by Rule 701.

18. On August 4, 2004, Google filed a Form S-1 with the Commission to register a rescission offer for the stock option grants and the purchase of shares upon the exercise of options made between September 2001 and June 2004 to Google's employees and consultants. The Form S-1 was declared effective on November 24, 2004. However, the rescission offer does not cure a violation of Section 5.

D. Legal Conclusion

19. Section 5(a) of the Securities Act prohibits the use of any means or instruments of transportation or communication in interstate commerce or of the mails to sell a security unless a registration statement is in effect as to such security. Section 5(c) of the Securities Act prohibits the use of any means or instruments of transportation or communication in interstate commerce or of the mails to offer to sell or offer to buy a security unless a registration statement has been filed as to such security.

20. Google offered to sell and sold its securities without a registration statement filed or in effect and without a valid exemption from registration. As a result of the conduct described above, Google violated, and Drummond caused Google to violate, Sections 5(a) and 5(c) of the Securities Act. The Commission previously has charged attorneys for

causing Section 5 violations. *See, e.g.,* In the matter of John L. Milling, Esq., Securities Act Rel. No. 33-8189 (Feb. 3, 2003).

E. Cooperation

21. In determining to accept Google and Drummond's offer of settlement, the Commission took into account their cooperation during the Commission staff's investigation.

IV.

In view of the foregoing, the Commission deems it appropriate to impose the sanctions agreed to in Respondents' Offer.

Accordingly, it is hereby ORDERED, pursuant to Section 8A of the Securities Act, that Respondents Google and Drummond cease and desist from committing or causing any violations and any future violations of Sections 5(a) and 5(c) of the Securities Act. By the Commission.

Jonathan G. Katz
Secretary

NOTES AND QUESTIONS

1. What was the nature of the problem that Google faced in connection with its IPO?
2. Based on the allegations contained in this settled order, why do you suppose the SEC brought this proceeding against Google's lawyer?
3. With respect to item 18 in the SEC's Order, why do you suppose that, to the best of our knowledge, no investors sought to rescind their purchase of Google stock?
4. What are the lessons to be learned from Google's experience?
5. What should lawyers do in the future when they find themselves in a situation similar to that of Google's lawyer (Drummond)?
6. As part of the SEC press release announcing the cease-and-desist order set forth above, Helane Morrison, then serving as the District Administrator of the Commission's San Francisco District Office, was quoted as saying, "Attorneys who undertake action on behalf of their company are no less accountable than any other corporate officers. By deciding Google could escape its disclosure requirements, and failing to inform the Board of the legal risks of his determination, Drummond caused the company to run afoul of the federal securities laws." SEC Press Release 2005-06 (Jan. 13, 2005). *Query:* What do these comments suggest is the proper role for the lawyer in ensuring that his or her client conducts its business and financial affairs in compliance with relevant provisions of the federal securities laws?

As you reflect on these questions, you may want to consider the insights offered by the author of the following article, who is himself an experienced securities lawyer:

Stanley Keller
Securities Enforcement: Searching Google for Meaning — Equity Compensation Pitfalls and a Changed Climate for Lawyer Responsibility

19 InSights 2 (August 2005)

Almost 20 years ago, I wrote an article on the so called no harm, no foul exemption frequently used by private companies before they become public to grant equity awards to employees.[1] In that article, I noted the need for the SEC to adopt a targeted exemption that would put private companies on a par with public companies that are able to use Form S-8 and, as a by-product, make honest people out of these companies and their lawyers. This article and follow-up on discussions with the SEC contributed to the adoption of Rule 701 (which, interestingly, went beyond my somewhat tentative suggestions).[2] Rule 701 was subsequently expanded and has become a highly useful exemption for equity awards by private companies, at least when used correctly.[3] However, it has its limitations.

Some 10 years later, I wrote an article that, among other things, identified ways to combine several exemptions to go beyond the then existing limits of Rule 701 without requiring registration under the Securities Act of 1933 and resulting public reporting under the Securities Exchange Act of 1934 (and, in today's parlance, becoming an "issuer" for purposes of the Sarbanes-Oxley Act of 2002).[4] These exemptions included, in addition to Rule 701 (which was then subject to a $5 million annual dollar limitation), (1) use of the private offering exemption, either under the statutory Section [4(a)(2)] exemption or the safe harbor under Rule 506 for accredited investors (such as executive officers) and up to 35 nonaccredited investors;[5] (2) Regulation S for offshore employees and, for good measure; (3) Regulation A for offerings of up to $2,500,000. Since the 1999 amendments to Rule 701 eliminating the $5 million annual limitation and substituting an information requirement, Rule 504 can be added to the list.[6]

This background is helpful because the recent enforcement action against Google and its general counsel involved, according to the SEC, use of the "no harm, no foul

---

1. Keller, "Employee Equity Incentive Arrangements," 19 *The Review of Securities and Commodities Regulation* 156 (June 25, 1986). I referred to it as the "see no evil, hear no evil, speak no evil" exemption, but it had the same import.

2. Release No. 33-6768 (Apr. 14, 1988).

3. Release No. 33-7645 (Feb. 25, 1999). *See also* Plimpton, "Form S-8 and Rule 701: Opportunities Shrink and Expand," 13 *Insights* No. 5, p. 7 (May 1999).

4. Keller, "When the Pay Includes Stock: An Overview of Employee Equity Compensation," *Business Law Today,* Nov./Dec. 1995, and "Overview of Employee Equity Compensation," *ALI-ABA Course of Study, Tax, Business and Succession Planning for the Growing Company* (Mar. 6, 1997).

5. Because the information requirements of Regulation D will be triggered for non-accredited investors, the Rule 506 exemption usually will be relied on only for accredited investors.

6. The amendment of Rule 701 in 1999 eliminating the dollar limitation was adopted pursuant to the SEC's blanket exemptive authority under Section 28 of the Securities Act, thus eliminating it as a Section 3(b) exemption that would be aggregated with the Rule 504 limit. See n.3 *supra*.

exemption" in awarding a large number of Google employees and consultants stock options allegedly without compliance with Rule 701 or any other exemption from registration. Therefore, according to the SEC, it resulted in violations of Section 5 of the Securities Act.[7] In fact, there was "no harm, no foul" to the Google option holders because of the substantial appreciation realized on the Google public offering. However, the same cannot be said for Google or its general counsel, both of whom suffered at least reputational harm. The Google enforcement order is instructive with respect to the SEC's attitude both toward strict compliance with Section 5 in the context of equity compensation awards by non-public companies and on the role and responsibility of counsel. It also indicates that the effort to produce an effective exemption for equity awards by private companies is not complete.

Background of the Google Offering

The Google 2004 IPO was one of the most successful and innovative offerings in recent years. It used a unique auction process and set new standards for electronic offerings. It also was something of a poster-boy for classic IPO problems, including gun jumping due to the notorious Playboy interview with the Google founders and a rescission offer for its stock options issued in violation of Section 5 of the securities Act. There were also issues of failure to register under Section 12(g) of the Exchange Act as a result of the number of option holders exceeding 500.

The Enforcement Order

Google and its general counsel consented to an enforcement order to cease and desist from further violations of Section 5. The facts are somewhat sketchy because they are derived from the agreed upon consent order. Therefore, there are many details of what happened that we just do not know.

The proceeding against the general counsel has raised the predictable concern among the bar, particularly since the general counsel was sanctioned for actions ostensibly taken in his capacity as a lawyer for the company after consulting outside counsel. However, a close reading of the order and subsequent statements by senior SEC officials indicates the presence of two critical elements that formed the basis for the SEC's proceeding against the general counsel: (1) advice that the SEC viewed as outside the bounds of reasonableness and, in fact, even as reckless disregard of legal compliance; and (2) actions by the lawyer as decision maker as opposed to adviser to the client.[9] As to the first element, the order refers to reliance on the absence of harm; as to the second, the order repeatedly notes the failure to inform the board of the risks of violating Section 5. Indeed, these references can also be viewed as the SEC's emphasizing the failure of the general counsel to observe proper corporate governance principles and to fulfill his professional responsibility to report possible securities law violations to the board.

---

7. *In the Matter of Google, Inc. and David C. Drummond,* Release No. 33-8523 (Jan. 13, 2005).
9. *See* n.17 *infra.*

Let's examine in more detail the two issues of (1) compliance with Section 5 in the award of equity to employees and consultants and (2) the responsibility of counsel.

Alternatives for Equity Awards Compliance

Google's problem was that its growth as a private company caused it to exceed the $5 million outstanding award threshold under Rule 701 (as it was amended in 1999) that required it to provide specified information to optionees including summary financial information in order to comply with the exemption. This disclosure, which understandably could not be counted on to remain confidential, would have deprived Google of a strategic advantage of being private. The only choice, absent an exemption from registration, would have been to curtail equity awards. This choice could have harmed the business and was inconsistent with Google's culture. Thus, Google faced a Hobson's choice, which drove the effort to find a solution in an exemption apart from Rule 701.

In the description in its August 18, 2004, IPO prospectus of the rescission offer to options and holders of shares acquired on the exercise of options, Google stated that it relied on the Section [4(a)(2)] private offering exemption but, because of the uncertainties associated with that exemption, it may have violated the securities Act. The SEC was more direct in the enforcement order, finding that Google's option grants did not qualify for the [Section 4(a)(2)] exemption and that it therefore violated Section 5 of the [1933] Act.[10]

Rule 701 was not relied on by Google because of the requirement to provide certain information about the issuer, including financial statements and risk factors, if more than $5 million in awards are made in any 12-month period and, in the case of options, any shares are issued upon exercise of the options during that period. Google had a large option program under which options were both exercised and outstanding so that by 2003 it was clear that the $5 million threshold for the need to provide information was exceeded. Rule 701, as amended, still has a limitation on the total amount of awards that may be made in reliance on it in a 12-month period but this limitation, which is based on total assets and percentage of outstanding shares, was not relevant to Google due to its size.

* * *

The Google experience suggests the need for the SEC to revisit whether the information requirement of Rule 701 really serves a necessary purpose in the compensatory context in view of the strategic disadvantages of the disclosure imposed on a private company. As the timeframe and size threshold for companies to go public increases due to market conditions and the expanded burdens imposed by the Sarbanes-Oxley Act, more private companies will face the dilemma Google confronted. . . .

* * *

---

10. Interestingly, the leading decision on the requirements for a private offering exemption under Section [4(a)(2)] involved offerings to employees. *See SEC v. Ralston Purina Co.*, 346 U.S. 119 (1953).

Attorneys as Enforcement Target

A significant aspect of the Google enforcement action is that the SEC targeted Google's general counsel for what ostensibly appears to have been legal judgments. However, the SEC's proceeding against Google's general counsel is best understood in the context of two strands of recent public statements by SEC officials.

The first is the SEC's stated emphasis on gatekeepers, such as lawyers, because, in the words of SEC officials, gatekeeper cases provide the "best bang for the buck" given a gatekeeper's ability to prevent numerous cases of fraud.[13] The other strand is found in statements of SEC officials explaining the Google enforcement action as relating to a combination of reckless disregard for legal compliance and the lawyer functioning as decision maker since he failed to disclose the legal risks to a higher corporate authority — the board in the case of Google.

. . . The [SEC's current] emphasis on enforcement actions against "gatekeepers," finding attorneys to be the "cause" of a violation,[15] and the adoption of [the SEC's] Rules of Professional Conduct[16] have changed the ground rules by which attorneys must play in the post-Sarbanes-Oxley era.

When lawyers themselves are actively involved in violations, there is no exemption from enforcement, and this has always been the case. What has changed is a greater willingness of the SEC to find a lawyer to be a participant in the violation and a need for lawyers to be more aware of their responsibilities in rendering advice to companies regarding legal compliance.

The most recent articulation of the SEC's current approach to enforcement actions against lawyers, especially in-house counsel, is found in an important and thoughtful speech by SEC General Counsel Giovanni Prezioso given April 28, 2005, to the Association of General Counsel, but only recently posted on the SEC's web site.[17]

General Counsel Prezioso notes the competing policy considerations involved regarding the central role lawyers play in preventing securities law violations, on the one hand, and the need to avoid chilling zealous advocacy and the ability of lawyers to advise clients without fear about the lawyer's own liability, on the other. This requires a delicate balance, which Prezioso states the SEC seeks to achieve by having greater involvement by the Office of the General Counsel in cases against lawyers.

His remarks emphasize the need to distinguish between SEC action sanctioning lawyers for violation of professional conduct standards and for participating as a principal in a securities law violation. In the first case, the emphasis is on the lawyer as adviser, while in the second it is primarily the lawyer as decision maker, although it can sometimes also involve the lawyer as adviser.

---

13. *See, e.g.*, statement of David Kornblau, Chief Litigation Counsel, SEC Division of Enforcement, at the PLI's 2005 SEC Speaks Conference, SEC Today, Mar. 11, 2005.

15. *See, e.g., SEC v. Fehn*, 97 F.3d 1276 (9th Cir. 1996); *SEC v. Woghin*, 04 Civ. 4087 (E.D.N.Y. Sept. 22, 2004); *In the Matter of Stanley Silverstein*, Release No. 34-49676 (May 11, 2004); *In the Matter of David C. Watt*, Release No. 34-46899 (Nov. 25, 2002).

16. *See* SEC Release No. 33-8185 (Jan. 29, 2003), adopting the final Part 205 Rules of Professional Conduct.

17. Prezioso, "Remarks before the Spring Meeting of the Association of General Counsel" (Apr. 28, 2005), located at *http://www.sec.gov/news/speech/spch042805gpp.htm.*

As an adviser, a lawyer is unlikely to be sanctioned for bad advice, even if that advice is negligent. On the other hand, if the lawyer knows the advice to be wrong or even is reckless in disregarding whether there is a violation, the lawyer can become a participant in the violation.

When the lawyer becomes the decision maker, he can be subject to enforcement like any other person. The failure to bring legal risks to the attention of an appropriate authority within the corporation can be an indicator that the lawyer is a decision maker rather than a legal adviser.

The Action Against Google's General Counsel

The Google enforcement action involved a combination of: (1) legal advice that, according to the consent order, appears to be outside the bounds of reasonableness amounting to reckless disregard of legal compliance; and (2) the lawyer as decision maker because of his failure to bring the legal risks to the board as the appropriate authority in connection with that matter.

If Google's general counsel had brought the legal risks to the attention of the board, it would have been a more difficult case, at least against the general counsel. If he fairly described the legal risks, and the board nevertheless authorized proceeding, it seems likely that he would not have been sanctioned as a violator. Even in those circumstances, however, the general counsel still would have had professional obligations, which could have included withdrawing from involvement in the matter and so informing the board, or even potentially resigning. Alternatively, if Google's general counsel had given reasonable legal advice in good faith that there was a basis, albeit not a certainty, for a claimed exemption from registration, even if that advice turned out to be wrong, and the board, based on that advice, chose to proceed, I believe he similarly would not have been sanctioned. We just do not know from the consent order whether Google's general counsel in fact, after consulting outside counsel, believed there was a legitimate basis for an exemption.[18] However, in view of the legal risks involved, the failure to bring those risks to the attention of the board when they were authorizing the option plan left Google's general counsel in the position of making the decision to proceed, and resulted in the SEC's decision to bring the enforcement action against him.

The failure to bring wrongdoing and consequent legal risks to the attention of an appropriate higher authority within the corporation, even when the lawyer's legal advice is not involved, also can form the basis for a securities law violation, as well as a violation of the SEC's Rules of Professional Conduct. Thus, in a proceeding against the general counsel of Electro Scientific Industries, Inc., the failure of that general counsel to inform the audit committee and auditors of the improper elimination of a pension plan expense as a result of an invalid termination of a foreign plan, enabling the company to make its numbers, was asserted to be a violation.[19] By permitting the improper accounting to continue, the general counsel became a cause of the company's violation.

---

18. One might surmise from the hypothetical used at the outset of Prezioso's speech that Google's outside counsel might have advised that the existence of an exemption from registration was doubtful.

19. *In the Matter of John E. Isselmann, Jr.*, Release No. 34-50428 (Sept. 23, 2004). Presumably, the SEC did not claim a violation of the Rules of Professional Conduct because the failure to report up occurred before those rules became effective. This enforcement action shows that a failure to report, under certain

Difficulties in Applying the SEC's Enforcement Policy

Although these principles appear straightforward, as General Counsel Prezioso acknowledges, difficult issues can exist in separating out (1) when the lawyer is engaged in advising and when he is making or substantially influencing the decision and (2) when the advice is being rendered in good faith and on a reasonable basis, even though it involves close calls, and when the advice is beyond the bounds of reasonable judgment. These determinations are especially difficult in the securities disclosure context, where the lawyer's role is central and tough materiality decisions and judgments regarding fair presentation are involved.

If the chilling of zealous advocacy is to be avoided and the ability of the corporate client to obtain disinterested legal advice is to be preserved, the SEC will have to keep these important policy objectives in mind and continue to exercise appropriate restraint in deciding when to pursue enforcement actions against lawyers, no matter how tempting leveraging the role of "gatekeepers" may be. This is not to question the appropriateness of the action against Google's or Electro Scientific's general counsel. Rather, it is to recognize the realistic difficulties in applying the principles outlined by General Counsel Prezioso and the consequences of appropriate restraint not being exercised by the SEC in deciding when to bring enforcement actions against lawyers in connection with their legal judgments.

Given the enhancement of disclosure processes and legal compliance procedures that have been put in place following enactment of the Sarbanes-Oxley Act, compliance with those procedures should be factors that permit the SEC to give the benefit of the doubt to lawyers who advise and reach legal conclusions in good faith, so long as they do so within the bounds of reasonable judgments and without disregard for the consequences of violations. Thus, the vetting of disclosure decisions with the company's disclosure committee, even though the lawyer is playing an active, and maybe even an influential role, should go some distance toward establishing that the lawyer was acting in a legal advisory capacity. Similarly, bringing difficult legal compliance issues to an appropriate higher level in the corporation, sometimes to the board or a board committee, should be a strong indicator that the lawyer is performing as legal counselor and thereby avoiding exposure as a violator. In this way, avoiding sanction as a participant and compliance with professional conduct obligations can be harmonized.

* * *

Conclusion

. . . There is a greater public demand in the post–Sarbanes-Oxley era for "gatekeepers" to meet their professional responsibilities. As a result, the SEC, with its stepped up enforcement efforts and its charge from Congress to oversee the professional conduct of lawyers, is more willing to sanction lawyers as participants in violations and for failure to comply with professional standards. Operating with these lessons as guiding principles

---

circumstances, can also constitute participation in a violation, apart from a violation of the Rules of Professional Conduct.

will go a long way toward meeting our legal and professional obligations, serving our client's interests and avoiding the pitfalls of regulatory sanctions.

NOTES AND QUESTIONS

1. In Chapter 6, we describe the mechanics of equity-based compensation in more detail. The discussion in Chapter 6 highlights tax and accounting issues, but it is always necessary for the company's lawyer to remember that equity-based compensation involves the offer and sale of securities to a potentially large group of potentially very unsophisticated people.

2. In what way does the SEC's proceedings against Drummond add to our understanding regarding where we should draw the line between purely "legal" vs. purely "business" decisions? As a practical matter, is there such as a thing as a "purely business" decision? This was a topic that we briefly touched on in Chapter 1. Does the case that the SEC brought against Google and its lawyer cause you to reconsider your views on this issue? How easy is it for the lawyer to "change hats" within the context of a board meeting?

3. As a public policy matter, why would the SEC use its (scarce) administrative resources to bring these proceedings against Google and its lawyer?

4. Do you agree with the author that there is a "gap" that needs to be filled for those companies that fear relying on the §4(a)(2) exemption but need to raise more than $5 million? How do you balance (the competing considerations of) the investor's need for disclosure while also protecting the company's competitive advantage?

5. The SEC's proceedings were based on facts that occurred before the SEC adopted its set of professional responsibility rules, generally referred to as Part 205, which was promulgated pursuant to the Congressional mandate set forth in SOX. 17 C.F.R. §§205.1-205.7. If these regulations had been effective, what would be required of Google's lawyers in order for the lawyers to have satisfied the requirements of Part 205?

6. Why do you suppose that Drummond did not inform Google's board of directors? Did that benefit Google in any way?

7. What do you think are the lessons that can be learned from the SEC's proceedings against Google and its lawyer?

8. Recall our discussion of the professional responsibility rules in Chapter 1. Following the SEC's proceedings against Drummond, we see that the lawyer's failure to observe gatekeeper responsibilities in our post-SOX era can lead not only to disciplinary proceedings by the Bar, but also sanctions can now be imposed by the SEC under certain circumstances. *Query*: How do the reforms adopted by SOX and the SEC's professional responsibility rules promulgated thereunder affect you as the lawyer for SoftCo?

C. Role of the Lawyer After SOX in Planning Financing Transactions

Mitchell E. Herr & Stephen P. Warren
Lawyer Liability: Why the SEC Should Clarify Policy on Its Actions Against Attorneys for Advising Clients

21 CORP. COUNS. WEEKLY (BNA) 200 (June 28, 2006)

For the last 25 years, the Securities and Exchange Commission has been exceedingly cautious about bringing actions challenging attorneys' legal advice and has repeatedly affirmed that it will not proceed against attorneys for mere professional negligence. Indeed, there has been a broad consensus that it would be an inappropriate exercise of its prosecutorial discretion for the SEC to do so. This consensus is grounded in the concern that suing securities attorneys for mere professional negligence would chill their exercise of independent judgment and cause them to pay undue attention to their self-preservation as they resolve the close questions of professional judgment that are their daily fare.

However, the SEC's recent decision in *In re Ira Weiss*[1] has the potential to create considerable confusion about whether the SEC has reversed course and now intends to sue securities lawyers whose mere professional negligence results in violations of the federal securities laws. If the SEC did not intend to reverse its course of the last 25 years — and presumably it did not — it should issue a formal policy statement clarifying its intent. In the absence of such a clarification, the *Ira Weiss* decision is bound to cause mischief in the SEC's enforcement program.

History of SEC Policy

Any discussion of the SEC's enforcement policy towards securities lawyers must start with its seminal 1981 decision in *Carter and Johnson*.[2] There, the SEC reversed an initial decision by an Administrative Law Judge that sanctioned two attorneys under former SEC Rule of Practice 2(e)[3] for aiding and abetting their client's violations of the federal securities laws by failing to correct misstatements contained in its press releases and SEC filings. In absolving the attorneys, the SEC made clear that it did not intend to sanction lawyers who make negligent errors in counseling their clients, even if those errors lead to, or fail to prevent, securities violations:

> If a securities lawyer is to bring his best independent judgment to bear on a disclosure problem, he must have the freedom to make innocent — or even, in certain cases, careless — mistakes without fear of legal liability or loss of the ability to practice before the Commission.

Over the years, the SEC, its commissioners, and its general counsel have reiterated this policy. For instance, in 1996, SEC Commissioner Norman Johnson stated that the *Carter and Johnson* decision "viewed the practice of law as to allow even negligence, as

---

1. 2005 WL 3273381 (Dec. 2, 2005).
2. 1981 WL 384414 (Feb. 28, 1981).
3. Now SEC Rule of Practice 102(e), 17 C.F.R. §201.102(e).

necessary to accomplish the Commission's larger purposes."[4] As recently as April 2005, SEC General Counsel Giovanni Prezioso stated that "the Commission ordinarily will not sanction lawyers under the securities laws merely for giving bad advice, even if that advice is negligent and perhaps worse."[5]

SEC's Current View

In September 2004, the Director of the SEC's Division of Enforcement warned that the SEC would target lawyer "gatekeepers" in its enforcement investigations:

> [P]ursuing gatekeepers [is] the most targeted and effective way of using the agency's limited enforcement resources. . . . Consistent with Sarbanes-Oxley's focus on the important role of lawyers as gatekeepers, we have stepped up our scrutiny of the role of lawyers in the corporate frauds we investigate.[6]

Since that speech, the SEC has brought a number of settled enforcement proceedings against attorneys based on their performance as lawyers.[7]

Most of these cases were brought against in-house general counsel of public companies who allegedly aided and abetted their company's securities violations.[8] Because aiding and abetting liability requires an actual awareness of improper conduct,[9] these cases are not grounded in mere professional negligence.

Additionally, the SEC recently brought two widely reported settled cease-and-desist proceedings against attorneys that were not based on aiding and abetting. In both cases, the SEC charged general counsel with "causing" their company's violations of the securities laws. Although mere negligence can sustain a "causing" charge, neither of these two cases was grounded in professional negligence.

In the first case, *In re Isselmann*,[11] a corporate general counsel was charged with "causing" his client to file an inaccurate quarterly report. The company's disclosure committee had considered a quarterly filing that reflected cost savings from terminating vested retirement and severance benefits belonging to employees in Asia, but the general counsel received legal advice that these benefits could not legally be terminated. Not only did the general counsel fail to speak up at the disclosure committee meeting and fail

---

4. Norman S. Johnson, Speech before the American Bar Ass'n Fed. Sec. Law Comm. (Nov. 8, 1996), at 4, *available at* http://www.sec.gov/news/speech/speecharchive/1996/spch137.txt.

5. Giovanni P. Prezioso, Remarks before the Spring Meeting of the Ass'n of General Counsel (Apr. 28, 2005), at 5, *available at* http://www.sec.gov./news/speech/spch042805gpp.htm.

6. Stephen M. Cutler, Speech before the UCLA School of Law (Sept. 20, 2004), at 4-5, *available at* http://www.sec.gov/news/speech/spch092004smc.htm.

7. The SEC has also brought a number of cases against securities laws violators who happened to be lawyers. *See, e.g., SEC v. Shlansky*, SEC Litigation Release No. 19332 (Aug. 10, 2005) (announcing settled insider trading charges against attorney). However, these cases do not implicate the policy concerns at play when a lawyer is charged with respect to the performance of professional duties.

8. *See, e.g., SEC v. Woghin*, SEC Litigation Release No. 18891 (Sept. 22, 2004), *In re Stanley P. Silverstein*, SEC Litigation Release No. 49676 (May 11, 2004), *In re Jonathan B. Orlick*, SEC Litigation Release No. 51081 (Jan. 26, 2005), *In re Leonard Goldner*, SEC Litigation Release No. 53375 (Feb. 27, 2006), *SEC v. Ferguson*, SEC Litigation Release No. 19552 (Feb. 2, 2006).

9. *Howard v. SEC*, 376 F.3d 1136, 1143 (D.C. Cir. 2004).

11. Release No. 50428 (Sept. 23, 2004).

to reveal this advice in response to an audit committee member's questions, but he signed the quarterly filing improperly reflecting these savings. Thus, the SEC's enforcement proceeding in *Isselmann* was based on the general counsel's actions and omissions in the face of actual knowledge, and not on mere negligence in rendering legal advice.

In the second case, *Google, Inc. and David C. Drummond*,[12] Google's general counsel was charged with "causing" Google's violation of the registration provisions of the securities laws. While the SEC's rules exempt only the issuance of $5 million of stock options during a 12-month period, Google issued over $80 million of unregistered stock options to its employees. On two occasions, Google's general counsel recommended that the board of directors continue issuing such options, but failed to disclose the legal basis for, and risks attendant upon, continuing to issue such options. Senior SEC staff have since made it clear that the SEC charged the general counsel because, in failing to give nothing more than his bottom-line conclusion to his client, the general counsel stepped out of his role as legal advisor to the company and became a corporate actor responsible for causing his company's violation.[13]

In contrast to the facts in the *Drummond* proceeding, bond attorney Ira Weiss was sued by the SEC for acting in a purely legal advisory role. Indeed, the SEC ultimately found that he had violated the securities laws by merely issuing an incorrect legal opinion. Moreover, the SEC did not find that Weiss knew his legal opinion was incorrect at the time he issued it, thus distinguishing the *Isselmann* decision. It is for these reasons that the *Ira Weiss* decision warrants closer scrutiny.

The "Ira Weiss" Decision

Ira Weiss, a seasoned bond counsel, was sued by the SEC for legal work performed in connection with a tax-exempt municipal bond offering by a Pennsylvania school district. Weiss had issued an unqualified legal opinion that the bonds had been validly issued and that the interest payable on the bonds would be exempt from the federal income tax. The IRS later determined, however, that the interest was taxable.

In April 2004, the SEC commenced administrative proceedings against Weiss for allegedly violating, and causing the school district to violate, Section 17(a) of the Securities Act of 1933 and Section 10(b) of the Securities Exchange Act of 1934. The charging document (or "Order Instituting Proceedings") alleged that Weiss had "knowingly or recklessly" issued his unqualified legal opinion in the face of information casting substantial doubt on the tax-exempt status of the offering. Weiss contested the SEC's charges.

Following a four-day hearing, an ALJ dismissed all of the charges against Weiss, concluding that Weiss had not violated the securities laws because he had "acted with the requisite standard of care" and had not caused the school district to violate the

---

12. Release No. 8523 (Jan. 13, 2005).

13. For example, in discussing the *Drummond* proceeding, SEC General Counsel Prezioso cautioned that "the lawyer's continuing participation in the activity without providing advice to others may, in some cases, constitute part of a course of conduct that effectively makes the ultimate business decision for the company." Giovanni P. Prezioso, Remarks before the Spring Meeting of the Ass'n of General Counsel (Apr. 28, 2005), *available at* http://www.sec.gov/news/speech/spch042805gpp.htm.

securities laws. The SEC staff appealed the ALJ's decision to the Commission of the SEC.

In December 2005, the SEC in effect reversed the ALJ's dismissal[14] and found that Weiss had violated the federal securities laws when he issued his unqualified legal opinion. Notably, the SEC staff had urged the SEC to find Weiss liable under Section 17(a)(1) of the Securities Act and Section 10(b) of the Exchange Act, both of which require proof of intentional or, at a minimum, reckless conduct.[15] However, the SEC grounded its opinion solely on Sections 17(a)(2) and 17(a)(3) of the Securities Act, which do not require proof of intentional or reckless conduct. Under these sections, mere negligence suffices to establish a violation. Indeed, on multiple occasions in its opinion, the SEC remarked that Weiss's conduct was "at least negligent" and that Weiss's conduct had "departed from the standard of reasonable prudence." The SEC could not cite any legal precedent for holding an attorney liable for violating the securities laws through mere professional negligence. Based on its finding that Weiss was "at least negligent," the SEC determined that he committed primary violations of Sections 17(a)(2) and 17(a)(3) of the Securities Act, ordered him to cease and desist from committing or causing similar violations in the future, and to disgorge his $9,509.63 legal fee, plus prejudgment interest.[17] Curiously, the SEC did not address, or even mention, the staff's contention that Weiss had violated Section 17(a)(1) of the Securities Act and Section 10(b) of the Exchange Act.

Intent Needs Clarification

At first blush, an observer might conclude from reading the *Ira Weiss* decision that it represents a sharp break with the SEC's well-established enforcement policy towards attorneys. It is not at all clear, however, that this would be an accurate conclusion. Although *Ira Weiss* arguably gives the SEC Staff a precedential basis for investigating and commencing enforcement actions against attorneys whose mere professional negligence results in a violation of the securities laws, the language used in *Ira Weiss* may simply be the product of compromise and may not reflect an intent to change the commission's enforcement program.

First, the fact that the *Ira Weiss* opinion repeatedly states that his conduct was "at least negligent" leaves open the possibility that at least some of the Commissioners believed that Weiss acted recklessly. Second, if the SEC had intended to depart from its 25-year policy of not pursuing enforcement actions against attorneys for professional negligence, it chose an odd platform to announce such a seismic shift in policy. The bond counsel community is a highly specialized subset of the securities bar.

---

14. On appeal from an ALJ's initial decision, the SEC conducts an independent *de novo* review of the evidentiary record. If the SEC does not agree with the ALJ's decision, the SEC issues its own decision and the ALJ's initial decision is effectively revoked.

15. Recklessness is defined as "an extreme departure from the standards of ordinary care . . . present[ing] a danger of misleading buyers or sellers that is either known to the [respondent] or is so obvious that the [respondent] must have been aware of it." *Sundstrand Corp. v. Sun Chem. Corp.*, 553 F.2d 1033, 1044–45 (7th Cir. 1977).

17. Weiss has appealed the SEC's decision to the U.S. Court of Appeals for the District of Columbia.

Predictably, the *Ira Weiss* decision has received scant attention from the mainstream securities press. Indeed, the only legal periodical which has covered the *Ira Weiss* proceedings in any depth is *The Bond Buyer*, a daily newspaper serving the municipal finance industry. Finally, senior enforcement officials from the SEC's Office of Municipal Finance responsible for investigating and prosecuting *Ira Weiss* have repeatedly reassured the municipal finance bar that they do not intend to pursue bond attorneys for mere professional negligence.[18]

All of these factors suggest that the SEC did not intend in *Ira Weiss* to reverse its enforcement policy of the last 25 years with respect to attorneys. Nevertheless, the SEC's wording in its opinion (i.e., "at least negligent" and "depart[ing] from the standard of reasonable prudence") may leave the SEC staff with the impression that they have the authority to investigate attorneys who they suspect gave negligent legal advice resulting in a violation of the securities laws. Indeed, some senior SEC officials have already indicated publicly that they view the *Ira Weiss* decision as opening the door to the investigation and prosecution of mere professional negligence. For example, former Commissioner Harvey Goldschmid is reported to have asked an SEC assistant general counsel at a conference earlier this year whether *Ira Weiss* opened lawyers to SEC enforcement action for mere negligent conduct. The assistant general counsel is reported to have responded that "lawyers . . . when they act negligently . . . can be liable."[19]

Given that it is unclear whether the SEC intended to cast aside its historic reluctance to prosecute attorney negligence, the SEC should issue a policy statement clarifying its intent.[20] If the SEC does intend to investigate and prosecute attorney negligence that results in securities violations, that is a matter of grave concern to the securities bar, and the SEC should clearly and unambiguously state that intent. If the SEC did not intend for *Ira Weiss* to usher in a brave new world of attorney liability, it is all the more imperative that the SEC issue a clarifying policy statement. In the absence of such a statement, *Ira Weiss* will cause considerable mischief in the SEC's enforcement program unless it is reversed on appeal. Given the SEC's continued focus on "gatekeepers," virtually every enforcement investigation today examines the conduct of the attorneys. The line level staff attorneys and their branch chiefs who conduct and guide these investigations will justifiably read *Ira Weiss* as indicating that it is appropriate to investigate and charge attorneys whose professional negligence results in violations of the securities laws. Even if senior enforcement division staff ultimately recommend against enforcement action, it will not be before the unfortunate attorney has been put to the unwarranted expense and considerable anxiety of defending his conduct in an enforcement investigation. A clear policy statement from the SEC would avoid such mischief.

---

18. Of course, SEC staff lack authority to speak for the commission and preface their remarks with an appropriate disclaimer.

19. Lynn Hune, *Weiss Called "Extremely Negligent,"* 355 Bond Buyer (USA) 1 (Mar. 6, 2006).

20. The SEC issues policy statements from time to time to clarify its position on a particular matter. For a compilation of the SEC's Policy Statements, *see* http://www.sec.gov/rules/policys.html.

NOTES AND QUESTIONS

1. The SEC's proceedings against Google's lawyer (and the other SEC enforcement cases against lawyers that were described in the preceding article) are not isolated cases. Indeed,

> in the past two years, the SEC has brought more cases against lawyers than in almost any comparable period in the agency's history.[1] In times of financial crisis and scandal, regulators often become more aggressive in the cases they bring against lawyers. For this reason, it seems safe to predict that the SEC's scrutiny of lawyers will only increase in response to the financial market turmoil of 2008.

W. Hardy Callcott & Abigail C. Slonecker, *A Review of Recent SEC Actions Against Lawyers*, 42 REV. SEC. & COMM. REG. 71 (Mar. 2009).

3. Is the SEC's ruling in the Ira Weiss matter consistent with the settlement order that was entered in the SEC's proceedings against Google and its lawyer?

4. Do you think that either Drummond (Google's lawyer) or Ira Weiss suffered reputational harm as a result of the proceedings that were brought against these lawyers by the SEC? (In this regard, it bears mentioning that Drummond currently serves as Chief Legal Officer for Google (as of this writing in fall 2013)). Also, recall that the ALJ originally dismissed the SEC's claims against Ira Weiss only to be reversed when he appealed this ruling to the full Commission.

5. As a public policy matter, should we care that the SEC is "going after the lawyers"?

6. How does the role of a lawyer differ from the role of a business, such as Standard and Poor's (S&P)? S&P is a credit rating agency that rates issuers' securities for a fee, which is paid by the issuer. In February 2013, the U.S. Justice Department filed a civil suit against S&P, alleging fraudulent practices on the part of S&P in connection with its ratings of certain financial products during the time period of September 2004 through October 2007. *See* Jean Englesham, Jeannette Neumann, and Evan Perez, *U.S. Sues S&P Over Ratings*, WALL STREET JOURNAL ONLINE, February 5, 2013, *available at* http://online.wsj.com/news/articles/SB10001424127887324445 90457828406400379514.2. *Query:* How does the scope of the lawyer's responsibilities in connection with issuing an opinion letter as part of a client's financing transaction (such as was reflected in *Ira Weiss*) differ from the scope of S&P's responsibilities when it was retained by an issuer to assign credit ratings to the issuer's securities?

---

1. Counting SEC cases against lawyers is not a science — a single case may be active in multiple years, and as discussed below, the activity of a lawyer may result in both injunctive and administrative cases. Simon M. Lorne, *An Issue-Annotated Version of the SOX Rules for Lawyer Conduct*, in 2 PREPARATION OF ANNUAL DISCLOSURE DOCUMENTS, at 337, 404-10 (P.L.I., 2009), counts eighteen such cases in 2007 and fifteen in 2008 (through September). For comparison, he counts only six such cases in 2001, and thirteen in 2006. *Id.*

PROBLEM

Ruiz served as general counsel to a broker-dealer firm, Goodgreed & Co. The SEC has alleged that, in his capacity as general counsel, Ruiz facilitated thousands of late trades in over 600 mutual funds on behalf of several large institutional clients. The SEC claims that this trading activity constitutes a violation of Rule 22c-1 promulgated pursuant to the Investment Company Act of 1940. Ruiz serves as the only full-time, licensed practicing lawyer on the staff at Goodgreed & Co. By his own admission, Ruiz knew nothing about broker-dealer regulation when he joined the firm in 2001. In 2002, Ruiz was asked to draft a contract setting forth the terms of mutual fund trading for a new institutional client. Ruiz drafted a contract using as precedent the sample form of agreement that had been provided to Ruiz by the new client. Using the sample agreement, Ruiz's early draft of the contract required the new client to submit its list of proposed transactions to Goodgreed & Co. by 3:30 P.M., New York time, and to confirm those trades by 4:00 P.M. However, at the direction of a senior executive from the new client, Ruiz changed those times to 4:15 P.M. and 4:45 P.M. These changes were later used by this new institutional client to engage in late trading in violation of the Investment Company Act.

Ruiz did not have any experience in the trading of mutual funds, nor did he fully understand how mutual funds were priced. By his own testimony, Ruiz admitted that he did not realize that the agreement contemplated violations of the Investment Company Act, nor did he ask any questions regarding the timing of the trading activity that was permitted as a result of the changes that the client requested to be made in the draft agreement.

In its administrative proceeding against Ruiz, the SEC's Enforcement Division claimed that Ruiz was negligent by virtue of not having the requisite knowledge of the federal securities laws (in particular, the Investment Company Act of 1940), and further, by failing to conduct an adequate inquiry into the trade-timing issues raised by the changes that were made to the draft agreement. Following a hearing on the SEC's allegations, the Administrative Law Judge (the "ALJ") found that the contract was ambiguous as to whether the agreement contemplated illegal late trading, as opposed to permissible late processing of orders that had been submitted to Goodgreed & Co. on a timely basis. The ALJ ultimately held that Ruiz did not act negligently in failing to spot the issue. As permitted by law, the SEC's Enforcement Division has appealed the ALJ's findings to the full Commission.

Assume that you are a member of the staff of the Chair of the SEC. The Chair has asked for your recommendation as to how to dispose of this appeal in a manner that is consistent with the precedent of the Commission (as described in this chapter). Also, please consider the lawyer's potential professional responsibility violations as well. Specifically, should these potential violations be subject only to state disciplinary proceedings, or is there a basis for SEC sanctions as well?

D. State Blue Sky Laws and the Uniform Limited Offering Exemption

In the case of most start-up financing transactions, perfecting a federal exemption is just the first step in planning the financing transaction. Issuers (and their lawyers) must then also analyze the applicability of state securities laws (more popularly referred to as "blue sky laws"), both in the case of registered offerings as well as any exempt financings. In the case of registered offerings, the impact of state blue sky laws has been significantly tempered by the enactment of NSMIA, which (briefly summarized) preempts state registration of offerings that are *registered* under Section 5 of the 1933 Act. With respect to offerings that are *exempt* from federal registration, things are a bit more complicated, as explained in the following excerpt:

> Even after NSMIA, many offerings exempt from federal registration remain subject to state regulation — namely those subject to the §3(b) small offering exemption (such as Rule 504, Rule 505, and Regulation A offerings), the statutory [§4(a)(2)] private placement exemption, . . . and the §3(a)(11) intrastate exemption. Although NSMIA does not preempt state registration of these offerings, state exemptions may still be available. These exemptions, which vary from state to state, are typically more restrictive than the federal exemptions and often impose the controlling conditions on the offering.
>
> * * *
>
> Many states exempt issuer "limited offerings" made pursuant to offers directed to no more than 10 persons (revised in many states to 25 persons) within the state in any 12-month period. [Uniform Securities Act (USA)] §402(b)(9) (1956 version); [USA] §202(14) (2002 version would cover both preorganization and operational financing). The exemption has no dollar ceiling, and specified institutional investors are often excluded from the 10-person (or 25-person) numerical limits. Some states, consistent with Regulation D, have revised their limited offering exemption to cap the number of actual *purchasers*, not *offerees*.
>
> * * *
>
> In 1983, to facilitate the use of Regulation D, the North American Securities Administrators Association (NASAA) promulgated the Uniform Limited Offering Exemption (ULOE) to create a uniform state exemption for Rule 505 and 506 offerings. As promulgated and adopted in many states, the ULOE is more demanding than Regulation D. While generally exempting offerings that meet the federal Rules 505 and 506 conditions, the ULOE contains investor "sophistication-suitability" requirements for Rule 505 offerings and "bad boy" disqualifiers for Rule 506 offerings. The future of the ULOE remains uncertain since NSMIA preempts any conditions imposed on Rule 506 offerings and Rule 505 offerings have become (by comparison) less attractive.
>
> * * *

. . . The following table shows the fit of Regulation D and current state exemptions:

	Federal exemption	State exemption
Small offerings	Rule 504 • no reporting companies, investment companies, or "blank check" companies • $1 million or less (12 months) • no general marketing • limits on resales • marketing and resale limits not applicable, if offering is state-registered or state-exempt because sold only to accredited investors	"Limited offering" exemption • less than 10 (or 25) investors • no restrictions or marketing • no limits on resales Model Accredited Investor Exemption • no [issuers subject to "bad actor" disqualifications] and no "blank check" companies • sold only to accredited investors • general announcements to accredited investors
Medium offerings	Rule 505 • no investment companies [and no issuers subject to "bad actor" disqualifications] • $5 million or less (12 months) up to 35 nonaccredited investors (must receive disclosure document) • no general marketing • limits on resales	"Limited offering" exemption • less than 10 (or 25) investors • no restrictions on marketing • no limits on resales Uniform Limited Offering Exemption • similar conditions as Rule 505 • all investors must meet sophistication and suitability requirements
Large offerings	Rule 506[(b)] • no issuers [who are subject to "bad actor" disqualifications] • unlimited amounts • up to 35 nonaccredited investors (must receive disclosure document, and must be sophisticated or have investor rep) • no general marketing • limits on resales	NSMIA preempts state [regulation, although the states may impose a Form D filing obligation and/or require payment of filing fees]

PALMITER, *supra*, at pp. 211-213.

CHAPTER 5

INCORPORATION PROCESS

A. Introduction: Choice of State of Incorporation

At this point, the founders, Joan and Michael, have decided to incorporate their new business, SoftCo, on the view that they want to plan ahead in anticipation of venture capital funding.

In Chapter 2, as part of our choice of entity discussion, we presented a broad overview of the issues that the transaction planner (i.e., the lawyer for the new business) must address in terms of the pros and cons of organizing a new business as a corporation. In this chapter, we specifically focus on the legal and business considerations that generally arise in connection with incorporating a start-up business. At the outset of this discussion, it bears emphasizing that by anticipating problems that are likely to arise in the course of growing a start-up business, the transaction planner will often help the founders structure the new corporation in order to minimize future obstacles and maximize the company's flexibility to take advantage of new opportunities.

Modern state corporation statutes generally offer the transaction planner wide flexibility in terms of establishing the organization of the new corporation. However, once the structure of the new corporation has been established, it generally takes on a life of its own and thus is not always easy to alter. Consequently, as part of the incorporation process, the founders are generally well-advised to carefully consider their short-term *and* long-term business objectives so that the transaction planner can organize the new corporation in a manner that will facilitate — rather than frustrate — the attainment of these objectives.

The first decision to be made in the incorporation process is to determine the state where the new business will incorporate. As a practical matter, this generally means deciding between incorporating in Delaware or in the state where the business will be physically located. In this chapter, we analyze two states: Delaware and California. Why? With respect to Delaware law, for the simple reason that many practitioners regard Delaware as providing an unparalleled corporate environment. Not only is [Delaware corporate law] flexible, it is constantly maintained and updated by a corporate bar dedicated to keeping the Delaware corporation law firmly in touch with business needs. The Delaware General Assembly routinely . . . [enacts] changes [to the state's statutes as] proposed by the state bar association without alteration. In turn, the Delaware judiciary . . . is marked by the highest standards of scholarship and integrity, . . . understands business issues and, as a result, has developed a nationally recognized expertise in corporate law. . . .

Wendell Fenton & Gregory Varallo, *Organizing a Delaware Corporation*, START-UP AND EMERGING COMPANIES (Gregory Smith, ed.) ch. 22, at page 22-3 (1997).

At the other end of the spectrum, California corporate law is not generally regarded by practitioners in nearly so favorable terms. "If there is a 'race to the bottom,' California was never in it. Instead, California corporate law has maintained shareholder protections and declined the adoption of a pro-management regime based on flexibility and simplicity, while stretching its application to foreign corporations having substantial connections with the state [by virtue of §2115 of the California Corporations Code]." Philip Peters, *The California Corporation: Legal Aspects of Organization and Operation*, vol. 31 CORPORATE PRACTICE SERIES A-1 (3d ed. 2003).

As you go through the materials in this chapter, you should be prepared to make your own assessment of the relative advantages of incorporating a new business in Delaware over that of California. You should also consider where your local jurisdiction lies on the continuum between Delaware and California. More specifically, you should review the materials in this chapter for purposes of forming a recommendation to the founders, Joan and Michael, as to whether it is in their best interests to incorporate their new business, SoftCo, in California or Delaware. Having done that analysis, you will be able to look at other clients and situations with a clearer perspective on the merits of the jurisdictional choices available to them and thus will be in a position to offer more informed advice. In addition, many new businesses decide to incorporate locally, for reasons that are described in this chapter. Since the corporation statutes of many states are based on the MBCA, reference will also be made to provisions of the Model Act where appropriate.

Regardless of which state you decide to recommend, the basic steps involved in the incorporation process are essentially the same. This chapter reviews the necessary steps, which generally are:

- Preparing and filing the articles (certificate) of incorporation
- Conducting the organizational meeting of the initial board of directors
- Preparing and adopting bylaws
- Issuing shares

We analyze each of these steps under both Delaware and California law. In addition, we analyze the respective roles of management (officers and directors) versus owners (shareholders) in operating the business as a corporation once it has been duly incorporated. As we shall see, certain differences in the law governing the operation of the corporation may influence the transaction planner's decision whether to incorporate in Delaware or California. At another level, discussion of these differences also will serve to highlight certain legal issues and business considerations that the founders (and their counsel) are generally well advised to address at the time of incorporation in order to maximize the founders' ability to achieve both the short-term and long-term objectives for the new corporation.

B. Preparing the Articles (Certificate) of Incorporation: Herein of "Private Ordering"

The charter document — that is, the key organizational document — for the modern corporation is known in California as the "Articles of Incorporation," and in Delaware, as the "Certificate of Incorporation." (For simplicity's sake, we will generally refer to this document as "the Charter" throughout this chapter.) In both states, the process of preparing the Charter requires the transaction planner to comply with various statutory requirements as to its contents. In this section, we review the key statutory provisions that the lawyer must consider in preparing this document. As you go through the materials in this chapter, specific references are made to the relevant statutory provisions of California and Delaware law. You should consult these statutes in order to be sure that your analysis of the issues is adequately informed in terms of making a recommendation to SoftCo.

1. Corporate Name

At the risk of stating the obvious, every state requires that the corporation be given a name. As a business matter, the founders will generally want to select a name that is distinctive and, if possible, bears some relationship to the company's proposed business activity. (As discussed further in Chapter 7, the corporate name also may serve as an identifying mark for the company's products or services, raising intellectual property issues that the transaction planner also must address as part of organizing the new business.) *Query*: As a business matter, do you see any practical problems in using the name of a founder as part of the corporate name? Can you think of any publicly traded companies that use the name of a founder as part of the corporate name? [*Hint*: Ford Motor Co.]

As a legal matter, most state corporation statutes require that the corporate name include a word or notation (such as "Company," "Corporation," "Corp.," or "Inc.") in order to reflect the corporateness of the new enterprise. Many states' statutes prohibit the use of certain words as part of the corporate name (such as "bank" or "insurance") unless certain requirements have been satisfied. *Query*: What are the requirements of Delaware and California? [*Hint*: *See* Del. §102(a)(1); and Calif. §201; *see also* Model Act §4.01.]

Once the founders have selected a name for their new corporation, then it must be "cleared," generally with the secretary of state's office, before filing the Charter in order to be sure that the chosen name is available for use. Many states prohibit the use of a name that is the same as or similar to the name of an existing corporation. If the name is "cleared" (i.e., determined by the secretary of state's office to be available), then generally for a fee it can be "reserved" by the applicant for a certain period of time, generally ranging from 30 days to 12 months depending on the state. *Query*: What is the process of "name reservation" under Delaware law? Under California law? [*Hint: See* Del. §102(e); and Calif. §201(c); *see also* Model Act §4.02.]

2. *Statutory Requirements: Mandatory vs. Optional Provisions*

The Charter must set forth all the provisions required by the relevant state statute; these are often referred to as the "mandatory" provisions. Over the years, state corporation statutes have relaxed the information that *must* be included in the Charter so that today, in most states, the bare minimum contents of the Charter (often referred to as a "plain vanilla" Charter) can usually be set forth on a single sheet of paper, often with room to spare. Although the set of "mandatory" provisions varies slightly from state to state, as a general rule, the modern corporation statute will require the Charter to set forth the following items of information:

- The corporate name
- The purposes (or general nature) of the business that the corporation is authorized to undertake, including, on occasion, the duration of the corporation's existence
- Information related to service of process on the corporation
- Identification of the incorporators and/or the initial board of directors
- A description of the types and amount of shares that the corporation is authorized to issue
- The proper execution of the Charter by the incorporators

We have already described the corporate name; we describe the other "mandatory" provisions in the next few sections of this chapter.

In addition to the mandatory provisions, the Charter *may* contain a broad range of other provisions, generally known as the "optional" provisions. The transaction planner will often include these optional provisions in order to "customize" the structure of the newly organized corporation to meet the particular needs of the participants in the new business. In this way, the transaction planner can vary the default rule that is set forth in the corporation statute and which would otherwise apply. As a result of this flexibility, modern corporation statutes are broadly referred to as "enabling," meaning that the statutory provisions apply in the event that the corporation does not specify otherwise, usually by including an appropriate provision in the Charter or the bylaws. Modern corporation statutes thereby allow for "private ordering," although certain provisions of the statute may be made mandatory and not subject to customization or modification.

Consequently, in drafting the Charter, the lawyer must be careful to identify not only which statutory provisions that may be varied, but also whether the modification of the statute's default rule *must* appear in the Charter to be effective, or alternatively, whether the modification can be set forth in *either* the Charter or the bylaws. "That is, in some instances the statutes expressly permit variations *only* in the [Charter]. In other instances, the variation *may* appear in either the [Charter] or the bylaws." JAMES COX & THOMAS HAZEN, CORPORATIONS at pg. 57 (2d ed. 2003) (emphasis added).

Although forming a corporation appears to be relatively straightforward and uncomplicated (at least when preparing a "plain vanilla" Charter), it should now be apparent that modern corporation statutes allow the organizers to create very complex business arrangements by including appropriate modification of the default rule in the company's

Charter. Viewed in this light, the Charter constitutes a contract between the corporation and its investors. In addition, the Charter represents a contract between the corporation (and its organizers) and the state, which grants the right to exist as a corporation. Taken together, this means that there is a hierarchy whereby the corporate statute is controlling unless appropriate modification is made in the Charter, although provisions that are "contrary to law" will not be enforced. What's more, as part of this hierarchy, bylaw provisions that conflict with either statutes or the Charter are void.

As you might imagine, this freedom to modify the relevant default rule often can lead to greater complexity in preparing the Charter. The remaining materials in this chapter describe the types of optional provisions that frequently are considered in the process of organizing a new business as a corporation. As we go through these materials, you should consider whether you would recommend that our client, SoftCo, include such a provision in its Charter, and whether your recommendation varies depending on whether the founders, Joan and Michael, decide to raise the necessary capital from a *Venture Capital* investor, or from *Friends and Family*, or alternatively, decide to *Go-It-Alone*.

3. *Agent for Service of Process*

Virtually every state corporation statute requires that the Charter set forth the name and address of the new company's initial registered agent for service of process. Generally speaking, the registered agent may be either an individual or a corporation, although the agent usually must be a resident of the state of incorporation. A registered agent can resign, usually by giving written notice to the secretary of state's office. Thereafter, a new agent is substituted through an appropriate filing with the secretary of state. *Query*: With respect to the initial agent for service of process, what is required as a matter of Delaware and California law? [*Hint: See* Del. §102(a); and Calif. §202; *see also* Model Act §2.02(a) and §5.04.]

4. *Statement of Purposes, Powers, and/or Duration*

Historically, state corporation statutes required that a corporation be formed to engage in a definite enterprise or line of business. This typically led the draftsman to recite a lengthy "multi-purpose" clause in order to assure that the corporation had the flexibility to expand the scope of its business activity in the future. This often led to Charters that were virtually unreadable, with purpose clauses that went on for several pages. Modern corporation statutes address this issue by authorizing the Charter to simply recite that the corporation's purpose is "to engage in any lawful business," without the need for any further elaboration. *Query*: What is required under the Delaware statute vs. the California statute with respect to the statement of corporate purpose? [*Hint: See* Del. §102(a); and Calif. §202; *see also* Model Act §2.02(b) and §3.01.]

Corporate "powers" generally refers to the methods available to the corporation to achieve its "purpose." So, for example, a business organized to manufacture furniture generally must have the "power" to contract with third parties as well as the "power" to borrow money in order to achieve its business "purpose." Historically, corporation statutes required that the Charter specifically enumerate the powers that a corporation was to possess, which often led to lengthy lists of powers for fear that something might be omitted. Today, however, such lists are unnecessary as most state statutes expressly grant broad powers that the corporation may exercise. *Query*: What does the Delaware statute provide as to the scope of the corporation's powers? What about the California statute? [*Hint: See* Del. §§102 and 121-123; Calif. §202; *see also* Model Act §§2.02 and 3.02-3.04.]

Finally, with respect to duration, we learned in Chapter 2 that the key attribute of the corporation is that it exists as a separate legal entity "with perpetual existence." As such, what must be included in the Charter with respect to duration as a matter of either Delaware or California law? [*Hint: See* Del. §102(b); and Calif. §204; *see also* Model Act §§2.02 and 3.02.]

5. *Statement of Authorized Capital*

Generally speaking, the Charter must set forth the aggregate number of shares that the corporation will have authority to "issue" (i.e., sell), the par value of these shares, and the class or classes into which these shares may be divided, if the founders desire to create more than one class of shares. *See, e.g.,* Del. §102(a); Calif. §202(d)-(e); Model Act §§2.02(a) and 6.01. The statement of authorized capital is widely regarded as the most important aspect of the modern Charter. So, it bears emphasizing that, if the corporation plans to issue more than one class of stock, then the Charter *must* recite the rights, preferences, and privileges to be conferred on each class of shares as well as the number of authorized shares in each class. The range of "rights, preferences, and privileges" that are typically considered by the transaction planner as part of the formation of a new corporation are briefly described in section D of this chapter. But remember, if not otherwise provided in the Charter, *all* shares will enjoy equal rights with respect to voting, dividend distributions, and distributions on dissolution of the corporation.

6. *Incorporators and Initial Directors*

Reminiscent of the old "chicken-and-egg" problem, there is a bit of a timing problem inherent in the legal mechanics of forming a corporation in that the corporation cannot function without electing its first board of directors. However, at the time of formation, there are no shareholders since there is no board of directors to decide whether the corporation should issue shares to investors. "The link between the inchoate corporation and the completed organization is often the incorporator." Cox & Hazen, *supra*, at pg. 55. At a minimum, the incorporator must sign the Charter, and, in most states today, an incorporator may be either an entity or a natural person.

However, if the Charter does not name the initial board of directors, then the incorporator is generally vested by statute with the authority to complete the process of organizing the new business as a corporation, which typically includes holding the organizational meeting (which is described in more detail later in this chapter). *Query*: What is required to be included in the Charter with regard to incorporators and/or initial directors under Delaware's and California's corporation statutes? [*Hint: See* Del. §§102(a) and 107-108; and Calif. §§200 and 204; *see also* Model Act §§2.01-2.02 and 2.05.]

7. *Signature*

The Charter must be signed by the incorporator. Once signed, the Charter must be filed with the secretary of state's office, along with the filing fee. Generally speaking, corporate existence begins once the Charter has been filed, although some states' statutes provide that the filing will become effective only after the Charter has been approved and accepted for filing by the secretary of state's office. Once the Charter is filed, it becomes a public document. *Query*: What do the Delaware and California statutes provide with respect to when the corporation comes into existence? [*Hint*: *See* Del. §§103 and 106; and Calif. §200; *see also* Model Act §2.03.] Along these same lines, why do lawyers generally advise that the organizational meeting should not take place *before* corporate existence has commenced?

8. *Optional Provisions*

As mentioned earlier in this chapter, many of the default rules set forth in the relevant corporation statute are subject to modification by an appropriate provision in the Charter (or in the bylaws, in some instances). While by no means exhaustive, some of the "optional" provisions that are frequently addressed in the process of drafting the Charter for a new corporation include the following:

Limitation on Director Liability.   In 1986, in response to the landmark decision of the Delaware Supreme Court in *Smith v. Van Gorkom*, 488 A.2d 858 (Del. 1985), and the ensuing crisis (or at the least the perception of a crisis) in the market for directors' and officers' insurance, Delaware amended its corporation statute to add Section 102(b)(7). This new section authorizes corporations, by including an appropriate provision in their certificate of incorporation, to limit the personal liability of directors for money damages to the corporation (or its stockholders) for conduct that amounts to a breach of fiduciary duty, subject to certain exceptions. Virtually all states followed and thus have adopted some form of exculpatory ("raincoat") statute, although the exceptions to the limitation (or elimination) of directors' personal liability vary from state to state. *See, e.g.*, Calif. §204(a)(10)-(11); and Model Act §2.02(b)(4)-(5). *Query*: What differences, if any, are there in the terms of Delaware's exculpatory provision as compared to California's provision?

As a general rule, these exculpatory provisions are not applicable by default, and therefore, corporations must "opt in" by making them a part of the company's Charter. As to existing corporations, this means that the Charter must be amended to include such a provision; the mechanics of amending the Charter are described later in this chapter. With respect to the process of forming a new corporation, this means that an appropriate provision must be included in the initial Charter submitted for filing with the secretary of state's office. *Query*: Would you recommend that SoftCo include such an exculpatory provision in its Charter?

Super-Majority Votes.   Like many states' corporation statues, Delaware's section 102(b)(4) permits the certificate of incorporation to include a provision that requires a "super-majority" vote to take corporate action. A super-majority vote requires a vote that is higher, but not lower, than what is otherwise required by the Delaware statute with respect to certain actions, such as approval of mergers, sales of assets, and dissolution of the corporation. To be effective, the super-majority vote must be included in the company's certificate and not its bylaws. *Query*: Does California permit "super-majority" votes for either shareholder approval (where such approval is required by statute), or for valid director action? [*Hint*: *See* Calif. §204(a); *see also* Model Act §6.01.] The rules that would otherwise govern the mechanics of board meetings and shareholder meetings are described later in this chapter. *Query*: Would you recommend that SoftCo include a provision requiring a super-majority vote as part of its Charter? If so, would you recommend that it extend to *all* matters that are subject to shareholder approval?

Denial of Right to Act by Written Consent.   Both California and Delaware permit shareholders to take action by written consent, thereby bypassing a formal meeting of the shareholders. *See* Del. §228; and Calif. §603; *see also* Model Act §7.04. As a practical matter, this means that Delaware permits stockholder action to be taken without a meeting, without prior notice, and without a vote *if* written consent to such action is given by the holders of stock sufficient to take such action at a meeting at which all shares entitled to vote on the matter are present and voted — that is, Delaware Section 228 requires approval by the written consent of a majority of outstanding shares *unless* the certificate of incorporation provides otherwise. *Query*: What does California require in order for action to be validly taken by written consent? Would you recommend that SoftCo modify the default rule allowing shareholder action by written consent by including an appropriate provision in its Charter? If so, what purpose is to be served by modifying the statute's default rule to limit the shareholders' right to act by written consent? [*Hint*: You may want to revisit this issue after you review the materials later in this chapter regarding shareholders meetings, where we discuss the mechanics of "written consent" in more detail.]

Anti-Takeover Statutes.   Delaware has adopted a form of "business combination" statute that comes into play in the event that a Delaware company with securities (i) listed on a national stock exchange, (ii) quoted on NASDAQ, or (iii) held by more than 2,000 stockholders is faced with the threat of an unfriendly takeover. Generally speaking, anti-takeover statutes protect corporations against the advances of an unwanted bidder. Delaware's Section 203 provides that if a "person" (i.e., an unwanted bidder) acquires 15 percent or more of the voting stock of a Delaware company, then that "person" (i.e., the unwanted bidder) may not consummate a merger or other specified transactions with the Delaware corporation unless (a) the "person" (i.e., the unwanted bidder) acquires 85 percent or more of the company's stock, or (b) the transaction is approved by the board of directors and at least two thirds of the shares other than the shares held by the "person" (i.e., the unwanted bidder) acquiring the stock. Unlike Delaware, California has not adopted an anti-takeover statute. *Query*: Does this difference influence your recommendation as to whether SoftCo should incorporate in California or Delaware?

Renouncement of Corporate Opportunity.   In 2000, Delaware amended its corporation statute to add Section 122(17), which, in essence, allows a Delaware certificate of incorporation to include a provision that permits the company's officers, directors, or shareholders to take advantage of "corporate opportunities"; that is, to take for themselves business opportunities that might be of interest to the corporation. California's corporation statute does not include a similar (exculpatory) provision. *Query*: Does this difference influence your recommendation regarding whether SoftCo should incorporate in California or Delaware?

Staggered Boards.   Delaware Section 141(d) permits the certificate of incorporation to include a provision that divides the board of directors into two or three classes to serve staggered terms of two or three years, respectively. As a practical matter, this means that if the board is divided into three classes, stockholders will be unable to replace the entire board in a single election. It is widely believed that for a company with publicly traded stock the use of a "staggered board" works to discourage unwanted bidders, and thus serves as an "anti-takeover" measure. *Query*: Does California permit the use of a "staggered board"? [*Hint*: See Calif. §§301(a) and 301.5; *see also* Model Act §8.06.] Will the use of a "staggered board" be of importance to the founders, Joan and Michael — or, for that matter, to the investors in SoftCo?

9. Amendments to the Charter

As a general proposition, the Charter can be amended after corporate existence begins by obtaining the requisite approval of both shareholders and directors. So, in most states, the board of directors must adopt a resolution setting forth the proposed amendment and recommending its adoption by the company's shareholders. Following director approval, the amendment must be submitted for shareholder approval. If the requisite shareholder approval is obtained, the amendment becomes effective once an appropriate certificate has been filed with the secretary of state setting forth the amendment. Also, corporations may approve an amended and restated Charter, which incorporates new amendments into a fully restated document. Alternatively, a corporation may simply restate its Charter without amendment, which sets forth in one document the entire Charter, as amended as of the date of filing, but includes no new amendments. *Query*: What is the amendment process required by Delaware's and California's statutes? [*Hint*: *See* Del. §242; and Calif. §902; *see also* Model Act §§10.01-10.03.]

One of the most important issues concerning the amendment of the company's Charter relates to the right of the shareholders to vote as a class, or what is commonly referred to as "class voting." The right to a "class vote" is relevant only in those situations where the company decides to issue more than one class of stock. Some states grant the shareholders the right to vote as a class in the case of certain types of Charter amendments, even in the absence of a provision in the company's Charter that grants the shares a right to vote. Irrespective of the right to vote as a class, there is also the issue of what number of shares must approve the proposed amendment in order for it to be validly approved. Most states today require approval by an absolute majority of shares — that is, by a majority of the outstanding shares entitled to vote — unless the Charter requires a higher percentage per a super-majority provision, as discussed earlier. Historically, many states imposed a super-majority voting standard for shareholder approval of Charter amendments, often requiring as many as two thirds of the outstanding shares to approve the Charter amendment. *Query*: What is the stockholder voting requirement under the Delaware statute with respect to amendments to the company's certificate of incorporation? Is it a different voting standard than the corresponding provision of the California statute? Does the statutory treatment of the process for amending the company's Charter influence your recommendation whether to incorporate SoftCo in Delaware or California?

C. Organizational Meeting

1. Initial Board of Directors

After the Charter is filed, there are still several formalities that need to be completed in order to get the business up and running. In general, the process of organizing the corporation is undertaken by the initial directors of the corporation, if they are named in the Charter. If they are not named, the incorporators must hold a meeting to elect directors and often to adopt bylaws. Thereafter, the initial directors must hold a meeting to appoint officers.

> . . . While the statute authorizes action at the initial meeting to include other matters necessary to perfect the organization of the corporation and to facilitate the commencement of its business, it is generally the practice that incorporators do no more than adopt bylaws and elect directors.
>
> Among the additional items [often referred to as "housekeeping details" that are] commonly dealt with at the organizational meeting are the designation of a depository [i.e., bank] for corporate funds, the acceptance of stock subscriptions, the approval of forms of seal and stock certificate, and the granting of authority to officers of the corporation to sign and issue such certificates to those persons from whom subscriptions [i.e., pledges made by prospective investors to purchase stock] have been accepted. If a meeting is held, minutes recording all actions should be filed with the corporate records.
>
> In most cases, no actual meeting is held; the organizers take advantage of [statutory provisions such as Del. §108(c),] which permits action that otherwise would have to be taken at an organizational meeting to be taken without a meeting if each incorporator or director, as the case may be, signs an instrument so stating and consenting to the action taken. Such a consent should be filed in the corporation's minute book.

A. Gilchrist Sparks & Frederick H. Alexander, *The Delaware Corporation: Legal Aspects of Organization and Operation*, vol. 1, CORPORATE PRACTICE SERIES (4th ed. 2006) at pg. A-10.

2. Preparing and Adopting Bylaws

As a general proposition, the bylaws set forth the rules for the internal operations of the corporation. Thus, bylaw provisions typically deal with such matters as how many officers the corporation will have; the functions of each office; the mechanics for calling and conducting shareholders' and directors' meetings; the formalities of shareholder voting (including voting by proxy); the qualifications of directors; the formation of board committees (such as executive or audit committees); and procedures for issuing and transferring shares (as well any limitations on such transfer). As you can see, the range of topics typically contained in the bylaws is quite broad. Indeed, many states' statutes allow the bylaws to "contain any provision, not in conflict with the law or the articles for the management of the business and for the conduct of the affairs of the corporation. . . ." Calif. §212; *see also* Model Act §2.06; and Del. §109(b). While extending broad freedom to customize its bylaws to fit the specific needs of the new business, this freedom is not completely open-ended. You will recall that bylaw provisions that conflict with mandatory statutory provisions or with the Charter or with public policy are void, given the hierarchical nature of corporate law.

3. Issuance of Shares

Generally speaking, one of the most important agenda items for the initial meeting of the board of directors concerns the issuance of shares. The board must set the consideration to be received for the shares (including a determination of the fair value of any non-cash consideration), and, by valid board action, authorize the issuance of such shares to the investors in the new company. The details involved in connection with the issuance of shares are described in the next section.

D. Capital Structure of the New Corporation

In Chapter 9, we discuss in more detail the various rights, preferences, and privileges that are typically going to be heavily negotiated terms in the case of preferred shares issued as part of a venture capital financing transaction. As a result, this section provides just a brief overview of the rights, preferences, and privileges that generally play an important role in tailoring the capital structure of a new corporation to accommodate the economic and managerial objectives of the interested parties. In keeping with the topic of this chapter, this discussion highlights the differences between California and Delaware law that may be relevant in deciding where to incorporate the new business. Bear in mind, though, that we revisit these attributes of preferred stock in considerably more detail in Chapter 9.

1. Number and Classes of Shares

The type and number of shares to be authorized in the company's Charter will usually be a matter of considerable negotiation among the company's founders. As a general rule of thumb, for a start-up company whose shares will be held by just a few owners, there is usually no reason to authorize more shares than are necessary to satisfy the proportional interests that the parties have agreed upon. *Query*: Can you identify any risks in authorizing more shares than are necessary in such a situation?

On the other hand, if the plan is to sell shares to the public, then a sufficient number of shares should be authorized in order to meet the expected demand of such a public offering. Finally, sufficient shares should be authorized to satisfy the terms of any prospective option plan that the company may be contemplating. In Chapter 6, we describe this type of equity incentive compensation plan in more detail.

2. *Consideration*

More often than not, shareholders pay cash to acquire their shares. But corporations are not limited to cash consideration; indeed, very often corporations will issue shares in exchange for services or property. Most state statutes set forth the types of consideration that the corporation may receive in order for its shares to be validly issued — or, as it is often expressed in modern corporation statutes, for the shares to be "fully paid and non-assessable." The traditional view is that shares may be issued for money, real and personal property (including intangible property), and labor done. Under this approach, promissory notes and contracts to work in the future (i.e., future services) are not valid forms of consideration. The clear growing trend, however, is to abolish this distinction between valid and invalid forms of consideration. *Query*: What are the permitted forms of consideration in California and Delaware? [*Hint: See* Del. §§152-154; and Calif. §409; *see also* Model Act §6.21.]

With respect to non-cash consideration, the board of directors generally will be called upon to fix the value of the property or services to be received by the corporation in exchange for its shares. Most states' corporation statutes rely on the "good faith rule," whereby the judgment of the board as to the value of the property or services received by the corporation is binding and conclusive "in the absence of fraud" (*see* Calif. §409(b)), or as expressed in Del. §152, "in the absence of *actual* fraud" (emphasis added). *See also* Model Act §6.21(c). *Query*: What must the board do in order to determine the "value" of non-cash consideration to be received by the company in connection with the issuance of its stock? Whose interests are to be protected by imposing this obligation on the company's board of directors?

3. *Par Value*

"Par value" is rapidly becoming an obsolete concept in most states. However, we talk about this outmoded concept because Delaware (the most popular state for incorporation) continues to embrace the concept of "par value." Historically, par value originated at common law in order to provide investors with some protection against unfair dilution by fixing a minimum issuance price (i.e., the par value) for the shares to be sold by the corporation to raise capital. In this way, prospective purchasers could be confident that the shares to be issued would not be sold for less than their stated par value. This concept, however, does not have any application to the resale of the shares by the purchasers. Thus investors in the secondary markets can trade the issuer's stock at whatever price they want without regard to the par value of the shares. In Delaware, this means that the aggregate par value of all of the issued shares will constitute the minimum amount of the corporation's "legal capital." If, as is usually the case, the par value is set at a nominal amount (i.e., $0.01) and the shares are sold for a price that is greater than their par value, then the excess over the par value is "capital surplus," a concept that shall become important as a matter of Delaware law later in this chapter when we discuss statutory limitations on the payment of dividends (and other distributions) by the corporation to its shareholders. *Query*: How does the California statute treat the concept of "par value?" [*Hint: See* Calif. §205.]

The concept of par value created certain difficulties for the corporation when, as a going concern, it sought to raise additional capital by issuing more shares *after* completing its original offering of stock. Unless the corporation had been successful at keeping the market price of its shares *above* the stated par value, the company generally would be precluded from issuing additional shares, as a practical matter. Why? To address this potential (and very real) problem, the practice grew up to set the par value at an arbitrarily low amount (i.e., $1 or even less), an amount that typically is way below the actual issuance price for the shares. *Query*: How does the use of nominal par value avoid problems for the issuer when it decides to issue more shares after completing its initial financing?

4. Issuance of Shares

In order for the shares to be validly issued, we know that the shares must be "authorized" by an appropriate provision in the company's Charter. Once the shares have been sold by the corporation, they are generally referred to as "authorized and issued shares." So long as they are not reacquired by the corporation — that is, so long as they remain in the hands of the shareholders — they are also "outstanding shares" (or what is generally referred to as "authorized, issued, and outstanding" shares). Shares that were "authorized and issued" but which are no longer "outstanding" are shares that were previously issued by the corporation, but subsequent to their issuance, the shares were reacquired by the corporation. In California and under the Model Act, those shares return to the pool of authorized and unissued shares, unless the articles of incorporation specifically states that reacquired shares of that class may not be reissued. *See* Calif. §510 and Model Act §6.31. Where reissuance is prohibited, the company should amend its articles of incorporation to reflect the reduction in the authorized shares of that class.

In some jurisdictions, such as Delaware, these reacquired shares are referred to as "treasury shares" or "treasury stock." The general rule in most states that utilize the concepts of par value and treasury stock is that a corporation may resell (i.e., issue) treasury shares for less than their par value. The notion is that once the shares were issued for an amount not less than their par value, they remain "issued" even though the corporation may later reacquire the shares. So long as these treasury shares are not retired (i.e., not cancelled), the shares remain "issued," but are treated as no longer "outstanding." When the treasury shares are subsequently "reissued," the notion is that the company has already received a contribution to capital (i.e., the "par value") for these shares, and this capital contribution was not eliminated. Consequently, when the company goes to "resell" treasury shares, this issuance has no impact on the corporation's "stated capital" (i.e., the aggregate par value of the company's issued shares). *Query*: As a matter of Delaware law, what is the status of "treasury shares"? In other words, can a Delaware company "resell" its treasury shares?

Very often a corporation's capital structure will consist of a single class of shares, known as "common shares." However, modern corporation statutes allow for much more complex capital structures by permitting the corporation to create additional and different classes of shares, generally known as "preferred shares" because they have some preference over the common shares. Thus, many practitioners refer to preferred shares as "senior securities" because of their stated preference over the common shares, which are then viewed as the residual layer of ownership in the corporation. However, the law is equally clear that preferred shares are "equity securities," and thus are distinct from debt. This distinction is important because the claims of the debtholders must be satisfied *before* any distributions may be made by the corporation to its equity holders (whether they hold preferred or common shares). (We describe this rule of "priority" in more detail later in this chapter as part of our discussion of liquidation rights.) The reason that things can get a little confusing is that practitioners often lump preferred stock and debt instruments (such as bonds and debentures) into the term "senior securities." In one sense, this is accurate in that both debt and preferred shares are "senior" to the common shares. However, it bears emphasizing that there is an important distinction between debt instruments (such as bonds and debentures) versus preferred shares — even though they may collectively be referred to as "senior securities" — because no distributions may be made to the preferred shareholders until the claims of *all* of the debtholders have been satisfied.

In order for preferred shares to be validly issued, the Charter must authorize these shares by an appropriate provision that sets forth the "rights, preferences and privileges" of each class of preferred shares to be sold by the corporation. On the other hand, with respect to debt, the "power" to issue bonds, debentures, and other debt obligations belongs to the board of directors (as the manager of the company's business affairs) in the absence of a provision to the contrary in the company's Charter. Thus, the power to issue debt is not dependent on express authorization by the company's Charter, unlike the issuance of preferred shares. In Chapter 9, we talk more about the use of debt financing as part of the capital structure of a start-up business (such as SoftCo).

The next few sections describe in very general terms the various types of "rights, preferences and privileges" that are widely used in connection with the issuance of preferred stock. These include: voting rights, dividend rights, liquidation rights, redemption rights, conversion rights, preemptive rights, and restrictions on the preferred shareholder's right to transfer ownership of such shares. The following description is set forth in very general terms because we discuss these "preferred stock attributes" in considerably more detail in Chapter 9.

5. *Voting Rights*

Most states' corporation statutes provide that each outstanding share is entitled to one vote, unless the Charter provides otherwise. *See, e.g.,* Del. §212; and Model Act §7.21. Thus, as a general proposition, the Charter may provide for classes of shares with a greater or lesser vote per share, or even for classes of shares that have no voting rights. While California follows essentially the same rule by permitting a class of shares to have full, limited, or no voting rights, at the same time no denial or limitation of voting rights is going to be effective under California law unless one or more classes of outstanding shares (either alone or in the aggregate) are entitled to full voting rights. *See* Calif. §400(a). "Notwithstanding this [statutory provision], however, the Department of Corporations tends to look with disfavor upon nonvoting equity securities. [*See* 10 Cal. Code Regs. §260.140.1.] The principal exception is preferred stock. . . ." Philip W. Peters, *The California Corporation: Legal Aspects of Organization and Operation*, vol. 31, Corporate Practice Series (3d ed. 2003) at pg. A-12. We describe the attributes of venture capital preferred shares, which very definitely include voting rights, in more detail in Chapter 9. *Query*: What is the Department of Corporations? In general, how do its functions differ from those of the secretary of state?

6. *Dividend Rights*

Generally speaking, dividends are *pro rata* payments by the corporation to its equity shareholders that may consist, among other things, of cash, property, common shares, or preferred shares. The decision to declare dividends is generally left to the discretion of the company's board of directors. No shareholder has a legally enforceable "right" to a dividend unless and until the board "declares" a dividend. Very often, preferred shareholders will be given a dividend preference, which means the stated amount of the dividend preference (e.g., $10 per year) must be paid to the preferred shareholders *before* any dividends can be paid to the common shareholders. Thus, the preferred shares are "senior" to the common shares. In addition, there are different types of dividend preferences (e.g., "cumulative" vs. "non-cumulative"), which are explored in more detail in Chapter 9.

Determining Validity of Dividends (and Other Distributions to Shareholders). The amount of dividends and other distributions by a corporation to its shareholders (such as payments made by the corporation to repurchase its shares) are subject to certain statutory limitations. As a general rule, states have long imposed limitations on distributions to shareholders, including dividends, in order to protect the interests of the company's creditors. *Query*: How can the interests of creditors be impaired by the board's decision to pay dividends to the company's shareholders?

The nature of these statutory restrictions has evolved over the years into a difficult and complex branch of corporation law. Of necessity, the discussion that follows will provide a brief introduction to this area of corporate law focusing primarily on the differing approaches followed by California and Delaware. By way of broad generalization, California (like many states today, including the Model Act states) follows what is often referred to as a "balance sheet" test, borrowing from generally accepted accounting practices (GAAP). Delaware, on the other hand, continues to follow what are traditionally known as the "legal capital rules" to determine the validity of a particular distribution by a Delaware company to its stockholders. In addition to these tests, virtually every state has adopted some form of "insolvency" limitation on the company's ability to make distributions to its shareholders.

California Law. California relies on accounting entries (as reflected on the company's balance sheet) to determine whether the company has sufficient funds legally available to pay the proposed distribution to shareholders. *See* Calif. §§500-502 (as amended in 2011). Briefly summarized, under California's balance sheet test, the statute allows the payment of dividends if immediately after the dividend distribution (1) total assets equal or exceed total liabilities, and (2) the payment does not endanger any liquidation preference. In the alternative, the California statute permits distributions if they satisfy a retained earnings test. *See* David M. Hernand and Abigail Hing Wen, *State Corner: California Amends Corporations Code to Liberalize and Streamline Legal Standards for Corporate Distributions and Dividends*, 25 INSIGHTS 29 (October 2011);

W. Alex Voxman, *California Corporations Code Provisions Governing Dividends and Distributions Amended and Streamlined with the Passage of AB 571*, BUSINESS LAW NEWS, State Bar of California, Issue 1 at pg. 1 (2012).

Delaware Law.   Delaware, following the legal capital rules, "limits dividends to the extent that there is sufficient surplus, which is defined . . . as the amount net assets or net worth is in excess of the legal capital. [Thus, Delaware permits] dividends out of surplus of any and all varieties, whether [it] is earned [surplus, i.e., retained earnings] or capital surplus." JAMES D. COX & THOMAS LEE HAZEN, CORPORATIONS (2d ed. 2003) at pp. 556-557; *see also* Del. §§154, 170(a), 173. In Delaware, the determination of a legally available source of funds for the payment of dividends (and other distributions to stockholders) is linked (in substantial part) to the concept of par value. As described earlier in this chapter, the excess of the purchase price paid to the corporation over the par value of the shares issued is generally allocated to capital surplus. Under Delaware law, both capital surplus and earned surplus (i.e., retained earnings) are equally available as a source of funds for shareholder distributions. *See* COX & HAZEN, *supra*, at 561. *Query*: What is earned surplus?

The Insolvency Test.   In addition to the tests used today in Delaware and California, the oldest form of limitation on the ability of the company to pay dividends is generally known as the "insolvency test." "Today, virtually all states have some form of balance sheet test [imposed by state statute] in addition to an insolvency limitation." COX & HAZEN, *supra*, at page 562; *see, e.g.*, Model Act §6.40. The insolvency test originated in equity, but today,

> [t]here are two rival definitions of "insolvency": (1) The commercial or equity test of an inability to meet debts and obligations promptly as they fall due;[4] and (2) the bankruptcy or "balance sheet" test, an excess of the amount of liabilities over the total value of the assets. It is not always clear in dividend statutes which of the two possible meanings of "insolvency" should be taken. The rule against impairment of capital should take care of the question of the total assets at least equaling the liabilities,[6] but, if the insolvency limitation is to have any additional force or effect, it should be drawn so as to cover some objective test of reasonable grounds for believing that the corporation will not be rendered unable to pay its debts and liabilities, both long- and short-term, as they fall due. Probably the most prevalent interpretation of prohibitions against insolvency in dividend statutes is the equity test.

COX & HAZEN, *supra*, at pp. 562-563.

Liability for Invalid Distributions.   Historically, directors were held strictly liable for approving an illegal distribution. Today, modern statutes generally have moved away from this standard of strict liability and will impose personal liability on directors who approved an illegal distribution only if the facts show that they did not act in good faith. "It would appear that [today the dominant public policy is to] protect directors [from

---

4. *See* . . . Cal. Gen. Corp. Law §501 (West 1990); . . .

6. Since rules against capital impairment operate on the theory that dividends will be paid out of the excess of net assets over liabilities and stated capital, such a rule requires the total assets to exceed total liabilities.

personal liability for a shareholder distribution] whenever they act in good faith and with the reasonable care that the circumstances require. If greater protection is demanded [by the company's creditors], this should and does occur through the loan agreements that lenders so frequently require for their protection." COX & HAZEN, *supra*, at pg. 570.

It is also possible for shareholders who receive an illegal distribution to be held liable to the corporation. Thus, under some statutes, the shareholder may be personally liable for the amount of the illegal distribution if the facts show that the shareholder knew the distribution was illegal at the time of its receipt. *See, e.g.*, Calif. §506 and Model Act §8.33(b)(2). Another potential source of liability in this area of shareholder distributions is fraudulent conveyance law, which (in the case of shareholder distributions) generally will allow creditors to recover from the shareholder directly if the distribution was made by the corporation when it is an insolvent debtor. *See, e.g.*, Uniform Fraudulent Transfer Act §§3-8.

7. *Rights on Dissolution: Herein of Liquidation Rights*

The equivalent of "corporate death" is known as "dissolution," which generally involves two legal steps. First comes the decision (either voluntary or involuntary) to terminate the existence of the corporation (i.e., cease doing business). Second comes the winding up of the company's business affairs, involving most notably the payment of creditors' claims against the company, to be followed by the distribution of the company's remaining assets, if there are any, to its shareholders. This is known as a "liquidating distribution." Before we discuss the second step (involving liquidation rights, which are very important in the context of venture capital investment), let us briefly describe the mechanics of the first step, the decision to terminate the existence of the corporation.

This decision can be made on a voluntary or involuntary basis. As to voluntary dissolution, every state has a statute that provides for voluntary dissolution when authorized by the requisite vote.

> . . . The proposal to dissolve is usually to be made in the first instance by the directors. Most states require an authorization by the directors before the shareholders may vote,[2] and only a few states do not mandate director approval.[3] Upon the requisite stockholders' vote at a meeting held upon the prescribed notice to all shareholders without regard to class or voting restrictions, the dissolution can proceed without any confirmatory court action.[4] The number of stockholder votes required varies widely among the states,[5] with most requiring a majority of the shares entitled to vote. . . . In some states, dissolution may be had upon the written [consent] of all or of a specified majority of the shares without a meeting.[7]

---

2. *E.g.*, Del. Code Ann. tit. 8, §275 (2001).

3. *E.g.*, Cal. Corp. Code §1900(a) (West 1990).

4. *E.g.*, Del. Code Ann. tit 8, §275 (2001). . . .

5. *See* Cal. Corp. Code §1900(a) (West 1990) (50 percent of the voting power); Del. Code Ann., tit. 8, §275 (2001) (majority of the shares entitled to vote).

7. *See, e.g.*, Del. Code Ann. tit. 8, §275(c) (2001). . . .

State statutes commonly authorize dissolution solely on the approval of the incorporators or the board of directors when the corporation either has not issued shares or has not commenced business.[8] Some jurisdictions so empower the incorporators or board of directors only if the corporation has not issued shares.[9] . . .

In most states only the voting shares have a voice as to dissolution under many corporation acts.[12] Filing of a certificate of dissolution and, in some states, the publication of notice are required steps. After the statement of intent to dissolve has been duly adopted and filed, notice thereof is generally required to be sent to all known creditors.[13] When a corporation has qualified to do business in several states, it must make appropriate filings for dissolution in each state.[14]

Cox & Hazen, *supra*, at pp. 706-707.

On the other hand, the decision to terminate the existence of the corporation may be made on an involuntary basis. For our purposes, more often than not, involuntary dissolution involves a judicially supervised proceeding in response to a shareholder petitioning the court to dissolve the corporation. Since most courts do not undertake this request lightly, generally speaking, there must be "grounds for dissolution." For reasons that are described at length in your introductory Business Associations course, the remedy of dissolution is most important in the context of the privately held corporation where there is no market for the shares. Consequently,

> . . . most corporation acts provide for involuntary dissolution in a suit by minority shareholders in some or all of the following four situations:[2] (1) when the directors are deadlocked, the shareholders cannot break the deadlock, and irreparable injury to the corporation is suffered or threatened; (2) when the directors, controlling managers, or majority shareholders are acting in an illegal, oppressive, or fraudulent manner; (3) when the shareholders are deadlocked and cannot elect directors; and (4) when corporate assets have been misapplied or wasted. The emphasis of such actions is the protection of the interests of the shareholders.

Cox & Hazen, *supra*, at pp. 710-711.

Once the dissolution decision has been reached, then the corporation remains in existence in order to complete the orderly winding up of its business affairs. This process has been described as follows:

> . . . During the course of these proceedings, the assets will be collected and realized upon, the claims of creditors will be settled, and the remaining assets will be distributed to the shareholders. The statutes of most states proscribe the winding-up process only in a general way. The most important questions are the rights of creditors. . . . It also is to be remembered that the directors of a corporation retain their fiduciary obligations during the winding-up process. . . .
>
> . . . The dissolution of a corporation, like that of a partnership, operates only with respect to future transactions. The corporation or partnership continues until all

---

8. *See, e.g.,* Del. Code Ann. tit. 8, §274 (2001).
9. *See* Cal. Corp. Code §1900(b)(3) (West 1990).
12. *See, e.g.,* Del. Code Ann. tit. 8, §275 (2001).
13. *See, e.g.,* Cal. Corp. Code §1903 (West 1990). . . .
14. *See* Cal. Corp. Code §§2112 & 2113 (West 1990).
2. *See, e.g.,* Cal. Corp. Code §1800 (West 1990); Del. Code Ann. tit. 8, §§226, 352 (2001). . . .

preexisting matters are terminated. The dissolution does not destroy the authority of a partner to act for his former associates and for creditors in winding up the business, as distinguished from carrying on the partnership's ordinary business.[6] Corporate agents have similar authority.

Today states commonly provide for continued existence of the corporation for winding-up purposes.[7] . . . In the eyes of the common law, the assets are a trust fund for creditors and shareholders, and a court of equity has the power to liquidate the assets. . . .

* * *

When a corporation is dissolved by expiration of the time specified in its [C]harter, by a voluntary dissolution, . . . or in any other manner, it ceases to exist unless there is some statutory provision continuing its existence. It no longer has the capacity or power to enter into contracts, to take, hold, or convey property, to sue or be sued, or to exercise any other power. Debts due to or by the corporation are not extinguished. Even in the absence of a statute, a court of equity can enforce collection of debts due to a corporation for the benefit of creditors and shareholders and will satisfy debts due from the corporation out of its assets. The property of the corporation belongs to the shareholders, subject to the corporate debts and the powers of the liquidators.

COX & HAZEN, *supra*, at pp. 712-714.

Once the orderly winding up of the company's business affairs has been completed and the claims of the company's creditors are satisfied, the remaining assets are distributed out to the company's shareholders, in what is generally known as a "liquidating distribution." In the context of a liquidating distribution, the remaining assets are distributed *pro rata* (either in cash or in kind) to the company's shareholders. However, the Charter may change that priority of payment by giving preferred shareholders ("senior" shares) a right to receive payment (i.e., a liquidating distribution) first, before any payments in liquidation can be paid to the common shareholders ("junior" shares). Again, if such a preference is to be conferred on a particular class of shares, this right must be specifically set forth in the Charter. *Query*: Why is it important to discuss the *end* of the corporation prior to the formation of the corporation — that is, *before* the Charter has even been filed?

8. Redemptions and Repurchases

Shareholders will often bargain for the right to force the company to repurchase their shares under certain circumstances, known as *redemption rights*. This right of redemption also may exist in favor of the corporation, whereby the company has the right to repurchase the shares, typically on the happening of certain events or during certain windows of time.

Since redemptions constitute a payment to shareholders (i.e., a distribution), there must be a legally available source of funds in order for the redemption to be valid. Consequently, all of the restrictions that were described in the previous

---

6. . . . Uniform Partnership Act §30 (1969); 2 Alan A. Bromberg & Larry E. Ribstein, Law of Partnership §7.15 (Supp. 1999).

7. *See, e.g.*, Cal. Corp. Code §2010 (West 1990). . . .

subsection — that limit the amount of dividend distributions that a company can validly pay — will apply in this context as well. The redemption price (i.e., the amount to be paid by the corporation to redeem out its shares) is typically set forth in the company's Charter, or it may be fixed in the discretion of the board.

9. Conversion Rights

Generally speaking, conversion rights give the shareholders the option to convert their shares into some other security of the corporation (e.g., preferred shares may be given the right to convert into common shares). The conversion right sometimes will be made exercisable only on the happening of certain events or only during certain periods of time. For example, outside the venture capital context, when investors purchase preferred shares that are not otherwise convertible, they will bargain for the right to convert to common shares if the corporation does not pay dividends for a specified number of consecutive years. The mechanics of exercising this right of conversion — where it exists by appropriate provision included in the company's Charter — are described at greater length in Chapter 9.

10. Preemptive Rights

Preemptive rights originated at early common law in order to:

. . . allow shareholders to acquire shares when the corporation issues new shares. This protects existing shareholders' proportional interest (voting and ownership) in the corporation's shares already issued and outstanding. For example, if a shareholder owns 300 of 1,000 outstanding common shares and the corporation proposes to issue 200 more common shares, a preemptive right would entitle the shareholder to acquire 60 more shares at the issue price, thus preserving the shareholder's 30 percent position.

Preemptive rights were once viewed as an inherent aspect of share ownership. . . . Over time this view became untenable, and preemptive rights are now generally a matter of statutory right. In some states they exist automatically unless the [Charter specifies] otherwise ("opt out"). In others, they do not exist unless the [Charter provides] for them ("opt in"). Preemptive rights make issuing new shares cumbersome, particularly if the firm's shares are publicly held. . . .

ALAN R. PALMITER, CORPORATIONS: EXAMPLES & EXPLANATIONS (7th ed. 2012) at pg. 68. While preemptive rights, set in the Charter and applicable to all shares of the class to which they apply, are now infrequently used, contractual preemptive rights granted to specific investors are a regular part of venture capital transactions. We examine the nature of these contractual rights as part of our discussion of Investor Rights Agreements in Chapter 10. *Query*: What is the default rule under the corporation statutes of California and Delaware with regard to preemptive rights? [*Hint*: *See* Del. §102(b) and Calif. §204(a); *see also* Model Act §6.30.]

11. Blank Check Shares

We can now see that very often corporations will want to issue shares that have different combinations of attributes. And we also know that in order to create these differences among classes of shares, the Charter must describe the rights, preferences, and privileges of each class of authorized shares.

> But it frequently happens that the terms of stock to be issued are subject to considerable negotiation between the corporation and the potential investors and that time is of the essence for all. Because it would jeopardize so many potential issuances of noncommon stock for the corporation to have to seek shareholder approval of an amendment to the [Charter] and would likewise be impossible to predict the precise terms of noncommon stock in advance so that those terms can be included in the [Charter] from the initial incorporation, [modern corporation] statutes provide that the [Charter] may include a provision authorizing more than one class (i.e., preferred as well as common) and more than one series of stock with such attributes as the board decides. The maximum number of noncommon shares must still be stated in the [Charter] but the terms of those shares can be decided later, as the corporation is prepared to sell them to an investor. Once the terms of the new stock have been agreed upon, the corporation's board of directors adopts a resolution setting out the terms and files that resolution with the Secretary of State [often referred to as a "Certificate of Determination"]. That resolution becomes a part of the [Charter] and thus a public record. A provision allowing this procedure is said to be one that authorizes *blank stock* or *blank check stock*.

ERIC CHIPPIANELLI, BUSINESS ENTITIES at pg. 185 (2006). *Query*: Does the corporation statute of either California or Delaware permit the use of "blank check stock"? [*Hint: See* Del. §102(a); and Calif. §§202 and 401(a); *see also* Model Act §§6.01-6.02.] Would you recommend that SoftCo include a provision authorizing the use of "blank check stock" as part of its Charter?

12. Restrictions on Transferability of Shares

Corporate shares are personal property. As such, they are freely transferable. However, frequently the founders of a new corporation will want to impose restrictions on the ability of shareholders to freely dispose of their shares. In practice, share transfer restrictions are found most often in the case of small, closely held corporations. Since we know from our discussion in Chapter 2 that there is a limited market (if any) for shares of a privately held corporation, why do you suppose investors continue to insist on imposing restrictions on the transfer of shares of a new start-up business, such as SoftCo? In reflecting on this question, you may want to consider the following observations:

> Participants in a close corporation may want to restrict the transferability of shares for a number of reasons. Because of the close working relationship that often exists among owners and managers, they may want to retain power to select future associates and thus be able to exclude persons who will not be congenial or will not fit into the management team. Further, the participants may desire to restrict the transferability of shares to prevent their purchase by competitors or other persons unfriendly to the corporation. They may also impose transfer restrictions to prevent any one shareholder from gaining absolute control of the corporation by purchasing colleagues' stock. Another reason for restricting the transferability of shares is to preserve the corporation's eligibility to elect the tax status provided by Subchapter S of the Internal Revenue Code[4] or its eligibility to

---

4. By preventing transfer to a shareholder who does not qualify under Subchapter S or who will refuse to consent to the corporation's election of Subchapter S. *See* I.R.C. §§1371-1373 (1988). Restrictions on the

elect to be governed by special close corporation legislation in a number of states requiring close corporations to restrict the transfer of their stock.

There are many different types of share transfer restrictions. The most widely used is the so-called first-option refusal [or right of first refusal], which grants the corporation or the other shareholders a right to purchase shares at a set price or at the price offered by a third party, respectively, if a holder decides to sell or otherwise transfer her shares. Other types of transfer restrictions are as follows: (1) absolute prohibitions against transfer; (2) prohibitions against transfer to designated classes of persons, such as competitors; (3) limitation of transfers to stated classes of persons — for example, descendants of the corporation's founders or residents of a designated American state; (4) "consent restraints" that prohibit the disposition of stock without approval of the corporation's directors or shareholders or a stated percentage of one of those groups; and (5) options giving the corporation or the other shareholders the right to purchase the shares of a holder on his death or disability, on the termination of his employment with the corporation, or on the occurrence of some other event. Somewhat related functionally to restrictions on the transfer of stock are buyout agreements, whereby the shareholder agrees to sell stock, and the corporation or the other shareholders agree to buy it, on the occurrence of a stated contingency, such as the shareholder's death or retirement. Such an agreement stipulates a transfer price or sets out a formula for determining price. . . .

Cox & Hazen, *supra*, at pp. 396-397.

Assuming that the founders and/or investors in the new company wish to impose limitations on the transferability of the newly issued shares, the next obvious question is whether those restrictions will be enforceable. Although the dominant public policy, as a matter of property law, is to promote full transferability, the general rule today as a matter of corporate law is to permit share transfer restrictions subject to a standard of reasonableness. Thus the modern view adopted by most courts is to enforce restrictions that are reasonable in light of all the circumstances, which of necessity involves a fact intensive inquiry. *Query*: Would you recommend that Joan and Michael impose stock transfer restrictions on shares to be issued by SoftCo? Should this restriction apply to *all* of the issued shares?

E. Role of Shareholders

The corporate norm mandates that the board of directors manages the business affairs of the corporation. As a direct corollary, the shareholders are passive investors with limited (if any) ability to involve themselves in questions of management policy within the corporation. However, the shareholders do have voting rights, and through the exercise of their voting rights, the shareholders (as owners of the corporation) do have an important, although indirect, influence on the management of the company's business affairs. This section offers a broad overview of the mechanics of shareholder meetings (including the voting process), the shareholders' election (and monitoring) of the

---

transfer of stock are also useful in implementing exemptions from the 1933 Securities Act's registration provisions.

board of directors, and finally, we consider the scope of shareholders' rights to information about the corporation and its business affairs.

1. Shareholder Meetings

The traditional view is that valid shareholder action requires a shareholder meeting with a modern statutory exception for action by written consent (discussed later in this section). There are two types of shareholder meetings: annual and special. California section 600(b) requires annual meetings of the shareholders. *See also* Del. §211(b); and Model Act §§7.01-7.02. Indeed, most modern statutes provide that each shareholder has a right to have the corporation hold an annual meeting for the election of directors. If the corporation fails to hold the annual meeting within a statutorily prescribed period, then generally speaking, any shareholder of the corporation may petition the court of appropriate jurisdiction for an order that such a meeting be held. *See* Del. §211(c); and Calif. §600(c); *see also* Model Act §7.03. Any meeting other than an annual meeting is generally referred to as a special meeting of the shareholders.

With respect to the annual meeting of the shareholders, the time and place is usually fixed in the company's bylaws. However, most modern corporation statutes require that notice be given to each shareholder entitled to vote within a certain minimum and maximum number of days before the scheduled meeting date, whether annual or special. As a general rule, the notice for an annual meeting must specify the date, time, and place of the meeting and that the purpose of the meeting is to elect directors and conduct any other business that is proper at such meetings. *See* Calif. §600(b); and Del. §222. In many states today, the relevant statute requires that the notice for a special meeting set forth the purpose of the meeting. This is important because, as a general rule, the business that can be transacted at a special meeting will be limited to the matters set forth in the required notice. *See, e.g.,* Calif. §601(a).

As a general rule, notice must be delivered to the shareholders of record entitled to vote. Most state corporation statutes authorize the board of directors (or, in some cases, the bylaws) to fix a record date for purposes of determining which shareholders are entitled to notice of, and to vote at, the meeting (whether annual or special). *See* Del. §213; and Calif. §601(b).

Compliance with the (statutorily) prescribed notice requirements is vitally important because insufficient notice generally renders any action taken at such a meeting voidable at the insistence of those who did not participate. However, most modern corporation statutes permit shareholders to waive any required notice. Such a waiver generally must be in writing, but may be executed at any time, either before or after the meeting. *See generally* Del. §229; Calif. §601; and Model Act §7.06(a). In addition, there may be implied waiver of the notice requirements in those cases where the shareholders who did not receive proper notice nonetheless attend and participate in the meeting without objection to the defect in the notice of the meeting. *See* Del. §229; and Calif. §601; *see also* MBCA §7.06(b).

In order to have a valid meeting of the shareholders, a quorum must be present. In most states a quorum consists of a majority of the outstanding shares entitled to vote, unless the Charter provides for a different percentage, although in many states the Charter may not reduce the quorum below some statutorily prescribed minimum number of shares. See, e.g., Calif. §602(a) (which prescribes that "in no event shall a quorum consist of less than one-third of the outstanding shares entitled to vote," with a limited exception for "close corporations," a concept that is described in more detail later in this section). *Query*: What are the notice and quorum requirements of the corporation statute of your state?

Once a valid quorum exists at a duly noticed meeting of the shareholders, then the corporate lawyer may be called upon to determine if valid shareholder action has been taken at such a meeting. This determination generally entails an analysis of the minimum number of shares that must approve a matter submitted for a shareholder vote in order for the vote to be binding. The requisite voting standard will depend on whether the shareholders voted on the election of directors or some other matter. Analysis of this issue further turns on whether shareholder action was taken by written consent in lieu of a meeting. As described in the following sections, shareholder voting for directors involves a different set of rules, which entails a thorough understanding of the differences between "straight voting" vs. "cumulative voting" in elections for directors.

2. *Action by Written Consent*

Most states' corporation statutes permit shareholder action to be taken (i.e., approved) without a meeting of the shareholders *if* the requisite number of shares submit written consent approving a proposed action. In some states action may be taken without a shareholders' meeting only by *unanimous* written consent. *See, e.g.,* Model Act §7.04(a). On the other hand, both California and Delaware permit an "absolute majority" of the shareholders to take action by written consent and without a meeting. *See* Del. §228; and Calif. §603(a). Under the Model Act, corporations may opt-in to written consent by an "absolute majority" with an authorizing provision in their articles of incorporation. *See* Model Act §7.04(b). *Query*: What are the advantages and disadvantages of modern statutes that dispense with the need to hold a shareholders' meeting by authorizing shareholder action to be taken by "written consent"? What is the voting standard required under the "written consent" provision of the corporation statute of your state? For example, can the shareholders elect directors by written consent? *See, e.g.,* Calif. §603(d).

3. *Shareholder Voting Process*

The requisite number of shares that must vote to approve a matter submitted to a vote of the shareholders is prescribed by the relevant corporation statute, although typically this default rule may be modified by an appropriate provision in the Charter, or sometimes even by an appropriate bylaw provision. As a general proposition, lawyers engaging in planning the capital structure of a new, small, closely-held corporation will often find that the participants in this new business will want to modify the traditional rules for shareholder voting in order to allocate managerial control — and perhaps even create liquidity — for the participants. This section generally describes the default rules for shareholder voting and then discusses some of the devices commonly used to modify these default rules, most notably the use of voting trusts, pooling agreements and buy-sell agreements.

Vote Required. As a general rule, each share is entitled to one vote, absent a contrary provision in the company's Charter. Moreover, the general rule is that a quorum consists of a majority of the shares entitled to vote (present either in person or by proxy) absent a contrary provision in the company's Charter. Once a valid quorum is established, then most corporation statutes provide that the quorum cannot be broken if a disgruntled group of shareholders should decide to walk out in the middle of the meeting. *See, e.g.,* MBCA §7.25(b). *Query*: How do the Delaware and California statutes treat this issue? [*Hint: See* Del. §216; and Calif. §602.]

Shareholders can attend a meeting in person, or alternatively, they can decide to vote by *proxy*. While virtually all states authorize voting by proxy, the mechanics of such voting are subject to varying regulation by local law. At a minimum, most states require that the proxy appointment be contained in a writing signed by the shareholder of record. *See, e.g.,* MBCA §7.22. The proxy creates an agency relationship in which the shareholder of record (i.e., the principal) grants the proxy holder (i.e., the agent) the power to vote his/her/its shares. As such, this agency relationship is generally freely revocable by the principal/shareholder, unless the proxy has been made irrevocable. *Query*: As a matter of California and Delaware law, when (if ever) may a proxy be made irrevocable? [*Hint: See* Del. §212; and Calif. §705.] Today, most states' statutes limit the duration of a proxy to 11 months, unless otherwise provided in the proxy, thus requiring the solicitation of a new proxy for each annual shareholders' meeting. *Query*: What is the default rule under Delaware and California regarding the duration of a proxy? (While beyond the scope of this casebook, it bears emphasizing that proxy voting in publicly traded companies is subject to detailed federal regulation under the SEC's proxy rules promulgated pursuant to the 1934 Securities Exchange Act, in addition to the state law provisions described above.)

Apart from the election of directors — which is governed by a different set of rules — modern corporation statutes generally limit mandatory shareholder voting to matters that constitute a fundamental, organic change. As a general proposition, these matters usually include removal of directors, amending the Charter, mergers, sales of substantially all of the company's assets not in the ordinary course of business, and voluntary dissolution. Under certain circumstances, shareholders may be asked by management to approve other matters, such as directors' conflict of interest transactions (*see, e.g.,* Del. §144; and Calif. §310; *see also* Model Act §8.63) or requests for indemnification submitted by the company's officers and/or directors (*see, e.g.,* Del. §145; and Calif. §317; *see also* Model Act §8.55), among other things. In the case of most small, start-up corporations, usually the minority interests (as part of their investment decision) may bargain to expand their voting rights beyond the matters described above.

In order to determine whether matters submitted for a vote of the shareholders have received the requisite level of shareholder approval, the following rules generally apply. Under many state statutes, valid shareholder action requires approval (i.e., yes votes) of an absolute majority of shares entitled to vote for certain fundamental changes to be approved, such as a merger. *See, e.g.,* Del. §251(c). Other statutes require that the yes votes constitute a majority of the shares actually voting. *See, e.g.,* MBCA §7.25(c).

Historically, many states required the favorable vote (i.e., yes votes) of a majority of shares present at a meeting (either in person or by proxy) as to those matters that do not involve a fundamental change. *See, e.g.,* Del. §216. As a final reminder, the transaction planner must consult the company's Charter since most states permit the Charter to require a super-majority vote rather than the statutorily prescribed minimum. *Query*: What is the voting standard required for valid shareholder action under Calif. §602(a) as to matters not involving a fundamental corporate change?

Pooling Agreements.   Very often — and especially in the context of closely held corporations — no one shareholder will own a sufficient number of shares to have voting control. In these cases, shareholders may agree to combine their voting strength by agreeing to vote their shares as a block. In general, pooling agreements are valid and enforceable so long as they relate to a matter on which shareholders may properly vote. (You recall, of course, the famous case of *McQuade v. Stoneham*, 189 N.E. 234 (N.Y. 1934), in which the court addresses the issue of when does a shareholder agreement relate to "non-shareholder" matters.) More often than not, shareholder pooling agreements relate to the election of directors. The Voting Agreements frequently used in venture capital transactions, and discussed in Chapter 10, are effectively pooling agreements.

Pooling agreements are contracts, and as such, are governed by the laws of contracts. In addition, some states specify the maximum duration of such agreements, while other states require notice of the agreement, while still other states limit the remedies available in the event of breach of a pooling agreement. *But see* Del. §218(c); Calif. §706(a) and (c); and Model Act §7.31, none of which limit these agreements in these ways. With respect to enforcement of a pooling agreement, the well-known *Ringling Bros.* case illustrates the importance of appropriate drafting so that the pooling agreement achieves the party's objectives. *Ringling Bros.-Barnum & Bailey Combined Shows, Inc. v. Ringling*, 53 A.2d 441 (Del. 1947); *see also Ramos v. Estrada*, 10 Cal. Rptr. 2d 833 (Cal. App. 1992) (where the California court upheld mandatory buy-sell provisions of a shareholder pooling agreement that were triggered when one shareholder group (who was a party to the pooling agreement) failed to vote their block of shares in the manner required under the terms of the agreement).

Voting Trusts.   Pooling agreements must be distinguished from voting trusts. In the case of a voting trust, shareholders actually transfer legal title to their shares to a voting trustee, unlike the pooling agreement, which does not involve the transfer of ownership of the shares. Under the terms of the voting trust agreement that establishes the voting trust, the trustee usually has exclusive voting power over the shares transferred into the voting trust. As to other attributes of share ownership — such as the right to receive dividends — the voting trust agreement will usually specify that these rights remain with the original shareholders, who now hold voting trust certificates as evidence of their equitable ownership interest in the voting trust.

Voting trusts have long been regulated by corporation statutes. While the relevant state corporation statute must be consulted to determine all of the state's requirements for a valid voting trust, most modern statues require: (i) a written trust agreement setting forth the trustee's obligations; (ii) the voting trust generally may not exceed 10 years, although its duration may be extended under certain circumstances; and (iii) a copy of the voting trust agreement usually must be delivered to the corporation at its principal office and thus made part of the company's books and records. *Query*: What are the requirements that must be satisfied as a matter of Delaware and California law in order to establish a valid voting trust? [*Hint*: *See* Del. §218; and Calif. §706(b); *see also* Model Act §7.30.]

4. Election of Directors

The number of directors to be elected is generally fixed in the Charter or bylaws. In the absence of a staggered board (a concept which was described earlier in this chapter), the general rule is that all directors stand for election at each annual shareholders' meeting. The general method for electing directors is by straight (i.e., plurality) voting — meaning that a separate election is held for each open seat, and the top vote-getter in each election wins. As a practical matter, where straight voting applies, this means that a shareholder (or group of shareholders) owning a majority of the company's shares can elect the entire board of directors.

On the other hand, many states, such as California, mandate the use of cumulative voting, and in other states cumulative voting is available if the company's Charter (or its bylaws) include an appropriate provision (i.e., the "opt-in" approach). As a matter of long-standing California law, the shareholders' right to vote cumulatively in the election for directors may not be eliminated by the company's articles of incorporation, unless the requirements of Calif. §301.5 are satisfied.

In cumulative voting, there is a single election to fill all the open seats. If there are three seats open, for example, the top three vote-getters win. However, if available, cumulative voting allows minority shareholders to accumulate all of the votes attributable to their shares and pile them on one (or even a few) board candidates. By allowing the minority to cumulate (i.e., "pile on") their votes, the assumption is that this will increase the likelihood that the minority will be able to elect a representative to the company's board of directors. It bears emphasizing that cumulative voting only applies in elections for directors and thus has no relevance in shareholder voting on other matters.

Cumulative voting can be a bit confusing. The first step is to determine how many votes a shareholder may cast and then the next step is to determine how to best allocate the votes attributable to that block of shares over the nominees for election to the board of directors. This analysis has been aptly described as follows:

> The operation of cumulative voting can be tricky and involves some arithmetic. Suppose that Alphonse has 70 shares and Byron 30 shares. Under cumulative voting in an election of five directors, Alphonse would have a total of 350 (70 [shares] times 5 [director positions to be elected]) votes to distribute among his candidates as he chooses; Byron would have 150 (30 [shares] times 5 [director slots to be filled]) votes. If Byron votes intelligently, cumulative voting assures him at least one director. If Byron casts all of his 150 votes for his candidate, Alphonse cannot [cast his votes in such a manner as to] prevent the candidate's election. But Alphonse, if careful, can cast his 350 cumulative votes to elect the four other directors.

Cumulative voting has pitfalls for the unwary. If Alphonse spreads his votes unevenly or too thinly, he might elect only three or even fewer directors. Suppose Alphonse casts his votes and Byron responds as follows:

Alphonse (350 votes)		Byron (150 votes)	
Agatha	150	Bernice	50
Arthur	150	Bertrand	50
Alexis	20	Beatrice	50
Andrew	20		
Astor	10		

The top five vote-getters are Agatha, Arthur, Bernice, Bertrand, and Beatrice. By this inept voting, Alphonse placed only a minority of directors on the board despite owning 70 percent of the voting shares. To avoid such surprises, many statutes require advance notice of cumulative voting. Either the notice of the shareholders' meeting must state that cumulative voting is authorized or a shareholder planning to exercise her cumulative voting right must give notice before the meeting. MBCA §7.28(d) (notice to shareholders must be "conspicuous" or shareholder must give notice within 48 hours of meeting).

ALAN R. PALMITER, CORPORATIONS: EXAMPLES & EXPLANATIONS (7th ed. 2012), at pp. 140-141. Consistent with the foregoing description of the mechanics of cumulative voting, the following formula is often used to determine the number of shares needed to elect one director:

$$\frac{S}{D+1} + 1$$

where "S" equals the total number of shares actually voting and "D" equals the number of directors to be elected. *Query*: Using this formula in the context of the Alphonse and Byron example described in the preceding excerpt, how would you recommend that the shareholders, Alphonse and Byron, allocate the votes attributable to their respective shareholdings in order to maximize their influence on the board of directors?

Cumulative voting is not the only mechanism available to assure that the minority interest gains representation on the board. In the context of privately held corporations, other mechanisms that are widely used (and which we have previously described in this chapter) include pooling agreements and issuing different classes of stock with different voting rights (sometimes referred to as "classified shares"). In the case of publicly traded companies, it is fairly unusual to have cumulative voting, even in California, long a bastion for mandatory cumulative voting. *See* Calif. §301.5; *see also* Model Act §7.28. *Query*: What are the pros and cons of straight versus cumulative voting for Joan and Michael in the context of incorporating SoftCo? Does your analysis of this question vary depending on whether SoftCo is to be financed by an institutional venture capital investor or by *Friends and Family*? What about Joan and Michael deciding to *Go-It-Alone*?

5. Removal and Resignation of Board Members: Filling Vacancies on the Board

Early common law allowed shareholders to remove directors only "for cause," which was generally defined to be egregious misconduct such as fraud, criminal activity, gross mismanagement, or self-dealing. Today, though, most states have liberalized their corporation statutes to allow shareholders to remove directors before their term expires — either with or without cause. Where shareholders seek (usually at a duly noticed special meeting) to remove a director (whether with or without cause), most states' statutes require that shareholders be given specific notice that removal of a director is to be considered at the meeting. What's more, directors who are to be removed for cause generally have the right to be informed of the reasons for removal and the right to respond to the accusations made. *Query*: What are the requirements under both Delaware and California law regarding the removal of directors? [*Hint: See* Del. §141(k); and Calif. §303; *see also* Model Act §8.08.]

What if the shareholders seek to remove a director that has been elected by the minority using cumulative voting? In order to prevent the majority from undermining the minority's use of cumulative voting to gain board representation,

> nearly all state statutes specify that a director elected under cumulative voting cannot be removed if any minority faction, with enough shares to have elected him by cumulative voting, votes against his removal. MBCA §8.08(c) (the Official Comment indicates that this restriction applies whether removal is with or without cause). For example, if 20 shares would have been enough to elect a director under cumulative voting, then he cannot be removed if 20 shares are voted against his removal.

PALMITER, *supra*, at pp. 144-145; *see also* Calif. §303.

In addition to vacancies created by removal of directors, vacancies on the board may also result from death or resignation of a director. No matter how the vacancy occurs, the next obvious question is *"Who fills vacancies on the board?"* The longstanding general rule is that either the board or the shareholders can fill such vacancies. Of course, shareholders can fill a vacancy on the board usually only by way of a duly noticed special shareholders' meeting. Today, however, some states limit the board's authority to fill vacancies, especially in those cases where the vacancy occurs because of removal of a director or where a vacancy results because the size of the board has been expanded to create new directorships. *Query*: What is the public policy premise underlying this statutory limitation on the board's ability to fill vacancies? As a matter of Delaware and California law, who fills vacancies on the board? [*Hint: See* Calif. §305; and Del. §223; *see also* Model Act §8.10.]

6. Shareholders' Rights of Inspection

To allow shareholders to exercise their voting rights on an informed basis, corporate law grants shareholders the right to receive certain information from the corporation. At early common law, shareholders generally had the right to inspect the company's books and records (either in person or by an agent) so long as the shareholder had a "proper purpose," which was generally taken to be a purpose related to the shareholders' interest as investors. Today, most states have codified this common law rule, usually carrying forward the "proper purpose" requirement that originated at common law. Under many states' statutes, certain records (such as the Charter, bylaws, and minutes of certain meetings) are available to shareholders as of right and without regard to a showing of proper purpose. Other corporate records, most notably accounting records and other types of financial information, are generally available for shareholder inspection only on a showing of "proper purpose." *See, e.g.*, MBCA §§16.01 and 16.02; Del. §220; and Calif. §1601. The general rule in most states continues to be that the shareholder requesting inspection of these types of more sensitive, proprietary corporate records must show a purpose that is reasonably related to the shareholder's interest in his/her/ its investment in the company. Most states also provide an enforcement mechanism in the event that the company denies shareholders access to the requested books and records, which very often takes the form of a judicially supervised summary proceeding. *See, e.g.*, MBCA §16.04; Del. §220(c); and Calif. §1603.

More recently, the MBCA has taken the rather dramatic step of requiring corporations to provide their shareholders with certain annual financial information, including a year-end balance sheet, income statement, and statement of changes in shareholders' equity. *See* MBCA §16.20. In the context of closely held corporations, this is often quite important since this may be the only source of mandatory disclosure imposed on the company. (You will recall that the SEC's periodic reporting requirements under the 1934 Securities Exchange Act extend only to publicly traded companies and do not apply to privately held corporations.) In a similar vein, California requires domestic corporations to file annual statements with the secretary of state, which must set forth certain required items of information. *See* Calif. §1502.

F. Role of Directors

It is axiomatic that the board of directors "manages the business affairs of the corporation." *See* Del. §141(a); and Calif. §300(a); *see also* Model Act §8.01. In this section, we review the basic mechanics required for valid board action, as well as the scope of directors' fiduciary duties and indemnification rights. In the process, we will also briefly describe the role of officers as part of the management hierarchy of the modern corporation.

1. Meetings of Directors

As described by a knowledgeable practicing California lawyer, California's (as well as most states') corporation statutes generally allow:

> . . . boards of directors to act [in one of the following ways:] by unanimous written consent,[35] at meetings conducted by means of conference telephone, facsimile,

---

35. Cal. Corp. Code §307(b). For transactions in which one or more directors has a conflict of interest, the transaction may be approved by written consent if the interested or common directors abstain in writing from providing consent, all required disclosures have been made to each non-interested or non-common

electronic mail or electronic video screen communication,[36] or at meetings held without notice or with defective notice if those not present waive notice.[37]

Moreover, committees can be delegated all the authority of the board, except the following:

- approving action that also requires shareholder approval;
- filling vacancies on the board or on any committee;
- fixing compensation of directors;
- amending, repealing, or adopting bylaws;
- amending or repealing any board resolution that by its express terms is not so amendable or repealable;
- authorizing a distribution to the shareholders except at a rate or in a periodic amount or within a price range set forth in the articles of incorporation or determined by the board; and
- appointing other committees of the board or members thereof.[38]

A majority of authorized directors constitutes a quorum, unless the articles of incorporation or bylaws provide [for] a lesser quorum, which lesser quorum shall be at least one-third the authorized number of directors but not less than two (unless there is but one director authorized, in which case the one director constitutes a quorum).[39] An act of the board typically requires concurrence of a majority of the directors present at a meeting that has a quorum; the articles or bylaws cannot reduce that requirement.[40] However, the articles can impose a higher requirement, and the bylaws can require a majority of the authorized directors for valid action (not just a majority of those at a meeting with a quorum).[41] A board meeting at which a quorum was initially present can continue to transact business after directors withdraw and break the quorum, but any action taken must be approved by at least a majority of the required quorum.[42]

Corporate Officers

A corporation must have a chairman of the board or a president or both, and unless otherwise provided in the articles of incorporation or bylaws, the president or the chairman of the board is the general manager and chief executive officer of the corporation. The corporation must also have a secretary and a chief financing officer, but any number of offices can be held by the same person unless the articles or bylaws provide otherwise.[43] Other officers and their titles and duties can be stated in the bylaws or determined by the board.

---

director before such director consents and these disclosures are included in the written consent. The foregoing provision expires on Jan. 1, 2011. *Id.* [*See* Del. §141.]

36. *Id.* §307(a)(6). For board meetings held by means of facsimile, electronic mail or electronic video screen communication, each board member must be able to communicate with all other board members concurrently and to participate fully in the meeting, including having the capacity to make proposals and objections with regard to corporate action.

37. Cal. Corp. Code §307(a)(3). [*See* Del. §141.]

38. Cal. Corp. Code §311. [*See* Del. §141.]

39. *Id.* §307(a)(7). The quorum requirement is based on the number of directors authorized and is therefore not reduced by a vacancy. [*See* Del. §141(b).]

40. Cal. Corp. Code §307(a)(8).

41. *Id.* §204(a).

42. *Id.* §307(a)(8). [*See* Del. §141(b).]

43. *Id.* §312(a). [*See* Del. §142.]

Indemnification of Directors, Officers, and Others

Statutory indemnification is permitted for the corporation's directors, officer, employees, and other agents. It is also permitted for persons who serve or have served in such capacities with any other enterprise at the request of the indemnifying corporation, as well as for the persons who served as such with any predecessor corporation.[44] . . . Indemnification is available in connection with civil, criminal, administrative, or investigative proceedings.[46] During the course of a proceeding, the corporation can advance a person's expenses upon an appropriate undertaking for repayment if it is ultimately determined that the recipient is not entitled to indemnification.[47]

The GCL ["General Corporate Law" of California] mandates indemnification for expenses in any case to the extent the individual has been successful on the merits.[48] Otherwise, the statute permits indemnification, in a derivative case [brought by a shareholder (or group of shareholders) on behalf of the corporation] for expenses and in a nonderivative case for expenses and also judgments, fines, settlements, and other amounts reasonably incurred, if the person acted in good faith and in a manner he or she believed to be in the best interests of the corporation.[49] In the case of a criminal proceeding, indemnification is permitted only if the person had no reasonable cause to believe the conduct of the person was unlawful.[50]

If a person has been adjudged liable in derivative proceedings, indemnification cannot be made unless the court determines that he or she is fairly and reasonably entitled to indemnity for expenses.[51] Either the disinterested directors, independent legal counsel if a quorum of disinterested directors is not available, the shareholders other than the person being indemnified, or the court can make the necessary determination whether the person has conducted himself or herself in a manner entitling him or her to indemnification.[52]

The corporation can provide and pay for liability insurance covering risks beyond the scope of the permitted indemnification described in the statute,[53] and under certain limited circumstances such insurance may even be obtained from a partially captive insurer.[54] In addition, the corporation can indemnify, and can purchase and maintain insurance on behalf of, any fiduciary of its employee benefit plans.[55] . . .

Philip Peters, *The California Corporation: Legal Aspects of Organization and Operation*, vol. 31 CORPORATE PRACTICE SERIES (3d ed. 2006) at pp. A-19–A-20.

---

44. *Id.* §317(a). [*See* Del. §145.]
46. Cal. Corp. Code §317(a). . . .
47. Cal. Corp. Code §317(f).
48. *Id.* §317(d). . . .
49. Cal. Corp. Code §317(b)-(c).
50. *Id.* §317(b).
51. *Id.* §317(c).
52. *Id.* §317(e).
53. *Id.* §317(i).
54. *Id.* . . .
55. Cal. Corp. Code §§207(f), 317(j).

2. *Fiduciary Duties of Directors, Officers, and Controlling Shareholders*

For many practicing lawyers, fiduciary duty law is an important factor in making a recommendation to the client as to the state in which it should incorporate. The following article chronicles the key differences between California and Delaware in this vitally important area of corporate law.

Edward Gartenberg
A *Review of Fiduciary Duties in California and Delaware Corporations*

State Bar of California, Business Law News, Oct. 2006

Introduction

The legal community and the press have focused much attention on the responsibilities of corporate officers and directors under the federal Sarbanes-Oxley Act. In addition, the daily press has been replete with examples such as the Enron litigation demonstrating the federal criminalization of corporate law. The advantages and disadvantages of the increasing federalization of the duties owed in the corporate context have been, and will continue to be, a source of debate. However, the business practitioner, and particularly, the business litigator in California, will most often look to the principles of state fiduciary duty law to evaluate potential claims within the corporate context. Given the historical predilection for incorporation in Delaware, the California lawyer practicing in this area should have familiarity with both Delaware and California law. This article seeks to present a brief summary of fiduciary duties in the corporate context under the laws of both states.

The corporation presents potential fiduciary duty issues for shareholders, directors, officers, employees, and promoters. It is often stated that shareholders do not owe a fiduciary duty in their capacity solely as shareholders to either the corporation or other shareholders. (See *Jones v. H.P. Ahmanson & Co.* (1969) 1 Cal. 3d 93.) The *Jones* case did identify certain circumstances in which a fiduciary duty may be imposed under California law: when a majority shareholder usurps a corporate opportunity from, or otherwise harms, the minority shareholder. (*Id.* at p. 108.; *Miles, Inc. v. Scripps Clinic and Research Foundation* (S.D. Cal. 1993) 810 F. Supp. 1091, 1099 (applying California law, "The general rule of limited liability of corporations is that shareholders do not owe each other a fiduciary duty."); *Ivanhoe Partners v. Newmont Min. Corp.* (Del. 1987) 535 A.2d 1334, 1344 (under Delaware law a shareholder owes a fiduciary duty only if it owns a majority interest in or exercises control over the business affairs of the corporation).

A careful analysis suggests that one must consider whether the corporation is closely held and whether the shareholder is a controlling shareholder. In both California and Delaware, as in other jurisdictions, it has been held that the controlling shareholder owes a fiduciary duty to both the corporation and the minority shareholders.

In closely held corporations, there are two principal views of the fiduciary duty of shareholders. Massachusetts and a number of other jurisdictions have adopted what has been characterized, probably improperly, as the "majority" view. This view holds that, at least in a closely held corporation, *all* officers, directors, and shareholders are fiduciaries of each other and, in that capacity, owe each other a heightened fiduciary duty, similar to that which partners owe each other in a partnership.

Delaware follows what has been characterized as the "minority" view that controlling shareholders, at least in closely held corporations, like officers and directors, owe fiduciary duties to the corporation. A shareholder need not own a majority of the corporation's share to be a "controlling shareholder." Thus, even if a shareholder owns less than 50% of the outstanding shares, if that shareholder exercises domination through actual control of corporate conduct, the shareholder can be deemed a controlling shareholder. The duties for controlling shareholders as expressed in at least some Delaware cases appear to be owed to the corporation only; California cases hold that the duties are owed to both the corporation and other shareholders. The controlling shareholder in a Delaware corporation, unlike a partner in a general partnership who owes a fiduciary duty to all other partners, does not owe a fiduciary to the other shareholders. Under Delaware law, however, a controlling shareholder may vote his shares in his own self-interest even if that interest is contrary to the corporation's best interest.

In both Delaware and California, the fiduciary duties owed by a controlling shareholder include the duties of loyalty and care. The application of those duties in Delaware are often presented in the context of alleged self-dealing transactions (i.e., where the controlling shareholder is effectively on both sides of the transaction). Self-dealing is not per se invalid under Delaware law, but rather is subject to the entire fairness test. By being on both sides of the transaction, the controlling shareholder bears the burden of proving the entire fairness of the transaction. Delaware courts also apply the entire fairness test wherever the fiduciary will receive a financial benefit from the transaction at issue that is not equally shared by all the stockholders. It has been held that the disparity must be more than a *de minimus* departure from equal treatment.

Entire fairness has two components: fair dealing and fair price. Fair dealing includes such factors as when the transaction was timed, how it was initiated, structured, negotiated, disclosed to the directors, and how approvals were obtained. Fair price relates to the economic and financial consideration for the deals. (See *Weinberger v. UOP, Inc.* (D. Del. 1983) 457 A.2d 701-703.)

California case law provides authority indicating that a controlling shareholder owes fiduciary duties to both the corporation and the minority shareholders. (See, e.g., *Jones v. Ahmanson & Co.* (Cal. 1969) 460 P.2d 464, 471 (holding that any use of the corporation or controlling power must benefit all shareholders equally).) In *Stephenson* [v. *Dreyer*, 16 Cal. 4th 1167 (1997)], a minority shareholder and former employee brought an action against the majority stockholder of a closely held corporation and two of its officers and directors for breach of fiduciary duty and misuse of corporate assets. The plaintiff was a party to a buy-sell agreement giving the corporation the right (and obligation) to repurchase the shares of the minority shareholder on the termination of his employment. The precise issue presented was whether the agreement, on its face, implied an intention to deny the minority shareholder his rights post-employment but before the shares were transferred. The California Supreme Court held it did not. The court explained that corporate shareholders have valuable property rights including the right to dividends voted by the boards. The court concluded that, since the plaintiff was the only minority shareholder, the directors and the majority shareholders had fiduciary duties to the minority shareholders:

Majority shareholders may not use their power to control corporate activities to benefit themselves alone or in a manner detrimental to the minority. Any use to which they put the corporation or their power to control the corporation must benefit all shareholders proportionately and must not conflict with the proper conduct of the corporation's business." [*Jones v. H.F. Ahmanson & Co.* (1969) 1 Cal. 3d 93, 108] adopted "the comprehensive rule of good faith and inherent fairness to the minority in any transaction where control of the corporation is material" (*id.* at p. 112), and declared broadly that "[t]he rule applies alike to officers, directors, and controlling shareholders in the exercise of powers that are theirs by virtue of their position and to transactions wherein controlling shareholders seek to gain an advantage in the sale or transfer or use of their controlling block of shares." (*Id.* at p. 110.)

Stephenson v. Dreyer (1997) 14 Cal. 4th at 1178.

* * *

In *Jones v. H.F. Ahmanson*, a minority stockholder in a savings and loan association brought a derivative action against a holding company formed by defendant majority stockholders and officers of the association. Essentially, the plaintiff contended that to take advantage of a bull market in savings and loan stock, the majority stockholders formed a holding company, transferring to it the control block of association stock in exchange for a considerably greater number of holding company shares, excluding the minority stockholders from participating therein, pledging the association's assets and earnings to secure the holding company's debt that had been incurred for their own benefit, and finally, having thus left the minority with stock whose potential market had been destroyed, using that very fact as a basis for offering to buy stock at an exchange rate less favorable than they themselves had enjoyed. In addition, the majority through the newly formed holding company caused the savings and loan association to cease paying dividends, other than the regular $4.00 per share annual dividend, although extra large dividends had previously been paid.

The California Supreme Court held that California no longer follows the rule recognizing the right of majority stockholders to dispose of their stock without the slightest regard to the wishes or knowledge of the minority. The prevailing rule is that of inherent fairness from the viewpoint of the corporation and of those interested therein, and majority stockholders may not use their power to control corporate activities to benefit themselves alone or in a manner detrimental to the minority. . . .

The court [in *Jones v. Ahmanson & Co.*] noted that the potential for oppression by the controlling shareholder may include the reduction or elimination of dividends. . . .

Directors

Both Delaware and California hold that directors owe fiduciary duties to the corporation and to its shareholders.

As is true for controlling shareholders in Delaware, the fiduciary duties provided for under Delaware law for directors include the duty of loyalty and the duty of care. (*Malone v. Brincat* (Del. 1998) 722 A.2d 5, 10.) However, Delaware's General Corporation Law allows corporations to grant their directors certain protections from monetary liability with respect to the duty of care. Section 102, subsection (b)(7) states:

[T]he certificate of incorporation may also contain . . . [a] provision eliminating [or] limiting the personal liability of a director to the corporation or its stockholders for monetary damages for breach of fiduciary duty as a director . . . provided that such provision shall not eliminate or limit the liability of a director: (i) for any breach of the director's duty of loyalty to the corporation or its stockholders; (ii) for acts or omissions not in good faith or which involve intentional misconduct or a knowing violation of law; . . . or (iv) for any transaction from which the director derived an improper personal benefit.

In California, waiver of corporate directors' and majority shareholders' fiduciary duties to minority shareholders, at least in private close corporations, has been held to be against public policy, and a contract provision in a buy-sell agreement purporting to effect such a waiver is void. Certain limitations on the duties of directors may, however, be permitted to limit monetary damages. (See Cal. Corp. Code, §204.) In addition, statutes in both California and Delaware provide a safe harbor for contracts with directors under certain circumstances.[4]

As in Delaware, it has been held in California that the fiduciary duties of directors include the duty of care and the duty of loyalty. The duties are reflected in Corporations Code section 309, subdivision (a) which provides,

A director shall perform the duties of a director, including duties as a member of any committee of the board upon which the director may serve, in good faith, in a manner such director believes to be in the best interests of the corporation and its shareholders and with such care, including reasonable inquiry, as an ordinarily prudent person in a like position would use under similar circumstances.

Some authorities also make reference to a duty of good faith. Good faith is arguably an obligation separate from the fiduciary duties of care and loyalty. Good faith is presumed and the party challenging it has the burden of rebutting that presumption. . . .

* * *

Under Delaware law, self-dealing transactions for directors (*i.e.*, where the director is effectively on both sides of the transaction) are subject to the entire fairness test. (*See Weinberger v. UOP, Inc.* (D. Del. 1983) 457 A.2d 70170.) In *Technicorp International II, Inc. v. H. Johnston* (Del. Ch. 2000) Westlaw 713750, the Delaware Chancery Court explained:

Corporate officers and directors, like all fiduciaries, have the burden of showing that they dealt properly with corporate funds and other assets entrusted to their care. Where, as here, fiduciaries exercised exclusive power to control the disposition of corporate funds and their exercise in challenged by a beneficiary, the fiduciaries have a duty to account for their disposition of those funds, *i.e.* to establish the purpose, amount and property of the disbursements. And where, as here, the fiduciaries cause those funds to be used for self-interested purposes, i.e., to be paid to themselves or to others for the fiduciary's benefit, they have the burden of establishing [the transactions'] entire fairness, sufficient to pass the test of careful scrutiny by the court. (*Id.* at p. 16.)

---

4. *See* Corp. Code, §310, and 8 Del. Code Ann., §144.

As a practical matter, in a claim by the corporation either directly, or, more commonly, in a derivative action, the application of the entire fairness test is likely to be crucial to success of a claim by a plaintiff. The alternative is the application of the business judgment rule. The business judgment rule embodies the deference that is accorded to managerial decisions of the board. . . .

The business judgment rule reflects a presumption that absent a breach of the fiduciary duties of care and loyalty, or a failure to act in good faith, directors act on an informed basis in the best interest of the corporation. If it is shown that a director breached the fiduciary duties of care or loyalty or did not act in good faith, the burden shifts to that director to demonstrate that the transaction or act at issue satisfies the entire fairness test.

* * *

The Delaware courts will under certain circumstances subject director's action to enhanced judicial scrutiny before the presumptive protection of the business judgment rule can be invoked. (*Omnicare, Inc. v. NCS Healthcare, Inc.* (D. Del. 2003) 818 A.2d. 914, 928.) These circumstances will most commonly arise when directors are often confronted with an "'inherent conflict of interest' such as contests for corporate control '[b]ecause of the omnipresent specter that a board may be acting primarily in its own interests, rather than those of the corporation and its shareholders.'" (*Unocal Corp. v. Mesa Petroleum Co.* (Del. 1985) 493 A.2d 946, 954.) Consequently, during contests for corporate control, under Delaware law directors have to satisfy the additional burden of enhanced judicial scrutiny before they are accorded the deference of the business judgment rule. Enhanced scrutiny consists of a two part test: (1) a *reasonableness test*, which is satisfied by a demonstration that the board of directors had reasonable grounds for believing that a danger to corporate policy and effectiveness existed; and (2) a *proportionality test*, which is satisfied by a demonstration that the board of directors' defensive response was reasonable in relation to the threat posed. Only if the directors are able to satisfy that burden are their actions accorded the deferential business judgment rule. If the directors are not able to satisfy that burden (or if the presumption of the business judgment rule is defeated for any other reason), the more critical entire fairness standard applies instead. This standard requires judicial scrutiny of both "fair dealing" and "fair price."

* * *

As is true under Delaware law, California case law has repeatedly stated that directors owe fiduciary duties to their corporations, which at a minimum include a duty of care and a duty of loyalty. Like Delaware courts, California courts at least claim that they afford directors the benefit of the business judgment rule, which provides a presumption the directors' decision [sic] are based on sound judgment. (*Guillard v. Natomas Company* (1989) 208 Cal. App. 3d 1250, 1269.) . . .

The Delaware courts' use of "enhanced judicial scrutiny" of directors in certain instances before determining whether to apply the business judgment rule is not frequently seen in California case law. It is not, however, entirely absent in California. The widespread use of the concept in Delaware decisions suggests that a similar argument in an appropriate California case might prove successful.

The director's duty of care in California is codified in Corporations Code section 309, which states:

(a) A director shall perform the duties of a director, including duties as a member of any committee of the board upon which the director may serve, in good faith, in a manner such director believes to be in the best interests of the corporation and its shareholders and with such care, including reasonable inquiry, as an ordinarily prudent person in a like position would use under similar circumstances.

(b) In performing the duties of a director, a director shall be entitled to rely on information, opinions, reports or statements, including financial statements and other financial data, in each case prepared or presented by any of the following:

(1) One or more officers or employees of the corporation whom the director believes to be reliable and competent in the matters presented.

(2) Counsel, independent accountants or other persons as to matters which the director believes to be within such person's professional or expert competence.

(3) A committee of the board upon which the director does not serve, as to matters within its designated authority, which committee the director believes to merit confidence, so long as, in any such case, the director acts in good faith, after reasonable inquiry when the need therefore is indicated by the circumstances and without knowledge that would cause such reliance to be unwarranted.

(c) A person who performs the duties of a director in accordance with subdivisions (a) and (b) shall have no liability based upon any alleged failure to discharge the person's obligations as a director. In addition, the liability of a director for monetary damages may be eliminated or limited in a corporation's articles to the extent provided in paragraph (10) of subdivision (a) of Section 204.

* * *

Also, under Delaware law, in some circumstances a director may owe a fiduciary duty not only to the corporation but also effectively to its creditors. Typically, Delaware law does not permit creditors to allege fiduciary duty violations against corporate directors. The Delaware courts reason that creditors have the protection of other legal tools, such as contract claims, the law of fraudulent conveyance, and federal bankruptcy law. However, when a corporation becomes insolvent, its creditors take on the same role as the corporation's shareholders: they become residual risk bearers. The possibility of insolvency exposes creditors to risks of opportunistic behavior. (*Credit Lyonnaise Bank v. Pathe Communications* (Del. Ch. 1992) Lexis 215 at 108 (unpublished opinion).) Thus, insolvency "creates fiduciary duties for directors for the benefit of the creditors." (*Geyer v. Ingersoll Publications Co.* (Del. Ch. 1992) 621 A.2d 784, 787.) Creditors are deemed to have an equity interest in an insolvent corporation's assets, and the directors of the insolvent corporation have a fiduciary duty to preserve capital for the benefit of the creditors. The application of fiduciary duties may apply to creditor relationship even before actual bankruptcy, if the corporation is in the "vicinity" of insolvency.

California also recognizes this duty to creditors. (*See Commons v. Schine* (1973) 35 Cal. App. 3d 141, 144) ("The corporate controller-dominator is treated in the same manner as a director of an insolvent corporation and thus occupies a fiduciary relationship to its creditors".) California state and bankruptcy courts cite to the United States Supreme Court's decision in *Pepper v. Litton* [308 U.S. 295 (1939)] for the proposition that a director of an insolvent corporation is a fiduciary whose obligation extends to creditors.[6]

Officers

Under both California law and Delaware law a corporate officer with management powers is a fiduciary of a corporation. . . .

* * *

Employees

The law concerning the status of employees who are not officers (whether in title or in fact) as fiduciaries is relatively sparse. However, commentators have concluded that in California, "employees who are not officers or directors are generally not considered to be fiduciaries and thus owe no fiduciary duty to their employers." (Chin, et al., Cal. Prac. Guide: Employment Litigation (The Rutter Group 2005) 14:33.) California case law supports this conclusion. (*See, e.g., Calvao v. Sup. Ct.* (Klippert) (1988) 201 Cal. App. 3d 921, 923 ("The superior court in its trial *de novo* believed there was a fiduciary relationship between the county and its employees. . . . However, this is an employment contract situation. There is no confidential or fiduciary relationship in this context."); *O'Byrne v. Santa Monica-UCLA Medical Center* (2001) 94 Cal. App. 4th 797, 811-812 ("[E]mployment-type relationships are not fiduciary relationships. In the absence of a fiduciary relationship, there can be no breach of fiduciary duty as a matter of law.")

These decisions in California stand in contrast to the broad language concerning fiduciary duties of employees which may be found in other jurisdictions. (*See, e.g., Eckard Brandes, Inc. v. Riley* (9th Cir. 2003) 338 F.3d 1082 (holding that regular employees owe their corporate employer a fiduciary duty in Hawaii).)

Notwithstanding the foregoing broad statements concerning the lack of a fiduciary status for ordinary employees in California, in particularly [*sic*] instances it may be appropriate to find a limited fiduciary relationship between an ordinary employee and his corporate employer. Similarly, in Delaware, there is case law referring to a fiduciary duty of employees in certain contexts. (*See, e.g., Science Accessories Corp. v. Summagraphics Corp.* (1980) 425 A.2d 957, 961.)

Promoters

In the context of corporations, California also recognizes that in certain circumstances even promoters, although they are not directors, officers, or controlling

---

6. Some jurisdictions have adopted "other constituency" statutes that provide for fiduciary duties for directors to constituencies including employees, customers, suppliers, and local communities.

shareholders, have fiduciary duties. Typically these cases arise where the promoter has obtained a secret undisclosed profit. Delaware has also recognized fiduciary duties in promoter cases.

Conclusion

While attention has properly been focused on the duties of directors under the Sarbanes-Oxley Act and other federal securities and criminal laws, state law in both Delaware and California continues to provide ample authority for regulating the conduct not only of officers and directors of corporations, but also corporate promoters, controlling shareholders, and employees.

G. Choice of State of Incorporation — Delaware vs. California

In this final section, as we bring the chapter to a close, we return to the fundamental issue that faces our client, SoftCo: *in which state to incorporate?* The materials in this chapter offered a broad overview of the various provisions of California and Delaware corporate law that usually influence this decision. The materials in this section are designed to help you think about this decision in the specific counseling context of founders (such as Joan and Michael) who have decided to incorporate their new business (SoftCo) in order to seek start-up financing from venture capital investors. At the end of this chapter, you should be prepared to make a recommendation whether to incorporate SoftCo in Delaware or California, taking into account all of the legal considerations previously outlined in this chapter, as well as the practical business considerations that are described in the following materials.

Guide to Starting a Corporation
Fenwick & West, LLP, Law Firm Memo (2013)*

Introduction

This guide describes certain basic considerations and costs involved in forming a Delaware or California corporation. Although Delaware and California law are emphasized, the legal concepts are much the same in other states. One important tip is that you should avoid making business decisions in a vacuum. Instead, consider how a decision may impact future alternatives. For example, an improperly priced sale of common stock to founders immediately followed by a sale of preferred stock may result in a significant tax liability to the founders. Another example is that converting a limited liability company into a corporation immediately before the business is acquired, rather than at an earlier time, may prevent the transaction from being tax-free.

* * *

---

* *Available at* http://www.fenwick.com/FenwickDocuments/Legal%20Resource%20Guide.pdf.

A. Selecting the Form of Business Organization

No single factor is controlling in determining the form of business organization to select, but if the business is expected to expand rapidly, a corporation will usually be the best alternative because of the availability of employee incentive stock plans; ease of accommodating outside investment and greater long-term liquidity alternatives for shareholders. A corporation also minimizes potential personal liability if statutory formalities are followed. The characteristics of a corporation are described below. . . .

1. Corporation

A corporation is created by filing [its Charter] with the Secretary of State in the state of incorporation. Corporate status is maintained by compliance with statutory formalities. A corporation is owned by its shareholders, governed by its Board of Directors who are elected by the shareholders and managed by its officers who are elected by the Board. A shareholder's involvement in managing a corporation is usually limited to voting on extraordinary matters. In both California and Delaware, a corporation may have only one shareholder and one director. A president/CEO, chief financial officer/treasurer and secretary are the officer positions generally filled in a start-up and, in fact, are required under California law. All officer positions may be filled by one person.

The reasons for using a Delaware corporation at start-up are the ease of filings with the Delaware Secretary of State in financings and other transactions, a slight prestige factor in being a Delaware corporation and avoiding substantial reincorporation expenses later, since many corporations which go public reincorporate in Delaware at the time of the IPO. Delaware corporate law benefits are of the most value to public companies. However, if the corporation's primary operations and at least 50% of its shareholders are located in California, many provisions of California corporate law may be applicable to a private Delaware corporation and such a company would pay franchise taxes in both California and Delaware. These considerations may result in such a business choosing to incorporate in California instead of Delaware. Another reason for keeping it simple and using a California corporation is the current non-existent IPO market which makes an acquisition a more likely exit for a start-up.

There is more flexibility under Delaware law as to the required number of Board members. When a California corporation has two shareholders, there must be at least two Board members. When there are three or more shareholders, there must be at least three persons on the Board. Under Delaware law, there may be one director without regard for the number of stockholders. Most Boards stay lean and mean in number as long as possible to facilitate decision-making. Since the Board is the governing body of the corporation, when there are multiple board members, a party owning the majority of the shares can still be outvoted on the Board on important matters such as sales of additional stock and the election of officers. Removing a director involves certain risks even when a founder has the votes to do so. Thus, a founder's careful selection of an initial Board is essential. You want board members whose judgment you trust (even if they disagree with you) and who can provide you with input you won't get from the management team.

A corporation is a separate entity for tax purposes. Income taxed at the corporate level is taxed again at the shareholder level if any distribution is made in the form of a dividend. The S Corporation election described below limits taxation to the shareholder level but subjects all earnings to taxation whether or not distributed. The current maximum federal corporate tax rate is 35%. The California corporate income tax rate is 8.84% and the Delaware corporate income tax rate is 8.7% but Delaware income tax does not apply if no business is done in Delaware and only the statutory office is there. There is also a Delaware franchise tax on authorized capital which can be minimized at the outset but increases as the corporation has more assets.

If the business fails, the losses of the initial investment of up to $1 million in the aggregate (at purchase price value) of common and preferred stock (so-called "Section 1244 stock") may be used under certain circumstances by shareholders to offset a corresponding amount of ordinary income in their federal income tax returns. An individual may deduct, as an ordinary loss, a loss on Section 1244 stock of up to $50,000 in any one year ($100,000 on a joint return).

If statutory formalities are followed, individual shareholders have personal liability only to the extent of their investment, i.e., what they paid for their shares. If the corporation is not properly organized and maintained, a court may "pierce the corporate veil" and impose liability on the shareholders. Both California and Delaware law permit corporations to limit the liability of their directors to shareholders under certain circumstances. The company can raise additional capital by the sale and issuance of more shares of stock, typically preferred stock when an angel or venture capitalist is investing. Though rare, the power of a court to look through the corporation for liability underscores the importance of following proper legal procedures in setting up and operating your business.

Filing fees, other costs and legal fees through the initial organizational stage usually total about $3,500 to $5,000, with a Delaware corporation being at the high end of the range.

* * *

B. S Corporations

A corporation may be an "S corporation" and not subject to federal corporate tax if its shareholders unanimously elect S status for the corporation on a timely basis. "S corporation" is a tax law label; it is not a special type of corporation under state corporate law. Like a partnership, an S corporation is merely a conduit for profits and losses. Income is passed through to the shareholders and is generally taxed only once. Corporate level tax can apply in some circumstances to an S corporation that previously had been a "C" corporation for income tax purposes. Losses are also passed through to offset each shareholder's income to the extent of his basis in his stock and any loans by the shareholder to the S corporation. The undistributed earnings retained in the corporation as working capital are taxed to a shareholder.

A corporation must meet certain conditions in order to be an S corporation, including the following: (1) it must be a U.S. corporation, (2) it must have no more than 100 shareholders, (3) each shareholder must be an individual, certain trusts, certain charitable organizations, employee stock ownership plans or pension plans, (4) no share-holder may be a nonresident alien, and (5) it can have only one class of stock outstanding (as opposed to merely being authorized). As a result, S corporation status will be termi-nated when a corporation sells preferred stock or sells stock to a venture capital part-nership, corporation or to an off-shore investor.

California and Delaware recognizes the S corporation for state tax purposes, which may result in additional tax savings. California, however, imposes a corporate level tax of 1.5% on the S corporation's income and nonresident shareholders must pay California tax on their share of the corporation's California income. In addition, only C corpora-tions and noncorporate investors are eligible for the Qualified Small Business Corpo-ration capital gains tax break. The benefit of this tax break is that if the stock is held for at least 5 years, 50% of any gain on the sale or exchange of stock may be excluded from gross income. This benefit may not be as important because of the reduction in the capital gains tax rate.

C. Choosing a Business Name

The name selected must not deceive or mislead the public or already be in use or reserved. "Inc.," "Corp." or "Corporation" need not be a part of the name in California but must be part of a Delaware corporate name. Name availability must be determined on a state-by-state basis through the Secretary of State. A corporate name isn't available for use in California merely because the business has been incorporated in Delaware. Several alternative names should be selected because so many businesses have already been formed. Corporate name reservation fees range from approximately $10-50 per state for a reservation period of 30-60 days. Exclusive state rights in a trade name can also be obtained indefinitely through the creation of a name-holding corporation, a corpo-ration for which [a Charter is] filed but no further organizational steps are taken.

D. Selecting the Location for the Business

This decision is driven by state tax considerations and operational need, for example, to be near customers or suppliers or in the center of a service territory. A privately-held corporation cannot avoid California taxes and may not be able to avoid the application of California corporate law if it is operating here and has most of its shareholders here. For example, Delaware law allows Board members to be elected for multiple year terms and on a staggered basis rather than on an annual basis. . . .

E. Qualifying To Do Business in Another State

A corporation may need to open a formal or informal office in another state at or near the time of founding. This requires a "mini" incorporation process in each such state. If a California business is incorporated in Delaware it must qualify to do business in California. The consequences of failing to do so range from fines to not being able to enforce contracts entered in that state. The cost of qualifying is approximately $1,000 per state. Some states, like Nevada, also charge a fee based on authorized stock, so the fee could be higher in such states.

F. Initial Capital Structure

1. Structure

The capital structure should be kept as simple as possible and be within a range of "normalcy" to a potential outside investor for credibility purposes. A common initial structure is to authorize 10 million shares of common stock and 4 million shares of preferred stock. Not all authorized shares of common stock are sold at the founding stage. After initial sales to founders, there are usually only about 3-5 million shares issued and outstanding and about 1-2 million shares reserved in the equity incentive plan. This is referred to as the "1X model" below.

While at the outset there may not seem to be any difference between owning 100 shares or 1 million shares, a founder should purchase all of the units of stock he desires at the time of founding. Thereafter, a founder will generally lose control over further issuances and stock splits, particularly once a venture capital financing occurs. In addition, the purchase price will usually increase.

The number of shares issued and reserved in the initial capital structure are driven by a desire to avoid a later reverse stock split at the time of an IPO because of excess dilution. The number of shares outstanding at the time of an IPO is driven by company valuation at IPO, the amount to be raised in the IPO and IPO price per share range (usually $10 to $15). The "pattern" for the business value at the time of the IPO can be reached by forward or reverse stock splits. For example, if a corporation has a market valuation at IPO time of $200 million, it would not be feasible for 40 million shares to be outstanding. A reverse stock split is needed. Reverse stock splits reduce the number of shares held. On the other hand, forward stock splits add shares to holdings. Neither changes the percentage ownership, but seeing the number of shares held decrease because of a reverse split is still hard on employee morale.

Because of the great demand for engineers during the Internet bubble, many corporations used a multiple of this 1X model in order to have more equity units available for employees. The immediate need for employees to increase the possibility of business success outweighed the potential consequence of a later reverse stock split. Currently, most start-ups use a 1X or 2X model to avoid excessive dilution.

2. Minimum Capital

Neither Delaware nor California law require a minimum amount of money to be invested in a corporation at the time of founding. The initial amount of capital, however, must be adequate to accomplish the purpose of the start-up business in order for shareholders not to have personal liability. For example, a corporation which will serve only as a sales representative for products or a consulting operation requires less capital than a distributor or dealer who will stock an inventory of products. A dealership or distributorship will require less capital than a manufacturing operation.

3. Legal Consideration

A corporation must sell its shares for legal consideration, i.e., cash, property, past services or promissory notes under some circumstances. A founder who transfers technology or other property (but not services) to a corporation in exchange for stock does not recognize income at the time of the transfer (as a sale of such property) under IRC Section 351 if the parties acquiring shares at the same time for property (as opposed to services) own at least 80% of the shares of the corporation after the transfer. Because of this limitation, Section 351 is generally available at the time of founding but not later. Since a party who exchanges past or future services for stock must recognize income in the amount of the value of the stock in the tax year in which the stock is received, it is the preferred practice to issue the shares at a low valuation for cash or property.

4. Valuation

The per share value at the time of founding is determined by the cash purchases of stock and the number of shares issued. For example, if one founder buys stock in exchange for technology and the other founder buys a 50% interest for cash, the value of the technology and the fair market value per share is dictated by the cash purchase since its monetary value is certain. Sales of the same class of stock made at or about the same time must be at the same price or the party purchasing at the lower price may have to recognize income on the difference.

Thereafter, value is determined by sales between a willing seller and buyer or by the Board of Directors based on events and financial condition. Value must be established by the Board at the time of each sale of stock or grant of a stock option. Successful events cause value to increase. Such determinations are subjective and there is no single methodology for determining current fair market value. There are pitfalls of hedging on the timing of forming corporation to save on expenses. The longer the delay in incorporating, the more difficult it is to keep the founders price at a nominal level if a financing or other value event is imminent.

A general objective is to keep the value of common stock as low as possible as long as possible to provide greater stock incentives to attract and keep key employees. Tax and state corporate laws generally require option grants to be made at current fair market value. IRC Section 409A has increased the diligence needed in determining pricing for stock option grants.

5. Use of Debt

Loans may also be used to fund a corporation. For example, if a consulting business is initially capitalized with $20,000, half of it could be a loan and the remaining $10,000 used to purchase common stock. Using debt enables the corporation to deduct the interest payments on the debt, makes the repayment of the investment tax free and gives creditor status to the holder of the debt. If a corporation is too heavily capitalized with shareholder's loans, as opposed to equity (usually up to a 3-1 debt/equity ratio is acceptable), however, these loans may be treated as additional equity for tax and other purposes. Debts owed to shareholders may be treated as contributions to capital or a second class of shares and subordinated to debts of other creditors. Eligibility for S corporation status is lost if a loan is characterized as a second class of shares.

NOTES AND QUESTIONS

1. If the founders (Joan and Michael) should decide to incorporate their new business (SoftCo) in Delaware but actually operate their business in California, then they will be required to "qualify" to do business in California as a "foreign corporation." In general, to "qualify" to do business in a state other than the state of incorporation requires the company to file a certified copy of its Charter, pay a filing fee, and appoint a local agent to receive service of process in that state. *See, e.g.*, Calif. §2101. What are the consequences if the company fails to "qualify" but nonetheless is "doing business" in a state other than its state of incorporation? While it varies slightly from state to state, more often than not the company will be subject to a fine and cannot bring lawsuits in the local courts of the foreign jurisdiction unless and until it has "qualified" to do business in that state and paid any penalties that were imposed. *See, e.g.*, Calif. §§2203, 2105, and 2258.

2. In the preceding article, the author makes an oblique reference to Calif. §2115. The nature of this provision, as well as the practical and legal implications of this California statute, are described in the *VantagePoint* case, which follows.

VantagePoint Venture Partners 1996 v. Examen, Inc.

871 A.2d 1108 (Del. 2005)

HOLLAND, Justice:

This is an expedited appeal from the Court of Chancery following the entry of a final judgment on the pleadings. We have concluded that the judgment must be affirmed.

Delaware Action

On March 3, 2005, the plaintiff-appellee, Examen, Inc. ("Examen"), filed a Complaint in the Court of Chancery against VantagePoint Venture Partners, Inc. ("Vantage Point"), a Delaware Limited Partnership and an Examen Series A Preferred shareholder, seeking a judicial declaration that pursuant to the controlling Delaware law and under the Company's Certificate of Designations of Series A Preferred Stock ("Certificate of Designations"), VantagePoint was not entitled to a class vote of the Series A Preferred Stock on the proposed merger between Examen and a Delaware subsidiary of Reed Elsevier Inc.

California Action

On March 8, 2005, VantagePoint filed an action in the California Superior Court seeking: (1) a declaration that Examen was required to identify whether it was a "quasi-California corporation" under section 2115 of the California Corporations Code[1]; (2) a declaration that Examen was a quasi-California corporation pursuant to California Corporations Code section 2115 and therefore subject to California Corporations Code section 1201(a), and that, as a Series A Preferred shareholder, VantagePoint was entitled to vote its shares as a separate class in connection with the proposed merger; (3) injunctive relief; and (4) damages incurred as the result of alleged violations of California Corporations Code sections 2111(F) and 1201.

Delaware Action Decided

On March 10, 2005, the Court of Chancery granted Examen's request for an expedited hearing on its motion for judgment on the pleadings. On March 21, 2005, the California Superior Court stayed its action pending the ruling of the Court of Chancery. On March 29, 2005, the Court of Chancery ruled that the case was governed by the internal affairs doctrine as explicated by this Court in McDermott v. Lewis, [531 A.2d 206 (Del.1987)]. In applying that doctrine, the Court of Chancery held that Delaware law governed the vote that was required to approve a merger between two Delaware corporate entities.

On April 1, 2005, VantagePoint filed a notice of appeal with this Court. On April 4, 2005, VantagePoint sought to enjoin the merger from closing pending its appeal. On April 5, 2005, this Court denied VantagePoint's request to enjoin the merger from closing, but granted its request for an expedited appeal.

Merger Without Mootness

Following this Court's ruling on April 5, 2005, Examen and the Delaware subsidiary of Reed Elsevier consummated the merger that same day. This Court directed the parties to address the issue of mootness, simultaneously with the expedited briefing that was completed on April 13, 2005. VantagePoint argues that if we agree with its position "that a class vote was required, then VantagePoint could pursue remedies for loss of this right, including rescission of the Merger, rescissory damages or monetary damages." Examen submits that "the need for final resolution of the validity of the merger vote remains important to the parties and to the public interest" because a decision from this Court

---

1. Section 2115 of the California Corporations Code purportedly applies to corporations that have contacts with the State of California, but are incorporated in other states. *See* Cal. Corp. Code §171 (defining "foreign corporation"); and Cal. Corp. Code §2115(a), (b). Section 2115 of the California Corporations Code provides that, irrespective of the state of incorporation, **foreign corporations' articles of incorporation are deemed amended** to comply with California law and are subject to the laws of California if certain criteria are met. *See* Cal. Corp. Code §2115 (emphasis added). To qualify under the statute: (1) the average of the property factor, the payroll factor and the sales factor as defined in the California Revenue and Taxation Code must be more than 50 percent during its last full income year; and (2) more than one-half of its outstanding voting securities must be held by persons having addresses in California. *Id.* If a corporation qualifies under this provision, California corporate laws apply "to the exclusion of the law of the jurisdiction where [the company] is incorporated." *Id.* Included among the California corporate law provisions that would govern is California Corporations Code section 1201, which states that the principal terms of a reorganization shall be approved by the outstanding shares of each class of each corporation the approval of whose board is required. *See* Cal. Corp. Code §§2115, 1201 [emphasis in original].

will conclusively determine the parties' rights with regard to the law that applies to the merger vote. We have concluded that this appeal is not moot.

Facts

Examen was a Delaware corporation engaged in the business of providing web-based legal expense management solutions to a growing list of Fortune 1000 customers throughout the United States. Following consummation of the merger on April 5, 2005, LexisNexis Examen, also a Delaware corporation, became the surviving entity. VantagePoint is a Delaware Limited Partnership organized and existing under the laws of Delaware. VantagePoint, a major venture capital firm that purchased Examen Series A Preferred Stock in a negotiated transaction, owned eighty-three percent of Examen's outstanding Series A Preferred Stock (909,091 shares) and no shares of Common Stock.

On February 17, 2005, Examen and Reed Elsevier executed the Merger Agreement, which was set to expire on April 15, 2005, if the merger had not closed by that date. Under the Delaware General Corporation Law and Examen's Certificate of Incorporation, including the Certificate of Designations for the Series A Preferred Stock, adoption of the Merger Agreement required the affirmative vote of the holders of a majority of the issued and outstanding shares of the Common Stock and Series A Preferred Stock, voting together as a single class. Holders of Series A Preferred Stock had the number of votes equal to the number of shares of Common Stock they would have held if their Preferred Stock was converted. Thus, VantagePoint, which owned 909,091 shares of Series A Preferred Stock and no shares of Common Stock, was entitled to vote based on a converted number of 1,392,727 shares of stock.

There were 9,717,415 total outstanding shares of the Company's capital stock (8,626,826 shares of Common Stock and 1,090,589 shares of Series A Preferred Stock), representing 10,297,608 votes on an as-converted basis. An affirmative vote of at least 5,148,805 shares, constituting a majority of the outstanding voting power on an as-converted basis, was required to approve the merger. If the stockholders were to vote by class, VantagePoint would have controlled 83.4 percent of the Series A Preferred Stock, which would have permitted VantagePoint to block the merger. VantagePoint acknowledges that, if Delaware law applied, it would not have a class vote.

Chancery Court Decision

The Court of Chancery determined that the question of whether VantagePoint, as a holder of Examen's Series A Preferred Stock, was entitled to a separate class vote on the merger with a Delaware subsidiary of Reed Elsevier, was governed by the internal affairs doctrine because the issue implicated "the relationship between a corporation and its stockholders." The Court of Chancery rejected VantagePoint's argument that section 2115 of the California Corporation Code did not conflict with Delaware law and operated only in addition to rights granted under Delaware corporate law. In doing so, the Court of Chancery noted that section 2115 "expressly states that it operates 'to the exclusion of the law of the jurisdiction in which [the company] is incorporated.'"

Specifically, the Court of Chancery determined that section 2115's requirement that stockholders vote as a separate class conflicts with Delaware law, which, together with

Examen's Certificate of Incorporation, mandates that the merger be authorized by a majority of all Examen stockholders voting together as a single class. The Court of Chancery concluded that it could not enforce both Delaware and California law. Consequently, the Court of Chancery decided that the issue presented was solely one of choice-of-law, and that it need not determine the constitutionality of section 2115.

VantagePoint's Argument

According to VantagePoint, "the issue presented by this case is not a choice of law question, but rather the constitutional issue of whether California may promulgate a narrowly-tailored exception to the internal affairs doctrine that is designed to protect important state interests." VantagePoint submits that "Section 2115 was designed to provide an additional layer of investor protection by mandating that California's heightened voting requirements apply to those few foreign corporations that have chosen to conduct a majority of their business in California and meet the other factual prerequisite of Section 2115." Therefore, VantagePoint argues that "Delaware either must apply the statute if California can validly enact it, or hold the statute unconstitutional if California cannot." We note, however, that when an issue or claim is properly before a tribunal, "the court is not limited to the particular legal theories advanced by the parties, but rather retains the independent power to identify and apply the proper construction of governing law." *Kamen v. Kemper Fin. Serv.*, 500 U.S. 90, 111 S. Ct. 1711, 114 L. Ed. 2d 152 (1991).

Standard of Review

In granting Examen's Motion for Judgment on the Pleadings, the Court of Chancery held that, as a matter of law, the rights of stockholders to vote on the proposed merger were governed by the law of Delaware — Examen's state of incorporation — and that an application of Delaware law resulted in the Class A Preferred shareholders having no right to a separate class vote. The issue of whether VantagePoint was entitled to a separate class vote of the Series A Preferred Stock on the merger is a question of law that this Court reviews *de novo*.

Internal Affairs Doctrine

In *CTS Corp. v. Dynamics Corp. of Am.*, the United States Supreme Court stated that it is "an accepted part of the business landscape in this country for States to create corporations, to prescribe their powers, and to define the rights that are acquired by purchasing their shares." 481 U.S. 69, 91, 107 (1987). In *CTS*, it was also recognized that "[a] State has an interest in promoting stable relationships among parties involved in the corporations it charters, as well as in ensuring that investors in such corporations have an effective voice in corporate affairs." *Id.* The internal affairs doctrine is a long-standing choice of law principle which recognizes that only one state should have the authority to regulate a corporation's internal affairs — the state of incorporation.

The internal affairs doctrine developed on the premise that, in order to prevent corporations from being subjected to inconsistent legal standards, the authority to regulate a corporation's internal affairs should not rest with multiple jurisdictions. It is now well established that only the law of the state of incorporation governs and determines issues relating to a corporation's internal affairs. By providing certainty and predictability, the internal affairs doctrine protects the justified expectations of the parties with interests in the corporation.

The internal affairs doctrine applies to those matters that pertain to the relationships among or between the corporation and its officers, directors, and shareholders. . . . Accordingly, the conflicts practice of both state and federal courts has consistently been to apply the law of the state of incorporation to "the entire gamut of internal corporate affairs."[14]

The internal affairs doctrine is not, however, only a conflicts of law principle. Pursuant to the Fourteenth Amendment Due Process Clause, directors and officers of corporations "have a significant right . . . to know what law will be applied to their actions" and "[s]tockholders . . . have a right to know by what standards of accountability they may hold those managing the corporation's business and affairs." Under the Commerce Clause, a state "has no interest in regulating the internal affairs of foreign corporations." Therefore, this Court has held that an "application of the internal affairs doctrine is mandated by constitutional principles, except in the 'rarest situations,'" e.g., when "the law of the state of incorporation is inconsistent with a national policy on foreign or interstate commerce."

California Section 2115

VantagePoint contends that section 2115 of the California Corporations Code is a limited exception to the internal affairs doctrine. Section 2115 is characterized as an outreach statute because it requires certain foreign corporations to conform to a broad range of internal affairs provisions. Section 2115 defines the foreign corporations for which the California statute has an outreach effect as those foreign corporations, half of whose voting securities are held of record by persons with California addresses, that also conduct half of their business in California as measured by a formula weighing assets, sales and payroll factors.

VantagePoint argues that section 2115 "mandates application of certain enumerated provisions of California's corporation law to the internal affairs of 'foreign' corporations if certain narrow factual prerequisites [set forth in section 2115] are met." Under the California statute, if more than one half of a foreign corporation's outstanding voting securities are held of record by persons having addresses in California (as disclosed on the books of the corporation) on the record date, *and* the property, payroll and sales factor tests are satisfied, then on the first day of the income year, one hundred and thirty five days after the above tests are satisfied, *the foreign corporation's articles of incorporation are deemed amended to the exclusion of the law of the state of incorporation.* If the

---

14. *McDermott Inc. v. Lewis,* 531 A.2d at 216 (quoting John Kozyris, *Corporate Wars and Choice of Law,* 1985 Duke L.J. 1, 98 (1985)). The internal affairs doctrine does not apply where the rights of third parties external to the corporation are at issue, *e.g.,* contracts and torts. *Id. See also Rogers v. Guaranty Trust Co. of N.Y.,* 288 U.S. 123, 130-31, 53 S. Ct. 295, 77 L. Ed. 652 (1933).

factual conditions precedent for triggering section 2115 are established, many aspects of a corporation's internal affairs are purportedly governed by California corporate law to the exclusion of the law of the state of incorporation.[22]

In her comprehensive analysis of the internal affairs doctrine, Professor Deborah A. DeMott examined section 2115. As she astutely points out:

> In contrast to the certainty with which the state of incorporation may be determined, the criteria upon which the applicability of section 2115 hinges are not constants. For example, whether half of a corporation's business is derived from California and whether half of its voting securities have record holders with California addresses may well vary from year to year (and indeed throughout any given year). Thus, a corporation might be subject to section 2115 one year but not the next, depending on its situation at the time of filing the annual statement required by section 2108.[23]

Internal Affairs Require Uniformity

In *McDermott,* this Court noted that application of local internal affairs law (here California's section 2115) to a foreign corporation (here Delaware) is "apt to produce inequalities, intolerable confusion, and uncertainty, and intrude into the domain of other states that have a superior claim to regulate the same subject matter. . . ." Professor DeMott's review of the differences and conflicts between the Delaware and California corporate statutes with regard to internal affairs, illustrates why it is imperative that only the law of the state of incorporation regulate the relationships among a corporation and its officers, directors, and shareholders. To require a factual determination to decide which of two conflicting state laws governs the internal affairs of a corporation at any point in time, completely contravenes the importance of stability within inter-corporate relationships that the United States Supreme Court recognized in *CTS.* . . .

* * *

State Law of Incorporation Governs Internal Affairs

In *McDermott,* this Court held that the "internal affairs doctrine is a major tenet of Delaware corporation law having important federal constitutional underpinnings."

---

22. If Section 2115 applies, California law is deemed to control the following: the annual election of directors; removal of directors without cause; removal of directors by court proceedings; the filing of director vacancies where less than a majority in office are elected by shareholders; the director's standard of care; the liability of directors for unlawful distributions; indemnification of directors, officers, and others; limitations on corporate distributions in cash or property; the liability of shareholders who receive unlawful distributions; the requirement for annual shareholders' meetings and remedies for the same if not timely held; shareholder's entitlement to cumulative voting; the conditions when a supermajority vote is required; limitations on the sale of assets; limitations on mergers; limitations on conversions; requirements on conversions; the limitations and conditions for reorganization (including the requirement for class voting); dissenter's rights; records and reports; actions by the Attorney General and inspection rights. *See* Cal. Corp. Code §2115(b) (1977 & Supp. 1984).

23. Deborah A. DeMott, *Perspectives on Choice of Law for Corporate Internal Affairs,* 48 LAW & CONTEMP. PROBS. 161, 166 (1985).

Applying Delaware's well-established choice-of-law rule — the internal affairs doctrine — the Court of Chancery recognized that Delaware courts must apply the law of the state of incorporation to issues involving corporate internal affairs, and that disputes concerning a shareholder's right to vote fall squarely within the purview of the internal affairs doctrine.

Examen is a Delaware corporation. The legal issue in this case — whether a preferred shareholder of a Delaware corporation had the right, under the corporation's Certificate of Designations, to a Series A Preferred Stock class vote on a merger — clearly involves the relationship among a corporation and its shareholders. As the United States Supreme Court held in *CTS*, "[n]o principle of corporation law and practice is more firmly established than a *State's authority* to regulate domestic corporations, including the authority to *define the voting rights of shareholders.*"[34]

In *CTS*, the Supreme Court held that the Commerce Clause "prohibits States from regulating subjects that 'are in their nature national, or admit only of one uniform system, or plan of regulation,'" and acknowledged that the internal affairs of a corporation are subjects that require one uniform system of regulation. In *CTS*, the Supreme Court concluded that "[s]o long as each State regulates voting rights *only in the corporations it has created*, each corporation will be subject to the law of only one State." Accordingly, we hold Delaware's well-established choice of law rules and the federal constitution mandated that Examen's internal affairs, and in particular, VantagePoint's voting rights, be adjudicated exclusively in accordance with the law of its state of incorporation, in this case, the law of Delaware.

Any Forum — Internal Affairs — Same Law

VantagePoint acknowledges that the courts of Delaware, as the forum state, may apply Delaware's own substantive choice of law rules. VantagePoint argues, however, that Delaware's "choice" to apply the law of the state of incorporation to internal affairs issues — notwithstanding California's enactment of section 2115 — will result in future forum shopping races to the courthouse. VantagePoint submits that, if the California action in these proceedings had been decided first, the California Superior Court would have enjoined the merger until it was factually determined whether section 2115 is applicable. If the statutory prerequisites were found to be factually satisfied, VantagePoint submits that the California Superior Court would have applied the internal affairs law reflected in section 2115, "to the exclusion" of the law of Delaware — the state where Examen is incorporated.

In support of those assertions, VantagePoint relies primarily upon a 1982 decision by the California Court of Appeals in *Wilson v. Louisiana-Pacific Resources, Inc.*, [138 Cal.

---

34. *CTS Corp. v. Dynamics Corp. of Am.*, 481 U.S. 69, 89, 107 S. Ct. 1637, 95 L. Ed. 2d 67 (1987) (emphasis added). *See* Restatement (Second) of Conflict of Laws §304 (1971) (concluding that the law of the incorporating State generally should "determine the right of a shareholder to participate in the administration of the affairs of the corporation").

App. 3d 216, 187 Cal. Rptr. 852 (1982)]. In *Wilson v. Louisiana-Pacific Resources, Inc.*, a panel of the California Court of Appeals held that section 2115 did not violate the federal constitution by applying the California Code's mandatory cumulative voting provision to a Utah corporation that had not provided for cumulative voting but instead had elected the straight voting structure set forth in the Utah corporation statute. The court in *Wilson* did not address the implications of the differences between the Utah and California corporate statutes upon the expectations of parties who chose to incorporate in Utah rather than California. As Professor DeMott points out, "[a]lthough it is possible under the Utah statute for the corporation's [Charter] to be amended by the shareholders and the directors, that mechanical fact does not establish California's right to coerce such an amendment" whenever the factual prerequisites of section 2115 exist.

Wilson was decided before the United States Supreme Court's decision in *CTS* and before this Court's decision in *McDermott*. Ten years after *Wilson*, the California Supreme Court cited with approval this Court's analysis of the internal affairs doctrine in *McDermott*, in particular, our holding that corporate voting rights disputes are governed by the law of the state of incorporation. Two years ago, in *State Farm v. Superior Court*, a different panel of the California Court of Appeals questioned the validity of the holding in *Wilson* following the broad acceptance of the internal affairs doctrine over the two decades after *Wilson* was decided.[46] In *State Farm*, the court cited with approval the United States Supreme Court decision in *CTS Corp. v. Dynamics* and our decision in *McDermott*. In *State Farm*, the court also quoted at length that portion of our decision in *McDermott* relating to the constitutional imperatives of the internal affairs doctrine.

Since *Wilson* was decided, the United States Supreme Court has recognized the constitutional imperatives of the internal affairs doctrine.[50] In *Draper v. Gardner*, this Court acknowledged the *Wilson* opinion in a footnote[51] and nevertheless permitted the dismissal of a Delaware action in favor of a California action in which a California court would be called upon to decide the internal affairs "demand" issue involving a Delaware corporation. As stated in *Draper*, we had no doubt that after the *Kamen* and *CTS* holdings by the United States Supreme Court, the California courts would "apply Delaware [demand] law [to the internal affairs of a Delaware corporation], given the vitality and constitutional underpinnings of the internal affairs doctrine." We adhere to that view in this case.

Conclusion

The judgment of the Court of Chancery is affirmed.

---

46. *State Farm Mut. Auto. Ins. Co. v. Superior Court*, 114 Cal. App. 4th 434 (2d Dist. 2003).

50. *E.g., Edgar v. MITE Corp.*, 457 U.S. 624, 102 S. Ct. 2629, 73 L. Ed. 2d 269 (1982); *CTS Corp. v. Dynamics Corp. of Am.*, 481 U.S. 69, 107 S. Ct. 1637, 95 L. Ed. 2d 67 (1987). *See also Kamen v. Kemper Fin. Serv.*, 500 U.S. 90, 111 S. Ct. 1711, 114 L. Ed. 2d 152 (1991).

51. *Draper v. Gardner*, 625 A.2d 859, 867 n.10 (Del. 1993).

1. What is the internal affairs doctrine?
2. Do you think that the court reached the right decision in this case?
3. Does the holding of this case influence your recommendation as to whether SoftCo should incorporate in California or Delaware?

When considering the decision whether to incorporate a new business (such as SoftCo) in Delaware, the transaction planner is well advised to take into account the observations in the following two articles:

Our Delaware Franchise Tax is WHAT?!?

The Corporation Secretary's Blog (July 22, 2013)*

Delaware has been preeminent as the place for businesses to incorporate since the early 1900s. Close to a million business entities are domiciled in Delaware, including more than one-half of the corporations that make up the Fortune 500.

Why do corporations choose Delaware? There are several reasons. First, the Delaware General Corporation Law is one of the most comprehensive, advanced and flexible corporation statutes in the nation. Second, Delaware's corporations court, the Court of Chancery, is highly respected because its judges are very knowledgeable and their decisions are well reasoned. The accumulated body of Delaware court decisions provides clarity and guidance in many of the situations that might arise in the realm of corporate governance or shareholder rights. Third, the state legislature is diligent about keeping Delaware's corporation statute current. And fourth, the Secretary of State's Office is not at all bureaucratic. Quite the contrary, it is efficient, helpful, and courteous. As one small example, Delaware was among the first states to accept corporate filings by fax.

Delaware's large body of corporation laws, including both statutes and court cases, allows a company to avoid lawsuits through better planning. The law is often much less clear in other states. Moreover, most corporate attorneys are familiar with Delaware corporation law in addition to the laws of the particular state where they are admitted to practice. A typical engagement letter from a law firm will say something like, "our practice is limited to the laws of [home state] and the Delaware General Corporation Law."

For all these reasons, many venture capital firms are more willing to invest in Delaware corporations, and entrepreneurs want to make their new businesses attractive to venture capital firms from the outset.

What are the disadvantages of incorporating in Delaware? There are two. First, the Delaware annual filing fee and annual franchise tax is an added expense because most

---

* *Available at* http://thecorpsecblog.com/2013/07/22/our-delaware-franchise-tax-is-what.

corporations (i.e., those located outside Delaware) must still register as a "foreign" corporation in the state where they are located and pay annual fees to that state. And second, the annual franchise tax in Delaware can come as a shock if the corporation is formed without adequate planning.

The Delaware annual franchise tax is calculated as follows (this is somewhat oversimplified — the exact calculation can be found at http://corp.delaware.gov/frtaxcalc.shtml):

If the authorized shares have *no par value*, the franchise tax is $75 for up to 5,000 authorized shares; an additional $150 for the next 5,000 authorized shares; and an additional $75 for each additional 10,000 authorized shares above the first 10,000 authorized shares. The maximum annual franchise tax is $180,000.

If the authorized shares have a *stated par value*, the corporation must calculate the "assumed par value", which is determined by dividing total gross assets of the corporation by the total number of *issued* shares. If this assumed par value is greater than the stated par value (which it almost always is), the assumed par value is multiplied by the number of authorized shares. The result is rounded up to the nearest million, then divided by a million, and then multiplied by $350. The minimum annual franchise tax is $350 and the maximum is $180,000.

Many entrepreneurs like to start their corporations with a huge number of authorized shares, hoping that they will need these shares for several rounds of future issuance: founders, new employees, family and friends, angels, venture capital investors and then the IPO. The problem is that a huge number of authorized shares, if not issued, can result in a very high annual franchise tax for a Delaware corporation, and the tax gets even higher as the gross assets of the corporation grow. . . .

The lesson here is that it can be very expensive for a Delaware corporation to authorize shares and not issue them. In most cases it would be better to start out with a small number of authorized shares and then later amend the certificate of incorporation to increase the number of authorized shares when a new issuance is planned.

Thomas E. Rutledge
State Law & State Taxation Corner: Going to Delaware

Journal of Passthrough Entities (July-Aug. 2013) at pp. 59-63

[There is wide consensus today that] Delaware dominates the "marketplace" for the organization of business organizations, whether they be publicly or privately held. . . . In fact, most business entities are organized under the laws of their home jurisdiction. To the extent that there is an analysis of the merits (or not) of organizing a particular venture in another jurisdiction, that other jurisdiction is almost always Delaware.

. . . [However,] all too many attorneys are of the belief that Delaware law is necessarily *better* without appreciating that Delaware is *different*; even when those differences are, to a greater or lesser degree, appreciated, *different* is all too often equated with *better*.

Now I do not mean to suggest that the Delaware business entity statutes and their supporting structures are not highly valuable and vitally important resources. . . . That is not to say, however, that Delaware's statutes are necessarily better. Rather, they are different, and sometimes that difference is beneficial. At other times, those differences may be detrimental.

Statutes

Undoubtedly the various Delaware business entity statutes are the most intensively scrutinized statutes of this nature in the country. Drafting committees focused upon the General Corporation Act, [and] the various unincorporated acts [such as the Delaware LLC statute] meet regularly to consider developments in practice and judicial developments and [then propose] amendments for presentation to the Delaware legislature for enactment. It is practically guaranteed that, on an annual basis, there will be a statutory update to most if not each of [the Delaware business entity statutes]. . . .

The Common Law in Parallel with Statutes

Another set of issues that also require consideration when organizing a venture in Delaware is the utilization in business organization law of the common law. To give but one example, while most business corporation acts define a standard of care applicable to corporate directors, [see, e.g., Calif. §309(a),] the fiduciary duty of care of a Delaware director is defined by common law. . . . Further, practitioners considering those common law implications in a state such as Delaware [where the courts issue a significant number of opinions each year], might find the task rather daunting.

In addition, counsel always needs to be aware that many of the organizational acts themselves incorporate the general common law.[4] This fact necessitates at least working knowledge of Delaware nonentity law. Further, in the unincorporated realm, where Delaware has strongly fixed its position as a "freedom of contract" jurisdiction,[5] it is necessary to know Delaware contract law when either crafting or interpreting a partnership/limited partnership/LLC agreement. Most attorneys would have some reluctance to draft a contract [that provides that the contract is to be] governed by the law of some state in which they are not resident and indeed are likely not even a member of the bar. Conversely, it is quite common for attorneys to draft contracts governed by Delaware law; those contracts are called partnership agreements, limited partnership agreements, LLC agreements and shareholder agreements. But honestly, if you have written those agreements, did you first research Delaware law [including Delaware case law with respect to the numerous] points of law that will impact on the [validity and] enforcement of the agreement?

One final thought with respect to the choice of business entity for a new business such as SoftCo: Do the founders, Joan and Michael, even need the services of a lawyer?

---

4. [See, e.g., §18-1104 of Delaware's LLC statute, which as we saw in Chapter 3, provides that "[i]n any case not provided for in this chapter, the rules of law and equity including the rules of law and equity relating to fiduciary duties and the law merchant, shall govern."].

5. See, e.g., DEL. CODE ANN tit.6, §18-1101(b) [of Delaware's LLC statute, which as we saw in Chapter 3, establishes broad freedom of contract in the drafting of limited liability company agreements.]; . . .

With the proliferation of online incorporation services (offered inexpensively and with just the swipe of a credit card), would today's entrepreneurs be well advised to forego the expense of retaining a lawyer?

Joel Beck
"We're Not Lawyers or Accountants, and Won't Give You Advice." Where's the Value in That? (Or, Why You Shouldn't Do Legal Work for Yourself Online)

The Beck Law Firm, LLC Blog (July 29, 2013)*

. . . [W]hile listening to a radio show [recently,] . . . [I heard] a commercial repeatedly played . . . that just left me scratching my head asking where the value was in this company's services.

I can't recall the company, but the advertisement talked about the need for business people to incorporate or form a LLC so that they could "protect" themselves and their assets from business problems. This company prominently stated that business owners would be most "protected" by ensuring they had a business entity filed with their state, and that they could handle the filing. The commercial continued to prominently state that the company was NOT providing any legal advice or accounting advice, but that it's goal was to simply help business owners be protected, and to protect their assets, by forming a legal entity in their own state. During the time I was [listening to the radio] — about an hour and a half or so — I heard this commercial at least 4 times. And it bothered me more each time I heard it. Why? Read on.

My problem with this company's commercial is that I think they're not providing real value to their clients. Sure, they can file online with a state to form a corporation or an LLC. Anyone can do that — it takes only a bare amount of know-how, a computer and internet connection and a credit card. But if they're not providing legal or accounting advice, what value are they actually providing? They're making money to file online something that the client could do themselves for less, and are . . . not providing the [client with] critical information needed [to make an appropriate business entity choice].

I've often said that a lawyer doesn't really provide value when we file a corporation or an LLC. Our value is instead provided when we analyze the proposed business and help the client choose the best entity type for their business, be it a corporation, a LLC, . . . Then, we provide value to the client by tailoring the initial books and records of the new business to the manner in which the business and its owners will operate, and then by giving them some information on how to operate the business and actually get the benefit of limited liability (to the extent possible under law) from this entity after it is formed. And this is something that actually requires the provision of legal advice. For example, lawyers [regularly] help newly formed businesses understand: how to sign contracts on behalf of the business entity and not the individual [so as] to bind only the business; how to transfer assets or property into the name of the business and how to have the business acquire additional assets; how to operate and observe the

---

* *Available at* http://www.bdlawblog.com/2013/07/.

required business formalities including separate accounts, annual shareholder meetings, corporate minutes, etc. to maintain the separate existence of the entity [in order] to help prevent the corporate "veil" from being pierced and [thereby] exposing the owner(s) to personal liability; and by providing information on all of the other start-up business issues that arise including licenses, permits, and the importance of establishing a relationship with a tax advisor to determine the tax status election, establish accounts with the [Department of Labor, the], IRS and [relevant] state taxing [authorities], etc. ([Note: This] isn't an exhaustive list, just some examples.)

Sometimes, there's just not a good replacement for actual legal advice, or accounting advice, when starting a new business. . . .

CHAPTER 6

EQUITY-BASED COMPENSATION: STOCK OPTIONS, INCENTIVE COMPENSATION, AND RELATED FOUNDER ISSUES

Having made the decision to incorporate SoftCo, and possibly to seek *Venture Capital* investment, Joan and Michael now face a number of issues regarding the potential use of company ownership interests as an incentive to attract employees, as well as the structure of their personal ownership relationship with SoftCo.

If Joan and Michael choose the venture capital financing pathway, they will, in effect, be choosing to build SoftCo as quickly as they can and to sell it in the next three to seven years. While we analyze the nature of venture capital investment in more detail in Chapter 8, the key point that Joan and Michael need to recognize now is that venture capital investors look to build a company's share value as quickly as possible, then seek a means of realizing on that increase in value (i.e., cashing out), usually by selling the company to a competitor or to the public in an IPO. Accepting venture capital investment will commit SoftCo to these twin objectives of building value and pursuing a means for its owners to cash out, but also will create an opportunity to use the potential future value of its stock as an element of its employee compensation. The prospect of stock ownership would be a meaningful compensation incentive when the intention is to create a high stock value in the future and to work toward a transaction where stockholders will have the ability to convert that value to cash. In contrast, should Joan and Michael decide to pursue *Friends and Family* financing or to *Go-It-Alone*, where the sale of SoftCo would not necessarily be a goal, using equity as a broad-based incentive compensation tool would be less practical. In those situations, with no clear intent to sell the business, a minority stock position in a privately held company probably would be seen by most potential employees as a dead end. This chapter looks at some common structures growth-oriented start-up companies use to offer equity incentives to their employees, non-employee directors, consultants, and independent contractors; basically to the range of individuals who provide them with services.

In addition to analyzing the prospect of using SoftCo's stock as a tool to attract and incentivize employees and other potential option grant recipients, Joan and Michael need to examine their personal stock ownership situations. They need to consider structuring their stock ownership positions in a way that will be attractive to venture capital investors, should they decide to seek venture financing. They need to understand the trade-offs between imposing restrictions on their ownership in anticipation of a venture capital investment versus waiting for the investment and negotiating restrictions then. They also need to understand how each of them may benefit from both of them agreeing to restrictions on their ownership regardless of whether venture capital investment ever occurs. This chapter looks at issues specific to founders and how some of the same mechanisms used for equity incentive programs can be applied by founders to their own ownership positions.

Equity-Based Compensation.   When considering the risks inherent in early-stage companies, the focus often is directed toward the investors. In fact, perhaps the greater risk-takers are the people who, instead of putting investment capital at risk, are accepting the uncertainty that the company will be around at the end of the month to honor their paychecks. To induce people to work for them, early-stage growth-oriented companies need to offer prospective employees something to compensate for the risk that the business may not succeed — the company may never attract financing, the product may not be as revolutionary as they had hoped, or there may be fewer customers in the marketplace than expected. What most venture capital–financed start-ups do, in addition to paying cash salaries and some level of benefits, is offer their employees an opportunity to share in the company's possible future growth by giving them stock or the right to buy stock, which is generally referred to as *equity-based compensation*.

The contents of this chapter relate to corporations only and specifically do not extend to LLCs, where partnership tax treatment means that equity incentive arrangements present markedly different issues, contain substantially different terms, and are very complex. In short, approaches presented in this chapter do not in any way translate into the LLC context.

In addition, this discussion is intended only as an introduction to private corporation equity incentives for the junior transactional lawyer. The focus of this chapter is on stock option and restricted stock mechanics and the basic tax, securities, and accounting rules that apply to these equity incentives and mechanisms when used in early-stage, privately held corporations. The reality is that these materials do not even begin to touch upon all the tax and accounting complexities relating to corporate equity incentives, so consultation with experts in those areas is an absolute must when dealing with equity incentive matters.

Section A introduces the basic mechanics of stock options. Section B addresses nonqualified stock options (NQSOs) as the default option form for incentive compensation, while section C looks at incentive stock options (ISOs) and the special rules applicable to this creature of tax law. Section D examines restricted stock, which can be used both as an equity incentive tool and as a means of addressing issues relating to the purchase of stock by the company's founders. Section E presents a brief overview of some other, less frequently used forms of equity-based compensation, and section F discusses a number of contractual variations that are frequently used as part of equity-based compensation plans as well as in stock purchase arrangements with company founders.

Notice that there is variation in the terminology and in the formats used for presenting share numbers, prices, and values in this chapter and in later chapters of this casebook. This is not an oversight. While consistent terminology and appropriate conventions of presentation are very important in legal documents, deal terms are expressed differently by different people in different contexts. One of the challenges for the business lawyer is being able to recognize and understand concepts no matter how they are expressed and then to select the clearest way to document the agreed-upon arrangement. The varying forms of expression and presentation commonly encountered in dealing with clients, accountants, and investment bankers, not to mention other lawyers, are used in this casebook intentionally in an effort to expose you, the prospective business lawyer, to what may be found in actual practice.

As you read the following materials, keep in mind that from a company's point of view, a successful equity incentive program allows it to attract employees in a tax-efficient manner at a reasonable cost — granting stock ownership is just as real a cost to a company's existing shareholders as paying cash compensation — with an acceptable level of administrative expense. From the employees' point of view, a successful equity incentive program provides meaningful potential value with limited investment risk, administrative complications, or surprise outcomes. While these viewpoints can be reconciled in some areas, they will conflict in others. Part of the business lawyer's role is to assist the company in evaluating and weighing the strengths and weaknesses of the various approaches available for providing equity-based compensation. In reading the remainder of this chapter, consider the effect of the issues raised both from the perspective of the company and of its future employees.

A. Stock Options Generally

1. What Is a Stock Option?

As the term is used in the equity compensation context, a *stock option* is the right to buy, over a specified period of time, a specified number of shares of common stock at a specified price. For example, SoftCo, Inc., could grant Emma, an employee, an option to buy 100 shares of SoftCo's common stock at $1.00 per share that is exercisable at any time over the next ten years. Therefore, no matter how high in value SoftCo's stock grows over the next ten years, Emma can buy 100 shares for $100 — even if the stock is worth $200 per share when Emma exercises her option. Stock options are granted by a company to people who provide it with services (such as an employee, consultant or other non-employee, or director) as supplemental compensation for those services. The purchase right may be exercised by the person, or "option holder," at the holder's discretion, in accordance with the terms of the option. The purpose is to offer individuals who provide services to a company an extra incentive by giving them the opportunity to buy the company's stock in the future, after the company has grown and its stock is more valuable, at a price set today, while the company is young and its stock has little value.

Options often are issued pursuant to an *option plan* (also called an *equity incentive plan*) that sets the terms and rules applicable to all options issued by the company under that plan. (That sounds circular because it is — a company can have multiple plans with different terms for different purposes and issue options under any of them.) Such a plan is normally approved by the board and shareholders, and it designates the number of common stock shares that are to be set aside from the company's authorized capital stock for issuance under the terms of the plan.

Options are securities that must be issued in compliance with federal securities laws as well as the state securities laws in both the state from which the company is issuing the options (generally the state where the company is headquartered) and the state where the recipient of the option is domiciled. As discussed in Chapter 4, the federal registration exemption applicable to securities issuances under equity incentive plans is SEC Rule 701. 17 C.F.R. §230.701. Most companies conform their plans to the requirements of Rule 701. State securities laws may impose additional terms on a plan.

2. Granting an Option

A company may grant options to anyone it wishes. Option plans are not subject to broad participation requirements, such as those that apply to pension plans or to tax-deferred defined contribution retirement plans, such as 401(k) plans. While a company's plan may include terms limiting those who may receive options to a defined class or group, and (as we shall see in section C of this chapter) specific restrictions apply to the grant of ISOs, the board of directors has discretion to grant options to people within that permitted group as it sees fit.

As a practical matter, because the federal securities law exemption provided by Rule 701 applies only to issuances to a defined range of permitted grant recipients, most equity incentive plans limit grants to the people specified by that Rule: employees; consultants, advisors, and other non-employees who are natural persons providing *bona fide* services not in connection with offering, selling, or trading the issuer's securities; and directors, regardless of whether they are employees or not. 17 C.F.R. §230.701(c)(1). ISOs may be granted only to employees. In the course of the following discussion, an option recipient often will be referred to as "the employee" simply as a convenience. However, it is important to keep in mind that NQSOs, in contrast to ISOs, typically may be granted to a broader class of individuals that provide services to a company, rather than just to employees. *Query*: Why would SoftCo want to grant options to its employees, especially considering that options potentially dilute the ownership interest of Joan and Michael?

The grant of an option is usually evidenced by an option agreement that incorporates by reference the terms of the plan and sets forth the specifics of the individual option grant (the number of shares that may be purchased, the price at which they may be purchased, and any vesting requirements) and, within the scope of terms permitted by the plan, provides for any special terms applicable to that particular option grant. Instead of an option agreement, some companies provide a "notice" of the option grant, which references the plan and contains the key terms of the grant. Alternatively, an option may be granted without a plan through a stand-alone agreement that provides all the terms applicable to the option.

Options very often are granted as part of the overall compensation package for new employees, but also are routinely granted to continuing employees. An option grant is made in consideration of on-going services, so no other payment is made by the employee to receive the option.

In private companies, options are granted by authorization of the corporation's board of directors or, if contemplated by the terms of the company's option plan, a committee of the board to which the responsibility has been delegated. While this is mechanically simple for grants to existing employees, it can be awkward for new employee grants because hiring may take place at any time and the board usually only meets monthly, or perhaps even quarterly. As a result of the board's unavailability on a day-to-day basis, in most venture capital-financed companies the board often will approve a budget for new-hire option grants based on a hiring plan developed to accommodate the company's planned growth. For each position to be filled, the hiring plan includes a projected level of cash compensation as well as an anticipated range in the size of the option grant expected to be necessary to attract qualified candidates.

When a job candidate is selected for hire, management frequently will present the candidate with an offer letter that describes the position, the offered compensation (including the grant of an option to purchase a stated number of shares), and the other terms of employment. But as to the option grant, the offer letter typically says that the described grant will be presented to the board for approval and is conditioned on that approval. Then at the board's next regular meeting, management will present each individual new hire's proposed option grant for approval. In circumstances where a prospective new employee will have to relocate, for example, or the hire is for a senior position and therefore involves a large compensation package, so the candidate wants confirmation at the time of the offer that the option grant will in fact be made, management may request that the board pre-approve the specific grant as part of the terms to be offered. In that case, the board normally will condition its authorization of the grant on the actual commencement of the candidate's employment.

It is important for the business lawyer to remind the client company of these formalities and of the fact that management is not authorized to make binding commitments regarding option grants absent specific authorization from the board of directors. Because setting terms for employment *is* within the scope of officers' authority generally, a compelling argument could be made that officers have apparent authority to communicate binding compensation terms. (You will recall, from your introductory Business Associations course, the essential principles of apparent and actual authority that are fundamental precepts of agency law.) So in circumstances where a prospective employee detrimentally relies on an unqualified promise to provide a specified option grant, by leaving a current job or by relocating, for example, the company may find itself bound to make the grant, even if it has not been approved by the board and is outside the budgeted size for that position.

3. *Term of an Option and Vesting*

Option Term.   Options have a fixed term that for employees, absent special circumstances, usually is ten years, subject to earlier termination. The practice of granting ten-year options reflects the fact that the various forms of special tax treatment applicable to options that the federal government has adopted over the years, the most recent being ISOs, have limited maximum terms to ten years. 26 U.S.C. §422(b)(3) (setting a maximum ISO term at ten years). If a holder fails to exercise the option by purchasing the company's shares at the price and on the terms specified before the option expires, that holder loses the chance to do so. Because we are discussing options granted as a form of supplemental non-cash compensation for services, the usual reason for an option to terminate early is that the services relationship between the company and the option holder ends — for example, upon termination of employment, completion of a consulting project, or failure to be reelected to the board. In that situation, the option holder usually has some period of time, post-termination, to exercise the option before it expires. For employees, who are likely to have had a lengthy opportunity during employment to exercise their options, that post-termination time period is usually 30 to 90 days. For consultants and directors, because they tend to provide services for a shorter period of time (particularly consultants), the post-termination exercise period often has a longer term, perhaps six months or one year, or sometimes even longer.

An additional early termination trigger is the sale of the company. When the company that issued an option is acquired, the acquiring company has the choice of offering a "substitute option" to some or all of the option holders. A substitute option has substantively equivalent terms and allows the option holder to roll over some or all of the existing option into an option to purchase shares of the acquiring company's common stock. As a substitute option is a negotiated contractual arrangement, its terms may vary and may be customized to achieve specific outcomes. For example, substitute options may be offered only to a small number of key employees. Often, no substitute options are offered. If the acquiror does not offer a substitute option to any particular option holder or holders, the options held by those holders typically expire immediately prior to the effective date of the acquisition. The result is that those option holders who are not offered a substitute option only have the choice of allowing their options to terminate without exercise or exercising them and participating in the sale of the issuing company as a common stock holder, receiving whatever consideration the common stock holders are entitled to from the buyer.

Vesting.   In addition to having a limited term, the right to purchase the common stock shares underlying an option typically "vests" over time. When an option is unvested, it cannot be exercised. In other words, "vesting" is the mechanism that switches on the right to exercise the option and therefore to purchase the underlying shares. Vesting is usually conditioned on continued employment or, for a consultant or board member, an ongoing services relationship with the company.

While the period of time over which an option vests may vary, a typical vesting term for new employees of venture capital-financed companies is four years, with no vesting occurring until the end of the first year of employment, when 25 percent of the option vests, and the remainder of the option vesting in 36 equal monthly installments over the next three years. For example, on March 1, 2014, SoftCo grants to employee Emily a ten-year option to buy 20,000 shares at $1.00 per share, with 25 percent of the option vesting on the one-year anniversary of the grant date, and the remaining option vesting thereafter in 36 equal monthly installments. On March 1, 2015, Emily's option will vest as to the right to buy 5,000 shares (20,000 shares x 25 percent). On the first day of each month thereafter, for the next 36 months, an additional 416.67 shares (the remaining 15,000 shares ÷ 36 months) will vest. As of March 1, 2018, Emily's option will be fully vested.

The extended period of time at the beginning of employment during which no shares vest, referred to as a "cliff" (in the foregoing example, a "one-year cliff"), represents a probationary period for new hires. Alternatively, options may be fully vested as of the time of the grant or may vest over the entire life of the option. Options granted to continuing employees often do not have the one-year cliff, as a probationary period is no longer relevant. Instead, they usually vest in equal monthly increments over a three- or four-year vesting term. *Query*: Why would a company want to impose a vesting "cliff"? What does a probationary period accomplish? For example, would you recommend that SoftCo impose a cliff in the grant of options to company employees?

Explaining option vesting is a good test of the business lawyer's ability to create documentation that is clear and unambiguous. An option agreement must clearly state the vesting terms so there can be no debate regarding the number of shares that may be purchased upon exercise of the option as of any specific date.

Fractional Shares.   Managing fractional shares (an ownership interest representing less than a single share) is a common issue when a company uses a standard vesting template, such as four-year vesting with a one-year cliff followed by 36 equal monthly installments. As we saw with Emily's option, the grant, divided by the number of installments, simply may not yield a whole number for each installment. Most companies find it administratively inefficient to issue fractional shares, so a vesting schedule that vests share fractions is a potential problem. The most common solution is to allow for fractional vesting but restrict the right to exercise the option to the number of whole shares that are vested at the time of exercise. An alternative is to round the number of shares that vest in each incremental vesting installment down to the next lower whole number and catch up the employee on the last installment.

Termination of Vesting Period.   If an option is not yet fully vested when the services relationship terminates, vesting virtually always stops on the effective date of the termination of employment or other end to the services provided by the option holder. The option holder then has the specified post-termination exercise period to exercise that portion of the option that was vested on the services termination date. To the extent that the option did not vest as to a portion of the shares covered by it, or it vested but was not exercised, the unpurchased shares return to the pool of shares available for issuance under the equity incentive plan.

QUESTIONS

1. Employee Emily receives an option grant from SoftCo on March 1, 2014, to buy 20,000 shares at $1.00 per share, with 25 percent of the option vesting on the one-year anniversary of the grant date, and the remainder of the option vesting thereafter in 36 equal monthly installments. She decides to celebrate her birthday on August 21, 2016, by exercising the then-vested portion of her option. How many shares may Emily buy? Assume that SoftCo's option plan allows option holders to exercise the number of whole shares vested on any particular date.

2. If SoftCo's option plan provides that periodic vesting (annual, quarterly, or monthly) shall not include any fractional share amounts, but instead each incremental vesting amount is to be rounded down to the nearest whole share number, with all fractional amounts aggregated and added to the final vesting installment, how does that change the number of shares Emily can purchase on August 21, 2016?

3. Emily gets an offer from an established software company in Washington state and terminates her employment with SoftCo on January 31, 2017. SoftCo's option plan gives employees 60 days following employment termination to exercise their options. Emily exercises her option on the sixtieth day, April 1, 2017. How many shares can she buy when she exercises her option?

4. Exercise Price

The per-share exercise price of an option (also referred to as the "strike price") is the price the option holder must pay to purchase the company's shares upon exercise of the option. For tax reasons, the exercise price almost always is set at the fair market value of the company's common stock as of the date the option is granted.

In Chapters 8 and 9, we look at how venture capital investors place a value on the preferred stock of a company in order to make an investment. That process assumes that all shares have equal value because it is based on the premise that the company ultimately will be wildly successful and the difference in rights and powers between the company's preferred stock and its common stock will be irrelevant. For purposes of stock options and other equity incentives, however, valuation is not a product of a projection of future success. As a result, the equity incentive value of a company's common stock, as the junior equity security, takes into account the effect of the priority rights and powers of the preferred stock. We detail the sorts of preferential rights typically granted to venture capital preferred stock in Chapter 9. Consequently, the value of the common stock is usually substantially discounted from the per-share price of the preferred stock. In many cases, the discount is 80 percent to 90 percent off the price paid by investors in the most recent issuance of preferred stock.

The common stock of publicly traded companies has an established market, so its fair market value often changes on a daily basis but is usually easily determined as of any given day. In contrast, the common stock of privately held companies typically does not change hands frequently nor does it have day-to-day changes in value.

Many private companies set the exercise price of their options based on the value of the common stock on the date of the meeting when the board is considering the proposed option grants. Given that months can pass between events that would cause a private company to revalue its shares, so long as the board meets frequently there should be little, if any, prejudice to the option grant recipients if the price is set as of the board meeting date rather than as of their employment commencement date. By setting the price as the fair market value of the company's common stock on the date of board approval, the company will conform to the tax rules as well as to the accounting rules for determining the "grant date" of the option. *See generally* Internal Revenue Code (I.R.C) §409A (25 U.S.C §409A) and related regulations and Financial Accounting Standards Board Statement No. 123(R). Section B.2 of this chapter provides more details on §409A and the process for setting the option exercise price.

The lower the exercise price, the greater potential benefit to the option recipient. The temptation to search for a low price date has resulted in highly publicized criminal "back-dating" prosecutions of public company officers. This is less of an issue in the private company context where the share price fluctuates less and typically the board meets more frequently. The best practice in either context is to have a consistent approach to fixing the date for pricing so that there is no temptation to distort the pricing decision. From company counsel's perspective, deviations from this approach should be strongly discouraged as they may result in a price that is later rejected by the IRS as not representing the fair market value of the company's stock on the date of the grant. Section B.2 below discusses the penalties that may be triggered by not adhering to the valuation requirements of I.R.C. §409A.

5. Exercising an Option

The mechanics for exercising an option (that is, purchasing some or all of the common stock underlying the option) are set forth in the option agreement or the plan. An option is usually exercised by the option holder providing the company with a notice of intent to exercise that indicates how many shares the option holder wishes to purchase at this time. Usually an option may be exercised to purchase any or all of the then-vested shares, but some companies, in order to limit the administrative cost of small exercises, will have a minimum number of shares that may be the subject of an exercise while the holder is employed. A minimum exercise amount might be, for example, the lesser of (i) 10 percent of the total number of shares making up the option grant or (ii) the remaining unpurchased shares available under the option.

Upon receiving a notice of exercise, the company usually provides the option holder with an execution copy of a Stock Purchase Agreement, filled in with the correct number of shares and the total purchase price to be paid, and information regarding the tax effects of the option exercise and how any tax obligations are to be met. The Stock Purchase Agreement (a form of which usually is attached to the option agreement when the grant is made, so that the option holder will be on notice of its terms) also will reflect any ongoing contractual restrictions or covenants that may apply to the shares after purchase. The option holder then signs the Stock Purchase Agreement and delivers it to the company with payment for the shares being purchased, together with any other documentation or tax payments that may be required under the terms of the plan, the option agreement, and the Stock Purchase Agreement, and the holder subsequently receives a certificate representing the purchased common stock shares. Some plans allow the option holder to make the exercise price payment by surrendering shares of the company's stock already owned by the option holder. However, the rules on "cashless exercise" by surrendering stock can be tricky and many companies simply require cash. For share ownership rights, as well as tax and securities holding periods, the shares normally are treated as purchased on the date that the required consideration and executed documents are delivered to the company. *Query*: What if, instead of happening simultaneously, these acts occur on different dates?

6. Accounting Treatment for an Option Grant

Historically, there was no accounting treatment applicable to an option grant; it simply was a non-event as far as the issuing company's income statement was concerned. This, in fact, was one of the primary advantages of using stock options as incentive compensation. While salaries and other compensation paid by a company must be shown as expenses on the company's income statement and, like all expenses, serve to reduce the profits that company earns, options were simply ignored. Of course, options must have some value or they would not be a desirable form of compensation. Many people were troubled by the fact that options deliver value to employees as part of a compensation package, but their value was not reflected as compensation expense in the issuer's financial statements.

In December 2004, the Financial Accounting Standards Board (FASB), the accounting profession's self-regulatory board, issued Financial Accounting Standards Board Statement No. 123 (Revised) *Share-Based Payment* (FASB 123(R)), which provides that, beginning upon the grant of an option, the "fair value" of that option must be recorded as a non-cash compensation expense over the "requisite service period" of the option and reflected on the company's income statement as a cost of the business for those reporting periods. Implementation of FASB 123(R) was delayed repeatedly but became generally applicable for financial statements covering periods beginning after December 15, 2005. In short, this means that the "fair value" of an option is recorded on the company's income statement as a compensation expense, pro-rated over a period of time (the "requisite service period") that is set when the option is granted and reflects the terms of that option as well as the likelihood that the options like it that have been granted by the company will actually vest and be exercised.

The "fair value" is determined by a financial calculation that may or may not have any connection with reality. The idea is that an ongoing right to buy a number of shares at a fixed price in the future must have some real, determinable current value. There are a number of complex financial models, the most famous of which is probably the Black-Scholes formula, that apply a series of financial variables in a multi-part equation to determine a fair price for an option and have been accepted as having predictive validity in setting an option's value. It is important to remember that the issue here is not setting the *exercise price* of the option, but rather determining the *financial value of the option itself* as a right to buy the company's stock at some future date. On a very simplified basis, these value analyses look at the range of potential outcomes for the market in general (or for the sector the company operates in), then look at how the particular company's stock historically has performed in relation to that broader market. Assuming that circumstances do not change dramatically (for example, no Great Recession occurs), the models predict a range of likely future outcomes for the company's stock price with some degree of confidence and assign probabilities to those outcomes. The likelihood that various profit outcomes will be realized upon exercise of the option, as well as the likelihood that no profit will be gained, can then be measured. Based on that information, a reasonable value can be assigned to *the option* as of the date it is granted — that is, the price an independent person would pay to purchase the option in light of the risks and potential for profit it offers.

For publicly traded companies these value assignment metrics can be quite useful, particularly when a company has a large trading base of shares and a substantial history showing predictable stock price movements in relation to changes in the general market. For private companies, however, the utility of this approach is much more problematic for the simple reason that in many cases the most likely outcome is that the company will fail and the value of the option will be zero.

For example, the stock market did better in the years from 2003 to 2007 than most financial experts predicted. As a result, there were some complaints in Congress that companies were recognizing relatively small compensation expenses when options were granted during that period, but later, when the options were exercised, those companies took advantage of significantly larger tax deductions for the gains actually recognized by the employees when those same options were exercised. The reason was simple: the "fair value" formulas underweighted the probabilities for positive outcomes because the market in general did better than expected. Thus, actual option outcomes were better than predicted. In contrast, options granted in 2007 and 2008 were significantly over-valued because the Great Recession beginning in 2008 was not adequately reflected in the formulas. As a result, companies during that time period recorded compensation expense for option grants that far exceeded the actual value of those options.

This valuation problem can be compared to actuarial theory. A life insurance company can look at actuarial information regarding life expectancy and price its policies to make money so long as it sells enough policies over a long enough period of time to make its outcome essentially match the statistically predictable outcome for the population as a whole. A narrow range of statistical variation will occur from year to year, but with a broad base of insured lives over a reasonable number of years, the outcomes are very predictable. The life insurer knows with a high degree of confidence that death will occur each year to a specific percentage of its hundreds of thousands of policy holders. On the other hand, it cannot say with any predictive confidence what will happen to a particular policy holder.

As a result, with imperfect data and a staggering range of potential outcomes in the private company context, the determination of the fair value of an option at the time of its grant that must be recorded as an expense is fundamentally imprecise. In practice, it generally ends up being the subject of negotiation between the company and its auditor, where the company simply wants to record the lowest possible "fair value" expense and the auditor needs to see a price that can be validated with an accepted financial model.

Requisite Service Period.   The "requisite service period" used in option accounting is based on a prediction of the likelihood that options granted by the company actually will vest and be exercised. Because of employee turnover, stock price fluctuations, and other factors, some portion of the options a company grants will never be exercised. Again, the accountants do not attempt to predict what will happen to each individual option, but rather do a general prediction of a company's option grants overall. The object is to recognize the financial cost of all compensation paid each month, quarter, and year. Thus, where an option vests over time based on services, the expense recognition of the fair value of the option is spread over a period of time that reflects a portion of the option vesting that is equal to the portion of the company's options in general that are likely to vest and be exercised.

Depending on the length of time employees tend to stay, a private company that grants options vesting in four years with a one-year cliff and monthly installments there-after may have a "requisite service period" applied to its option grants of somewhere between 18 months and three years. Thus, the compensation expense for the option grant is recorded in equal increments on a monthly basis over the requisite service period that, in the end, adds up to the "fair value" of the option when granted.

While the application of the "fair value" accounting treatment may be complex, FASB 123(R) in many ways simplified the potential accounting outcomes; the adoption of FASB 123(R) actually eliminated a number of variations in the way option grants had been treated for financial reporting. In the past, for example, a grant to a non-employee director received different accounting treatment from an identical grant to a director who also was an employee. That being said, option accounting, including the treatment of amendments to outstanding options, obviously is very complex. Deloitte & Touche, LLP, one of the major international accounting firms, has provided its professionals and clients a "roadmap" to applying FASB 123(R) that is over 275 pages long and disclaims the generality of its contents! *See* DELOITTE, FASB STATEMENT NO. 123(R), SHARE-BASED PAYMENT: A ROADMAP TO APPLYING THE FAIR VALUE GUIDANCE TO SHARE-BASED PAYMENT AWARDS (2d ed. Apr. 2006, last updated Oct. 29, 2009), *available at* www.iasplus.com/dttpubs/0605fas123guidance.pdf. Before making any changes in a company's option plans, in addition to the obvious need to seek assistance from a tax expert, a business lawyer always should consult with a knowledgeable accountant to understand what the accounting implications of the contemplated action will be so that no surprises result.

QUESTIONS

1. Why do companies worry so much about the accounting treatment of the options that are granted to their employees?
2. What are some of the major accounting concerns that an issuer faces in deciding whether to grant stock options to its employees?

B. Nonqualified Stock Options

1. The Default Form of Option

A *nonqualified stock option* is any stock option that does not meet the requirements of an incentive stock option. The NQSO is, therefore, the default form of option and, as the basic option model, is a useful foundation point for looking at stock options and equity incentives. The terms required for an option to receive ISO treatment are outlined in section C below.

The first issue to clear up is the naming protocol. NQSOs are called "nonqualified" because the Internal Revenue Code used to provide for "qualified" options before that scheme was abandoned and "incentive stock options" were created. Apparently, as an effort to avoid the awkwardness of a "non-incentive" option, the "nonqualified" terminology survived the death of the "qualified" option. NQSOs are also referred to as "non-statutory options," again as a contrast to those authorized under the federal tax statutes that create ISOs, which are sometimes referred to as "statutory stock options."

2. Tax Treatment of NQSOs

When an issuer grants an NQSO, the option recipient does not recognize any taxable income and the issuer (i.e., the company) does not receive a tax deduction. The value of the option is too speculative for a tax to be assessed at this time. However, as noted in section A.6's accounting discussion, the company does have to record a compensation expense, for financial accounting purposes, based on the "fair value" of the NQSO at the time of the grant. When an NQSO is exercised, the option holder recognizes ordinary income equal to the difference between the exercise price paid and the fair market value of the common stock so purchased, and the company receives a tax deduction for compensation expense in that amount.

Taxes Assessed upon Exercise. Section 83 of the Internal Revenue Code generally provides that property transferred to a person (the "property" here is the stock) in connection with the performance of services is taxable to the recipient as ordinary income. The Internal Revenue Code applies ordinary income tax to payments made as compensation for services, regardless of the form of the payment.

When an NQSO is exercised, the value of stock received, less the price paid to exercise the option, is taxable income to the option holder. For example, if an employee exercised an NQSO on December 31, 2014, to purchase 30,000 shares for $0.10 per share, and the fair market value of the company's common stock at that time was $1.00 per share, the employee would recognize ordinary income in the amount of $27,000 (($1.00 value of each share of the stock minus the $0.10 exercise price per share equals $0.90 gain per share) x 30,000 shares) on the date of the exercise.

Any ordinary income the employee recognizes in connection with an NQSO exercise is deemed "wages." The company is required to deduct and withhold federal and state income tax from its employees' "wages," including employment related taxes, such as Social Security and Medicare taxes. The company may withhold the required tax amounts from the employee's wages, salary, bonus, or other income to which the employee would otherwise be entitled. Or, at the company's election, the employee may be required to pay money to the company in the amount the company is required to withhold and pay to the federal and state governments on the employee's behalf. An additional alternative is that, as an accommodation to the employee, the company may allow the employee to surrender a portion of the stock purchased and credit that value toward the employee's tax obligation. In the case of many start-up companies, this is a significant accommodation because the company then must come up with the cash to pay the withholding taxes.

This points up a major distinction between public company options and private company options. In the public company context, where there is an active trading market for the company's shares, options often are exercised in broker-assisted transactions in which a stock broker makes a short-term loan of the exercise price to the employee. The broker pays the loan amount to the company to exercise the option and the shares are issued to the broker for the benefit of the employee; then immediately upon completion of the exercise, the broker sells a sufficient number of the shares in the market to generate enough cash to cover the exercise price loan plus the tax withholding amounts. The broker uses that cash to repay itself, with interest, for the loan, plus collects a fee for the service, and reports the transaction and taxable income amount to the company. It delivers additional cash from the stock sale to the company to take care of the withholding, then forwards any remaining cash and the unsold shares to the employee. The employee, then, does not have to use any of his or her cash to exercise the option; instead, he or she uses a portion of the shares being purchased to finance the entire transaction and receives the net value after the exercise price, taxes, and the broker's charges have been paid.

In the private company context, the shares being purchased are not liquid unless an option is exercised on the eve of a cash acquisition of the company. Therefore, in most circumstances, because there typically is no easy way to convert the shares into cash, the employee has to come up with the exercise price and pay the tax obligations from his or her own resources. If the income recognized is relatively small, that may not be a problem. However, if, in our example, instead of an option grant of 30,000 shares, the option is for 300,000 shares, the employee is looking at a $30,000 exercise price (based on a $0.10 purchase price times 300,000 shares purchased upon the exercise of this option) and a tax obligation based on $270,000 of ordinary income, calculated as follows: $1.00 stock value minus $0.10 exercise price = $0.90 of gain on each share, which is then multiplied by 300,000 shares. In this example, the combined state and federal withholding taxes on the $270,000 of ordinary income will be at least $67,500, based on a flat federal supplemental wage withholding rate of 25 percent. *See* 26 U.S.C. §3402; Treas. Reg. §§31.3402(g)-1(a)(5) to (7). Employment taxes and any state tax withholding would be in addition to that amount. Given time, the employee may be able to find a buyer for some or all of the stock to cover the exercise price and the tax obligation, but cash in those amounts has to be paid to the employer immediately, not in weeks or months. In short, if the gain on the option is substantial, that gain may make it impossible for the employee to exercise the option unless the employee has the financial resources to pay the required tax withholding amounts.

Because the employee is receiving taxable income, the company will be entitled to an income tax deduction equal to the amount the employee recognized as ordinary income.

Stock acquired upon the exercise of an NQSO that is later sold is taxed again on that sale. The employee will recognize long-term capital gain or loss if the sale is made after one year from the date of the option exercise. If the employee transfers the shares within one year of the option exercise, the employee will owe short-term capital gain tax, which is payable at the same rate as ordinary income tax. As of November 2013, the maximum federal long-term capital gain tax rate is 23.8 percent, which is significantly lower than the maximum 39.6 percent rate applicable to ordinary income.

Continuing the prior example, if the employee were to sell the 30,000 shares bought for $0.10 per share on December 31, 2014, in a transaction on or after December 31, 2015, for $2.75 per share, the employee would recognize $52,500 of long-term capital gain (i.e. ($2.75 − $1.00) x 30,000 shares). That is, the proceeds, $2.75 per share, less the employee's tax basis of $1.00 per share (representing the $0.10 paid, plus the $0.90 of ordinary income per share on which the employee has already paid tax at the time the option was exercised) multiplied by the number of shares sold in the transaction. The company has no withholding responsibility on a transfer; rather, the employee is then responsible for reporting the gain or loss as part of his or her annual income tax return.

If the employee sold the shares during 2016 for only $0.50 per share, the employee would recognize a $15,000 long-term capital loss instead of a gain (i.e. (the $0.50 sale price less the $1.00 tax basis) x 30,000 shares that were sold). In that case, the employee would have paid $3,000 to purchase the shares, recognized $27,000 of ordinary income on the option exercise (which required the employee to pay combined state and federal taxes in the range of perhaps $9,000 to $13,000), then had a long-term capital loss of $15,000 when the shares were later sold. Thus, the employee would be out of pocket approximately $12,000 to $16,000 (exercise price plus taxes) and would have a $15,000 long-term capital loss, which can be used to reduce other capital gains, with up to $3,000 of any excess loss deductible against ordinary income and the remainder carried over to future years.

This illustrates an additional important point about options, particularly in the private company context where the shares purchased may not be easily sold. Despite the option holder's hope that he or she will be able to sit on the option and only exercise it when it has value and the shares being purchased are liquid, options are not without risk. The employee may feel compelled to exercise the option, despite the absence of any means of selling the shares, because the shares have increased in value and a termination in employment has triggered a "use it or lose it" situation. Yet, after he or she scrapes up the money to exercise the option and pay the withholding taxes based on the then-current share value, the company still may fail to realize its potential, and the shares may turn out to be worthless. Like any other securities purchase, an option exercise is an investment decision and, especially while the company is at an early stage, carries with it all the risks of owning the illiquid stock of a high-risk, private company.

3. Effect of I.R.C. §409A

Historically, the exercise price of NQSOs sometimes was set lower than the fair market value of the company's common stock on the date of the grant. This was a means of giving optionees an (often unvested) extra benefit, but since the adoption of I.R.C. §409A, substantial tax penalties now exist for issuing under-priced options.

Section 409A was enacted in response to Enron Corp.'s collapse and its bankruptcy filing in December 2001. At that time, executives were permitted to defer compensation to themselves without being taxed, so long as the company's payment obligation to them was unsecured and any assets set aside to pay the compensation were exposed to the claims of the company's creditors. Yet, in the weeks prior to bankruptcy, the Enron executives, in accordance with the deferred compensation rules in place at the time, were able to accelerate deferred compensation payments from Enron to themselves and draw out of the company (and away from its creditors) approximately $53 million. In response, Congress concluded that the mechanisms controlling informal deferred compensation arrangements were inadequate and enacted §409A in 2004 to establish a broadly written regulatory framework for permitted deferral arrangements and to harshly penalize any nonconforming deferred compensation plans and agreements. The statute contemplated that the IRS would develop detailed rules for implementing the new restrictions across the range of regulated compensation arrangements.

The full regulatory scheme ultimately was implemented effective as of the beginning of 2009.

Nonconforming deferred compensation payments are subject to a 20 percent penalty tax over and above regular taxation (which almost always is at ordinary income rates), plus interest. Similar state penalties apply in many jurisdictions, which means that a nonconforming deferred compensation arrangement may face taxation at a combined federal and state rate potentially of 70–85 percent, plus interest. While these rates and penalties are assessed against the employee or other compensation recipient, the company is required to withhold the mandated taxes, and further, may be held liable to the employee for its failure to construct its compensation arrangements in conformity with the law.

Stock options, which are deferred compensation arrangements by their very nature, do not conform to the §409A standards for unpenalized deferred compensation. By following certain rules, however, NQSOs may be excluded from their scope. Primary among those rules is the requirement that a stock option must be granted with an exercise price that is not less than the fair market value of the underlying stock on the date of the grant. Treas. Reg. §1.409A-1(b)(5)(i)(A)(1). In addition, the underlying stock must be common stock, and if a company has more than one type of common stock, then the options must be exercisable into the type that has the greatest value. Treas. Reg. §1.409A-1(b)(5)(iii)(A).

In the past, one of the elements of NQSOs that made them attractive in contrast to ISOs was that they could be granted with an exercise price below the then–fair market value of the underlying common stock. Thus, on the date of the grant, the NQSO could have "built-in value" because the stock was already worth more than the exercise price of the option. Although the grant recipient faced ordinary income tax recognition on the date of the grant on the difference between the fair market value of the underlying shares and the option exercise price, many companies found the practice useful in providing a built-in price gain to an employee. For reasons just described above, the penalties imposed under §409A now make that practice completely uneconomical.

Section 409A requires not only that NQSOs must have an exercise price at least equal to the fair market value of the company's common stock at the time of the grant, but also that the fair market value must be determined by "the reasonable application of a reasonable valuation method." *See* Treas. Reg. §1.409A-1(b)(5)(iv)(B)(1). The IRS has defined three "safe harbor" methods that private companies may use to value their common stock. If a company uses one of these three methods, the valuation will be deemed presumptively reasonable unless the IRS can establish it was grossly unreasonable or that the method was applied in a grossly unreasonable way. Treas. Reg. §1.409A-1(b)(5)(iv)(B)(2). Companies are permitted to use any other "reasonable valuation method," but no other method will be presumed reasonable and, should the IRS question the valuation, the company would bear the burden of proof to show that the method it used was reasonable and was reasonably applied. Treas. Reg. §1.409A-1(b)(5)(iv)(B)(3).

The three safe harbor valuation methods for private companies are:

(i) *An Independent Appraisal* — An independent appraisal of the company's stock value will be deemed reasonable for a period of one year from the time of the appraisal, absent any material change in the business or its prospects.

(ii) *An Existing Buyback Formula* — If a company has agreements with its principal shareholders providing for the repurchase of their shares at a fair market value price based on a formula, the company may use that formula.

(iii) *A Valuation Expert's Opinion* — Companies with illiquid stock that have been in business for less than ten years may rely on a written report from a valuation expert, who need not be independent, that addresses certain factors identified by the IRS. The valuation expert should have at least five years of experience in business valuation or appraisal, financial accounting, investment banking, private equity, securities lending, or other comparable experience in the industry segment in which the company does business. This method cannot be used if the company intends to complete an IPO within 180 days or a sale of the business within 90 days, or if the stock underlying the company's options is subject to certain types of put, call, or repurchase arrangements. Treas. Reg. §1.409A-1(b)(5)(iv)(B)(2).

An independent appraiser typically charges between $5,000 and $15,000 for a "409A valuation" and the process usually takes at least a few weeks to complete.

The safe harbor based on buyback plans that match a formula used by principal shareholders seems to be based on the assumption that if the price is good enough for the big holders, it should be good enough for option grant recipients generally, and if it is too sweet a deal, the major holders will choose some other valuation method for the general population.

The "valuation expert" alternative, as it does not require independence, often means that the company's chief financial officer can prepare a report addressing the factors required by the IRS and allow the company to avoid the fee an independent appraiser would charge. Although valuing companies is part of the day-to-day business of the venture capitalists who often serve on the company's board of directors, the inherent conflict of interest makes them reluctant to take on this responsibility. The prohibition on using a valuation expert if the stock is subject to puts, calls, or repurchase arrangements does not apply to the typical "at cost" repurchase rights that are often used by venture capital-financed companies and are discussed in section D below.

If one of the listed safe harbor methods is to be used, or if the company decides to forego the safe harbor and use some other method, the IRS will consider the degree to which the selected method addresses the following factors, to the extent each is relevant in the circumstances, in order to determine whether the valuation method is reasonable: (i) the value of the company's tangible and intangible assets; (ii) the present value of projected future cash flows; (iii) the market value of comparable companies that have a readily calculable value; (iv) recent arm's length transactions in the company's common stock; and (v) other relevant factors like minority interest discounts and illiquidity discounts. Treas. Reg. §1.409A-1(b)(5)(iv)(B)(1).

The IRS also will consider the following factors as weighing against the reasonableness of a valuation method: (i) does it fail to take into account all relevant information in ascertaining the company's value; (ii) does it fail to take into account events that have taken place since the formal valuation was completed; and (iii) is it more than 12 months old. *Id.*

As noted, if the IRS is applying these pro and con factors to a safe harbor method, then *the IRS* bears the burden of showing that the method used (or its application) is grossly unreasonable. In contrast, if the method is outside the safe harbor, *the company* bears the burden of demonstrating the reasonableness of the method used in the face of the IRS's analysis of these factors. Treas. Reg. §1.409A-1(b)(5)(iv)(B)(2)-(3).

It is important for the business lawyer to remind the board of directors that the fact that a valuation opinion has been obtained does not mean that the board is no longer responsible for determining the fair market value of the company's common stock. A valuation is a snapshot taken at a particular time. As the company's circumstances and the financial markets change, that snapshot becomes less and less useful. The board of directors needs to use its judgment in determining whether, and how much, to tweak the per-share exercise price to update the valuation or whether a new valuation is needed even if the current valuation is less than one year old.

In practice, when setting NQSO exercise prices, most venture capital-financed companies obtain an independent appraisal or have an internal valuation expert render a valuation opinion. For the next year, the board of directors relies on that opinion, carefully reviewing subsequent events (with specific application of those events to the five "reasonableness" factors listed above being reflected in the board meeting minutes) and perhaps making some minor adjustments to the exercise price it sets in light of those events. If a subsequent event undercuts the criteria used in the formal valuation, even if a year has not passed, the board typically seeks a new valuation opinion. It goes without saying that the method a company relies upon must be fully documented.

QUESTIONS

1. Assume that SoftCo completes its first round of venture capital investment in late 2013. It orders an independent 409A valuation, which is delivered on February 15, 2014. On October 30, 2014, SoftCo's engineers make a major breakthrough in the data transfer rate, a critical performance criterion, for what is expected to be the company's primary software product. At the November 2014 board meeting, management presents NQSO grants to the board for approval. How would you advise the board regarding setting the fair market value of the common stock?

2. Continuing the foregoing timeline, on January 18, 2015, SoftCo completes a new round of funding at a four-times increase in the company's valuation compared to SoftCo's first round of venture capital investment. Following the completion of that financing, SoftCo intends to issue NQSOs to new employees. What is your advice at this point about SoftCo's §409A compliance?

C. Incentive Stock Options

1. Special Requirements for ISO Treatment

An *incentive stock option* is an option that meets the requirements of §422 of the Internal Revenue Code. Briefly stated, the result of qualifying as an ISO is that no tax is directly assessed upon exercise of the option and there is the potential that all value realized on the sale of the shares received upon exercise of the ISO will be taxed as long-term capital gain. We explore what that means and the significant barriers to actually achieving ISO treatment later in this chapter.

In order to qualify as an ISO, the option must conform to the nine factors displayed in italics and discussed below:

> (i) *Have an exercise price at least equal to the fair market value of the company's common stock at the time of the grant of the option, provided, however, that if the option recipient owns more than 10% of the voting power of the company's stock at the time of the grant, the exercise price must at least equal 110% of that fair market value.* 26 U.S.C. §422(b)(4) and (c)(5).

ISOs are specifically not subject to the §409A requirements, hence, the valuation rules promulgated under that section do not apply. *See* Treas. Reg. §1.409A-1(b)(5)(ii). Section 422 simply requires that the fair market value of the common stock underlying the option be determined by the company's board of directors in good faith. *See* 26 U.S.C. §422(c)(1). However, because ISOs can be granted only to employees and companies typically want to be able to grant options to consultants and directors as well, most companies adopt plans that allow for the issuance of both ISOs and NQSOs (or they adopt separate plans for each type). Since an NQSO plan would be subject to §409A and it would be difficult to explain why the board in good faith reached a different fair market value exercise price result for the ISO grants, compliance with §409A's valuation methods has become the de facto standard for all option grants.

> (ii) *Be granted to an employee (i.e., not a consultant or a non-employee director) of the issuing company, its parent or a subsidiary company.* 26 U.S.C. §422(a)(2).

This seemingly straightforward requirement that ISO recipients must be employees (including directors who also are employees, but not non-employee directors) can become surprisingly complex in light of the flexibility of services arrangements today. The expansion of part-time employment, "contract employment," and employee leasing, for example, makes this more difficult than it might otherwise seem.

> (iii) *Be nontransferable, other than by will or the laws of descent and distribution upon the death of the holder.* 26 U.S.C. §422(b)(5).

This requirement is less significant following the adoption of Rule 701, which you will recall from our discussion in Chapter 4 also broadly prohibits option transfers in order to preserve its exemption from the 1933 Act registration obligation. As a result, virtually all stock options generally have very limited transferability. The distinction is that Rule 701(c) allows transfers to "family members who acquire such securities . . .

through gifts or domestic relations orders," while the only transfer permitted to the option holder under the ISO rules is upon death.

(iv) Have a term of no more than 10 years (five years if the option recipient holds more than 10% of the corporation's voting power). 26 U.S.C. §422(b)(3) and (c)(5).

The ISO rules require that the option state that it terminates in ten years or less from the date of grant. While shorter time periods are permitted, the maximum term, being the most beneficial to the employee, is typically used for stock options generally.

(v) Require exercise within three months of the termination of the employee's employment (within one year if the termination was the result of a permanent and total disability, and prior to the expiration of the option if the termination was because of death). 26 U.S.C. §422(a)(2), (c)(5), and (c)(6); Treas. Reg. §1.421-2(c)(1).

Absent death or permanent total disability, the maximum post-employment time period during which a former employee may exercise an ISO is three months. The option plan or agreement may provide for a shorter term. If the employment is terminated as the result of permanent total disability, the maximum post-employment exercise term is one year. No time limit is set by statute if the employment terminates as the result of death (other than the expiration of the option); however, the plan or agreement may set one, and many plans use the same post-employment time period for both disability and death.

The question of when employment terminates can become difficult. Leaves of absence, for instance, may or may not end the employment relationship for purposes of ISOs, depending on the facts. Some employers may be required by law to provide leaves while others (with fewer employees, for example) are exempt, or leaves may be simply a matter negotiated into the employment contract. In general, if a leave is for not more than three months, or if it is longer but the employee has a statutory or contractual right to continued employment, the leave will not constitute a termination of employment, and an employee taking such a leave will continue to be eligible to hold and exercise an ISO. *See* Treas. Reg. §1.421-1(h)(2).

Perhaps the most frequent situation where employment becomes an issue is where an employee shifts to a consulting relationship. In this case, the tax law is clear that the change in status is a termination of employment and the ISO must be exercised within the option plan's post-termination exercise window or it will expire. The option may, however, be amended to allow it to remain outstanding as an NQSO and continue in force during the consultancy relationship.

(vi) Not provide for more than $100,000 in stock value (measured by the exercise price) to vest in any calendar year. 26 U.S.C. §422(d).

An ISO may not contain terms that allow for the right to purchase more than $100,000 in stock value to become vested in a calendar year. Stock value is calculated by multiplying the exercise price times the number of shares that become vested during a calendar year. For example, consider an ISO granted to an employee on March 1, 2014, permitting the purchase of 500,000 shares at $1.00 per share, with four-year vesting set as a one-year cliff followed by 36 equal monthly increments. On March 1, 2015, 125,000 shares (25 percent of 500,000 shares) with a value of $125,000 (125,000 shares times the $1.00 exercise price) will vest, which will immediately put the employee over the $100,000 statutory limit for calendar year 2015. In addition, monthly installments of 10,416.67 shares will vest starting on April 1, 2015, and will continue for the next three years (500,000 shares minus 125,000 shares leaves 375,000, which, divided by 36 monthly installments, equals 10,416.67 shares per month). As a result, in 2015, the employee will have far more than $100,000 in value becoming vested. Further, in each of 2016 and 2017, 12 installments of 10,416.67 shares will vest, which again will push the employee over the $100,000 limit in those years. Only in 2018, when just three monthly installments will vest, will the option comply with the $100,000 per year limit.

The result of exceeding the limit is that the option loses ISO treatment with respect to all *excess* shares and becomes an NQSO with respect to those shares. In our prior example, with an exercise price of $1.00 per share, on March 1, 2015, when the one-year cliff installment of 125,000 shares vests, the option to purchase only 100,000 shares, representing $100,000 in value (shares vesting times exercise price), will be eligible for ISO treatment. The option to purchase the excess 25,000 shares will be treated as an NQSO. Further, each monthly installment from April 1 through December 1, 2015, also represents the vesting of options in 2015 to purchase shares in excess of the $100,000 value threshold, so they all will be NQSOs. In 2016, the first nine monthly installments will stay under the $100,000 limit for that year, totaling 93,750 shares (nine installments of 10,416.67 shares at $1.00 per share). The installment that vests on October 1, 2016, however, will qualify as an ISO only as to 6,250 shares ($100,000 minus $93,750 in share value already vested in that year), and the option to purchase the remaining 4,166.67 shares vesting on October 1, 2016, will be treated as an NQSO.

Any separate, additional purported ISO grants that provide for vesting during the same time period are aggregated, which means that the $100,000 per year limit applies collectively to all ISO grants to an employee rather than on a grant-by-grant basis. An alternative to avoid losing ISO treatment because of the $100,000 per year vesting limitation would be to modify the option terms in the prior example so that the cliff vesting is the right to purchase 100,000 shares on December 31, 2014, rather than 125,000 shares on March 1, 2015, which moves $100,000 in value into 2014. You then could reduce the vesting during 2015, 2016, and 2017 to the right to buy shares having an exercise price of $100,000 per year, catch up the employee's vesting on January 1, 2018, and allow the remainder of the option to vest on February 1 and March 1, 2018. While delaying vesting that otherwise would have occurred by the end of 2017 by pushing $100,000 in value over to 2018, these vesting modifications would accomplish ISO treatment for the entire option grant. The question is whether this mix of accelerating and delaying vesting to achieve ISO treatment is economically wise for the employee. Section C.2 below discusses the tax advantages and shortcomings of ISOs.

(vii) Not, by its terms, explicitly disavow its ISO status. 26 U.S.C. §422(b).

An option cannot be an ISO if it says it is not an ISO. This strange requirement is the direct result of the IRS taking the position at one time that it would treat an option that met the requirements of an ISO as an ISO whether it said it was one or not. This "inadvertent ISO" treatment threatened to cause tax recognition in certain circumstances as a result of violating an ISO rule where taking the same action on an NQSO would have no tax consequence. Many lawyers then, as now, generate option plans that allow for the issuance of both NQSOs and ISOs and, for convenience, set the terms for both option types at the more restrictive ISO standards, then provide their clients with a single form of option agreement with a blank to fill in stating whether the particular option is intended to be an ISO or an NQSO. The "inadvertent ISO" analysis said that if the option conformed to the ISO rules, even if it said it was not an ISO, it would be treated as an ISO. For a while, lawyers trying to grant NQSOs were forced to put into their option agreements at least one substantive term that violated ISO treatment, such as a post-employment exercise period of three months and one day. *See* the discussion regarding post-termination exercise above at item *(v)*. This silliness stopped when Congress amended §422(b) to provide that ISO treatment would not apply to any option that by its terms provided, at the time of the grant, that it would not be an ISO.

> *(viii) Be granted pursuant to a written plan adopted by the board of directors and approved by the shareholders within 12 months of the board's adoption of the plan, which must state the number of shares that may be issued through option grants under the plan and must specify the class of employees eligible to receive ISOs.* 26 U.S.C. §422(b)(1).

ISOs may be granted only under the terms of a written plan that has been adopted by a company's board of directors and approved by the shareholders within one year (either before or after) of the board's adoption. The plan must state the number of shares that may be issued through the grant of ISOs. If the plan provides for the issuance of both ISOs and NQSOs, a numerical breakout between the two is not required so long as all the shares reserved for issuance under the plan may be issued as ISOs. If the company has more than one plan under which ISOs may be issued, each plan must specify the number of shares that may be issued under it — a single pool applying to all the plans is not permitted. *See* Treas. Reg. §1.422-2(b)(3)(i) and (iv).

While the board may amend most of the terms of the plan and of options granted under the plan without shareholder approval, any increase in the number of shares that may be issued through the grant of ISOs must be approved by the shareholders within one year (before or after) of the board's approval of the increase. In addition, the identification of the class or group of employees entitled to receive ISOs must be approved by the shareholders and any change to that group also must be resubmitted to the shareholders for approval. The statement of eligible recipients does not need to be detailed or even very restrictive. A plan may provide that ISOs may only be granted to "executive officers," to "key employees," or even to "employees" of the company. Regardless of the group of employees designated as eligible to receive ISOs under the plan, the board retains the discretion to determine which employees within that group will receive what options.

> *(ix) Have been granted within 10 years of the earlier of the adoption of the ISO plan by the company's board of directors or the approval of the plan by its shareholders.* 26 U.S.C. §422(b)(2).

In addition to the maximum ten-year term for each ISO grant, the plan itself may have a term of no more than ten years. In other words, ISOs may be granted under a plan over a period of ten years after the earlier of the plan's adoption by the board or its approval by the shareholders. At the expiration of the plan's ten-year term, the plan will continue to be valid with respect to the outstanding options already granted under its terms, but no additional option grants may be made.

QUESTIONS

1. You are counsel to SoftCo, which has adopted an ISO plan and decided it will not grant NQSOs. At a board meeting, one director raises the issue of obtaining a 409A valuation opinion to support the board's determination of a fair market value option exercise price. He reports that a risk management consultant who made a presentation to his venture fund recommended getting a 409A valuation opinion. Another director objects, saying the valuation opinion is not required. She adds that when you add the price of the opinion to the value of the management time needed to gather the financial data required and manage the process, the cost of the whole thing would pay the salary for a junior engineer for six months. All eyes turn to you. What do you advise?

2. SoftCo has an employee, Eloise, who has been called to active duty by the National Guard. Despite the fact that her service could extend to over a year, the company has given her a letter stating that her job will be available to her so long as she returns to SoftCo within 45 days after the expiration of her call to duty. Eloise received an ISO grant seven months ago. Will the option's ISO treatment survive this interruption in her employment with SoftCo?

3. Continuing with the same hypothetical facts, SoftCo's CFO, Bruce, who has designed a nifty, self-updating spreadsheet for monitoring option vesting schedules, asks you what he should tell Eloise regarding her ISO's vesting schedule as a result of her leave of absence. He needs to know if he should reprogram his spreadsheet. Your search of the Internal Revenue Code and related regulations leads you to the conclusion that the statutes and regulations do not mandate a particular outcome on this issue. The language of SoftCo's ISO option agreement does not address a leave of absence. What do you advise?

---

2. Tax Treatment of ISOs and Disqualifying Dispositions

When an ISO is granted, the option recipient does not recognize any taxable income, and the company does not receive a tax deduction. In this regard, an ISO is the same as an NQSO. As noted in the accounting discussion in section A.6 above, however, the company does have to record a compensation expense for financial accounting purposes, which is spread over the "requisite service period" and based on the "fair value" of the ISO at the time of the grant. In contrast to the NQSO, there is no tax applied to the option holder and no withholding requirement upon the exercise of an ISO. The company does not receive a tax deduction at that time. If the shares are held for at least one year from the date of exercise of the ISO *and* two years from the date of the option grant, the entire difference between the option exercise price and the sale price realized on the eventual transfer of the shares will be taxed as a long-term capital gain (or loss). 26 U.S.C. §422(a)(1) (applying taxation pursuant to 26 U.S.C. §421(a)). Given that in 2013, the maximum federal ordinary income tax rate was 39.6 percent and the maximum long-term capital gain rate was 23.8 percent, this treatment can be a very meaningful benefit to the employee.

The Alternative Minimum Tax.   Unfortunately, what the tax code gives with one hand, it takes away with the other. The spread between the exercise price and the value of the common stock at the time of the exercise of the ISO (that is, the amount that would have been taxed as ordinary income upon exercise if the option had been an NQSO), while not subject to "regular" income tax, is treated as "preference income" under the Alternative Minimum Tax (AMT).

The purpose of the AMT originally was to ensure that the idle rich were paying at least a minimum of ordinary income tax. A taxpayer calculates his or her normal tax then recalculates the tax liability after adding back into income certain deductions not permitted under the AMT rules and including certain income not recognized under the standard tax rules, referred to as "preference income." The larger amount from the two calculations is the tax owed. When it was adopted as part of the 1986 Internal Revenue Code amendments, the maximum ordinary income tax rate was approximately 50 percent; at such a high regular tax rate, few people were affected by the AMT. As the maximum rates have trended downward over the last 25 years to 39.6 percent, the difference between the effective AMT rate (26 percent on the first $175,000 of income and 28 percent thereafter) and the effective regular tax rate, given the graduated scale of regular rates, has become quite small. As a result of this process and the decrease in the normal income tax rate, many salaried employees making less than $200,000 per year are now paying extra tax because of the AMT. This is particularly the case for people who are subject to high state income taxes, as state tax payments are one of the disallowed deductions under the AMT calculation.

As an example of how the AMT would apply to an ISO, assume that employee Erma received an ISO grant on December 31, 2010, with an exercise price of $0.10 per share and exercised the ISO on January 5, 2013, to purchase 30,000 shares. At that time, the fair market value of the company's common stock was $1.00 per share. Under the normal tax rules, Erma would recognize no ordinary income. However, upon recalculating her taxes for the AMT, Erma would have to include as AMT preference income the amount of $27,000 (($1.00 value per share of the stock at the time of exercise, less the $0.10 exercise price equals a gain per share of $0.90) x 30,000 shares) deemed to have been received on the date of the exercise.

At the end of 2013, the employer would have to send a report to Erma and the IRS providing details on the ISO exercise. In the past, a stock issuer was required only to provide information to its employees in order to assist them in preparing their taxes, but rules adopted in 2008 now require that ISO exercise data also be given to the IRS on Form 3921. Like Forms W-2 and 1099, which report normal income, this mechanism will allow the IRS to track reporting of the ISO preference income as part of the employee's AMT calculation. When Erma prepares her 2013 tax return for filing on April 15, 2014, after she calculates her normal income tax owed, she will have to prepare an AMT calculation including the $27,000 of ISO exercise preference income. Depending on her other income during 2013 and the nature of her deductions, Erma may end up paying more tax as a result of her AMT calculation.

The good news about the AMT is that the ISO spread is not considered wages, as it would be with an NQSO, so no additional employment tax obligations apply. In addition, there is no withholding obligation on AMT, so the employee does not have to deal with an immediate tax obligation. Instead, the AMT tax is paid when the tax return for that year is due (as long as the employee has provided for the minimum level of withholding — generally 110 percent of the prior year's tax for higher-income taxpayers — so that the taxpayer is not required to make quarterly estimated payments). In our example, which happens to be the best case, Erma's return would be filed more than a year after she exercised the ISO, which gives her a significant period of time to plan for the future payment of the tax obligation. Finally, the maximum incremental ordinary income tax rate for 2013 is 39.6 percent, while the maximum AMT rate is applied at 26 percent to 28 percent on recalculated taxable income over an exemption amount. As a result, at least the amount payable under the AMT typically is less than what would be assessed under the regular tax if the gain at the time of exercise had been included in regular income and taxed at the marginal rate, as would be the case if the option were an NQSO.

Continuing the example, assume that Erma sells the 30,000 shares bought on January 5, 2013, for $0.10 per share in a transaction on January 15, 2014, for $2.75 per share. This is more than one year from the date of exercise of the ISO and more than two years from the date of grant, so Erma would recognize $79,500 of long-term capital gain (($2.75 − $0.10) x 30,000 shares). (That is, the proceeds, $2.75 per share, less the exercise price of $0.10 per share, multiplied by the number of shares.) The company has no withholding or reporting responsibility on a shareholder's subsequent transfer consistent with the ISO rules; instead, Erma is then responsible for reporting the gain as part of her annual income tax return.

The result is that Erma, after calculating her tax obligation under the AMT, may have paid extra tax under the AMT on her 2013 return on the increase in per-share value from $0.10 to $1.00 (at a current maximum rate of 28 percent). Now she will pay long-term capital gain tax on her 2014 return on the increase in per-share value from $0.10 to $2.75 (at a current maximum rate of 23.8 percent). While there appears to be a double tax on the first $0.90 of gain, most, if not all, of the AMT amount paid with the 2013 return may be credited against future capital gain tax liability and in some cases can be recovered. Despite this credit, the obligation to pay the AMT amount effectively constitutes a "prepayment" of some portion of the capital gain tax to be paid on the disposition of the shares. As one of the fundamental principles of tax planning is to pay taxes later rather than sooner, the application of the AMT system to ISO exercises undercuts what is intended to be a primary advantage to ISOs, both in terms of financial effect as well as pure complexity.

An additional AMT disadvantage occurs when the value of the shares drops between the time the ISO is exercised and the time the shares purchased are ultimately sold. The tax paid as a result of the AMT treatment on the ISO exercise is not refunded upon a subsequent sale of the shares at a price lower than the value of the stock at the time of the option exercise. In general, the later sale at a price lower than that used to calculate AMT preference income has limited relevance to the AMT obligation.

For example, if Erma had exercised the ISO for 30,000 shares on January 5, 2013, when they were worth $3.50, her preference income recognition would have been $102,000 (($3.50 − $0.10) x 30,000). If she sold the 30,000 shares on January 15, 2014, for $1.00 per share, since that is more than one year from the date of exercise of the ISO and more than two years from the date of grant, she would recognize $27,000 in long-term capital gain (($1.00 − $0.10) x 30,000 shares; that is, the proceeds, $1.00 per share, less Erma's exercise price of $0.10 per share, multiplied by the number of shares). In the end, between the AMT obligation resulting from the preference income of $102,000 and the capital gain on the ultimate sale at $27,000, Erma is likely to pay more in tax than she received in proceeds from the sale of the shares.

Disqualifying Dispositions.   If an employee does not hold the shares purchased upon exercise of an ISO for the requisite holding periods (i.e., two years from the date of the ISO grant and one year from the date of exercise, as provided in 26 U.S.C. §422(a)(1)), then the sale of the shares is treated as a "disqualifying disposition" and the ISO treatment is lost. Instead, the employee will be treated as having ordinary compensation income in the tax year the disqualifying disposition was made in an amount equal to the lesser of the "spread" (being the value of the shares less the exercise price) at the time of the exercise of the ISO or the gain amount actually realized on the disqualifying sale of the shares, *plus* a capital gain (probably short term and therefore also taxed at ordinary income rates) equal to any increase in the value of the shares at the time of sale versus their value at the time of exercise. In short, the ISO treatment is unwound and the exercise and sale of the shares are treated as though the option were an NQSO. Any AMT paid in a prior tax year is effectively applied against the ordinary income being recognized in the current tax year. If AMT was to be paid in the same year as the disqualifying disposition, it is inapplicable and ordinary income tax applies.

Additional Rules for ISOs.   In addition to the numerous requirements applicable to ISOs, there also are rules for amendments to outstanding ISOs that, if not followed, will disqualify the option from ISO treatment. For example, if an employee leaves the company following an injury, but does not meet the ISO definition of disabled, and the company amends the employee's option term to give the employee a few extra months post-termination to exercise, that amendment destroys ISO treatment for the option. The option from then on will be an NQSO.

In addition, any amendment that gives the ISO holder increased benefits under the option, with certain specified exceptions, is considered a "modification" of the option. When a modification occurs, the option is treated as though it were being re-granted and all the ISO rules must be met again, including the requirement that the exercise price equal the fair market value of the shares at the time of the re-grant. If a disqualifying modification is offered to an employee and rejected or revoked within 30 days, the ISO treatment of the option is not terminated. Also, should a change be made, then recognized as being a modification destroying ISO treatment and withdrawn, the ISO treatment is not terminated. The primary exception to the modification rules is that the company may accelerate the vesting of an option at its discretion.

As discussed in section A.3 of this chapter, sometimes upon an acquisition of a company, the acquiring company chooses to issue "substitute options" to the acquired company's employees to purchase its own stock. The ISO rules allow the substitution of ISOs if the acquiring company's options conform to the ISO requirements other than the fair market value requirement, which does not need to be met as of the date of the acquisition. The fair market value exercise price set at the time of the original issuance of the ISO is preserved in the roll-over into a substitute option.

Tax Comparison to NQSOs.   By now it should be obvious why general business lawyers need to tread carefully and consult tax and accounting experts when dealing with equity incentive plan issues. The primary tax advantage to ISOs for option recipients is that the spread when they are exercised (i.e., the difference between the fair market value of the shares purchased and the exercise price of the option) is not treated as wages and subject to ordinary income taxation requiring immediate withholding, as would be the case upon an NQSO exercise or if the employee had just received a cash bonus. On the other hand, that same spread is subject to taxation as preference income under the AMT, which often offsets a major portion of that advantage.

The application of AMT to the ISO exercise spread may encourage employees to exercise their ISOs as soon as they vest in order to minimize their AMT exposure should the company's stock value go higher (as hoped). While that may work to reduce AMT payments, employees should never forget that exercising an option is investing in a security; the tax tail should not wag the investment dog. If the options have a low exercise price and represent a relatively small cash outlay, then perhaps quick exercise makes sense as an affordable risk. A major investment, however, should be made based on the ability to realize a gain, not on a tax timetable.

Private companies present a particular problem in this area because their shares, once purchased, normally are very difficult to sell. The reality is that most ISO grants do not ultimately achieve ISO treatment. Most private companies do not go public. Instead, successful venture capital–funded companies more often than not are acquired. So, in most cases, options are exercised on the eve of the acquisition and the shares immediately sold in the acquisition, thereby failing compliance with the ISO two-year/one-year holding periods. As a result, the options are treated as NQSOs because the immediate sale of the shares gives rise to a disqualifying disposition. (Refer to the preceding discussion regarding disqualifying dispositions.)

From the company's point of view, the primary advantage to NQSOs is that the company gets an immediate tax deduction based on the ordinary income recognized by the employee upon the exercise of the option. Most early-stage companies are not taxpayers. Instead, they are building net operating losses that can be carried forward and deducted against future income. Therefore, the usefulness of an additional tax deduction is perhaps remote, but still has value. In addition, the company's ability to deduct net operating losses against future income can be substantially limited by an "ownership change," which may occur as a consequence of a large capital infusion such as a venture capital investment. While the "ownership change" rules are beyond the scope of this discussion, that limitation may make the company a taxpayer sooner than it otherwise would be, which means that the NQSO exercise deduction could be meaningful sooner than one might expect.

QUESTIONS

1. On November 19, 2014, SoftCo employee Edgar and director Dave are each granted stock options to purchase 10,000 shares at $0.10 per share, vesting over five years, with a 20 percent cliff after one year and four years of monthly vesting thereafter.

Edgar is a full-time employee. Dave is a retired executive recruited to serve on the company's board of directors as an outside director. Edgar's option is an ISO and Dave's is an NQSO. Why the distinction?

2. On January 14, 2017, when the fair market value of SoftCo's common stock is $0.60 per share, Edgar and Dave both exercise the then-vested portions of their options. What are the tax treatments and obligations applicable to each of them?

3. In November 2018, Big Bad Software and SoftCo announce an all-cash acquisition of SoftCo at $6.35 per share, projected to close on November 21, 2018. Neither Edgar nor Dave is offered substitute options, and under the terms of SoftCo's option plan they are given notice that they must exercise any vested options outstanding no fewer than ten days prior to the acquisition's projected closing date. Any options not exercised by that deadline will terminate. How many shares can Edgar and Dave exercise on that date?

4. Upon the November 21, 2018, sale of SoftCo for $6.35 per share, what is the tax treatment applicable to the shares Edgar purchased in January 2017? What federal income tax does he owe? What is the tax treatment applicable to the shares Dave purchased on that date? What federal income tax does he owe?

5. What is the tax treatment applicable to the shares Edgar and Dave bought when they exercised their remaining vested options pursuant to SoftCo's notice of the acquisition under the terms of its option plan? Upon the November 21, 2018, sale of SoftCo for $6.35 per share, what is the tax treatment on the sale of the shares just purchased by Edgar? By Dave?

D. Restricted Stock

Restricted stock refers to shares of a company's common stock issued to an employee or other provider of services that the company has the right to take back, by refunding the amount paid for it, upon termination of the holder's services relationship with the company. The company's repurchase right normally applies to most or all of the shares when the restricted stock is issued and lapses over a vesting term, ultimately expiring as to all the shares by the end of the vesting term. As the company's right to repurchase the shares expires, the shareholder's rights in the shares vest, which means that when the repurchase right has expired completely, the shareholder's ownership in the shares is fully vested. (Contrast this with the term *restricted securities*, which was discussed earlier in Chapter 4 in connection with shares that are issued in a transaction exempt from the registration requirements of federal securities laws and thus are restricted as to resale into a public stock market.) It is important to note that the company's right to repurchase is an *option* on the part of the company, *not an obligation*. The company typically wants to preserve the flexibility of deciding whether to exercise its right to repurchase on a case-by-case basis, selecting the course of conduct that it believes is fair and appropriate based on the facts of each restricted stock holder's situation without having to conform to any defined pattern of behavior. *Query*: Does this seem fair to the employee? Does this seem fair to the company?

Stock certificates representing restricted stock shares often are not delivered to the shareholder when the shares are purchased, but rather are held in escrow, sometimes by the corporate secretary, until the shares are fully vested. This expedites the company's ability to repurchase unvested shares without having to rely on the cooperation of the recently terminated shareholder.

One way to look at restricted stock is that it is issued as partial compensation for, and in anticipation of, services that the company will receive over a period of time. If the share purchaser does not provide all those services, the company retains the right, in essence, to "unwind" that portion of the compensation that has not yet been earned. This unwind occurs by the company's taking back the unearned shares and refunding the purchase price paid for those shares. In using its discretion on whether to exercise that right, the company must consider the fairness to the company, the fairness to the employee or other optionee, and the effect its choice is going to have on all the other employees, non-employee directors, and independent contractors holding options, who most certainly are watching and taking note.

1. Restricted Stock Compared to Stock Options

Restricted stock, as an equity incentive mechanism, clearly shares the same basic elements as a stock option and achieves basically the same ultimate result, although the order of events and mechanical processes are different. An option grant might provide a right to buy 30,000 shares at $0.10 per share, with 25 percent vesting after one year and the remaining 75 percent vesting in 36 equal monthly installments, based on continued employment, such that the option is fully vested on the fourth anniversary of its grant. A restricted stock grant might provide the right to buy 30,000 shares today at $0.10 per share, with all the shares subject to the company's right to repurchase at a price of $0.10 per share without regard to the fair market value of the shares at the time of the repurchase. The repurchase right would lapse based on continued employment as to 25 percent of the shares after one year and as to the remaining 75 percent of the shares in 36 equal monthly installments, such that the restricted stock shares would be fully vested (i.e., no longer "restricted") on the fourth anniversary of the grant.

The two main differences between a restricted stock issuance and a stock option grant are that the restricted shares are acquired immediately and a different tax treatment applies.

A restricted stock grant gives the employee a short period of time from the date the grant is approved by the company's board of directors (generally 10 to 30 days) to accept the grant. Like options, restricted stock may be granted to new hires as well as to individuals already proving services to the company. The recipient usually accepts the grant by signing a form of purchase document, often called a "Restricted Stock Purchase Agreement," and delivering to the company the executed agreement together with any required payment for the shares. The Restricted Stock Purchase Agreement will set forth the terms for the purchase and vesting of the restricted stock, as well as for any escrow arrangement and other matters, such as a prohibition on transfers of unvested shares and any continuing transfer restrictions applicable after the shares have vested. See the discussion below in section F.1 of this chapter regarding contractual transfer restrictions.

The fact that the employee typically pays the purchase price for restricted stock up front is the primary disadvantage of using restricted stock as an equity incentive, particularly after the company has grown and its shares begin to have significant value. Buying restricted stock, like exercising a stock option, requires the employee to make an investment decision about the company. With stock options, the time of that investment decision is deferred. With restricted stock, the employee is required to buy the early-stage, privately held company's illiquid, high-risk stock at the time of the grant in the hope that it will someday have a realizable value. While some employers like the idea of key employees having "skin in the game," the employee must realize that if the company ultimately is not successful, the amount paid for the restricted stock may be completely lost.

However, when the company is at a very early stage and its stock has a nominal per-share value, restricted stock can be an effective means of getting equity incentive shares into the hands of a key employee, non-employee director, or consultant. When the share value is low, a restricted stock grant of significant size might call for investment of only a few hundred or thousand dollars, which may be small enough for the employee to justify making the high-risk investment decision. But as the company grows and its shares increase in value, accepting a restricted stock grant may mean having to invest a more meaningful amount, which might make the investment decision (that is, the appropriateness of putting that sum of money at risk) more problematic.

In contrast, a stock option grant requires no cash outlay by the grant recipient. Unless a termination of employment puts the option holder in a "use it or lose it" position, the employee can sit on the option and wait to exercise until the very eve of an event that will cause the underlying stock to have realizable value, such as a sale of the business. While the resulting profit on the option, based on an exercise and immediate sale, will be taxed at ordinary income rates, the employee bears no investment risk. If the option is never exercised, the employee will have had nothing at risk and will have lost nothing.

2. Application of §83

What are the advantages of issuing restricted stock as a form of equity-based compensation? First and foremost, restricted stock can be very tax efficient and can provide a way to deliver shares at a price below fair market value to an employee or other option plan participant. In addition, the purchase of the restricted stock shares starts the clock running on holding periods for tax law purposes.

Tax Treatment.   As briefly mentioned in section B.2 of this chapter, §83 of the Internal Revenue Code requires that the value of any property (in this case, stock) transferred in connection with providing services is taxable as ordinary income to the person who received the property. In short, if a company pays for services by a transfer of some tangible property or an issuance of stock, rather than with cash, the tax law does not consider the form of payment, but regards the value of the property as taxable income to the person who received it. The amount of taxable income recognized is to be reduced by any amount the recipient paid for the property. 26 U.S.C. §83(a).

While it might seem obvious that §83 should apply when the person receiving the property is simply being paid for services by delivery of property or stock in lieu of cash, it is important to recognize that the tax treatment set out in §83 applies even when the person receiving the property pays full price for it. "Congress made section 83(a) applicable to . . . property transferred 'in connection with . . . services' not just compensation for employment." *See Alves v. Commissioner*, 734 F.2d 478, 482 (9th Cir. 1984), *aff'g* 79 T.C. 864 (1982) (quoting from 26 U.S.C. §83(a)).

Section 83 recognizes that, whether paid for or not, sometimes stock or other property received in connection with services may be forfeited if the services are not fully provided. This contingency is captured in §83 by the concept of "substantial risk of forfeiture." The §83 tax does not apply at the time stock is received in connection with services if that stock is subject to a substantial risk of forfeiture when issued. The right of the company to buy back shares of restricted stock at the original issuance price upon a termination of services, without regard to the actual value of the shares at the time of the repurchase, is considered a "substantial risk of forfeiture" imposed on the share purchaser at the time of the purchase. 26 U.S.C. §83(c)(1). For example, if the stock is issued at $0.10 per share, and when the repurchase right is triggered, the stock is worth $5 per share, the company has the right to repurchase the shares as to which its repurchase right has not yet lapsed at $0.10 per share.

In this case, taxable income is recognized under §83 not when the shares are received but in the tax year in which any substantial risk of forfeiture lapses. The idea is that, for purposes of assessing tax under §83, the shareholder does not enjoy the full benefits of ownership until the forfeiture risk lapses. The amount of income recognized at the time the substantial risk of forfeiture lapses (in other words, when the company's repurchase right expires and the shares vest) is the difference between the price paid for the stock and its fair market value at the time the shares vest.

Looking again at an employee who receives a restricted stock grant of 30,000 shares at a purchase price of $0.10 per share, let's assume that the company's repurchase right is fixed as the original issue price and expires as to 25 percent of the shares in one year and monthly in 36 equal installments thereafter, such that full lapse of the repurchase right (or, from the employee's point of view, full vesting of the shares) will take place on the fourth anniversary of the grant. At the time the restricted stock is purchased, all the shares are subject to a substantial risk of forfeiture because none of the shares have vested. As a result, there is no taxable event. On the one-year anniversary of the grant, the company's repurchase right lapses as to 7,500 shares (25 percent of 30,000 shares) and the shareholder no longer faces a forfeiture risk as to those shares; they have "vested." If the fair market value of the shares has then risen to $0.25 per share, the employee is considered to have received $1,125 of ordinary income (the $0.25 per-share fair market value minus the $0.10 per-share purchase price, equaling $0.15 in per-share gain, times 7,500 vested shares). In addition, in each of the next 36 months thereafter, the employee will "receive" ordinary income as the company's repurchase right lapses on each installment of 625 shares (30,000 shares minus 7,500 shares equals 22,500 shares divided by 36 monthly installments equals 625 shares per month). The amount of monthly income considered to be received by the employee will be based on the difference between the fair market value of each installment of those shares when they vest and the $0.10 per share originally paid for them.

This normally is not a good outcome in the private company context because the employee is facing the prospect of paying an increasing amount of income tax on illiquid shares. The employee is being forced to recognize income, and pay tax on it, when the value of the shares is not yet realized and may not be realizable for some time to come, if it ever is.

3. The §83(b) Election

The Internal Revenue Code offers a solution to this problem in §83(b), which is popularly referred to as the §83(b) election. Section 83(b) provides that the recipient of property in connection with services that is subject to a substantial risk of forfeiture may elect to pay all tax due in the tax year in which the property was received, rather than when the substantial risk of forfeiture lapses. In our example, the employee purchased 30,000 shares by paying $0.10 per share, for a total of $3,000. If the fair market value of the shares at the time of the purchase was in fact $0.10 per share, the employee paid the full value of the shares. The employee would report to the IRS on a "Section 83(b) election" form that the employee received property subject to a substantial risk of forfeiture in the current tax year (the property being common stock of the company subject to repurchase at the issuance price) with a value of $3,000, and that the employee paid $3,000 for that property.

With that filing, the employee has agreed to pay *ordinary income* tax in the current year on the value of the property received in excess of the amount paid for it, and has informed the IRS that no income will be reported with respect to the restricted stock on the employee's current-year tax return because the employee paid full value for the shares. As a result of electing to pre-pay taxes in the current year, the employee will not have to recognize income over the next four years as the company's repurchase right lapses. When the shares are ultimately sold by the employee, they will be subject only to a capital gain tax based on the difference between the $0.10 purchase price and the ultimate sale price.

In terms of setting fair market value, even though restricted stock as described is not subject to §409A and its valuation process, if the company has an NQSO plan, the company will have to do a §409A valuation for that plan, and there is no good reason why shares issued as restricted stock would have a different fair market value from shares issuable upon exercise of an NQSO. Section 83 specifically provides that the fair market value of the stock issued as a restricted stock grant is not diminished by reason of being subject to a repurchase right constituting a substantial risk of forfeiture. Absent a §409A valuation, the company is to determine fair market value in good faith. *See* I.R.C. §83(a)(1).

Unlike options, which must be issued at fair market value, restricted stock may be issued at a discount or at no cost. If the employee in our example, instead of paying the $0.10 per-share fair market value to buy the 30,000 restricted stock shares, paid only $0.0333 per share, the §83(b) election form would note that the value of the stock was $3,000 and $1,000 was paid, so that $2,000 of ordinary income will be recognized during the current tax year and taxed. The employee would later recognize capital gain tax on the sale of the shares based on the proceeds of the sale in excess of tax basis of $0.10 per share ($0.0333 per share paid plus $0.0666 per share recognized as ordinary income and previously taxed). If the employee received the shares for free, the current federal and state tax would be based on all $3,000 in value received, and upon the future sale of the stock, the employee's tax basis again would be $0.10 per share.

What that means, then, is that the employee can pay nothing to buy the shares, make a §83(b) election and pay ordinary income tax in the current year on the value of the shares, and get capital gain treatment on the future sale of the shares. The employee can get $3,000 of stock by paying approximately $1,000 in taxes, and receive capital gain treatment on the gain or loss on the later disposition of the stock.

As should be clear, the availability of the §83(b) election can make restricted stock very attractive for tax purposes. In fact, when dealing with restricted stock, making the §83(b) election is *almost always* very beneficial for the employee, unless there would be *both* (i) a significant income recognition triggered by the election at the time of the grant (meaning the shares' issuance price was substantially below their value), and (ii) the shares when vested would be liquid and so could be sold to cover the tax recognized as each increment of the repurchase right lapsed.

Disadvantages of the §83(b) Election.   Making a §83(b) election upon the issuance of restricted stock does present some potential disadvantages. As previously discussed, the purchase of restricted stock is an investment decision and creates the risk of loss of the entire investment amount if the company fails. The amount paid for the stock plus any amount recognized as ordinary income would be the tax basis in the shares, and should the stock become worthless, the loss of that amount would be recognizable as a capital loss.

Where the employee paid nothing for $3,000 of stock, then paid approximately $1,000 in ordinary income taxes on the $3,000 in value received, if the stock turns out to be worthless, the employee would recognize a capital loss of $3,000 (the tax basis created by recognizing that amount as ordinary income when the stock was issued and paying ordinary income tax on it). On the other hand, if that employee were terminated before any of the shares vested and the company exercised its repurchase right as to all the shares, he or she would receive no loss deduction for the $3,000 of income recognized and the ordinary income tax paid. So, essentially, that employee would be out of pocket for the taxes paid as a result of making the §83(b) election upon receipt of the restricted stock and would receive no tax adjustment on the forfeiture of the shares.

In addition, the §83(b) election must be filed with the IRS by the restricted stock recipient within 30 days of the share issuance. There are no extensions, and failure to make the filing on a timely basis can destroy a large part of the financial benefit of the transaction to the employee. Often the company will include the §83(b) election form with the Restricted Stock Purchase Agreement in order to reduce the risk that the employee will miss the deadline.

The consequences of failing to file the §83(b) election form on a timely basis are potentially so significant that venture capital investors in a company sometimes require that the company make a representation to them (as part of their investment transaction) that all §83(b) elections have been made on a timely basis. These investors recognize that if key employees or founders should have made a §83(b) election but failed to do so, the company will generally end up having to "solve" the problem in some way to protect those key employees from the tax liabilities they otherwise would face and provide them with a suitable equity incentive going forward. That solution might be seriously complicated by the fact that the value of the company's shares may have gone up since the original incentive arrangement was set. In short, the company's "solution" will generally involve paying money to the employee to cover taxes or issuing additional shares to make up for the lost value of the equity incentive, or both. There are circumstances, of course, where the company will decline to assist an employee who failed to file a §83(b) election in a timely manner. Yet, if that person truly is key to the company's potential success, the incentive probably will be redone to preserve the net value to the employee from the original incentive grant, which could result in a significant expense to the company.

In summary, a well constructed and operated restricted stock incentive program can provide employees, employee directors, non-employee directors, and independent contractors with capital gain treatment on the entire increase in value of the restricted shares over their original value. This is a more comprehensive tax benefit than is available for stock options, which recognize the increase in value of the shares between grant and exercise as ordinary income "wages" for an NQSO or as AMT preference income for an ISO. Further, in contrast to an ISO, the steps needed to achieve capital gain treatment for restricted stock are taken up front rather than being dependent on conforming behavior by the company and option holder over a period of years.

QUESTIONS

1. Employee Eldrick receives a restricted stock grant at no cost in connection with services, files a §83(b) election form, and includes in his income for that year the value of the stock. He pays, out of pocket and in cash, the tax owed on the value of the stock received. Later, when the value of the company's stock has increased, but before any of his restricted stock has vested, Eldrick is terminated and the company repurchases all his restricted stock at its original value. Eldrick is unhappy that he paid taxes, never got the benefit of the appreciation in the value of the repurchased stock, and got no tax deduction or loss recognition when the shares were repurchased for less than their then-current value. Was the tax treatment that applied to Eldrick fair (or at least logical)? How would you explain the outcome to Eldrick?
2. The inherent tension in using restricted stock is seen in its use in providing large equity incentives to highly compensated senior executives. Why does that use of restricted stock highlight both the primary strength and the major risk of the restricted stock form of equity incentive?

Holding Period Advantage. In addition to its tax treatment, the purchase of restricted stock offers other advantages, particularly regarding the capital gain holding period.

To receive long-term capital gain treatment, shares must be held for one year before being sold. While options give an employee or other option holder the ability to reduce investment risk by waiting to exercise the options until immediately prior to a point where the shares become liquid, the trade-off for eliminating the investment risk is that the shares are sold within a few days of their purchase, resulting in a short-term capital gain, so the profit (or "spread") is taxed at ordinary income rates. A restricted stock equity incentive with a §83(b) election starts the holding period up front on all the shares received, before vesting occurs, and therefore increases the likelihood that long-term capital gain treatment ultimately will apply.

In addition, a special capital gain treatment might apply to a company's stock generally if its shares meet the definition of "qualified small business stock." I.R.C. §1202(c). Briefly stated, the primary requirements of §1202(c) are:

- the shares must be acquired directly from the company (rather than upon a transfer from another holder);
- the company must be a C corporation that does not provide financial or professional services or engage in other prohibited areas of business; and
- it must have less than $50 million in assets at all times prior to the issuance (including the proceeds received at the time of the issuance).

If the shares and the company meet these requirements, among others, and the shares are held for five years, the share owner is entitled to exclude from income half of the gain on the eventual disposition of those shares. In addition, if the shares are sold and the proceeds reinvested in another qualified small business, the gain can be "rolled over" to the tax basis for the new stock and not recognized until that stock is sold (and its proceeds are not rolled over). If the company's stock is eligible for this treatment, purchasing restricted stock and filing a §83(b) election starts the clock running on the five-year holding period. *Query*: What are the advantages and disadvantages of this treatment?

QUESTIONS

1. Assume that you are representing a venture capital fund contemplating an investment in a company that has issued restricted stock to its employees. What representations would you want from the company in the stock purchase agreement your client will be entering into upon its investment?
2. The reading addresses a repurchase right at the restricted stock's original issuance value as being a "substantial risk of forfeiture." Would a repurchase right at the stock's fair market value at the time of the repurchase represent a substantial risk of forfeiture? As company counsel, would you advise that such a repurchase right successfully implements the objectives of a restricted stock incentive program?
3. Employee Ervin is offered a restricted stock incentive consisting of the opportunity to buy 20,000 shares at $0.10 per share, the stock's current fair market value. The shares will vest in 48 equal monthly installments starting on the first monthly anniversary following their purchase. Erwin buys the restricted stock and files a timely §83(b) election. After 26 installments have vested, Ervin leaves the company and the company exercises its repurchase option as to all the then-unvested shares. Six months later, the company is acquired for $3 per share. What are Erwin's financial transactions, tax obligations, and gains or losses?

4. Assume that Erwin receives the same restricted stock, makes a §83(b) election, and pays the tax. Then, after 26 months, the company fails, liquidates its assets to pay off its creditors, and no value is left for equity owners. In this case, what are Erwin's financial transactions, tax obligations, and gains or losses?

5. The reading describes some conditions where a §83(b) election would be ill advised. Under what circumstances would those conditions exist in real life?

6. Assume that you have been offered a position as general counsel of SoftCo. As part of your compensation package, you are offered an equity incentive of 50,000 shares, which currently have a fair market value of $0.50 per share. What form would you like your incentive to take — an NQSO, ISO, or restricted stock — and why? How valuable is capital gain treatment of restricted stock versus the downside of having to put money at risk up front? How valuable is the potential ability to wait to exercise an option until the shares have value and that value can be cashed out, versus knowing that ordinary income tax rates will apply to that income? How valuable are the potential tax benefits of an ISO versus the complication and low likelihood of realizing those benefits?

4. Application of Restricted Stock Concepts to Founder's Stock

Founder's Stock Issues Generally.   *Founder's stock* has no distinguishing characteristics other than the fact that it is the stock issued when the company is formed or, if not at formation, before the company begins to conduct its business. The significance of that timing is that founder's stock typically is issued when the company has minimal assets and little or no business operations. As a result, the price paid for founder's stock is usually nominal and often somewhat arbitrarily set. Further, upon formation of a company, the founders, by definition, divide up the entire ownership of the company and each receives a large percentage of the company's stock.

Generally speaking, the IRS will apply §83 to founder's stock if it concludes that the founders are in fact receiving their stock in exchange for services. However, as to a start-up business that just incorporated, with a small group of individuals who each contributed consideration amounting to a few hundred or a few thousand dollars, the practical problem facing the IRS is one of valuation — who can say whether these founders paid a fair price for their shares? At this point in time, the company may be unformed as a business and truly worth no more than the pieces that went into it, which often totals only a few thousands of dollars of value. Once the company comes together, begins to put its assets to work, and becomes a viable, stand-alone business, its value quickly increases at a dramatic rate. As a result, someone who is hired only a few months after the company was formed may be joining a real business, rather than the concept that the founders put together based on little more than a belief in their shared future. As a consequence, while the founders may have collectively paid only a few thousand dollars in exchange for their stock, and thus the total paid for all the company's stock issued to the founders may not reach five figures, the per-share price applicable to someone who joins only a few months later may be much higher and, if multiplied by all the company's stock then outstanding, might easily impute a value on the entire business in the hundreds of thousands of dollars or even the millions. (In Chapter 8 we see how venture capital investors use this imputed value process to set a "pre-money valuation" on a company they intend to invest in.)

The fact that founder's stock is typically really cheap gives rise to a number of issues regarding company valuation and the timing of formation, some of which are addressed below in section F.3 of this chapter. What we focus on here is the fact that the founders end up with very large ownership interests in the company, but while they may have invested a lot of effort ("sweat equity"), they might actually have very little at risk in the business in terms of money or hard assets. As a result, if a founder ends up failing to provide the services and expertise he or she was expected to contribute to building the business, how are the other founders going to feel about that person's ownership position? Similarly, if a major investor were to invest cash to own some portion of the company's equity and a non-performing founder leaves the company shortly thereafter with a large block of stock, how is that investor going to react? The company must find someone to fill that founder's key role and likely will have to give that new person a significant equity incentive in the company. This reduces the ownership interests of the other holders, and the departed founder basically is a free-rider on the efforts and money others invest in the company. *Query*: What if the departed founder is truly departed — does the death of a founder change the issues faced by the company or an investor?

As a result of concerns like these, whether it is the founders protecting themselves from each other, or an investor protecting its investment, it is very typical to see restricted stock concepts applied to shareholders who received founder's stock.

Repurchase Rights on Founder's Stock.   In the case of founders, outside of the equity incentives context but as a result of the same basic desire to be sure that an equity ownership position is "earned," a founder's stock purchase agreement often includes a company repurchase right at the original purchase price that lapses over time. While section F.2 of this chapter considers some issues that apply specifically to a restricted stock mechanism for founders, in contrast to subsequent hires as part of an equity incentive program, the basic structure operates the same way that restricted stock does. If continued services are not provided over the entire vesting period, the company has the right to repurchase from the founder those shares that remain unvested (as to which the repurchase right has not lapsed) at a price equal to the original issuance price of the shares.

Looking at SoftCo, Joan and Michael would be well served to consider what would happen to the company if one of them turns out to be unwilling or unable to continue to participate in the business. Would either one find it appropriate for the other to be able to leave the business and take half the company's ownership with him or her? While neither may be happy with the idea of putting a repurchase right on his or her own stock, it should be pretty apparent that it is an appropriate concept when looking at the situation from the point of view of the founder who is left behind but who will keep trying, alone, to make the business succeed.

In addition to addressing their position vis-à-vis each other, founder's stock purchase agreements with a repurchase right in favor of the company may also be to Joan and Michael's advantage in dealing with subsequent investors. First, if the founders have already agreed and adhered to reasonable restrictions on their own shares, the investors may be inclined to leave those restrictions in place rather than renegotiate them.

Second, even if the investors want a new set of restrictions put in place as part of their investment deal, the fact that the founders set a vesting schedule and have clocked time on that schedule may lead the investors to give the founders credit for that time under the new restriction structure, rather than making them start again from zero.

If Joan and Michael impose repurchase restrictions on themselves at the time they form the company and purchase their founder's stock, they will be taking their shares in connection with the performance of services, even though they paid its fair market value. They should therefore file §83(b) elections on a timely basis, being sure to reflect that the price paid was the full value of those shares.

Joan and Michael might decide to form SoftCo and issue shares to themselves with no company repurchase right. Then later, after deciding to seek a venture capital investment, they might agree to accept repurchase restrictions and vesting on their shares if the investors require it as a condition to the investment transaction. In that case, a §83(b) election would not be required because the transfer of the property (i.e., their receipt of stock when SoftCo was formed) occurred in the past and was not subject to a *substantial risk of forfeiture* when it happened. Later imposition of vesting requirements in a separate event does not change the terms of an earlier share issuance. *See* Revenue Ruling 2007-49, 2007-31 I.R.B. 237.

If, however, Joan and Michael form SoftCo after they have begun discussions with a venture capital investor, even if they wait to agree to repurchase restrictions until after the investment is complete, they should take care to file their §83(b) election forms because the IRS may not view that sequence of events as resulting in a separate, subsequent imposition of the forfeiture risk.

Some counsel believe that, even when there is a clear separation in time and substance between the share issuance and the imposition of vesting requirements, it is prudent for the purchasers to file a §83(b) election on a "protective" basis, even though it is clear one is not required. These lawyers take the position that, in essence, the original shares, issued without vesting requirements, have been exchanged for new shares that are subject to vesting. The surrendered shares are treated as having the full value of the new, restricted shares, so the §83(b) election form would show no income in the current tax year. Other lawyers believe this is unnecessary and confuses the tax basis and holding period of the founder's stock. While the IRS has said explicitly that an election is not required where the founder's stock is issued in a wholly separate transaction from the imposition of repurchase restrictions, its guidance is based on analysis of a sample fact pattern that presented a three-year time lapse from the original share issuance to the imposition of vesting restrictions. *Id.*

Of course, that gives rise to the question, what if the transactions are separated by only a year? By six months? Regardless of the lack of connection between the formation of a company and the subsequent imposition of vesting requirements, is there some time frame that is just too short? Even if there is good evidence for the non-connection between the events, when the time period is short, is it better to bear the risk of confusion created by filing a protective §83(b) election simply to avoid the cost of an IRS inquiry?

A §83(b) election filing by founders has the same consequences that apply in the equity incentive context, including the fact that any tax paid on extra value received at the time the shares were purchased over the consideration paid for the shares will have only the off-setting $3,000 per year ordinary income deduction resulting from a capital loss in the event the shares are later sold for a loss or are abandoned as worthless. Further, if tax was recognized on the purchase of the shares and the company exercised its repurchase right on an employment termination, no tax deduction at all would apply. *See* "Disadvantages of the §83(b) Election" in section D.3 of this chapter.

An additional factor that founders have to take into account is that the IRS is not the only referee that must be satisfied regarding the value and nature of the consideration that the founders pay for their shares. As noted in Chapter 5, state law enumerates the forms of appropriate consideration that may be used to purchase stock from the issuing company. In addition to satisfying the IRS regarding the value and nature of consideration paid for their stock, the founders also must ensure that the consideration delivered to the company is consistent with the statutory requirements in their state of incorporation. This typically is not a concern in the equity incentives context because usually option or restricted stock plans designate cash or the surrender of previously owned shares as the only permitted forms of consideration.

E. Other Equity Incentive Mechanisms

Private companies typically provide equity incentives in the forms we already have discussed — stock options and restricted stock. These are well-established incentive mechanisms that generally are more efficient from a tax, financial accounting, and cash perspective than the other available alternatives. Stock options are still the most commonly used equity incentive mechanism, even with the negative effects of FASB 123(R), which requires the company to record a compensation expense when it grants options, and §409A, which imposes a significant set of restrictions on NQSOs, particularly the requirement that the exercise price be set at fair market value, as determined according to its requirements.

Despite the general popularity of stock options and restricted stock, other equity (and "virtual" equity) incentive plan structures also are used from time to time, and a business lawyer should be generally familiar with them.

1. Employee Stock Purchase Plan

An *employee stock purchase plan* (ESPP) is a mechanism to encourage broad stock ownership among a company's employees. Because of the structural limitations of ESPPs, they are generally viewed as supplementary to a company's equity incentive program rather than as a direct alternative to an option or restricted stock plan.

ESPPs are not available to consultants or non-employee directors, but are open to almost all employees of a company, including parent and subsidiary company employees (subject to probationary periods, limitations on part-time, seasonal, and non-U.S. employees, employees that hold more than 5 percent of the company's stock, and highly compensated employees — which, as of January 1, 2014, is defined as employees earning more than $115,000 per year. *See* Press Release, Internal Revenue Service, "IRS Announces 2014 Pension Plan Limitations" (IR-2013-86, Oct. 31,2013), *available at* http://www.irs.gov/uac/IRS-Announces-2014-Pension-Plan-Limitations;-Taxpayers -May-Contribute-up-to-$17,500-to-their-401%28k%29-plans-in-2014. Plan participants designate after-tax amounts they want withheld from their wages. These withholdings are accumulated over an offering period. Under most plans, just prior to the end of the offering period, the employees must opt either to purchase shares of the company's common stock or have their cash distributed to them. The stock purchase then would take place at the end of the offering period. Under typical ESPP terms, stock may be purchased at the lower of 85 percent of the value of the shares at the beginning or at the end of the offering period. Offering periods may be as long as 27 months, but most plans provide for a 6- or 12-month term so that employees may purchase shares at least once or twice each year. The ESPP must be adopted by the board and approved by the shareholders, and may provide for a maximum annual stock purchase by any employee of $25,000.

ESPPs may be set up to conform to Internal Revenue Code §423, which makes an ESPP grant, like an ISO, a "statutory option." While the following discussion focuses on §423-compliant ESPPs, they also may be structured as not conforming to §423, and in that case are referred to as "non-qualified" plans. Since ESPPs are used almost exclusively by companies with publicly traded shares, this gross overlap of terminology with stock options will not be a major concern for our purposes. However, ESPPs are frequently adopted by newly public companies and are a fairly common equity benefit that the business lawyer should be aware of and generally understand.

The tax treatment of shares purchased under an ESPP is quite complicated. So long as the shares are held for one year from the date of purchase and two years from the beginning of the offering period applicable to the purchase, when the shares are ultimately sold the employee will recognize ordinary income in an amount equal to the lesser of (i) the difference between the stock's fair market value at the beginning of the offering period and the price actually paid to purchase the shares and (ii) the difference between the proceeds of the sale and the purchase price paid. Any additional gain is taxed as a capital gain. If the shares are sold for a loss, then item (ii) is zero, so no ordinary income is recognized and the entire loss is a capital loss. If the holding periods are not met (i.e., the stock is sold in a "disqualifying disposition"), the spread at the time of the purchase between fair market value and the price actually paid is treated as ordinary income and the spread between the fair market value at the time of the purchase and the proceeds of the disqualifying disposition of the shares is a capital gain or loss. If shares are issued under a non-qualified ESPP, the transaction is treated like a NQSO.

Under FASB 123(R), if the ESPP allows a purchase price that is less than 95 percent of the fair market value of the stock on the purchase date (as most do), or fails to meet certain other criteria, the difference between the fair market value of the stock on the purchase date and the amount paid for the stock by the employee must be recorded on the purchase date as a compensation expense by the company for financial reporting purposes.

2. Phantom Equity Plans

A *phantom equity* plan usually is a cash compensation plan that pays bonuses based on changes in the value of the company's stock. It is intended to establish an incentive for employees to increase the company's stock value by setting a cash bonus formula for plan participants tied to increases in the company's stock price without requiring the company to issue actual shares of stock. This type of plan sometimes is referred to as a "Phantom Stock Plan," "Stock Appreciation Rights Plan," or "Performance Unit Plan." Usually participation is limited to senior executives, but non-employees may be included. Each participant is given a "phantom grant" of a number of shares of the company's common stock. Under the terms and restrictions of the plan, the participant is later permitted to "sell" the phantom holdings back to the company and receive the gain in cash. The participant gets to keep the increase in stock value without ever actually buying or selling the stock. Under some plans, the participant is given the alternative of taking the gain in shares of the company's stock (with a value equal to the gain amount) rather than cash.

The different plan forms can be structured to emulate an NQSO or a restricted stock grant, or simply to provide a cash payment based on a change in some company metric, such as gross margins or revenues, that the company wishes to improve. Some companies like these plans because they allow key personnel to participate in the growth of the company without the company having to give them actual stock and deal with the equity dilution and other issues (legal and administrative) that granting, selling, and repurchasing stock would entail. For the plan participant, the good news is that there is no risk of loss because he or she never actually puts investment dollars at risk. The bad news is that any benefits the participant receives under these plans are taxed as ordinary income.

Phantom plans must be carefully constructed to avoid creating "deferred compensation" subject to the penalties under §409A. If structured correctly, plan participants pay tax only when the compensation is actually paid to them and the company gets a corresponding tax deduction at that time.

From the company's perspective, phantom plans are simply cash bonus plans with the bonus amounts typically being determined based on changes in the company's stock value. A plan that is settled in stock rather than cash (that is, in which the gain is paid by issuing shares to the participant) can be more attractive to a company than a stock option plan because it involves tying up fewer shares; the company only issues shares representing the gain in the value of the stock, while under a restricted stock plan the full number of shares would be issued and, when the shares appreciate, only part of the value of each share represents gain. In addition, grants get made and unvested shares get repurchased — all those extra shares that just go in and out of an equity incentive plan would not have to be set aside.

Unfortunately, phantom plans have two significant negative attributes from the company's perspective. First, plans that must be settled in cash may require a significant cash outlay at a time when the company may prefer to use its cash for other purposes. If, for example, the plan participants see the prospect of a negative turn in the business ahead, they could all rush to realize their vested plan value at a time when, if they are correct about negative future prospects, the company would be well served to conserve its available cash.

Second, these plans are treated as "liability awards" rather than "equity awards" under FASB 123(R). With an equity award, a "fair value" is set once, at the time of the grant, and is charged as a compensation expense proportionately over the "requisite service period" associated with that type of award for that company. Refer to section A.6, above, for a discussion of FASB 123(R). With a "liability award," however, the "fair value" is adjusted in each accounting period based on changes in the stock price and the likelihood that the plan participants' rights will actually vest or be forfeited. As a consequence, if changes in a company's prospects result in fluctuations in its stock value, the accounting expense adjustments for these plans can be large enough to distort the company's financial reporting. Before one of these plans is adopted, management needs to have a clear and direct conversation with the company's accountants or auditors in order to understand what the plan's accounting treatment will be so that no untoward surprises appear in the company's financial statements.

QUESTIONS

1. Should Joan and Michael consider adopting either an ESPP or a Phantom Equity Plan for the employees of SoftCo? What are the advantages and disadvantages of each type of equity incentive plan in the context of SoftCo? Does your analysis of these issues vary depending on which financing alternative Joan and Michael decide to pursue for SoftCo?
2. In what way do these equity incentive and other plans present hidden costs for a company, such as SoftCo?

F. Common Contractual Variations for Stock Options and Restricted Stock

1. Equity Incentive Plan Options and Restricted Stock

In addition to the basic terms previously reviewed, equity incentive plans often include a number of variations. While these plans are guided by concepts arising from securities, tax, employment, and corporate law, as well as accounting rules, they are delivered through plans and agreements that constitute contracts. These contracts often have additional terms that vary the basic incentives or that address other issues that are intended to make the equity incentive more effective from the perspective of the company as well as the grant recipient. As you may have noted, the tax and accounting issues applicable to equity incentives are layered and complex, so even a seemingly innocuous change to an equity incentive plan's terms could have serious unintended consequences. Expert tax and accounting advice always should be sought when drafting and before changing an equity incentive contract.

Combining Options and Restricted Stock — the "Early Exercise" Option.   One common contract variation links options to restricted stock. The option might allow, for example, the holder to wait for vesting to take place before exercising the option in the normal way. Plus, it also might allow the holder to exercise the option without regard to its vesting schedule, but in that case, upon exercise the holder would receive restricted stock that would vest on the same schedule that otherwise would have applied to the option.

The benefit is that the option holder has the right to *early exercise*; that is, the holder may exercise the option without having to wait for it to vest, and therefore can buy the shares at a time when the income tax liability triggered by the purchase will still be small. In addition, with an early exercise the option holder can start the holding period for capital gain treatment on the shares before he or she otherwise would have had the right to buy the shares. The company, on the other hand, still has the protection provided by the full vesting schedule; early exercise simply shifts vesting from the option to the restricted stock.

If the option holder were able to exercise before a major event that would cause the value of the company's shares to increase significantly, the holder could reduce the tax liability triggered by the exercise. On an early exercise, the holder receives restricted stock, vested to the same degree that the option was vested, and almost always should file a §83(b) election disclosing the difference between the exercise price and the fair market value of the stock purchased at the time of purchase. Under the NQSO rules, the employer would withhold the tax on that amount in the ordinary course. Under the ISO rules, there would be no regular tax, but AMT income recognition is addressed by the same §83 structure. As a result, by filing the election, the ISO holder is agreeing to include the spread (i.e., fair market value of the purchased shares less the exercise price for those shares) at the time of the exercise in AMT income for the current year and is avoiding AMT recognition of income as the restricted stock vests in the future.

The downside of this approach is that the tax treatment is complex and often not fully understood by option holders, which leads to unexpected results. Many companies try to limit this problem by providing early exercise rights only to senior officers or directors. Early exercise encourages option holders to exercise in order to minimize the tax recognized on exercise. As noted, one of the major advantages to options is the holder's ability to avoid putting any investment dollars at risk until it is clear that a profit can be quickly obtained. Early exercise leads some option holders to let the tax tail wag the investment dog.

Also, from the company's point of view, early exercise must be used with caution when the option granted is an ISO. Recall the earlier discussion in (vi) of section C.1, regarding the $100,000 maximum stock value that may become vested in any calendar year. When an ISO is granted with early exercise rights, the entire option can be exercised immediately so that all of it will be counted against the $100,000 cap in the calendar year of the grant — the fact that the shares would be restricted stock is simply not relevant for the ISO rules. As a result, if the number of shares times the exercise price per share of the ISO is greater than $100,000, then ISO treatment will apply to the option only to the extent of $100,000 of exercise price and the remainder of the option above $100,000 will be treated as an NQSO. This treatment applies regardless of whether the employee actually takes advantage of the early exercise right.

An additional complication that arises when options allow for the purchase of restricted stock is managing the timing of post-termination exercise rights. As an option grant typically allows the option holder some period of time post-termination to exercise the option, the period of time during which the company may repurchase the restricted stock shares needs to contemplate that there may be some delay before the option holder exercises the option. A company's right to repurchase unvested shares that expires 30 days after an employee is terminated would not be useful if the employee has

60 days post-termination to exercise an outstanding option allowing the purchase of unvested stock. When options allow for early exercise, often the company's restricted stock repurchase right is coordinated so that it runs from the later of the services termination date or the post-termination exercise of an option.

Accelerated Vesting.   Because the eventual sale of the company is frequently the objective of an early-stage business, equity incentive programs often provide for the *acceleration of vesting* should the company be acquired. While other events also may cause an acceleration of vesting, a sale of the company, or a termination of employment in association with a sale of the company, are the most common trigger events. A vesting acceleration contract provision might say that upon a trigger event, all or some portion of the unvested incentive will immediately vest. Alternatively, it might say that the equity incentive holder will have extra service time added to the time that actually has passed under the incentive's vesting schedule, thus giving the holder credit for more vesting.

Accelerated vesting triggered by the sale of a business offers benefits to a company's incentive holders while fulfilling two purposes that are useful to the company. First, it corrects a potential disincentive that a vesting schedule might create. Vesting is intended to make an employee want to stay with the company for an extended period of time in order to reap a reward for building company value. While a sale of the company may represent a realization of that growth in value, if the employee has a large block of unvested options or restricted stock, he or she actually may be discouraged from working toward a sale of the company now as opposed to a few years from now. In short, an immediate sale could be perceived as creating a loss of value to the employee holding unvested options. Accelerated vesting, effective immediately prior to the acquisition, mitigates this disincentive.

Second, the sale of the company is a change and change creates uncertainty. Employees in particular do not like uncertainty; they often fear they will lose their jobs after the acquisition, which may lead to the decision that they would be better off looking for new jobs now. Accelerated vesting thus acts as a retention bonus in that it rewards employees for staying with the company through the sale transaction.

Constructing a vesting acceleration mechanism requires that a number of potential outcomes be considered. For example, if a company uses a four-year vesting schedule and one employee has been with the company for six months while another has been working for three years, how would each be affected if a sale of the company triggered full vesting acceleration (i.e., all unvested incentives vest)? *Query:* Would the employee who has put in three years think his or her treatment is fair in comparison to that of the other employee?

What if, in order to allay employees' fear of termination on a sale of the company, the acceleration provision instead called for 50 percent of the outstanding unvested incentive to vest if an employee is terminated within six months of an acquisition? Consider two employees who received equal option grants when they were hired four months prior to the acquisition. One is terminated effective upon the acquisition, triggering vesting of half of that employee's option, and the other is offered a replacement option to purchase shares of the new company, none of which is yet vested. *Query:* Which employee got the better deal — the key person who has been kept on or the one who has been let go?

In order to achieve an outcome that is perceived as fair by the new employee as well as the veteran, and the fired employee as well as the one retained, accelerated vesting terms are often broken into sub-elements. One frequent outcome is that every employee gets a small vesting acceleration upon an acquisition, while employees who get terminated in connection with the acquisition receive a second incremental acceleration. In addition, the size of the acceleration may be capped. For example, the acceleration provision might say that on a sale of the business one half of any unvested incentive shall be vested, but that the acceleration may not exceed one year of vesting.

Even when a company does not provide vesting acceleration upon a sale to its employees generally, it often will provide at least some acceleration for senior executives. One of the benefits of combining two companies is reducing employment costs by eliminating one set of managers. As the acquiring company tends to like to keep its own management team, the acquired company's management often is terminated. A vesting acceleration provision gives those people an incentive to work diligently toward their own job loss.

A "sale of the company" for these purposes is usually defined as a transaction in which the owners of the company immediately prior to the transaction end up after the transaction no longer holding at least 50 percent of the ownership of the company. This is frequently referred to as a "change of control" transaction. In general, but more particularly when addressing the concerns of senior management, an acceleration provision will make a distinction between a change of control transaction that is a sale of the company and a transaction that is for the purpose of financing the company.

Generally speaking, the proceeds of a sale transaction go into the pockets of current owners, while the proceeds of an investment transaction stay in the company and are used to build the company. Sale transactions and financing transactions can be difficult to distinguish, but sale transactions often result in employment terminations for senior management while financing transactions usually are an endorsement of the capability of senior management to continue to build the company. While it is reasonable for executives to seek some mitigation against the risks that may result from a sale, it is perhaps not appropriate to get those protections in the case of a financing. Consequently, vesting acceleration terms often exclude transactions that fall under the definition of a sale but actually are done for financing purposes.

Fair Market Value Repurchase Right.   Companies sometimes will include in their option and restricted stock agreements the right to repurchase the *vested* shares from an equity incentive participant upon the termination of that person's services. In contrast to the right to repurchase unvested restricted stock at the original issue price, which represents a "substantial risk of forfeiture" to the incentive recipient, this right gives the company the ability to repurchase otherwise unrestricted shares at their then-current fair market value. Its purpose is to allow the company to prevent a departing employee from walking away with any shares of the company's stock, while giving that employee the benefit of any gain so far in the shares' value.

The contract terms usually mirror the terms of a restricted stock repurchase right; that is, they are triggered by termination of services, are at the discretion of the company, and must be exercised within a relatively short period of time (usually 30 days) following employment termination.

When a company has both an original issue price repurchase right on unvested shares and a fair market value repurchase right on vested shares, the company typically has the same exercise term for both repurchase rights following termination of the shareholder's employment or other services. As noted in the early exercise context, the post-termination time period applicable to the company's repurchase right on vested shares purchased upon the normal exercise of stock options has to take into account the fact that the options usually will have a post-termination exercise term.

One substantive difference in these repurchase provisions is that the fair market value repurchase right applicable to vested shares often is assignable by the company to a shareholder or perhaps pro rata to a class or group of shareholders. This allows the company to ensure that the right may be exercised and the shares stay in friendly hands, even if the company does not have the cash resources or fails to meet the legal standards necessary to make the share purchase itself. *See* section D.6 of Chapter 5, addressing limitations on distributions to shareholders. We discuss those statutory limitations in the context of share repurchases in Chapter 9, section E.1.

Like restricted stock, share certificates representing stock subject to a fair market value repurchase right often are held in escrow until the company determines to waive its repurchase right.

While employers generally favor these provisions because they give the company the ability to pull shares back from someone who has turned hostile to the company, employees often object. They see the repurchase right as an effort to take away the long-term upside potential of their vested shares. *Query:* Why would the fair market value right to repurchase vested shares be assignable by the company, but the original purchase price repurchase right, applicable to unvested shares, not? [*Hint:* Consider the magnitude of the transaction from the company's perspective. Separately, as to each type of repurchase right, consider the economic value of that right if assigned to a shareholder or group of shareholders.]

QUESTIONS

1. What do you think a company such as SoftCo should take into consideration in deciding whether to include a fair market value repurchase right as part of its option plan for its employees?
2. What are the competing interests that a company such as SoftCo must address in this context?
3. What other legal issues are raised by a fair market value repurchase right? (*Hint:* Refer to section D.6 of Chapter 5.)

Right of First Refusal on Transfers.   In order to control the dispersion of its shares, a company often will include a section in its option exercise or restricted stock purchase documents giving the company a *right of first refusal on transfers* (i.e., sales, gifts, charitable donations, etc.) of any stock that was received as an equity incentive. Under these terms, should an employee decide to transfer the shares, he or she may find a buyer and negotiate a deal, but then must bring that deal to the company and allow the company to step into the place of the buyer and buy the shares itself. If the company does not exercise its right within a defined period of time, the employee may then sell the shares to the buyer under the disclosed terms.

Often a right-of-first-refusal provision allows the company to assign its right to a shareholder or group of shareholders, in the same manner as just described for a fair market value repurchase right applicable to vested shares, and for the same reasons.

A right of first refusal usually survives termination of the shareholder's employment and only expires if and when the company's shares are registered for trading under the 1934 Act. If, however, the shareholder notifies the company of a proposed sale and the company chooses not to exercise its right of first refusal, under some agreements the buyer of the shares takes the shares free of any continuing application of the right. Other companies provide that the transferee must take the shares subject to the ongoing right of first refusal.

Usually a right of first refusal provides for a limited range of "permitted transfers" by the shareholder that do not trigger the company's right. These typically are limited to estate planning or intra-family transfers where the shareholder, or the shareholder's immediate family, continues to beneficially own the shares. However, most permitted transfer provisions do require the new registered owner of the shares to enter into a joinder agreement (an agreement causing a new party to "join" an existing set of contractual commitments) providing that the new owner will be bound by the terms of the company's right of first refusal. The idea is that so long as the shareholder (or immediate family) continues to have a beneficial interest in the shares and they remain subject to the right of first refusal, the company can accommodate the transfer without losing the ability to supervise the dispersion of its stock.

If the company has other concerns about the dispersion of its shares, it may add other provisions to these agreements to address specific circumstances. The problem, however, is tying up the shares too tightly; the terms of a right of first refusal should not be overreaching or they may be self-defeating for the company. The general issue with a right of first refusal is that it is a restriction on the alienability of the stockholder's property interest in the shares, which is generally viewed unfavorably as a matter of property law. The argument in favor of a right of first refusal is that it permits the company to supervise its shares while allowing the shareholder to realize the value of its property rights by selling the stock. While the company's interest is legitimate, if the shareholder's ability to transfer the shares is restricted by overly burdensome procedures, excessively long exercise periods, or other constraints that create too great a barrier to an actual sale of the shares, the company's right of first refusal may not be enforceable as a matter of law.

The reality is that rights of first refusal are a powerful chill on the shareholder's ability to sell the covered shares. Many buyers are not willing to invest the time and money necessary to do the diligence on a company in order to evaluate the appropriateness of making an investment in its shares if they know the company can step in and prevent the sale from being completed. Many view the right of first refusal as a "sucker's bet," since if the buyer offers a low price, the company will step in and purchase the shares. As they see it, the only time that the buyer is likely to be successful in purchasing the shares is when the company thinks that the buyer is overpaying.

Right of first refusal provisions often are accompanied by terms that automatically void any transfer made in violation of the transfer restrictions. In addition, they may include self-executing purchase terms for the benefit of the company. This means that if the company provides the selling shareholder with notice of its desire to exercise its right and makes the payment available in accordance with the agreement's terms, it will be deemed to have purchased the shares, regardless of whether the shareholder collects the money or surrenders the stock certificate. In short, a lack of cooperation by the shareholder will not prevent the company from completing the share purchase.

Market Stand-Off.   Equity incentive documents regularly include a *market stand-off* or *lock-up* provision. This term provides that in the event of an underwritten public offering of the company's stock (and virtually all public offerings are underwritten) the shareholder agrees not to sell the shares into the public market (or engage in any transaction that constructively results in a sale) for a defined period of time following the offering. This lock-up period is usually 180 days following an IPO (plus additional time the company or underwriter may request for regulatory compliance), although a shorter period may apply to later offerings.

The market stand-off gives the company and the underwriter comfort that shareholders who received their stock through an equity incentive program will not rush to cash out immediately after the company goes public, creating an excess supply of shares and driving down the company's stock price. The underwriter wants, and it is in the company's best interests, to allow a trading market to become established before people who got their shares in private issuances start selling into the market.

Many lawyers include market stand-off terms in every agreement they prepare that involves a private stock issuance. They do so because they know that if the company has the opportunity to go public, the underwriter will want as many as possible of the shares outstanding pre-IPO to be subject to a market stand-off. Further, since a public offering usually is a long way away, the term will not be controversial early in the company's life, and stock purchasers tend just to accept it. On the eve of an IPO, shareholders asked to sign a market stand-off may be less cooperative.

2. Variations for Repurchase Rights Applied to Founder's Stock

Founder's stock repurchase rights documents often have a few distinctions from the pure restricted-stock-as-equity-incentive model. At the most fundamental level, founder's stock is not issued as part of an equity incentive plan. As a result, the founder's stock purchase agreement has to include the securities representations and other exemption requirements of a §4(a)(2) or Regulation D, rather than a Rule 701, transaction. Recall the discussion in sections B.2 and B.3 versus B.6 of Chapter 4 regarding the specific terms of these securities issuance exemptions from the registration requirements of the 1933 Act.

As was previously suggested, at the time of a venture capital investment, the investors may leave in place a self-imposed vesting program already adopted by the founders or, if the investors want something different, they may be willing to give vesting credit for "time served" under a self-imposed restriction program. In addition, founders often are not subjected to the probationary period imposed by a vesting schedule that includes a cliff; their shares typically vest in monthly increments from the outset. If a cliff does apply, it often is used in connection with a relatively short vesting term.

In the equity incentive context, vesting stops and repurchase is triggered when employment terminates, which generally means any cessation of employment, regardless of the reason or lack of a reason. With founders, the ownership interest involved is usually large enough to cause the founder some concern that an arbitrary termination may be prompted by the company's desire to get the shares back. Of course the company is concerned that the founder will perform poorly or lose interest in the long effort to build the company, making the company better off without him or her around. How to balance this tension is one of the primary matters for negotiating an effective repurchase right on founder's stock.

Often the result of these negotiations is that different treatments apply to the company's repurchase of founder's stock upon a termination *for cause* versus a termination *without cause*, or upon a termination that results from disability or death, or a termination that is connected with an acquisition of the business. Thus, the usual outcome in founder's stock purchase agreements is that "cause" is narrowly defined — a crime, act of dishonesty, fiduciary duty violation, direct insubordination, or contract breach — and triggers the company's right to repurchase all unvested shares. A termination "without cause" usually is defined simply as a termination where "cause" does not apply. The founder is usually entitled to accelerate vesting for some (or even all) shares on a termination "without cause."

Dealing with the death or disability of a founder can be difficult, as the moral turpitude of a "for cause" termination does not apply, but on the other hand, what advantage does the company obtain from "without cause" treatment resulting in a larger block of shares going to a founder's survivors? It is extremely doubtful that they will be able to assume the departed founder's role and provide value to the company. *Query:* Would the company be better off repurchasing all those unvested shares so it has equity to offer as an incentive to the person who will have to replace the departed founder?

An additional employment termination concept in this mix is resignation for *good reason*. While walking away from the job is usually treated as a "for cause" termination, what if the company changes the job situation and, in effect, compels the founder to leave? While contracts vary, "good reason" usually includes the employee quitting because of a negative change in compensation, authority, or responsibilities, or a change in the primary job site that makes a home relocation necessary. Termination by the founder for "good reason" typically is treated the same as a "without cause" termination. In order to protect itself from an inadvertent act triggering "good reason," a company sometimes will require the employee to give notice of the "good reason" factor within some period of time after becoming aware of it so that the company may correct the issue if it wishes. In addition, the company may limit "good reason" treatment to a time period following the notice; if the employee does not leave within the contractual window of time, the "good reason" basis will be deemed to have lapsed.

QUESTIONS

1. Assume that SoftCo is in its formation stages and planning its approach to founder's stock and equity incentives. Joan and Michael have asked you, as company counsel, whether a right of first refusal on transfers of equity incentive or founder's stock

should be used where the shareholder seeks to make a donation of shares to a charity. How would the right of first refusal work? Would the company want it to apply? What is the shareholder's competing interest? What is your advice to SoftCo regarding covering charitable contributions within the scope of a right of first refusal?

2. Continuing the same facts, should charitable contributions or other gifts be treated the same way as "permitted transfers" to family members or for estate planning purposes? What are the similarities and distinctions?

3. What are the pros and cons of having the corporate secretary hold in escrow shares issued under a restricted stock agreement or subject to a right of first refusal on transfers? From the company's perspective? From an employee's? Would you advise SoftCo to use an escrow arrangement? For both restricted stock and stock subject to a right of first refusal on transfers?

4. As SoftCo's counsel, do you think it would be prudent to include a market stand-off provision in Joan's and Michael's founder's stock purchase agreements? In SoftCo's employee equity incentive plan?

5. In listing the factors that should give rise to a resignation for "good reason," how relevant is the fact that SoftCo is just in its formation stage, and so bound to undergo significant changes over the next few years? How might the list be different from one you would prepare for a mature, publicly traded company?

6. What is the argument from the employee's perspective that death and disability should be treated as a termination without cause? What is the argument from the company's side that it should be able to repurchase all the unvested shares in either case? Is there a middle ground?

3. Other Founder's Stock Issues

Founder's stock may be made subject to the contract variations discussed previously in section F.1 of this chapter, particularly with respect to accelerated vesting on a sale of the company and a right of first refusal on transfers. In addition, a market stand-off provision is very standard.

Separately, founders have some unique issues that apply to their share purchases. Assume that Joan and Michael form SoftCo by contributing their intellectual property (which is valued by the IRS based on the cost of producing it rather than its market worth) and some equipment and cash. The total value of those assets may be in the tens, or maybe hundreds, of thousands of dollars. For purposes of discussion, let's assume that the value of this consideration is $100,000.

What if, three weeks later, a venture capital fund makes a $5 million investment in SoftCo and is issued convertible preferred stock that represents half the ownership of the company? We deal with company valuations and venture capital convertible preferred stock in more detail in Chapters 8 and 9, but as a matter of simple logic, if the venture capital investor paid $5 million for half of the company, and Joan and Michael own the other half, does that suggest that their half is also valued at $5 million? Obviously their ownership interest is illiquid, so its realizable value is inherently speculative, and the venture capital investor is paying extra for special rights and preferences, but still, the venture capital investor's payment of hard cash into SoftCo in exchange for the ownership of a portion of the company allows a value to be imputed on the entire company and, therefore, on the portion of the company owned by Joan and Michael.

From the point of view of the IRS, Joan and Michael paid in $100,000 to SoftCo three weeks ago, and now Joan and Michael's shares are worth $5 million. Since the investor is a third-party, arms-length professional putting real money at risk, the IRS probably will not question the valuation it put on SoftCo in that transaction. Instead, however, it might take the position that Joan and Michael's stock must have been worth close to $5 million when they bought it, and since they only contributed about $100,000 in asset value, the only other thing they might have contributed that could account for that huge difference in value is their pre-incorporation services to SoftCo. Accordingly, the IRS might reason that the stock must have been issued in large part for services and, as a result, §83 applies, thereby resulting in Joan and Michael owing ordinary income tax on approximately $4.9 million in stock value.

Keep in mind that the IRS has up to a six-year statute of limitations, so it does not need to bring this claim against Joan and Michael until after SoftCo becomes incredibly successful and is acquired by Big Bad Software (regretting the joint venture went awry) four years after formation for $650 million. With the benefit of that hindsight, the IRS might well assert that tax, interest, and penalties are owed.

As a result, in order to protect clients that intend to seek outside investment from this ugly result, it often is prudent for lawyers representing formation-stage companies to advise the founders to set a business entity structure in place early to create as much separation in time as possible between the issuance of the cheap founder's shares and the higher-priced stock issued to other investors. Basic incorporation documentation is relatively inexpensive, and getting the company set up and putting initial ownership into the hands of the founders as early as possible can significantly reduce the tax risk by allowing time for the company to legitimately grow in value before an investment occurs.

Alternatively, in Joan's and Michael's circumstances, with no employees and limited exposure to third party liability (hopefully true as to intellectual property!), they may be well served by just continuing to develop their products and acknowledging that they are, and have been for some time, operating as a general partnership. Refer to the discussion in sections A.2 and B of Chapter 2 regarding general partnerships.

If Joan and Michael create even informal documentation for their partnership, this could help establish that they contributed assets and intellectual property to their partnership back when it originally was formed. Later, when they are prepared to take on a *Friends and Family* or other form of outside investment, or the development of the business makes it appropriate from a liability protection standpoint, Joan and Michael could form a corporation and contribute their partnership interests into the corporation as consideration for their shares. Since Joan and Michael would be the only owners of the corporation when it is formed (their partnership interests being contributed for all the stock of the corporation), the "acquisition" of their partnership by their corporation would be a non-taxable event. They could then go forward as shareholders with a tax basis in their stock equal to the value of their original contributions to their partnership.

The roll-over of ownership from the partnership to the corporation establishes the amount of their original contributions to the partnership, *and the time those contributions were made,* as the relevant measuring points for their tax position in the corporation. Taking on an investor soon after the corporation is formed should not pose a problem, then, because the original "purchase" of their ownership interests now would be treated as having taken place back when the partnership was formed. Sufficient time would have passed since then to make the valuation of the company imputed by the outside investment not reflect an underpayment for their stock.

As before, this is a tax issue and should not be pursued without the advice and involvement of a tax specialist. In addition, this scenario may be appropriate for Joan and Michael to use, but only because it reflects the facts of their situation. If a company's founders actually had just met two weeks before their corporation was formed, this outline would not solve their problem because it simply would not be true.

As a business lawyer, you frequently have to create documents dated "as of" some time in the past. Occasionally it can be to the client's great advantage to document correctly some undocumented or improperly documented history. In contrast, you cannot falsify history to make it, as things turned out, what would have been nice if it had happened. The good business lawyer never ignores the distinction between documenting history and creating it.

CHAPTER 7

INTELLECTUAL PROPERTY PROTECTION — A PRIMER FOR THE NON-EXPERT

A. What Is Intellectual Property?

Valuable intellectual property (IP) can be created in almost any business. At a minimum, virtually every company wants to have its products or services clearly identified as being its own. Whether a business is a dry cleaner or a technology company like SoftCo, establishing and protecting a recognizable identity is often a key to attracting and building a customer base. How can a business grow and retain its customers if they cannot distinguish it from its competitors?

Further, some types of businesses develop special techniques or processes that make their products unique and useful. A company like SoftCo not only has to do that, but also has to deliver a recorded expression of the sequence of computer instructions that make up its software. SoftCo will want to preserve its exclusive use of the inventive approaches taken in creating its products as well as protect the product itself from duplication. Whether a company makes software, jewelry, romance novels, handbags, or thousands of other products, it will want to ensure that its creative efforts are not simply replicated by a competitor.

As you read the following materials and begin to appreciate the breadth of the potential forms of IP and some of the practical steps a company may take to protect its IP, consider SoftCo's situation and how, as it grows, these various subjects may come into play. Does your perspective change depending on the course SoftCo takes to obtain financing? Consider also the IP issues and risks arising in SoftCo's relationship with its employees, suppliers, customers, investors and, perhaps most importantly, Joan and Michael themselves.

1. Introduction to Intellectual Property

In common parlance, IP refers to inventions, ideas, plans, methods, creations, secrets, and symbols that have economic value either in use or in sale. As a legal matter, IP is a range of creations that, because they have value, are given specific legal protections through property rights. From the point of view of a business, the key issue with IP is having the ability to commercially exploit it while preventing unauthorized people from obtaining the economic advantage of like exploitation. IP protection divides into two basic types: (i) inventions and other new creations, and (ii) identity in the marketplace. Generally, the former are protected through restrictions on use, such as monopoly rights to prohibit unauthorized use (patents), exclusive rights to reproduce (copyrights), and measures to preserve secrets (trade secret laws). Identity in the marketplace — specifically product or service marks, names, and other identifications that foster an association with a particular provider — is protected as trademarks and trade dress. *See* HOWARD C. ANAWALT, IP STRATEGY: COMPLETE INTELLECTUAL PROPERTY PLANNING, ACCESS AND PROTECTION §I.A (2006).

The existence of legal protections for IP is at the foundation of a successful free enterprise system. Without the ability to protect economically useful creations and identifiers, there would be little incentive to develop those things. The most aggressive and reactive competitors simply would duplicate and use or sell each new meaningful product development or identifier as it made its appearance in the marketplace. IP laws encourage invention and technological advancement by providing the creators of new and different things the ability to control the commercial exploitation of their creations. Some companies, such as biotech research firms, have no product to sell other than their intellectual property. Without IP protection, SoftCo, for example, would never have been offered the opportunity to develop a business relationship with Big Bad Software. Instead, Big Bad Software just would have waited for the release of SoftCo's products into the marketplace and then simply copied them.

Furthermore, without marketplace identity protections, purchasers would have difficulty identifying the provider of a product or even distinguishing one product from another. IP protections level the playing field in the marketplace by penalizing parties who seek to mislead purchasers by falsely associating their products or services with those of a known provider of products or services.

In this chapter, we look at what IP is and how it is protected by law. We first examine protections of inventions and creations, then turn to marketplace and identity protections. After that introduction, we consider some of the practical measures corporate counsel should be familiar with in order to assist clients in protecting their IP rights. Of course, this is only the briefest introduction to IP, which is a complex and highly specialized area of law with many subspecialties. The important thing to recognize is that a company does not have to be in a technical or creative business in order to face IP issues. A business lawyer needs a basic awareness of what IP protections are afforded by law because, in representing new businesses, IP matters *will* arise.

2. Trade Secrets

Even the least paranoid business is likely to have reports, procedures, techniques, systems, or other business information that it considers private and does not want its competitors to know. The Uniform Trade Secrets Act, which has been adopted in most states, codifies a long history of common law protection for trade secrets. It defines a *trade secret* as information, without regard to form, that is valuable because it is not generally known or readily ascertainable by proper means and is the subject of reasonable efforts to protect its secrecy. Unif. Trade Secrets Act §1 (1985) (defining "trade secret"). Examples include formulas and manufacturing processes, financial information, marketing or product development plans, production techniques, employee evaluations, and compensation arrangements. Information that is of value to a business operation but does not meet the terms of the definition of a trade secret is sometimes referred to as "know-how," which may exist in both the positive and the negative. "Negative know-how" is understanding what does not work, which can be valuable because you can save money by knowing which solutions *not* to try. This whole range of information is often generally referred to as "proprietary" or "confidential" information.

The singular element of a trade secret is that it truly is a secret and is treated as one. As we all learned by the second grade, the best way to keep a secret is not to tell anyone. Unfortunately, in business, secrets often must be shared with at least some employees as well as certain outsiders, such as a key part, equipment, or materials supplier, or a customer, and maybe some service providers. Given that some people have to know a trade secret, the owner's ability to obtain legal protection for it depends on whether the owner, as a practical matter, used reasonable efforts under the circumstances to protect the information as a secret. *See id.* What constitutes "reasonable efforts" depends on the nature of the secret and its use. And, of course, the legal protection only applies to the degree to which it really is a secret in the first place. In many trade secret lawsuits, it ultimately is determined that the plaintiff's case must fail because there simply was no secret.

The common law on trade secrets developed as an element of torts. Although in more recent years legislation such as the Uniform Trade Secrets Act has moved to the forefront, to understand the ideas behind current trade secret law it is useful to examine how it developed in the context of torts. This also brings home the fact that trade secrets are not necessarily technology; instead, they often are business information.

Background.　In 1939, the Restatement (First) of Torts set forth some factors to be used to ascertain whether information constitutes a trade secret:

> (1) the extent the information is known outside the . . . business; (2) the extent to which it is known by employees and others involved in the business; (3) the extent of measures taken . . . to guard the secrecy of [the] information; (4) the value of the information to [the business] and to its competitors; (5) the amount of effort or money expended . . . in developing the information; and (6) the ease or difficulty with which the information could be properly acquired or duplicated by others.

4 RESTATEMENT (FIRST) OF TORTS §757 (1939).

Item (1) addresses whether the information really is a secret. Items (2) and (3) relate to the internal protections used by the business — whether knowledge of the information is restricted to those who need to use it, and what measures generally are taken to maintain confidentiality. Items (4), (5), and (6) approach the issue of the commercial value of the information from different directions — how hard was it to come up with (and therefore how hard will it be for a competitor to duplicate) and does it really have competitive value? The foundation for the Uniform Trade Secrets Act definition of "trade secret" summarized at the beginning of this discussion is clearly based on this set of factors published before World War II.

Establishing Trade Secret Protection.　The first step in a company's trade secret protection efforts is identifying its trade secrets. In fact, as each form of IP protection requires a different set of procedures, this is fundamental to implementing not just trade secret protection, but IP protections generally. Specialized IP counsel often can provide an IP audit of a company, which can be very useful not only in identifying the existence of trade secrets (and other IP) but also their location and how they are used. With this knowledge, a program for protecting a company's trade secrets and other IP can be developed and implemented.

The sort of practical measures a company can take to protect its trade secrets may include:

- Limiting access to its facility (and/or to certain areas within the facility) through key cards and the like;
- Storing secret data in locked storage areas;
- Marking secret information as "confidential" and limiting physical access to it;
- Shredding old copies of confidential documents; and
- Creating password-protected data access systems.

In addition, a company may separate portions of information if the secret requires more than one data set, or alternatively, it may isolate groups of employees who have separate pieces of the secret information.

For example, a company with a secret recipe or formula may combine elements of the mix in preliminary steps in separate facilities or operations so that the entire recipe is never being manipulated in one place (a technique famously employed by KFC Corporation to protect its secret blend of 11 herbs and spices). Imagine dividing a recipe for a cake into three parts and giving the dry ingredients part to one person and the wet to another, and then having someone pick up their prepared mixes and take them to the home of another person, who combines the prepared ingredients and has the baking directions. Each person involved would end up with some idea of what went into the final product, but no one would know exactly.

A training program setting out the company's processes for protecting trade secrets, combined with a signed pledge or certification from each employee upon completion of training, also may be used. Ongoing training can be useful for policy enforcement — without regular reminders, employees are likely to regress to what is convenient and fail to adhere to even slightly burdensome processes.

The difficulty is that, since the legal standard applied to a company's protective actions is what is "reasonable" in light of the circumstances, a company can never know before a lawsuit whether it has done enough. The temptation is to beef up protections, but if a company implements overly stringent security processes to the point where security interferes with productivity, employees will begin to sidestep cumbersome procedures. As a legal matter, companies generally want to avoid that outcome because the value of having security protocols is seriously undercut by evidence that they are routinely ignored or bypassed.

The other mechanism companies typically use to protect their trade secrets is confidentiality agreements. We look in depth at confidentiality agreements later in this chapter, but it is important to keep in mind that contractual protection often is the only barrier a company can have under circumstances where it simply must share its trade secrets with certain employees or other business relations.

Trade secrets are misappropriated when they are acquired, disclosed, or used without the consent of the owner. Unif. Trade Secrets Act §1 (1985) (defining "misappropriation"). While industrial espionage exists, most often a company's trade secrets are misappropriated by someone who once had legitimate access to them, such as a former employee of the company.

When misappropriation of a trade secret occurs, both injunctive relief and monetary damages (for actual loss or unjust enrichment) may be available. In addition, the court may impose a "reasonable royalty" on the unlawful use or disclosure. Where willful and malicious misappropriation exists, the court may award exemplary damages of up to two times any monetary damages assessed and may award attorneys' fees. Attorneys' fees also may be awarded against a plaintiff who brings a misappropriation claim in bad faith. Unif. Trade Secrets Act §§3, 4 (1985). In addition, criminal penalties may be available for trade secret theft under the Economic Espionage Act of 1996, 18 U.S.C. §§1831-1839.

One of the significant state-by-state differences in trade secret law is that in some states, such as California, it is necessary for a plaintiff to identify with "reasonable specificity" the secrets alleged to have been misappropriated, while in others, such as Texas, the plaintiff can plead the misappropriation generally and initiate discovery without having to specify the exact subject of the claim. The argument for allowing a "general pleading" by the plaintiff is that, if the secret had to be specified, the lawsuit would be self-defeating as it would announce the secret to the world as well as deliver it to the competitor suspected of misappropriating it. The counterargument is that a general pleading allows a plaintiff to go on a fishing expedition throughout a competitor's IP, based on an assurance to the court that there is a misappropriation in there somewhere and we will tell you what it is when we find it. Yet, even in states where the secret is supposed to be identified in the complaint, the intent of that requirement is often undercut by liberal pleading rules that allow a plaintiff to adjust its identification of the secrets allegedly stolen as the case proceeds. Because of the concerns litigants typically have about disclosing their trade secrets, often mechanisms are set in the litigation process to segregate from each party the details of their opponent's trade secrets.

The ability to bring an action without specifying what got stolen can lead to abuse by large, well-financed plaintiffs who seek to beat their competitors in court because they are losing in the marketplace. A fully litigated trade secret lawsuit can take several years and cost each side millions of dollars, putting a small business at a major disadvantage. Despite the use of litigation as a competitive tactic, courts seem to be very willing to find a basis for a colorable claim on almost any subject and thus aggressive plaintiffs are often able to avoid paying exemplary damages or legal fees. This can allow the loser in court to win in the marketplace by forcing a threatening upstart company to direct its time and money toward litigation rather than product development and marketing. *Query*: If a small start-up company (such as SoftCo) receives a complaint alleging trade secret misappropriation from a large competitor (such as Big Bad Software), what are the start-up company's options?

Another significant state-by-state variation in trade secret protection is the adoption or rejection of the "inevitable disclosure" doctrine. This doctrine provides that a holder of trade secrets, usually a former employer, is entitled to presume that a person who knows that employer's trade secrets or other confidential information cannot help but disclose that information in a new job working for a competitor. This doctrine has been accepted in a number of states (*see, e.g., PepsiCo, Inc. v. Redmond*, 54 F.3d

1262 (7th Cir. 1995) (applying Illinois law)), while the doctrine has been flatly rejected in other jurisdictions (*see, e.g., Schlage Lock Co. v. Whyte*, 101 Cal. App. 4th 1443 (2002) (applying California law)).

In some states, such as New York, the inevitable disclosure doctrine has been applied narrowly in limited situations, for example, where a high-level employee has accepted employment with a direct competitor in a position similar to the one previously held and the former employee is expected to make decisions that directly relate to the subject matter of the former employer's confidential information. In this sort of situation, the former employer has been able to enjoin the new employment of the former employee, even in the absence of an agreement not to compete. *See, e.g., Marietta Corp. v. Fairhurst*, 301 A.D.2d 734 (N.Y. App. Div. 2003); and *Merck & Co. v. Lyon*, 941 F. Supp. 1443 (M.D.N.C. 1996). More recently, however, the Federal District Court applied a broader interpretation, making no distinction between an employee's expertise and his or her knowledge of trade secrets:

> The harm to IBM, however, is more likely to derive from inadvertent disclosure of the IBM trade secrets that have defined Mr. Papermaster's long career. Put another way, what other base of technical know-how could Mr. Papermaster draw upon to perform his/her new and important job?

Int'l Bus. Machines Corp. v. Papermaster, No. 08-CV-9078 (KMK), 2008 WL 4974508, *8-10 (S.D.N.Y. Nov. 21, 2008).

Two key elements of that case, and perhaps critical aspects generally to a court's willingness to apply the inevitable disclosure doctrine, are (i) the degree to which the secrets known by the departing employee are foundational to the old employer's business and central to the job duties at the new company, and (ii) the extent to which the employee engaged in questionable behavior regarding those secrets. In *Bimbo Bakeries USA, Inc. v. Botticella*, 613 F.3d 102 (3rd Cir. 2010), the court applied Pennsylvania law and used the inevitable disclosure doctrine to affirm the lower court's injunction to prevent an employee leaving Bimbo from becoming a bakery operations vice president at Hostess Brands, Inc. The employee, Botticella, had run five Bimbo bakery facilities where Thomas' English Muffins were made. That product line generated about $500 million in annual sales for Bimbo. Botticella had access to Bimbo's formula and process code books for all Bimbo products and was one of only seven people who possessed all the information to replicate Thomas' "nooks and crannies" texture. Furthermore, after accepting the offer to join Hostess, Botticella continued to work at Bimbo without disclosing his agreement with Hostess, downloaded sensitive Bimbo documents, and attempted to restore deleted documents that had been downloaded previously.

In contrast, where the employee's knowledge of the old employer's secrets is not central to the new job, and the employee (as well as the new employer) has treated the old employer's IP with respect in the transition process and in the very design of the new job duties, a different result may occur. *See, e.g., Int'l. Bus. Machines Corp. v. Visentin*, 2011 WL 672025 (S.D.N.Y. Feb. 16, 2011) (denying a preliminary injunction).

Regardless of the applicability of the inevitable disclosure doctrine in a given jurisdiction, the prudent course is to restrict employees' use of a company's confidential information through an appropriate confidentiality and invention assignment agreement, which will be discussed in more detail later in this chapter.

QUESTIONS

---

1. What steps should a start-up company such as SoftCo take to reduce the risk of its trade secrets being disclosed when its proprietary trade secret information gives it a strong competitive advantage?
2. Considering the "reasonable specificity" versus "general pleading" doctrines, from SoftCo's perspective in bringing a misappropriation action, under what circumstances might it want to have the case tried in a reasonable specificity jurisdiction? In a general pleading jurisdiction?
3. Review the quoted language from *Int'l Bus. Machines Corp. v. Papermaster,* where the court enjoined Papermaster from going to work for Apple, Inc. Do you agree that there is no distinction between the former employee's "technical know-how" and the former employer's trade secrets?

---

3. Patents

A *patent* is an exclusive property right granted to an inventor in exchange for sharing the details of an invention with the world. That is important to keep in mind — the contents of a patent application will be published. Seeking a patent, therefore, is largely incompatible with maintaining a trade secret.

Three types of patents exist: *utility* patents (the most common and widespread by far, which will be explored more thoroughly in the next few paragraphs); *design* patents (for new, original, and ornamental designs for functional items) (35 U.S.C. §171); and *plant* patents (for invented or discovered and asexually reproduced distinct plant varieties) (35 U.S.C. §161). Utility patents can cover four areas: processes, machines, articles of manufacture, or compositions of materials. These categories, together, cover most everything people make and the means for their manufacture. Abstract ideas and laws of nature, physics, or mathematics are not patentable. A "process" primarily applies to industrial or technical acts or methods. 35 U.S.C. §§100(b) and 101. Process patents have been the focus of some significant recent developments in patent law (to be touched on later in this section under the heading "Developments in Patent Law") as they often lie at the intersection between patentable inventions and abstract ideas or mere human activities.

The authority of the U.S. government to award patents is set in the Constitution:

> The Congress shall have Power . . . To promote the Progress of Science and useful Arts, by securing for limited Times to Authors and Inventors the exclusive Right to their respective Writings and Discoveries;

U.S. Const. art. I, §8.

It is important to emphasize that, unlike other types of IP, no patent rights result simply from the creation or use of a patentable invention. The only way to obtain a U.S. patent is by filing an application with the U.S. Patent and Trademark Office (USPTO). In fact, disclosure of an invention or its introduction into commerce has serious legal implications, which are discussed in the next few paragraphs.

What Can Be Patented?   Federal law provides a definition of what is "patentable." The relevant statute provides: "Whoever invents or discovers any new and useful process, machine, manufacture, or composition of matter, or any new and useful improvement thereof, may obtain a patent therefore, subject to the conditions and requirements of this title." 35 U.S.C. §101.

A patentable invention must be novel, useful, and non-obvious. 35 U.S.C. §§101-103. "Novel" means that the invention was not known to others before the effective filing date of the patent application. In the patent application, the applicant is required to disclose to the USPTO "prior art" known to him/her/it. "Prior art" is the term used in patent law to refer to publicly available information about previously existing inventions that are related to the invention upon which the patent is now being sought. The current invention has to be effectively distinguished from the prior art, otherwise it will fail the "novel" requirement.

The "useful" requirement is intended to restrict patents to practical inventions, not theories or ideas. The patent application must show how the invention can be manifested in reality and that it actually *does* something.

The third requirement, that the subject of the application be "non-obvious," is measured against the knowledge of a person having ordinary skill in the invention's area of technology. The purpose of the standard is to require patents to be appreciably different from the prior art; a new invention cannot just rearrange the pieces from the prior art without making any substantive difference.

The Leahy-Smith America Invents Act.   As of March 16, 2013, with the effectiveness of all elements of the amendments to Article 35 of the U.S. Code adopted through the Leahy-Smith America Invents Act (AIA), the U.S. shifted from a "first to invent" patent system to a "first inventor to file" system. The difference in the systems can be seen in an example: Inventor Carlos creates an invention in May, works on it while preparing a patent application, then files the application in August. Inventor Elizabeth independently creates the same invention (no copying) in June and files her patent application in July. Under the pre-2013 system, Carlos, with good record keeping, could show he was the first to invent and be awarded the patent. Under the AIA, however, Elizabeth, as the first inventor to file, would be awarded the patent.

An exception to this outcome under the AIA would be triggered if, after the May creation of the invention, Carlos published a paper on it or showed it to potential customers at a trade show, and either act took place before Elizabeth filed her patent application in July. The result of this sequence of events is that Carlos's application would be honored and Elizabeth's would be rejected. The reason is that the disclosure, use, or sale of an invention by an inventor anywhere in the world is "prior art" as to other inventors. While that disclosure, use, or sale starts a one-year clock running for Carlos to make an effective patent filing, it has the advantage for Carlos of being prior art to others, *but not to him*. However, after one year, the disclosure becomes prior art to everybody, including Carlos, if he does not get his application on file by the one-year deadline, rendering the invention not patentable *by anyone*. 35 U.S.C. §102(a) and (b).

These deadline rules for filing a patent application are important for the non-IP counsel to know and communicate to the client. Matters are complicated by the fact that disclosure, use, or sale by the inventor can be an advantage under U.S. law by precluding other inventors from making effective filings, but can be problematic outside the United States, where the general rule is that a patent application has to be on file *on or before* the date the invention is disclosed or introduced into commerce.

Obtaining a Patent. Because the AIA's transition to a "first inventor to file" system creates a race to the filing window at the USPTO, the initial patent filing often is made using a "provisional application," which can be shorter and less formal (and thus less expensive) than a non-provisional application, although it still must meet all the disclosure requirements of a non-provisional application. The provisional application establishes an effective filing date for the application, so long as it is supplemented with a full, non-provisional application within one year. 35 U.S.C. §111(b).

Preparing a patent application and responding to comments from the examiner at the USPTO is referred to as "patent prosecution." It is a highly specialized legal task that should be left to experts registered with the USPTO as patent lawyers or "agents" (non-lawyer application-preparers and prosecutors). The application sets forth the "claims"; that is, the elements of the invention for which patent protection is sought. A patent application may have only a few separate claims that make up the patentable elements of the invention, or it may have hundreds. After review, comment (normally followed by revision and supplementation), and publication of the application, which usually takes at least two years and often quite a bit longer, the USPTO may grant a patent. Patents are valid for 20 years from the date of the original filing, so the longer it takes to convince the USPTO that the patent should be issued, the shorter the time the patent is effective. 35 U.S.C. §154(a)(2). The life of the patent can be extended, however, if a delay in issuing the patent was caused by inaction at the USPTO. 35 U.S.C. §154(b).

As a property right, generally speaking, a patent may be used, asserted against an alleged infringer, sold, licensed, pledged as security, or simply abandoned. The specific right granted by a U.S. patent is the right to exclude others from making, using, offering for sale, or selling the invention within the United States, or importing the invention into the United States. 35 U.S.C. §271(a). Significantly, the grant of a patent does not give the inventor the right to make or use the invention. The grant of a patent does not circumvent other patent holders' rights or other laws that may make the manufacture or sale of an item illegal. Instead, a patent merely protects the IP involved from unauthorized use.

A patent is effective only in the jurisdiction in which it was issued. An important strategic consideration, then, is *where* to file patent applications. As each application requires separate legal and filing fees, pursuing worldwide patent coverage quickly becomes an expensive proposition. In addition, after a patent is issued, most jurisdictions require payment of periodic "maintenance fees" that increase over the life of the patent. *See* 35 U.S.C. §41(c). Failure to pay these fees on a timely basis causes the issuing jurisdiction to treat the patent as having been abandoned and terminate its effectiveness. Deciding where to file patent applications is normally based on a handful of considerations, including the nature of what is being patented; where the product will be sold;

where the product will be used; where competitive products are manufactured; and where patent rights, once obtained, can be effectively enforced.

A general business counsel needs to remind clients that the right to file a patent application is *owned by the inventor.* Ownership of IP is of particular importance in the business world, where companies act through the work of their employees. Contrary to what may seem obvious, the fact that a company paid someone to create something does not necessarily mean the company owns that creation; the employer or principal must have obtained an assignment to the rights under a patent application from the inventor-employee or contractor. This assignment is an important element of the typical confidentiality agreement used by many companies, which will be examined later in this chapter. Clear and exclusive ownership to a patent is important because if a patent is jointly owned, each owner has full authority to utilize or license the patent without the consent of the other owners. 35 U.S.C. §262.

In addition to adhering to the U.S. and foreign deadlines for getting patent applications on file and establishing a system for obtaining assignments of invention rights from employees and consultants, the general business counsel should note that a client can inadvertently infringe on patents belonging to others. Knowledge of the third party's patent is not necessary to infringe. 35 U.S.C. §271. As a result, a client is well advised to be aware of the patents that apply in the general area of its business so that it may avoid infringement, for example, in developing new products.

It should be apparent that the applicable law is complex and technical, so the advice of a patent specialist is needed whenever a patent is relevant to the operation of a business. Inventors and transactional lawyers can find free patent information at the following websites:

- USPTO: http://patft.uspto.gov/
- Google: http://www.google.com/?tbm = pts&hl = en

The USPTO also maintains Patent and Trademark Depository Libraries throughout the United States and provides a list of their locations on its website at http://www.uspto.gov/products/library/ptdl/locations/index.jsp.

Remedies.   Remedies for patent infringement include injunctive relief as well as damages — no less than a reasonable royalty — that may be trebled at the court's discretion where the infringement is willful. Attorneys' fees also may be awarded. 35 U.S.C. §§283-285.

The threat of treble damages for willful infringement has led to the practice of obtaining non-infringement or invalidity opinion letters from IP counsel. When a company becomes concerned that it may be engaging in infringing activity, it can retain an IP counsel to look at the relevant patents and the potentially infringing activity and provide a legal opinion on infringement, which may address the validity of the outstanding patents. If an opinion concluding that there is no infringement is done with care and is properly presented, it can provide evidence later that the infringement was not willful. One cannot, however, infer willfulness from the absence of an opinion.

Developments in Patent Law.   The entire arena of patent law and practice has changed dramatically since the advent of the semiconductor and the technology associated with computers and the Internet. As these massive technology shifts really began to hit over the same time period that lawyer compensation in private practice increased perhaps fivefold, the USPTO has struggled to adapt, to recruit staff, and, basically, to keep up. In addition, the USPTO has become understaffed simply in comparison to the number of applications received. For example, 108,648 patent applications were filed in 1978, while in 2012, the USPTO received 576,763. U.S. PATENT AND TRADEMARK OFFICE, U.S. PATENT STATISTICS CHART CALENDAR YEARS 1963–2012, *available at* http://www.uspto.gov/web/offices/ac/ido/oeip/taf/us_stat.htm.

As a consequence of those struggles, the quality and sophistication of the USPTO's review of some patent applications over the last 30 years has been wanting, and some patents were issued that are difficult to justify. One particularly touchy area is "business method" patents, where the USPTO was lax in allowing basic business behaviors to be deemed patentable. The USPTO also has been criticized for not grasping what is obvious in the evolution of emerging technologies. Litigation (such as *KSR International Co. v. Teleflex Inc.*, 550 U.S. 398 (2007) (*KSR*)) and the USPTO's nonbinding guidelines (*see* MANUAL OF PATENT EXAMINING PROCEDURE (MPEP) §2141) show that the "nonobvious" requirement has become more difficult to meet. The *KSR* opinion, which is quoted in the guideline, states: "A person of ordinary skill in the art is also a person of ordinary creativity, not an automaton." *KSR* at 421. "[I]n many cases a person of ordinary skill will be able to fit the teachings of multiple patents together like pieces of a puzzle." *Id.* at 420; *see also* MPEP §2141, paragraph II.C. Note that the MPEP guidelines, as of February 2014, have not been updated to address the AIA's new terms.

Problems like these, as well as others, at the USPTO have encouraged the rise of an economic subculture referred to as "patent trolls" or, more politely, "non-practicing entities" (NPEs). These are people and companies who buy up old patent portfolios, often from insolvent or inactive companies, with no intention of actually using ("practicing") the IP productively. Instead, they examine the portfolios for any claims that may be more broadly applicable than was considered at the time the patent was issued, or that otherwise are arguably infringed. For example, do patent claims regarding television sets potentially apply to computer display devices? Does an early technique for translating global positioning system (GPS) coordinates onto a map apply to all navigation systems? The patent troll then identifies everyone that might be infringing on the broadly interpreted claim and begins filing lawsuits, using contingency fee counsel. Usually, the defendants quickly settle, acquiring licenses to the patent for relatively small amounts of money, but all those small sums can add up to hundreds of thousands, millions, or even hundreds of millions, of dollars across an entire industry.

Patent trolls are the bane of legitimate businesses in many industries, as they use the threat of high-cost litigation to shake down a payment from an accused "infringer." Unfortunately, there is usually not much a general business counsel can do when a client is sued by a patent troll other than urge the client to get past the outrage and settle for as little as possible. While fighting the suit on principle may seem correct, it is difficult to justify the business decision to spend several million dollars on litigation that can be settled for significantly less money.

A number of bills introduced in Congress during 2013 attempt to make it more difficult for NPEs to conduct litigation or more simple for operating companies to defend themselves. However, the political clout that is being brought to bear to thwart this proposed legislation may be insurmountable. First, definitional boundaries between litigation brought by trolls and by operating companies may be difficult to set in light of a recent series of expensive acquisitions of historical IP portfolios by "legitimate" companies, such as Google's $12.5 billion acquisition of Motorola's IP library. And, more cynically, too many members of the patent bar are making too much money from troll activity to make reform likely in the near future.

One step taken in the AIA addresses the quality of previously issued patents. The AIA creates new, streamlined, post-grant reviews that allow an accused infringer to more easily challenge the validity of patent claims that form the basis of the infringement claim. 35 U.S.C. §§311-329. In addition, the AIA gave the USPTO rulemaking authority to create additional patent review processes. Under that authority, the USPTO created an eight-year "Transitional Program for Covered Business Method Patents" (the "Transitional Program"), which allows a party sued for infringement to challenge the validity of an existing financial business methods patent in what is hoped will be a relatively short and definitive proceeding. *See Changes to Implement Inter Partes Review Proceedings, Post-Grant Review Proceedings, and Transitional Program for Covered Business Method Patents*, 77 Fed. Reg. 48680 (Aug. 14, 2012) (to be codified at 37 C.F.R. pt. 42). The Patent Trial and Appeals Board recently issued its first decision under the Transitional Program, nine months after the petition for review was filed. The opinion invalidated a number of patent claims it characterized as "[nothing] other than conventional, routine steps that are a consequence of implementing the abstract idea." *SAP America, Inc. v. Versata Development Group, Inc.*, CBM2012-0001, slip op. 32 (P.T.A.B. June 11, 2013).

In terms of new patent grants, one effort by the USPTO to rein in the scope of patent coverage can be seen in *Bilski v. Kappos*, 130 S. Ct. 3218, 561 US __, 177 L. Ed. 2d 792 (2010). The case arose after the USPTO denied a patent application on a technique to hedge for weather-related risks in commodities trading. The Supreme Court was unanimous in concluding that the process underlying the patent application was a non-patentable abstract idea. Unfortunately, three separate opinions present divided views on why that conclusion is correct. The Court rejected the notion that the exclusive test for patentability of a process turns on whether the invention: (i) is tied to a particular machine or apparatus (*Parker v. Flook*, 437 U.S. 584, 589 n.9 (1978)); or (ii) transforms a particular article into a different state or thing (*Diamond v. Diehr*, 450 U.S. 175, 192 (1981) and *Gottschalk v. Benson*, 409 U.S. 63, 67 (1972)). While the justices agreed that this "machine or transformation" test is not the exclusive inquiry on process patentability, all three opinions acknowledge that it is important, and perhaps often dispositive.

Thus, *Bilski* is clear in rejecting the patentability of human activity in gathering data and making calculations in the execution of an abstract idea. It does not, however, provide the hoped-for clarity on how the patentability of a process is to be analyzed. *Query*: The abstract idea addressed in the *Bilski* patent application was financial hedging. What would be the practical (and public policy) implications if financial hedging were determined to be patentable?

4. Copyrights

The same constitutional provision that establishes the authority of the U.S. government to grant patents, quoted at the beginning of the patent discussion above, also provides the authority to establish *copyrights*. Unlike patents, however, copyrights also exist in common law, outside the statutory registration requirements. The federal statutory basis for copyrights and copyright ownership is the U.S. Copyright Act, 17 U.S.C. §§101 et seq.

Copyright protection applies to original works of authorship that are presented in a fixed medium. *Id.* §102(a). The types of things covered include works involving words, graphics (including art and non-functional design), sounds, dramatic works, computer programs, sculpture and architecture. *Id.* The standard for "original" is minimal — quality is not an issue and only some modicum of originality is required. A compilation of public data, such as a phone book, would not be subject to copyright protection, nor would a multiplication table. *See, e.g., Feist Publications, Inc. v. Rural Telephone Service Co.*, 499 U.S. 340 (1991). However, these materials can be presented in formats, designs, or other graphic or audio means that may be copyrightable, even if their primary content is not. The fixed medium requirement means that the expression must exist for more than a transitory period of time. *See* U.S. COPYRIGHT OFFICE, CIRCULAR 1: COPYRIGHT BASICS (Mar. 1992).

Even if a company is not in the business of creating art, drama, architecture, or narrative works, it still may create marketing materials, advertising, instructional manuals, or other material where copyright protection may be appropriate.

Expressions vs. Ideas. The key issue regarding copyright protection is the distinction between the "expression," which is protectable, and the "idea," which is not. This is particularly important in dealing with computer software, where many lines of code simply state standardized commands for the tasks embodied in the software. The appearance of the program in operation, use of non-generic terminology, and unique approach taken to accomplish what the software does are subject to copyright protection. Copyright protection would not extend more generally to the way that the program addresses a particular routine task or to standard programming practices required by the operating environment.

A separate example of this distinction is two painters sitting side by side, painting the same rural scene. The content of the scene depicted in their paintings is not protectable, but the particular approach to expressing that content used by each artist is subject to copyright protection.

The Copyright Act and Registration. The Copyright Act establishes the rights of a copyright owner, the most significant of which are the right to reproduce and distribute a copyrighted work and the right to prepare derivative works, that is, works in a different form that are derived from or based on the original work, such as a movie from a play, or vice versa. 17 U.S.C. §106.

The Copyright Act also creates a process for registering copyrights and provides a set of statutory damages that allow a plaintiff to avoid having to prove up actual damages. *Id.* §§412, 502-505. A copyright registration must be filed before an infringement suit may be brought in federal court, *id.* §411, and registration must occur either before the infringement or not more than three months after the first publication by the owner in order to be able to obtain statutory damages with respect to an infringement. Registration also provides a rebuttable presumption of ownership and allows the owner to enlist government assistance in blocking the importation of infringing materials.

The process of registering a copyright is very straightforward and inexpensive compared to that of filing a patent application. Registration forms generally can be prepared and filed online with the U.S. Copyright office at http://www.copyright.gov at a nominal cost per registration of $35. The Copyright Office reviews the filing only to confirm that the correct registration form was used and properly completed, the material for which the copyright is sought has been provided, and the fee has been paid. There is no substantive examination for originality or novelty. Registration is effective upon completion of the filing, even though a certificate of registration may take a few months or longer to be delivered. However, it is important to keep in mind that the certificate is the evidence of registration, which is necessary in order to bring an action in federal court. For an additional fee, the Copyright Office will expedite examination and delivery of the certificate.

A copyright registration, unlike a patent filing, accommodates the trade secret elements of computer software by allowing a registrant to inform the Copyright Office that trade secrets are involved and to provide a redacted filing of the program source code, blocking the secret elements, or a filing of only a portion of the source code.

Different countries have different copyright laws, but a number of international accords have sought to make the global process of putting others on notice of a claimed copyright interest fairly uniform. In general, using the copyright symbol, "©", followed by the year of publication and the name of the owner, is sufficient in most jurisdictions to put recipients of the material on notice that a copyright is asserted. *See* 17 U.S.C §§406-410. Under the terms of the Universal Copyright Convention, it also is prudent to add "All Rights Reserved" if the material will be used outside the United States.

For works created on or after January 1, 1978, the duration of a copyright for an individual author is the life of the author plus 70 years. If the author is a corporation (see the "work-for-hire" discussion below), the copyright protection lasts for 95 years from first publication or 120 years from creation, whichever expires first. Other time periods apply to other situations — a chart detailing the various duration periods is provided at http://copyright.cornell.edu/resources/publicdomain.cfm.

Determining the identity of the author is important not only for the duration issue but also because the author is the owner of the copyright and, as such, the only party that may seek to register it, unless ownership has been assigned to another party. 17 U.S.C. §408. As with patents, joint owners each may exploit or license this IP property right. *See* 17. U.S.C. §101 (defining "joint work"); and §106 (regarding rights of ownership).

"Work-for-Hire" Doctrine.   As noted in the patent discussion, companies work through their employees but IP laws generally contemplate that the creator of a new thing is the owner of that thing. It is important, therefore, that a company have a mechanism for obtaining ownership of new IP that has been created for it by an employee. The Copyright Act sets out a number of rules for what it defines as "work-for-hire" that, without a further assignment, belongs to the employer. The most important of these rules is that work prepared by an employee within the scope of his/her employment belongs to the employer. *Id.* §101 (defining "work made for hire"). As more companies use contract labor, this can be more problematic than might first appear. Regarding non-employees, the definition provides that the work must be one of a list of items (consisting of a contribution to a collective work, part of a motion picture or audio visual work, a translation, a supplementary work, a compilation, an instructional text, a test, answer materials for a test, or an atlas) and that the parties must have a written agreement reciting that the work is a "work-for-hire." If the work does not appear on the list, the employer or contractor must obtain an assignment in writing of the copyright interest in the work created. *Id*.

Note that the list does not include computer programs or stand-alone works of authorship. Companies routinely use third-party service providers to prepare things like advertising copy, graphic designs, and computer programs. Software companies frequently use independent-contractor "coders" who take a functional outline for a program and do all the tedious work of preparing the pages and pages of step-by-step program instructions that accomplish the tasks shown in the outline. Yet, despite the fact that the company explained to the service provider or independent contractor exactly what it wanted, and paid for the result, it is not the "author" and therefore is not the owner of the copyright to that work product, absent an assignment in writing.

While the Copyright Act provides protections to employers through the "work-for-hire" doctrine, an appropriate agreement between a company and its employees is still very useful in order to close the door on any later argument that a company's "work-for-hire" claim is somehow defective. And because the doctrine has very limited application outside of the employer/employee relationship, the discussion below on confidentiality and invention assignment agreements is particularly important when a company relies on non-employees to develop portions of its IP. *Query*: How will the "work-for-hire" doctrine affect Joan and Michael and SoftCo?

Copyright Infringement.   *Copyright infringement* is the unauthorized exercise of one or more of the copyright holder's rights, which usually means copying or making derivative works. Unlike patent infringement, copyright infringement requires proof of copying. The key elements to proof of copying are access to the protected work and substantial similarity between the protected work and the allegedly infringing work. Remember, copyright protects against the expression of an idea, not the idea itself. As a result, similar works may be created without infringement if they were done independently. If, however, works are substantially similar and the alleged infringer had access to the protected work, a strong case for infringement exists.

In identifying infringing acts, there are a couple of concepts to keep in mind. When you buy Avenged Sevenfold's "Hail to the King," you own a copy of that work, but do not own a copyright to it. You may sell your copy, but you may not reproduce its contents for resale unless you fall under the "fair use" doctrine. "Fair use" includes reproducing material for purposes of criticism, comment, news reporting, research, or education. 17 U.S.C. §107. The factors considered in determining if a use is "fair" are the nature of the use (commercial versus nonprofit educational); whether the work is factual or fictional (facts can only be expressed in certain ways, so in non-fiction more similarity may be permissible); the extent of the copying (the larger the portion of the whole, the greater the risk of it not being fair); and the effect on the commercial market or value of the copyrighted work.

DJs, for example, can "sample" songs without infringement because the pieces used are short and the use probably enhances the commercial value of the original work. A library at a nonprofit law school has broad ability to copy a law review article for dissemination to students or faculty, but a law firm copying the same article for the lawyers in the firm may well be infringing. As there is no bright-line test for "fair use," it is an infringement defense that may be relied upon only with caution.

One way software developers try to produce competitive products without copyright infringement is through a "clean room." Using this method, a company buys a copy of the software product it wants to compete with and has a team of its people work with it extensively in order to identify its features and characteristics. They then prepare a summary of the product's key elements and meet with IP counsel to confirm that nothing in their product summary terms or processes represents a violation of the software license or protectable rights of the software's creator. Having determined that they have prepared a non-infringing product outline, they deliver it to management, who has put together a separate developer team of software engineers, each of whom has sworn that he or she has not seen or used the product upon which the new development will be based.

The developer group, working in an isolated environment — no contact with any people or circumstances that might contaminate their perfect lack of knowledge regarding the product they are trying to emulate — then independently creates a functionally equivalent product. They are physically segregated from other employees in a "clean room" for the duration of the project and periodically reaffirm non-access to the third-party product. Using a management intermediary for communication (to avoid direct contact between the first team and the clean-room group), and in consultation with IP counsel to avoid instructions that could lead to infringement, management provides the product criteria to the developer team. So long as the information and specifications they are given is carefully managed, the developers can create a knock-off product without infringement because they have never seen the expression of the original product and therefore are not copying it.

Damages.   If a registered copyright owner is able to show infringement, it may seek actual damages or statutory damages (up to $30,000 per infringement, or $150,000 if the infringement is willful); obtain injunctive relief, including impoundment and destruction of the infringing materials and the apparatus for duplication (molds, master sets, etc.); and be awarded legal fees at the court's discretion. 17. U.S.C §§502-505.

5. Trademarks

The final major area of IP rights is trademark and trade dress law, which protects the goodwill associated with the source of a product or service. A *trademark* is a name, symbol, device, or design used in commerce to indicate the source of goods and to distinguish them from goods from another source. A service mark is the same thing, just applicable to services, but the rights are effectively the same. When we refer to trademarks or "marks" or branding, we mean to include service marks, and to avoid repetition, when we refer to products or goods we mean that to include services. Trade dress is a close cousin of trademark. It relates more generally to aspects of the appearance of a product or package that symbolizes the source of the product.

The purpose of a trademark is to prevent others from confusing the marketplace regarding the source of a product. It is important to keep in mind that marks must be associated with goods. A corporation's name usually is treated under trademark law as a "trade name" and is not, standing alone, subject to trademark protection. 15 U.S.C. §1127. However, a corporate name, when used to identify goods, can be protected as a trademark. It usually is prudent, then, in selecting an enterprise name to pick one that may be used as a trademark when attached to the company's products. It also is important to recognize that trademarks go to identity of source only — they do not protect against the creation of similar products.

Unlike in most other countries, where registration of a trademark is required in order to protect it, in the U.S. trademark rights are created by the use of the mark and can be maintained by its ongoing use. However, use of a mark creates protection for it only within the geographic area of its use. As a consequence, prior to the advent of effective Internet search engines, it was very difficult to be sure that an unregistered mark was not in use by someone else somewhere across the country.

Trademark Registration.   In the United States, trademarks may be unregistered, registered on a state-by-state basis (though not all states issue registrations), or registered federally. Federal registration is done with the USPTO and is usually appropriate if a company intends to operate in multiple states. Any business using a website for sales should view its business as multi-state. When a new business intends to use its corporate name in association with its products, it may register that branding once the mark is in use with the products or it may register the mark earlier through an "intent to use" application.

An "intent to use" application allows the company to get the registration process moving before the products are ready. Having a trademark registration on file provides constructive notice to the public that the registrant claims ownership of the mark so that it may be protected while the product development is completed.

Another advantage to registering a mark is that it establishes a legal presumption of the registrant's ownership and exclusive right to use the mark nationwide in association with the products or services listed on the application. That presumption can be overcome, however, by another person's demonstration of continuing use of a mark from a time preceding the date of the registration filing.

In addition, a federally registered mark may be enforced though an infringement action in federal court and may be filed with the U.S. Immigration and Customs Enforcement office to prevent the importation of infringing goods.

Having filed for U.S. registration also can be useful for foreign registrations. Most countries use a "first to register" system, in contrast to the "first to use" approach used in the United States, so that prior use, which creates rights to the mark in the United States, does not apply internationally. If another person makes an earlier filing, then that person is presumed to have prior rights. However, if a foreign registration is filed within six months of the U.S. registration filing, under treaty, most countries will treat the filing with their trademark office as having been made on the date of the U.S. filing.

A trademark may be asserted simply by putting the designation "TM" (or "SM" for service marks) next to the mark. This puts an observer of the mark on notice that the user of the mark claims a trademark interest. The symbol "®" or the term "registered" may be used only after a trademark has been registered by the USPTO. Those designations may not be used while the application is pending, nor may they be used with respect to any product or mark other than what was covered in the registration.

The validity of a trademark rests on its distinctiveness in identifying the origin of the products it is associated with. This means that valid trademarks for the same, or very similar, marks can exist where they are associated with unrelated products because the likelihood of confusion in the marketplace is low. Also, a mark that may be unprotectable when associated with one product may receive strong protection when identifying another product. The word "apple," for example, in 1976 would be unprotectable as a fruit identifier; a strong mark for computers; and an infringing mark if used in connection with music publication, as the Beatles had already been using it in their music business for over ten years.

Before adopting a mark, it is a very good idea to do a trademark search. You can search the USPTO's registry or use a professional search firm, which, while representing an out-of-pocket expense, can be a very useful investment. It also is fruitful to search the Internet for use of the desired mark. These steps will prevent the investment of time and money in an inherently unprotectable or infringing mark. When filing for a federal registration, the application requires the applicant to certify (to its knowledge, subject to punishment by fine or imprisonment) that no one has the right to use the applied-for mark in a way such that the mark would create confusion for that prior, rightful user.

When an application to register a mark is filed, the USPTO checks the registry of existing marks to see if there is any conflict in using the mark to identify the products named in the application. The standards used to determine whether a mark is distinctive enough to be granted trademark protection are (i) whether there is a similarity with an existing mark and (ii) the commercial relationship between the products or services listed in the application and those to which the existing mark applies. The USPTO can reject an application even if the applied-for mark is not the same as an existing mark or if the products the marks are associated with are different. The issue is whether there is a likelihood of confusion. Similar marks and generally related goods are enough to deny a registration.

"Weak" vs. "Strong" Trademarks. When selecting or developing a mark, as a corollary to the question of whether the mark will be valid and a registration successful, the client should consider whether the selected mark will be "strong," that is, highly protectable, or "weak," or less protectable. Trademark law has developed a continuum of "distinctiveness" factors that measure whether a valid mark may be created and, if so, how protectable it will be. Starting with the least distinctive, these factors begin with *generic terms*. Generic terms are not protectable, which is why "apple" cannot be trademarked when used for fruit. This can become a trap for the successful because when a product name begins to be used to describe the product category, it is going down the path towards becoming generic, charmingly referred to as "genericide." The words *aspirin* and *escalator* were trademarks at one time. The people who make Kleenex® worry that their brand leadership could cause them to lose trademark protection for their tissues. There must be mixed feelings at the Google, Inc. headquarters when they hear people referring to searching the Internet as "googling."

The next category of distinctiveness is *descriptive terms*. Trademark protection does not extend to terms that are merely descriptive as to an aspect, quality, ingredient, purpose, or use of a product. This limitation exists even where the descriptive terms do not accurately describe the product. If Joan and Michael wanted to call their business

"Software, Inc." they would run into the descriptive terms problem in seeking to use that name as a trademark. Even "SoftCo" might be viewed as descriptive. If they wanted to call the company "Flowers by the Bunch," they would have the same problem, even though the description is not very apt for a software business. It might be possible, however, for them to establish a valid trademark if the term has "secondary meaning," that is, if they have used "Flowers by the Bunch" in connection with their products for over five years and they can present persuasive evidence that customers associate the products with that mark and connect the products with the company. 15 U.S.C. §1052(f). They also could argue that the name is arbitrary (which we will address in a moment) in light of its total misdescription of the product. Descriptiveness is a problem companies like International Business Machines Corporation have had to overcome.

Somewhere in this region of the continuum are things like geographic descriptions and surnames. These terms are normally useable as trademarks, but only because registered rights are not often pursued because they are not very protectable. To the extent a geographic reference is descriptive — "Illinois-Wisconsin Trucking Service" — it probably will not be protectable. A name like United States Steel Corporation also is difficult to use as a trademark as it suffers from being both descriptive and geographic. A surname is often not a good trademark, but long and exclusive association with a particular product can make a surname protectable. It would be difficult for a Mr. Johnson, for example, just getting into the household products business, to use his name for a trademark on his wax. The same would be true of a new car manufacturer named Ford. However, Mr. Johnson and Ms. Ford might be able to use their surnames if either were to go into, for example, the computer printer business.

Moving into the range of more easily protectable marks, next on the continuum are *suggestive terms*. Suggestive terms do not describe the product, but instead allow the observer's imagination or association to reach a conclusion regarding the nature of the product. They are less direct than descriptive terms, yet allow a name to reflect an aspect of the product. Eveready® batteries and Vise-Grip® tools are examples of suggestive terms. To the extent that a geographic reference is used to suggest something other than merely geography, such as an attitude, or style, or a product characteristic, geography can slide along the continuum into a more protectable "suggestive term" position. For example, Outback Steakhouse™ uses a regional association for style and attitude and Shasta® beverages, named after a snow-covered mountain, suggest cool refreshment.

At the most protectable end of the continuum are *arbitrary and fanciful* terms. These are the most protectable as trademarks because they have no meaning associated with the product, or have no meaning at all, other than to serve as identifiers. Joan and Michael might argue that Flowers by the Bunch is an arbitrary name rather than descriptive. They would assert that if they were florists, it would be descriptive, but for software, it is arbitrary. Red Bull® (drinks), Quaker® (foods), and Apple® (computers) are all terms used arbitrarily to describe a product having nothing to do with the terms. Fanciful terms are those that are made up. Pepsi-Cola®, Exxon®, and Google® are examples. These can be very strong trademarks, but the risk is that, having no meaning, potential customers will not understand them and cannot be trained to associate them with the product.

Trademark Infringement and Other Causes of Action.   There are several causes of action possible under trademark law. Trademark infringement occurs when a person uses a product identification that "is likely to cause confusion, or to cause mistake, or to deceive as to the affiliation, connection, or association of such person with another person . . ." 15 U.S.C. §1125(a)(1)(A). The issue of what is "likely to cause confusion" has been litigated repeatedly. Often quoted for setting forth the factors to be considered is the Federal Circuit Court of Appeals decision in *In re du Pont de Nemours & Co.*, 476 F.2d 1357 (C.C.P.A. 1973). The court reversed the decision of the Trademark Trial and Appeal Board refusing to allow DuPont to acquire trademark rights in the name "Rally" for a car wax because of an existing "Rally" trademark registration for an all-purpose detergent.

In its decision in *In re du Pont*, the court asserted that the issue of confusion relates to the products in the marketplace, regardless of the nature of the marks themselves. It listed 13 factors — without specifying any priority or weighting — that should be taken into account in determining if there is a likelihood of confusion, including the similarity of the marks; the similarity of the products; the similarity of the means of distribution of the products and the nature of the buying decision for each product; the fame of the prior mark, the range of products it is used on, and the existence of other similar marks; actual evidence of confusion or the lack thereof by customers and the potential extent of confusion; and the course of conduct between the registrant and the owner of the existing mark. *Id.* at 1361. The purpose of the listed factors is to look at the practical effect of the use of the marks in the marketplace.

In addition to infringement, another avenue for trademark liability is a false designation of origin, false or misleading description of fact, or false or misleading representation of fact, which:

> in commercial advertising or promotion, misrepresents the nature, characteristics, qualities, or geographic origin of his or her or another person's goods, services or commercial activities . . .

15 U.S.C. §1125(a)(1)(B).

This reflects strongly the marketplace protection aspect of trademark law, to the point where it abuts the Federal Trade Commission's oversight of unfair trade practices and false labeling matters. The quoted language in part relates to the trademark version of "fair use," which allows a person to use another's trademark in comparative advertising. Significantly, this requirement that all statements must be factually accurate and not misleading applies to *both* products. Other "fair use" frequently seen is in news coverage and speech protected by the First Amendment.

Trademark Dilution.   In addition, a cause of action lies in trademark "dilution." Dilution occurs when, after a mark has become famous, someone acts to diminish the uniqueness of the well-known trademark and that conduct:

> is likely to cause dilution by blurring or dilution by tarnishment of the famous mark, regardless of the presence or absence of actual or likely confusion, of competition, or of actual economic injury.

Id. §1125(c)(1).

In contrast to infringement, where there is a likelihood of confusion regarding the source of the product, dilution is aimed at unauthorized-party use of "famous" marks for other purposes. "Dilution by blurring" is defined as "association arising from the similarity between a mark or trade name and a famous mark that impairs the distinctiveness of the famous mark." *Id.* §1125(c)(2)(B). One of the elements the statute directs courts to consider in determining if dilution by blurring exists is the extent to which "the owner of the famous mark is engaging in substantially exclusive use of the mark." *Id.* §1125(c)(2)(B)(iii). Finally, "dilution by tarnishment" is defined as an "association arising from the similarity between a mark or tradename and a famous mark that harms the reputation of the famous mark." *Id.* §1125(c)(2)(C).

It is unlikely that someone would be confused regarding the source of Exxon computer printers, so it would be difficult for ExxonMobil Corporation to argue trademark infringement. On the other hand, Exxon is a well-known name that does not exist in nature, so there is no reason for anyone to use it other than to take advantage of the public's general familiarity with the name. Because the unique nature and value of the Exxon® mark is diluted by blurring when it is used by others, and might be diluted by being tarnished if the Exxon printers are low quality junk that amount to little more than a fraud on consumers, even if the other party's use is not confusing, ExxonMobil is entitled to seek injunctive relief to halt the dilutive behavior, as well as damages if they exist, without having to show that there was any intention to infringe.

QUESTIONS

1. Would you recommend that Joan and Michael reconsider naming their company "SoftCo" in light of trademark concerns? What are the arguments against using a name like SoftCo?
2. If Joan and Michael chose a "fanciful" name, while it would make a stronger mark, what problems (and potential costs) might result from such choice?

B. Protecting Intellectual Property by Contract

In the preceding discussion, particularly on the topic of trade secrets, we noted a number of physical restrictions and protection policies that companies often use to restrict access to and dissemination of their confidential information. While implementing sensible restrictions on access to proprietary information is useful in preventing its inappropriate dissemination, the earlier discussion noted that sometimes IP simply has to be used or shared. Under these circumstances, prudence and practical restrictions often must be combined with a set of contractual constraints so that key proprietary information can be used or shared under a set of rules and penalties that reduces the risks to the disclosing entity. We look first at the way this situation is handled with third parties, including vendors, customers, and potential strategic partners, and then we turn to employees, contractors, and other ongoing service providers.

1. *Third-Party Non-Disclosure Agreements*

A company may find it necessary to disclose confidential information to third parties under a number of situations. It may have to provide confidential information to a vendor of materials, parts, or of manufacturing services, for example, in order to ensure that the vendor can properly meet the company's requirements. Particular specifications for materials supplied can involve communication of trade secrets that a company would not want a vendor sharing with its other customers (who may be competitors). Even order quantities could provide a competitor with information about confidential sales projections or inventory levels, and information that may have to be disclosed in just a month or two in a public company periodic financial disclosure, for example, still may have proprietary value until the time of that disclosure. The vendor may have to disclose to the customer techniques, quality control systems, production schedules, and capacity information, and the parties may agree to pricing, delivery schedules, and other data that they may mutually wish to protect.

When a company is not the customer but instead is the vendor, it may find it necessary to share its own confidential information during the sales process. If a company sells some sort of component or system that is to be included in a larger product, such as a disc brake caliper assembly for a car, both the company and its customer may have to provide confidential information regarding other related systems or assemblies, quantities, pricing, specifications, delivery timing, and other business information.

In either case, as part of ordinary commerce, it is likely to be in *both* parties' best interests to treat shared information as confidential. While a supply agreement, volume purchase agreement, specialty manufacturing agreement, private label product supply agreement, or whatever the final contractual arrangement might be called, is the best place to address these concerns on an ongoing basis, how do the parties start the conversation? How do the parties get comfortable with sharing enough data to know if they can do business together? How about a strategic relationship that may go beyond a simple supply arrangement?

In each of these situations, the parties typically enter into a *Non-Disclosure Agreement* (NDA). This is a usual and customary document that allows the parties to share information for the purpose of exploring a potential business relationship based on their mutual agreement not to use or disclose anything confidential that they may learn about each other in the course of their discussions. If the relationship is consummated, then the definitive agreements documenting the relationship normally will supersede the NDA and address confidentiality as well as a whole range of other IP-related issues. If the parties decide that they do not want to go forward together, the NDA provides them with rules, protections, and remedies regarding the confidential information they shared during their preliminary discussions.

In the discussion that follows, we work through the sample NDA that begins on page 722 in Appendix B (the "Sample NDA").

Parties and Purpose.   The first issues to resolve in preparing an NDA are to get the parties right and to express clearly the permitted use of the information being delivered under the agreement. Getting the parties right means knowing what entity you are dealing with and ensuring that the correct entity is contractually bound. Concern about binding a corporate group or the corporate entity that has the assets is typically addressed in the provisions addressing internal disclosure and use. (*See* §8 of the Sample NDA.) So long as that provision requires every recipient of confidential information to take it subject to the terms of the NDA, it should not be necessary to enter into a separate NDA with every entity in a corporate group that might be involved in a preliminary discussion.

Looking at the terms of the Sample NDA, you will see that the purpose of the NDA is generally stated in the Recitals, while the specific restrictions on use and dissemination of confidential information are set forth in Section 3. As part of the Recitals, some lawyers (particularly when representing the party receiving most of the confidential information) like to include a sentence stating more specifically the point of the parties' meetings, rather than a generic reference to a "business relationship," so that reasonable use is linked with a more direct statement of why the information was shared in the first place.

The Scope of "Confidential Information."   The "Confidential Information" definition in Section 1 of the Sample NDA lists some non-exclusive categories of information that are to be deemed Confidential Information. While the defined term might be "Proprietary Information" or "Restricted Information," the issue is to be sure that the scope of the coverage is sufficient. Where the company is in a specialized business, such as medical devices or machine tools, conforming language to the applicable industry terminology will be needed. Further, even when it seems that the parties' discussions will be very technical, it is entirely likely that business information will be discussed (plans, customer identities or needs, costs, development schedules, identities of key personnel, and so on) so the agreement should be broad enough to protect both technical and business information.

The Confidential Information definition ends by including the sort of information:

> that is disclosed by one party (the "Disclosing Party") to the other party (the "Receiving Party") or that is otherwise learned by the Receiving Party in the course of its discussions or business dealings with, or physical or electronic access to Confidential Information of, the Disclosing Party . . .

Note that this provision redefines the parties based on their conduct. They are each given short-titles in the introductory paragraph of the Sample NDA, but here they are redefined as "Disclosing Party" and "Receiving Party," and each party is expected to fall under both defined terms. This is a drafting approach that emphasizes the mutuality of the obligations and rights under the agreement by attaching those obligations and rights to the conduct of the parties rather than repeating identical personal obligations and rights for each party.

In contrast to this bilateral approach, a unilateral agreement can be appropriate where one side is doing all the disclosing and the other is just receiving, but bilateral agreements, perhaps because of the inherent ring of fairness the arrangement implies, are most often used. The reality in most prospective relationships is that both sides discuss what they are doing and how it might fit in with what the other side is doing, so even where most of the information is likely to flow in one direction, a bilateral agreement is usually appropriate.

The language quoted above provides that the NDA covers anything "disclosed" or "otherwise learned" in the course of the parties' dealings. The purpose of these words is to sweep up what may be observed simply by being at the other party's facility or getting limited access to its computer network. Sometimes things that are simply seen (for example, the nature of security and what is secured) can provide an informed party with some insight into what might be going on.

This language is usually closely negotiated because once the NDA gets away from covering stuff that can be put into a file, stamped "confidential," and locked up, parties get nervous that the scope of their obligations is beginning to get fuzzy. Note that the language of Section 1 of the Sample NDA continues from the quote above to say:

> and that has been identified as being proprietary and/or confidential or that by the nature of the circumstances surrounding the disclosure or receipt ought to be treated as proprietary and confidential.

Many parties will insist that any Confidential Information must be marked "confidential" (or the like) or it will not be covered. They do not want to be in the position of guessing what must be kept secret and not used. Often, in fact, this provision has additional language stating that, in order to be covered by the NDA, anything discussed or otherwise not delivered in a fixed medium that can be stamped "confidential" must be the subject of a follow-up communication within 30 days that "reduces to writing" the disclosure or "describes in reasonable detail" what the extra Confidential Information was. As it is virtually impossible to itemize each and every conceivably relevant element of the information that came up in a discussion, the requirement of reducing the disclosed Confidential Information to writing can become the point of dispute in litigation: Did the follow-up writing detail the confidential aspects of the discussion, demonstration, or whatever, with sufficient specificity? The "describes in reasonable detail" approach is usually seen as more practical.

In the negotiating process, a company has to keep in mind that if it is not comfortable with the contract terms, it may have to solve the problem by managing the process of sharing the company's information with a third party. If a company wanted, but was unsuccessful in negotiating for, the broad "otherwise learned" language, it should not invite the other side's representatives to visit its facility. There are plenty of hotels, airports, even law firms, with conference rooms that would be neutral sites where the parties could meet without fear of disclosing something unintentionally. And when the company's representatives go to that meeting, everything they take should be stamped "confidential" and one of the members of their party should be assigned the task of tracking all topics discussed and immediately following up with the required written notice identifying any supplemental Confidential Information that may have been delivered orally. Also, electronic files may have to be copied and delivered off-line so there is no potential for information delivery through even limited access to the company's computer network. Of course, these restrictions may inhibit the ability of the parties to conduct their inquiries and investigations, but if that is the case, it should become obvious to both sides and perhaps an amendment to the NDA with more flexible language may be agreed upon.

Section 2 of the Sample NDA separates out "Product Samples" as a distinct deliverable by a Disclosing Party. Other than emphasis, there is no major reason to have a separate provision for this subject; Product Samples could be covered in Section 1 by simply adding them to the list of Confidential Information.

Restrictions on Use and Disclosure.   Section 3 of the Sample NDA explicitly prohibits unauthorized disclosure of received Confidential Information or any use that is inconsistent with the purpose of the delivery of that information. It also prohibits any actions that are inconsistent with the Disclosing Party's ownership interest in the disclosed materials and specifies that no imputed license is created by delivering the Confidential Information, other than for use consistent with the purpose that led the parties to enter into the NDA. The issue is that the Disclosing Party does not in any way want to suggest that the disclosure terminates its exclusive proprietary interest in the disclosed materials. In connection with this issue, recall that as part of the trade secret discussion earlier in this chapter, we described the need for a company to take reasonable steps to protect its secrets.

Section 3, entitled "Use and Ownership of Confidential Information and Product Samples," states that:

(a) The Receiving Party, except as expressly provided in this Agreement, will not disclose Confidential Information to anyone without the Disclosing Party's prior written consent.

(b) The Receiving Party, except as expressly provided in this Agreement, will not distribute to anyone, disassemble, damage, destroy, reverse engineer, or otherwise treat any Product Samples in any way inconsistent with the Disclosing Party's ownership rights in such Product Samples.

(c) The Receiving Party will take all reasonable measures to protect and avoid the disclosure, dissemination or unauthorized use of Confidential Information or Product Samples including, at a minimum, those measures it takes to protect its own confidential information or products or goods of similar nature.

(d) The Receiving Party will not use, or permit others to use, Confidential Information or Product Samples for any purpose other than to evaluate the potential of a business relationship . . . [with the Disclosing Party].

(e) All Confidential Information and Product Samples will remain the exclusive property of the Disclosing Party, and the Receiving Party will have no rights, by license, or otherwise, to use the Confidential Information or Product Samples except as expressly provided herein.

These restrictions are typical and reflect the threefold concern a party has in disclosing its Confidential Information; namely, that (i) it will be used in an unauthorized way; (ii) it will be disclosed and used by a third party or become part of the public flow of information; and (iii) the Disclosing Party will lose its exclusive property rights to it, including the ability to continue to use it on an exclusive basis.

The standard of care set forth in subsection (c) is typical for these agreements, in that it calls for the Receiving Party to take reasonable measures (some would object to the word "all") to protect the Disclosing Party's Confidential Information, including at least those steps that are consistent with what the Receiving Party does to protect its own proprietary information of an equivalent nature.

Section 4 of the Sample NDA provides limitations on the obligations and duties with respect to Confidential Information provided in Section 3. The carve-outs listed in

Section 4 present the full range of what one normally sees in NDAs. Item (i) exempts information that is publicly available, which obviously is not truly confidential. This term protects the Receiving Party against the Disclosing Party that, in an abundance of caution, has over-used the "confidential" stamp.

Item (ii) of Section 4 provides that the restrictions of Section 3 do not apply to information that:

> can be shown by documentation to have been known to, or developed by, the Receiving Party prior to its receipt from the Disclosing Party;

This is the "we already had that" carve-out. Large organizations want this because they often do not know what people are doing in all their facilities around the world and do not want to be blocked from pursuing something that they already knew or had previously created.

Item (iii) is a "level playing field" provision, carving out information that:

> is rightfully received from a third party who did not acquire or disclose such information, goods or products by a wrongful or tortious act;

This means that if someone else out there has this supposedly Confidential Information on an unrestricted basis and the Receiving Party rightfully gets it from them, it will not have to treat it as Confidential Information. In other words, the NDA will not be a tool to restrict the use or disclosure of information that the Disclosing Party has already given to others without restriction.

Item (iv) provides a carve-out for "independent development," which is where the information:

> can be shown by documentation to have been developed by the Receiving Party without reference to any Confidential Information or Product Samples.

An "independent development" carve-out makes many Disclosing Parties very uncomfortable, partly because of activities like the "clean room" development described in the earlier copyright discussion. (Refer to section A.4, above.) While that scenario presumes the use of publicly available information to avoid copyright infringement and would clearly violate the terms of an NDA if it were applied to information received on a restricted-use basis, Disclosing Parties still get nervous about the prospect that the smallest exposure to their Confidential Information may lead to a shift in thinking that allows the Receiving Party to create the same discovery. On the other hand, why should a company be prohibited from using something that is later independently created for it, perhaps in a subsidiary thousands of miles away, by people who did not know about the discussions contemplated by the NDA? Again, this provision is often insisted upon by large organizations and most smaller companies end up agreeing to this carve-out, so long as the NDA's terms for internal dissemination of the Disclosing Party's Confidential Information and materials provide for access and disclosure only on a "need to know" basis and the Receiving Party documents who has access to the Confidential Information. Those caveats at least allow the Disclosing Party to examine later just how "independent" any subsequent independent development really was.

A related provision is Section 10, which expands on the idea that independent development, without violation of the NDA, is possible and that the NDA should not be interpreted as suggesting otherwise. Again, large organizations often request these sorts of provisions, perhaps for their notice value and to head off any unrealistic expectations that by signing an NDA they are barred from a particular product area.

Another limitation sometimes demanded by the Receiving Party's lawyers is a "Residuals" carve-out. This type of carve-out goes more to the scope of what constitutes Confidential Information rather than to the restrictions on use and disclosure of Confidential Information. This provision would say that, notwithstanding the NDA's restrictions on use of Confidential Information, the Receiving Party will be free to use "Residual Information" retained by its employees who had access to the Confidential Information. It would then go on to distinguish Residual Information from Confidential Information by defining Residual Information as:

> General information relating to ideas and techniques derived from or contained in the Confidential Information related to Receiving Party's products and activities that is retained in the memories of individual employees without external aids containing any of the Confidential Information.

The premise underlying this provision is that people cannot erase their memories. While that may be correct, this provision undermines the rest of the NDA by allowing a Receiving Party to say — "Yes, this product is derived from your Confidential Information, and no, we cannot show that we developed it independently or prior to seeing your materials, but we definitely did not breach the agreement because we gave back everything you gave us and only used what we remembered." Once the bologna starts getting sliced this thin ("ideas and techniques . . . contained in the Confidential Information" can be used because they were remembered instead of contained in written notes), protecting the Confidential Information becomes very difficult and, at the very least, the evidentiary issues become a litigation nightmare. *Query:* In what ways does a Residuals carve-out embody the concepts of the "inevitable disclosure" doctrine previously outlined in the trade secrets discussion in section A.2 of this chapter?

Non-Solicitation and No-Hire Covenants.   Section 5 of the Sample NDA is a fairly typical employee "non-solicitation" covenant. Some jurisdictions permit going a step further: a "no-hire" covenant. These restrictions assume that the discussions under the NDA will make it apparent who the key people are on both sides (those developing what is disclosed and those analyzing what is received), which is, itself, Confidential Information. Each party will have to show who its experts are, and neither wants the other to target those people for hiring. The "non-solicitation" provision is milder than a "no-hire" covenant, which in some jurisdictions (California, for example) is deemed an unfair trade practice. However, in jurisdictions that enforce employee non-compete agreements, no-hire covenants may be more favorably received. Although the non-solicitation provision prohibits targeting specific employees, if one of them should respond to a general posting on a web-based job site, then that employee was not solicited and the hiring cannot be stopped. Under a no-hire provision, however, the former employer would be able to enjoin even a hire initiated by the employee.

Additional Covenants.   Section 6 acknowledges that disclosure of Confidential Information may be required in some circumstances, most often by a court. The Receiving Party who is compelled by a court or other government authority to deliver information or material that is Confidential Information under the NDA does not violate the NDA by doing so if it discloses the minimum amount of Confidential Information necessary to honor the order of the compelling authority and gives the Disclosing Party notice and the opportunity to seek a protective order or other remedy. This provision is usually not controversial.

Section 7 requires compliance with laws, particularly export laws, in the retention and control by a Receiving Party of Confidential Information. Since it is generally acknowledged that law enforcement seizure of the delivered Confidential Information or Product Samples would not enhance the maintenance of confidentiality, this provision is not seen as controversial.

"Need to Know" and Management of Received Confidential Information. Section 8 of the Sample NDA, which limits access to Confidential Information to specific persons or entities, is a very important element of securing the information delivered to the Receiving Party. A number of different approaches can be taken to this section and it often is one of the most closely negotiated terms in an NDA. The version in the Sample NDA provides:

> The Receiving Party will restrict the possession, knowledge, development and use of Confidential Information and Product Samples to its employees, agents, subcontractors and entities controlled by or controlling it who have a need to know Confidential Information or require access to the Product Samples in connection with the purposes set forth in Section 3(d) above (collectively, "Personnel"). The Receiving Party's Personnel will have access only to the Confidential Information or Product Samples they need for such purposes. The Receiving Party will ensure that the Personnel comply with this Agreement and will promptly notify the Disclosing Party of any breach of this Agreement.

The first sentence requires the Receiving Party to limit access to the Delivering Party's materials only to those who have a "need to know" in connection with the potential relationship opportunity that prompted the parties to enter into the NDA in the first place. The next sentence hones in on the issue, saying those people who have a need to know may only have access to what they need for those limited purposes. The final sentence makes the Receiving Party responsible for the conduct of the "Personnel" (regardless of the nature of the formal relationship between those people and the Receiving Party) and also requires that it give notice to the Disclosing Party if it becomes aware that a breach has occurred.

An additional element often added to the first sentence is that the authorized Personnel all must have a confidential relationship with the Receiving Party. What the Disclosing Party usually is looking for is the existence of a confidentiality agreement between the Receiving Party and each person or entity having access to its Confidential Information. While the third sentence makes the Receiving Party responsible for all these people's acts, many lawyers find comfort in the fact that an existing confidential relationship means that the Personnel are on notice that they have a duty of confidentiality with respect to the Disclosing Party's Confidential Information. The language typically sought by the Disclosing Party states that access to the Confidential Information will be limited to:

employees, agents, subcontractors, and entities controlled by or controlling it, each having confidentiality obligations to the Receiving Party that are substantially of the same scope as those required by the NDA, and each having a need to know in connection with the evaluation of, or require access to, the Confidential Information and Product Samples in the furtherance of the purposes set forth in Section 3(d) above (collectively, the "Personnel").

For even more protection, some lawyers also want the Personnel to individually acknowledge that their access to the Confidential Information is subject to the terms of the NDA, which shall bind the conduct of the persons granted access. This can be accomplished through a sign-out sheet, with the NDA attached, providing that to get access to the restricted data, all prospective Personnel must sign up to honor the standards required by the NDA. Since access presumably would be in furtherance of each person's employer's objectives and therefore within the scope of employment, this sort of provision gives the Disclosing Party a basis for a claim against the employers of any Personnel who are not employed directly by the Receiving Party.

The additional benefit of this approach is that it is only a short step away from an access log, which requires (or allows) the Receiving Party to track who reviewed or used the restricted material. A log can provide useful evidence of both the Receiving Party's supervision of its obligations as well as the identities of the people who saw the restricted information. As noted previously, that information can support, or may undercut, a subsequent claim of "independent development."

Section 9 of the Sample NDA provides that, upon the written request of the Disclosing Party, all materials containing Confidential Information are to be returned or destroyed, as directed by the Disclosing Party. Often only samples and devices are returned, while all media on which hard copy or electronic copies of the materials that were delivered, as well as notes and analyses prepared by the Receiving Party, are destroyed. A variation on this requires a signed certification from the Receiving Party that it has in fact destroyed all materials not returned to the Disclosing Party.

Remedies — Injunctions. Section 11 of the Sample NDA provides for remedies in case the NDA is breached, including, in addition to all other remedies that may be available, the right to injunctive relief. Injunctive relief is critical in confidentiality situations because of the need to control the exclusive right to use the information, which means stopping any unauthorized use and any conduct that may lead to further dissemination of the information. The relevant provision provides:

> The Receiving Party acknowledges that [unauthorized disclosure or use of Confidential Information] could cause irreparable harm to the Disclosing Party for which monetary damages may be difficult to ascertain or an inadequate remedy. The Receiving Party therefore agrees that the Disclosing Party will have the right, in addition to its other rights and remedies, to injunctive relief for any such violation of this Agreement without posting bond, or by posting bond at the lowest amount required by law.

Recall that, generally stated, the standard for injunctive relief is irreparable harm, including the inadequacy of monetary damages, and an appropriate likelihood of prevailing on the merits. This provision provides a contractual agreement that the first two elements exist, leaving the alleged breaching party with the right to contest only the likelihood of prevailing on the merits. While these terms are typical, some lawyers object to conceding irreparable harm and the inadequacy of monetary damages, arguing that there could be minor breaches that would not result in, for example, the wholesale dissemination of the proprietary information. If this argument is made in the course of negotiations regarding an agreement where the remedies provision provides for injunctive relief on *any* breach of the NDA, a response often is to include the quoted provision and then limit the concession on the elements needed to obtain equitable relief to *fundamental* breaches of the non-use and non-disclosure terms.

Term of the NDA.   Section 14 provides the term of the NDA and the duration of the confidentiality and non-use obligations. These are different concepts: the first relates to how long the parties will share information and discuss a business relationship, whereas the second relates to how long the NDA's restrictions on use and disclosure of the Confidential Information will continue to apply.

The term of the NDA is often fairly short — perhaps only three or six months. Sometimes this provision has an extension mechanism built in so that if discussions go on longer than expected, the term is easy to extend. If the decision is made to move forward with an ongoing relationship, the parties also have to decide whether they will continue to share information and keep the NDA alive or whether they will wait for definitive documentation of that relationship to be signed and rely on the confidentiality provisions included in that subsequent agreement.

The protections provided by an NDA usually run throughout the specified term of the NDA, plus a stated length of time following its termination (a "tail"). The Sample NDA starts the term of the tail at the time the agreement expires or is terminated. Having a single date that applies to everything disclosed under the NDA (rather than having a separate confidentiality obligation term that applies to each disclosure and begins on the date each disclosure is made) is simpler administratively. In addition, having the termination date rather than the date of the NDA start the clock on the tail means that a party cannot effectively shorten the term of the restrictions by slowing the ongoing discussions.

As a basic rule, the term of the tail should rationally reflect how long keeping the Confidential Information confidential continues to have economic value. Once sufficient time has passed to make the information no longer valuable, the tail term should be winding up. If the purpose of the NDA is to discuss an acquisition of one private company by another, and the information is primarily financial, perhaps a tail of only a few years is appropriate. In contrast, if the subject for discussion is fundamental technology, a longer tail may be necessary.

An appropriate tail length is also influenced by the nature of the IP protection that is otherwise available to protect the Confidential Information. Typically, however, even if the information relates to a patentable technology or a copyrighted computer system, there will be associated trade secrets involved that usually will drive the decision on the tail term. In general, of course, the party doing most of the disclosure will want a long tail term and the Receiving Party will want a short term.

The other issue to keep in mind is the management of what a Disclosing Party actually discloses. Even though the parties have agreed to talk and enter into an NDA, remember again that the best way to keep a secret is not to tell anyone. Careful management of what actually is shown to other parties is probably the most important means of protecting Confidential Information.

Miscellaneous Provisions.   While all the miscellaneous provisions presented in the Sample NDA are useful, one of the most important is the attorneys' fees clause. Intellectual property litigation is extremely fact driven and can be very technical. As a result, it can be lengthy and shockingly expensive. So from the point of view of an early-stage company client, an attorneys' fees clause is critical. While it may present a theoretical risk of having to pay a large company's fees, the more likely outcome is that an attorney's fees provision will cause the large company to think twice about using its greater resources to grind down a smaller company.

In addition, many companies want to see a prohibition on any assignment of the contractual rights under the NDA. They may be comfortable with the party they are talking to, but do not want the NDA assigned to a different competitor. In some jurisdictions, a contract is assignable unless it expressly prohibits assignment by its terms. As a result, when the choice of law is set, that will determine the default on assignability, so a specific provision prohibiting assignment is usually prudent. And, of course, governing law is important for many other reasons, including variations in the substantive law of trade secrets, as well as in basic contract law.

QUESTIONS

1. Some large companies, as well as most venture capitalists, refuse to enter into NDAs because they deal with so much overlapping confidential information that they see themselves as easy targets for litigation. What aspects of the Sample NDA would present problems for a large company or an investor?

2. In the context of SoftCo's proposed arrangement with Big Bad Software, would you recommend the use of an NDA? How does your analysis of this issue vary depending on whether you are SoftCo's counsel or Big Bad Software's? Which party is likely to insist on signing an NDA?

3. In considering the provisions customarily included in an NDA, what advice would you give SoftCo on these issues? If you were Big Bad Software's counsel, what advice would you give your client on these matters? In considering this question, you may want to reflect on the following, which are typically addressed in any NDA:

   - Are the parties competitors (or potential competitors)? Why does this make a difference in negotiating terms of the parties' NDA?
   - What is the scope of the parties' obligations under the terms of the NDA? Does it go beyond a simple non-disclosure obligation? Should there be a prohibition on the use of confidential information that has been shared by the parties during the course of their negotiations and the due diligence process?
   - Should the NDA include a restriction on the solicitation and/or hiring of any employees?

- Should the NDA include any restrictions on each party's right to contact or otherwise communicate with the other's customers or vendors?
- How long should the terms of the NDA be binding on the parties?

4. From SoftCo's perspective, the IP risks involved in the proposed joint venture with Big Bad Software were pretty apparent. What would the risks be in simply entering into a "bundling agreement," where SoftCo's products would be packaged and sold by a third party as part of a suite of related software products?

5. If SoftCo were to enter into a bundling and distribution agreement with the U.S. sales unit of a large, multinational technology company based in Europe, what terms from the Sample NDA would SoftCo insist upon in order to protect against losing control of its information when it is shared with the people "back at headquarters"?

6. Joan and Michael want to start talking with venture capital investors but are dismayed to discover that they will not sign NDAs. They are nervous about pitching their business plan on a non-confidential basis. How do you advise them?

2. Confidentiality and Invention Assignment Agreements

The *Confidentiality and Invention Assignment Agreement* is a fundamental element of a company's IP protection program. This agreement, which often is called a "Proprietary Information and Invention Assignment Agreement," addresses issues that the employee brings with him or her from the time preceding the employment relationship, that arise during the term of employment, and that extend after the employment terminates. The following discussion focuses on employers and employees, but these agreements are equally, if not more, important when dealing with consultants and independent contractors. A later section addresses some specific issues that are particular to consultants and independent contractors.

Overview of Terms. A Confidentiality and Invention Assignment Agreement (CIAA) is important to a company for three reasons. First, it demonstrates diligence in supervising the use of the company's (and others') proprietary information, which, as we have discussed, is an important element of trade secret protection. By addressing issues related to the employee's prior employment, it establishes the company's policy of not using the confidential information of others. By also asking the employee to segregate any IP previously developed and owned by the employee, a CIAA avoids any mixing of the employee's IP with (and thus jeopardizing the employer's exclusive control of) the employer's IP. Also, by requiring compliance with the employer's agreements with third parties (such as NDAs, as the result of which the employee may be exposed to an outside party's confidential information), it strengthens the record that the company has fulfilled those contractual obligations. Further, a demonstration of diligence in supervising IP is important to potential investors, lenders, and acquirors, each of whom wants to see that the company is in control of its IP issues.

Second, a CIAA protects the company's confidential information by setting restrictions on its use during employment and after the relationship terminates. It also establishes specific rules for controlling the employer's confidential information, such as requiring that company materials be returned upon the employee's departure and often prohibiting the solicitation of employees on behalf of a competitor.

Third, it assigns to the employer ownership of any inventions or creations that the employee may develop during the course of the employment relationship that relate to the nature of the employment. To do this, it takes the principles underlying the "work-for-hire" doctrine in copyright law and makes that concept a contract right of the employer that applies regardless of the character of the IP that is created.

In reviewing the issues and terms that are part of a CIAA, we refer to the Sample form at page 817 of Appendix B (the "Sample CIAA"). The Sample CIAA represents an effort by the drafting lawyer to prepare a short, comprehensible document that covers the subject, but is not so technical or complex that it might be confusing to the employee. This typifies a problem that lawyers constantly face in daily practice — that is, balancing the use of "legalese" and detailed language, on the one hand, with plain, understandable language on the other. One of the factors to be considered when resolving that issue is the nature of the document's users. In many companies, a CIAA must be signed by all employees. To many lawyers, that argues for something more generally comprehensible. On the other hand, IP law is detailed, complex, arcane, and filled with large amounts of specialized terminology. Some lawyers argue that if you do not use that terminology, you cannot be confident that you have created a legally sufficient agreement. Of course, case law is all over the place on this issue, so the debate is ongoing. Regardless of where your views and inclinations put you in this discussion, the important thing is to be aware of its existence and its influence on approaches to drafting agreements.

Many attorneys urge that a CIAA should be used by every company with every employee. Regardless of the nature of the business, if it has employees, those employees will learn confidential information about the business or create something that may be useful to the business and, from time to time, some will become former employees. A CIAA defines from the onset the employee's and the employer's rights and obligations regarding confidential information and things created for the company during the term of the employment.

Consideration.   Most companies present the CIAA as an employment intake document. It must be completed and signed, along with a W-9, an I-9, and a receipt for a copy of the employee handbook, for example, as a condition to employment. This is done partly for practical reasons — to ensure the terms apply from the start of the relationship — and partly for legal reasons. The CIAA requires the employee to assign all rights to anything the employee may create during the course of employment that is employment related. As a result, the employee is entitled to some consideration for agreeing to forego the rights of authorship or inventorship the employee otherwise would hold. While some states allow archaic recitations of covenant exchanges to demonstrate sufficient consideration, many require something more tangible than setting "hands and seals to this pledge and covenant." *See, e.g., Marine Contractors Co. v. Hurley*, 310 N.E.2d 915 (Mass. 1974) (addressing consideration for a non-compete covenant from an employee). If the restrictions and agreements embodied in the CIAA are entered into as part of the commencement of the employment relationship, then the new employment relationship itself is sufficient consideration for the agreement.

If, however, a CIAA is presented to an existing employee, what then is the consideration? Continued employment generally is not enough. In circumstances where a CIAA was not put in place as part of the employee intake process, most companies will present the agreement in connection with a *discretionary* change in employment compensation, such as a raise, an equity incentive grant, a promotion, special training, or access to an educational benefit, since a non-trivial change in the terms of employment usually is sufficient consideration. Care must be taken, however, in presenting a CIAA to an employee who is the recipient of, for example, a non-discretionary, across-the-board raise. *Query*: In that situation, is the employee receiving the full value of the agreed-upon benefit to be shared by all employees because of the presentation of the CIAA?

The best practice is to include the CIAA form with company information provided with an offer letter or other employment offer. In this way it is part of the accepted offer of employment. If a copy is not provided, mention of the CIAA, together with other normal details of employment, in the offer letter or other offer materials also is very useful for establishing the agreement as an element of the initial terms of employment. Then, as noted earlier, the employee should sign the CIAA as part of the basic employee intake process.

Relationship to Employment Arrangement.   The Sample CIAA begins with a provision disavowing any amendment to the employee's term of employment or otherwise modifying the concept of "at-will" employment:

> 1. No Term of Employment. I acknowledge and agree that my employment with the Company is not for any fixed term, and that my employment will continue only at the will of both the Company and me. I agree that this means my employment may be terminated at any time for any reason or for no reason, either with or without cause, either by me or the Company.

This Section 1 is intended to avoid any argument that because the CIAA creates ongoing obligations on the part of the employee, it creates a presumption that the employer is agreeing to provide ongoing employment in contravention of the "employment-at-will" doctrine.

The employment-at-will doctrine exists in every state in one form or another. It provides that absent a specific agreement otherwise, including, for example, a collective bargaining agreement, an employment relationship has no fixed term and may be terminated by either party at any time for any reason or for no reason. RESTATEMENT (THIRD) OF EMPLOYMENT LAW §2.01 (2009). There are limitations, of course, including discriminatory actions and other terminations that violate a range of public policies. *See id.* Moreover, there are two common exceptions to the doctrine that are applicable in an overwhelming majority of states: obligations to provide ongoing employment under implied contracts and under covenants of good faith and fair dealing. While the standards for demonstrating that either of these exceptions apply in a particular situation vary, rights or obligations that are collateral to the basic employment engagement, such as those created in a CIAA, can be used to support a claim for ongoing employment under either of these grounds for exception.

Even when a company has entered into an employment agreement with a particular employee, unless there is a union contract in place or it is hiring actors or athletes, the company normally does not intend that agreement to modify the employment-at-will doctrine. Most employment agreements in fact are nothing more than agreements setting compensation and rights on termination; indeed, as a practical matter, they typically contain provisions very much like Section 1 of the Sample CIAA. It is good practice, therefore, when drafting *any* document relating to the employment relationship to specify that ongoing rights or duties should not be used to infer a modification of the employee's employment-at-will status.

If an employment agreement has been entered into that specifically provides for a defined term of service or lists specific grounds for termination, or a collective bargaining agreement is in place, Section 1 of the Sample CIAA will need to be amended to conform to the terms of that other agreement.

Prior Employers and Others.   Section 2 of the Sample CIAA looks both backwards and forwards. In it, the employee represents that the current employment relationship does not conflict with any obligations to former employers and the employee has not brought to the current employer any confidential information or other materials belonging to a prior employer. The employee further covenants that he or she will not bring to the current employer any confidential information or property belonging to others in the future:

> 2. No Conflicts with Prior Employment. I represent that my employment with the Company will not conflict with any obligations I have to former employers or any other persons. I specifically represent that I have not brought to the Company (and will not bring to the Company) any materials or documents of a former employer or other person, or any confidential information or property of a former employer or other person.

This provision addresses a number of objectives. First, as a practical matter, it asks the employee to report any ongoing obligations to a "former employer or other person." An "other person" might be someone the employee did consulting work for, a former business partner, or perhaps a university where the employee was a student. The obligations could include non-competition agreements, which, if the terms are reasonable, are enforced in some jurisdictions as a means of protecting IP. A new employer has a legitimate interest in understanding what ongoing confidentiality obligations apply to a new employee. Second, it provides evidence that the Company respects the confidential information of others. There is a credibility issue if a company seeking to protect its own information in court appears to view others' confidential information as "free for the taking." Finally, it shows the company's effort to supervise the use and flow of unauthorized confidential information as part of its general oversight of its own IP rights. As noted earlier, however, management has to take these matters seriously. If a company is going to ignore these terms or even encourage its employees to violate them, it might very well be better not to have them at all.

In Section 2, the employee represents that he or she has not "brought to the Company," and further covenants that he or she "will not bring to the Company," "materials or documents or any confidential information or property of a former employer or other person." "Brought" and "bring" have to be read as "to the new employer for use," whether in tangible form or by the employee's actions in carrying out his or her employment duties. If the employee has not brought any other person's property to the new employer, then the employee cannot use that property, so this language covers both possession and use of another party's IP.

Longer provisions may itemize various forms of "disclosure or use" of materials from the former employer or others, and may attempt to catalog what those things may be. Lawyers who use detailed provisions often say that something on the list of potentially confidential items from the former employer may trigger a question from a new employee and allow for a quick resolution of what otherwise could have been a problem. But many lawyers think a short, broad statement, such as the one in the quoted section, is better than one attempting to be all-inclusive, which inevitably will result in leaving something out.

Alternative provisions also may provide, in addition to a commitment not to use anyone else's confidential information, an ongoing covenant by the employee to use only information that is well known to persons acquainted with the relevant industry, that is in the public domain, or that has been developed by or legally provided to the new employer. Some lawyers find this language to be too restrictive and point out that employers often *want* to hire employees that know and can use more than what is "well known." This gets back to an issue that arose in the earlier discussion of inevitable disclosure (see section A.2, above) where the quoted language from the *Papermaster* case suggested this result and therefore that an employee's expertise may not exist outside of the trade secrets that employee has learned regarding a former employer's business. All of this raises the question of whether it is possible for an employee to have expertise that is more than what is generally known in an industry but does not require infringement of a former employer's IP rights.

Segregating Prior Inventions.   Section 3 of the Sample CIAA excludes from the agreement's invention assignment provisions any "discoveries and inventions" that existed prior to the commencement of the new employment relationship. Note that the terms "discoveries and inventions" is intentionally left broad and vague in order to elicit disclosure of IP rights the employee claims to have an interest in:

> 3. Prior Inventions. As a matter of record, and in order to assist the Company in determining its rights to any intellectual property interests in connection with my engagement, I have listed (at the end of this Agreement) all inventions, copyrighted or trademarked material, patents and patent applications and any other protectable intellectual property rights I own (or have any interest in) that were conceived of, or first reduced to practice, prior to the date hereof, all of which are excluded from the provisions of Section 5 of this Agreement ("Prior Inventions"). If nothing is listed below, I agree that the Company may conclusively assume that I am not retaining any Prior Inventions outside of the Company. I will not use any Prior Inventions in the course of my engagement with the Company.

Note that the default position is that unless an employee's creation is listed as a Prior Invention, the Company will assume that the assignment section of the CIAA applies to it. The second sentence of the quoted section creates that default by specifying that if no Prior Inventions are identified, then there are none. Hence, if the employee's creation is subsequently identified and relates to the nature of the employment duties, it belongs to the employer. For the hiring employer, this is the beauty of the Prior Inventions structure; it puts the onus on the employee to identify the exceptions, while leaving everything else as the employer's property. *Query*: Do you see any contractual fairness issues that might arise as a result of this business practice?

The last sentence provides the covenant that no Prior Inventions will be used in the employee's discharge of his or her obligations to the Company. This shows the Company's supervision of its IP — making sure that there is no outside material mixed with its own — but it also sets the presumption that the employee will have no ownership interest in what he or she does for the Company, because the employee will not use Prior Inventions and anything that is used is assigned under Section 5. If the employee uses Prior Inventions in the course of employment, then the employee has violated this agreement.

Alternative provisions might set out in more detail what an IP ownership interest might be in order to create an interest in a Prior Invention, or provide for specific mechanisms for disclosing Prior Inventions that have confidential contents (in order to avoid any confidentiality breach). The quoted Section 3 above avoids that latter question by focusing on patentable and copyrightable creations, having already addressed trade secrets through the treatment of confidential information in Section 2.

One situation that arises from time to time involves an employee with numerous Prior Inventions that relate to the business of a Company, such as a university professor forming a company with some graduate students. As an example, let's assume for a moment that there are three founders of SoftCo, Joan, Michael, and the professor who was their primary academic supervisor. Since the professor's job at Caltech is to research and develop new advances in the professor's field, the Prior Inventions concept can be a problem. One response is to turn it around: to set the Prior Inventions section to say that Prior Inventions exist, but *no* Prior Inventions are being delivered *other than* any interest the professor has in the listed IP, which is the foundation of what SoftCo is using, and with respect to that IP, it is hereby assigned. The result is that instead of creating a list of *excluded* IP with a covenant not to use any of it, the Prior Inventions mechanism would create a list of *assigned* IP, together with a covenant that no other Prior Inventions will be used in the business.

The shortcoming of this approach is that it does not preserve the simple beauty of the Prior Inventions structure, which is to provide that the Company owns everything except what the employee specifically carves out. It does, however, provide a clear demarcation of what belongs to the Company and puts the professor/employee, in this special circumstance, on notice of where his or her academic research and other activities must end and the Company's rights begin.

An additional variation addresses what happens if an employee violates this agreement and uses a Prior Invention in furtherance of the employment relationship with the Company. The Company could be in an uncomfortable situation if that Prior Invention becomes imbedded in the Company's product and the employee claims an ownership interest in the Company's resulting product or seeks to forbid the Company from using "his" or "her" technology. The Company's first line of defense is to structure the CIAA so that the employee's actions constitute a violation of the CIAA; the law does not encourage people to be enriched by their own contract breaches. Additional protection would be provided by language addressing and heading off this potentiality, such as the following:

If, notwithstanding the terms of this Agreement, I incorporate a Prior Invention into my work on a Company process, product or device, I hereby grant the Company a perpetual, non-exclusive, fully-paid, irrevocable, worldwide license (including the right to sublicense) to make, have made, modify, use or sell that incorporated Prior Invention.

Finally, some CIAA forms do not use the concept of Prior Inventions at all; rather, they simply prohibit the employee's use of any confidential information or other IP belonging to any party other than the Company. In short, if the employee uses a Prior Invention for work, it gets assigned to the employer.

Confidentiality Obligation.   Section 4 of the Sample CIAA covers four issues:

- First, it establishes that the employee will have access to the Company's Confidential Information, and in fact personally may create new Confidential Information, and that the Company's Confidential Information has value to the Company;
- Second, it uses broad language to define what the Company's "Confidential Information" is;
- Third, it provides the employee's (i) acknowledgement that all Confidential Information belongs to the Company and (ii) agreement that he or she will use that information only for the Company's purposes and will not disclose it; and
- Finally, it adds the employee's agreement to adhere to any additional confidentiality obligations that the Company might have with a third party, such as through an NDA.

In addressing these matters, the language of Section 4 of the sample CIAA reads as follows:

> 4. Confidential Information. I understand that as part of my employment with the Company I am expected to make new contributions of value to the Company. I also acknowledge that, during my employment, I will learn information relating to the Company, its business and products, that has commercial value to the Company and that the Company desires to keep confidential. This confidential information will include such things as trade secrets, techniques, processes, know-how, technical specifications, discoveries, inventions, marketing information, business strategies, information regarding customers and suppliers, and any other information (not necessarily in writing) that may be useful to the Company, and that is not generally available to the public (all of this information is referred to in this Agreement as "Confidential Information"). I agree that all Confidential Information will be the sole property of the Company and I agree that I will not disclose any Confidential Information to any other person (except solely in performing my duties as an employee of the Company), and that I will otherwise keep all Confidential Information in strictest confidence and not use it for any purpose other than in connection with the furtherance of the interests of the Company. Also, I will comply with the terms of agreements entered into by the Company from time to time relating to the protection of the proprietary information of other parties.

Some agreements go beyond this version's simple acknowledgment of the existence of the Company's interest in and rights to the Confidential Information. They may include, for example, a statement of the potential civil and criminal penalties that may apply to a misappropriating employee under applicable state law or the Economic Espionage Act of 1996, 18 U.S.C. §§1831-1839, as noted in the discussion of trade secrets earlier in section A.2.

Any definition of Confidential Information, such as that in the Section 4 language just quoted, should always be broad enough to cover both technical and business information. Certain industries may require special variations of the definition to reflect the terminology used in that industry. Some lawyers put the definition of Confidential Information (which may be called "Proprietary Information" or another like term) into a separate section, which leaves behind in the Sample CIAA's Section 4, and therefore emphasizes, the covenants undertaken by the employee regarding Confidential Information. Regardless of how comprehensive the list of things that are included in the definition is, virtually every agreement makes it clear that the list merely provides examples and the definition covers everything a company treats as confidential, whether mentioned or not.

As we discussed earlier in this chapter, a company's treatment of its confidential information is, to a large extent, self-fulfilling. Put another way, in large part, a company's confidential information is protectable only to the extent that it is protected. Note that the quoted Section 4 language uses a "catch-all" as part of the definition of Confidential Information:

> and any other information (not necessarily in writing) that may be useful to the Company, and that is not generally available to the public.

If the Company makes an effort to keep something useful from becoming generally available to the public, then the Company can treat it as Confidential Information. If the Company is lax in protecting information, it will have a hard time asserting later that it is Confidential Information. In short, a company's use of an effective, comprehensive, and rational approach to identifying and protecting its confidential and proprietary information makes it more likely that it will be able to successfully enforce its confidentiality rights.

Another common approach to this catch-all is reflected in the language of the following provision:

> and any other information that may be designated by the Company as Confidential Information.

While this has the advantage of creating a bright line — that is, something is either on the Company's list of confidential materials or information or it is not — some lawyers do not like this approach because it elevates an inadvertent omission from the Confidential Information category, or the failure to put a legend on a file or document, to a presumption of intentional non-inclusion. In addition, many lawyers want the CIAA to provide a general basis for what is Confidential Information rather than to rely upon the conclusory determination of the Company. They believe treating the Company's designation as dispositive allows an alleged misappropriater to call into question the Company's process for designating material as confidential. The concern is that the argument may be made that the Company is over-inclusive in treating things as confidential, which will have the potential to shift the focus of the inquiry away from the misappropriated material to the Company's practices in designating material as Confidential Information.

Also, some agreements may include an assignment provision in this section relating to modifications or contributions to any Confidential Information. The idea is that if there is any basis for the employee to claim an ownership interest in the Company's Confidential Information, and that interest is not sufficiently addressed by the invention assignment provision of the agreement (perhaps because the definition of an "invention" is narrow), that gap will be filled here.

For example, if the employee's job is to prepare financial analyses and reports, that work product would be Confidential Information created by the employee even though it does not constitute an "invention." Some lawyers want to make it abundantly clear that, should the employee's efforts in creating that work product result in any arguable property rights for the employee, those rights are assigned to the employer. Other lawyers see a very limited risk of this sort of right arising and view this as overkill, but the response to that comment is always: "What's the harm?" This gets us back to the fundamental debate as to whether it is better to use short, broad definitions and general terminology to avoid the risk that a detailed, technical list has omitted something, trusting that a court will be inclined to enforce a comprehensible, straightforward document that uses "any and all" to mean just that, as opposed to detailed, comprehensive descriptions that try to anticipate all conceivable outcomes in order to be sure that any required references or judicially required "magic words" (i.e., specific references or recitations necessary for an agreement to be effective as to a specific item or subject) have been covered. *Query*: In considering the advantages and disadvantages of each of the methods described above, which variation would you recommend to SoftCo?

Invention Assignment.   Having addressed the requirement that the Company's proprietary information be treated confidentially, the Sample CIAA next moves to its second function, which is having the employee assign to the Company any inventions, developments, or discoveries the employee creates during the course of the employment relationship:

> 5. Inventions During Employment. I agree that all discoveries and inventions relating in any manner to the business or the future business of the Company and conceived, reduced to practice, authored or made by me (either alone or with others) during my employment with the Company, will constitute work product of my employment, will be the sole property of the Company and will become part of the Company's Confidential Information. I will promptly disclose these discoveries and inventions to the Company in writing, and I will not disclose these discoveries and inventions to any other persons other than in the performance of my duties as an employee of the Company. I hereby assign to the Company all my right to such discoveries and inventions, and I will sign such additional documents as the Company from time to time considers advisable in order to complete this assignment and to apply for patent, copyright or other protection in the name of the Company. I agree that, for purposes of this Agreement, the term "discoveries and inventions" shall have the broadest meanings, including new products, machines, methods, processes, works of authorship (including software programs), improvements, compositions of matter, and designs or configurations.

In keeping with the Sample CIAA's strategy of using general descriptions, note that the first few lines of Section 5 refer to "discoveries and inventions" that are "conceived, reduced to practice, authored or made." The section also ends with an acknowledgment by the employee that "discoveries and inventions shall have the broadest meanings. . . ." A criticism of the Sample CIAA is that it is weak on trade secrets because it never directly says they are included in "discoveries and inventions."

An alternative approach is to run through the elements that make something protectable under patent, copyright, and trade secret law, as well as the Semiconductor Chip Protection Act (17 U.S.C. §§901-914) and anything else that may be relevant, and provide for their assignment. The more comprehensive option is to provide a laundry list of anything that might be considered a discovery or invention, or a "development" or "creation," and have the assignment apply to anything on that list.

While the employee is required to keep his or her discoveries and inventions confidential, Section 5 also requires the employee to disclose them in writing promptly to the Company, presumably so that the Company can then take appropriate steps to protect the newly created IP. These requirements are not controversial, although some lawyers will put a "tail" on this notice obligation, causing it to continue to apply for some period of time, usually ranging from six months to a year, after the termination of the employment relationship. The reasoning is that even when an employee has returned all the employer's documents and materials, the employee may still have ideas based on the employer's IP that have not become fully formed, or that that do not come into being, until after the employment relationship ends, so the old employer still needs the ability to supervise discoveries and inventions that relate to its business and that should be assigned to it. Other lawyers think this is over-reaching and basically an effort to interfere with the departed employee's relationship with a new employer. *Query*: Does this constitute a reasonable protection or is it overreaching?

The assignment language of Section 5 includes the employee's acknowledgement of the Company's ownership of the employee's work product, the actual assignment of his or her rights, and a covenant to sign any further documents necessary to allow the Company to perfect its property interest in the new discovery or invention. This covenant is used because some IP interests lodge in the "inventor" or "author" (as noted in the prior discussions of patents and copyrights) and the Company would like to have the employee sign a specific assignment of the rights covered by a particular copyright registration or patent application rather than rely on a generic assignment of future creations. Some lawyers omit this language, apparently out of concern that it might give the employee the idea that he or she can refuse to sign an inventor's rights assignment associated with a patent application, for example, as a leverage issue. In fact, there does not appear to be any U.S. authority to suggest a specific assignment is anything other than a neatness issue.

The other element of Section 5 is that its assignment provision is limited to:

> discoveries and inventions relating in any manner to the business or the future business of the Company. . . .

This partly comes from the "work-for-hire" concept in copyright law, which restricts the application of that doctrine to things authored within the scope of employment. It also reflects the basic fairness of the idea that an employer has no legitimate interest in claiming an interest in anything created by an employee on private time that is unrelated to the company's business (for example, the copyright to a mystery novel written at night and on the weekends by an employee working in a telemarketing call center).

As employees are assigning potentially significant IP property rights by signing a CIAA, a court's willingness to enforce the assignment partly depends on the employer's reasonableness in setting the scope of that grant of rights. An overreaching employer could find itself with nothing.

State law actually varies on the scope of the interest it permits an employer to legitimately have in the creative work of its employees. For example, §§2870 through 2872 of the California Labor Code set additional constraints on the employer's rights. Section 2870 sets forth in detail the permitted scope of invention assignments and §2872 requires that employees be given notice of the limitations set by §2870. The common practice, then, in California is to quote the relevant portion of §2870 in the CIAA (or in an exhibit thereto) and to include a statement saying that by presenting the language in the agreement, the company has given the employee the notice required by §2872. In the Sample CIAA, which is written to conform to California law, this is done in the second paragraph of Section 5:

> I understand that the Company is hereby advising me that any provision in this Agreement requiring me to assign my rights in any invention does not apply to an invention that qualifies fully under the provisions of Section 2870 of the California Labor Code. That section provides that the requirement to assign inventions "shall not apply to an invention that the employee developed entirely on his or her own time without using the employer's equipment, supplies, facilities, or trade secret information except for those inventions that either: (1) relate at the time of conception or reduction to practice of the invention to the employer's business, or actual or demonstrably anticipated research or development of the employer; or (2) result from any work performed by the employee for the employer." BY SIGNING THIS AGREEMENT, I ACKNOWLEDGE THAT THIS PARAGRAPH SHALL CONSTITUTE WRITTEN NOTICE OF THOSE PROVISIONS OF SECTION 2870.

Interestingly, §2871 provides that §2870 does not restrict the ability of an employer to require confidential disclosure "of *all* the employee's inventions made solely or jointly with others during the term of his or her employment." (Emphasis added.) Thus, while §2870 prohibits the employer from seeking an assignment of IP created outside of the scope of employment, the employer nevertheless can require the employee to disclose that new IP to it on a confidential basis. This allows the employer to supervise IP created during the term of employment and intervene if it believes that a particular bit of creativity is within the scope of its assignment interest.

Note that the Sample CIAA does not take full advantage of this authority. The scope of Section 5's notification language reaches the same inventions and discoveries that the assignment provision does ("I will promptly disclose these discoveries and inventions . . ."). A variation, then, for California documents is to separate the notice provision into its own section where it is not subjected to the limitations of §2870 that apply to assignments.

Other Obligations During Employment.   Section 6 of the Sample CIAA restricts the employee from engaging in other activities during the term of employment:

> 6. Certain Further Agreements. I agree that, since my employment with the Company involves a relationship of confidence and trust, during my employment I will not engage in any other employment or business activities that are competitive

with or otherwise conflict with the interests of the Company, and I will not plan or organize any such competing business activity.

This is a fairly tame "anti-moonlighting" provision in that it only reaches to competitive or conflicting activities or employment. Some agreements flatly prohibit other employment, while others allow only uncompensated charitable and community service activities. This sort of provision sets a loyalty requirement, seeks to avoid distractions, and recognizes that employees working more than one full-time job may well be overtired and unable to perform effectively. In addition, an employer would argue that an anti-moonlighting provision also acts to keep employees out of potentially conflicting situations. More cynically, it prohibits employees from setting up their next job, whether with a new employer or as an entrepreneur, while still working at their current one.

The quoted restriction would be more appropriate than a flat prohibition on other work when the CIAA is for a part-time employee or perhaps even a full-time, hourly employee. Anti-moonlighting restrictions are more frequently seen in contracts associated with senior management and professional positions (such as in engineering or technical development) where "full time" usually means more than "9 to 5."

Post-Employment Obligations.   Section 7 of the Sample CIAA includes three post-employment obligations: first, to return all Confidential Information and materials (which really is to occur at termination rather than after) and to not take or use any of that material; second, to not use any Confidential Information and to keep it all confidential for three years; and third, to not solicit any of the Company's employees to work for a competitor for one year:

> 7. Certain Obligations Upon Termination of Employment. In the event of the termination of my employment by me or by the Company for any reason, I will promptly deliver to the Company all documents, data and other materials of any nature or media pertaining to my work with the Company that contain any Confidential Information or any discoveries and inventions, I will not take with me nor use any such documents or materials (or any copies of them), and I will continue to keep all Confidential Information in strictest confidence as required by paragraph 4, above, for a period of three years following the termination of my employment. I also agree that, in recognition of my position of confidence and trust with the Company during my employment, for a period of one year following such termination I will not solicit any of the Company's employees to work for a competitive company.

Requiring the return of the Company's materials is a good practice generally for IP protection. By putting it into the CIAA, the Company has bound the employee with an enforceable covenant that can give rise to a legal remedy should it turn out that the employee retained Confidential Information.

The length of the post-termination confidentiality obligation depends on the nature of the Confidential Information. If the information is more business-oriented, a shorter term is appropriate, as that sort of information changes fairly rapidly and often becomes outdated in only a couple of years. If the employee has been exposed to technology that is the foundation of the Company's business, a longer term would be reasonable. Some agreements do not require that a time frame be specified, but simply let the constraint expire as the information ceases to be confidential or to have commercial value. Under that approach, it becomes a question of fact whether the information is still subject to the agreement's restrictions. While it is true that the agreement should apply so long as the information is confidential, some lawyers see that formulation as an effort to intimidate employees by creating uncertainty regarding their legal responsibilities. The post-employment obligation sometimes is folded directly into the general confidentiality obligation like that of Section 4, rather than presented separately. *Query*: As SoftCo's legal counsel, would you prefer to set a defined term or leave it open-ended and rely upon a court's interpretation?

The non-solicitation provision is an option that a good number of companies use in jurisdictions where employee "non-competes" are not enforceable. In those states, since former employees cannot be prohibited from going to work for a competitor, their agreement not to solicit their former co-workers at least prevents someone with inside knowledge of who the key employees are from targeting them for the benefit of a new, competitive employer. A stronger provision, which is not enforceable in all states, is a "no-hire" covenant. This would flatly prohibit a former employee from hiring the Company's other employees or aiding a third party (i.e., a new employer) in targeting, soliciting, or hiring those employees.

A variation along the same lines adds a provision on non-solicitation of customers after termination of employment. As this limitation is grounded in the Company's authority to protect its Confidential Information, this restriction would not be applicable if customer identity or the details of the sales relationship with each customer are not confidential. Even if provisions like these are not included in the CIAA, soliciting employees and customers using the former employer's Confidential Information also can be construed as a tortious interference with the employer's contractual or business relationship with those employees or customers. *Query*: As counsel to SoftCo, why would you want to include a section in its CIAA that prohibits "poaching" the company's customers?

One of the major regional differences you see in the CIAAs used by emerging growth companies, particularly those with professional venture capital investors, is the use of employee non-compete covenants. Non-competition provisions are very rare on the West Coast but are very typical on the East Coast for senior or technical or creative employees. In California, for example, §16600 of the Business and Professions Code, which prohibits contracts in restraint of trade, includes a prohibition on non-compete agreements that arise from the employment relationship (and do not involve the purchase of entity good will).

In contrast, Massachusetts, for example, allows covenants not to compete so long as they are used to protect the legitimate business interests of the employer and are reasonable in terms of the applicable time period, the geographical scope, and the breadth of the prohibited conduct. *See, e.g., Marine Contractors Co., Inc. v. Hurley*, 310 N.E.2d 915, 920 (Mass. 1974). As every state provides by statute the right of IP owners to protect their proprietary rights, protection of confidential information and trade secrets clearly is a legitimate business interest of the employer. A typical non-competition provision might read:

> For one year after the termination of my employment with the Company, I will not, whether as an employee, proprietor, partner, contractor, agent or owner of any business or company, in the geographic areas where the Company actively does business or is

pursuing plans to do business, engage in any business activity that is in competition with the products or services of the Company in effect at the time of the termination of my employment with the Company.

A reasonable geographic scope is usually limited to where the employer is currently doing business or pursuing plans to expand the business. Some states require a list of the restricted areas. This is a problem for Internet vendors, as they are, to some extent, doing business everywhere. The nature of the prohibited conduct should be no broader than is appropriate to protect the interests of the employer. Some contracts simply prohibit providing services to a competitor of the employer, while others identify the specific industries in which services may not be provided.

The length of time the covenant is in effect following termination is a key aspect of the reasonableness of the entire covenant. The states that enforce covenants not to compete often balance the merits of enforcement against the reasonableness of prohibiting the employee from practicing his or her trade or occupation. Often, if a court believes that the covenant reaches too far in prohibiting work that does not present a risk to the former employer's Confidential Information or trade secrets, the court will throw out the entire covenant or modify its scope to make it reasonable.

Injunctive Relief.   Since preventing the continued dissemination or unauthorized use of its Confidential Information is often the Company's first priority, injunctive relief is a critical right. Note that Confidential Information often is leaked out slowly, or put to use gradually, by a former employee for the benefit of a new employer. Once the former employer sees the leakage start, it wants to put a stop to it quickly. After the problem is stopped, monetary damages can be sorted out, but halting the improper behavior must happen first. Section 8 of the Sample CIAA provides that, in addition to other remedies, the parties have reached certain agreements regarding injunctive relief:

> 8. Specific Performance. I acknowledge and agree that irreparable injury to the Company may result in the event I breach any covenant and agreement contained in this Agreement and that the remedy at law for the breach of any such covenant will be inadequate. Therefore, if I engage in any act in violation of the provisions of this Agreement, I agree that the Company shall be entitled, in addition to such other remedies and damages as may be available to it by law or under this Agreement, to injunctive relief to enforce the provisions of this Agreement.

Generally speaking, as discussed previously regarding NDAs in section B.1 of this chapter, the standards for injunctive relief are irreparable harm, together with the inadequacy of monetary damages, and a substantial likelihood of prevailing on the merits. Section 8 provides a contractual agreement that the irreparable harm and inadequacy of monetary damages exist, leaving the breaching employee to contest only the likelihood of prevailing on the merits.

The reality is that, even where there is no covenant not to compete, if a former employee moves to a competitor and takes a position where the former employer's Confidential Information is at risk, such as a similar position to that held at the former employer, the former employer's first action often is to send a letter to the employee, copying the new employer. That letter will set forth the former employer's grave concerns regarding the potential misuse of its Confidential Information, cite the employee's continuing obligations under the CIAA, and state the specific aspect of the new position that causes the former employer's level of concern to be so high. If the jurisdiction has adopted the inevitable disclosure doctrine, the risk of inevitable disclosure would be raised. (Refer to section A.2, above.) If not, the former employer will point out that the significant overlap in job responsibilities creates an almost certain likelihood that the former employer's Confidential Information will come into use in the new position. The letter will demand immediate assurance that the new employer's procedures and oversight systems will reduce the risk that the former employer's IP will be disclosed or used.

If the response is prompt and demonstrates a responsible attitude towards protecting the former employer's Confidential Information, including the implementation of some protective measures, perhaps the matter will end. If the response is slow or not satisfactory, the former employer might deliver a firm demand for protection of its Confidential Information. If that does not result in a prompt response indicating a change in the new employer's appreciation of the seriousness of the issue, the next step would be filing for a temporary restraining order to protect the Confidential Information while an injunction is sought. The former employer must press the issue and show urgency at each step, or else the court will not see the need to grant a restraining order pending the hearing on the request for an injunction. As with any litigation, this is an expensive and unpredictable path to pursue, so the former employer must be fully, calmly, and rationally committed to the decision that it is in the best interests of the company to go forward by way of formal litigation. *Query*: How can the new employer prevent this from occurring?

Miscellaneous Provisions.   The Sample CIAA has little in the way of miscellaneous provisions, only an integration clause in Section 9, which is useful in preventing an argument that the employee's obligations were controlled by some prior understanding.

Many companies do not include an attorneys' fees clause because they do not believe they would be able to recover their fees from the employee even if they won and had the fees awarded. As a result, they view the clause as only working for the benefit of the prevailing former employee. Some companies see it as extra leverage against the employee, however, and want it included in their document.

The Sample CIAA also does not have a choice of law provision, although it is clear from the California-specific terms that it contemplates California law will apply. It may be that this form originally was prepared for a single-location, California-based company. To the extent that a company has facilities in more than one state, it may seek to have one of those state's laws apply to all its employee agreements. On the other hand, a substantial number of courts will protect an employee who is a resident of their state and works at a location in their state by examining the law of their state that governs the employment relationship (since applying the state's interest in regulating employment within its borders means using local law regardless of any choice of law provision), and then interpreting the attempt to use the law of another jurisdiction as an abuse of power by the employer.

Many employment lawyers routinely put arbitration clauses in employment documents, although arbitration seems to go in and out of favor. If an arbitration clause is used in a company's employment documents generally, or if the company's employee handbook calls for arbitration, it would be best for the CIAA to have a conforming provision so that all disputes involving an employee can be resolved coherently in one forum.

To the extent there is anything "aggressive" in the CIAA, a severability clause would be prudent. This provision states that if any portion of the agreement is unenforceable, it is to be severed from the agreement and the remainder of the agreement is to be enforced. Some severability clauses state that the court shall modify the unenforceable provision to produce the most similar, but enforceable, result.

A waiver provision (i.e., "Any waiver of a breach shall not be construed as a waiver of a subsequent breach") may be more important than normal in a CIAA because so much of the company's ability to protect Confidential Information is based on prior conduct and diligent enforcement of protection policies. A company would not want a single waiver of a right to be treated as broadly precedential. *Query*: How can a company monitor for breaches of the CIAA?

Companies often want an assignment provision allowing the company to assign its interest in the CIAA to an entity that takes over its operations, together with a successors' provision on the part of the employee. An assignment provision for the benefit of the company allows an acquirer to step into the company's shoes regarding the employer's rights under the CIAA. A provision binding any successor of the employee allows the company to pursue recovery of company confidential materials against the estate of a deceased employee, for example. State law varies on what the default rule is concerning whether contracts are assignable: in some states, if the contract is silent, it is assignable; in others, the contract must state that it may be assigned in order for it to be assignable.

Consultants and Contractors.   It is particularly important that CIAAs be used with non-employees like consultants and independent contractors because they typically are retained to work on specific projects that require them to have access to some amount of confidential information. As noted earlier in the "work-for-hire" discussion in the copyright section (see section A.4, above), the work-for-hire doctrine provides that an employer owns the copyright interest in works of authorship created by its employees. But unless consultants and contractors are retained to prepare an item on the statutory list, the "work-for-hire" doctrine will not apply. That list does not include software or stand-alone works of authorship, like advertising copy, graphics or web designs, logos, schematics, and lots of other things that companies typically turn to independent contractors to prepare.

Since a company is paying for a result it intends to use in its business, it is completely appropriate for it to insist that a consultant keep the company's confidential information confidential, and it is also completely appropriate for the company to expect the consultant to assign any rights in the work product delivered to the company.

The problem is that the consultant is selling expertise and know-how. It may be very difficult for the consultant to agree that *all* rights in the work product belong to the company because that work product may incorporate some built-in know-how that the consultant needs to be able to use again and again. Sometimes, however, this problem can be solved with the company getting a virtually unlimited right to *use* the work product, but with the embedded IP being retained by the consultant. This situation, however, can quickly grow into a problem that is beyond the scope of services that a general business lawyer should be providing.

The bottom line is that, in a world of outsourced business functions, leased employees, contract employees, and self-employed contract service providers, IP protection has to be even more carefully supervised and scrupulously documented. And of all the things that a company can mess up, control of its IP is one of the very few that is very hard, and sometimes impossible, to fix down the road.

C. Intellectual Property Protection and the Early-Stage Company

Regardless of the nature of a new business, IP will be a relevant issue. Whether it extends only to selecting the entity name or perhaps a logo, or whether it rests at the core of the business, virtually every company has to deal with IP issues. Even the lowest of low-tech businesses, with no naming issues, might still have confidential information regarding suppliers and supplier pricing; customers and special accommodations and arrangements with them; compensation, revenues, margins, and other financial data; or plans and projections.

A business lawyer needs to be sensitive to the existence of IP and alert to measures that should be undertaken for its protection. While professional "best practices" materials may provide lists of hundreds of actions a company may take to secure the confidentiality of its physical and electronic information — and "security consultants" will be happy to sell a new company elaborate and complex access and monitoring systems — the business lawyer has to be sensitive to expense and practicality.

SoftCo, for example, does not need elaborate physical security to protect its IP when it is operated from Joan's parents' house by Joan and Michael alone. Their biggest risks are power failures, the house burning down, and casual burglars who will break in looking for something they can sell for $50. So SoftCo's initial security plans should address those problems rather than theoretical issues that will not come into being for a long time. That does not mean, however, that deeper IP protection issues should be ignored at this point. Joan and Michael need to be sensitive to unintended dissemination and unauthorized access issues, and need to build into their business right from the start an evolving set of practices that will limit those risks and adjust to each change in the way the business operates.

Joan and Michael would be wise to get a briefing from an IP specialist on how to avoid contaminating or losing control of their ownership interests in their IP, particularly as they begin to work with contractors or start to take on employees. A well-meaning employee who includes someone else's property in SoftCo's product, such as an "open source" software utility, can create massive headaches (and potentially significant legal problems) later for Joan and Michael.

Joan and Michael (and you, as SoftCo's counsel) also will need to deal with potential IP issues SoftCo has with its founders, in terms of documenting exactly how their prior work became the property of SoftCo, as well as resolving the overhanging issue regarding the work they did while students and postdocs at Caltech.

While it is not appropriate to look for trouble where it does not exist, IP issues are much easier to resolve in the early stages of a company's life than on the eve of a major financing transaction, the company's IPO, or a sale of the business. Thus, the role of the business lawyer is to anticipate where problems might arise and deal with them while they are still manageable.

QUESTIONS

1. At a stage where Joan and Michael are SoftCo's only employees, what are SoftCo's greatest risks in terms of IP protection? What sorts of protective measures would you recommend that SoftCo implement?

2. How will those risks change once SoftCo moves into its own facility and starts hiring employees? How should SoftCo's IP protection strategy change at that point? What about when it has customers?

3. Does your recommendation as to the scope of the company's IP protection plan vary depending on what financing scenario SoftCo should decide to pursue?

4. What recommendations do you have for understanding and addressing Joan and Michael's IP issues with Caltech? What plan of action would you present to them in order to gather the information needed to evaluate that issue? What kind of information will your investigation need to uncover in order to assess the issues?

5. What if, in addition to doing development work at Caltech, Joan had previously worked for Microsoft? Microsoft, like Caltech, has every right to protect its intellectual property. Since SoftCo is seeking to develop and market operating system software utilities for the personal computer user, and Microsoft is widely recognized as the world's leader in personal computer operating system software, what would you need to know as SoftCo's counsel? What information would you need from Joan to get a handle on the risks and offer a plan of action?

6. Alternatively, suppose that before getting involved with Joan and starting SoftCo, Michael had started another software company with a different friend, though they later had a falling out and abandoned the business. As SoftCo's counsel, what might you want to find out then? What do you suppose "abandoned" actually means in this situation?

7. Joan and Michael will need to enter into assignment agreements with SoftCo that transfer into SoftCo their property rights in the IP they have developed. As SoftCo's counsel, should you advise that they be required also to sign a form of CIAA? Why?

CHAPTER 8

OVERVIEW OF VENTURE CAPITAL

As Joan and Michael look at the possibility of pursuing the *Venture Capital* financing scenario for SoftCo, they need to consider what a venture capital investment entails. They need to consider what the process of finding, negotiating, and taking on a venture capital investment means and how it relates to the other choices available to them. In this chapter, we review the need for capital, the sources that might be available, and the forms of consideration a company might have to deliver in order to obtain it. We then look more closely at the venture capital industry. We examine how venture capital funds are structured and how the valuation and investment process works. We then consider the steps a company seeking venture capital should take to make itself ready to move into the world of venture capital.

A. Capital: What Is It and Who Needs It?

1. Introduction to Capital

For our purposes, *capital* means the financial and other resources required to obtain the necessary assets — money, labor, or property — to launch a business, as well as to pay for the operations of the business until it generates enough revenue to pay for itself as a going concern. A "capital asset" can be defined as an asset obtained and used on an ongoing basis for the purpose of generating revenue. For example, in a manufacturing business, capital assets might include factory equipment; in a retail business, display cases; and in a technology business, lab and test equipment. An investor in a business usually delivers "capital" in the form of money, but as we saw in SoftCo's potential joint venture transaction with Big Bad Software, as well as in Joan and Michael's founder investments, capital can be contributed "in kind" — that is, in the form of existing property or rights, rather than in cash.

2. The Need for Capital

Virtually every new business needs capital — some more than others, some much more — although the amount of capital usually depends on the nature of the business. Generally speaking, service businesses need less investment in capital assets, while manufacturing businesses need more. Businesses involving large-scale, complex processes (electricity generation, automobile manufacture, oil refining) as well as high-volume, technically difficult manufacturing (semiconductors) may require very large amounts of capital. For these businesses, the plant and equipment are expensive to build or purchase and time consuming to set up, test, and calibrate. Furthermore, operating costs must be funded from invested capital for an extended period of time until the business begins to produce enough revenue to fund itself. These businesses bear the double burden of large capital asset needs as well as a lengthy and costly term to reach profitable operations.

In contrast, consider a service business, such as a hairdresser. Opening a customized, high-end shop may entail many thousands of dollars of equipment and furnishings, tools, accessories, and products (both for use in the business and for retail sale), as well as the costs of staffing, advertising, and keeping the doors open long enough for business to build to a sustainable level. But many hairdressers get started in their homes with only a few inexpensive tools and some consumable products. Even taking into account the cost of cosmetology school and obtaining a license, the capital assets needed are few and the path to revenue can be very short, so the capital requirements may be quite modest and may not present a significant barrier to entering the field.

In short, the amount of "capital" required to start a business is a function of the type of "capital assets" the business needs, together with the length of time needed to fund the operating costs of the business as it moves from concept to profit-generating operations.

Of course, beyond our focus on early-stage companies, there are many circumstances where the availability of capital is critical to an established business. As examples, capital may be needed for retooling and building a new production line for its next generation of products, opening a new store, acquiring a competitor, or simply expanding operations in order to improve cost efficiencies.

B. Capital: Where Do You Find It?

In all these cases, the circumstances of the business and the desires and goals of its owners dictate what sources and forms of capital are available and most suitable. We touched on this subject in the choice of entity analysis in Chapter 2 and now revisit these questions in order to put venture capital in its proper place among an entrepreneur's range of funding choices.

In the context of our client, Joan and Michael have to ask themselves what they envision for their future and the future of SoftCo. Do they want to build their company and then sell it? Do they want to take it public? Can they stand the idea of having additional "partners" in the business — people who are going to look over their shoulders and want to participate in management decisions? Or do they want to operate it with little outside interference for the remainder of their working lives? Do they want to pass it to their (presently hypothetical) children?

In addition to their personal objectives, Joan and Michael have to look at the nature of their business. Is SoftCo a business that is best suited to growth or to a stable level of operations? Does the company need to be large to make its products relevant in the marketplace?

Joan and Michael need to acknowledge their own objectives and understand the range of strategies for their business before they look at sources and forms of capital. Only when they have those criteria clearly in mind can they properly evaluate the pros and cons of the various sources and structures of investment capital available to them.

In considering the relative advantages and disadvantages of the potential sources of capital available to our client, let's look again at the three basic hypothetical capital-raising scenarios for the development of SoftCo.

1. Self-Funding

Joan and Michael, after the unsuccessful effort to capitalize SoftCo through a joint venture with Big Bad Software, might think that they do not want to deal with the difficulties of raising capital for SoftCo, so maybe they should just return to the *Go-It-Alone* plan and fund the business themselves. Unless one of them were clever enough to have selected rich parents, or otherwise had amassed a personal fortune, self-funding may mean using the business to generate the cash needed for its own growth. This is often referred to as "bootstrapping," particularly when it involves subordinating the longer-term objectives of the business to whatever will generate cash now. Funding a business's growth from internally generated cash from normal operations is often called "organic growth."

For Joan and Michael, if they do not have other assets, perhaps *Going-It-Alone* means they will need to take on consulting work or development projects to generate cash while they work on SoftCo's product development in whatever spare time they may have. The downside, of course, is the passage of time. The rest of the operating system software utilities world will not come to a stop because Joan and Michael have to do an unrelated consulting project. Without the time and money to focus on the development of SoftCo's products, the window of opportunity for the business may slip away. In addition to the distraction and the delay, the excess cash they will be able to generate themselves from these outside projects — the cash they will be able to devote to SoftCo — will be limited, so to the extent that they need coding personnel, test equipment, or other resources that more money would make readily available, progress will be slow.

Using personal resources to fund a start-up business presents several other disadvantages. Many entrepreneurs get themselves into serious financial trouble by investing more than they can afford in a new business. Very often, an entrepreneur will run up the balances on multiple credit cards and mortgage his or her house, but then run out of money before the business is successful, ending up facing personal financial ruin as well as a failed business. Thus, a major issue with self-funding is that most people's resources are limited and the needs of the business may be (and usually are) larger than predicted. In addition, while Joan and Michael may be brilliant software architects and engineers, they may not be experienced business managers, so by *Going-It-Alone* they are losing the potential collaborative benefits they could get from a sophisticated, experienced investor who is deeply engaged in their specific industry. This is the trade-off of not having to deal with other owners; the fact is that other owners may well have something positive to contribute to the success of the business.

On the other hand, one of the primary advantages of self-funding is that it will allow Joan and Michael to maintain full ownership of SoftCo while they build its value. They will avoid the time-consuming and difficult process of looking for capital, which they already have gotten a taste of, and will have the luxury of not having to deal with the potential disruption of other owners participating in their business. Down the road, if they do decide to take on other investors, or even to sell the business, they will have retained a larger ownership interest while they built the business and will be likely to attract a higher valuation than if they had not invested any capital or had tried to bootstrap the business without making an investment of personal wealth. In addition, personal investment shows commitment to the business and is generally viewed positively by outside investors.

2. Friends and Family Financing

The second scenario for SoftCo is investment from *Friends and Family*, which founders may pursue from the outset or may resort to after exhausting their self-funding resources. *Friends and Family* investment involves some of the same benefits as *Going-It-Alone* while increasing the pool of resources available to the company. Friends and family tend to invest from motivations outside of pure financial return, so they often will accept a smaller ownership position for their investment than a true outsider would require. For the same reason, they generally are not interested in being involved in the management of the business and so may interfere less in day-to-day operations.

However, there are disadvantages to friends and family financing. The first problem with friends and family as a financing source is that they usually offer a fairly small, one-time opportunity. In addition, they may not be sophisticated or experienced investors and so may be willing to invest more than a prudent portfolio mix would suggest is appropriate for their particular circumstances. Experienced lawyers have seen friends and family investments in unsuccessful companies that have led to the estrangement of family members and the destruction of friendships. An entrepreneur needs to be cautioned to think carefully before taking a widowed aunt's life savings for the business — imagine how Thanksgiving dinner will go for the rest of that entrepreneur's life should things not work out well!

QUESTIONS

---

1. Consider the pros and cons to SoftCo of *Going-It-Alone* versus seeking *Friends and Family* investment. How would you help Joan and Michael evaluate those two alternatives?
2. Would your answer change depending on whether venture capital investment is in SoftCo's plan as the next step? If so, how?

---

3. Outside Investors — Alternatives to Professional Venture Capital

The third scenario for SoftCo, which we are calling *Venture Capital* financing, actually refers more broadly to outside investment by unrelated, previously unknown parties. Although professional venture capital investment funds are probably the best known source of outside investment for early stage companies, there are other options we should examine. Several financing alternatives offer significant opportunities to obtain capital but, like everything in the real world, have advantages and disadvantages.

Strategic Investors.   Joan and Michael have already pursued one source of outside investment — a strategic investor. A *strategic investor* is one that invests not only for direct financial gain, but also to further its own business objectives. The first plan Joan and Michael considered was to use a joint venture with Big Bad Software as a means of bringing investment dollars into SoftCo. Big Bad Software apparently was interested in making the investment because it felt the distribution rights to SoftCo's products, when linked to sales of its own operating systems, would lead to more operating systems sales. However, that option collapsed, primarily as a result of the problems of allocating management and decision-making authority between the parties, as well as concerns regarding the sharing of financial risks and benefits and controlling intellectual property rights. These are typical issues that arise when a strategic relationship is used to obtain capital.

The cost, both financial and opportunity, of a strategic partner as a source of capital has to be examined carefully in light of the constraints that may be imposed as a result of the issues arising from the broader aspects of the parties' business relationship, including exclusivity obligations and intellectual property license rights. The LLC operating agreement issues presented in the proposed Big Bad Software joint venture raised only a few of the difficulties that would typically arise from the joint venture relationship taken as a whole. For example, other matters to be addressed might include intellectual property licensing and use agreements, employee leasing and other human resources agreements, production and support agreements, and product distribution agreements, not to mention operating plans, budgets, and agreements on administrative logistics. Consequently, the capital-raising transaction costs can be high because of all the collateral issues that must be addressed in a complex, multi-part relationship.

In addition, while the motives of the strategic partner may be relatively pure, they may not closely match those of the entrepreneurs. The Big Bad Softwares of the world enter into these strategic relationships generally because they want to control the product or technology as part of their own business objectives. If SoftCo's objectives happen to be aligned, then the relationship may be mutually beneficial. But if the parties' interests diverge, then the party with the power in the relationship will usually drive the outcome. Further, even nicely aligned strategic goals may diverge over time. Large organizations are famous for internal restructurings that may leave a financing joint venture with no internal sponsors or, worse, under the authority of someone who opposed the program from the beginning. In addition, product strategies may shift, government incentives may be withdrawn or new mandates implemented, or myriad other changes in circumstance may arise that would undercut the good intentions that brought the joint venturers together in the first place.

Private Placements.   SoftCo could try raising money in a transaction that is exempt from the registration requirements of the 1933 Act by selling its securities to accredited investors found for it by an investment banker or a finder. By reaching beyond friends and family, the pool of available investment resources is expanded still further. This situation may be referred to as a "broad-based private placement" because it includes a larger network of individuals than just the founders' friends and family. An investment banker, typically having a broker/dealer license, can assist in structuring an offering document, developing the terms of the security, and negotiating with the investors. A finder, however, is unlicensed and so must avoid doing those things, as they require a broker/dealer license. Thus, the finder's role usually is limited solely to introducing potential investors to a company.

While a lot of people are willing to charge a handsome fee for rounding up individual investors tempted by the prospect of getting in on the ground floor of "The Next Big Thing," this path has many potential potholes.

Wealth is not synonymous with investment savvy, so even properly vetted accredited investors may resemble friends and family in this regard and have limited private-company investment experience and sophistication. Further, the investment strategies previously outlined often are pursued with informational materials that consist of little more than an informal business plan, a budget, and a list of warnings on what could go wrong. In contrast, a company would be foolish to pursue previously unknown, individual investors through a broad-based private placement offering without a carefully constructed Private Placement Memorandum (PPM), which is expensive to prepare and requires detailed attention from management to get right. As developed in Chapter 4, a PPM is a key securities law compliance document that provides a description of the investment opportunity, information on the business and industry, financial data, and the risks of the investment. The PPM acts as both a sales and marketing tool for the investment and as an insurance policy. In a broad-based private placement, a thorough and thoughtful exploration of the terms and the risks of the investment, both those that are within and those outside the company's control — that is, the insurance function of the PPM — is critical.

Joan and Michael should expect to spend a lot of time dealing with shareholder questions, commentary, and problems over the next several years if they take this route. Even if the finder or investment banker has not overhyped the company in an effort to earn its fees, and despite prominent warnings that their investment will be illiquid, some private placement investor invariably will call the company within a few months of closing and ask to have his or her money back. And, despite explicit disclosure that the company will use all its cash for development of its business and the investors are likely to see no return on their investment unless and until the company is sold or a public offering occurs, within the first year someone will call the company and ask why no dividends have been paid.

Although the PPM's disclosures of potential risks help protect the company from legal liability for claims on these issues (the insurance function), it cannot solve the underlying investor relations problem. The company must go forward with investors who did not understand what they were doing and now regret having made the investment, and unfortunately, there is typically little the company can do to placate these disgruntled people. In short, the broad-based private placement as a means of raising money has high transaction costs, is time-consuming to complete, and can result in the company being presented with potential investors who are difficult to screen and just may not be well suited to a risky, illiquid investment. The primary advantage of the broad-based private placement is that the pricing and terms of the offering usually are not aggressively negotiated, so a company that can deal with the vagaries of the process can obtain capital while selling a relatively small portion of its ownership.

Angel Investors.   Another outside-investor capital source is *angel investors.* While the name comes from the theatre (financial backers of plays are referred to as "angels"), many angel investors are retired entrepreneurs or business executives who invest in the industries they spent their careers in and offer their experience as well as their money for the development of new businesses. They often can use their excellent industry knowledge and contacts to become important contributors to a start-up business. There are a growing number of active angel investment groups, and some have highly formalized systems for online submission of business plans for the individual angels to review. In addition, angel groups regularly collaborate on investments in order to gather more capital and expertise and to spread risk. While no definitive dollar ranges exist, angel investors typically have more financial resources than friends and family and so frequently will make a collective investment in a company of several hundred thousand dollars. They also usually have much more industry sophistication, and often more investment sophistication, than either friends and family or people who invest in a company through a broad-based private placement.

On the limitations side, despite significant growth in angel investing in recent years, angels still are hard to find and are very selective in their investment choices. They will drive a much harder bargain than any of the previously discussed alternatives. They will ask for more risk-protection terms for their investment and will require a larger portion of the company's ownership in order to make an investment. Their desire for a more complex and detailed set of rights than is usually needed for the other alternatives we have reviewed means that there will be more negotiation on terms and multiple document drafts prepared and revised as the deal is resolved. Deal negotiation and document revision require expensive lawyer time, so transaction costs will be high. (Remember the old adage, "when there is only one lawyer in town, the lawyer starves; when there are two, they both get rich.") Also, like all capital-raising efforts directed at individual people, angels often are good for one investment round but do not have the resources to make substantial additional investments. Finally, as with any company/investor relationship, personal compatibility is important, and even more so here as the angel very likely will want to be involved in management, often including a seat on the board of directors.

Franchising.   There may be other sources of capital that Joan and Michael are aware of and might want to explore. While these may not be appropriate for SoftCo, their legal counsel must know enough to discuss them with Joan and Michael. They might ask about franchising, for example. In brief, a franchisor sells a template for a business to a franchisee, so when the franchised business opens, it looks and operates just like every other business under the franchisor's brand. The franchisor grows its business using investment capital obtained from the franchisee. The franchisee invests capital and gets a head start on a successful business. In addition to the initial franchise fee, the franchisee pays a percentage of ongoing revenues, as well as the cost of supplies, inventory, and customized equipment and furnishings, all of which are purchased from the franchisor. The franchisor in a well-run operation uses the scale of the franchise network to obtain high-volume prices from vendors, passing though that pricing advantage to its franchisees, and works with them to address problems in their businesses. If the system is well constructed, the fee from the franchisee's operations is the profit motive for the franchisor, and if the franchisee operates the business in accordance with the franchisor's guidelines, the franchisee also should make a nice profit.

In short, the franchisor uses the franchisee's capital, in lieu of its own, to open a new outlet. The franchisor strengthens its brand and increases its sales by having more distribution points without incurring the capital cost itself of opening them. The franchisee gets a template for a well-run business, leverages on the whole operation's economies of scale in purchasing its inventory and supplies, and benefits from the broader brand awareness of the franchise's identity.

Problems arise when an unscrupulous franchisor makes its money not off the fee from revenues, but rather from selling the franchises and materials, equipment, and supplies to its franchisees. Instead of benefitting from the scale of the franchise chain, the franchisee is compelled by the franchise agreement to buy things at prices that the franchisor relies on for its profits. Under these circumstances, the franchisees are almost predestined to fail. Their businesses never become profitable and they lose the capital they paid to the franchisor in buying the franchise and related capital assets, as well as the money spent supporting the business while it was operating at a loss. The franchisor often will then repossess the equipment and sell it to the next franchisee.

While a legitimate franchisor can set up a system where everyone makes money, problems can still arise. The template for the franchised business may be flawed and it may not work in an economic downturn. Or, the franchise may become a victim of its own success — it may over expand, with sales cannibalized by other outlets of the same chain. The franchisee is making a capital investment in the franchised business and is undertaking the costs of the franchise in order to reduce some of the risks inherent in starting a business. On the other hand, the franchisee is taking on some risks regarding the franchisor that would not exist in an independent business, or perhaps with a different franchisor.

What does this have to do with SoftCo? As a practical matter, not much. Franchising is a means of raising capital for the franchisor, allowing it to expand its brand by using the franchisees' capital to set up multiple, duplicate businesses within an overall brand identity. SoftCo, being a developer of unique software products rather than the operator of, say, a fast food restaurant, does not fit into that structure. Franchising is not an appropriate means for SoftCo to find capital.

However, be aware that franchise law is a highly specialized area and expert assistance should be sought in any situation where a client might end up creating or purchasing into a franchise relationship. There is no federal franchise law and state laws vary, as does the quality of the states' oversight of the franchise process. In general, many states treat as a franchise any business where a fee is charged in order to do business within an organization. Some states distinguish between franchises and a lower tier of "seller-assisted marketing plans," but the bottom line is that, if someone must pay a fee (however disguised) to get into a business relationship, it probably is regulated as a franchise or franchise-like business. And under the laws of many states, to sell a franchise, the franchisor must provide substantial disclosure, akin to that required for a securities offering, and make extensive informational filings with state authorities.

Public Offerings. Perhaps Joan and Michael have heard that small companies sometimes go straight to the stock market to raise money from the general public. Why wade through all this private financing mess when instead you can just "go public"? Indeed, if going public is the long-term objective of the company, then why not just do it? The analogy, unfortunately, is: Why not get married when you are 12 years old? There may be places in the world where you could do it, but is it a good idea? Just as a 12-year old does not have the maturity or the capacity to meet the responsibilities and obtain the benefits of marriage, a start-up company is not prepared to meet the obligations of the public market, nor is it situated to receive the benefits of being a public company. Like marriage, being a public company is not an end, but a new set of obligations, challenges, and benefits.

Public offerings are expensive and a start-up company would not attract a large amount of money. Imposing that high expense on a small offering means that transaction costs will be significant relative to the amount of money raised. In addition, absent extraordinary circumstances, public offerings for pre-operations companies usually are organized by promoters who charge substantial fees and, with the investors they have brought aboard, take a large ownership position in the newly public entity. Further, once the company is public, it faces the burden of the time-consuming and expensive information delivery obligations required of public companies as well as enhanced exposure to shareholder liability. Finally, small companies that have very little total share value trading in the market find it very hard to attract news reporting or investment banker "analyst" coverage. Without some means of making the world aware of the company's existence and the opportunity it presents, the company will not attract much buying interest in the stock. The result is that very small public companies sometimes can go weeks without any trades in their stock.

In short, the small public company has all the burdens of being public without getting many of the benefits. Of course, it can be done; there are reputable people who can set up the transactions, and some companies do get their capital this way and achieve some level of success. But to take on public-company obligations at a premature stage is an expensive, distracting, and risky means of raising capital.

The final outside source of capital we look at is professional venture capital, which is addressed in detail later in this chapter. However, in reviewing the various potential sources of capital for SoftCo, we have not yet discussed what a company has to give up in order to convince investors to provide it with the capital it needs to launch its new business. As that discussion also is relevant to venture capital, we will address that next.

C. Capital: What Must You Give to Get It?

The two basic inducements a company can offer to potential investors are (i) agreeing to pay the money back together with a fee (interest), which means taking the investment as a loan, or "debt," or (ii) selling part of its ownership, or "equity," to the investor.

A company that borrows money and agrees to pay it back is undertaking a debt to the lender. It can accomplish the transaction either by entering into a personal contract, such as a promissory note or a credit agreement with a bank, or by selling a debt security to one or more investors. Recall the discussion in Chapter 4 distinguishing borrowing as a personal transaction from the issuance of a debt security. As a reminder, a debt that satisfies the criteria set forth by the Supreme Court in *Reves v. Ernst & Young*, 494 U.S. 56 (1990), will be treated as a security for purposes of the 1933 Act. A plain-vanilla example of a personal loan that is not treated as a "security" under the *Reves* test is a mortgage loan obtained to complete the purchase of a new home. Whether entering into a personal contract or issuing securities, the company in either case is borrowing money and agreeing to the terms on which it is to be paid back.

A company that gives up ownership in the business in exchange for capital does so by issuing to the investor an equity interest in the business. As discussed in Chapter 2, depending on the company's business form, that interest may be a personal contractual right (a partner's interest upon joining a partnership) or an equity security. For corporations, and usually for limited partnerships, as well as for LLCs that are not member-managed, that interest is an equity security. The simplest form of equity security is common stock, but equity ownership can take many other shapes and forms, as described in more detail later in this chapter.

1. Capital for Debt

A loan would have the great advantage of providing money without reducing the founders' ownership interest in SoftCo. When one thinks of a loan, one often thinks of a bank. The first issue with bank debt, however, is that it probably would not be available to a start-up company with limited assets and no current revenue. Even in the strongest of economies, banks simply do not make loans involving that level of risk. To the extent that a bank might be willing to make a loan, it probably would be a personal loan to Joan or Michael based on their individual assets and creditworthiness. In other words, the borrower personally will be responsible for repaying the loan regardless of what happens to SoftCo, which means the limited liability protection of the corporate form would be sacrificed in order to obtain the loan. Even if SoftCo had begun operations and had revenue, it is unlikely that a bank would make a loan of any size to SoftCo without personal guarantees from both Joan and Michael, which once again would put their personal assets at risk in the event of a default.

In addition, debt normally requires ongoing monthly payments through the life of the loan. This means SoftCo would have to begin repaying the loan regardless of whether its operations have begun to generate revenue. In essence, SoftCo would have to use part of the loan proceeds to pay back the loan until its revenues are sufficient to make payments from operating cash flow. Despite that major disadvantage to the start-up borrower, there are two significant reasons for the lender to insist on an ongoing repayment stream. First is the fundamental business issue that delaying collection of any loan increases the risk that the loan will never be fully repaid. Second, the IRS treats accrued interest in many circumstances as taxable when it is "earned," regardless of whether a current interest payment is actually received or is deferred until a later date (*see, e.g.*, Treas. Reg. §1.451-1(a)). This means that even if a lender agreed to postpone SoftCo's obligation to make payments on the loan, it probably would have to recognize as income and pay taxes on interest that it "earned" annually over the life of the loan, even without receiving any actual cash payments until the loan is repaid.

Selling debt securities to individual investors is not a solution. In many cases, those investors face the same tax issues on earned but unpaid interest that banks or other lending institutions do. They also face the same increased risk of never collecting on the debt if there are no current payments.

This situation gives rise to one of the key considerations involved in structuring a suitable capital-raising transaction for a start-up business. We touched upon this problem in the prior discussion of strategic investors and individual investors. While some entrepreneurs would like to believe that any capital is good capital, there is a distinct problem when the capital source has different needs or objectives from the company. We earlier reviewed some of those disconnects in our discussion of strategic investors. Another common misalignment occurs when the capital source expects a current payment stream from a company without revenues, as when investors call about their dividend checks or a lender looks for monthly payments. That investor objective means that this source (or form) of capital is not well suited to a start-up company. Thus, the start-up company must do its homework in selecting the most appropriate capital-raising transaction in light of these considerations.

A start-up company seeking venture capital funding typically is at a stage where it is moving from (i) a demonstrated prototype or an experimentally or empirically validated technology or concept to (ii) the creation of a fully formed, working, manufacturable, or duplicable product that can be sold to third parties. The start-up stage involves significant cash expenditures in the course of transforming an idea or a technology from something that can be demonstrated to work to something that can be produced on a large scale at a reasonable cost and sold in meaningful numbers for a reasonable profit. It represents the transition from a viable idea to a business.

The start-up stage involves investment over a period of months or years in capital assets as well as in the expenses involved in creating a business around the idea or product being developed. During this time, when the company's need for cash is paramount but it is not generating any internally, a capital source or investment structure that requires ongoing repayment just is not suitable. Under these circumstances, that investor's or lender's expectations fundamentally conflict with the company's goals, and that conflict most likely will result in an unworkable relationship. A start-up company needs investors who are looking for potentially big returns, are willing to wait a long time, are tolerant of high levels of risk of total loss of their investment in exchange for the opportunity for a big profit, and do not require ongoing cash flows. And, as we turn later in this chapter to professional venture capital as a potential source of start-up funds, we unfortunately will have to look again at the problems that arise when investor objectives diverge from those of the founders.

2. *The Structural Limitation of Debt*

Debt is simply not well suited for a very high-risk investment in a start-up company. The limitation is inherent in the structure of borrowing. Money received through a loan must be repaid, together with a defined premium (the interest), to compensate the lender for the risk incurred in lending the money. The rate of interest is explicitly expressed. While it may adjust, there is always a calculable amount of interest that must be repaid. Even if the company could pay more, it does not have to, and, if it cannot make the payments, it defaults. As a result, the lender is taking the risk that less than the full amount of the debt will be repaid. But on the flip side, the lender has no mechanism for increasing the amount it receives (beyond the principal amount of the loan plus interest) should the company be wildly successful. Consequently, for creditors, this situation presents high risk and very limited reward.

In contrast, an investor in the equity of a company takes a certain number of shares that the investor believes will have an acceptable projected value if the company grows within a predicted range of success. If the company's success is below that range, the stock will be worth less than predicted, but if the company is very successful, the stock may be worth much more than predicted, and the equity investor gets that extra value. In other words, equity offers the potential for large rewards in exchange for taking significant risks.

A very large percentage of start-up companies fail, so any investor must accept a very high risk of losing everything. Even though (as you will recall from your introductory Business Associations class) in liquidation, creditors have the right to be paid before equity owners, if the lender has not received an ongoing payment stream and then the company fails, there is a high likelihood that the lender will lose some, if not all, of its investment. Given the structural limit on the upside, the high risk on the downside is simply too great for most investors to conclude that the opportunity for profit on debt justifies the risk of loss.

3. Capital for Common Stock

Since raising capital through debt presents the combined problems of being unattractive to the company because of the need for a current payment stream and unattractive to the investor because of the structural limitation on balancing high risk with a reasonable prospect of a suitable return, let's look at equity as a capital source. The simplest equity investment vehicle is common stock. What should be the response when Joan and Michael point out, correctly, that all this is getting rather complicated, and what is wrong with just issuing common stock to a capital provider?

The answer turns on pricing. In a company liquidation, equity securities get paid only after the creditors have been satisfied, and common stock has the last right to payment among equity securities. However, it also is the security that holds the company's residual value. Thus, in the event of a liquidation or sale of the company, after paying creditors and everyone holding equity securities with a priority that entitles the holders to a fixed return on their investment (e.g., preferred stockholders), the remaining value of the company, if any, no matter how little or much, goes to the common stock holders. Common stock is the highest risk security by virtue of being last in priority, but because it gets all the extra value in the company, it holds the equity upside.

The risk in common stock makes it the cheapest security, on a per-share basis, the company can sell. Low price per share means more shares per dollar of investment received. As a result, if SoftCo sells common stock to raise capital, it will have to sell a lot of shares per dollar of capital raised. That means Joan and Michael, as the founders and current shareholders of SoftCo, will have to give up a large portion of the ownership of SoftCo if the company raises capital by issuing new shares of its common stock.

If, however, SoftCo sells a higher-priority security to raise capital — that is, one that combines some of the aspects of debt (high priority) with the equity upside that common stock provides — it can charge a higher price per share relative to common stock. That means fewer shares would need to be issued and the investors would end up with a smaller ownership portion of SoftCo after the investment, so Joan and Michael's portion, therefore, would be larger. In addition, if capital is raised with a higher-priority, higher-priced security, then SoftCo could provide its management and employees with common stock at a discount price from what the investors paid for their "better" (i.e., higher-priority) stock without creating the kind of §83 tax problem that was discussed in Chapter 6.

4. *Capital for a Debt/Equity Combination*

Convertible Debt. A possible alternative to common stock is a hybrid debt and equity security. An example of such an instrument is convertible debt, which is a loan whose outstanding balance can be converted into common or preferred stock instead of being repaid in cash, at the investor's discretion. A convertible debt security gives the investor the higher priority of a debt holder (in the event the company fails) and the ability to charge an interest rate, plus the right to exchange the security for a defined number of shares of stock to take advantage of the equity upside.

In general, convertible debt is not favored by start-up companies because some payment stream is often required by the terms of the deal. If payments are deferred, investors are uncomfortable with the treatment of imputed interest as taxable income over the life of the debt. In short, creating a hybrid debt/equity security gives the investor an equity upside, but does not overcome the other problems (previously discussed) that are inherent with debt.

Debt with a Warrant. Another alternative is debt with a warrant or other detachable equity instrument (a "sweetener" or "equity kicker") that allows the debt to be repaid while leaving in place a continuing right to receive equity. A *warrant* is the functional equivalent of an option: a right to buy a stated number of shares of stock at a defined price during a specified period of time. Depending upon the circumstances, the number of shares or the price could be set by formulas rather than fixed numbers. Either way, at any given time, the exact number of shares and per-share price must be calculable.

Again, this approach presents the same structural limitations that apply to debt. Because the debt has a fixed return, the equity element usually is counted as supplemental consideration (which is why it is called a "sweetener"), so the value allocation between the debt portion and the equity right does not fully address the investor's objectives (not enough shares are purchasable through the warrant to offset the upside limitation on the debt). Further, from the company's point of view, it does not eliminate the problem of an ongoing payment obligation.

In addition, issuance of debt with a warrant gives rise to a tax problem called Original Issue Discount (OID). Section 1273 of the Internal Revenue Code requires that the purchase price paid for debt and warrants (if the two securities are not separately priced) be allocated between those two securities based on their fair market value. *See* 26 U.S.C. §1273. Thus, a portion of the investment amount is deemed to be paid for the debt instrument and a portion for the warrant, despite the fact that the amount to be repaid under the debt terms is equal to the entire investment amount. Since the "real" amount paid for the debt instrument, per the IRS, is the amount of the total investment less the value of the warrant, a portion of the repayment proceeds that the parties labeled as repayment of principal the IRS sees as extra interest. The upshot of OID is that the investor has to recognize this imputed additional interest as taxable income during each year the loan is outstanding. In this circumstance, the warrant's value probably is not high, but the tax recognition of the OID amount means the lender faces either an increase of the effective current tax rate on the interest payments in fact received, or taxation on an additional amount of income recognized without any actual interest payments being received.

As a simple example, assume that a lender loans $1 million at 12 percent per annum and receives a warrant to buy shares of the borrower's stock. Under the terms of the loan, the lender is to receive repayment over five years in 60 equal monthly payments that are fully amortized (that is, like a classic home mortgage, the payments are a shifting mix of principal and interest). If the IRS views the warrant as being worth $100,000, then the IRS will tax the transaction as though the lender loaned $900,000 and paid $100,000 for the warrant. As a result, the IRS will ignore the stated interest rate and loan balance and look at the payments as though they repay a $900,000 loan. Because the IRS sees the loaned amount as smaller, part of the monthly repayment the lender designated as return of principal is treated by the IRS as extra interest and is taxed at ordinary income rates.

There is an exception to the application of OID where the value of the warrant is *de minimis*, meaning its value is less than one fourth of 1 percent of the stated amount to be repaid as principal at maturity of the debt, multiplied by the number of full years to maturity. Thus, on a $1 million debt and warrant investment, if the note required repayment of $1 million over five years, then 0.0025 times $1 million times 5 equals $12,500. If the value of the warrant is less than $12,500, then no OID is applied. The regulations under §1273 used to provide guidance on how value should be calculated, but that is no longer the case. However, in light of the stock option valuation requirements of §409A of the Internal Revenue Code, discussed in section B-3 of Chapter 6, it is likely that any warrant valuation approach used for OID purposes that varies from that used for stock options to comply with Section 409A will be viewed by the IRS with suspicion. Although some practitioner guides (*see, e.g.,* HALLORAN ET AL., VENTURE CAPITAL & PUBLIC OFFERING NEGOTIATION at pp. 6-11 (3d ed. Supp. 2011)) provide language for claiming this *de minimis* exemption, it is difficult to conceive in the venture capital context (outside of a very short-term "bridge loan," to be discussed in the next few paragraphs) that a warrant would be for so few shares relative to the value of the note that a credible argument for the *de minimis* exemption could be made.

In summary, debt securities, even with equity kickers, have limitations as mechanisms for investment in early stage companies for at least two fundamental reasons. First, they have the structural limitation of not commanding sufficient opportunity for a return that investors would view as appropriate in light of the risk of investing in early stage companies. Second, their basic requirement of some level of ongoing repayment makes them unsuitable for a company that is not yet generating cash from operations.

Bridge Loans. Though less suitable for long-term investment, convertible debt or debt with a warrant frequently is used for short-term loans, generally referred to as "bridge loans," which are loans that are not outstanding long enough for the problems inherent with debt to become meaningful. A bridge loan is a short-term financing vehicle, typically used by a company's existing investors, that provides the company with enough capital to "bridge the gap" between where it is now and where it needs to be in order to attract new equity investment. A bridge loan effectively is an advance on the next round of investment and so explicitly provides that it is to be repaid within a period of months, either with cash (which is unlikely) or by the issuance of shares in the next round of investment. Since the bridge loan investor is taking the risk that there will not be another round of investment, repayment by a share issuance often involves a discount on the per-share price paid by new investors to buy the same securities — the longer the loan is outstanding, the bigger the discount. In other words, the investor, who is bearing a high risk of default, will be enticed to take this risk because the share price discount (more shares for the money) offers the potential for a better return on the next equity investment. If the next round of investment does not take place and the company fails, the bridge loan, as debt, gives the investor the priority of a creditor in the distribution of the company's assets.

From the investor's perspective, a bridge loan offers the priority of a debt instrument with the upside of an equity investment should things work out. Bridge loans typically are outstanding for only a few months, so the problems with debt discussed earlier in this section are minimized. From the company's point of view, a bridge loan is a way to buy time to accomplish key short-term goals and postpone setting an equity investment value on the company until after those goals have been accomplished. (We look at equity investment and company valuation in the next part of this chapter.) Outside of this limited application, debt generally is not a favored instrument for early-stage venture capital investment.

What is left, not surprisingly, is the usual mechanism for early stage capital investment: the issuance of convertible preferred stock. This security is at the top of the priority group among equity securities and includes a range of protective mechanisms that are similar to debt, while retaining a strong equity character. It is typically "permanent," meaning that it is not subject to a debt-like fixed repayment obligation. It also improves a company's creditworthiness because it adds assets (cash) to the business without an offsetting liability (debt to a lender). Convertible preferred stock is the traditional, though evolving, form for private, high-risk capital investment and generally is perceived by investors as providing the best mix of priority and potential return. The details and significance of these factors will be explored in the following sections.

D. Venture Capital and the Venture Capital Investor

1. Introduction to Venture Capital

Overview. Venture capital is private investment capital in high-risk ventures. It has existed for most of modern history. Indeed, one classic example was Queen Isabella's personal financing of Christopher Columbus's voyage to find a faster route to the Indies.

Venture capital is an investment arena that accurately can be called "private equity," as it typically takes the form of investment in the equity securities of privately held companies. Yet while venture capital partnerships share many structural similarities with private equity funds, as do hedge funds, their market segments are distinguished by their investment strategies. Hedge funds nominally are designed to act as a counterbalance to the risks inherent in investment in certain industries or markets, although in some notorious cases they seem to operate as highly leveraged, unregulated mutual funds. While venture capital funds invest in earlier-stage, high-risk companies, private equity funds tend to focus on more established, later-stage companies. In addition, private equity often is used to finance acquisitions (the money goes to existing owners of the company in exchange for the transfer of their ownership interests) instead of investments (the money goes into the company in exchange for the issuance of new ownership interests).

While the term *venture capital* describes in general all of the investment alternatives realistically available to SoftCo, we are using it to mean professionally managed venture capital investment funds. In that light, venture capital investing is more of a multifaceted process than a specific financial act. But, simply stated, venture capitalists seek very high levels of long-term capital appreciation through stock investments (together with active management participation) in high-risk, growth-oriented companies with outstanding management that have some kind of protectable head start on providing a game-changing product or service in a growing industry.

Very few businesses qualify for financing under the strict criteria used by venture capitalists. Despite the drawbacks of the investment sources outlined earlier in section B of this chapter, most businesses are funded by the founders and/or their friends and families. Usually those sources, perhaps together with government grants and subsidized loans, are sufficient to get the vast majority of businesses to the level where they can be self-sufficient enough to grow organically or perhaps qualify for a line of credit from a traditional lending institution.

But, as we have reviewed, those sources typically have limited funds. While they may be sufficient for businesses with relatively low capital needs that can afford to (or want to) grow slowly, what about the company that seeks to enter a fast-moving industry and needs a substantial amount of capital soon? A company like SoftCo may have only a brief window of opportunity to hit the marketplace with its products before the market moves on to something else. If SoftCo does not come to the market with its products when a lot of people are looking for the very solution those products offer, it may never succeed. If SoftCo is too late, potential customers may have already chosen a different company's solution to their problem. Once that occurs, even if SoftCo's products are better, it would be in the position of having to displace an existing solution provider rather than entering an open market. As a result, SoftCo's best opportunity for success may be getting into the market as large and in as an advanced a stage as possible, and doing so as quickly as possible. That means it will need a substantial amount of capital very early on in order to grow fast. While SoftCo might develop into a successful business if Joan and Michael pursue the *Go-It-Alone* or the *Friends and Family* financing scenarios, really big success is most likely to come from growth to a size — and at a rapid speed — that only a large investment from a venture capitalist can provide.

It is important to remember that venture capital represents only a fraction of the private investment capital deployed in the United States each year. Because it is high profile and at the top of the private risk capital food chain, it gets attention that is vastly disproportionate to its size. Venture capital is useful to look at, however, because it occupies one end of the continuum of private capital investment sources, with self-funding from the founders at the other end. It is the most sophisticated, well-developed approach to high-risk private company equity capital investment. As a consequence, a lawyer working with an early-stage company that seeks financing would be well-served by understanding how venture capital funds work, and how venture capital convertible preferred stock and a typical venture capital transaction each are structured. Awareness of the issues, forms, and solutions used in professional venture capital financing will give any transactional lawyer, even one who may never deal with an actual venture capital fund, a head start at advising on, negotiating, and documenting a private company financing transaction.

Advantages and Disadvantages.   Just as we did with other potential sources of investment capital, let's look at the pros and cons of venture capital financing. First, as we have noted, venture capital investors have deep pockets. They can invest large sums and, while their resources certainly are not unlimited, when they choose a company to invest in, they plan to make subsequent investments, earmarking additional funds for that purpose from the very start. By providing access to large amounts of capital, venture capital offers a start-up company the opportunity to grow quickly and to achieve more rapidly the success that can come from early arrival in the market as a fully formed, sizable business.

In addition, venture capital investors often can provide extremely useful industry knowledge and contacts. Venture capital funds tend to focus their investments on a fairly narrow area in which they have particular expertise. While larger funds may reach across a range of industries, this usually reflects the number and diversity of their investment professionals rather than some unique, renaissance capability. Their typically narrow focus means that venture capitalists, like well-qualified angel investors, are deeply immersed in their selected industries. They know who is doing what, who is working where, who is losing talented employees, and who is hiring. They know the specific industry problems that growth companies have to overcome. They have seen companies clear those hurdles and companies that have stumbled. They understand where a company's product or technology fits into the broader landscape of the industry as a whole. Venture capital investors make their knowledge, contacts, and expertise available to their portfolio companies and consult with and assist management on almost every key decision the company faces, which can be of invaluable assistance to the company. The other side of that coin is that venture capital investors do insist on playing a major, active role in the management of the company and its business.

Venture capital investors also will demand a large portion of the company's ownership for taking the financial risks and for devoting their time to becoming an investor and active participant in a company. Along with a greater equity share, venture capital investors often will sit on the board and thereby introduce a new and more demanding level of oversight. This can lead to personality and management clashes between the founders and the investors. In addition, a venture capital-financed company not only *can* progress more quickly — venture capital investors will *insist* on rocket-speed growth. That speed itself entails risks. Processes will be pursued in parallel. Decisions may be forced based on achieving a time line that turns out to be unrealistic. Management skills will be tested and additional management will be brought to the company, perhaps significantly diminishing the roles of the founders. It can be a turbulent and awesome ride when it works and a massive train wreck when it does not.

2. Recent History of the Venture Capital Industry

The growth of venture capital investing over the last 40 years has been nothing short of dramatic. Annual U.S. venture capital investments grew from several hundred million dollars in the late 1970s to approximately $4 billion in 1994, the last year preceding the run-up to the tech bubble of the late 1990s. After spiking up to a little over $100 billion in 2000, the level of annual investment dropped to around $19 billion in 2003. From 2004 to 2007, venture capital investments grew at an increasing rate, topping $30 billion in 2007, falling off in 2009 to approximately $20 billion as a result of the Great Recession, then slowly recovering to approximately $27 billion in 2012. THE 2012 MONEY-TREE™ REPORT by PricewaterhouseCoopers/National Venture Capital Association based on data from Thomson Reuters (PwC/NVAC 2012 MONEYTREE REPORT). Among a range of technological, social, and regulatory causes, part of this growth is the result of basic economics, which dictates that money flows to where returns are highest. In addition, tax law has been kind to venture capital investors and to venture capitalists. Since they make equity investments, most of their returns are realized as capital gains, which in recent times, other than a few years in the 1980s, have been taxed at significantly lower rates than ordinary income.

Deregulation of financial institutions, particularly pension funds and investment banks, has lowered investment barriers, thus allowing those institutions to make high-risk investments. These regulatory changes have resulted in more money being available for venture capital investment. In addition, because the public stock markets represent an attractive means for venture capital investors to sell their shares and realize on their gains, greater acceptance of smaller, growth-oriented public companies, as evidenced by the emergence of the NASDAQ market, has been a boon to venture capital. Unfortunately, the initial public offering market was hit hard by the Great Recession. While 86 venture-backed companies had IPOs in 2007, only 20 went public in 2008 and 2009 combined — the lowest two-year total since 1974-1975. PwC/NVCA 2009 MONEYTREE REPORT. In each of 2011 and 2012, approximately 50 venture-backed IPOs occurred, while the first two quarters of 2013 yielded 29 IPOs thanks to a particularly strong market interest in biotech companies. *See* Press Release, Thompson Reuters/National Venture Capital Association, *Venture-Backed IPO Exit Activity More Than Doubles in Q2'2013 with Strongest Quarter for Biotech Offerings Since 2000* (July 1, 2013), *available at* http://thomsonreuters.com/press-releases/pdf/Q2-13-Exits-Release. For a quarter-by-quarter report covering the last five years of mergers and acquisitions (M&A) and IPO exits, *see* http://nvcatoday.nvca.org/index.php/industry-stats/venture-backed-ipo-exit-activity-more-than-doubles-in-q22013-with-strongest-quarter-for-biotech-offerings-since-2000.html.

E. The Venture Capital Fund

1. Fund Structure

Limited Partnership. Venture capital funds typically are organized as limited partnerships with a limited liability entity, such as an LLC, serving as the general partner. The actual venture capitalists — that is, the venture capital organization whose name is on the fund — control the general partner, which, in the limited partnership structure, gives them virtually total control over the entity. The limited partnership form, with a limited liability entity as the general partner, creates limited liability for all the participants in the venture capital fund. Also, recall the discussion in Chapter 2 regarding pass-through "partnership" (as opposed to "corporate") tax treatment. In the context of a venture capital fund, the tax treatment is significant not only in that income and loss are allocated to the partners (in accordance with the terms of the partnership agreement) and then recognized on their tax returns rather than on the partnership's return, but also in that assets may be distributed out to the individual partners without taxation. In an asset distribution, the partners receive the assets with the tax basis the partnership had, and no taxable event occurs until the partner sells the asset and, usually, a capital gain is recognized. With a venture capital fund, the assets distributed out to the individual partners usually consist of the stock received by the fund in exchange for its investments in the companies it has funded.

The limited partnership agreement for a venture capital fund generally specifies that the fund has a limited life, typically ten years. However, the agreement usually gives the partners the right to extend the partnership's (i.e., the fund's) life by one to three years in order to allow any remaining investments in the fund to mature before being distributed out to the partners upon liquidation of the partnership.

Generally, the venture capitalists, acting through their general partner entity, invest 1 percent of the fund's total capital (although they may invest more, but not often more than 5 percent), with the limited partners putting in the remaining 99 percent. In addition, the individuals making up the general partner also may invest more funds through a separate entity that invests as a limited partner. Unlike the limited partners, the venture capitalists often invest only 10 percent of their general partner capital commitment in cash. The remainder of their investment obligation is covered by a reduction in the annual management fee the general partner would otherwise be entitled to receive. As an example, if the projected fund size is $100 million, the venture capitalists, in their roles as operators of the general partner entity, might commit to invest $1 million, with $100,000 to be delivered in cash and the remaining $900,000 delivered through foregoing a portion of the annual management fee. Essentially, the bulk of the general partner's financial contribution to the fund is paid by an offset against its annual management fee.

General Partner Compensation. The venture capitalists make their money in two ways. First, for operating the fund's general partner, they receive an annual management fee, which is often set at 1.5 to 3 percent of the total amount committed for investment in the fund. In the foregoing example, with $100 million committed to the fund, a 2 percent management fee would mean $2 million paid by the limited partners to the general partner each year. Sometimes, after several years, the basis for the fee calculation shifts from committed capital to the amount actually invested. This provides a steady source of fees to support the cost of looking for and screening investment possibilities during the earlier years of the fund, when those activities are more intense. After, say, four to six years, when the focus of the fund has shifted to managing and supporting its existing portfolio of companies, the limited partnership agreement may provide that the formula for the management fee changes to a percentage of the actual fund investment. This fee structure protects the limited partners from paying large fees throughout the life of the fund to a general partner that only invested a portion of the committed capital.

As noted, a portion of the management fee often is waived by the general partner in connection with a corresponding reduction in the amount of investment in the fund required to meet the general partner's capital contribution commitment. While tax issues are generally beyond the scope of our discussion, it bears emphasizing that this mechanism for reducing the management fee has to be structured carefully so that the general partner is not treated for tax purposes as having earned the entire annual fee (which would be taxable as ordinary income), then invested a portion of it back into the limited partnership.

The second way the venture capitalists make money is from an override interest in the fund's profits, often referred to as the "*carry*" or the "*carried interest*." As the owners of the entity serving as the general partner (e.g., an LLC), which is investing, say, 1 percent of the partnership's capital, the venture capitalists are entitled to receive 1 percent of any returns of invested capital. That is, they will receive a proportionate return of the dollars invested in the fund (ignoring for the moment the capital contribution through the waiver of its management fee) until all investors, including the limited partners who put up 99 percent of the money, are paid back all of the money they put in. At that point, any additional distributions shift from being a return of investment capital to a sharing out of profits, and now the general partner's portion steps up from 1 percent to 20 percent of the proceeds. This override on profits can be extremely lucrative to the venture capitalists if the fund is very successful. In some venture funds the profits have to exceed an annualized "*hurdle*" rate before the general partner's override kicks in. The hurdle is a pre-set rate of annualized profit that the limited partners must receive, in addition to getting their original investment amounts back, before the 1-99 percent allocation shifts to 20-80 percent.

While limited partners like the concept of a hurdle, some venture capitalists argue that it actually ends up decreasing the overall return of the fund. They assert that it encourages the general partner to focus excessively on investments likely to turn a short-term profit in order to quickly surpass the hurdle and get to the 20-80 percent allocation instead of holding out for better long-term results. This position is difficult to accept because the venture capitalists share most in high-return outcomes; it seems contradictory that a hurdle would make them shift to a shorter-term, lower-return outlook when doing so is contrary to their own interests. A more realistic basis for their objection is that a hurdle requires them to forego their 20 percent share in the first profits the fund returns.

In any case, the carry, with or without a hurdle, can be a very complex matter to draft into the limited partnership agreement. Consider that a venture capital fund invests varying amounts of money in a number of companies over a period of years. In addition, as we examine more closely in a moment, investment commitments to a venture capital fund actually are fulfilled in pieces over a period of years. Plus, the stock purchased by the fund is not necessarily sold in the same order as the investments were made, and returns can vary wildly from one investment to another.

In light of all these variables, at what point does the general partner's carry kick in? In other words, using our earlier example, let's say that the $100 million venture fund is early in its life and has collected only $40 million of the committed capital from the limited partners. Further assume that one of the fund's first investments is for $8 million, and that company was sold in the second year of the fund in a transaction that pays back the $8 million plus a $42 million profit. Should the carry be triggered? On a current basis, the fund already has returned more than it has invested and it still has $32 million outstanding in ongoing investments. But what if the remaining outstanding investments, as well as all the subsequent investments of the fund, turn out to be worthless? In that case, the limited partners will have invested $99 million and received back only $49.5 million (($8 million plus $42 million) times 99 percent). When you throw in a hurdle, the calculation gets even more problematic.

In short, if the limited partners agree to allow the general partner to be paid on the carry based on achieving early profitability, there must be a mechanism for the partnership to retrieve those funds and reallocate them on the 1-99 percent basis if the perceived profitability evaporates in the face of subsequent losses. That mechanism is called a "clawback." The carry, hurdle, and clawback mechanisms often are the most closely negotiated and carefully drafted provisions in the limited partnership agreement for a venture capital fund.

Tax Controversy.   The general partner's carry also raises some controversial tax policy issues. While the details, and the ebb and flow of the regulations and positions of the Internal Revenue Service, must be left to a tax course, tax law has been clear for years that the grant of an interest in partnership capital in exchange for services is taxable as ordinary income. *See* Treas. Reg. §1.721-1(b)(1). However, it also has long been the case that the grant of an interest in future partnership profits in exchange for services is *not* taxable as ordinary income because the value of that interest is just too speculative to be taxed when granted. *See Campbell v. Commissioner of Internal Revenue*, 943 F.2d 814 (8th Cir. 1991). *Query*: How does this treatment compare with the Section 83 income recognition problem (discussed in Chapter 6) that arises when a stock interest is granted in exchange for services?

Therefore, the venture capital fund is structured so that the general partner is entitled to be paid back its invested capital in proportion with the return of the capital invested by the limited partners, all of which conforms to Treas. Reg. §1.721-1(b)(1). In addition, at the onset of the fund's life, the general partner is granted an excess interest in future partnership profits, the value of which in fact will flow from the quality of the general partner's management activities on behalf of the partnership. That is, the general partner, in exchange for future services, gets a grant of a future profit interest that has a completely speculative value. Thus, under the court's ruling in *Campbell*, no taxable event occurs on the grant of that carried interest.

The real rub occurs as a result of the second element of the tax policy issue, which is how to characterize the income received by the venture capitalist as a result of the carry.

The character of partnership income is determined at the partnership level and it is then attributed (i.e., passed through) to the partners in that form. *See* IRC §702. Thus, if a partnership purchased a capital asset, such as the stock of a start-up company, then some years later sold that stock at a profit and distributed the proceeds to its partners, because the partnership held the shares as a capital asset and the sale qualified for long-term capital gains tax treatment, the realization of the gain on the sale would be taxed to the partners at the lower long-term capital gains rate. In short, the carry is not taxed as ordinary income when it is granted in exchange for services (since the value is too speculative) and, when the carry is later triggered, the general partner, like the limited partners, pays taxes on it at lower capital gain rates because profit distributions from the fund are typically made in the form of capital gains. Thus, some argue, that the carry is a mechanism to achieve capital gain tax treatment on income paid for services. *See, e.g.,* Victor Fleischer, *Two and Twenty: Taxing Partnership Profits in Private Equity Funds,* 83 N.Y.U. L. REV. 1 (2008).

Most private equity and hedge funds have similar general partnership compensation structures, and hedge funds in particular have taken the brunt of the outrage on this issue because many of them hold billions of dollars in assets. Their size can make for eye-popping sums of tax dollars "lost" to the government when hedge fund managers receive tens or hundreds of millions of dollars, or even billions, through their carry but pay taxes on these distributions at relatively low capital gain rates. *See, e.g.,* Victor Fleischer, *Taxing Blackstone,* 61 TAX L. REV. 89 (2008). The Barack Obama administration has made some attempt to address this: a line item entitled "Tax carried (profits) interests as ordinary income" has been included in its budget proposal for several years, but no action has been taken to implement this significant change in tax treatment. OFFICE OF MGMT & BUDGET, EXEC. OFFICE OF THE PRESIDENT, FISCAL YEAR 2014 BUDGET OF THE U.S GOVERNMENT, at pg. 18 (2013), *available at* http://whitehouse.gov/sites/default/files/omb/budget/fy2014/assets/budget.pdf. The same is included in the 2013 budget on pg. 222, *available at* http://whitehouse.gov/sites/default/files/omb/budget/fy2013/assets/budget.pdf, and in the 2012 budget on pg. 186, *available at* http://whitehouse.gov/sites/default/files/omb/budget/fy2012/assets/budget.pdf. Similar entries for 2011 and 2010 are *available at* http://www.gpo.gov/fdsys/browse/collectionGPO.action?collectionCode = BUDGET. *Query*: What is your view of the public policy issues surrounding this tax controversy? Remember, if you apply ordinary income tax to a big hedge fund manager's carry, do you also apply it to Workerbee's share of the profits of The Pizza Joint's sale? Is that the right result?

2. *The Limited Partners*

The Role of Limited Partners.   The limited partners provide most of the money to venture capital funds and rely on the venture capitalists to manage the limited partnership. Limited partners typically are financial institutions and money managers at pension funds, trust funds, and foundations who are seeking to diversify their portfolios by allocating a small amount of money to high-risk, potentially high-return, equity investments. Other investors might include corporations, wealthy individuals, and business associates of the venture capital organization. These latter investors often are looking to build (or cement) their business relationship with the venture capitalists or perhaps just hope to obtain early access to the venture fund's portfolio companies.

What about the people who invest in broad-based private placements or as angel investors? Do they also participate as venture capital fund limited partners? Usually not. One reason may be the compensation structure previously outlined. Angel investors with strong industry knowledge and executive experience may believe that they do not require the expertise of the venture capitalists, and they particularly do not need (or want) it at that price. Generally, these investors believe that they, or their investment advisors, have enough industry and investment savvy that they can eliminate the venture capitalist middleman and invest directly.

Securities Issues Regarding Limited Partners.   There are legal constraints on who can invest in venture capital partnerships. The sale of limited partnership interests in a venture capital fund is a sale of securities. As with a company selling its stock to raise capital, a venture capital fund selling its limited partnership interests either must file a registration statement under the 1933 Act or must qualify for a registration exemption. This alone would not preclude investment from most of the individuals described in the preceding discussion, as they typically meet the accredited investor standard of Rule 501(a) of Regulation D. The problem comes not from the 1933 Act, but from its lesser-known securities regulation sibling, the Investment Company Act of 1940. 15 U.S.C. §§80a-1 through 80a-64. In looking at the regulatory application of the Investment Company Act, the following paragraphs are in no way meant to be comprehensive. Instead, they simplify the statutory language of the definitions and exemptions of the Investment Company Act in order to focus on its relevance to a typically structured venture capital limited partnership.

The Investment Company Act regulates "investment companies," which, simply stated, includes securities issuers that are primarily engaged in the business of investing, reinvesting, owning, holding, or trading in securities that have a value representing more than 40 percent of the issuer's total assets. *See generally* 15 U.S.C. §§80a-3(a)(1)(A), 80a-3(a)(1)(C), and 80a-3(a)(2). As a venture capital fund is issuing securities (i.e., limited partner interests) in order to pursue the business of investing in and holding securities (i.e., the stock of its portfolio companies, which represents substantially all of the fund's total assets), a venture capital fund falls squarely within the statutory definition of "investment company." Unless an exemption applies, an "investment company" is subject to a number of enhanced fiduciary duty requirements, limitations on transactions with affiliates, restrictions in making changes to certain management policies or making cash distributions without seeking investor approval, and administrative and bookkeeping requirements that are supervised (and enforced) by the SEC. Since those obligations and restrictions add to the cost of the venture fund's operations and complicate management's responsibilities, most funds seek an exemption from the regulatory requirements of the Investment Company Act.

Two exemptions typically are used. First, §3(c)(1) exempts private securities issuers whose outstanding securities are held by 100 or fewer investors. 15 U.S.C. §80a-3(c)(1). Second, §3(c)(7) exempts a private issuer that sells its securities only to "qualified purchasers." 15 U.S.C. §80a-3(c)(7). Venture funds normally rely on Rule 506(b) of Regulation D as the 1933 Act registration exemption for the issuance of their securities, which satisfies the requirement in each of the referenced exemption sections that the funds be *private* securities issuers. Turning to the second element of the

§3(c)(1) exemption, as is typical with various provisions of the federal securities laws that restrict the number of permitted investors, the difficulty lies in determining *who* you must count. The Investment Company Act provides a maze of provisions that address who is to be counted and under what circumstances the venture fund must "look through" an entity making an investment in the fund and count the owners of that entity. For example, the owners of an investing entity must be counted separately if that entity was formed for the purpose of investing in that particular venture fund, or if the entity will have 10 percent of the voting interests of the venture fund and is relying upon the same two exemptions to address its own Investment Company Act issues. *See* 15 U.S.C. §80a-3(c)(1)(A). As this requires a layered, factual inquiry, some funds simply apply a worst-case outcome approach and treat suspect entities as though the "look through" requirements will apply. The result is that many funds, in an abundance of caution, over-count their investors.

The consequence of relying on the §3(c)(1) exemption is that a fund needs to raise a lot of money per limited partner since the fund is permitted to have a maximum of 100 counted investors. Our $100 million fund, therefore, being conservative on its count, would have to raise an average of over $1 million per investor. While the fund may be willing to allocate some of its counted slots to individuals who are each interested in committing $500,000, or even $250,000, it very well might not accept smaller commitments. In addition to being inefficient in terms of dollars per counted investor, more investors means higher administrative costs, plus a greater risk that one or more investors may default on their capital commitment. From the investor/limited partner perspective, an individual investor may be perfectly comfortable making a series of $10,000 to $50,000 investments directly in small companies over a period of years, recognizing them to be long-term, high-risk, illiquid investments, because the investor knows he/she can stop at any time if, for example, the economic outlook or the investor's personal circumstances change. In contrast, committing $250,000 to a venture capital fund can take away that discretion for seven to ten years (i.e., the term of the fund's investment activity). The bottom line is that the §3(c)(1) exemption acts to severely limit participation by individual investors in a venture fund, unless they are very wealthy.

The §3(c)(7) exemption applies to funds where *all* investors are "qualified purchasers." As applied to individuals, this means a person owning at least $5 million in investment value, which is defined by the SEC to exclude a principal residence. The "accredited investor" standard of Rule 501(a) of Regulation D also excludes the principal residence's value, but it requires only $1 million of net worth (subject to periodic adjustment, as addressed in Chapter 4, section B-3). Many wealthy people who make private investments as "accredited investors" simply do not meet the higher "qualified purchaser" standard and, therefore, are not eligible to invest in a venture fund that relies on the §3(c)(7) exemption. *Query*: Why is the exemption net worth threshold for investing in a venture capital fund under the §3(c)(7) exemption higher than that for a Regulation D private placement?

While these two Investment Company Act exemptions are separate, sometimes funds will seek to meet the requirements of both in the hope that if they are unsuccessful in their compliance efforts on one, the other will provide a fall-back exemption. Thus, a fund accepting only qualified purchasers may hedge its position by also staying at or below 100 investors, just in case a purchaser it thought was qualified actually was not.

(Recall the "Burden of Proof" discussion in section B of Chapter 4 regarding the diligence obligation imposed on an issuer of securities to investigate the appropriateness of prospective investors in order to establish the relevant exemption from registration.) Alternatively, a venture capital group may set up parallel funds: a large, lead fund for clearly qualified purchasers where the investor count does not matter, relying on the §3(c)(7) exemption; and one or more smaller funds, each under 100 limited partners, relying on the §3(c)(1) exemption, for smaller investors, friends, and strategic relations of the venture capitalists. Because of the inherent conflict-of-interest issue faced by venture capitalists in managing multiple funds, often when parallel funds invest in a company, the venture capitalists who manage them will divide the total investment among the group members based on their proportionate committed capital amounts. This takes the funds through life in lockstep, so there can be no question of favoring one over another.

3. Operating the Fund

Set-up and Strategy.   Setting a venture capital fund in motion is much like starting any other business. A team of qualified people forms a strategy and seeks to raise the capital necessary to execute on the strategy. In venture capital, experienced investment professionals get together and determine in what industries and at what stage of a company's development they will invest. Industries are selected based on prospective growth and the capacity for rapid change. Usually, the venture capitalists have extensive experience as investors in or managers of businesses in the target industries. In deciding what stage of company development the fund will target, venture capitalists combine their expertise and experience with an economic calculation. In general, the earlier in a company's life the fund invests, the longer the time until a return-achieving exit will occur and thus the greater the risk of failure. High risk and a long period of illiquidity before any payoff is the rule for all venture investing, and it means the projected growth in the value of the investment must be very high to justify making the investment in the first place.

There is no fixed set of names or definitions for the stages in a company's development. In part, this is because the stages vary by industry and even may not consistently apply within an industry, depending on the product and other circumstances. Having said that, the stages may be described as follows:

- At the *seed* stage, the business consists of a credible person with an idea, but with little or no "company."
- At the *start-up* stage, depending on the industry, the company has either a demonstrable technology, a prototype, a mock-up, or some other proof of value; the core of a management team has assembled; and the business structure is beginning to exist or at least is well planned.
- By the *early* stage, the product or service is well fleshed out or perhaps already available for sale, and the company is turning its activities from internal development outward, by adding marketing efforts and the build-up of sales to its focus. The basic risk of the company during this stage begins to shift from its conceptual viability to its ability to execute its business plan.

- During the *expansion* stage, the company has revenue, is building its market presence with an expanded sales and marketing staff, and perhaps is rolling out its second-generation product or service offerings.
- *Later*-stage companies are continuing the expansion stage but need more growth and seasoning in order to be an attractive acquisition target or public offering candidate.

The expertise and, frankly, the time a venture capitalist will be called on to provide to a seed-stage company is very different from what will be needed at the expansion or later stage. So the venture fund's management team has to be well suited to the risks, the timing, and the services required, given its targeted industry and business stage.

As a company moves through these stages, the risks shift from the viability of the concept — *Can we create a viable product or service from this idea?* — to the execution of the business model — *Can this product or service be sold in a way that makes money?* As the components of risk are progressively overcome during the growth and development of a company, the risk discount investors apply to the company's value decreases. In other words, the value of the company goes up as it grows and accomplishes more, thus narrowing the scope of the risks its investors face. The upshot is that funds that focus on the seed and start-up stages face higher levels of risk and, therefore, will invest only in companies that can be projected to provide very high levels of return, perhaps in the range of 60 to 75 percent per annum. If a company is in an early stage, the required projected annualized rate of return might be 40 to 60 percent. Expansion and later stage companies present lower risk, but still may need to show 30 to 50 percent annual returns. These numbers, like the stages, are not fixed or consistently applied. The important thing to recognize is that, no matter the stage, the increases in projected value these companies are expected to attain through venture capital investment are absolutely staggering.

Once an investment team and a strategy are set, the venture capitalists begin the task of gathering the investors who will provide the fund with its capital. They prepare a PPM explaining their strategy, describing their team, and providing the financial and structural details of the fund. As with the PPM for any new securities issuer raising funds, that document also serves an insurance function and so describes the risks and the consequences of negative developments. The venture capitalists also prepare the limited partnership agreement, form their general partner entity if it does not already exist, and set the target fund size (the amount of money they hope to get committed to the fund) and the minimum fund size.

The size of the fund is a function of the company stage it intends to focus on and the number of venture capital professionals making up the fund's management. Usually one of the fund's venture capitalists is responsible for overseeing the relationship with each company the fund invests in. Earlier-stage companies require smaller initial investments but need more support time, so each fund manager handles less money and fewer companies. Funds focusing on earlier-stage companies tend to be smaller. Later-stage companies usually involve larger investments, but these companies are fairly well-established institutions that require less fund manager time, which means more money and more companies per fund manager. These funds tend to be larger.

Since the process of raising capital commitments from prospective limited partners can take a year or more, a minimum total commitment amount is set by the fund.

This means that when the fund has received commitments at least equal to the minimum, it can ask those investors to actually deliver a portion of their committed investment and it can start operations. As other investors decide to join, they can be added to the partnership until the target amount is reached or the venture capitalists simply decide to quit raising money. The limited partnership agreement, as well as the PPM, set out the minimum so the prospective investors are aware of the terms. Setting a minimum amount assures the initial investors that they will not be called upon to contribute capital until there are enough investors providing enough capital to make the fund viable.

QUESTIONS

1. Based on the definitions provided in the foregoing discussion, what stage is SoftCo in? Does it have a workable technology? Does it have a product? Does it have an assembled management team?
2. Because venture capital funds tend to focus on specific industry areas, SoftCo most likely would look for a venture fund that has a lot of experience in software. Would a fund that has made significant investments in digital effects software for James Cameron movies (e.g., *Terminator, Titanic, Avatar*) be a good potential investor candidate? What about a company that creates software for ring tones and cell phone applets? How would you evaluate the suitability of a venture capital fund's software experience?

Capital Commitments.   The limited partners make an investment commitment to the venture capital fund, which actually is the maximum amount they may be called upon to deliver over the life of the fund. The fund may call less than the entire commitment, but it may not call more. The limited partners do not deliver all their money at the outset because most of it would just sit in the fund's account waiting for the venture capitalists to find the companies to invest in. Instead, the limited partners deliver their investment commitment to the fund in pieces over the life of the fund in response to "capital calls" made by the general partner.

The general partner may call on the limited partners to provide the committed investment amount based on a set schedule over time, or upon notice sent from time to time as needed in order to make company investments, or by some combination of the two. The key point is that responding to a capital call by the fund is not an opt-in/opt-out decision for the limited partners. The limited partners have made a commitment to deliver up to a specified amount of money under the terms of the limited partnership agreement, and they are expected to honor that commitment. A default on a capital call would be very disruptive and harmful to the venture capital fund and the other limited partners. As a result, in addition to the usual range of breach-of-contract remedies, the limited partnership agreement often will provide that a limited partner defaulting on a capital call is (i) barred from making further investments, and (ii) required to forfeit to the other limited partners some or all of its already invested interest in the fund.

The capital call mechanism is used not only to allow the limited partners to hold on to their money and put it to work in other ways prior to the time it is needed by the fund, but also because the venture fund does not want the money until it is ready to use it. The reason is that the performance of a venture fund is determined by a calculation of the fund's "internal rate of return" or "IRR," which for this purpose is the annualized effective return rate on the limited partners' investment in the fund. Public stock markets provide a liquid investment opportunity and have averaged an approximately 7 percent per annum return from the crash of 1929 until 2013. Venture capital investing involves high-risk and long, illiquid investments, so venture capital funds need to offer the prospect of a significantly higher rate of return in order to attract investment capital. Since the internal rate of return on an investment is strongly affected by the period of time the investment is outstanding, it makes no sense for the venture fund to collect money from its limited partners — starting the IRR time period running — before it is ready to actually invest that money.

An investment that doubles in value in one year has an IRR of 100 percent, but if that doubling takes place over seven years, the IRR is just 10 percent. An investment would have to return 128 times the original invested amount in order to achieve a 100 percent annualized rate of return over seven years! (As a simple example, $1 needs to be $2 at the end of year one, $4 at the end of year two, $8 at the end of year three, $16 at the end of year four, $32 at the end of year five, $64 at the end of year six, and $128 at the end of year seven in order to achieve a targeted annualized rate of return of 100 percent.) Another way to look at it is that the longer the investment is outstanding, the higher the outcome has to be to meet the fund's targeted rate of return. The venture fund wants to put its investors' money to work when it locates investment opportunities that it thinks can return 40 percent, or 60 percent, or higher, on an annual basis, so that, in the end, when all the success and failures are totaled up, it can deliver to its investors overall returns of perhaps 15 percent, or maybe 20 percent, per annum. Having to achieve those levels of return, the venture fund does not want to call money and have the IRR clock ticking while that money sits in an account earning paltry money market rates.

4. The Economics of Venture Capital Investing

Venture capital investing is a subjective mix of qualitative and quantitative analysis that is more art than science. The fundamental issue for the lawyer to grasp in order to understand how venture capitalists decide whether to invest in a company is the time value of money. The lesson is that, given the extremely high return rates targeted by venture capital funds: (i) money should not be invested in a company until it actually can be used to increase that company's value, and (ii) the faster a company can get to a point where the investment can be cashed out, and the proceeds paid to the limited partners, the better the annualized return on that investment will be.

Time Value of Money.   As an example, let's assume that a venture capital fund is targeting a 40 percent annualized return on each investment it makes and has identified a company it thinks has a good chance to be really successful. After careful analysis, the venture capitalists decide that the company will need approximately $10 million in investment and five years of development to grow into an attractive acquisition candidate.

The question is whether the company will be worth enough in five years to produce an annualized rate of return of at least 40 percent on the $10 million investment. Let's further assume that the venture capitalists have used their business school skills to run a bunch of different financial models to project a future value for the company. These models, depending on the assumptions made, may show a huge range of potential values for the company, but because the fund would not even consider investing if it did not believe in the qualitative parts of its analyses (for example, that management is sound — for the company's current needs, at least — the product is real, and the industry is growing fast enough) its assumptions probably will skew towards projecting success. Finally, let's assume that after much discussion and argument among the venture capitalists, they agree that the lower end of the projections points to this company being an acquisition target in five years at a price in the range of $45-$50 million. Given that the company needs $10 million in investment, does a projected sale in that price range achieve the targeted 40 percent per annum return on that investment amount? The answer depends in large part on when money actually is put into the company.

If the venture fund were to invest all $10 million at the outset, then an annual return on capital of 40 percent would require that the fund get $53,782,400 when the company is sold five years later. The calculation is simple: multiply the value at the beginning of each year by 1.4 (100% = 1, and 40% = 0.4, therefore a 40% annual return is the value multiplied by the sum of 1 plus 0.4, or 1.4) to find what the value at the end of that year must be, then repeat that process for each year involved. So, the projected value of an up-front investment of $10 million after one year is $14 million ($10 million times 1.4); after two years, $19,600,000 ($14 million times 1.4); after three years, $27,440,000 ($19,600,000 times 1.4); after four years, $38,416,000 ($27,440,000 times 1.4); and after five years, $53,782,400 ($38,416,000 times 1.4). This growth shows the effect of compounding, where the increase is added to the base of the next calculation. An annualized rate of return on an investment — or a venture capital fund's aggregate IRR on all its investments — is essentially a compounded interest calculation. In contrast, $10 million invested at a "simple" interest rate of 40 percent per annum would produce an unchanging $4 million each year. After five years, the $10 million would have grown by $4 million per year, or $20 million, to a total of $30 million.

So, to return to the original question: will the $10 million investment get the venture fund its desired 40 percent annualized return if the company's sale at the end of year five must yield proceeds to the venture fund of at least $53,782,400? Because the fund's models project a sale price for the company of only $45-$50 million, the answer is no, so the fund should not make this investment.

But what if all the venture fund's money were not invested up front? What if the investment were cut into pieces, or "tranches" (which comes from the French word *trancher*, meaning to slice), and spread out over time? As an example, assume that the company's budgets and growth plans show that it really only needs $1 million right away, but it will need an additional $2 million in the beginning of the second year, $2 million more at the beginning of the third year, and $5 million at the beginning of the fourth year. Using the same calculation as before, to achieve a 40 percent annualized return, the projected value of an up-front investment of $1 million after one year is $1,400,000 ($1 million times 1.4). At the beginning of the second year, $2 million more is invested, so at the end of the second year, we have $2 million times 1.4 for the new investment amount, which is $2,800,000, plus an additional year on the $1,400,000 we had at the end of year one (multiply by 1.4), which is $1,960,000, for a total of $4,760,000.

At the beginning of the third year, another $2 million is invested, so at the end of the third year, we have $2 million times 1.4 for the new invested amount, which is $2,800,000, plus an additional year on the $4,760,000 we had at the end of year two (multiply by 1.4), which is $6,664,000, for a total of $9,464,000. At the beginning of the fourth year, $5 million is invested, so at the end of the fourth year, we have $5 million times 1.4 on the new invested amount, which is $7 million, plus an additional year on the $9,464,000 we had at the end of year three (multiply by 1.4), which is $13,249,600, for a total of $20,249,600. There is no new tranche at the beginning of year five, so to determine the value at year-end, we have only to multiply our year-four total by 1.4 ($20,249,600 times 1.4) to arrive at a year-five required value of $28,349,440.

Thus, if the $10 million were invested in tranches on the schedule outlined above, a 40 percent annualized return would require proceeds to the venture fund on the sale of the company at the end of year five in the amount of $28,349,440. This company has a range of projected prices on sale of $45-$50 million according to the venture capitalists' models/calculations. This means that the fund should consider making this investment if, as is addressed in the next section, its ownership interest in the company will give it a large enough portion of those total projected sale proceeds to meet its targeted return.

Similarly, when the venture fund is calculating its IRR on this investment in order to report on how well it has invested its limited partners' capital contributions, would the fund report a better rate of return to its limited partners if it had made one capital call up front for $10 million, or if it had made four smaller capital calls on the outlined schedule? The principle is the same: the fund can present a higher annualized rate of return to its investors (i.e., its limited partners) by calling their money in pieces over time because the time value of money issues the fund applies in making its investments apply equally to the limited partners' investments into the fund.

QUESTIONS

1. Assume that a venture capital fund is targeting a 50 percent annualized rate of return. It is looking at a potential investment in a company that needs $5 million of capital. The venture capitalists project that their interest in the company could be sold after four years for $20 million. Should they make the investment?

2. Upon additional analysis, the venture capitalists decide that instead of investing $5 million at once, they could invest $1 million, and after one year invest another $1 million. At the end of the second year, they would then need to invest the remaining $3 million. How does that change the investment decision?

Investment Amounts.   We have shown how a venture capital investment's rate of return is a function of the amount invested, the length of time the investment remains outstanding, and the amount ultimately paid back on the investment in the future. The prior discussion focused on the impact of the period of time an investment remains outstanding. We turn now to the issues of the amount invested and the amount recovered on the investment in the future.

The amount invested is determined by the company's capital needs in order to achieve its business plan. Companies with extremely large initial capital needs that will not produce a return for an extended period of time often are viewed as unsuitable for venture capital, in part for the reasons just reviewed. The venture capital investment model prefers that large capital expenses be deferred until later in the company's life so the large investments required will not be outstanding for a lengthy period of time and, even better, other forms of financing might be available to the then more mature company. As we have seen, a venture investment can produce a higher annualized return if it is structured in tranches that reflect the company's actual cash needs over time rather than delivered as a lump sum at the outset. The lower limit on the size of each tranche and the time scheduled to elapse between tranches is set by the need to allow room for variations in the company's projections and other changes in its business plans, the administrative and legal cost of documenting and completing frequent investments, and the fact that the company must be able to present itself to the world as an adequately funded, viable entity. This last element is particularly important in convincing a landlord to rent an office, employees to join, and tradespeople to do business with, and extend normal commercial credit to, the company. Thus, while there may be a temptation to micro-manage the delivery of investments into a company, venture investors in most circumstances expect in each tranche to deliver enough money to meet the company's cash needs for at least 12 to 18 months.

Company Valuation.   The remaining aspect of the investment decision process that we have not examined is how much ownership the venture capital investor gets in the company in exchange for the fund's investment. In the earlier discussion of capital, we noted that venture capital funds generally receive convertible preferred stock in exchange for their investments. While we analyze the terms of that security in more detail in Chapter 9, our question for now is what portion of the total ownership interest in the company will the venture capital investor receive in exchange for putting its money at risk. This is determined through a process called *valuation*. It is an essential component of the venture capitalist's rate-of-return projection because the value the fund anticipates it will get on the future sale of the company, or on the sale of its shares in (or following) a public offering of the company's stock, depends on what portion of the company the venture fund owns.

Note that in the prior discussion of a 40 percent annualized return, the projected proceeds of $45-$50 million were referred to as the sale price of the company. In order to simplify that earlier example, we did not address a key variable — the venture fund's ownership in the company at the time of its sale. If the venture fund owned half of the equity of the company (and thus was entitled to half of the proceeds of the sale), then if the company were sold for $45-$50 million, the venture fund would receive only $22.5-$25 million. If the venture fund owned half the company and were looking for proceeds of $45-$50 million, the sale price of the company would need to be $90-$100 million. If the venture fund were targeting proceeds of $45-$50 million and owned only one third of the equity of the company, then the company's sale price would have to be $135-$150 million. It is clear, then, that projecting the future payback on a venture fund's investment is a matter of predicting both the future value for the company at the time of a liquidity event (such as its sale) and also knowing what portion of that value will belong to the venture fund. The venture fund's future ownership portion of a company is determined by its starting ownership portion, which then must be adjusted to reflect changes that occur within the company during the life of the investment.

The portion of a company the venture capital fund buys with its investment is set by the "valuation" applied to the company at the time of the investment. The valuation process involves two related values: the pre-money valuation and the post-money valuation. The *pre-money valuation* is the value of the company before it receives the contemplated investment. The *post-money valuation* is the value of the company after the investment is made in the company. Hence, the pre-money valuation of a company, plus the investment amount, equals the company's post-money valuation, which can be expressed as the following equation:

$$\textit{Pre-Money Valuation} + \textit{Investment Amount} = \textit{Post-Money Valuation}$$

If we assume that the company will need one investment from the fund, that it will never need any additional investment capital, and that the shares needed for founders and for equity incentives as the company grows can all be built into the equity ownership structure (the company's *capitalization*) at the time of the investment, meaning that the portion of ownership of the company the venture fund receives for its investment will not change through the life of the company and will still be in place when the company is sold, then the valuation process is simple.

Using our prior example, if the company needs an investment of $10 million up front, and the projected proceeds of the company's sale after five years are $45-$50 million, how much of the company would the fund need to own in order to justify the investment? We determined that if the fund is targeting a 40 percent annualized rate of return, then the value of its $10 million investment after five years needs to be at least $53,782,400. Thus, the projected sale price range for the company simply cannot deliver enough money to justify the investment.

As another alternative, what if the sale proceeds after five years were projected to be $70-$90 million? If the company were sold for $70 million, the venture fund would need to own at least 76.832 percent of the company to hit its desired return target ($53,782,400 is 76.832% of $70 million). Similarly, if the company were sold for $90 million, the fund would need to own at least 59.7582 percent of the company ($53,782,400 is 59.7582% of $90 million).

Based on this information, we essentially back into the company's pre-money and post-money valuations based on the amounts imputed by these potential transactions. Recall that post-money valuation is the pre-money valuation plus the investment amount; it is the total value of the company after the investment has been made. If the venture fund projects a $70 million sale price for the company, then it must get at least 76.832 percent of the company for its $10 million investment in order to achieve its targeted IRR over five years of ownership. So, what is the value of the entire company immediately after the investment (the post-money valuation) if the venture capital fund paid $10 million to buy 76.832 percent of the company? Using simple algebra:

$10 million = 76.832% of $X, where $X is the post-
money valuation of the company, or, restated,
$10 million = .76832 times $X.

Dividing both sides of the equation by .76832, we have
$10 million divided by .76832 = $X, or
$13,015,410.25 = $X.

Under this calculation, the post-money valuation is $13,015,410.25. Because the post-money valuation is equal to the pre-money valuation plus the investment amount, and given that the investment amount is $10 million, then $13,015,410.25 minus $10 million is $3,015,410.25, which is the pre-money valuation. What this means is that by deciding it needs to own almost 77 percent of the company in order to hit its target return on its $10 million investment based on its assumptions and projections, the venture fund is attributing a value to the remaining ownership of the company at the time of its investment of $3,015,410.25. That amount is the pre-money valuation: the value of the company immediately before the venture investment, as imputed by the amount of the investment and the portion of the company the venture capital investor is to receive for the investment.

At the other end of the venture capitalists' projected sale price range in our example, the price was $90 million and the venture fund needed to own at least 59.7582 percent of the company in order to hit its 40 percent per annum target. In light of these assumptions, how are the pre-money and post-money valuations changed? In this case, the equation is:

$10 million = 59.7582% of $X, or
$10 million = .597582 times $X.

Dividing both sides by .597582, we have
$10 million/.597582 = $X, or
$16,734,105.11 = $X.

Under this calculation, the post-money valuation, $16,734,105.11, based on the same investment amount of $10 million, means the pre-money valuation of the company is $6,734,105.11. Thus, if the venture investors decide they need to own a little less than 60 percent of the company in exchange for their $10 million investment, then the value they are attributing to the rest of the company before the investment is $6,734,105.11. From the point of view of the shareholders of the company prior to the investment, note that changing the venture capital investors' projected sale outcome to $90 million from $70 million, and nothing else, means the pre-money valuation (that is, the value placed on the interests of the pre-investment owners of the company), would be over $6.7 million rather than just about $3.0 million. *Query*: What does the pre-investment, pre-money valuation mean to Joan and Michael and their contributions to SoftCo? How much of this process seems rather arbitrary?

In real life, venture capital investments rarely are made in one piece and rarely do companies require no additional investment, so this example is extremely simplified. In addition, for sale proceeds at the lower end of the projected range ($70 million) the venture investor would have to take over three-quarters of the ownership of the company, which leaves little ownership for the founders and key employees and, thus, is more than most funds are comfortable taking at the outset. Therefore, it is likely that the fund would not do the investment. Or, as the venture capitalists might express it, the financial projections simply do not justify a pre-money valuation that supports a $10 million investment.

In addition, with the company's financial need divided into a number of pieces addressed in separate rounds of investment over time, so many things can change the predicted outcome that these valuation projections become extremely complicated and perhaps so speculative as to be of little use. Many companies also have multiple venture capital investors and, as a company advances through the various stages of development, the mix of ownership among the investors may shift, plus new investors may join. As an investor's projections of future value are based wholly on estimates and assumptions, some investors try to simplify the process by, for example, looking in growing industries to find companies they think can grow faster than the rest of the industry. Or a seed stage venture investor might look at the start-up stage financings in a particular industry and decide that if a company has several specific criteria in place, it can attract a predictable range of venture capital valuations as a start-up. This type of venture capital investor may determine, then, that its objective should be to finance seed stage companies at a price that will yield a target rate of return based on hitting those start-up stage criteria and valuations. In short, they invest by targeting not the exit transaction but instead only the next step in the investment sequence.

The valuation process is repeated each time the company takes on a new "round" of investment capital. A note on terminology is in order. A single investment by a venture capital fund may be sequenced over time in tranches, while each new decision to make an investment and to set a value on the company is referred to as a *round* of investment. Each round of investment is typically done by issuing a new series of preferred stock. Despite the examples discussed earlier, it is unlikely that an investment by a particular venture capital fund would be tranched over four years at one valuation. Instead, new money would be delivered at a new valuation in a new round of investment using a new series of preferred stock. If things go well, with each round of investment the company's valuation will grow; that is, the pre-money valuation of each subsequent financing round will be greater than the post-money valuation of the prior round. As you will recall, the pre-money valuation is the value attributed by the investors to the existing ownership of the company immediately prior to their investment. So the pre-money valuation for a second round of funding applies to the ownership of the company immediately prior to that investment, which is the ownership after the first round and, therefore, includes the venture capital investor from the first round. If the pre-money valuation on that second round is higher than the post-money valuation on the first round of investment, then the value of the company has increased. If the company's growth takes longer than expected, so that, for example, the investment money that was supposed to get the company to completion of a manufacturable product has been spent and the company is still doing research and development, then the valuation may go down. *Query*: How can an investor ensure that a company stays on track? In turn, how can a company like SoftCo ensure that its business stays on track?

Venture investors understand that a company's value does not grow on a straight-line basis, but rather it stair-steps its way up as the company accomplishes certain milestones and addresses outstanding risks. As a result, the amount of money delivered in an investment round, in addition to reflecting the other considerations already discussed, often is specifically set to provide enough funds to support the company for a sufficient period of time (i.e., enough "runway") to get it past the next step-up in value. That way, when the company is looking for new capital in another round of financing, it can present itself to prospective new investors as deserving a higher valuation, having accomplished a major milestone or addressed a fundamental risk.

Why would venture capital investors want the price to go up for the next round of investment? Recall that as a company moves from one stage of development to the next, its pool of potential investors will include a new set of venture funds that focus on companies at that stage. The prior venture capital investors will continue to invest (i.e., to "support the company") but will look for substantial investment from new venture capital investors. If new investment comes in at a higher price, then fewer shares have to be issued to the new investors, and accordingly, the prior investors, founders, and employees will experience a smaller decrease in their percentage ownership in the company.

From the lawyer's perspective, this is an example of the shifting constituencies that make up a corporate client. The venture capital investors that company counsel negotiated against in the last financing round became shareholders upon the completion of that financing and thus are part of the company when it comes to negotiating the terms of the next round of financing. Moreover, in that next round, those venture funds not only may have representatives sitting on the company's board of directors but also may be investors in that new round, with separate legal counsel negotiating on their behalf. Company counsel must represent the company in the face of this shifting cast of characters and manage the inevitable conflicts of interest that result from these changes.

QUESTIONS

1. If SoftCo is given a pre-money valuation of $4 million by a venture capital fund, and the anticipated investment amount is $5 million, what is the post-money valuation of SoftCo? What percentage of SoftCo's value will be held by the investor upon completion of the transaction?

2. If SoftCo's venture capital investors buy 55 percent of SoftCo for $6 million in a one-time, lump-sum investment, what is the pre-money valuation? The post-money valuation? If the venture capital fund targets a 45 percent annual rate of return and SoftCo, with no further investment or other share issuances, is sold after three years for $40 million, will the investors hit their target?

3. If company counsel had taken common stock in lieu of fees at the time that the company was being formed, how would that complicate the issue of multiple

stakeholders in the company? Alternatively, what if company counsel made a small investment in the prior round of preferred stock financing?

4. What fiduciary duty issues arise in obtaining corporate approval of the second round of funding in light of the board and shareholder roles played by the first-round investors? Do those issues change if those first round investors are also investing in the second round? If they are the only investors in the second round?

Shares "Deemed" Outstanding and Fully Diluted Shares.   One aspect of the venture capital approach to valuation is that it treats all the ownership interests of the company as having equal value. It ignores the fact that some shares may be common stock and some preferred stock. In contrast, recall the discussion in section A.4 of Chapter 6 of the disparity in value between venture capital preferred stock and common stock arising from the different rights embodied in each.

In addition, some shares counted for the valuation process are not even issued, but just set aside for employee options. In the venture capital valuation process, all of these shares are treated as *deemed outstanding* on a *fully diluted basis*. By ignoring any distinction between the forms of ownership interests, this approach to valuation defines all shares as having equal per-share value. It assumes that in a successful company, all preferred stock will be converted to common stock, all outstanding options and warrants will be exercised, and the end result will be that everyone will hold identical common stock shares. As a result, percentages of ownership are treated as equal to percentages of value. Thus, the venture investor who buys 59.7582 percent of the value of the company in a cash investment of $10 million also buys 59.7582 percent of the post-money fully diluted shares, or the post-money capitalization, of the company.

If a venture investor were to approach SoftCo with a proposal to invest $4 million on a $5 million pre-money valuation, we would know that the venture fund is proposing to own $4 million of the $9 million post-money valuation of the company. That also means that the venture investor expects to receive 4/9, or 44.44 percent, of the ownership of SoftCo. It also suggests that Joan and Michael, assuming they hold all the pre-money ownership, would have 5/9 of the ownership of SoftCo, or 55.56 percent, and thus would hold 5/9 of the post-money valuation of the company. Unfortunately for Joan and Michael, even with no other shareholders, that ownership interest is probably not a realistic assumption.

Venture investors typically want a company to have a pool of common stock shares set aside for equity incentives. As the company grows and hires new employees, it often will provide those employees with the opportunity to have an ownership interest in the company as an additional element of compensation along with salary and benefits. A typical equity incentive plan set-aside (or *reservation*) is 15 to 20 percent of the post-money capitalization. Now, since we know the venture investor has determined how much of the company it seeks to own after making its investment, we should not be surprised that it has no intention of letting the company take that incentive pool from its portion of the ownership of the company. The only other place it can come from is Joan and Michael's share.

In the foregoing example, if the venture capital investor seeks to invest $4 million on a $5 million pre-money valuation, and the investor wants the pre-money valuation to include a reservation for equity incentives equal to 20 percent of the post-money shares, what does that mean to Joan and Michael? In short, it means that the preferred stock issued to the venture investor will still represent 44.44 percent of SoftCo, but that 20 percent of the total "deemed outstanding" post-money shares will be an equity plan reservation. Thus, Joan and Michael, instead of owning 55.56 percent of the post-money capitalization of the company, would have only 35.56 percent. So 20 percent of SoftCo's post-money shares deemed outstanding would be shares not actually issued, but rather only set aside for an equity incentive program.

In addition to shares reserved for an option plan, not yet issued but "deemed outstanding" shares normally include the shares issuable upon the exercise of any outstanding options or warrants or upon conversion of any outstanding convertible securities. The underlying idea is that these shares either have already been paid for, so the money already is in the company, or that the price to be paid for them in the future will be low, so the issuance of these shares will not add any capital value to the company. As a result, these shares should be treated as already outstanding.

The concept of shares being *deemed* to have been issued arises in a number of contexts in venture financing. As a result, it is important to recognize the difference between the shares that *actually* are outstanding versus those *deemed* outstanding. For example, consider the venture investor in SoftCo who proposed to get 44.44 percent of the fully diluted capitalization. Because the equity incentive reservation is only *deemed* outstanding (until the shares in fact are issued), the venture investor owns 55.56 percent of the *actually outstanding* shares. (Only 80% of the "deemed" outstanding shares making up the post-money capitalization of the company are actually outstanding and $44.44 \div 80 = 55.56\%$.) The result is that the venture investor, with only 44.44 percent of the fully diluted shares, actually owns outright control of the company.

QUESTIONS

1. What are the implications for Joan and Michael of treating SoftCo's "deemed outstanding" shares as part of its pre-money valuation?
2. SoftCo is told by a venture capital fund that it should have an option plan reservation equal to 20 percent of the post-money capitalization of the company, and that reservation will be part of the pre-money capitalization for that fund's investment. SoftCo's employee-hiring budget, as built into its business plan, shows that the proceeds of the venture capital investment will fund the company for 18 months and allow it to hire employees only using half of those reserved shares. Is 20 percent an appropriate inclusion in the pre-money calculation?

Fund Performance.   Venture capital funds are businesses just like SoftCo in the sense that they seek to provide a sufficiently attractive rate of return on their limited partners' investments in order to reflect the risks and illiquidity inherent in private risk capital investments. Venture capital funds are different in that, unlike most corporations, they have a planned limited life and their general partners usually plan to organize more funds in the future, which they hope will be invested in by satisfied limited partners from the current fund. In light of the phenomenal run-up in venture fund performance in the late 1990s, the disastrous returns following the tech bubble crash in 2000-2001, with the subsequent recovery followed the by the downturn beginning in 2008 as a result of the Great Recession, it may not be useful to try to offer an average annual return for venture investing. Remember that venture capital investments are long-term and illiquid, so a profit-recognition transaction in a particular year may reflect more on the opportunity to achieve an exit from a company in that year than the quality of the original investment.

In addition, venture funds are privately operated and their results are self-reported, so they probably are not completely transparent in the details of their results. Not surprisingly, when funds are doing well, the number of responses to performance surveys is very high. In difficult business environments, as during the second half of 2009, survey responses become less reliable. For example, for the third quarter of 2009, *Dow Jones VentureSource* reported that the amount of new commitments from investors to venture capital funds was approximately $3.5 billion, up from $2.3 billion of investment capital raised in the second quarter. *See* Dow Jones VentureSource Third Quarter, 2009 Report. In marked contrast, however, the *PricewaterhouseCoopers/National Venture Capital Association's MoneyTreeReport* says the amount raised in the third quarter was approximately $1.6 billion, down from $2.0 billion in the second quarter. *See* PwC/NVCA Q3-2009 MoneyTree Report.

That said, venture funds as a whole showed lackluster performance for the ten years from 2003 to the end of 2012. Based on data through March 31, 2013, the S&P 500 (a broad index of public company stock values) outperformed venture investment for the then-most-recent quarter, year, 3-year, 5-year, and 10-year periods. *See* Cambridge Associates LLC U.S. Venture Capital Index® and Selected Benchmark Statistics (March 31, 2013), *available at* www.NVCA.org/index.php?option = com_docman&task = doc_download&gid = 997&Itemid = 317.

Venture capital funds target overall performance at annualized rate of return percentages in the teens or low twenties. These returns compensate investors for the illiquidity and uncertainty inherent in long-term, high-risk private equity investments. However, potential venture capital fund investors will turn to other, more liquid investment choices when those disadvantages are not offset by better performance.

Trying to boil down venture investing and fund performance into one number, however, does not do the subject justice. As was the case in looking at a fund's IRR for a particular investment, the final overall performance reported by the fund does not tell you much about what happened in between. A successful 40 percent IRR investment made in the first year of a fund's life may actually have required the limited partners to contribute funds pursuant to capital calls made on several occasions over, say, six years, with a big return in year eight. That investment, on a year-to-year basis, had zero or negative cash returns for seven years in a row (based on capital outflows for the initial and subsequent investments), before providing a big payoff in year eight. In addition, during the first seven years, the limited partners would have been called upon to pay in money for management fees and for other investments made by the venture fund, some of which will have failed.

A well-known maxim in venture investment is that "the dogs die before the runners win." That is to say, a well-managed fund will cut off money to companies that are not progressing (i.e., the "dogs") and take the loss rather than pour in good money after bad. The consequence is that limited partners tend to get nothing but bad news for the first several years of a fund's life, then, as the "runners" start to come on after a few years, those results begin to reverse themselves. The key to venture fund performance, simply put, is the "runners" and how well they run.

The standard wisdom on venture investing, particularly in earlier-stage companies, is that out of ten investments, five will end up valueless, four will provide a partial return of capital or perhaps a small profit, and, hopefully, one will be spectacular. Venture capitalists live for those few spectacular companies they find for their funds. A single big winner can turn a fund from losing half its invested capital to beating the annualized stock market index returns. A second winner can put results into the stratosphere for the fund generally and, in light of the 20 percent carry, make the venture capitalists very wealthy indeed.

This expected high rate of failure is the reason venture capital investors look only at companies that have the potential of being big winners. The target IRR a fund uses in vetting its potential investments is not really a goal for an investment in a single portfolio company. The venture capitalists know very well that the companies they invest in will not *all* perform as predicted. Instead, the target return is more a required threshold of potential success. There is no point in investing in a company that — even if it does everything right — simply does not have the potential to deliver a big payoff.

The cautionary aspect to these fund performance facts for companies seeking investment capital and their counsel is that the venture capitalist is managing a portfolio for the benefit of the limited partners and the venture capitalists running the fund. Thus, it is relatively easy for a venture fund manager to look at a struggling company the fund has invested in and just walk away. From the venture capitalist's perspective, cutting losses by letting "the dogs die" is simply a matter of running the fund properly. The cruel truth is that the fund's bottom line is driven by winners. Putting time and energy into a company that, with effort, may just survive and return the capital invested, or maybe even a little extra, will not materially change the fund's results and takes away time and energy that could be applied to finding the next runner that wins big. The problem from the founders' point of view, of course, is that they do not have a portfolio. They have this one company, which at some time may no longer satisfy the objectives and constraints of venture capital investment.

Furthermore, the kinds of disconnects discussed earlier in section B also may arise. A company's early success may encourage the founders to want to sell the company and take their profits, but just as likely may encourage the venture investors to put in more money in order to grow the company further in the hope of a big win. Nice returns are not the goal of venture capital investors, so they may well prefer to put in more money, roll the dice, and reach for the spectacular outcome.

The upshot is that venture capital investors have goals and criteria for making investments and for managing their funds that, generally speaking, do not always align perfectly with the interests of the owners of their portfolio companies. The point is not to malign venture capitalists. Rather, as counsel to a company seeking venture capital, or any other source of investment for that matter, it is important to remind the company's shareholders to choose an investment source whose motives best match their own objectives. While some of the investor's goals may be perfectly in sync with those objectives, there are likely to be others that are not, and those potential disconnects need to be understood at the outset.

QUESTIONS

---

1. After the foregoing tour of the world of venture capital investing, how would you counsel Joan and Michael when they ask you whether it is worth the tradeoffs?
2. How would Joan and Michael avoid the divergence of goals that may hamper their relationship with SoftCo's venture capital investors?
3. How does SoftCo keep its venture capital investors engaged with and positive about the company? Sure, the easy answer is to be very successful, but what about beyond that?

F. Taking on a Venture Capital Investment

1. Preparing a Company for Venture Capital Investment

Goals of the Founders.   As counsel to a company about to seek venture capital investment, or any other source of outside capital, the first task to focus on is clarifying the goals of the company's founders and current shareholders. For our discussion, we will focus on a company like SoftCo, whose founders, Joan and Michael, own the entire company.

In order to prepare most companies for investment, a number of steps must be undertaken over a period of months. Those steps are detailed in section F.2 below, and include creating the outline of a business plan, strengthening the management and professional team, developing a detailed business plan, and "draining the swamp," which means formalizing a range of internal procedures and eliminating the known "deal killers" in the business as it presently stands. While a very early stage company like SoftCo may find those tasks less complex than an older, more advanced business, whatever the stage of the company, the founders have to conclude honestly that they can take on those tasks, with the inconvenience, delay, frustration, and inefficiency necessarily involved. Once the founders begin to actively pursue outside investment, they will have to be willing to devote their time to a lengthy series of pitch meetings to potential investors who may be arrogant and egotistical or, worse, may not like the company. Interested investors will require diligence investigations and may seek fundamental revisions to the company's business plan. The actual investment itself will involve negotiations, a raft of indecipherable documents, and probably more money in lawyer's fees than the company has spent since its inception.

Once the investment is in place, it is inevitable that the dynamic of the business's operation will be changed forever. Taking outside capital means taking on a partner, in one form or another, and having to deal with a lot of people who were never involved in the business before. In addition to requiring a lot more process, formalized systems, and information development and dissemination, the new partner is going to impose restrictions on how the business is operated and how the new capital it has just invested is to be spent, which might include demanding a veto power on major decisions or a seat on the board of directors or some other formal role in management of the business. Further, owner compensation and management authority will come under scrutiny, perhaps for the first time. In short, the founders will find themselves doing a lot more explaining, pitching, cajoling, and selling than ever before, all within their own business. They may feel like they have been saddled with some kind of bizarre joint custody order on their child.

At the risk of sounding like a parody on psychotherapy, the founders must face the question: "How do you feel about that?"

We touched on these issues in the materials presented at the beginning of this chapter (as well as in Chapter 1), but we are now returning to consider these issues in the context of venture capital investment because this type of start-up financing involves a particularly difficult, time-consuming, and paradigm-shifting undertaking for the founders. While some entrepreneurs may be able to tolerate the dislocation of minor outside investment, taking on venture capital investment is a more comprehensive test of character and commitment.

For reasons described in more detail in Chapter 1, some entrepreneurs set up their own business specifically to avoid dealing with exactly these issues. Entrepreneurs whose personalities require that they control, supervise, and review every aspect of their business's operations should think carefully before taking on any outside capital. They need to consider seriously whether their mental health will survive the process of finding investors or, more so, taking their money. Should they decide to go forward, they will need to delegate the legwork of the pre capital-raising and capital-raising processes to a trusted subordinate, although the ideas of "delegate" and "trusted" may be enough to push some entrepreneurs to the brink. If they can survive the time-wasting foolishness, in their eyes, of the capital-seeking process, they will need to find very passive investors who want very little voice in the business and, even then, will need someone to take on the responsibility of interacting, even at that light level, with these new investors.

Ironically, when entrepreneurs like these can survive the process, they often are very successful at attracting investment. Their driving confidence and clear vision, which in regular life might be derided as stubborn pigheadedness, can be very compelling attributes for leading a business. Usually, these people are best at attracting money from individuals who do not expect (nor, perhaps desire) to provide industry knowledge and executive expertise to the company. However, these entrepreneurs usually do not fare as well with angel investors and venture capitalists because typically they are not collaborative managers, so they do not delegate well. The first weakness leads to arguments and general unpleasantness within the ranks of company management, and the second limits the growth potential of the company. When all management actions have to pass through an entrepreneur's hands, that entrepreneur soon becomes the bottleneck to growth. While a founder with this style can be very successful at starting a business, getting it on its feet, and selling it, the exit is often at too early a stage to make the path attractive to venture capital investors, who are looking for huge returns.

Beyond examining the personality fit, founders also must acknowledge their fundamental goals for the business. Founders who want to build their business slowly, and make a nice living doing it, are not well suited for investors who are looking for rapid growth and an exit. The same is true if the founders want to create a legacy for their children, bringing them up in the business and eventually transferring control to the next generation.

As a final point, our discussion of these issues has assumed for convenience that the founders of SoftCo think and act in lockstep on these issues. But what if Joan were 62 years old with a family and had gone back to school to pursue her lifelong interest in software after 30 years as an aerospace engineer, while Michael is a typical 27-year-old newly minted Ph.D. who has never had a job for longer than a summer? Would their different circumstances give them different inclinations on what the best outcome for SoftCo might be? Even if they were both typical, young, new Ph.D.s, they would need to make sure their goals are the same, or at least compatible.

These issues are made that much more complicated where there are already other shareholders in addition to the founders — employees, perhaps, or friends and family investors who have a small interest in the company. On what basis did they acquire their shares? Were they clear-eyed, experienced investors, who understood the risks inherent in being a minority investor? Or were they relatives who just wanted to support these really smart and creative individuals whom they know and trust? What are the founders' responsibilities to them legally as directors? What about simply as shareholders? *See, e.g., Sterling v. Mayflower Hotel Corp.*, 93 A.2d 107 (Del. 1952).

QUESTIONS

1. How can you, as company counsel, assist Joan and Michael, who are inexperienced in dealing with investors, to decide whether they are ready to handle professional investors such as venture capitalists?
2. If there are other shareholders in SoftCo, on what basis could Joan and Michael have legal liability to those shareholders as a result of taking investment from venture capitalists?
3. If those additional SoftCo shareholders are key employees, should you counsel Joan and Michael on their moral obligations to them, regardless of any actionable legal duty? Why? What happens to SoftCo if those employees are not comfortable with the shift from a slow and steady growth model, with the business run by individuals whom they know and trust, to a company that now plans to take on venture capital and go for greatness? What are the ramifications of having employee shareholders who are not enthusiastic about the founders' plans?
4. What impact does a change in financing plans have on friends and family shareholders? (Remember Thanksgiving dinner!) Are there circumstances where the founders would be best served to find a way to buy them out?
5. How do founders balance the priorities of fundraising and devoting the time necessary to grow and manage their business? How do they decide whether the trade-off is worth it?

2. Making Venture Capital Investment Work

Once a company has made the decision to seek investment from venture capitalists, it must prepare itself to embark on the process, which often takes several months. Understanding what venture capitalists look for in their portfolio companies in general is just the first step; then the company needs to identify which venture funds specialize in its industry and figure out the best way to present itself to them. Attracting venture capital investment requires application and discipline in the pre-financing stages, the financing transaction itself, and the follow-on operations of the business with a venture capital investor in place. While many of these steps were described in more general terms in Chapter 1, the discussion that follows focuses on this process from the specific perspective of seeking professional venture capital to finance a start-up business.

Preparations before Seeking Investors.   First, the founders have to exercise the discipline to prepare the outline of a business plan. Most venture capital investment is made on the basis of a business plan. While founders who have not gone through the venture investment process may not be able to prepare a fully developed plan without help, they need to begin that process. There are many books and on-line resources, as well as materials prepared by the major accounting and consulting firms, that provide the basics of what a business plan should cover.

While Chapter 1 provides information about business plans generally, an effective business plan for a company seeking venture capital financing typically covers the following topics:

  (i) *The Company*: including the current status of the business, its short- and long-term objectives, and very importantly, its management, with brief summaries of their relevant experience, naming companies and positions;

 (ii) *The Market and Competition*: including a basic introduction to the company's product and what problem it solves, a knowledgeable analysis of the market the product will compete in, a description of who the customers will be and how they are currently addressing their needs, the alternatives available (i.e., the competition), and an insightful projection of both the short- and long-term future of the market;

(iii) *The Product*: including what it does and how, its uniqueness and how that is protected, and its state of development;

(iv) *The Business Model*: stating clearly the revenue model and the means for marketing and selling the product;

 (v) *The Operation of the Business*: describing in detail management's command of the operational elements of the business (for example, manufacturing); and

(vi) *The Financials*: presenting actual results to date and management's projections based on obtaining the needed financing, including the specific uses of the proceeds of the targeted financing.

The business plan should be fewer than 40 pages in length; have a cover sheet with the company's name and contact information for the CEO; a table of contents with chapter and subheadings; numbered pages; and an appendix for back-up materials on the financial projections, management biographies, and other supplemental information supporting the plan presentation. Each copy should be numbered so that the company can keep track of who has a copy at any given time.

Without question, in seeking venture capital financing, the most important part of the business plan is the two pages that follow the cover sheet and precede the table of contents, entitled "Executive Summary." This overview is often the tool used by venture capital investors to preliminarily screen the hundreds of business plans that come in each week. As a result, the Executive Summary must deliver the goods by clearly summarizing key information from the entire plan and concisely communicating the objectives and prospects of the company. If the prospective investor does not understand by the second paragraph the market being targeted, the problem the customers in that market have, and the reasons why this company's products are the solution to that problem, he or she probably will read no further.

The founders have to begin the process of preparing this plan, not to create a polished document, but to start the process of analyzing the company and planning its future in the way a venture investor will require. Sometimes, founders look at the scope of the plan and the depth of analysis it requires and decide that they simply do not want to devote the time and effort needed to prepare it, so they hire a consultant to do the work. After all, they have a business to run. This is a fatal error. Dwight D. Eisenhower said, regarding the plan for the D-Day invasion, "Plans are nothing; planning is everything." The value of a plan is that it comes from working through the planning process. Founders who apply themselves to the preparation of a business plan discover that, by going through the steps it requires, they learn more about their business than they ever knew before. Hiring a consultant to prepare the company's business plan typically results in delivery of a bad plan to founders who are no better prepared to raise capital.

Having begun a serious planning effort, the founders often identify areas where they need expert support for the business, both in the form of outside professional services and additional management. Strengthening the professional services to the company usually means retaining securities counsel and a financial advisor or chief financial officer who are experienced in working with companies seeking venture capital financing. These experts can assist both in supporting the preparation of the business plan and in negotiating the investment transaction. In addition, having this expertise on hand shows that the founders are serious. They also can provide introductions to their contacts in the investor community and other professional services that may be needed by the company as it grows. As to strengthening management, by preparing the business plan, the founders often discover that there are gaps in the business model that they need to start filling by obtaining additional managers with expertise in areas like marketing, sales, manufacturing, or engineering, depending on what the founders' backgrounds are. Often, these people will not be prepared to join a start-up before it gets funding, but they may be willing to offer their expertise with the objective of making the move as things progress further. The benefit of having begun the planning process is that the founders gain a better idea of what their needs are and, when they start talking to people to fill those needs, they are more educated and better prepared for those conversations so, consequently, a positive outcome is more likely.

With a strong team in place, or at least in the process of being assembled, the founders need to use that added expertise to complete a polished business plan so that they are prepared to approach potential investors. At the same time, the founders need to "drain the swamp." That is, they need to address the shortcuts they have taken and correct problems in their business they have been ignoring. They need to pay for completing documentation on formation of the business entity and issuing the ownership interests in it. They need to document delivery of ownership in and appropriate protection of the business's key intellectual property. This process also includes eliminating any outstanding problems that will be seen by venture capital investors as "deal killers." These might include tax delinquencies, retirement account funding shortfalls, related-party transactions that will not survive close scrutiny, or illegal or improper payments to or from suppliers, distributors, or customers. They also may include contractual commitments that could restrict the growth of the business, such as agreements to buy from only one supplier or to sell to only one distributor; licenses or territory agreements that overly restrict the markets the company may sell into; or long-term obligations to earlier strategic partners or customers that are not consistent with the growth of the business. An additional area that has become critical in the past several years is compliance with applicable state laws on employee overtime and wage and hour rules.

These are all issues that quickly will become apparent to a potential investor and, if not cleaned up, almost certainly will cause that investor to walk away. Experienced legal counsel, doing a diligence investigation of their own client, are critical to the completion of this step in preparing the company to seek outside investment from professional venture capitalists. Only *after* the swamp has been drained should the company start presenting itself to potential venture capital funds.

Identifying Suitable Investors.   There are hundreds and hundreds of venture capital funds. You can find them on the Internet or through directories, such as PRATT'S GUIDE TO PRIVATE EQUITY & VENTURE CAPITAL SOURCES (Thomson Financial, 2013 ed.), which is also available online (subscription required) at http://www.prattsguide.com. Unfortunately, a bulk mailing to all of them is not appropriate, so the first step in finding a suitable potential investor is to comb through the choices with an understanding of the criteria that the various venture funds use in selecting companies.

The first issue is location. Venture capitalists definitely do not like to waste their time sitting on airplanes. Some operate on the "one-day rule." If getting to the company's office, attending a three- to four-hour board meeting, and getting back home cannot be done in a day, the company is not a suitable investment for that fund. Location is an issue that may require some creative analysis. The fund may not provide detailed data regarding the scope of acceptable locations on its website or directory listings. Does that mean they do not have any such criteria? Maybe. It can be informative, however, to take a look at the list of portfolio companies that almost all funds provide on their websites. If geographic information is not provided, they almost always provide links to the companies' websites, which usually have "Contact Us" information. If all the companies identified as part of a fund's portfolio are located within 50 miles of the fund's headquarters, then that does not necessarily indicate that the fund will not invest in a company farther away, only that it is not likely.

Next, does the venture fund invest in the company's industry? Again, this factor requires more research than initially might meet the eye. The directory listing or website description of a fund's investment focus is intended to encourage businesses seeking capital to contact the fund. Unless there are specific areas that the fund absolutely will not invest in (entertainment content, retail, or oil and gas production, for example), the venture capitalists generally do not want to discourage people from sending in their plans. Remember, they make their money on the big winners. This means that they do not want to miss a great business because they appeared lukewarm on that industry. Further, when describing their industry focus, they will use broad, vague terms. Once more, the good data is in the portfolio listings. *Query*: Is a fund that says it invests in software potentially a good fit for SoftCo? What if an examination of its portfolio shows that its only software investments are in online game companies?

The company then must find the venture capital funds that invest in companies in its stage of development. This can be tricky, as the funds often appear open to all stages, and sometimes it is hard to glean from the portfolio listings what stage a particular company was in when the fund made its first investment in that company. The "News" section of the fund's website often will be helpful in this regard, as the blurbs on recent investments often give more information about the investment transactions. In addition, services such as VentureDeal (http://www.venturedeal.com) provide information on investment activity by financing round and industry segment.

The final criterion for the company to use in sorting out potential venture capital investors is whether they will "lead." Depending on the size of a company's capital needs, it may need only one investor, or it may need several. If the investment amount required is fairly small, then the company should identify funds that will make that kind of investment alone. On larger investments, venture funds often prefer to share the risk by forming informal groups (or *syndicates*) to make an investment. If, for example, a company needs $4 million and a venture fund likes the company but, as a general rule, does not like to make early-stage investments that large, it may seek one or two other funds to join it in a deal syndicate. The investor that takes that role is referred to as the *lead investor*. While there is usually no long-term agreement among the members of a deal syndicate, the members do agree on how much they each will invest, and usually that the lead investor will take the primary role in negotiating the deal terms and providing the management oversight of the company. What this means is that the company needs to determine whether the venture funds it is talking to will be able to do the investment by themselves or, if a syndicate is needed, whether they are willing to lead the syndicate. Some venture funds prefer to "follow" and therefore should not be targeted. While a "following" fund that really likes a business plan may call the plan to the attention of the lead funds it invests with, it is usually more efficient for the company to approach those lead funds in the first place. Again, the "News" section of the funds' websites often is most helpful in figuring out if a fund will make an investment without a syndicate, and if there is one, whether it will lead.

The final consideration on this subject is that once a company has identified venture capital funds it thinks might be suitable investors, what is the best way to get in touch with them? Here, the company runs up against the unspoken rule of venture capital investors: no cold calls. Simply stated, cold calling a venture fund, or sending an unsolicited email to a fund, with the business plan attached and a "Dear Sir or Madam" cover message, is almost always pointless. In fact, on some venture fund websites, the e-mail contact links go to addresses the venture capitalists do not really use for their day-to-day business. In most cases, "over the transom" plans, if they are read at all, will be looked at by a junior person. There is a strong belief in the venture capital world that there is a self-selection process going on, and therefore those entrepreneurs who send out plans blindly generally do not know how to raise money and are unlikely to know how to put together a suitable business.

The reality is that venture capital investors rely on their network of contacts to keep them apprised of new investment opportunities. This includes other venture capitalists, investment bankers and private equity investors, lenders, lawyers, accountants, and anyone else who frequently deals with companies in the industry and stage the fund is interested in. Perhaps the most important network group for many funds is the members of management in their current and past portfolio companies.

The result is that, in addition to doing their own research to identify suitable investors, the founders, in parallel, need to start canvassing their network of lawyers, accountants, financial advisors, former professors, former co-workers, and so on, to find people with links to potential investors. When they are scanning the portfolio company information on the funds' websites, as suggested earlier in this section, they need to note any companies where a friend or former associate now works. The founders need to hook into the networks that will lead them to the funds they have identified as potential investors. They need to use those relationships to make an introduction for them and get their business plan onto the priority pile for that particular fund.

Investors that are interested by the business plan will contact the company and set up a meeting to learn more. In addition to being ready to go with a 20- to 30-minute presentation, and making sure the product prototype they are bringing actually works, the founders need to remember that they have rights in this process too. Just like a student on a job interview, they often get so focused on getting selected that they do not pay enough attention to the fact that they are making a selection as well. They should do as much diligence as they can on the fund, its people, and its prior investments. This not only better prepares them for the meeting, it also may provide the founders with some insight on whether these venture capitalists are the ones the founders want as their business partners for the next three to seven years. Personal fit should never be undervalued. If the first meeting goes well, there will be follow-on meetings and additional information requested, and the internal approval process at the venture fund may continue for several months after the first meeting.

For additional resources on these subjects, there are a number of good books on preparing for venture investment, the business plan, and personal presentation process of venture capital, including the pre-Internet, but still outstanding, BUSINESS PLANS THAT WIN $$$ — LESSONS FROM THE MIT ENTERPRISE FORUM (Stanley R. Rich & David E. Gumpert, eds., 1987). Another highly regarded resource is *www.foundersatwork.com*, which collects insights from company founders regarding their experiences with venture capital investors. As to the transaction itself, the terms of the preferred stock to be issued to the venture capital investors are described at length in Chapter 9 and the documentation of this investment transaction is addressed in Chapter 10.

Living with Venture Capitalists.   As should be clear, venture capital investors generally become very active in the management of their portfolio companies. After investing, their normal avenue for involvement is through the board of directors. Typically, they will require that the company have monthly board meetings. They will have representatives on the board of directors and even the funds that do not have a seat on the board will insist on "observation rights." That is, they will want notice and the opportunity to attend all board meetings and to receive all informational material provided to the company's board of directors. Thus, venture investors will participate in virtually all major decisions going forward and particularly will be involved in filling key management slots as the company grows. However, absent special circumstances — usually some sort of serious trouble within the company — the venture capitalists do not want to take on operational management authority. One of the key factors in their investment decisions is the management team, and they expect management to operate the business. On the company's side, management should expect to devote a significant level of attention to interacting with their venture investor partners.

Finding an equilibrium between keeping the venture investors sufficiently informed and involved in the company without constraining day-to-day management activities and decision-making can require some time and experience. Management must convey to the company's employees, as well as to its investors, that it is in charge. The CEO needs to set the agenda for the board meetings and run the meetings. It is common courtesy, though, to circulate a well-considered agenda draft a week before meeting and request additions or suggestions. Virtually all boards request that copies of the handouts or presentation deck sent to them at least a couple of days before the meeting date to allow them to prepare. It also is normal in the first several meetings after an investment for members of management to make departmental presentations, such as engineering or finance, and at the end, turn to the investors and ask: "Is this what you need to hear?" "Is the presentation format useful?" "Would you like other data or to have this data analyzed differently?" Management should expect the venture investors to have preferences and requirements on these presentations and should seek to conform to them. In terms of maintaining healthy investor relationships, it is always better for management to request that input than to wait to be told.

Put simply, effective and open communications between the company and its venture investors is critical to the venture capital investors playing a constructive and supportive oversight role. The credibility of management is something that, once lost, probably can never be regained. Inexperienced management sometimes will treat the board like a customer that must be sold to each month. That approach will not be tolerated for long, and if management cannot (or will not) adjust, then the investors may well decide that perhaps new management is needed.

Many CEOs schedule a mid-month call (between board meetings) with each of their venture investors in order to keep them apprised of what is happening and to talk through open matters and priorities. Further, if something has become delayed, or other bad news is to be delivered to the board, most CEOs find it more effective to contact their board members (plus the additional venture capital investors who do not have board seats but do have "observation" rights) before any formal meeting and before the information package for the next meeting is sent out. They tell their directors personally and give them the opportunity to consider the problem before arriving at the board meeting. As a result, the board meeting can focus on solutions rather than on grasping the problem. In fact, many CEOs take the view that directors should learn nothing new at the board meeting, other than the greater knowledge that results from discussing known issues with members of management.

Legal counsel to a company receiving start-up capital from venture capital funds can offer meaningful assistance to the client by reviewing these norms before the first post-investment board meeting. Every company and board is different, so each situation will involve a feeling-out process. Many corporate attorneys find it valuable to attend all their clients' board meetings, and often they will waive their normal fees in order to be there. Once there, counsel frequently records the minutes of the meeting.

Attending board meetings sends an important message to everyone involved with the company. Company counsel represents the company, not management. Both management and the non-management board members need to be reminded of this fundamental fact. As the board is responsible for the operation of a corporation, it is the best human manifestation of the legal construct of a "corporation." But, as with management, company counsel does not represent the board.

In addition, a lawyer is better able to advise the company when he or she knows what management is telling the board and how the board is directing management. As board meetings are major information delivery events, a lawyer who attends and studies the data provided to the board can learn an immeasurable amount about the company and its industry. And, as a practical matter, the company is well served by having counsel on the spot and ready to offer important advice when decisions are being made, so that no time and momentum are lost by having to circle back later to correct a legal defect.

The lawyer who understands the nature of venture capital and the drivers for venture capital investors is better prepared to support a company's management through the process of planning for and seeking venture capital investment. While the legal services in the venture capital transaction itself are very important, the issues this chapter outlines regarding the pre-investment steps, seeking the investment, and managing the post-investment relationship with the venture capitalists can make the difference to the lawyer between being a technical advisor on legal matters and being a trusted counselor to the company.

QUESTIONS

1. Why would it be worth your (unbilled) time to go through the package of materials provided to the members of the company's board? Why, for example, should you read the description of the hiring and compensation plan for the new sales force?
2. In this casebook, questions regarding the role of the business lawyer have arisen repeatedly. Do you find the scope of the business issues addressed in this chapter surprising? Disturbing?

CHAPTER 9

VENTURE CAPITAL FINANCING — PREFERRED STOCK ATTRIBUTES

As Joan and Michael move forward with the prospect of launching SoftCo with funds raised through a *Venture Capital* financing, we must turn to a review of the rights, preferences, and privileges typically granted to venture capital convertible preferred stock. We need to advise Joan and Michael, as the board, management, and common stock holders of SoftCo, on the economic and management control features that venture capital investors normally expect in their preferred stock. Further, Joan and Michael need to understand the impact of the preferred stock on their rights as common shareholders and on their roles as directors and management.

A. Overview of Convertible Preferred Stock

In Chapter 8, we discussed and eliminated a range of debt and equity security options as being unsuitable for high-risk investment in early stage companies, and concluded that convertible preferred stock is the most appropriate investment vehicle for this particular purpose. In this chapter, we look at why the venture capital investment community came to that conclusion by examining the attributes of venture capital convertible preferred stock in detail. We examine the hybrid nature of this security, which holds debt-like rights that give it first priority among equity securities as well as common stock-like rights that allow it to share in what we have previously referred to as the "equity upside."

The rights, preferences, and terms we discuss are negotiable, so the specifics of any agreed-upon deal, as well as the documentation of that deal, will vary from transaction to transaction. In order to comprehend the implications of differing language, a lawyer needs to understand the underpinnings of the fundamental rights that may be granted to a preferred stock. Whether representing a company like SoftCo, a venture capital fund making an investment in a company like SoftCo, or any company or investor in a private financing deal outside of professional venture capital, a lawyer with a strong foundational knowledge of the basic attributes of convertible preferred stock will have acquired some important tools for structuring any given financing transaction.

1. Classes of Equity Securities

The first thing to understand about the form of preferred stock that is used in venture capital financing is that it is an "equity" security, which means that it represents an ownership interest in the issuing corporation. The residual equity ownership in a corporation resides in the common stock. Generally speaking, common stock is stock that does not have priority (i.e., a right to be paid *first*) over any other equity security with respect to payments of dividends or the distribution of assets on liquidation of the corporation.

If a stock has a priority over another equity security on either of those rights, it is a *preferred stock. See, e.g.*, Cal. Corp. Code §§159 and 176 (defining common and preferred stock, respectively); and Del. GCL §151(c) and (d) (governing dividend and distribution rights). The Model Act rejects the designation of a stock as "preferred," but contemplates the authorization of shares with preference rights. *See* Model Act §6.01. Thus, after all the corporation's debts have been repaid in full and all the equity securities having prior rights have received the payments to which they are entitled, any remaining dividends or liquidation distributions are paid to the holders of common stock. This does not mean the residual right is exclusive; the common stock holders may have to share their residual right with other equity security holders who have bargained for a share of it.

Different types of stock are referred to as "classes" of stock, and a class of stock can be subdivided further into "series." A company may divide its class of common stock into separate series. For example, a corporation's common stock might be divided into two series, with Series A common stock having a right to receive two-thirds of any dividend or liquidation distribution and Series B common stock having the right to one-third. Note that the Series A is not a preferred stock because its right is to a larger portion of a shared distribution, not a right to be paid first.

A corporation's stock is authorized in its Certificate (or Articles) of Incorporation. As you will recall from Chapter 5, this is the document filed with the secretary of state of the state where the corporation is incorporated that, upon its acceptance for filing, causes the corporation to exist. Because the terminology varies by state, and because under some circumstances other documents, called Certificates of Designation or Certificates of Determination, may be filed and become part of the Certificate or Articles of Incorporation, respectively, we will refer to this document as the "Charter." A corporation's Charter must state the number of shares it is authorized to issue and what classes of stock are authorized.

The details of applicable state laws vary. Delaware, for example, requires a statement of the total number of shares authorized, and then requires that the total be divided among the authorized classes. It also requires the stock to be designated as having a stated par value or as being without par value. *See* Del. GCL §102(a)(4). On the other hand, California requires a statement of the total number of shares only if there is just one class, but if there is more than one, it requires a statement of just the number of shares in each class. *See* Cal. Corp. Code §202(e). California has no par value requirement. *See* Cal. Corp. Code §205. The Model Act uses the Delaware approach by requiring a statement of the number of authorized shares as well as of the number of shares in each class or series. *See* Model Act §§2.02(a)(2) and 6.01(a). Although par value has no special meaning under the Model Act, it provides that the Articles of Incorporation may set a par value for the shares. *See* Model Act §2.02(b)(iv).

The Charter must also establish any distinctions between a corporation's classes of stock or among the series within a class. In other words, the Charter must set forth the special powers, preferences, and rights of a particular class or series of stock in order to distinguish that class or series from the others having other rights. If no distinction is made or preferential rights set, then all classes or series share in the statutory default right for that particular matter (i.e., "Unless otherwise provided in the [Charter], each share/ stockholder . . ."). *See, e.g.,* Del. GCL §§102(a)(4) and 151(a); Cal. Corp. Code §203; and Model Act §6.01.

Fundamentally, as to stock rights, by default all shares of a corporation's stock are the same and all are common stock, unless the Charter creates a separate class or series and sets forth its distinguishing rights. If the Charter creates a separate class or series, then all shares of that class or series participate equally in its separate set of rights. Within a class of stock that is not divided into series, every share is the same. If a class has been divided into series, then every share within a particular series has identical rights.

As mentioned in our discussion of equity incentives in section A.4 of Chapter 6, the fact that preferred stock has preferential rights that set it above common stock is important in a venture capital financing not simply because of the rights themselves. In addition, the special rights of a preferred stock create a value disparity between it and the common stock (i.e., a premium over the common stock). Notwithstanding the valuation process described in section E.4 of Chapter 8, where all shares are treated as common stock equivalents, by having an extra set of rights, a company's preferred stock justifies a higher per-share price than its common stock. As a result, a company can issue fewer shares (thereby selling a smaller ownership percentage) in its capital-raising trans-actions by using preferred stock rather than cheaper common stock. Further, as detailed in section A.4 of Chapter 6, the price difference between preferred stock and common stock allows the company to offer its lower-priced common stock in equity incentive programs to management and employees.

2. Preferred Stock — Charter vs. Contract Rights

While preferred stock is generally distinguished by having the right to receive dividends or liquidation distributions before common stock, the set of potential preferential rights, or "preferences," that may be granted to a preferred stock is far broader. A venture capital preferred stock typically also has special rights regarding voting and conversion into common stock. In addition, a significant minority of companies issuing venture capital preferred stock also provide redemption rights. These types of preferential rights, which are the subject of this chapter, are all addressed in the Charter because (i) they must appear there in order to establish a difference from the statutory defaults that exist for those rights, and (ii) they usually are expressed in relation to, and in distinction from, the rights of the common stock. It bears emphasizing that our discussion focuses on these preferential rights and Charter provisions as they apply to venture capital preferred stock financings and does not represent a comprehensive examination of the laws and Charter terms as they might apply in other contexts. State corporate laws typically have specific provisions addressing how these rights are established in the Charter and what their permissible scope may be. By setting out these rights in the Charter, they become part of the structure of the preferred stock and apply equally to all shares of the preferred stock (or, if the preferred stock is divided into series, to all shares of the applicable series).

In addition to the rights that are built into the structure of the preferred stock, various additional rights typically are granted to the purchasers of venture capital preferred stock by the issuing company and, often, by the founders or other key common stock holders. Those rights are usually set forth in the Investor Rights Agreement, Right of First Refusal and Co-Sale Agreement, and Voting Agreement, all of which are addressed in Chapter 10. The rights granted in these agreements are established separately by contract because they are not subject to statutory defaults that can only be modified in a corporation's Charter. While some could be put into the Charter, as they apply to corporate governance or shareholder rights and would not conflict with a state's corporations code generally, they usually are not, for a number of reasons.

The first reason is privacy. The Charter is a public document, while the secondary contracts in a venture capital transaction are private and may be kept confidential. While there is a huge social benefit in providing transparency as to the inner workings of publicly traded companies, people outside of a company and its direct business relationships have very little legitimate interest in the workings and arrangements of a private business.

Second, rights set forth in the Charter are part of the stock itself and must apply to all holders of a class or series of stock in the same way. In contrast, contractual rights are *personal* rights held by the *holders* of the stock. Thus, a contract may exclude some holders from certain rights. In addition, an agreement may set forth the company's covenant granting a right to the holders of its preferred stock, but then also may provide that the preferred shareholders shall designate one of their number to exercise that right on behalf of all preferred shareholders. Personal rights, or rights that only exist based on holding a minimum number of shares of a particular stock, are perfectly appropriate in a private contract, but as they distinguish among the owners of the same series of preferred stock, they may well be contrary to applicable law if placed in the Charter. *See, e.g.* Model Act §6.01(a) ("Except to the extent varied as permitted by this section, all shares of a class or series must have terms, including preferences, rights and limitations, that are identical with those of other shares of the same class or series.") *See* also Cal. Corp. Code §400(b) (to the same effect regarding "voting, conversion and redemption rights and other rights, preferences, privileges and restrictions").

This chapter focuses on the attributes of preferred stock that are addressed in the Charter because they are driven by statute. These attributes of preferred stock are products of law. The preferred shareholder rights provided through the agreements discussed in Chapter 10 may be widely used as a matter of custom and tradition in venture capital investing, but the breadth of potential contractual arrangements that parties may construct in coming to an agreement is limited only by the scope of the creativity of business people assisted by their lawyers. Rather than try to corral an endless variety of potential contract terms that may apply to preferred stock investors, this chapter concentrates on the rights that are a part of the preferred stock itself.

B. Dividend Preferences

1. Dividends Generally

A *dividend* is broadly defined as a distribution by a corporation of its stock, cash, or other property on a proportionate basis to its shareholders. Dividends of a corporation's own stock present a separate set of issues (see the anti-dilution discussion below in section D.3), so the focus here is on dividends of cash or other corporate assets. Generally speaking, these dividend distributions are a means for the shareholders of a corporation to share in the company's profits while still leaving their ownership interests unchanged.

Restrictions on Dividend Payments.   State law imposes restrictions on the payment of dividends. While the specific rules vary, the basic requirement is that the corporation, after payment of the dividend, still must be in a financial condition that would allow it to meet its obligations as they come due. States approach this standard in different ways. Delaware requires that dividends be paid only from surplus or from net profits. *See* Del. GCL §§170(a), 174, 154, and 244 (discussing provisions regarding the authority to grant dividends and the definitions for the appropriate sources). In contrast, both California law and the Model Act provide that a dividend falls within the general category of a "distribution to its shareholders" by a corporation. *See* Cal. Corp. Code §166; and Model Act §140. Both of the latter two statutory structures provide a set of rules, including solvency and financial statement tests, for determining the validity of a particular shareholder distribution. *See* Cal. Corp. Code §§500 *et seq.*; and Model Act §6.40. As the statutory approach to determining when dividends are permitted tracks the approach used for redemptions, and redemptions tend to involve much larger payments and thus are more likely to bump against statutory limitations, details on the specifics of these standards are developed more fully below in section E.1, entitled "The Statutory Treatment of Redemption."

The purpose of these restrictions is to protect creditors. A corporation is a limited liability entity, which means that its shareholders are liable for the debts of the corporation only to the extent of their ownership interest in the corporation. Put another way, a corporation's creditors have the right to require a corporation to deliver its assets to repay its debt obligations to them before the shareholders may receive their proportionate interest in those assets; thus, creditors have a priority right over shareholders to the assets of the corporation. It would be manifestly unfair (fraudulent, even) to permit a corporation to distribute its cash or assets to its shareholders if doing so would leave it unable to pay its debts. This would allow the shareholders, effectively, to jump ahead of the creditors on the priority list and receive value to which the creditors were entitled. Therefore, before any dividends are paid, careful compliance with the state law prerequisites is required.

Dividend Terminology.   A specific set of terminology applies to dividends. A dividend is said to have been "declared" when the company has obligated itself to pay that dividend. The board of directors "declares" the dividend, which then obligates the company to pay it. Dividends are usually declared by the board of directors some time (often around 60 days) before they are actually "paid." A dividend is paid (that is, the funds or assets actually get distributed to the shareholders) at a future date that is generally set by the board when it declares the dividend. If a dividend has been declared but not yet paid, it is said to be "accrued," which indicates that it is an outstanding obligation of the company. A "cumulative" dividend, which will be discussed in more detail in the following section, accrues periodically, usually quarterly or annually, without having to be declared. It simply accrues, or "accumulates," period by period, until it is paid. Depending on the specific language used in creating the cumulative dividend, the amount may accumulate on a compound or simple basis. (Recall our discussion of the time value of money on a compound versus a simple basis in section E.4 of Chapter 8.)

Dividends in the Venture Capital Setting.   As we discussed in Chapter 8, venture capital financed companies are looking to grow quickly and therefore usually are not generating enough cash to pay for that growth; indeed, often they are "pre-revenue" and generating no cash at all. In light of those cash flow limitations, we discussed the inappropriateness of any investment form that requires an ongoing repayment stream to the investor. So why are we now talking about dividends, which are just another form of payment to the investors?

One of the primary objectives underlying the set of preferential rights a venture investor insists upon in exchange for its capital investment is to establish the right of the preferred shareholders to get their money out of the company before any other equity holders. While it is true that a venture capital-financed company is not likely actually to pay dividends, a dividend is a potential means for value to come out of the company to its shareholders. Therefore, even though it probably will never happen, the preferred shareholders need to ensure that, if dividends are paid, they will be first in line.

In addition, a right to dividends can be a way to increase the return on investment in the preferred stock at a future sale of the company or upon redemption of the preferred stock. We will return to this issue as we address those topics later in this chapter.

Our discussion of the dividend preference introduces a common mechanism that is part of the hybrid nature of venture capital preferred stock. This convertible preferred stock is designed to bridge the gap between the higher priority rights of a debt security while still maintaining the equity upside opportunity that is inherent in the lowest-priority security, common stock. The result is that the dividend preference often reflects a debt-like "priority" right — that is, a right to first payment before any payments to any other stock — plus a common stock-like "participation" right. We will first address the dividend priority preference.

2. The Dividend Priority Preference

A corporation's Charter typically will have a provision that reads something like the following:

Charter Sample 9.1. No dividend shall be declared on the Common Stock until each share of the Preferred Stock has received a dividend equal to _____% of its original per-share purchase price, when, as and if declared by the Board of Directors. This Preferred Stock dividend right shall be non-cumulative.

This language sets the *priority* right of the preferred shares by requiring that some percentage of the original purchase price of the preferred stock must be paid on each share of the preferred stock prior to any dividend payment to the holders of common stock. Rather than expressing the dividend rate as a percentage of the original price per share paid for the preferred stock, the provision could state a specific dollar amount per share as the dividend priority right. Another approach might be to state that the preferred stock is to receive a certain amount (whether equal to a percentage of its per-share purchase price or a stated dollar amount) annually, prior to any payment to the holders of common stock. The result of that approach is that over a period of one year, the priority provision would cap the dividend payment on the preferred stock to that annualized amount.

The "when, as and if declared" language included in this provision means that there is no requirement that the company actually declare any dividends at all, ever. This is important because, historically, preferred stock was a very debt-like instrument. It had the right to be redeemed and to receive dividends, and very few other common stock-like rights. In the context of the historic style of preferred stock (which is still used by many public companies), the expectation is that dividends will be declared on a set schedule and paid if the company is legally able to do so.

As dividends in mature companies are typically paid out of earnings, or profits, meeting the legal standard for making a dividend payment is sometimes expressed as the dividend being "earned." There is case law holding that if the company is legally able to declare a scheduled dividend (i.e., the dividend was earned) and the company does not declare and pay the stated dividend, then the dividend is considered cumulative, even if the company's Charter specifically provides that dividends are non-cumulative. In Sanders v. Cuba Railroad Co., 120 A.2d 849, 850 (N.J. 1956), the court faced a Charter provision stating that the preferred stock:

> shall be entitled to receive from the net profits . . . a non-cumulative dividend up to, but not exceeding six percent.

Nevertheless, the court held that the "non-cumulative" reference applied only to unearned dividends. In light of the debt-like nature of that style of preferred stock, which often includes limited or no voting rights, the court supported its view that earned dividends that are not paid should carry the financial price of being treated as cumulative by stating:

> This much is quite apparent — if the common stockholders, who generally control the corporation and will benefit most by [not declaring] the dividends on the preferred stock, may freely achieve that result without any [accumulation] consequences, then the preferred stockholders will be substantially at the mercy of others who will be under temptation to act in their own self-interest.

Id.

The line of New Jersey cases reflecting this view has been rejected in most other jurisdictions. For example, in Guttman v. Illinois Central R. Co., 189 F. 2d 927, 930 (2d Cir. 1951), *cert. denied*, 342 U.S. 867 (1951), Judge Frank observed that nothing in the ordinary non-cumulative preferred stock contract provides for a:

contingent or inchoate right to arrears of dividends. The notion that such a right was promised is, rather, the invention of lawyers or other experts, a notion stemming from considerations of fairness, from a policy of protecting investors in those securities. But the preferred stockholders are not — like sailors or idiots or infants — wards of the judiciary.

In contrast to this traditional form of preferred stock, venture capital preferred stock is more of a "supersized" common stock. It has a powerful mix of "debt-like" and "common stock-like" rights, but it normally does not provide the expectation of a payment stream because the company usually needs to retain any cash it generates in order to grow the business. As a result, in order to break cleanly from these historical issues, the typical approach with non-cumulative venture capital preferred stock is to explicitly state that the shares are not cumulative, and further, to explicitly state that a dividend is completely discretionary on the part of the company's board of directors. In the sample charter provision quoted above, this latter result is achieved by using the "when, as and if declared" language.

Priority dividend rights typically are part of the preferred stock rights granted by companies in venture capital transactions. The annualized dividend rate can vary, but something in the range of 6 to 10 percent of the preferred stock's original issuance price would be very typical. Again, the expectation is that dividends normally will not be paid by the company, so this priority right is not often called into effect.

3. The Dividend Participation Right

In contrast to the debt-like priority right entitling the preferred stock to first payment on dividends, the other aspect of the hybrid nature of venture capital preferred stock is represented by the common stock-like *participation* right. A preferred stock has a participation right on dividends when, after it has been paid its priority dividend right (if it has one), it then has the separate right to share (i.e., participate) in any dividend paid on the common stock. If the preferred stock has this right, it is referred to as "participating" on dividends; if it does not, it is referred to as "non-participating."

As with the idea of priority, this participation concept is relevant to several rights typically granted to venture capital preferred stock. Participation is important because it allows the holders of the preferred stock, in essence, to have it both ways; in addition to the priority right to get paid first among the equity securities, they also participate in the common stock's residual rights. While the priority right can be seen as protective, in case the company does not grow in value as projected, the participation right allows the holders of preferred stock to share in the company's potential upside.

A participating dividend preference might be written in the Charter as follows:

Charter Sample 9.2. After payment of the [priority dividend amount], any additional dividends shall be paid to the holders of the Preferred Stock and the Common Stock *pro rata* based on the number of shares of Common Stock then outstanding, assuming conversion in full of the Preferred Stock.

If there is no priority right, the participating provision would need to be revised to begin, perhaps, with the following language:

> When, as and if declared by the Board of Directors, dividends shall be paid to the holders of the Preferred Stock and the Common Stock *pro rata*. . . .

Note that doing away with the priority dividend right by simply striking the priority right provision that we examined in Charter Sample 9.1 also deletes the language that provides that dividends are not cumulative. As a drafting issue, revising a document to eliminate a right must be done carefully in order to ensure that no other substantive provisions (or key procedural steps) are inadvertently lost in the deletion.

Participation on an "As-Converted" Basis.   The mechanism used to translate the preferred stock's participation right on dividends into dollars and cents is something that will arise repeatedly as we look at the rights and interests of venture capital preferred stock. The dividend participation right gives the preferred stock the right to share with the common stock on an *as-converted basis*. This means that the preferred stock is treated as though its holders have exercised their right of conversion and converted it all into common stock. (The conversion right is dealt with in detail later in section D of this chapter.) It is important to keep in mind, however, that, to take advantage of a participation right, the preferred stock *does not actually convert* into common stock; it is simply treated as if it had.

For purposes of participating in a dividend to be paid to the common stock, the preferred stock is treated as representing the number of common stock shares *issuable* upon exercise of the preferred stock's right to convert into common stock. The number of common stock shares issuable upon conversion is sometimes referred to as the number of *common stock equivalent* shares (or *CSE* shares) represented by the preferred stock. Further, the number of common stock shares actually outstanding, plus the number *deemed outstanding* by looking at the preferred on an as-converted basis, is sometimes referred to as the "total common stock deemed outstanding" (or the "total common stock equivalent shares outstanding"), even though in those cases, the shares referred to include a mix of (i) actually outstanding common stock shares and (ii) as-converted common stock shares.

Example 9.2-A: Dividend Priority and Participation Rights.   To illustrate how the dividend participation right works, let's assume that after its first venture capital financing, SoftCo has 5 million shares of common stock outstanding and 5 million shares of Series A Preferred Stock outstanding, and the preferred stock has both priority and participation rights on dividends. If SoftCo wished to declare a dividend, it first would pay the priority dividend in the amount required by the Charter to the holders of the Series A Preferred Stock, based on the number of preferred shares outstanding. After that payment, it could then pay a dividend to Joan and Michael and its other common stock holders, but in doing so, it must allow the holders of the Series A Preferred Stock to participate in that dividend on an "as-converted basis." If each share of the Series A Preferred Stock were convertible into one share of common stock, then for the common stock dividend SoftCo would have a "deemed" total of 10 million shares of common stock outstanding, and each share would receive an equal dividend. If, after paying the preferred stock's priority dividend preference, SoftCo had $1 million lawfully available that it wished to pay as a dividend on its common stock, then each of the 5 million shares of common stock actually outstanding, as well as each of the 5 million additional shares "deemed outstanding" (by virtue of treating the preferred stock on an "as-converted basis"), would receive a dividend distribution of $0.10.

Example 9.2-B: Dividend Priority but No Participation Right. On the other hand, if SoftCo's Series A Preferred Stock had been non-participating on dividends, it would have received its priority right, and no more. The dividend to the common stock then would have been paid only to the holders of outstanding common stock, who would then receive $0.20 per share, since there are only 5 million shares of common stock outstanding.

Example 9.2-C: Variation on Dividend Priority and Participation Rights. Alternatively, let's assume that SoftCo's Series A Preferred Stock provides both a priority right and a participation right, *and* it has the right to convert at a rate of three shares of common stock for each share of preferred stock. In this case, the preferred stock first would receive its dividend under its priority right. Then, for the common stock dividend, counting the preferred stock on an as-converted basis, 20 million common stock shares would be deemed outstanding (i.e., the 5 million common stock shares actually outstanding, plus 15 million common stock shares deemed outstanding in treating the preferred stock on an as-converted basis). Under this scenario, with the same $1 million being distributed, each share of the 20 million shares of common stock deemed outstanding would receive a dividend distribution of $0.05.

It is important to note that the priority right is based on the number of shares of preferred stock outstanding. The participation right, in contrast, is based on the number of shares of common stock into which the preferred stock may be converted.

In each of the hypothetical dividend grants described in Examples 9.2-A, B, and C, the preferred stock dividend on its "priority" right is the same. In contrast, the "participation" dividend amounts changed from $0.10 to zero to $0.05 per as-converted common share. The amounts also changed, and changed differently, when looked at in terms of the amounts received per share of outstanding preferred stock. In Example 9.2-A, the participation right yielded $0.10 per as-converted share. Since the preferred stock converted at a one-for-one rate, the preferred stock holders received $0.10 per share of preferred stock. In Example 9.2-B, the preferred stock holders had no participation right, so they received nothing. In Example 9.2-C, the preferred stock holders received $0.05 per share on an as-converted basis, but because the preferred stock converted at a three-for-one rate, the preferred stock holders received $0.15 per share of preferred stock. As Example 9.2-C shows, when looking at preferred stock rights, it is important to track whether a particular right is based on the number of preferred stock shares or, alternatively, whether it is based on the number of common stock shares issuable upon the conversion of the preferred stock.

The Vanishing Priority. Sometimes company counsel, being told that the preferred stock is to receive, say, a $0.10 per share priority on dividends and then is to participate in further distributions, will draft a Charter provision along the following lines:

Charter Sample 9.3. No dividends shall be paid on the Common Stock during any given year until the Preferred Stock shall have been paid a dividend in that year of $0.10 per share. Thereafter, the Preferred Stock shall participate in dividends paid on the Common Stock, on an as-converted basis, in an amount per share (including the priority amount payable pursuant to this provision) equal to the amount paid per share to the Common Stock. Dividends shall not be cumulative.

Although this provision may appear to provide priority and participation rights to the preferred stock, it does not. It establishes the priority right to $0.10 per share, but then counts that priority amount as part of the participation right. The parenthetical "including the priority amount payable pursuant to this provision" means that when calculating the "equal" amount the preferred stock is entitled to receive under its participation right, the amount paid under the priority right is included. The result is what we will call a vanishing priority right.

Example 9.3-A: The Vanishing Priority Right.   For example, if SoftCo's preferred stock is convertible at a one-for-one rate, and the company wants to pay a dividend of $0.12 per share on the common stock, under the terms of this Charter provision, the company would pay the preferred stock $0.10 per share (the priority right), but then would count that $0.10 towards the participation right, which would limit the additional amount paid under the participation right to $0.02 per share. The total preferred stock dividend paid, then, would be $0.12. Thus, the preferred stock would receive only an amount equal to what a participation right alone would have given it — that is, the same dividend as paid to the common stock. The priority amount, in essence, vanished. In contrast, under the priority and participation structure shown in Charter Sample 9.2, the preferred stock would receive $0.10 per share on the priority right and $0.12 on the participation right (assuming the company had sufficient legal funds available) for a total dividend distribution of $0.22 per share.

While the vanishing priority approach shown in Charter Sample 9.3 may serve the company nicely by limiting the preferred stock dividend preference, and of course the parties can agree to whatever terms they like, it is not an intellectually coherent package of rights when taken as a whole. First, it allows the priority right to be set off against the participation right, and so does not provide the full set of rights agreed upon. Further, it mixes the priority right, which is granted on a per-share basis on the preferred stock, with the participation right, which is granted on a per-share basis on the shares of common stock issuable upon conversion of the preferred stock, which can create anomalous outcomes.

Example 9.3-B: The Vanishing Priority Right — Varying Conversion Rates. We have seen that this formulation will not produce the result intended in a simple example, but if the conversion rate is greater than one-for-one, or less than one-for-one, the outcome can get even stranger. For example, if the preferred stock were convertible on a three-for-one basis, then each share first would get its $0.10 per preferred stock share priority amount. Then we are faced with interpreting the language: "on an as-converted basis, in an amount per share equal to or greater than the amount paid per share to the Common Stock." Since each share of preferred stock represents three shares of common stock "on an as-converted basis," each of those as-converted common stock shares would have received $0.0333 per share based on their priority right. Then, in order to determine a participation amount "on an as-converted basis" equal to what each share of outstanding common stock would receive (i.e., $0.12), each as-converted common share would have to receive $0.0867 ($0.12 common stock dividend amount minus $0.0333 (i.e., $0.10 divided by 3) per as-converted share from the priority dividend = $0.0867). The outcome would be that the preferred stock would get $0.12 per share on each as-converted share, for a total of $0.36 on each preferred stock share. That amount is what the preferred stock would have received on its participation right under the more standard construction, but its $0.10 per preferred stock share priority right has vanished once again.

If the preferred stock were convertible on a one-half-for-one basis (which means each share of preferred stock is convertible into one-half share of common stock, so that it takes two shares of preferred stock to convert into one share of common stock), then the preferred stock would receive its $0.10 per share priority amount, but on an as-converted basis, that $0.10 would be $0.20 per issuable share of common stock ($0.10 per half share is $0.20 per share). Under these circumstances, the preferred stock would not have a participation right because it already has received more, on a per-share, as-converted basis, than the per-share amount payable on the outstanding common stock shares. Consequently, the preferred shares would not be paid any more dividends until the dividend paid to the common stock exceeded $0.20 per share.

Using the standard construction presented in Charter Sample 9.2, the dividend would have been $0.10 per preferred stock share plus $0.12 per share of as-converted common stock. Since each share of preferred stock is convertible into one-half share of common, the participation dividend per share of preferred stock would be one-half of $0.12, making the total dividend $0.16 per share of preferred stock ($0.10 priority plus $0.06 participation).

We look at these examples not because the vanishing priority right is a common, or even an appropriate, construction; it is an unintended result of sloppy drafting. The purpose of our examination is that the vanishing priority right effectively illustrates the importance of recognizing that priority rights apply to each share of preferred stock outstanding, while participation rights are based on the number of shares of common stock issuable upon conversion of the preferred stock. By confusing the elements of the two preferential rights, these examples create muddled outcomes that do not remotely match the terms of the deal described in the introduction to Charter Sample 9.3, which consisted of a priority right of $0.10 per share plus a right to participate in dividends paid on the common stock.

As to the market today, venture capital preferred stock typically has a straightforward participation right on dividends along the lines presented in Charter Sample 9.2.

4. Cumulative Dividends

The dividends addressed so far have been non-cumulative. As previously discussed, a "cumulative dividend" is treated as though it is declared automatically, so the dividend amount accumulates over the life of the preferred stock. As start-up companies typically do not want to pay dividends (and even if they wanted to, most could not meet the statutory tests for valid payment), they usually would have to let the dividends accumulate. When a cumulative dividend is accumulated on a compounded basis, it can result in a significant value shift to the preferred stock over its lifetime.

Cumulative dividend language in the Charter might read as follows:

Charter Sample 9.4. The holders of the Preferred Stock shall be entitled to annual dividends in an amount equal to 8% of (i) the original purchase price of the Preferred Stock (as may be adjusted for stock dividends, splits and the like), plus (ii) all dividends then accrued [or accumulated], prior to and in preference to any dividend payment to Common Stock.

This provision sets a priority right to dividends for the preferred stock; calls for those dividends to be cumulative; and, by multiplying the 8 percent each year by the sum of the preferred stock price *plus* prior dividends not yet paid, provides for the dividends to compound.

Unlike the non-cumulative dividend, the accumulation of a cumulative dividend is not discretionary. It does not simply disappear if the year passes and the board of directors takes no action on dividends. It also accrues, or accumulates, regardless of whether the company had sufficient assets to pay a dividend at the time it was scheduled in the Charter provision.

Note that the language of Charter Sample 9.4 does not require that the dividend be declared or paid on a periodic basis. It simply says that there is an annual right to a dividend based on a percentage of the original purchase price of the Preferred Stock, plus any previous dividend right that has not yet been paid. As a result, unless the dividend is declared and paid, the amount the Preferred Stock holders are entitled to receive accumulates on a "compounded" basis.

The statutory financial tests that are a prerequisite to paying a dividend are typically applied as of the time the dividend is declared. *See, e.g.*, Del. GCL §170(a) (setting forth the legal sources from which the directors of a corporation may "declare and pay" a dividend); and Cal. Corp. Code §166 (stating that the "time of any distribution by way of dividend shall be the date of declaration thereof"). The cumulative dividend language presented above addresses the amount of the dividend without requiring that it be periodically declared, thus avoiding the need to satisfy the statutory tests for declaring a dividend. The obligation simply accumulates or accrues as if it had been declared, even though it was not.

The obligation to pay an accrued or accumulated dividend can be triggered by payment of a dividend on the common stock, which is not highly probable for business reasons that we have previously described. The more likely trigger is a liquidation or redemption, when the accrued amount is added to the liquidation preference or redemption price. As we discuss later regarding those rights, accrued but unpaid dividend amounts are commonly added to those preferred stock preference rights. The result is that, with the passage of time and compounded rates, a cumulative dividend can make the value of those rights grow significantly over the life of the preferred stock.

Venture capital investors like cumulative dividends, since they add a built-in, time-value-of-money adjustment to the preferred stock's preferential rights on a liquidation or redemption. However, in practice, only a small minority of venture capital transactions actually provide for cumulative dividends, although there is significant regional variation. According to several years of data reported in the FENWICK & WEST VENTURE CAPITAL SURVEY, the percentage of Silicon Valley venture capital transactions calling for cumulative dividends typically is in the single digits, ranging generally from 2 to 8 percent of deals, with occasional spikes as high as 11 percent. *See* FENWICK & WEST VENTURE

CAPITAL SURVEY (2nd Quarter 2013), *available at* http://www.fenwick.com/publications/ Pages/Silicon-Valley-Venture-Survey-Second-Quarter-2013.aspx. (These surveys present data over a rolling period of eight quarters. Earlier surveys are *available at* http://www .fenwick.com/Topics/pages/topicsdetail.aspx?topicname = VC%20Survey.) On the other hand, on the East Coast, the percentage of deals with cumulative dividends is reported to be as high as 50 percent or more, depending on the stage of financing. *See, e.g.*, VALU-ATION AND DEAL TERM DATABASE – DEAL ANALYSIS (2nd Quarter 2013) Private Equity Data Center — A VCExperts.com Product, *available at* http://pedatacenter.com/; and the May 26, 2010, post by author Dave Broadwin to the very informative Emerging Enter-prise Center Blog, published by Foley Hoag LLP, reporting on the experience of his Boston-based firm with New England transactions, *available at* http://www.emerging enterprisecenterblog.com/activity-levels/is-the-venture-economy-back-or-do-we-just-think -so (May 26, 2010) (copy on file with authors).

QUESTIONS

---

1. Using Charter Sample 9.4 to establish a cumulative dividend right, assume the original issue price of the preferred stock was $4.35 per share, and upon a corporate liquidation, each share of preferred stock has a priority right to be paid its original issue price plus all accrued or cumulated and unpaid dividends. If a liquidation were to occur six years after the preferred stock issuance, what is the amount of the per-share priority right of the preferred stock?
2. Why would so few West Coast venture capitalists take advantage of a cumulative dividend preference when it clearly can substantially alter their monetary stake in a company?

C. The Liquidation Preference

The liquidation preference is set of rights built into preferred stock that provides for a special claim on the proceeds of a sale of the company. As with the dividend preference, the liquidation preference normally consists of a priority right coupled with a partici-pation right. The priority right is normally based on the original purchase price of the preferred stock, plus accrued but unpaid dividends. The participation right is normally based on the number of common stock shares issuable upon conversion of the preferred stock.

The fundamental purpose of the liquidation preference is to allow the preferred stock holders to get back their invested funds on a sale of the business before any amounts are paid to other equity security (i.e., common stock) holders. This is accomplished through the priority liquidation right. In addition, the liquidation participation right often gives the preferred stock holders the ability to participate in the equity upside on a sale of the business, while balancing their interests with those of the founders, employees, and other common stock holders.

1. A "*Liquidation*"

Literally, a *liquidation* is the conversion of a company's assets to cash and a distribution of that cash (after meeting all debt and other higher-priority obligations) to the shareholders in the course of a dissolution and winding up of a corporation. A *liquidation preference* governs the scope of the claim a preferred stock holder would have on the disposition of the company's assets.

However, as it actually is used in the venture capital context, a liquidation preference is intended to apply to a much broader swath of transactions. Again, the first purpose of this preference is to make sure the preferred stock holders get their money out of the company before payments are made to any other equity holders. As a result, a liquidation preference is usually structured to cover any merger or reorganization transaction, sale of a large portion of the company's stock, or sale or other disposition (including a lease or exclusive license, for instance) of all or substantially all of the company's assets.

Often, the liquidation preference section of the Charter contains a lengthy defined term that may be a "Liquidation Event" or a "Deemed Liquidation." This definition is intended to sweep up the full range of transactions that functionally represent a sale of the business with proceeds going to its owners. An example might read as follows:

Charter Sample 9.5. For purposes of this Section, a "**Liquidation Event**" shall include (A) the closing of the sale, transfer or other disposition of all or substantially all of this corporation's assets, (B) the consummation of the merger or consolidation of this corporation with or into another entity (except a merger or consolidation in which the holders of capital stock of this corporation immediately prior to such merger or consolidation continue to hold at least 50% of the voting power of the capital stock of this corporation or the surviving or acquiring entity), (C) the closing of the transfer (whether by merger, consolidation or otherwise), in one transaction or a series of related transactions, to a person or group of affiliated persons (other than an underwriter of this corporation's securities), of this corporation's securities if, after such closing, such person or group of affiliated persons would hold 50% or more of the outstanding voting stock of this corporation (or the surviving or acquiring entity), or (D) a liquidation, dissolution or winding up of this corporation; *provided, however,* that a transaction shall not constitute a Liquidation Event if its sole purpose is to change the state of this corporation's incorporation or to create a holding company that will be owned in substantially the same proportions by the persons who held this corporation's securities immediately prior to such transaction. Notwithstanding the prior sentence, the sale of shares of Preferred Stock in a financing transaction shall not be deemed a "Liquidation Event." The treatment of any particular transaction or series of related transactions as a Liquidation Event may be waived by the vote or written consent of the holders of a majority of the outstanding Preferred Stock (voting together as a single class and not as separate series, and on an as-converted basis).

As we analyze the language in the Charter Samples, if there are defined terms, such as "Liquidation Event," that are useful in our discussion of the Charter Sample language, they will be capitalized and should be read in the context of the relevant Charter Sample. When the discussion turns to rights and terms more generally, those defined terms will no longer be used.

In this "Liquidation Event" definition, item (A) addresses a sale of the company's assets. The language "all or substantially all" is the term of art used to acknowledge that the sale may not include 100 percent of the company's assets. The intention is to capture sales of capital assets rather than inventory or assets that are sold in the ordinary course of operating the business.

Item (B) addresses merger transactions. "Merger," "consolidation," and "reorganization" are all terms used to describe a change in the legal interests that make up an entity. As the particular terms used, and their specific meanings, vary from state to state, we will use the term "merger" to address this concept. In a simple two-party corporate merger, the ownership interests of one or both of the entities involved are changed. In this kind of merger, the acquiring corporation and the target corporation make a joint filing with the secretary of state providing that, on the effective date of the merger, the shares of the target corporation will be transformed into the right to receive cash, shares of the acquiring corporation, or both; the target corporation will cease to exist; and the acquiring corporation will become the owner of the target corporation's assets and the obligor on all its debts. The end result is that the acquirer gets the business of the target and the target disappears, while its shareholders' stock is transformed into the right to receive a payment from the acquirer.

The difficulty is that the complex structures used in some merger transactions may cause form and substance to diverge. For example, sometimes the acquirer disappears and the target survives, but it is owned by the acquirer's shareholders. As the purpose of a liquidation preference is to give the preferred stock holders the right to receive their money first, before any other payments are made to other equity security (i.e., common stock) holders, a merger involving payment to a company's shareholders in exchange for a transfer of the business needs to be covered by the liquidation preference. Thus, item (B) is broadly written to avoid the liquidation preference being limited to any particular merger form or structure.

However, the parenthetical language in item (B) carves out from the definition of Liquidation Event a merger where the owners of the corporation end up owning at least 50 percent of the voting power of the entity that survives the merger. The point is to exclude mergers that are used for financing the company, or to acquire rights or assets from a third party (where the company is the acquirer rather than the target). As a result, the mere fact that a "merger" has taken place should not be enough to trigger a liquidation preference. To be a Liquidation Event, a merger, however it is structured, must result in the owners of the corporation (i.e., the shareholders) ending up with less than 50 percent of the voting power in the surviving entity. Basically, the liquidation preference is triggered when the substance of a merger involves a sale of the business to new majority owners, regardless of the form of transaction used.

Item (C) addresses a "transfer," however it is structured, of the corporation's securities that results in a new person (or group of related persons) owning 50 percent or more of the voting securities of the corporation. Note that a *transfer* is a conveyance of existing outstanding shares from their owner to another person. This is distinct from an *issuance*, which is the sale of newly issued shares by a corporation to the initial owner of those shares. Item (C) addresses transfers — not issuances and not changes in form through a merger — that result in voting control of the corporation being held by a new party or affiliated group. Specifically excluded is a transfer to an underwriter for purposes of a public offering of the corporation's securities. You will recall, from our discussion of the federal securities laws in Chapter 4, that the typical structure of an underwritten public offering calls for the company to sell its shares to an underwriter, who then resells them to the public through the registered public offering transaction. The shares that the underwriter resells to the public may be newly issued shares from the corporation, or alternatively, they may be shares that were previously held by existing shareholders of the company, or they may be some combination of the two. As a public offering is a means of obtaining shareholder liquidity separate from a sale of the business, it should not trigger the liquidation preference merely because of the structure of the underwriting transaction.

Item (D) is a classic liquidation upon the dissolution of the corporation.

Following item (D), the *"provided, however,"* language included at the end of this list carves out from the definition of Liquidation Event any transaction — even if it would otherwise fall within one of the (A) through (D) terms — if the "sole purpose" is to reincorporate the corporation in a different state, or to create a holding company whose ownership is substantially the same as the existing corporation's. While these transactions may be done in preparation of a public offering or of a transaction that might qualify as a Liquidation Event, they by themselves do not change the fundamental ownership proportions of the company, and therefore should not be enough to trigger the liquidation preference.

The next sentence of Charter Sample 9.5 following item (D) reads:

> [N]otwithstanding the prior sentence, the sale of shares of Preferred Stock in a financing transaction shall not be deemed a "Liquidation Event."

The "prior sentence" is the entire definition up to that point, so this concept could have been added to the previous sentence as another "provided, however." Perhaps the drafter decided that sentence was long enough already, or perhaps the object was to highlight the financing transaction issue by giving it its own sentence. At any rate, this provision excludes from all prongs of the Liquidation Event definition any transaction whose purpose is a financing rather than a sale. While it does not define what a "financing transaction" is, generally speaking, in a financing transaction the money stays in the company for use in the business, rather than being paid out to the owners of the business. The impact of this particular carve out is that if a transaction occurs that otherwise would fit the terms of one of items (A) through (D), so long as the proceeds of that transaction stay in the company, the financing transaction does not trigger the liquidation preference even if it results in a majority of voting power being acquired by a new party.

The final sentence of the Liquidation Event definition provides one final exception that grants the preferred stock holders the ability to decide, by majority vote, that a transaction should not be treated as triggering the liquidation preference, even if it otherwise falls within the Liquidation Event definition. This ability to "opt out" is a reflection of the fact that corporate transactions have grown to be very complex and convoluted, which has caused the definition of Liquidation Event to be drafted in very broad terms. Thus, Charter Sample 9.5 sensibly provides a "saving clause" that gives the holders of the preferred stock (who, after all, are the beneficiaries of the liquidation preference rights) the power to determine whether those rights should not apply in a particular instance.

Some lawyers separately define "transfer of ownership" transactions, where the proceeds are paid to the shareholders, versus "sale of assets" transactions, where the proceeds are paid to the company and then distributed out to the shareholders. Some lawyers use very long, comprehensive definitions of everything they believe should be included as triggering the liquidation preference, while others use simple, broad definitions and focus on tightly crafted terms for the carve-outs. Regardless of the drafting approach taken, the liquidation preference is intended to give the holders of the preferred stock the right to get their money back first. As a result, any transaction that may constitute a sale of the business should be swept in and scrutinized in order to determine whether it should trigger the preferred stock's liquidation preference.

Often, the Liquidation Event definition (or whatever term the drafter uses) is followed by a provision that addresses how to determine the value of non-cash assets to be distributed in a liquidation transaction. Some lawyers use detailed terms applying varying valuation approaches to different classes of assets, while others simply state that the corporation's board of directors will make a good faith determination of the fair market value of the assets as of the date of distribution. Whichever approach is taken, the end result is that the liquidation preference right is expressed in dollars, so that whatever (other than cash) is actually distributed out to the shareholders must be assigned a monetary value in order to demonstrate conformity to the liquidation preference.

2. The Liquidation Priority Preference

The priority element of the liquidation preference states that the preferred stock is entitled to receive a defined amount before any proceeds of the liquidation can be paid to any other equity securities. A liquidation priority preference provision in the Charter might read as follows:

> **Charter Sample 9.6-A.** In the event of any Liquidation Event [as defined in Charter Sample 9.5], either voluntary or involuntary, the holders of each series of Preferred Stock shall be entitled to receive, prior and in preference to any distribution of the proceeds of such Liquidation Event (the "**Proceeds**") to the holders of Common Stock by reason of their ownership thereof, Proceeds in an amount per share equal to the sum of the applicable Original Issue Price (as defined below) for each series of Preferred Stock, plus declared but unpaid dividends on such share.

This preference provision is triggered by a Liquidation Event. The version of that defined term we looked at in Charter Sample 9.5 covered the full range of events that would trigger liquidation rights. But sometimes the Charter's definition of this term will not include a basic liquidation, dissolution, or winding up of the corporation. As a result, the preference provision has to refer to "a liquidation, dissolution or winding up, or other Liquidation Event." As another alternative, the preference provision may just refer to a liquidation, dissolution, or winding up, "which, as used herein, shall include . . ." and then provide a list of all the additional triggering events identified in the "Liquidation Event" definition. So, when using another company's Charter as precedent to modify your client's liquidation preference terms, it is important to make sure that each document uses the same approach to setting out what constitutes the triggering events. Otherwise, carelessly imported language may inadvertently result in narrowing the scope of the liquidation preference or may result in a redundant provision.

The "voluntary or involuntary" reference in the example above is an acknowledgement that state corporate statutes dealing with dissolution may provide for different processes in a voluntary dissolution (i.e., when the corporation liquidates on its own initiative) versus an involuntary dissolution (i.e., when the corporation is compelled to liquidate by a third party bringing an action in court). The purpose of the reference is to clarify that the liquidation priority preference applies regardless of what prompts the liquidation.

Pari Passu Priority Rights.   The Charter Sample 9.6-A liquidation preference provision goes on to say that each series of Preferred Stock is entitled to receive "Proceeds" from the Liquidation Event, in preference to any payment made to the holders of Common Stock, in a per-share amount equal to their applicable "Original Issue Price" plus declared but unpaid dividends. The "each series" reference means that multiple series of preferred stock have the same degree of priority preference. They are referred to as *pari passu* — in Latin, "with equal step" — meaning none of the series is ahead, or preferred, over any other. This formulation means that the Proceeds are allocated out proportionately to the preferred holders of each outstanding series of Preferred Stock simultaneously, so that with each additional dollar of proceeds received in liquidation of the company, each shareholder moves proportionately closer to receiving its stated preference amount.

Example 9.6-A: Liquidation Priority Right.   For example, let's assume that SoftCo has completed a second round of financing and has 5 million shares of Series A Preferred Stock outstanding with an Original Issue Price of $0.10 per share, and 10,000 shares of Series B Preferred Stock outstanding with an Original Issue Price of $150 per share, and has declared no dividends. The liquidation priority preference would be $500,000 for the Series A Preferred Stock (5 million times $0.10) and $1.5 million for the Series B Preferred Stock (10,000 times $150), equaling the total amounts invested in each financing round, for an aggregate liquidation priority preference of $2 million. If SoftCo were to be sold for $5 million, under the *liquidation waterfall* (a term of art used to refer to the flow of proceeds, disbursed from the highest priority down to the lowest) in this example, the preferred stock would get the first $2 million ($500,000 paid to the Series A Preferred Stock and $1.5 million paid out to the Series B Preferred Stock), and the remaining $3 million would be distributed in accordance with the participation rights granted in the Charter, which are discussed in the next section.

But what if the proceeds available on liquidation of the company were, for example, only $1.28 million? The Charter has to address how the two series of *pari passu* preferred stock are going to divide up liquidation proceeds when the amount available is not enough to pay the full preference amounts to each outstanding series of preferred stock. Clearly, all of the proceeds on sale of the company will go to the preferred stock, but how much will each share get when there is more than one series of preferred stock outstanding?

Would it be fair, for instance, simply to divide the proceeds on a per share basis? The Series A Preferred Stock, with 5 million shares outstanding, represents 99.8 percent of the total preferred stock shares. If it got 99.8 percent of the $1.28 million of proceeds, that would be far more than its $500,000 preference right. So maybe the Series A Preferred Stock should be paid out of the sale proceeds on a per share basis until it reaches its preference amount, then the rest of the sale proceeds would be paid out to the Series B Preferred Stock. But if we did that the shares would not really be treated *pari passu*, would they? Why? Because the Series A Preferred Stock would have been paid the full amount of its stated preference while the Series B Preferred Stock would have received only about half of its preference.

Pari Passu Pro-Rata Liquidation Priority Right.   The typical approach to this dilemma is to provide for a proportionate allocation to each share of preferred stock based on the relative preference amount of each series of preferred stock. The language used in the Charter for a *pari passu* liquidation priority right, after stating the priority preference amounts (which in this case would be $150 per share to the Series B Preferred Stock and $0.10 per share to the Series A Preferred Stock), therefore might read:

> **Charter Sample 9.6-B.** . . . provided, however, that if the assets and funds thus distributed are insufficient to permit the payment of those full preferential amounts, then the entire assets and funds of the Corporation legally available for distribution pursuant to this subsection shall be distributed among the holders of the Preferred Stock ratably in proportion to the full preferential amounts each holder would be entitled to receive pursuant to this subsection.

Example 9.6-B: Pari Passu *Pro-Rata Distribution*.   Continuing with the facts presented in Example 9.6-A, to calculate the distribution allocation under Charter Sample 9.6-B, we know that of $2 million of total preference, the Series A Preferred Stock is entitled to one fourth ($500,000 divided by $2 million) and the Series B Preferred Stock is entitled to three fourths ($1.5 million divided by $2 million). That means that if we ratably divide each dollar of SoftCo's sale proceeds so that one fourth goes to the Series A Preferred Stock and three fourths goes to the Series B Preferred Stock, when we have paid out $2 million of the sale proceeds, each series will have received its full preference right and each shareholder will have gotten his or her full preference amount of $0.10 or $150, per share, as applicable.

Example 9.6-C: Pari Passu *with Inadequate Proceeds*.   Now let's apply Charter Sample 9.6-B to the situation where less than the full preference amount is available to distribute on liquidation of the company. We know that under the language of this Charter provision, one fourth of our $1.28 million in sale proceeds goes to the Series A Preferred Stock, or $320,000, and three fourths goes to the Series B Preferred Stock, or $960,000. But each series has a different number of shares outstanding, so we have to go one step further and calculate the correct amount to distribute *per share* for each series. Only in that way can we allocate the correct preference amounts among the individual shareholders. There are 5 million Series A Preferred Stock shares outstanding, so $320,000 divided by 5 million shares means each share gets $0.064. As to the Series B Preferred Stock, $960,000 divided by 10,000 shares is $96 per share.

Fig. 9.1 Liquidation waterfall with *pari passu* priority rights

Proceeds of Sale	$5,000,000	$1,280,000
Priority payment to Series A Preferred Stock	− 500,000	− 320,000
Priority payment to Series B Preferred Stock	−1,500,000	− 960,000
Remaining Available for Distribution to junior securities (i.e., common stock)	$3,000,000	$ 0

To confirm that our calculations result in distributing the liquidation proceeds ratably in proportion to the preference amounts of each series, we start with the fact that there was $1.28 million in available proceeds for distribution versus a total preference right of $2 million. Proceeds of $1.28 million divided by the total preference amount of $2 million, equals 0.64, or 64 percent. This tells us that the proceeds were 64 percent of the preferential rights. As to the Series A Preferred Stock preference, we see that $320,000 is 64 percent of $500,000 and $0.064 is 64 percent of $0.10. With respect to the Series B Preferred Stock preference, we see that $960,000 is 64 percent of $1.5 million and $96 is 64 percent of $150. Thus, we can conclude that each share of each series got its proportionate allocation of the total amount available for distribution in liquidation of the company.

Layered Priority Rights.   What happens if, instead of *pari passu* treatment, one series of preferred stock is given a priority over another series of preferred stock? For example, assume that the Series B Preferred Stock investors, who invested in SoftCo after the Series A Preferred Stock at a much higher price, negotiated for the right to get their money out first on liquidation of the company. In this situation, the Charter would have to contain separate liquidation priority provisions that sequentially address each series and preference amount, such as the following:

Charter Sample 9.7. Upon a Liquidation Event [as defined in Charter Sample 9.5] all funds, assets, or proceeds available for distribution shall be distributed in the following order of priority:

(a) First to the holders of the Series B Preferred Stock in the amount of $150.00 per share, plus declared and unpaid dividends thereon (as adjusted for stock splits, stock dividends, combinations and the like). If, upon the occurrence of a Liquidation Event, the funds, assets, or proceeds legally available for distribution to the holders of the Series B Preferred Stock shall be insufficient to permit a payment of that full preferential amount, then all available funds, assets, or proceeds shall be paid ratably among the holders of the Series B Preferred Stock in proportion to the preferential amount each holder is otherwise entitled to receive.

(b) Then, upon completion of the distribution required by subsection (a), any remaining funds, assests or proceeds next shall be distributed to the holders of the Series A Preferred Stock in the amount of $0.10 per share . . .

This process is continued until all the priority rights have been addressed in their order of seniority, ending with the common stock's residual right in remaining proceeds.

At each liquidation priority level, in addition to stating the per-share preference amount or amounts that apply to the one or more series of preferred stock at that level, the Charter language also has to make clear what happens if the proceeds are not sufficient to pay the full amount of the stated liquidation preference. In Charter Sample 9.6-B, we looked at a proportionate allocation for two *pari passu* series of outstanding preferred stock. If there is no *pari passu* sharing between or among series at a priority stage, then the Charter normally states that if proceeds are insufficient to pay the full preference to the series at that priority stage, then all the funds available are to be paid to that series ratably on a per-share basis. This is simpler than the *pari passu* calculation because all the shares from one series have the same per-share preference amount, so this allocation is just made on an equal, per-share basis.

Example 9.7: Layered Liquidation Priority Preferences. Returning to our hypothetical sale of SoftCo at $1.28 million, if the Series B Preferred Stock had a first priority among preferred stock series on liquidations, how would the distribution outcomes change versus the *pari passu* result shown in Fig. 9.1, above? Since the liquidation waterfall would flow first to the Series B Preferred Stock and we know that this series has a priority preference of $1.5 million, and since the Proceeds are less than that amount, all the Proceeds would go to the Series B Preferred Stock. The amount paid out would be $128 per share and the Series A Preferred Stock (as well as the Common Stock) would receive nothing. You will recall that in the earlier *pari passu* hypothetical with the sale price of $1.28 million, the Series B Preferred Stock received $96 per share and the Series A Preferred Stock received $0.064 per share.

Fig. 9.2 Liquidation waterfall with layered priority rights when Series B has first priority

Proceeds of Sale	$1,280,000
Priority payment to Series B Preferred Stock	−1,280,000
Remaining Available for Distribution to junior securities:	0
Priority payment to Series A Preferred Stock	— 0
Remaining Available for Distribution to junior securities (i.e., common stock)	$ 0

PROBLEM

How would our analysis of these facts change if the Charter provided that the first priority on a liquidation of SoftCo was held by the Series A Preferred Stock? The liquidation waterfall is partially constructed as Fig. 9.3. Please fill in the missing numbers. What would the first priority preference amount be and to whom is it payable? What amount would be left and what priority rights would apply? What would the per-share distribution amounts be to the Series A Preferred Stock and to the Series B Preferred Stock?

Fig. 9.3 Liquidation waterfall with layered priority rights when Series A has first priority

Proceeds of Sale	$1,280,000
Priority payment to:	$
Remaining Available for Distribution to junior securities Priority payment to:	$
Remaining Available for Distribution to junior securities (i.e., common stock)	$ 0

The Liquidation Priority Preference Amount — Stock Splits.   Our basic liquidation priority preference provision, Charter Sample 9.6-A, referred to a definition for *Original Issue Price* (sometimes called "Original Purchase Price" or "Liquidation Preference Amount"), which states an exact per-share amount for each series of preferred stock equal to the original per-share purchase price of the shares of that series. A provision containing that definition might read as follows:

> **Charter Sample 9.8.** In the event of any Liquidation Event [as defined in Charter Sample 9.5], either voluntary or involuntary, the holders of each series of Preferred Stock shall be entitled to receive, prior and in preference to any distribution of the proceeds of such Liquidation Event (the "Proceeds") to the holders of Common Stock by reason of their ownership thereof, Proceeds in an amount per share equal to the sum of the applicable **Original Issue Price** (which shall be $0.10 for each share of Series A Preferred Stock and $150 for each share of Series B Preferred Stock, as adjusted for any stock splits, stock dividends, combinations or the like), plus declared but unpaid dividends on such share.

Under these terms, the amount of the preference is the sum of the "Original Issue Price" per share plus declared but unpaid dividends on such share. If the shares of a particular series of preferred stock are split or combined, the price will adjust proportionately. The purpose of this proportionate adjustment is to make sure that the aggregate Original Issue Price for any given series of preferred stock will remain unchanged by a split or combination of the shares of that series. For example, if the preferred stock is split two-for-one, then there are twice as many shares outstanding, but the total price paid for those shares did not change, so, therefore, the total liquidation preference should not change. In order to prevent the liquidation preference from expanding in the case of a stock split (or contracting in the event shares are combined), the per-share preference needs to adjust proportionately so that, in this example, with twice as many shares outstanding, each share's stated liquidation preference is half as much.

Example 9.8-A: Liquidation Priority Preference — Effect of Stock Split.   Looking again at our hypothetical sale of SoftCo for $1.28 million, what would be the result if, one year prior to the sale transaction, the Series B Preferred Stock had been split on a one hundred-for-one basis? In the aggregate, the Series B Preferred Stock preference of $1.5 million would not change. But because the Original Issue Price adjusts proportionately to reflect the stock split, when the number of Series B Preferred shares went from 10,000 to 1 million, the Original Issue Price per share adjusted from $150 to $1.50. Thus, in the situation where the Series B Preferred Stock had a first priority, it would get the same $1.28 million in proceeds, but since that amount would be divided over 1 million shares rather than 10,000, its per-share proceeds would be $1.28 rather than $128. (See Fig. 9.2.) Where the Series A Preferred Stock had the first priority and the proceeds payable to the Series B Preferred Stock were $780,000 (one of the missing amounts from Fig. 9.3!), the Series B Preferred Stock per-share amount following the stock split would be $0.78 rather than $78.

The Liquidation Priority Preference Amount — Dividends.   The preference amount in Charter Sample 9.8 also includes any declared but unpaid dividends. Since dividends are a means of distributing value to the shareholders, if a holder is entitled to a dividend that has not been paid, to ignore that dividend right at the time of liquidation would deprive that shareholder of a portion of the value of the company that was owed to the shareholder. It bears emphasizing that this formulation refers to "any declared but unpaid" dividends. This language is intended to forestall any argument that a cumulative dividend right exists, and therefore, an accrued amount should be paid on liquidation. In the venture capital context, since the statutory financial tests for valid dividend distributions often are not satisfied until many years into a company's growth, *declaring* a dividend is an extraordinary event. As discussed in section B.2 of this chapter, cumulative dividends are designed to accumulate without being declared. If the Charter contemplated cumulative dividends, this provision might instead read as follows:

> plus accrued but unpaid dividends, whether or not declared.

Example 9.8-B: Liquidation Priority Preference — Effect of Dividends.   Now let's return to our hypothetical sale of SoftCo, which we know has outstanding 5 million shares of Series A Preferred Stock with a $0.10 per share Original Issue Price and 10,000 shares of Series B Preferred Stock with a $150 per share Original Issue Price. Assume that before the Series B Preferred Stock was issued (so we are not distracted by the relative dividend rights of the two series), a dividend was declared on the Series A Preferred Stock in the amount of $0.02 per share, but was never paid. SoftCo is now being sold for $5 million. What are the liquidation priority rights? The Original Issue Price of the Series B Preferred Stock is $150 per share, so we know that the Series B Preferred Stock shares are still entitled to a total priority preference of $1.5 million. The Original Issue Price of the Series A Preferred Stock also is unchanged at $0.10 per share, but now the shares of that series are entitled to an additional $0.02 per share as a result of the declared but unpaid dividend. Consequently, the $500,000 in priority preference for the Series A Preferred Stock increases to $600,000 ($500,000 + ($0.02 × 5 million shares) = $600,000) and the total preferred stock priority preference has increased to $2.1 million. After payment of $2.1 million to the preferred stock, the remaining $2.9 million of liquidation proceeds would be paid in accordance with the participation rights in SoftCo's Charter. See Fig. 9.4, below.

Example 9.8-C: Pari Passu *Liquidation Priority Preference — Effect of Dividends.* The same declared but unpaid dividend on the Series A Preferred Stock also would change the *pari passu* allocation we previously calculated when the proceeds are less than the total preference amount. Returning to the facts of our *pari passu* Examples 9.6-A and B, we see that instead of the priority preference allocation being three quarters to the Series B Preferred Stock and one quarter to the Series A Preferred Stock, it would now be five-sevenths to the Series B Preferred Stock ($1.5 million out of $2.1 million is 15/21, or 5/7) and two-sevenths to the Series B Preferred Stock ($600,000 out of $2.1 million is 6/21 or 2/7). Therefore, on the sale of SoftCo for $1.28 million, the *pari passu* allocation to the Series B Preferred Stock would be $914,285.7143 (5/7 of the proceeds, or $91.42857143 per share) and the allocation to the Series A Preferred Stock would be $365,714.2857 (2/7 of the proceeds, or $0.073142857 per share). In contrast, without the dividend, as we saw in Example 9.6-C, the per-share distribution would have been $96 on the Series B Preferred Stock and $0.064 on the Series A Preferred Stock.

Fig. 9.4 Liquidation waterfall with *pari passu* preferred stock priority rights when Series A is entitled to declared but unpaid dividend of $0.02 per share

Proceeds of Sale	$5,000,000	$1,280,000
Priority payment to Series A Preferred Stock	− 600,000	−365,714.29
Priority payment to Series B Preferred Stock	−1,500,000	−914,285.71
Remaining Available for Distribution to junior securities (i.e., common stock)	$2,900,000	$ 0

A Note on "Rounding." This calculation raises the question of how many decimal places you should use. The answer is purely practical: you should use enough to minimize the effect of rounding. The more powers of ten in share numbers you are dealing with, the more decimal places you need. It often is a good idea to communicate to the interested parties on a liquidation transaction that the preference allocations will be calculated out to a specific number of decimal places. If you do not make this clear at the outset, invariably a representative of one of the parties will call with slightly different numbers because their spreadsheet was set at four decimal places and you used eight. Getting an accord on decimal places up front may well save the client spending legal fees on recalculating and recirculating the shareholder allocations in order to reconcile a few pennies' difference in rounding.

Example 9.8-D: Pari Passu *Liquidation Priority Preference — Effect of Cumulative Dividends.* Let's do another example, but now let's assume that part of the reason the investors paid such a high price for the Series B Preferred Stock is that it earns a cumulative dividend at a compounded annual rate of 8 percent. Assuming that the stock has been outstanding for five years and accrued dividends, whether declared or not, are now part of the liquidation priority preference, what impact does that cumulative dividend have on our sale of SoftCo for $5 million? To find out, we first have to determine the amount of the accumulated dividend obligation. On a per-share basis, we multiply the

Original Issue Price of $150 times 1.08 to determine what the liquidation preference amount (defined as the Original Issue Price plus accrued dividend at 8 percent) would be at the end of the first year, which gives a total liquidation preference amount of $162 per share. Because the dividend compounds, we multiply that amount by 1.08 to determine the preference amount at the end of the second year, giving us $174.96 per share. Then, we repeat this process, multiplying each successive outcome by 1.08 for each successive year, which gives us $188.9568 per share for year three, $204.073344 per share for year four, and $220.3992115 per share for year five.

With this information, we now know that the $150 per share Original Issue Price of the Series B Preferred Stock has been supplemented by an accumulated per-share dividend of $70.3992115 by the end of the fifth year. As a result, when running the sale proceeds through the liquidation waterfall, the liquidation priority preference for the Series B Preferred Stock now aggregates $2,203,992.115, making the total priority preference of the preferred stock, including the $500,000 to the Series A Preferred Stock, $2,703,992.115. Thus, after paying out that amount to the preferred stockholders, the balance of $2,296,007.885 in sale proceeds remaining in the liquidation waterfall would then be distributed in accordance with the liquidation participation rights set forth in SoftCo's Charter. See Fig. 9.5, below.

Example 9.8-E: Pari Passu *Liquidation Priority Preference, Inadequate Proceeds — Effect of Cumulative Dividends.*   With *pari passu* liquidation priority preferences and a sale price for SoftCo of $1.28 million (which is less than the total preferred stock preference amount), the Series B Preferred Stock would be allocated 81.50882 percent of the total priority preference ($2,203,992.115 divided by $2,703,992.115) and the Series A Preferred Stock would have the remaining 18.49118 percent ($500,000 divided by $2,703,992.115). Therefore, the proportionate allocation to the Series B Preferred Stock would be $1,043,312.896 (that is, $1.28 million times .8150882), or $104.3312896 per share, and the payment to the Series A Preferred Stock would be $236,687.104 (that is, $1.28 million times .1849118), or $0.0236687104 per share. To confirm that this results in a ratable proportionate distribution: $1,280,000 is 47.337416 percent of $2,703,992.115 (the sale proceeds available as a percentage of the total preference); $1,043,312.896 is 47.337416 percent of $2,203,992.115 (the Series B Preferred Stock allocation as a percentage of its preference); and finally, $236,687.104 is 47.337416 percent of $500,000 (the Series A Preferred Stock allocation as a percentage of its preference).

Fig. 9.5 Liquidation waterfall with *pari passu* preferred stock priority rights when Series B is entitled to five years of 8% accumulated dividends

	$5,000,000.00	$1,280,000.00
Proceeds of Sale		
Priority payment to Series A Preferred Stock	− 500,000.00	− 236,687.10
Priority payment to Series B Preferred Stock	−2,203,992.12	−1,043,312.90
Remaining Available for Distribution to junior securities (i.e., common stock)	$2,296,007.88	$ 0

PROBLEMS

1. Revisit the facts of Examples 9.8-B and C. We saw the impact of unpaid dividends where the two series of preferred stock were *pari passu* in their liquidation preferences and saw the waterfalls in Fig. 9.4. What would the liquidation waterfalls and per-share proceeds be under those facts for SoftCo's preferred stock shareholders if they had layered priority rights and the Series A Preferred Stock had the first priority right? *Hint*: Use the waterfall layout shown in Fig. 9.3.
2. This time revisiting the facts in Examples 9.8-D and E and Fig. 9.5, what would the liquidation waterfalls look like if, instead of *pari passu* rights, the Series B Preferred Stock had the first priority right?

The Liquidation Priority Preference Amount — Multiples. The priority preference amount on liquidation of the company, regardless of the variations we have explored, is based on the Original Issue Price of the preferred stock. Absent accrued or accumulated dividends, the preferred stock holder's priority preference is the number of dollars invested to buy the share of preferred stock. The amount of the priority preference can vary, however; a common alternative is to have the preference amount stated as some multiple of the Original Issue Price. To reflect this variation, the Charter's liquidation priority preference provision might read, for example:

> **Charter Sample 9.9.** In the event of any Liquidation Event [as defined in Charter Sample 9.5], either voluntary or involuntary, the holders of each series of Preferred Stock shall be entitled to receive, prior and in preference to any distribution of the proceeds of such Liquidation Event (the "Proceeds") to the holders of Common Stock by reason of their ownership thereof, Proceeds in an amount per share equal to the sum of *two times* the applicable Original Issue Price (as defined below) for each series of Preferred Stock, plus declared but unpaid dividends on such share.

This would mean that each share of preferred stock would be entitled to twice its Original Issue Price, plus declared but unpaid dividends, before any funds could be distributed to the holders of the common stock.

Example 9.9: Liquidation Priority Preference — Effect of Multiples. Using our hypothetical sale of SoftCo for $5 million, what would the impact be if the Series B Preferred Stock had a "2X" (i.e., two times) liquidation priority right? Recall that SoftCo has outstanding 5 million shares of Series A Preferred Stock with a $0.10 per share Original Issue Price and 10,000 shares of Series B Preferred Stock with a $150 per share Original Issue Price. Assuming no splits or dividends, under the terms of Charter Sample 9.9, the *pari passu* priority liquidation preference for the preferred stock would increase from $2 million to $3.5 million because the Series B Preferred Stock preference would increase from $1.5 million to $3 million. As a result, the liquidation waterfall on a $5 million sale would provide for the first $3.5 million to flow to the preferred stock ($500,000 to the Series A Preferred Stock and $3 million to the Series B Preferred Stock), with the remaining $1.5 million in proceeds available to be distributed out pursuant to the participation rights in the SoftCo Charter.

Fig. 9.6 shows that in the *pari passu* allocation, when the Series B Preferred Stock has a 2X priority, it now has six-sevenths ($3 million of $3.5 million) of the priority liquidation preference right. In addition, the portion of the liquidation waterfall siphoned off by the priority preference has grown, which means that there is less available for all junior shares. The result is that a priority preference amount set as a multiple of the Original Issue Price significantly devalues the common stock. If multiple preferences are given to several series of preferred stock, soon the total preference amount is so daunting that the common stock is usually perceived as being essentially worthless.

Fig. 9.6 Liquidation waterfall with *pari passu* preferred stock priority rights when Series B has a 2X priority

Proceeds of Sale	$5,000,000	$1,280,000
Priority payment to Series A Preferred Stock	− 500,000	− 182,857
Priority payment to Series B Preferred Stock	−3,000,000	−1,097,143
Remaining Available for Distribution to junior securities (i.e., common stock)	$1,500,000	$ 0

Multiple liquidation preferences, not surprisingly, tend to be used more frequently when investment money is hard to find and venture capital investors are concerned about the prospects for exiting the investment. In general, the percentage of Silicon Valley deals with multiple liquidation preferences ranges from the teens to the low twenties, with occasional blips up or down. *See* Fenwick & West Venture Capital Survey (2nd Quarter 2013), *available at* http://www.fenwick.com/publications/Pages/Silicon-Valley-Venture-Survey-Second-Quarter-2013.aspx. (Earlier surveys are *available at* http://www.fenwick.com/Topics/pages/topicsdetail.aspx?topicname = VC%20Survey.) As the Fenwick & West Venture Capital Survey reports, the most common multiples consistently are two times the Original Issue Price or less (usually 1.5 times), with multiples over three being very rare. In the difficult days after the tech bubble burst, multiples of up to five were occasionally seen. In New England, multiple preferences are less common. *See, e.g.,* Valuation and Deal Term Database — Deal Analysis (2nd Quarter 2013) Private Equity Data Center — A VCExperts.com Product, *available at* http://pedatacenter.com/.

When writing a multiple liquidation preference, the drafter must take special care when using a defined term such as Original Issue Price. This term sometimes is presented as the price originally paid for the stock, as adjusted for splits or combinations, *plus accrued dividends*, but a multiple liquidation preference normally is not intended to include a multiple of accrued dividends. In a cumulative preferred situation, multiplying the accrued dividends could result in a very significant shift in value to the preferred stock holders. *Query:* Why would common stock holders agree to the use of multiples in subsequent series of preferred stock issuances? When does a company have the most — and the least — leverage on the use of multiples?

1. SoftCo has outstanding 5 million shares of Series A Preferred Stock with a $0.10 per share Original Issue Price and 10,000 shares of Series B Preferred Stock with a $150 per share Original Issue Price. The Series B Preferred Stock has a first priority liquidation preference, but the Series A Preferred Stock has a 3X multiple preference for its liquidation priority right. What does the liquidation waterfall look like? What are the per-share proceeds on a sale of SoftCo for $5 million? For $4 million?

2. Assume the same facts, except that the Series B Preferred Stock has a 4 percent cumulative dividend payable upon a Liquidation Event and the Series B Preferred Stock has been outstanding for four years. What does the liquidation waterfall look like? What are the per-share proceeds on a sale of SoftCo for $5 million? For $4 million?

Funds Available for Distribution.   Look again at Charter Sample 9.9 and note that it includes the definition for the term "Proceeds." Its somewhat circular definition, as "the proceeds of a Liquidation Event," is an effort to draft around a fundamental issue in liquidation transactions. The problem is that a "Liquidation Event" covers many transaction forms, and the liquidation rights need to work in all of them. For example, in a literal liquidation (see item (D) in the Liquidation Event definition in Charter Sample 9.5), which might follow a sale of all or substantially all the company's assets (see item (A) in that definition), the "Proceeds" would come from the funds the company received on the sale of its assets. After honoring more senior obligations, such as taxes and debts, those funds would then be available for distribution as "Proceeds" to the shareholders of the company in accordance with their rights in liquidation. In contrast, upon a merger or a stock transfer transaction (see items (C) and (D) in the Liquidation Event definition), the proceeds from the sale of the business would be paid by a third party or parties directly to the company's shareholders. Those "Proceeds" would not get paid to the company and distributed out in the process that is used in a literal liquidation (or dissolution) of the company.

Many liquidation preference provisions are drafted to conform to the statutory requirements for an asset distribution by a corporation to its shareholders. The problem is that the terminology and processes contemplated by the governing statutes simply do not apply to all the potential transaction forms that are typically listed as triggering events in the Charter's definition of "Liquidation Event." Of course, as the following case demonstrates, when a company is going though a liquidation transaction, money (or assets) are being distributed and any failure to clearly define the relative stock class rights will be seized upon by someone who would be advantaged by a different interpretation.

Mathews v. Groove Networks, Inc. et al.

(Del. Ch. 2005)

William B. CHANDLER, III, Chancellor.

The parties to this case disagree about how to interpret the Certificate of Incorporation ("COI") of Groove Networks, Inc. ("Groove Networks"). Plaintiff argues that the liquidation preference in Article IV(B)(3) of the COI (the "Liquidation Preference") does not apply to merger proceeds in the event of a merger. Plaintiff is one of the common stockholders of Groove Networks who, as a result of the Liquidation Preference, received nothing in the March 2005 merger between Groove Networks and Microsoft Corporation.

* * *

[The COI] creates the Liquidation Preference — a distribution preference in favor of the preferred shareholders. The Liquidation Preference governs the distribution of the assets upon the occurrence of any "Liquidation Event." A number of different events qualify as "Liquidation Events," including "any liquidation, dissolution, or winding up" as well as "any reorganization, merger or consolidation" of Groove Networks.

The Liquidation Preference states that, in the event of a merger, the preferred stockholders are to be paid from Groove Networks' "Distributable Assets." The Distributable Assets are defined as the company's assets, "whether from capital, surplus or earnings."[footnote omitted] The COI clarifies the definition of Distributable Assets in Article IV(B)(3)(d)(i) where the COI states: "In the event of a sale of a Majority of the Assets, the Distributable Assets shall be the net proceeds of such sale." The COI does not contain a corollary statement clarifying what constitutes Distributable Assets in the event of a merger. Based on this bit of silence, plaintiff takes the position that merger consideration was not intended to be part of the assets of the corporation and so the Liquidation Preference does not govern the distribution of merger consideration.

* * *

[Article IV(B)(3)(a) of the COI] provides that one of the rights of the preferred stock is that in the event of a merger of Groove Networks, the assets shall be distributed according to the Liquidation Preference.

* * *

Plaintiff would have me read the COI so that it states that the Liquidation Preference applies in the event of a merger only with respect to the assets owned and controlled by the corporation. I decline to adopt this interpretation because it makes little sense. The assets of the corporation in the sense of capital, surplus and earnings are not distributed to target shareholders in the event of a merger; they are transferred to the acquiring corporation in return for cash or other consideration paid to the [target corporation] shareholders. If I were to adopt plaintiff's interpretation, the Liquidation Preference would be interpreted so that it applied in the event of a merger but it would have no effect.

Plaintiff's interpretation fails for another reason: It renders portions of the COI inoperative. Article IV(3)(a)(i) provides that:

> When paid, the Series F Liquidation Preference shall be paid in cash or, at the option of the Corporation . . . (ii) if the Corporation is acquired by a public company, the Corporation may, at its option, pay 100% in registered common stock of the *acquiring* company . . . [emphasis in original]

The COI states in Article IV(3)(a)(i) that the preference scheme can be paid in stock of the acquiring corporation in the event of a merger. The COI must, therefore, have intended that stock of the acquiring corporation be considered one of the "assets of the corporation" available to satisfy the preference scheme. If I adopt plaintiff's reading and read "assets of the corporation" to not include merger consideration, then this portion of the COI would be interpreted so that it was nonsensical.

For the above reasons I conclude that defendants' interpretation is the correct one. Accordingly, I grant defendants' motion for summary judgment.

IT IS SO ORDERED.

QUESTIONS

1. If the Liquidation Preference is to be paid from Groove Networks' "Distributable Assets," does Chancellor Chandler's order render "nonsensical" the COI's definition of "Distributable Assets," which are defined by the COI as the company's assets, "whether from capital, surplus or earnings," in order to make sense of the language defining Liquidation Events as including mergers?
2. In the context of the LLC, we saw in Chapter 3 an article written by Delaware Supreme Court Chief Justice Steele, making it clear that the contract (i.e., the operating agreement) strictly controls in determining rights in LLCs. Similarly, "[provisions of Sections 151(c) and (d) of the Del. GCL regarding preferred stock rights] are consistent with a long line of Delaware cases stating that the rights of preferred stockholders are contract rights and any preferences or special rights must be clearly and unambiguously set out in the certificate of incorporation." DAVID A. DREXLER ET AL., DELAWARE CORPORATION LAW AND PRACTICE §17.01[3] (2008). Is the Chancery Court applying the same standard when interpreting an Operating Agreement contract versus Groove Network's Certificate of Incorporation contract?

NOTE

Despite the free pass granted to sloppy drafters by the court in *Groove Networks*, many practitioners, perhaps not confident that the courts of their states would come to the same conclusion, or perhaps concerned that different specific language in their Charter might lead to a different result, have sought to draft around the problem of the source of proceeds upon the sale of the business. One approach is to cover the waterfront by using a broadly defined term, such as "Proceeds," in Charter Sample 9.9. Another is to address the problem explicitly by including in the Charter language such as the following:

The assets and funds of the Corporation deemed available for distribution pursuant to [the liquidation preference] shall include the aggregate consideration received by holders of capital stock of the Corporation (in the event of a merger, reorganization, transfer or similar transaction) or the aggregate consideration received by the

Corporation together with all other available assets of the Corporation (in the event of a sale of assets or similar transaction).

The result of both of these drafting approaches is that sums paid directly to the shareholders by the company's buyer are deemed part of the liquidation distribution made by the company and, therefore, must be allocated in accordance with the stated liquidation preference set forth in the company's Charter.

3. *The Liquidation Participation Preference*

As stated in the introduction to liquidation preferences at the beginning of section C of this chapter, the opportunity of the preferred stock holders to share in liquidation proceeds after receiving their priority preference is referred to as the *participation right*. There are three basic approaches to the liquidation participation right: a preferred stock can be *non-participating*, *fully participating*, or *participating with a cap*. Perhaps because each approach has pros and cons, all are in common use today. Although the concept of "participating" also applies to dividends, when this term is used without explanation, it generally refers to the liquidation preference granted to the preferred shares.

Non-Participating Preferred.   A non-participating preferred stock has no participation preference on liquidations. After receiving its priority amount, these shares are paid nothing more. When the preferred stock has no liquidation participation right, the Charter might read:

> **Charter Sample 9.10.** Upon completion of the [Preferred Stock's priority preference] distribution, all of the remaining Proceeds available for distribution to stockholders shall be distributed to the holders of Common Stock pro rata based on the number of shares of Common Stock held by each.

This approach was very common in the early days of venture capital and still is widely used. Today, across all regions of the United States, typically 40 to 50 percent (and occasionally even more) of venture capital transactions involve non-participating preferred stock. *See* Fenwick & West Venture Capital Survey (2nd Quarter, 2013) *available at* http://www.fenwick.com/publications/Pages/Silicon-Valley-Venture-Survey-Second-Quarter-2013.aspx; Valuation and Deal Term Database — Deal Analysis (2nd Quarter 2013), from Private Equity Data Center — A VCExperts.com Product, *available at* http://pedatacenter.com/; and Venture Perspectives: New England Edition (1st Quarter 2013), *available at* http://www.foleyhoag.com/publications/alerts-and-updates/2013/july/venture-perspectives-first-quarter-2013. The consequence of owning a non-participating preferred stock is that the holders must choose, prior to a liquidation, whether to be paid in the liquidation of the company as preferred stock holders, receiving their priority preference and no more, or alternatively, whether to convert their preferred stock into common stock, which means they will forego their priority preference, and instead share in the liquidation proceeds with the common stock holders.

Example 9.10-A: Non-Participating Preferred.   Let's look at some potential outcomes for an investor buying a non-participating preferred. Continuing our ongoing example, assume that SoftCo has outstanding 5 million shares of Series A Preferred Stock, each with a $0.10 per-share liquidation priority preference; 10,000 shares of Series B Preferred Stock, each with a $150 per-share liquidation priority preference; and 5 million shares of common stock. Assume further that no dividends have accrued and each series of the outstanding preferred stock has *pari passu* liquidation priority rights, is non-participating on liquidations, and is convertible one-for-one into common stock.

If SoftCo were sold for $5 million, the choice for the Series A Preferred Stock holders would be easy; rather than take their total liquidation preference of $500,000, they would convert and share with the common stock. Why? Following the dollars over the liquidation waterfall, we see that, in this scenario, the Series B Preferred Stock is the only remaining stock with a liquidation preference, so it will be paid its $1.5 million priority amount first. The remaining $3.5 million of proceeds from the sale of the company will then be shared among the 10 million common stock shares outstanding following the conversion of the 5 million Series A Preferred Stock shares on a one-for-one basis. Each share of common stock will be paid $0.35 (that is, the balance of the sale proceeds of $3.5 million, divided by 10 million common shares outstanding), so the Series A Preferred Stock, by converting to common stock and foregoing its priority preference, traded a $0.10 preference per share for a $0.35 payment per share. Note that this situation does not involve a "deemed conversion" or an "as-converted" treatment — rather, the Series A Preferred Stock *actually must convert* and go through the liquidation process as common stock in order to receive these proceeds. Further note that the preferred stock cannot convert part-way through the liquidation. The choice to the preferred shareholders is a "one or the other" proposition, meaning that the Series A Preferred Stock must go through the liquidation waterfall either as preferred stock or as common stock.

Fig. 9.7 Liquidation waterfall for a $5 million sale when *pari passu* preferred stock is non-participating; Series A converts into common stock

	Total	Per Share
Proceeds of Sale	$5,000,000	
Priority payment to Series A Preferred Stock	— 0	$ 0.00
Priority payment to Series B Preferred Stock	−1,500,000	$ 150.00
Remaining Available for Distribution to common stock, including converted Series A Preferred Stock	$3,500,000	$ 0.35

Example 9.10-B: Non-Participating Preferred.   What about the Series B Preferred Stock? Its priority liquidation preference is $150 per share. Should it convert? Absolutely not. By converting, the 10,000 shares of Series B Preferred Stock would lose their priority preference of $1.5 million, and instead would share the $5 million in proceeds with 10 million other shares of common stock. All the shareholders would then be paid

$0.4995 per share (that is, $5 million sale proceeds divided by 10,010,000 common shares), which would mean the Series B Preferred Stock, by converting, would be trading a $150 per share preference for a paltry $0.4995.

The difference in the positions between the Series B Preferred Stock and the Series A Preferred Stock on the eventual sale of SoftCo is a function of the valuations they placed on SoftCo when making their investments. It appears that, with regard to a $5 million sale of SoftCo, the Series A Preferred Stock investors made a decent, while not spectacular, pricing decision that would earn 4.85 times their money back. (We cannot calculate an IRR since we do not know how long before the sale they invested in SoftCo.) The holders of Series B Preferred Stock at a $5 million sale, in contrast, by keeping their preference would be paid back the amount they invested in SoftCo and no more. To put into perspective the valuation these holders placed on their shares, the Series B Preferred Stock would not make the choice to convert their preferred shares into common stock until SoftCo's sale price was over $1.5015 billion (10,010,000 outstanding common shares times $150 per share equals $1,501,500,000). A $5 million sale represents less than 1/300 of that price. As it turns out, the holders of the Series B Preferred Stock hugely overpaid for their shares.

Example 9.10-C: Non-Participating Preferred — The Black Hole.   What if SoftCo ultimately is sold for $2.4 million? The top of the liquidation waterfall does not change in that the Series B Preferred Stock will still keep its preferred stock position in order to be paid its $1.5 million preference. What are the options available to the Series A Preferred Stock? If it does not convert, it will get its $500,000 preference ($0.10 per share times 5 million shares). After $2 million to the preferred stock, the remaining sale distribution will be $400,000 for the common stock. With 5 million shares outstanding, the common stock will receive $0.08 per share.

Fig. 9.8A Liquidation waterfall for a $2.4 million sale when *pari passu* preferred stock is non-participating and does not convert

	Total	Per Share
Proceeds of Sale	$2,400,000	
Priority payment to Series A Preferred Stock	− 500,000	$ 0.10
Priority payment to Series B Preferred Stock	−1,500,000	$150.00
Remaining Available for Distribution to common stock, assuming no preferred stock has converted	$ 400,000	$ 0.08

On the other hand, what if the Series A Preferred Stock holders were to change the waterfall by foregoing their preference and converting their preferred shares into common stock? After the $1.5 million distribution to the Series B Preferred Stock, there would then be $900,000 left for distribution to the 10 million common stock shares then outstanding, yielding a per share payment of $0.09. The Series A Preferred

Stock holders would lose $0.01 per share by converting, so they would choose not to convert.

Fig. 9.8B Liquidation waterfall for a $2.4 million sale when *pari passu* preferred stock is non-participating and Series A Preferred Stock converts

	Total	Per Share
Proceeds of Sale	$2,400,000	
Priority payment to Series A Preferred Stock	– 0	$ 0.00
Priority payment to Series B Preferred Stock	−1,500,000	$ 150.00
Remaining Available for Distribution to common stock, including converted Series A Preferred Stock	$ 900,000	$ 0.09

While the Series B Preferred Stock holders might breathe a sigh of relief to have gotten their invested capital out, especially after so grossly overpaying for their stock, a sale at this price would be particularly frustrating to the holders of the Series A Preferred Stock in that they are getting their money out with no gain on their invested capital.

What is especially irritating about this scenario to the Series A Preferred Stock holders is that they know the founders paid a pittance for their common stock. While employees hired after the investors originally bought the Series A Preferred Stock most likely paid higher prices for their equity incentive shares, those purchases were still probably substantially discounted from the Series A Preferred Stock price, as we discussed in section A.4 of Chapter 6. The result is that Joan and Michael might each walk away with, say, $150,000 or more in gain on their founders' stock, while other employees might share in up to another $100,000. While Joan and Michael invested "sweat equity" through their work in SoftCo's business, they were paid salaries for their services. In the meantime, the Series A Preferred Stock investors, who invested hard cash in exchange for their shares and were supposed to occupy a preferential position, only managed to get back the dollars they invested in SoftCo.

If the Series A Preferred Stock holders would be irritated with this outcome, just imagine how the Series B Preferred Stock holders would feel if SoftCo sold for, say, $200 million. The Series B shareholders would get paid back their invested dollars (i.e., $1.5 million), while Joan, Michael, and the other employee shareholders would receive half of $198.5 million. (The Series A Preferred Stock would convert, so there would be 10 million common stock shares outstanding, 5 million of them owned primarily by the founders and employees.) The effect is exaggerated by the outrageous valuation set in the Series B Preferred Stock transaction, but the Series B Preferred Stock holders only would get their investment back while management and the employees would be receiving a life-changing gain on the sale of SoftCo.

Fig. 9.9 Liquidation waterfall for a $200 million sale when preferred stock is non-participating and Series A converts

	Total	Per Share
Proceeds of Sale	$200,000,000	
Priority payment to Series A Preferred Stock	− 0	$ 0.00
Priority payment to Series B Preferred Stock	− 1,500,000	$ 150.00
Remaining Available for Distribution to common stock, including converted Series A Preferred Stock	$198,500,000	$ 19.85

In short, non-participating preferred stock is a blunt tool. Forcing the preferred stock to take its priority or convert can lead to tension among the shareholders. In section E.4 of Chapter 8, we discussed the potential misalignment of interests between founders and investors, and we described how early success might encourage the founders to look for a sale of the company while encouraging the investors to "double down" and go for the big win. Non-participating preferred exacerbates that problem by creating what is colloquially referred to as a "black hole" in the liquidation preference — a range of company sale prices where the preferred stock holder gets its money out with its liquidation priority, but no more, and gets less by converting, while the common stock holders make a profit.

QUESTIONS

1. How broad is the "black hole" for the Series A Preferred Stock? In other words, at what sale price for SoftCo does the Series A Preferred Stock first get all its invested money back (which is where the black hole begins), and at what sale price is the Series A Preferred Stock better off foregoing its preference rights and converting to common stock?

2. Having answered the preceding question, ask yourself now where the money is going as the proceeds from the sale of SoftCo cause the Series A Preferred Stock to hit the black hole until the black hole ends? *Hint:* This is why the common stock holders refer to the black hole as the "catch-up."

Fully Participating Preferred. The opposite extreme from non-participating is "fully participating" preferred stock. Fully participating shares are the ultimate in "having it both ways" on liquidation rights. After receiving its liquidation priority right, a fully participating preferred stock then shares in all remaining liquidation proceeds with the common stock on an as-converted basis. The Charter provision for a "fully participating" preferred stock might read as follows:

> **Charter Sample 9.11.** [After payment of the Preferred Stock priority rights, remaining liquidation proceeds shall be paid] ratably among the holders of the Preferred Stock and the Common Stock according to the number of shares of Common Stock (A) then held, with respect to holders of the Common Stock, and (B) into which the outstanding shares of Preferred Stock are then convertible.

The effect of fully participating preferred stock is that the holders never face the "convert/not convert" choice in a liquidation because they *always* receive more by not converting. Since fully participating preferred always provides the best outcome for the investor, full participation provides more value to the preferred stock investor than non-participation and, hence, should justify a higher valuation on the company when the investment is made. In other words, the preferred stock investors are taking less risk, so they should pay a higher price per share and receive fewer shares in the company.

Note that the participation right applies "ratably . . . according to the number of shares" (sometimes expressed as *pro rata* on a per-share basis), which means each share gets an equal amount. Contrast this to the *pari passu* treatment we examined earlier (review Examples 9.6-A, B, and C), where the multiple series of preferred stock shared the proceeds proportionately based on their liquidation priority amount. In the *pari passu* situation, liquidation proceeds were divided so each preferred stock series reached its priority preference amount at the same time. In the participation context, however, that is not possible because the common stock is involved and it does not have a preference amount. As a result, the participation proceeds are allocated on an equal amount per share basis.

Example 9.11-A: Fully Participating Preferred.   Let's return to our hypothetical in order to examine the impact of full participation. We looked at some sale prices for SoftCo assuming its Series A Preferred Stock and Series B Preferred Stock were non-participating. (See Examples 9.10-A through C and Figs. 9.7, 9.8A, 9.8B, and 9.9.) What happens if the only factor we change is that the preferred stock is now made fully participating? Once again, let's assume that SoftCo has outstanding 5 million shares of Series A Preferred Stock, each with a $0.10 per-share liquidation preference, 10,000 shares of Series B Preferred Stock, each with a $150 per-share liquidation preference, and 5 million shares of common stock, and further assume that no dividends have accrued and each series of the preferred stock is fully participating on liquidations on a *pari passu* basis and convertible one-for-one into common stock.

If the sale price for SoftCo were $5 million, the liquidation waterfall would start with the preferred stock priority preferences of $1.5 million paid to the Series B Preferred Stock and $500,000 paid to the Series A Preferred Stock. Thereafter, with the preferred stock fully participating, the remaining $3 million in proceeds would be shared among 10,010,000 "common stock equivalent" or "deemed outstanding" common stock shares (i.e., the 5 million common stock shares actually outstanding plus the 10,000 common stock shares deemed outstanding by treating the Series B Preferred Stock on an "as-converted" basis plus the 5 million common stock shares deemed outstanding by treating the Series A Preferred Stock on an "as-converted" basis), yielding $0.2997 per share

($3 million divided by 10,010,000 deemed outstanding or common stock equivalent shares).

Fig. 9.10 Liquidation waterfall for a $5 million sale when preferred stock is fully participating

	Total	Per Share
Proceeds of Sale	$ 5,000,000	
Priority payment to Series A Preferred Stock (5 million shares)	− 500,000	$ 0.10
Priority payment to Series B Preferred Stock (10,000 shares)	−1,500,000	$150.00
Remaining Available for Distribution to common stock deemed outstanding, treating Series A and Series B on an as-converted basis (5 million common + 5 million Series A + 10,000 Series B = 10,010,000 shares)	$ 3,000,000	$0.2997

Under this hypothetical, the holders of the Series B Preferred Stock would get their $150 per share priority plus an additional $0.2997 participation per share, for a per-share total of $150.2997. With non-participating preferred, their per-share total was $150. A $5 million sale is such a poor outcome for the Series B Preferred Stock that their participation rights in liquidation are trivial when compared to their priority amount.

The holders of the Series A Preferred Stock, on the other hand, would be paid their $0.10 per share priority plus $0.2997 per share, for a total payment of $0.3997 per share. You will recall from Example 9.10-A and Fig. 9.7 that in the non-participating situation, they would have converted to common stock and would have been paid $0.35 per share. In contrast to the Series B Preferred Stock, a $5 million sale is a rather decent outcome for the Series A Preferred Stock, but its priority preference still represents about 25 percent of its distribution amount (in that its priority preference of $0.10 is approximately 25 percent of the $0.3997 paid per share).

In this scenario, the holders of the common stock would be paid $0.2997 per share. In the liquidation waterfall with non-participating preferred stock, where the Series B Preferred Stock would not convert and the Series A Preferred Stock would, the holders of common stock would have received $0.35 per share. However, making the preferred stock fully participating reduced the liquidation proceeds available for payment to the common stock because the priority amounts on both series of preferred stock were paid first and, with both series participating on an "as-converted basis," more common stock equivalent shares were outstanding to share what remained at the bottom of the waterfall. A $5 million sale price for SoftCo would be a nice outcome for the common stock holders, but it needs to be emphasized that preserving payment of the Series A Preferred Stock priority preference and dividing up the residual proceeds with more common stock equivalent shares clearly had an impact on the common stock holders' per-share proceeds. In contrast, the Series A Preferred Stock investors, with both priority and participation rights, made four times their investment. While this outcome may not result in a homerun for the Series A investors, nonetheless, the common stock holders might well resent having to divert a meaningful portion of their proceeds to cover the Series A priority right.

PROBLEM

In the non-participating liquidation preference hypotheticals discussed in Examples 9.10-A, B, and C, we noted that the Series B Preferred Stock would not convert until SoftCo's sale price reached $1.5015 billion ($1,501,500,000 divided by 10,010,000 shares is $150 per share). Thus, on a $1.5 billion sale of SoftCo, the Series B Preferred Stock would not convert because it would still be in the black hole and could get more by staying with its stated $150 per share priority preference. What would happen in a $1.5 billion sale if all the preferred stock were fully participating? *Hint:* Use the waterfall structure offered by Fig. 9.11.

Fig. 9.11 Liquidation waterfall for a $1.5 billion sale when preferred stock is fully participating

	Total	Per Share
Proceeds of Sale	$1,500,000,000	
Priority payment to Series A Preferred Stock	$	$
Priority payment to Series B Preferred Stock	$	$
Remaining Available for Distribution to common stock, treating Series A and Series B on a CSE basis	$	$

Example 9.11-B: Fully Participating Preferred. Earlier, in Example 9.10-C, we examined the terms of a liquidating distribution that assumed SoftCo was sold for $2.4 million and the preferred stock was non-participating. (See Fig. 9.8A.) In that situation, we saw that the preferred stock would take its priority distribution, for a total of $2 million. But if the preferred stock had full participation rights, the liquidation waterfall then would divide the remaining $400,000 in proceeds among all the shares on a fully diluted basis (that is, with the preferred stock included on an as-converted basis). The per-share distribution after the priority rights payments then would be $0.03996 (i.e., $400,000 divided by 10,010,000 common stock equivalent shares).

Fig. 9.12 Liquidation waterfall for $2.4 million sale when preferred stock is fully participating

	Total	Per Share
Proceeds of Sale	$2,400,000	
Priority payment to Series A Preferred Stock (5 million shares)	− 500,000	$ 0.10
Priority payment to Series B Preferred Stock (10,000 shares)	−1,500,000	$ 150.00
Remaining Available for Distribution to common stock deemed outstanding, treating Series A and Series B on an as-converted basis (5 million common + 5 million Series A + 10,000 Series B = 10,010,000 shares)	$ 400,000	$ 0.03996

As we previously discussed, these few extra pennies are trivial to the Series B Preferred Stock holders because they horrendously overpaid for their shares when they invested in SoftCo. But remember the irritated Series A Preferred Stock holders? While they probably still are not thrilled with the sale of SoftCo for $2.4 million, they might be mollified by getting $0.13996 per share (i.e., their $0.10 priority plus $0.03996 participation per share) instead of just their investment back. As to the common stock holders, a comparison of Fig. 9.8A and Fig. 9.12 shows that their return basically would be halved, going from $0.08 per share when the preferred stock was non-participating down to $0.03996 with the preferred stock fully participating, because, after the priority payments, they would have to share the proceeds available with all the preferred stock's common stock equivalent shares.

This final hypothetical shows why venture capital investors like fully participating preferred. As we have seen, making the preferred shares fully participating does not change anything when the liquidation proceeds are not sufficient to cover the priority right, and may not be meaningful when the company does really well (assuming that there is no multiple on the priority right), but in the in-between, slightly profitable, sale situation, full participation allows the preferred stock investors to get more than just their money back and reduces what they may perceive as the unjust enrichment of the common stock holders. On the other hand, common stock holders see fully participating preferred as a little piggish, particularly when it is combined with a priority right that provides for a multiple return on the preferred stock's original investment amount. Essentially, the view of the common stockholder is: "We can understand that if you only got your investment amount back through your priority right, you would want participation rights to cover the "in-between" situation, but on a great outcome, why do you still need a priority right? Why not have everyone go through the liquidation as common stock and all get the same thing? After all, isn't that how the valuation process worked when you set the price for your investment in our company?" *Query:* Which option seems more fair, considering the respective investment risks of the venture capitalists and the founders (and employees) of the company?

Capped Participation.   The effort to balance these competing concerns has led to the development of *capped participation*. A preferred stock with a capped participation right first is paid its priority right when the company is sold, then participates on an as-converted basis with the common stock until each share of preferred stock has received an additional, defined amount. Usually that additional amount is some multiple of the Original Issue Price. Once each share of preferred stock has received that maximum amount, then the participation right of the preferred shares ceases to exist and the preferred stock is paid nothing more. All remaining proceeds go to the common stock. A capped participation provision in the company's Charter might read as follows:

Charter Sample 9.12. After the payment of the full liquidation priority preference of the Preferred Stock as set forth above, the remaining assets of the Corporation legally available for distribution (or the consideration received in such transaction), if any, shall be distributed ratably to the holders of the Common Stock and Preferred Stock (as if such holders of Preferred Stock had converted their shares in accordance with the provisions of [the conversion section]) until the holders of Preferred Stock have received, in addition to the amount of the full liquidation priority preference of the

Preferred Stock as set forth above, an amount equal to two times (2X) the Original Issue Price (as adjusted for any stock splits, combinations, recapitalizations and the like with respect to such shares) for each share of Preferred Stock held by such holders. Thereafter, the remaining assets of the Corporation legally available for distribution (or the consideration received in such transaction), if any, shall be distributed ratably to the holders of the Common Stock.

Under this provision, each share of preferred stock is paid its priority preference on liquidation of the company and then participates until it has received an additional amount that is equal to two times its Original Issue Price. At that point, the preferred stock's participation ends, and all remaining proceeds are distributed to the common stock (which may include other series of preferred stock that has full participation rights or rights capped at a higher level).

Two important drafting issues routinely arise in connection with capped participation provisions. The first is the need to be explicit about whether the capped amount includes the priority preference or is in addition to the priority amount. The language in Charter Sample 9.12 is clear in stating that the two-times (2X) participation cap is *in addition* to the priority preference. The confusion often arises in conversation or in a term sheet, where an expression such as "a liquidation preference with a 2X cap" might be used. This vagueness calls into question whether the amount of the cap refers to the entire preference or just the participation portion.

The second important drafting issue concerns the need to be clear about how the cap is calculated. The language in Charter Sample 9.12 specifically states that the cap is based on the Original Issue Price, as adjusted for splits, etc., and no more. Thus, as was the case with the multiple priority preferences discussed earlier, accumulated or declared but unpaid dividend amounts are part of the priority preference, but not part of the base that is multiplied to calculate the cap. In addition, the participation continues until the capped amount is received in respect of "each share of Preferred Stock." This is important because the number of common stock shares issuable upon conversion of a preferred stock may change over the life of the preferred stock. We address conversion rate adjustments in section D of this chapter when we turn to the conversion right and anti-dilution protections. Are changes in the number of common stock equivalent shares represented by a share of preferred stock intended to change the participation cap amount? The short answer usually is no. The amount of the cap is set by the amount invested in exchange for the preferred shares, not the common stock equivalent shares owned, and so is based on the Original Issue Price. Regardless of how changes in the conversion rate of the preferred stock may change the number of common stock equivalent shares counted for purposes of the participation right and, hence, the proceeds to be paid per as-converted share, the cap is reached when a multiple of the Original Issue Price has been distributed per share of preferred stock.

Example 9.12-A: Capped Participation Liquidation Preference.   Returning to our hypothetical sale of SoftCo for $5 million, let's assume once again that there are 5 million shares of Series A Preferred Stock outstanding, each with a $0.10 per share liquidation preference, 10,000 shares of Series B Preferred Stock outstanding, each with a $150 per share liquidation preference, and 5 million common stock shares outstanding; further assume that no dividends have accrued, the preferred stock is *pari passu* as to liquidation priority, and, consistent with Charter Sample 9.12, each series of the preferred stock has a capped two-times (2X) participation right on liquidations and is convertible one-for-one into common stock. The liquidation waterfall starts with $5 million, of which $2 million is paid out to satisfy the preferred stock's preference rights. The remaining $3 million is then allocated, *pro rata*, on a per share basis, among the 10,010,000 common stock shares deemed outstanding until a series of preferred stock reaches its participation right cap. (Reminder: "deemed outstanding," "common stock equivalent," and "CSE" shares all refer to common stock issuable upon conversion of the preferred stock, as well as those shares combined with actually outstanding common stock.)

The Series B Preferred Stock will reach its two-times cap after it receives $300 per share in participation proceeds, which appears unlikely to occur. The Series A Preferred Stock, however, will reach its cap upon receipt of $0.20 of participation proceeds per share. This means that we need to calculate at what level of proceeds that cap is reached so that we then can adjust the waterfall to exclude the Series A Preferred common stock equivalent shares from any further distribution of the remaining sale proceeds. This calculation involves simple algebra requiring us to divide the unknown proceeds amount by the number of common stock equivalent shares outstanding, which gives us proceeds per share. Because the capped amount is $0.20 per share for the Series A Preferred Stock, we can solve for the unknown amount of sale proceeds that yields a participation preference distribution to the Series A Preferred Stock of $0.20 per share.

$$X \text{ (the unknown proceeds)} \div 10{,}010{,}000 \text{ (total CSE shares)} = \$0.20$$

We multiply both sides by 10,010,000 in order to solve for X and this yields:
$$X = \$0.20 \text{ times } 10{,}010{,}000 \text{ and, thus,}$$
$$X = \$2{,}002{,}000$$

Stated as a mathematical equation:
$$X = \text{unknown proceeds}$$

$$\frac{X}{10{,}010{,}000} = \$\,0.20$$
$$X = \$\,0.20 \times 10{,}010{,}000$$
$$X = \$\,2{,}002{,}000$$

Going back to our liquidation waterfall, it shows $3 million in proceeds remaining available for distribution after payment of the liquidation priority amounts. We now know that after paying out $2,002,000 of those proceeds in equal amounts per participating share, the Series A Preferred Stock will have received enough participation proceeds to hit its $0.20 per share cap. As a consequence, the Series A Preferred Stock's 5 million common stock equivalent shares will not participate in the distribution of additional proceeds. The remaining $998,000 of proceeds, therefore, will be shared on a per-share basis between the holders of the Series B Preferred Stock and the common stock, who together hold 5,010,000 common stock equivalent shares. Each will receive $0.1992 per share (that is, $998,000 divided by 5,010,000 shares).

Fig. 9.13 Liquidation waterfall for a $5 million sale when Series A Preferred's participation has a 2X cap

	Total	Per Share
Proceeds of Sale	$5,000,000	
Priority payment to Series A Preferred Stock	− 500,000	$ 0.10
Priority payment to Series B Preferred Stock	−1,500,000	$150.00
Available for Distribution to common stock deemed outstanding until a preferred stock's cap is reached	$3,000,000	
Allocation: Series A on an as-converted basis	−1,000,000	$ 0.20
Series B on an as-converted basis	− 2,000	$ 0.20
Common stock outstanding	−1,000,000	$ 0.20
Available for Distribution to common stock deemed outstanding (excluding preferred stock that has reached its cap) until another preferred stock cap is reached	$ 998,000	
Allocation: Series B on an as-converted basis	− 1,992	$ 0.1992
Common stock outstanding	− 996,000	$ 0.1992

To review the results of the capped participation waterfall, looking first at the Series B Preferred Stock, we see that it received its priority right of $150 per share. The Series B Preferred Stock then received $0.20 per share among the 10,010,000 CSE participating shares, which is where the Series A Preferred Stock hit its cap and was eliminated from any further participation. The Series B Preferred Stock then received an additional $0.1992 per share as the only continuing participant with the common stock, for a total amount of $150.3992 paid per share.

The Series A Preferred Stock received its priority amount of $0.10 per share, then was paid its full participation cap of $0.20 per share and no more. Its total return was $0.30 per share. The common stock began to share in the liquidation proceeds only after the priority amounts were paid. Then each share of the common stock was paid $0.20 per share, sharing with everyone (i.e., both the Series A and the Series B Preferred Stock on an as-converted basis), plus another $0.1992 per share after the Series A Preferred Stock hit its cap, for a total of $0.3992 paid per common share. Note that at four decimal places, we have an $8.00 rounding error in dividing these proceeds over 10,010,000 shares.

If the preferred stock had been fully participating on this $5 million sale, as we saw in Example 9.11-A and Fig. 9.10, after its priority amounts had been paid, the remaining $3 million in proceeds would have been shared *pro rata* on a per-share basis among the 10,010,000 common stock equivalent shares, amounting to a per-share participating distribution to the preferred stock, and total distribution to the common stock, of $0.2997 per share. In that case, the Series B Preferred Stock would have received a total of $150.2997 per share (i.e., the $150 priority plus the $0.2997 participation) and the Series A Preferred Stock a total of $0.3997 per share ($0.10 priority plus $0.2997 participation).

In contrast, on a $5 million sale of the company with the preferred stock non-participating, as we saw in Example 9.10-A, the priority amounts would still be paid out first, that is, $150 per share to the Series B Preferred Stock and $0.10 per share to the Series A Preferred Stock. But the remaining proceeds of $3 million would all go to the common stock, yielding a distribution of $0.60 per share ($3 million divided by 5 million shares) unless the Series A Preferred Stock decided to forego its priority and convert in order to go through the liquidation waterfall as common stock, which it clearly would do. In that case, presented in Fig. 9.7, after payment of the Series B Preferred Stock's priority amount, the remaining proceeds of $3.5 million would be divided among the 10 million common stock shares that would be outstanding after the Series A Preferred Stock converted, with each share receiving $0.35.

Example 9.12-B: Capped Participation Liquidation Preference — Convert or Not. Now let's look at our hypothetical from the perspective of the Series A Preferred Stock that has negotiated for a 2X participation cap. We find that the Series A Preferred Stock faces the same "convert/not convert" dilemma that is inherent in non-participating preferred. As we shall see in the discussion below, the major difference for the capped participation is that a higher level of proceeds is needed to trigger the decision to convert.

As we saw in Example 9.10-A, and as Fig. 9.7 shows, where the Series A Preferred Stock is non-participating, then on the sale of SoftCo for $5 million, the Series A Preferred Stock ends up being paid $0.35 per share if it converts. As we saw in Example 9.12-A, the Series A Preferred Stock with a 2X participation cap that did not convert received its priority amount of $0.10 per share, then was paid its full participation cap of $0.20 per share, for a total return of $0.30 per share. How does a 2X capped participation right change the "convert/not convert" decision for the Series A Preferred Stock? If the Series A Preferred Stock converts, then after the Series B Preferred Stock gets its $150 per-share priority right, the remaining $3.5 million in proceeds is divided among the 10 million common stock shares outstanding plus the 10,000 as-converted Series B Preferred Stock shares, yielding $0.34965 per share in proceeds (that is, $3.5 million divided by 10,010,000 shares). Thus, the Series A Preferred Stock with the 2X capped participation right would receive $0.30 per share based on its priority right plus its capped participation if it did not convert, but would receive $0.34965 per share if it converted and went through the liquidation as common stock.

Fig. 9.14 Liquidation waterfall for a $5 million sale when Series A Preferred's participation has a 2X cap and Series A converts to common stock

	Total	Per Share
Proceeds of Sale	$ 5,000,000	
Priority payment to Series A Preferred Stock	− 0	$ 0.00
Priority payment to Series B Preferred Stock	− 1,500,000	$ 150.00
Distribution to common stock deemed outstanding	$ 3,500,000	
Allocation: Series A converted to common	−1,748,251.70	$0.34965
Series B on an as-converted basis	− 3,496.50	$0.34965
Common stock outstanding	−1,748,251.75	$0.34965

Since the maximum amount payable to the Series A Preferred Stock with the 2X capped participation is $0.30 per share, it would be better off converting whenever it could obtain proceeds in excess of $0.30 per share by converting to common stock. In real life, the exact amount of proceeds that will provide more than $0.30 per share will be affected by other preferred stock rights (here, the rights of the Series B Preferred Stock), any accrued dividend distributions captured in the liquidation process, and the conversion rates of the preferred stock. But staying with the assumptions used in our earlier hypo, we can solve for the amount of proceeds that will provide the Series A Preferred Stock with $0.30 per share after converting using the same formula as before:

X (the unknown proceeds) divided by 10,010,000 shares = $0.30 per share

We multiply both sides of the equation by 10,010,000 to solve for X and get
X = $0.30 times 10,010,000 and, thus,
X = $3,003,000 of proceeds available for distribution to the common stock holders.

Stated mathematically:
$$X = \text{unknown proceeds}$$
$$\frac{X}{10,010,000} = \$0.30$$
$$X = \$3,003,000$$

This result means that when the sale proceeds available for distribution to shareholders are sufficient to cover the other preferred stock's priority preferences (in our hypo, $1.5 million) as well as to provide a common stock distribution in excess of $3,003,000, which, in our hypo, means a total distribution of more than $4,503,000, then the Series A Preferred Stock should convert.

In contrast, in the earlier Example 9.10-A, involving non-participating preferred stock as shown in Fig. 9.7 (assuming that all the other factors remain the same), the conversion point for the Series A Preferred Stock was lower; that is, any time the Series A Preferred Stock could obtain more than $0.10 per share as common stock, it should convert. Using the same equation as above, but with 10 million common stock shares outstanding following conversion of the Series A Preferred Stock (the Series B Preferred Stock would not convert at these prices), we find that $1 million in proceeds available for distribution to the common stock is the trigger point for conversion. That is, with 10 million common stock shares outstanding, at $1 million in proceeds, the converted Series A Preferred Stock would receive $0.10 per share ($1 million ÷ 10 million shares = $0.10 per share). Therefore if the available proceeds (after payment of the other preferred stock priority preferences) are greater than $1 million, the Series A Preferred Stock would receive more than its priority amount and should convert.

Comparing Participation Rights.   At the beginning of this discussion, we noted that a driving purpose of the capped participation approach was balancing the venture capital investors' desire to avoid the low-priced "convert/not convert" decision compelled by non-participation and thereby share in profits in a marginally successful company against the common shareholders' desire that the preferred stock with full participation forego its priority preference when there is a reasonable level of profit to share. We see these issues arising in connection with our hypos for the sale of SoftCo, for reasons discussed below.

First, looking at the per-share distributions to the Series A Preferred Stock and the common stock, we see that with $5 million in proceeds from the sale of SoftCo and fully participating preferred, the Series A Preferred Stock would be paid $0.3997 per share and the common stock would receive $0.2997 per share. (See Example 9.11-A and Fig. 9.10.) With non-participating preferred, however, those proceeds are well over the trigger point for the Series A Preferred Stock to convert, so it would convert, and both it and the common stock would receive $0.35 per share. (See Example 9.10-A and Fig. 9.7.) Finally, in the case of preferred stock with a 2X participation cap, the results are almost the same, with the Series A Preferred Stock converting and receiving — along with the common stock — payment of $0.34965 per share (the slightly lower amount being the result of the participation right of the 10,000 common stock equivalent shares represented by the Series B Preferred Stock). (Compare Example 9.12-A and Fig. 9.13 with Example 9.12-B and Fig. 9.14.) These numbers show that fully participating preferred receives more sale proceeds because it always retains its priority right, never having to choose between (i) keeping its priority and foregoing additional participation or (ii) relinquishing its priority in order to obtain additional participation. It always gets its full measure of both.

Fig. 9.15 Per-share distributions for Series A and common on a $5 million sale with different participation rights

	Fully Participating Preferred	Non-Participating Preferred	Preferred has 2X cap; Series A converts
Series A Preferred Stock	$ 0.3997	$ 0.35	$ 0.34965
Common Stock	$ 0.2997	$ 0.35	$ 0.34965

In contrast, recall our earlier hypos involving a sale price for SoftCo of $2.4 million. There, in Example 9.10-C and Figs. 9.8A and 9.8B, we found that the non-participating Series A Preferred Stock would receive its $0.10 per share priority amount — the amount invested — and no more, while the common stock would be paid $0.08 per share. Even with the common stock getting a meaningful distribution, the Series A Preferred Stock would be paid less by converting and thus would be caught in the "black hole." With fully participating preferred (and the result is the same with capped participation since the amounts are well under the cap) in this marginal success situation (a $2.4 million sale), Example 9.11-B and Fig. 9.12 show that the Series A Preferred Stock would be paid $0.13996 per share, representing an almost 40 percent profit on its investment on a "cash in/cash out basis" (that is, ignoring the time value of money), and the common stock's distribution would drop to $0.03996 per share. The range of these outcomes is compared in Fig. 9.16, below.

Fig. 9.16 Per-share distributions on a $2.4 million sale with different participation rights

	Fully Participating and 2X Capped Preferred; No Conversion	Non-participating Preferred; Series A Converts	Non-participating Preferred; Series A Does Not Convert
Series A Preferred Stock	$ 0.13996	$ 0.09	$ 0.10
Common Stock	$ 0.03996	$ 0.09	$ 0.08

The trade-off of a capped participation right for the preferred stock is that, in the case of a marginal outcome on the sale of the company, it will receive more than just its money back by participating, but when the sale proceeds grow and its cap on participation compels it to convert, it loses its priority right and therefore a part of the bigger pay-out. The mirror image of this is experienced by the common stock; capped participation causes it to trade some profit in the marginal outcome in exchange for eliminating the preferred stock's priority right in the case of a big win, where it gets a bigger share. While there is pushing and shoving on the details (i.e., 2X or 3X cap?), capped participation is an accommodation that often works to address the concerns of both groups.

PROBLEMS

1. Assume once again that SoftCo has 5 million shares of Series A Preferred Stock outstanding, each with a $0.10 per-share liquidation preference, 10,000 shares of Series B Preferred Stock outstanding, each with a $150 per-share liquidation preference, and 5 million common stock shares outstanding. Further assume that no dividends have accrued, the preferred stock is *pari passu* as to liquidation priority, and, consistent with Charter Sample 9.12, each series of the preferred stock has a capped two-times (2X) participation right on liquidations and is convertible one-for-one into common stock. What is the liquidation waterfall, including the per-share proceeds for each series of preferred stock and the common stock, if the proceeds available for distribution upon the sale of SoftCo are $3.5 million?

2. Use the same assumptions as in Problem 1, except assume that each series of the preferred stock has a 2X priority multiple and is non-participating. What is the liquidation waterfall, including the per-share proceeds for each series of preferred stock and the common stock, if the proceeds available for distribution upon the sale of SoftCo are $3.5 million?

3. Use the new assumptions presented in Problem 2, except assume that the Series B Preferred has a first priority on liquidations. What is the liquidation waterfall, including the per-share proceeds for each series of preferred stock and the common stock, if the proceeds available for distribution upon the sale of SoftCo are $3 million?

4. Go back to the assumptions in Problem 1, except assume that the Series B Preferred Stock has a 9 percent per annum accumulated dividend right that does not compound, and assume further that the Series B Preferred Stock was issued six years ago. What is the liquidation waterfall, including the per-share proceeds for each series of preferred stock and the common stock, if the proceeds available for distribution upon the sale of SoftCo are $3.5 million?

5. Use the same assumptions as in Problem 1, except assume the participation cap for the Series A Preferred Stock has a 4X cap on its participation right (with the right otherwise as provided in Charter Sample 9.12). What is the liquidation waterfall, including the per-share proceeds for each series of preferred stock and the common stock, if the proceeds available for distribution upon the sale of SoftCo are $5 million?

6. Continue with the new assumptions in Problem 5, except assume also that the Series B Preferred Stock has a 2X priority preference and is non-participating. What is the liquidation waterfall, including the per-share proceeds for each series of preferred stock and the common stock, if the proceeds available for distribution upon the sale of SoftCo are $5 million?

The "Either/Or" Liquidation Priority.   Another alternative developed in order to eliminate the "convert/not convert" dilemma with non-participating or capped participation preferred stock is to build an "either/or" structure into the liquidation preference. To implement this approach in a situation where the preferred stock is non-participating, the Charter might read as follows:

> **Charter Sample 9.13.**[Upon a Liquidation Event,] the holders of Preferred Stock shall be entitled to receive from Liquidation Proceeds, prior to any distribution or payment to the holders of Common Stock, for each share of Preferred Stock held by them an amount per share equal to the greater of (i) the Original Issue Price plus all declared and unpaid dividends thereon or (ii) the amount per share that would have been payable had each share of Preferred Stock been converted into Common Stock pursuant to the provisions of [the conversion provisions of this Charter] immediately prior to the Liquidation Event.

By this means, the "convert/not convert" issue is rendered moot. Instead, the company is charged with delivering proceeds based on whichever approach would provide the bigger distribution to the preferred stock. The company, assuredly subject to close review by the preferred stock holders, would run alternative liquidation waterfall calculations based on the preferred stock keeping its preference rights versus being treated as if it had converted into common stock immediately prior to the Liquidation Event.

This "whichever is greater" arrangement has some appeal for preferred stock holders in situations where the exact amount of liquidation proceeds is contingent on later events. The preferred stock holders are protected against having to make a choice in an uncertain situation and take their chances. The effect is that the non-participating preferred stock gets the right to receive liquidation proceeds as if it had converted, without actually converting, and thus it still keeps its full set of other preference rights.

However, this "either/or" approach also creates uncertainty on payment of liquidation rights. For example, a portion of the sale proceeds of private companies often is placed in an escrow account to facilitate resolution of any post-sale indemnity claims that may be asserted against the seller. After the passage of a year or more, any amounts remaining in the escrow account typically are then released to the seller and thus are available for distribution under the liquidation waterfall. This set of facts leads to the question: what is the liquidation distribution to be made at the time of the sale if the amount in the escrow account would make the sale proceeds cross over the preferred stock's conversion point? Stated another way, what happens if the proceeds to be distributed immediately are low enough to cause the preferred stock not to convert, but if the amount in escrow were to be distributed, the preferred stock would convert?

Some lawyers argue that no distributions can be made until the amounts and the means of calculating the preferred stock preference rights are determined. Others argue that a "least common denominator" amount should be released as proceeds are available, even if it is not clear which half of the "either/or" approach will ultimately apply.

This "either/or" provision also can present some tricky drafting problems when the preferred stock has a capped participation right. In this situation, the "either/or" choice must present the "stay-as-preferred-stock" outcome squarely against the "convert-to-common-stock" outcome. Thus, the description of the proceeds the preferred stock would receive as preferred stock must be carefully drafted to include both the priority right amount *plus* the capped participation amount. That amount must then be contrasted to what the proceeds would be if the preferred stock converted and passed through the liquidation waterfall as common stock.

The "either/or" right is typically presented as the preferred stock's priority right. Liquidation priority and participation rights are usually addressed in successive sections of the Charter, and the participation right is usually expressed as sharing in the common stock's residual right. However, when the "either/or" approach is used, the participation right has to be part of the "either/or" right and therefore built into the priority right. If not done successfully, the preferred stock's priority right provision might say that it is entitled to receive its "either/or" amount (consisting of the greater of (i) its original issue price plus a capped participation amount or (ii) what it would receive if it converted to common), then be followed by a capped participation right provision. If so drafted, the preferred stock would have been given two separate participation rights, one in the priority provision and one in the participation provision, and the liquidation preference would have an unintended, and nonsensical, outcome.

PROBLEM

We saw in Example 9.10-C and Figs. 9.8A and 9.8B that the conversion of the preferred stock changes the proceeds available to the common stock. Revisit the waterfall presented in Fig. 9.8A, but assume that the sale proceeds had been $2.7 million and $500,000 had been held back in a two-year escrow account. If the $2.2 million available for immediate distribution had been paid out, how much would have gone to the common stock? Assume that, after two years, the remaining $500,000 in sale proceeds becomes available. How would that distribution affect the "convert/not convert" decision of the Series A Preferred? What happens to those proceeds? Is that delay in payment fair to the common stock holders? Without an "either/or" provision, the Series A Preferred Stock holders would have to decide whether to convert without knowing what will happen to the escrowed proceeds. Is it fair to force the preferred stock holders to make a "convert/not convert" decision before the entire outcome of the transaction is known?

D. The Conversion Right and Anti-Dilution Protection

Venture capital preferred stock, as previously described, is a hybrid security intended to give the holder first-in-line priority rights combined with the opportunity to participate in the growth of a company's value. Its priority rights exist through its preferred stock character, and its ability to share in a company's equity upside potential exists through its convertibility to common stock.

As we have seen in looking at dividend and liquidation preferences, venture capital preferred stock can have a right of participation in the distribution allocation to common stock holders without actually converting into common stock. Thus, the number of shares of common stock issuable upon its conversion plays a major role in determining the rights of venture capital preferred stock throughout its life, regardless of whether it actually ever converts.

While the right to convert and the process of conversion are fairly straightforward, the rate at which the preferred stock converts is subject to a few typical adjustments and processes that, while not necessarily complex, can add a good amount of length to the Charter. In the case of most companies issuing venture capital preferred stock, the Charter document will typically be about 14 pages long, with some longer and some shorter; however, it is safe to assume that fully half the document will address conversion rights.

1. *The Conversion Right*

Generally.   The ability of a corporation to issue a security with a *conversion right* is established by statute. *See, e.g.,* Del. GCL §151(e); Cal. Corp. Code §403; and Model Act §6.01(c)(2). While the typical conversion right for venture capital preferred stock is the ability to convert into common stock, the authority of a corporation to establish a right to convert may not be limited to conversion having this sort of "downstream" movement (i.e., moving from preferred stock, a more senior security, into common stock, the residual layer of ownership in the corporation). While it would rarely arise, a company could establish a right to convert common stock into preferred stock, in what is referred to as an "upstream" conversion. Contra, *see* N.Y. Bus. Corp. Law §519(a)(1) (prohibiting "upstream" conversions).

The fact that a security is *convertible*, and the terms of the conversion right, must be set forth in the issuing corporation's Charter. While most state statutes do not provide extensive details on the mechanics of how conversion must work, most do provide a list of actions that may trigger a conversion. Generally speaking, conversion may take place at the option of the holder of the convertible security; upon the occurrence of a specified event; or upon a vote of the shares of the class (or series) of stock having the conversion right. While the latter is not specifically addressed in either Delaware or the Model Act, it appears that a vote to convert is contemplated as being within the scope of both statutes, either as a "specified event" (*see, e.g.,* Del. GCL §151(e); and Model Act §6.01(c)(2)(i)); or as an action by "another person" (*see* Model Act §6.01(c)(2)(i)). In addition, many states' conversion statutes provide that the corporation may be authorized to trigger a conversion, although this authority is limited under California law (*see* Cal. Corp. Code §403(a)(2) and (3)) and not often seen in connection with preferred stock issued in the venture capital financing context.

The other terms of conversion that must be set forth in the Charter are the type of security into which the convertible security is to be converted, the rate of conversion and any process for adjustments thereto, and finally, the mechanics of the conversion process. The rate of conversion and adjustments to that rate are the subject of the next section, which addresses "anti-dilution."

Voluntary Conversion.   The basic right of conversion is the ability of a holder of convertible preferred stock to convert those shares into common stock whenever the holder chooses. This is characterized as the right of *voluntary conversion*. The Charter provision providing for voluntary conversion often is the same provision establishing the basic right to convert. It may read something like the following:

> **Charter Sample 9.14.** Each share of Preferred Stock shall be convertible at the option of the holder thereof, without payment of additional consideration, at any time after the date of issuance of such share. Each share of Preferred Stock initially shall convert into one (1) fully paid and nonassessable share of Common Stock.

This provision clearly makes the Preferred Stock convertible into Common Stock. The phrase "at the option of the holder thereof" simply establishes that each holder controls the right to convert his/her/its Preferred Stock into Common Stock at any time. In addition, this provision establishes that each share of Preferred Stock converts into one share of Common Stock, at least initially.

Voluntary Conversion Including Conversion Rate. Typically, a Charter provision establishing the basic right to convert also will introduce the concept of the *Conversion Rate*:

> **Charter Sample 9.15.** The number of shares of Common Stock into which one share of Preferred Stock is convertible is hereinafter referred to as the "**Conversion Rate**." The Conversion Rate shall be subject to adjustment from time to time as provided for in [the anti-dilution provisions,] below.

This provision defines "Conversion Rate" and further specifies that it actually is subject to adjustment. How the Conversion Rate adjusts is the primary issue addressed in the anti-dilution discussion below.

Both Charter Samples 9.14 and 9.15 allow for Preferred Stock to consist of more than one series, and they each use general terms and structures so that additional series of Preferred Stock may be authorized and included within these rights without tedious repetition of the conversion right and mechanism as to each additional series. It is likely that both provisions would be accompanied by a definitions section that sets forth the Original Issue Price for each series of the Preferred Stock.

Automatic Conversion. In addition to voluntary conversion, venture capital financings typically provide for the *automatic conversion* of preferred stock (sometimes referred to as "mandatory conversion") upon an underwritten public offering of the company's common stock that meets certain specifications or, alternatively, upon a vote of the class or series of convertible shares. A Charter provision providing for automatic conversion might read:

> **Charter Sample 9.16.** Each share of Preferred Stock automatically shall be convertible into fully paid and nonassessable shares of Common Stock at the then applicable Conversion Rate upon either (i) the closing of a firm commitment underwritten public offering pursuant to an effective registration statement under the Securities Act covering the offer and sale of Common Stock (for the account of the Corporation, the account of one or more stockholders of the Corporation, or a combination thereof) at an aggregate offering price of not less than $25,000,000 and at a public offering price (prior to underwriters' commissions and expenses) equal to or exceeding $2.00 (as adjusted for any stock dividends, combinations, or splits with respect to such shares) per share of Common Stock (a **"Qualified IPO"**) or (ii) the affirmative vote by written consent of holders of a majority of the then outstanding shares of Preferred Stock voting together as a separate class. In the event of such an automatic conversion of the Preferred Stock as aforesaid, the conversion of Preferred Stock shall be deemed to have occurred automatically as of the closing of such sale of securities or the giving of such written consent, as applicable.

The first alternative under this automatic conversion provision provides that all the Preferred Stock will convert if there is a public offering of the company's common stock involving $25 million in share value at a price of at least $2.00 per share. As these same criteria often are used as a benchmark in more than one document in a venture capital financing (see the discussion in Chapter 10 regarding the Investor Rights Agreement), it often is given a title in the Charter such as *Qualified IPO*. The purpose of these terms is to require a company's preferred stock to convert if the company has the opportunity to complete a satisfactory initial public offering. The reality is that it is extremely difficult to find an underwriter who will do an IPO if the preferred stock will continue to remain outstanding. The belief is that the preferred stock's rights are so powerful that the common stock will have a limited value so long as the preferred stock continues to exist. By accepting this Charter provision, the preferred stock holders agree from the outset that they will convert if the public offering meets the specified size and price criteria. *Query*: Why do the venture capital investors seek to define the term "Qualified IPO"? Whose interests are protected by defining this term?

In most venture capital transactions, the minimum acceptable size of the IPO (i.e., the "aggregate offering price") is between $20 and $50 million, and the minimum offering share price generally is between 3 and 10 times the Original Issue Price of the preferred stock. Usually the share price multiple required by the venture capitalists is at the higher end of the range in an earlier stage investment and comes down as the valuation of the company rises in later rounds of financing. These numbers are negotiated, and they are intended to require an offering of substantial size that represents an attractive value increase over the latest series of preferred stock's Original Issue Price. "Substantial size" is necessary, so there is an active and efficient trading market after the offering. If those circumstances exist, the holders of the preferred stock should find the Qualified IPO and the subsequent public trading market an attractive exit and thus should readily agree to give up their preferential rights and convert their shares to common stock. The reality is that a public offering between $20 and $50 million is quite small and investors should be better served by offering size thresholds atleast two or three times larger.

Note the last sentence of Charter Sample 9.16, which provides that:

> In the event of such an automatic conversion . . . the conversion of Preferred Stock shall be deemed to have occurred automatically as of the closing of such sale of securities. . . .

This language is intended to provide the preferred stock holders with the comfort of knowing that mandatory conversion is conditioned on the Qualified IPO actually being completed. If the offering should be terminated for some reason, and many reasons are possible, the conversion would be terminated and they would go forward as preferred stock holders.

The second automatic conversion alternative included in Charter Sample 9.16 reads as follows:

> the affirmative vote by written consent of holders of a majority of the then outstanding shares of Preferred Stock voting together as a separate class.

This provision generally applies in two circumstances. First, it gives the preferred stock a right to a class vote to approve conversion in the face of a public offering that does not meet the Qualified IPO criteria but, because it is the best financing opportunity available, is supported by the holders of a large majority of the preferred stock. If the company had to rely on voluntary conversion to remove the outstanding preferred stock, which as previously mentioned would be required by most underwriters, a minority holder who objected would have extraordinary leverage on the company (or the other preferred stock holders) to extract a high price for agreeing to convert. Automatic conversion by a vote of the preferred stock holders can eliminate that potential roadblock. If a sufficient number of preferred stock holders believe the offering to be in the company's (and their) best interests, their vote can cause *all* of the outstanding preferred stock to convert and the public offering could go forward. If they are not convinced of the offering's merit, they could vote no and the continued existence of their preferred shares would, in all likelihood, quash the transaction.

The second circumstance in which a vote might be used is an informal, voluntary restructuring of a company's capitalization. As an example, the preferred stock holders, facing a company that has underperformed, may determine to do a "restart" of the company by agreeing to treat all investments to date as effectively worthless. In this case, they would agree to convert their existing preferred stock into common stock (thus eliminating all the existing liquidation and other preferences), reduce the number of the then-outstanding common stock shares by a reverse split (i.e., proportionately reducing the number of shares outstanding), set a low valuation on the "new" company, invest new money, and create a new, post-reverse-split pool of shares for employee equity incentives. The provision allowing for an automatic conversion by a vote of the preferred stock, as in the non–Qualified IPO situation, prevents a minority holder of the preferred stock from blocking this type of informal restructuring by refusing to voluntarily convert.

Of course, one person's obstreperous minority gadfly is another's beleaguered defender of honesty and fair dealing. As a result, the terms of any vote that would trigger automatic conversion have to be examined carefully, particularly when more than one series of preferred stock is outstanding. Charter Sample 9.16 provides that all of the outstanding Preferred Stock is to vote together as a single class, with majority approval required. Where there are multiple series of preferred stock outstanding, each series may have a separate approval right on its conversion. We will look at voting issues more closely later in this chapter.

QUESTIONS

1. In the hypothetical SoftCo capitalization we used in our discussion of liquidation preferences earlier in this chapter, we assumed that the Series A Preferred Stock had invested $500,000 and received 5 million shares, while the Series B Preferred Stock had invested $1.5 million and received 10,000 shares. Based on those facts, how would a vote of the preferred stock, voting as a single class with majority approval required, work?

2. Would some other means of measuring shareholder approval be more appropriate? What would you want as counsel to the Series A Preferred Stock? What if you were counsel to the Series B Preferred Stock? Counsel to the company?

As a final issue to consider on automatic conversion, look again at the last sentence of Charter Sample 9.16, where the relevant language provides the following:

> In the event of such an automatic conversion . . . the conversion of Preferred Stock shall be deemed to have occurred automatically as of . . . the giving of such written consent. . . .

This wording creates a bit of a process trap for company counsel. Instead of providing that the automatic conversion will be effective in accordance with *the terms* of the written consent, which would allow the parties to agree on an effective time for the conversion and give their approval for its implementation at that specified time, this provision says the conversion is effective *when the consent is given*. Under most state statutes, a written consent is effective when enough favorable votes are delivered to the company. *See, e.g.*, Del. §228(c); Cal. Corp. Code §603(a); and Model Act §7.04(a) and (b) (regarding shareholder action in lieu of a meeting). Since neither company counsel nor the preferred stockholders wants the conversion to occur at a random time based on when preferred stock holder signatures are delivered to the company, the quoted Charter provision means the written consent resolutions addressing the conversion should state that they become effective as of the designated time the conversion is intended to occur.

Mechanics of Conversion — Share Surrender and Reissuance.   The seemingly mundane mechanics of how a conversion is done and when it takes effect can be of crucial importance in determining shareholder rights. In order to facilitate our review of the details of the conversion process, let's break a typical "mechanics" provision into its pieces. A typical Charter provision regarding conversion might begin as follows:

Charter Sample 9.17-A. A holder of Preferred Stock voluntarily may convert the same into shares of Common Stock by surrendering the certificate or certificates therefor, duly endorsed, at the office of this corporation or of any transfer agent for the Preferred Stock, and giving written notice to this corporation at its principal corporate office of the election to convert and stating therein the name or names in which the certificate or certificates for shares of Common Stock are to be issued. This corporation shall, as soon as practicable thereafter, issue and deliver at such office to such holder of Preferred Stock, or to the nominee or nominees of such holder, a certificate or certificates for the number of shares of Common Stock to which such holder shall be entitled, together with cash in lieu of any fraction of a share.

Under the terms of this provision, the converting preferred stock holder must deliver its stock certificate to the company, or transfer agent, and notify the company of its intent to convert. If the holder wishes the common stock to be issued to a person other than the one who held the preferred stock shares, it must so specify in its notice.

The expression "duly endorsed" means the back of the stock certificate must be signed by the holder, much as one would endorse a check. Many stock certificates have an endorsement legend printed on the back that designates an attorney-in-fact, usually the company counsel, corporate secretary, or the transfer agent, with the authority to cancel the certificate and issue a new one. In some cases, the endorsement is done on a separate form, often entitled "Stock Assignment Separate from Certificate" but generally referred to as a "Stock Power." The use of a Stock Power allows the unendorsed stock certificate and the endorsement to be delivered separately for security purposes (one is of little value without the other). Like an endorsed check, an endorsed stock certificate is effective evidence of a transfer of legal rights. As a result, some lawyers are more comfortable not asking the shareholder to sign the certificate, preferring instead to prepare a separate endorsement document and then requiring delivery of both for the transfer to become effective. In addition, because the text of the Stock Power can be word processed, it is easier to set out detailed directions or make corrections there, rather than on the back of the stock certificate itself. In the private company context, many attorneys will treat a signed letter accompanying the stock certificate (referenced in Charter Sample 9.17-A as a "written notice") as sufficient endorsement and instruction for the cancellation and reissuance of the stock certificate, but Charter Sample 9.17-A requires actual endorsement.

A "transfer agent" is an independent service provider that maintains a company's stock ledgers and handles its stock certificate changes. Professional transfer agent companies are used by virtually every publicly traded company, but are not widely employed by privately held companies where share transfers are infrequent and stock certificate administration generally is less burdensome. Private companies often rely on the corporate secretary, who frequently is the chief financial officer or another senior administrative official, or outside counsel to manage their stock matters. This task typically does not require much ongoing attention and is important enough that many private companies are very willing to pay for their counsel's time in order to improve the probability that it will be done correctly.

The company is required to prepare (or cause the transfer agent to prepare) appropriate common stock certificates (and perhaps a replacement preferred stock certificate if the holder is converting only a portion of the preferred shares represented by the certificate the holder has turned in) and to deliver the new certificates "as soon as practicable." This formulation means promptly but without undue administrative urgency. As a courtesy to the company's shareholders and out of respect for the corporate formalities, stock certificates should be issued without unreasonable delay. The fact is, however, that the corporation's "share ledger," which also may be referred to as the "share register" or "shareholder record," is the official record of share ownership. A stock certificate represents the ownership interest, and it may be endorsed and delivered to transfer legal title. In addition, it may convey information on its face or reverse regarding the company or the stock holder rights it represents, putting the holder on notice of restrictions and limitations applicable to the interest. However, particularly as a result of the development of electronic trading markets, the stock certificate has become more and more obsolete. Many publicly traded companies actually charge a fee if you make them go to the trouble of preparing and delivering a paper certificate.

Note that Charter Sample 9.17-A provides that, in lieu of issuing fractional shares, the company is to deliver their value in cash. Cleaning fractional shares off a company's stock ledger by delivering their cash value is authorized in many states. *See, e.g.* Del. GCL §155; Cal. Corp. Code §407; and Model Code §6.04. Most corporations prefer to cash out fractional shares because carrying fractional ownership interests on the company's stock ledger can be administratively awkward. Paying out their cash value eliminates this inconvenience. However, this means that the fractional value remaining for each shareholder, after issuance of the largest possible whole number of shares to that shareholder, must be calculated carefully to the nearest penny, checks for each shareholder must be prepared, and the checks and new stock certificates then must be delivered to each shareholder. Because fractional share payments are, by definition, less than the value of one share, if the share value is low and there are a lot of shareholders, this process can result in preparing a significant number of checks that are each payable for only a few cents. In a large-scale conversion, in order to avoid the cost of preparing, tracking, and processing so many small dollar-value checks, some companies provide postage stamps (do they count as "cash"?), and on one recent closing, company counsel delivered new stock certificates and closing document sets with the required number of pennies taped to the cover of each document binder.

Mechanics of Conversion — Effective Time.   A conversion mechanics Charter provision typically would go on to address the effective time of the conversion:

> **Charter Sample 9.17-B.** Such conversion shall be deemed to have been made immediately prior to the close of business on the date (i) of the later of such surrender of the shares of Preferred Stock to be converted and the delivery of written notice to this corporation, or, with those completed, a later date, if so specified in the written notice, or (ii) as specified in [the automatic conversion provision] above, and the person or persons entitled to receive the shares of Common Stock issuable upon such conversion shall be treated for all purposes as the record holder or holders of such shares of Common Stock as of such date.

The provision states exactly when the conversion is effective and that, as of that time, the former preferred stock will cease to exist and the new common stock will be outstanding. Having a clear transition point is important so that there is no question about the scope of shareholder rights that exist at any given point in time. For example, in a voluntary restructuring of a company, an automatic conversion by vote often will be scheduled to coincide with the delivery of money in a new financing transaction. Knowing which event happens when, and what shares are outstanding at each given moment in the course of a transaction, is the only way to ensure that proper shareholder approvals actually have been obtained.

Mechanics of Conversion — Effective Time of IPO.   A Charter provision on conversion mechanics often addresses the timing of mandatory conversion in the event of a public offering by providing as follows:

> **Charter Sample 9.17-C.** If the conversion is in connection with an underwritten offering of securities registered pursuant to the Securities Act of 1933, as amended, the conversion will be conditioned upon the closing with the underwriters of the sale of securities pursuant to such offering, in which event the persons entitled to receive the Common Stock upon conversion of the Preferred Stock shall not be deemed to have converted such Preferred Stock until immediately prior to the closing of such sale of securities.

PROBLEM

Charter Sample 9.17-C raises exactly the same issue that we discussed in reviewing the automatic conversion terms of Charter Sample 9.16; in fact, you may have noticed that this "mechanics" provision provides the same result as the last sentence of Charter Sample 9.16. If that automatic conversion provision were used with this mechanics provision as precedent to draft a new Charter, what would the result be? What language would you use? Why?

Cutting and pasting provisions without using diligent care in drafting the Charter can lead to overlapping terms that, here, are simply duplicative, but in other cases could create an inconsistency in setting the rights of a class of stock.

Mechanics of Conversion — Effective Time of Conversion by Vote.   A mechanics provision also often addresses the timing of an automatic conversion that is triggered by a vote by providing as follows:

> **Charter Sample 9.17-D.** If the conversion is in connection with Automatic Conversion [by vote], such conversion shall be deemed to have been made on the conversion date described in the shareholder consent approving such conversion, and the persons entitled to receive shares of Common Stock issuable upon such conversion shall be treated for all purposes as the record holders of such shares of Common Stock as of such date.

The language here avoids the "process trap" for company counsel that we discussed earlier in this chapter regarding the last sentence of Charter Sample 9.16, which provided that an automatic conversion upon a vote by written consent would be effective upon the "giving" of the consent. Charter Sample 9.17-D, in contrast, contemplates that the effective time of the conversion can be set in the resolution presented to the shareholders for a vote, rather than having the conversion occur when the consent is given.

The Conversion Rate.   Charter Samples 9.14 through 9.17 established the right to convert, provided for voluntary conversion, and used the defined term "Conversion Rate." In contrast to the general terms we saw in Charter Sample 9.15, here is a more detailed provision that defines "Conversion Rate" and explains how it works:

> **Charter Sample 9.18.** Each share of Preferred Stock shall be convertible, at the option of the holder thereof, at any time after the date of its issuance, into a number of fully paid and nonassessable shares of Common Stock as is determined by dividing the applicable Original Issue Price for such series by the applicable Conversion Price (as defined below) for such series (the conversion rate for a series of Preferred Stock into Common Stock is referred to herein as the "**Conversion Rate**" for such series), determined as hereafter provided, in effect on the date the conversion takes place. The initial Conversion Price per share for each series of Preferred Stock shall be the Original Issue Price applicable to such series of Preferred Stock (the "**Conversion Price**"); provided, however, that the Conversion Price for the Preferred Stock shall be subject to adjustment as set forth in subsection (d), below.

The Conversion Rate is the number of shares of common stock into which each share of a particular series of preferred stock converts. As a result, the Conversion Rate, multiplied by the number of shares in a series of preferred stock, equals the number of shares of common stock issuable upon conversion of that series of preferred stock.

The Conversion Rate is calculated by dividing the Original Issue Price per share of the preferred stock by the "Conversion Price," which can be expressed mathematically as follows:

$$\text{Conversion Rate} = \frac{\text{Original Issue Price}}{\text{Conversion Price}}$$

Both the Original Issue Price and the initial Conversion Price for each series of preferred stock must be set forth in the Charter. The Original Issue Price (another frequently used defined term is "Original Purchase Price") is equal to the per-share price paid by the investors to buy the preferred stock shares of that series from the company. The Conversion Price is the mechanism by which the Conversion Rate is adjusted, so it is initially set so that each share of preferred stock will convert into the negotiated number of shares of common stock. In venture capital transactions, the initial Conversion Rate is almost always one-for-one (i.e., each share of preferred stock converts into one share of common stock). As a result, the initial Conversion Price normally is set as an amount equal to the Original Issue Price.

For example, if the preferred stock was issued for $3.00 per share, the Conversion Price would be set at $3.00 so that the Conversion Rate would be 1: $3.00 (the Original Issue Price) divided by $3.00 (the Conversion Price) equals 1.

$$1 \text{ (Conversion Rate)} = \frac{\$3.00 \text{ (Original Issue Price)}}{\$3.00 \text{ (Conversion Price)}}$$

If the transaction terms call for an initial Conversion Rate other than 1, the initial Conversion Price may not be so obvious. And since the Conversion Price is the element of the equation that changes in order to set a different Conversion Rate, we have to know how to solve for the Conversion Price algebraically. Let's say that the deal terms set the Conversion Rate at 2 and the Original Issue Price at $3.00. We need to solve for X, the unknown Conversion Price:

$$2 = \frac{\$3.00}{\$X}$$

Using simple algebra, we first multiply both sides of the equation by $X and get the following result:

$$2 \times \$X = \$3.00$$

We then divide both sides of the equation by 2 to solve for X, the Conversion Price:

$$\text{Conversion Price} = \frac{\$3.00}{2}$$
$$\text{Conversion Price} = \$1.50$$

Going back to the Conversion Rate formula, we see:

$$\text{Conversion Rate} = \frac{\$3.00}{\$1.50}$$

Because $3.00 divided by $1.50 is 2, which was the Conversion Rate set by the deal terms, we know that the correct Conversion Price for this transaction is $1.50.

PROBLEMS

1. As an alternative to the previous scenario, if the terms of the preferred stock issued by the company provided that it would convert at a four-for-one rate, then what would the initial Conversion Price set in the Charter be for that series of preferred stock if the Original Issue Price was $2.00? *Hint*:

$$\text{Conversion Rate} = \frac{\text{Original Issue Price}}{\text{Conversion Price}}$$

   If 100,000 shares of this preferred stock were issued, they then would convert into how many common stock shares in total?

2. As you are doing diligence on a company into which your venture capital fund client is considering making an investment, you discover a "Certificate of Adjustment"

from the company to its shareholders informing them that the Conversion Price of the company's Series A Preferred Stock has been adjusted to $1.16. On further investigation you discover that the Original Issue Price of the Series A Preferred Stock is $0.9728 and there are 1,541,941 shares of Series A Preferred Stock outstanding. What is the Conversion Rate of the Series A Preferred Stock and how many common stock equivalent shares does that stock represent?

After the preferred stock shares are issued, the Charter almost always will provide for adjustments to the Conversion Rate by adjusting the Conversion Price. The important thing to remember is that absent a rare split or reverse split of the preferred stock, the Original Issue Price does not change. Adjusting the Conversion Rate is linked to adjusting the Conversion Price, as we examine in the next section.

2. The Effect of Dilution

Adjustments to the Conversion Rate are made as a result of a set of preferred stock preference rights that are commonly called *anti-dilution* protections. In order to address how anti-dilution works, we first have to look at what "dilution" is and under what circumstances a preferred stock investor expects to be protected from dilution.

"Good" Dilution. Most broadly, *dilution* is the effect of an increase in the number of shares of stock a company has outstanding. When a company issues more shares of stock, the existing shareholders are "diluted" because, unless they received the new shares, their percentage ownership of the company is decreased by the fact that more shares are now outstanding.

Dilution occurs each time new shares are issued, and it is not necessarily bad. If the new shares are issued at a higher per-share price than was paid for the existing shares, then the new investor receives fewer shares per dollar invested than the existing investors received when they invested. The existing investors clearly are better off if the company can issue new shares for more money per share than the existing shareholders paid for their investment because the price rise indicates that the value of their investment has increased.

Example 9.19-A: Good Dilution, SoCal Ventures Investment. As an example, let's assume that SoftCo has 2 million common stock shares outstanding that were issued to Joan and Michael in exchange for the few thousand dollars of cash and property that they paid into the company when they formed it. Now SoftCo is able to attract $4 million in investment from SoCal Ventures at a $4 million pre-money valuation. (Recall that we discussed the term *pre-money valuation* in section E.4 of Chapter 8.) Each share of the existing capitalization of SoftCo is now deemed to be worth $2.00 ($4 million pre-money valuation divided by 2 million pre-money shares outstanding). By agreeing to invest $4 million at a $4 million pre-money valuation, SoCal Ventures has agreed to pay $2.00 per share and will purchase 2 million shares of a new Series A Preferred Stock, which will be convertible into common stock at a one-for-one rate. So at the conclusion of the investment, SoftCo will have 4 million shares outstanding (2 million common stock shares plus 2 million Series A Preferred Stock shares) and a post-money valuation of

$8 million ($4 million pre-money valuation plus $4 million investment). This can be summarized mathematically as follows:

$$\text{Pre-Money Valuation} + \text{Investment Amount} = \text{Post-Money Valuation}$$
$$\$4 \text{ million} + \$4 \text{ million} = \$8 \text{ million}$$

Further, SoftCo's outstanding shares will be divided equally between the common stock holders and the investor. The fraction below shows the value per share that is imputed on the pre-money outstanding shares, as well as the price per share to be paid by the investor:

$$\frac{\text{Pre-Money Valuation}}{\text{Pre-Money Shares Outstanding}} = \text{Price Per Share}$$

$$\frac{\$4 \text{ million Pre-Money Valuation}}{2 \text{ million Pre-Money Shares Outstanding}} = \$2.00 \text{ Price Per Share}$$

Thus, $2.00 is the imputed value per share of each of the outstanding common shares and the price per share for the investment. Because the investment is $4 million, we know that 2 million Series A Preferred Stock shares will be issued ($4 million investment divided by $2.00 as the price per share).

This can be summarized in the following chart:

Fig. 9.17 SoCal Ventures Investment

	SoftCo Pre-Money	+ New Investment	= SoftCo Post-Money
Valuation	$4 million	$4 million	$8 million
Shares outstanding	2 million existing: 2M common	2 million newly issued shares of Series A = 2M CSE	4 million CSE shares: 2M common, 2M Series A = 2M CSE
Price per share	$2.00 imputed value	$2.00 price paid	$2.00
Ownership	100% common stock	100% SoCal Ventures	50% common stock 50% Series A

As a result of this financing transaction, Joan and Michael have gone from owning 100 percent of SoftCo to owning only 50 percent of the company's stock, yet the 2 million shares they bought for only a few thousand dollars now have an imputed value, based on the price SoCal Ventures paid to acquire its shares, of $4 million. *Query:* Joan and Michael have suffered significant dilution, but have they been harmed?

Example 9.19-B: Good Dilution, LAVC Investment. Next, let's assume that two years later, SoftCo is doing really well and L.A. Venture Capital ("LAVC") offers to invest $10 million at a $20 million pre-money valuation. SoftCo has 4 million pre-money shares outstanding (i.e., 2 million common stock shares plus 2 million Series A Preferred Stock shares, which convert on a one-for-one basis), so the per-share value imputed by the transaction is $5.00 (i.e., $20 million pre-money valuation divided by

4 million shares outstanding) and LAVC will pay $5.00 per share for its Series B Preferred Stock, which also converts on a one-for-one basis. At the conclusion of this financing round, SoftCo will have 6 million shares outstanding (i.e., 2 million common stock shares plus 2 million Series A Preferred Stock shares plus 2 million Series B Preferred Stock shares), a post-money valuation of $30 million (i.e., $20 million pre-money valuation plus $10 million investment by LAVC), and will be owned evenly in thirds by the common stock holders and each of the two venture capital investors, as reflected in the following chart:

Fig. 9.18 LAVC Investment

	SoftCo Pre-Money	+ New Investment	= SoftCo Post-Money
Valuation	$20 million	$10 million	$30 million
Shares outstanding	4 million existing: 2M common, 2M Series A = 2M CSE	2 million newly issued shares of Series B = 2M CSE	6 million CSE shares: 2M common, 2M Series A = 2M CSE, 2M Series B = 2M CSE
Price per share	$5.00 imputed value	$5.00 price paid	$5.00
Ownership	50% common stock 50% Series A	100% LAVC	33.3% common stock 33.3% Series A 33.3% Series B

As a result of this additional round of investment, Joan and Michael, as the common stock holders, and SoCal Ventures, as the Series A Preferred Stock holder, each have been diluted, going from 50 percent ownership to 33.33 percent ownership, as LAVC has purchased 33.33 percent of the company. However, have they been harmed by that dilution? They had stock that was valued in the last round of financing at $2.00 per share but is now valued at $5.00 per share. The total value of the common stock is now $10 million. The value of the Series A Preferred Stock is also now $10 million. Each set of shareholders now holds a smaller portion of the SoftCo ownership pie, but that pie is now very much larger, so their portions are worth much more. *Query:* While the valuation attributable to the ownership interests of Joan, Michael, and SoCal Ventures has increased, their percentage of ownership has decreased. What are the drawbacks of this decline?

This is another example of good dilution. The founders, Joan and Michael, and SoCal Ventures all should be pleased because the valuation increase on their shares has vastly outweighed the dilution in their percentage ownership of SoftCo. There is no anti-dilution adjustment applicable to this kind of dilution, nor should there be since their ownership interests have increased in value.

"Bad" Dilution.   But what if the dilution is not accompanied by an off-setting value increase?

Example 9.20-A: Bad Dilution — Stock Split. Let's assume that after LAVC's investment, SoftCo's board of directors determines that its future equity incentive offerings for new employees (no option plan shares have yet been set aside for this purpose) would have a stronger motivational impact if the company were able to offer more shares at a lower price. As a result, the board decides to split the common stock shares by a factor of 4, so that instead of 2 million common stock shares outstanding, there are now 8 million. Does that mean the common stock, which at this point in our hypo is still wholly owned by Joan and Michael, now represents 66.67 percent of SoftCo's ownership (i.e., 8 million common shares out of 12 million shares outstanding), and the preferred stock investors, who each previously owned 33.33 percent of the company, now each own only 16.67 percent (i.e., 2 million as-converted common shares divided by 12 million total shares deemed outstanding)?

The preferred stock holders still have the same number of shares of Series A Preferred Stock and Series B Preferred Stock, with their original priority rights on dividends and liquidation, but what has happened to their participation rights? We know from our earlier discussion of dividend and liquidation preferences that participation rights are based on the preferred stockholder's "as-converted" ownership of common stock. But now, suddenly, there are many more common stock shares outstanding following this stock split, which means the value of the participation rights has been diluted. As we will see later in this chapter, voting rights are set on the same as-converted basis as participation rights, so what has happened to the preferred stock's voting rights? The preferred stock's anti-dilution protections are intended to correct for this kind of dilution to the participation rights of the preferred stock.

Example 9.20-B: Bad Dilution — "Down-Round" Financing.   Another example of "bad" dilution is a so-called "down round" of financing. A "down round" occurs when the pre-money valuation put on a company by the new investors is lower than the post-money valuation at the completion of the prior round of financing. Let's assume, for instance, that SoftCo does not enjoy continued growth and the common stock split posited in Example 9.20-A. Instead, things go very badly with the launch of SoftCo's generation 2.0 operating system products, and the company now finds itself (a) with a line-up of products no one wants to buy and (b) out of money. Let's further assume that SoftCo finds an investor willing to take a chance, Lemonade Ventures, but they are only offering to invest $3 million in Series C Preferred Stock at a $2 million pre-money valuation. That would mean that the existing 6 million shares would have a value of $0.3333 each (i.e., $2 million pre-money valuation divided by 6 million pre-money shares). Based on that price, after the transaction, Lemonade Ventures would own 9 million shares (i.e., $3 million divided by $0.3333 price per share) out of a total of 15 million post-money shares (i.e., 9 million Series C Preferred Stock shares plus 6 million pre-money shares). Lemonade Ventures would therefore end up owning 60 percent of SoftCo (i.e., 9 million common stock equivalent shares divided by 15 million shares, or $3 million divided by a post-money valuation of $5 million), and the common stock, Series A Preferred Stock, and Series B Preferred Stock would each own 13.33 percent (i.e., 2 million common stock equivalent shares divided by 15 million shares, or $666,666.67 divided by $5 million), all of which can be summarized in the following chart:

Fig. 9.19 Lemonade Ventures Investment

	SoftCo Pre-Money	+ New Investment	= SoftCo Post-Money
Valuation	$2 million	$3 million	$5 million
Shares outstanding	6 million total shares: 2M common, 2M Series A = 2M CSE, 2M Series B = 2M CSE	9 million newly issued shares of Series C = 9M CSE	15 million CSE shares: 2M common, 2M Series A = 2M CSE, 2M Series B = 2M CSE, 9M Series C = 9M CSE
Price per share	$0.3333 imputed value	$0.3333 price paid	$0.3333
Ownership	33.3% common stock 33.3% Series A 33.3% Series B	100% Lemonade Ventures	13.33% common stock 13.33% Series A 13.33% Series B 60% Series C

In looking at Fig. 9.19, how do you suppose Joan and Michael, SoCal Ventures, and LAVC feel about the dilution they have suffered following this "down round" of financing? In this case, their ownership interests have gotten smaller *and* have become less valuable. While there is no anti-dilution adjustment for Joan and Michael as common stock holders — the downside of owning the residual value of the company is that the common stock holders take on more risk — the preferred stock holders, when negotiating the terms of their original investment, will usually insist on anti-dilution protections to mitigate the harm that results from exactly this kind of dilution of value.

In terms of the preferred stock anti-dilution adjustments that venture capital investors typically bargain for, we will examine first the protection against *dilution of participation rights*. Next, we will turn our attention to protection against *dilution to economic value*, also referred to as "price protection anti-dilution" rights. In each case, these protections change the effective Conversion Price, causing the Conversion Rate to adjust.

3. *Dilution to Participation Rights*

Dilution to the preferred stock's participation rights occurs whenever the common stock is restructured so that the proportionate relationship between the common stock and preferred stock is shifted. The events that cause this to happen do not involve new money coming into the company or value leaving the company. They represent only an internal reconfiguration of the company's ownership interests.

Common Stock Splits and Stock Dividends. Dilution to the participation right is triggered when the common stock is split or a dividend payable in the common stock is declared. A dividend payable in common stock (or some other security convertible into common stock) has the same practical effect as a split of the common stock, which is why we did not discuss stock dividends in our previous analysis of preferred stock dividend preferences. The typical venture capital preferred stock preference structure treats stock dividends as an anti-dilution issue instead of as a dividend issue.

A split of the common stock is accomplished by filing a Charter amendment with the secretary of state stating that, effective on its filing (or as of a specified time), each share of the corporation's common stock shall be split into a designated number of shares (2, 3, 10, or even 1,348 — whatever the company decides as a business matter that the split factor should be). That Charter amendment also adjusts the authorized number of shares of common stock to ensure a sufficient number of authorized common shares will be available on a post-split basis.

A split will apply to all common stock shares of the company, whether outstanding, underlying a convertible security, reserved for issuance upon the exercise of an option or a warrant, or even just promised as an equity incentive in an employment offer letter. For example, if a company has 5 million authorized common stock shares and 2 million shares outstanding, and wants to split its outstanding common stock by two, it could do so without increasing the number of its authorized shares. Its outstanding shares would go to 4 million, so it would have only 1 million remaining shares available for future issuance. As part of its split process, it also could double the number of authorized common stock shares, thereby keeping its post-split outstanding shares and the available number of authorized but unissued shares at the same proportionate relationship they had before the stock split became effective. The company also could change its authorized shares to any number (above the 4 million shares outstanding following the split) that it likes.

A common stock dividend is done without a Charter amendment by using existing authorized common stock shares, which obviously limits the size of a permitted stock dividend to the number of common shares that are authorized but unissued or unreserved. To effect a stock dividend, the corporation's board of directors passes a resolution calling for a dividend of a designated number of common shares (1, 2, 9, 1,347, or whatever the dividend rate is to be) for each share of common stock outstanding.

Note that in these two examples the same result is obtained; in other words, a two-for-one stock split has the same economic effect as a stock dividend of one share per outstanding share. In the end, for each share previously outstanding, there are now two. A ten-for-one split has the same effect as a dividend of nine shares per share. In each case, where there was one share, there are now ten.

Splits are used when a company decides that it needs more common stock shares outstanding or it needs to reduce the per-share value of its common stock (which is an inevitable by-product of having more shares outstanding). A company might want to reduce its per-share price because it believes potential employees will be more attracted by stock options covering more shares at a lower price. Or, the company may believe that its shares would be more attractive to investors at a lower per-share price.

Example 9.21-A: *Effect of Common Stock Split.*   Let's assume that Joan and Michael actually had issued to themselves only 50 SoftCo common stock shares each before SoCal Ventures invested its $4 million on a $4 million pre-money valuation in Example 9.19-B. (See Fig. 9.18.) With only 100 shares outstanding, the $4 million pre-money valuation would have meant that each share was worth $40,000 ($4 million pre-money valuation divided by 100 shares outstanding). That means each share would represent a fairly large piece of SoftCo's value. If we further assume that the company established an equity incentive plan and offered shares to its employees at 20 percent of the preferred stock price, each share would have an $8,000 value. (Refer to the discussion in section A.4 of Chapter 6 regarding pricing equity incentives.) Almost all venture capital financed early stage companies prefer to offer employees equity incentives with very low purchase prices, often $0.10 or below, both because of the psychological value of grants made up of large share numbers and because if each share has a small value, management has the ability to fine-tune the value of equity incentives among employees. If each share is worth $8,000, little fine-tuning is possible. To make the share price more manageable and more attractive to its employees, SoftCo could opt to split its shares on a one-into-20,000 basis before the SoCal Ventures investment, resulting in Joan and Michael together owning 2 million shares and making the per-share value a more manageable $2.00 per share.

Reverse Common Stock Split.   A reverse split simply goes the other way. Instead of outstanding common stock shares being divided into more shares, they are "combined" into fewer shares. A reverse split is accomplished by filing a Charter amendment with the secretary of state saying that each common share is reverse split into 1/2 share, 1/3 share, 1/10 share, or 1/1,348 share. The amendment can leave the authorized number of common shares alone or may reduce it to reflect the number needed after the reverse split.

Example 9.21-B: Effect of Reverse Common Stock Split.   A reverse split is used to decrease the number of shares of common stock or, as its natural and inevitable consequence, to increase the per-share value of the common stock. Reverse splits are used when the per-share price has dropped too low. In the Lemonade Ventures investment presented in Example 9.20-B and Fig. 9-19, what would have been the outcome if the prior two rounds of preferred stock investments had been at $0.20 and $0.50 per share, respectively, for 20 million shares in each round? Lemonade Ventures, then, would have been paying $0.03333 per share to buy 90 million shares. Following the Series C Preferred Stock investment round, there would have been 150 million shares outstanding with a value of $0.03333 per share. That would represent a substantial number of outstanding shares at a very low per-share price. For an equity incentive plan, using an 80 percent discount from the preferred stock price, the per-share price would be less than a penny. In this situation, a reverse split would bring the number of shares down and the per-share price up to more manageable, less awkward levels.

The key thing to keep in mind about stock splits, stock dividends, and reverse splits is that they are closed-universe actions. That is to say, no new owners become involved with the company and no new value is delivered into or taken out of the company. The only thing that happens is that the number of ownership units (i.e., shares) gets multiplied or divided.

Looking back at the stock split scenario described in Example 9.20-A, we had Soft-Co's board of directors deciding, after the LAVC investment, that SoftCo should split its common stock in preparation for creating and adopting an equity incentive plan and setting aside (i.e., reserving) common stock shares in order to implement that plan. We further assumed that SoftCo would split its common stock on a four-for-one basis. The stock split would result in 8 million common stock shares outstanding, 2 million Series A Preferred Stock shares and 2 million Series B Preferred Stock shares. Each series of preferred stock, convertible on a one-for-one basis, instead of representing 33.33 percent of SoftCo's ownership (i.e., 2 million divided by 6 million pre-split outstanding CSE shares) would now represent only 16.67 percent (2 million divided by 12 million post-split outstanding CSE shares). After giving effect to the split, SoftCo's capitalization could be presented as follows:

Fig. 9.20 Effect of 4-for-1 common stock split after LAVC Investment

	SoftCo after LAVC investment	SoftCo after 4-for-1 common stock split
Valuation	$30 million	$30 million
Shares outstanding	6 million CSE shares: 2M common, 2M Series A = 2M CSE, 2M Series B = 2M CSE	12 million CSE shares: 8M common, 2M Series A = 2M CSE, 2M Series B = 2M CSE
Ownership	33.3% common stock 33.3% Series A 33.3% Series B	66.67% common stock 16.67% Series A 16.67% Series B

Query: Is this an appropriate outcome for a closed-universe transaction? In other words, how do you imagine the venture capital funds feel about the dilution of their ownership interests that inevitably results from this type of stock split (especially since no value has come into the company or left the company)? What is the effect on the preferred stock's participation and voting rights?

Common Stock Split — Anti-Dilution Adjustment. A typical Charter provision providing for a proportionate anti-dilution adjustment upon a common stock split or stock dividend might read as follows:

Charter Sample 9.22. In the event this corporation should at any time or from time to time after the Filing Date effectuate a split or subdivision of the outstanding shares of Common Stock or a dividend or other distribution payable to the Common Stock holders in additional shares of Common Stock or other securities or rights convertible into, or entitling the holder thereof to receive directly or indirectly additional shares of, Common Stock (hereinafter referred to as "**Common Stock Equivalents**") without payment of any consideration by such holder for the additional shares of Common Stock or the Common Stock Equivalents (including the additional shares of Common

Stock issuable upon conversion or exercise thereof), then, as of the date of such dividend distribution, split or subdivision, the Conversion Price of each series of the Preferred Stock shall be appropriately decreased so that the number of shares of Common Stock issuable on conversion of each share of such series (i.e. the Conversion Rate) shall be increased in proportion to such increase of the aggregate of shares of Common Stock outstanding and those issuable with respect to such Common Stock Equivalents.

Before discussing the mechanics of anti-dilution protection, it is important to emphasize that the goal of this Charter provision is to determine how many shares of common stock are being issued by split or dividend, regardless of how many steps it takes before these common shares are, in fact, outstanding. In the end, the adjustment provides that the Conversion Price is to be "appropriately decreased" so that the number of shares issuable upon conversion of each share of preferred stock, that is, the Conversion Rate, is "increased in proportion" to the increase in the number of common stock shares outstanding.

The "Filing Date," or simply "upon the effectiveness of this Amended and Restated [Charter]," is the time the Charter provision becomes effective, which means no adjustment is made for any events that took place before that date. Sometimes the defined term is the "Preferred Stock Purchase Date" or "Original Issue Date," which usually is a day or two later, given the natural delay between the Charter filing and the delivery of signature pages and money to complete the share issuance, but that difference usually is not meaningful. The result is that adjustments for any prior dilutive events are being waived by the preferred stock, or alternatively, the adjustments from those events are built into the financial terms of the current preferred stock investment. "Common Stock Equivalents" are defined as the common stock shares issuable upon the exercise, exchange, or conversion of other outstanding or reserved securities. This is consistent with the way that defined term has been used in this chapter in our discussion of dividend and liquidation preferences. But here, in the context of anti-dilution protections, this defined term specifically addresses the common stock issuable upon exercise or conversion of a security issued as a dividend.

The language "without payment of any consideration" to convert or exercise the Common Stock Equivalents into common stock is intended to separate out situations that are not closed-universe and, therefore, do not trigger this form of anti-dilution protection. For example, if a warrant is issued by dividend to the common stock holders, but the shareholders must pay money to exercise the warrant, then the common stock underlying the warrant would not be considered a dividend since it is issuable only after payment of a price.

Example 9.22: Anti-Dilution Adjustment — Common Stock Split.   Now, let's turn to the mechanics of anti-dilution protection so that we can better understand how the goal of this Charter provision is implemented as a practical matter. Looking at our hypo presented in Example 9.19-A (as reflected previously in Fig. 9-17), we know that SoCal Ventures' Series A Preferred Stock was issued at a price of $2.00 per share, which is, therefore, its Original Issue Price, and, because it initially was convertible on a one-for-one basis, we know that its Conversion Price is also $2.00. Looking again at the formula presented earlier, the mathematical calculation of the Conversion Price is:

$$\text{Conversion Rate} = \frac{\text{Original Issue Price}}{\text{Conversion Price}}$$

$$1 = \frac{\$2.00}{\$X}$$

$$1 \text{ times } \$X = \$2.00$$

$$\$X = \$2.00$$

$$\text{Conversion Price} = \$2.00$$

To find the new Conversion Rate after giving effect to the four-for-one stock split described in Example 9.20-A, we must make a proportionate adjustment to the existing Conversion Price, so we divide it by the rate of the split, according to the following calculation:

New Conversion Price = Old Conversion Price divided by Rate of Split
Old Conversion Price = $2.00
Rate of Split = 4
New Conversion Price = $2.00 divided by 4
New Conversion Price = $0.50

Plugging these numbers into our original formula allows us to determine the new Conversion Rate after giving effect to this stock split:

$$\text{New Conversion Rate} = \frac{\text{Original Issue Price}}{\text{New Conversion Price}}$$

$$X = \frac{\$2.00 \text{ (Original Issue Price)}}{\$0.50 \text{ (New Conversion Price)}}$$

$$X = \frac{\$2.00}{\$0.50}$$

$$X = 4$$

These calculations establish that the new Series A Preferred Stock Conversion Price is $0.50, which results in a New Conversion Rate of 4.

Thus, every share of Series A Preferred Stock now converts into four shares of common stock rather than into one. The Conversion Price of the Series A Preferred Stock has been proportionately adjusted to $0.50 as a result of the stock split, which results in a new Conversion Rate of 4.

Now, let's consider what will happen under Charter Sample 9.22 to the Series B Preferred Stock after giving effect to the four-for-one stock split. The Series B Preferred Stock was originally issued at $5.00 per share and is also convertible on a one-for-one basis. Refer to Example 9.22 and Fig. 9.20. Going through the same process as for the Series A Preferred Stock, what are the New Conversion Price and New Conversion Rate for the Series B Preferred Stock? *Hint*:

$$\text{New Conversion Price} = \text{ Old Conversion Price divided by Rate of Split}$$

$$\text{New Conversion Rate} = \frac{\text{Original Issue Price}}{\text{New Conversion Price}}$$

This leads to the obvious question: How can we confirm that all of these calculations, which are called for by the terms of Charter Sample 9.22, actually serve to implement the original goal, which was to preserve the proportionate relationship between the preferred stock and the common stock? Returning to the facts of Example 9.22, we see that Fig. 9.20 reflects SoftCo's capitalization after giving effect to the four-for-one common stock split with no anti-dilution adjustment. However, with the proportionate Conversion Price adjustment, while the number of preferred stock shares outstanding has not changed, the New Conversion Rate on both series has changed from 1 to 4, and the number of common stock shares issuable upon conversion of the preferred stock has thereby increased by a factor of 4. Thus, the common stock equivalent shares outstanding have increased, and the proportional relationship between the preferred stock and the common stock has been returned to the pre-split balance, thereby achieving the stated goal of proportionate anti-dilution protection, all of which is reflected below:

Fig. 9.21 Effect of anti-dilution adjustment after 4-for-1 common stock split following LAVC Investment

	SoftCo after LAVC investment and 4-for-1 common stock split	SoftCo after 4-for-1 common stock split and preferred stock conversion rate adjustment
Valuation	$30 million	$30 million
Shares outstanding	12 million CSE shares: 8M common, 2M Series A = 2M CSE, 2M Series B = 2M CSE	24 million CSE shares: 8M common, 2M Series A = 8M CSE, 2M Series B = 8M CSE
Ownership	66.67% common stock 16.67% Series A 16.67% Series B	33.3% common stock 33.3% Series A 33.3% Series B

If we compare this outcome with the result of the split without this adjustment, as shown previously in Fig. 9.20, we see that the preferred stock's anti-dilution adjustment has resolved the otherwise inappropriate result from the stock split.

Reverse Common Stock Splits.   What if, instead of a stock split, SoftCo decided to do a reverse stock split, thereby causing each common stock share to become one fifth of a share? In this case, the number of common stock shares would be reduced from 2 million to 400,000 and, if no conversion rate adjustment were made, suddenly the preferred stock would own a greater percentage of the company than the parties bargained for, as reflected in the following table:

Fig. 9.22 Effect of reverse 1-for-5 common stock split after LAVC Investment

	SoftCo after LAVC Investment	SoftCo after 1-for-5 common stock split
Valuation	$30 million	$30 million
Shares outstanding	6 million CSE shares: 2M common, 2M Series A = 2M CSE, 2M Series B = 2M CSE	4.4 million CSE shares: 400,000 common, 2M Series A = 2M CSE, 2M Series B = 2M CSE
Ownership	33.3% common stock 33.3% Series A 33.3% Series B	9.1% common stock 45.5% Series A 45.5% Series B

Even though this reverse stock split works to the benefit of the preferred stock holders, the investors recognize that the common stock holders would never agree to a reverse split if this would be the outcome. Because reverse splits often can be useful to the company, and further, because a proportionate adjustment in this circumstance is just as appropriate as it was when the common stock was split, the Charter typically includes language such as the following:

> **Charter Sample 9.23.** If the number of shares of Common Stock outstanding at any time after the Filing Date is decreased by a combination of the outstanding shares of Common Stock, then, following the record date of such combination, the Conversion Price for the Preferred Stock shall be appropriately increased so that the number of shares of Common Stock issuable on conversion of each share of such series (i.e. the Conversion Rate) shall be decreased in proportion to such decrease in outstanding shares.

We see that this adjustment goes the other direction from the adjustment for a stock split, which we saw in Charter Sample 9.22; that is to say, when there is a reverse common stock split, in order to maintain the relationship between the number of preferred and common shares, the preferred stock's Conversion Price is appropriately *increased* in order to proportionately *decrease* the Conversion Rate consistent with the rate of the reverse split. One important factor to note is that this is the *only circumstance where a Conversion Price actually is increased*, thereby causing the Conversion Rate to go down.

All other anti-dilution adjustments decrease the Conversion Price, causing the Conversion Rate to go up.

Example 9.23: Reverse Common Stock Split — Anti-Dilution Adjustment.   In the case of a reverse common stock split, we will use the same formula that we used earlier in Example 9.22 for the adjustment to SoCal Ventures' Series A Preferred Stock when there was a common stock split. Again, we start by dividing the old Series A Preferred Stock Conversion Price ($2.00) by the rate of the stock split to find the new Conversion Price. Because we are dealing with a reverse stock split, the rate of the stock split will be less than one, as reflected in the following calculation:

New Conversion Price = Old Conversion Price divided by Rate of Split
Old Conversion Price = $2.00
Rate of Stock Split = 1-for-5 (or 1/5, or 0.20)
New Conversion Price = $2.00 divided by 0.20
New Conversion Price = $10.00

Once again, we use the basic formula, plugging in the New Conversion Price, to determine the New Conversion Rate for the preferred stock after giving effect to this reverse common stock split:

$$\text{New Conversion Rate} = \frac{\$2.00 \text{ (Original Issue Price)}}{\$10.00 \text{ (New Conversion Price)}}$$

$$\text{New Conversion Rate} = \frac{\$2.00}{\$10.00}$$

$$\text{New Conversion Rate} = \frac{1}{5}$$

$$\text{New Conversion Rate} = 0.20$$

Thus we see that the Series A Preferred Stock's New Conversion Price is $10.00, which results in a New Conversion Rate of 0.20. After this adjustment, every share of Series A Preferred Stock now converts into one-fifth of a share of common stock, or to put it another way, every five shares of Series A Preferred Stock converts into one share of common stock.

PROBLEM

Now, let's consider what will happen under Charter Sample 9.23 to LAVC's Series B Preferred Stock after giving effect to the reverse common stock split. As described in Example 9.19-B, the Series B Preferred Stock was originally issued at $5.00 per share and is also convertible on a one-for-one basis. Going through the same process as we did above in connection with the Series A Preferred Stock, what are the New Conversion Price and New Conversion Rate for the Series B Preferred Stock?

As reflected below in Fig. 9.23, we see that, following the proportionate adjustment in the Conversion Price called for in the anti-dilution provisions of Charter Sample 9.23, the number of preferred stock shares outstanding has not changed, but the Conversion Rate of the preferred stock has decreased proportionately to reflect the reverse stock split of the company's common stock. As a consequence, the proportionate relationship between the preferred stock and the common stock has been returned to the pre reverse-split balance, as reflected below:

Fig. 9.23 Effect of anti-dilution adjustment after 1-for-5 reverse common stock split following LAVC Investment

	SoftCo after LAVC investment after 1-for-5 common stock reverse split	SoftCo after 1-for-5 common stock split and preferred stock conversion rate adjustment
Valuation	$30 million	$30 million
Shares outstanding	4.4 million CSE shares: 400,000 common, 2M Series A = 2M CSE, 2M Series B = 2M CSE	1.2 million CSE shares: 400,000 common, 2M Series A = 400,000 CSE, 2M Series B = 400,000 CSE
Ownership	9.1% common stock 45.5% Series A 45.5% Series B	33.3% common stock 33.3% Series A 33.3% Series B

If we then compare this outcome with Fig. 9.22 above, which reflects the result of the reverse split after the LAVC investment without making a proportionate adjustment in the Conversion Rate of the preferred shares, we see that the adjustment corrects the otherwise inappropriate consequence of the reverse split of the common stock.

Again, these adjustments apply in the case of common stock splits, reverse common stock splits, and distributions of stock dividends that presently or ultimately result in the issuance of common stock without consideration. Similar provisions often are used to address share exchanges or other recapitalization transactions. It is important to recognize that in all these instances, no new owners are investing their capital into the company and none are withdrawing their capital from the company. These adjustments involve *only* existing shareholders and their relative interests in the company. As we said at the outset of this discussion, the purpose of these adjustments is to prevent the division or combination of the common stock's ownership interest in the company from having an effect on the preferred stock's proportionate interest in the company and thereby impacting the preferred holders' participation and voting rights.

These proportionate adjustments are so fundamental that they sometimes are presented in a very cursory fashion. For example, instead of detailing the distinction between splits and the like (decreasing the Conversion Price) and reverse splits (increasing the Conversion Price) in separate provisions, as presented in Charter Samples 9.22 and 9.23, respectively, a Charter may contain just one provision that references all the triggering events together – splits, stock dividends, reverse splits, and so on – and simply states that upon any such an event, the Conversion Price of the existing preferred stock will be proportionately adjusted. The business lawyer who understands the underlying rationale for these proportionate adjustments to the Conversion Price is not flummoxed by this sort of minimalist drafting and can implement the necessary change.

Preferred Stock Split.   The foregoing changes address the preferred stock's anti-dilution adjustment if there is a split or reverse split of the common stock. As a separate matter, however, what happens if there is a split or reverse split of the preferred stock? You will recall from our earlier discussion of liquidation priority preferences, as presented in Charter Sample 9.8, that when the Original Issue Price is defined, a separate price is set for each series of the company's preferred stock and that price explicitly adjusts proportionately for subsequent splits, reverse splits, and the like of that particular series of preferred stock. As a result, using again SoftCo's Series A Preferred Stock purchased by SoCal Ventures, first introduced in Example 9.19-A, in the event of a four-for-one split of the Series A Preferred Stock, its Original Issue Price automatically adjusts from $2.00 to $0.50. Since the Charter does not tell us to adjust it, the Conversion Price remains unchanged at $2.00 following this stock split, and the Series A Preferred Stock now would convert at a rate of 1/4. You reach this result by doing the following calculation:

$$\text{New Conversion Rate} = \frac{\$0.50 \ (\text{Adjusted Original Issue Price})}{\$2.00 \ (\text{Conversion Price})}$$

$$\frac{1}{4} = \frac{\$\ 0.50}{\$\ 2.00}$$

Thus, each share of Series A Preferred Stock now converts into one-fourth of a share of common stock instead of one share, or stated in slightly different terms, it takes 4 shares of Series A Preferred Stock to convert into one share of common stock. As there are now four times as many Series A Preferred Stock shares outstanding, this results in the Series A Preferred Stock representing an unchanged number of common stock equivalent shares.

On the other hand, if the objective actually is to change the proportionate interest of a series of preferred stock, perhaps as an equitable adjustment done to effectively re-price the preferred stock, the Charter amendment implementing the split would need to manually re-set both the Original Issue Price and the Conversion Price for that series.

If the common stock and the preferred stock are both being split, we must calculate both the proportionate adjustment to the Conversion Price as a result of the common stock split and the Original Issue Price adjustment as a result of the preferred stock split.

If both classes were split at the same rates, then when all is said and done, these proportionate adjustments would result in no change to the Conversion Rate from the rate before the split, but there will be more shares outstanding.

For example, if the Series A Preferred Stock and common stock were both split two-for-one, the proportionate adjustment to the old Conversion Price ($2.00) would cause the New Conversion Price to be $1.00. This means that each share of Series A Preferred Stock would now convert into two shares of common stock (Original Issue Price of $2.00 divided by New Conversion Price of $1.00). But, as a result of the split of the Series A Preferred Stock, there are now twice as many Series A Preferred Stock shares outstanding, so the Original Issue Price is adjusted from $2.00 to $1.00. As a result, with the Original Issue Price and the Conversion Price each now at $1.00, the preferred stock's Conversion Rate properly reverts to 1. Since the number of preferred stock shares was split by the same rate as the common stock split, the number of shares outstanding will have increased, but relative proportions of the ownership of the company held by each class will have been preserved.

Note, however, that if the Original Issue Price is being adjusted, it is critical to confirm that the per-share preferred stock preferential rights based on the Original Issue Price (typically dividends, liquidation, and redemption) also adjust proportionately. The point is that the aggregate preferential amounts (the number of preferred stock shares multiplied by the per-share preference amount) should not change unless a modification in the aggregate amount was the objective. In a well-drafted Charter, those per-share preferred stock preferential rights should be linked to the Original Issue Price so that when the latter changes, they automatically adjust with it, and the aggregate preferential amount does not change.

PROBLEMS

1. Assume that SoftCo issues 100,000 common stock shares as founder's stock to each of Joan and Michael. Prior to a first round of venture capital financing, SoftCo does a 10-for-1 common stock split. The investors buy 1 million shares of SoftCo's Series A Preferred Stock, initially convertible at a one-for-one rate, at a price of $2.35 per share. Two years later, SoftCo implements a three-for-one common stock split. Following that split, what are the common stock equivalent shares outstanding, and what are the conversion rate and conversion price of the Series A Preferred?

2. Assume that SoftCo issues 100,000 common stock shares as founder's stock to each of Joan and Michael. Prior to a first round of venture capital financing, SoftCo declares a common stock dividend of 7 shares per outstanding share. The investors buy 661,376 shares of SoftCo's Series A Preferred Stock, initially convertible at a one-for-one rate, at a price of $1.89 per share. Two years later, SoftCo adopts a four-for-one stock split. Following that split, what are the common

stock equivalent shares outstanding and what are the conversion rate and conversion price of the Series A Preferred?

3. Assume that SoftCo issues 10,000,000 common stock shares as founder's stock to each of Joan and Michael. In a first round of venture capital financing, the investors buy 25 million shares of SoftCo's Series A Preferred Stock, initially convertible at a one-for-one rate, at a price of $0.20 per share. Two years later, SoftCo adopts a ten-into-one reverse stock split. Following that split, what are the common stock equivalent shares outstanding and what are the conversion rate and conversion price of the Series A Preferred?

4. Dilution to Economic Value — Price Protection

The discussion in this section addresses the second kind of "bad" dilution, which has an immediate and negative economic impact. Dilution to "economic value" is the adverse result that follows when the company sells new shares at a price lower than the price that was paid by the existing preferred stock holders. When this happens, which typically occurs when the company is not growing as quickly as originally anticipated, it means that the existing preferred stock holder originally paid too much for its shares. While venture capital investment is high risk, the means for setting price is so imprecise that investors seek protection against getting it wrong. Price protection anti-dilution adjustments are intended to confront this problem.

Issuance of Shares Below Conversion Price. Recall the situation discussed earlier as Example 9.20-B (and illustrated in Fig. 9.19), where things went so badly on the launch of SoftCo's generation 2.0 operating system products that the company found itself "dead in the water" and out of money. Thereafter, the company found an investor, Lemonade Ventures, who was willing to invest $3 million in Series C Preferred Stock, convertible one-for-one, at a $2 million pre-money valuation. As we saw, that $2 million pre-money valuation made the existing 6 million shares worth only $0.33 each ($2 million pre-money valuation divided by 6 million pre-money shares). Thus, after completing the transaction, Lemonade Ventures would own 9 million shares ($3 million divided by $0.33 price per share) out of a total of 15 million post-money shares (9 million Series C Preferred Stock shares plus 6 million pre-money shares). In the end, Lemonade Ventures would own 60 percent of SoftCo (its 9 million as-converted shares divided by 15 million shares, or $3 million investment divided by a $5 million post-money valuation), and the common stock, Series A Preferred Stock, and Series B Preferred Stock would each own 13.33 percent (2 million divided by 15 million shares, or $666,667 divided by $5 million). The capitalization of SoftCo following completion of this financing transaction is reflected in the following table:

Fig. 9.24 Down-round financing that triggers anti-dilution price protection

	SoftCo Post-Money (post-LAVC)	SoftCo Pre-Money (pre–Lemonade Ventures)	SoftCo Post-Money (post–Lemonade Ventures)
Valuation	$30 million	$2 million	$5 million
Shares outstanding	6 million CSE shares: 2M common, 2M Series A = 2M CSE, 2M Series B = 2M CSE	6 million CSE shares: 2M common, 2M Series A = 2M CSE, 2M Series B = 2M CSE	15 million CSE shares: 2M common, 2M Series A = 2M CSE, 2M Series B = 2M CSE, 9M Series C = 9M CSE
Price per share	$5.00 price paid	$0.33 imputed value	$0.33
Ownership	33.3% common 33.3% Series A 33.3% Series B	33.3% common 33.3% Series A 33.3% Series B	13.33% common stock 13.33% Series A 13.33% Series B 60% Series C

This is called a "down-round" financing; that is, an investment in which the pre-money valuation by the new investors is lower than the post-money valuation at the completion of the prior round of financing. In our example, this financing is also at a lower valuation than the post-money valuation of SoftCo's first round of financing, as shown in Fig. 9.17. It triggers, then, the price protection anti-dilution rights of both the Series B Preferred Stock and the Series A Preferred Stock. From the perspective of SoCal Ventures, the Series A Preferred Stock investor, and LAVC, the Series B Preferred Stock investor, the company has not performed up to their expectations; in other words, it has not used their investment funds effectively. This inability to perform means that these venture capital investors over-paid for their shares. Anticipating this risk, they have built into SoftCo's Charter a price adjustment to remedy at least part of the harm that results from this type of "down-round financing." This section focuses on the alternative forms and mechanics of this kind of price adjustment anti-dilution protection.

Economic value (or price) anti-dilution protection is triggered when a company sells shares of stock at a price lower than the Conversion Price of the existing preferred shares. We saw in our earlier discussion of participation right dilution that the Conversion Price was adjusted proportionately and the Conversion Rate recalculated. During the course of that discussion, it might have occurred to you that a proportionate change to the Conversion Price mathematically results in an identical proportionate change in the Conversion Rate. So why not just adjust the Conversion Rate directly? In other words, why bother figuring out the New Conversion Price? The reason is that economic value anti-dilution protection requires that we know what the Conversion Price is at any time. This anti-dilution adjustment comes into play whenever a new share issuance is at a per-share price lower than the then-applicable Conversion Price of a preferred stock. It causes the Conversion Price on that stock to be adjusted downward, which results in that stock's Conversion Rate going up. The result of this adjustment is to cause the preferred stock to convert into a larger number of common stock shares.

The nature of the price protection anti-dilution adjustment depends on the terms of the Charter that are negotiated between the company and the investors. In venture capital financing transactions, there are two basic approaches typically used: *ratchets* and *weighted average* formulas.

Ratchet Anti-Dilution Adjustments.   Let's look at a typical Charter provision providing for price protection through "ratchet" anti-dilution protection:

Charter Sample 9.25. If this corporation shall issue, on or after the Filing Date, any Additional Stock (as defined below) without consideration or for a consideration per share less than the Conversion Price of a series of Preferred Stock in effect immediately prior to the issuance of such Additional Stock, the Conversion Price for such series in effect immediately prior to each such issuance shall be adjusted to the amount of the per-share consideration of the Additional Stock.

First, note that this adjustment is triggered if, after the effective date of the Charter, the company issues "Additional Stock" (which we address in reviewing Charter Sample 9.30, below) without consideration or, alternatively, for inadequate consideration when compared to a Preferred Stock's Conversion Price. As to the adjustment, ratchet anti-dilution protection is refreshingly straightforward. With a ratchet, the Conversion Price of the existing preferred stock is simply adjusted to equal the price of the new share issuance. More specifically, this is a *full ratchet*, the most typically used ratchet, so-called because it adjusts all the way to the new stock's price. Existing investors are effectively treated retroactively as though they had invested at any new, lower price paid in a subsequent share issuance.

Alternatively, a ratchet may be expressed as a percentage of the difference between a preferred stock series' existing Conversion Price and the new stock's issue price. For example, if the preferred stock has a Conversion Price of $2.00 and a 75 percent ratchet, and new shares are issued at $1.00 per share, the difference between the two prices is $1.00 and the Conversion Price would adjust by 75 percent of that difference, or $0.75. By subtracting $0.75 from the existing Conversion Price of $2.00, the New Conversion Price, therefore, would be $1.25.

Example 9.25-A: Full Ratchet Anti-Dilution Adjustments.   It is important to understand that a full ratchet is a powerful adjustment. Looking again at SoftCo's Series C Preferred Stock investment round, as originally presented in Example 9.20-A and in Fig. 9.19 and (for your convenience) repeated below as Fig. 9.25, what would happen to the Series A Preferred Stock upon Lemonade Venture's investment at $0.33 per share? With a full ratchet, the Conversion Price for the Series A Preferred Stock simply would adjust to $0.33. As a result, the Series A Preferred Stock Conversion Rate would be:

$$\text{New Conversion Rate} = \frac{\text{Original Issue Price}}{\text{New Conversion Price}}$$

$$\text{New Conversion Rate} = \frac{\$\,2.00}{\$\,0.33}$$

$$\text{New Conversion Rate} = 6$$

Looking at the effect of the Lemonade Ventures investment at $0.33 per share on SoftCo's capitalization, recall that, with no anti-dilution adjustments, our chart before and after the transaction looked like this:

Fig. 9.25 Lemonade Ventures investment without price protection anti-dilution adjustment

	SoftCo Pre-Money	+ New Investment	= SoftCo Post-Money
Valuation	$2 million	$3 million	$5 million
Shares outstanding	6 million CSE shares: 2M common, 2M Series A = 2M CSE, 2M Series B = 2M CSE	9 million newly issued shares of Series C = 9M CSE	15 million CSE shares: 2M common, 2M Series A = 2M CSE, 2M Series B = 2M CSE, 9M Series C = 9M CSE
Price per share	$0.3333 imputed value	$0.3333 price paid	$0.3333
Ownership	33.3% common 33.3% Series A 33.3% Series B	100% Lemonade Ventures	13.33% common stock 13.33% Series A 13.33% Series B 60% Series C

However, with the Series A Preferred Stock entitled to full ratchet price protection and converting into 12 million shares (i.e., 2 million preferred shares times the New Conversion Rate of 6, as calculated above), and further assuming that the Series B Preferred Stock has no anti-dilution adjustment right, then the company's adjusted, common stock equivalent, or CSE, capitalization chart would look like this:

Fig. 9.26 Lemonade Ventures investment with Series A full ratchet adjustment

	SoftCo Pre-Money	SoftCo Post-Money with Series A Full Ratchet Adjustment
Valuation	$2 million	$5 million
Shares outstanding	6 million CSE shares: 2M common, 2M Series A = 2M CSE, 2M Series B = 2M CSE	25 million CSE shares: 2M common, 2M Series A = 12M CSE, 2M Series B = 2M CSE, 9M Series C = 9M CSE
Ownership	33.3% common stock 33.3% Series A 33.3% Series B	8% common stock 48% Series A 8% Series B 36% Series C

As a result of its full ratchet price protection, the Series A Preferred Stock actually *increased* its ownership percentage from 33.33 percent before the Series C Preferred Stock investment to 48 percent after the Series C Preferred Stock financing transaction.

Full ratchet price protection also can have extreme outcomes in small transactions. As we have seen, a full ratchet causes the existing preferred stock's Conversion Price to move to the per-share price of the share issuance transaction that triggered the anti-dilution protection. It does this regardless of the number of shares issued at that lower price.

Example 9.25-B: Full Ratchet Anti-Dilution Adjustments.   As an illustration of the power of a ratchet, let's further assume that, after Lemonade Ventures bought its Series C Preferred Stock, SoftCo found a finance company to lend it money based on pledging some of the company's test equipment as collateral. As part of the loan, the finance company asked, as an equity sweetener, for a warrant to buy 50,000 common stock shares at $0.05 per share. Unless that issuance was exempted from the anti-dilution protections in SoftCo's Charter (because of the "Additional Stock" definition presented in Charter Sample 9.30, below), the Conversion Price of the Series A Preferred Stock, using a full ratchet adjustment, would immediately drop to $0.05. As a result, its New Conversion Rate would now be $2.00 divided by $0.05, or 40, meaning the 2 million Series A Preferred Stock shares would now convert into 80 million shares of common stock!

The lesson to be learned from these examples is that a ratchet anti-dilution adjustment can be a wildly erratic tool. While venture capital deals almost always use a broad-based, weighted average formula (to be discussed next), full ratchets are used with some regularity in "pre-venture" transactions. These are investments, usually by individuals, maybe angel investors, in very early stage companies that are intended to get the companies, within a few months, or at least within a year, to a point where they are ready for a seed-stage investment from venture capital investors. Because these companies are so early in their development, their valuations are somewhat arbitrary, to say the least. Thus, these investors often will insist on a full ratchet for price protection. That way, if venture capital investors later set a lower price for the issuance of their shares, then the earlier investors can adjust down to that price. As a practical matter, the earlier investment is seen as an advance on the later round of venture capital financing.

Another context where a ratchet is used regularly is when a company has some major issue to resolve in the next, say, 45 days, but is out of money. In this situation, the company desperately needs money but does not want to engage in a full-scale financing round because that would require it to issue too many shares at too low a price in light of the pressing business issues it faces. As a result, the company might work with an investor that is willing to invest a small amount at a price that takes into account the probability that the problem can be overcome, or the needed milestone reached, using the cash raised from the stock purchased by that investor. The price, therefore, would reflect some risk, but would not predict failure. If the problem is addressed successfully on a timely basis, the investor will have gotten a good price without gouging the company (through a large, low-priced purchase) while having gotten a better deal than new investors coming into the company after everything is in good shape. But if the milestone cannot be reached and the company has to find new money based on the existence of the continuing problem, the investor will have overpaid — perhaps drastically — for its shares. In this case, the investor may insist on a full ratchet but may agree that it will be in effect only for a short time. The idea is that the ratchet will cover the present price uncertainty, which will be resolved within the term of the ratchet. After the stated time period, the anti-dilution adjustment will revert to a weighted average share formula. *Query:* If you were recommending an investment with a full ratchet, would you put a time horizon on it? If so, for how long? What factors influence this decision?

Absent these sorts of high uncertainty/short time frame investments, where the ratchet is directed to a specific outcome rather than creating an ongoing right, ratchets are typically viewed as being extreme enough to inhibit the willingness of subsequent investors to put money into a company. As a result, outside of these unique circumstances, full ratchets are used rarely in venture capital financing.

Broad-Based Weighted Average Formula Anti-Dilution Adjustments.   Absent special circumstances, price protection anti-dilution adjustments in venture capital transactions are accomplished through a *weighted average formula* conversion price adjustment. While *narrow-based* formulas are occasionally used, by far the most typical price protection adjustment is *broad-based*. The meanings of, and distinctions between, these terms will become clear as we examine how they work. The Charter provision setting forth a broad-based formula might read as follows:

> **Charter Sample 9.26.** Whenever the Conversion Price is adjusted pursuant to this subsection, the new Conversion Price shall be determined by multiplying the Conversion Price then in effect by a fraction, the numerator of which shall be the number of shares of Common Stock Outstanding (as defined below) immediately prior to such issuance plus the number of shares of Common Stock that the aggregate consideration received by this corporation for such issuance would purchase at such Conversion Price; and the denominator of which shall be the number of shares of Common Stock Outstanding (as defined below) immediately prior to such issuance plus the number of shares of such Additional Stock.

As with Charter Sample 9.25's ratchet, Charter Sample 9.26 provides that whenever a transaction occurs involving the issuance of shares at a price below the existing preferred stock's Conversion Price, a New Conversion Price is set. The difference lies in the means of the adjustment. Here, the formula for determining the New Conversion Price can be expressed as follows, where NCP means "New Conversion Price" and ECP means "Existing Conversion Price."

$$\text{NCP} = \text{ECP times} \quad \frac{\text{\# Shares Outstanding plus \# Shares Issuable at ECP}}{\text{\# Shares Outstanding plus \# Shares Actually Issued}}$$

This seemingly daunting fraction is actually very simple once you get past the repetition. The idea is to multiply the Existing Conversion Price by an adjustment fraction. The fraction's numerator is the total number of shares outstanding plus the number of shares that would have been issued in the current transaction if the issuance price had been the Existing Conversion Price for an outstanding series of preferred stock. In other words, you divide the amount of money invested in the transaction that triggered this anti-dilution protection by the Existing Conversion Price to determine how many shares would have been issued if the transaction had been priced at the Existing Conversion Price. The denominator in this fraction is the sum of the number of shares outstanding plus the number of shares that are actually issued in the transaction that triggered this anti-dilution protection. Remember, this price protection anti-dilution adjustment applies only when new shares are issued at a price below the Existing Conversion Price.

Reduced to its essence, the left half of the fraction in both the numerator and denominator is simply the total number of shares outstanding, which represents the "weighted" part of the formula. This part of the fraction puts the magnitude of the new share issuance into the context of the company's existing capitalization.

On the other hand, the right half of the fraction addresses the number of shares that *should have been issued* if the issuance price had been the Existing Conversion Price versus the number of shares that are *actually issued* in the triggering share issuance. We look at the number of shares that "SHUDDA" been issued at the Existing Conversion Price because that is the lowest price that does not trigger an adjustment. What we are comparing, then, is the number of shares that SHUDDA been issued at the lowest permitted price versus what actually happens in the share issuance by the company.

Thus a translation of this formula that might make it easier to remember is:

$$\text{NCP} = \text{ECP times} \quad \frac{\text{\# Shares Outstanding plus \# SHUDDA Shares}}{\text{\# Shares Outstanding plus \# Actual Shares}}$$

Example 9.26-A: Broad-Based Weighted Average Formula Conversion Price Adjustments. Let's run some numbers through this formula in order to see how this form of anti-dilution protection actually works. Assume that the weighted average formula anti-dilution adjustment rights of Series A Preferred Stock investor SoCal Ventures and Series B Preferred Stock investor LAVC are being triggered by SoftCo's financing transaction with Lemonade Ventures. In that transaction, described in Example 9.20-B and Fig. 9.19, Lemonade Ventures is purchasing 9 million shares (the formula's Actual Shares) for $3 million, or $0.33 per share (9 million shares divided by $3 million investment). Because the existing preferred stock series have not had any previous Conversion Price adjustments, their Conversion Prices are equal to their Original Issue Prices; thus the Series A Preferred Stock Conversion Price is $2.00 and the Series B Preferred Stock Conversion Price is $5.00 (in our formula, this represents the ECP for each investor). Immediately prior to the issuance of the Series C Preferred Stock to Lemonade Ventures, we know that there were 6 million shares outstanding (in our formula, this is the # Shares Outstanding).

Looking first at the Series A Preferred Stock, we work through the formula for the price adjustment triggered by this transaction as follows:

$$\text{NCP} = \text{ECP times} \quad \frac{\text{\# Shares Outstanding plus \# SHUDDA Shares}}{\text{\# Shares Outstanding plus \# Actual Shares}}$$

$$\text{NCP} = \$2.00 \text{ times} \quad \frac{6 \text{ million shs} + (\$3 \text{ million divided by } \$2.00) \text{ shs}}{6 \text{ million shs} + 9 \text{ million shs}}$$

$$\text{NCP} = \$2.00 \text{ times} \quad \frac{6 \text{ million shs} + 1.5 \text{ million shs}}{15 \text{ million shs}}$$

$$\text{NCP} = \$2.00 \text{ times} \quad \frac{7.5 \text{ million shs}}{15 \text{ million shs}}$$

$$\text{NCP} = \$2.00 \text{ times} \quad \frac{1}{2}$$

$$\text{NCP} = \$1.00$$

Knowing that the New Conversion Price is $1.00, we now can calculate the New Conversion Rate for the Series A Preferred Stock, using the same formula we previously used:

$$\text{New Conversion Rate} = \frac{\text{Original Issue Price}}{\text{New Conversion Price}}$$

$$\text{New Conversion Rate} = \frac{\$2.00}{\$1.00}$$

$$\text{New Conversion Rate} = 2$$

As a result of its weighted average anti-dilution protection, each share of the Series A Preferred Stock now converts into two shares of common stock rather than one. With 2 million shares outstanding, the Series A Preferred Stock now converts into 4 million shares of common stock. As we saw in Example 9.25-A, the full ratchet formula moved the Conversion Rate from 1 to 6 (compare Figs. 9.25 and 9.26), whereas it moved only to 2 using a broad-based, weighted average formula for anti-dilution price protection.

PROBLEM

Use the same steps to calculate the Conversion Price adjustment for the Series B Preferred Stock triggered by the $3 million financing transaction with Lemonade Ventures. Recall that there are 2 million shares of Series B Preferred Stock outstanding with an Original Issue Price of $5.00 and, prior to the Lemonade Ventures transaction, it converted on a one-for-one basis. What is the new Series B Preferred Stock Conversion Price? What is the resulting new Conversion Rate? How many shares of common stock will the post-adjustment Series B Preferred Stock convert into? *Hint:*

$$\text{NCP} = \text{ECP} \text{ times} \ \frac{\text{\# Shares Outstanding plus \# SHUDDA Shares}}{\text{\# Shares Outstanding plus \# Actual Shares}}$$

and

$$\text{New Conversion Rate} = \frac{\text{Original Issue Price}}{\text{Conversion Price}}$$

As you work through this problem, you will note that because the Existing Conversion Price of the Series B Preferred Stock was higher than for the Series A Preferred Stock (i.e., $5.00 versus $2.00), the application of the broad-based anti-dilution adjustment formula to the Series B Preferred Stock produces a bigger difference between the SHUDDA shares and the Actual shares. Consequently, it yields a larger adjustment than in the case of the Series A Preferred Stock.

However, a closer examination of these numbers provides some interesting observations about this form of anti-dilution protection. Because the 6 million shares outstanding and the 9 million shares actually being issued to Lemonade Ventures did not change in the adjustment calculations for the two existing series of preferred stock, the only difference in applying this formula was in the number of shares that SHUDDA been issued had the $3 million from Lemonade Ventures been invested in the company at the applicable Existing Conversion Price rather than at $0.33 per share. In applying the price adjustment formula to the Series A Preferred Stock, we see that the number of these shares (i.e., the "SHUDDA" number in the numerator of the fraction) is 1.5 million, while for the Series B Preferred Stock it is 600,000. The difference between these "SHUDDA" share numbers, which results from their different Existing Conversion Prices, forms the basis for the difference in the New Conversion Prices for each series.

The "weighted average" aspect of this formula comes from the fact that the new shares issued to Lemonade Ventures — which is the number reflected in the numerator at the ECP as the "SHUDDA" shares and in the denominator at the actual price as the "Actual" shares — are each being added to the total number of shares outstanding immediately prior to the transaction. If there had been only a few shares outstanding, then the financing with the Lemonade Ventures transaction would represent an even bigger portion of the company and, therefore, would be even more dilutive. Consequently, as we shall see next, a larger price protection anti-dilution adjustment would occur.

Example 9.26-B: Broad-Based Weighted Average Formula Conversion Price Adjustments.   Looking at the Series A Preferred Stock adjustment calculation, if instead of 6 million shares outstanding, SoftCo has only 3 million shares outstanding, the Lemonade Ventures transaction would be larger relative to SoftCo's existing capitalization, and the formula would work as follows:

$$NCP = \$2.00 \text{ times} \quad \frac{3 \text{ million shs} + (\$3 \text{ million divided by } \$2.00) \text{ shs}}{3 \text{ million shs} + 9 \text{ million shs}}$$

$$NCP = \$2.00 \text{ times} \quad \frac{3 \text{ million shs} + 1.5 \text{ million shs}}{12 \text{ million shs}}$$

$$NCP = \$2.00 \text{ times} \quad \frac{4.5 \text{ millions shs}}{12 \text{ million shs}}$$

$$NCP = \$2.00 \text{ times} \quad \frac{3}{8} \text{ or } 0.375$$

$$NCP = \$0.75$$

Applying the New Conversion Price of $0.75 to its Original Issue Price of $2.00, the New Series A Preferred Stock Conversion Rate would be:

$$\frac{\$2.00}{\$0.75} \quad \text{or } 2.6667, \text{ instead of } 2.$$

Thus we see that with a weighted average formula, the fewer shares outstanding prior to the transaction, the greater the impact of the transaction, and the price protection anti-dilution adjustment is larger.

PROBLEM

If instead of 6 million shares, SoftCo had 20 million shares outstanding immediately prior to the Lemonade Ventures investment, what would the Series A Preferred Stock's New Conversion Price be? What would the Series A Preferred Stock's New Conversion Rate be, and how many common stock equivalent shares would the Series A Preferred Stock now represent?

NOTE

In summary, Example 9.26-B and the Problem illustrate that, with fewer shares outstanding, the current issuance has more impact and the anti-dilution adjustment is larger. In contrast, with more shares outstanding, the current issuance has less impact and the anti-dilution adjustment is smaller. Thus the outcome of the weighted average share formula is driven by the price per share in the new financing transaction relative to the Existing Conversion Price of the outstanding preferred stock, and by the size of the new financing transaction relative to the existing capitalization of the company.

Turning our attention back to the Lemonade Ventures transaction with SoftCo, we see that, as a result of the adjustments made to their Conversion Rates by their weighted average anti-dilution protection, the Series A Preferred Stock and the Series B Preferred Stock now represent more common stock equivalent shares. The following chart reflects the impact on SoftCo's capitalization as a result of the anti-dilution adjustments that are triggered by Lemonade Ventures' investment:

Fig. 9.27 Lemonade Ventures investment with weighted average anti-dilution price protection

	SoftCo Pre-Money	SoftCo Post-Money without Adjustment	SoftCo Post-Money with Anti-Dilution Adjustment
Valuation	$2 million	$5 million	$5 million
Shares outstanding	6 million CSE shares: 2M common, 2M Series A = 2M CSE, 2M Series B = 2M CSE	15 million CSE shares: 2M common, 2M Series A = 2M CSE, 2M Series B = 2M CSE, 9M Series C = 9M CSE	19.54 million CSE shares: 2M common, 2M Series A = 4M CSE, 2M Series B = 4.54M CSE, 9M Series C = 9M CSE
Ownership	33.3% common 33.3% Series A 33.3% Series B	13.33% common 13.33% Series A 13.33% Series B 60% Series C	10.23% common stock 20.47% Series A 23.26% Series B 46.05% Series C

Fig. 9.27 shows that the anti-dilution adjustment significantly increases the existing preferred stock's relative ownership of SoftCo after the issuance of the Series C Preferred Stock to Lemonade Ventures. Compared to what their positions would have been without economic value anti-dilution protection, the Series A Preferred Stock's common stock equivalent ownership goes from 13.33 percent to 20.47 percent and the Series B Preferred Stock's goes from 13.33 percent to 23.26 percent. While neither set of investors went back to the 33.33 percent ownership interest that they had before the Lemonade Ventures investment, the dilutive impact of the "down round" on both was mitigated. Also, as previously noted, the higher-priced Series B Preferred Stock was more seriously affected by the transaction than the Series A Preferred Stock, and as a result, its Conversion Price adjustment was larger, so now the Series B Preferred Stock represents more common stock equivalent shares than the Series A Preferred Stock.

On the other hand, the common stock, which represented a 33.33 percent ownership interest in SoftCo before the Lemonade Ventures "down-round" financing and just 13.33 percent afterward, has been whacked still further by these anti-dilution adjustments and now has only a 10.23 percent interest. *Query:* The SoftCo common stock holders, Joan and Michael, have seen their ownership interests significantly diminish as a result of the "down round" and the prior investors' anti-dilution adjustments. How might this influence the founders' decision whether to support a "down round" of financing? Note the impact on the common stock resulting from the Lemonade Ventures investment versus the anti-dilution adjustment it triggers — which is more dilutive for Joan and Michael?

As a final observation, we see that the ownership interest being purchased by Lemonade Ventures is almost a quarter smaller, going from 60 percent to 46.05 percent as a result of the Conversion Rate adjustments to the existing preferred stock.

The bottom line is that Lemonade Ventures, like any new investor coming in at a low price, has to take into account the impact of any anti-dilution adjustment rights of the existing preferred stock when it negotiates and structures its financing transaction with the company. If the new investor prices its investment proposal with the understanding that it will end up with 46.05 percent of SoftCo's ownership after giving effect to the adjustments that are triggered by this new round of financing, then it will be ready to go forward. But if the new investor truly intends to end up with a 60 percent ownership interest in SoftCo, then it will inform SoCal Ventures and LAVC that its investment will be conditioned on their waiving their anti-dilution adjustments.

Often, the actual outcome of these negotiations lies somewhere in between. The negotiation in these circumstances can cover a range of ways to accommodate the existing and the new investors, including, among other things:

- allowing the existing preferred stock to keep some portion of its anti-dilution adjustment;
- inviting the existing preferred stock holders to put in more money in the current financing in order to maintain a larger ownership position by being both the dilutor as well as the diluted;
- allowing those existing holders who invest a minimum amount in the new financing to keep their anti-dilution adjustment, while requiring those that do not make that minimum investment to waive it;

- inviting the existing investors to make a separate, competing investment proposal; and
- restructuring the common stock position in the company to provide enough opportunity to make founder share ownership and employee equity incentives meaningful.

This last issue — concerning equity incentives for employees on a going-forward basis — can create an interesting negotiating dynamic, particularly if the existing preferred stock holders are suffering from "investor fatigue" and are not inclined to invest more funds, or perhaps are willing to invest only a small additional amount. What can happen in this situation is that the new investor and management can "gang up" on the company's existing shareholders. That is to say, on the facts of our hypothetical, Lemonade Ventures might tell SoftCo's management that it wants to support them and would like to include a large "refresh" of the employee option pool as a condition to its investment in the company. Of course, that share reservation for equity incentives would need to be built into the pre-money capitalization, which would make it dilutive to the existing shareholders rather than to Lemonade Ventures. That means that management's current interests would be diluted even more heavily, but they would get "topped up" (or "refreshed") by virtue of the new shares that will be available through the increase to the option pool, so the real impact from the additional dilution would be to the existing preferred stock holders and those common stock holders who are no longer with the company (and, hence, not eligible to be refreshed). So, for example, if Joan and Michael have moved on (or got pushed out) from SoftCo, they would not be eligible to participate in ongoing management equity incentive programs. If they left with a large portion of the common stock, existing management, whose equity incentive grants would be refreshed after the investment, would improve its relative position over Joan and Michael by going along with Lemonade Ventures and having the existing common stock owners take the brunt of the dilution.

Another interesting aspect of the negotiation dynamic in this context lies in obtaining the requisite approvals for the new round of financing. If the preferred stock holders have structured their voting rights well (we address voting rights in section F later in this chapter), their consent will be required in order for SoftCo to go forward with the creation and issuance of the Series C Preferred Stock. If they are not interested in investing more money, they may face the unappealing choice of either using their approval rights to block the deal, force a liquidation and thereby salvage what they can, or alternatively, allowing the investment to go forward, knowing that the value of their ownership in the company will be seriously diminished.

Comparing Broad-Based Weighted Average Formula Adjustments with Full Ratchet Anti-Dilution Adjustments.   By way of concluding our discussion of price protection anti-dilution, let's contrast the impact of broad-based weighted average adjustments with full ratchet adjustments. Recall Example 9.25-B, where SoftCo issued a $0.05 per share warrant to purchase 50,000 shares of common stock to a lender as an "equity sweetener." We saw that with a full ratchet, the Conversion Rate for the Series A Preferred Stock would have gone to 40, which would result in the Series A Preferred Stock then converting into 80 million shares of common stock.

Example 9.27: Comparing Anti-Dilution Adjustments.   Let's now contrast that outcome with what would have happened under the same circumstances immediately following the LAVC Series B Preferred Stock investment in SoftCo, assuming the Series B Preferred Stock had been granted a broad-based weighted average formula anti-dilution adjustment right. Since the Series B Preferred Stock's Existing Conversion Price would still be equal to its Original Issue Price, the ECP is $5.00. The total number of outstanding shares is 6 million and the number of shares being "issued" by the grant of the warrant is 50,000 at $0.05 per share, representing a total price of $2,500. The formula for the Series B Preferred Stock's Conversion Price adjustment would be:

$$\text{NCP} = \text{ECP times} \quad \frac{\text{\# Shares Outstanding plus \# SHUDDA Shares}}{\text{\# Shares Outstanding plus \# Actual Shares}}$$

$$\text{NCP} = \$5.00 \text{ times} \quad \frac{6 \text{ million shs} + (\$2{,}500 \text{ divided by } \$5.00) \text{ shs}}{6 \text{ million shs} + 50{,}000 \text{ shs}}$$

$$\text{NCP} = \$5.00 \text{ times} \quad \frac{6 \text{ million shs} + 500 \text{ shs}}{6{,}050{,}000 \text{ shs}}$$

$$\text{NCP} = \$5.00 \text{ times} \quad \frac{6{,}000{,}500 \text{ shs}}{6{,}050{,}000 \text{ shs}}$$

$$\text{NCP} = \$5.00 \text{ times} \quad 0.9918$$

$$\text{NCP} = \$4.9591$$

Knowing that the New Conversion Price for the Series B Preferred Stock is $4.9591, we now can determine its New Conversion Rate as follows:

$$\text{New Conversion Rate} = \frac{\text{Original Issue Price}}{\text{New Conversion Price}}$$

$$\text{New Conversion Rate} = \frac{\$5.00}{\$4.9591}$$

$$\text{New Conversion Rate} = 1.008247$$

This tells us that the number of common shares underlying the warrant is so small in relation to the existing capitalization of SoftCo that, using a weighted average formula adjustment, the Conversion Price for the Series B Preferred Stock would change only from $5.00 to $4.9591. This, in turn, would adjust the Series B Preferred Stock Conversion Rate from 1 to 1.008247. The 2 million shares of Series B Preferred Stock, previously convertible into 2 million common stock shares, now would convert into 2,016,494 shares. However, the 2 million Series A Preferred Stock shares, still assuming they had full ratchet price protection, would convert into 80 million shares.

This illustrates the dramatic differences that can result from a weighted average formula and a full ratchet. The first puts the new issuance into the overall context of the company's capitalization, while the second does not. In fact, given the trivial impact a small issuance might have, depending on the surrounding facts, most Charters providing for a weighted average formula also state that adjustments to a Conversion Price will not be made in an amount less than $0.01.

So, we see that weighted average formula anti-dilution protection is a partial remedy at best and that any anti-dilution adjustment is going to affect the ownership interest of some other investor. While the anti-dilution adjustment may be a right of the existing series of preferred stock, it frequently is not exercised as a result of a negotiation among the parties regarding the company's capitalization after the new investment.

"Common Stock Outstanding." Different Charter provisions may have different titles for this concept, but they all address the same thing, which is defining the number of shares outstanding or deemed outstanding that must be included in the left half of the weighted-average adjustment fraction. Recall that the adjustment formula is

$$\text{NCP} = \text{ECP times } \frac{\text{\# Shares Outstanding plus \# Shares Issuable at ECP}}{\text{\# Shares Outstanding plus \# Shares Actually Issued}}$$

In the Charter, immediately following the provisions of Charter Sample 9.26, which established the terms of the weighted average anti-dilution adjustment, this issue of what is counted as outstanding might be addressed as follows:

Charter Sample 9.28-A. For purposes of this subsection, the term "**Common Stock Outstanding**" shall mean and include the following: (1) outstanding Common Stock, (2) Common Stock issuable upon conversion of outstanding Preferred Stock, (3) Common Stock issuable upon exercise of outstanding stock options, (4) Common Stock issuable upon exercise (and, in the case of warrants to purchase Preferred Stock, conversion) of outstanding warrants, and (5) Common Stock issuable, whether directly or indirectly, upon the conversion, exercise, or exchange of any security of this corporation that may be outstanding from time to time, but without regard for any potential anti-dilution adjustments. Shares described in (1) through (5) above shall be included whether vested or unvested, whether contingent or non-contingent, and whether exercisable or not yet exercisable.

This defined term refers to "common stock" that is "outstanding"; however, it is important to read neither "common stock" nor "outstanding" literally. As we see from the text of Charter Sample 9.28-A, it means common stock *issued* or *issuable* (upon the conversion, exercise, or exchange of the described securities). This is another example of the "deemed outstanding" or "common stock equivalents" concept.

In our earlier Example 9.20-B, involving Lemonade Venture's investment in SoftCo, it was fairly easy to determine the common stock outstanding (using the definition above) because there were 2 million common stock shares and 4 million preferred stock shares (all convertible one-for-one) outstanding immediately prior to this round of financing. Therefore, we simply included 6 million in the numerator and denominator (as the "number of shares outstanding") in order to make up the left half of the fraction and moved on to focus on the right half of the fraction. But what happens to the left side of this fraction if we make the facts more complicated by assuming that SoftCo had employee incentive options, or warrants, or some convertible debt outstanding? The outcome will turn on the Charter's definition of "Common Stock Outstanding."

Charter Sample 9.28-A presents a "broad-based" definition of "Common Stock Outstanding." In essence, it provides that you count every common stock share outstanding, plus every share issuable as a consequence of an outstanding security, as of the date immediately prior to the adjustment-triggering transaction. Why? Because the numbered items (1) though (4) in Charter Sample 9.28-A refer to securities that existed as of the date the Charter containing the quoted provision became effective, and item (5) sweeps up anything else. Moreover, the last sentence of the provision makes it clear that any vesting or contingencies to exercise, convert, or exchange are to be ignored; if a security is outstanding as of the date immediately prior to the triggering transaction and it somehow translates into shares of common stock, you are to count those shares for purposes of this definition. This expansive determination of which securities are to be considered "outstanding" is what makes this adjustment approach "broad-based."

Interestingly, it is not as "broad-based" as it could be. Recall our discussion of shares "deemed" outstanding for valuation purposes in Chapter 8, section E.4. When a venture capital investor puts a valuation on a company, it counts as outstanding — in addition to all the shares identified in Charter Sample 9.28-A — the entire pool of common stock shares set aside for the equity incentive plan. The venture capital investor counts the entire pool, not just the options outstanding, as part of its determination of "fully diluted" or "deemed outstanding" shares. By deeming those shares as outstanding, the venture capital fund makes the company's existing ownership look larger, which makes the ownership interest it is to receive look smaller.

However, in the context of anti-dilution protection, the venture capital investor is negotiating a bigger adjustment for itself by having a smaller number of shares deemed outstanding. Pursuant to Charter Sample 9.28-A, the common stock shares reserved for the employee option pool are ignored, and we are to count only the shares issuable upon exercise of options that are actually outstanding. These inconsistent treatments simply reflect the bargaining power of the party with money (i.e., the venture capital investor) versus the party that needs money (i.e., the company) and further illustrate why it is extremely important that lawyers read these documents very carefully in order to be sure that they understand how all the pieces fit together.

"Common Stock Outstanding" — Multiple Closings.   Since the shares included in the left half of the adjustment formula fraction set the "weight" of the weighted average, a variation on the "Common Stock Outstanding" definition adds language addressing how to count the shares issued in a transaction that calls for *multiple closings*. In other words, how should we handle the adjustment in the situation where the lower-priced security is being sold on more than one date, but at the same price and under the same terms as part of the same overall financing transaction? If investors in a round of financing are to put their money into the company at more than one time, so the transaction has, for example, two closings, should you run the anti-dilution formula as of the date of each closing? To do so would reduce the adjustment at the second closing because of the increase in the Common Stock Outstanding resulting from the first closing. A more accurate approach might, therefore, be to revisit the entire adjustment at the later closing, re-running the formula as though all the new shares had been issued as of the date of the first closing. Charter language addressing this common problem could be added at the end of the "Common Stock Outstanding" definition and might read as follows:

Charter Sample 9.28-B. For purposes of adjusting the Conversion Price of a series of Preferred Stock, the grant, issue or sale of Additional Stock consisting of the same class of security issued or issuable at the same price at two or more closings held within a six-month period shall be aggregated and shall be treated as one sale of Additional Stock occurring on the earliest date on which such securities were granted, issued or sold.

As a final note, the language in item (5) of Charter Sample 9.28-A specifically excludes from the count of outstanding shares the effect of "any potential anti-dilution adjustments." This is an important concept. As we saw when we ran the formulas for each outstanding series of SoftCo's preferred stock, we treated the adjustment for each preferred stock series as a stand-alone event and separately calculated the adjustment for each series. In short, to fill in the fraction in the weighted average anti-dilution adjustment formula, you must take a snapshot of the company's capitalization immediately before the share issuance that triggers the adjustment and look at the terms of the below-price issuance, but you ignore any other adjustments that may be taking place to any other series of preferred stock because of the same investment transaction.

On the other hand, if there has been a prior anti-dilution adjustment made to a security, then, of course, you must take that into account when filling in the formula because it reflects the capitalization of the company as of immediately prior to the current financing transaction. But potential adjustments, such as those mentioned in item (5), as well as simultaneous adjustments triggered by the same transaction, must be ignored. The consequence of setting up a structure that flaunts this rule is an endless series of adjustments — the change made to one series is counted when adjusting the other, and that change in turn increases the first series' adjustment, which in turn increases the adjustment for the second series, and so on to infinity.

Narrow-Based Weighted Average Formula Anti-Dilution Adjustments. Having explored broad-based adjustments, it should be no surprise that a "narrow-based" weighted average formula is pretty much the same, except the definition of "Common Stock Outstanding" simply is narrower. As we have seen, by decreasing the "weight" part of the fraction (i.e., by having fewer shares "outstanding"), the transaction that "triggers" the adjustment is relatively larger, which means the adjustment to be made is larger.

As a practical matter, there is no norm or convention for the definition of "outstanding shares" as that term is used in narrow-based formulas. Probably the most typical definition just counts actually outstanding shares, including shares issuable upon "price-less conversion" of outstanding securities (meaning conversion or exchange without payment), but ignoring options or warrants. This usually represents a fairly mild cutback from a broad-based formula, since companies typically do not have a substantial number of options and warrants outstanding.

More dramatically, some narrow-based formulas treat as outstanding *only* the shares of the series of preferred stock that is to be adjusted. Under this formulation, the idea is that the existing investor sees the price of the new issuance as being the price that should have applied to *its* round, so a weighted average price of the two rounds is a fair adjustment.

Example 9.29: Narrow-Based Weighted Average Formula Anti-Dilution Adjustments. Looking back at the conversion adjustment that we did in Example 9.25-A for

SoftCo's Series A Preferred Stock that was triggered by the Lemonade Ventures investment, recall that, with a full ratchet adjustment, the Series A Preferred Stock Conversion Rate increased from 1 to 6. When we re-ran the anti-dilution adjustment in Example 9.26 using a broad-based weighted average formula based on 6 million outstanding shares, we ended up with the Conversion Rate increasing from 1 to 2. Now, let's consider what would happen if SoftCo's Charter provided that the Series A Preferred Stock had anti-dilution protection based on a narrow-based formula that treated only the 2 million shares of Series A Preferred Stock as being outstanding:

$$NCP = \$2.00 \text{ times } \frac{2 \text{ million shs} + (\$3 \text{ million divided by } \$2.00) \text{ shs}}{2 \text{ million shs} + 9 \text{ million shs}}$$

$$NCP = \$2.00 \text{ times } \frac{2 \text{ million shs} + 1.5 \text{ million shs}}{11 \text{ million shs}}$$

$$NCP = \$2.00 \text{ times } \frac{3.5 \text{ million shs}}{11 \text{ million shs}}$$

$$NCP = \$2.00 \text{ times } .318182$$

$$NCP = \$0.636364$$

Knowing the New Conversion Price is $0.636364, we now can adjust the New Conversion Rate for the Series A Preferred Stock as follows:

$$\text{New Conversion Rate} = \frac{\text{Original Issue Price}}{\text{New Conversion Price}}$$

$$\text{New Conversion Rate} = \frac{\$2.00}{\$0.636364}$$

$$\text{New Conversion Rate} = 3.142855$$

With this narrow-based formula, we see that the Conversion Rate for the Series A Preferred Stock adjusted not to 2, but to approximately 3.14. This is clearly a better outcome for SoCal Ventures as the Series A Preferred Stock holder, but whether it would actually happen is still subject to the practical limitations on the exercise of anti-dilution rights we previously have discussed.

What is counted as outstanding for a narrow-based formula, as suggested, can be pretty arbitrary. In addition to the approaches noted above, some narrow-based anti-dilution formulas count the series of preferred stock being adjusted and the common stock that is actually outstanding. In general, there really is no logical basis for using these alternatives other than they make for a larger conversion adjustment and thus may be requested by an investor.

When presented with an anti-dilution formula, it is imperative that an attorney understand how to use it and be comfortable with what is and is not to be included in the calculation. From the company's point of view, the broader the base the better. An investor, however, is benefited by having a narrower base of "outstanding" shares. Despite that benefit, the overwhelming majority of venture capital deals are done with broad-based weighted average anti-dilution formulas. This may be recognition by investors that these adjustments, while they are actually used from time to time, more often are renegotiated when a new transaction is being structured, so there is no reason to make them a crucial deal point. It is important to emphasize that the mere fact that an anti-dilution right exists generally will assure that the prior preferred stock investors will have a seat at the table when a "down-round" financing is imminent, which often is all they really want.

QUESTIONS

1. In reviewing the Charter Samples, Examples, and Problems in the preceding discussion of economic value anti-dilution adjustments, or price protection, we saw at least part of the possible range of outcomes in Example 9.29. There, after previously determining the Series A Preferred Stock's adjustment upon the Lemonade Ventures investment under a full ratchet and a broad-based weighted average formula, we calculated the adjustment resulting from a narrow-based weighted average formula. Which approach strikes you as the most reasonable? The most intellectually sound? Do you come to the same answer for each of those questions? Why?

2. The preceding question assumes that price protection anti-dilution adjustments actually do have a logical underpinning. An investor would support price protection by arguing that it invests in the company based on the company's projections of what the company can do to be successful and how long it would take. Economic value anti-dilution protection only applies when the company so completely fails to hit its projections that, despite the money invested and spent, the company actually ends up being worth less. In that case, investors would argue, the most likely reason is that the company misrepresented (as a business matter, if not in the legal sense) its potential and the time and money needed to achieve that potential. In that light, is some price protection for the investor in the event of a later "down-round" financing appropriate? What other factors might prevent a company from reaching its potential in the projected time frame?

3. Contrast the appropriateness of economic value anti-dilution protection with the proportionate adjustments applicable upon common stock splits and reverse stock splits. Which is easier for you to intellectually support?

Triggering Price Anti-Dilution Adjustments — "Additional Shares of Common Stock." Having looked at the approaches for economic value, or price, anti-dilution protection, the final issue to address is what type of transaction will trigger the adjustment, and what will not. The answer generally is that the adjustment is triggered by an issuance of "Additional Shares of Common Stock" at a price below the then-current Conversion Price of a series of preferred stock. The key, then, is the definition of *Additional Shares of Common Stock* (also called *Additional Stock* or other similar term). Understanding this definition can be tricky because it operates in the negative by detailing the exceptions to the transactions that trigger an adjustment. In short, it provides that "Additional Stock" means everything *except* shares described on the stated list, which itemizes the issuances that are to be *excluded* from those that constitute anti-dilution trigger events. A usual provision might read as follows:

> **Charter Sample 9.30.** "**Additional Stock**" shall mean any shares of Common Stock issued (or deemed to have been issued pursuant to [the terms of this Charter]) by this corporation on or after the Filing Date *other than*:
>
> (A) Common Stock issued pursuant to a split or stock dividend transaction resulting in a proportionate Conversion Price adjustment as provided herein;
>
> (B) Common Stock issued to employees, directors, consultants and other service providers for the primary purpose of soliciting or retaining their services pursuant to plans or agreements approved by this corporation's Board of Directors and designated by this corporation's Board of Directors (whether before or after the issuance) as meeting the requirements of this subsection (B);
>
> (C) Common Stock issued pursuant to a Qualified Public Offering;
>
> (D) Common Stock issued pursuant to the conversion of the Preferred Stock or the conversion or exercise of convertible or exercisable securities outstanding on the Filing Date;
>
> (E) Common Stock issued or deemed issued as a result of a decrease in the Conversion Price of any series of Preferred Stock resulting from the operation of [the anti-dilution adjustment provisions of this Charter triggered by the same Additional Stock];
>
> (F) Common Stock issued in connection with a bona fide business acquisition of or by this corporation, whether by merger, consolidation, sale of assets, sale or exchange of stock or otherwise, approved by this corporation's Board of Directors and designated by this corporation's Board of Directors (whether before or after the issuance) as meeting the requirements of this subsection (F);
>
> (G) Common Stock issued pursuant to any equipment leasing arrangement or debt financing from a bank or similar institution approved by this corporation's Board of Directors and designated by this corporation's Board of Directors (whether before or after the issuance) as meeting the requirements of this subsection (G); or
>
> (H) Common Stock issued to any entity as a part of a business relationship with that entity in pursuance of a joint venture, licensing or other cooperative arrangement; a supply, distribution or manufacturing arrangement; or other strategic arrangement not for the purpose of raising capital; the terms of such arrangement having been approved by this corporation's Board of Directors and designated by this corporation's Board of Directors (whether before or after the issuance) as meeting the requirements of this subsection (H).

Looking at this definition on a paragraph-by-paragraph basis, we start with the introductory language, which tells us that we are dealing with shares of Common Stock issued or deemed to have been issued on or after the Filing Date. Often, the Charter provision is not explicit about "deemed" issuances, so the fact that they are included has to be read into its terms.

The concept of when common stock is "deemed" to have been issued takes us back to our earlier discussion of the concept of "common stock equivalent." For anti-dilution adjustment purposes, common stock is deemed to have been issued when a security has been issued that is exercisable, convertible, or exchangeable into common stock (or into another security that is then exercisable, convertible, or exchangeable into common stock). When that security is issued — no matter how many intermediate steps may be required to be taken by the security holder in order to receive the actual common stock — the underlying common stock nonetheless is deemed to have been issued. In short, Additional Stock is new common stock that is issued or is deemed to be issued.

Having worked through some price protection weighted-average formula Conversion Price adjustments, we know that the information needed regarding the triggering transaction is how many shares were actually issued and what was the price per share. In a straightforward stock issuance, these numbers are obvious. However, because of the potential complexity and variation in the terms of the equity securities that a company might issue, a Charter's anti-dilution provisions entitled *Deemed Issuances of Additional Stock* or the like, which sets out when Additional Stock are deemed to have been issued, and *Determination of Consideration* or the like, which sets out what the price per share is for the deemed-issued shares, can run on for several pages. These provisions must address a broad range of variables, such as what happens if the share numbers or prices are subject to adjustment or to contingencies, or if, for example, a warrant causing a deemed issuance expires without the share issuance actually occurring.

The other important element of this introductory paragraph is that it limits Additional Stock to issuances (or deemed issuances) that take place after the "Filing Date." As noted earlier in this chapter, as part of our discussion of Charter Sample 9.22, the Filing Date (the time also may be the preferred stock's "Original Issue Date," should the Charter be filed some time prior to the preferred stock transaction) cuts off adjustments for past events as of that defined time. The idea is that prior adjustments to outstanding series of preferred stock are either waived or have been built into the Conversion Prices of those series and, therefore, have been incorporated into the terms of this particular version of the company's Charter. Accordingly, as for adjustments, we are to look only to post-Filing (i.e., future) events.

It is important to define this concept of the "Filing Date" with care. If it is the filing date of the current Charter amendment, are there any other intended share issuances scheduled between the time of the Charter filing and the issuance of the newly created preferred stock? That time gap is normally only a few days, but in a recapitalization transaction, for example, share issuances that are part of the same transaction may occur prior to the preferred stock issuance. If so, it would be unfortunate if those planned issuances were to unintentionally trigger an anti-dilution adjustment. Also, if the Charter designates this measurement date as the preferred stock's "Original Issue Date," and new preferred stock is to be issued in a transaction that contemplates more than one closing, it must be clear that "Original Issue Date" means the first issuance of shares of that series of preferred stock, so that all shares of that series will wind up receiving equal anti-dilution treatment.

Paragraph (A) of Charter Sample 9.30 excludes from "Additional Stock" issuances resulting from a common stock split or dividend payable in common stock that has already resulted in a proportionate adjustment to the preferred stock Conversion Price. Having been addressed separately, those share issuances do not need to be included in the price protection adjustments.

Paragraph (B) excludes from "Additional Stock" options or rights, or the underlying common stock, issued under the terms of the company's equity incentive plan. These shares are excluded because they already were counted as being outstanding in the company valuation process that was used to price the preferred stock in this round of financing. To count them again as they actually are issued (or are deemed issued) pursuant to the terms of the company's plan would, in effect, constitute a "double dip." Further, the holders of the preferred stock generally agree that equity incentive plans are in the company's best interests, so increases in the number of shares reserved for the incentive plan often are included within this exemption.

One frequent Delaware variation of this exclusion is to require that not only the board of directors generally approve any increase in the shares reserved for an option plan, but also to require the approval of those directors designated in the Charter as elected by the holders of preferred stock. Their approval is treated as being an approximate proxy for approval by the holders of preferred stock. *See* Del. GCL §141(d) (providing for different voting powers for directors elected by different classes of shares). We describe voting rights that are typically granted to preferred stock in more detail in section F of this chapter. California and the Model Act provide no statutory authority for this type of variation in voting power among directors and, in fact, the California secretary of state will reject the filing of Articles of Incorporation that contain variations in the voting powers of directors. *See* Cal. Corp. Code §307(a)(8) (an act by a majority of the directors is an act of the board).

Paragraph (C) excludes from the "Additional Stock" definition shares that are issued as part of a Qualified Public Offering. A Qualified Public Offering is usually defined as a public offering at a per-share price at least several times higher than the Original Issue Price (and Conversion Price) of the most recent series of preferred stock. As a result, it very rarely is at a price below a preferred stock's Conversion Price, so this carve-out seldom comes into play as a practical matter.

Paragraph (D) excludes from the definition of "Additional Stock" those shares of common stock that were issued upon the conversion or exercise of any convertible or exercisable security that was outstanding when the current version of the Charter was filed. As was the case with the shares that were reserved for the employee stock option plan, these shares were included in the pre-money capitalization when the preferred stock was priced, so counting them again when the underlying common stock actually is issued would again constitute a "double dip." Issuances of convertible or exercisable securities *after* the "Filing Date" are "deemed issuances" of common stock and, therefore, will trigger an anti-dilution adjustment if the consideration payable per share of issuable common stock is below the Conversion Price of an outstanding series of a preferred stock. But the later issuance of the underlying common stock shares will be ignored, given that the anti-dilution adjustment has already occurred.

Paragraph (E) excludes from "Additional Stock" any deemed issuances resulting from anti-dilution adjustments. As previously noted following the discussion of Example 9.28, allowing an adjustment to one series of preferred stock to trigger an adjustment to another series would lead to an endless series of adjustments to both. There, we saw that anti-dilution adjustments to other preferred stock triggered by a present transaction were not included in the definition of "Common Stock Outstanding," as shown in Charter Sample 9.28. Paragraph (E) of Charter Sample 9.30 is a parallel provision specifically providing that new common stock shares deemed issued as a result of an anti-dilution adjustment to another preferred stock will not trigger an anti-dilution adjustment. However, as was also previously noted, the increased shares issuable upon the conversion of a series of preferred stock as a result of an anti-dilution adjustment usually will be part of the broad-based "Common Stock Outstanding" of the company for purposes of a *subsequent* anti-dilution calculation.

Paragraph (F) excludes from "Additional Stock" any issuance of the company's securities in connection with an acquisition. The modifier "bona fide" probably is an effort to distinguish a financing transaction structured as an acquisition from an acquisition that advances the strategic objectives of the company. Share issuances in acquisitions conserve cash and frequently are issued in exchange for consideration that is difficult to value. While this carve-out is often used, it typically has size or other qualifiers added so that if the acquisition transaction is material in size, the preferred stockholders affirmatively would have to waive their anti-dilution protection.

Paragraphs (G) and (H) each excludes from the definition of "Additional Stock" those share issuances or deemed issuances that occur as part of some strategic relationship or other business action taken by the company. These events are excluded because they often are relatively small issuances, are fundamental to the company's business strategy, and, therefore, are generally undertaken in the best interests of the company. Moreover, these issuances or deemed issuances are often linked to additional consideration that may be quite difficult to value.

The potentially open-ended nature of the exclusions presented in paragraphs (F), (G), and (H) often leads to terms providing additional safeguards for the preferred stock including, for Delaware corporations, the separate approval of the directors elected by the holders of preferred stock. An additional provision used from time to time is a clause setting a maximum number of shares that may be issued individually or collectively under these (or other identified) exemptions.

These definitional carve-outs truly represent a key element of a Charter's anti-dilution protections. From the lawyer's perspective, these provisions must be read carefully in order to avoid a transaction that would inadvertently trigger a right to an adjustment. When a company has venture capital preferred stock outstanding and is engaging in *any* transaction where a securities issuance or a right to a securities issuance is involved, company counsel must carefully review the "Additional Shares of Common Stock" definition in the company's Charter.

NOTES

1. At some point, most every junior corporate lawyer falls afoul of "Additional Shares of Common Stock," or comes close to doing so. For example, paragraph (B) of Charter Sample 9.30 is broadly worded and forgiving. It provides that virtually any equity incentive arrangement designated by the board as not triggering an anti-dilution adjustment is excluded from "Additional Shares of Common Stock." On the other hand, this provision could refer only to equity incentives issued pursuant to the terms of a specific plan. It might limit its terms to equity incentives granted to employees. Or, it might limit equity incentive grants to a maximum aggregate number of shares. An attorney who "knows how these things work" and fails to check the applicable provision in the Charter, at some point will trip over an unexpected restriction.

The result will require some serious explaining — to the company, the company's shareholders, the law firm, and perhaps the malpractice insurance company.

2. Paragraph (G) of Charter Sample 9.30 excludes from "Additional Shares of Common Stock" any issuances in connection with a debt or leasing arrangement with an institutional lender. Occasionally, the Charter provision on this subject is not limited to banks or other institutions. In that circumstance, a loan by insiders, with a large, cheap equity issuance attached to it, would not trigger an anti-dilution adjustment.

Anti-Dilution Rights — Conclusion. Charter provisions establishing anti-dilution protections for holders of preferred stock can be complicated and lengthy because they have to address a wide range of contingencies. The elements that are most heavily negotiated between the parties are generally the items to be excluded from the price protection triggering events by virtue of being carved out of the Charter's definition of Additional Stock, or other similar definition. Occasionally, the nature of the price protection adjustment (i.e., weighted-average formula versus full ratchet) will be an issue, but overwhelmingly, across the United States, venture capital investors accept broad-based weighted average formula protection. *See* FENWICK & WEST VENTURE CAPITAL SURVEY (2nd Quarter, 2013) *available at* http://www.fenwick.com/publications/Pages/Silicon-Valley-Venture-Survey-Second-Quarter-2013.aspx; and VALUATION AND DEAL TERM DATABASE — DEAL ANALYSIS (2nd Quarter 2013), from Private Equity Data Center — A VCExperts.com Product, *available at* http://pedatacenter.com. Proportionate adjustments protecting the preferred stock's participation right are virtually always seen as non-controversial, mechanical corrections whose substantive terms do not vary.

From the perspective of the lawyer in reviewing the conversion and anti-dilution sections of the Charter, it is important that the document make clear that the price protection adjustments apply *only* when a new share issuance (or deemed issuance) is at a price below the then-effective Conversion Price of a series of preferred stock. The Charter also must specify clearly what shares are included in the elements of the price protection adjustment formula (i.e., what is "outstanding") and what events constitute an issuance or deemed issuance that triggers the price protection adjustments. Finally, the Charter document also must allow for only one adjustment per issuance. While that adjustment may be modified by subsequent events, a share of common stock, no matter how many intermediate forms, conversions, or exercises it took to become that share, should be counted only once.

The remaining Charter provisions that deal with conversion and anti-dilution rights normally address how to deconstruct complex or layered transactions to determine the number of shares that were issued in a particular transaction and the effective price per share, as well as set forth certain procedural rights. Typically included among the latter provisions are the facts that the price protection anti-dilution adjustment only decreases, and never increases, a Conversion Price; adjustments of less than 1 cent are not recognized; and a formal notification of any Conversion Price adjustment (sometimes certified by the company's auditors) must be provided to all affected preferred stock holders.

E. Redemption Rights

Venture capital preferred stock may be issued with a *redemption right*, which means that the company either *may* or *must* repurchase all shares of the applicable series or class. Redemption is different from a contractual repurchase right that, for example, a company might receive as part of the share issuance agreement with a founder or employee. In contrast to that type of personal contract, which applies to specific shares based on the owner's identity and the company's relationship with that owner, a redemption right is set forth in the company's Charter and applies to all shares of a particular class or series of the company's stock.

1. The Statutory Treatment of Redemption

As touched on in the discussion of dividends earlier in section B.1 of this chapter, payments made to shareholders have the potential for upending the priority rights of those with senior claims on a corporation's assets, including debt-security holders, creditors generally, and holders of more senior equity securities. Consequently, most modern state corporation statutes specifically, if perhaps not clearly, address the circumstances in which a redemption may validly take place.

California and the Model Act. Like dividends of cash and property, under California law and the Model Act, a redemption falls within the general category of a "distribution to its shareholders" by a corporation. *See* Cal. Corp. Code §166; and Model Act §140. Both of these statutory schemes address the designation of shares as redeemable. *See* Cal. Corp. Code §402(a); and Model Act §6.01(c)(2). They also provide a set of rules, including solvency and financial statement tests, for validly completing any of these distributions to the company's shareholders. *See* Cal. Corp. Code §§500 *et seq.*; and Model Act §6.40.

Under §500(a) of the California Corporation Code, a redemption payment may be made out of retained earnings if:

> The amount of the retained earnings of the corporation immediately prior thereto equals or exceeds the amount of the proposed distribution.

Alternatively, the statute provides a balance sheet test: a redemption payment is permitted if, following the proposed payment, the assets of the corporation would be equal to or greater than its liabilities plus the amount of any distribution rights held by senior securities. *See* Cal. Corp. Code §500(b).

The California Corporations Code provides that the financial terminology it uses should be interpreted as those terms are defined under generally accepted accounting principles (GAAP) as promulgated by the Financial Accounting Standards Board (FASB), subject to certain specified treatments required by a particular statute. *See* Cal. Corp. Code §114. (The FASB is the U.S. accounting profession's self-regulatory group that establishes standards for appropriate accounting practices.) Section 500(c) of the California Corporations Code creates an exception to the application of GAAP for this balance sheet test by providing that a board of directors may use financial statements based on accounting practices deemed reasonable under the circumstances, a fair valuation, or any other method that is reasonable under the circumstances.

In addition, California applies an equitable solvency standard, prohibiting any corporation from making a distribution if the corporation:

> is, or as a result thereof would be, likely to be unable to meet its liabilities . . . as they mature.

Cal. Corp. Code §501.

The Model Act does not use retained earnings as a basis for making distributions to shareholders. Instead, it calls for a balance sheet test that prohibits a distribution if, afterwards:

> the corporation's total assets would be less than the sum of its total liabilities plus . . . the amount that would be needed, if the corporation were to be dissolved at the time of the distribution, to satisfy the preferential rights upon dissolution of shareholders whose preferential rights are superior to those receiving the distribution.

Model Act §6.40(c)(2).

The Model Act's balance sheet test is equivalent to California's test. The quoted Model Act section, consistent with the approach taken in California, also addresses the rights of a holder of a senior equity security by requiring the corporation to retain additional assets in excess of its liabilities sufficient to pay the liquidation preference of that senior security.

The Model Act also has an equitable solvency requirement, to the same effect as California's, that prohibits distributions if, afterwards:

> the corporation would not be able to pay its debts as they become due in the usual course of business. . . .

Model Act §6.40(c)(1).

The Model Act, however, does not adopt GAAP as the basis for its financial standards, providing instead that a corporation's board of directors may rely on financial statements that have been:

> prepared on the basis of accounting practices and principles that are reasonable in the circumstances or on a fair valuation or other method that is reasonable in the circumstances.

Model Act §6.40(d).

The Official Comments to §6.40 of the Model Act further clarify that a board of directors should in all circumstances be entitled to rely on financial statements prepared in accordance with GAAP, but the Act does not insist that this is the only appropriate standard.

Both these statutory approaches reflect a fairly modern view of corporate finance, particularly in their recognition of the usefulness of GAAP and the rejection of any attempt to create special financial standards by statute. As the overwhelming majority of companies prepare financial statements based on GAAP, these statutes apply the same information a company uses for its other operating and financial needs. Because accounting standards regularly evolve and statutes are amended only slowly, statutory standards soon become obsolete. In addition, to demonstrate compliance with special statutory accounting standards, particularly as GAAP financial accounting moves away from those standards, a company must maintain parallel financial records reflecting the statutory requirements, or at least prepare special financial statements applying statutory standards.

Delaware.   With respect to Delaware's statutory provisions regarding redemptions and other forms of stockholder distributions, we encounter one important disadvantage that is an (inevitable) by-product of a long-established body of corporate law. While the Delaware General Corporation Law ("Delaware GCL") is constantly evolving and frequently updated, it is grounded in a view of corporate finance that was developed in the 1899 version (or perhaps even earlier versions) of the law and, unfortunately, survived the significant 1967 revision of the Delaware GCL. Despite later clean-ups, Delaware's statutory provisions regarding stockholder distributions remain particularly challenging.

Delaware does not have a general concept of "distributions to stockholders," preferring instead to set out separate rules for dividends and redemptions. Accordingly, §151(b) of the Delaware GCL authorizes the creation of redemption rights with respect to a particular class or series of stock. Actually redeeming shares is authorized by §160(a), which prohibits a redemption if "the capital of the corporation is impaired" or if the redemption would cause it to become impaired. This statutory provision requires us first to understand what "capital" is, and, as a matter of Delaware corporate law, the answer is rooted in the archaic concept of "par value."

Under §154, absent action by the board of directors, the aggregate par value of the shares issued by a Delaware corporation constitutes the company's *capital*, and any additional amounts paid to the corporation for those shares is *surplus*. In other words, the difference between the amount paid for stock and its par value constitutes "surplus," although the board of directors may attribute more value to "capital" if it so desires. A corporation's board of directors may, from time to time, determine to increase "capital" by moving amounts from "surplus" to "capital," or it may reduce "capital" by moving "capital" value to "surplus," but it may only reduce "capital" when the assets of the corporation exceed its liabilities. *See* Del. GCL §§154, 244.

"Surplus" also includes the amount of *net assets* the corporation has in excess of its capital. "Net assets" are the amount by which total assets exceed total liabilities. If a stock purchaser paid $10 for shares with a $1 par value, the company would have assets of $10 in cash and a capital account of $1, hence its surplus would be $9. If the company then obligated itself to pay $5 in wages and taxes (which create no directly offsetting assets), its surplus would be reduced to $4.

A corporation's capital is impaired if it has a negative surplus. *See*, e.g., *In re International Radiator Co.*, 92 A. 255, 256 (Del. Ch. 1914). In other words, if, as a result of the company's business operations, a company has lost asset value or generated liabilities faster than it has created new assets, its surplus is decreased. Looking at a company from the perspective of the investment originally made by its stockholders, if the company's losses or liabilities are more than its surplus, the surplus will be consumed and its capital will be impaired. The end result is that redemption payments generally may be made only from surplus.

The problem with all this is that, in the modern world, par value is totally arbitrary. As a result, "surplus" — defined by Delaware statute as the payment for shares in excess of the par value of those shares — does not reconcile with "surplus," as customarily defined to be the excess of "net assets" over "capital." In other words, Delaware's statutory concepts of "capital" and "surplus" are not consistent with modern financial accounting. If, in the prior example, the par value were $10 instead of $1, the company's capital would become impaired when it lost its first penny instead of after it lost 90 percent of its net asset value. Despite there being no difference in the company's obligations or resources, if par value were set at $10, then any redemption would be prohibited, while if par value were set at $1, then redemptions would be permitted up to the remaining surplus.

It seems that the only issue many lawyers take into account when setting par value for a class or series of stock in Delaware is its impact on the state's franchise tax calculation, which rather than being a flat fee like many other states, is based on the par value (or an alternate imputed par value calculation) of a company's authorized shares. In the end, Delaware's "capital," "surplus," and "par value" approach is of very little use in determining whether a company has enough money to make a distribution to its stock holders and still meet its obligations to its creditors and senior security holders. Furthermore, this is the extent of Delaware's statutory scheme; there is no separate statutory provision addressing the need to maintain equitable solvency.

Returning to the language of §160(a) of the Delaware GCL, we see that, after setting the standard of "no capital impairment," the statute goes on to provide an exception for redemptions of preferred stock, which it says may be made from capital. However, §244(b) prohibits reductions in capital (that is, reductions in the "capital" account by the capital amount designated for the redeemed shares) when the company has no net assets (i.e., total assets are less than total liabilities). Furthermore, when a company is not permitted to reduce its capital, it also is prohibited from "retiring" its shares under §243(c) of the Delaware GCL. As redemption provisions typically provide that, once redeemed, the subject stock may not be reissued, they must be "retired" (in this case meaning eliminated from the company's authorized shares) and the company's capital reduced. Thus, it is not clear precisely what the §160(a) exception for preferred stock actually means, since it appears unusable. The better practice clearly would be that redemptions and other distributions to stock holders should be made only from surplus.

Having mastered the Delaware issues regarding redemptions, unfortunately, there is a final wrinkle specific to California. The wrinkle is the "quasi-California corporation" treatment of corporations incorporated in foreign jurisdictions but primarily doing business in California. Under this controversial doctrine, California applies its own financial sufficiency tests (*see* Cal. Corp. Code §§500 *et seq.*) to any corporation that it deems to have sufficient California contacts. *See* Cal. Corp. Code §2115. Thus, in the case of a "quasi-California corporation," before a dividend, redemption, or other distribution may be made to a shareholder, the lawyer (other than one who seeks the opportunity to create a test case on the enforceability of the quasi-California doctrine!) must analyze the company's compliance both with California's statutory standards as well as any tests applied by the company's jurisdiction of incorporation in order to determine the validity of the proposed distribution.

Potential Tax Issue with Redemption.   The price paid to redeem stock is usually expressed in relation to its (by now familiar) Original Issue Price and often is that amount, plus accumulated dividends or, where dividends do not cumulate, plus declared but unpaid dividends and a defined "redemption premium," which is basically an interest factor. Obviously, repayment of the original investment plus an interest factor makes redemption a very debt-like right.

The concept of a "redemption premium" takes us back to the issue of the historic debt-like nature of preferred stock. Recall the discussion in Chapter 8, section C.1, of the taxation of "earned" but unpaid interest on debt. Because traditional preferred stock is very debt-like in its rights, the IRS applies the same tax treatment it uses for interest on debt to distributions on traditional preferred stock in excess of a return of capital (i.e., in excess of repayment of the Original Issue Price). Thus, the IRS imputes income as a result of the premium to be paid upon redemption and assesses ordinary income tax on that imputed income over the life of the security. As a result, any holder of a form of traditional preferred stock, who is entitled to receive, for example, a compounded 8 percent per annum premium on redemption, would have to recognize the amount of that premium annually as ordinary income so long as the holder owns the shares. *See* IRC §305 and related regulations.

However, there are a couple of exceptions to that general rule. For our purposes, the most important of these exceptions hinges on whether the security receiving the distribution is treated by the IRS as "common stock" rather than "preferred stock." For this analysis, venture capital preferred stock wants to be treated as "common stock" because of the more favorable capital gains (versus ordinary income) tax treatment accorded to "common stock" by the IRS on returns in excess of the invested amount. For IRS purposes, a "preferred stock" means stock that is both preferred and limited in its equity-like rights. The key determining factor is the stock's ability to participate in the growth in value of the corporation (what we have been referring to as "the equity upside"). However, under IRS regulations, a conversion right is not sufficient to remove the venture capital preferred stock from the IRS' category of "preferred stock." From the perspective of the IRS, the conversion right does allow the preferred stock to change form (i.e., convert to common stock), but the issue is whether, in its preferred stock form, it provides any equity upside.

In contrast, if the preferred shares are granted a participation right on liquidation, the IRS views this as representing an element of equity upside while the preferred stock is still preferred stock. As such, the IRS views preferred stock with participation rights on liquidation as being sufficiently "equity-like" to take the preferred stock out of that "almost-debt" category and thus exempt it from taxation of earned but unpaid distributions. According to the terminology that the IRS uses, this results in treating venture capital preferred stock as "common stock" rather than as "preferred stock." *See* IRC §305 and related regulations.

This tax issue clearly argues against combining a redemption right with a non-participating liquidation preference. But what about capped liquidation participation? Will that be sufficient for the venture capital preferred stock to qualify for treatment by the IRS as "common stock"? Absent direct authority, it would probably be wise for that capped participation to be bundled together with a nice package of other participation rights in order to make sure that the IRS does not perceive the stock's equity-like rights as being too limited.

In short, when structuring a redeemable preferred stock, it is particularly important to take careful note of the stock's other preferences in order to avoid creating an inadvertent tax problem. The tax rules are complex and vary depending on the facts and circumstances of the redemption right and other preference rights, so whenever a redeemable preferred stock is contemplated, even if it does not appear to stray too far from the norm, it is highly advisable to consult with a tax expert, and this is true regardless of whether one is counsel to the company or to the investor.

2. Redemption as Part of Venture Capital Financing

Redemption rights are included in a significant minority of venture capital financings on the West Coast, ranging from 20 to 33 percent since the beginning of 2004, after a spike into the 40 percent range in the immediate aftermath of the collapse of the tech bubble. *See* Fenwick & West Venture Capital Survey (2d Quarter 2004 to 2nd Quarter 2013) (copies on file with authors). In contrast, a clear majority of venture capital deals on the East Coast include redemption rights. *See, e.g.,* Valuation and Deal Term Database — Deal Analysis (2nd Quarter 2013), from Private Equity Data Center — A VCExperts.com Product, *available at* http://pedatacenter.com; and David Broadwin's blog post *Redemption and Misunderstanding* (August 12, 2012), *available at* http://www.emergingenterprisecenterblog.com/deal-terms/redemption-and -misunderstanding (copy on file with authors). Regardless, for reasons that we review below, venture capital preferred stock is rarely actually redeemed.

Triggering a Redemption and Payment. A stock that is redeemable is to be repurchased by the issuing company, usually either at its instigation or at the instigation of the holders, at a defined future time (or during some future window of time), and at a defined price. Redemption also may be mandatory; that is, as of a particular date, the company *must* redeem the preferred stock. The form of consideration to be paid upon a redemption typically is not restricted by statute. Thus, the redemption price may be paid in cash, assets, securities, or debt, though typically it is paid in cash. *See* Del. GCL §160(a)(1); Cal. Corp. Code §180; and Model Act §6.01(c)(2)(ii).

The party or parties entitled to initiate a redemption, or the fact that a mandatory redemption will occur on a specified date, must be set forth in a company's Charter. California law provides that redemptions may be at the option of the corporation, upon the occurrence of a specified event, at the option of the holder, or upon the vote of at least a majority of the class (or series) of shares to be redeemed. *See* Cal. Corp. Code §402(a). Under the Model Act, redemption may be at the option of the corporation, the shareholder, another person (such as the company's shareholders), or upon the occurrence of a specific event. *See* Model Act §6.01(c)(2)(i). Under Delaware law, a redemption may occur at the option of the corporation or the holders of the redeemable shares, or upon the occurrence of a specified event. *See* Del. GCL §151(b).

There appears to be no meaningful distinction between these various statutory provisions. That is to say, they all provide for a *call* right on the part of the company that issued the shares, which simply means that the Charter's redemption provision may allow the company to *call the shares back from* the stock holders. They also provide for a *put* right, meaning the Charter may allow the holders of the stock to *put their shares back to* the company, thereby forcing the redemption to occur. The differences among the statutes regarding whether that put right belongs to an individual holder or all the holders of the shares (that is, whether it is a personal right or a group right) seem inconsequential since all of the statutes provide that a redemption may be triggered by the occurrence of a specified event. It is not difficult to draft a Charter provision to include the approval of a majority of the shares or the request of any individual share-holder as an event that triggers redemption.

Redemption as Leverage.   Once the parties to a venture financing transaction have agreed that the shares being issued will be redeemable, designating the party that will control the trigger has significant consequences. From the company's point of view, having the ability to "call" the preferred stock shares gives the company the power to impose its will on its shareholders by eliminating an entire class or series of stock. In contrast, allowing the shareholders to "put" their shares to the company gives the shareholders tremendous power to disrupt the financial viability of the business.

In the venture capital context, the preferred stock is rarely, if ever, redeemable at the option of the company. That outcome would be totally unacceptable to the venture capital investors. They would not want the company to have the right to buy out their shares for merely their original investment amount plus an interest factor. In fact, it is where the company has the financial strength to afford to pay the price of redemption that the investors particularly do not want to be redeemed. Under those circumstances, the company, by definition, has achieved a certain level of success. Given that success, rarely would the redemption price on the preferred stock be as attractive an exit as selling the business or taking the company public.

Instead, the investors want to keep for themselves the ability to control the potential demand for a redemption of their shares. They want that authority in order to potentially exercise the right, not when the company is doing well, but when the company is struggling. Even then, they do not want the company actually to redeem their shares. Instead, the preferred stock holders just want management to have to face the fact that the preferred stock holders have the *power* to force the company to redeem their shares.

In point of fact, preferred stock holders generally use their right of redemption as a threat to push management to build the company to an acceptable exit or face the consequences. Traditionally, exit strategies consist of an IPO (i.e., "going public") or, alternatively, a sale of the company. Redemption rarely presents an attractive mechanism for the preferred stock investors to achieve their exit. In reality, a cash redemption of the preferred stock would be a practical impossibility for most rapidly growing companies. These companies consume large amounts of cash in order to pay for the growth of their businesses — indeed, their need for cash was the reason they took money from the venture capital investors in the first place.

Even for those companies that could afford it, redemption usually would consume a large portion of the company's cash on hand and, therefore, would be tremendously disruptive to its business. So, as a practical matter, venture capital investors use the prospect of forcing a redemption to drive management towards accomplishing an orderly sale of the company. *Query:* Looking back to Chapter 8, why would a redemption be an undesirable choice for a venture capital preferred stock investor?

3. *Redemption Provisions in the Charter*

The Authority to Redeem.   A Charter provision providing for redemption of a series of preferred stock when the redemption right is held by the holders might contain the following terms:

Charter Sample 9.31. The Series A Preferred Stock shall be redeemed as follows:

From and after [five years from the issuance date], upon the written approval of the holders of at least two thirds (2/3) of the shares of Series A Preferred Stock then outstanding, the Corporation shall redeem all the Series A Preferred Stock then outstanding. The holders of at least two thirds (2/3) of the shares of Series A Preferred Stock shall demand redemption by delivery of a written notice to the Corporation demonstrating the requisite level of approval for such redemption (the "**Redemption Notice**"). Within fifteen (15) days after the date of receipt of a Redemption Notice (the "**Date of Receipt**"), the Corporation shall deliver written notice to all holders of Series A Preferred Stock informing each such holder of (1) the receipt of such Redemption Notice, (2) the Date of Receipt, (3) the number of shares of Series A Preferred Stock held by each holder thereof and therefore subject to redemption, (4) the total number of shares of Series A Preferred Stock outstanding as of the Date of Receipt, and (5) the date upon which the redemption is to take place (the "**Redemption Date**"), which shall be within ninety (90) days of the Date of Receipt. At the Corporation's option, the redemption may take place in up to four (4) equal installments, each proportionately applied among the holders of the Series A Preferred Stock, with the first installment taking place on the Redemption Date and the additional three (3) installments occurring every one hundred eighty (180) days following the initial Redemption Date (the time of each installment shall be an additional "**Redemption Date.**") The shares of Series A Preferred Stock so redeemed are referred to herein as the "**Redemption Shares.**" The Corporation shall redeem the Redemption Shares at a price per share equal to the Original Purchase Price of the Series A Preferred Stock (as adjusted for stock splits, stock dividends, combinations and the like), plus any declared but unpaid dividends, if any, for each such share as of the applicable Redemption Date, plus a redemption premium sufficient to yield an eight percent (8%) annually compounded return from [the date of the first issuance of Series A Preferred Stock] to the applicable Redemption Date (the "**Redemption Price**"). The Corporation shall pay for shares redeemed hereunder by delivery of cash in the amount of the Redemption Price on the respective Redemption Dates to a designated trust account, to be held there awaiting surrender of the certificates representing the Redemption Shares.

In venture capital financings, redemption usually is triggered by the request of the holders of a majority (or a supermajority) of the redeemable preferred stock and then applied to *all* the shares on a pro-rata basis. Venture capital investors, in order to manage, as well as to maximize, the power to require the company to repurchase their shares, typically want to exercise that right collectively. If the right were held by individual shareholders, a minority of holders requesting redemption could cause a "run on the bank" and deplete the assets of the company, despite the desires of a majority of the preferred stock holders.

An alternative would be a true mandatory redemption, where the Charter would state that, as of a particular date, the company *shall* redeem the preferred stock. This is not frequently used because it is inflexible and the large cash outflow requirement may inhibit the company's ability to raise equity from future investors or to borrow. In addition, investors are uncomfortable with mandatory redemption because in a situation where the company is doing well it may require them to convert, losing their preferred status, to avoid being bought out at a relatively low price. Venture capital investors usually want the discretion to delay the timing of a redemption and, if a mandatory approach is used, often will couple it with a provision allowing for a waiver or postponement of the redemption upon the requisite vote of a majority (or super-majority) of the redeemable preferred stock.

In the first sentence of Charter Sample 9.31, the words in brackets give the time period during which the stock may be redeemed, providing that redemption may only take place five years after the initial issuance of Series A Preferred Stock. Five years is a typical length of time because it is long enough to make the investment "permanent," and therefore equity-like, rather than "temporary" and more debt-like. Note that this provision is completely open-ended. For however long the Series A Preferred Stock remains outstanding after the fifth anniversary of its issuance, the holders are permitted to act on their redemption right. A typical alternative is to give the holders a window of opportunity when they can exercise the right, for example a year (or two years) after the fifth anniversary of the issuance of the shares.

After a description of the specific process the company must follow to carry out the redemption, Charter Sample 9.31 defines "Redemption Date" and then provides that redemption may take place in up to four equal installments 180 days apart, creating four "Redemption Dates" over an eighteen-month period. Some provisions require full redemption on one date, while others provide for scheduled installments that may extend over a period of several years. Probably the most typical redemption provision allows for redemption by the company in three installments over two years.

These differences can be significant. Recall that, by statute, a snapshot of the company's financial status takes place immediately prior to any payment to its shareholders in order to determine whether it can distribute out that amount of value legally. By dividing up a redemption into a series of smaller payments and stretching them out over an extended period of time, it might actually become affordable to the company. (Would you prefer to pay cash for your new Audi, or would 48 monthly payments be more affordable?) The preferred stock investors, of course, want to limit the number of installments and keep as short as possible the time period over which redemption can occur so as to maintain the "gun to the head of management" aspect that is inherent in their right to require a redemption. By spreading the redemption payments over time in installments, the company is able to mitigate the leverage this right of redemption otherwise gives to the investors.

Referring back to the language of Charter Sample 9.31, note that the option to redeem in multiple installments requires that each installment be "proportionately applied" to the Series A Preferred Stock holders. This means of allocating the application of a partial redemption is also the method normally used when the company does not have enough money legally available to make the full distribution. While other approaches may be permitted by law, by far the most usual way to deal with inadequate funds is a partial redemption on a pro-rata basis. *See, e.g.,* Cal. Corp. Code §402(b) (providing also for selection by lot, at the discretion of the board, or upon such other terms as are specified in the Charter). A pro-rata redemption preserves the voting balance among the holders of the redeemable shares and eliminates any temptation to target the redemption at (or away from) a particular shareholder or group of shareholders, which would give rise to obvious fiduciary duty issues.

The end of Charter Sample 9.31 sets the Redemption Price and explicitly states that the redemption will be paid for in cash. As of the Redemption Date, the company must pay into a trust account a cash amount sufficient to meet its redemption obligation, and the effectiveness of the redemption is contingent on the delivery of those funds. Under the terms of this Charter provision, the Redemption Price is the sum of the Original Issue Price, plus any unpaid dividends, plus a redemption premium that is equal to 8 percent per annum of the Original Issue Price, compounded annually to the applicable Redemption Date.

Insufficient Funds and the "Vampire Scenario."   Whenever a company issues redeemable stock, its Charter must include terms to deal with the possibility that the company will have insufficient funds legally available to accomplish the redemption when required. A Charter provision addressing the possibility of partial redemptions very typically will contain something like the following:

> **Charter Sample 9.32.** If the funds of the Corporation legally available for redemption of shares of Series A Preferred Stock on any applicable Redemption Date are insufficient to redeem the total number of such shares to be redeemed on such date, then the Corporation shall redeem a pro-rata portion of each holder's redeemable shares of such Series A Preferred Stock out of funds legally available therefor, based on the respective amounts which would otherwise be payable in respect of the shares to be redeemed if the legally available funds were sufficient to redeem all such shares. The shares of Series A Preferred Stock not redeemed shall remain outstanding and entitled to all the rights and preferences provided herein. At any time thereafter when additional funds of the Corporation are legally available for the redemption of shares of Series A Preferred Stock, such funds immediately shall be used to redeem additional shares of Series A Preferred Stock until the Corporation has redeemed the balance of the shares the Corporation has become obliged to redeem on any applicable Redemption Date but that it has not yet redeemed in accordance with the foregoing provisions.

The language of this provision presents what some commentators refer to as the "vampire scenario." It provides that if there are insufficient funds legally available to complete a redemption, the company is to buy back as many shares as its financial condition permits. Those shares that are not redeemed on the Redemption Date then remain outstanding, retaining their full preferred stock rights, until more funds become legally available, which then immediately must be used by the company to redeem more of the preferred shares. If those funds still are not sufficient to redeem the balance of the preferred shares, additional shares will be redeemed until the maximum amount legally available has been used up, and the then-remaining preferred shares continue to be outstanding. When more funds become legally available, the process repeats, and it continues to repeat until the redemption obligation has been met in full. Each partial redemption is done on a pro-rata basis, so all holders of the preferred stock are bought out proportionately over the life of the redemption.

In other words, like a vampire keeping its victim barely alive and sucking out its life force whenever the victim regains strength, the redemption obligation keeps the company in a state of living death. The company is unable to grow its business because all of its excess cash now must be put towards fulfilling its redemption obligation. It is difficult for the company to raise new equity capital under these circumstances because the preferred stock that is being redeemed will be at the top of the equity distribution chain until it is fully paid off. In addition, potential lenders likely will stay away, disliking the periodic sweep of excess assets out of the company to pay for the redemption.

This vampire scenario underscores the leverage that a redemption right provides to the preferred stockholder. Rather than subject the company to this living death, management would be strongly motivated to put up the company for sale.

A final issue regarding insufficient funds is the nature of the claim that the holder of redeemable shares has against the company if the shares are not redeemed in accordance with the Charter's provisions. Certainly, when funds are legally available and the company simply breaches its obligation to redeem, the shareholder becomes a creditor of the corporation, with a claim for the past-due redemption payment.

But what if the company is unable to complete the redemption because it is not legally permitted to distribute the cash to its shareholders? Logically, the shareholder cannot become a creditor under those circumstances. Incurring a debt to a shareholder means creating an enforceable obligation to pay the shareholder, which is functionally equivalent to making a payment to a shareholder. Treating the redemption obligation as a debt establishes the obligation to pay while simply postponing the time for delivering the cash. If the financial capacity test applied to shareholder distributions prohibits the redemption payment, it most likely also prohibits incurring a debt obligation on behalf of the company to make a future payment to that shareholder. When a company is obligated to redeem shares and has insufficient assets to do so, it is understandable that shareholders holding shares subject to redemption would have a priority over other equity holders to the assets of the company, but it is difficult to see how they could jump up the priority ladder and obtain equal priority rights with the company's creditors.

Redemption Mechanics. The Charter must include a number of provisions addressing the mechanics of a redemption. For example, what happens to the shares being redeemed? When do they cease being shares and represent only the right to receive the redemption payment? To address these details, a provision in the company's Charter might read as follows:

> **Charter Sample 9.33-A.** From and after each applicable Redemption Date, unless there shall have been a default in payment of the applicable Redemption Price, all rights of the holders as to the shares of Series A Preferred Stock so redeemed (except the right to receive the applicable Redemption Price without interest upon surrender of their certificate or certificates) shall cease with respect to such shares, and such shares shall not thereafter be transferred on the books of the Corporation or be deemed to be outstanding for any purpose whatsoever.

This provision makes clear that if the company has provided sufficient funds for the redemption and otherwise honored the required procedures, even if the certificates remain in the shareholders' possession, the shares are no longer stock of the company as of the Redemption Date and thus retain only the right to receive the redemption payment. *See also* Model Act §7.21(d) (prohibiting such shares from voting).

The process customarily used in redemptions calls for the company to deliver the redemption payment to a trust account and then directs the holders of the redeemed shares to deliver their certificates to the trustee for cancellation and distribution of the redemption payment. This causes the redemption to occur as of a date certain and puts the onus on the shareholders to surrender their certificates to collect their money.

Charter Sample 9.33-A then goes on to specifically provide that shares called for redemption are not transferable. This is an effort to reduce the risk that a purchaser of the shares might be defrauded by getting only the right to the redemption payment rather than an equity interest in the company.

Additional Redemption Mechanics.   An additional provision often seen in conjunction with a redemption right states that once the preferred shares are delivered to the company, they cannot be reissued. This results in the same treatment for redeemed shares of preferred stock as for those shares that are converted into common. As such, this provision might be found in either or both of the conversion or redemption sections of the Charter or presented as a separate section:

> **Charter Sample 9.33-B.** No shares of Preferred Stock redeemed, purchased or acquired by the Corporation or converted into Common Stock shall be reissued, and all these shares shall be canceled and eliminated from the shares the Corporation shall be authorized to issue.

This approach is in direct contrast to the typical treatment of shares of common stock that are reacquired by a company pursuant to a contractual repurchase right, or upon the expiration of an unexercised equity incentive grant. In those cases, the shares usually are returned to the pool of authorized but unissued shares that are then available for future issuance.

As a fundamental matter, in drafting or reviewing a Charter section providing for redemption, it is important for the lawyer to confirm that the mechanics are unambiguously set forth. Statutory default provisions on redemption processes often are very limited. (*Contra, see* Cal. Corp. Code §509.) As a consequence, if the directions given in the Charter are inadequate or unclear, the statutory default rules most likely will not provide much guidance. As is the case when implementing other rights granted in the Charter, and in contracts generally, the mechanics provisions must provide clear instructions for a situation where the parties may have strongly competing interests. *Query:* In drafting these provisions, how can the lawyer ensure that the mechanics, as written, will work as intended? *Hint:* Why do you think, earlier in this chapter, you were asked to work through so many liquidation waterfalls and anti-dilution adjustments?

Careful drafting is particularly important when a company has more than one series of preferred stock subject to redemption. Coordinating the competing redemption rights in order to maintain the agreed-upon priority of one series over another, or the *pari passu* treatment of two series, requires careful construction of the rights and processes for each series. This is particularly true in the situation where multiple series of preferred stock have separate rights that overlap as to the time of performance. For example, if the Series A Preferred Stock is redeemable in installments over a three-year period and in the second year, the Series B Preferred Stock becomes redeemable, how are those rights to be reconciled? If there is enough money for one series to be redeemed, but not both, then what happens?

Another coordination issue involves whether the Charter will set a deadline for preferred stock holders to opt out of a redemption by converting to common stock. If the preferred stock to be redeemed is convertible right up to the date of the redemption, and the redemption is effective upon delivery of sufficient funds to an escrow account, how does the company know how many shares it will have to redeem and therefore how much money will be required? In order to fix what otherwise can be something of a moving target, a Charter provision often will state that the right to convert is suspended a certain number of days (say three, or five, or seven) prior to a Redemption Date. In this way, the company can determine exactly how many shares will be outstanding as of the Redemption Date. The company then can calculate the correct number of shares to be redeemed and, therefore, deposit into escrow the correct amount of funds.

Additional details that might be seen in a Charter's redemption provisions include the processes for surrendering redeemed shares and delivering payment to the holders of those shares. These are often omitted and dealt with in an instruction letter to the shareholders from the trustee or redemption agent handling the procedure. Also, redemption provisions often make it clear that the right of redemption is not intended to be the exclusive means by which the company may acquire the particular preferred stock. This is the typical statutory default position, but sometimes it is expressly set forth in the Charter. *See* Del. GCL §160; Cal. Corp. Code §402(d); and Model Code §6.31(a) (broadly permitting the reacquisition of its shares by a company without exclusion of shares subject to redemption).

A final note on redemption mechanics is in order. Since redemptions rarely occur in the venture capital context, many company Charters have redemption provisions that were not reviewed adequately when the Charter was drafted. Even though it is unlikely that these terms will ever be invoked, the mechanics still need to work. So, as a practice pointer, when reviewing a draft of a proposed Charter, do not let the fact that there is only a remote chance that the redemption will occur cause you to reduce the care of your review. Also, while a prudent lawyer always carefully reviews provisions he or she intends to use as precedent, for the same reason, an extra level of care is appropriate when choosing redemption terms.

QUESTIONS

1. One of the observations regarding venture capital on the East Coast versus the West Coast is that on the East Coast, investment terms tend to be more debt-like. This is supported by the fact that preferred stockholder redemption rights are significantly more common on the East Coast. What other preferred stock terms would you expect to see more often on the East Coast than in a West Coast deal?

2. You are representing a potential Series B Preferred Stock venture capital investor in a company that has redeemable Series A Preferred Stock outstanding. The terms of the company's Charter regarding the Series A Preferred Stock state that the redemption may be initiated in a little over three years from the time your client is contemplating its investment. Your client informs you that it also wants a redemption right. What is your strategy on negotiating redemption rights on behalf of your client and who are you going to be negotiating with?

F. Voting Rights

When a company has more than one class of stock, or when a class is divided into series, the voting rights (or lack thereof) of each class or series need to be set out in the Charter. *See* Del. GCL §151(a); *but see* §212(a) (providing for one vote per share if the Charter is silent); Cal. Corp. Code §400(a); and Model Code §6.01(b) and (c). A class or series of shares may be given full, limited, or no voting rights (subject to certain statutory limitations on the complete denial of voting rights) and may be given voting rights on matters where a shareholder vote is not otherwise required by statute. *See* Del. GCL §151(a); Cal. Corp. Code §400(a); and Model Code §6.01(b) and (c).

In the venture capital context, preferred stock almost always has broad, general voting rights, plus it typically is granted a set of special voting rights that address the election of directors and the right to approve certain specified corporate actions.

1. Voting as a Participation Right

A typical Charter provision setting out the preferred stock's general voting right might read:

> **Charter Sample 9.34.** At all meetings of the stockholders of the Corporation and in the case of any actions of stockholders in lieu of a meeting, each share of Common Stock shall be entitled to one vote, and each share of Preferred Stock shall be entitled to that number of votes equal to the number of shares of Common Stock into which each share is then convertible (in accordance with [the conversion and anti-dilution provisions] hereof) on the record date set for the meeting or action or, if no record date is set, on the date of the meeting or the date the action is taken. Except as otherwise expressly provided in this [Charter], or as required by law, the holders of Common Stock and Preferred Stock shall vote together as a single class in accordance with the preceding sentence, and neither the Common Stock nor the Preferred Stock shall be entitled to vote as a separate class on any matter to be voted on by stockholders of the Corporation.

Under these terms, the Preferred Stock gets one vote for each share of Common Stock into which it is convertible, and has the right to vote together with the Common Stock as a single class. In short, the Preferred Stock votes with the Common Stock on an as-converted basis on anything that may be presented to the stockholders for their approval.

Sometimes investors will be confused by the grant of a general voting right to the preferred stock, whether to the class as a whole or to a specific series of preferred stock, thinking that this may somehow limit the voting rights of the preferred stock by putting these shares on a par with the common stock. To the contrary, the importance of a provision like this is that it sets out the fact that the preferred stock has the right to vote on *anything* that may be presented to the company's shareholders for a vote. Since the rights of separate classes must be designated in the Charter, it is necessary to have a Charter provision establishing that the preferred stock has full voting power. The additional, preferential voting powers granted to the preferred stock are acknowledged by the "[e]xcept as otherwise provided in this Charter" introductory phrase in the last sentence of Charter Sample 9.34. Occasionally, counsel will want to reference the specific voting rights provisions of the Charter, but this can become unwieldy where the preferred stock has the right to vote on a wide variety of matters, such as whether to trigger an automatic conversion, or to waive "Liquidation Event" treatment, or to implement a redemption, among other things. The result is that the cross reference may need to refer to five or six sections, and what happens if a specific voting right gets overlooked? Rather than create potential ambiguity through an administrative error with an incomplete cross reference, the "otherwise provided" carve-out encompasses the entire Charter document.

In addition, Charter Sample 9.34 sets a limitation on the voting rights of the common stock by specifically disavowing any class-by-class votes, as opposed to votes taken together as a single class, except those required by law or specifically provided for in the Charter. As the rights "required by law" cannot be taken away by a provision in the company's Charter, and since the rights "expressly provided" in the Charter address preferential preferred stock rights, the common stock is left with the general right to vote, but no more.

One final, rather technical matter with regard to the language of Charter Sample 9.34 bears mentioning here. The end of the first sentence refers to the "record date" set for a meeting or written consent, and offers a default if no date is set. If the shareholders are granted the right to vote (as in this example), to receive a dividend, or be eligible for a redemption, it is necessary to know exactly which shareholders have that right and how many shares each of those holders owns. A "record date" is a snapshot of who the shareholders of a corporation are at the end of the business day on a specific date. Shares may be transferred, or a conversion rate adjustment may have taken effect, around the time of a shareholder vote. If shares are converted before a record date, then they are common stock as of the record date. If they are converted after that date, then they were preferred stock as of the record date. (Recall our earlier discussion, in reviewing Charter Sample 9.17-B, of the importance of clearly specifying when a conversion takes effect.)

Corporations codes tend to provide defaults for setting record dates, and those defaults frequently are repeated in a company's bylaws. In privately held companies, there is usually little activity that would make it difficult to ascertain the stockholders as of the record date for a vote, dividend, or redemption. For companies with publicly traded shares where the ownership of stock is constantly shifting, however, knowing who is eligible to vote at a shareholder meeting or is entitled to receive a dividend, for example, is critical. The shares continue to trade, but holders who bought after the record date acquire the shares without the right to vote or to receive a dividend based on the past record date.

Despite the fact that these issues are more remote in the private company context, they still can arise, and most often do so in potentially adversarial situations, such as recapitalizations as part of a "down-round" financing. When, for example, an existing preferred stock holder is being forced by other preferred stock holders into an automatic conversion as the penalty for not supporting the company with new investment funds, you can be very sure that the corporate formalities of record dates and effectiveness of conversion will be closely scrutinized for any flaws. It is critical, then, to make sure that the interaction between the record date and transfer mechanics as set forth in the company's bylaws and the dividend, liquidation, conversion, redemption, and voting provisions set forth in the company's Charter do not give rise to some ambiguity regarding the ownership, rights, or character of a particular share of stock on any given date. Whenever a record date for a corporate event is set, the company must be able to specify who owns how much of what on that date.

2. Director Election Rights

A typical venture capital preferred stock voting preference is the right to elect a specified number of directors. Since control of the board effectively amounts to control of the corporation, the right to fill director positions is usually a matter that is closely negotiated. While some investors are reluctant to exercise actual control, wanting instead the ability to veto acts they object to, others insist on the right to be the decider in every single significant decision a company makes after their investment is completed.

Allocating Board Seats.   A Charter provision creating special preferred stock director election rights might read:

Charter Sample 9.35. So long as a majority of the Series A Preferred Stock originally issued remains outstanding, the holders of such shares of Series A Preferred Stock shall be entitled to elect two (2) directors of this corporation (each a "**Series A Director**") at any election of directors. The holders of outstanding Common Stock shall be entitled to elect two (2) directors of this corporation at any election of directors. The holders of Series A Preferred Stock and Common Stock (voting as separate classes) shall be entitled to elect by the approval of each class any remaining directors of this corporation.

This provision begins with a limitation on the preferential right of the Series A Preferred Stock to elect directors. The right only applies so long as a threshold number of Series A Preferred Stock shares remain outstanding. If a sufficient number of shares of Series A Preferred Stock are, for example, redeemed or converted to Common Stock, the special director election right terminates. This sort of limitation prevents a relatively small number of remaining Series A Preferred Stock shares from exercising rights that have become disproportionate to the ownership interest in the company represented by those shares. More specifically, it limits the ability of the Series A Preferred Stock to seek to obtain through conversion a controlling voting interest of the Common Stock class while retaining all its preferential voting rights.

Charter Sample 9.35 grants to the holders of the Series A Preferred Stock the right to elect two directors, so long as a sufficient number of those preferred shares remain outstanding. It then goes on to provide to the holders of the Common Stock the right to elect two directors, and then provides that any remaining directors are to be elected by all the holders, voting as separate classes, upon the approval of each class. This is a classic compromise allocation of director positions in that each class of shares — the preferred stock being the investors and the common stock being management and the founders — has the right to elect an equal number of directors, with any additional directors mutually elected.

However, there are a couple of aspects to Charter Sample 9.35 that may not be apparent upon an initial read. First, the size of the board is not stated (apparently it is addressed in the bylaws, which needs to be confirmed), so the Charter has to deal with the fact that the board size could change and that a procedure for electing additional directors must exist. To address this possibility, the final sentence of the provision, therefore, provides for the classes to elect mutually "any remaining directors. . . ."

The fact that the Charter gives the Series A Preferred Stock and the Common Stock each the right to elect two directors sets an effective floor on the board size of four, so long as the requisite number of Series A Preferred Stock shares are outstanding; if not, the floor drops to two. Those minimums would apply even if the bylaws stated a lower number because the Charter grants specific rights to the stock classes and, in a conflict, the Charter controls over the bylaws.

If the number of Series A Preferred Stock shares outstanding drops to half or less of the originally issued number, this provision provides that the class right to elect two directors terminates. What about the right to mutually approve "remaining directors"? Given that the threshold number of shares qualifier is drafted to apply to the first sentence of the provision but not the third, the right of the Preferred Stock to mutually approve remaining directors appears to continue so long as any Series A Preferred Stock remains outstanding.

What if no remaining shares of Series A Preferred Stock are outstanding, all having been converted, for example? How do director elections work then? Under Charter Sample 9.35, the right of the Preferred Stock to elect directors no longer applies and the Common Stock has the right to elect two directors. As to "remaining directors," though, there is a problem in that the Charter specifies that their election requires the affirmative vote of a class of shares that no longer exists. As impossibilities generally are not enforceable, most lawyers would conclude that the "remaining directors" can be elected by the Common Stock. This conclusion is supported by the fact that no shareholders are being disenfranchised by that course of action. However, the best practice would be to eliminate doubt by amending the Charter promptly to delete the reference to the preferred stock right.

A director election provision that self-corrects in the event the Preferred Stock's voting right expires has practical virtues, in that the ability of the corporation to fill out its board is not impaired by unintended voting power limitations on the remaining shares. Further, there are legal considerations. Under California law, for example, the minimum number of authorized directors in a corporation having three or more shareholders is three. Cal. Corp. Code §212(a). As a consequence, if a California corporation has three or more shareholders, any director election rights provision it uses must provide, under all circumstances, for a mechanism to elect at least three directors. If it does not, the California secretary of state likely will reject the Charter filing.

If Charter Sample 9.35 had begun with a statement that the board of directors shall consist of, say, five members, then the mutual election provision might have said the two classes would elect "the fifth director," the "final director," or "one director." Where the

Charter sets the board size, it often addresses the election of exactly that number of directors. But, because Charter Sample 9.35 is silent, the board size must be fixed by an appropriate provision in the company's bylaws. Consequently, the approval required in order to modify the bylaws and change the size of the board might be different from the approval required to change the Charter. Thus, the Charter terms have to be open-ended to accommodate a change in the designated number of directors.

A second aspect of Charter Sample 9.35 that should be considered carefully is the mechanism for electing "remaining directors." The relevant language reads as follows:

> The holders of Series A Preferred Stock and Common Stock (voting as separate classes) shall be entitled to elect by the approval of each class any remaining directors. . . .

This means that the "remaining directors" are elected upon the separate approval of each class. Each class would vote on a nominated director. If a majority of each class voted in favor of that director, then he or she would be elected. When described casually, or perhaps in a term sheet, the quoted provision might be expressed as "two directors elected by the preferred, two by the common, and the remainder mutually elected." The "mutual" aspect, however, is not always clear. Would a vote of the preferred stock and the common stock, together as a single class, qualify as "mutually elected"? The lawyer representing the party with a majority of the votes of the combined classes would probably argue yes, while the lawyer representing the party with the minority voting interest in the combined classes would probably argue that his or her client being outvoted does not qualify as "mutually electing." *Query*: Would mutual election by all shares voting together as a single class solve the problem discussed above regarding the ability to elect "remaining directors" after full conversion of the Series A Preferred Stock?

This is yet another reminder that when reading a Charter provision or other contract right, it is often necessary to work through how the provision actually operates in order to decide if the provision really does work as intended and if it is fairly reflecting the agreement reached by the parties.

Additional provisions frequently seen as part of the Charter dealing with the election of directors include terms on filling vacancies on the board and removing directors. However, because state laws vary on how vacancies are to be filled (*see, e.g.*, Del. GCL §223; Cal. Corp. Code §305; and Model Code §8.10), and on the ability to restrict the right of the shareholders generally to remove directors without cause (*see, e.g.*, Del. GCL §141(k); Cal. Corp. Code §§303 and 304; and Model Act §8.08), and because shareholders of a class representing a minority of the total outstanding shares generally do not want their ability to elect directors potentially undercut by the majority's ability to remove those directors or fill vacancies, there appears to be a trend towards addressing these issues (i.e., filling director vacancies and accomplishing director removals) through mechanisms that are set forth in a separate Voting Agreement. (See the discussion of Voting Agreements in Chapter 10, section B.7.)

Through contractually agreed-upon procedures set forth in a Voting Agreement, the shareholder class having the right to elect a director can control the removal of that director (other than for cause) and can manage the process for filling any vacancies among the directors that class elected. If, for example, the applicable law requires a vote of all the shareholders together as a single class to remove a director without cause, a Voting Agreement might provide that upon an affirmative vote of the class of shareholders who elected a director to remove that director, the other shareholders agree to join in that vote, thereby achieving the requisite measure of statutory approval in order to remove that director validly while not undercutting the class election right.

Effect on Cumulative Voting.   The applicability of cumulative voting in director elections varies widely from state to state. *See* Del. GCL §214 (cumulative voting applies only if so provided in the Charter); Cal. Corp. Code §708(a) (any shareholder may request application of cumulative voting, *but see* §301.5 allowing "listed companies" to adopt Charter provisions eliminating cumulative voting); and Model Act §7.28 (cumulative voting applies only if so provided in the Charter *and* notice of its application or a shareholder request precedes the vote). If cumulative voting applies, and the Charter provides that a particular number of directors are to be elected by a specific class of shares, then cumulative voting would apply within that class vote. *See* Cal. Corp. Code §708(c) (referring to prevailing candidates as those "receiving the highest number of affirmative votes of the shares entitled to be voted for them . . ."); and Model Code §7.28 (referring to cumulative voting by "voting groups" as provided in §8.04). As previously noted, in the venture capital financing context, shareholder voting typically is governed by the terms of a Voting Agreement, which normally results in near-unanimous approval of director nominees. This aspect of shareholder voting is discussed at greater length in section B.7 of Chapter 10.

Voting Shift.   In situations where the preferred stock has the right to elect a minority of the directors, occasionally the venture capital investors want a practical remedy in the event that a dividend is not paid when required, a redemption payment is missed, or some other fundamental obligation is not honored by the company. In these circumstances, the venture capital investors may request a *voting shift*, or *voting switch*, provision in the Charter, essentially providing that, upon an enumerated "default event," the holders of the preferred stock immediately shall have the right to call a shareholder meeting in which they shall have the power to elect the smallest number of directors representing a majority of the board. This special right to elect a majority of the board should end with the "cure" of the default event.

The nature of the "default events" that trigger this right must be carefully drafted in order to avoid ambiguity or an inadvertent default. Since the provision is reducing the voting rights of, typically, the common stock class, it often contains special shareholder meeting quorum requirements so that common stock holders may not thwart the preferred stock's right to elect additional directors by boycotting the shareholder meeting, leaving the preferred stock with less than a quorum and thereby preventing the convening of a valid shareholder meeting. In addition, a voting shift provision always should have a "sunset clause" or an end date. That is to say, once the crisis triggering the special voting rights has been successfully addressed, the special voting powers should end and the normal director election process should be reestablished.

QUESTIONS

1. Charter Sample 9.34 establishes the general right of the preferred stock to vote and sets the basis on which the number of votes held by the preferred stock is determined. Review that provision and reflect on your reaction to the proportionate, ratchet, and weighted average anti-dilution adjustments addressed earlier in this chapter. Does Charter Sample 9.34 cause you to reassess your view of those anti-dilution rights? How?

2. Charter Sample 9.35 provides that the right to elect two directors applies only "so long as a majority of the Series A Preferred Stock originally issued remains outstanding." After *half* the Series A Preferred Stock is converted or redeemed, that election right is still valid. Does "a majority" seem like an appropriate standard? What would you suggest? Does it matter if the Series A Preferred Stock is redeemable? If the redemption terms call for two installments? For three installments?

3. Should the holders of the Series A Preferred Stock have the right to consent to the "remaining directors," as provided in Charter Sample 9.35, for so long as there are *any* remaining Series A Preferred Stock shares outstanding?

4. The discussion following Charter Sample 9.35 mentioned the election of the "remaining directors" and expressed concern about what would happen if there were no Series A Preferred Stock shares left outstanding. Would the problem be solved if the last sentence of Charter Sample 9.35 began: "So long as any shares of Series A Preferred Stock remain outstanding . . ."?

3. Protective Provisions

A second category of preferential voting right typically granted to venture capital preferred stock holders is a special approval right that applies to a list of specified corporate actions. These "protective provisions" are simply an additional set of voting rights but, for reasons probably buried in the past, they often are drafted as a separate article of the Charter rather than as part of the voting provisions.

The effect of the protective provisions is creation for the preferred stock of a defined class (or series) approval right over specified events. As was briefly discussed in Chapter 5, the existence of statutory class voting rights, as well as the terms of those rights, varies widely by jurisdiction. Preferred stock investors usually seek, therefore, to have their class or series voting rights specifically set forth in the Charter so that they are not left dependent on the vagaries of state law for their voting rights.

Preferred Stock Protective Provisions. A Charter's protective provision section may begin as follows:

Charter Sample 9.36-A. So long as a majority of the Preferred Stock originally issued remains outstanding, this corporation shall not (by amendment, merger, consolidation, or otherwise) without first obtaining the approval (by vote or written consent, as provided by law) of the holders of a majority of the then outstanding shares of Preferred Stock (voting together as a single class and not as separate series, and on an as-converted basis): [a list of the acts requiring approval then follows]

Just as with the director election right, we see that a threshold number of shares of Preferred Stock must remain outstanding in order to maintain these special approval rights. The reasons are the same as those previously discussed. This provision prevents the Preferred Stock from having disproportionate voting power after significant redemption or conversion, as well as prevents the holders of the Preferred Stock from attempting to keep their protective provision rights while also converting a large number of their shares to common stock and simultaneously controlling that class of voting shares.

Charter Sample 9.36-A also provides for approval upon the affirmative vote of a majority of the Preferred Stock shares. Care must be taken in setting the required level for approval. It is important to consider the spread of the preferred stock shares among the holders and the relationship among those holders in order to measure the impact of a majority versus various potential supermajority approval requirements.

As a closely related issue, note also that this provision requires that the Preferred Stock vote together as a single class. Company counsel usually resists series-by-series protective provisions because they can result in personal veto powers in the hands of one or more major holders in each series. While a general consensus of the preferred shareholders is conceded as being appropriate, a maze of series approval rights can put undue leverage in the hands of an excessive number of parties. Each situation will be governed by its particular facts and circumstances, but company counsel often is more comfortable having a supermajority requirement for approval by the entire preferred stock class rather than majority requirements on a series-by-series basis.

Also important to note is the first parenthetical of Charter Sample 9.36-A, providing that the actions requiring approval may not be undertaken "by amendment, merger, consolidation, or otherwise. . . ." This is a direct response to the *Benchmark* case, which we examine later in this chapter after reviewing a list of events and actions that are typically included as part of a preferred stock's protective provisions.

Protective Provisions Relating to Preserving the Preferred Stock's Preferences.   The actions typically included in a Charter's protective provisions can be divided into groups of events that have similar outcomes. The corporation, for example, may be prohibited from doing any of the following without approval of the holders of the preferred stock:

Charter Sample 9.36-B. (a) alter or change the rights, preferences or privileges of the shares of Preferred Stock;

(b) increase or decrease (other than as a result of redemption or conversion) the total number of authorized shares of Preferred Stock (or any series thereof) or Common Stock;

(c) authorize or issue, or obligate itself to issue, any equity security (including any other security convertible into or exercisable for any such equity security) having a preference over, or being on a parity with, any series of Preferred Stock with respect to dividends, liquidation or redemption, other than the issuance of any authorized but unissued shares of Series A Preferred Stock designated in [this Charter] (including any security convertible into or exercisable for such shares of Preferred Stock);

(d) change the authorized number of directors of this corporation;

(e) amend the [Charter] or the Bylaws of this corporation;

These items are grouped together because they all relate to preserving the effectiveness and value of the Preferred Stock's preferences and ownership interest in the company. Item (a) does this by prohibiting any change to the Preferred Stock, other than potentially some administrative change that is not part of the rights, preferences, and privileges of the Preferred Stock. Likewise, item (b) prohibits changing the number of Preferred Stock or Common Stock shares. This prevents swamping the Preferred Stock's rights by the creation and issuance of a huge number of new shares. It also prevents, for example, changing an agreed-upon plan for future financing by reducing the number of authorized shares so as to make that plan impossible to implement. Item (c) also prevents diluting the Preferred Stock's rights by creating any additional stock that shares those rights on a *pari passu* basis. It further prohibits the creation of senior stock that would have a priority over the Preferred Stock.

Item (d) protects the preferred stock's preferential right to elect a specified number of directors against being diluted by expanding the size of the board. Item (e) is a catch-all that overlaps items (a), (b), most of (c) (not including the "issue, or obligate itself to issue" portion), and (d), as well as prohibits any other change in the Charter or bylaws. Changes not covered by (a), (b), and (c), but that (e) would cover might include the grant of specific rights, such as class voting rights, to the Common Stock.

Item (d), regarding changes in board size, may not be completely overlapped by the catch-all of item (e) because, while board size is typically stated in a corporation's Charter or bylaws, most state corporations codes allow the establishment of a variable board size, designating the minimum and maximum number of directors, but permitting the exact size to be determined by a board or shareholder action. Depending upon how the variable board size provision is written, that board or shareholder action might be incorporated into the bylaws, but it might not. If the bylaws set a variable board size, for example, with a minimum of four and a maximum of seven, they may state:

> The exact number of Directors shall be fixed from time to time, within the limits specified in this section, by an amendment of this section adopted by the Board of Directors. The exact number of directors shall be five (5) until changed as provided in the preceding sentence.

On the other hand, the bylaws might just say that the exact number shall be "set by resolution of the board of directors from time to time," without designating that act as an amendment to the bylaws. As a result, item (d) is necessary as a separate protective provision if the board size can be set by either board or shareholder resolution. If, however, board size is designated in the Charter or requires a bylaw amendment to change, then the catch-all of item (e) covers this issue.

Provisions like these give the holders of preferred stock the ability to protect the value and utility of their negotiated preferential rights. These provisions go further, however, since no new equity security can be created without the specified separate approval of the preferred stock. As a result, the effect of these protective provisions is to place virtually any future equity financing of the company at the discretion of the holders of the preferred stock.

Protective Provisions Relating to Payments or Distributions. Another group of events that the preferred stock investors usually want to approve is anything that involves money leaving the company and going into the hands of an equity security holder. A set of provisions such as the following is commonly used to address this concern:

> **Charter Sample 9.36-C.** (f) redeem, purchase or otherwise acquire (or pay into or set aside for a sinking fund for such purpose) any share or shares of Preferred Stock or Common Stock; provided, however, that this restriction shall not apply to (i) the repurchase of shares of Common Stock from employees, officers, directors, consultants, or other persons performing services for this corporation or any subsidiary pursuant to agreements under which this corporation has the option to repurchase such shares upon the occurrence of certain events, such as the termination of employment or service; (ii) repurchases pursuant to this corporation's exercise of a contractual right of first refusal as approved by the Board of Directors; or (iii) redemption of the [series of preferred stock] as provided in this Charter;
>
> (g) declare or pay any dividend on any equity securities of this corporation;

These provisions ensure that the holders of the Preferred Stock have the right to approve or veto any distributions of money or assets to a shareholder as a dividend or to repurchase shares. The carved-out events are intended to allow acts that usually are viewed as being in the best interests of the company and all its shareholders, or that are part of the Charter as negotiated by the Preferred Stock holders.

It is important to highlight the interaction of these approval rights with the preferred stock's dividend preferences. Some lawyers argue that if the preferred stock has the right to approve any dividend, then it does not need a dividend preference. The preferred stock can simply use its approval right as leverage to negotiate whatever dividend terms it wants before allowing any other dividend to be paid. That is undoubtedly correct, but having a dividend preference in addition to an approval right establishes that those negotiations are going to start from the premise that the preferred stock is already entitled to something. This is a recurring theme in crafting preferred stock rights, as we saw with redemption — that is, the stated preferences create leverage by setting the starting point for the next round of negotiations.

Protective Provisions Relating to Liquidation.   A third set of protective provisions often seen gives the preferred stock the right to vote on any transaction that would trigger the preferred stock's liquidation rights under the terms of the company's Charter. As liquidation represents a division of the value of the company and, almost always, the cessation of any continuing ownership interest in the company by the preferred stock holders, it is only to be expected that they would want the right to approve any event that triggers liquidation. A typical provision might read:

> **Charter Sample 9.36-D.** (h) effect any sale, lease, assignment, transfer or other conveyance (including without limitation a transfer or conveyance in the form of an assignment of intangible assets or an exclusive license or sublicense of intellectual property rights) of all or substantially all of the assets of the Corporation, or any merger, consolidation or conversion or any other transaction or series of transactions involving the Corporation in which the stockholders of the Corporation immediately before such transaction or transactions do not hold a majority of the shares or voting power of the surviving entity immediately thereafter, or any dissolution, liquidation or winding up of the Corporation;

This language generally summarizes those events that might trigger the preferred stock's liquidation preferences. It is absolutely necessary to integrate this provision with the actual definition of a "liquidation" (as set forth in the liquidation preference section of the company's Charter), so that there is no disconnect between the two sets of terms.

An alternative approach, where a defined term has been used to cover all triggering events, is simply to use that defined term, as reflected in the language of the following provision:

(h) commit the corporation to, or consummate a Liquidation Event;

As discussed in reviewing liquidation rights (such as the "Liquidation Event" definition in Charter Sample 9.5) and in the preceding paragraph, regardless of the approach taken to drafting the language of this particular protective provision, it is important for counsel to make sure that the events it describes that trigger the voting rights of the preferred stock are all of the events that trigger the preferred stock's liquidation rights.

Miscellaneous Protective Provisions.   The last set of protective provisions is a miscellaneous collection that might be seen as comparable to the affirmative and negative covenants that a lender might impose on a borrower. These are events that might involve a change in circumstances for the company, or are just significant management decisions in which the preferred stock holders simply want a voice. Examples of these events that might appear at the end of the Charter's list of protective provisions include:

Charter Sample 9.36-E. (i) effect any material change in the nature of the business in which the Corporation is engaged;

(j) take an action that would result in the taxation of the Preferred Stock under §305 of the Internal Revenue Code of 1986, as amended;

(k) incur any indebtedness exceeding $500,000;

(l) cause or effect the sale, transfer or other disposition (in a single transaction or a series of related transactions) of any material assets of the Corporation or any direct or indirect subsidiary of the Corporation, unless such sale, transfer or other disposition has been unanimously approved by the Board of Directors;

(m) authorize or approve any increase in the number of shares of Common Stock reserved for issuance under the Corporation's [Equity Incentive Plan] or create any similar equity incentive or benefit plan, or make any single grant of stock options equal to or greater than one percent (1%) of the Corporation's then fully diluted capitalization, in each case unless approved by a majority of the Board (including the Series A Directors);

Company counsel very often will object to item (i) because what constitutes a "material change in the nature of the business" is not defined and may not be definable. For example, assume that a software company goes from selling individual, full-use licenses to its software by delivering of a copy of the software to the user, to instead putting the software on a website and charging anyone who wants to use it on a per-use basis. These are certainly very different revenue models that involve a very different sales process and a very different set of tasks for the successful operation of the company, but the company is still selling the same software. In this case, there might have been "material changes" to the company's business model, but are they "material" to "the nature of the business"? Does the company need to seek Preferred Stock approval? Should the company face, effectively, a "no-confidence" vote on every potentially material decision? *Query*: Should legal counsel just leave this out altogether, or alternatively, should counsel attempt to define "material change" as part of the Charter's provisions?

Item (j) is normally not controversial because the things the company can do to cause the Preferred Stock to be treated by the IRS as debt-like "preferred stock" rather than as equity-like "common stock" without the approval of the holders of the Preferred Stock under the other protective provisions are fairly limited. (Recall the discussion in section E.1 of this chapter of the tax treatment issues on "preferred stock" that may be triggered by a redemption right.) Company counsel will object when the provision reads "allow any action . . ." because they see that as an open-ended indemnity of the Preferred Stock regarding its tax treatment regardless of whether the change in the treatment was triggered by an act of the company or by the holders of the Preferred Stock themselves.

Items (k) and (l) are simply major events that, unlike item (i), are more readily definable. The debt provision of item (k) is sometimes expanded to include leases treated as "financing" rather than "operating" leases under GAAP, as a financing lease often is the functional equivalent of borrowing. Note that item (l) addresses sales of assets not in the ordinary course of business, but not meeting the level of a liquidation by sale of all or substantially all the assets of the company. The unanimous board approval exception from the asset sale restrictions of item (l) is a surrogate for approval by the preferred stock holders, as it requires the directors elected by the preferred stock to conclude that the sale is in the best interests of the company. Contrast this standard with that used in item (m). We will return to this in a moment.

Item (m) restricts the reservation of additional shares of Common Stock for issuance under the terms of the company's equity incentive plan or of any additional incentive plan. Moreover, it restricts the size of the incentives that may be granted to any particular plan participant without board approval, which must include approval of the directors elected by the preferred stock.

A protective provision like item (m) has to be integrated with the definition of "Additional Shares of Common Stock" in the anti-dilution provisions. Usually, one of the issuances that does *not* trigger an anti-dilution adjustment is an equity incentive grant under the company's plan. (See Charter Sample 9.30, above, and the discussion thereafter.) If that anti-dilution carve-out is limited to a maximum number of shares, then the triggering of an anti-dilution adjustment is a practical roadblock to setting aside more shares for equity incentives. If the Charter has to be amended to increase the permitted shares under the anti-dilution carve-out, and the protective provisions give the preferred stock a vote on that change, then many lawyers would view item (m) as not necessary. As to the terms of, or limitations on, specific option grants, these more often are addressed as company covenants in the Investor Rights Agreement with the preferred stock holders. See Chapter 10, section B.5, for a fuller discussion of the provisions typically included in the Investor Rights Agreement. What's more, company counsel often will object to the inclusion of any of these issues in the Charter, taking the position that addressing these issues by contract is more private and more flexible than dealing with them in the company's Charter.

A final issue to be discussed in connection with protective provisions is raised by the requirement of director approval as set forth in items (l) and (m). As noted above in the discussion of item (l), these provisions can be used as a proxy for separate approval by the preferred stock — in other words, if the directors elected by the preferred stock approve it, no vote of preferred stock holders should be needed. While it sounds simple and efficient to rely on approval by the board, including the directors elected by the preferred stock, as opposed to going to the administrative trouble of soliciting and documenting approval of the holders of a requisite majority of the preferred stock, this approach needs to be considered carefully.

In looking at item (l), it is entirely possible that, for a company in a distressed financial situation, a sale of certain assets would allow the company to generate some cash that might keep it funded for several months of continued operations. It may be the view of the preferred stock investors, however, that the best time to sell the company is *now*, before any of the company's productive assets are disbursed. On the other hand, the common stock holders, often employees, may be more interested in preserving their pay checks for as long as possible and, because of the preferred stock liquidation preferences, may have no realistic prospect of getting any proceeds from a sale of the company at this point in time.

It is important to remember that a director owes fiduciary duties to the entire company, not just to the shareholders who elected him or her. A shareholder, on the other hand, absent control situations, typically has no fiduciary duties to the company or other shareholders. (Recall the reference at the beginning of this voting rights discussion to the fact that some venture capital investors avoid taking any investment position that involves outright voting control of the company, seeking instead only veto powers — now we can see one of the important reasons why venture capital investors adopt this approach to their portfolio companies.) In short, by using a board vote as a proxy for a class or series shareholder approval, the preferred stock holders may find their choices limited by virtue of the fiduciary responsibilities placed on their elected directors. Thus, by holding out for an actual vote of their series or class, they may allow their elected board members to meet their fiduciary responsibilities (or at least avoid a claim that they did not do so) by voting in favor of the asset sale, while as shareholders they would then vote against it.

A second aspect of this issue is presented in the different approaches taken to board approval in items (l) and (m). A preferred stock vote is triggered unless the event is, per item (l), "unanimously approved" or, as provided in item (m), "approved by a majority of the Board (including the Series A Directors)." These different approaches are the product of differences in state law. Under §141(d) of the Delaware GCL, the Charter may designate the right to elect directors by class or series and may designate the voting powers of those directors. As a result, Delaware permits the special requirement in item (m) that the director approval include the vote of "the Series A Directors." In many other jurisdictions, all directors have equal powers and item (m) would not be an acceptable Charter provision. *See, e.g.,* Cal. Corp. Code §307(a)(8) (providing that an action of the board occurs upon the approval of a majority of a quorum unless a higher approval standard is set forth in the Charter pursuant to §204(a)(5)). In those jurisdictions, attorneys take the approach used in item (l) in order to conform to the relevant state law requirements. Setting a supermajority or unanimity requirement for board approval presents a separate set of issues, however, and the veto powers entailed need to be carefully considered before that avenue is taken.

The *Benchmark* Case.   A widespread revision to the "protective provision" precedent files maintained by practicing lawyers took place as a result of the Delaware Chancery Court's decision in the *Benchmark* case, below. In *Benchmark*, a holder of a junior preferred stock, based on the holder's protective provisions, sought to enjoin a transaction that amended the company's Certificate of Incorporation in order to amend the terms of the holder's shares and thereby create equity ownership interests that were senior to the holder's. The court denied the request.

Benchmark Capital Partners IV, L.P. v. Vague

Del. Ch., C.A. No. 19179 (July 15, 2002)
2002 WL 1732423 (Del. Ch. 2002)

NOBLE, Vice Chancellor.

Introduction

This is another one of those cases in which sophisticated investors have negotiated protective provisions in a corporate charter to define the balance of power or certain economic rights as between the holders of junior preferred stock and senior preferred stock. These provisions tend to come in to play when additional financing becomes necessary. One side cannot or will not put up more money; the other side is willing to put up more money, but will not do so without obtaining additional control or other diminution of the rights of the other side. In short, these cases focus on the tension between minority rights established through the corporate charter and the corporation's need for additional capital.

In this case, Plaintiff [Benchmark] invested in the [Series A Preferred and Series B Preferred] of the defendant Juniper Financial Corp.'s ("Juniper") preferred stock. When additional capital was required, Defendant Canadian Imperial Bank of Commerce ("CIBC") was an able and somewhat willing investor. As a result of that investment [in Series C Preferred], Benchmark's holdings were relegated to the status of junior preferred stock and CIBC acquired a controlling interest in Juniper by virtue of ownership of senior preferred stock [and holding a majority of the preferred stock class]. The lot of a holder of junior preferred stock is not always a happy one. Juniper's Fifth Amended and Restated Certificate of Incorporation (the "Certificate") contains several provisions to protect the holders of junior preferred stock from abuse by the holder of senior preferred stock. Two of those provisions are of particular importance here. The Certificate grants the junior preferred stockholders a series vote on corporate actions that would "[m]aterially adversely change the rights, preferences and privileges of the [series of junior preferred stock]"[the "First Protective Provision"]. In addition, the junior preferred stockholders are entitled to a class vote before Juniper may "[a]uthorize or issue, or obligate itself to issue, any other equity security . . . senior to or on a parity with the [junior preferred stock]"[the "Second Protective Provision"].

The Certificate provides that those provisions protecting the rights of the junior preferred stockholders may be waived by CIBC [because the series of preferred stock vote on the protective provisions together as a single class and CIBC owns a majority of the entire class — this is referred to by the parties as the "Series C Trump"]. CIBC may not, however, exercise this power "if such amendment, waiver or modification would . . . diminish or alter the liquidation preference or other financial or economic rights" of the junior preferred stockholders or would shelter breaches of fiduciary duties.

[Upon realizing that its efforts to raise additional capital would be thwarted by the invocation of the junior preferred protective provisions, Juniper] elected to structure a more complicated transaction that now consists principally of a merger and a sale of Series D Preferred Stock to CIBC. The merger is scheduled to occur on July 16, 2002 with a subsidiary merging with and into Juniper that will leave Juniper as the surviving corporation, with a restated certificate of incorporation that will authorize the issuance of a new series of senior preferred stock and new junior preferred stock with a reduced liquidation preference and will cause a number of other adverse consequences or limitations to be suffered by the holders of the junior preferred. . . . Juniper will not obtain approval for these actions from the holders of the junior preferred stock. It contends that the protective provisions do not give the junior preferred stockholders a vote on these plans and, furthermore, in any event, that CIBC has the right to waive the protective provisions through the Series C Trump.

Benchmark, on the other hand, asserts that the protective provisions preclude Juniper's and CIBC's heavy handed conduct and brings this action to prevent the violation of the junior preferred stockholder's fundamental right to vote on these corporate actions as provided in the Certificate and to obtain interim protection from the planned evisceration of its equity interest in Juniper.

* * *

1. General Principles of Construction

Certificates of incorporation define contractual relationships not only among the corporation and its stockholders but also among the stockholders. Thus, the Certificate defines, as a matter of contract, both the relationship between Benchmark and Juniper and the relative relationship between Benchmark, as a holder of junior preferred stock, and CIBC, as the holder of senior preferred stock. For these reasons, courts look to general principles of contract construction in construing certificates of incorporation. . . .

[A court's function in ascertaining the rights of preferred stockholders] is essentially one of contract interpretation against the background of Delaware precedent. These precedential parameters are simply stated: Any rights, preferences and limitations of preferred stock that distinguish that stock from common stock must be expressly and clearly stated, as provided by statute. Therefore, these rights, preferences and [limitations] will not be presumed or implied.

These principles also apply in construing the relative rights of holders of different series of preferred stock.

2. Challenges to the Merger

Benchmark presents two distinct challenges to the merger. First, it argues that [the junior preferred's First Protective Provision] preclude[s] the merger without a series vote because the merger "[m]aterially adversely changes the rights, preferences and privileges" of [the junior preferred]. Second, Benchmark asserts that the merger cannot go forward, without a class vote by the holders of the [junior preferred], because of [the Second Protective Provision], which precludes the authorization of a senior preferred stock without such a vote. The Series D Preferred Stock, when issued, will have rights superior to the [junior preferred]. Because the merger agreement provides the mechanism for the authorization of the Series D Preferred Stock through the accompanying restatement of Juniper's certificate of incorporation, if falls within the reach of [the Second Protective Provision's limitation on authorization of a senior security], or so Benchmark argues.

a. Merger as Changing the Rights, Preferences and Privileges

Benchmark looks at the Series D Preferred financing and the merger that is integral to that transaction and concludes that the authorization of the Series D Preferred Stock and the other revisions to the Juniper certificate of incorporation accomplished as part of the merger will materially adversely affect the rights, preferences, and privileges of the junior preferred shares. Among the adverse affects to be suffered by Benchmark are a significant reduction in its right to a liquidation preference, the authorization of a new series of senior preferred stock that will further subordinate its interest in Juniper, and a reduction in other rights such as dividend priority. These adverse consequences will all be the product of the merger. Benchmark's existing [junior preferred] shares will cease to exist as of the merger and will be replaced with new [junior preferred shares], warrants, common stock and a small amount of cash. One of the terms governing the new junior preferred stock will specify that those new junior preferred shares are not merely subordinate to Series C Preferred Stock, but they also will be subordinate to the new Series C Preferred Stock. Thus, the harm to Benchmark is directly attributable to the differences between the new junior preferred stock, authorized through the merger, and the old junior preferred stock, as evidenced by the planned post-merger capital structure of Juniper.

Benchmark's challenge is confronted by a long line of Delaware cases which, in general terms, hold that protective provisions drafted to provide a class of preferred stock with a class vote before those shares' rights, preferences and privileges may be altered or modified do not fulfill their apparent purpose of assuring a class vote if adverse consequences flow from a merger and the protective provisions do not expressly afford protection against a merger. This result traces back to the language of 8 *Del.* C. §242(b)(2), which deals with the rights of various classes of stock to vote on amendments to the certificate of incorporation that would "alter or change the powers, preferences, or special rights of the shares of such class so as to affect them adversely." That language is substantially the same as the language ("rights, preferences and privileges") of the [First Protective Provision]. Where the drafters have tracked the statutory language relating to charter amendments in 8 *Del.* C. §242(b), courts have been reluctant to expand those restrictions to encompass the separate process of merger as set forth in 8 *Del.* C. §251, unless the drafters have made clear the intention to grant a class vote in the context of a merger.

* * *

The draftsmen of this language — the negotiators to the extent it has actually been negotiated — must be deemed to have understood, and no doubt did understand, that under Delaware law (and generally) the securities whose characteristics were being defined in the certificate of designation could be converted by merger into "shares of or other securities of the corporation surviving or resulting from [a] merger or consolidation" or into cash property, rights or securities of any other corporation." 8 *Del. C.* §251(b). . . .

I can only conclude that it is extraordinarily unlikely that the drafters . . . who obviously were familiar with and probably expert in our corporation law, would have chosen language so closely similar to that of §242(b)(2) had they intended a merger to trigger the class vote mechanism of that section.

The range of [the First Protective Provision] is not expressly limited to changes in the Certificate [pursuant to §242]. However, given the well established case law construing the provisions of certificates of incorporation and the voting rights of classes of preferred stockholders, I am satisfied that the language chosen by the drafters (i.e., the "rights, preferences, and privileges") must be understood as those rights, preferences and privileges which are subject to change through a certificate of incorporation amendment under the standards of 8 *Del.* C. §242(b) and not the standards of 8 *Del.* C. §251.

* * *

In short, to the extent that the merger adversely affects the rights, preference and privileges of [the junior preferred stock], those consequences are the product of a merger, a corporate event which the drafters of the protective provision could have addressed, but did not.

Accordingly, I am satisfied that Benchmark has not demonstrated a reasonable probability of success on the merits of its claim that [the First Protective Provision's terms] require a series vote on the merger contemplated as part of the Series D [preferred financing].

b. Authorization of Series D Preferred Shares Through the Merger Process

Benchmark's straightforward argument that it is entitled to a class vote on the authorization of the Series D Preferred Stock through the merger can easily be set forth. By [the Second Protective Provision], the holders of the [junior preferred stock] have the right, unless that right is properly waived by CIBC, to a class vote on the authorization of a senior preferred security. The Series D Preferred Stock will be on parity with the Series C Preferred Stock and, thus, will be senior to the existing junior preferred and the newly created junior preferred that will be created as part of the merger. The protective provisions of the Certificate do not distinguish between authorization through amendment of the Certificate under 8 *Del.* C. §242(b) and those changes in the Certificate resulting from a recapitalization accompanying a merger pursuant to 8 *Del.* C. §251. Thus, according to Benchmark, it matters not how the result is achieved. Moreover, [the Second Protective Provision] does not track or even resemble the "privileges, preferences and special rights" language of 8 *Del.* C. §242(b) that was important to the analysis [applied to the First Protective Provision]. Benchmark thus argues that the clear and unambiguous words of the [Second Protective Provision] guarantee (at least in the absence of an effective waiver by CIBC) it and the other holders of [junior preferred shares] a class vote before the Series D Preferred Stock may be authorized. While Benchmark has advanced an appealing and rational analysis, I conclude, for the reasons set forth below, that it has failed to demonstrate a reasonable probability of success on the merits of this argument.

In ascertaining whether a class of junior preferred stockholders has the opportunity to vote as a class on a proposed corporate action, the words chosen by the drafters must be read "against the background of Delaware precedent." For example, *Sullivan Money Management, Inc. v. FLS Holdings, Inc.* involved the question of whether a class vote was required in order to change critical rights of preferred shareholders "by amendment to the Certificate of Incorporation of [FLS Holdings, Inc.] or otherwise.'" In interpreting the charter of FLS Holdings, Inc., the Court was urged to treat the phrase "or otherwise" as including mergers. The Court, in rejecting this contention, set forth the following:

> The word "merger" is nowhere found in the provision governing the Series A Preferred Stock. The drafters' failure to express with clarity an intent to confer class voting rights in the event of a merger suggests that they had no intention of doing so, and weighs against adopting the plaintiff's broad construction of the words "or otherwise."

[Delaware cases] demonstrate that certain rights of the holders of preferred stock that are secured by the corporate charter are at risk when a merger leads to changes in the corporation's capital structure. To protect against the potential negative effects of a merger, those who draft protective provisions have been instructed to make clear that those protective provisions specifically and directly limit the mischief that can otherwise be accomplished through a merger under 8 *Del.* C. §251.

* * *

General language alone granting preferred stockholders a class vote on certain changes to the corporate charter (such as authorization of a senior series of stock) will not be read to require a class vote on a merger and its integral and accompanying modifications to the corporate charter and the corporation's capital structure. To reach the result sought by Benchmark, the protective rights "'must . . . be clearly expressed and will not be presumed.'" Unfortunately for Benchmark, the requirement of a class vote for authorization of a new senior preferred stock through merger was not "clearly expressed" in the Certificate. Against this background, I am reluctant both to presume that protection from a merger was intended and, perhaps more importantly, to create uncertainty in a complex area where [Delaware case law] has set down a framework for consistency.

3. Obligation to Issue and Issuance of Series D Preferred Shares

Under [the Second Protective Provision, providing for a class vote before Juniper may "authorize or issue, or obligate itself to issue" a senior security, Benchmark's claim regarding authorization has been addressed, but] Juniper is also required to obtain class approval, unless effectively waived by CIBC, from its junior preferred holders before it can issue or obligate itself to issue a senior preferred stock. Juniper plans to issue its Series

D Preferred stock after the merger and at a time when the new [junior preferred] shares will be outstanding. The shares will not be issued as the result of the merger, but instead will be issued pursuant to the Purchase Agreement between CIBC and Juniper. Because the merger is not implicated by the issuance of the shares, there is no "background" precedent against which this act must be evaluated in the same sense as the case law addressing the consequences of mergers. These facts bring Juniper's proposed issuance of its Series D Preferred Stock squarely within the scope of the restrictions imposed by [the Second Protective Provision as incorporated into] the post-merger certificate. Specifically, to paraphrase that provision, so long as any shares of the new [junior preferred] are outstanding, Juniper may not, without the class vote or class consent of the new [junior preferred] stockholders, issue any senior security. While the restrictions of the [Second Protective Provision] may be subject to the Series C Trump and, thus, may yet not prevent the issuance of the Series D Preferred Stock without the approval of the holders of the junior preferred stock, I am satisfied that [the Second Protective Provision] applies, from the plain and unambiguous language of its text, to the issuance of the Series D Preferred Stock when and as planned by Juniper.

* * *

Because [the Second Protective Provision] will entitle the holders of the new [junior preferred] to a class vote on the issuance of the Series D Preferred Stock, it becomes necessary to determine whether exercise of the Series C Trump would allow CIBC to waive the right of the junior preferred stockholders to a class vote.

All of the class voting rights conferred upon the junior preferred holders by [the Second Protective Provision] are subject to waiver by CIBC through the proper exercise of its Series C Trump. The Series C Trump is broad and (for present purposes) is restricted in application only if the corporate action for which the class vote is waived would "diminish or alter the liquidation preference or other financial or economic rights" of the holder of the junior preferred stock. Issuance of the Series D Preferred stock will not "diminish or alter" Benchmark's liquidation preference — that was accomplished through the merger. The question thus becomes one of whether the issuance of a previously authorized senior preferred security "diminish[es] or alter[s]" the junior preferred shares' "financial or economic rights."

In some very general sense, when shares of a security with a higher priority are issued, the financial and economic rights of the holders of junior securities are adversely affected. On the other hand, that broad of a reading of "financial or economic rights" would make it difficult to find a valid waiver under the Certificate because all of the rights at issue — liquidation preferences, dividend rights, redemption rights, and even voting rights — in some sense implicate financial or economic right and interests. In this analysis, the Court, of course, must seek to give meaning to all of the relevant provisions of the Certificate and interpret the Certificate "as a whole."

One approach to interpreting the critical language can be drawn from the line of cases addressing the vexing issues associated with authorization of a new senior security without a class vote under 8 *Del.* C. §242 such as whether that creation of a new security with a priority can be construed to alter or change the preferences, special rights or powers given to any particular class of stock through the certificate of incorporation and whether that creation of a new senior security also can be deemed to affect such class adversely. Under the analytical approach suggested by [Delaware case law], the issuance of shares of a security that has priority will not adversely affect the preferences or special rights of a junior security. The argument, in general, is that the terms and powers of that particular class of junior security have not themselves been changed. That another security with priority has been issued is said to "burden" it, but its particular rights have not been modified, and thus those rights are not perceived as having been "diminished or altered." I tend toward this reading because it does interpret the preferred stock protective provisions against the "background of Delaware precedent" and because "financial and economic rights" appear in a list with other items such as liquidation preferences and registration rights which are more fairly viewed as technical and specific (as opposed to broad and general) rights.

* * *

Both sides agree that the Series C Trump, absent the exception, would provide CIBC with the authority it claims. Accordingly, the effectiveness of any exercise of the Series C Trump in this context depends upon the scope to be given to the exception. Benchmark suffers, in this context, because it must rely on the exception; terms of preferred shareholders' protective provisions "must . . . be clearly expressed and will not be presumed"; and it bears the burden as the moving party on its motion for a preliminary injunction.

No words of explicit import clearly express the voting right the plaintiffs claim exists in this case. No positive evidence supports the claim that the drafters intended to create such a right. Although one might argue (as plaintiffs do) that that right exists by implication, it does not exist by *necessary* implication. To adopt the plaintiffs' position would amount to presuming a preferential voting right. In the present case, however, where (at least) an ambiguity exists, our law requires that it be resolved *against* creating a preference.

A preliminary injunction necessarily involves an initial determination on less than complete record and that limitation precludes a detailed consideration of extrinsic evidence. In light of the foregoing, I conclude that Benchmark has not demonstrated a reasonable probability of success on the merits of its claim that the waiver should not be available to CIBC.

* * *

Therefore, for the foregoing reasons, Benchmark's motion for a preliminary injunction is denied.

QUESTIONS

1. Who are the parties to the case and what are their positions relative to each other?
2. Having read through to the end of the court's opinion, consider again the first paragraph, setting the context of the case as "the tension between minority rights established through the corporate charter and the corporation's need for additional

capital." How does Delaware law treat "minority rights established through the corporate charter"?

3. In the first two paragraphs under the heading "2.a. Merger as Changing the Rights, Preferences and Privileges," the court quotes from the First Protective Provision and acknowledges that the creation of the Series D Preferred "[m]aterially adversely changes the rights, preferences and privileges" of Benchmark's shares. It then associates that language with 8 Del. C. §242(b), which addresses amendments to a company's certificate of incorporation that "alter or change the powers, preferences, or special rights of the shares of such class so as to affect them adversely." Do you agree with the court's conclusion that the language of the First Protective Provision and the statute are "substantially the same"?

4. While the court does not quote the full text of the protective provisions set forth in the company's certificate, the court does describe, under the heading "Introduction," the First Protective Provision as granting "the junior preferred stockholders a series vote on corporate actions that would '[m]aterially adversely change the rights, preferences and privileges of'" the series of junior preferred stock. If the First Preference Provision actually said "corporate actions," do you think that should have been part of the court's analysis of whether the protective provision was limited to amendments to the certificate of incorporation as contemplated by 8 Del. C. §242(b)? Would you treat a merger as a "corporate action"?

5. Under the heading "2.a. Merger as Changing the Rights, Preferences and Privileges," what do you think of the court's conclusion that the First Protective Provision's reference to "rights, preferences and privileges" "must be understood as those rights, preferences and privileges which are subject to change through a certificate of incorporation amendment under the standards of 8 *Del.* C. §242(b) and not the standards of 8 *Del.* C. §251."? Is the court really referring to two different mechanisms for amending one set of rights, preferences, and privileges?

6. The court looks to the opinion in *Sullivan Money Management, Inc. v. FLS Holdings, Inc.*, noting that the court there determined that a protective provision addressing changes in the preferred shareholders' rights "by amendment to the Certificate of Incorporation of [FLS Holdings, Inc.] or otherwise" did not apply to changes in the preferred shareholder's rights through a merger. The *Sullivan* court is quoted, noting that the word "merger" did not appear in the relevant provision of the company's certificate, and further rejecting any "broad construction of the words 'or otherwise.'" How would you read "by amendment . . . or otherwise"?

7. Under the heading "3. Obligation to Issue and Issuance of Series D Preferred Shares," what is the court's conclusion regarding the existence of the approval right arising from the "issue or obligate to issue" language of the Second Protective Provision? Does the protective provision create a right to vote?

8. Five paragraphs from the end of the text quoted from the court's opinion, the court discusses changes that "burden" the rights of a class or series of stock, versus those changes that amend or alter those rights. This analysis is predicated on those cases that interpret the class voting rights provisions of Del. GCL §242(b). This statute provides for a class vote when the certificate of incorporation is amended to, among other things, "alter or change the powers, preferences, or special rights" of the shares of that class "so as to affect them adversely." Look again at Charter Sample 9.36-B's

protective provisions. For a Delaware corporation, with the limited statutory class voting rights provided by §242(b), which of those protective provisions are duplicative of the statutory rights? Which are designed to remove the "affect them adversely" qualifier in the statutory right? Which of those provisions in Charter Sample 9.36-B are intended to provide a class vote where the preferred stock is merely "burdened"?

9. After the merger and the issuance of the Series D Preferred, the junior preferred holders' voting power in Juniper will fall from 29 percent to approximately 7 percent and CIBC's will rise from approximately 67 percent to more than 90 percent. In light of those facts, what is your reaction to CIBC's ability to exercise its voting rights (the Series C Trump)? Does CIBC have a conflict of interest? Is there anyone in the preferred stock vote under the protective provisions that does not have a conflict of interest?

10. Looking at the *Benchmark* case together with the *Groove Networks* case, which follows Problem 9.9-B, above, do both of them look at preferential rights set forth in the certificate of incorporation as terms that "must be expressly and clearly stated, as provided by statute[.] [T]herefore, these rights, preferences and [limitations] will not be presumed or implied."? Does it make a difference that *Benchmark* examines the grant of "minority rights"?

11. Having waded around in this case for so long, are you *ever* going to let a protective provision get by you without including the magic words "by amendment, merger, consolidation, or otherwise"?

4. Blank Check Provisions

As we observed in Chapter 5, a "blank check" provision is a statutorily created mechanism that allows a company's board of directors to designate the rights, preferences, and privileges of one or more new series of preferred stock without shareholder approval. *See* Del. GCL §102(a)(4) and §151(g); Cal. Corp. Code §202(e)(3); and Model Code §6.02. The board's authority to designate stock terms is limited to authorized but unissued shares. The board may designate the terms for an entire class of shares, or may use authorized but unissued shares to create multiple new series of stock, each having a new set of rights. The rights of existing shareholders cannot be changed through the blank check mechanism.

A blank check provision either must be in a company's original Charter or, if adopted after shares are issued, it must be approved by the shareholders. In the same way, the authorized but unissued shares available, upon which the board may apply its powers under the blank check provision, must also be included in the corporation's original Charter or must have been authorized by a vote of the shareholders.

The company's authorized capital must, of necessity, include extra shares. If it has 10 million preferred shares authorized, of which 1 million are designated Series A Preferred Stock, there would be 9 million authorized but unissued shares of preferred stock upon which the board may apply its blank check powers. Also, if the new preferred stock series is to be convertible, the company must have extra authorized common stock shares available for issuance upon that conversion.

When a company has no blank check provision, the board must approve the designation of each new series of preferred stock and set forth its terms, and then submit those terms to the company's shareholders for approval. Upon the requisite vote, the company's officers make a filing with the secretary of state, usually called a "Certificate of Amendment," including the new terms. Alternatively, the entire Charter may be restated, incorporating in the new terms, and this document is referred to as an "Amended and Restated" Charter. With a blank check, the board applies its power to approve the designation of the new series and its terms, then authorizes the officers to make a filing with the secretary of state that may be called a "Certificate of Determination" or a "Certificate of Designation." That document describes the rights, preferences, and privileges of the new security and becomes part of the company's Charter, but it may not change any other aspect of the Charter.

The effect of a blank check in the venture capital context is to eliminate the right of the common stock to vote on future preferred stock issuances. As we have seen, preferred stock typically has protective provisions that give it the authority to vote on new share authorizations and issuances without regard to statutory approval requirements. As a result, the ability to use a blank check can be a very powerful tool for a preferred holder who has a controlling position on the board.

The fact that the board may not change any existing Charter term can make a blank check a bit tricky to use. As an example, assume that a company has an existing Series A Preferred Stock with a liquidation preference that says the proceeds of a Liquidation Event shall be paid "First to the holders of the Series A Preferred Stock" until the priority amount is paid, "then all remaining proceeds shall be paid to the Series A Preferred Stock and Common Stock, pro rata." With those terms, it would not be possible to wedge in a liquidation preference for a Series B Preferred Stock without amending the rights of the Series A Preferred Stock.

The result is that a lot of surplus language needs to go into the board-authorized blank check filing to create the "hooks" that allow the terms for each additional series to be set into place without changing any other Charter terms. For example, the briefly summarized Series A Preferred Stock liquidation preference from the previous paragraph instead might say:

> After payment of liquidation preferences to shares of series of preferred stock designated as senior to the Series A Preferred Stock as to liquidation preferences, it, together with shares of all series of preferred stock designated as being *pari passu* with the Series A Preferred Stock as to liquidation preferences, shall receive its proportionate share of available liquidation proceeds [until it reaches its priority amount,] then, after payment to shares of series of preferred stock designated as junior to the Series A Preferred Stock as to liquidation preferences, the Series A Preferred Stock, together with the common stock and all other shares designated as participating with respect to liquidation distributions, on a pro-rata per share basis with respect to funds available.

Under the language of this provision, each new series of preferred stock is then designated in relation to the prior series, but without amending the prior series. As a result, each series has a separate statement of its rights, which can make for some difficult integration problems when an event occurs that means the scope of those separate rights have to be determined collectively and then exercised. And, again, the designation authority may only be applied to already authorized but unissued shares. Authorizing more shares requires shareholder approval.

Blank Check Provision.   A blank check Charter provision might read as follows:

Charter Sample 9.37. The remaining shares of Preferred Stock may be issued from time to time in one or more series as the Board of Directors of this Corporation may determine. The Board of Directors is hereby authorized, subject to any approval required by [the preferred stock protective provisions], to determine and alter the rights, preferences, privileges, and restrictions granted to and imposed upon any wholly unissued series of Preferred Stock, and to fix the number of shares of any such series of Preferred Stock and the designation of any such series of Preferred Stock. As to any series of Preferred Stock, the number of shares of which is authorized to be fixed by the Board of Directors, the Board of Directors is further authorized, within the limits and restrictions stated in any resolution or resolutions of the Board of Directors originally fixing the number of shares constituting any such series, to increase or decrease (but not below the number of shares of such series then outstanding) the number of shares of any such series subsequent to the issuance of shares of that series.

After an introductory sentence, which includes a reminder that the authority of the board of directors applies only to authorized but unissued shares, the language of this blank check provision addresses the authority of the board of directors to determine and alter the rights of any wholly unissued series of Preferred Stock and to fix the number of shares and the designation (that is, the name) of that series. The right applies to "wholly unissued" series because once the shares are issued, subject to the limited additional authority of the board of directors under the blank check, any amendment to that series would be an amendment to the Charter requiring shareholder approval. In addition, the language of this blank check provision acknowledges that the preferred stock's protective provisions may give them a voting right despite the authority otherwise granted by this provision to the company's board of directors. This is often seen in venture capital financed companies but may be more unusual outside of that context.

Some lawyers include a separate reference to the establishment of voting rights and the scope or limits on the new series' rights regarding voting. This seems to be the result of some older case law in Delaware holding that voting is not a preferential right. *See, e.g., Telvest, Inc. v. Olson*, CA 5798, Del. Ch. (Mar. 8, 1979), *but see National Education Corp. v. Bell & Howell Co.*, CA 7278, Del. Ch. (Aug. 23, 1983). While that may be more of an issue in the context of using "blank check" provisions as the basis for creating anti-takeover devices — which today is probably the most common use of blank check preferred — it is less of a concern in the venture capital context, where there is little question that a preferred stock might be seen as a sham security intended to shift voting power and nothing more.

The blank check provision quoted as Charter Sample 9.37 goes on to provide that when the board of directors is authorized to fix the number of shares of a series, it can later change that number unless it denied itself that authority when it authorized the series of stock in question. So the board of directors can increase the number of shares in that series or decrease the number down to the number actually outstanding. The shares "undesignated" as part of a series then reassume the character they had before they were designated, which is authorized but unissued preferred stock. It bears emphasizing that this authority only applies to series previously designated by the board of directors. If there are unused shares in a series that was designated through the conventional board and shareholder approval process, the board has no authority to change those share numbers.

Occasionally, language will be included in the blank check provision stating that when the board decreases the number of shares designated in a series, those "decreased" shares return to their former character (i.e., authorized but unissued and undesignated shares). That is the outcome provided for by statute in Delaware and California, and the Model Act gives the board authority to designate shares as it determines, so this additional language seems unnecessary in those jurisdictions. *See* Del. GCL §151(g); Cal. Corp. Code §202(e)(3); and Model Code §6.02(a)(2) and (3).

Another alternative that is useful in Delaware is a Charter provision that takes advantage of a carve-out to the class voting terms set forth in §242(b)(2) of the Delaware GCL by providing:

> The authorized number of shares of Common Stock may be increased or decreased (but not below the number of shares of Common Stock then outstanding) by the affirmative vote of the holders of the shares of stock of the corporation representing a majority of the votes represented by all outstanding shares of stock of the corporation entitled to vote, notwithstanding the provisions of §242(b)(2) of the General Corporation Law.

This provision provides that class approval of the Common Stock is not required to increase or decrease the number of authorized Common Stock shares. Section 242(b)(2) provides that if a provision, such as the preceding paragraph, was in place *before* the Common Stock was issued, or was subsequently approved by a majority of the Common Stock in a class vote, no further class vote is required to increase or decrease the number of shares of the Common Stock.

This type of Charter provision is useful in the venture capital context because the preferred stock designated under the blank check provision normally is convertible. As noted at the start of this discussion, this means counsel not only has to make sure that there are authorized but unissued preferred stock shares available, but also that there are enough common stock shares available for the preferred stock to convert into. As the purpose of the blank check in the venture capital context is to avoid the need to obtain common shareholder approval for a new series of preferred stock, this mechanism is a handy tool to make sure the common stock pool remains sufficient to accommodate the conversion of all outstanding preferred stock.

The fact is that many venture capital investors do not like to include blank check provisions in the Charters of their portfolio companies. Some are concerned that the provision may be used against them. Others worry about the fiduciary duties of the board members in a contested situation. While a blank check can be very useful in forcing a change to a company's capitalization over the objection of the common stock holders, it is often a tool of last resort. In fact, the Charters of most venture capital funded companies do not include a blank check provision until they are on the eve of an IPO. At that point, the provision is put in place as a potential anti-takeover tool to be used in its future as a public company.

NOTES AND QUESTIONS

1. In considering venture capital as a financing mechanism, a company's founders, such as Joan and Michael, face the prospect of granting a set of lengthy and complex rights to the venture capital investors that, in many ways, act to subordinate the founders' rights and interests. There are positive trade-offs, but the founders have to understand what they are giving up. As discussed in Chapter 8, they must be psychologically, as well as intellectually, prepared for a very different working environment and a dramatic change in lifestyle.

2. One of the maxims of preferred stock transactions, mentioned a number of times in this chapter, is that the rights agreed upon may never be used. The main value of the documents you have carefully negotiated and drafted most likely will be that they will represent the starting point for the next round of negotiations. An additional maxim of venture capital investment is that once a company gives a right to its preferred stock investors, no matter how many additional rounds of financing that company may have, it will have to give away that right in every subsequent round. In short, if you give it once, you will have to give it every time. This fact of life adds an extra dimension of meaning when, as counsel to an early stage company, you are reviewing the provisions of competing Series A Preferred Stock term sheets.

3. Assume that Joan and Michael came to you as SoftCo's counsel and said they were going to go forward with the *Friends and Family* scenario for financing the company. What investor rights, of those examined in this chapter, would you recommend they offer to their family members and friends? A priority right on dividends? A dividend participation right? Cumulative dividends? Would you suggest a liquidation priority? A multiple priority right? A liquidation participation right? What about convertibility — would you offer that? Any anti-dilution protection? Proportionate for splits? Price protection? Would you suggest that Joan and Michael offer a redeemable security? What about board seats — would you suggest that Joan and Michael offer any? Would you give the *Friends and Family* any protective provisions? Which ones? Why?

4. As you read through this chapter, were there any preferred stock investor rights or terms that made you think "Why would anyone agree to give that right away?" If not, ask yourself that question again as, in Chapter 10, we examine the additional contractual rights typically required by venture capital preferred stock investors.

DOCUMENTING THE TRANSACTION; VENTURE CAPITAL FINANCING AGREEMENTS

A. "Pre-Contract" Contracts: Use of Letters of Intent and Non-Disclosure Agreements

1. Overview

In negotiating the terms of a business transaction, there often comes a point where the parties wish to commit to paper the deal points they have been discussing. Reasons for doing so are many and quite varied. Sometimes the writing is intended to serve as a discussion outline for future negotiations. In other instances, it memorializes those key terms on which the parties have reached agreement and identifies those items on which they will continue to negotiate. A writing also may be used when one party faces other obligations (often public company disclosure requirements imposed by the federal securities laws or the rules of a stock exchange or other such self-regulatory organization) and, before making any disclosures, either one (or both) of the parties wants the other to demonstrate its commitment to the transaction by signing some writing.

In these situations, the parties customarily sign a *letter of intent* (LOI), which also may be referred to as a *memorandum of understanding* or *term sheet*, or by other similar names. While the format and scope of these documents may vary, they all aim to capture the fundamental deal issues and record some understandings as to how the parties will behave during the negotiation process. Generally speaking, an LOI expressly provides that it is *not* binding on either party, *except for the parts that are specifically made binding.* As a result of its almost schizophrenic nature, there is a wide divergence of opinion among practicing lawyers as to the LOI's usefulness and desirability in many circumstances.

Early stage companies are frequently presented with LOIs as they develop basic business relationships with key suppliers, distributors or marketing partners, or customers. In addition, preliminary deal terms very typically are assembled in LOIs in private financing transactions. In the venture capital context, the LOI is usually called a *term sheet* and is almost a universal prerequisite to moving forward with the preparation of definitive investment transaction documents.

2. Use of Non-Disclosure/Confidentiality Agreements

Even in those situations where there is no LOI, the parties usually enter into a *confidentiality agreement*, or as it is frequently called, a *Non-Disclosure Agreement* (NDA). In certain cases, the parties' agreement on confidentiality is made part of the LOI, in which case it is considered one of the provisions that is binding on the parties. Alternatively, the NDA may be the subject of a separate, freestanding written agreement between the parties to a proposed transaction. (*See* Chapter 7, section B.1, which addresses some of the typical terms of an NDA.) Again, for early stage and emerging companies, NDAs are frequently a part of the process of developing key business relationships necessary for the company's growth.

In the venture capital financing context, it is important to note that venture capital investors almost universally refuse to enter into NDAs. Their position is that they focus on specific industries and are presented with thousands of business plans relating to those industries that, by necessity, have overlapping content or are essentially duplicative. As a result, it is impossible for them to manage an effective information segregation system. Further, because they tend to focus on a few fairly narrow industry segments, it would be impractical as a business matter for them to enter into any agreement that would preclude them from investing in a particular technology, product, or market.

As suggested in the NDA discussion earlier in Chapter 7, companies dealing with venture capital investors need to address their disclosure issues through management of the information delivery process, since a contract is not possible. The scope and content of information provided to a potential venture capital investor must strike a balance between enough details to attract interest and too much itemization of the company's secrets.

Even so, at some point prior to completion of an investment, the company will have to disclose more than it would like to the potential investor. It then will be relying upon the integrity of the investor, which among credible venture capital funds is a serious matter. The overwhelming majority of venture capital investors are very sensitive to their need to respect the confidentiality interests of the companies that they evaluate as potential investment opportunities. These venture capital funds understand that their ability to obtain the trust of the next company that they may want to invest in, and every one thereafter, can be destroyed by a single example of inappropriate information sharing.

3. Issues Regarding the Letter of Intent

The potential pitfalls of signing an LOI, even where it expressly provides that it is non-binding, are reflected in the following decision of the Delaware Supreme Court.

SIGA Technologies, Inc., v. PharmAthene, Inc.

67 A.3d 330 (Del. 2013)

Steele, Chief Justice:

A Delaware corporation appeals from the Vice Chancellor's finding that it breached a contractual obligation to negotiate in good faith and is liable under the doctrine of promissory estoppel. We reaffirm that where parties agree to negotiate in good faith in accordance with a term sheet, that obligation to negotiate in good faith is enforceable.

Where a trial judge makes a factual finding, supported by the record, that the parties would have reached an agreement but for the defendant's bad faith negotiation, we hold that a trial judge may award expectation damages. We reverse the Vice Chancellor's promissory estoppel holding because a promise expressed in a fully enforceable contract cannot give rise to a promissory estoppel claim. We also reverse the Vice Chancellor's equitable damages award based on his factual conclusion that the parties would have reached an agreement, so that he may reconsider the award in light of this opinion.

I. Factual and Procedural History[1]

A. Facts

Plaintiff–Appellee PharmAthene, Inc., and Defendant–Appellant SIGA Technologies, Inc., are both Delaware corporations engaged in biodefense research and development. In 2004, SIGA acquired an antiviral drug for the treatment of smallpox, ST-246. At that time, the drug's viability, potential uses, safety, and efficacy were all unknown, but the drug had enormous potential.

By late 2005, SIGA had experienced difficulty developing the drug and was running out of money. NASDAQ threatened to delist SIGA's shares and SIGA's largest shareholder, MacAndrews & Forbes (MAF), was unwilling to invest additional money. SIGA estimated it needed approximately $16 million to complete the development process.[2]

As a result of SIGA's difficulties, SIGA's management began discussing a possible collaboration with PharmAthene. Thomas Konatich, SIGA's Chief Financial Officer, contacted Eric Richman, PharmAthene's Vice President of Business Development and Strategies. Richman desired a merger between the two companies, but SIGA resisted because of its past experience with PharmAthene.[3] According to Richman's contemporaneous notes, SIGA insisted on framing a license agreement before discussing a merger because of that past experience and because SIGA needed an immediate cash infusion to stabilize its financial situation. By the end of 2005, both SIGA's and PharmAthene's conservative estimates valued ST-246 at approximately $1 billion.

In late 2005 and early 2006, Konatich and Richman outlined the terms of a license agreement. Konatich kept Donald Drapkin, Chairman of SIGA's Board of Directors and MAF's Vice Chairman, well informed about the negotiations. Konatich and Richman also assembled negotiation teams on behalf of their companies. On January 3, 2006, Richman sent Konatich and Dr. Dennis Hruby, SIGA's Chief Scientific Officer, a proposed term sheet based on his discussions with SIGA about a license agreement for ST-246. On January 4, Hruby replied: "Thanks for the prompt response. We are most interested in trying to make this a mutually agreeable term sheet and moving on to the next step."

---

1. The facts in this section are taken primarily from the Vice Chancellor's posttrial opinion below, *PharmAthene, Inc. v. SIGA Techs., Inc. (PharmAthene III)*, 2011 WL 4390726 (Del.Ch. Sept. 22, 2011).

2. SIGA also lacked much of the institutional experience necessary to take a drug to market successfully. For example, SIGA lacked employees with expertise in regulatory or government affairs, quality assurance, quality control, clinical trials, manufacturing, and business development.

3. Near the end of 2003, SIGA and PharmAthene had discussed a potential merger, but those discussions failed as a result of PharmAthene's board members' reservations.

Konatich and Richman continued to exchange draft term sheets. Much of the negotiation focused on upfront cash payments and funding guarantees. On January 16, Richman sent Konatich a revised term sheet that provided for a total deal size of $16 million, an increased upfront payment of $6 million, and significant cash milestone payments. When Konatich forwarded this term sheet to Drapkin, he recommended that Drapkin speak directly to Richman to present SIGA's Board of Directors' position on PharmAthene's proposal.

On January 17, the Vice Chancellor found that Drapkin and Richman discussed the term sheet during a telephone call and Drapkin requested that Richman make two changes. Richman testified that Drapkin told him that if the changes were acceptable to PharmAthene, then "[w]e have got a deal on the term sheet, and it's ready to present to your board for approval." At a January 18 PharmAthene board meeting, Richman presented the January 16 term sheet and explained Drapkin's proposed changes. Jeffrey Baumel, PharmAthene's outside counsel, drafted the minutes for that board meeting. The term sheet was not signed, however, and the minutes do not state that the board approved the term sheet.[7]

On January 19, Richman again spoke with Drapkin and told him that the PharmAthene board had approved the license agreement term sheet with Drapkin's two proposed changes. While PharmAthene alleges that by this time, the parties had "a deal" and could move on to discussing a merger, Richman did not send a copy of the revised term sheet to Drapkin until February 10, 2006.

On January 26, a clean copy was made of the two-page license agreement term sheet incorporating Drapkin's two changes (the LATS). The LATS recites that the parties intended to "establish a partnership to further develop & commercialize [ST-246] for the treatment of [s]mallpox and orthopox related infections and to develop other orthopox virus therapeutics." The LATS also sets forth terms relating to, among other things, patents covered, licenses, license fees, and royalties. However, the LATS was not signed, and a footer on both pages states, "Non Binding Terms."

The Vice Chancellor summarized the LATS in his posttrial opinion:

> Without attempting to cover all the details, the LATS contemplates a license agreement along the following lines to support the further development and commercialization of ST-246 for the treatment of smallpox. First, SIGA would grant to PharmAthene "a worldwide exclusive license and [sic] under the Patents, Know–How and Materials to use, develop, make, have made, sell, export and import Products in Field. The right to grant sublicenses shall be specifically included in the license." Second, the license would cover ST-246 and all other related products worldwide covered by the patents and know-how relating to ST-246 and its development and manufacture. Third, the LATS described the makeup of a research and development committee, which would include representatives from both PharmAthene and SIGA. The parties identified twelve categories of tasks relevant to that committee and assigned responsibility for each one to either SIGA or PharmAthene. In addition, PharmAthene agreed to fund the research and development based on a defined budget.

---

7. The Vice Chancellor found that Baumel credibly testified that the minutes do not mention the term sheet because he does not incorporate documents into the minutes until they are signed.

Fourth, the LATS included economic terms. PharmAthene was scheduled to pay a "License Fee" of $6 million in total, which consisted of $2 million cash up front, $2.5 million as a deferred license fee to be paid twelve months after execution of a license agreement if certain events occurred, and $1.5 million after SIGA obtained financing in excess of $15 million. In addition, the LATS contained a provision under which PharmAthene would pay an additional $10 million based on the achievement of specific milestones relating to certain sales targets and regulatory approvals. The LATS also provided for PharmAthene to make annual royalty payments of 8% on "yearly net sales of Patented Products" of less than $250 million, 10% on sales greater than $250 million, and 12% on sales greater than $1 billion. Lastly, the LATS stated that, "[i]n addition, SIGA will be entitled to receive 50% of any amounts by which net margin exceeds 20% on sales to the U.S. Federal Government."

On January 18, 2006, [in addition to approving the LATS,] the PharmAthene board decided that it preferred a merger with SIGA instead of a license agreement, so representatives of PharmAthene and SIGA met to begin merger discussions on January 23 at MAF's office in New York City. Because of SIGA's precarious financial position, SIGA asked PharmAthene to provide bridge financing so that SIGA could continue developing ST-246 while merger negotiations proceeded. Richman and two other PharmAthene representatives testified that PharmAthene agreed to consider raising funds for a bridge loan on the condition that PharmAthene would obtain at least a license for ST-246 if merger negotiations fell through.

On February 10, 2006, David Wright, PharmAthene's Chief Financial Officer, sent Drapkin a draft merger term sheet that included the following provision regarding a license agreement:

> SIGA and PharmAthene will negotiate the terms of a definitive License Agreement in accordance with the terms set forth in the Term Sheet . . . attached on Schedule 1 hereto. The License Agreement will be executed simultaneously with the Definitive [Merger] Agreement and will become effective only upon the termination of the Definitive [Merger] Agreement.

* * *

On February 22, 2006, the parties once again met at MAF's office. Drapkin and another SIGA board member attended. Baumel reiterated PharmAthene's desire to execute simultaneously a merger agreement and a license agreement (in case the merger did not close). Relying on testimony from Baumel, Richman, and Wright, the Vice Chancellor found that Drapkin told PharmAthene he was not going to pay lawyers to draft a formal license agreement and suggested PharmAthene just attach the LATS to the merger agreement. Relying on Baumel's testimony, the Vice Chancellor found that Drapkin told PharmAthene that "this approach would be as good as a license agreement and would guarantee PharmAthene, at a minimum, a license if negotiations for a merger fell through."

The PharmAthene board reviewed a final merger term sheet on March 1, 2006. That term sheet specifically referred to the LATS and included a copy of the LATS as an exhibit. Again relying on testimony from Baumel, Richman, and Wright, the Vice Chancellor found that during a March 6 meeting, "Drapkin reiterated that 'in any case, if the merger doesn't close, [PharmAthene] will get [its] license.'" On March 10, the parties signed a merger letter of intent and attached the merger term sheet and the LATS.

On March 20, 2006, SIGA and PharmAthene entered into a Bridge Loan Agreement in which PharmAthene loaned SIGA $3 million for expenses relating to the merger, developing ST-246, and overhead. . . . It also specifically contemplates that the parties might not ultimately agree on either a merger or a license agreement. Bridge Loan Agreement Section 2.3 obligates the parties to negotiate in good faith a license agreement in accordance with the terms of the LATS if the merger is terminated:

> Upon any termination of the Merger Term Sheet . . . , termination of the Definitive Agreement relating to the Merger, or if a Definitive Agreement is not executed . . . , SIGA and PharmAthene will negotiate in good faith with the intention of executing a definitive License Agreement in accordance with the terms set forth in the License Agreement Term Sheet attached as Exhibit C and [SIGA] agrees for a period of 90 days during which the definitive license agreement is under negotiation, it shall not, directly or indirectly, initiate discussions or engage in negotiations with any corporation, partnership, person or other entity or group concerning any Competing Transaction without the prior written consent of the other party or notice from the other party that it desires to terminate discussions hereunder.

With the Bridge Loan Agreement signed, PharmAthene provided SIGA with financial and administrative support while the parties redevoted attention to their proposed merger terms. On June 8, 2006, PharmAthene and SIGA signed the Merger Agreement, which selects Delaware law as its choice of law. Merger Agreement Section 12.3 is substantively identical to Bridge Loan Agreement Section 2.3 and provides that if the merger is terminated, the parties agree to negotiate in good faith a definitive license agreement in accordance with the LATS's terms. Section 13.3 stipulates that each of the parties must use their "best efforts to take such actions as may be necessary or reasonably requested by the other parties hereto to carry out and consummate the transactions contemplated by this Agreement." Section 12.4 provides that those provisions, among others, survive the Merger Agreement's termination. The Merger Agreement had a drop-dead date of September 30, 2006.

The Vice Chancellor found that SIGA's key representatives understood that PharmAthene and SIGA were likely to enter into a lasting relationship, either by a merger or a license agreement. Several comments by SIGA representatives indicate that SIGA began experiencing seller's remorse after SIGA received a $5.4-million-dollar grant from the National Institutes of Health. As the parties continued preparing for the merger, SIGA achieved several milestones. For example, SIGA's Audit Committee approved an agreement with a clinical trial organization to perform the first human trial of ST-246. In September 2006, the National Institutes of Health awarded SIGA $16.5 million to develop the drug. After receiving this grant, SIGA representatives expressed remorse over having agreed to the merger.[18]

---

18. *See id.* at *9 ("For example, after receiving the NIH grant, Hruby stated in an email to Drapkin (which he later acknowledged to be an exaggeration) that, 'I have grave concerns about the merger as it is currently going forward in that the merged company will not be . . . [Small Business Innovation Research Program] compliant. In that case we would have to shut down [$]30 million in current grants and contracts.'

As the Merger Agreement's September 30 drop-dead date approached, the SEC still had not approved SIGA's draft proxy statement. PharmAthene asked SIGA to extend the drop-dead date. On October 4, SIGA's Board of Directors met and decided to terminate the Merger Agreement. Shortly after terminating the Merger Agreement, SIGA publicly announced it had received the $16.5 million NIH grant and that ST-246 provided 100% protection against smallpox in a primate trial. After that announcement, SIGA sold two million shares of its stock at $4.54 per share, more than three times SIGA's 2005 share price.

After SIGA terminated the Merger Agreement, PharmAthene hired attorney Elliot Olstein to draft a licensing agreement with SIGA. On October 12, 2006, Baumel sent PharmAthene's Proposed License Agreement to SIGA's outside counsel, James Grayer. On October 26, Olstein emailed Nicholas Coch, another outside attorney for SIGA, and stated that PharmAthene was ready to sign the Proposed License Agreement because it contained "all the essential terms of a license agreement and is completely consistent with the [LATS]." Coch responded that SIGA would not provide a revised license agreement before the parties met, because the "nature of the negotiations required under the Merger Agreement" necessitated "a robust discussion."

Meanwhile, as the Vice Chancellor found, SIGA had internally discussed alternative structures for a definitive license agreement. SIGA's controller emailed Konatich and several other SIGA representatives a financial analysis concluding that total past and future development costs equaled $36.66 million, and that a $40 million upfront license fee would support a 50-50 profit split.

On November 6, the parties met to discuss the license agreement. Given the clinical progress made since the parties last negotiated, PharmAthene emphasized the need to revise some of the LATS's economic terms. PharmAthene's representatives expressed confusion about SIGA's new emphasis on a partnership and maintained that the LATS's terms bound the parties. Nevertheless, PharmAthene was willing to listen to SIGA's proposal in order to avoid a dispute. SIGA then proposed a $40–45 million upfront payment and a 50-50 profit split. SIGA agreed to draft a formal proposal and send it to PharmAthene.

On November 21, 2006, SIGA sent PharmAthene a 102–page Draft LLC Agreement. The Vice Chancellor contrasted the LATS to the Draft LLC Agreement thusly:

[T]he Draft LLC Agreement included the following economic changes: (1) the upfront payment from PharmAthene to SIGA increased from $6 million to $100 million; (2) the milestone payments to SIGA increased from $10 million to $235 million; (3) the royalty percentages owed to SIGA increased from 8%, 10%, and 12% depending on the amount of sales to 18%, 22%, 25%, and 28%; and (4) SIGA would receive 50% of any remaining profit whereas the LATS provided for profit sharing only from U.S. government sales having a margin of 20% or more. In addition, several noneconomic terms were revised to favor SIGA heavily and to undermine PharmAthene's control of ST-246. These provisions included: (1) SIGA's right to resolve disputes unilaterally; (2) SIGA's ability to block any distribution to PharmAthene; (3) PharmAthene's obligation to fund fully the

---

In response to this email, Steven Fasman, an in-house lawyer at [MAF], asked, 'should SIGA continue with its merger plans or should it try to go it alone?'" (some alterations in original) (footnote omitted)).

LLC's costs, despite having to split profits 50/50; and (4) SIGA's right to terminate the LLC under certain conditions, with PharmAthene having no right to cure and with all rights to the product reverting to SIGA.

Olstein and Coch exchanged letters discussing SIGA's Draft LLC Agreement throughout November and December. Olstein asserted that the Agreement's terms were "radically different from the terms set forth in the [LATS]," but that PharmAthene was "willing to consider" changes to the LATS, including a 50/50 profit split. SIGA disputed that the LATS was binding because of the "Non Binding Terms" footer, and it never addressed PharmAthene's proposed profit split. Coch issued an ultimatum on December 12: unless PharmAthene responded by December 20 that it was prepared to negotiate "without preconditions" regarding the LATS's binding nature, the parties had "nothing more to talk about." On December 20, 2006, PharmAthene filed suit in the Court of Chancery.

B. Procedural History

* * *

In January 2011, the Vice Chancellor presided over an eleven-day trial in this action. After extensive posttrial briefing . . . the Vice Chancellor made posttrial findings of fact and conclusions of law on both PharmAthene's amended complaint and SIGA's counterclaim. [In *PharmAthene III*],[23] [the Vice Chancellor] determined that: . . . , (2) SIGA was liable for breach of its obligation (under the Bridge Loan and Merger Agreements) to negotiate in good faith a definitive license agreement in accordance with the LATS's terms . . . and (4) the proper remedy was an equitable payment stream approximating the terms of the license agreement to which he found the parties would ultimately have agreed. . . .

. . . SIGA appeals the Vice Chancellor's orders. . . .

* * *

III. Analysis

* * *

B. SIGA breached its contractual obligation to negotiate in good faith.

SIGA argues that the Vice Chancellor erred when he concluded that SIGA breached an obligation to negotiate in good faith under the Bridge Loan and Merger Agreements. SIGA argues it is inconsistent to hold that the LATS is not a binding license agreement and at the same time conclude that SIGA's obligation to negotiate in good faith requires that SIGA only propose terms substantially similar to the LATS. We disagree.

---

23. *PharmAthene III*, 2011 WL 4390726 (Del.Ch. Sept. 22, 2011).

. . . Although [we acknowledge that before our 2012 decision in *Titan Investment,*][43] some ambiguity existed concerning whether an obligation to negotiate in good faith was enforceable,[44] . . . we now reaffirm that an express contractual obligation to negotiate in good faith is binding on the contracting parties.

* * *

RGC International Investors, LDC v. Greka Energy Corp.[54] is instructive [with respect to the scope of this duty to negotiate in good faith]. In *RGC International*, a Vice Chancellor addressed whether a defendant breached an obligation to negotiate a definitive agreement based on a term sheet. The Vice Chancellor noted that the term sheet did "not include language that the parties explicitly reserved the right not to be bound."[56] He concluded that, "[a]t the very least, after signing the [t]erm [s]heet, neither party could in good faith insist on specific terms that directly contradicted a specific provision found in the [t]erm [s]heet."[57]

Similarly, although applying New York law, a Southern District of New York judge concluded that where parties "bind themselves to a concededly incomplete agreement in the sense that they accept a mutual commitment to negotiate together in good faith in an effort to reach final agreement within the scope that has been settled in the preliminary agreement,"[58] a party to that agreement may demand that "his counterparty negotiate the open terms in good faith toward a final contract incorporating the agreed terms."[59] While "good faith differences in the negotiation of the open issues may prevent a reaching of final contract," a counterparty cannot "insist[ ] on conditions that do not conform to the preliminary agreement."[60]

The express contractual language in the Bridge Loan and Merger Agreements obligated the parties to "negotiate in good faith with the intention of executing a definitive License Agreement in accordance with the terms set forth in the" LATS. The question becomes whether the language "in accordance with the terms set forth" means that the parties had a duty, as the Vice Chancellor found, "to negotiate toward a license

---

43. *Titan Inv. Fund II, LP v. Freedom Mortg. Corp.*, 58 A.3d 984, 2012 WL 6049157, at *3 (Del. Dec. 5, 2012) (ORDER).

44. *See Great–W. Investors LP v. Thomas H. Lee Partners, L.P.*, 2011 WL 284992, at *9 (Del.Ch. Jan. 14, 2011) (citations omitted) ("[A]n agreement to negotiate in good faith *may* be binding under Delaware law, however, and specific performance could, in theory, be an appropriate remedy for breach of such a provision." (emphasis added)).

54. 2001 WL 984689 (Del.Ch. Aug. 22, 2001), *overruled on other grounds by Scion Breckenridge Managing Member, LLC v. ASB Allegiance Real Estate Fund,* _____ A.3d _____, 2013 WL 1914714 (Del.2013).

56. *Id.* at *13 n. 79.

57. *Id.* at *14.

58. *Teachers Ins. & Annuity Ass'n. of Am. v. Tribune Co.*, 670 F.Supp. 491, 498 (S.D.N.Y.1987) (citations omitted). Federal courts interpreting New York law recognize this as a Type II preliminary agreement. *See Fairbrook Leasing, Inc. v. Mesaba Aviation, Inc.*, 519 F.3d 421, 426–27 (8th Cir.2008) (citations omitted). [With respect to Type I and Type II preliminary agreements, *see infra* note 82 and accompanying text.]

59. *Teachers*, 670 F.Supp. at 498.

60. *Id.*

agreement with economic terms substantially similar to the terms of the LATS"[61] (or at least not inconsistent with the LATS's terms) or whether the parties intended the LATS merely as a "jumping off point."[62]

Although the LATS itself is not signed and contains a footer on each page stating "Non Binding Terms," the record supports the Vice Chancellor's factual conclusion that "incorporation of the LATS into the Bridge Loan and Merger Agreements reflects an intent on the part of both parties to negotiate toward a license agreement with economic terms substantially similar to the terms of the LATS if the merger was not consummated."[63] The Vice Chancellor recognized that while "the economic terms [SIGA] proposed in the Draft LLC Agreement may not have 'directly contradict[ed]' the LATS . . . , they differed dramatically from the LATS in favor of SIGA"[64] to the extent that they "virtually disregarded the economic terms of the LATS other than using them as a skeletal framework for the *types* of payments that would be made without giving any meaningful weight to the dollar amounts or percentages [SIGA] had negotiated earlier."[65]

SIGA notes that requiring parties to propose terms "substantially similar" to those in a term sheet introduces some uncertainty and litigation risk into negotiations. Because a trial judge must find both that a party's proposed terms are substantially dissimilar and that the party proposed those terms in bad faith, we think SIGA overstates the litigation risk. Under Delaware law, "bad faith is not simply bad judgment or negligence, but rather it implies the conscious doing of a wrong because of dishonest purpose or moral obliquity; it is different from the negative idea of negligence in that it contemplates a state of mind affirmatively operating with furtive design or ill will."[66] Not only did SIGA's negotiating position differ substantially from the LATS's terms, but also the Vice Chancellor also correctly concluded that SIGA took that position in bad faith.

The record supports the Vice Chancellor's finding that "SIGA disregarded [the LATS's] terms and attempted to negotiate a definitive license agreement that contained

61. *PharmAthene III*, 2011 WL 4390726, at *22 (Del.Ch. Sept. 22, 2011).

62. *Id.* (describing SIGA's position that "the parties intended the LATS simply to provide a 'jumping off point' by specifying the basic structure of a potential licensing agreement or partnership").

63. *Id.* The Vice Chancellor found that "[t]he extent to which the parties negotiated the economic terms of the LATS in January 2006 and the inclusion of the LATS in the Bridge Loan and Merger Agreements buttresses the conclusion that they intended those terms to be more than a mere 'jumping off point' in later negotiations." *Id.* at *23. He found it unlikely, especially in light of SIGA's cash needs at the time, "that the parties would have wasted time and money negotiating specific economic terms for the LATS without intending to give those terms significance in later negotiations." *Id.* He also found it "unlikely that the parties would have incorporated the LATS into the subsequent Bridge Loan and Merger Agreements if they intended the LATS to provide only a rough and easily modified outline of the basic structure of the licensing agreement." *Id.* As support for his factual conclusions, the Vice Chancellor credited, among other things, "the testimony and documentary evidence PharmAthene adduced that it would not have loaned $3 million to SIGA without an assurance from SIGA that PharmAthene reasonably could expect to control ST-246 through either a merger or a license agreement in accordance with the terms of the LATS." *Id.*

64. *Id.* at *26.

65. *Id.*

66. *CNL–AB LLC v. E. Prop. Fund I SPE (MS REF) LLC*, 2011 WL 353529, at *9 (Del.Ch. Jan. 28, 2011) (quoting *Desert Equities, Inc. v. Morgan Stanley Leveraged Equity Fund, II, L.P.*, 624 A.2d 1199, 1208 n. 16 (Del.1993)) (internal quotation marks omitted).

economic and other terms drastically different and significantly more favorable to SIGA than those in the LATS."[67] The Vice Chancellor also found that Drapkin "abdicated" his responsibility to remind SIGA of the terms to which it agreed in the LATS "and resorted instead to a selective and biased memory of the parties' negotiations. Drapkin apparently took no active role in the post-September 2006 licensing negotiations other than to offer his counterfactual recollection that the LATS [was] nothing but a 'jumping off point.'"[68] The Vice Chancellor further found that "Drapkin, and SIGA for that matter, essentially left the negotiations of the license agreement to those who either had no involvement in the previous negotiations and agreements . . . or acting in their own self-interest . . . were more than happy to disregard the economic importance of the LATS."[69] Evidence that "SIGA began experiencing 'seller's remorse' during the merger negotiations for having given up control of what was looking more and more like a multi-billion-dollar drug" bolsters the Vice Chancellor's finding that SIGA failed to negotiate in good faith for a definitive license agreement in accordance with the terms of the LATS.[70] Therefore, we affirm the Vice Chancellor's conclusion that SIGA acted in bad faith when negotiating the license agreement in breach of its contractual obligations under both the Merger Agreement and the Bridge Loan Agreement.

* * *

D. Proper Remedy

We now turn to the question of what is the proper contractual remedy for breach of an agreement to negotiate in good faith where the court finds as fact that the parties, had they negotiated in good faith, would have reached an agreement. Our decisions have not clearly answered this question. In *Titan Investment Fund II, LP v. Freedom Mortgage Corp.*, we reversed the Superior Court judge's award of a one-percent commitment fee for breach of an agreement to negotiate in good faith.[75] We noted that it was "fatally inconsistent" for the trial judge to conclude "that the contract would not have closed[,] even absent Freedom's breach," and at the same time award damages "that presupposed the opposite conclusion, namely, that the deal would have closed."[76] We concluded that given the plaintiff's "inability to establish that the . . . [c]ontract would have closed but for [the defendant's] breach, [the plaintiff was] not entitled to damages measured on a 'benefit-of-the-bargain' basis. Rather, [the plaintiff] was entitled only to its 'reliance' damages, measured by its actually-incurred costs and expenses."[77]

* * *

---

67. *PharmAthene III*, 2011 WL 4390726, at *22. . . .

68. *Id.* at *25. In making this factual determination, the Vice Chancellor made credibility judgments which deserve deference. *Id.* at *25 n. 129. . . .

69. *Id.* at *25.

70. *Id.* at *24;. . . .

75. *Titan Inv. Fund II, LP v. Freedom Mortg. Corp.*, 58 A.3d 984, 2012 WL 6049157, at *3 (Del. Dec. 5, 2012) (ORDER).

76. *Id.*

77. *Id.*

Even though our choice of law analysis mandates that we apply Delaware law, we find other courts' analyses instructive. Federal courts interpreting New York law recognize two types of binding preliminary agreements, "Type I" and "Type II."[82] Parties create a Type II preliminary agreement when they "agree on certain major terms, but leave other terms open for further negotiation."[83] "[T]he parties can bind themselves to a concededly incomplete agreement in the sense that they accept a mutual commitment to negotiate together in good faith in an effort to reach final agreement within the scope that has been settled in the preliminary agreement."[84] A Type II agreement "does not commit the parties to their ultimate contractual objective but rather to the obligation to negotiate the open issues in good faith in an attempt to reach the alternate objective within the agreed framework."[85]

* * *

Our decision in *Titan Investment* leaves open the question of whether expectation damages are available where the trial judge makes a factual finding that the parties would have reached agreement but for the defendant's breach. In fashioning his remedy, the Vice Chancellor noted the lack of consensus. We now hold that where the parties have a Type II preliminary agreement to negotiate in good faith, and the trial judge makes a factual finding, supported by the record, that the parties would have reached an agreement but for the defendant's bad faith negotiations, the plaintiff is entitled to recover contract expectation damages.[99]

In this case, the Vice Chancellor made two key factual findings, supported by the record: (1) "the parties memorialized the basic terms of a transaction in . . . the LATS, and expressly agreed in the Bridge Loan and Merger Agreements that they would negotiate in good faith a final transaction in accordance with those terms"[100] and

---

82. *Fairbrook Leasing, Inc. v. Mesaba Aviation, Inc.*, 519 F.3d 421, 426–27 (8th Cir. 2008) (citations omitted). A Type I agreement "is a fully binding preliminary agreement, which is created when the parties agree on all the points that require negotiation (including whether to be bound) but agree to memorialize their agreement in a more formal document. Such an agreement is fully binding . . . ." *Adjustrite Sys., Inc. v. GAB Bus. Servs., Inc.*, 145 F.3d 543, 548 (2d Cir.1998) (citations omitted).

83. *Adjustrite*, 145 F.3d at 548.

84. *Teachers Ins. & Annuity Ass'n of Am. v. Tribune Co.*, 670 F.Supp. 491, 498 (S.D.N.Y.1987) (citations omitted).

85. *Id.* A Type II agreement "does not guarantee" the parties will reach agreement on a final contract because of "good faith differences in the negotiation of the open issues" may preclude final agreement. *Id.* A Type II agreement "does, however, bar a party from renouncing the deal, abandoning the negotiations, or insisting on conditions that do not conform to the preliminary agreement." *Id.*

99. An expectation damages award presupposes that the plaintiff can prove damages with reasonable certainty. *Callahan v. Rafail*, 2001 WL 283012, at *1 (Del.Super. Mar. 16, 2001) (citation omitted) ("It is well-settled law that 'a recovery for lost profits will be allowed only if their loss is capable of being proved, with a reasonable degree of certainty. No recovery can be had for loss of profits which are determined to be uncertain, contingent, conjectural, or speculative.'").

100. *PharmAthene III*, 2011 WL 4390726, at *35. The Vice Chancellor ultimately found that the Bridge Loan and Merger Agreements "required the parties to negotiate in good faith a license agreement with economic terms substantially similar to those contained in the LATS." *Id.* at *23. He also found "that the parties also recognized that the negotiations probably would introduce new terms and lead to some adjustment of terms expressly embodied in the LATS, while other terms in the LATS were almost certain to remain." *Id.* at *35.

(2) "but for SIGA's bad faith negotiations, the parties would have consummated a license agreement."[101] The Vice Chancellor's factual conclusions support a finding that SIGA and PharmAthene entered into a Type II preliminary agreement and that neither party could in good faith propose terms inconsistent with that agreement. Because we had not previously addressed whether Delaware recognizes Type II preliminary agreements [and thus would permit] a plaintiff to recover expectation damages, . . . we reverse the Vice Chancellor's damages award and remand the case for reconsideration of the damages award consistent with this opinion.

* * *

1. What type of transaction is at issue in this case? Who are the parties to the transaction at issue in this case? How was the proposed transaction to be structured?
2. What do you suppose was the business incentive for SIGA Technologies, Inc. to enter into this transaction?
3. What do you suppose was the business incentive for PharmAthene Inc. to enter into this transaction?
4. What is the difference between a "Type I" and a "Type II" binding preliminary agreement?
5. What is the appropriate remedy for breach of an agreement to negotiate in good faith? Do you agree with the result reached by the court in this case?
6. What are the advantages to entering into a letter of intent? What are the disadvantages of entering into this kind of written agreement, even if it specifies that it is non-binding?

1. **What is "Bad Faith"?** At least one leading law firm has concluded that the SIGA *Technologies* decision adds

> to the level of uncertainty and risk for parties negotiating a transaction. The Delaware Court addressed this concern head-on and found it overstated, explaining that "a trial judge must find *both* that a party's proposed terms are substantially dissimilar and that the party proposed those terms in bad faith." [*SIGA Technologies* at pg. 39 (emphasis added).] We are not as convinced as the Court on this point, particularly because one person's "bad faith" may be another's tough negotiating style. While the facts in *SIGA Technologies* may illustrate a level of bad faith — what the Court referred to as "seller's remorse" — the definition of bad faith is far from cut and dry. Under

---

101. . . . *PharmAthene III*, 2011 WL 4390726, at *40, *42.

Delaware law, bad faith is defined using ambiguous terms such as "dishonest purpose or moral obliquity" and "furtive design or ill will." [*Id.* Accordingly, in the wake of the *SIGA Technologies* decision, the parties must be aware] that even in the absence of a signed definitive agreement, one party may be required to pay the other the full benefit of the bargain for a deal that was contemplated but ultimately did not reach finality if they agreed in a term sheet or letter of intent to negotiate in good faith.

Clients should also be aware that state laws vary widely in their treatment of term sheets, letters of intent, and agreements to negotiate in good faith, as do the available remedies for breach of those agreements. Parties should carefully consider the choice of law clause when entering into such agreements, and draft the agreements with precision to make clear whether the parties intend to enter into a binding agreement to negotiate, an exclusivity agreement, or another type of preliminary agreement. With this decision [in *SIGA Technologies*], the Delaware Supreme Court made clear that so-called non-binding "agreements to agree" can in fact be interpreted as enforceable contracts and the breach of those contracts can have substantial financial ramifications if they previously agreed to negotiate in good faith.

Stephen M. LaRose and Kathleen Burns, *"But I Thought We Were Just Negotiating" — Are the Good Faith Provisions in a Term Sheet or Letter of Intent Enforceable Upon the Parties?* Nixon Peabody, LLP, Client Memo (July 24, 2013), *available at* http://www.nixonpeabody.com/beware_good_faith_provisions_can_be_enforceable_contracts. *Query*: Do you think the facts of *SIGA Technologies* reflect "bad faith" or just a "tough negotiating style"?

2. **What is the Appropriate Remedy?** "The most important aspect of the [*SIGA Technologies*] decision is the court's holding that benefit of the bargain, rather than reliance, damages are available where a court finds that a deal would have been reached but for the defendant's bad faith. This raises the stakes significantly. . . ." Jones Day Alert, *Delaware Update: Supreme Court Awards Expectation Damages for Failure to Negotiate in Good Faith*, Law Firm Memo (July 2013), *available at* http://www.jonesday.com/delaware-update-supreme-court-awards-expectation-damages-for-failure-to-negotiate-in-good-faith-07-09-2013/. *Query*: What is the difference between the reliance measure of damages vs. expectation damages (which also are often referred to as "benefit of the bargain" damages)? Why is this distinction so important?

> . . . Benefit of the bargain damages are meant to compensate a party with what it would have received had the contract been finalized and fully performed. It is usually measured in terms of reasonably expected profits. The reliance measure of damages, in comparison, provides reimbursement to the non-breaching party for expenses it incurred in reliance on the contract.
>
> The *SIGA* court's decision is notable for the remedies it contemplates, *i.e.*, expectation damages, not for its determination that a party can be held liable for breaching a duty to negotiate in good faith. Numerous courts have recognized a cause of action for breach of a duty to negotiate in good faith.[1] In fact, at least one California court

---

1. *Goodstein Constr. Corp. v. City of New York*, 604 N.E.2d 1356 (N.Y. 1992); *Venture Associates Corp. v. Zenith Data Systems Corp.*, 96 F.3d 275 (7th Cir. 1996) (applying Illinois law); *Brady v. State*,

has gone so far as to recognize a cause of action for breach of the implied covenant of good faith and fair dealing in a case where the parties' term sheet did *not* expressly impose an obligation to negotiate in good faith. *Copeland v. Baskin Robbins U.S.A.*, 96 Cal. App. 4th 1251 (2002) [emphasis added]. But these prior court rulings have typically favored reliance, [not the expectancy measure of] damages.[2]

Robert Burwell and Howard Miller, *When a Non-Binding Term Sheet Becomes Binding*, Mintz, Levin, Cohn, Ferris, Glovsky, and Popeo, PC, Law Firm Memo (July 8, 2013), *available at* http://www.mintz.com/newsletter/2013/Advisories/3203 -0713-NAT-COR/index.html. *Query:* Which measure of damages — expectancy or reliance — is more likely to result in a larger damages award? From a transactional lawyer's point of view, why is it important to understand this difference?

3. ***What are the Practical Implications of* SIGA Technologies?** Admittedly, the facts of *SIGA Technologies* are rather unusual and thus may be limited to the specific facts of the underlying dispute in that case. *Query:* Do you think that the Delaware Supreme Court would reach the same result in a situation where there was a stand-alone term sheet (or LOI) clearly stating that it was non-binding and was not incorporated into a separate agreement between the parties?

In thinking about the scope and usefulness of term sheets in connection with SoftCo's proposed arrangement with Big Bad Software, you may want to consider the observations of an experienced practitioner as set forth in the following article:

---

965 P.2d 1, 11 (Alaska 1998) ("Many courts enforce promises to negotiate in good faith. . . . Most courts that do so limit relief to reliance damages.").

   Promises to negotiate are not, however, universally enforced. *See Chambers v. Gold Medal Bakery, Inc.*, 83 Mass. App. Ct. 234, 247-248 (Mass. App. Ct. 2013) ("[A] mere commitment to negotiate in good faith is of limited enforceability. Even if such an agreement were deemed to have some incremental force beyond a mere agreement to agree, it ultimately would be unenforceable if either party credibly could claim that a good faith dispute remained."); *485 Lafayette St. Acquisition, LLC v. Glover Estates, LLC*, 2012 Mass. Super. LEXIS 207, 20 (Mass. Super. Ct. May 14, 2012), citing *Schwanbeck v. Federal-Mogul Corp.*, 412 Mass. 703, 706, 592 N.E.2d 1289 (1992) (language in a letter of intent calling for the parties to "proceed to negotiate in good faith a definitive Joint Venture Agreement is merely a promise made with an understanding that it is not to be legally binding, but only a statement of present intention. . . . 'An expression of present intent is not a contract.'").

   2. For example, the New York Court of Appeals held that New York law limits a plaintiff to reliance damages for breach of a duty to negotiate. *See Goodstein Constr. Corp.*, 604 N.E.2d at 1360. *See also Copeland*, 96 Cal. App. 4th at 1263-64 (applying California law); *L-7 Designs, Inc. v. Old Navy, LLC*, 647 F.3d 419, 431 (2d Cir. N.Y. 2011) (citing *Goodstein*) (lost profits not available where no agreement is reached).

   Although the *SIGA* decision appears to represent the first case in which a state's highest court has ruled in favor of expectancy damages for breach of a duty to negotiate in good faith, federal courts and lower state courts, including the Delaware Court of Chancery, have found expectancy damages to be appropriate in certain circumstances. For example, in 1996, Judge Richard Posner, writing for the Seventh Circuit and applying Illinois law, stated in dicta that "[d]amages for breach of an agreement to negotiate may be . . . the same as the damages for breach of the final contract that the parties would have signed had it not been for the defendant's bad faith." *Venture Associates*, 96 F.3d at 278-79. *See also RGC Int'l Investors, LDC v. Greka Energy Corp.*, 2001 Del. Ch. LEXIS 107, 53 (Del. Ch. Aug. 22, 2001) overruled on other grounds by *Scion Breckenridge Managing Member, LLC v. ASB Allegiance Real Estate Fund*, 2013 Del. LEXIS 235, 48 (Del. May 9, 2013); *Milex Products, Inc. v. Alra Laboratories, Inc.*, 237 Ill. App. 3d 177 (Ill. App. Ct. 1992).

Gregory Gosfield
It's a Question of What's Binding: A Look at Letters of Intent
Bus. L. Today 55 (July/Aug. 2004)

Thus, for example, an instrument which expressly states that it is a gentleman's agreement or otherwise not a binding commitment will generally not be treated as creating contractual duties, although it is nevertheless an agreement.

Williston, A TREATISE ON THE LAW OF CONTRACTS §1.3.

That a letter of intent is not a useless document, but it is not, in principle, a contract, except perhaps a contract to continue bargaining in good faith.

Corbin, CORBIN ON CONTRACTS, §1.16.

Though these are eminent authorities, their conclusions are representative of the conventional wisdom about letters of intent. But, they confuse the true function of the document.

A letter of intent is a contract preceding and enhancing the negotiation phase of the business transaction. As a contract, however, it is different from most traditional contracts. The unique difference, and the one that is probably the most confusing and peculiar, is that the letter is binding at least in one part — sometimes most parts, but never all parts. The traditional contract, to the contrary, is supposed to be binding in all parts. Which part of the letter is binding and which part is not is the issue that the parties need to agree on.

Binding or nonbinding. Letters of intent can be grouped into four general classes. The classifications range from least binding to most binding.

One group is comprised of letters that are used solely to list the most essential business terms and which bluntly disclaim any contractual effect. These letters are generally term sheets. They would seem to disclaim all contractual effect; but they actually should preserve contractual effect as to the disclaimer.

A second group is comprised of letters that are used to lay the ground rules for negotiation. This is probably the most effective and efficient use for the letters.

A third group is comprised of letters that are used to identify all of the significant business terms, as well as make sufficient reference to other terms so as to permit a competent drafter to complete final documentation without a tremendous amount of additional negotiation. In theory, these letters are missing only one essential element to make them binding as transaction contracts. That is the satisfaction of a condition subsequent of a kind that should be easy to evidence, such as the approval by a party's board of directors or the signature by the necessary executive officer. Loan commitments frequently fall into this group.

The last group of letters is comprised of letters of intent that have failed. To call them letters of intent at all is technically a mischaracterization. They have failed because these kinds of letters are actually binding transaction contracts, albeit letter contracts, for the negotiated transactions.

When two parties start to negotiate a letter of intent, even when they hesitate from ambivalence, they expect that they will agree on at least one term: that they should not be bound by any other terms. When one of the parties seemingly pulls an about face and complains that the true intent was either at that time, or over time, that the parties be contractually bound, then the court is brought in to interpret the relationship of the parties.

The court does not so much interpret what the parties later say they had originally intended; rather the court finds as a matter of fact what the parties did, and construes the legal effects of their acts. To reduce the risk of litigation, the single most important provision of the letter of intent is to disclaim contractual effect as to all but specifically preserved terms, a key one being the disclaimer itself.

That is why having a letter of intent is better than "going straight to documents." The path to documentation may result in contractual effect before one of the parties is certain it wants to be bound. With or without letters of intent, contractual liability can be deemed to arise from a number of acts that involve no writing: oral agreements, agreements implied-in-fact, substantial partial performances, and prior course of conduct. Recognizing that contractual effect can arise before the transaction contract is signed, a careful drafter trying to contain that risk can use the letter as a helpful tool, imperfect though it may be.

Take-aways. A number of intrinsically significant issues can be laid out between the two extreme approaches to letters of intent, between those considered almost completely nonbinding and those considered almost completely binding. The issues that especially apply to letters of intent are listed in the take-away points below. Of them, the issues of exclusivity, standards of negotiation, and the trigger of contractual effect are most essential.

Letters of intent should disclaim any contractual effect as to the particular business terms of the transactions, except for terms expressly identified as binding. The nonbinding terms, as a section, should be conspicuously separated from the binding terms, as a section.

Letters of intent should confirm contractual effect with respect to rules of negotiation during the negotiation phase. Those rules, and the provisions that substantiate their binding qualities, can include:

- exclusivity of negotiation,
- standards of effort and cooperation to be used in conducting the negotiation,
- determination of which conditions are deemed consummation or abandonment of contractual effect — the events that signal the achievement of the final formal definitive transaction contract,
- confidentiality of materials and information provided by the owner for the prospect,
- access to materials and information provided by the owner for the prospect,
- allocation of expenses between the parties, with a possible reimbursement to the prospect for the cost of materials turned over to owner if the transaction contract does not get signed,
- performance milestones with conditional rights to extend performance dates in the event of supervening circumstances,
- specially contained remedies, such as injunctive relief against the owner for breach of the negotiation covenant, or injunctive relief against the prospect for breach of confidentiality and access covenants.

The letter of intent is binding in part, specifically as to those points raised above. As to them, the letter is a contract. As to that portion of the letter that has contractual effect, it can be further improved with additional standard contractual provisions that would apply in any contract: representations as to due organization, due authority and no conflicts; covenants as to notifications of change, nonassignability, survival, notice procedures, integration, choice of law, venue and service of process; conditions as to consents, approvals and no change in circumstances; and, disclaimers, releases, waivers and indemnifications.

Exclusivity. Some prospects consider that their paramount goal is to prevent owners from negotiating with the prospects' competitors. Other prospects are undaunted by the auction-type process. But what exactly should be included and what excluded from the concept of exclusivity is a challenge for the drafter.

Exclusivity can mean that the owner does not actively market, privately solicit, encourage inquiry, respond to proposals, discuss proposals, analyze proposals, retain proposals, or even receive proposals. Therefore, the prospect would want to establish exclusivity as a binding provision, notwithstanding that the rest of the letter of intent (other than the disclaimer) would have no contractual effect.

An exclusive may fail in its contractual effect if it is unlimited in time. However, it can be reasonably limited in several ways. The exclusivity could end prior to the expiration of the letter, then the letter's other binding terms would continue, but the owner could undertake parallel negotiations with the prospect as well as the prospect's competitors.

The exclusive could be co-terminous with the effective period of the letter. The exclusive could survive termination of the letter, so that if the owner sought to continue to bring the transaction to the market — or received a compelling proposal within a set period of time after the letter's expiration — the prospect's exclusive rights would revive, similarly to the way a right of first refusal can revive.

Some owners add variety to the restrictions on exclusivity. If a prospect receives a purchase inquiry, the owner may prohibit the prospect from responding and may require the prospect to pass the information along to the owner so as to prevent a "flip" of the transaction. Sometimes the prospect has to pay for exclusivity or extensions of exclusivity.

Sometimes the owner has options to buy out the prospect's right to exclusivity, so that the exclusive is either extinguished or at least limited as to specifically designated third parties. Sometimes the buyout is based on the owner and the prospect sharing increases in profits above those that the owner would have earned if it had completed the transaction with the prospect. This is basically sharing the "flip."

Standards. A [second] important issue that the parties face is setting ground rules as to what standards should apply to negotiation. Some courts believe the standards of good faith, fair dealing and commercial reasonableness should apply to all contracts including letters of intent. Other courts adopt the proposition that these standards apply to contracts, but because letters of intent are not binding, the standards do not apply to those letters. Some courts take a reasoned middle ground, that if the letters contain express contractual requirements that compel negotiation, then a duty to negotiate in good faith will be imposed.

Should the standard of negotiation be best efforts, reasonable efforts or no effort at all? Some courts have concluded that an agreement to negotiate using "best efforts" is unenforceable for indefiniteness unless the agreement delineates a clear set of guidelines by which the parties' efforts can be measured. Those courts lambaste forward-looking agreements as unenforceable agreements to agree.

"Best efforts" has the ring of superlative virtue, but like most virtues its achievement is subjective and subject to contention. Some courts hold that the "best efforts" standard imposes a peer standard of performance, measured against a similar party in a similar situation. Other courts look to an "objective" test based on a prudent business person rule. Some courts equate "best efforts" with "good faith efforts" — though equating the two devalues "best efforts" by limiting it to the even more subjective "pure heart, empty head" rule: The performance may be awful, but it is excused if it was done with sincerity.

"Good faith" has been championed most famously in Judge Cardozo's opinion, that the presence of an implicit obligation of good faith abides in all commercial contracts, claiming that "a promise may be lacking, and yet the whole writing may be 'instinct with an obligation' imperfectly expressed." (Wood v. Lucy, Lady Duff-Gordon, 222 N.Y. 88, 91 118 N.E. 214 (1917).)

The Uniform Commercial Code expressly codifies a duty of good faith in all contracts it governs, requiring as well "commercially reasonable standards of fair dealing" meaning that the party is under a duty to act fairly, not commercially reasonably. (UCC revised §1-201(b)(20) (2002), and §9-102(a)(43), but compare §1-302(b) which permits contractual alteration of the duty.)

In the end, the concept of "good faith" exasperates some courts as much as "best efforts" because of this vagueness. The upshot of this uncertainty is that the careful drafter will try to describe the important indicia of the obligation. An "industry" standard would speak to customary practices in the industry generally. A "peer" standard would narrow the standard to what parties of similar size in similar segments of the industry would do. It could be further confined by specific geographical characteristics or locations.

Whatever standard is adopted, its limits on time and expense should also be identified — such as confirming that there is no duty to expend extraordinary effort or cost, or that all expenditures are subject to a maximum limit on time and cost, or that no party is obligated to use efforts that would diminish its own rights. Limitations on liability can also be made express.

A flat disclaimer of the duty to negotiate, meaning the implicit duty to negotiate in good faith, may be the most direct. But if the parties agree to some level of negotiation, an implicit standard of unconditional good faith can be ameliorated by an explicit agreement otherwise. The parties can agree that their duty to negotiate is subject to express contractual rights and privileges that might otherwise be considered bad faith: the right to break off negotiations, the right to revisit any issue until all issues are resolved, the right to withhold information, the privilege to be free from any duty to correct misimpressions and misassumptions, and the estoppel by each party that it proceeds at its own risk and cost.

The debilitating effect of bad faith is caused by hiding the detrimental act and misleading the victim. It can be prevented by the exercise of effective disclosure and disclaimer.

As a general rule, a duty to negotiate in good faith does not include a duty to advocate for approval. The careful drafter would want to include in the parties' duties that each party's representatives diligently pursue approvals in the most efficacious manner and advocate for approval of the target transaction. These undertakings could include a series of milestones, both in the application for approval as well as in the timing of periodic progress reports.

Consummation. The [third] major issue is the most dangerous one: When does the event of contractual effect as to the transaction occur? Sometimes the parties to the letters push the letters beyond their presumptive function — to try to make them approach the state of total contractual effect — by fixing business terms and not just proposing them. These letters generally have agreements as to terms, but no contractual agreement that the business terms are binding.

They hold out contractual effect until a conspicuous unambiguous condition is met, such as,

- board approvals, or
- execution of a definitive transaction contract, or
- some other objectively discernible event has occurred.

These letters are in the greatest peril of being recharacterized as binding; sometimes because they ineffectually disclaim binding intent. The theory that throws these letters into that dangerous zone is that the courts through their findings of fact, and not the parties, determine the existence of contractual effect. Though a court will frequently try to deduce intent, and for that purpose will closely examine the written statements of the parties, the court will also readily conclude contractual effect if all necessary contractual elements are in force, even if the parties originally may have had no intent to be bound.

Williston in another provocative gesture quotes Judge Learned Hand's severe postulate about contractual effect: "A contract has, strictly speaking, nothing to do with the personal, or individual, intent of the parties. A contract is an obligation attached by the mere force of law to certain acts of the parties . . . . If, however, it were proved by 20 bishops that either party, when he used the words, intended something else than the usual meaning which the law imposes upon them, he would still be held. . . ." (1 WILLISTON ON CONTRACTS §3.5.)

The compelling public policy championed by legal formalists is that no court should try to find a "meeting of the minds" because that would require exploration of a party's mental state, a hidden, subjective and murky terrain. Any investigation of mental states could be easily manipulated and therefore would be extremely unreliable. Put another way, for the pragmatist, if it looks like a contract and works like a contract, then it will be binding, even though in their innermost thoughts the parties may have originally thought they were not being bound.

Confidentiality and access. Two other provisions that are frequently part of the letter-of-intent process are access and confidentiality provisions. The owner's goal is to induce the prospect to spend time and money to the point it feels too invested in the undertaking to abandon it lightly. The prospect usually wants to find out as quickly as possible whether to pursue or abandon the negotiation of the transaction.

To do that requires that the owner expose its business information and physical assets to the prospect. Before exposing its private information to review by a stranger, the owner also needs to govern the use of the information and the universe of people who can gain access to it. What governs is the separate confidentiality provision. Both in access and in confidentiality, the owner would need to build in injunctive remedies to prevent violation of the privilege granted.

Ambiguity or duplicity. Ambiguity is frequently used in letters of intent to avoid confrontation. Ambiguity can be created intentionally in different ways: purposeful multiple meanings, vagueness or omissions are common tactics. The parties may initially be lured to use ambiguity to create the semblance of an agreement. The semblance is naturally unstable and the letter's function can degenerate into dysfunction. Then, when the parties are battling over whether an agreement came into existence, raising ambiguity as a defense may be too sharp a practice to be respected or enforced by courts.

When there is ambiguity because of conflicting provisions, or because of conflicts between the statements of the parties and their acts, or simply from silence, then the courts are called on to find intent or the lack of it. From the pragmatic view, trying to discover intent can be impossible, especially when the parties had multiple conflicting intents, or worse, when they were ambivalent and had no idea what their intents were.

Consequently, the courts fall back on the more external analysis of manifestations, to determine what the parties actually did rather than what they thought they intended.

The letter of intent is a contract in part, preceding the negotiation phase of the transaction contract. It is, in short, a prenegotiation contract with the limited but focused purpose of framing negotiations. It is a separate and distinct tool in the life of a business transaction. If disregarded or misused, it can be construed by courts in ways that are inconsistent with the parties' expectations.

But used properly, it functions to dispel confusion, avert unwanted outcomes and clarify the undertaking of negotiations.

NOTES AND QUESTIONS

1. How does the author distinguish a "term sheet" from a "letter of intent"? While the business and legal communities have not adopted the definitional model the author presents (documents entitled "Term Sheet" often include detailed provisions that are intended to be enforceable), did the continuum of non-binding to binding clarify your understanding of the enforceability issue?

2. What prompts the parties to prepare a term sheet? In other words, why would the parties to a financing transaction decide to prepare a term sheet?

3. The end of the preceding article touches on confidentiality terms. Compare the Non-Disclosure Agreement discussion in section B.1 of Chapter 7. Note the specific provisions there regarding treatment of confidential information, remedies, and the post-agreement "tail" term. What are the advantages and disadvantages of integrating

confidentiality and non-disclosure terms into a term sheet versus separating the documents?

4. In light of the observations made in this article, has your view changed as to whether the Delaware Supreme Court reached the correct result in *SIGA Technologies*?

B. Venture Capital Investment Documents

1. *Overview*

Venture capital investment transactions typically are memorialized through the use of five primary documents: a Preferred Stock Purchase Agreement (SPA), an Amended and Restated Charter (A&RC), an Investor Rights Agreement (IRA), a Right of First Refusal and Co-Sale Agreement (ROFR), and a Voting Agreement (VA). While their names may vary and the content sometimes is consolidated into fewer agreements (for example, the ROFR and the VA may be consolidated into a Shareholder Agreement), the provisions we address in reviewing these agreements typically are incorporated into most venture capital transactions. The following discussion specifically focuses on venture capital investments and may be applied only with care to other stock issuance transactions; while forms of such agreements are used for other purposes, practice and convention vary in different contexts.

The norm in venture capital financing is for a new SPA to be created for each round of financing but for each of the other major documents to be amended and restated from its prior form. By this mechanism, each of the other documents adds the new investors in with all the earlier investors in one comprehensive and integrated set of rights and terms. The short-titles used in this chapter refer to these agreements in their original form or as amended and restated agreements as a result of subsequent rounds of investment.

Despite the fact that the content and mechanisms of agreements vary depending on their purposes, most business transaction documents follow some basic patterns that are useful to recognize. For this reason, you should review both the Sample Loan Agreement and the Sample Acquisition Agreement in Appendix B in connection with reading this section of Chapter 10. The object is to give you a feel for the basic geography of a transactional document, even though specific content that is typical in a loan, acquisition, or venture capital deal may be completely inappropriate in another context.

To give a sense of perspective, a brief overview of the scope of the key documents in a venture capital transaction is in order. First, the SPA serves a dual purpose in that it acts to document the issuance and sale of the company's preferred stock as well as operates as the master agreement for the entire transaction. The A&RC amends and restates the company's Charter to include the rights, preferences, and privileges granted to the new series of preferred stock, as discussed in detail in Chapter 9. The IRA provides a set of ongoing covenants from the company to the venture capital investors. The ROFR sets forth agreements between the founders (and other large common stock holders) and the investors that give the investors certain rights against those other holders' common stock. Finally, the VA sets forth those same parties' agreement on how board representation is to be allocated among the various share ownership groups, what board nomination rights will be granted to individual investors, as well as how all the shareholder-parties will vote under specified circumstances.

2. *The Preferred Stock Purchase Agreement*

The SPA documents the company's issuance and sale of its equity securities to the investors. Because it refers to *all* of the other documents required for the entire investment transaction — the completion and delivery of which typically are conditions to its own effectiveness — the SPA acts as the control document in that it manages all the elements that make up the transaction as a whole. Despite variations in specific terms, the basic architecture used to create an SPA is consistent and recognizable across deals, states, and law firms. More frequently than not, a venture capital SPA will have the following provisions, usually set forth in the following order:

   (i) *Introductory provisions* — consisting of the name and date of the agreement, the names of the parties, and the recitals (i.e., the "Whereas" provisions) setting the parties' premises for entering into the agreement;

  (ii) *Statement of the transaction* — stating the parties' agreement to issue and sell and to buy, respectively, the stock at a specified price under the terms of the SPA, and setting the time and place for the completion of the transaction;

 (iii) *Representations and warranties of the company* — providing the investors with factual assurances that they rely on in making their investment;

 (iv) *Representations and warranties of the investors* — giving the company confirmation that it may rely on selected exemptions under federal and state securities laws for the share issuance, and addressing any issues that may be specific to a particular investor or group of investors;

  (v) *Conditions to the investors' obligations at closing* — listing those things the company (or others) must do before the investors' obligations under the SPA become effective;

 (vi) *Conditions to the company's obligations at closing* — listing those things the investors (or others) must do before the company's obligations under the SPA become effective;

(vii) *Miscellaneous terms* — spelling out the usual general contract and other miscellaneous terms (e.g., governing law, venue, etc.); and

(viii) *Signature page* — with signature blocks set up for execution by authorized representatives of the company and each stock purchaser.

In addition, some SPA forms include a *covenants* section that may precede or follow the *conditions to closing* sections, where the company provides ongoing promises to the investors and sometimes the investors make some promises back to the company. The much more common practice, however, is to put all the company's covenants in the IRA.

Some SPA forms have a separate section setting forth the statutory restrictions on transfer of the purchased securities, while others simply include those restrictions in the form of acknowledgement provisions included in the *representations and warranties of investors* section. Also, some forms of SPA include a separate section reciting the list of things that must be delivered by the company and the investors at the closing, while others include these items in the sections dealing with *conditions to closing*.

Reviewing the Provisions of the SPA.   As we review these provisions in more depth, it is important to consider not just their contents, but also the role each plays in the process of establishing and documenting the rights, obligations, and responsibilities of the parties arising from the transaction.

The *introductory provisions* and *statement of the transaction* are mechanical terms. The *introductory provisions* must accurately and specifically identify the contract, the parties, and the premises upon which the parties have come together (if any are relevant and useful in understanding the SPA and the context of the transaction). The premises, normally presented in a list of "Recitals" or "Whereas" clauses, can help readers understand what the document does and how it (or the transaction generally) relates to other agreements or relationships between the parties. In addition, it often defines key terms in the course of identifying the parties to the transaction and describing important background facts. Unlike in an acquisition or loan agreement, where the introductory provisions often are followed by a "definitions" section (which also may appear at the very end of the document or in an exhibit to the agreement), an SPA usually embeds its definitions within its provisions.

As venture capital investment transactions typically involve more than one investor, the statement of the purchase of the stock by the investors must reflect the fact that, while they may be defined as a group (as "the Purchasers," for example), their obligations to the company are individual and are not linked together. For convenience, the investors are often listed on a *Schedule of Purchasers* or similar attachment to the SPA that names each individual or entity purchasing shares, often including a contact person and address for each (which, among other things, assists in establishing residence for blue sky compliance), and states the amount being invested, the form of the investment (usually cash or conversion of an outstanding bridge note), and the number of shares each investor is purchasing.

The *statement of the transaction* attests that the securities exist and that the company is authorized to issue and sell them, then provides that under the terms of the SPA, "the company hereby sells and the investors hereby buy" the preferred stock at the specified price. It then goes on to address the mechanics of collecting funds from the investors and issuing the shares by the company at the "closing." It also explains whether there will be more than one closing and, if so, what the arrangements are for the additional closing(s).

A *closing* actually is a transactional methodology concept that has little application in the standard venture capital transaction. The "closing" is when the obligations of the parties under the terms of the contract are performed and value is exchanged. Most venture capital investments are "sign and close" transactions, where the contract is signed and the parties fulfill their obligations (that is, the closing occurs) simultaneously.

In contrast, a "delayed closing" transaction contemplates that the agreement will be signed now, but the parties' obligations will not be completed until some later date (by which time, for example, shareholder approval will have been solicited and obtained, or debt financing arranged and the lender will be ready to disburse the funds needed to complete the transaction). Delayed closings are very common in the world of acquisitions. The "Specialty Recordkeeping Materials" Sample Acquisition Agreement included in Appendix B is an example of a delayed closing agreement. It is for an acquisition in which the acquirer is buying the target through the purchase of all the target's shares owned by its sole shareholder.

A delayed closing agreement often has an additional section of covenants that are to be completed prior to closing. These covenants may include obtaining a governmental permit required for the transaction, for example. If the requisite permit is not obtained, the covenant is not met and the other party is excused from closing on the transaction. These pre-closing covenants represent tasks that must be accomplished *prior* to the parties' completion of the transaction. The consequence of failing to fulfill them is what fundamentally distinguishes pre-closing covenants from covenants that continue to have effect *following* the closing, such as those described in the IRA discussion below.

Even though venture capital investments usually are "sign and close" transactions, the mechanism of a "closing" is still used in the documentation because it is a convenient contract structure, and it is possible that the parties may decide later to sign and delay the closing. In addition, venture transactions frequently contemplate one, or often more than one, subsequent closing. If the latter is the case, the conditions or milestones for completing each closing must be clear — are there any special conditions that apply only to the "initial closing" or only to a "subsequent closing"? On the other hand, do the general conditions to closing apply equally to every closing? Aside from the possible variations in the conditions to closing that are applicable when multiple closings are contemplated, it is important to recognize that all of the other terms of the SPA (and the other transaction documents) will apply to every investor at each closing. In other words, the company is issuing the same security to each investor at every closing under the same terms through a single SPA. Because every investor under a given SPA is getting the same thing at the same price, a significant passage of time between the initial closing and a subsequent closing could substantially benefit later investors, who might learn new information that did not exist at the time of the initial closing. Consequently, SPAs usually provide that subsequent closings must occur within a relatively short time frame (often 60 or 90 days) following the initial closing.

The *representations and warranties of the company* are a series of factual statements that the company, as the seller, makes to the investors, as the buyers, in order to induce the latter to deliver their money and purchase the company's stock. The primary purpose of the company's "reps and warranties" in an SPA for a venture capital transaction is disclosure.

The reps and warranties are to be correct upon the closing. If any are not, the company must provide additional information on a *Schedule of Exceptions* or *Disclosure Schedule* that becomes part of the SPA and modifies and supplements the representations and warranties contained in the agreement. As the Schedule of Exceptions effectively amends the provisions of the SPA and reports that certain parts of the reps and warranties are not true, the additional disclosures, inconsistencies, and risks must be acceptable to the investors. If the investors do not accept the Schedule of Exceptions, they can walk away from the transaction.

The SPA typically contains a lengthy set of company reps and warranties for the purpose of requiring the company to provide further information on the Schedule of Exceptions regarding its history or any facts that may be problematic for the investors. Because they are intended to elicit disclosure of information that may be useful for the investors to know, these reps and warranties often are expressed in a way that cannot possibly be true. For example, an early stage company may be asked to represent that it has not entered into any contracts having a value of more than $10,000. The point is not that the investors object to larger contracts — they just want to be aware of the company's significant obligations. That representation is intended to stimulate disclosure (on the Schedule of Exceptions) of all contracts over $10,000 in value, and the negotiation issue is whether $10,000 is the appropriate threshold for requiring disclosure.

To the extent that the SPA allows for more than one closing, it usually requires that the company's reps and warranties, as modified by the Schedule of Exceptions, must be correct at each closing, which means that the Schedule of Exceptions has to be reviewed and updated for each subsequent closing. It also means that any change to the Schedule of Exceptions may be a contract modification that gives the investors the ability to balk at putting in additional funds at that later closing. In practice, venture capital investors routinely accept disclosures that reflect ordinary course changes in the business and raise issues only where an unanticipated adverse event has occurred that might materially affect the company's situation or prospects.

The convention on negotiating the wording of representations and warranties in SPAs is to leave them generally intact, with minor modifications, then to provide disclosure in the Schedule of Exceptions. The investors normally want even the most seemingly irrelevant representations — their attitude being "Well, if it is irrelevant, there should not be any problem telling us that you have nothing to disclose." This does not mean, however, that company counsel should not object to representations that are unduly burdensome (for example, a representation that seeks disclosure of every agreement, written or oral, that the company has ever entered into), cover irrelevant time periods, or are directed toward a business area that simply has nothing to do with the company (e.g., a representation regarding adequate, bonded refrigerated warehousing capacity would not be appropriate for SoftCo).

Negotiation on the company's representations and warranties usually centers on the extent to which they will be cut back by "materiality" qualifiers and "knowledge" limitations. Materiality qualifiers are intended to insulate the company from penalties or damages resulting from insignificant deviations from the representations. For example, a representation that the company has all necessary permits to operate its business typically has a materiality qualifier so that the company is not in breach of the agreement because it failed to obtain a $5 city business license and then forgot to mention it as an exception. The mechanism for applying materiality qualifiers is often the defined term "material adverse effect," which usually means something that would cause a material adverse effect to the company, its business, prospects, or financial condition. For example, a representation might provide that the company has all permits necessary to operate its business, "other than as would not have a material adverse effect."

Knowledge limitations (i.e., adding "to the company's knowledge" as a lead-in to a representation) have to be defined so that all the parties are comfortable regarding whose knowledge is going to be relied upon. Knowledge should not be based on one person, if possible, but on the key people who are involved on a daily basis with the company's operations. A knowledge limitation is appropriate, for example, where a company is asked to represent that it has no litigation pending or, to the company's knowledge, threatened. Obviously, if the key officers of the company are aware of threatened litigation, the investors want to know. If they are not aware of any, then the investors simply have to take the risk that someone is out there intending to file an action.

Investors want knowledge and materiality qualifiers used judiciously. They especially dislike "doubling up" on materiality. That is, if the SPA already requires that all company representations and warranties must be true and correct "in all material respects" at the closing in order for the investors to be obligated to complete the financing, then the investor usually will be less willing to accept materiality qualifiers as part of individual representations set forth in the SPA.

In addition, sometimes knowledge is simply not an appropriate limitation. Some representations are intended to be statements of knowable fact, while others are instead an undertaking of responsibility for a set of facts that may not be knowable. For example, the investors may want a representation that a real estate management company is in compliance with all its material lease obligations, and the company may respond that it wants a knowledge qualifier because it is a party to a lot of leases and it would be difficult to know of every possible violation. In these circumstances, the investors may point out that they already are qualifying the representation with materiality and insist on no knowledge limitation, arguing that because the company is responsible for managing its leases, it should not be excused from responsibility for failure to conform to its material obligations simply because it is not aware of the problem. In short, if the company is in breach of a lease, it has a potential liability problem whether it knows it or not, and the investors want it clear that the existing owners of the company are responsible for that problem.

Having said that, risk allocation is less important in a venture capital financing transaction than in an acquisition, where representations provide disclosure but also serve an important risk allocation function. In other words, in an acquisition agreement, representations serve to assign responsibility between the sides to the agreement for problems that emerge after the transaction closes. The reason for this distinction is a simple product of the relationship between the parties involved in an investment transaction versus an acquisition. In the investment context, the purchaser is getting in the boat with the company's existing owners, so to speak. On the other hand, in an acquisition, the purchaser is paying the previous owners of the business money to get out of the boat, and then the buyer sails on alone. Suing to recover money paid to a departed owner for an untrue statement of fact regarding the company allows the purchaser to recover the consideration paid to the seller of the business. However, suing the company that the investors have now invested in reduces the chance that the company ever will have any value. This outcome is self-defeating for the investor as it effectively results in the company using the invested money to pay for the litigation expenses incurred by the company in defending against the investors' own claims. Any damages recovered also will be subsidized by the investment. In sum, the practical absence of an effective means of recovering damages from the company for breaches of its representations and warranties makes their use in allocating responsibility for risks less important in a venture capital investment. Even on the East Coast, where the founders often make personal representations in the SPA in addition to the company's representations, it is unusual for venture capital investors, absent a clear instance of fraud, to bring legal action against the company's founders.

That is not to say that risk allocation is not relevant in venture capital investment transactions. Even if venture capital investors are reluctant to litigate, there is still a meaningful allocation of responsibility going on through the representations and warranties in the SPA. The fact is just that the negotiation over the scope of the remedies tends to be more grounded in equity than in contract damages. If the founders of a company misled the investors, the harm often is mitigated by repricing the investment. That may mean directly changing the terms of the investors' preferred stock to give them more shares for the money they paid (perhaps by increasing the conversion rate), or it may mean asking the responsible management or founders to forfeit some of their shares back into the company. As the people responsible for the company's representations in the SPA, presumably, it seems only fair that they should bear a price for their misstatements by having a diminished ownership position. In addition, that forfeiture would result in fewer shares outstanding, so the investors' stock would thus represent a larger portion of the company, which has the same effect as reducing the price of their shares.

The *representations and warranties of the investors* have a completely different purpose than those made by the company. Investor representations typically are used to provide the company with a factual basis to conclude that it has met the terms of an exemption from the 1933 Act's transaction registration requirements. Because a venture capital investment involves an issuance of securities regulated by the 1933 Act, as discussed in Chapter 4, the company must register the transaction with the SEC unless an exemption applies. The exemptions typically used for a venture capital transaction are those available under Regulation D. The company confirms the facts required by the exemption by obtaining representations from each of its investors (severally, not jointly) regarding the nature of the transaction, the conduct of the sale, their investor qualifications, and their understanding of the nature of the securities purchased.

In addition, depending on the circumstances, the company may want the investors, or a specific investor, to make representations addressing other issues. A strategic investor, for example, may be asked to make representations regarding its related activities and the absence of any restrictions on its ability to enter into the strategic relationship.

The *conditions to the investors' obligations at closing* is a list of the facts or actions that must be in place or completed for the investors to be obligated to close. The *conditions to the company's obligations at closing* is a parallel list of the things that must be true or in place for the company to be obligated to close. This may seem like an odd mechanism since a "sign and close" agreement is not binding until it is signed and, as a result, the investors or the company can walk away without closing at any time. The utility of this "conditions to closing" approach is more obvious in a "delayed closing" agreement, when the parties sign the agreement and agree to a list of things that each must do before the other is committed to close. Some facts or actions will be within the parties' control, while others will depend on the act of a third party. For example, in SoftCo's situation, one condition may be that Caltech shall have agreed upon a license arrangement with SoftCo regarding any interest it may have in SoftCo's technology. Caltech's refusal to provide this license would affect SoftCo's prospects so seriously that, in that case, it would be reasonable to allow the investors to withdraw (i.e., refuse to close).

In a "sign and close" situation, however, the "conditions to closing" essentially serve as a checklist of the things that must be done before the agreement is signed. They could just as easily be presented in the SPA as representations, since they must be true as of the closing. Using the "conditions to closing" mechanism serves to highlight those matters that are not yet in place as the SPA is being negotiated and must be resolved before the agreement can become effective. It creates emphasis by providing a to-do list, rather than letting outstanding items be buried in the representations section.

Both "conditions to closing" sections should include *all* the actions needed to put the parties in a position to complete the transaction and its documentation. When the listed conditions have been satisfied, the parties should then be willing to sign the agreement and do what is described in the *statement of the transaction* section — that is, issue and sell the securities against delivery of the funds, and deliver the funds to buy the securities.

The *miscellaneous terms* at the end of the SPA cover the range of general contract terms that are sensible and appropriate in the context of the transaction. They should provide a coherent, non-redundant, useful set of rules and provisions that relate to the purpose and context of the agreement. For example, a "Choice of Law" provision would be appropriate if out-of-state investors are involved. On the other hand, a "Construction of Titles and Subtitles" provision, indicating that section titles and subtitles are for convenience and are not substantive, should be modified if the SPA's format has no subtitles. Sometimes, when the investors are from out of state and the company is a Delaware corporation, investors' counsel might suggest using Delaware law as a "compromise." The problem with this approach arises when the investors require company counsel to provide a legal opinion as to the enforceability of the transaction documents. While Delaware corporate law may be something that many corporate lawyers are willing to practice from out of state, the same is not true of Delaware contract law, and thus company counsel may be unwilling or unable to provide that opinion. In addition, without a jurisdiction and venue provision providing for adjudication in Delaware, any dispute is going to be heard in front of a local judge. As a result, best practice is usually to elect to be governed by the law of the jurisdiction where the company resides.

QUESTIONS

1. After receiving a draft SPA from the investor's counsel for SoftCo's first round of venture financing, Joan and Michael call you as SoftCo's counsel (the company still is just the two of them, and no entity has been formed) and tell you that the SPA requires that they deliver audited financial statements. Not only do they not have financial statements, let alone audited ones, they do not have any financial records. They have been meaning to buy a small business accounting software product but have not yet gotten around to it. SoftCo does not even have a bank account. What is your advice regarding the representation in the SPA?

2. Joan and Michael are very honorable people who take pride in doing things correctly and ethically. They inform you that they want to set up SoftCo and operate the company so there never will be the need to take any exceptions to the normal representations that a venture capital investor would expect SoftCo to make. What is your response?

3. Due Diligence and the SPA

Due diligence is the investor's obligation to adequately inform itself regarding the securities issuer and transaction. It is called "due" because the level of inquiry varies based on the circumstances; an investor needs to perform that level of inquiry that is appropriate, or "due." While an investor engages in various forms of diligence investigation (e.g., financial, technological, market, commercial), our focus is on the investor's *legal diligence* and the lawyer's role in that process.

Venture capital transactions are different from acquisitions or later-stage "private equity" investments in that they typically are done relatively quickly with somewhat standardized documents, and there is a significant emphasis on holding transaction costs to a minimum. While some observers might argue that this makes a venture capital practice simple and routine, the counter argument is that it is an area of law that puts a premium on the quality of the legal services provided because it discourages quantity. Discovering the potential problems with a transaction by flooding it with legal resources to examine every possible risk is not an option in most venture capital deals.

Legal fees for investors' counsel almost always are capped in the SPA, perhaps as low as $10,000 to $15,000 in early stage transactions under $1 million (with variations around the country), and often in the $25,000 to $40,000 range in larger transactions. Because the standard practice is for the company to pay the "reasonable" fees of investors' counsel upon completion of the transaction, and the company often has absolutely no ongoing relationship with the investors' counsel, in addition to dealing with the capped fee amount, investors' counsel can be confident that its bill will be carefully reviewed by the company for any inefficiencies. In addition, the firm representing the company also can be confident that its bills will be carefully scrutinized. In short, whether the lawyer is representing the investors or the company, a venture capital practice is, to say the least, fee sensitive.

How, then, does a lawyer meet his or her diligence responsibilities to the client in an environment where there is so much concern about transaction costs? The answer lies, in part, in the transaction structure that has developed in venture capital practice.

As suggested in the discussion of the SPA above, venture capital investors seek to protect themselves by relying on documents that are fairly standardized as to form and substance and are designed to spur disclosure on the Schedule of Exceptions, and then focusing their legal resources on examining the documents and circumstances that are disclosed. Accordingly, these investors insist on representations that might otherwise appear to be overly comprehensive as an effective way to reduce transaction costs. Since venture capital financed companies tend to be fairly young and relatively small, the range of issues that should come to light in the disclosure process is fairly predictable.

In addition, while the SPA is being prepared, investors' counsel normally gives the company a *due diligence request list* of material company documents that investors' counsel needs to review. Again, in order to control costs, investors' counsel should focus the requests in an efficient way, asking, for example, for samples of equity incentive documents rather than for copies of each outstanding contract. Sample forms, together with a report of incentives outstanding and their vesting schedules, which the company should be maintaining as part of its normal recordkeeping activities, provide investors' counsel the necessary information without unduly burdening the company's staff (or its photocopiers), while still allowing counsel to identify any anomalies that require additional investigation.

The key for investors' counsel is to focus on issues that are material to the investors. Accordingly, investors' counsel should ask the company (and its counsel) to deliver only information that is directly relevant to those issues. In the end, the diligence effort should give investors' counsel the opportunity to review everything that appears on the Schedule of Exceptions, as well as other key corporate records. The reality is that small, early stage companies often have not devoted significant resources to legal administration and, consequently, many of these administrative matters may need to be cleaned up. (Recall the discussion in Chapter 8, section F.2, regarding "draining the swamp.") Investors' counsel, however, needs to focus on what *must* be done to manage the investors' risk, not what is ideal.

Diligence time and money is limited and so lawyers must focus on the things that are likely to be expensive or difficult to fix later. In general, these fall into two basic areas: (i) issues regarding ownership interests in the company and (ii) issues regarding the company's ownership of (or rights to) its intellectual property or other agreements (or rights) that may affect the company's ability to pursue its business.

As to ownership interests, many companies poorly document founders' stock issuances and other equity incentives granted early in the company's life. Unlike SoftCo, some companies have been operating for some time, having incorporated using a self-help legal document service and a stock option plan downloaded from the Internet. Common errors include failure to comply with relevant securities laws, failure to make timely Section 83(b) election filings, and acceptance of illegal consideration for shares.

In addition, equity ownership interests, whether in a stock purchase agreement, warrant, or other document, sometimes include vague or improper rights that must be corrected. For example, a venture capital investor would never agree to the continued existence of a warrant that permits someone else to buy a fixed percentage of the company's equity at a fixed price. Before the venture capital investment goes forward, the investor would insist that the warrant holder agree to exchange that security for something stating a fixed number of shares that may be purchased, with the existing shareholders bearing the cost of that exchange. Another common problem with equity ownership arises when a security holder has been granted specific approval rights on corporate actions or preemptive rights on any future share issuance by the company. Venture capital investors typically want those rights terminated or, at a minimum, conformed to the similar contractual rights granted to them.

While investors' counsel should focus on resolving these sorts of issues, problems that can be fixed later, or where perfect compliance is not critical (such as the inclusion of market standoff terms in each previous equity issuance), should be given a lower priority. Investors' counsel would be better off making sure the company represents that holders of all outstanding shares have market standoffs in place, and perhaps reviewing major shareholder agreements, but leaving implementation (and appropriate documentation) of those arrangements to company counsel.

As to intellectual property (IP) issues, the fact is that, if the company depends on IP, it *must* own (or have exclusive rights to use and/or commercially exploit) every key element of its intellectual property. This means that the company should have Confidentiality and Invention Assignment Agreements in place with every employee, consultant, or contractor who contributed to the IP. While the ideal is that everyone who should have entered into such an agreement has done so, errors inevitably occur. The key to the diligence investigation is that the lawyers must ensure that proper agreements were and are in place for those people or entities who might otherwise have a meaningful claim on the IP the company is depending on for its future. If non-compete covenants are enforceable against the employees in the company's jurisdiction, the same evaluation process should be applied.

Other potential claimants to the company's IP, if any, need to be identified and dealt with. The company's IP protection mechanisms need to be reviewed and determined to be adequate. If the nature of the business makes it appropriate, IP counsel may be retained to examine, for example, the scope and enforceability of the company's patent portfolio. Any IP issues that the company discloses have to be carefully examined. In short, if there is any taint on the company's ability to use its IP as planned, making an investment could be nothing more than buying into years of costly litigation. Counsel's goal in pursuing his or her diligence inquiry on behalf of the investors is to minimize that risk.

Another IP-related issue concerns restrictions on the company's ability to pursue its business. For example, a "field of use" restriction in a key license might make it impossible for the company to expand its business. Thus, if SoftCo has a license to a key product component that is restricted to home computer users, prospective investors would legitimately worry about whether SoftCo may be barred from pursuing the commercial user market. As another example, a territorial restriction in a strategic marketing agreement, particularly in light of the Internet and the emergence of a global marketplace, could unduly hinder the company's future business prospects. Likewise, a "most favored nation" pricing clause in a key customer agreement might undercut future price increases and restrict profitability. An inartfully worded "change of control" provision in a key contract that might allow the other party to terminate as a result of the share ownership shift inherent in a venture capital investment could harm the company's cost structure or profit outlook. An exclusivity agreement with a strategic partner could have broader implications as the company's product line grows. If any of these issues exist, they must be identified and evaluated. If any of these issues need to be corrected or eliminated, the changes typically should be done before the investment occurs, i.e., before closing on the transaction.

Beyond these two categories of problems, most other issues that arise in diligence, or are disclosed on the Schedule of Exceptions, can be corrected with only a routine level of attention and effort. From the investors' point of view, however, anything that might affect their ability to own the portion of the company they set out to buy, or that might constrain the company in its commercial exploitation of its intellectual property or the growth of its business, is likely to be a deal killer.

QUESTIONS

1. Joan and Michael have received a "Due Diligence Request List" from investor's counsel, which asks for copies of all "technology licenses" to which SoftCo is a party. They have been looking for a printout of their Microsoft Windows 8® license and cannot find it, but they assure you that it came with their national brand computer. They also tell you that they cannot find their copy of their technology transfer license with Caltech, which gives them the right to commercially exploit the work that they did while at Caltech. Given your knowledge of the goals and purposes of the diligence inquiry, which document should be the focus of their records search and why?

2. While, as SoftCo's counsel, you are preparing documents to respond to the investor's diligence request, Michael calls you and embarrassedly informs you that he has a felony conviction for business fraud. He tells you that, 15 years ago, while in high school, he and some friends designed and built a device that would manipulate access to the standard long-distance switching equipment used by telephone companies so that he and his friends could make international telephone calls without paying for them. He says the telephone company was very upset when they discovered the infraction and pressed charges. Because of his age, he did community service and was on probation for seven years, which was all completed long ago. He tells you that the device was cool, but he never understood all the fuss because, as a high school student, who was he going to call overseas? He is concerned about what will happen if the investors find out he is a felon. What is your advice?

4. The Amended and Restated Charter

The A&RC sets forth the rights, preferences, and privileges that make up the terms of the preferred stock the venture capital investors will purchase. The portions of the A&RC that present those preferred stock terms are addressed in detail in Chapter 9. The mandatory Charter terms that also must be addressed, as well as a number of the optional terms that may be included in the Charter, are addressed in Chapter 5.

In preparing an A&RC, a lawyer must check the statutory requirements in the jurisdiction where it will be filed, as they may vary from state to state. Delaware, for example, requires that an Amended and Restated Certificate of Incorporation must recite:

> "the corporation's present name, and, if it has been changed, the name under which it was originally incorporated, and the date of filing of its original certificate of incorporation. . . ."

Del. GCL §245(c).

The secretary of state's website in many states provides sample forms and instructions for various types of corporate filings, which can be very helpful in drawing a lawyer's attention to the unique requirements of a particular filing. In addition, the forms and instructions also can be very useful with respect to signature page requirements, including who must sign, the declaration (if any) that must accompany the signatures, the nature of any attestation (usually by the corporate secretary) that must be provided, and the nature of the physical signature the secretary of state needs to see (i.e., original, facsimile, or conformed). Those requirements sometimes are scattered throughout a corporate code and many secretaries of state websites provide very useful assistance that can help the attorney avoid the embarrassing problem of having to ask the company officers to re-sign the A&RC because the signature page was not set up correctly.

5. *The Investor Rights Agreement*

The IRA is a collection of covenants provided by the company to the preferred stock investors. While covenants could be included in the SPA, the better practice is to put them in the IRA, unless the covenants relate to some matter specific to the immediate preferred stock issuance. The reason is that, while there is no problem putting a group of covenants into the first-round SPA (for the Series A Preferred) — since all the company's preferred stock holders presumably will be parties to that agreement — what happens when the company wants to issue its Series B Preferred Stock in a subsequent transaction? The Series B investors, of course, will enter into a new SPA for their share purchase transaction, but what is to be done about the covenants that were part of the Series A transaction? In other words, are there to be separate agreements and separate terms regarding the company's ongoing contractual rights to the preferred stock holders?

Typically, the answer is no. The company's ongoing covenants to its preferred stock investors are separated from the SPA and, upon each round of investment, the rights of each set of investors are reconciled and integrated into a single document signed by the company and effective as to all the preferred stock investors. The IRA from the Series A Preferred Stock investment round is revised to become the Amended and Restated IRA upon the Series B Preferred Stock issuance. A sufficient majority of the Series A Preferred Stock holders, who are the parties to that original IRA, agree (per the terms of the amendment section of that agreement) to amend and restate the IRA as to all the Series A Preferred Stock holders in connection with the Series B Preferred Stock transaction, and the company and the Series B Preferred Stock investors all enter into the new Amended and Restated IRA, which takes effect upon the closing of the Series B Preferred Stock issuance. The result is that the company has one integrated set of covenants to its investors, which reduces the risk of inconsistency, conflict, or other ambiguity.

Registration Rights.   As an introduction to registration rights, we should first review the securities law constraints that apply to shares issued in a private transaction. Venture capital investors make investments with the intention of seeing their preferred stock shares grow in value over time and then cashing out. Normal avenues for liquidity include the sale of the business or an IPO, where the company typically issues shares of its common stock to the public in a registered transaction under the 1933 Act and also registers its common stock for public trading under the 1934 Act. As described in Chapter 9, section D.1, depending on the size and terms of the IPO, the venture capital investors may be required to convert their preferred stock to common stock under the terms of their shares' "automatic" (or "mandatory") conversion provision. Alternatively, they may voluntarily convert their shares. Unfortunately, even after the venture capital investors convert their shares to common stock, the fact that the company's common stock is now publicly traded does not magically entitle *all* of the company's common shares to be sold into the public market.

As was also discussed in Chapter 4, the ability of an owner of preferred stock that was privately issued to resell those shares (or the common stock issued upon conversion of those shares) into a public trading market is restricted by federal securities laws. Section 5 of the 1933 Act prohibits sales of stock to the public other than in a registered transaction, unless an exemption is available. That prohibition applies not only to new issuances by a company but also to resales of privately issued shares by the current holders of those shares. Unless the resale of privately issued shares to the public is in a registered transaction, or an exemption from registration applies to the resale, the holder of those shares is prohibited from selling the shares into the public market.

The primary means for selling privately issued stock into the public market is through the resale exemption provided by Rule 144 under the 1933 Act. Under Rule 144, "non-affiliate" shareholders may resell their stock into the new public trading market (subject to minor restrictions) after holding their shares for six months and with virtually no restrictions after holding their shares for at least one year. Officers, directors, 10 percent shareholders, and other "affiliates" (as loosely defined in Rule 144(a)(1)) also may sell their shares (subject to the restrictions described in footnotes 2-5 in the following article) after six months, but for them, these restrictions continue to apply no matter how long they hold their shares, so long as they remain affiliates (and for 90 days thereafter).

Since venture capital investors may be sizable shareholders at the time of the company's IPO, or may continue to have a partner from the fund sitting on the company's board of directors, they often fall under the definition of "affiliate." As such, the primary Rule 144 restriction they are concerned about is the limitation on the number of shares that they may sell during any three-month period, referred to as the "volume restrictions" (or the "dribble out" rules), which are described more fully in footnote 3 of the following article.

In light of the Rule 144 volume restrictions, the only way for major shareholders, such as venture capital funds, to resell large amounts of their shares to the public is through a registered transaction under the 1933 Act. Registered transactions are complex and expensive and virtually impossible to accomplish without the cooperation and involvement of the company. So, when preferred stock is sold in a venture capital investment, it is customary for the issuing company to grant to the preferred stock purchasers the right to require the company to assist them in selling their converted shares into the public market through one or more registered transactions, through what are commonly referred to as *registration rights*.

The grant of *registration rights* to the company's preferred stock investors is the longest and most technically complex provision in most IRAs. The following article addresses many of the major issues regarding registration rights that are typically included in an IRA, although it is primarily directed at registration rights granted in acquisitions or private equity investments (i.e., a majority or near-majority ownership investment in more established companies). It, therefore, refers to "registration rights agreements," because in those transactions registration rights often are addressed in a stand-alone document. The exercise of registration rights following an acquisition or major private equity investment is not unusual because there often is one very large shareholder who is seriously limited by Rule 144's volume restrictions. On the other hand, venture capital registration rights are rarely used. Venture capital investment is done in pieces over time and often involves multiple investors, so usually no one investor ends up after the IPO with a huge percentage ownership in the company. As a result, the time and expense involved in a registered public offering can make exercising registration rights inefficient. Also, in an early-stage investment, the potential exercise of registration rights is a long way off. Most lawyers use their limited time and fee budget on more immediate issues and defer focus on registration rights terms to a third or fourth round transaction, when an IPO actually might be on the horizon.

The grant of registration rights, however, appears in virtually every IRA, and when the public market is highly receptive to growth-company offerings, the rights actually may be used. Further, "piggyback" rights often are requested by lenders in their equity sweetener warrants and by strategic partners for their equity shares. Consequently, the business lawyer needs to be familiar with how the rights are structured and what the key issues are.

Throughout the following article, italicized references have been inserted in brackets directing you to relevant sections of the Sample Investor Rights Agreement ("Sample IRA") that appears in Appendix B, and comments or questions have been added to allow you to examine the terms of that sample agreement in light of the issues the authors discuss in this article.

Valerie Ford Jacob, Stuart H. Gelfond, Michael A. Levitt, & David A. Kanarek
Key Considerations in Drafting a Registration Rights Agreement from the Company's Perspective

41 Rev. Sec. & Comm. Reg. 113 (May 21, 2008)

Registration rights are contractual rights that are intended to provide future liquidity to investors by establishing a mechanism to register securities purchased in a private placement. Under Section 5 of the Securities Act of 1933, investors generally may not publicly resell securities they purchased in a private offering unless the resale is registered or the resale is subject to an exemption from registration. Investors negotiate for registration rights so that they may sell their securities to the public in an underwritten or other public offering without limitation, including the resale restrictions imposed by Rule 144 of the Securities Act of 1933.[1]

Even after exemptions to resell securities become available under Rule 144, registration rights enable investors to sell large blocks of securities to the public. This is

---

1. The Securities Act restricts the sale of (i) restricted securities (whether debt or equity), which are securities that were acquired from a company, or from an affiliate of a company, in a transaction or chain of transactions not involving a public offering and (ii) control securities (whether debt or equity), which are any securities (whether restricted or otherwise) of a company that are held by an affiliate of that company. Sales of restricted and control securities are permitted if the sale is registered pursuant to an effective registration statement or an exemption is available. The SEC established Rule 144 to provide a safe harbor for sales of restricted securities and control securities. If the seller complies with Rule 144, the sale will not violate the registration requirements of the Securities Act. Rule 144 imposes certain holding period, informational, volume, manner of sale and notice obligations in certain situations and for certain stockholders. The application of the obligations are described more fully in footnotes 2-6, *supra*.

preferred, notwithstanding the [amendments to Rule 144 that became effective February 15, 2008] eliminating most requirements for non-affiliates and shortening holding periods, because a selling entity may prefer to sell its interest through an underwritten public offering. Further, registration rights agreements set forth the procedures for the registration of securities at the outset, which can avoid issues during an offering and thus provide comfort to the issuer and the underwriters that the offering can occur smoothly.

While the broad terms of registration rights are often negotiated in the context of an acquisition or investment, there is frequently significantly less thought given to the mechanics set forth in the registration rights agreement to implement the registration rights. Often business persons agree to have a "customary" registration rights agreement and negotiate only certain items, such as the number of times registration rights may be exercised and the allocation of expenses. "Customary" agreements may not work mechanically and technical points that are glossed over as boilerplate can have a significant impact on the parties when the agreement actually has to be implemented. Further, these agreements and the mechanics therein may be negotiated by one group of merger and acquisition ("M&A") lawyers while a different group of securities lawyers will actually handle the registration and any subsequent offering. When investors do focus on the mechanics, they may seek complete flexibility at the company's expense without regard to how to best benefit the company (and ultimately such investors) and the actual offering that may occur. The company representatives may often have little say or experience in registration rights agreements negotiated between big investors and are left with a document that can impose unnecessary burdens on the process to register investors' securities. In particular, often registration rights are provided to multiple small holders (which can number 100 or more) who do not need registration rights, particularly given the new shortened holding periods under Rule 144. In the context of an underwritten offering, coordinating registration rights for each of these holders can lead to delays in timing, failure to be able to price deals during market windows, and significant additional costs.

It is in the company's, as well as the investors', best interest to make the registration rights agreement work mechanically so as to eliminate unnecessary costs and delay in registering the securities and providing liquidity. This article will address key provisions companies and their counsel should consider in order to draft a registration rights agreement that actually works for the company and follows the contours and business realities of a registered offering. This article is not intended to summarize or address all of the provisions of a registration rights agreement; rather, it is intended to provide practice points for companies and their counsel in order to make the actual public offering process and the use of registration rights more manageable for the company.

Registration Rights

The Securities Act restricts the sale of restricted securities, which are securities that were acquired from a company (or an affiliate of a company) in a transaction not involving a public offering. [*"Restricted securities," as used in this article in reference to federal securities laws, means privately issued securities. This casebook uses the latter term because "restricted" has different meanings in different contexts (see the equity incentives discussion in section D of Chapter 6, for example*.] Sales of restricted securities are permitted if the sale is registered pursuant to an effective registration statement or an exemption is available. The Securities and Exchange Commission established Rule 144 to provide a safe harbor for sales of restricted securities. If the seller complies with Rule 144, the sale will not violate the registration requirements of the Securities Act.

Under Rule 144 non-affiliated holders of restricted securities of a non-reporting company [*that is, a company whose securities are not registered for public trading under the 1934 Act*] must wait a minimum of one year from the time the securities were last owned by the company or an affiliate of the company before they can freely sell the restricted securities. Affiliates of a non-reporting company may sell after the one-year period subject to certain information requirements,[2] volume limitations,[3] manner of sale,[4] and notice obligations.[5] For reporting companies, non-affiliates may sell restricted securities after six months subject only to certain information requirements[6] and freely without regard to Rule 144 compliance after one year. Affiliates of a reporting company may sell after six months subject to the information requirements, volume limitations, manner of sale, and notice obligations discussed above. [*See Sample IRA §1.10, where the company agrees that, after its shares are registered for public trading under the 1934 Act, it will use its best efforts to meet the conditions to Rule 144 that are within its control.*]

Given that the only requirement imposed by Rule 144 on a non-affiliated stockholder is a six-month holding period (one year for non-reporting companies), there may be little reason to provide registration rights to such holders. Registration rights may be

---

2. To satisfy the informational requirement, a non-reporting company must make certain information publicly available as specified in Rule 15c2-11 of the Exchange Act. Such information includes, among other things, the nature of the company's business, products, or services and facilities, balance sheets, and profit and loss and retained earnings statements and information regarding securities outstanding. *See* §240.15c2-11(a)(5)(i)-(xiv), (xvi).

3. The maximum amount of securities that may be sold under Rule 144 during any three-month period may not exceed the greater of (i) one percent of the outstanding securities of the same class, (ii) the average weekly trading volume of that class on all exchanges or as reported through an automated quotation system for the four calendar weeks prior to the filing of the notice of sale, or if no such filing is required, the date of receipt of the order to execute the transaction by the broker or the date of execution made directly with a market maker and (iii) with respect to debt securities only, 10% of the tranche of debt securities. Rule 144 also contains various requirements concerning aggregation of sales by certain related parties, including the aggregation of shares to be sold by two or more affiliates or other persons acting in concert.

4. Generally, sales of securities under Rule 144 must be made in customary unsolicited "broker's transactions," transactions directly with a "market maker," or in "riskless principal transactions" (a principal transaction where, after having received from a customer an order to buy, a broker or dealer purchases the security as principal in the market to satisfy the order to buy or, after having received from a customer an order to sell, sells the security as principal to the market to satisfy the order to sell).

5. If the amount of securities to be sold in reliance upon Rule 144 during any three-month period exceeds 5,000 in number or $50,000 in aggregate sales price, the selling security holder must file a notice of sale on Form 144 with the SEC concurrently with the placing of the broker's order to sell, or upon the execution of the sale directly with a market maker. Any person submitting such notice must have a bona fide intention to sell such securities within a reasonable time after the filing of Form 144.

6. To satisfy the informational requirement, a reporting company must have been subject to reporting requirements under the Securities Exchange Act of 1934 for at least 90 days and must be current in the filing of its reports thereunder for the preceding 12 months or such shorter period for which it has been a reporting company. The company will meet this requirement as long as it remains current in filing its periodic reports after the expiration of such 90-day period.

less attractive to such holders since they will not offer any advantages over an unregistered transaction under Rule 144, including the speed of execution. In particular, investors who agree to a six-month lock-up period from the date of the investment would be able to freely sell under Rule 144 after six months and thus not need registration rights unless such investors wanted the ability to sell securities in an underwritten deal. Many deals do not provide registration rights for a period of time after the securities are purchased [*see Sample IRA §1.2(a)(ii)(B)*], and once holders can demand a registration, it can take several months to go through the SEC process to have the registration statement declared effective before the holders can proceed with the transaction. If registration rights are granted, the agreement should provide that such rights lapse for securities other than those held by affiliates once the Rule 144 holding period expires. [*See Sample IRA §1.13, terminating registration rights for "Investors" who can sell their shares without restriction under Rule 144 or whose holdings are small enough that all of their shares may be sold without being affected by the volume limitations of Rule 144. It also terminates registration rights altogether five years after the company has a "Qualified Public Offering." Some agreements terminate registration rights as early as three years following any registered offering.*]

Because the Rule 144 exemption is not always available, particularly for affiliates, registration rights provide a mechanism for restricted securities to be registered under the Securities Act and sold in a public offering. Furthermore, even if Rule 144 is available, registration rights would be needed by large investors who want to sell in underwritten offerings. There are two types of registration rights: demand and piggyback. Demand registration rights enable the stockholder to require the issuer to register all or a portion of its shares. [*See Sample IRA §§1.2 and 1.4, which are both demand rights, but §1.4 separately addresses registrations on Form S-3. Section 1.2 contemplates the use of Form S-1 but does not explicitly require it, leaving open the ability of the company to use Form S-3. Note that the definition of "Registrable Securities" in §1.1 applies only to common stock issued upon conversion of the venture capital preferred stock.*] Piggyback registration rights allow a stockholder to include shares in a registration being effected by the issuer either for its own account or for the benefit of other selling stockholders. With piggyback registration rights, the stockholder cannot trigger the registration process. [*See Sample IRA §1.3, referring to the right to participate in "company registrations."*]

Demand Registration Rights

A holder with demand registration rights can compel the company to file a registration statement with the SEC on the holder's request. Filing a registration statement and causing it to become effective is an expensive proposition and exposes the company to potential federal securities law liabilities associated with a registered offering and the restrictions placed on a company "in registration." As a result, from the company's perspective the number of demands should be limited to two or three demands unless the holder has a significant amount of stock. [*See Sample IRA §1.2(a)(ii)(E), which limits the Investors as a group to the right to demand three registrations under that Section. In the venture capital context, three demands is at the high end of the normal range. The reality, however, is that demands are rarely used because of the expense and disruption involved in a registered transaction on Form S-1. Most venture capital registration rights exercises are piggybacks or S-3 registrations.*]

Stockholders should not be able to demand an initial public offering (an "IPO") generally because if the company is not ready, a premature IPO will not result in good execution and in all likelihood will not be successful. It may be appropriate to allow an IPO demand if the holders have held the stock for a long period of time (*e.g.*, five years) or for private equity investors who may need an IPO as their exit strategy. [*See Sample IRA §1.2(a)(ii)(B), which allows demands only after a period of five years or six months after an IPO. A period of up to one year following the IPO is normally used — one year being the minimum time after which registration on Form S-3 may become available.*] Liquidity for investors is one of many factors a company should consider when deciding to go public. Being a public company increases administrative expenses and workload, creates reporting requirements, and requires compliance with provisions of the Sarbanes-Oxley Act, SEC regulations, and requirements of an exchange or trading market. The exercise of demand rights for an IPO should not benefit one demand holder to the detriment to the long-term interests of the company and the remaining stockholders.

To insure that a demand registration is made for the mutual benefit of the company and the holders, a minimum percentage of shares holding demand rights should be required in order to initiate the demand (*e.g.*, 25%). [*See Sample IRA §1.2(a) and the defined term "Initiating Investors," which requires a demand from holders of at least 50 percent of the shares having registration rights — 25 percent is at the low end of the normal range, with the top being perhaps 66.7 or 75 percent. Query: How might the distribution of shares among holders of Registrable Securities affect the negotiation between the company and the Investors in setting this threshold?*] A dollar threshold pegged to the minimum public float amount for a particular exchange (e.g., $60 million for the New York Stock Exchange or $70 million for the NASDAQ Global Select Market) may be more appropriate. This will insure that a company is not required to incur the time and expense of registering a small number of shares and incur the costs of being a public company. [*See Sample IRA §1.2(a), which provides that the shares to be registered must have an expected aggregate offering price of not less than $5 million. What the authors say is completely valid, but venture capital transactions typically have very low threshold transaction size requirements. In addition, as discussed in section D.1 of Chapter 9, venture capital transactions sometimes also require that the proposed public offering anticipate a threshold per-share price like the one in Sample IRA §1.1's definition of a "Qualified IPO."*]

The Filing and Effectiveness Periods

Time periods set forth in the registration rights agreement as to when a registration statement must be filed following a demand should be very specific (*e.g.*, 90 days). It should not use language similar to the following: "as soon as practical but within 90 days." Although this language is typical in most registration rights agreements, it is too imprecise and can cause disagreements as to when a company is obligated to file. Fluctuations in the company's stock price and the capital markets generally can compound disagreements surrounding a company's efforts to file "as soon as practical" and can lead to litigation. As a general matter, companies not yet public should be given at least 90, if not 120, days to file their registration statements with the SEC, and already public companies should get at least 60 days. [*See Sample IRA §1.2(a)(ii), which provides that the company shall "as soon as practicable, use its best efforts to effect the registration. . . ." Query: Do you think the authors typically represent investors demanding registration or the companies receiving the demands?*]

The agreement should not provide for short, specific time periods for the SEC to review and declare a registration statement effective (*e.g.*, 30 or 60 days). The company cannot control the SEC process and should not be contractually bound to complete a process that is unpredictable at best. That said, the company can agree to a shorter time period if it is a well-known seasoned issuer (a "WKSI")[7] since the WKSI registration statement on Form S-3 will become effective without SEC review. The time period provisions for WKSIs should not apply when the company ceases to qualify as a WKSI. [Query: *What do you think is the likelihood that a venture capital financed company will become a WKSI before all or virtually all the registration rights expire under the terms of §1.13 of the Sample IRA?*]

The company should agree to keep the registration statement effective for 60 to 90 days rather [than] indefinitely (although for a shelf registration statement, a longer effectiveness period would be more appropriate). [*See Sample IRA §1.7(a), providing for 90 days, and §1.7(b), providing for post-effective amendments to keep the registration effective for up to 180 days. In practice, most registrations, other than on Form S-3, are firmly underwritten and, therefore, are completed immediately, so the provision for keeping the registration effective usually is only meaningful for Form S-3 or shelf registrations.*] While indefinite effectiveness is required by many registration rights agreements, there are burdens on the company to keep a registration statement effective in perpetuity, including the updating responsibility to file post-effective amendments or supplements to reflect material developments and monitoring when black-out periods are appropriate. The updating responsibility normally lasts until the distribution of shares is completed. Typically, if a company is current in filing its Exchange Act reports and proxy statements the registration statement on Form S-3 will likewise remain current. However, there may be situations in which a material development is not required to be disclosed in periodic filings because the development does not fall under the requirements of Form 8-K, but a company would not feel comfortable selling securities at such time. In such a case, the company must be able to impose a black-out period on resales.[8]

---

7. A WKSI is any company that meets the following criteria: (a) it meets the registrant requirements under Form S-3 or F-3 and (b) meets one of the following two tests: (1) the worldwide market value of its outstanding voting and non-voting common equity held by non-affiliates is U.S. $700 million or more or (2) during the last three years it issued at least U.S. $1 billion aggregate principal amount of non-convertible securities, other than common equity, in primary offerings for cash registered under the Securities Act. Further, the following categories of issuers are deemed not to be WKSIs: ineligible issuers, voluntary filers, asset-backed issuers, registered investment companies, business development companies, and Schedule B issuers (a foreign government or political division of a foreign government).

8. It is incumbent upon a company to appropriately tailor its contractual obligation to keep a registration statement current to account for the possibility that it might engage in activities such as merger negotiations which would necessitate the suspension of trading under a registration statement. *See* TheraTx v. Duncan, No. 99-11451, 2000 U.S. App. LEXIS 38558 (11th Cir. 2000).

If the company has to impose such a black-out period, demand holders would know there exists material, non-public information about the company. In fact, to comply with Regulation FD, the company may be required to prematurely disclose the relevant information.[9] Further, the legal and accounting costs of preparing a registration statement on Form S-3 may not be insignificant. As a compromise, the company can agree to unlimited shelf registration statements until the first anniversary of the issuance of the shares.[10] This limitation should not adversely affect investors if they are able to sell under Rule 144 and will limit overhang in the market. [*Registration on Form S-3 allows a company to incorporate by reference disclosure it has filed previously with the SEC, thereby reducing the cost of the registered transaction. While the authors are correct that the cost may not be trivial, it almost certainly will be significantly less than a registration on Form S-1, the default form. A venture capital term sheet often will provide for unlimited Form S-3 registrations, but no more than one each six months. See Sample IRA §1.4(b)(iii), which allows for no more than one registration every six months.*]

Black-Out Periods

Demand holders control the timing of a registration, not the company. However, a holder may inadvertently pick an inopportune time to demand registration due to ongoing negotiations, uncertainties, contingencies, pending projects, or other issues that can be problematic to disclose or would make it undesirable for the company to complete a registration at that time. Investors typically prefer one very limited black-out period (*e.g.*, 60 days per year) and only for specific items (*e.g.*, merger negotiations). However, there are circumstances where a company could be forced into premature disclosure, held liable to investors under a registration rights agreement, or unable to enter into negotiations or material business agreements.[11] As a result, from a company's perspective, the agreement should provide for multiple black-out periods each year (many deals allow only one) and permit each period to be at least 75 days (that is the SEC standard for preparing *pro forma* financial information).

Also, from a company's perspective, the company should be able to block a demand for a period of time per year (90 or 180 days) if the company believes it would have a material adverse effect on the company or any material transaction contemplated by the

---

9. Under the SEC's Regulation FD, if a company, or any person acting on its behalf, intentionally discloses material, non-public information to an analyst or an institutional investor, or to any other investor where it is "reasonably foreseeable" that the person to whom the information is disclosed will trade on the basis of that information, then the information must be disseminated to the public simultaneously with such disclosure. Disclosure for purposes of Regulation FD may be made on Form 8-K, in broadly disseminated press releases, through open or webcast conference calls (assuming adequate notice), or through other SEC filings. Failure to disclose information as required by Regulation FD could result in loss of a company's Form S-3 or F-3 eligibility or, if the recipient trades on the information, insider trading violations.

10. The first anniversary mirrors the Rule 144 holding period requirements imposed on holders of restricted securities of non-reporting companies. For securities sold by reporting companies, a six-month period may be more appropriate.

11. *See e.g.*, United Telecomm. v. American Television & Comm. Corp., 536 F.2d 1310 (10th Cir. 1976) (the company was in breach of an agreement granting registration rights to an investor by entering into negotiations that led to a merger agreement because it resulted in an inability to cause a then-pending registration statement to become effective).

company. [*See Sample IRA §1.2(a)(ii)(F), providing for a 90-day deferral for any reason that is seriously detrimental to the company or its shareholders, but usable only once during any 12-month period. The deferral term is sometimes as long as 180 days, but 90 or 120 days are more common.*]

The reason for being able to invoke a black-out period should be in the reasonable judgment of the company. [*See Sample IRA §1.2(a)(ii)(F), providing for "the good faith judgment" of the board.*] As described above, many deals provide that a company can only invoke a blackout if there is material, nonpublic information in the hands of the company of a specific type (e.g., merger discussions) and the company informs the holders of the reason to impose a black-out period. However, after the company signs and announces a material transaction, it may not have sufficient information (*e.g., pro forma* financial information) to make the registration statement complete. Also, the company may be a party to an SEC investigation or a litigation that is disclosed in general terms but that the company may not want to, or be able to, provide sufficient disclosure from a registration statement point of view. It is not possible to anticipate all the potential business reasons why a company could be in need of a blackout.

Once a registration statement has been declared effective, the company should have the right to require that holders suspend their sales if the company invokes a black-out period. If the company has new material, nonpublic information and it would not be desirable to amend or supplement the registration statement with the information, the registration statement will no longer be current and holders should rightly suspend their sales. [*See Sample IRA §§1.7(b) and 1.7(f) — is the objective noted by the authors accomplished by the interaction of these two provisions?*]

In addition, demand holders should not be able to use a demand within 180 days of any company stock offering. Since a company can usually only do one deal every six months, a company may be unable to raise capital appropriately if a demand holder is able to trump a company stock offering by delivering a notice first. This would clearly not be in the best interest of the remaining stockholders. [*See Sample IRA §§1.2(a)(ii)(C) and (D).*] One provision that is not currently included in registration rights agreements but which would give a company flexibility would be to give the company the ability to conduct its own offering when it gets a demand notice (either prior to or simultaneously with the offering demanded).

Piggyback Registration Rights

Piggyback holders do not have the right to initiate the registration process. [*Sometimes, piggyback rights are given to a particular set of investors who do not receive demand rights (for example, lenders who receive warrants as an equity sweetener may be granted piggyback rights for the shares issuable upon exercise of the warrants). Venture capital investors typically get both.*] It is, nevertheless, important to regulate piggyback rights. Piggyback rights are significantly time consuming in the context of an offering, can cause delays in the registration process, and can complicate pricing and marketing efforts if holders can withdraw from a transaction at any time. Many deals provide unlimited piggyback rights to all stockholders into perpetuity even after the shares are freely tradable. This makes every offering mechanically difficult since the company will have to keep trying to track down holders with piggyback rights who would have no incentive to participate in a registered deal and may not even own any stock. Coordinating with sometimes hundreds of selling stockholders becomes a full-time job for internal and outside counsel at the company. [*See Sample IRA §1.13. Query: Does that provision distinguish between piggyback versus demand registration rights?*]

The company itself should have piggyback rights on deals resulting from a demand exercise by the stockholders. Often the company is second in right to the selling stockholders initiating the demand. As discussed above, it will be in the best interest of remaining stockholders if the company is first in priority in any offering and those negotiating registration rights agreements should carefully consider providing for that. [*See Sample IRA §1.2(b). Query: Does the agreement contemplate the company's participation in demand registrations?*]

In negotiating initial registration rights agreements, it is important for those representing the company to keep in mind that the company will want the ability to provide new holders with equivalent piggyback rights without needing the consent of existing holders of registration rights, since consent may be hard to get. This can often be a contentious provision and the existing stockholders may demand significant concessions. However, without this provision, the company may not be able to raise money when needed. [*The authors' observation is appropriate in looking at public companies or later stage private companies, but see Sample IRA §1.5. Query: Does that approval right surprise you, given that venture capital preferred stock holders generally have approval rights on any new financing?*]

Piggyback rights should only apply to the registration of equity securities by the company or a selling stockholder (other than shares being registered on Form S-4 [*for business combinations*] or S-8 [*for equity incentive plans*], or shares issued in an acquisition or debt securities). Many registration rights agreements inadvertently permit debt and equity holders to piggyback on any securities offering even if not for a similar security. [*Note that the Sample IRA applies to "Registrable Securities." Query: Given the definition of that term in §1.1, should you be concerned about this issue under the Sample IRA?*]

Companies may consider limiting piggyback rights to affiliates and other large stockholders, given that the requirements imposed by Rule 144 have been significantly reduced, as discussed above. Small, nonaffiliated stockholders who have no need to register large block sales will be able to sell their shares in the market without restriction after the Rule 144 holding period lapses (such period depends on the reporting status of the company but is either six months or one year, as discussed above). As a result, small stockholders will have no need to participate in a public offering and pay the higher fees charged by an underwriter as compared to the typical broker's fee in a Rule 144 trade. Otherwise, offering a large group of holders the option to exercise piggyback rights will be quite onerous on the company and may threaten to delay an offering to the detriment of larger stockholders participating in the offering.

Notices to Piggyback Holders

Registration rights agreements typically entitle piggyback holders to advance notice of a proposed registration statement filing and require the piggyback holder to exercise its rights within a period of time after receipt of the intention to file. These notice provisions are actually quite crucial, particularly if there are multiple small piggyback holders. There is often a great deal of marketing pressure not to miss an opportunity to file and consummate a deal within certain windows of time in a company's reporting calendar (*e.g.*, before the company's financial statements go "stale") or to take advantage of market opportunities, and the notice provisions can be an unnecessary delay in the process. We have worked on deals with more than 100 piggyback holders, many of whom are no longer connected to the company, and the cost of compliance with these provisions can run into the hundreds of thousands of dollars. Some companies simply do not fully comply with these provisions, leading to potential litigation claims. Others comply with each requirement of the registration rights agreement, which can delay the offering and result in potentially missing market windows. Piggyback holders may also not want notice of an offering too early in the process as they will have to decide whether or not to participate at that time and it may limit their options during the process. Nevertheless, investors at the outset typically negotiate for notice as early as possible, which is often not in their, or the company's, best interest. [*See Sample IRA §1.3(a).*]

Registration rights agreements should be drafted to provide that notices should *not* be required to be sent prior to filing (*e.g.*, 20 days before filing) but should be tied to printing red herrings (*e.g.*, 20 days before printing). Virtually all deals tie the notice period to the pre-filing period even though this makes little practical sense and companies generally do not want to provide notice before the deal happens. In the first instance, the deal may never happen. Second, and perhaps more importantly, the company may be deemed to be sharing material, non-public information by sending the notice. This may trigger Regulation FD disclosure (when an issuer discloses material, non-public information to certain individuals or entities, the issuer must make public disclosure of that information) and can block the recipients of the notice from selling until the registration statement is filed. To avoid such a situation, registration rights agreements should include a confidentiality provision. Further, if the notice does not block piggyback holders from selling, early notice can result in recipients selling their stock. Also, the notice can easily be leaked even if provided on a confidential basis.

Delaying the notice and response period is also beneficial to piggyback holders. Piggyback holders will want to delay the decision on whether or not to participate in an offering until the last possible moment, given the volatility of securities markets. This desire to delay is especially strong if there is a limitation on the number of times that piggyback rights may be exercised. Holders also will not want material, nonpublic information that can restrict their ability to trade.

If possible, we suggest that the notice period should be 10 to 15 days before red herrings are printed in IPO situations, and five to 10 days for non-IPO situations. If the SEC does not review a filing, the deal can happen within 10 days of filing with the SEC and a longer notice period may delay the deal. Furthermore, if the company is WKSI-eligible, the registration statement becomes effective automatically, so the longer the notice period the more market risk for the transaction, particularly if the notice is not delivered before filing.

From a piggyback holder's perspective, the exercise of piggyback rights should not be required until pricing terms are determined. Most deals require holders to decide quickly to participate but will let them withdraw at any time until pricing. However, if the holder can withdraw up until pricing, the mechanics of actually completing the offering will be quite difficult. For example, the underwriters will not know how many shares to sell. Further, the participating holders will need to be available at pricing to confirm they are still in the deal. A fair position is to permit holders to give a conditional notice whereby they will participate above a specified price and that they cannot withdraw above that price. That will enable the company and the underwriters to organize the deal and know the parameters by which the piggyback holders will participate. It will also set the expectations of the holders and limit their ability to withdraw from the offering once pricing terms become available.

Withdrawal Rights

As discussed above, most deals are either silent on withdrawal rights or effectively let stockholders withdraw from an offering up until pricing. This makes a deal unmanageable in the days leading up to pricing since the company would have to be in constant contact with all participating holders (which could be over 100 holders in some cases).

In an ideal world from the company's point of view, participating selling stockholders (particularly small holders) invoking piggyback rights should not be able to withdraw shares once the red herring is printed (particularly if the deal prices within the range in an IPO). While the withdrawal of one holder from the offering may not require a recirculation of the preliminary prospectus, the downsizing of the deal may be a negative signal to potential or existing investors or may cause embarrassment to the company. Further, it may decrease the size of the offering to a point at which the shares could have been sold in a Rule 144 transaction, which would have saved the company the additional time and expense of pursuing an underwritten offering.

If it is not possible to eliminate withdrawal rights once the red herring is printed, we suggest that withdrawal should be allowed only in connection with the conditional exercise of piggyback rights based on a minimum price, as discussed above. [*The Sample IRA provides for early notice to piggyback rights holders and allows them to withdraw up to the point of execution of the underwriting agreement, which happens on the very eve of the offering. (See Sample IRA §§1.3(a) and 1.3(b).) The Sample IRA does not provide for the mechanisms recommended by the authors to manage piggyback participants, so implementing those procedures would be voluntary on the part of the piggyback rights holders.*]

Offering Mechanics

Requirements to Participate

Most standard registration rights agreements have a provision that requires any stockholder that wants to participate in the offering to do so on the terms required by the underwriters for all holders (including delivering opinions, executing powers of attorney and custody agreements, and executing a customary underwriting agreement). Otherwise, the deal becomes unmanageable. If company officers are given powers of attorney by the selling stockholders, the company will be able to sign the underwriting agreement on behalf of the selling stockholders, thereby eliminating the need to have each selling stockholder sign the agreement at the time of pricing.

The most favorable provision for the deal process is to have the selling stockholders provide the company or the lead selling stockholder with the authority to price the deal (the other stockholders would sell at the same price) or at least agree to a minimum price so that the company or the underwriters do not have to check with every stockholder at the time of pricing.

Each selling stockholder should further be required to timely complete a questionnaire to provide information for inclusion in the registration statement about that selling stockholder. [*Participating shareholder information is required by §1.9 of the Sample IRA.*]

Cutback Provisions; Priority on Registration

As a general matter, the company should come first in any sale (other than certain demand right situations). After the company, all stockholders who have first-priority registration rights should be treated equally rather than having the stockholder who initiated the demand go before all other stockholders as is the case in some deals. If the party who delivers the demand had the right to sell all of its shares first, there becomes a race to deliver the demand and the deal may happen at the wrong time since holders may prefer to sell first at a sub-optimal price than be stuck holding shares while others sell their shares at a sub-optimal time.

A cutback provision will provide that if all the shares cannot be sold in an orderly manner, then the company and the underwriters can cut back the number of shares to be sold in the offering. It is critical to the company to define this provision in a way that it will be able to implement. We have worked on many deals where the standard is so unclear that it is difficult for advisors to determine if a cutback is permissible (*e.g.*, company can cut back if the number of shares to be offered would impact the marketability of the deal). In some circumstances, an amendment to the registration rights agreement may be required. A fair standard for the company and the holders should require the underwriters to include shares that can be sold "in an orderly manner at a price that is acceptable to the company or the relevant stockholders." Further, although not typical in current agreements, we believe the company or a lead stockholder should be able to apply the standard in its sole discretion. They should be able to invoke a cutback before the marketing of the offering begins, which will provide more flexibility than many registration rights agreements that appear only to allow a cutback at the time of pricing. It may also be helpful to allow cutbacks of all or some of the selling stockholder shares if the underwriters determine it would be adverse to have any selling stockholder shares (*e.g.*, in an IPO). [*The cutback provisions of the Sample IRA are in §1.2(b) for demand registrations and §1.3(b) for piggyback registrations. Note that §1.2(b) says that "Other Investors" are cut back first. They are participants in the offering who do not have registration rights under the Sample IRA, often lenders holding equity sweeteners or large founder or management shareholders. Cutbacks are a negotiated term and often will be referenced in the venture capital term sheet. Query: How are the Sample IRA's piggyback cutback terms different for the company's IPO versus subsequent registered offerings?*]

The standard to invoke the cutback provision should not be tied to the numbers of shares that can be sold. Shares can always be sold at some price.

In addition, the agreement should not require the investment bank to provide written advice for cutbacks. In our experience they are reluctant to do so. [*Note that cutbacks on demands in §1.2(b) require written notice from the managing underwriter, while §1.3(b) says on piggybacks that cutbacks may take place merely if the managing underwriter determines that they should.*]

Holdback Agreements (Lock-Ups)

The holdback or lock-up agreements should cover both the initial public offering and, for certain stockholders, future offerings. The lock-up for the initial offerings should be for 180 days from the date of the underwriting agreement and for follow-on offerings 7-14 days before, and 90 days after, the underwriting agreement. [*See Sample IRA §1.12, which provides for a 180-day standoff only on the IPO. The lock-up terms noted by the authors for subsequent offerings are frequently seen in venture capital transactions.*] Also consider whether lock-up agreements should not be required after the first deal or two, or for holders with less than a specified number of shares. This will reduce the paperwork needed to consummate follow-on offerings and provide flexibility to smaller holders whose sale of shares will not adversely affect the market price of the stock. Note, however, that without additional lock-up agreements, all the shares held by non-affiliates could be sold after the 180-day period for initial offerings since the six-month holding period imposed by Rule 144 will also lapse. Accordingly, it may be in the company's and the remaining stockholders' interest to require the lock-up agreements to extend beyond the currently standard 180 days for those shareholders that can sell under Rule 144. This would be a departure from market practice.

Historically, many deals did not lock up securities that were freely tradeable. However, since the revised Rule 144 permits shares to be sold after being held for six months or one year, most securities sold by a company before an IPO would be freely tradeable when the company completes its IPO. Accordingly, companies may want to have lock-ups apply even when shares are no longer registrable under the registration rights agreement. [*See Sample IRA §1.12. Query: Does it address only shares with registration rights or is its coverage broader?*]

The holdback for the company should permit the company to issue shares in acquisitions (whether or not pursuant to an S-4, which is the typical carve-out) and permit registration for those shares to be sold.

The holdback should include the standard 17-day extension periods required by underwriters to comply with applicable NASD and NYSE conduct rules regarding research.[13] Very few registration rights agreements have this provision because it is

---

13. If (1) during the last 17 days of the holdback period the company issues an earnings release or material news or a material event relating to the company occurs or (2) prior to the expiration of the holdback period, the company announces that it will release earnings results or becomes aware that material news or a material event will occur during the 16-day period beginning on the last day of the holdback period, the holdback restrictions imposed should continue to apply until the expiration of the 18-day period beginning on the issuance of the earnings release or the occurrence of the material news or material event. Without this extension period, analysts would not otherwise be able to publish research reports on material

new and the professionals who negotiate this provision may not be aware of it. [*Often, the extension is set at 18 days — see the text of footnote 13.*]

The registration rights agreement should not include carve-outs for the selling stockholders since the underwriters may not agree with them, or only allow carve-outs to the extent the underwriters agree.

Selling stockholders often request a "most favored nation" provision for their lock-up. It may enable the company to get stronger lock-ups up front since the stockholders know they will not be treated worse than the "most favored" stockholder. [*See Sample IRA §1.12(b).*] However, if any stockholder receives a carve-out, all other stockholders automatically will receive the same carve-out and therefore it is unlikely that any stockholder will receive one — even for ordinary course sales or transfers to charities.

The company will also often be asked to use reasonable efforts to get its officers, directors, and 5% stockholders to execute lock-ups. The company should not guarantee these people would sign (particularly 5% holders), but rather should use its reasonable efforts to get its directors and officers to sign. The company usually has no way to influence third-party institutional holders, like mutual funds or pension funds, to sign lockups. [*In the venture capital context, where the company is more apt to be in a position to implement market standoffs on all its future share issuances, provisions like §1.12(b) are not unusual, although for the reasons the authors note, later stage companies usually resist them.*]

Selection of Underwriters

The agreement should be drafted to provide that the company will choose the underwriter if it is selling any shares. Another option is to have selling stockholders choose if they are exercising a demand right (many deals incorporate this option even if the company also sells). If the company is not selling in the offering, the majority of the selling stockholders should choose the underwriter. The company should always have a consent right not to be unreasonably withheld, other than perhaps in a block trade scenario. [*Sample IRA §§1.2(b) and 1.3(b) explicitly provide that the parties will enter into an underwriting agreement with the managing underwriter selected by the company.*]

Providing Documents to Selling Stockholders

The company can also agree to provide copies of the registration statement and amendments after they are filed to stockholders and perhaps copies of the SEC's staff comments to the registration statement. Since the documents will be available on the SEC's website through EDGAR, this provision is not necessary. In addition, although it seems reasonable to provide the comments (though they too will eventually become available on EDGAR), it is unlikely that the company will actually send the comments to all the selling stockholders and seek their input if there are multiple sellers. [*See Sample IRA §1.7(c).*]

The company should agree to reasonably consider the selling stockholders' comments on the registration statement, but should not give the selling stockholder final approval

---

events or earnings releases per FINRA rules that limit publication 15 days prior to and after the expiration of a lockup. *See* NASD Conduct Rule 2711(f)(4); NYSE Member Regulation Rule 472(f)(4).

over the disclosure (except perhaps for disclosure specifically relating to the selling stock-holder). The company will have ultimate responsibility for the disclosure, but many deals provide that the company must accept the selling stockholder comments. [*The Sample IRA has no such requirement.*] If the selling stockholders are allowed to comment on the registration statement, the registration rights agreement should include limited time per-iods in which to provide such comments. Further, the agreement should be drafted to provide that the selling stockholders must deliver to the underwriters adequate documen-tation so that the underwriters may satisfy their due diligence defense.

Comfort Letter and Opinions

The company should only be required to use reasonable efforts to have appropriate comfort letters provided and addressed to the underwriters and the selling stockholders (if the accountants permit). The company should not be required to contractually agree to timely deliver a comfort letter because the company does not control either its own accountants or the accountants of acquired entities, particularly in situations where the company has changed accountants. [*See Sample IRA §1.7(e)(ii).*]

Underwriters will not do a deal without receiving standard legal opinions. The company may agree to pay the selling stockholders' legal fees associated with the opinions if they agree to use a predetermined law firm. [*See Sample IRA §1.6(a) and the definition of Registration Expenses in §1.1.*] This will facilitate the offering as the under-writers will only have to negotiate the opinions with one firm and the company will be able to control the process of delivering the opinions. If the company has not agreed to pay these costs in advance, they may be uncomfortable doing so.

Costs

The costs of filing a registration statement, causing it to go effective and doing an underwritten offering can be quite high (even for an already public company). Typically, the company will pay for all costs of the selling stockholders, which disincentivizes selling stockholders to control costs. To limit the costs of registration and the offering, the following provisions should be considered:

- The number of counsel for selling stockholders should be limited to one for all of the stockholders combined (this will also make communications with the selling stockholders easier) [*See Sample IRA definition of Registration Expenses in §1.1.*];
- If the company starts the registration process, such action should count as a demand even if the selling stockholders later withdraw (as an alternative, the action would not count as a demand if the selling stockholders pick up the costs) [*See Sample IRA §1.6(a).*];
- The stockholders should have a limited window (*e.g.*, 60 or 90 days) to do an underwritten deal once the registration statement has been through the SEC process so that the company does not need to keep updating the document (and paying lawyers and accountants to do so) while the selling stockholders wait for favorable market conditions. We are aware of deals where the company

has had to keep updating the registration statement for a year or more. [*As noted, §1.7(b) of the Sample IRA provides for 180 days.*]

Other Provisions

Best Efforts

As a general matter, many registration rights agreements modify promises made by the company to cause things to happen (*e.g.*, to file the registration statement, to cause it to become effective, to market the shares to the public) by "best efforts," "reasonable best efforts," "commercially reasonable efforts" or similar language. Often the standards are based on the precedent used and the use of different standards throughout the agreement is not given careful thought. While it may be true that it is not clear how these standards are measured under New York law,[14] an agreement containing multiple standards provides a sliding scale as to how each standard should be interpreted. As a result, the agreement should have one consistent standard for the company's efforts (*e.g.*, commercially reasonable efforts) and should not use multiple standards, which may be interpreted by a court to require extraordinary efforts where a higher efforts standard is used. The company should never have a "flat" standard to make something happen (*e.g.*, cause the registration statement to become effective) for items outside its control (*e.g.*, effectiveness). If the company or the investor wants a specific action to occur (*e.g.*, file the registration statement in 30 days), the agreement should specifically require the action to occur and not use an "efforts"-based standard. [Query: *What is the standard used in the Sample IRA? Is it used consistently?*]

Confidentiality

The agreement should contain a specific confidentiality provision for non-public information provided to the parties pursuant to the registration rights agreement. Information about a black-out period under the registration rights agreement, or perhaps notice of an anticipated registered offering, may be material and may not be permitted to be provided to stockholders under Regulation FD absent a specific agreement to keep the information confidential. [*See Sample IRA §2.3. Query: Do the terms of this provision limit its effect to information provided under §2?*]

Applicable Shares

Once shares become freely tradeable under Rule 144 (*i.e.*, shares that are not subject to the holding period, but that may otherwise be subject to information requirements, volume limitations, manner of sale, and notice obligations), they should not generally be covered by the registration rights agreement (although it may be desirable to be able to lock up shares once they become freely tradable after the requisite Rule 144 holding

---

14. David N. Shine, "*Best Efforts*" *Standards Under New York Law: Legal and Practical Issues*, M&A Law. (Mar. 2004).

periods lapse, as discussed above). Otherwise the company will be required to provide piggyback notices to stockholders who would not ordinarily need to participate in a registered offering in order to sell its shares. Also, the shares held by these holders may be inadvertently locked up under the holdback provisions. If the continued coverage of shares is deemed of critical benefit to the company even after they become freely tradeable under Rule 144, the shares should not be covered by the registration rights agreement after they have been sold. [*See Sample IRA §§1.11, 1.12, and 1.13. Query: Does the Sample IRA address the concerns the authors raise? How does §1.11 address the authors' concerns regarding the proliferation and dispersion of registration rights?*]

Marketing Rights

Often the marketing section of a registration rights agreement includes boilerplate language and requires management to do whatever is asked of them. The registration rights agreement should be drafted to require management to participate in the marketing of an underwritten offering of selling stockholder shares within reason. Management should control the timing of an underwritten offering such that it does not conflict with key business initiatives or preparing other public filings.

Some deals are silent or have minimal discussion on marketing. [*The Sample IRA is silent on marketing.*] This hurts all involved in the process. Unclear requirements can unduly burden management and, from the selling stockholders' point of view, may not require enough from management to result in a successful offering.

Conclusions

The considerations discussed in this article are meant to focus companies and their counsel on the mechanics of registration rights and assist with drafting more effective registration rights agreements. All sides will benefit from having a registration rights agreement that works and reflects legal and commercial realities.

In addition to registration rights, the following covenants are also frequently included in the IRA.

Information Rights. Information rights are very typically provided by the company to its preferred stock investors. (*See* Sample IRA §§2.1-2.5.) In addition to addressing the understandable desire of investors for information on their investments, information rights fulfill the requirement imposed by some limited partners in venture capital funds (such as pension funds and other regulated companies) that the fund demonstrate it has management rights with respect to its portfolio companies. Information rights are considered positive evidence that the venture capital fund plays an active role in managing its investments.

The major negotiating issues on the scope of information rights generally relate to the specifics of what is to be provided, to whom, and when. Section 2.1 of the Sample IRA begins with a definition of "Major Investor" and limits the company's information delivery obligations to Major Investors. The term used may be "Significant Holders" or something similar, but the key idea is to limit the company's disclosure obligations to a defined subgroup of preferred shareholders that own more than some threshold number of shares. Some agreements call for delivering annual and perhaps quarterly financial information to all preferred shareholders (as in §2.1(a) and (c) of the Sample IRA), although most will limit monthly reports and operating plan deliveries to Major Investors. (*See* Sample IRA §2.1(b) and (d).) This limitation is a product of both administrative ease as well as a desire to restrict the circulation of immediately current confidential company information. The right to "additional information" (as set forth in §2.2 of the Sample IRA) is almost always limited to Major Investors for the same reasons. As should be obvious, where the line is drawn for Major Investor status can have a significant impact on a particular investor's rights, especially since the Major Investor distinction often is applied to additional important rights granted in the IRA.

Section 2.1(a) of the Sample IRA calls for annual financial statements to be audited by a nationally recognized public accounting firm. Early stage companies often do not have their financials audited, and even later stage companies no longer use nationally recognized public accounting firms. Since the advent of the Sarbanes-Oxley Act of 2002, national public accounting firms have been strongly focused on serving their public company clients and have had less of a presence in the early stage, private company market. Many audits are now being done by local firms or, when done by a national firm, often are delayed until May or June, when the busy public company filing and tax seasons are over. In the latter situation, the audited annual financials provision might say that audit-ready financials will be delivered within 90 to 120 days after the end of the year and the audit completed by, perhaps, June 30.

Section 2.3 of the Sample IRA requires that all *nonpublic information* obtained from the company be kept confidential, subject to specified limitations. It is important to remember that shareholders have no fiduciary duties to the companies in which they are invested. While self-interest might encourage a shareholder to keep company information confidential, it also could push an investor towards using that information in a way that is contrary to the best interests of the company. Establishing a confidentiality obligation in association with the company's information delivery obligations, therefore, is a normal and prudent act.

Preferred investors' information rights should end as soon as they conflict with that company's public disclosure obligations. Regulation FD (17 C.F.R. §§243.100-243.103) seeks to level the information playing field among investors by prohibiting public companies from engaging in special disclosure to selected shareholders. The information rights section of the IRA, therefore, should terminate once the company is subject to public reporting and disclosure requirements. Section 2.4 of the Sample IRA addresses this issue.

Sample IRA §2.5 allows investors that own their shares in more than one entity to aggregate their holdings for purposes of determining their status as a Major Investor. Venture capitalists often allocate their investments among a number of parallel funds based on agreements with their limited partners. As an example, the signature page to the Sample IRA shows that the fictional Menlo Park Ventures has invested through three separate funds, each having the same general partner. When a venture investor uses multiple funds, it does not want its rights restricted because its holdings are divided.

In practice, information delivery obligations are often not strictly enforced so long as the company is applying appropriate effort and achieving reasonable quality in its information preparation. For example, most IRAs require that an operating plan for the following year be delivered prior to the end of the current year, yet most operating plans seem to be completed sometime during the first quarter of the year to which they apply. Similarly, the speed at which an auditor completes the audit process is not within the company's control, so deadlines on the delivery of audited financials often are not met.

In addition to understanding the impact of the threshold number of shares for Major Investor status, an additional barrier to that status that counsel needs to be sensitive to arises when the company has a strategic investor. To the extent that a strategic investor also may be a competitor, the company's management needs to have the discretion to exclude trade secrets or other proprietary information from the materials provided to that investor.

Right of First Refusal. Venture capital transactions very often include the company's covenant to the preferred stock investors that it will not issue new securities without first offering them the right to buy at least a portion of the new issuance. There is an administrative burden and transactional cost issue if the company has a large number of small preferred investors, many of whom will not exercise the right anyway. Because a burdensome right of first refusal can impede the company's ability to raise new investment funds, this right often is limited to Major Investors.

Section 3.1 of the Sample IRA, after a long list of excluded securities issuances, states the right of the Major Investors to participate in a new issuance of the company's securities. Note the consistency between the list of excluded transactions and the carve-outs from the preferred stock's price protection anti-dilution rights. (*See* section D.4 of Chapter 9 in the discussion of Charter Sample 9.30 — "Additional Shares of Common Stock.") These exclusions are often negotiated and can vary significantly from company to company.

As provided in §3.2 of the Sample IRA, the right of first refusal gives each Major Investor the right to buy its pro-rata portion of a covered issuance so that the Major Investor may maintain its percentage ownership interest in the company. As an example, if the preferred holders own 65 percent of the company's shares, they will have the right to buy 65 percent of a new issuance, so 35 percent is unburdened by the right of first refusal and can be sold to new investors. In essence, the company may sell to new investors a percentage of the new offering equal to the portion of the company that is owned by shareholders not participating in the right of first refusal.

Section 3.2 provides that the company must give notice to the Major Investors at least 10 days before a covered securities issuance (that is, one that is not excluded by §3.1). The Major Investors then have 20 days to respond in order to express their intention to exercise their right to buy, in all or in part, their proportionate piece of the new issuance. To the extent that the entire part of the offering that is subject to the right of first refusal is not taken up by the Major Investors — that is, some Major Investors decline their opportunity to buy — the participating Major Investors may allocate among themselves the part not taken within five days. This latter, second allocation among participating Major Investors is referred to as a "gobble-up" provision, as it allows the participating investors to divide up any portion of the right not exercised by their fellow investors. Any portion of the offering that is not taken by exercise of the right of first refusal may be sold to new investors.

The time period for investors to respond to a right of first refusal is normally kept short so that the company is not delayed in completing a needed financing. While some IRAs require that all rights of first refusal be resolved before any securities may be issued, §3.2 of the Sample IRA provides that notice may be given to the Major Investors as few as 10 days before an issuance, but allows them up to 25 days to decide how much of the issuance they want to purchase. This is not a warp in the space-time continuum. It simply lets the company take money from a new investor while sorting out the first refusal rights of its existing preferred stock holders. In this way, the company can issue shares to the new investor at a first closing, and then meet its obligations to its existing investors at a second closing. In pursuing this course, the company obviously has to make sure it sets aside enough shares to meet its first refusal obligations to the Major Investors.

One important issue is how each Major Investor's proportionate interest is calculated for the right of first refusal. In the case of the Sample IRA, §3.2 provides that the Major Investor is deemed to own the as-converted number of shares represented by the securities it holds, plus the similar shares owned by its affiliates. That number is divided by the fully diluted shares of the company to determine percentage ownership. Some agreements limit the denominator to all as-converted shares outstanding, which does not include shares reserved but yet unused under an option plan. That change would decrease the denominator and, therefore, increase the percentage interest the Major Investor could purchase under the right of first refusal.

The right of first refusal gives investors their best true anti-dilution protection, but it is not free. They have the right to avoid dilution from a new securities issuance only by putting up the money to maintain their percentage ownership interest in the company. While companies are usually just as willing to take money from existing investors as from new, the company's concern always is that the right of first refusal is going to interfere with its ability to raise significant new investment capital because the existing holders will limit the portion of the company the new investor can buy. A new investor, for example, might offer to invest $35 million to buy 45 percent of a company, but if the exercise of the first refusal right limits its investment to $17 million for 27 percent of the company, it may not be interested.

It bears mentioning also that the last sentence of §3.2 of the Sample IRA allows the Major Investor to apportion the securities purchased using the first refusal right among its partners and affiliates as it sees fit. In short, related shareholders get to aggregate their shares for purposes of calculating the extent of their rights, and then allocate the exercise of that right freely among members of the affiliated group. Setting aside the fiduciary issues this might trigger within a Major Investor group, this mechanism makes exercise of the right of first refusal more flexible and, therefore, easier for an affiliated group of entities to use, so it is an investor-favored term.

In addition, §3.2 of the Sample IRA allows the right to be exercised on an "all-or-part" basis, which also increases flexibility for investors by allowing partial exercise. An alternative is to make the right "all or none" as to each Major Investor. Investors will resist this approach as it restricts their ability to exercise because an investor with a

$500,000 allocation, but who is only willing (or able) to invest $100,000, probably will decide to invest nothing rather than come up with the extra $400,000.

Similarly, the existence of the "gobble-up" right increases the probability that the right of first refusal will be more fully exercised and so is often objected to by the company. Regardless, the provision is commonly included as part of the IRA.

The final issue on the right of first refusal we will consider is the termination provision. Section 3.3 of the Sample IRA provides that the right will terminate immediately prior to a Qualified Public Offering, which means that it will survive a smaller public offering. Item (ii) of §3.1 of the Sample IRA says that the right would not apply to the shares issued in the public offering (it would present some awkward securities problems if it did), but the continued existence of the right might make an underwriter unwilling to attempt that public offering. Some IRAs provide that the right terminates on any public offering.

Additional Covenants.   After registration rights, information rights, and the right of first refusal, which typically appear in most IRAs, the remaining covenants are usually the subject of negotiation. Some IRAs have none, while others go on for pages. The trend seems to be for more covenants to be added. Perhaps venture capital investors have found shortcomings in relying on their participation on boards of directors as the mechanism for setting certain company policies and behaviors. Regardless of what prompts them, these covenants tend to fall into a handful of categories.

The first category is covenants relating to specific employee issues. Turning to the Sample IRA, §4.1 sets forth a Key-Employee Insurance covenant. When the company has personnel that are critical to the execution of its business plan, it is typical for the investors to insist on insurance for the benefit of the company should one of those key employees die. Given that replacing such an important part of the business could take time and delay the growth of the company, the insurance proceeds could be very useful in dealing with the unexpected costs caused by such a tragedy. Often having the insurance in place is a condition to closing in the SPA and this covenant requires the company to keep the policy in effect. The Sample IRA's provision is silent on the company's duty to maintain the policy, although the duty to procure it is ongoing. A better provision would require the company to procure *and* maintain a policy, with any changes in the policy or any company-initiated cessation in coverage made subject to approval by the board of directors, including the directors elected by the preferred stock.

Sections 4.2 and 4.4 of the Sample IRA are also common covenants in this category, addressing contractual matters between the company and its employees. As discussed in Chapter 7, section B.2, confidential information and invention assignment agreements are an important element of the company's management and protection of its intellectual property. Section 4.2 creates an ongoing obligation to enter into those agreements with future employees and consultants. Section 4.4 sets a template for equity incentive vesting terms that may only be deviated from with unanimous board approval. Both put management on notice of the investors' expectations for employment terms that are to be offered in recruiting new key personnel.

Sections 4.3, 4.5, 4.7, 4.9, and 4.13 of the Sample IRA are fundamental premises and deal preservation covenants. Sections 4.3 (qualified small business), 4.7 (flow-through entity), and 4.13 (SBIC investors) all relate to maintaining basic corporate characteristics and circumstances that made the original investment suitable for the investors. These covenants prohibit changes to these facts and circumstances, as well as mandate continued compliance with the investors' expectations regarding these issues. Sections 4.5 and 4.9 address company conduct needed to preserve some of the basic deal terms set by the transaction documents. Section 4.5 provides that if the company has any rights of first refusal with regard to any of its stock and is not going to exercise that right, it will, to the extent permitted, assign that right pro rata to the preferred shareholders. Section 4.9 deals with large equity incentive grants. It requires that becoming a party to the ROFR and the VA be made a condition to receiving equity incentive grants above a certain size. This term preserves the restrictions and agreements those documents place on large common stock holders. Particularly where founders are no longer part of the management team and new senior management has received sizable equity incentives, it is important to monitor which shares are addressed by those documents to be sure that their purposes (discussed in the following sections of this chapter) are being fulfilled.

The next category of company covenant is represented by §§4.6 (reimbursement of board meeting expenses), 4.8 (indemnity agreements with directors), 4.11 (existence and basic makeup of board compensation committee), and 4.12 (existence and basic makeup of board audit committee), which address the company's obligations regarding its board of directors. These all are matters that relate, directly or indirectly, to the participation of the preferred stock holders on the board of directors.

The final covenant type might be described, for lack of a better term, as *banker covenants*. Sections 4.10 (compliance with laws), 4.14 (notice of major events), 4.15 (transactions with affiliates), and 4.16 (payment of taxes) are covenants addressing the ongoing conduct of the company's business. They are known collectively as banker covenants because they are very much like what a bank would require under the terms of a loan. In fact, referring back to the Sample Loan Agreement included in Appendix B, you will see that each of these covenants appears in one form or another in that document. Along these same lines, maintenance of general liability insurance, maintenance of properties and assets, changes in the business, incurrence of debts or encumbrances, and investments in or dispositions of assets — all of which appear in general terms under that Sample Loan Agreement — are also covenants that might appear in an IRA. Other covenants might include limitations on employee compensation, customer credit policies, or frankly anything that an investor might feel is an important constraint on company conduct. Of course, the company can be expected to resist what it might perceive as micromanagement by covenant.

Section 4.17 provides that the covenants of Section 4 will terminate when the company becomes subject to the public company reporting requirements. Some IRAs use the Qualified IPO standard defined for that deal, allowing the covenants to survive a small IPO.

Additional and Miscellaneous Terms. Beyond the foregoing covenants, an IRA may include any provision that relates to the relationship between the company's preferred stock holders and the company. For example, an IRA may include a "play or pay" provision that requires certain preferred stock holders to purchase all or a specified portion of their pro-rata allocation of future investment rounds or have their shares automatically converted to common stock. These types of provisions can be done by contract (e.g., the IRA) or by operation of the company's Charter. A Charter provision provides ease of enforcement but also less flexibility in tailoring the deal to the needs of, or to accommodate, specific groups of stockholders. Another shortcoming is that the Charter is a public document, which means that private deal terms must be revealed.

Finally, the IRA contains a set of miscellaneous terms, some of which are particularly important if the document is to serve its purpose as the consolidated repository of the company's ongoing covenants to *all* of its preferred stock holders. Perhaps primary among these terms is the section on amendments. The intent is to amend and restate the IRA upon each successive round of financing, so the rights of the new investors are folded in with and reconciled to the continuing rights of the earlier investors in one comprehensive set of covenants. Having reviewed the typical IRA terms, you should be able to see the shortcomings of a company having three or four separate sets of registration rights or rights of first refusal. As a result, the IRA needs an amendment provision that allows the company and a majority (or supermajority) in interest of the preferred stock holders to amend it, and that causes the amendment to be binding on all the existing parties to the agreement, whether they voted in favor of the amendment or not.

Section 6.1 of the Sample IRA addresses this need by providing that a written waiver or amendment approved by the company and the holders of 60 percent of the converted or as-converted preferred stock shall be effective as to all parties to the agreement. An exception is provided for any amendment that eliminates a specific holder's rights, including the holder's information right or rights of first refusal.

Another important part of §6.1 is its last sentence, which allows additional "Investors" who buy preferred stock in a subsequent closing under the terms of the current SPA to be added to the IRA without their addition constituting an amendment to the agreement. This provision reduces transaction costs by simplifying subsequent closing procedures in reliance on the fact that subsequent closings under the current SPA have been approved by the preferred stock holders and that Investors in those closings will be in the same position as Investors from earlier closings.

Other miscellaneous provisions are basically a product of appropriate contract drafting. Sections providing for counterpart signatures and the effectiveness of facsimile signatures are crucial for completing a timely closing as the number of parties grows, not to mention the sanity and administrative convenience of the company's lawyer. A counterparts provision, such as §6.5, allows each party to sign a separate signature page and for those pages to be assembled and to constitute execution of one complete document. A facsimile signatures provision, such as §6.6, allows the transaction to be completed when signature pages are electronically delivered, rather than when hard copies eventually arrive by snail mail.

QUESTIONS

1. Joan and Michael are confused by registration rights. The term sheet they got talked about piggyback rights, but they have read the "registration rights" section of the IRA draft and that term does not appear. Since the term sheet calls for "unlimited piggyback rights," they are concerned. What is your response?

2. Joan and Michael wonder if giving the preferred stock investors a right of first refusal on new, capital-raising securities issuances may limit the amount a new investor can buy and, therefore, constrain SoftCo's future ability to raise capital. As a practical matter, how realistic is this concern?

3. After reading the covenants section of the IRA, Joan and Michael ask you about the "Key Employee" insurance requirement. Joan says she saw a documentary on how some companies buy life insurance policies on their employees in order to cash in on untimely deaths. She recalls that these are labeled "dead peasant" policies and is offended that an investor would suggest that SoftCo should have insurance on her life or on Michael's. What is your response?

---

6. Right of First Refusal and Co-Sale Agreement

Overview.   The ROFR sets forth agreements by the major common stock holders for the benefit of the preferred stock investors and, to a lesser extent, the company. The investors seek to accomplish two basic objectives with the ROFR: first, supervision of the dissemination of the company's shares; and second, ensured participation in any liquidity opportunity that becomes available to the common stock holders.

As a result, if a major common stock holder should decide to transfer all (or a portion) of his or her shares, a ROFR provides that the preferred stock investors have two options. First, they may take the place of the prospective purchaser and buy the shares themselves under the negotiated terms (the *right of first refusal*). Alternatively, if they choose not to exercise their right of first refusal, the preferred shareholders may compel the selling shareholder to include in the proposed sale some of the preferred investors' shares in place of some of his or her own (the *co-sale right*).

In terms of the mechanics of the agreement, the right of first refusal typically is applied first. A common holder who proposes to sell shares is required to give the company and the preferred shareholders notice of the proposed transfer, including the basic terms of the transaction. The company then has the first right to step in front of the purchaser and buy the shares under the proposed terms. Should it decide not to, or should it not have the financial capacity to make the purchase, then the right passes to the preferred stock investors on a pro-rata basis. Should the preferred shareholders decide not to exercise the right to step into the shoes of the purchaser under the proposed terms of sale, then the co-sale right applies. The co-sale right allows the preferred stock investors to inform the selling shareholder that they wish to sell some of their shares with him or her. The common holder is then required to reduce the number of shares he or she is selling to the purchaser and substitute instead shares owned by the preferred investors. Upon exercise of the co-sale right, the transaction goes forward unchanged from the purchaser's point of view — in fact, the exercise of the co-sale right may be structured so that it is completely invisible to the purchaser. Should neither the right of first refusal nor the co-sale right be exercised, the selling shareholder then has a window of time during which he or she may complete the negotiated transaction with the proposed purchaser.

As was discussed in Chapter 6, section F.1, the function of a right of first refusal is to control the dispersion of the company's shares. In fact, the basic terms described there, in the context of founder stock purchase or employee equity incentive agreements, apply equally to the right of first refusal as it generally appears in the ROFR. The terms are so similar, in fact, that most ROFR agreements contain a provision asserting that their right of first refusal terms supersede the terms of any previous agreements between the company and the common shareholders who are parties to the ROFR.

The co-sale portion of the ROFR (sometimes referred to as a *tag-along* right) is one component of the preferred stock's right to be first in line in cashing out of the company. To the extent that a major common shareholder has found someone interested in making a substantial investment in the company, the preferred investors have two legitimate arguments as to why the common shareholder should not be permitted to go forward with the sale of his or her shares. First, a potential investor in the company's stock really should be considered a corporate opportunity that should be directed to the company so all of its shareholders benefit from the cash the investor is willing to spend to buy shares. That is, from the perspective of the preferred shareholders, the proposed purchaser of the common shareholder's interest should be buying newly issued shares from the company. A right of first refusal and a co-sale right make a transfer from a common shareholder slower and more complicated, which might lead that investor to look to the company as a better source for the purchase of an equity interest in the business.

Second, the only reason the common shareholder's shares have real value is because the preferred stock investors put hard cash into the company. Moreover, at the time this investment was made, the common shareholders specifically agreed that the preferred stock would have the first right to proceeds upon a liquidation, and that promise went into the Charter. For a common shareholder now to seek to transfer shares privately to a prospective buyer is to attempt an end-run around the preferred stock investors' right to get their money out first. As a consequence, if the transfer transaction is to go forward, at the very least the preferred shareholders should have the right to participate in the sale, consistent with their right to get their money out of the company before any holders of common stock.

In practice, ROFRs are a very common element of venture capital transactions. While the investors occasionally do not insist on one, it is certainly the norm that the company's major common stock holders agree to bind their shares by the ROFR's terms as a necessary element of attracting venture capital investment to the company. Despite the fact that ROFRs are used regularly, common stock transfers that trigger the terms of a ROFR are relatively rare. Instead of *despite*, perhaps the absence of triggering transfers *results* from the common usage of ROFRs. As noted in the Chapter 7 discussion, the existence of a right of first refusal, with its attendant delay and complication, is a major impediment to finding a potential transferee and completing a transfer. Few buyers are willing to invest time and money pursuing a private stock purchase when the company, as well as the existing preferred stock investors, are in a position to step in and take the benefit of the bargain if it is a good one. The further addition of the co-sale right in a ROFR, with its additional delay and complexity, simply exacerbates the problem.

Parties to the ROFR.   To better understand the basic terms of a ROFR, we examine the Sample Right of First Refusal and Co-Sale Agreement in Appendix B (the "Sample ROFR"). First, note that the parties to the Sample ROFR are the "Company," the "Series A Investors," and certain holders of the Company's "Common Stock," identified in §1.5 as *Significant Shareholders* (sometimes called *Key Holders* or *Major Common Holders*). Note that the recitals report that this agreement is being entered into concurrently with the issuance and sale of the Company's Series A Preferred Stock to the Series A Investors. Unlike the Sample IRA, then, this is a first-round document that has not yet been amended and restated — it is the initial ROFR for these parties. Note also that although the Sample ROFR is to be executed by all the Series A Investors, it also defines "Major Investors" in §1.3 and limits the rights granted under the agreement to the Major Investors.

The Significant Shareholders are defined in §1.5 to include holders of Common Stock (or of options or rights to buy Common Stock) representing more than 1 million shares in the aggregate. Section 1.5 adds that any person who meets that standard in the future shall become a party to the agreement, and any person who was a Significant Shareholder but ceases to hold more than 1 million shares of Common Stock shall be excused from its terms, subject to being re-included should that person's holdings later increase above the 1 million-share threshold.

Historically, it was typical to see the common shareholder parties to ROFRs defined as the "Founders" for the simple reason that the founders usually held a large portion of a normal venture capital financed company's common stock. As venture capital has proliferated and "professional venture managers" have proliferated with it, and as major economic up-turns and down-turns have led to wild shifts in company values and an increased likelihood that a company will go through at least one capitalization restructuring in the course of its financing life, it has become more common for founders to have a relatively small interest in their companies, and for "experienced management," hired later, to end up with a larger ownership interest than the founders. As a result, particularly in the years following the collapse of the technology bubble, ROFRs moved away from application to founders alone towards application to any common stock or equity incentive holder with a threshold number of shares (or the right to buy that number of shares). The threshold is frequently presented as a percentage, rather than a number, of the company's fully diluted shares, often 1 or 2 percent, but sometimes as high as 5 percent.

Note also that Sample ROFR §1.5 links the status of Significant Shareholder to the covenant in §4.9 of the Sample IRA referred to above. In that section, the company covenanted that any equity incentive grant that would cause the grant recipient to hold the threshold number of shares (or, with the shares he or she holds, have the right to buy an additional number that would, in the aggregate, exceed the threshold) would be conditioned upon the grant recipient becoming a party to the ROFR. (Because the Sample IRA came at a later time than the Sample ROFR in this particular company's life, note that it is amended and restated, and the threshold number of shares for Significant Shareholder status has changed from what applied at the time of the first round of investment shown in the Sample ROFR.)

Right of First Refusal.   The right of first refusal terms are set forth in §2 of the Sample ROFR. Section 2.1 provides the general restriction that any Significant Shareholder transfer must be made in conformity with the terms of the Sample ROFR. Section 2.2 details the information (including the identity of the proposed buyer and the price to be paid) to be provided in the notice of a proposed transfer that a Significant Shareholder must deliver to the Company and the Major Investors in the event a prospective sale is negotiated with a third party.

Under §2.3, the Company has 15 days before it must provide a notice to the selling Significant Shareholder and the Major Investors stating whether it will buy "all of the Offered Stock" at the "same price and on substantially equivalent terms" as described in the proposed transfer notice. Note that the Company's right of first refusal precedes the Major Investors' right of first refusal. This is almost always the case, and company counsel typically insists that the company have the right to act on behalf of all its shareholders to exercise the right of first refusal before that right is shifted to a select few shareholders. As a result of the sequence of notices and resulting decisions that have to be made under the terms of a ROFR, the time periods for notices and responses tend to be short.

Under the language of §2.3, the Company has the right to buy *all* the shares proposed to be transferred. A requirement like this — mandating that the right be exercised as to "all the shares or none" — is usually viewed as less of an impediment on transfers. A right that allows the company or preferred shareholders to purchase less than all the shares proposed to be transferred makes the right of first refusal an even larger disincentive for a prospective buyer because the likelihood of a partial exercise is greater than that of a full exercise. In addition, it puts the selling shareholder in a position of having to go forward following the right of first refusal exercise as to a portion of the shares, only to see the prospective buyer then decline to buy the smaller number of remaining shares. A provision sometimes seen (but not appearing in the Sample ROFR) allows a company with an all-or-none right to determine that it will exercise a portion of its right, but that exercise will be effective only if the preferred shareholders take up all the remaining shares by exercising their right of first refusal. The result is that the company and the preferred stock investors share in the purchase of *all* of the shares, thus satisfying the all-or-none requirement, and the terms of the selling common shareholder's negotiated transaction are preserved.

An additional significant element of §2.3 is the fact the Company must exercise the right of first refusal at the "same price" presented in the notice, but the other transfer terms need only be "substantively equivalent." This is a compromise that allows the Company to avoid any personal terms a prospective buyer might offer that could not be equaled but could be substantively matched. At the same time, as price is the most critical term, the Company is required to pay the same price offered. Some agreements say that the company must meet the same price *and* terms offered by the prospective buyer. Others say the company only must meet *substantively equivalent* price and terms. Any room for deviation between the specifics of the prospective buyer's offer and the terms of the company's exercise of the right is a breeding ground for dispute and can lead to a claim either that the company is abusing its contractual rights in an effort to block the transfer without honoring the purchase terms or that the selling shareholder has negotiated idiosyncratic terms to thwart the company's efforts to match the proposed transaction. In any event, regardless of the language, the Company should be prepared to match the proposed transfer terms as nearly as possible.

Finally, §2.3 requires that the Company, upon giving notice that it will exercise its right of first refusal, must be ready and able to complete the purchase within five business days. This short term to closing takes away the Company's ability to (i) string the

Significant Shareholder along until the prospective buyer gets frustrated and withdraws, then (ii) not purchase the shares. Short time periods are seen, then, as reducing the constraint on sale inherent in a right of first refusal. Some agreements do not impose a time limit on the company's purchase, instead relying on the fact that the company is to match the terms offered by the prospective buyer, including the timing of closing the transfer. Many lawyers see that as inadequate, so most agreements require the company to move promptly to complete the transaction.

Should the Company choose not to exercise its right of first refusal, the Major Investors next are given their opportunity. Section 2.4 lays out the Major Investors' right of first refusal, again with a short response time (15 days) and the same exercise requirements that applied to the Company (all or none, same price, substantively equivalent terms). To the extent that any of the Major Investors choose not to exercise their right, a gobble-up provision allows those that do to take up the remaining shares.

The Sample ROFR differs from some agreements in that it requires the Company to send its notice regarding exercise or waiver of its rights to the selling Significant Share-holder and to the Major Investors. Many agreements have the company give its response only to the selling common shareholder, who must then send a second notice to the preferred investors holding the right of first refusal. Given that delivery of that notice starts the time period running on the Major Investors' right, and electronic communications often are not permitted by the notice provisions of legal documents, that additional step can add several days of delay to the resolution of the ROFR rights.

As previously mentioned, §2.4 also provides that the terms of the Sample ROFR supersede those of any existing right of first refusal, such as in a founder stock purchase agreement or an equity incentive plan stock purchase agreement. As the Sample ROFR represents a written agreement entered into by (presumably) the parties to any prior right of first refusal agreement (i.e., the Company and the several Significant Shareholders), that provision probably is effective as an amendment to a prior agreement. In addition, the language at the very end of §2.4 specifically references certain agreements containing rights of first refusal as being superseded, which, absent a very unusual amendment section in the referenced agreements, almost certainly will be effective as to the referenced agreements. Section 2.5 is intended to eliminate any assumption that, by superseding the rights of first refusal on transfers in any prior agreements, the Sample ROFR also terminates any of the Company's restricted stock repurchase rights that may be set forth in those agreements with respect to any Significant Shareholder shares.

If the Company and Major Investors do not exercise their first refusal rights, the Significant Shareholder still must clear the hurdle of the co-sale right in Section 3 before the transfer may be completed.

Rights of Co-Sale.   Upon completion of the right of first refusal mechanics, assuming the right is not exercised, the shares proposed to be sold also must pass through the Sample ROFR's co-sale procedures in §3.2 before they may be transferred. The Company does not share in the Major Investors' co-sale rights. The key elements of the co-sale rights are time frames, the formula for allocating the opportunity to co-sell, and whether any gobble-up right is provided. As was true for the right of first refusal, the Significant Shareholders want the time allotted for the Major Investors to make up their minds as short as possible. Section 3.2(a)(ii) gives them only 5 days following expiration of the right of first refusal to deliver notice of their election to participate in the sale. Either 10 business days or 15 days probably is a more common standard.

Section 3.2(a)(i) sets out the allocation formula, with the percentage of the proposed transfer that may be taken by a Major Investor equaling the number of common stock equivalent shares held by that Major Investor divided by the total number of Major Investor common stock equivalent shares plus the number of common stock equivalent shares owned by the Significant Shareholder who is proposing the transfer. Some ROFRs will limit the denominator by including only the number of shares the selling common shareholder proposes to transfer, rather than all the shares held. If the transaction represents the selling common shareholder's entire share interest in the Company, this difference has no impact. But if the transfer is only a portion of the seller's shares, by including all the common stock equivalent shares held, the selling common shareholder retains a larger allocation.

The other factor that can reduce the portion of the sale left for the Significant Shareholder who negotiated it is the gobble-up right for participating Major Investors provided in §3.2(a)(iii). To the extent that some of the Major Investors believe that exercising the co-sale right is in their interests, this provision allows them to take up the entire portion of the transfer that is subject to the co-sale right.

The Major Investors participating in the co-sale exercise their right in accordance with §3.2(a)(ii) by delivering to the Company a written election and endorsed share certificates (common or preferred). The Company then handles the mechanics of the transfer. To the extent that the parties choose to do so, by having the Company orchestrate the mechanics of the transfer, including the conversion of preferred shares into common, the operation of the co-sale can be kept invisible from the prospective purchaser. Alternatively, some agreements have the preferred holders deliver common or preferred stock certificates to the selling common shareholder and charge him or her with managing the logistics of the sale.

Should the co-sale right not be exercised, §3.3 of the Sample ROFR gives the Significant Shareholder 60 days from the initial notice of the proposed transfer to complete the sale to the prospective buyer under the terms described in that initial notice. Selling shareholders are usually provided a window of between 30 and 90 days to complete the sale. If the transfer is not completed within that window, or if the terms upon which the sale is to be completed are reset, the shares must go through the entire process again. Section 3.3 provides that, once sold, the shares are taken free and clear of the terms of the Sample ROFR. While some ROFRs are not explicit that the transferred shares are free of the continuing application of the ROFR, those documents usually do not include any mechanisms for having the transferee become a party to the ROFR, which results in the same outcome.

Prohibited Transfers.   In the event that a common stockholder who is bound by a ROFR does not follow the document's terms and provide the preferred stock investors the benefit of their co-sale right, those investors typically get a *put right* or a *put option* under the terms of the ROFR. Section 3.4 of the Sample ROFR, after reserving all other remedies for the Major Investors, establishes the put option elaborated in §3.5 as an additional remedy. Section 3.5 provides that each Major Investor will have the right to require the defaulting Significant Shareholder to buy, at the price and terms of the breaching transfer, that number of shares that the Major Investor would have been able to sell under its co-sale right. Separately, §3.5(d) states that any breaching transfer will be void and requires the Company to not give effect to the transfer on its register of shareholders. Terms like these are fairly typically in ROFRs, although their enforceability is a question very few courts have addressed.

As a practical matter, a breaching transfer would be unusual. The common shareholders who are parties to a ROFR typically have legends placed on their stock certificates (*see* §5.1 of the Sample ROFR), which should put the Company, its transfer agent (*see* §5.2), and the prospective purchaser on notice that a problem exists when the certificate is delivered upon consummation of the sale or for reissuance in the new holder's name. Even so, some ROFRs go further and create a mechanical bar to unauthorized transfers by requiring the common shareholders covered by the agreement to deliver their share certificates into escrow, typically with the company's corporate secretary, for so long as the shares remain subject to the ROFR's terms.

Exempt Transfers.   Share transfers by common shareholders typically are exempt from a ROFR's terms if they fall into one of three categories: (i) family gifts or estate planning transfers where the recipient person or entity (a family trust, for example) agrees that the shares will continue to be bound by the ROFR's terms (*see* §4.1 of the Sample ROFR); (ii) transfers of a *de minimis* number of shares (*see* §4.2(i) of the Sample ROFR); and (iii) transfers that do not conflict with the "preferred get liquidity first" purpose of the ROFR, such as transfers made as part of an acquisition of the company, a liquidation of the company, or to the public as part of the company's IPO (*see* §4.2(ii), (iii) and (iv) of the Sample ROFR).

Some ROFRs do not include a *de minimis* sale exemption, and for those that do, the limit is usually set as a percentage of the number of shares held by the common stock holder. The Sample ROFR provides for sales representing up to 5 percent of a Significant Shareholder's shares, but many exemptions are as low as 2 or 3 percent.

Termination and Miscellaneous Terms.   Section 4.3 of the Sample ROFR sets forth the circumstances upon which the Significant Shareholder is released from that agreement's terms. At a minimum, a ROFR should terminate when the company is sold or dissolved or upon a Qualified IPO. Most ROFRs terminate upon any public offering (*see* §4.3(ii)). The Sample ROFR treats a transfer of Common Stock in connection with an acquisition or dissolution of the Company as exempt (*see* §4.2), and as those transactions fundamentally change the Company, they effectively terminate the agreement.

The Sample ROFR has some less frequently seen provisions in that it terminates on any of the following: (i) after a fixed number of years (*see* §4.3(i) setting termination after ten years); (ii) upon approval of the Company and a vote of the Investors (*see* §4.3(iii), setting termination upon the same threshold vote required to amend the agreement per §6.4, which might suggest that it is not needed, but note that an amendment also must be approved by a majority in interest of the Significant Shareholders); and (iii) when the Major Investors cease to hold at least 20 percent of the shares originally issued to them (*see* §4.3(iv)).

Since the Sample ROFR applies only to common shareholders who own a threshold number of shares (*see* §1.5), it automatically terminates as to a particular holder who falls below a material ownership level. Agreements that apply simply to a named group of common shareholders need to have a mechanism for excusing any one of them when his or her interests become small enough that the restrictions on his or her stock no longer provide a meaningful benefit to the preferred stock investors.

As to miscellaneous terms, the same issues that apply to the IRA and are discussed above are relevant here. In fact, because the IRA and ROFR are expected to be amended and restated with each new financing round and to continue side by side, together with the VA (discussed in the next section), it is particularly prudent for the drafter to coordinate the miscellaneous provisions of the three agreements so there is no administrative awkwardness arising, for example, from different definitions of what constitutes valid notice and when it is deemed delivered.

QUESTIONS

1. One of the arguments for why a right of first refusal on transfers is not unduly burdensome to someone like a Significant Shareholder under the terms of the Sample ROFR is that it does not restrict the ability of the common shareholder to complete a transfer under the terms that were negotiated — in short, the transferring common shareholder's negotiated deal is preserved. How accurate is that argument when the right of first refusal on transfers is an "all or nothing" right? An "any or all" right?

2. The same argument cannot be made for the co-sale right, as the selling common shareholder has to "share" the sale with the preferred shareholders. Which of the right of first refusal on transfers and the co-sale right do you find most intellectually, practically, and ethically sound from the perspective of the Significant Shareholders? From the perspective of the preferred stock investors? If the question were broken into three parts based on each of those standards of evaluation individually, would you have different answers from each perspective for "intellectually," "practically," and "ethically"?

3. Is restricting the right of first refusal and the co-sale right to "Major Investors" in the Sample ROFR really an administrative convenience, or is it actually a power and value grab by the big investors? Does your answer depend on how many preferred stock investors there are and how many are excluded by the "Major Investors" definition?

4. The exempt transfers permitted by Section 4 of the Sample ROFR do not include a charitable donation. What would happen if a Significant Shareholder wanted to donate some of his or her shares to the American Diabetes Association? Should that transfer be exempt from the terms of the Sample ROFR? Why? If it is not an exempt transfer, what is the consideration offered for the shares for purposes of the right of first refusal on transfers? (We probably can assume that the co-sale right will not come into play.)

7. *Voting Agreement*

A VA is a statutorily authorized mechanism to bind shareholder votes. Similar agreements in the public company context may be called "pooling agreements." VAs are wholly distinct from proxies and voting trusts (*see, e.g.*, Del. GCL §218(c); Cal. Corp. Code §706; and Model Act §7.31) in that they are agreements on how the parties will vote rather than direct means for actually voting. A VA typically is an agreement among a company's preferred stock investors and its major common stock holders to vote their shares in specified ways in board of director elections and, in some cases, on other key matters presented to the shareholders for approval. The parties to the VA usually are all the preferred stockholders, the company, and the same large common stock holders that are parties to the ROFR. Because the purpose of the VA is to manage the outcome of shareholder votes, the venture capital preferred stock investors want the holders of an overwhelming majority of all classes of a company's stock to be bound by the VA.

Typically used as a way to ensure that certain shareholders gain representation on the company's board, the VA often gives named shareholders the personal right to nominate directors and memorializes the other parties' agreement to vote their shares for those nominees. In addition, the VA can establish the obligation of all parties to vote their shares in favor of actions meeting specified criteria, which at a minimum can mean approval by a designated portion or subset of the preferred shareholders. These latter *drag-along* rights can be particularly significant in jurisdictions where a class vote by the common stock is necessary to approve a major corporate event. (*See, e.g.*, Cal. Corp. Code §1201(a), providing for shareholder approval by class (subject to exceptions) in the event of a reorganization; and Model Act §10.04(a)(5), providing for approval by a class upon the creation of a class or series of shares having higher-priority liquidation rights.) A drag-along right does not change the need for a class vote; it simply is a means to ensure in advance what the outcome of that vote will be.

Drag-along rights seem to be appearing in a growing number of venture capital transactions in recent years. If this trend continues to develop, it will represent a significant deviation from other investor rights, in that drag-alongs grant the power to *cause* a defined action. In contrast, the corporate governance rights and preferences attained through protective provisions, described in Chapter 9, section F.3, are *veto* powers.

In summary, a VA takes the shareholders' authority to vote under applicable state law and the company's Charter and, within the voting procedures required by state law and the company's bylaws, sets forth agreements among a major portion of the company's shareholders on how they will vote their shares in specified circumstances. VAs implement and sometimes expand on voting rights existing in a company's Charter but cannot conflict with those rights.

Director Elections.   Following a venture capital investment, a company's Charter normally reflects some negotiated allocation of the right to elect directors between the holders of the preferred stock and common stock. See examples in Chapter 9, section F.2. In the absence of a VA, the procedures for director nominations and elections would take place simply in accordance with applicable state law and the company's bylaws. A VA typically adds details on how the company's directors will be nominated and elected by the holders of the preferred stock, the common stock, and, if applicable, mutually by the two classes. The new preferred stock investors normally will have negotiated among themselves and with the prior preferred stock investors the allocation of the preferred stock's board election rights and the number of preferred stock shares each investor granted the right to designate a board member must maintain in order to keep that right.

In turning to the Sample Voting Agreement in Appendix B (the Sample VA), we see that it is an amended and restated agreement entered into in connection with a Series B Preferred Stock financing. Recital A records the acknowledgement of the parties to the Prior Agreement (the VA entered into as part of the Series A Preferred Stock issuance) that the present Sample VA amends and supersedes that Prior Agreement. This language indicates that the parties to the Sample VA include *all* the parties to the Prior Agreement, whether or not they execute the Sample VA. They are all bound because the Sample VA is an amendment to the Prior Agreement approved by the requisite holders under the terms of the Prior Agreement's amendment provision. In addition, each Series B Preferred Stock purchaser is required to become a party to the Sample VA as a condition to its investment.

The Sample VA's Recital B lays out the allocation of director election rights authorized in the Restated Certificate, noting that the holders of the Series A Preferred Stock are entitled to elect two directors, the Series B Preferred Stock one director, and the Preferred Stock and Common Stock, voting together as a single class, are to elect two directors. Recital B does not state that the Preferred Stock's director election rights in the Restated Certificate are conditioned on any threshold number of shares of the Preferred Stock remaining outstanding. For threshold language, look back at Charter Samples 9.35 and 9.36-A in Chapter 9, which limit the preferred stock rights to circumstances where a majority of the originally issued preferred stock continues to be outstanding. If the voting rights were limited by a threshold in the Restated Certificate, and the Sample VA ignored that threshold, then, so long as the Sample VA did not violate the terms of the Restated Charter, it could establish rights that go beyond the negotiated terms of the investment. So, when the Charter sets a threshold level of outstanding preferred stock as a prerequisite to director election rights, it should be noted in the VA's recitals, and the VA's director election terms should be qualified as applying only so long as the preferred stock's director election rights, as set forth in the Charter, continue in effect.

Section 1.1 of the Sample VA contains the parties' agreement to vote their shares to maintain a five-member board of directors. This provision might be redundant if the Restated Certificate set the board size at five and included a protective provision requiring the affirmative vote of the Preferred Stock in order to amend the Restated Certificate. Alternatively, no matter whether the board size is set in the Restated Certificate or the bylaws, the Restated Certificate could have a protective provision requiring that the Preferred Stock approve any change in the size of the board. In either case, the board's size could not change without the approval of the Preferred Stock holders and §1.1 would not be needed. Since §1.1 appears in the Sample VA, we would expect the Preferred Stock's protective provisions in the Restated Certificate to be narrowly drawn and not address changes in board size, although that would be unusual where director election rights are allocated in the Charter among classes. Board representation is such an important part of a preferred stock investor's involvement in the management of a company that when director election rights are set it would be surprising to have no

Charter provision preventing those rights from being diluted by an increase in the size of the board.

Section 1.2 establishes each party's agreement to vote to elect directors nominated in accordance with that section's provisions. Sections 1.2(a), (b), and (c) give specific Investors the right to nominate the two Series A Directors and the one Series B Director. Section 1.2(d) specifies the nominees for the two jointly elected board seats as the Company's CEO and an Outside Director not affiliated with the Company or any Investor. The result is that four of the five board positions are to be nominated by a specific investor or held by the person occupying the position of CEO. The only board nomination that is not locked in by §1.2 is the Outside Director, and if the mechanism for nominating that director set forth in §1.2(d) is not successful, that position is to go vacant until the deadlock is resolved and a nomination can be made. Note that the Preferred Stock nominates three of the five board positions, which means that the venture capital investors would have a majority of the quorum at a meeting of directors even if only four seats were filled. The Sample VA, therefore, reflects a situation where the preferred stock investors have a powerful level of control over the election of directors.

In examining a VA's board nomination and election provision, company counsel should confirm that the election rights do not act to expand the allocation of board seats agreed upon in the Charter. For example, as previously noted, the nomination and election provision should be subject to the same threshold that applies to the preferred stock's continuing right in the Charter to elect a specified portion of the board. Consequently, §1.2 of the Sample VA should cease to apply if the Restated Certificate no longer gives the Preferred Stock special director election rights.

Separately, the personal rights granted in each of §1.2(a), (b), and (c) by their terms apply only so long as each of the holders of those rights continues to own half of the Preferred Stock shares held by it as of the date of the Sample VA. For example, the Company could have a "play or pay" provision in its Restated Certificate or its IRA that requires its Investors to invest their pro-rata portions of future preferred stock issuances and, upon failing to do so, provides that their Preferred Stock shall be converted to Common Stock. An Investor with a board nomination right under §1.2(a), (b), or (c) who fails to support the Company in its next financing round and is forced to convert its Preferred Stock shares would lose that nomination right. Even if the Preferred Stock holders still had the required threshold number of shares outstanding to retain their right to elect board seats, if a threshold exists in the Restated Charter, nonetheless the personal right of the now-converted Preferred Stock Investor to nominate a director would have terminated. Note further that, despite losing its nomination right, given the definition of "Shares" in §1.1 and the wording of the voting obligation in the lead-in paragraph of §1.2, that Investor would still be bound to vote its Common Stock shares as provided in the Sample VA.

The Sample VA recognizes in Recital B that the Preferred Stock and Common Stock director election rights are separate but obligates all parties to vote "in whatever manner as shall be necessary" to implement the election of the nominees designated under the terms of §1.2. Some VAs have separate provisions requiring the preferred stock holders to vote their shares per the VA terms in elections in which the preferred stock holders vote and requiring the defined "major common stock holders" to vote per the agreement in elections in which the common stock holders vote. This approach must be taken with great care. In the event that, as just posited, a preferred stock holder is forced to convert to common stock as the result of a play or pay provision, is that holder then bound to vote its common stock in the same manner as the defined "major common stock holders" are bound? Does that holder fall within that defined group? Probably not. As a result, the question becomes whether the agreement addresses that holder's change in status. As a preferred stock investor upon a forced conversion may become the largest, or at least one of the largest, single holders of common stock, and may no longer be a supportive participant in the company, the goals of the VA would be seriously undercut if that investor, post-conversion, were not held within the control of the VA.

Section 1.3 of the Sample VA is an unusual, but potentially useful, provision that addresses what happens if a party with director nomination rights simply fails to make a nomination. It states that if a nomination is not made after two written notices to the nomination right holder, that stockholder waives its right to nominate and the general terms of the Company's corporate governance documents apply to making a nomination and filling the director position. Under many VAs, no mechanism addresses how the board seats are to be filled if a stockholder with nomination rights fails to act when called upon to nominate a director candidate. After the major downturns in the venture capital industry, when the tech bubble burst at the turn of this century and following the Great Recession beginning in December 2007, some venture capital funds simply went out of business. In some cases, while winding up their affairs, they cut down on staffing so dramatically that they no longer had sufficient personnel to serve on their portfolio companies' boards. In addition, in some circumstances, nomination rights may be given to large individual investors or to a founder who holds a major common stock position, and individuals can die or disappear. In any of these cases, the company needs a means of electing a board of directors if the people with nominating rights are no longer alive, available, or capable of exercising their nomination rights or otherwise overseeing their ownership interest in the company.

Section 1.4 of the Sample VA reconciles the right to remove directors with the rights granted in §1.2 to nominate them, including the effect of cumulative voting on the removal process. Section 1.5 exculpates shareholders from liability for nominating a director or voting for that nominee in accordance with the terms of the Sample VA as a consequence of that nominee's acts or omissions after being elected as a director. Both are normal parts of a VA.

QUESTIONS

1. A VA grants director nomination rights to specific investors and provides that all parties will vote their shares to elect the nominated persons. Under the terms of the Sample VA, if one of the Investors with the right to nominate a director were

penalized by a play or pay provision and forced to convert its Preferred Stock to Common Stock, how would that board position be filled?

2. How would board nominations and elections work under the terms of the Sample VA if *all* the Preferred Stock were converted to Common Stock?

3. How would board nominations and elections work under the Sample VA after conversion of all the Preferred Stock to Common Stock if §1.2(a), (b), and (c) did not have the requirement that each nominating party must continue to own 50 percent of the Preferred Stock owned on the date of the Sample VA?

Drag-Along Rights.   A drag-along provision requires all the parties to a VA to vote their shares in the same way as some designated person or group in specific circumstances. Its purpose usually is to give an investor group the right to require a majority of a company's stockholders to join them in approving or disapproving a major corporate event. As previously noted, drag-along provisions can be particularly meaningful if the company is incorporated in a jurisdiction where the common stock has a class approval right on, for example, a sale of the business. The negotiating issues are what major transactions it covers, what approval triggers the right, and what related approval activities are required of the "dragged" stockholders.

Section 3.1 defines the type of transaction triggering the drag-along right as either a sale of a majority of the stock of the Company by its current stockholders to new stockholders or an acquisition of the Company that triggers the "Deemed Liquidation Event" provision in the liquidation rights section of the Restated Certificate. Section 3.2 provides that if one of these "Sale of the Company" transactions is presented to the Company and a majority in interest of Common Stock issued or issuable upon conversion of the Preferred Stock *and* the Board approves the transaction, all parties to the Sample VA will vote in favor of the transaction.

In addition to the narrowly defined triggering transaction, probably the most important element of §3.2 to the Common Stock holders under the Sample VA is that a qualifying Sale of the Company must be approved by the Board. The reason is that the members of the Board have fiduciary duties to all the Company's stockholders. Some drag-alongs are triggered only by approval of some percentage or group of the preferred shareholders. But, as shareholders, preferred shareholders have no fiduciary responsibility to the holders of common stock, other than in very narrow circumstances, so they are broadly allowed to vote in their personal interests without regard to the impact on other shareholders. A board has different responsibilities and duties, however, so adding its approval as part of the triggering equation provides significant protection to the "dragged" shareholders.

The remainder of §3.2 details what related approval activities "voting in favor" requires, including voting for any Restated Certificate amendment the transaction requires, voting against any proposal presented to the stockholders that is adverse to the transaction, executing and delivering any documents reasonably related to approving the transaction, not exercising dissenter's rights, and accepting cash in lieu of stock if the shareholder is not an accredited investor and that status is required in order to receive acquirer stock by the terms of the transaction.

These broad obligations to approve future deals and sign documents usually make common stock owners very nervous. As a result, many drag-along agreements have a group of exceptions and restrictions, such as those in §3.3 of the Sample VA, to give the common stock holders comfort that all shareholders will be treated equally in the transaction and, to the extent any shareholder guaranties or indemnities are required, they will be several and not joint, and they will be proportionate. As these are common shareholder-friendly protections, many drag-along terms prepared by investors' counsel will not include them, and company counsel must negotiate in order to have them added to the VA.

Section 3.4 protects the Investors by requiring all parties to engage in a Sale of the Company transaction only when the participation of all the Preferred Stock holders is allowed and with proceeds allocated in accordance with the liquidation preference rights in the Restated Certificate.

QUESTIONS

1. The Sample VA provides that a Sale of the Company transaction triggering the drag-along right must be approved by the Company's Board and "the holders of at least a majority of the outstanding shares of Common Stock *issued or issuable* upon conversion of the [Preferred Stock]" (emphasis added). What are the arguments for and against using that measure of shareholder approval as opposed to approval only by the shares of Common Stock *issuable* upon conversion of the Preferred Stock?

2. Under the terms of the Sample VA's drag-along right, would a founder/significant common stockholder have to enter into a personal non-compete agreement with an acquirer as part of his or her obligation to "execute and deliver all related documentation . . . in support of the Sale of the Company" pursuant to §3.2(c)?

Remedies and Enforcement.   Section 4 of the Sample VA presents two levels of special remedies, without waiving any other remedies at law or in equity. Section 4.2 is the grant by each party to the Sample VA of a proxy to the President and the Treasurer of the Company and, if applicable, to a designee of the preferred shareholder group whose approval of a transaction triggered the drag-along vote, to vote their shares in accordance with the requirements of §1, 2, or 3 of the Sample VA. This bit of self-help is recognition that resort to the courts, even an action for injunctive relief, in order to enforce an internal corporate procedure is slow and expensive. A proxy grant puts the onus of obtaining injunctive relief on a party that wants to stop the vote or the effect of the vote while giving the company and the preferred stockholders a mechanism to move forward. The proxy terms and duration must conform to the proxy statutes in the company's jurisdiction of incorporation.

Section 4.3 sets out the basis for obtaining equitable relief, which despite its limitations is probably the only reasonable remedy at hand, other than the proxy grant, to enforce the voting obligations under the Sample VA.

Section 5 of the Sample VA provides for the Agreement to terminate upon the earliest of: (i) the Company's IPO; (ii) a Sale of the Company; (iii) the vote of the parties to the Sample VA, as provided in §6.8; or (iv) ten years from the date of the Sample VA. The first three are all consistent with the absence of any continuing need or the appropriateness of a VA following those events. As to the last item, in addition to setting a date certain for the end of the Agreement, a stated termination date also may be necessary under the proxy laws of a company's jurisdiction of incorporation.

Miscellaneous Provisions.   The miscellaneous terms of the Sample VA have many similarities with those of the Sample IRA and the Sample ROFR, although this particular example was specifically included in these materials because it does not come from the same document set as those agreements and reflects different approaches to adding new significant common stock holders, choice of law, venue and jurisdiction, dispute resolution, notices, and the other normal miscellaneous terms. Since the VA is part of a package of rights and obligations together with the SPA, the IRA, and the ROFR, the drafter must ensure that all of the miscellaneous terms of these agreements work seamlessly together. It is very frustrating to find, for example, that a notice given under the terms of one of these documents is not effective under the terms of another. As the significant common stock holders who are parties to the VA normally should be the same common stock holders who are parties to the ROFR, the mechanism for sweeping in new significant holders needs to work across both agreements. And, of course, since the intention with the VA, like the IRA and ROFR, is to amend and restate the document with each new round of financing, the amendment provision of the VA is very important for the reasons outlined previously as part of the IRA discussion, above.

One of the special issues that arises in the VA context is whether it is possible for a personal board nomination right to be terminated without the consent of the holder of that right. The restrictions on amending the nomination rights given to named Investors in the Sample VA that appear in §6.8(iv), (v), and (vi) are very typical. Yet most VAs do not include the waiver concept in the case of a party's prolonged failure to nominate presented in §1.3 of the Sample VA. The result is that a non-responsive (or perhaps even deceased) holder of the nomination right is required to sign off on the termination of the right, which simply may not be possible. Similarly, the Sample VA works in the event of a sale of an Investor's shares or the forced conversion scenario because the Investors with nomination rights are required to maintain ownership of at least half the Preferred Stock held by them on the date of the Sample VA in order to retain their nomination rights. However, many VAs do not have a threshold ownership requirement for maintaining those rights. In those cases, there is often *no mechanism at all* for ending the personal rights to nominate, even after that right has been abandoned.

From the perspective of company counsel, establishing a way to validly elect a board of directors is essential. A company cannot have its ability to function placed at risk by an agreement that might end up blocking the election of a full board. Further, investors are not well served by having one or more of their negotiated board seats remain unfilled simply because there is no mechanism for moving a party's nomination right to someone who will act upon it.

The Sample VA addresses this issue more comprehensively than many frequently used VA forms, but the use of VAs in general, and the approaches taken by lawyers in drafting them, seem to be still evolving. It is important to realize that statutory authorization of, and judicial comfort with, voting agreements is a recent development in some jurisdictions. In California, for example, the statutory authority was not explicit until 1997.

Finally, in reviewing a VA, a business lawyer needs to track carefully the rights and obligations of the parties and how they are changed (or unchanged) on a share conversion or a corporate recapitalization. A VA must be integrated carefully with the terms of a company's Charter, as well as the other documents that are part of the investment transaction. Defined terms have to be set with precision and managed with care in order for the agreement to work successfully. Indeed, a VA can be very fertile ground for the law of unintended consequences.

QUESTIONS

1. Review the definition of "Shares" in §1.1 of the Sample VA. What happens if a preferred stock holder converts to common stock? What happens if one of the Key Holders gets a restricted stock equity incentive grant? Are those newly held securities subject to the terms of the Sample VA? Should they be?
2. Given the scope of voting agreements such as the Sample VA, how frequently do you suppose venture capital financed companies with VAs in place actually have formal shareholder meetings?

8. *Closing Checklist*

It is good practice for a business lawyer to develop a closing checklist for each transaction he or she is involved in so that all the elements needed for the closing can be pursued in parallel and completed on a timely basis. A closing checklist is a helpful process management tool and a precedent file of deal checklists also can provide the business lawyer with helpful memory cues for elements necessary to the current transaction that, so far, may be missing. One of the most difficult tasks in reviewing transaction documents is to recognize the things that are not there. Scanning through a precedent file of closing checklists can be very useful in reminding a lawyer what all the pieces were in other deals in order to support the analysis of whether the current document drafts are complete and comprehensive.

The Sample Closing Checklist in Appendix B is organized in four columns that:

- Name the document or action taken or to be taken;
- Identify the parties who are required to sign each named document;
- Report on the status of each document or task; and
- Identify the most recent draft of each relevant document.

Because the Sample Closing Checklist is for a Series C Preferred Stock transaction, virtually all the documents it lists are to be prepared by company counsel. If the checklist were for a Series A Preferred Stock deal, it would not be unusual for the primary transaction documents to be drafted by investors' counsel. However, once a preferred stock document set is in place at a company, subsequent investment rounds normally are based on that existing documentation. As noted earlier, the SPA is created anew for each transaction round, but usually the A&RC, IRA, ROFR, and VA all are amended and restated with each new round of investment so that each contains all relevant rights and obligations in one integrated document.

In looking at the Sample Closing Checklist, we can see the role of the SPA as the transaction control document. The closing deliverables primarily consist of exhibits to the SPA and other documents (e.g., corporate approvals and closing certificates) that typically are listed in the "Conditions to Closing" sections of the SPA.

Compliance Certificate.   Of the closing documents shown on the Sample Closing Checklist that we have not addressed directly, note first Document 6, the "Compliance Certificate." This is normally a one-page certification signed by the company's CEO, and perhaps the CFO, reporting that the company is in compliance with the SPA's conditions to the investors' obligation to close. In other words, the certificate confirms that all those closing documents or actions requested by the investors have been completed or met and the company therefore is prepared to close the transaction. This document is essential in a delayed closing transaction, as it communicates that a party has met its pre-closing obligations and is ready to close. In a sign-and-close structure, the type typically used in venture capital transactions, a Compliance Certificate is of questionable substantive value at an initial closing. The reality is that the same effect results from simply signing the SPA. Subsequent closings contemplated by the SPA, however, often are conditioned on the continued correctness of the company's representations and warranties, as well as on the other conditions to the investors' obligation to close. The Compliance Certificate provides a mechanism to confirm that the company is prepared to issue additional securities in a subsequent closing.

Legal Opinions.   Documents 7 and 8 are, respectively, the opinion of the company's legal counsel and a factual certificate given to the company's counsel by the company's officers that supports the factual assumptions made in the legal opinion. A legal opinion normally is given in the form of a letter from the company's counsel to the investors. It is a set of representations from the law firm to the investors. Typically, it provides comfort that the securities issuance has been properly approved by the company; the preferred stock shares (as well as the common stock issuable upon conversion of the preferred stock), when issued, will be fully paid and nonassessable; and the transaction documents have been properly approved and, when executed and delivered, will represent enforceable obligations of the company.

Opinions are highly formalized documents, and larger firms often have required templates for each typical transaction type and, within each template, pre-approved acceptable variations in terminology. Virtually all law firms require a partner to approve an opinion, and most require a second, independent partner's review and approval. In larger firms, that independent review function often is achieved through an opinion committee or a designated set of partners, one of whom must approve any opinion before it may be issued.

The negotiation on opinions typically is concerned with the details of what the opinion is to address. To state it succinctly, legal opinions should address legal issues. In recent years, the scope of legal opinions in investment transactions has been narrowed as lawyers have become more resistant to giving what amounts to factual representations. In addition, many lawyers are objecting to putting together the mix of facts and legal conclusions necessary to reach some opinions. For example, an opinion on the number of fully paid and nonassessable shares a company has outstanding used to be commonly given. Many law firms now resist providing that opinion on behalf of the company, as the legal analysis is minor compared to the reliance that must be placed on facts taken from company documents that just as easily can be reviewed and confirmed by investors' counsel.

There is a growing trend in venture capital transactions away from routinely providing a legal opinion at closing. Where the company, investors, and all legal counsel are domiciled in the same state, and the company is domestically incorporated or incorporated in Delaware, and no special circumstances exist that would call for heightened diligence, many transactions are closed without legal opinions.

Good Standing Certificates.   Document 9 is "good standing" certificates from the secretary of state and the tax authority in the company's state of incorporation indicating that its corporate status has not been suspended or revoked. If the company were not a domestic corporation (for example, if it were incorporated in Delaware), the company also would need a confirmation of good standing as a qualified foreign corporation in the state where it primarily does business. In some jurisdictions, a company's contracts are voidable if they were entered into while the company was not in good standing. The tax authority certificate is to be provided by the collector of annual state franchise taxes and does not relate to filing returns for and paying income, sales, or other operations taxes. In many jurisdictions, companies have to pay their annual fee and file a short disclosure or information statement with the secretary of state's office. Absent some major systemic problem, the most common reason companies become "not in good standing" seems to be that they failed to file the annual information statement form. Many states send out the form as filed during the prior year as a courtesy, but if a company has moved offices and the postal service is no longer forwarding mail, filing the form frequently falls through the cracks. The prudent business lawyer orders "good standing" certificates from his or her attorney service company several days prior to the planned transaction closing so that if an unforeseen problem arises, it can be addressed and cured without delaying the closing.

Corporate Approvals.   Documents 10 and 11, consisting of the necessary board and shareholder approvals, are usually delivered as exhibits to a Secretary's Certificate, although one was not required in the transaction for which the Sample Closing Checklist was prepared. A Secretary's Certificate is a straightforward certification from the corporate secretary that the attached records of corporate actions are part of the official books and records of the company and have not been revised, superseded, or terminated. In the present situation, the board and shareholder approval documents simply are being delivered to the investors accompanied by representations in the SPA that they are accurate, complete, and effective.

Right of First Refusal Documents.   Documents 12 and 13 are not required for all closings but relate to a right of first refusal to participate in the Series C Preferred Stock issuance that was offered to some or all of the company's shareholders in this particular transaction. As discussed earlier in section B.6 of this chapter, these rights often are part of the company's covenants in an IRA. Based on the description of Document 12, it appears that the cover letter transmitting the shareholder consent included a disclosure of the right of first refusal and an invitation to provide confirmation of accredited investor status and an indication of interest in participating in the transaction. Because the Document 12 entry notes that the indication of interest relates to participation in a "Second Closing," it appears that the company is moving forward with some investors at a first closing, the subject of this checklist, while reserving a portion of the potential investment for the right of first refusal holders at a second closing. Document 13 is the form by which interested shareholders would confirm their accredited investor status and their desire to invest in the Series C Preferred Stock transaction.

Management Rights Letter.   Document 14 is a special requirement that some venture capital funds may be required to obtain by *their* investors if they have, for example, regulated pension funds among their limited partners. A "management rights letter" provides the necessary confirmation that the venture capital fund has the right to actively participate in the management of the company.

Stock Certificates.   In the post-closing obligations shown at the end of the Sample Closing Checklist, Document 15 is the stock certificates representing the Series C Preferred Stock shares issued in the transaction. While some private companies (and virtually all public companies) use transfer agents to take care of certificate mechanics, most often the stock certificates have to be prepared by the company's law firm. The contents of a stock certificate are mandated by the corporate law of the company's state of incorporation. From the business lawyer's point of view, other than careful proofreading, the key issues regarding stock certificates are that the shareholder names and share numbers be exactly correct, and that the legends on the back of the certificate conform to the requirements of all the relevant transaction documents.

Oddly, stock certificates are frequently a forgotten element of a stock issuance. A business lawyer should prepare and distribute the certificates promptly following the completion of the transaction. (Preparing them beforehand is often unproductive because, as often happens in the real world, some portion of an investor group will change the entity being used for the investment at the last minute, or will decide to adjust the share allocation among their investment entities.) It is always prudent to send the certificates by a delivery service that requires a signature upon receipt. Investors are notorious for misplacing their stock certificates, and when they cannot find them, their first response is almost always to complain that they never got them in the first place.

Securities Filings.   Document 16 is the required securities exemption filings. A Form D filing usually must be made with the SEC and state filings are required in the jurisdiction from which the company issued its shares and in each jurisdiction in which a purchaser of those shares resides. It is important to note that if the transaction is a

Rule 506 exempt issuance, then conformity with state securities laws is not required. Despite this fact, a copy of the Form D must be filed in every state where state law otherwise would have to have been complied with, and whatever fee the state would have collected with its own filing requirements and compliance procedures must be paid when the Form D is filed. The SEC now requires that all Form Ds be filed online and has established, at least for small, early-stage companies, a ridiculously complex registration procedure that must be navigated before the filing can be completed. The SEC's website does not provide an "as-filed" copy of the Form D, nor does it allow for direct electronic filing with state securities departments, so it is important to remember to print a copy of the completed Form D before hitting the "file" button.

Closing Binders.   After closing a transaction like the Series C Preferred Stock investment described in the Sample Closing Checklist, and completing the post-closing documents and actions, the final task to be completed is the preparation of "closing binders." Usually handled by a junior lawyer or paralegal and often put off as mere cleanup in the natural letdown following the euphoria (or relief, or exhaustion) of a closing, preparing a closing binder is a necessary exercise, both for the parties and their lawyers. Each party that signs a document should receive a copy of it signed by all the other parties thereto, and everyone involved in a deal needs a complete set of the final documents as evidence of the definitive agreements that were finally reached after innumerable drafts were circulated.

Even with the common use of electronic document delivery, a closing binder, whether in hard copy or a "virtual binder" on a CD or an emailed zipfile, is still an important element of a properly documented transaction. Little is as frustrating as, a few years after a transaction, trying to track through a series of email exchanges to sort out which iteration of each document was actually the final, signed version.

A well-prepared closing checklist can simplify the headache of assembling the materials for closing binders by serving the additional function of providing a draft table of contents. While some extra documents might be needed to complete the closing binders, the closing checklist should be a very useful tool for organizing and assembling the materials for the binders. Copies of all the documents listed on the closing checklist (other than the Officer's Certificate in Support of the Legal Opinion, which is needed for the closing and may be reviewed by investors' counsel, but is not delivered) typically are gathered with original signature pages from each signatory. The sets are either copied and bound for more convenient reference and storage or scanned, burned onto a CD, and stored.

Transactional lawyers often have rows of thick closing binders weighing down their bookshelves. In addition to being handy and important transaction records, they are frequently consulted later in advising investors and the company on their respective rights and obligations. Also, like precedent files, they are useful sources of information for future deals and are regularly referred to in subsequent drafting projects. Clients, alas, not realizing that a properly documented transaction is a thing of beauty, tend never to open them.

HOMEWORK ASSIGNMENTS

HOMEWORK ASSIGNMENT #1

To: Associate

From: Partner

Re: Term Sheet

[Assignment will be given orally in class.]

HOMEWORK ASSIGNMENT #2

HYPOTHETICALS — ANALYZING THE MECHANICS OF LLC OPERATING AGREEMENTS

Appendix B includes the California LLC Operating Agreement (the "Operating Agreement") for The Pizza Joint, LLC (the "Company"), which was prepared on behalf of four individuals (Moneybags, Greenbacks, Dollarbills, and Workerbee) who decided to start a new pizza restaurant business to operate under the name "The Pizza Joint." The first three of the individuals will each contribute the same amount of cash and each will receive a 25% interest. The fourth, Workerbee, will contribute no money but will receive his 25% interest in exchange for his services in managing the day-to-day business operations of The Pizza Joint.

Below are several Hypotheticals that raise the sort of issues a client might face when involved in such a business. These Hypos ask you to analyze the terms of the Operating Agreement in order to figure out how to advise the client regarding the issues raised in each Hypo.

Using the Operating Agreement and the applicable California statutes, please prepare a short memo (no more than two pages) and be ready to discuss at our meeting next week the advice you would give (and a brief description of the basis for your advice/recommendation) in connection with each of the following Hypotheticals.

HYPO No. 1:

Moneybags offers his friend Jenny a job as cook at The Pizza Joint, which is the restaurant owned by the Company. If Jenny accepts the offer, is the Company bound to hire Jenny?

HYPO No. 2:

In an effort to increase business on the weekends, Moneybags and Greenbacks want to hire Buck, a musician, to perform live music on Friday and Saturday nights at The Pizza Joint. Workerbee balks at this suggestion, claiming that it will drive away the family business clientele that he has been trying to develop. Can Moneybags and Greenbacks force the Company to hire Buck?

HYPO No. 3:

On his way to work at The Pizza Joint, Workerbee suffers a fatal heart attack. What happens to his interest in the Company?

HYPO No. 4:

As part of his estate planning, Dollarbills has been advised that he should transfer his interest in the Company to Donna, his 25-year-old daughter. Donna is quite excited at the prospect of joining the Company — having just completed her MBA, she is full of ideas that she thinks will improve the profitability of The Pizza Joint. The other three LLC members are insisting that Donna should not be involved in operating The Pizza Joint. How do you advise?

HYPO No. 5:

A representative of Pizza Hut, Inc. has approached Workerbee and made an offer to purchase The Pizza Joint at a very attractive price. Workerbee is interested in selling the Company to Pizza Hut and has consulted you for advice as to how to arrange for the sale of the business to Pizza Hut.

HOMEWORK ASSIGNMENT #3

HYPOTHETICALS — FIDUCIARY DUTIES IN LLCs

In connection with each of the following Hypotheticals, you are to advise the client, The Pizza Joint, LLC, using the terms of the sample California LLC Operating Agreement included in Appendix B. Please prepare a short memo (no more than two pages) that sets forth your analysis and the recommendation you would make. In addition, please be prepared to discuss at our meeting next week how this recommendation might change (if at all) assuming that the business was organized under Delaware law using the terms of the Generic LLC Operating Agreement also included in Appendix B. Use the two operating agreements and the relevant statutes for your analysis. It would be useful to begin with a review of California Corporations Code §17704.09 and Delaware Limited Liability Company Act §§18-1101 and 18-1104.

HYPO No. 1:

Dollarbills was recently approached by The Pizza Joint's Landlord, a personal friend, for advice on who might be interested in buying the restaurant building and the attached lease. Without informing the other LLC members, Dollarbills negotiates an agreement with the Landlord to buy the restaurant building for his own account. Has Dollarbills violated his fiduciary duties to the LLC and its members?

(a) Would it affect your answer if, instead of being a stand-alone building exclusively used by The Pizza Joint, the building in question was a strip mall and The Pizza Joint was one of 20 tenants occupying the 20 storefronts that made up this strip mall?

(b) Would it affect your answer if Dollarbills had notified each of the other three LLC members in writing — before joining the LLC — that he would become a member of the LLC only if it was agreeable for Dollarbills to continue to pursue outside business ventures with his personal friend, The Pizza Joint's Landlord, and no one objected?

HYPO No. 2:

The Company has decided to expand by opening a second The Pizza Joint restaurant and has proposed to lease the second location from Greenbacks' brother, Lance. If the Company signs the lease with Lance — without knowing that its new landlord is Greenbacks' brother — has Greenbacks breached his fiduciary duty to the LLC and its members?

HYPO No. 3:

To fulfill their student loan commitments, Dollarbills and Workerbee joined the National Guard. Their unit has been called for a year of active duty. While Greenbacks and Moneybags worked their respective ways through medical school working in local pizza parlors, they had never managed a restaurant before. So they decided to hire a manager to operate The Pizza Joint during the week and paid him a salary substantially higher than the salary paid to Workerbee. On the weekends, the two doctors managed The Pizza Joint. Moneybags and Greenbacks spent lavishly for radio and print advertising and offered 2-for-1 weekend specials that resulted in an operating loss for the Company. On their return from military duty, Dollarbills and Workerbee consult you for advice as to whether they can sue Moneybags and Greenbacks for breach of fiduciary duty. What do you advise?

HYPO No. 4:

Dollarbills reads in the newspaper that the owners of a well-known local pizza parlor are retiring. Dollarbills calls the owners, who confirm that they are retiring and that they are going to put their pizza restaurant up for sale. Dollarbills makes the owners an all-cash offer that they cannot refuse and purchases the pizza parlor for himself. Dollarbills then approaches Maya, the current manager of The Pizza Joint, and makes her a very attractive offer to leave The Pizza Joint and come to work for Dollarbills in his new pizza parlor. Has Dollarbills violated his fiduciary duty to the LLC and its members?

HYPO No. 5:

After enjoying some modest initial success, profits have grown stagnant at The Pizza Joint. Dollarbills, Greenbacks, and Moneybags believe that a new manager needs to be brought in to reinvigorate the business. So they propose to remove Workerbee as the manager of The Pizza Joint and replace him with an outsider.

(a) Under the terms of the Operating Agreement, how do they go about implementing their plan to terminate Workerbee?
(b) Following his termination, Workerbee feels that the decision to let him go was made by the others in an effort to acquire his interest at an unfair price and, further, to deprive him of salary, bonus, and future participation in the Company's very successful business. Would Workerbee be successful on a suit for breach of fiduciary duty?

HOMEWORK ASSIGNMENT #4

To: **Associate**
From: **Partner**
Re: **SoftCo — Choice of State of Incorporation**

As you know, our software client to be formed by Joan Smith and Michael Jones ("SoftCo") is examining its entity formation alternatives. While it is likely that a pass-through entity would make the most sense as the entity to act as a member of the strategic LLC SoftCo is now pursuing, your analysis of the draft LLC agreement makes it clear that the parties have a lot of ground to cover to reach a meeting of the minds on that arrangement.

We need, therefore, to be prepared to discuss the alternative entity choices for SoftCo in the event the strategic joint venture doesn't come together. Should that happen, it is likely that SoftCo will seek to raise venture capital and hence should be organized as a corporation.

Under those circumstances, Joan and Michael will need help in understanding whether they should form a California or a Delaware corporation. They have heard conflicting things on this issue from various entrepreneur colleagues and potential investors and are looking to us for guidance. They intend to locate the business in Los Angeles and at least initially all of SoftCo's employees will be located in California. SoftCo's products (hopefully) will be sold all over the country and, for that matter, the world.

I would like you to think about this question and be prepared to discuss it with SoftCo at our next meeting. Please prepare a short memo (no more than two pages) to assist you in being ready to discuss the main differences between incorporation in California and Delaware and be prepared to recommend to SoftCo a course of action and the reasons for your recommendation.

HOMEWORK ASSIGNMENT #5

EQUITY-BASED COMPENSATION HYPOTHETICALS

1.   On July 1, 2012, Generous Corporation (the "Corporation") gave Mary Smith, one of its employees, an option to purchase 100,000 shares of the Corporation's common stock at an exercise price of $0.10 per share. The option vested over a four-year period, with one quarter (12/48th) of the shares vesting at the end of one year (that is, no shares vested until the end of the first year) and the remainder vesting one forty-eighth (1/48th) upon each of the thirty-six subsequent monthly anniversaries of the date of grant.

On September 10, 2014, Mary left her employment at the Corporation. At the time she left, how many shares of the Corporation's stock was Mary entitled to purchase pursuant to the July 1, 2012 option grant? Mary mistakenly thought that after the one year cliff, the remaining shares would vest daily rather than monthly. If calculated according to her understanding of the option, how many shares would she be entitled to purchase as of her departure date?

2.   On May 31, 2015, the Corporation gave Bob Jones, a member of the board of directors who also has provided consulting services to the Corporation from time to time, an incentive stock option to purchase 50,000 shares of its common stock at an exercise price of $0.10 a share. The option vested over a four-year period, with equal amounts exercisable on each monthly anniversary date of the grant after a six-month cliff (that is, 6/48th vested after six months).

On April 30, 2016, the fair market value of the Corporation's common stock was $0.30 per share and Bob decided to exercise his option with respect to all shares that had vested. How many shares could Bob purchase on April 30, 2016, pursuant to the May 31, 2015 grant? Did Bob have any tax liability at the time of exercise? Why or why not?

3.   Mark Johnson is a key software engineer who was one of the Corporation's first employees hired. On February 1, 2011, he was awarded a properly granted incentive stock option to purchase 200,000 shares of the Corporation's common stock at an exercise price of $0.01 per share. The option vested over four years, with the first twenty-five percent (25%) vesting at a one-year cliff and the remaining shares monthly thereafter. In addition to this vesting schedule, the Corporation's option plan also allowed for the early exercise of all options.

On February 1, 2015, Mark exercised his February 1, 2011 option with respect to all 200,000 shares. The fair market value of the Corporation's common stock on that date was $3.00 per share. In order to qualify for preferential ISO tax treatment, Mark decided to hold his stock for one year from the date of exercise. He sold it all on February 2, 2016, for $2.00 per share. If Mark had come to you at the time of sale, how would you have described his tax position to him? Based upon the facts presented, in hindsight, could Mark have made more after-tax money on his shares? If so, how?

HOMEWORK ASSIGNMENT #6

To: Associate
From: Partner
Re: SoftCo — Potential VCs

Thank you for your previous work with SoftCo (the "Company"). You did a great job and something else has come up that I think you can handle.

Now that its joint venture with Big Bad Software has fallen through, the Company has decided to pursue its original plan of raising a round of venture capital financing. In that regard, it has asked for our assistance in identifying some local venture capital firms that might make a good fit.

Using the Internet and whatever other sources you can find, please do some research on the local VC community and pick out three firms that might be interested in making an early-stage investment in the Company. Remember that its business is platform-agnostic operating system utilities software, the Company will be based in Los Angeles, and that it will be seeking at least $5,000,000, and perhaps as much as $15,000,000, in this initial venture round. You, therefore, will need to be sure that the firms you identify are large enough to handle this amount, as well as additional investments that might be called for in subsequent rounds.

I plan to make some inquiries about your choices among my own sources before recommending them to the Company. So please have your list ready for our next meeting, with names, addresses, and a brief notation of why each firm might be appropriate for our client. Thanks.

HOMEWORK ASSIGNMENT #7

DIVIDEND AND LIQUIDATION PREFERENCE HYPOTHETICALS

1.   You are a Maynard & Warren, LLP attorney representing GoingToBeBig, Inc., in its first venture capital financing. GoingToBeBig has good prospects and is fortunate to have received two term sheets from competing VCs. Both offer to invest $5,000,000, but at differing valuations. Term Sheet #1 offers the $5,000,000 investment at a pre-money valuation of $5,000,000 with a noncumulative 8% dividend payable when, as and if declared. Term Sheet #2 offers the $5,000,000 investment at a pre-money valuation of $6,000,000 with a cumulative 8% dividend compounding annually. In addition, both offers contain a 1x, plus all accrued but unpaid dividends, fully participating liquidation preference, which is triggered upon a sale or merger of GoingToBeBig. All other terms are identical.

Our client has asked for our help in evaluating these offers. Assuming that it is sold for $20,000,000 in one year, which offer would be most advantageous to GoingToBeBig? Assuming a sale of $20,000,000 in three years, which would be best? Assuming a sale of $20,000,000 in five years, which would be best? You can assume that, at the time of the VC investment, GoingToBeBig has 5,000,000 shares of common stock outstanding. You may also assume that no dividends will have been declared at the time GoingToBeBig is sold.

2.   You are the Maynard & Warren attorney representing Los Angeles Ventures ("LA Ventures"), a large local venture capital fund, in its investment in WeMadeIt, Inc. LA Ventures previously invested $15,000,000 (out of a preferred stock investment round of $25,000,000) in WeMadeIt, which is now in the process of being sold to Motorola for $150,000,000. The preferred stock held by LA Ventures has a liquidation preference of 2x (two times the original purchase price) and then participates on an as converted basis with the common stock. However, the certificate of incorporation provides that the participation with common stock ceases at 4x (four times the original purchase price, inclusive of the 2x preference).

LA Ventures needs help in determining whether they should go with their liquidation preference or convert to common stock and forego the liquidation preference. WeMadeIt has 10,000,000 shares of stock outstanding, 5,000,000 of which are common and 5,000,000 of which are preferred. There is only one series of preferred stock, so it all has the same liquidation preference. All 5,000,000 shares of preferred were issued in connection with the $25,000,000 round of financing already mentioned and all the preferred stock into common at a one-to-one rate. Also note that WeMadeIt's certificate of incorporation contains a provision allowing a simple majority of the preferred to force a conversion of the whole series, so if LA Ventures determined to convert its shares into common, it could cause all preferred stockholders to convert.

How would you advise our client to proceed? What would you recommend if WeMadeIt were being sold for $250,000,000?

HOMEWORK ASSIGNMENT #8

ANTI-DILUTION HYPOTHETICALS

1. You are a Maynard & Warren, LLP, attorney representing SureHopeItWorks, Inc. (the "Company"). As a start-up, the Company raised its first professional venture capital round of financing 18 months ago. At that time, the Company sold its Series A Preferred Stock to Los Angeles Ventures ("LA Ventures") for $2.00 a share. (Rest assured, M&W made the proper disclosures and got the proper informed waivers prior to its engagement by the Company, and LA Ventures was represented by one of the other firms it regularly uses when it invested in the Company.) LA Ventures invested $10,000,000 in the Company and received 5,000,000 Series A Preferred shares in exchange. At the time of the investment, the Company had a pre-money valuation of $10,000,000 and had 5,000,000 shares outstanding (all common stock). As a condition to investing, and in addition to standard proportionate anti-dilution adjustments from the initial one-for-one conversion rate, LA Ventures insisted on full ratchet anti-dilution protection for the Series A Preferred and, feeling certain it would not need to raise additional money, the Company agreed. Approximately six months later, the Company did a two-for-one split of its common stock. A year later, the Company realized its product development was taking longer than expected and it needed to raise more money in order to continue operations. After searching high and low for new investors, the Company finally received a term sheet from Sand Hill Ventures ("Sand Hill"), which offered to purchase $5,000,000 of a new Series B Preferred Stock, priced at $1.25 a share.

The Company has asked us to determine if this new investment by Sand Hill would trigger the anti-dilution protection of the Series A Preferred Stock and, if so, what the resulting capitalization of the Company would be.

2. After making the analysis requested above and discussing it with the Company, management now informs you that, because of deteriorating market conditions, Sand Hill has lowered the price it is willing to pay for Series B Preferred Stock to $0.90 a share. The good news is that Sand Hill will increase its investment in the Company to $6,000,000, but in exchange, it is insisting that its investment must give it 25% of the Company, post-transaction.

The Company must do this deal in order to stay in business. It wants to know how this new structure plays out with respect to the anti-dilution protection of the Series A Preferred and has asked your advice regarding how they should proceed.

HOMEWORK ASSIGNMENT #9

To: Associate
From: Partner
Re: SoftCo, Inc.

Thank you for your previous good work for SoftCo, Inc. Our client has contacted us concerning a new matter and you have been doing such a good job understanding the issues it faces that I would like you to do the analysis as well as participate in the discussion when we present our conclusions to Joan and Michael.

SoftCo just received term sheets from two venture capital firms that are willing to invest in its initial round of financing, though on rather different terms. The client has asked for help in comparing the pros and cons of each and a recommendation regarding which one to choose. (To save some trees, I didn't copy the signature pages.)

I have scheduled a conference call for a week from today and want you to join in. Let's plan to meet about a half hour before the call so you can prep me first — but if you have any questions before then, just ask. It would be very helpful to have a one-page summary of the key differences between the term sheets and your recommendation. Thanks.

SUMMARY OF DRAFT TERMS SOFTCO, INC. SERIES A CONVERTIBLE PREFERRED STOCK INVESTMENT

This memorandum summarizes the principal terms of a proposed Series A-round venture capital financing ("Investment") in SoftCo, Inc. ("Company"), which was incorporated in _____ on _____ _____, 201____. This term sheet is an expression of intent only, and with the exception of the "No Solicitation" and "Confidentiality" sections below, which are intended to be binding obligations of the parties governed by Delaware law, this term sheet is not to be construed as a binding agreement. All financing terms and expressions of interest are subject to completion of due diligence and execution and delivery of definitive agreements.

KEY PROVISIONS

Investors

Sand Hill Ventures (an "Investor" and, with other purchasers of Series A Preferred, one of the "Investors").

Security

Series A Convertible Preferred Stock of SoftCo, Inc. ("Series A Preferred").

Price per Share

$ [TBD — *based on $10,000,000 pre-money valuation*] ("Original Price").

Aggregate Proceeds

$5,000,000.

Expected Closing Date

_____ _____, 201__ ("Initial Closing"). Additional closings may be held at the option of the Company within 90 days after the Initial Closing, at times selected by the Company (together, "Closings").

TERMS OF SERIES A PREFERRED STOCK

Dividend Provisions

Annual 8% per share dividend on the Series A Preferred when, as, and if declared by the Company's Board of Directors ("Board"). Dividends are not cumulative.

For any other dividends or distributions, Series A Preferred participates with the Company's common stock ("Common") on an as-converted basis.

Liquidation Preference

First pay Original Price plus accrued dividends on each share of Series A Preferred. Thereafter, holders of Series A Preferred and Common shall share proceeds on a pro rata (as converted) basis until the holders of Series A Preferred have received five times their Original Price. Balance of proceeds paid to Common.

A consolidation or merger of the Company or sale of all or substantially all of its assets shall be deemed a liquidation or winding up for purposes of the liquidation preference.

Redemption	The Company shall, unless the holders of more than 50% of the Series A Preferred otherwise agree in writing, redeem the Series A Preferred for a redemption price equal to (i) the Original Price, plus (ii) an amount equal to an 8% dividend compounded annually, less (iii) any dividend amounts actually paid to the Series A Preferred holders. Such redemption shall occur in three equal annual installments beginning five years after the Initial Closing.
Conversion	Each share of Series A Preferred shall be convertible at any time at the option of the holder into one share of Common (subject to anti-dilution adjustments).
Automatic Conversion	Series A Preferred shall be automatically converted into Common, at the then-applicable conversion price, (i) in the event of an underwritten public offering of shares of the Common at a price per share that is not less than four times the Original Price and an aggregate offering price of $15,000,000 ("Qualifying IPO") or (ii) at the time of, or upon a date designated by, the vote for or consent to such conversion by the holders of more than 50% of the then-outstanding shares of Series A Preferred.
Anti-dilution Provisions	Series A Preferred shall be entitled to proportional anti-dilution protection for stock splits, stock dividends, etc. In addition, the conversion ratio shall be adjusted on a full ratchet basis for one year; thereafter, adjustments will occur on a broad-based weighted average basis.
Voting and Protective Provisions	Series A Preferred shall vote on an as-converted-to-Common basis and, so long as more than 25% of the originally issued Series A Preferred shares remain outstanding, also shall have a class vote, by more than 50%, on:

1) Altering, changing or amending the preferences, privileges or rights of Series A Preferred;

2) Authorizing, creating and/or issuing any new class or series of equity securities, other than an issuance pursuant to the Company's existing employee option pool or conversion of any of its outstanding debt to equity;

3) Engaging in any business other than the business engaged in by the Company at the time of the Initial Closing;

4) Increasing or decreasing the authorized number of directors constituting the Board;

5) Any consolidation, sale, or merger of the Company or other transaction in which control of the Company is transferred;

6) Amending or waiving any provision of the Company's Articles/Certificate of Incorporation or Bylaws;

7) Redeeming, repurchasing, or declaring a dividend with regard to any security of the Company prior to the fifth anniversary of the Initial Closing, without written approval of more than 50% of the holders of Series A Preferred. This provision shall not apply to the Company's repurchase of stock granted or purchased pursuant to a stock incentive plan.

TERMS OF INVESTOR RIGHTS AGREEMENT

Right of First Offer on Subsequent Issuances

Holders of at least fifty percent (50%) of the shares of Series A Preferred shall have the right, in the event the Company proposes to offer equity securities to any person (other than pursuant to stock incentive plans or acquisitions, in each case as approved by the Board, including any directors elected by the Series A Preferred) to purchase on a pro rata basis all or any portion of such securities. Any securities not subscribed for by an Investor may be reallocated among the other Investors. If the Investors do not purchase all of the securities, that portion that is not purchased may be offered to other parties on terms no less favorable to the Company for a period of sixty (60) days.

This right shall not apply to the issuance by the Company of up to [_____] shares of Common to employees, officers or directors of, or advisors or consultants to, the Company pursuant to its stock incentive plan or plans. It shall also not apply to Common issued in connection with strategic alliances or other partnering arrangements approved by the Board.

This right shall terminate immediately prior to (i) the closing of a Qualifying IPO, or (ii) the closing of any merger or consolidation of the Company.

Registration Rights — Demand Rights

Beginning on the earlier of the third anniversary of the Initial Closing or six months after initial registration of the Common, the Company shall grant two demand registrations, to be effected upon initiation of Investors holding at least 50% of the (i) outstanding shares of Series A Preferred on an "as converted" basis plus (ii) outstanding Common issued on conversion of the Series A Preferred (together, "Registrable Securities"), with minimum aggregate offering price to the public of not less than $5,000,000.

The Company shall have the right to delay such registration under certain circumstances for two periods not in excess of ninety (90) days each in any twelve (12) month period.

Company Registrations

Holders of Registrable Securities shall have unlimited "piggyback" registration rights subject to pro rata cutback at the underwriters' discretion. Full cutback may occur on the initial public offering of the Company's Common ("IPO"), but 25% minimum inclusion shall occur thereafter. If the Investors are cut back, however, no party shall sell shares in such registration other than the Company or the shareholders, if applicable, invoking a demand registration.

No stockholder of the Company shall be granted piggyback registration rights that would reduce the number of shares includable by the holders of the Registrable Securities in such registration without the consent of the holders of more than fifty percent (50%) of the Registrable Securities.

S-3 Registration Rights

Unlimited registrations on Form S-3; minimum offering size of $1,000,000.

Company may defer an S-3 filing for up to 90 days once during any 12-month period. No more than two (2) S-3 registrations shall be permitted during any one twelve (12)–month period.

Termination of Registration Rights

The foregoing registration rights shall terminate (i) five (5) years after the Company's IPO, or (ii) when all shares held by an Investor can be sold under Rule 144 within a 90-day period.

No future registration rights may be granted without consent of a majority of Investors holding registration rights unless such rights are subordinate to those of the Investors.

Expenses of Registration

The Company shall bear registration expenses (exclusive of underwriting discounts and commissions) of all such demand, piggyback, and S-3 registrations (including the reasonable expense of one special counsel of the selling shareholders).

Transfer of Rights

Registration rights may be transferred to (i) any partner or retired partner of any holder of Series A Preferred that is a partnership, (ii) any family member or trust for the benefit of any individual holder, or (iii) any transferee who acquired at least [_____] shares of Registrable Securities; provided the Company is given written notice thereof.

Standoff Provision

No Investor shall sell shares of the Company's stock within 180 days of the effective date of the Company's IPO if all officers and directors are similarly bound.

Board Representation and Meetings

The authorized number of directors making up the Board initially shall be five. The Series A Preferred shall be entitled to elect two directors and the Common (voting as a class) shall be entitled to elect two. The remaining director shall be elected by the Series A Preferred and Common (voting together as a single class) and shall be an independent director. The Board shall meet at least monthly. Effective upon the Closing, the members of the Board shall be [INSERT NAMES].

Inspection and Information Rights

For so long as an Investor holds at least [_____] shares of Series A Preferred ("Major Investor") such Major Investor shall have the right to inspect the Company's premises and books at times convenient to both parties. Such Major Investor shall have the right to receive unaudited monthly financial statements (including income statements, balance sheets, cash flow statements, and summaries of bookings and backlog) and management commentary within thirty (30) days of the close of each month, and audited annual financial statements within ninety (90) days of the close of the fiscal year, in each case showing changes from the applicable budget for the corresponding period. Prior to the beginning of each fiscal year (and prior to the Initial Closing), the Company shall prepare and forward to the Major Investors detailed monthly financial projections for the year. These rights shall end upon consummation of the Company's IPO.

TERMS OF PREFERRED STOCK PURCHASE AGREEMENT

Representations and Warranties

The Investment shall be made pursuant to a Stock Purchase Agreement reasonably acceptable to the Company and the Investors, which shall contain, among other things, appropriate representations, warranties, and covenants of the Company reflecting the provisions set forth herein and other standard provisions, and appropriate conditions to closing including a customary legal opinion of Company counsel regarding the Investment.

Expenses

The Company and the Investors shall each bear their own legal and other expenses with respect to the Investment except that, upon the successful completion of the Investment, the Company shall pay the reasonable legal fees of Namath, O'Brien, & Testaverde LLP, counsel to the Investors, up to a maximum of $25,000, plus reasonable expenses. Every effort shall be made to minimize these fees and expenses.

FOUNDERS AND EMPLOYEE AGREEMENTS

Stock Vesting

All Company stock incentives issued after the Closing to employees, directors and consultants shall be subject to vesting as follows: 25% to vest at the end of the first year following such issuance, with the remaining 75% to vest monthly over the next three years. The Company's standard incentive grant terms shall provide that upon termination of the services to the Company by the shareholder, with or without cause, the Company or its assignee (to the extent permissible under applicable securities law qualification) shall have the right to repurchase at cost any unvested shares held by such shareholder.

Common Stock Transfer Restrictions

No transfers of unvested shares shall be allowed.

Market Standoff

Holders of Common and options to buy Common must, at the request of the Company or an underwriter involved in the Company's IPO, agree not to sell or otherwise transfer any securities of the Company during a period of up to 180 days following the effective date of the registration of such IPO.

Proprietary Information and Inventions Assignment Agreement

Each current and former officer, employee, and consultant of the Company shall enter into a proprietary information and inventions assignment agreement in a form reasonably acceptable to the Investors.

Key-Person Insurance

As soon as reasonably possible after the Closing, the Company shall procure key-person life insurance policies on each of Joan Smith and Michael Jones, each in the amount of $1,000,000, naming the Company as beneficiary.

Co-Sale Rights

Each holder of the Series A Preferred shall have the right to participate on a pro-rata basis in transfers of Common shares for value by Joan Smith or Michael Jones.

OTHER PROVISIONS

Expiration

If not accepted by the Company by the close of business on the fifth day after the date hereof, this term sheet shall expire.

No Solicitation

Upon the acceptance of this term sheet for a period of 60 days from the date hereof, the Company, its officers, members of the Board, and stockholders agree not to enter into any direct or indirect discussions, negotiations, or offer solicitations regarding the sale of any equity securities (or securities convertible into equity securities) of the Company, other than with regard to potential participation as an Investor in the transaction contemplated by this term sheet.

Confidentiality

The Company will not disclose or discuss the terms hereof with any person other than its officers or members of the Board, its financial advisors, accountants, attorneys, or potential Investors without the written consent of a majority in interest of the Investor signatories hereto, except as required by law or specifically contemplated hereby. Notwithstanding the foregoing, the Company may distribute this term sheet and discuss its terms with existing stockholders (and their confidential advisors) solely in order to complete the transaction contemplated hereby. Absent consent as specified above, the Company shall not make any public statement regarding this term sheet or the transaction contemplated hereby, and shall not use any Investor's name in any manner (including links to websites, documents, etc.).

Finders

The Company and each of the Investors shall represent and warrant that it has no obligation to pay any finder's fee and shall indemnify the other parties to this transaction for any breach of this representation.

Closing Conditions

The Initial Closing shall be subject to the negotiation of definitive legal documents and completion of legal and financial due diligence by the Investors.

SUMMARY OF DRAFT TERMS SOFTCO, INC. SERIES A CONVERTIBLE PREFERRED STOCK INVESTMENT

This memorandum summarizes the principal terms of a proposed Series A-round venture capital financing ("Investment") in SoftCo, Inc. ("Company"), which was incorporated in _____ on _____ _____, 201____. This term sheet is an expression of intent only and, with the exception of the "No Solicitation" and "Confidentiality" sections below, which are intended to be binding obligations of the parties governed by Delaware law, this term sheet is not to be construed as a binding agreement. All financing terms and expressions of interest are subject to completion of due diligence and execution and delivery of definitive agreements.

KEY PROVISIONS

Investors   Stone Partner Ventures (an "Investor" and, with other purchasers of Series A Preferred, one of the "Investors").

Security   Series A Convertible Preferred Stock of SoftCo, Inc. ("Series A Preferred").

Price per Share $ [TBD — *based on $11,500,000 pre-money valuation*] ("Original Price").

Aggregate Proceeds $5,000,000.

Expected Closing Date   _____ _____, 201__ ("Initial Closing"). Additional closings may be held at the option of the Company within 120 days after the Initial Closing, at times selected by the Company (together, "Closings").

TERMS OF SERIES A PREFERRED STOCK

Dividend Provisions   Annual 8% per share dividend on the Series A Preferred. Dividends payable if, as and when determined by the Company's Board of Directors ("Board"). Dividends are cumulative.

For any other dividends or distributions, Series A Preferred participates with the Company's common stock ("Common") on an as-converted basis.

Liquidation Preference   First pay Original Price plus accrued dividends on each share of Series A Preferred. Thereafter, holders of Series A Preferred and Common shall share proceeds on a pro rata as-converted to Common basis.

A consolidation or merger of the Company or sale of all or substantially all of its assets shall be deemed a liquidation or winding up for purposes of the liquidation preference.

Redemption

The Series A Preferred shall not be redeemable.

Conversion

Each share of Series A Preferred shall be convertible at any time at the option of the holder into one share of Common (subject to anti-dilution adjustments).

Automatic Conversion

Series A Preferred shall be automatically converted into Common, at the then-applicable conversion price, (i) in the event of an underwritten public offering of shares of the Common at a price per share that is not less than two times the Original Price and an aggregate offering price of $7,500,000 ("Qualifying IPO") or (ii) at the time of, or upon a date designated by, the vote for or consent to such conversion of by the holders of at least 66 2/3% of the then-outstanding shares of Series A Preferred.

Anti-dilution Provisions

Series A Preferred shall be entitled to proportional anti-dilution protection for stock splits, stock dividends, etc. In addition, the conversion ratio shall be adjusted on a full ratchet basis in the event of a dilutive issuance. Dilutive issuances shall not include the sale of Common reserved for employees, consultants and the like or shares issued pursuant to partnering arrangements, leaselines, or other standard exceptions.

Voting and Protective Provisions

Series A Preferred shall vote on an as-converted-to-Common basis and, so long as more than 25% of the originally issued Series A Preferred shares remain outstanding, also shall have a class vote, by two-thirds (2/3) majority, on:

1) Altering, changing, or amending the preferences, privileges, or rights of Series A Preferred;

2) Authorizing, creating, and/or issuing a senior or *pari passu* class or series of equity securities, other than an issuance pursuant to the Company's existing employee option pool or conversion of any of its outstanding debt to equity;

3) Increasing or decreasing the authorized number of directors constituting the Board;

4) Any consolidation, sale, or merger of the Company or other transaction in which control of the Company is transferred;

5) Amending or waiving any provision of the Company's Articles/Certificate of Incorporation or Bylaws;

6) Redeeming, repurchasing, or declaring a dividend with regard to any security of the Company without written approval of a majority of the holders of Series A Preferred. This provision shall not apply to the Company's repurchase of stock granted or purchased pursuant to a stock incentive plan.

TERMS OF INVESTOR RIGHTS AGREEMENT

Right of First Offer on Subsequent Issuances

Holders of at least fifty percent (50%) of the shares of Series A Preferred shall have the right, in the event the Company proposes to offer equity securities to any person (other than pursuant to stock incentive plans or acquisitions, in each case as approved by the Board, including any directors elected by the Series A Preferred) to purchase on a pro rata basis all or any portion of such securities. Any securities not subscribed for by an Investor may be reallocated among the other Investors. If the Investors do not purchase all of the securities, that portion that is not purchased may be offered to other parties on terms no less favorable to the Company for a period of sixty (60) days.

This right shall not apply to the issuance by the Company of up to [_____] shares of Common to employees, officers or directors of, or advisors or consultants to, the Company pursuant to its stock incentive plan or plans. It shall also not apply to Common issued in connection with strategic alliances or other partnering arrangements approved by the Board.

This right shall terminate immediately prior to (i) the closing of a Qualifying IPO, or (ii) the closing of any merger or consolidation of the Company.

Registration Rights — Demand Rights

Beginning on the earlier of the third anniversary of the Initial Closing or six months after initial registration of the Common, the Company shall grant two demand registrations, to be effected upon initiation of Investors holding at least 50% of the (i) outstanding shares of Series A Preferred on an "as converted" basis plus (ii) outstanding Common issued on conversion of the Series A Preferred (together, "Registrable Securities"), with minimum aggregate offering price to the public of not less than $5,000,000.

The Company shall have the right to delay such registration under certain circumstances for two periods not in excess of ninety (90) days each in any twelve (12) month period.

Company Registrations

Holders of Registrable Securities shall have unlimited "piggyback" registration rights subject to pro rata cutback at the underwriters' discretion. Full cutback may occur on the initial public offering of the Company's Common ("IPO"), but 25% minimum inclusion shall occur thereafter. If the Investors are cut back, however, no party shall sell shares in such registration other than the Company or the shareholders, if applicable, invoking a demand registration.

No stockholder of the Company shall be granted piggyback registration rights that would reduce the number of shares includable by the holders of the Registrable Securities in such registration without the consent of the holders of at least two-thirds (2/3) of the Registrable Securities.

S-3 Registration Rights

Unlimited registrations on Form S-3; minimum offering size of $1,000,000.

Company may defer an S-3 filing for up to 90 days once during any 12-month period. No more than two (2) S-3 registrations shall be permitted during any one twelve (12) month period.

Termination of Registration Rights

The foregoing registration rights shall terminate (i) five (5) years after the Company's IPO, or (ii) when all shares held by an Investor can be sold under Rule 144 within a 90-day period.

No future registration rights may be granted without consent of a majority of Investors holding registration rights unless such rights are subordinate to those of the Investors.

Expenses of Registration

The Company shall bear registration expenses (exclusive of underwriting discounts and commissions) of all such demand, piggyback, and S-3 registrations (including the reasonable expense of one special counsel of the selling shareholders).

Transfer of Rights

Registration rights may be transferred to (i) any partner or retired partner of any holder of Series A Preferred that is a partnership, (ii) any family member or trust for the benefit of any individual holder, or (iii) any transferee who acquired at least [_____] shares of Registrable Securities; provided the Company is given written notice thereof.

Standoff Provision

No Investor shall sell shares of the Company's stock within 180 days of the effective date of the Company's IPO if all officers and directors are similarly bound.

Board Representation and Meetings	The authorized number of directors making up the Board initially shall be five. The Series A Preferred shall be entitled to elect three directors and the Common (voting as a class) shall be entitled to elect two. The Board shall meet at least monthly. Effective upon the Closing, the members of the Board shall be [INSERT NAMES].
Inspection and Information Rights	For so long as an Investor holds at least [_____] shares of Series A Preferred ("Major Investor") such Major Investor shall have the right to inspect the Company's premises and books at times convenient to both parties. Such Major Investor shall have the right to receive unaudited quarterly financial statements (including income statements, balance sheets, cash flow statements, and summaries of bookings and backlog) and management commentary within thirty (30) days of the close of each quarter, and audited annual financial statements within one hundred twenty (120) days of the close of the fiscal year, in each case showing changes from the applicable budget for the corresponding period. Prior to the beginning of each fiscal year (and prior to the Initial Closing), the Company shall prepare and forward to the Major Investors detailed monthly financial projections for the year. These rights shall end upon consummation of the Company's IPO.

TERMS OF PREFERRED STOCK PURCHASE AGREEMENT

Representations and Warranties	The Investment shall be made pursuant to a Stock Purchase Agreement reasonably acceptable to the Company and the Investors, which shall contain, among other things, appropriate representations, warranties, and covenants of the Company reflecting the provisions set forth herein and other standard provisions, and appropriate conditions to closing including a customary legal opinion of Company counsel regarding the Investment.
Expenses	The Company and the Investors shall each bear their own legal and other expenses with respect to the Investment except that, upon the successful completion of the Investment, the Company shall pay the reasonable legal fees of Namath, O'Brien & Testaverde LLP, counsel to the Investors, up to a maximum of $25,000, plus reasonable expenses. Every effort shall be made to minimize these fees and expenses.

FOUNDERS AND EMPLOYEE AGREEMENTS

Stock Vesting

All Company stock incentives issued after the Closing to employees, directors, and consultants shall be subject to vesting as follows: 25% to vest at the end of the first year following such issuance, with the remaining 75% to vest monthly over the next three years. The Company's standard incentive grant terms shall provide that upon termination of the services to the Company by the shareholder, with or without cause, the Company or its assignee (to the extent permissible under applicable securities law qualification) shall have the right to repurchase at cost any unvested shares held by such shareholder.

Common Stock Transfer Restrictions

No transfers of unvested shares shall be allowed.

Market Standoff

Holders of Common and options to buy Common must, at the request of the Company or an underwriter involved in the Company's IPO, agree not to sell or otherwise transfer any securities of the Company during a period of up to 180 days following the effective date of the registration of such IPO.

Proprietary Information and Inventions Assignment Agreement

Each current and former officer, employee, and consultant of the Company shall enter into a proprietary information and inventions assignment agreement in a form reasonably acceptable to the Investors.

Key-Person Insurance

As soon as reasonably possible after the Closing, the Company shall procure key-person life insurance policies on each of Joan Smith and Michael Jones, each in the amount of $1,000,000, naming the Company as beneficiary.

Co-Sale Rights

Each holder of the Series A Preferred shall have the right to participate on a pro-rata basis in transfers of Common shares for value by Joan Smith or Michael Jones.

OTHER PROVISIONS

Expiration

If not accepted by the Company by the close of business on the fifth day after the date hereof, this term sheet shall expire.

No Solicitation

Upon the acceptance of this term sheet for a period of 60 days from the date hereof, the Company, its officers, members of the Board, and stockholders agree not to enter into any direct or indirect discussions, negotiations, or offer solicitations regarding the sale of any equity securities (or securities convertible into equity securities) of the Company, other than with regard to potential participation as an Investor in the transaction contemplated pursuant to this term sheet.

Confidentiality   The Company will not disclose or discuss the terms hereof with any person other than its officers or members of the Board, its financial advisors, accountants, attorneys, or potential Investors without the written consent of a majority in interest of Investor signatories hereto, except as required by law or specifically contemplated hereby. Notwithstanding the foregoing, the Company may distribute this term sheet and discuss its terms with existing stockholders (and their confidential advisors) solely in order to complete the transaction contemplated hereby. Absent consent as specified above, the Company shall not make any public statement regarding this term sheet or the transaction contemplated hereby, and shall not use any Investor's name in any manner (including links to websites, documents, etc.).

Finders   The Company and each of the Investors shall represent and warrant that it has no obligation to pay any finder's fee and shall indemnify the other parties to this transaction for any breach of this representation.

Closing Conditions   The Initial Closing shall be subject to the negotiation of definitive legal documents and completion of legal and financial due diligence by the Investors.

DOCUMENTS*

* These documents are presented to supplement the discussion included in the text of this book, as well as for use in connection with the suggested homework and writing assignments provided to augment the text. In many cases, the purpose of including particular documents is to explore their shortcomings. Thus, these forms should not be considered endorsed templates. Anyone using any of these documents as precedent should do so only with the utmost care.

SAMPLE CONFIDENTIALITY/NONDISCLOSURE AGREEMENT:

MUTUAL NONDISCLOSURE AGREEMENT

This Mutual Nondisclosure Agreement (this "Agreement") is dated as of _____ _____, 20_____ between [COMPANY], Inc., a California corporation (the "Company"), and _____, a _____ ("_____").

RECITALS

WHEREAS, in connection with the evaluation and pursuit of certain mutually beneficial business opportunities, the Company and _____ may disclose valuable proprietary information to each other relating to their respective operations and business;

WHEREAS, in connection with the evaluation and pursuit of those certain mutually beneficial business opportunities, the Company and _____ may disclose valuable proprietary technology, in the form of product samples or design specifications to each other relating to their respective products or research and development initiatives;

WHEREAS, the Company and _____ would, among other things, like to protect the confidentiality of, maintain their respective rights in and prevent the unauthorized use and disclosure of such proprietary information; and

WHEREAS, the Company and _____ would, among other things, like to protect the confidentiality of, maintain their respective rights in and protect their proprietary rights to their product samples or design specifications.

NOW THEREFORE, the Company and _____ hereby agree as follows:

1. <u>Confidential Information</u>. As used in this Agreement, "Confidential Information" means all information of either party that is not generally known to the public, whether of a technical, business or other nature (including, without limitation, information with respect to their business opportunities, trade secrets, know-how and information relating to the technology, customers, business plans, promotional and marketing activities, finances and other business affairs of such party), that is disclosed by one party (the "Disclosing Party") to the other party (the "Receiving Party") or that is otherwise learned by the Receiving Party in the course of its discussions or business dealings with, or its physical or electronic access to Confidential Information of, the Disclosing Party, and that has been identified as being proprietary and/or confidential or that by the nature of the circumstances surrounding the disclosure or receipt ought to be treated as proprietary and confidential. Confidential Information also includes all information concerning the existence and progress of the parties' dealings and the identity of each party's clients, vendors and strategic partners, regardless of whether any such information is marked or otherwise identified in writing as confidential.

2. <u>Product Samples</u>. As used in this Agreement, "Product Samples" means all goods or products, which incorporate any proprietary information, design, technology, know-how or intellectual property owned or leased by the Disclosing Party, which is generally not known by the public, which is delivered to the Receiving Party in an effort to promote any potential beneficial business opportunities between the Delivering Party and the Receiving Party.

3. <u>Use and Ownership of Confidential Information and Product Samples</u>.

(a) The Receiving Party, except as expressly provided in this Agreement, will not disclose Confidential Information to anyone without the Disclosing Party's prior written consent.

(b) The Receiving Party, except as expressly provided in this Agreement, will not distribute to anyone, disassemble, damage, destroy, reverse engineer, or otherwise treat any Product Samples in any way inconsistent with the Disclosing Party's ownership rights in such Product Samples.

(c) The Receiving Party will take all reasonable measures to protect and avoid the disclosure, dissemination or unauthorized use of Confidential Information or Product Samples, including, at a minimum, those measures it takes to protect its own confidential information or products or goods of a similar nature.

(d) The Receiving Party will not use, or permit others to use, Confidential Information or Product Samples for any purpose other than to evaluate the potential of a business relationship between the Company and _____ and, if desired, the negotiation and consummation of a business transaction involving both parties.

(e) All Confidential Information and Product Samples will remain the exclusive property of the Disclosing Party, and the Receiving Party will have no rights, by license or otherwise, to use the Confidential Information or Product Samples except as expressly provided herein.

4. <u>Exceptions</u>. The provisions of Section 3 will not apply to any information, goods, or products that (i) is or becomes publicly available without breach of this Agreement; (ii) can be shown by documentation to have been known to, or developed by, the Receiving Party prior to its receipt from the Disclosing Party; (iii) is rightfully received from a third party who did not acquire or disclose such information, goods or products by a wrongful or tortuous act; or (iv) can be shown by documentation to have been developed by the Receiving Party without reference to any Confidential Information or Product Samples.

5. <u>Non-Solicitation</u>. Each party agrees that it shall not, without prior written consent of the other party, directly or indirectly, solicit for hire any person who is employed by the other party, provided however, that such party may solicit persons employed by the other party pursuant to a newspaper, Internet, or other general advertisement or solicitation in which such person is not specifically identified.

6. <u>Disclosures to Governmental Entities</u>. If the Receiving Party becomes legally obligated to disclose Confidential Information or Product Samples by any governmental entity with jurisdiction over it, the Receiving Party will give the Disclosing Party prompt written notice to allow the Disclosing Party to seek a protective order or other appropriate remedy. Such notice must include, without limitation, identification of the information to be so disclosed or the products or goods to be remitted, as well as a copy of the order. The Receiving Party will disclose only such information, or remit only such products or goods, as is legally required and will use its reasonable best efforts to obtain confidential treatment for any Confidential Information or Product Samples that are so disclosed or remitted.

7. <u>Compliance with Laws; Exportation/Transmission of Confidential Information and Product Samples</u>. Both parties will comply with all applicable federal, state, and local statutes, rules and regulations, including, but not limited to, United States export

control laws and regulations as they currently exist and as they may be amended from time to time.

8.   <u>Receiving Party Personnel</u>. The Receiving Party will restrict the possession, knowledge, development, and use of Confidential Information and Product Samples to its employees, agents, subcontractors and entities controlled by or controlling it who have a need to know Confidential Information or require access to the Product Samples in connection with the purposes set forth in Section 3(d) above (collectively, "Personnel"). The Receiving Party's Personnel will have access only to the Confidential Information or Product Samples they need for such purposes. The Receiving Party will ensure that the Personnel comply with this Agreement and will promptly notify the Disclosing Party of any breach of this Agreement.

9.   <u>Return of Confidential Information and Product Samples</u>.

(a)   Upon the Disclosing Party's written request, the Receiving Party promptly will return or destroy (or, in the case of electronic embodiments, permanently erase) all tangible material embodying Confidential Information (in any form and including, without limitation, all summaries, copies and excerpts of Confidential Information) in its possession or under its control.

(b)   Upon the Disclosing Party's written request, the Receiving Party promptly will return all Product Samples, without exception, that were delivered to the Receiving Party pursuant to this agreement. The Product Samples shall be returned in substantially the same condition in which they were delivered, in keeping with the terms of Section 3(b) above.

10.   <u>Independent Development</u>. The Disclosing Party acknowledges that the Receiving Party may currently or in the future be developing products or information internally, or receiving information from other parties, that is similar to the Confidential Information, or relates to the Development of goods or products similar to the Product Samples. Accordingly, nothing in this Agreement will be construed as a representation or agreement that the Receiving Party will not develop, or have developed for it, goods, products, concepts, systems or techniques that are similar to or compete with the products, concepts, systems or techniques contemplated by or embodied in the Confidential Information or Product Samples, provided that the Receiving Party does not violate any of its obligations under this Agreement in connection with such development.

11.   <u>Injunctive Relief</u>. The Receiving Party acknowledges that (i) disclosure or use of Confidential Information, or (ii) damage to, the destruction of, loss of, or reverse engineering of Product Samples, in violation of this Agreement, could cause irreparable harm to the Disclosing Party for which monetary damages may be difficult to ascertain or an inadequate remedy. The Receiving Party therefore agrees that the Disclosing Party will have the right, in addition to its other rights and remedies, to injunctive relief for any such violation of this Agreement without posting bond, or by posting bond at the lowest amount required by law.

12.   <u>Cumulative Obligations</u>. Each party's obligations hereunder are in addition to, and not exclusive of, any and all of its other obligations and duties to the other party, whether express, implied, in fact or in law.

13.   <u>Entire Agreement; Amendment</u>. This Agreement constitutes the entire agreement between the parties relating to the matters discussed herein and supersedes all prior oral and written understandings with respect to any information disclosed or received

under this Agreement. This Agreement may be amended or modified only with the mutual written consent of both parties.

14.   Term and Termination. This Agreement is intended to cover Confidential Information and/or Product Samples disclosed or received by either party prior or subsequent to the date of this Agreement. Unless otherwise earlier terminated, this Agreement automatically will expire _____ (_____) years from the date first written above; provided, however, that each party's obligations with respect to the other party's Confidential Information and/or Product Samples disclosed or received prior to termination or expiration of this Agreement will survive for _____ (_____) additional years following the expiration or termination of this Agreement.

15.   Non-waiver. Any failure by either party to enforce the other party's strict performance of any provision of this Agreement will not constitute a waiver of its right to subsequently enforce such provision or any other provision of this Agreement.

16.   Attorney Fees. In the event that any court action is commenced by one party against the other, the substantially prevailing party is entitled to recover its court costs, out-of-pocket expenses, and reasonable attorneys' fees. The cost of in-house legal staff will be valued at market rates for comparable services from private practitioners.

17.   Governing Law; Etc. This Agreement will be governed by the internal laws of the State of California, without reference to its choice of law rules. Each party hereby waives its right to a jury trial for any claims that may arise out of this Agreement. If a provision of this Agreement is held invalid under any applicable law, such invalidity will not affect any other provision of this Agreement that can be given effect without the invalid provision. Further, all terms and conditions of this Agreement will be deemed enforceable to the fullest extent permissible under applicable law, and, when necessary, the court is requested to reform any and all terms or conditions to give them such effect.

18.   Counterparts. This Agreement may be executed in any number of counterparts, each of which shall be an original and all of which together shall constitute one instrument.

19.   Facsimile Signatures. Any signature page delivered by a telecopy machine shall be binding to the same extent as an original signature page, with regard to any agreement subject to the terms hereof or any amendment thereto. Any party who delivers such a signature page agrees to later deliver an original counterpart to any party which requests it.

IN WITNESS WHEREOF, the parties have executed this Agreement on the date first written above.

[COMPANY], INC.,   _____
a California corporation   a _____

By: _____   By: _____
    Name: _____   Name: _____
    Title: _____   Title: _____

SAMPLE TERM SHEETS — EMPLOYMENT AGREEMENTS:

DAVID DENNIS, TENET HEALTHCARE CORP.

TERM SHEET

Name:	David Dennis
Position:	Vice Chairman, Chief Corporate Officer and CFO
Reports to:	Chairman and CEO
Start Date:	March 1, 2000
Base Salary:	$600,000
Next Salary Review:	June 1, 2001

Annual Incentive Plan

Target Award:	60% (78% if 162(m) executive for FY 2001) Award will be pro rated for balance of FY 2000.
Stock Options:	Multi-year grant of 450,000 non-qualified options vesting 1/3 each year with the first third vesting one year from the date of grant. The next scheduled grant to be three years from initial grant.
Tendex:	Will be given opportunity to buy into Tendex at next round at same level as former CFO but at then current price.
Auto Allowance:	$23,500 per year
Executive Medical Plan:	$10,000 annual maximum benefit
SERP:	Will receive two years of service credit for each year of actual service during first five years in SERP.
Change of Control:	Will be eligible for benefit of two times base salary plus target bonus for qualifying termination following a change of control of Tenet. All options vest on change of control.
Benefits:	Will be eligible to participate in all other standard employee benefits, including health, life, dental, vision, long-term disability, 401(K) retirement savings, Executive Deferred Compensation and Employee Stock Purchase Plan.
Club Memberships:	Will receive reimbursement for annual membership fee for country club, Regency Club, Jonathan Club and appropriate Santa Barbara club.
Relocation:	To be determined based upon need.

MARK WATTLES, HOLLYWOOD ENTERTAINMENT CORP.

OFFER OF EMPLOYMENT TERM SHEET

The Employment Agreement shall be fully documented in a formal agreement to be signed by both parties, however, the following term sheet will be fully binding upon the Company upon its acceptance by Mark Wattles.

Title: President and Chief Executive Officer

Salary: 975,000.00 annual to be effective January, 2001

Bonus:

To be determined by board tied to the same performance criteria as other executives as well as additional bonuses based on certain key goals, such as completion of the amended bank facility.

Stock and Options:

— 3,000,000 share grant as approved by the full board. Wattles will sign a Lock-Up Agreement to not sell the any of the shares granted for 360 days from the date of grant with a performance review at 180 days to consider releasing 50% of the shares from the lock-up. The shares will also be subject to the normal restrictions under Rule 144.
— 3,000,000 options are hereby granted to Wattles as part of the options being granted to senior management under the management retention program. The exercise price will be at today's closing price (01/25/01). 1/3 vesting on 2/25/02 and 1/6 vesting every six months thereafter. Once options have vested they will not expire until end of the 10-year option term regardless of whether or not Wattles is still employed by Hollywood. The option grant is effective today at today's price, but will be contingent upon the approval by the shareholders of the 2001 Stock Incentive Plan adopted by the Board today. There can be no assurance that the shareholders will approve the plan in which case the options will not be issued.

Travel:

Use of company owned or leased aircraft for travel between Las Vegas and Portland and all business related travel.

Las Vegas Office:

Continuation in Las Vegas, NV of office space and required equipment and services to conduct business on behalf of Hollywood as Mr. Wattles's primary office.

Non-compete:

For a minimum of one year from the date of this term sheet and if the 3,000,000 options are finalized upon the approval of the option plan by shareholders, for a period of two years from the end of Wattles's employment with the Company, Mr. Wattles may not be employed by any competitor, unless such competition operates as a franchisee of the Company. Wattles and the Company will enter into a franchise agreement with financial terms to be agreed upon but at least sufficient to cover the Company's costs associated with the franchisee which allows for the building of a video chain which does not compete with the Company's locations and adds to the Company's leverage and brands. Competition would be defined as any company that owns or operates video specialty stores where 10% or more of such company's video stores operate within 2 miles of the Company's stores.

Term:

The Employment Agreement with Mr. Wattles shall be for 1 year if only the 3,000,000-share grant is effective. The Employment Agreement will increase to 3 years upon approval of the 2001 Stock Incentive Plan by the shareholders and completion of documentation and issuance of the 3,000,000 options.

Change of Control:

Upon a change in control all options will immediately vest, any lock-up remaining up will be cancelled and the remaining pay for the term remaining under the Employment Agreement will paid at the time of the Change of Control. If the term remaining on the Employment Agreement is less than two years then an amount equal to two years' pay will be paid. If the 3,000,000 options were not yet granted or could not be granted then Wattles will receive an amount in cash equal to the in the money value of the options had they been granted and vested as outlined above.

"Change of Control" for the Employment Agreement shall, in addition to the definition contained in the Company's Change of Control Plan, include change of ownership of 25% or more of the Company's common stock or securities convertible into common or other changes in securities causing 25% or more of the vote to be under the control of an entity or related group or a change in the board causing the current members or remaining current members as a group to not compose a majority of the board.

Entered into this 25th day of January 2001.

Hollywood Entertainment Corporation Compensation Committee of the Board of Directors

_____   _____
James N. Cutler Jr.   Doug Glendenning

_____
William P. Zebe

Accepted by Mark Wattles effective this 25th day of January 2001

_____
Mark Wattles

STEVEN LIPSCOMB, WORLD POKER TOUR, LLC

April 14, 2004

Re: Employment Agreement Terms

Dear Steve:

This term sheet sets forth the understandings with respect to the terms and conditions of your proposed employment with WPT Enterprises, Inc. ("WPT"). The parties agree that this term sheet represents the good faith intention of the parties to enter into a long form employment agreement that is consistent with the terms set forth below (the "Employment Agreement"). Until such a long form agreement is executed and delivered, this term sheet shall be binding on both parties.

1. TERM: 3-years commencing on December 29, 2003.
2. TITLE: Founder, President and Member, Board of Directors of WPT.
3. SALARY AND BENEFITS: $500,000 per year, subject to increase at the discretion of the Board. Salary change will be effective as of December 29, 2003 and any shortfall in the salary you received since December 29, 2003 will be paid to you as soon as practicable following execution of this letter agreement. You will also be entitled to the benefits and perquisites which WPT provides to its employees generally, as determined by WPT's board of directors (or a committee thereof) in its discretion.
4. BONUSES: You will be entitled to receive annual bonuses during the term of the Employment Agreement as follows:
   - You will continue participation in the 10% bonus pool described in the Section 3 of the Management Contract and Contribution Agreement between you and World Poker Tour, LLC dated March 4, 2002 (the "Prior Management Agreement"), and Section 10.17 of the World Poker Tour Limited Liability Company Agreement dated March 4, 2002 (10% of profits for the first five years of business); and
   - For each fiscal year, you will be entitled to 5% of the Profits (as such term is defined in the World Poker Tour Limited Liability Company Agreement dated March 4, 2003) in excess of $3,000,000 that is realized by WPT from and after the closing date of the initial public offering. In the event your employment with WPT is terminated either by you or by WPT for Cause (as defined in Section 8 hereof) prior to the end of a fiscal year in which you are entitled to receive this bonus, you will be entitled to receive a pro-rata portion of this bonus based on the portion of the applicable fiscal year during which you were employed.
5. STOCK OPTIONS: You will receive an option (the "Option") to purchase 600,000 shares of WPT common stock on the closing date of the IPO at an exercise price equal to the per share IPO price of the common stock. The Option will vest in equal installments over three years, commencing on December 29, 2004. All limited liability company units you currently hold in World Poker Tour, LLC shall be converted to proportional shares of WPT common stock, with the forfeiture

restrictions on such shares lapsing on the same schedule outlined in the Prior Management Agreement.

6. INTERNAL REVENUE CODE MATTERS AND NASDAQ LISTING REQUIREMENTS: Each of the bonus arrangements set forth in paragraph 4 above and the stock option grant contemplated by paragraph 5 above will be structured to ensure (i) qualification for expense deduction thereof by WPT under Section 162(m) of the Internal Revenue Code of 1986, and (ii) compliance with applicable Nasdaq Marketplace Rules (including without limitation Rule 4350(c)).

7. EXCLUSIVITY: During the term of the Employment Agreement, you agree not to compete with WPT in connection with poker and gaming related television and film projects (the "Restricted Projects"). In addition, during the term of the Employment Agreement, you will advise the Board in advance of pursuing any television and film projects that are non-Restricted Projects and offer any such non-Restricted Projects to WPT, which the Board may accept or reject within ten (10) days in its sole discretion. If the Board rejects a non-Restricted Project, you may pursue such project individually. It is understood that your current "Psycho Bunnies," "Big Pitch with Norman Lear," and "The Music Man" projects will not be considered Restricted Projects and you will be able to pursue these projects individually without obtaining Board approval. In no event shall your individual pursuit of a non-Restricted Project rejected by the Board interfere with your duties under the Employment Agreement.

8. SEVERANCE: Upon termination without Cause, you will be entitled to receive all salary and any applicable bonus amounts through the term of the Employment Agreement and the vesting of all previously unvested portions of the Option will accelerate. "Cause" will be defined as (i) your willful and continued failure to substantially perform your duties as reasonably assigned, (ii) your indictment for a criminal offense related to theft or embezzlement from WPT, which charges are not dismissed, or of which you are not acquitted within one (1) year, or (iii) your indictment for any felony offense that is not the result of actions performed by you within the scope of activities approved by the Board, which charges are not dismissed, or of which you are not acquitted, within one (1) year.

If this term sheet is consistent with your understanding, please so confirm by executing and returning the attached copy of this term sheet to Timothy Cope, c/o Lakes Entertainment, Inc., 130 Cheshire Lane, Minnetonka, Minnesota 55305.

WORLD POKER TOUR, LLC

By: /s/ Lyle Berman

Lyle Berman, Chief Executive Officer

Accepted and agreed to on
April 14, 2004.

/s/ Steven Lipscomb

SAMPLE LLC OPERATING AGREEMENTS:

CALIFORNIA FORM

OPERATING AGREEMENT
of
THE PIZZA JOINT, LLC

This Operating Agreement (this "Agreement") is entered into this 14th day of September, 2014, by and among DR. BOB MONEYBAGS, an individual ("MONEYBAGS"), DR. FRED GREENBACKS, an individual ("GREENBACKS"), RICHARD F. DOLLARBILLS, III, an individual ("DOLLARBILLS"), and SAM WORKERBEE, an individual ("WORKERBEE").

R E C I T A L S

The parties have agreed to organize a limited liability company in accordance with the terms and subject to the conditions set forth in this Agreement.

A G R E E M E N T

NOW, THEREFORE, the parties agree as follows:

Article I
Defined Terms

The following capitalized terms shall have the respective meanings specified in this Article I. Capitalized terms not defined in this Agreement shall have the meanings specified in the Act.

"*Act*" means the California Revised Uniform Limited Liability Company Act, as amended from time to time.

"*Affiliate*" means (a) a Person directly or indirectly controlling, controlled by, or under common control with another Person; (b) a Person owning or controlling 10 percent or more of the outstanding voting securities or beneficial interests of another Person; (c) an officer, director, partner, or member of the immediate family of an officer, director or partner, of another Person; and/or (d) any affiliate of any such Person.

"*Agreement*" means this Operating Agreement, as amended from time to time including each exhibit hereto.

"*Assignee*" means the Person who has acquired an Economic Interest in the Company but is not a Member.

"*Capital Account*" means the account to be maintained by the Company for each Interest Holder in accordance with Treasury Regulations Section 1.704-1(b)(2)(iv).

"*Capital Transaction*" means any transaction not in the ordinary course of business which results in the Company's receipt of cash or other consideration other than Contributions, including, without limitation, proceeds of sales, exchanges, or other dispositions of property not in the ordinary course of business, financings, refinancings, condemnations, recoveries of damage awards, and insurance proceeds.

"Cash Flow" means all cash derived from operations of the Company (including interest received on reserves), without reduction for any non-cash charges, but less cash used to pay current operating expenses and to pay or establish reasonable reserves for future expenses, debt payments, capital improvements, and replacements as determined by the Members. Cash Flow shall not include Capital Proceeds but shall be increased by the reduction of any reserve previously established.

"Code" means the Internal Revenue Code of 1986, as amended, or any corresponding provision of any succeeding revenue law.

"Company" means the limited liability company formed in accordance with this Agreement.

"Company Minimum Gain" shall have the meaning ascribed to the term "Partnership Minimum Gain" in the Treasury Regulations Section 1.704-2(d).

"Contribution(s)" means any money, property, or services rendered, or a promissory note or other binding obligation to contribute money or property, or to render services as permitted in this title, which a Member contributes to a Limited Liability Company as capital in that Member's capacity as a Member pursuant to an agreement between the Members, including an agreement as to value.

"Default Interest Rate" means a variable rate of interest adjusted quarterly on the last day of each calendar quarter equal to fifteen percent (15%) per annum, compounded annually, or the highest rate of interest permitted by law, whichever is less.

"Economic Interest" means a person's right to share in the Net Profits, Net Losses, deductions, credit, or similar items of, and to receive Distributions from, the Company, but does not include any other rights of a Member including, without limitation, the right to vote or to participate in management, or any right to information concerning the business and affairs of the Company.

"Financial Member" means the member who shall be charged with keeping the books and records of the Company and who shall be responsible for writing all Company checks and establishing and maintaining the Company's bank accounts. Initially the Financial Member shall be DR. BOB MONEYBAGS. The Financial Member may be changed upon Majority Approval of the Members.

"Interest Holder" means any Person who holds an Economic Interest, whether as a Member or as an Assignee of a Member.

"Majority Approval" means the approval of Members holding a majority (i.e. greater than fifty percent (50%)) of the Percentage Interests, whether such approval is evidenced by vote of the Members at a meeting of the Members, by execution by Members holding such a majority of a written consent in lieu of a meeting of the Members, or by execution of an agreement, instrument or other document requiring such approval by Members holding such a majority.

"Majority Interests" means Members holding a majority of the Percentage Interests in question.

"Member" means any person who executes a counterpart of this Agreement as a Member and any Person who subsequently is admitted as a Member of the Company.

"Membership Interest" means a Member's rights in the Company, collectively, including the Member's Economic Interest, any right to vote or participate in management, and any right to information concerning the business and affairs of the Company.

"*Member Nonrecourse Debt*" shall have the meaning ascribed to the term "Partnership Nonrecourse Debt" in Treasury Regulations Section 1.704-2(b)(4).

"*Member Nonrecourse Deductions*" shall mean items of Company loss, deduction, or Code Section 705(a)(2)(B) expenditures which are attributable to Member Nonrecourse Debt.

"*Nonrecourse Liability*" shall have the meaning set forth in Treasury Regulations Section 1.752-1(a)(2).

"*Percentage*" or "*Percentage Interest*" means, as to a Member, the percentage set forth after the Member's name on *Exhibit* A, as amended from time to time, and as to an Interest Holder who is not a Member, the Percentage or part of the Percentage that corresponds to the portion of a Member's Economic Interest that the Interest Holder has Acquired, to the extent the Interest Holder has succeeded to that Member's interest.

"*Person*" means and includes an individual, corporation, partnership, association, limited liability company, trust, estate, or other entity.

"*Positive Capital Account*" means a Capital Account with a balance greater than zero.

"*Secretary of State*" means the Secretary of State of the State of California.

"*Transfer*" means, when used as a noun, any sale, hypothecation, pledge, assignment, attachment, or other transfer, and, when used as a verb, to sell hypothecate, pledge, assign, or otherwise transfer. "*Transferor*" means one who Transfers, and "*Transferee*" means the recipient of a Transfer.

"*Treasury Regulations*" shall mean the final or temporary regulations that have been issued by the U.S. Department of Treasury pursuant to its authority under the Code, and any successor regulations.

"*Voting Power*" means the power to vote on any matter at the time any determination of voting power is made and shall be based on the Percentage Interests held by the Members entitled to vote on the issue.

Article II
Formation and Name; Office; Purpose; Term

2.1.   *Organization*. The parties hereby organize a limited liability company pursuant to the Act and the provisions of this Agreement. The Company shall cause Articles of Organization to be prepared, executed, and filed with the Secretary of State.

2.2.   *Name of the Company*. The name of the Company is THE PIZZA JOINT, LLC. The Company shall do business under the fictitious business name "The Pizza Joint." The Members shall cause to be filed, if required by applicable law, a Fictitious Business Name Statement and cause the same be filed in the Office of the County Clerk of such counties in which the Company does business.

2.3.   *Purpose*. The Company is organized solely to purchase, acquire, buy, sell, own, trade in, hold, manage and operate one or more retail "Pizza Joint" pizza franchise restaurants, and to do any and all things necessary, convenient, or incidental to that purpose, as well as to engage in any other lawful business activities.

2.4.   *Term*. The Company shall continue in existence until December 31, 2044, unless sooner dissolved as provided by this Agreement or the Act.

2.5.   *Principal Place of Business.* The Company's Principal Place of Business shall be located at 99 Elm Avenue, Suite 219, Littletown, California 80704, or at any other place within the State of California upon which the Members agree.

2.6.   *Resident Agent.* The name and address of the Company's resident agent in the State of California are Dr. BOB MONEYBAGS 99 Elm Avenue, Suite 219, Littletown, California 80704.

2.7.   *Members.* The name, present mailing address, taxpayer identification number, and Percentage of each Member are set forth on *Exhibit* A.

Article III
Members; Capital; Capital Accounts

3.1.   *Initial Contributions.* Upon the execution of this Agreement, the Members shall contribute to the Company the following Initial Capital Contributions:

Designated Member	Designated Dollar of Contribution
DOLLARBILLS	$20,000.00
MONEYBAGS	$20,000.00
GREENBACKS	$20,000.00

It is understood that no Initial Capital Contribution shall be required from WORK-ERBEE. It is further understood that WORKERBEE is the Member who shall be required to render full-time services to the Company as provided elsewhere in this Agreement. WORKERBEE shall, however, be responsible for making any Additional Capital Contributions to the same extent as other Members in accordance with his Percentage Interest.

3.2.   *No Additional Contributions.* No Member shall be required to contribute any additional capital to the Company, and no Member shall have personal liability for any obligation of the Company except as expressly provided by law. None of the Members shall be required to and no Member shall has the right to make any Additional Capital Contributions to the Company, except as provided below in this Section 3.2.

3.2.1   If the Members, by a Majority Approval determine, at any time and from time to time, that it is in the best interests of the Members that the Company receive additional capital (including, without limitation, to pay the amount of any **Mandatory Capital Distribution**, as that term is defined in Section 4.6 below), then the Finance Member shall deliver to the Members a notice (an **"Additional Capital Requirement Notice"**) specifying the additional amount of capital so determined to be required and each Member's *pro rata* share of such additional amount.

3.2.2   Each Member shall contribute its *pro rata* share of the required Additional Capital Contribution (defined in section 4.1.1) within fifteen (15) days after the delivery to the Members of the Additional Capital Requirement Notice.

3.2.3   If one or more Members (**"Defaulting Member(s)"**) shall fail to make an Additional Capital Contribution pursuant to an Additional Capital Requirement Notice (the **"Initial Tier Capital Call"**) as and when required to be made by each such Member pursuant to Section 3.2.2 (the total amount which all Members fail to pay pursuant to such a call shall be referred to as the **"Initial Tier Defaulted Amount"**), then the other Members (**"Contributing Members"**) shall be required to contribute to the Company within 15 days of receipt of a subsequent capital call notice (**"Subsequent Tier Capital Call Notice"**) such Contributing Member's *pro rata* share of the Initial Tier Defaulted Amount (based on relative Percentage Interests), such that the aggregate Contributions made by the Contributing Members pursuant to this sentence equals the total amount of the Initial Tier Capital Call.

In the event a Contributing Member fails to contribute his *pro rata* share of the Initial Tier Defaulted Amount of the Defaulting Members, such Contributing Member shall be deemed a Defaulting Member with respect to such Subsequent Tier Capital Call Notice, and the remaining Members shall be required to contribute to the Company Additional Capital in the same manner as applied to the initial Additional Capital Call Notice, and the process shall continue to repeat itself until such time as the total amount specified in the Additional Capital Requirement Notice has been paid.

A Majority in Interest of the Contributing Members with respect to the Initial Tier Defaulted Amount shall elect whether such amount shall be treated either as a **"Substituted Contribution"** (as defined below) or as a **"Default Loan"** (as defined below) to the Defaulting Member(s). Similarly, a Majority in Interest of the Contributing Members with respect to each Subsequent Tier Defaulted Amount shall make a similar election.

If the Contributing Members' Contributions with respect to any tier of Capital Call are to be treated as **"Substituted Contributions"**, and the Defaulting Member has a Positive Capital Account as of the date of the Company's most recent financial statement dated prior to the date that tier's Defaulted Amount was due, as adjusted by any subsequent distributions and Additional Capital Contributions made to, or by, such Defaulting Member (including Additional Capital Contributions made with respect to the Initial Tier or other prior tier Defaulted Amount) (**"Updated Adjusted Capital Account"**), then the Defaulting Member's Percentage Interest shall be reduced to equal the percentage obtained by dividing the amount of the Defaulting Member's Updated Adjusted Capital Account by the sum of the total Updated Adjusted Capital Accounts of all Members and 120% of the amount of the Additional Capital Contributions made by the Contributing Members with respect to the tier of the Capital Call to which the Defaulted Amount applies, and the Percentage Interest of each Contributing Member with respect to such tier of Capital Call shall be increased pro rata such that the total of the Percentage Interests of all Members continues to equal 100%.

In the event the Defaulting Member has a negative Updated Adjusted Capital Account, then the Defaulting Member's Percentage Interest shall be reduced to equal the percentage obtained by dividing the amount of the Defaulting Member's total Adjusted Invested Capital (including Additional Capital Contributions made with respect to the Initial Tier or other prior tier Defaulted Amount) (**"Updated Adjusted Invested Capital"**), by the sum of the total Updated Adjusted Invested Capital of all Members and 120% of the amount of the Additional Capital Contributions made by the Contributing Members with respect to the tier of the Capital Call to which the Defaulted Amount applies, and the Percentage Interest of each Contributing Member with respect to such tier of Capital Call shall be increased pro rata such that the total of the Percentage Interests of all Members continues to equal 100%, then each Defaulting Member's Percentage Interest with respect to such tier of Capital Call will be reduced to equal the percentage.

If the Contributing Members' Contribution is treated as a Default Loan, then such Default Loan shall bear interest at the Default Interest Rate, and shall be secured by collateral deemed adequate by a Majority in Interest of the Contributing Members. Until the Default Loan is fully repaid, the Contributing Members shall be entitled to receive, *pari passu*, an amount equal from the Company equal to the amount of the distribution to which the Defaulting Member would otherwise have been entitled, with such amounts so paid to be applied first, to accrued interest on the Default Loan, and only thereafter, to reduce the outstanding principal. **"Contributing Member"** means any Member other than the Defaulting Member.

3.3. *Preferred Return on Contributions.* Members or Interest Holders shall be entitled to a preferred return ("Preferred Return") on Adjusted Invested Capital (as defined in Section 4.1 below), equal to a percentage rate per annum equal to thirteen and one-half percent (13.5%), not compounded.

3.4. *Return of Contributions.* Except as otherwise provided in this Agreement, no Member nor Interest Holder shall have the right to receive the return of any Contribution or withdraw from the Company, except upon the dissolution of the Company.

3.5. *Form of Return of Capital.* If a Member or an Interest Holder is entitled to receive the return of a Contribution, the Company may distribute in lieu of money, notes, or other property having a value equal to the amount of money distributable to such Person.

3.6. *Capital Accounts.* A separate Capital Account shall be maintained for each Member and Interest Holder.

3.7. *Loans and Other Business Transactions.* Any Member may, at any time, make or cause a loan to be made to the Company in any amount and on those terms upon which the Company and the Member agree. Members may also transact other business with the Company and, in doing so, they shall have the same rights and be subject to the same obligations arising out of any such business transaction as would be enjoyed by and imposed upon any Person, not a Member, engaged in a similar business transaction with the Company.

Article IV
Allocations of Net Profits and Net Losses and Distributions

4.1   Definitions.

For purposes of this Agreement, the terms:

4.1.1 *"Additional Capital Contribution(s)"* shall mean all Contributions made by any Member other than pursuant to Section 3.1 hereof.

4.1.2 *"Adjusted Invested Capital"* shall mean the Initial Capital Contribution made by a Member to the Company, plus all Additional Capital Contributions which such Member may make from time to time to the Company, less all distributions made by the Company to such Member with respect to his interest in the Company (except distribution made in payment of Unreturned Preferred Return);

4.1.3 *"Initial Capital Contribution(s)"* shall mean the Contributions made by the Members pursuant to Section 3.1 hereof.

4.1.4   *"Preferred Return"* shall have the definition set forth in Section 3.3 (which provides that a preferred return is the return on such Member's Adjusted Invested Capital equal to 13.5% per annum (not compounded) accrued on the amount of each such Member's Adjusted Invested Capital).

4.1.5   *"Net Profits"* and *"Net Losses"* shall mean the income, gain, loss, deductions, and credits of the Company in the aggregate or separately stated, as appropriate, determined in accordance with the method of accounting at the close of each fiscal year employed on the Company's information tax return filed for federal income tax purposes.

4.1.6   *"Unreturned Preferred Return"* of a Member shall mean the amount of the Preferred Return earned by such Member as reduced (but not below zero) by all prior cash distributions to such Member pursuant to Section 4.6.2.1 which do not represent a return of a Member's Initial Capital Contribution.

4.2   *Allocation of Net Profits.* Net Profits shall be allocate among the Members in the following order of priority:

4.2.1   First, if any Member's Capital Account has an aggregate credit balance less than the sum of the amount of such Member's Adjusted Invested Capital and Unreturned Preferred Return, then Net Profits shall be allocated pro rata (i.e., based on the difference between the credit balance in such Member's Capital Account and the sum of the amount of the Adjusted Invested Capital and Unreturned Preferred Return for such Member) to all such Members until the credit balance in each Member's respective Capital Accounts is increased to the sum of their respective Adjusted Invested Capital and Unreturned Preferred Return amounts.

4.2.2   Second, and thereafter, Net Profits shall be allocated in proportion to their Percentage Interest.

4.3   <u>Allocation of Net Losses</u>. Net Losses shall be allocated among the Members in the following order of priority:

4.3.1   First, Net Losses shall be allocated among the Members in accordance with their Percentage Interests provided, however, that, first, Net Loss allocations to a Member shall be made only to the extent that such Net Loss allocations will not create a deficit Capital Account balance for that Member in excess of an amount, if any, equal to such Member's share of Company Minimum Gain that would be realized on a foreclosure of the Company's property and second, no such allocation shall cause the balance in any Member's Capital Account to be less than the sum of the amount of such Member's Adjusted Invested Capital and Unreturned Preferred Return to the extent any other Member has a Capital Account balance in excess of the sum of such other Member's Adjusted Investor Capital and Unreturned Preferred Return.

Any Net Loss not allocated to a Member because of the foregoing provisions shall be allocated to the other Members (to the extent that other Members are not limited in respect of the allocation of Net Losses under this Section 4.3.1). Any Net Loss reallocated under this Section 4.3.1 shall be taken into account in computing subsequent allocations of items of income and loss pursuant to this Article IV, so that the net amount of any item so allocated and the Net Income and Net Losses allocated to each member pursuant to this Article IV, to the extent possible, shall be equal to the net amount that would have been allocated to each such Member pursuant to this Article IV if no reallocation of Net Losses had occurred under this Section 4.3.1.

4.4.   *Special Allocations.* Notwithstanding Section 4.3:

4.4.1.   *Minimum Gain Chargeback.* If there is a net decrease in Company Minimum Gain during any fiscal year, each member shall be specially allocated items of Company income and gain for such fiscal year (and, if necessary, in subsequent fiscal years) in an amount equal to the portion of such Member's share of the net decrease in Company Minimum Gain that is allocable to the disposition of Company property subject to a Nonrecourse Liability, which share of such net decrease shall be determined in accordance with Treasury Regulations Section 1.704-2(g)(2). Allocations pursuant to this Section 4.4.1 shall be made in proportion to the amounts required to be allocated to each member under this Section 4.4.1. The items to be so allocated shall be determined in accordance with Treasury Regulations Section 1.704-2(f). This Section 4.4.1 is intended to comply with the minimum gain chargeback requirement contained in Treasury Regulations Section 1.704-2(i)(f), and shall be interpreted consistently therewith.

4.4.2.   *Chargeback of Minimum Gain Attributable to Member Nonrecourse Debt.* If there is a net decrease in Company Minimum Gain attributable to a Member Nonrecourse Debt during any fiscal year, each member who has a share of the Company Minimum Gain attributable to such Member Nonrecourse Debt (which share shall be determined in accordance with Treasury Regulations Section 1.704-2(i)(5)) shall be specially allocated items of Company income and gain for such fiscal year (and, if necessary, in subsequent fiscal years) in an amount equal to that portion of such Member's share of the net decrease in Company Minimum Gain attributable to such Member Nonrecourse Debt that is allocable to the disposition of Company property subject to such Member Nonrecourse Debt (which share of such net decrease shall be determined in accordance with Treasury Regulations Section 1.704-2(i)(5)). Allocations pursuant to this Section 4.4.2 shall be made in proportion to the amounts required to be allocated to each Member under this Section 4.4.2. The items to be so allocated shall be determined in accordance with Treasury Regulations Section 1.704-2(i)(4). This Section 4.4.2 is intended to comply with the minimum gain chargeback requirement contained in Treasury Regulations Section 1.704-2(i)(4) and shall be interpreted consistently therewith.

4.4.3.   *Nonrecourse Deductions.* Any nonrecourse deductions (as defined in Treasury Regulations Section 1.704-2(b)(1)) for any fiscal year or other period shall be specially allocated to the Members in proportion to their Percentage Interests.

4.4.4.   *Member Nonrecourse Deductions.* Those items of Company loss, deduction, or Code Section 705(a)(2)(B) expenditures which are attributable to Member Nonrecourse Debt for any fiscal year or other period shall be specially allocated to the Member who bears the economic risk of loss with respect to the Member Nonrecourse Debt to which such items are attributable in accordance with Treasury Regulations Section 1.704-2(i).

4.4.5.   *Qualified Income Offset.* If a Member unexpectedly receives any adjustments, allocations, or distributions described in Treasury Regulations Section 1.704-1(b)(2)(ii)(d)(4), (5) or (6), or any other event creates a deficit balance in such Member's Capital Account in excess of such Member's share of Company Minimum Gain, items of Company income and gain shall be specially allocated to such Member in an amount and manner sufficient to eliminate such excess deficit balance as quickly as possible. Any special allocations of items of income and gain pursuant to this Section 4.4.5 shall be taken into account in computing subsequent allocations of income and gain pursuant to this Article IV so that the net amount of any item so allocated and the income, gain, and Net Losses allocated to each Member pursuant to this Section 4.4.5 to the extent possible, shall be equal to the net amount that would have been allocated to each such Member pursuant to the provisions of this Article IV if such unexpected adjustments, allocations, or distributions had not occurred.

4.5. *Code Section 704(c) Allocations.* Notwithstanding any other provision in this Article IV, in accordance with Code Section 704(c) and the Treasury Regulations promulgated thereunder, income, gain, loss, and deduction with respect to any property contributed to the capital of the Company shall, solely for tax purposes, be allocated among the Members so as to take account of any variation between the adjusted basis of such property to the Company for federal income tax purposes and its fair market value on the date of Contribution. Allocations pursuant to this Section 4.5 are solely for purposes of federal, state and local taxes. As such, they shall not affect or in any way be taken into account in computing a Member's Capital Account or share of Net Profits, Net Losses, or other items of distributions pursuant to any provision of this Agreement.

4.6 *Distribution of Assets by the Company.* Subject to applicable law and any limitation contained elsewhere in this Agreement, Members holding a majority of the Percentage Interest shall cause the Company to make distributions in accordance with the terms of this Section 4.6.

    4.6.1   <u>Definitions</u>.

        4.6.1.1   *Cash Flow.* For purposes of this Agreement the term **"Cash Flow"** shall mean cash funds generated from operations of the Company for each fiscal year as determined through the use of the cash receipts and disbursements method of accounting, applied on a consistent basis, except that (i) charges for depreciation shall not be considered a deduction, and (ii) the amortization of principal with respect to loans, including loans secured by Company assets, shall be considered as a deduction. For purposes of this Agreement, the term **"Cash Available for Distribution"** shall mean Cash Flow less the following:

        (a)   The Company's share of all costs and expenses of acquiring, developing, operating, improving, preserving and disposing of any of the Company's assets, including all limited or general partnership interests in other partnerships or membership interests in other limited liability companies held by the Company, if not financed from Contributions or financing or refinancing proceeds;

        (b)   All operating or other expenses and expenditures of the Company, including Mandatory Capital Distributions, paid during the fiscal year.

        (c)   All amounts set aside in the judgment of the Members as necessary or appropriate for the creation or restoration of reserves for the purchase, development, improvement, replacement, operation, preservation or disposition of the Company's assets, increases in working capital and other contingencies, and otherwise to pursue and achieve the Company's specific purposes and objectives; and

        (d)   All amounts paid or set aside for payment to the Company's lenders for payment of interest, fees and charges with respect to the

Company debt and for repayment of principal whether at or prior to maturity of such loans.

4.6.1.2 *Mandatory Capital Distributions.* For purposes of this Agreement the term **"Mandatory Capital Distribution"** shall mean a monthly distribution to each Member equal to the amount necessary to pay the Initial Capital Contribution of each Member in thirty-six equal monthly installments, plus the amount of each such Member's Unreturned Preferred Return as of the time of each such monthly distribution.

4.6.1.3 *Unreturned Mandatory Capital Distributions.* For purposes of this Agreement the term **"Unreturned Mandatory Capital Distribution"** for each Member shall mean the amount of Mandatory Capital Contributions which are due or past due for each such Member.

4.6.2 Distributions of Company Cash

4.6.2.1 At the end of each calendar month, the Company shall distribute to each Member cash in an amount equal to the sum of the amount of that Member's Unreturned Mandatory Capital Distribution.

4.6.2.2 In addition to the distributions which are required to be made pursuant to section 4.6.2.1 hereof, Cash Available for Distribution shall be distributed the Members in the following order of priority:

4.6.2.2.1 First, to such Members as have a credit balance of their Adjusted Invested Capital, pro rata to each such Member based on the amount of the credit balance of such Adjusted Invested Capital of such Member, until the amount of such Adjusted Invested Capital is reduced to zero;

4.6.2.2.2 Second, to such Members, the amount of whose Positive Capital Account as a percentage of the aggregate amount of the Positive Capital Accounts of all Members (**"Member Positive Capital Account Percentage"**), is in excess of the percentage of their Percentage Interest, pro rata based on the amount of such excess for each such Member, until the percentage of each Member's Percentage Interest equals such Member's Member Positive Capital Account Percentage; and

4.6.2.2.3 Third, to the Members in accordance with their Percentage Interests.

The foregoing provisions of this Section 4.6.2.2 are not intended to give rise to any kind of a guaranteed return to the Members but shall be construed solely as a formula for distribution.

4.6.3 *Timing of Distributions and Distribution of Reserves.* All distributions shall be made at such times and in such amounts as may be determined in accordance with Section 4.6.4 of this Agreement. In the event a reserve is established under Section 4.6.1, which reserve is deducted in computing Cash Available for Distribution and, subsequently, all or any part of said reserve is not needed for the purpose for which said reserve was established and is not needed as a reserve for other working capital needs of the Company or otherwise to provide funds for acquisition, development, improvement, operation, restoration, preservation or disposition of the assets of the Company or any other reasonable contingency of the Company, the amount of said reserve found not to be necessary shall be added to the Cash Available for Distribution for the year in which such reserve becomes unnecessary.

4.6.4 *Determination of Effective Date and Amounts of Distributions of Company Funds.* The Members shall determine the effective date upon which Cash Available for Distribution shall be distributed to the Members, provided that Cash Available for Distribution shall be distributed no less frequently than once each fiscal quarter. Distributions to the Members shall be made only to those Members who are owners of record of an interest in the Company, as reflected on the books and records of the Company, upon the effective date of such distributions.

4.6.5 *Changes in Capital Interests and Transfer of Company Interests.* If there are changes in the Percentage Interests of the Members during any fiscal year, then Cash Available for Distribution and Company, and Net Profits or Net Losses shall be deemed to have accrued ratably over the quarterly period in which such change occurred, and the allocation of Cash Available for Distribution and Company Net Profits and Net Losses shall be charged, credited or distributed to the Members in proportion to the Percentage Interest held by each of them during the period prior to and after such change within such quarter, using a mid-month convention for allocating distributions, Net Profits and Net Losses relating to the month in which the change occurred.

4.6.6 *Liquidating Distributions.* Distribution of assets of the Company upon dissolution, winding up and termination shall be made in accordance with Article VII of this Agreement.

Article V
Management: Rights, Powers, and Duties

5.1 *Management.*

5.1.1. *Management by Members.* The Company shall be managed by the Members. Except as specifically provided otherwise in this Agreement, each Member shall have the right to act for and bind the Company in the ordinary course of its business.

5.1.2. *Decisions Requiring Majority Approval.* The following decisions affecting the business and affairs of the Company are examples of matters outside the ordinary course of business which shall therefore require Majority Approval of Members: Any decision to:

5.1.2.1. acquire by purchase, lease, or otherwise, or sell, dispose, trade, or exchange any real property, or any personal property with a value in excess of $5,000.00;

5.1.2.2. enter into agreements, contracts or other obligations which obligate the Company for more than $5,000 or which are not terminable on 90 days or less notice, or which are otherwise not in the ordinary course of business;

5.1.2.3. borrow money for and on behalf of the Company, and, in connection therewith, execute and deliver instruments;

5.1.2.4. execute or modify leases with respect to any real property, or any personal property with a value in excess of $5,000.00;

5.1.2.5. enter into, grant, prepay, in whole or in part, refinance, amend, modify, or extend any mortgages or deeds of trust which may affect any asset of the Company and in connection therewith to execute for and on behalf of the

Company any mortgages or deeds of trust, or extensions, renewals, or modifications of such mortgages or deeds of trust;

    5.1.2.6. any Capital Transaction;

    5.1.2.7. any loan of the Company's money or other assets if the amount of such transaction exceeds $10,000.00;

    5.1.2.8. the admission of a Member to the Company;

    5.1.2.9. causing the Company to engage in business in any jurisdiction which does not provide for the registration of limited liability companies; and

    5.1.2.10. causing the Company to exercise any option to purchase a Member's Membership Interest pursuant to Article VI.

    5.2. *Meetings of and Voting by Members.*

    5.2.1. A meeting of the Members may be called at any time by any two or more of the Members. Meetings of Members shall be held at the Company's principal place of business. Not less than ten (10) nor more than sixty (60) days before each meeting, the Person or Persons calling the meeting shall give written notice of the meeting to each Member entitled to vote at the meeting. The notice shall state the time, place, and purpose of the meeting. Notwithstanding the foregoing provisions, each Member who is entitled to notice may waive notice, either before or after the meeting, by executing a waiver of such notice, or by appearing at and participating, in person or by proxy in the meeting. Unless this Agreement provides otherwise, at a meeting of Members, the presence in person or by Proxy of Members holding Percentages which aggregate to not less than fifty-one percent (51%) constitutes a quorum. A Member may vote either in person or by written Proxy signed by the Member or by the Member's duly authorized attorney in fact.

    5.2.2. Except as otherwise provided in this Agreement, the affirmative vote of Members holding a majority of the aggregate Percentages present at the meeting in person and by proxy shall be required to approve any matter coming before the Members.

    5.2.3. In lieu of holding a meeting, the Members may take action by written consents specifying the action to be taken, which consents must be executed and delivered to the Company by Members whose combined Voting Power constitutes not less than 75% of the total Voting Power of all Members. Any such approved action shall be effective upon the date set forth or provided for in the written consent. The Company shall give prompt notice to all Members of any action approved by Members by less than unanimous consent.

    5.2.4. The following matters shall require the vote or consent of the Percentage Interest of Members indicated after each such item for such action to be approved by the Members:

    (a) A decision to continue the business of the Company after dissolution of the Company (100%);

    (b) Approval of the transfer of a Membership Interest and admission of an Assignee as a Member (100%);

    (c) An amendment to the Articles of Organization or this Agreement (100%), except that an amendment which changes this Company from a member managed Limited Liability Company to a manager managed Limited Liability Company, and in connection therewith specifies the identity of the Manager, and such manager's level of authority and rights and obligations may be adopted by vote by Members whose combined Voting Power constitutes not less than 75% of the total Voting Power of all Members.

5.3. *Personal Service.* No Member shall be required to perform services for the Company solely by virtue of being a Member. Unless approved by Majority Approval of the Members, no Member shall perform services for the Company or be entitled to compensation for services performed for the Company. However, upon substantiation of the amount and purpose thereof, a Member shall be entitled to reimbursement for expenses reasonably incurred, and advances reasonably made, in furtherance of the business of the Company. Notwithstanding the foregoing, the Members hereby approve the employment by the Company of WORKERBEE at a starting salary of $3,000 per month under terms to be specified herein and in a written employment contract between WORKERBEE and the Company.

5.4. *Duties of Parties.*

5.4.1. WORKERBEE shall devote full time to the business and affairs of the Company. WORKERBEE shall be responsible for doing all things necessary on behalf of the Company to cause to be opened and operated a Pizza Joint franchise restaurant to be acquired by the Company (the **"Restaurant"**) and any additional Pizza Joint franchise restaurants (or other restaurants) as the Company shall from time to time identify. WORKERBEE shall report to the Members but shall have the authority, subject to the limitations set forth above to do the following:

(a) to obtain on the Company's behalf business licenses, liquor licenses, and other governmental licenses and approvals as are necessary to open and operate the Restaurant;

(b) to hire sufficient employees to fully staff the Restaurant;

(c) to purchase necessary inventory of supplies, equipment and food to operate the Restaurant;

(d) to obtain all property and liability insurance as is customary in connection with the operation of the Restaurant;

(e) to cause the Restaurant to be maintained in good and clean condition and repair and cleanliness;

(f) to make recommendations to the Members regarding agreements which the Company should enter into in connection with the operation of the Restaurant including without limitation any franchise agreements, advertising or other promotional agreements, equipment or real property leases, and any other agreements necessary for the successful operation of the Pizza Joint Restaurant; and

(g) to make recommendations to the Members regarding any and all other acts that may be necessary or appropriate for the successful operation of the Restaurant or any subsequent restaurants which the Company shall elect to open upon receipt of Majority Approval.

5.4.2. Except as otherwise expressly provided in *Section* 5.4.3, nothing in this Agreement shall be deemed to restrict in any way the rights of any Member, or of any Affiliate of any Member, to conduct any other business or activity whatsoever, and no Member shall be accountable to the Company or to any other Member with respect to that business or activity even if the business or activity competes with the Company's business. The organization of the Company shall be without prejudice to the

Members' respective rights (or the rights of their respective Affiliates) to maintain, expand, or diversify such other interests and activities and to receive and enjoy profits or compensation therefrom. Each Member waives any rights the Member might otherwise have to share or participate in such other interests or activities of any other Member or the Member's Affiliates.

5.4.3.   The only fiduciary duties a Member owes to the Company and the other Members are the duty of loyalty and the duty of care set forth in subdivisions (a) and (b):

(a)   A Member's duty of loyalty to the Company and the other Members is limited to the following:

(1)   To account to the Company and hold as trustee for it any property, profit, or benefit derived by the Member in the conduct or winding up of the Company's business or derived from a use by the Member of Company property, including the appropriation of a Company opportunity, without the consent of the other Members;

(2)   To refrain from dealing with the Company in the conduct or winding up of the Company business as or on behalf of a party having an interest adverse to the Company without the consent of the other Members; and

(3)   To refrain from competing with the Company in the conduct of the Company business before the dissolution of the Company without the consent of the other Members.

(b)   A Member's duty of care to the Company and the other Members in the conduct and winding up of the Company business is limited to refraining from engaging in grossly negligent or reckless conduct, intentional misconduct, or a knowing violation of law.

5.5.   *Indemnification of Each Member.*

5.5.1.   Each Member shall not be liable, responsible, or accountable, in damages or otherwise, to any Member or to the Company for any act performed by such Member within the scope of the authority conferred on such Member by this Agreement, and within the standard of care specified in Section 5.5.2.

5.5.2.   The Company shall indemnify each Member for any act performed by the Member within the scope of the authority conferred on the Member by this Agreement, unless such act constitutes grossly negligent or reckless conduct, intentional misconduct, or a knowing violation of law.

Article VI
Transfer of Interests and Withdrawals of Members

6.1.   *Transfers.* Except as provided herein, no Member may Transfer all, or any portion of, or any interest or rights in, the Membership Interest owned by the Member. Each Member hereby acknowledges the reasonableness of this prohibition in view of the purposes of the Company and the relationship of the Members. The attempted Transfer of any portion or all of a Membership Interest in violation of the prohibition contained in this Section 6.1 shall be deemed invalid, null and void, and of no force or effect, except any Transfer mandated by operation of law and then only to the extent necessary to give effect to such Transfer by operation of law.

6.1.1.   A Member may Transfer all or any portion of or any interest or rights in the Member's Economic Interest if each of the following conditions ("**Conditions of Transfer**") is satisfied:

6.1.1.1.   the Transfer may be accomplished without registration, or similar process, under federal and state securities laws;

6.1.1.2.   the transferee delivers to the Company a written agreement to be bound by the terms of Article VI of this Agreement;

6.1.1.3.   the Transfer will not result in the termination of the Company pursuant to IRC Section 708;

6.1.1.4.   the Transfer will not result in the Company becoming subject to regulatory oversight pursuant to the terms of the Investment Company Act of 1940, as amended;

6.1.1.5.   the transferor or the transferee delivers the following information to the Company: (i) the transferee's taxpayer identification number (including evidence reasonably satisfactory to the Company demonstrating the validity of that taxpayer or employer identification number); and (ii) the transferee's initial tax basis in the transferred Membership Interest; and

6.1.1.6.   the transferor complies with the provisions of *Section 6.1.3*.

6.1.2.   If the Conditions of Transfer are satisfied, the Member may Transfer all or any portion of the Member's Economic Interest. The Transfer of an Economic Interest pursuant to this Section 6.1 shall not result in the Transfer of any of the transferor's other Membership rights. The transferee of the Economic Interest shall have no right to: (i) become a Member; (ii) exercise any Membership rights other than those specifically pertaining to the ownership of an Economic Interest; or (iii) act as an agent of the Company.

6.1.3.   *Right of First Refusal.*

6.1.3.1.   If a Member (a "**Transferor**") receives a bona fide written offer which the Member desires to accept (the "**Transferee Offer**") from any other Person, including another Member (a "**Transferee**") to purchase all or any portion of or any interest or rights in the Transferor's Economic Interest (the "**Transferor Interest**") then, prior to any Transfer of the Transferor's Interest, the Transferor shall give the Company written notice (the "**Transfer Notice**") containing each of the following:

6.1.3.1.1.   the Transferee's identify;

6.1.3.1.2.   a true and complete copy of the Transferee Offer; and

6.1.3.1.3.   the Transferor's offer (the "**Offer**") to sell the Transferor Interest to the Company for consideration equal to that contained in the Transferee Offer or, if the consideration specified in the Transferee Offer is not specified as cash, then for consideration in U.S. Dollars equal in value to the consideration specified in the Transferee Offer (the "**Transfer Purchase Price**").

6.1.3.2.   The Offer shall be and remain irrevocable for a period (the "**Offer Period**") ending at 11:59 P.M. local time at the Company's principal office, on the sixtieth (60th) day following the date the Transfer Notice is given to the Company. At any time during the Offer Period, the Company may accept the Offer by giving written notice to the Transferor of its acceptance (the "**Offeree Notice**").

The Transferor shall not be deemed a Member for the purpose of the vote on whether the Company shall accept the Offer. If the Company accepts the Offer, the Offeree Notice shall fix a closing date (the **"Transfer Closing Date"**) for the purchase, which shall not be earlier than ten (10) or more than sixty (60) days after the expiration of the Offer Period.

6.1.3.3.   If the Company accepts the Offer, the Transfer Purchase Price shall be paid on the Transfer Closing Date.

6.1.3.4.   If the Company does not accept the Offer in its entirety within thirty (30) days after the Offer Date, the Company shall give immediate notice to that effect (the **"Remaining Members Notice"**) to each Member, other than the Transferor (the **"Remaining Members"**). Such notice to the Remaining Members shall include a copy of the Transfer Notice and inform the Remaining Members of their right to purchase all, or a portion, of the Transferor Interest for a pro rata portion of the Transfer Purchase Price.

6.1.3.5.   The Remaining Members Notice shall be and remain irrevocable for the remainder of the Offer Period. At any time during such period, a Remaining Member may accept the offer by notifying the Transferor in writing that the Remaining Member intends to purchase all, but not less than all, of the Transferor Interest. If two (2) or more Remaining Members desire to accept the Offer, then, in the absence of an agreement between or among them, each such Remaining Member shall purchase the Transferor Interest in the proportion that such Member's respective Percentage bears to the total Percentages of all of the Remaining Members who desire to accept the Offer, adjusted to reflect the portion, if any, of the Transferor Interest to be purchased by the Company.

6.1.3.6.   If the Company and/or the Remaining Members (collectively, the **"Purchasers"**) have accepted the Offer prior to the end of the Offer Period, any Purchaser may give written notice to that effect to the Transferor specifying a closing date (the **"Transfer Closing Date"**) for the purchase which shall be no earlier than ten (10) nor later than sixty (60) days after the expiration of the Offer Period.

6.1.3.7.   On the Transfer Closing Date the Purchasers shall pay the Transfer Purchase Price.

6.1.3.8.   If neither the Company nor any Remaining Member accepts the Offer (within the time and in the manner specified in this Section), then the Transferor shall be free for a period (the **"Permitted Transfer Period"**) of thirty (30) days after the expiration of the Offer Period to Transfer the Transferor Interest to the Transferee, for the same or greater price and on the same remaining terms and conditions as set forth in the Transfer Notice. The Transfer shall be subject, however, to the Conditions of Transfer (other than Section 6.1.1.6). If the Transferor does not Transfer the Transferor's Interest within the Permitted Transfer Period, the Transferor's right to Transfer the Transferor Interest pursuant to this Section shall cease and terminate.

6.1.3.9.   Any Transfer by the Transferor after the last day of the Permitted Transfer Period or without strict compliance with the terms, provisions, and conditions of this Section and the other terms, provisions, and conditions of this Agreement, shall be null and void and of no force or effect.

6.2.   *Withdrawal of a Member.*

6.2.1.   No Member shall have the right or power to Voluntarily Withdraw from the Company except that WORKERBEE may withdraw as a Member if he desires to cease fulfilling his employment obligations to the Company. Such withdrawal by WORKERBEE shall be done by sending written notice to all of the Members. Such withdrawal shall be without prejudice to the rights of the Company and the Member under any contract to which WORKERBEE and the Company are parties, including, without limitation the provisions of Section 6.5 below.

6.2.2   *"Involuntary Withdrawal"* means, with respect to any Member, the occurrence of any of the following events:

(i)   the Member makes an assignment for the benefit of creditors;

(ii)   the Member is bankrupt;

(iii)   the Member files a petition seeking for the Member any reorganization, arrangement, composition, readjustment, liquidation, dissolution, or similar relief under any state law;

(iv)   the Member seeks, consents to, or acquiesces in the appointment of a trustee for, receiver for, or liquidation of the Member or of all or any substantial part of the Member's properties;

(v)   if the Member is an individual, the Member's death or adjudication by a court of competent jurisdiction as incompetent to manage the Member's person or property;

(vi)   if the Member is acting as a Member by virtue of being a trustee of a trust, the termination of the trust;

(vii)   if the Member is a partnership or limited liability company, the dissolution and commencement of winding up of the partnership or limited liability company;

(viii)   if the Member is a corporation, the dissolution of the corporation or the revocation of its charter;

(ix)   if the Member is a partnership, limited liability company or corporation, a change in control of such entity;

(x)   if the Member is an estate, the distribution by the fiduciary of the estate's entire interest in the Company; or

(xi)   if the Member files an action seeking a decree of judicial dissolution pursuant to Section 17707.03 of the Act.

6.3.   *Optional Buy-out in Event of Involuntary Withdrawal.*

6.3.1.   If the Members elect to continue the Company after an Involuntary Withdrawal or a Voluntary Withdrawal of WORKERBEE, the withdrawn Member or the successor in interest to such Member (the **"Withdrawn Member"**) shall be deemed to offer for sale to the Company (the **"Withdrawal Offer"**) all of the Membership Interest of the withdrawn Member (which in the case of WORKERBEE shall be determined after the application of Section 6.5 below) (the **"Withdrawal Interest"**).

6.3.2.   The Withdrawal Offer shall be and remain irrevocable for a period (the **"Withdrawal Offer Period"**) ending at 11:59 P.M. local time at the Company's principal office on the sixtieth (60th) day following the date the Members elect to continue the Company. At any time during the Withdrawal Offer Period, the

Company may accept the Withdrawal Offer by notifying the Withdrawn Member of its acceptance (the "**Withdrawal Notice**"). The Withdrawn Member shall not be deemed a Member for the purpose of the vote on whether the Company shall accept the Withdrawal Offer.

6.3.3. If the Company accepts the Withdrawal Offer, the Withdrawal Notice shall fix a closing date (the "**Withdrawal Closing Date**") for the purchase which shall be not earlier than ten (10) or later than ninety (90) days after the expiration of the Withdrawal Period.

6.3.4. If the Company accepts the Withdrawal Offer, the Company shall purchase the Withdrawal Interest for the price equal to the amount the Withdrawn Member would receive if the Company were liquidated and the amount equal to the Appraised Value were available for distribution to the Members pursuant to Section 4.4 (the "**Withdrawal Purchase Price**"). The Withdrawal Purchase Price shall be paid in cash on the Withdrawal Closing Date.

6.3.5. If the Company fails to accept the Withdrawal Offer, then the Withdrawn Member, upon the expiration of the Withdrawal Offer Period, thereafter shall be treated as the unadmitted assignee of a Member.

6.4. *Appraised Value.*

6.4.1. The term "**Appraised Value**" means the appraised value of the Company as hereinafter provided. Within fifteen (15) days after demand by either one to the other, the Company and the Withdrawn Member shall each appoint an appraiser to determine the value of the Company. If the two appraisers agree upon such value, they shall jointly render a single written report stating that value. If the two appraisers cannot agree upon the value of the Company, they shall each render a separate written report and shall appoint a third appraiser, who shall appraise the Company, determine its value, and render a written report of his or her opinion thereon. Each party shall pay the fees and other costs of the appraiser appointed by such party, and the fees and other costs of the third appraiser shall be shared equally by both parties.

6.4.2. The value contained in the aforesaid joint written report or written report of the third appraiser, as the case may be, shall be the Appraised Value; provided, however, that if the value of the equity contained in the appraisal report of the third appraiser is more than the higher of the first two appraisals, the higher of the first two appraisals shall govern; and provided, further, that if the value of the equity contained in the appraisal report of the third appraiser is less than the lower of the first two appraisals, the lower of the first two appraisals shall govern.

6.5 *WORKERBEE'S Interest.* Except to the extent otherwise specified in a written employment contract between WORKERBEE and the Company, WORKERBEE's employment status with the Company is that of an "at-will" employee. Subject to any rights specified in such an employment contract, WORKERBEE may be terminated as an employee upon Majority Approval of the Members and may be voluntarily terminated by WORKERBEE at any time. To the extent that either party desires to terminate WORKERBEE's employment relationship, such party shall give notice to all of the Members including WORKERBEE. In the event of any such termination, or in the event of any Involuntary Withdrawal of WORKERBEE, WORKERBEE's Percentage Interest shall be adjusted as follows:

(a) if such termination occurs on or before March 31, 2016, then WORKERBEE's Percentage Interest shall be adjusted to zero percent.

(b) if such termination occurs at any time on or after April 1, 2016, then WORKERBEE's Percentage Interest shall be adjusted to an amount equal to WORKERBEE's Percentage Interest at the time of Withdrawal times a fraction, the numerator of which is the amount of distributions previously made to MONEYBAGS, DOLLARBILLS, and GREENBACKS in return of their Initial Capital Contributions (exclusive of amounts distributed to the Contributing Members as payment for the Preferred Return); and the denominator of which shall be $60,000.00.

The foregoing adjustment to the Percentage of WORKERBEE shall take effect as of the date of termination. As of said date, the Percentages of the Members other than WORKERBEE shall be adjusted upward in proportion to the Percentages held by them so that the total Percentage is equal to 100%. In the event that WORKERBEE's Percentage becomes zero at the time of termination, then he shall no longer be a Member of the Company. In such event, the Company shall pay to WORKERBEE any positive Capital Account balance and WORKERBEE shall pay to the Company the amount of any negative Capital Account balance, in each case within ninety days of the date of termination. In the event that WORKERBEE's Percentage becomes an amount that is greater than zero, unless the optional buy-out provisions of Section 6.3 are exercised (which the parties agree may be exercised as to WORKERBEE, in the event of the termination, voluntarily or involuntarily of his employment with the Company), he shall remain a Member with the new Percentage taking effect upon the date of termination and his Capital Account remaining in place.

<h2 style="text-align:center">Article VII
Dissolution, Liquidation, and Termination of the Company</h2>

7.1. *Events of Dissolution.* The Company shall be dissolved upon the happening of the first to occur of an event specified in Section 17707.01 of the Act or any of the following events:

    7.1.1. the date fixed for its termination in Section 2.4;

    7.1.2. the happening of any event of dissolution specified in the Articles;

    7.1.3. entry of a judicial dissolution decree under Section 17707.03 of the Act;

    7.1.4. the vote of a majority in interest of the Members;

    7.1.5. the sale of all or substantially all of the assets of the Company.

7.2. *Procedure for Winding Up and Dissolution.* If the Company is dissolved, the Members shall wind up its affairs. On winding up of the Company, the assets of the Company shall be distributed, first to creditors of the Company, including Interest Holders who are creditors, in satisfaction of the liabilities of the Company, and then, to the Members in accordance with Section 4.6 of this Agreement.

7.3. *Filing of Certificate of Cancellation.* Upon completion of the affairs of the Company, any two Members shall promptly file a Certificate of Cancellation of Articles of Organization with the Secretary of State. If there are not two Members, then the remaining Member shall file the Certificate of Cancellation; if there are no remaining Members, the last Person to be a Member shall file the Certificate; if there are no remaining Members, nor any Person who last was a Member, the legal or personal representatives of the Person who last was a Member shall file the Certificate.

Article VIII
Books, Records, Accounting, and Tax Elections

8.1.   *Bank Accounts.* All funds of the Company shall be deposited in a bank account or accounts opened in the Company's name. The Financial Member shall determine the financial institution or institutions at which the accounts will be opened and maintained, the types of accounts, and the Persons who will have authority with respect to the accounts and the funds therein.

8.2.   *Books and Records.*

8.2.1.   The Financial Member shall keep or cause to be kept complete and accurate books, records, and financial statements of the Company and supporting documentation of transactions with respect to the conduct of the Company's business. The books, records, and financial statements of the Company shall be maintained on the cash method of accounting. Such books, records, financial statements, and documents shall include, but not be limited to, the following:

(1)   a current list of the full name and last known business or residence address of each Member and Interest Holder, in alphabetical order, with the Contribution and the share in Net Profits and Net Losses of each Member and Interest Holder specified in such list;

(2)   the Articles of Organization, including all amendments; and any powers of attorney under which the Articles of Organization or amendments were executed;

(3)   federal, state, and local income tax or information returns and reports, if any, for the six most recent taxable years;

(4)   this Agreement and any amendments thereto; and any Powers-of-Attorney under which this Agreement or amendments were executed;

(5)   financial statements for the six most recent years;

(6)   internal books and records for the current and three most recent years; and

(7)   a true copy of relevant records indicating the amount, cost, and value of all property which the Company owns, claims, possesses, or controls.

8.2.2.   Such books, records, and financial statements of the Company and supporting documentation shall be kept, maintained, and available at the Company's office within the State of California.

8.3.   *Right to Inspect Books and Records; Receive Information.*

8.3.1.   Upon the reasonable request of a Member for a purpose reasonably related to the interest of that Member of the Company, the Company shall promptly deliver to the requesting Member at the expense of the Company a copy of this Agreement, as well as the information required to be maintained by the Company under subparagraphs (1), (2), and (4) of Section 8.2.1.

8.3.2.   Each Member has the right upon reasonable request, and for purposes reasonably related to the interest of that Member of the Company, to do the following:

(1) to inspect and copy during normal business hours any of the records required to be maintained by the Company under Section 8.2.1 of this Agreement; and

(2) to obtain from the Company promptly after becoming available, a copy of the Company's federal, state, and local income tax or information returns for each year.

8.3.3. If the Company has more than 35 Members, Members representing at least 5 percent of the voting interests of all Members, or three or more Members, may make a written request to a Members for an income statement of the Company for the initial three-month, six-month, or nine-month period of the current fiscal year ended more than 30 days prior to the date of the request, and a balance sheet of the Company as of the end of that period. The statement must be delivered or mailed to the Members within 30 days thereafter. The financial statements referred to in this Paragraph shall be accompanied by the report thereon, if any, of the independent accountants engaged by the Company or, if there is no report, the certificate of Financial Member that the financial statements were prepared without audit from the books and records of the Company.

8.3.4. If the Company has more than 35 Members, the Members shall cause an annual report to be sent to each Member of the Company not later than 120 days after the close of the Company's fiscal year. Such report must contain the Company's balance sheet as of the end of the Company's fiscal year and an income statement and statement of changes in financial position for such fiscal year. The financial statements referred to in this Paragraph shall be accompanied by the report thereon, if any, of the independent accountants engaged by the Company or, if there is no report, the certificate of the Financial Member that the financial statements were prepared without audit from the books and records of the Company.

8.3.5. The Company shall send or shall cause to be sent to each Member or Interest Holder within 90 days after the end of each fiscal year of the Company: (i) such information as is necessary to complete federal and state income tax or information returns, and (ii) if the Company has 35 or fewer Members, a copy of the Company's federal, state, and local income tax or information returns for the fiscal year.

8.3.6. Unless otherwise expressly provided in this Agreement, the inspecting or requesting Member shall reimburse the Company for all reasonable costs and expenses incurred by the Company in connection with such inspection and copying of the Company's books and records and the production and delivery of any other books or records.

8.4. *Annual Accounting Period.* The annual accounting period of the Company shall be its taxable year. The Company's taxable year shall be selected by the Members, subject to the requirements and limitations of the Code.

8.5. *Tax Matters Partner.* The Financial Member shall be the Tax Matters Partner for purposes of IRC Section 6231(a)(7), and shall have all the authority granted by the Code to the Tax Matters Partner, provided that the Financial Member shall not have the authority without first obtaining the consent of the Members to do any of the following: (i) Enter into a settlement agreement with the Internal Revenue Service that purports to bind the Members; (ii) File a petition as contemplated in IRC Section 6226(a) or IRC

Section 6228; (iii) Intervene in any action as contemplated in IRC Section 6226(b)(5); (iv) File any request contemplated in IRC Section 6227(b); or (v) Enter into an agreement extending the period of limitations as contemplated in IRC Section 6229(b)(1)(B).

8.6.   *Tax Elections*. The Financial Member shall have the authority to make all Company elections permitted under the Code, including, without limitation, elections of methods of depreciation and elections under IRC Section 754.

8.7.   *Title to Company Property*. All real and personal property acquired by the Company shall be acquired and held by the Company in the Company's name.

Article IX
General Provisions

9.1.   *Assurances*. Each Member shall execute all certificates and other documents and shall do all such filing, recording, publishing, and other acts as the Members deem appropriate to comply with the requirements of law for the formation and operation of the Company and to comply with any laws, rules, and regulations relating to the acquisition, operation, or holding of the property of the Company.

9.2.   *Notifications*. Any notice, demand, consent, election, offer, approval, request, or other communication (collectively a "notice") required or permitted under this Agreement must be in writing and either delivered personally or sent by certified or registered mail, postage prepaid, return receipt requested. Any notice to be given hereunder by the Company shall be given by the any two of the Members. A notice must be addressed to an Interest Holder at the Interest Holder's last known address on the records of the Company. A notice to the Company must be addressed to the Company's principal office. A notice delivered personally will be deemed given only when acknowledged in writing by the Person to whom it is delivered. A notice that is sent by mail will be deemed given three (3) business days after it is mailed. Any party may designate, by notice to all of the others, substitute addresses or addressees for notices; and, thereafter, notices are to be directed to those substitute addresses or addressees.

9.3.   *Specific Performance*. The parties recognize that irreparable injury will result from a breach of any provision of this Agreement and that money damages will be inadequate to fully remedy the injury. Accordingly, in the event of a breach or threatened breach of one or more of the provisions of this Agreement, any party who may be injured (in addition to any other remedies which may be available to that party) shall be entitled to one or more preliminary or permanent orders (i) restraining and enjoining any act which would constitute a breach or (ii) compelling the performance of any obligation which, if not performed, would constitute a breach.

9.4.   *Complete Agreement*. This Agreement constitutes the complete and exclusive statement of the agreement among the Members. It supersedes all prior written and oral statements, including any prior representation, statement, condition, or warranty. Except as expressly provided otherwise herein, this Agreement may not be amended without the written consent of all of the Members.

9.5.   *Applicable Law*. All questions concerning the construction, validity, and interpretation of this Agreement and the performance of the obligations imposed by this Agreement shall be governed by the internal law, not the law of conflicts, of the State of California.

9.6. *Article and Section Titles.* The headings herein are inserted as a matter of convenience only and do not define, limit, or describe the scope of this Agreement or the intent of the provisions hereof.

9.7. *Binding Provisions.* This Agreement is binding upon, and to the limited extent specifically provided herein, inures to the benefit of, the parties hereto and their respective heirs, executors, administrators, personal and legal representatives, successors, and assigns.

9.8. *Jurisdiction and Venue.* Any suit involving any dispute or matter arising under this Agreement may only be brought in the Superior Court of the State of California in Los Angeles County. All Members hereby consent to the exercise of personal jurisdiction by any such court with respect to any such proceeding.

9.9. *Terms.* Common nouns and pronouns shall be deemed to refer to the masculine, feminine, neuter, singular, and plural, as the identity of the Person may in the context require.

9.10. *Separability of Provisions.* Each provision of this Agreement shall be considered separable; and if, for any reason, any provision or provisions herein are determined to be invalid and contrary to any existing or future law, such invalidity shall not impair the operation of or affect those portions of this Agreement which are valid.

9.11. *Counterparts.* This Agreement may be executed simultaneously in two or more counterparts, each of which shall be deemed an original and all of which, when taken together, constitute one and the same document. The signature of any party to any counterpart shall be deemed a signature to, and may be appended to, any other counterpart.

9.12. *Estoppel Certificate.* Each Member shall, within ten (10) days after written request by any Member, deliver to the requesting Person a certificate stating, to the Member's knowledge, that: (a) this Agreement is in full force and effect; (b) this Agreement has not been modified except by any instrument or instruments identified in the certificate; and (c) there is no default hereunder by the requesting Person, or if there is a default, the nature and extent thereof.

IN WITNESS WHEREOF, the parties have executed, or caused this Agreement to be executed, under seal, as of the date set forth hereinabove.

MEMBERS:

DR. BOB MONEYBAGS, an individual _____

DR. FRED GREENBACKS, an individual _____

RICHARD F. DOLLARBILLS, III, an individual _____

SAM WORKERBEE, an individual _____

EXHIBIT A

Social Security Number Name and Address	Percentages	Date Admitted
DR. BOB MONEYBAGS 999-99-9999 52 Maple, Suite 219 Littletown, California 80705	25%	September 14, 2014
DR. FRED GREENBACKS 999-99-9999 99 Elm Littletown, California 80705	25%	September 14, 2014
SAM WORKERBEE 999-99-9999 15 Main Drive Laguna Niguel, California 80677	25%	September 14, 2014
RICHARD F. DOLLARBILLS, III 999-99-9999 20 Fifth Dr. Oceanside, CA 80056	25%	September 14, 2014

GENERIC FORM

OPERATING AGREEMENT

DATE: *

PARTIES: *, *, and *

RECITAL:

The parties to this agreement (the "Members") are entering into this agreement for the purpose of forming a limited liability company under the Limited Liability Company Act of the state of * (the "Act").

AGREEMENTS:

1.1 Name. The name of this limited liability company (the "Company") is *.

1.2 Articles of Organization. Articles of organization for the Company were filed with the Secretary of State for the state of * on *.

1.3 Duration. The Company will exist until dissolved as provided in this agreement.

1.4 Principal Office. The Company's principal office will initially be at *, but it may be relocated by the Members at any time.

1.5 Designated Office and Agent for Service of Process. The Company's initial designated office will be at *, and the name of its initial agent for service of process at that address will be *. The Company's designated office and its agent for service of process may only be changed by filing a notice of the change with the Secretary of State of the state in which the articles of organization of the Company were filed.

1.6 Purposes and Powers. The Company is formed for the purpose of engaging in the business of *. The Company has the power to do all things necessary, incident, or in furtherance of that business.

1.7 Title to Assets. Title to all assets of the Company will be held in the name of the Company. No Member has any right to the assets of the Company or any ownership interest in those assets except indirectly as a result of the Member's ownership of an interest in the Company. No Member has any right to partition any assets of the Company or any right to receive any specific assets on liquidation of the Company or on any other distribution from the Company.

2. MEMBERS, CONTRIBUTIONS AND INTERESTS

2.1 Initial Members. The names and addresses of the Members of the Company, the amounts of their initial capital contributions, and their initial Ownership Interests are:

Name and address	Contribution	Ownership Interest
*	$*	*%
*		
*		
*	$*	*%
*		
*		
*	$*	*%
*		
*		

The initial capital contribution of each Member will be paid to the Company, in cash promptly following the full execution of this agreement. Each Member's Ownership Interest at any time will be determined by the ratio of that Member's aggregate capital contributions to the aggregate capital contributions of all Members.

2.2 Initial Capital Contributions. The initial capital contributions of * and * must be paid to the Company, in cash, immediately after all parties have signed this agreement. The initial capital contribution of * must be made by *'s transferring the assets listed on the attached Exhibit A to the Company. The transfer of the assets must be made immediately after all parties have signed this agreement by *'s executing and delivering to the Company such documents as may be necessary to transfer the assets listed on the attached Exhibit A to the Company free and clear of all liens and encumbrances. The transfer documents must include warranties of title and good right to transfer.

2.3 Additional Members. Except as otherwise provided in the section of this agreement relating to substitution, additional Members of the Company may be admitted only with the consent of all Members.

2.4 Additional Contributions. Except as otherwise provided in the Act, no Member is required to contribute additional capital to the Company. Additional capital contributions to the Company may be made by the Members only with the Members' unanimous approval. If the Members approve additional capital contributions, the Members must set a maximum amount for such contributions that will be accepted from the Members. Each Member will then have the right, but not the obligation, to contribute a pro rata share of the maximum based on the Member's Ownership Interest. If any Member elects to contribute less than the Member's pro rata share, the other Members may contribute the difference on a pro rata basis in accordance with their Ownership Interests or on any other basis they may agree on.

2.5 No Interest on Capital Contributions. No interest will be paid on capital contributions.

2.6 Capital Accounts. An individual capital account must be maintained for each Member. A Member's capital account will be credited with all capital contributions made by the Member and with all income and gain (including any income exempt from federal income tax) allocated to the Member. A Member's capital account will be charged with the amount of all distributions made to the Member and with all losses and deductions (including deductions attributable to tax-exempt income) allocated to the Member. Members' capital accounts must be maintained in accordance with the federal income tax accounting principles prescribed in Treasury Regulations §1.704-1(b)(2)(iv).

3. ALLOCATION OF PROFITS AND LOSSES

3.1 Determination. The net profit or net loss of the Company for each fiscal year will be determined according to the accounting principles employed in the preparation of the Company's federal income tax information return for that fiscal year. In computing net profit or net loss for purposes of allocation among the Members, no special provision will be made for tax-exempt or partially tax-exempt income of the Company, and all items of the Company's income, gain, loss, or deduction required to be separately stated under IRC §703(a) will be included in the net profit or net loss of the Company.

3.2 Allocation of Net Profits and Net Losses. The net profit or net loss of the Company for a fiscal year will be allocated among the Members in proportion to their Ownership Interests.

3.3 Allocations Solely for Tax Purposes. In accordance with IRC §704(c) and the corresponding regulations, income, gain, loss, and deduction with respect to any property contributed to the capital of the Company must be allocated among the Members, solely for income tax purposes, so as to take into account any variation between the adjusted basis of the property for federal income tax purposes in the hands of the Company and the agreed value of the property as set forth in this agreement, or in any document entered into at the time an additional contribution is made to the Company. Any elections or other decisions relating to the allocations to be made under this section will be made by action of the Members. The allocations to be made under this section are solely for purposes of federal, state, and local income taxes and will not affect, or in any way be taken into account in computing, any Member's capital account, allocable share of the net profits and net losses of the Company, or right to distributions.

3.4 Prorates. If a Member has not been a Member during a full fiscal year of the Company, or if a Member's Ownership Interest in the Company changes during a fiscal year, the net profit or net loss for the year will be allocated to the Member based only on the period of time during which the Member was a Member or held a particular Ownership Interest. In determining a Member's share of the net profit or net loss for a fiscal year, the Members may allocate the net profit or net loss ratably on a daily basis using the Company's usual method of accounting. Alternatively, the Members may separate the Company's fiscal year into two or more segments and allocate the net profits or net losses for each segment among the persons who were Members, or who held particular Ownership Interests, during each segment based on their Ownership Interests during that segment.

4. DISTRIBUTIONS

4.1 Distributions to Pay Taxes. To enable the Members to pay taxes on income of the Company that is taxable to the Members, the Company must make cash distributions to the Members. During each fiscal year, the Company must distribute an amount equal to the product of (a) the highest aggregate rate of federal, state, and local income and self-employment tax imposed on the Company's income for that fiscal year (taking into account the deductibility of state and local income taxes for federal income tax purposes) allocated to any Member who was a Member for the full fiscal year times (b) the amount of the taxable income of the Company allocated to all Members for that fiscal year. Distributions must be paid at least quarterly during each fiscal year at times that coincide with the Members' payment of estimated taxes, and the amount of each distribution must be based on the anticipated taxable income of the Company for the fiscal year of the distribution and the anticipated tax rates of Members, as determined at the time the distribution is made. The Company's obligation to make distributions under this section is subject to the restrictions governing distributions under the Act.

4.2 Additional Distributions. Subject to the restrictions governing distributions under the Act, additional distributions of cash or property may be made from time to time by the Company to the Members, at such times and in such amounts as the Members determine.

4.3 Allocation of Distributions. All distributions to pay taxes and additional distributions must be made to Members in proportion to their Ownership Interests.

5. ADMINISTRATION OF COMPANY BUSINESS

5.1 Management. All Members have the right to participate in the management and conduct of the Company's business. Subject to the limitations imposed by this agreement or by action of the Members, each Member is an agent of the Company and has authority to bind the Company in the ordinary course of the Company's business.

5.2 Actions by Members. Except as otherwise provided in this agreement, all decisions requiring action of the Members or relating to the business or affairs of the Company will be decided by the affirmative vote or consent of Members holding a majority of the Ownership Interests. Members may act with or without a meeting, and any Member may participate in any meeting by written proxy or by any means of communication reasonable under the circumstances.

5.3 Approval of Other Members Required. In addition to the other actions requiring unanimous Member approval under the terms of this agreement, no Member has authority to do any of the following without the prior written consent of all other Members:

5.3.1 To sell, lease, exchange, mortgage, pledge, or otherwise transfer or dispose of all or substantially all of the property or assets of the Company;

5.3.2 To merge the Company with any other entity;

5.3.3 To amend the articles of organization of the Company or this agreement;

5.3.4 To incur indebtedness by the Company other than in the ordinary course of business;

5.3.5 To authorize a transaction involving an actual or potential conflict of interest between a Member and the Company;

5.3.6 To change the nature of the business of the Company; or

5.3.7 To commence a voluntary bankruptcy case for the Company.

5.4 Devotion of Time; Outside Activities. Each of the Members must devote so much time and attention to the business of the Company as the Members agree is appropriate. Members may engage in business and investment activities outside the Company, and neither the Company nor the other Members have any rights to the property, profits, or benefits of such activities. But no Member may, without the consent of all other Members, enter into any business or investment activity that is competitive with the business of the Company, or use any property or assets of the Company other than for the operation of the Company's business. For this purpose, the property and assets of the Company include, without limitation, information developed for the Company, opportunities offered to the Company, and other information or opportunities entrusted to a Member as a result of being a Member of the Company.

5.5 Compensation and Reimbursement. Members who render services to the Company are entitled to such compensation as may be agreed on by the Members from time to time. Any compensation paid to a Member for services rendered will be treated as an expense of the Company and a guaranteed payment within the meaning of IRC §707(c), and the amount of the compensation will not be charged against the share of profits of the Company that would otherwise be allocated to the Member. Members are also entitled to reimbursement from the Company for reasonable expenses incurred on behalf of the Company, including expenses incurred in the formation, dissolution, and liquidation of the Company.

5.6 Self Interest. A Member does not violate any duty or obligation to the Company merely as a result of engaging in conduct that furthers the interest of the Member. A Member may lend money or transact other business with the Company, and, in this case, the rights and obligations of the Member will be the same as those of a person who is not a Member, so long as the loan or other transaction has been approved or ratified by the Members. Unless otherwise provided by applicable law, a Member with a financial interest in the outcome of a particular action is nevertheless entitled to vote on such action.

6. ACCOUNTING AND RECORDS

6.1 Books of Account. The Members must keep such books and records relating to the operation of the Company as are appropriate and adequate for the Company's business and for the carrying out of this agreement. At a minimum, the following must be maintained at the principal office of the Company: (a) financial statements for the three most recent fiscal years; (b) federal, state, and local income tax returns for the three most recent fiscal years; (c) a register showing the current names and addresses of the Members; (d) a copy of the Company's articles of organization and any amendments thereto; (e) this agreement and any amendments thereto; (f) minutes of any meetings of

Members; and (g) consents to action by Members. Each Member will have access to all such books and records at all times.

6.2 Fiscal Year. The fiscal year of the Company will be the calendar year.

6.3 Accounting Reports. Within 90 days after the close of each fiscal year, the Company must deliver to each Member an unaudited report of the activities of the Company for the preceding fiscal year, including a copy of a balance sheet of the Company as of the end of the year and a profit and loss statement for the year.

6.4 Tax Returns. The Company must prepare and file on a timely basis all required federal, state, and local income tax and other tax returns. Within 90 days after the end of each fiscal year, the Company must deliver to each Member a Schedule K-1, showing the amounts of any distributions, contributions, income, gain, loss, deductions, or credits allocated to the Member during the fiscal year.

6.5 Tax Matters Partner. Anytime the Company has more than 10 Members, any Member is an entity other than an estate or a C corporation, or any Member is a nonresident alien individual, the Members must designate one of the Members as the tax matters partner of the Company in accordance with IRC §6231(a)(7) and keep such designation in effect at all times.

7. DISSOCIATION AND DISSOLUTION

7.1 Withdrawal. A Member may withdraw from the Company only after giving notice of withdrawal to the other Members at least 90 days prior to the effective date of the withdrawal.

7.2 Expulsion. A Member may be expelled from the Company by an affirmative vote of the Members holding a majority of the Ownership Interests held by Members other than the expelled Member if the expelled Member has been guilty of wrongful conduct that adversely and materially affects the business or affairs of the Company, or the expelled Member has willfully or persistently committed a material breach of the articles of organization of the Company or this agreement or has otherwise breached a duty owed to the Company or to the other Members to the extent that it is not reasonably practicable to carry on the business or affairs of the Company with the expelled Member. The right to expel a Member under the provisions of this section does not limit or adversely affect any right or power of the Company or the other Members to recover any damages from the expelled Member or to pursue other remedies permitted under applicable law or in equity. In addition to any other remedies, the Company or the other Members may offset any such damages against any amounts otherwise distributable or payable to the expelled Member.

7.3 Events of Dissolution. Except as otherwise provided in this agreement, the Company will dissolve on the earliest of the following events: (a) the death, incompetence, withdrawal, expulsion, bankruptcy, or dissolution of any Member; (b) approval of a dissolution of the Company by unanimous consent of the Members; or (c) at such time as the Company has no members.

7.4 Effect of Member's Dissociation. Within 120 days following the death, incompetence, withdrawal, expulsion, bankruptcy, or dissolution of a Member, the other Members (whether one or more) may elect to continue the Company by themselves or with others, and to cause the Company to purchase the interest of the dissociating Member pursuant to the provisions of the sections of this agreement relating to purchase price and payment for member's interest. Making the election is in the sole discretion of the other Members and requires the consent of other Members holding a majority of the Ownership Interests held by the other Members. Notice of the election must be given in writing to the dissociating Member or the dissociating Member's successor in interest promptly after the election is made. If the other Members do not so elect, the Company will be dissolved.

7.5 Purchase Price. If the other Members elect to cause the Company to purchase the interest of a dissociating Member [under the section of this agreement relating to effect of member's dissociation,] the purchase price of the dissociating Member's interest in the Company will be determined by agreement between the other Members (acting by vote) and the dissociating Member. If an agreement on the purchase price is not reached within 30 days following the election to purchase the interest of the dissociating Member, the interest must be valued by a third party appraiser selected by the other Members who is reasonably acceptable to the dissociating Member, and the purchase price will be the value determined by that appraisal. In appraising the interest to be purchased, the appraiser must determine the fair market value of the interest as of the date of the event of dissociation. In determining the value, the appraiser must consider the greater of the liquidation value of the Company or the value of the Company based on a sale of the Company as a going concern. The appraiser must also consider appropriate minority interest, lack of marketability, and other discounts. If the appraisal is not completed within 120 days following the election to purchase the interest of the dissociating Member, either the other Members or the dissociating Member may apply to a court of competent jurisdiction for the appointment of another appraiser, in which case the court-appointed appraiser must appraise the interest of the dissociating Member in accordance with the standards set forth in this section, and the purchase price will be the value determined by that appraisal.

7.6 Payment for Member's Interest. The purchase price for the interest of a Member purchased under the section of this agreement relating to effect of member's dissociation will be paid as follows:

7.6.1 The purchase price will bear interest from the date of the election of the other Members to purchase the dissociating Member's interest at the prime rate of interest in effect on the date of the election as quoted in The Wall Street Journal or, if that publication is not available, another reputable national publication selected by the other Members that is reasonably acceptable to the dissociating Member.

7.6.2 The purchase price will be payable in accordance with the terms of a promissory note of the Company providing for the payment of the principal amount in 60 equal monthly installments, including interest on the unpaid balance, with the first installment to be due one month after the date of closing and an additional installment to be due on the same day of each month thereafter until the promissory note is paid in full. The promissory note will bear interest from the date of the closing at the rate specified in the preceding subsection. The promissory note must provide that if any installment is not paid when due, the holder may declare the entire remaining balance, together with all accrued interest, immediately due and payable. Partial or complete prepayment of the remaining balance due under the promissory note will be permitted at any time without penalty, provided that any partial pre-payment will not affect the amount or regularity of payments coming due thereafter.

7.6.3 The purchase must be closed within 30 days following the determination of the purchase price. At the closing, the dissociating Member must sign and deliver to the Company a written assignment transferring the entire interest of the dissociating Member in the Company to the Company free and clear of all encumbrances. Such assignment must contain warranties of title and good right to transfer. At the closing, the Company must pay the accrued interest on the purchase price then due to the dissociating Member, and the Company must also deliver its promissory note to the dissociating Member. Each of the other Members must sign and deliver to the dissociating Member a security agreement granting a security interest to the disso-ciating Member in that percentage of the interest of each of the other Members in the Company equal to the Ownership Interest of the dissociating Member being purchased by the Company. The security agreement must be in a form reasonably acceptable to the attorney for the dissociating Member and will secure payment of the promissory note by the Company. The security agreement must provide that if there is a default in the payment of the promissory note by the Company and the security interest is foreclosed or the interest in the Company is retained by the secured party in satisfaction of the indebtedness, the interest may be transferred without the necessity of tendering the interest to the Company under the section of this agreement relating to tender of interest and the person acquiring the interest in the Company will be admitted as a member of the Company without further consent of the Members being required.

As an example of the operation of this provision, if the Ownership Interest of a dis-sociating Member was 25% and there are three other Members, each with an Own-ership Interest of 33-1/3% after the purchase of the dissociating Member's Ownership Interest by the Company, each of the other Members will be required to grant the dissociating Member a security interest in an Ownership Interest of 8-1/3%.

7.7 Effect of Purchase of Member's Interest. A dissociating Member will cease to be a Member when the other Members elect to cause the Company to purchase the disso-ciating Member's interest pursuant to the section of this agreement relating to effect of member's dissociation. After that, the dissociating Member will have no rights as a Member in the Company, except the right to have the dissociating Member's interest purchased in accordance with the terms of this agreement.

7.8 Successor in Interest. For purposes of this section relating to dissociation and dis-solution, the term "dissociating Member" includes the dissociating Member's successor in interest.

8. WINDING UP AND LIQUIDATION

8.1 Liquidation on Dissolution. Following the dissolution of the Company, the Mem-bers must wind up the affairs of the Company unless the dissolution results from the dissociation of a Member and the other Members elect to continue the Company under the provisions of this agreement relating to effect of member's dissociation. If the affairs of the Company are wound up, a full account must be taken of the assets and liabilities of the Company, and the assets of the Company must be promptly liquidated. Following liquidation of the assets of the Company, the proceeds must be applied and distributed in the following order of priority:

8.1.1 To creditors of the Company in satisfaction of liabilities and obligations of the Company, including, to the extent permitted by law, liabilities and obligations owed to Members as creditors (except liabilities for unpaid distributions);

8.1.2 To any reserves set up for contingent or unliquidated liabilities or obligations of the Company deemed reasonably necessary by the Members, which reserves may be paid over to an escrow agent by the Members to be held by such escrow agent for disbursement in satisfaction of the liabilities and obligations of the Company, with any excess being distributed to the Members as provided in the following subsection; and

8.1.3 To Members in proportion to the positive balances of their capital accounts, after taking into account all adjustments made to capital accounts for the fiscal year during which the distributions to Members are made.

8.2 Distribution of Property in Kind. With the unanimous approval of the Members, property of the Company may be distributed in kind in the process of winding up and liquidation. Any property distributed in kind must be valued and treated for the Company's accounting purposes (and not tax purposes) as though the property distributed had been sold at fair market value on the date of distribution, as provided in Treasury Regulations §1.704-1(b)(2)(iv)(e)(1). The difference between the fair market value of the property and its adjusted tax basis will, solely for the Company's accounting purposes and to adjust the Members' capital accounts, be treated as a gain or loss on the sale of the property and will be credited or charged to the Members' capital accounts in the manner specified in the section of this agreement relating to capital accounts.

8.3 Negative Capital Accounts. If any Member has a negative balance in the Member's capital account on liquidation of the Company, the Member will have no obligation to make any contribution to the capital of the Company to make up the deficit, and the deficit will not be considered a debt owed to the Company or any other person for any purpose.

9. TRANSFER OF MEMBERS' INTERESTS

9.1 General Restrictions. No Member may transfer all or any part of such Member's interest as a member of the Company except as permitted in this agreement. Any purported transfer of an interest or a part of an interest in violation of the terms of this agreement will be null and void and of no effect. For purposes of this section a "transfer" includes a sale, exchange, pledge, or other disposition voluntarily or by operation of law.

9.2 Permitted Transfers. A Member may transfer all or a part of the Member's interest in the Company with the prior written consent of all other Members. If the other Members do not consent to a particular transfer, the Member may transfer all or a part of the Member's interest if the interest or part has been tendered for sale to the Company in accordance with the section of this agreement relating to tender of interest, the tender has not been accepted within the time limit set forth in that section, the transfer is made to the transferee named in the notice of tender within 180 days after the notice of tender is effective, and the transfer is at a price and on terms no more favorable to the transferee than those set forth in the notice of tender.

9.3 Tender of Interest. If a Member wishes to transfer all or part of the Member's interest in the Company and the other Members do not consent, the interest or the part to be transferred must be tendered to the Company by giving written notice of such tender to the Company. The notice must contain the name and address of the proposed transferee, the price to be paid by the proposed transferee for the interest, if any, and the terms of the proposed transfer. If a Member's interest is transferred by operation of law, the successor in interest to the transferring Member may give the required notice of tender to the Company at any time following the transfer, and the successor in interest will be deemed to have given the notice of tender at the time any other Member gives notice to the successor in interest and to all other Members of the failure to give the notice of tender. Within 30 days after a notice of tender is given, the other Members may accept the tender on behalf of the Company and have the Company purchase the interest tendered for the lesser of the price set forth in the notice of tender (if the proposed transfer is to be by sale) or the price applicable to the purchase of a Member's interest pursuant to the section of this agreement relating to the effect of member's dissociation. The tender must be accepted on behalf of the Company by giving notice of acceptance to the transferring Member or the transferring Members successor in interest. The purchase may, at the option of the other Members, be on the terms set forth in the notice of tender, if any, or the terms set forth in the section of this agreement relating to payment for member's interest. For purposes of those provisions, the date of the acceptance of tender will be deemed to be the date on which the other Members elected to purchase the interest of a dissociating Member.

9.4 Effect of Tender. The Member tendering an interest will cease to be a Member with respect to the tendered interest when the tender is accepted by the Company. Thereafter, the Member tendering the interest will have no rights as a Member in the Company, except the right to have the tendered interest purchased in accordance with the terms of this agreement.

9.5 Substitution. If the interest of a Member is transferred, the transferee of the interest may be admitted as a Member of the Company if the transferee executes and delivers to the Company a written agreement to be bound by all of the terms and provisions of this agreement. But the transferee is entitled to be admitted as a Member only if all of the other Members consent to the admission of the transferee as a Member, and this consent may be withheld reasonably or unreasonably. If a Member who is the only member of the Company transfers the Member's entire interest, the transferee will be admitted as a Member of the Company effective on the transfer without the requirement of an agreement to be bound by this agreement or consent. If the transferee is not admitted as a Member, the transferee will have the right only to receive, to the extent assigned, the distributions from the Company to which the transferor would be entitled. Such transferee will not have the right to exercise the rights of a Member, including, without limitation, the right to vote or inspect or obtain records of the Company.

10. INDEMNIFICATION AND LIABILITY LIMITATION

10.1 Indemnification. Except as otherwise provided in this section, the Company must indemnify each of the Members to the fullest extent permitted under the law of the state in which the Company's articles of organization have been filed, as the same exists or may be amended in the future, against all liability, loss, and costs (including, without limitation, attorneys' fees) incurred or suffered by the Member by reason of or arising from the fact that the Member is or was a member of the Company, or is or was serving at the request of the Company as a manager, member, director, officer, partner, trustee, employee, or agent of another foreign or domestic limited liability company, corporation, partnership, joint venture, trust, benefit plan, or other enterprise. The Company may, by action of the Members, provide indemnification to employees and agents of the Company who are not Members. The indemnification provided in this section does not supercede any other rights of any person to indemnification under any statute, agreement, resolution of Members, contract, or otherwise. But despite any other provision of this agreement, the Company has no obligation to indemnify a Member for:

10.1.1 Any breach of the Member's duty of loyalty to the Company;

10.1.2 Acts or omissions not in good faith that involve intentional misconduct or a knowing violation of law;

10.1.3 Any unlawful distribution under the Act; or

10.1.4 Any transaction in which the Member derives improper personal benefit.

10.2 Limitation of Liability. No Member of the Company is liable to the Company or to the other Members for monetary damages resulting from the Member's conduct as a Member except to the extent that the Act, as it now exists or may be amended in the future, prohibits the elimination or limitation of liability of members of limited liability companies. No repeal or amendment of this section or of the Act will adversely affect any right or protection of a Member for actions or omissions prior to the repeal or amendment.

11. MISCELLANEOUS PROVISIONS

11.1 Amendment. The Members may amend or repeal all or part of this agreement by unanimous written agreement. This agreement may not be amended or repealed by oral agreement of the Members.

11.2 Binding Effect. The provisions of this agreement will be binding on and will inure to the benefit of the heirs, personal representatives, successors, and assigns of the

Members. But this section may not be construed as a modification of any restriction on transfer set forth in this agreement.

11.3 Notice. Except as otherwise provided in other sections of this agreement, any notice or other communication required or permitted to be given under this agreement must be in writing and must be mailed by certified mail, return receipt requested, with postage prepaid. Notices addressed to a Member must be addressed to the Member's address listed in the section of this agreement relating to initial members, or if there is no such address listed for a Member, the address of the Member shown on the records of the Company. Notices addressed to the Company must be addressed to its principal office. The address of a Member or the Company to which notices or other communications are to be mailed may be changed from time to time by the Member's or the Company's giving written notice to the other Members and the Company. All notices and other communications will be deemed to be given at the expiration of three days after the date of mailing.

11.4 Litigation Expense. If any legal proceeding is commenced for the purpose of interpreting or enforcing any provision of this agreement, including any proceeding in the United States Bankruptcy Court, the prevailing party in such proceeding will be entitled to recover a reasonable attorney's fee in such proceeding, or any appeal thereof, to be set by the court without the necessity of hearing testimony or receiving evidence, in addition to the costs and disbursements allowed by law.

11.5 Additional Documents. Each Member must execute such additional documents and take such actions as are reasonably requested by the other Members in order to complete or confirm the transactions contemplated by this agreement.

11.6 Counterparts. This agreement may be executed in two or more counterparts, which together will constitute one agreement.

11.7 Governing Law. This agreement will be governed by the law of the state in which the articles of organization of the Company have been filed.

11.8 Severability. If any provision of this agreement is invalid or unenforceable, it will not affect the remaining provisions.

11.9 Third-Party Beneficiaries. The provisions of this agreement are intended solely for the benefit of the Members and create no rights or obligations enforceable by any third party, including any creditor of the Company, except as otherwise provided by applicable law.

11.10 Authority. Each individual executing this agreement on behalf of a corporation or other entity warrants that he or she is authorized to do so and that this agreement constitutes a legally binding obligation of the corporation or other entity that the individual represents.

11.11 Counsel. This agreement has been drafted by * (the "Attorney"), who represents * in connection with the creation of the Company. * and * each understand that the Attorney can represent only one party in connection with this matter, that the Attorney represents * and does not represent them, and that they have been advised by the

Attorney that they should retain attorneys of their own choice in connection with this matter.

*_____   *_____

*_____

FORM 2.3 COMMENTARY

Operating Agreement for Member-Managed LLC with Straight-Up Allocations

This is a basic form of operating agreement for a member managed limited liability company. The form is based on a partnership model of management and operation and is appropriate for use if there are a limited number of members of the LLC, all of whom are actively involved in the business. The form is designed to be used in a situation in which each member of the LLC will contribute money or property in an amount proportionate to the members share of the profits and losses, and no member will contribute services for his or her interest.

Since state LLC statutes vary, the applicable state LLC statute should always be consulted to verify the appropriateness of the provisions contained in this form. In some cases, modifications of the provisions of the form will be necessary.

The following comments on the provisions contained in the form are designed to provide further guidance.

1. FORMATION

1.1 Name. The name of the LLC is to be inserted in this section. State LLC statutes typically require that the name contain the term "limited liability company" or an abbreviation of the term. In addition, the name generally may not be the same as, or deceptively similar to, the name of any LLC, corporation, or limited partnership, or limited liability partnership that is organized under the law of the state or is qualified to transact business in the state.

1.2 Articles of Organization. The date of filing of the articles of organization for the LLC is to be inserted in this section. If the operating agreement is being signed before the articles of organization are filed, this section should be modified to so indicate. In that case, it is important to include language prohibiting the LLC from engaging in business before the articles are filed.

1.3 Duration. This section assumes that the LLC will continue until the occurrence of an event causing its dissolution. If the LLC is to exist only for a specified period of time, as may be the case if the LLC is formed as a joint venture to complete a single project, this section will need to be modified to so indicate. The limited duration should also be set forth in the articles of organization. If the LLC has a limited duration, Section 7.3 of the operating agreement relating to the events of dissolution, will need to be modified to reflect the limited term.

1.4 Principal Office. The address of the LLC's principal office is to be inserted in this section. Since the principal office is typically the place where the applicable state LLC statute requires the books and records to be maintained, this provision should identify the location of the business office of the LLC rather than the location where most of the LLC's operations are conducted, if those locations are different.

1.5 Designated Office and Agent for Service of Process. This section specifies the location of the LLC's designated office and the identity of its agent for service of process. The agent for service of process is called a registered agent in many states. This section reminds the members that the designated office and agent for service of process can only be changed by a state filing.

1.6 Purposes and Powers. The business of the LLC is to be inserted in this section. While it is possible to indicate that the LLC is authorized to engage in all businesses that may be lawfully engaged in by an LLC, this is ordinarily undesirable in the context of an LLC with more than one member because the members have the authority to act for the LLC in the ordinary course of its business, and unless the business is described with particularity, the authority of the members may be extremely broad.

1.7 Title to Assets. The LLC is a separate entity that owns its own assets. Failure to maintain a separation between the LLC's assets and those of the members might provide a court with justification to hold the members personally liable for liabilities and obligations of the LLC under the doctrine of piercing the corporate veil. This section also reminds members that they own interests in the LLC, not the assets of the LLC.

2. MEMBERS, CONTRIBUTIONS AND INTERESTS

2.1 Initial Members. It is desirable to include the names and addresses of the members and the amounts of their contributions in the operating agreement because many LLC statutes require this information to be maintained as part of the LLC's books and records at its principal place of business. In addition, it is desirable to document the fact that the LLC is adequately capitalized to forestall possible attacks on the limited liability of members.

If the names or addresses of all members, or the amounts of their contributions, are not known at the time the operating agreement is prepared, this information can be moved to an exhibit to facilitate its completion at the time the operating agreement is signed.

This form has been prepared for an LLC in which all members make capital contributions that are proportionate to their profit and loss sharing ratios a so-called "straight up" arrangement. For example, if there are three members, each member will contribute one-third of the capital and will be entitled to one-third of the profits and losses. If any member's capital contribution is disproportionate to his or her profit and loss percentage, because, for example, the member is contributing past or future services, there will be a special allocation of profits and losses for federal income tax purposes. In this case, the operating agreement should contain provisions supporting the special allocation that are not included in this form.

2.2 Initial Capital Contributions. This form provides that one member is contributing property. The agreed value of the property should be inserted in this section as the dollar value of the member's contribution. The agreed value will be used to establish the member's capital account, which will affect the amount the contributing member is entitled to receive on liquidation of the LLC. If the property is contributed to the LLC in a tax-free exchange under IRC §721, the member's tax basis in his or her interest and the LLC's tax basis of the contributed property will both be based on the member's adjusted tax basis in the property at the time of the contribution under IRC §§722 and 723. If the LLC's tax basis in the contributed property is different from its agreed value, special allocations of depreciation, depletion, gain, and loss must be made with respect to the contributed property for federal income tax purposes under IRC §704(c)(1). Provision is made for these allocations in Section 3.3 of the operating agreement.

2.3 Additional Members. Since this member managed LLC functions like a partnership, members have a strong interest in being able to approve the admission of new members. New members will have the right to actively participate in the management of the LLC and will have authority to act on behalf of the LLC. In addition, the admission of new members will affect existing members' ownership interests, and therefore their profit and loss sharing ratios. In view of the members' strong interest, this provision requires approval of all members for the admission of new members.

2.4 Additional Contributions. The issue of how to address additional capital needs is often knotty. It can be difficult to anticipate the capital needs of a business, and members may not have the resources or desire to commit substantial capital in addition to their initial contributions. At the same time, if members' profit and loss sharing ratios depend on their capital contributions, additional capital contributions can change the members' respective profit and loss shares, so members may be reluctant to allow others to make capital contributions.

This form provides that additional capital contributions can be made only if all members agree. If the members so agree, the members have the right to make any additional capital contributions in proportion to their initial capital contributions, but they are not required to do so. If any member does not make his or her proportionate additional contribution, the others may make the contribution and increase their percentage ownership interests.

2.5 No Interest on Capital Contributions. Ordinarily, interest is not paid on capital accounts because capital accounts represent equity investments in the LLC. In some situations where one member contributes capital and another contributes services or expertise, the member contributing capital is entitled to a preferred return on the member's contribution. A number of additional provisions, including provisions supporting special allocations, are required in an LLC's operating agreement if one or more members will receive a preferred return.

2.6 Capital Accounts. This provision requires the members' capital accounts to be maintained in accordance with the regulations under IRC §704(b). So maintaining capital accounts is a prerequisite to the recognition of any special allocation of income, gain, loss, deduction, or credit provided for in the operating agreement for federal income tax purposes. But requiring that capital accounts be maintained in accordance with Treasury Regulations is desirable even if special allocations are not contemplated at the outset because special allocations may occur in the future, for example as the result of disproportionate distributions made to members. Moreover, the capital account maintenance rules of the Treasury Regulations are consistent with the partnership accounting rules of general application.

3. ALLOCATION OF PROFITS AND LOSSES

3.1 Determination. The form assumes that the LLC will be taxed as a partnership for federal income tax purposes in accordance with the default rule under Treasury Regulations §301.7701-3. This section defines profits and losses in income tax terms and provides for inclusion of tax-exempt income and separately stated items in the calculation. This section lumps all items of the LLC's income, gain, loss, and deduction together, in order to determine a net profit or net loss figure, and the net profit or net loss is then allocated between members in accordance with their ownership interests under Section 3.2 of the operating agreement. This lumping is used only for allocation purposes. For purposes of preparing the LLC's partnership income tax return and the K-1s for each member, the items of income, gain, loss, and deduction will be reported separately, and tax-exempt income will be recognized as such.

3.2 Allocation of Net Profits and Net Losses. Net profits and net losses are allocated among the members based on their ownership interests, which are defined in Section 2.1 of the operating agreement based on the members' proportionate capital contributions. If profits and losses are to be allocated on some other basis, such as percentages that do not reflect the members' proportionate capital contributions, the result will be a special allocation for federal income tax purposes. If a special allocation is made, a number of additional provisions need to be included in the operating agreement to support the special allocation.

3.3 Allocations Solely for Tax Purposes. IRC §704(c)(1) requires that tax items, such as depreciation and gain, on property contributed to the LLC be allocated between the members so as to take into account the difference between the agreed value of the property for purposes of establishing capital accounts and the adjusted basis of the property for income tax purposes. Under the regulations, several alternative methods are available to make this allocation, and this section provides that the allocation method to be used by the LLC is to be selected by vote of the members. The allocation method chosen can have a material impact on the members' income taxes. Accordingly, if property contributions will be substantial and there is a large difference between agreed value and adjusted basis, the members may want to consult with their tax advisors and agree in advance about how the required allocations are to be made. Any such advance agreement should be reflected in this section of the operating agreement.

3.4 Prorates. If ownership interests change in midyear, as the result of a transfer of a member's interest, admission of a new member, or redemption of a member's interest, profits and losses must be allocated for the year of the ownership change under IRC §706(d)(1) and the regulations. This provision seeks to maintain maximum flexibility in making this allocation, and allows it to be made by either closing the LLC's books on the date of the ownership change or by prorating the gain or loss for the year of the ownership change.

4. DISTRIBUTIONS

4.1 Distributions to Pay Taxes. LLC members' profit and loss allocations are not the same as their rights to distributions. Members are taxed on their allocable share of the LLC's profits whether or not any of the profits are distributed to them. This section is designed to insure that the members receive enough by way of distributions to pay the taxes on their allocated shares of the LLC's profits. Since members' tax rates may vary, the amount of the required distribution is computed based on the rate of the member with the highest current tax rate.

The distributions are made to members in proportion to their ownership interests as provided in Section 4.3 of the operating agreement. The result is that some members may receive more than the amount required to pay their taxes. While distributions could be based on each member's needs rather than the member's ownership interest, the result would be to cause capital accounts to be out of balance with ownership interests, which would, in turn result in an allocation of profits and losses based on ownership interests being special allocations. In this basic form of agreement, this complexity is avoided by requiring all distributions to be made in proportion to ownership interests.

All distributions, including distributions to pay taxes, are subject to restrictions imposed by the applicable state LLC statute. Such statutes typically prohibit distributions that would render the LLC insolvent and may also prohibit distributions that would deprive members of their preferential rights to liquidating distributions. The latter prohibition may, for example, preclude distributions that create disproportionate negative balances in members' capital accounts.

4.2 Additional Distributions. This section permits additional distributions to be made on a majority vote of the members. Such a provision is generally appropriate for an LLC in which all members are active participants. If some members are passive investors, they may want the operating agreement to require the LLC to distribute excess cash not needed for the operations of the LLC.

4.3 Allocation of Distributions. In this basic form of operating agreement, with straight-up allocations, all distributions are made in proportion to ownership interests. This maintains parity between the members' capital accounts. If some other allocation scheme is desired, special allocations will result, in which case it will be necessary to use an operating agreement form with provisions supporting special allocations.

5. ADMINISTRATION OF COMPANY BUSINESS

5.1 Management. This operating agreement is based on a partnership model. All members have the right to participate in management of the LLC, and all have authority to act for the LLC in its ordinary course of business.

5.2 Actions by Members. Members' voting rights are proportionate to their ownership interests under the terms of this section. Some LLC statutes adopt a one member, one vote rule, which is ordinarily consistent with members' expectations if all members make equal capital contributions and share profits and losses equally. If capital contributions and profit and loss sharing percentages are unequal, voting by ownership interests, as is provided for in this section, may be more consistent with the members' expectations.

In keeping with the partnership model on which this form is based, the provisions of this section relating to member meetings and actions create a very informal structure. This provision can be modified to create a more formal structure for meetings and decision making if the members so desire.

5.3 Approval of Other Members Required. This section lists those actions that require the consent of all members. Consistent with a partnership model, these actions, which are outside the ordinary course of the LLC's business, require unanimous written consent of the members. The list of actions requiring approval of the other members can be modified as the members desire, and consideration should be given to the requirements of applicable state law for actions outside the ordinary course of business.

5.4 Devotion of Time; Outside Activities. This provision contemplates that members will have outside business activities but prohibits members from competing with the LLC. In LLCs engaged in personal service businesses, it is common to require that members devote their full time and attention to the LLC's affairs.

5.5 Compensation and Reimbursement. If one or more members will be performing significant services for the LLC and one or more others will perform few if any services, salaries can be used to compensate the members providing services without changing profit and loss sharing ratios. This section permits such an arrangement to be made.

5.6 Self Interest. This section permits members to engage in transactions with the LLC, subject to approval by the other members. If specific transactions are contemplated, such as use of affiliates of members to manage real property owned by the LLC, such specific transactions might be addressed in the operating agreement.

6. ACCOUNTING AND RECORDS

6.1 Books of Account. The specific requirements of the applicable state LLC statute should be consulted in drafting this provision. The records that this section requires the LLC to maintain at its principal office are those typically required by LLC statutes, but these statutes do vary.

6.2 Fiscal Year. Most LLCs with individuals as members will want to use a calendar year as its fiscal year. Under the general rule applicable to entities taxed as partnerships, the entity's tax year must be the same as that of a majority in interest of its members. If a majority of the members are calendar year taxpayers, a fiscal year ending September 30 or later can be elected, but a deposit must be made with the IRS in connection with the election that approximates the tax that will be deferred.

6.3 Accounting Reports. If there are two or more members of an LLC, it is important that financial statements be prepared so that all members can monitor the activities of the LLC. If one or more members are not active in management, more elaborate provisions for budgets and more frequent financial reports may be appropriate.

6.4 Tax Returns. LLCs are ordinarily taxed as partnerships, and a calendar year partnership must file a partnership information income tax return by April 15 following the end of each tax year. Partnership income and loss pass through to the partners to be reported on the members' tax returns. Accordingly, LLC members must each be provided a Form K-1 indicating the amount of the LLC's income, gain, loss, deduction, and credit to be reported on the member's income tax return.

6.5 Tax Matters partner. If there are 10 or more members of the LLC, or if any member of the LLC is a nonresident alien individual or an entity other than an estate or C corporation, the LLC will be subject to entity level audits for federal income tax purposes under IRC §6221. In this case, a tax matters partner will have authority to represent the LLC in dealing with the Internal Revenue Service. This section provides for the designation of a tax matters partner for the LLC by the members. If a tax matters partner is not designated, one will be selected under the default rules of the regulations under IRC §6231(c)(7).

7. DISSOCIATION AND DISSOLUTION

7.1 Withdrawal. This form is based on a partnership model and permits members to withdraw on 90 days' notice. If the withdrawal of a member may impair the LLC's ability to operate, as may occur for example during its formative years, withdrawal might be prohibited for a period of time or the notice period might be extended.

7.2 Expulsion. Although the remedy is not used often, expulsion of members is an issue that should be addressed in the operating agreement because the alternative may be costly and time consuming litigation to remove a troublesome member.

7.3 Events of Dissolution. This operating agreement follows a partnership model and provides that the LLC will dissolve on the occurrence of certain events. The specified events are those that cause the dissolution of a partnership — death, incompetence, withdrawal, expulsion, bankruptcy, or dissolution of a member, or consent of the members. A dissolution also results if the LLC has no members. In Massachusetts, where an LLC must have at least two members, this latter provision can be modified to provide that dissolution results if the LLC has less than two members.

Dissolution by consent of members requires unanimous approval. This could be changed to require only majority approval, but if less than all of the members want to liquidate their interests in the LLC, they can accomplish this by withdrawing.

7.4 Effect of Member's Dissociation. If an event of dissociation of a member occurs, the other members have the right, under the terms of this section, to continue the LLC by causing the LLC to purchase the interest of the dissociated member. It is possible to draft this provision to permit the other members, rather than the LLC, to purchase the interest of the dissociated member. Allowing the LLC to make the purchase is ordinarily preferable, however, because the LLC typically will be the source of the cash to make the purchase, and the LLC may be in a position to deduct interest paid in connection with an installment purchase, whereas the members may not. In addition, a redemption by the LLC will not be counted for purposes of determining whether there has been a sale or exchange of 50 percent or more of the ownership interests in a 12-month period, triggering a termination of the LLC for income tax purposes under IRC §708. In the corporate context, a cross purchase of stock may be advantageous because the purchasing shareholders receive a stepped up basis, whereas there is no basis step up if the corporation redeems stock. But in the case of an LLC taxed as a partnership, the basis step up will be available under IRC §734 even if the LLC makes the purchase, so long as an IRC §754 election is made or is in effect.

7.5 Purchase Price. This section provides that if the interest of a dissociated member is to be purchased, the value of the interest is to be determined by the parties at the time of the purchase. If the parties are unable to agree on a price, the price will be the fair market value of the interest as determined by an appraisal conducted by a single appraiser. There are other ways to determine the purchase price of a member's interest for this purpose, including use of a stipulated value and determination of the price based on a formula.

This section provides that minority interest and lack of marketability discounts are to be used in valuing a member's interest. In some cases, the members may prefer that these discounts not be used, and this section can be modified to so provide.

7.6 Payment for Member's Interest. This section specifies the terms of payment for the interest of a dissociated member if the other members elect to have the LLC purchase the member's interest. The provision provides for payment of the purchase price over five years in monthly installments with no down payment. These terms can be modified to suit the desires of the members.

The purchase price is to be secured with membership interests. Since the interest of the dissociating member is being redeemed and will no longer exist, the security is provided by the other members. Each of the other members is to pledge that percentage of his or her membership interest equal to the ownership interest of the dissociating member. This way, if the LLC defaults on the payment of the purchase price and the dissociating member reacquires an interest in the LLC, the dissociating member will wind up with the same percentage interest as was sold to the LLC.

7.7 Effect of Purchase of Member's Interest. If the interest of a dissociated member is purchased by the LLC, the member is considered to remain a member for income tax purposes under IRC §736 until the purchase price is paid in full. This provision makes it clear that the member does not remain a member for substantive law purposes.

8. WINDING UP AND LIQUIDATION

8.1 Liquidation on Dissolution. This section deals with the winding up of the business of the LLC and its liquidation following its dissolution. Questions are often raised about Subsection 8.1.3 of the operating agreement, which provides for the distribution of the remaining assets of the LLC in accordance with the capital accounts of members. If capital accounts are maintained in accordance with the Treasury Regulations referred to in Section 2.6 of the operating agreement, the amount available for distribution will always equal the amount in the members' capital accounts. Accordingly, it is not necessary to draft for the situations in which the amount available for distribution exceeds or falls short of the amount of the members' capital accounts.

8.2 Distribution of Property in Kind. This section permits property to be distributed in kind with member approval. Property distributed in kind is accounted for as if it were sold for its fair market value, but only for purposes of determining the interests of members, and not for purposes of computing the LLC's gain or loss on the liquidation.

8.3 Negative Capital Accounts. Members might have negative balances in their capital accounts on liquidation if the liabilities of the LLC exceed the value of its assets. In order to preserve the members' limited liability, this provision states that members have no obligation to make up negative balances in their capital accounts.

In general partnership agreements, it is common to require partners to make up negative balances in their capital accounts, particularly if special allocations are made because such a requirement gives the special allocations substantial economic effect for purposes of IRC §704(b). Such a provision has no impact on partners' liability for partnership debts and obligations because general partners are always personally liable for these items. Use of a negative capital account make up provision in an LLC operating agreement is inadvisable, however, because it may have the effect of creating personal liability of members for debts and obligations of the LLC.

9. TRANSFER OF MEMBERS' INTERESTS

9.1 General Restrictions. By statute, membership interests in an LLC are typically transferable, although the transferee may acquire only the transferor's economic rights and not the rights to participate in management or to inspect the LLC's records. This agreement seeks to restrict transfers and provides that transfers in violation of these restrictions do not need to be recognized by the LLC.

9.2 Permitted Transfers. An absolute prohibition on transfer of member interests may be unenforceable as an unreasonable restraint on alienation. Accordingly, this section permits transfers of members' interests if the other members have either consented to the transfer or declined to exercise a right of first refusal to acquire the interest.

In some situations, such as family owned LLCs, transfers to particular persons, such as other family members, are permitted, and this section can be modified to so provide. If transfers to particular persons are permitted, it is ordinarily desirable to modify Section

7.4 of the operating agreement to provide that the death of a member will not dissolve the LLC if the decedent's interest passes to persons to whom transfers are permitted.

This section assumes that all members are active participants in the affairs of the LLC and that the securities laws are not applicable to the transfer of members' interests. If the securities laws may be applicable, appropriate restrictions on transfer should be inserted.

9.3 Tender of Interest. This section provides the other members with an opportunity to cause the LLC to exercise a right of first refusal if a member desires to transfer his or her interest. This provision may be drafted to give the right of first refusal to the other members or to the LLC. But for the reasons discussed in connection with Section 7.4 of the operating agreement, allowing the LLC to make the purchase is ordinarily preferable.

9.4 Effect of Tender. This section makes it clear that a member whose interest is to be purchased in accordance with the right of first refusal ceases to be a member on the LLC's exercise of its option to purchase. As a result, the transferring member is not entitled to vote, participate in management, or receive distributions from the LLC after the option has been exercised.

9.5 Substitution. Consistent with the partnership model on which this form is based, the transferee of a member's interest is to be admitted as a substituted member in the place of the transferor only if all other members consent. If the transferee is not admitted as a member, the transferee obtains only the transferor's economic rights in the transferred interest. In a member managed LLC, all members have the right to participate in the management of the LLC and authority to act as agents of the LLC. Accordingly, each member has a strong interest in who the other members are, and this provision gives each member a veto power over the admission of new members.

The transferee is, however, admitted without consent if the entire interest of a sole member is transferred. This latter provision is designed to prevent a dissolution.

10. INDEMNIFICATION AND LIABILITY LIMITATION

10.1 Indemnification. This section provides that members are to be indemnified for any liability incurred as members of the LLC or in acting on behalf of the LLC, except in certain specified situations involving bad faith or breaches of clear duties.

10.2 Limitation of Liability. This section prevents members from being liable to the LLC or other members for actions taken as a member. The limitation on liability is consistent with members' limited liability to third parties under most LLC statutes.

11. MISCELLANEOUS PROVISIONS

11.1 Amendment. The operating agreement may be amended only by unanimous agreement of the members. This provision is consistent with a partnership model and protects the interests of minority members, whose rights might otherwise be subject to change without their consent.

11.2 Binding Effect. This agreement binds the successors in interest of the members and may, for example, require the successor in interest of a member to tender the interest for sale to the LLC under the buy-sell provisions of the operating agreement.

11.3 Notice. This section specifies the means by which notice is to be given to the members and the LLC.

11.4 Litigation Expense. This provision, which provides for the recovery of attorneys fees in any action involving this operating agreement, can be deleted at the option of the drafter. Some drafters prefer to substitute an arbitration provision.

11.5 Additional Documents. The members may need to sign additional documents to complete the organization of the LLC or to complete contributions to capital, and this section requires them to do so.

11.6 Counterparts. This provision permits the members to sign separate copies of the operating agreement.

11.7 Governing Law. The law controlling the organization and operation of an LLC is that of the state in which the LLC is organized.

11.8 Severability. If any provision of the operating agreement is declared invalid, the other provisions are not affected.

11.9 Third Party Beneficiaries. This provision seeks to prevent creditors of the LLC or of members from seeking to enforce the terms of the operating agreement.

11.10 Authority. This provision attests to the authority of any person signing on behalf of an entity that is a member. If all members of the LLC will be individuals, this section can be omitted.

11.11 Counsel. This provision seeks to address the conflict of interest issues that may be present if counsel for one member prepares the operating agreement. It can be omitted if the attorney drafting the operating agreement represents the LLC and has not represented any of the individual members in the past.

SAMPLE LOAN AGREEMENT

This **LOAN AND SECURITY AGREEMENT** (this "Agreement") dated March _____, 20____ between SILICON VALLEY BANK ("Bank") and FIBER COMMUNICATIONS CORPORATION ("Borrower"), provides the terms on which Bank will lend to Borrower and Borrower will repay Bank. The parties agree as follows:

1. ACCOUNTING AND OTHER TERMS

Accounting terms not defined in this Agreement will be construed following GAAP. Calculations and determinations must be made following GAAP. The term "financial statements" includes the notes and schedules. The terms "including" and "includes" always mean "including (or includes) without limitation" in this or any Loan Document. Capitalized terms in this Agreement shall have the meanings set forth in Section 13.

2. LOAN AND TERMS OF PAYMENT

2.1   Credit Extensions. Borrower will pay Bank the unpaid principal amount of all Credit Extensions and interest on the unpaid principal amount of the Credit Extensions in accordance with the terms and conditions hereof.

2.1.1   Equipment Advances.

(a)   Subject to the terms and conditions of this Agreement, Bank agrees to lend to Borrower, from time to time prior to the Commitment Termination Date, equipment advances (each an "Equipment Advance" and collectively the "Equipment Advances") in an aggregate amount not to exceed the Committed Equipment Line. When repaid, the Equipment Advances may not be re-borrowed. The proceeds of the Equipment Advances will be used solely to reimburse Borrower for the purchase of Eligible Equipment purchased on and after 90 days prior to the making of an Equipment Advance, provided, however, with respect to the first Equipment Advance hereunder *only* (and *only* if such Equipment Advance is made substantially concurrently with the execution of this Agreement), the proceeds of such Equipment Advance may be used to reimburse Borrower for the purchase of equipment purchased on and after November 1, 20____.

(b)   To obtain an Equipment Advance, Borrower will deliver to Bank a completed supplement in substantially the form attached as Exhibit C (the "Loan Supplement"), copies of invoices for the Financed Equipment, and such additional information as Bank may request, all at least five (5) Business Days before the proposed funding date (the "Funding Date"). On each Funding Date, Bank will specify in the Loan Supplement for each Equipment Advance, the Basic Rate, the Loan Factor, and the Payment Dates. If Borrower satisfies the conditions of each Equipment Advance specified herein, Bank will disburse such Equipment Advance by internal transfer to Borrower's deposit account with Bank. Each Equipment Advance may not exceed 100% of the Original Stated Cost of the proposed Financed Equipment. For purposes hereof, the minimum amount of each Equipment Advance is $50,000 and there shall be no more than one (1) Equipment Advance per month.

(c)   Bank's obligation to lend the undisbursed portion of the Committed Equipment Line will terminate if, in Bank's sole discretion, there has been a material adverse change in the general affairs, management, results of operation, condition (financial or otherwise) or the prospects of Borrower, whether or not arising from transactions in the ordinary course of business, or there has been any material adverse deviation by Borrower from the most recent business plan of Borrower presented to and accepted by Bank prior to the execution of this Agreement.

2.2   Interest Rate; Payments.

(a)   <u>Principal and Interest Payments On Payment Dates</u>. Borrower will repay each Equipment Advance on the terms provided in the Loan Supplement relating thereto. Borrower will make payments monthly of principal and accrued interest for each Equipment Advance (collectively, "Scheduled Payments") on the last Business Day of the month in which the Funding Date occurs with respect to such Equipment Advance and continuing thereafter during the Repayment Period on the last Business Day of each calendar month (each of such dates being referred to herein as a "Payment Date"), in an amount equal to the Loan Factor multiplied by the Loan Amount for such Equipment Advance. All unpaid principal and accrued and unpaid interest are due and payable in full on the last Payment Date with respect to such Equipment Advance. Payments received after 12:00 noon Pacific time are considered received at the opening of business on the next Business Day. An Equipment Advance may only be prepaid in accordance with the terms hereof.

(b)   <u>Interest Rate</u>. Borrower will pay interest on the Payment Dates (as described above) at the per annum rate of interest equal to the Basic Rate determined by Bank as of the Funding Date for each Equipment Advance in accordance with the definition of the Basic Rate. Any amounts outstanding during the continuance of an Event of Default shall bear interest at a per annum rate equal to the Basic Rate plus five percentage points (5%). If any change in the law increases Bank's expenses or decreases its return from the Equipment Advances, Borrower will pay Bank upon request the amount of such increase or decrease.

(c)   [Reserved]

(d)   <u>Prepayment Upon an Event of Loss</u>. If any Financed Equipment is subject to an Event of Loss and Borrower is required to or elects to prepay the Equipment Advance with respect to such Financed Equipment pursuant to Section 6.7, then such Equipment Advance shall be prepaid to the extent and in the manner provided in such Section.

(e)   <u>Mandatory Prepayment Upon an Acceleration</u>. If the Equipment Advances are accelerated following the occurrence of an Event of Default or otherwise (other than following an Event of Loss), then Borrower will immediately pay to Bank (i) all unpaid Scheduled Payments (including principal and interest) with respect to each Equipment Advance due prior to the date of prepayment, (ii) all remaining Scheduled Payments (including principal and interest unpaid) due after such date, (iii) all accrued unpaid interest, including the default rate of interest, to the date of the prepayment, but without duplication of any other payment item included herein; and (iv) all other sums, if any, that shall have become due and payable hereunder with respect to this Agreement.

(f)   Permitted Prepayment of Loans. If the Bank consents in writing, Borrower shall have the option to prepay some or all of the Equipment Advances (but in any event no repayment of a portion of any Equipment Advance shall be permitted) advanced by Bank under this Agreement, provided Borrower (i) provides written notice to Bank of its request to prepay the Equipment Advances at least thirty (30) days prior to such prepayment, (ii) Bank consents thereto, and (iii) Borrower pays, on the date of the prepayment (l) all unpaid Scheduled Payments (including principal and interest) with respect to each Equipment Advance due prior to the date of prepayment; (2) all remaining Scheduled Payments due after such date discounted to present value at 4%; (3) all other unpaid accrued interest to the date of the prepayment (but without duplication of any sum in item (1) hereof); and (4) all other sums, if any, that shall have become due and payable hereunder with respect to this Agreement.

2.3   Request to Debit. Bank may debit any of Borrower's deposit accounts for principal and interest payments or any amounts Borrower owes Bank when due. Bank will notify Borrower when it debits Borrower's accounts. These debits are not a set-off.

2.4   Fees. Borrower will pay to Bank:

(a)   Facility Fee. Borrower shall pay to Bank a fee of $15,000 concurrently herewith, which shall be in addition to interest and to all other amounts payable hereunder and which shall not be refundable.

(b)   Bank Expenses. All Bank Expenses (including reasonable attorneys' fees and expenses) incurred through and after the Closing Date when due.

2.5   Additional Costs. If any law or regulation increases Bank's costs or reduces its income for any loan, Borrower will pay the increase in cost or reduction in income or additional expense.

3.   CONDITIONS OF CREDIT EXTENSIONS

3.1   Conditions Precedent to Initial Credit Extension. Bank's obligation to make the initial Credit Extension is subject to the condition precedent that it receive the agreements, documents and fees it requires.

3.2   Conditions Precedent to all Credit Extensions. Bank's obligations to make each Credit Extension, including the initial Credit Extension, is subject to the following:

(a)   the satisfaction of the conditions set forth in Section 2.1.1 hereof with respect to the making of an Equipment Advance; and

(b)   the representations and warranties in Section 5 hereof must be materially true on the date of the submission of the Loan Supplement relating to the proposed Equipment Advances and on the effective date of each Credit Extension and no Event of Default may have occurred and be continuing, or result from the Credit Extension. Each Credit Extension is Borrower's representation and warranty on that date that the representations and warranties in Section 5 remain true.

4.   CREATION OF SECURITY INTEREST

4.1   Grant of Security Interest. Borrower grants Bank a continuing security interest in all presently existing and later acquired Collateral to secure all Obligations and performance of each of Borrower's duties under the Loan Documents. Any security interest will be a first priority security interest in the Collateral. If the Agreement is terminated, Bank's lien and security interest in the Collateral will continue until Borrower fully satisfies its Obligations.

5.   REPRESENTATIONS AND WARRANTIES

Borrower represents and warrants as follows:

5.1   Due Organization and Authorization. Each of Borrower and its Subsidiaries is duly existing and in good standing in its state of formation and qualified and licensed to do business in, and in good standing in, any state in which the conduct of its business or its ownership of property requires that it be qualified. The execution, delivery and performance of the Loan Documents have been duly authorized, and do not conflict with Borrower's formation documents, nor constitute an event of default under any material agreement by which Borrower is bound. Borrower is not in default under any agreement to which or by which it is bound in which the default could cause a Material Adverse Change.

5.2   Collateral. Borrower has good title to the Collateral, free of Liens except Permitted Liens. The Accounts are bona fide, existing obligations, and the service or property has been performed or delivered to the account debtor or its agent for immediate shipment to and unconditional acceptance by the account debtor. All Inventory is in all material respects of good and marketable quality, free from material defects.

5.3   Litigation. Except as shown in the Schedule, there are no actions or proceedings pending or, to Borrower's knowledge, threatened by or against Borrower or any Subsidiary of Borrower in which an adverse decision could cause a Material Adverse Change.

5.4   No Material Adverse Change in Financial Statements. All consolidated financial statements for Borrower and its Subsidiaries delivered to Bank fairly present in all material respects Borrower's consolidated financial condition and Borrower's consolidated results of operations. There has not been any material deterioration in Borrower's consolidated financial condition since the date of the most recent financial statements submitted to Bank.

5.5   Solvency. The fair salable value of Borrower's assets (including goodwill minus disposition costs) exceeds the fair value of its liabilities; the Borrower is not left with unreasonably small capital after the transactions in this Agreement; and Borrower is able to pay its debts (including trade debts) as they mature.

5.6   Regulatory Compliance. Borrower is not an "investment company" or a company "controlled" by an "investment company" under the Investment Company Act. Borrower is not engaged as one of its important activities in extending credit for margin stock (under Regulations T and U of the Federal Reserve Board of Governors). Borrower has complied with the Federal Fair Labor Standards Act. Borrower has not violated any laws, ordinances or rules, the violation of which could cause a Material Adverse Change. None of Borrower's or any of its Subsidiary's properties or assets has been used by Borrower or such Subsidiary or, to the best of Borrower's knowledge, by previous Persons, in disposing, producing, storing, treating, or transporting any hazardous substance other than by legally doing so. Each of Borrower and its Subsidiaries has timely filed all required tax returns and paid, or made adequate provision to pay, all material taxes. Each of Borrower and its Subsidiaries has obtained all consents, approvals and authorizations of, made all declarations or filings with, and given all notices to, all government authorities that are necessary to continue its business as currently conducted.

5.7   Subsidiaries. Borrower does not own any stock, partnership interest or other equity securities except for Permitted Investments.

5.8   Full Disclosure. No representation, warranty or other statement of Borrower in any certificate or written statement given to Bank contains any untrue statement of a material fact or omits to state a material fact necessary to make the statements contained in the certificates or statements not misleading.

6.   AFFIRMATIVE COVENANTS

Borrower will do all of the following:

6.1   Government Compliance. Borrower will maintain its corporate existence and good standing in its jurisdiction of incorporation and maintain qualification in each jurisdiction in which the failure to so qualify could have a material adverse effect on Borrower's business or operations. Borrower will cause each of its Subsidiaries to maintain such Subsidiary's corporate existence and good standing in its jurisdiction of incorporation and maintain qualification in each jurisdiction in which the failure to so qualify could have a material adverse effect on such Borrower's business or operations. Borrower will comply, and will cause each of its Subsidiaries to comply, with all laws, ordinances and regulations to which it is subject, the noncompliance with which could have a material adverse effect on Borrower's business or operations or cause a Material Adverse Change.

6.2   Financial Statements, Reports, Certificates.

(a)   Borrower will deliver to Bank: (i) as soon as available, but no later than 30 days after the last day of each month, a company prepared consolidated balance sheet and income statement covering Borrower's consolidated operations during the period, in a form acceptable to Bank and certified by a Responsible Officer; (ii) as soon as available, but no later than 120 days after the end of Borrower's fiscal year, commencing with the fiscal year ending December 31, 20____, audited consolidated financial statements prepared under GAAP, consistently applied, together with an unqualified opinion on the financial statements from an independent certified public accounting firm acceptable to Bank; (iii) a prompt report of any legal actions pending or threatened against Borrower or any Subsidiary that could result in damages or costs to Borrower or any

Subsidiary of $100,000 or more; and (iv) budgets, sales projections, operating plans or other financial information Bank requests.

(b)   Within 30 days after the last day of each month, Borrower will deliver to Bank with the monthly financial statements a Compliance Certificate signed by a Responsible Officer in the form of Exhibit D.

(c)   Bank has the right to audit the Collateral from time to time at Borrower's expense.

6.3   Inventory; Returns. Borrower will keep all Inventory in good and marketable condition, free from material defects. Returns and allowances between Borrower and its account debtors will follow Borrower's customary practices as they exist at the Closing Date. Borrower must promptly notify Bank of all returns, recoveries, disputes and claims that involve more than $50,000.

6.4   Taxes. Borrower will make, and cause each of its Subsidiaries to make, timely payment of all material federal, state, and local taxes or assessments and will deliver to Bank, on demand, appropriate certificates attesting to the payment.

6.5   Insurance. Borrower will keep its business and the Collateral insured for risks and in amounts, as Bank requests. Insurance policies will be in a form, with companies, and in amounts that are reasonably satisfactory to Bank. All property policies will have a lender's loss payable endorsement showing Bank as an additional loss payee and all liability policies will show the Bank as an additional insured and provide that the insurer must give Bank at least 20 days' notice before canceling its policy. At Bank's request, Borrower will deliver certified copies of policies and evidence of all premium payments. Without limitation of Section 6.7 (a) below, Borrower will keep its business and the Collateral insured for risks and in amounts standard for Borrower's industry, and as Bank may reasonably request. Insurance policies will be in a form, with companies, and in amounts that are satisfactory to Bank in Bank's reasonable discretion. All property policies will have a lender's loss payable endorsement showing Bank as an additional loss payee and all liability policies will show the Bank as an additional insured and provide that the insurer must give Bank at least 20 days' notice before canceling its policy. At Bank's request, Borrower will deliver certified copies of policies and evidence of all premium payments. Proceeds payable under any policy will, at Bank's option, be payable to Bank on account of the Obligations.

6.6   Primary Accounts. Subject to the Transition Provision (as defined below), Borrower will maintain its primary banking and investment account relationships with Bank, which relationships shall include Borrower maintaining deposit and investment account balances in accounts at or through Bank representing at least 85% of all such account balances of Borrower at any and all financial institutions. With respect to non-Silicon Valley Bank banking and investment accounts of Borrower, Borrower shall notify Bank in writing of all pertinent information relating thereto (including amounts, instrument numbers, maturities and applicable institutions) and Borrower shall update such information on a regular basis, if any changes occur or new accounts are opened, with its monthly reporting to the Bank pursuant to Section 6.2 hereof. Borrower hereby represents and warrants that the schedule relating to the foregoing delivered in connection with this Agreement and attached hereto as Schedule 6.6, is a complete and accurate listing of all bank and investment accounts at institutions other than the Bank (referred to herein as the "Other Accounts"). To the extent that Borrower would suffer a monetary penalty for terminating the Other Accounts in order to comply with the foregoing 85% covenant as of the date hereof, Borrower shall only be required to terminate and transfer to the Bank the balances in any such Other Accounts upon the current maturity thereof and thus comply with the foregoing 85% covenant at such time (the "Transition Provision").

6.7   Loss; Destruction; or Damage.

Borrower will bear the risk of the Financed Equipment being lost, stolen, destroyed, or damaged. If during the term of this Agreement any item of Financed Equipment is lost, stolen, destroyed, damaged beyond repair, rendered permanently unfit for use, or seized by a governmental authority for any reason for a period equal to at least the remainder of the term of this Agreement (an "Event of Loss"), then in each case, Borrower:

(a)   Prior to the occurrence of an Event of Default, at Borrower's option, will (i) pay to Bank on account of the Obligations all accrued interest to the date of the prepayment, plus all outstanding principal; or (ii) repair or replace any Financed Equipment subject to an Event of Loss provided the repaired or replaced Financed Equipment is of equal or like value to the Financed Equipment subject to an Event of Loss and provided further that Bank has a first priority perfected security interest in such repaired or replaced Financed Equipment.

(b)   During the continuance of an Event of Default, on or before the Payment Date after such Event of Loss for each such item of Financed Equipment subject to such Event of Loss, Borrower will, at Bank's option, pay to Bank an amount equal to the sum of: (i) all accrued and unpaid Scheduled Payments (with respect to such Equipment Advance related to the Event of Loss) due prior to the next such Payment Date, (ii) all regularly Scheduled Payments (including principal and interest) due after the date of such payment, plus (iii) all other sums, if any, that shall have become due and payable, including interest at the Default Rate with respect to any past due amounts.

(c)   On the date of receipt by Bank of the amount specified above with respect to each such item of Financed Equipment subject to an Event of Loss, this Agreement shall terminate as to such Financed Equipment. If any proceeds of insurance or awards received from governmental authorities are in excess of the amount owed under this Section, Bank shall promptly remit to Borrower the amount in excess of the amount owed to Bank.

6.8   Financial Covenant.
Borrower will maintain a ratio, determined as of any determination date from time to time, of: (i) the sum of Borrower's unrestricted cash and cash equivalents plus accounts receivable of Borrower to (ii) Adjusted Current Liabilities of at least 1.50 to 1.0. Borrower shall comply with the foregoing financial covenant at all times during the term of this Agreement and, at the request of Bank from time to time, Borrower shall provide evidence of compliance thereof.

6.9   Further Assurances.
Borrower will execute any further instruments and take further action as Bank requests to perfect or continue Bank's security interest in the Collateral or to effect the purposes of this Agreement.

7.   NEGATIVE COVENANTS

Borrower will not do any of the following without the Bank's written consent, which will not be unreasonably withheld:

7.1   Dispositions. Convey, sell, lease, transfer or otherwise dispose of (collectively a "Transfer"), or permit any of its Subsidiaries to Transfer, all or any part of its business or property, other than a Transfer (i) of Inventory in the ordinary course of business; (ii) of nonexclusive licenses and similar arrangements for the use of the property of Borrower or its Subsidiaries in the ordinary course of business; or (iii) of worn-out or obsolete Equipment, other than for Financed Equipment.

7.2   Changes in Business, Ownership, Management or Business Locations; Location of Equipment. Engage in or permit any of its Subsidiaries to engage in any business other than the businesses currently engaged in by Borrower or reasonably related thereto or have a material change in its management or a material change in its ownership of greater than 25% (other than by the sale of Borrower's equity securities in a public offering or to venture capital investors so long as Borrower identifies the venture capital investors prior to the closing of the investment). Borrower will not, without at least 30 days' prior written notice, relocate its chief executive office or add any new offices or business locations in which Borrower maintains or stores over $5,000 in Borrower's assets or property.

7.3   Mergers or Acquisitions. Merge or consolidate, or permit any of its Subsidiaries to merge or consolidate, with any other Person, or acquire, or permit any of its Subsidiaries to acquire, all or substantially all of the capital stock or property of another Person, except where: (i) no Default or Event of Default has occurred and is continuing or would result from such action during the term of this Agreement; (ii) such transaction would not result in a decrease of more than 25% of Tangible Net Worth; and (iii) upon the acquisition of any other Person as otherwise permitted pursuant to the terms of this Section, such Person become an appropriate obligor relating to the Obligations hereunder, as the Bank may determine, and shall execute such agreements, documents and instruments as are reasonably necessary or appropriate, as the Bank may determine, in order to evidence such debt obligations and to establish a first priority security interest in the personal property assets of such Person in favor of Bank, subject to Permitted Liens. A Subsidiary may merge or consolidate into another Subsidiary or into Borrower as long as no Default or Event of Default is occurring prior thereto or arises thereafter.

7.4   Indebtedness. Create, incur, assume, or be liable for any Indebtedness, or permit any Subsidiary to do so, other than Permitted Indebtedness.

7.5   Encumbrance. Create, incur, or allow any Lien on any of its property, or assign or convey any right to receive income, including the sale of any Accounts, or permit any of its Subsidiaries to do so, except for Permitted Liens, or permit any of Collateral that is subject to the Bank's first priority security interest in the Collateral to change, subject only to Permitted Liens.

7.6   Investments; Distributions. (i) Directly or indirectly acquire or own any Person, or make any Investment in any Person, other than Permitted Investments, or permit any of its Subsidiaries to do so; or (ii) pay any dividends or make any distribution or payment or redeem, retire or purchase any capital stock of the Borrower.

7.7   Transactions with Affiliates. Directly or indirectly enter or permit any material transaction with any Affiliate, except transactions that are in the ordinary course of Borrower's business, on terms less favorable to Borrower than would be obtained in an arm's-length transaction with a non-affiliated Person.

7.8   Subordinated Debt. Make or permit any payment on any Subordinated Debt, except under the terms of the Subordinated Debt, or amend any provision in any document relating to the Subordinated Debt, without Bank's prior written consent.

7.9   No Further Negative Pledge Agreements. Borrower shall not enter into or otherwise be bound by any agreement or provision that restricts or otherwise affects Borrower's ability to create, incur, or allow any Lien on or otherwise transfer any of its intellectual property assets or any proceeds thereof.

7.10   Compliance. Undertake as one of its important activities extending credit to purchase or carry margin stock, or use the proceeds of any Advance for that purpose; fail to meet the minimum funding requirements of ERISA, permit a Reportable Event or Prohibited Transaction, as defined in ERISA, to occur; fail to comply with the Federal Fair Labor Standards Act or violate any other law or regulation, if the violation could have a material adverse effect on Borrower's business or operations or cause a Material Adverse Change, or permit any of its Subsidiaries to do so.

8.   EVENTS OF DEFAULT

Any one of the following is an "Event of Default" hereunder:

8.1   Payment Default. Borrower fails to pay any of the Obligations within 3 days after their due date. During the additional period the failure to cure the default is not an Event of Default (but no Credit Extensions will be made during the cure period);

8.2   Covenant Default. If Borrower does not perform any obligation in Section 6 or violates any covenant in Section 7; or

If Borrower does not perform or observe any other material term, condition or covenant in this Agreement, any Loan Documents, or in any agreement between Borrower and Bank and as to any default under such other term, condition or covenant that can be cured, has not cured the default within 10 days after it occurs, or if the default relating thereto cannot be cured within 10 days or cannot be cured after Borrower's attempts within 10 day period, and the default may be cured within a reasonable time, then Borrower has an additional period (of not more than 30 days) to attempt to cure the default. During the additional time, the failure to cure the default is not an Event of Default (but no Credit Extensions will be made during the cure period);

8.3   Material Adverse Change. (i) A material impairment in the perfection or priority of the Bank's security interest in the Collateral or in the value of such Collateral which is not covered by adequate insurance occurs; (ii) a material adverse change in the business, operations, or condition (financial or otherwise) of the Borrower occurs;

or (iii) a material impairment of the prospect of repayment of any portion of the Obligations occurs (any of the foregoing is referred to herein as the a "Material Adverse Change");

8.4   Attachment. (i) Any material portion of Borrower's assets is attached, seized, levied on, or comes into possession of a trustee or receiver and the attachment, seizure or levy is not removed in 10 days; (ii) Borrower is enjoined, restrained, or prevented by court order from conducting a material part of its business; (iii) a judgment or other claim becomes a Lien on a material portion of Borrower's assets; or (iv) a notice of lien, levy, or assessment is filed against any of Borrower's assets by any government agency and not paid within 10 days after Borrower receives notice. These are not Events of Default if stayed or if a bond is posted pending contest by Borrower (but no Credit Extensions will be made during the cure period);

8.5   Insolvency. (i) Borrower becomes insolvent; (ii) Borrower begins an Insolvency Proceeding; or (iii) an Insolvency Proceeding is begun against Borrower and not dismissed or stayed within 30 days (but no Credit Extensions will be made before any Insolvency Proceeding is dismissed);

8.6   Other Agreements. If there is a default in any agreement between Borrower and a third party that gives the third party the right to accelerate any Indebtedness exceeding $100,000 or that could cause a Material Adverse Change;

8.7   Judgments. If a money judgment or judgments in the aggregate of at least $50,000 is rendered against the Borrower and is unsatisfied and unstayed for 10 days (but no Credit Extensions will be made before the judgment is stayed or satisfied);

8.8   Misrepresentations. If Borrower or any Person acting for Borrower makes any material misrepresentation or material misstatement now or later in any warranty or representation in this Agreement or in any communication delivered to Bank or to induce Bank to enter this Agreement or any Loan Document; or

8.9   Guaranty. Any guaranty of any Obligations ceases for any reason to be in full force or any Guarantor does not perform any obligation under any guaranty of the Obligations, or any material misrepresentation or material misstatement exists now or later in any warranty or representation in any guaranty of the Obligations or in any certificate delivered to Bank in connection with the guaranty, or any circumstance described in Sections 8.4, 8.5 or 8.7 occurs to any Guarantor.

9.   BANK'S RIGHTS AND REMEDIES

9.1   Rights and Remedies. When an Event of Default occurs and continues Bank may, without notice or demand, do any or all of the following:

(a)   Declare all Obligations immediately due and payable (but if an Event of Default described in Section 8.5 occurs all Obligations are immediately due and payable without any action by Bank);

(b)   Stop advancing money or extending credit for Borrower's benefit under this Agreement or under any other agreement between Borrower and Bank;

(c)   Settle or adjust disputes and claims directly with account debtors for amounts, on terms and in any order that Bank considers advisable;

(d)   Make any payments and do any acts it considers necessary or reasonable to protect its security interest in the Collateral. Borrower will assemble the Collateral if Bank requires and make it available as Bank designates. Bank may enter premises where the Collateral is located, take and maintain possession of any part of the Collateral, and pay, purchase, contest, or compromise any Lien which appears to be prior or superior to its security interest and pay all expenses incurred. Borrower grants Bank a license to enter and occupy any of its premises, without charge, to exercise any of Bank's rights or remedies;

(e)   Apply to the Obligations any (i) balances and deposits of Borrower it holds, or (ii) any amount held by Bank owing to or for the credit or the account of Borrower;

(f)   Ship, reclaim, recover, store, finish, maintain, repair, prepare for sale, advertise for sale, and sell the Collateral. Bank is granted a non-exclusive, royalty-free license or other right to use, without charge, Borrower's labels, patents, copyrights, mask works, rights of use of any name, trade secrets, trade names, trademarks, service marks, and advertising matter, or any similar property as it pertains to the Collateral, in completing production of, advertising for sale, and selling any Collateral and, in connection with Bank's exercise of its rights under this Section, Borrower's rights under all licenses and all franchise agreements inure to Bank's benefit; and

(g)   Dispose of the Collateral according to the Code or otherwise pursuant to law.

9.2   Power of Attorney. Effective only when an Event of Default occurs and continues, Borrower irrevocably appoints Bank as its lawful attorney to: (i) endorse Borrower's name on any checks or other forms of payment or security; (ii) sign Borrower's name on any invoice or bill of lading for any Account or drafts against account debtors, (iii) make, settle, and adjust all claims under Borrower's insurance policies; (iv) settle and adjust disputes and claims about the Accounts directly with account debtors, for amounts and on terms Bank determines reasonable; and (v) transfer the Collateral into the name of Bank or a third party as the Code permits. Bank may exercise the power of attorney to sign Borrower's name on any documents necessary to perfect or continue the perfection of any security interest regardless of whether an Event of Default has occurred. Bank's appointment as Borrower's attorney in fact, and all of Bank's rights and powers, coupled with an interest, are irrevocable until all Obligations have been fully repaid and performed and Bank's obligation to provide Credit Extensions terminates.

9.3   Accounts Collection. When an Event of Default occurs and continues, Bank may notify any Person owing Borrower money of Bank's security interest in the funds and verify the amount of the Account. Borrower must collect all payments in trust for Bank and, if requested by Bank, immediately deliver the payments to Bank in the form received from the account debtor, with proper endorsements for deposit.

9.4   Bank Expenses. If Borrower fails to pay any amount or furnish any required proof of payment to third persons Bank may make all or part of the payment or obtain insurance policies required in Section 6.5, and take any action under the policies Bank deems prudent. Any amounts paid by Bank are Bank Expenses and immediately due and payable, bearing interest at the then applicable rate and secured by the Collateral. No payments by Bank are deemed an agreement to make similar payments in the future or Bank's waiver of any Event of Default.

9.5   Bank's Liability for Collateral. If Bank complies with reasonable banking practices, it is not liable or responsible for: (a) the safekeeping of the Collateral; (b) any loss or damage to the Collateral; (c) any diminution in the value of the Collateral; or (d) any act or default of any carrier, warehouseman, bailee, or other person. Borrower bears all risk of loss, damage or destruction of the Collateral.

9.6   Remedies Cumulative. Bank's rights and remedies under this Agreement, the Loan Documents, and all other agreements are cumulative. Bank has all rights and remedies provided under the Code, by law, or in equity. Bank's exercise of one right or remedy is not an election, and Bank's waiver of any Event of Default is not a continuing waiver. Bank's delay is not a waiver, election, or acquiescence. No waiver is effective unless signed by Bank and then is only effective for the specific instance and purpose for which it was given.

9.7   Demand Waiver. Borrower waives demand, notice of default or dishonor, notice of payment and nonpayment, notice of any default, nonpayment at maturity, release, compromise, settlement, extension, or renewal of accounts, documents, instruments, chattel paper, and guaranties held by Bank on which Borrower is liable.

10.   NOTICES

Unless otherwise provided in this Agreement, all notices or demands by any party relating to this Agreement or any other agreement entered into in connection herewith shall be in writing and (except for financial statements and other informational documents which may be sent by first-class mail, postage prepaid) shall be personally delivered or sent by a recognized overnight delivery service, by certified mail, postage prepaid, return receipt requested, or by telefacsimile to Borrower or to Bank, as the case may be, at its addresses set forth below:

If to Borrower:	Fiber Communications Corporation
	1151 Oxford Road
	San Marino, California 91108
	Attention: President
	FAX: _____
If to Bank:	Silicon Valley Bank
	10585 Santa Monica Boulevard, Suite 140
	Los Angeles, California 90025
	Attn: Manager
	FAX: _____

11.   CHOICE OF LAW, VENUE AND JURY TRIAL WAIVER

California law governs the Loan Documents without regard to principles of conflicts of law. Borrower and Bank each submit to the exclusive jurisdiction of the State and Federal courts in Los Angeles County, California. **BORROWER AND BANK EACH WAIVE THEIR RIGHT TO A JURY TRIAL OF ANY CLAIM OR CAUSE OF**

ACTION ARISING OUT OF OR BASED UPON THIS AGREEMENT, THE LOAN DOCUMENTS OR ANY CONTEMPLATED TRANSACTION, INCLUDING CONTRACT, TORT, BREACH OF DUTY AND ALL OTHER CLAIMS. THIS WAIVER IS A MATERIAL INDUCEMENT FOR BOTH PARTIES TO ENTER INTO THIS AGREEMENT. EACH PARTY HAS REVIEWED THIS WAIVER WITH ITS COUNSEL.

12.   GENERAL PROVISIONS

12.1   Successors and Assigns. This Agreement binds and is for the benefit of the successors and permitted assigns of each party. Borrower may not assign this Agreement or any rights or Obligations under it without Bank's prior written consent which may be granted or withheld in Bank's discretion. Bank has the right, without the consent of or notice to Borrower, to sell, transfer, negotiate, or grant participation in all or any part of, or any interest in, Bank's obligations, rights and benefits under this Agreement, the Loan Documents or any related agreement.

12.2   Indemnification. Borrower will indemnify, defend and hold harmless Bank and its officers, employees and agents against: (a) all obligations, demands, claims, and liabilities asserted by any other party in connection with the transactions contemplated by the Loan Documents; and (b) all losses or Bank Expenses incurred, or paid by Bank from, following, or consequential to transactions between Bank and Borrower (including reasonable attorneys' fees and expenses), except for losses caused by Bank's gross negligence or willful misconduct.

12.3   Time of Essence. Time is of the essence for the performance of all Obligations in this Agreement.

12.4   Severability of Provision. Each provision of this Agreement is severable from every other provision in determining the enforceability of any provision.

12.5   Amendments in Writing, Integration. All amendments to this Agreement must be in writing signed by both Bank and Borrower. This Agreement and the Loan Documents represent the entire agreement about this subject matter, and supersedes prior or contemporaneous negotiations or agreements. All prior or contemporaneous agreements, understandings, representations, warranties, and negotiations between the parties about the subject matter of this Agreement and the Loan Documents merge into this Agreement and the Loan Documents.

12.6   Counterparts. This Agreement may be executed in any number of counterparts and by different parties on separate counterparts, each of which, when executed and delivered, is an original, and all taken together, are one Agreement.

12.7   Survival. All covenants, representations and warranties made in this Agreement continue in full force while any Obligations remain outstanding. The obligations of Borrower in Section 12.2 to indemnify Bank will survive until all statutes of limitations for actions that may be brought against Bank have run.

12.8   Attorneys' Fees, Costs and Expenses. In any action or proceeding between Borrower and Bank arising out of the Loan Documents, the prevailing party will be entitled to recover its reasonable attorneys' fees and other costs and expenses incurred, in addition to any other relief to which it may be entitled, whether or not a lawsuit is filed.

13.   DEFINITIONS

"**Accounts**" are all existing and later arising accounts, contract rights, and other obligations owed Borrower in connection with its sale or lease of goods (including licensing software and other technology) or provision of services, all credit insurance, guaranties, other security and all merchandise returned or reclaimed by Borrower and Borrower's Books relating to any of the foregoing.

"**Adjusted Current Liabilities**" shall mean, as of any date of determination, the aggregate amount of Borrower's Total Liabilities regarding the Equipment Advances hereunder together with those other Total Liabilities of Borrower which mature within one (1) year from the date of determination, provided any Subordinated Debt shall be excluded from the foregoing for purposes of this definition.

"**Affiliate**" of a Person is a Person that owns or controls directly or indirectly the Person, any Person that controls or is controlled by or is under common control with the Person, and each of that Person's senior executive officers, directors, partners and, for any Person that is a limited liability company, that Person's managers and members.

"**Bank Expenses**" are all audit fees and expenses and reasonable costs and expenses (including reasonable attorneys' fees and expenses) for preparing, negotiating, administering, defending and enforcing the Loan Documents (including appeals or Insolvency Proceedings).

"**Basic Rate**" is, as of the Funding Date, a per annum fixed rate of interest (based on a year of 360 days) equal to the sum of (a) the Prime Rate in effect as of such date, plus (b) the Loan Margin, <u>provided</u> that the Basic Rate shall under no circumstances be deemed less than a rate equal to 7.00% per annum.

"**Borrower's Books**" are all Borrower's books and records including ledgers, records regarding Borrower's assets or liabilities, the Collateral, business operations or financial condition and all computer programs or discs or any equipment containing the information.

"**Business Day**" is any day that is not a Saturday, Sunday or a day on which the Bank is closed.

"**Closing Date**" is the date of this Agreement.

"**Code**" is the Uniform Commercial Code, as applicable.

"**Collateral**" is the property described on <u>Exhibit A</u>.

"**Committed Equipment Line**" is a line of credit of up to $3,000,000.

"**Commitment Termination Date**" is December _____, 20____.

"**Contingent Obligation**" is, for any Person, any direct or indirect liability, contingent or not, of that Person for (i) any indebtedness, lease, dividend, letter of credit or other obligation of another such as an obligation directly or indirectly guaranteed, endorsed, co-made, discounted or sold with recourse by that Person, or for which that Person is directly or indirectly liable; (ii) any obligations for undrawn letters of credit for the account of that Person; and (iii) all obligations from any interest rate, currency or commodity swap agreement, interest rate cap or collar agreement, or other agreement or arrangement designated to protect a Person against fluctuation in interest rates, currency exchange rates or commodity prices; but "Contingent Obligation" does not include endorsements in the ordinary course of business. The amount of a Contingent Obligation is the stated or determined amount of the primary obligation for which the Contingent Obligation is made or, if not determinable, the maximum reasonably anticipated liability for it determined by the Person in good faith; but the amount may not exceed the maximum of the obligations under the guarantee or other support arrangement.

"**Credit Extension**" is each Equipment Advance and each other extension of credit by Bank for Borrower's benefit.

"**Current Assets**" are amounts that under GAAP should be included on that date as current assets on Borrower's consolidated balance sheet.

"**Current Liabilities**" are the aggregate amount of Borrower's Total Liabilities which mature within one (1) year.

"**Default**" means any event which with the passing of time or the giving of notice or both would become an Event of Default hereunder.

"**Eligible Equipment**" shall mean mission critical equipment and test equipment, workstations, computers and other mission critical semiconductor design machinery (the foregoing are collectively referred to herein as the "Hard Costs"), and Other Equipment, subject to (1) the limitations set forth below in the definition thereof and (2) provided that any such Other Equipment complies with all of Borrower's representations, warranties and covenants in favor of the Bank and which is acceptable to Bank in all respects. All Equipment financed with the proceeds of Equipment Advances shall be new when purchased, provided that Bank, in its sale discretion, may finance used equipment.

"**Equipment**" is all present and future machinery, equipment, tenant improvements, furniture, fixtures, vehicles, tools, parts and attachments in which Borrower has any interest.

"**Equipment Advance**" and "**Equipment Advances**" are defined in Section 2.1.1.

"**Event of Loss**" shall have the meaning set forth in Section 6.7 hereof.

"**Financed Equipment**" is defined in the Loan Supplement.

"**Funding Date**" shall have the meaning ascribed to such term in Section 2.1.1 hereof.

"**GAAP**" is generally accepted accounting principles.

"**Guarantor**" is any present, if existing, or any future guarantor of the Obligations.

"**Hard Costs**" shall have the meaning ascribed to such term in the definition of Eligible Equipment.

"**Indebtedness**" is (a) indebtedness for borrowed money or the deferred price of property or services, such as reimbursement and other obligations for surety bonds and letters of credit, (b) obligations evidenced by notes, bonds, debentures or similar instruments, (c) capital lease obligations and (d) Contingent Obligations.

"**Insolvency Proceeding**" are proceedings by or against any Person under the United States Bankruptcy Code, or any other bankruptcy or insolvency law, including assignments for the benefit of creditors, compositions, extensions generally with its creditors, or proceedings seeking reorganization, arrangement, or other relief.

"**Inventory**" is present and future inventory in which Borrower has any interest, including merchandise, raw materials, parts, supplies, packing and shipping materials, work in process and finished products intended for sale or lease or to be furnished under a contract of service, of every kind and description now or later owned by or in the custody or possession, actual or constructive, of Borrower, including inventory temporarily out of its custody or possession or in transit and including returns on any accounts or other proceeds (including insurance proceeds) from the sale or disposition of any of the foregoing and any documents of title.

"**Investment**" is any beneficial ownership of (including stock, partnership interest or other securities) any Person, or any loan, advance or capital contribution to any Person.

"**Lien**" is a mortgage, lien, deed of trust, charge, pledge, security interest or other encumbrance.

"**Loan Amount**" is the aggregate original amount of each Equipment Advance.

"**Loan Documents**" are, collectively, this Agreement, any note, or notes or guaranties or third party suretyship obligations in favor of Bank executed by Borrower or other Persons, as applicable, and any other present or future agreement between Borrower and/or for the benefit of Bank in connection with this Agreement, all as amended, extended or restated.

"**Loan Factor**" is the percentage which results from amortizing the Equipment Advance over the Repayment Period, using the Basic Rate as the interest rate.

"**Loan Margin**" is 250 basis points.

"**Loan Supplement**" has the meaning ascribed to such term in Section 2.1.1 hereof.

"**Maturity Date**" is, with respect to each Equipment Advance, the last day of the Repayment Period for such Equipment Advance, or, if earlier, the date of acceleration of such Equipment Advance by Bank following an Event of Default.

"**Obligations**" are debts, principal, interest, Bank Expenses and other amounts Borrower owes Bank now or later, including Equipment Advances, and including interest accruing after Insolvency Proceedings begin and debts, liabilities, or obligations of Borrower assigned to Bank.

"**Original Stated Cost**" is (i) the original cost to the Borrower of the item of new Equipment net of any and all freight, installation, tax or (ii) the fair market value assigned to such item of used Equipment by mutual agreement of Borrower and Bank at the time of making the Equipment Advance.

"**Other Equipment**" shall mean mission critical software, "stand alone" software, application software bundled into computer hardware, hand held items, furnishings, tenant improvements and other items of a similar nature that the Bank determines to be acceptable in its discretion. Unless otherwise agreed to by Bank in writing: not more than 20% of the Committed Equipment Line shall relate to and be based on Other Equipment.

"**Payment Date**" shall have the meaning ascribed to such term in Section 2.2(a) hereof.

"**Permitted Indebtedness**" is:

(a) Borrower's indebtedness to Bank under this Agreement or any other Loan Document;

(b) Indebtedness existing on the Closing Date and shown on the Schedule;

(c) Subordinated Debt;

(d) Indebtedness to trade creditors incurred in the ordinary course of business; and

(e) Indebtedness secured by Permitted Liens.

"**Permitted Investments**" are:

(a) Investments shown on the Schedule and existing on the Closing Date; and

(b) (i) marketable direct obligations issued or unconditionally guaranteed by the United States or its agency or any State maturing within 1 year from its acquisition, (ii) commercial paper maturing no more than 1 year after its creation and having the highest rating from either Standard & Poor's Corporation or Moody's Investors Service, Inc., and (iii) Bank's certificates of deposit issued maturing no more than 1 year after issue.

"**Permitted Liens**" are:

(a) Liens existing on the Closing Date and shown on the Schedule or arising under this Agreement or other Loan Documents;

(b) Liens for taxes, fees, assessments or other government charges or levies, either not delinquent or being contested in good faith and for which Borrower maintains adequate reserves on its Books, if they have no priority over any of Bank's security interests;

(c) Purchase money Liens (i) on Equipment acquired or held by Borrower or its Subsidiaries incurred for financing the acquisition of the Equipment, or (ii) existing on equipment when acquired, if the Lien is confined to the property and improvements and the proceeds of the equipment;

(d) Licenses or sublicenses granted in the ordinary course of Borrower's business and any interest or title of a licensor or under any license or sublicense, <u>if</u> the licenses and sublicenses permit granting Bank a security interest;

(e) Leases or subleases granted in the ordinary course of Borrower's business, including in connection with Borrower's leased premises or leased property; and

(f) Liens incurred in the extension, renewal or refinancing of the indebtedness secured by Liens described in (a) through (c), <u>but</u> any extension, renewal or replacement Lien must be limited to the property encumbered by the existing Lien and the principal amount of the indebtedness may not increase.

"Person" is any individual, sole proprietorship, partnership, limited liability company, joint venture, company association, trust, unincorporated organization, association, corporation, institution, public benefit corporation, firm, joint stock company, estate, entity or government agency.

"Prime Rate" is Bank's most recently announced "prime rate," even if it is not Bank's lowest rate.

"Repayment Period" shall mean (a) 36 months with respect to Equipment Advances regarding Hard Costs and (b) 24 months with respect to Equipment Advances regarding Other Equipment.

"Responsible Officer" is each of the Chief Executive Officer, the President, the Chief Financial Officer and the Controller of Borrower.

"Schedule" is any attached schedule of exceptions.

"Scheduled Payments" shall have the meaning ascribed to such term in Section 2.2(a) hereof.

"Subordinated Debt" is debt incurred by Borrower subordinated to Borrower's indebtedness owed to Bank and which is reflected in a written agreement in a manner and form acceptable to Bank and approved by Bank in writing.

"Subsidiary" is for any Person, or any other business entity of which more than 50% of the voting stock or other equity interests is owned or controlled, directly or indirectly, by the Person or one or more Affiliates of the Person.

"Tangible Net Worth" is, on any date, the consolidated total assets of Borrower and its Subsidiaries <u>minus</u>, (i) any amounts attributable to (a) goodwill, (b) intangible items such as unamortized debt discount and expense, patents, trade and service marks and names, copyrights and research and development expenses except prepaid expenses, <u>and</u> (c) reserves not already deducted from assets, <u>and</u> (ii) Total Liabilities.

"Total Liabilities" is on any date of determination, obligations that should, under GAAP, be classified as liabilities on Borrower's consolidated balance sheet, including all Indebtedness, and current portion of Subordinated Debt allowed to be paid, but excluding all other Subordinated Debt.

IN WITNESS WHEREOF, the parties hereto have caused this Agreement to be executed as of the date first above written.

BORROWER: BANK:

FIBER COMMUNICATIONS   SILICON VALLEY BANK
CORPORATION

By _____   By _____
Title _____   Title _____

EXHIBIT A

The Collateral consists of all of Borrower's right, title, and interest in and to all of Borrower's personal property, including without limitation the following:

All goods and equipment now owned or hereafter acquired, including, without limitation, all machinery, fixtures, vehicles (including motor vehicles and trailers), and any interest in any of the foregoing, and all attachments, accessories, accessions, replacements, substitutions, additions, and improvements to any of the foregoing, wherever located;

All inventory, now owned or hereafter acquired, including, without limitation, all merchandise, raw materials, parts, supplies, packing and shipping materials, work in process and finished products including such inventory as is temporarily out of Borrower's custody or possession or in transit and including any returns upon any accounts or other proceeds, including insurance proceeds, resulting from the sale or disposition of any of the foregoing and any documents of title representing any of the above;

All contract rights and general intangibles now owned or hereafter acquired, including, without limitation, goodwill, trademarks, servicemarks, trade styles, trade names, patents, patent applications, leases, license agreements, franchise agreements, blueprints, drawings, purchase orders, customer lists, route lists, infringements, claims, computer programs, computer discs, computer tapes, literature, reports, catalogs, design rights, income tax refunds, payments of insurance and rights to payment of any kind;

All now existing and hereafter arising accounts, contract rights, royalties, license rights and all other forms of obligations owing to Borrower arising out of the sale or lease of goods, the licensing of technology or the rendering of services by Borrower, whether or not earned by performance, and any and all credit insurance, guaranties, and other security therefor, as well as all merchandise returned to or reclaimed by Borrower;

All documents, cash, deposit accounts, securities, securities entitlements, securities accounts, investment property, financial assets, letters of credit, letter-of-credit rights, commercial tort claims, certificates of deposit, instruments and chattel paper now owned or hereafter acquired and Borrower's Books relating to the foregoing; and

All copyright rights, copyright applications, copyright registrations and like protections in each work of authorship and derivative work thereof, whether published or unpublished, now owned or hereafter acquired; all trade secret rights, including all rights to unpatented inventions, know-how, operating manuals, license rights and agreements and confidential information, now owned or hereafter acquired; all mask work or similar rights available for the protection of semiconductor chips, now owned or hereafter acquired; all claims for damages by way of any past, present and future infringement of any of the foregoing; and

All Borrower's Books relating to the foregoing and any and all claims, rights and interests in any of the above and all substitutions for, additions and accessions to and proceeds thereof.

Notwithstanding the foregoing, the Collateral shall not be deemed to include any copyrights, copyright applications, copyright registration and like protection in each work of authorship and derivative work thereof, whether published or unpublished, now owned or hereafter acquired; any patents, patent applications and like protections including without limitation improvements, divisions, continuations, renewals, reissues, extensions and continuations-in-part of the same, trademarks, servicemarks and applications therefor, whether registered or not, and the goodwill of the business of Borrower connected with and symbolized by such trademarks, any trade secret rights, including any rights to unpatented inventions, knowhow, operating manuals, license rights and agreements and confidential information, now owned or hereafter acquired; or any claims for damage by way of any past, present and future infringement of any of the foregoing (collectively, the "Intellectual Property"), except that the Collateral shall include the proceeds of all the Intellectual Property that are accounts, (i.e. accounts receivable) of Borrower, or general intangibles consisting of rights to payment, if a judicial authority (including a U.S. Bankruptcy Court) holds that a security interest in the underlying Intellectual Property is necessary to have a security interest in such accounts and general intangibles of Borrower that are proceeds of the Intellectual Property, then the Collateral shall automatically, and effective as of the Closing Date, include the Intellectual Property to the extent necessary to permit perfection of Bank's security interest in such accounts and general intangibles of Borrower that are proceeds of the Intellectual Property.

Further, notwithstanding the foregoing, the Collateral shall not include the items of equipment explicitly identified as excluded on Schedule I hereto.

EXHIBIT D
COMPLIANCE CERTIFICATE

TO: SILICON VALLEY BANK

FROM: Fiber Communications Corporation

The undersigned authorized officer of Fiber Communications Corporation certifies that under the terms and conditions of the Loan and Security Agreement between Borrower and Bank (the "Agreement"), (i) Borrower is in complete compliance for the period ending _____ with all required covenants except as noted below and (ii) all representations and warranties in the Agreement are true and correct in all material respects on this date. Attached are the required documents supporting the certification. The Officer certifies that these are prepared in accordance with Generally Accepted Accounting Principles (GAAP) consistently applied from one period to the next except as explained in an accompanying letter or footnotes. The Officer acknowledges that no borrowings may be requested at any time or date of determination that Borrower is not in compliance with any of the terms of the Agreement, and that compliance is determined on an ongoing basis and not just at the date this certificate is delivered.

Please indicate compliance status by circling Yes/No under "Complies" column.

Reporting Covenant	Required	Complies	
Monthly Financial Statements and Compliance Certificate	Monthly within 30 days	Yes	No
Annual Financials (Audited beginning with the 12/31/__ fiscal year)	FYE within 120 days	Yes	No

Financial Covenant	Required	Actual	Complies	
Maintain at all times: Minimum Quick Ratio (Adjusted)	X.XX:1.00	_____:1.00	Yes	No

Comments Regarding Exceptions:
See Attached.

Sincerely,

FIBER COMMUNICATIONS
CORPORATION

By:_____

    Title: _____

Date: _____

BANK USE ONLY

Received by: _____
                AUTHORIZED SIGNER

Date:_____

Verified:_____
                AUTHORIZED SIGNER

Date:_____

Compliance Status: Yes No

SAMPLE ACQUISITION AGREEMENT

SPECIALTY RECORDKEEPING MATERIALS, INC.

ACQUISITION AGREEMENT

By and Among

THE ACQUIRING CORP., INC.,

THE FOUNDER FAMILY TRUST,
DATED JANUARY 15, 1993, AS AMENDED

and

FOUNDER

Dated as of July 15, 20__

ACQUISITION AGREEMENT

This Acquisition Agreement ("Agreement") is made in Orange County, California as of July 15, 20____, by and among The Acquiring Corp., Inc. a California corporation (the "Buyer"), Founder, as trustee of The Founder Family Trust, dated January 15, 1993, as amended, the sole shareholder of Specialty Recordkeeping Materials, Inc. (the "Trust"), and Founder, as an individual ("Founder," and collectively with the Trust, the "Sellers").

R E C I T A L S

A.   The Trust desires to sell to the Buyer, and the Buyer desires to purchase and acquire all of the outstanding equity securities (the "Stock") of Specialty Recordkeeping Materials, Inc., a New Jersey corporation ("Target").

B.   Prior to the date hereof, Target and the Buyer have entered into that certain Nondisclosure Agreement dated February 23, 20____ (the "Nondisclosure Agreement") and Target, the Buyer and Buyer's CEO have entered into that certain Confidentiality/ Non-Piracy Agreement dated July 8, 20____ (the "Confidentiality Agreement").

C.   The parties desire, by this Agreement, to set forth the terms and conditions of the purchase and sale of the Stock.

THEREFORE, in consideration of the mutual covenants, agreements and provisions herein contained, the parties agree as follows:

1.   <u>Purchase of the Stock</u>. On the Closing Date (as hereinafter defined), the Trust shall transfer to the Buyer, and the Buyer shall purchase from the Trust, the Stock.

2.   <u>Consideration for Transfer to the Buyer</u>. The consideration to be received by the Trust for the transfer of the Stock to the Buyer shall be paid in cash or by wire transfer and shall be Two Million Dollars ($2,000,000) (the "Purchase Price").

3.   <u>Documentation of Transfer</u>. In order to fully effectuate the transfer contemplated by Section 1 hereof, the Trust agrees to execute and deliver at the Closing (as hereinafter defined) the certificates representing its shares of the Stock, together with executed forms of stock assignment separate from certificate, in a form reasonably acceptable to the Buyer, in order to vest in and confirm to the Buyer all right, title and interest in and to the Stock, free and clear of any mortgage, pledge, lien, charge, security interest or other right, interest or encumbrance thereon or restriction on voting or transfer, other than as may be imposed by federal or state securities laws.

4.   <u>Sellers' Participation</u>. The completion of the transactions contemplated by this Agreement is subject to a number of conditions being satisfied as set forth in Section 10, below. In addition, the Buyer's obligation to buy the Stock shall be effective only upon the participation of the Sellers in this Agreement, and Founder's participation in the Noncompetition Agreement and the Consulting Agreement contemplated in Sections 10(a)(viii) and 10(b)(iii), below, and the collateral documents necessary to complete the transfer of the Stock. Without the satisfaction of all the Conditions to Closing set forth in Section 10(a), below, the Buyer shall have no obligation to the Sellers to purchase any portion of the Stock.

5.   <u>Closing</u>. The time of the delivery and satisfaction of the items referred to in Sections 2, 3 and 10 of this Agreement is herein called the "Closing Date," and the acts of

delivery in satisfaction of the conditions of closing are sometimes referred to as the "Closing." The Closing Date under this Agreement shall be not later than ninety (90) days after the date of this Agreement, subject to postponement from time to time as the parties may mutually agree, such that this Agreement may be entered into with Closing to occur at a later date. If so, the transactions contemplated hereby shall be deemed to have occurred on the Closing Date. The Closing shall be held at the offices of Founder's Counsel, LLP, 611 Anton Boulevard, Costa Mesa, California at 10:00 a.m. on the Closing Date, unless another time or place is mutually agreed upon by the parties.

6. <u>Representations and Warranties of the Sellers</u>. The Sellers jointly and severally represent and warrant to the Buyer that:

(a) <u>Organization, Standing, Capitalization</u>. Target is a corporation duly organized, validly existing and in good standing under the laws of the State of New Jersey, and is duly qualified to do business in each jurisdiction where its operations or assets require it to be so qualified, including, but not limited to, the State of Ohio. Target has not received written notice regarding a failure to be qualified to do business from any jurisdiction where it maintains operations or assets. Target has all requisite power and authority to own, lease and operate its properties and to carry on its business, as such has in the past been conducted. The Stock held by the Trust represents all the outstanding equity securities of Target. There are no options, rights, agreements or obligations on the part of Target or the Sellers regarding the issuance of additional equity securities of any kind or the transfer of any interest in the Stock presently owned by the Trust.

(b) <u>Authority</u>. The execution and delivery hereof, and the consummation of the transactions contemplated hereby, constitute valid and legally binding obligations of the Sellers, enforceable against them in accordance with its terms. There is no litigation, proceeding or investigation pending or, to the best of the Sellers' knowledge, threatened, that questions the validity or enforceability of this Agreement or seeks to enjoin the consummation of any of the transactions contemplated hereby. Neither the execution and delivery hereof nor the consummation of the transactions contemplated hereby nor compliance with any of the provisions hereof will (i) conflict with or result in a breach of or default under any of the terms, conditions or provisions of Target's Articles of Incorporation or Bylaws, or any material agreement, instrument or obligation to which the Sellers or Target are a party, or by which the Sellers or Target or its properties or assets may be bound or affected, (ii) result in the violation of any order, writ, injunction, decree, statute, rule or regulation applicable to the Sellers or Target or its properties or assets, or (iii) create any lien or encumbrance on the Stock or upon any of Target's assets.

(c) <u>Ownership of the Stock</u>. The Stock is owned by the Trust free and clear of any mortgage, pledge, lien, charge, security interest or other right, interest or encumbrance, or restriction on voting or transfer, other than as may be imposed by federal or state securities laws. Upon the consummation of the transfer of the Stock, the Buyer will acquire good and marketable title to the Stock, without restriction, other than as may be imposed with respect to the transactions contemplated hereby or by federal or state securities laws.

(d) <u>The Assets and the Liabilities</u>. The Schedule of Assets and Liabilities, attached hereto as item 6(d) of the Schedule of Disclosure, contains a complete and accurate listing as of June 30, 20____ and as of the Closing Date of the assets (including intellectual property assets and excluding miscellaneous assets having a nominal value that in the aggregate do not exceed $5,000) and liabilities of Target. Except as set forth as item 6(d) of the Schedule of Disclosure, with respect to the equipment listed in item 6(d) of the Schedule of Disclosure that is material to the operation of Target's business, such equipment is in good operating condition and repair as of the date hereof and will be as of the Closing Date, reasonable wear and tear excepted. Target has good and marketable title to all of the assets it uses in the operation of its business, free and clear of all mortgages, liens, pledges, encumbrances or security interests, and claims of others, of any nature whatsoever, other than as indicated in item 6(d) of the Schedule of Disclosure hereto. To the best of the Sellers' knowledge, except as set forth as item 6(d) of the Schedule of Disclosure, there are no claims or threatened claims asserting infringement as a result of Target's use of its intellectual property, nor has Target made any claim that any third party is infringing upon its rights.

(e) Copies, Descriptions and Lists. The Sellers shall have provided to the Buyer, and set forth in the Schedule of Disclosure, Exhibit A hereto, the following, all of which shall be accurate and complete as of the date hereof and as of the Closing Date:

(i) copies of Target's Articles of Incorporation, Bylaws and minute books, showing copies of all material Board of Directors and shareholder actions;

(ii) copies of all material written contracts, leases or other agreements between Target and any independent sales representatives, vendors, landlords, or other providers of goods or services relating to Target's business;

(iii) copies of forms of invoices, warranties, representations or terms and conditions, customarily used by Target, any material special agreements or terms provided to customers, and any material written agreements relating to future delivery obligations to, work in process for and executory agreements with customers, that are effective on the date of this Agreement;

(iv) copies of all employee benefit plans, profit sharing, deferred compensation, 401(k), bonus, vacation pay and accrual, holiday pay, and other compensation arrangements, together with all employment or severance agreements between Target and any of Target's employees;

(v) a list of Target's insurance policies in effect as of the date hereof and as of the Closing Date, and copies of declaration pages thereof; and

(vi) a list of all bank and depository or investment accounts where cash or investments of Target have been deposited.

(f) Validity of Contracts; Relationships with Customers and Suppliers. Except as set forth as item 6(f) of the Schedule of Disclosure, all of the contracts made available pursuant to subparagraph (e) above, are valid and in full force and effect. Except as set forth as item 6(f) of the Schedule of Disclosure, Target has fully performed in all material respects to date under all such contracts and has not received any payments under any of such contracts for services or other obligations which have not already been performed by Target.

(g) Financial Statements; Undisclosed Liabilities. The Sellers have delivered to the Buyer compiled (unaudited, unreviewed and without notes, disclosures or footnotes) balance sheets of Target as of September 30, [2 years ago], September 30, [last year], March 31, [of this year], and June 30, [of this year] (when available), and the related statements consisting of income, retained earnings and supplemental financial information. These financial statements are derived from the books and records of Target, were prepared in accordance with GAAP, except with respect to footnote disclosure and as described in item 6(g) of the Schedule of Disclosure, on a consistent basis and fairly present the financial position and results of operations of Target at the date thereof and for the one-year periods, the six-month period and the nine-month period then ended. Except as disclosed on item 6(g) of the Schedule of Disclosure, Target has incurred no material liabilities or obligations not presented in the financial statements delivered pursuant to this Section 6(g), unless in the ordinary course of Target's business.

(h) Litigation or Proceedings. Except as set forth as item 6(h) of the Schedule of Disclosure, Target is not engaged in, or a party to, or, to the Sellers' knowledge, threatened with any governmental investigation or claim or legal action or other proceedings before any court, arbitrator or any administrative agency relating to its business. Except as set forth as item 6(h) of the Schedule of Disclosure, there are no outstanding rulings, decrees, judgments or stipulations to which Target or the Sellers are a party that relate to Target's business or the Trust's ownership of, or the right of either of the Sellers to transfer, the Stock.

(i) Compliance with Laws. With regard to the business, assets, business practices, and products of Target's business, Target has obtained and maintained, and set forth in item 6(i) of the Schedule of Disclosure, all material permits and, except as set forth on the Schedule of Disclosure in item 6(i), complied in all material respects with all applicable laws, regulations, orders and other requirements of governmental authorities.

(j) Taxes. Except as set forth as item 6(j) of the Schedule of Disclosure, Target has (i) timely filed or caused to be filed all material tax returns required to be filed by it, and all such returns were true, correct and complete in all material respects when filed, and (ii) paid or accrued for all material taxes shown to be due on its tax returns other than taxes being contested in good faith for which a reserve has been set. For the fiscal year ending September 30, [last year], Target filed state and local tax returns in the following jurisdictions: California, Colorado, Florida, Georgia, Illinois, Mississippi, Missouri, New Jersey, Ohio, Tennessee, and Texas. Sellers shall be responsible for all deficiencies (including interest and penalties) finally determined to be due or owing with regard to any federal, state, or local tax filing, payment or obligation, relating to events which occurred prior to the Closing Date. Sellers retain the right to defend themselves against any deficiency, such as described in this subparagraph (j), finally determined owing for any period prior to the Closing Date. In connection with this defense, Sellers shall be granted reasonable access to the relevant records of Target. Copies of all federal, state and local tax returns filed by Target for the five (5) most recently ended tax years have been delivered to the Buyer. To the best of the Sellers' knowledge, there are no pending or threatened federal, state, local, or foreign audits or examinations of any of Target's tax returns, nor are there any outstanding agreements or requests to extend the statutory period of limitations applicable to the assessment of any material taxes or deficiencies against Target. There are no agreements, closing agreements or letter rulings that bind Target as to the content or nature of its reporting on any returns due for filing after the Closing Date. None of the assets of Target are subject to an election or consent to the application of Section 341 of the Internal Revenue Code or of any predecessor provision with respect to collapsible corporations. There have not been, and as of the Closing Date there will not be, any payments (or agreements to make payments) in connection with a change of control of Target that would constitute "excess parachute payments" under Section 280G of the Internal Revenue Code.

(k) <u>Labor Matters</u>. Except as set forth as item 6(k) of the Schedule of Disclosure, Target is not a party to, nor is it bound by, any collective bargaining agreement or other understanding with a labor organization. Except as set forth as item 6(k) of the Schedule of Disclosure, to the best of the Sellers' knowledge, there are no controversies existing or threatened between Target and any of its current or former employees and, to the best knowledge of the Sellers, no facts that could reasonably be expected to result in such a controversy. Except as set forth as item 6(k) of the Schedule of Disclosure, Target has no liability for any past due wages, bonuses or compensation, or any penalties for failure to pay wages, bonuses or compensation when due, nor has it discharged any such liabilities or penalties during the twelve months preceding the Closing Date.

(l) <u>Environmental Matters</u>. Target is in compliance in all material respects with all laws, rules, regulations, orders or decrees now in effect that regulate or relate to the protection or clean-up of the environment and apply to its operations or facilities. Except as set forth as item 6(l) of the Schedule of Disclosure, Sellers have no knowledge of the existence or prior existence of any hazardous substance on the "Property," as defined in Section 10(a)(ix). Except as set forth as item 6(l) of the Schedule of Disclosure, Target has received no notices of any alleged, actual or potential responsibility for, or any written notice or inquiry regarding an investigation concerning any violation of, an environmental protection law or any asserted environmental injury or damage.

(m) <u>Brokers and Finders</u>. Neither Target nor the Sellers have employed any broker, agent or finder in connection with the transactions contemplated by this Agreement.

(n) <u>Statements True and Correct; Further Representations and Warranties</u>. The statements contained in this Agreement and in any written documents or schedules prepared and delivered by or on behalf of the Sellers pursuant to the terms hereof are true and correct in all material respects, and such documents or schedules do not omit any material fact required by the terms hereof or thereof to be stated therein or necessary to make the statements contained therein not misleading. Further, the internally prepared fiscal budget (the "Internal Budget") (October 1, [last year] through September 30, [this year]) has been prepared in good faith, using facts known to the Sellers and based upon assumptions reasonably believed by the Sellers to be reasonable and appropriate at the time those projections were prepared. The Buyer understands and acknowledges that due to Target's smaller size, the Internal Budget is not a formal forecast document including assumptions and footnotes; rather, it is prepared as an informal, internal planning tool. To the best of the Sellers' knowledge, the Internal Budget contains no material or adverse omissions. To the extent that the Internal Budget is revised taking into account actual [results during the applicable time period], a copy of the revised Internal Budget shall be delivered to the Buyer.

(o) <u>No Knowledge of Breach</u>. As of the Date of Closing, the Sellers will disclose to the Buyer any breach of the representations and warranties of the Buyer set forth herein.

7. <u>Representations and Warranties of the Buyer</u>. The Buyer represents and warrants to the Sellers that:

(a) <u>Organization, Standing, etc</u>. The Buyer is a corporation duly organized under the laws of the State of California and is in good standing under the laws of the

State of California. The Buyer has all requisite power and authority to own, lease and operate its properties and to carry on its business as such business is now being conducted.

(b) <u>Authority</u>. The execution and delivery of this Agreement and the consummation of the transactions contemplated hereby have been duly and validly authorized by all necessary corporate action on the part of the Buyer and this Agreement constitutes the valid and legally binding obligation of the Buyer, enforceable against the Buyer in accordance with its terms. There is no litigation, proceeding or investigation pending, or to the best of the Buyer's knowledge threatened, which questions the validity or enforceability of this Agreement or seeks to enjoin the consummation of any of the transactions contemplated hereby. Neither the execution and delivery hereof nor the consummation of the transactions contemplated hereby nor compliance with any of the provisions hereof will (i) conflict with or result in a breach of or default under any of the terms, conditions or provisions of the Articles of Incorporation or Bylaws of the Buyer or any agreement, instrument or obligation to which the Buyer is a party or by which the Buyer or any of its properties or assets may be bound or affected, or (ii) result in the violation of any order, writ, injunction, decree, statute, rule or regulation applicable to the Buyer or its properties or assets.

(c) <u>Brokers and Finders</u>. The Buyer has not employed any broker, agent or finder in connection with the transactions contemplated by this Agreement.

(d) <u>Validity of Agreement</u>. This Agreement, the Consulting Agreement set forth as Exhibit B hereto, and the Noncompetition Agreement set forth as Exhibit C hereto constitute the legal, valid and binding obligations of the Buyer, enforceable against the Buyer in accordance with their terms.

(e) <u>No Knowledge of Breach</u>. As of the Date of Closing, the Buyer will disclose to the Sellers or Target, or both, any breach of the representations and warranties of the Sellers and Target set forth herein.

(f) <u>Solvency</u>. On the date of entering into this Agreement, and after giving effect to all obligations of the Buyer hereunder, including, but not limited to, the payment of the Purchase Price, and the payments required under the Noncompetition Agreement and the Consulting Agreement, (i) the Buyer will be able to pay its obligations as they become due and payable; (ii) the present fair saleable value of the Buyer's assets exceeds the amount that the Buyer will be required to pay on its probable liabilities as the same become absolute and matured; and (iii) the sum of the Buyer's property at fair value exceeds its indebtedness.

8. <u>Covenants of the Parties</u>.

(a) <u>Consents and Approvals</u>. The parties will use their reasonable and best efforts to obtain all consents and approvals of other persons and governmental and regulatory authorities necessary to the consummation of the transactions contemplated by this Agreement.

(b) <u>Fulfillment of Conditions</u>. The parties will use their reasonable and best efforts to perform, comply with and fulfill all obligations, covenants and conditions required by this Agreement to be performed, complied with or fulfilled by the parties prior to, at or following the Closing Date.

(c) <u>Notice</u>. Prior to the Closing Date, each party will give prompt notice to the other parties of the occurrence, or failure to occur, of any event of which any party has knowledge that the parties reasonably determine would cause any representation or warranty contained in this Agreement to be untrue or inaccurate in any material respect.

(d)   <u>Confidentiality</u>. The Sellers, unless required to do so by court order, will not disclose, reveal or publish to any third party, or in any way utilize their knowledge of the terms of this Agreement (other than in the furtherance of this Agreement) for a period of five (5) years either following the Closing Date, or the date this Agreement is terminated if Closing does not occur; provided, however, that the Sellers will be able to use their knowledge of this Agreement for personal tax reasons. If this Agreement is consummated, the Sellers' obligations under this Section 8(d) will cease if, and only to the extent that, Buyer makes a public disclosure of any of the terms of this Agreement. If this Agreement is terminated, neither the Sellers nor the Buyer, unless required to do so by court order, will disclose, reveal or publish to any third party, or in any way utilize their knowledge of the terms of this Agreement (other than in the furtherance of this Agreement); provided, however, that the Sellers and Buyer will be able to use their knowledge of this Agreement for personal tax reasons. The parties hereby affirm all terms, provisions and conditions of the Nondisclosure Agreement and the Confidentiality Agreement.

(e)   <u>Taxes</u>.

(i)   <u>Fiscal Year Ended September 30, [this year]</u>. If the Closing Date is later than September 30, [this year], the Sellers, on a basis consistent with past practice and subject to the Buyer's reasonable judgment, shall prepare and file all tax returns required to be filed by Target with respect to Target's most recent completed fiscal year and Target shall pay all taxes shown to be due on Target's tax returns.

(ii)   <u>Proceeds</u>. The Sellers are responsible for reporting the proceeds of the sale of the Stock and the payments received under the other agreements and relationships contemplated by this Agreement to the appropriate tax authorities. The Sellers will report all tax obligations created as a result of this Agreement in a manner consistent with the terms of this Agreement and of the agreements giving rise to other payments or compensation received under this Agreement.

(f)   <u>Real Estate</u>. The Buyer and the Sellers agree that prior to the Closing Date, the parties shall obtain, and equally share the cost of, a Phase 1 Environmental Site Assessment for the real property set forth of Exhibit D hereto (the "Property") and any relevant adjoining properties (the "Phase 1"). If, in the Sellers' reasonable judgment, the Phase 1 indicates a substantial risk of a material liability to the Sellers, the Sellers may elect to terminate this Agreement.

9.   <u>Access to Records and Properties</u>. Subject at all times to the terms, provisions and conditions of the Nondisclosure Agreement and the Confidentiality Agreement, the parties acknowledge that prior to the Closing Date, through its employees, agents and representatives, the Buyer shall have the opportunity to make or cause to be made such investigation as it deems necessary or advisable of the assets, liabilities and business of Target, but such investigation shall not affect the Sellers' representations and warranties hereunder. The Sellers agree to permit the Buyer and its employees, agents and representatives to have access to Target's properties, on reasonable notice, and to all of the books and records, contracts and other documents with respect thereto, and to furnish to the Buyer such information with respect to Target's business as the Buyer has from time to time reasonably requested. The Sellers shall cause Target to authorize its key

employees, agents and representatives to cooperate with the employees, agents and representatives of the Buyer in the Buyer's due diligence.

10.   <u>Conditions to Closing</u>. The obligations of the parties to consummate and effect the purchase and sale of the Stock on the Closing Date are subject to the satisfaction in all material respects, on or before the Closing Date, of the following conditions (unless waived in writing by the party for whose benefit the condition is to be met):

(a)   <u>The Buyer</u>. The obligations of the Buyer are subject to the following conditions:

(i)   <u>Representations and Warranties of the Sellers; Performance</u>. The representations and warranties of the Sellers set forth herein shall be accurate in all material respects on and as of the Closing Date as though made on that date and the Sellers shall have performed all material obligations required to be performed prior to the Closing Date.

(ii)   <u>Consents</u>. The Sellers or Target shall have obtained all consents or waivers of any governmental authority, or the consent or waiver of any person in any contractual relationship with the Sellers or Target necessary to permit the transfer to the Buyer of all of the Stock and to give the Buyer the ability as the owner of Target to exercise Target's rights under the contracts listed in the Schedule of Disclosure, except such contracts as to which the Buyer shall have expressly waived this condition.

(iii)   <u>Stock Assignments Separate from Certificate</u>. The Trust shall have delivered to the Buyer executed Stock Assignment(s) Separate from Certificate, together with certificates representing the Stock, or other instruments of transfer respecting the sale, conveyance, transfer and assignment of the Stock from the Trust to the Buyer.

(iv)   <u>No Litigation</u>. No legal action or other proceedings to restrain or prohibit the consummation of the transactions contemplated by this Agreement or to obtain other relief in connection with this Agreement or the transactions contemplated hereby shall be pending or threatened.

(v)   <u>Adverse Changes</u>. There shall not have been instituted or threatened any litigation which materially affects Target's business or prospects, and there shall not have occurred any loss or destruction of any material part of the Target's assets taken as a whole, or any material adverse change in the financial condition, business or prospects of Target. The policies and practices of Target regarding compensation and payment to related parties shall be unchanged, such that the results of Target's operations since October 1, [last year] shall be reflected in Target's assets and liabilities on the Closing Date; provided, however, that on or before September 30, [this year], Target shall grant and pay a bonus of One Hundred Thousand Dollars ($100,000) to Founder (the "Bonus").

(vi)   <u>Due Diligence Investigation</u>. The Buyer shall have approved the results of its due diligence conducted pursuant to Section 9, above.

(vii)   <u>Financial Condition</u>. Target's stockholder's equity as of the most recent month end preceding the Closing Date shall not have changed by more than five percent (5%) from the Five Hundred Ninety-One Thousand Five Hundred and Nine Dollars ($591,509) stockholder's equity shown on Target's Balance Sheet as of September 30, [last year]; provided, however, that the percentage referenced above shall be computed without regard to (1) Target's [4 year old] Toyota Previa, (2) Target's [one year old] Toyota Camry, or (3) the Bonus.

(viii) <u>Noncompetition, Consulting and Employment Agreements</u>. On the Closing Date, Founder shall simultaneously enter into a Consulting Agreement substantially in the form of Exhibit B hereto and a Noncompetition Agreement substantially in the form of Exhibit C hereto with the Buyer (collectively, the "Ancillary Agreements").

(ix) <u>Real Estate</u>. Buyer and the Trust agree that prior to the Closing Date, the Trust shall notify the Buyer in writing as to whether it will (1) lease the Property to the Buyer at fair market value on mutually agreeable terms and based upon that certain Standard Industrial/Commercial Single-Tenant Lease — Net substantially in the form of Exhibit E attached hereto (the "Lease") or (2) offer the Property for purchase by the Buyer for Two Hundred Fifty Thousand Dollars ($250,000) in cash or by wire transfer on the Closing Date pursuant to that certain Standard Offer, Agreement and Escrow Instructions for Purchase of Real Estate (the "Purchase Agreement") substantially in the form and content of Exhibit F attached hereto. If the Buyer elects to purchase the Property pursuant to the Trust's offer, the purchase shall be entered into by the Trust and the Buyer on or before the Closing Date. If the Trust does not offer the Property for purchase by the Buyer, or if the Buyer does not elect to purchase the Property, and if the parties mutually agree as to the terms of the Lease, the parties shall enter into the Lease on or before the Closing Date. If the parties do not mutually agree as to the terms of the Lease, this Agreement shall be terminated.

(x) <u>Schedule of Disclosure</u>. The Schedule of Disclosure prepared in connection with this Agreement shall be delivered on or prior to the Closing Date and is hereby incorporated by reference.

(b) <u>The Sellers</u>. The obligations of the Sellers are subject to the following conditions:

(i) <u>Representations and Warranties of the Buyer; Performance</u>. The representations and warranties of the Buyer set forth herein shall be accurate in all material respects on and as of the Closing Date as though made on that date and the Buyer shall have performed all material obligations required to be performed prior to the Closing Date.

(ii) <u>No Litigation</u>. No legal action or other proceedings to restrain or prohibit the consummation of the transactions contemplated by this Agreement or to obtain other relief in connection with this Agreement or the transactions contemplated hereby shall be pending or threatened; and

(iii) <u>Consulting and Noncompetition Agreements</u>. On the Closing Date, the Buyer shall have entered into a Consulting Agreement and a Noncompetition Agreement with Founder, substantially in the form of Exhibit B and Exhibit C hereto, and the Lease or the Purchase Agreement (as provided in Section 10(a)(ix)).

11. <u>Satisfaction of Conditions Precedent</u>. Each of the parties hereto hereby agrees to use its good faith, diligent efforts to cause the satisfaction of the conditions specified in Section 10 hereof.

12. <u>Expenses</u>. Unless specifically addressed by this Agreement, all expenses incurred by any party hereto in connection with the transactions contemplated by this Agreement, including but not limited to legal and agent's expenses, shall be borne by such respective party.

13. Indemnification and Survival.

(a) <u>Indemnification by the Sellers</u>. Subject to the terms and conditions of this Section 13, in the event (i) that the Sellers breach any of the covenants contained in this Agreement, in any of the Ancillary Agreements or in the Lease or Purchase Agreement, or (ii) there is any inaccuracy in any representations or warranties made by the Sellers in this Agreement, in any of the Ancillary Agreements or in the Lease or Purchase Agreement, then the Sellers shall indemnify, defend and hold harmless the Buyer, its directors, officers, employees or agents, from and against any claim affecting the Buyer as a result of or relating to the matters specified in the foregoing subparts of this Section 13(a).

(b) <u>Indemnification by the Buyer</u>. Subject to the terms and conditions of this Section 13, in the event that (i) the Buyer breaches any of its covenants contained in this Agreement, in any of the Ancillary Agreements or in the Lease or Purchase Agreement, (ii) there is any inaccuracy in any representations or warranties made by the Buyer in this Agreement, in any of the Ancillary Agreements or in the Lease or Purchase Agreement, or (iii) there is any failure of the Buyer to pay, perform or discharge any of the obligations contained herein, in any Ancillary Agreement or in the Lease or Purchase Agreement, then the Buyer shall indemnify, defend and hold harmless the Sellers from and against any claims affecting the Sellers as a result of or relating to the matters specified in the foregoing subparts of this Section 13(b).

(c) <u>Direct Claims</u>. In the event the Buyer or the Sellers (the "Claimant"), desires to make a claim for indemnification pursuant to Sections 13(a) or (b) against the other (the "Indemnitor"), the Claimant shall give prompt written notice of the claim to the Indemnitor, describing, in reasonable detail, the nature of the claim. Failure to give such notice shall not affect the indemnification provided hereunder except to the extent that such failure shall have actually and materially prejudiced the Indemnitor as a result thereof.

(d) <u>Third Person Claims</u>.

(i) If any third person shall notify the Buyer or the Sellers (the "Indemnified Party") with respect to any matter (a "Third Person Claim") that may give rise to a claim for indemnification against the Buyer or the Sellers (the "Indemnifying Party") under this Section 13, then the Indemnified Party shall promptly notify each Indemnifying Party thereof in writing. Failure to give such reasonable notice shall not affect the indemnification provided hereunder except to the extent that such failure shall have actually and materially prejudiced the Indemnitor as a result thereof.

(ii) Except as otherwise provided in this Section 13, any Indemnifying Party will have the right to assume and thereafter conduct at his, hers or its own expense the defense of the Third Person Claim with counsel of his, hers or its choice, which counsel shall be reasonably satisfactory to the Indemnified Party; <u>provided</u>, <u>however</u>, that the Indemnifying Party will not consent to the entry of any judgment or enter into any settlement with respect to the Third Person Claim without the prior written consent of each Indemnified Party. If the Indemnifying Party assumes the defense then the Indemnified Party may participate in, but not control, any such defense or settlement, at the Indemnified Party's sole cost and expense.

(iii) Unless and until an Indemnifying Party assumes the defense of the Third Person Claim as provided in Section 13(d)(ii), the Indemnified Party may defend against the Third Person Claim in any manner he or it reasonably deems appropriate.

The costs of such defense shall be included in determining the losses relating to the Third Person Claim.

(iv)   In no event will the Indemnified Party consent to the entry of any judgment or enter into any settlement with respect to a Third Person Claim without the prior written consent of each of the Indemnifying Parties, which consent shall not be unreasonably withheld.

(e)   <u>Limitations; Survival</u>. All of the representations and warranties of the Buyer and the Sellers contained in Sections 6 and 7 of this Agreement, and any representations and warranties of the Buyer and the Sellers contained in the Ancillary Agreements, shall survive the Closing hereunder and the purchase and sale of the Stock and continue in full force and effect for a period of two (2) years after the Closing Date regardless of the inspections or examinations, if any, made on behalf of the other party, except that the representations and warranties contained in Sections 6(h), 6(j) and 6(l) shall survive until sixty (60) days after the expiration of the longest applicable period of limitations, if any, applicable to the matters therein represented (as such period may be extended pursuant to the request of the appropriate governmental authorities); provided, however, that as to knowing intentional misrepresentations upon which the Buyer materially and detrimentally relies, or other knowing intentional breaches of this Agreement that are material, individually or in the aggregate, such terms, conditions, warranties, representations and agreements shall survive for a period of two and one half (2½) years after the Closing Date. Notwithstanding anything to the contrary herein, no claim for indemnification under this Section 13 shall be made with respect to any representation or warranty herein after the survival period for such representation or warranty. The representations and warranties contained in this Agreement shall not be valid if the Buyer is then in material uncured default hereunder, under the Noncompetition Agreement or under the Consulting Agreement. Additionally, each representation or warranty is made solely for the exclusive benefit of the Buyer and all representations and warranties shall cease and be of no further effect upon a transfer by the Buyer to a third party who is not controlled or under the common control by or of the Buyer of all or any part of the Stock.

(f)   <u>Total Liability</u>. The total liability of the Sellers pursuant to this Agreement shall in no event exceed an aggregate amount of Two Million Dollars ($2,000,000).

(g)   <u>Liability Threshold</u>. Notwithstanding anything to the contrary in this Agreement, no indemnification pursuant to Section 13 shall be payable to the Buyer unless the total of all claims for indemnification pursuant to Section 13 shall exceed in the aggregate a threshold amount of Twenty Thousand Dollars ($20,000), whereupon the Sellers shall indemnify the Buyer for all claims in excess of such amount. Notwithstanding anything to the contrary in this Agreement, the Sellers shall have no liability to the Buyer, its successors or assigns for any loss or claim arising out of or due to the manner of the operation of the business after the Closing Date.

14.   <u>Termination</u>.

(a)   <u>Termination of Agreement</u>. This Agreement and the Lease or Purchase Agreement may only be terminated as provided below:

(i)   The parties may terminate this Agreement by mutual written consent at any time prior to the Closing;

(ii)   The Buyer may terminate this Agreement by giving written notice to the Sellers at any time prior to the Closing (A) if the Sellers have breached any of the covenants contained in this Agreement or if there is any material inaccuracy in the representations or warranties made by the Sellers in this Agreement, the Buyer has notified the Sellers of such breach or inaccuracy, and the breach or inaccuracy has not been cured within a fifteen (15) day period after such notice; or (B) if the Closing shall not have occurred within ninety (90) days after the date of this Agreement by reason of the failure of any condition precedent under Section 10 hereof (unless the failure results primarily from the Buyer breaching any covenant or misrepresenting any representation or warranty contained in this Agreement).

(iii)   The Sellers may terminate this Agreement by giving written notice to the Buyer at any time prior to the Closing (A) if the Buyer has breached any of its covenants contained in this Agreement or if there is any material inaccuracy in the representations or warranties made by the Buyer contained in this Agreement, the Sellers have notified the Buyer of such breach or inaccuracy, and the breach or inaccuracy has not been cured within a fifteen (15) day period after such notice; or (B) if the Closing shall not have occurred within ninety (90) days after the date of this Agreement by reason of the failure of any condition precedent under Section 10 hereof (unless the failure results primarily from the Sellers or persons under their control breaching any covenant or misrepresenting any representation or warranty contained in this Agreement).

(iv)   This Agreement shall terminate without any action by the parties upon the effectiveness of any final order binding upon any party and prohibiting consummation of the transactions contemplated by this Agreement.

(b)   <u>Effect of Termination</u>. If any party terminates this Agreement pursuant to subparts (i)–(iv) of Section 14(a) or Section 14(c), all rights and obligations of the parties hereunder, except the obligations with respect to (i) indemnification created under Section 13, (ii) the termination fee payable as a result of termination pursuant to Section 14(c) and (iii) confidentiality created under Section 8(d), shall terminate without further liability of any party to any other party.

(c)   <u>Termination Fee</u>.

(i)   <u>Termination Fee Payable by the Sellers</u>. Subject to the exceptions set forth in subparts (i), (iii) and (iv) of Section 14(a), if this Agreement is terminated by the Sellers, and if the conditions to closing set forth in Section 10(a) have been met to the satisfaction of, or waived by, the Buyer, and if the conditions to closing set forth in Section 10(b) have been met by the Buyer, the Sellers shall pay to the Buyer an aggregate of One Hundred Thousand Dollars ($100,000) in immediately available funds.

(ii)   <u>Termination Fee Payable by the Buyer</u>. Subject to the exceptions set forth in subparts (i), (ii) and (iv) of Section 14(a), if this Agreement is terminated by the Buyer, and if the conditions to closing set forth in Section 10(a) have been met by the Sellers, and if the conditions to closing set forth in Section 10(b) have been met to the satisfaction of, or waived by, the Sellers, the Buyer shall pay to the Sellers an aggregate of One Hundred Thousand Dollars ($100,000) in immediately available funds.

15.   <u>General Provisions</u>.

(a)   <u>Attorneys' Fees</u>. The Sellers, on the one hand, and the Buyer, on the other hand, agree to pay to the other all reasonable attorneys' fees, costs and other expenses incurred by such other party in successfully enforcing any provision of this Agreement against such other party.

(b)   <u>Entire Agreement; Modifications; Waiver</u>. This Agreement supersedes any and all written and oral agreements heretofore made relating to the subject matter hereof, and constitutes the entire agreement of the parties relating to the subject matter hereof. None of the parties has made any representation or warranty other than as expressly stated herein. This Agreement may be amended only by an instrument in writing signed by all of the parties hereto. Inspection of documents or the receipt of information pursuant to this Agreement shall not constitute a waiver of any representation, warranty, covenant or condition hereunder. No waiver shall be binding unless executed in writing by the party making such waiver.

(c)   <u>Severability</u>. If any clause or provision of this Agreement shall be held invalid or unenforceable, such clause or provision shall be fully severable and this Agreement and that separate clause or provision shall be construed and enforced as if such invalid or unenforceable clause or provision had never comprised a part of this Agreement, and the remaining provisions of this Agreement shall remain in full force and effect and shall not be affected by the invalid or unenforceable clause or provision or by its severance from the Agreement.

(d)   <u>Successors and Assigns</u>. This Agreement shall be binding upon and inure to the benefit of each of the parties hereto, and their successors and assigns.

(e)   <u>Captions</u>. The paragraph headings contained herein are for the purpose of convenience and are not intended to define or limit the contents of said paragraphs.

(f)   <u>Counterparts</u>. This Agreement may be executed in several counterparts, each of which shall be deemed an original, and all of which together shall constitute one and the same instrument.

(g)   <u>Governing Law; Jurisdiction; Venue</u>. This Agreement shall be governed by and construed in accordance with the laws of the State of California. The Sellers hereby consent to the jurisdiction of any State or Federal Court within the County of Orange, State of California and irrevocably agrees that all actions or proceedings arising out of or relating to this Agreement shall be litigated in such courts. The Sellers expressly submit and consent to the jurisdiction of the aforesaid courts and waive any defense of forum non conveniens.

(h)   <u>Notices</u>. All notices required or desired to be given hereunder shall be given in writing and signed by the party so giving notice, and shall be effective when actually received; when personally delivered; when delivered by a professional overnight courier service, receipt acknowledged; when delivered by facsimile transmission, with receipt acknowledged (so long as delivery occurs during regular business hours, otherwise notice shall be deemed given at the beginning of the next business day); or 72 hours after deposit with the United States Postal Service, as certified or registered mail, return receipt requested, first class postage and fees prepaid, addressed as set forth below. A notice not delivered in a manner described in the preceding sentence shall be deemed given when actually received by the party to whom it is given. Any notice required to be given to, or by, the Sellers shall be sufficient if given to, or by, Founder, so long as Founder continues as the sole trustee of the Trust.

The Trust: The Founder Family Trust, dated January 15, 1973, as amended

c/o Founder, Trustee
2100 Orangewood Avenue
Orange, CA 92868
Telephone: (714) xxx-xxxx
Facsimile: (714) xxx-xxxx

Founder: Founder
2100 Orangewood Avenue
Orange, CA 92868
Telephone: (714) xxx-xxxx
Facsimile: (714) xxx-xxxx

With a copy to: Paula Lawyer
Founder's Counsel, LLP
611 Anton Boulevard
Costa Mesa, CA 92626
Telephone: (714) xxx-xxxx
Facsimile: (714) xxx-xxxx

The Buyer: The Acquiring Corp, Inc.
15800 Ventura Blvd.
Encino, CA 91403
Attention: President
Telephone: (818) xxx-xxxx
Facsimile: (818) xxx-xxxx

With a copy to: Sandy Solicitor
Maynard & Warren, LLP
919 Albany Street
Los Angeles, CA 90015
Telephone: (213) xxx-xxxx
Facsimile: (213) xxx-xxxx

The time or manner of delivery of copies to counsel shall not affect the time of delivery or the effectiveness of notice to a party under this Agreement.

Any party from time to time may change such party's address for giving notice by giving notice thereof in the manner outlined above.

(i) <u>Further Assurances; Good Faith</u>. Subject to the terms and conditions set forth herein, each party agrees to cooperate in good faith with the other and execute and deliver such further documents and perform such other acts as may be reasonably necessary or appropriate to consummate and carry into effect the transactions contemplated by this Agreement. The Parties to this Agreement agree that their obligations hereunder are subject to the covenant of good faith and fair dealing which is implied under California law with respect to the relationship created hereunder.

(the remainder of this page intentionally left blank; signature page follows)

IN WITNESS WHEREOF, the parties hereto have executed this Agreement as of the date first above written.

THE BUYER:

THE ACQUIRING CORP., INC.

By: _____

CEO Guy, President

THE TRUST:

THE FOUNDER FAMILY TRUST,
DATED JANUARY 15, 1993, AS AMENDED

By:_____

Founder, Trustee

FOUNDER:

_____

Founder

EXHIBITS

SAMPLE CONFIDENTIALITY AND INVENTION ASSIGNMENT AGREEMENT

<u>Confidentiality and
Invention Assignment Agreement</u>

I hereby acknowledge and agree as follows with [COMPANY] Inc. (the "Company") in connection with my employment or the continuance of my employment (as the case may be) with the Company.

1.   <u>No Term of Employment</u>. I acknowledge and agree that my employment with the Company is not for any fixed term, and that my employment will continue only at the will of both the Company and me. I agree that this means my employment may be terminated at any time for any reason or for no reason, either with or without cause, either by me or the Company.

2.   <u>No Conflicts with Prior Employment</u>. I represent that my employment with the Company will not conflict with any obligations I have to former employers or any other persons. I specifically represent that I have not brought to the Company (and will not bring to the Company) any materials or documents of a former employer or other person, or any confidential information or property of a former employer or other person.

3.   <u>Prior Inventions</u>. As a matter of record, and in order to assist the Company in determining its rights to any intellectual property interests in connection with my engagement, I have listed (at the end of this Agreement) all inventions, copyrighted or trademarked material, patents and patent applications, and any other protectable intellectual property rights I own (or have any interest in) that were conceived of, or first reduced to practice, prior to the date hereof, all of which are excluded from the provisions of Section 5 of this Agreement ("Prior Inventions"). If nothing is listed below, I agree that the Company may conclusively assume that I am not retaining any Prior Inventions outside of the Company. I will not use any Prior Inventions in the course of my engagement with the Company.

4.   <u>Confidential Information</u>. I understand that as part of my employment with the Company I am expected to make new contributions of value to the Company. I also acknowledge that, during my employment, I will learn information relating to the Company, its business and products, that has commercial value to the Company and that the Company desires to keep confidential. This confidential information will include such things as trade secrets, techniques, processes, know-how, technical specifications, discoveries, inventions, marketing information, business strategies, information regarding customers and suppliers, and any other information (not necessarily in writing) that may be useful to the Company, and that is not generally available to the public (all of this information is referred to in this Agreement as "Confidential Information"). I agree that all Confidential Information will be the sole property of the Company and I agree that I will not disclose any Confidential Information to any other person (except solely in performing my duties as an employee of the Company), and that I will otherwise keep all Confidential Information in strictest confidence and not use it for any purpose other than in connection with the furtherance of the interests of the Company. Also, I will comply with the terms of agreements entered into by the

Company from time to time relating to the protection of the proprietary information of other parties.

5.   <u>Inventions During Employment</u>. I agree that all discoveries and inventions relating in any manner to the business or the future business of the Company and conceived, reduced to practice, authored or made by me (either alone or with others) during my employment with the Company, will constitute work product of my employment, will be the sole property of the Company and will become part of the Company's Confidential Information. I will promptly disclose these discoveries and inventions to the Company in writing, and I will not disclose these discoveries and inventions to any other persons other than in the performance of my duties as an employee of the Company. I hereby assign to the Company all my right to such discoveries and inventions, and I will sign such additional documents as the Company from time to time considers advisable in order to complete this assignment and to apply for patent, copyright or other protection in the name of the Company. I agree that, for purposes of this Agreement, the term "discoveries and inventions" shall have the broadest meanings, including new products, machines, methods, processes, works of authorship (including software programs), improvements, compositions of matter, and designs or configurations.

I understand that the Company is hereby advising me that any provision in this Agreement requiring me to assign my rights in any invention does not apply to an invention that qualifies fully under the provisions of Section 2870 of the California Labor Code. That section provides that the requirement to assign inventions "shall not apply to an invention that the employee developed entirely on his or her own time without using the employer's equipment, supplies, facilities, or trade secret information except for those inventions that either: (1) relate at the time of conception or reduction to practice of the invention to the employer's business, or actual or demonstrably anticipated research or development of the employer; or (2) result from any work performed by the employee for the employer." BY SIGNING THIS AGREEMENT, I ACKNOWLEDGE THAT THIS PARAGRAPH SHALL CONSTITUTE WRITTEN NOTICE OF THOSE PROVISIONS OF SECTION 2870.

6.   <u>Certain Further Agreements</u>. I agree that, since my employment with the Company involves a relationship of confidence and trust, during my employment I will not engage in any other employment or business activities that are competitive with or otherwise conflict with the interests of the Company, and I will not plan or organize any such competing business activity.

7.   <u>Certain Obligations Upon Termination of Employment</u>. In the event of the termination of my employment by me or by the Company for any reason, I will promptly deliver to the Company all documents, data and other materials of any nature or media pertaining to my work with the Company that contain any Confidential Information or any discoveries and inventions, I will not take with me nor use any such documents or materials (or any copies of them), and I will continue to keep all Confidential Information in strictest confidence as required by paragraph 4, above, for a period of three years following the termination of my employment. I also agree that, in recognition of my position of confidence and trust with the Company during my employment, for a period of one year following such termination I will not solicit any of the Company's employees to work for a competitive company.

8.   <u>Specific Performance</u>. I acknowledge and agree that irreparable injury to the Company may result in the event I breach any covenant and agreement contained in this Agreement and that the remedy at law for the breach of any such covenant will be inadequate. Therefore, if I engage in any act in violation of the provisions of this Agreement, I agree that the Company shall be entitled, in addition to such other remedies and damages as may be available to it by law or under this Agreement, to injunctive relief to enforce the provisions of this Agreement.

9.   <u>Entire Agreement</u>. This Agreement is the entire agreement between the Company and me regarding the above matters, and I represent that I am not relying upon any contrary statements or understandings between me and the Company with regard to these matters.

Dated: _____, _____.

[COMPANY] INC.
By: _____

Its: _____

EMPLOYEE

_____
(printed name of employee)

_____
(signature of employee)

Prior Inventions (if any) — see paragraph 3 above:

_____

_____

_____

_____

_____

_____

_____

_____

_____

_____

_____

_____

_____

_____

_____

_____

_____

(Attach additional pages if necessary)

SAMPLE VOTING AGREEMENT

LEARNING INC.

AMENDED AND RESTATED VOTING AGREEMENT

THIS AMENDED AND RESTATED VOTING AGREEMENT (the "**Agreement**") is made and entered into as of July 10, 20____, by and among Learning, Inc., a Delaware corporation (the "**Company**"), each holder of the Company's Series A Preferred Stock, $0.0001 par value per share ("**Series A Preferred Stock**") and of the Company's Series B Preferred Stock, $0.0001 par value per share (the "**Series B Preferred Stock**," referred to collectively with the Series A Preferred Stock, as the "**Preferred Stock**") listed on <u>Schedule A</u> (together with any subsequent investors, or transferees, who become parties hereto as "Investors" pursuant to <u>Sections 6.1(a)</u> or <u>6.2</u> below, the "**Investors**") and those certain stockholders of the Company listed on <u>Schedule B</u> (together with any subsequent stockholders or option holders, or any transferees, who become parties hereto as "Key Holders" pursuant to <u>Sections 6.1(b)</u> or <u>6.2</u> below, the "**Key Holders**," and together collectively with the Investors, the "**Stockholders**").

<u>RECITALS</u>

A.   Concurrently with the execution of this Agreement, the Company and certain of the Investors are entering into that certain Series B Preferred Stock Purchase Agreement (the "**Purchase Agreement**") providing for the issuance and sale of shares of the Series B Preferred Stock. Certain of the Investors are parties to the Amended and Restated Voting Agreement dated January 18, 20____ by and among the Company and the parties thereto (the "**Prior Agreement**"). The parties to the Prior Agreement desire to amend and restate that agreement to provide those Investors purchasing shares of the Company's Series B Preferred Stock with the right, among other rights, to elect certain members of the board of directors of the Company (the "**Board**") in accordance with the terms of this Agreement.

B.   The Amended and Restated Certificate of Incorporation of the Company (the "**Restated Certificate**") provides that (a) the holders of record of the shares of the Company's Series A Preferred Stock, exclusively and as a separate class, shall be entitled to elect two (2) directors of the Company (each, a "**Series A Director**") and the holders of record of shares of Series B Preferred Stock shall be entitled to elect one (1) director of the Company (the "**Series B Director**" and together with the Series A Director, the "**Preferred Directors**"); and (b) the holders of record of the shares of common stock of the Company, $0.0001 par value ("**Common Stock**") and the Preferred Stock, together as a class, shall be entitled to elect two (2) directors of the Company.

C.   The parties also desire to enter into this Agreement to set forth their agreements and understandings with respect to how shares of the Company's capital stock held by them will be voted on, or tendered in connection with, an acquisition of the Company and an increase in the number of shares of Common Stock required to provide for the conversion of the Company's Preferred Stock.

NOW, THEREFORE, the parties agree as follows:

1. <u>Voting Provisions Regarding Board of Directors</u>.

    1.1   <u>Size of the Board</u>. Each Stockholder agrees to vote, or cause to be voted, all Shares (as defined below) owned by such Stockholder, or over which such Stockholder has voting control, from time to time and at all times, in whatever manner as shall be necessary to ensure that the size of the Board shall be set and remain at five (5) directors. For purposes of this Agreement, the term "**Shares**" shall mean and include any securities of the Company the holders of which are entitled to vote for members of the Board, including without limitation, all shares of Common Stock, Series A Preferred Stock and Series B Preferred Stock, by whatever name called, now owned or subsequently acquired by a Stockholder, however acquired, whether through stock splits, stock dividends, reclassifications, recapitalizations, similar events or otherwise.

    1.2   <u>Board Composition</u>. Each Stockholder agrees to vote, or cause to be voted, all Shares owned by such Stockholder, or over which such Stockholder has voting control, from time to time and at all times, in whatever manner as shall be necessary to ensure that at each annual or special meeting of stockholders at which an election of directors is held or pursuant to any written consent of the stockholders, the persons nominated in accordance with this Section 1.2 shall be elected to the Board:

    (a)   Ocean Venture Partners ("**Ocean**") may nominate one Series A Director so long as Ocean holds at least fifty percent (50%) of the shares of Series A Preferred Stock (as adjusted for any stock splits, stock dividends, recapitalizations or the like) held by them as of the date of this Agreement, which individual shall initially be Akinobu Yorihiro;

    (b)   TransPacific Venture Partners and/or its affiliated entities ("**TransPacific**") may nominate one Series A Director so long as TransPacific holds at least fifty percent (50%) of the shares of Series A Preferred Stock (as adjusted for any stock splits, stock dividends, recapitalizations or the like) held by them as of the date of this Agreement, which individual shall initially be Alexandre Sood;

    (c)   Joseph Technology Partners ("**JTP**") may nominate one Series B Director so long as JTP holds at least fifty percent (50%) of the shares of Series B Preferred Stock (as adjusted for any stock splits, stock dividends, recapitalizations or the like) held by them as of the date of this Agreement, which individual shall initially be Alexander Suh; and

    (d)   At each election of directors in which the holders of the Common Stock and the Preferred Stock, voting together as a single class, are entitled to elect two (2) directors of the Company (i) one individual not otherwise an Affiliate (defined below) of the Company or of any Investor (the "**Outside Director**"), who shall initially be Dorothy Pavloff, provided that if she becomes unavailable to serve as the Outside Director, a replacement shall be nominated who is mutually acceptable to (A) the holders of a majority of the Preferred Stock and (B) the holders of a majority of the Common Stock shares held by the Key Holders, and if a mutual nominee cannot be agreed upon, such position shall remain vacant until that deadlock can be resolved; and (ii) the Company's then-current Chief Executive Officer, who shall initially be Tracy R. Roman (the "**CEO Director**"), provided that if for any reason the CEO Director shall cease to serve as the Chief Executive Officer of the Company, each of the Stockholders shall promptly vote their respective Shares (A) to remove the former Chief Executive

Officer from the Board if such person has not resigned as a member of the Board and (B) to elect such person's replacement as Chief Executive Officer of the Company as the new CEO Director.

To the extent that any of Ocean, TransPacific or JTP shall (i) transfer to any person or entity other than its own affiliate, more than fifty percent (50%) of the shares of Preferred Stock held by such entity as of the date of this Agreement; or (ii) no longer hold (as a consequence of conversion, merger or otherwise) the number of shares of Preferred Stock requisite to the continuation of the nomination rights set forth in Sections 1.2(a), (b) and (c), respectively, then the applicable Investor shall lose its right to nominate a director under this Section 1.2, and any member of the Board who would otherwise have been nominated in accordance with the terms hereof shall instead be nominated and voted upon by all the stockholders of the Company entitled to vote thereon in accordance with, and pursuant to, the Company's Restated Certificate and its Bylaws.

For purposes of this Agreement, an individual, firm, corporation, partnership, association, limited liability company, trust or any other entity (collectively, a **"Person"**) shall be deemed an **"Affiliate"** of another Person who, directly or indirectly, controls, is controlled by or is under common control with such Person, including, without limitation, any general partner, officer, director, or manager of such Person and any venture capital fund now or hereafter existing that is controlled by one or more general partners of or shares the same management company with such Person.

1.3   Failure to Designate a Board Member. In the absence of any nomination from a Person with the right to designate a director as specified in Section 1.2, above, if a Person entitled to make a nomination pursuant to this Agreement continues to fail to make a nomination after sixty (60) days following delivery of written notice from the Company, with a copy of such notice also delivered to the director previously designated by that Person, and a second delivery of such notices thirty (30) days following delivery of the first notice, then the applicable Person shall have waived its right to nominate a director under this Section 1.2, and any member of the Board who would otherwise have been nominated in accordance with the terms of Section 1.2 shall instead be nominated and voted upon by all the stockholders of the Company entitled to vote thereon in accordance with, and pursuant to, the Company's Restated Certificate and its Bylaws.

1.4   Removal of Board Members. Each Stockholder also agrees to vote, or cause to be voted, all Shares owned by such Stockholder, or over which such Stockholder has voting control, from time to time and at all times, in whatever manner as shall be necessary to ensure that:

(a)   except as set forth in Section 1.2(d) and Section 1.3, no director elected pursuant to Section 1.2 of this Agreement may be removed from office unless (i) such removal is directed or approved by the affirmative vote of the Person, or of the holders of a majority of the shares of stock entitled under Section 1.2 to nominate that director or (ii) the Person originally entitled to nominate or approve such director pursuant to Section 1.2 is no longer so entitled to nominate or approve such director;

(b)   any vacancies created by the resignation, removal or death of a director elected pursuant to Section 1.2 or Section 1.3 shall be filled pursuant to the provisions of this Section 1; and

(c)   upon the request of any Person entitled to nominate a director as provided in Section 1.2(a), (b) or (c) to remove such director, such director shall be removed.

All Stockholders agree to execute any written consents required to perform the obligations of this Agreement, and the Company agrees at the request of any Person entitled to nominate a director to call a special meeting of stockholders for the purpose of electing directors. So long as the stockholders of the Company are entitled to cumulative voting, if less than the entire Board is to be removed, no director may be removed without cause if the votes cast against his or her removal would be sufficient to elect such director if then cumulatively voted at an election of the entire Board.

1.5   No Liability for Election of Nominated Directors. No Person, nor any Affiliate of any such Person, shall have any liability as a result of nominating a candidate for election as a director for any act or omission by such nominated director in his or her capacity as a director of the Company, nor shall any Person have any liability as a result of voting for any such nominee in accordance with the provisions of this Agreement.

2.   Vote to Increase Authorized Common Stock. Each Stockholder agrees to vote or cause to be voted all Shares owned by such Stockholder, or over which such Stockholder has voting control, from time to time and at all times, in whatever manner as shall be necessary to increase the number of authorized shares of Common Stock from time to time to ensure that there will be sufficient shares of Common Stock available for conversion of all of the shares of Preferred Stock outstanding at any given time.

3.   Drag-Along Right.

3.1   Definitions. A "**Sale of the Company**" shall mean either: (a) a transaction or series of related transactions in which a Person, or a group of related Persons, acquires from stockholders of the Company shares representing more than fifty percent (50%) of the outstanding voting power of the Company (a "**Stock Sale**"); or (b) a transaction that qualifies as a "**Deemed Liquidation Event**" as defined in the Restated Certificate.

3.2   Actions to be Taken. In the event that the holders of at least a majority of the outstanding shares of Common Stock issued or issuable upon conversion of the shares of Preferred Stock (such holders, the "**Selling Investors**") and the Board approve a Sale of the Company in writing, specifying that this Section 3 shall apply to such transaction, then each Stockholder hereby agrees:

(a)   if such transaction requires stockholder approval, with respect to all Shares that such Stockholder owns or over which such Stockholder otherwise exercises voting power, to vote (in person, by proxy or by action by written consent, as applicable) all Shares in favor of, and adopt, such Sale of the Company (together with any related amendment to the Restated Certificate required in order to implement such Sale of the Company) and to vote in opposition to any and all other proposals that could delay or impair the ability of the Company to consummate such Sale of the Company;

(b)   if such transaction is a Stock Sale, to sell the same proportion of shares of capital stock of the Company beneficially held by such Stockholder as is being sold by the Selling Investors to the Person to whom the Selling Investors propose to sell their Shares, and, except as permitted in Section 3.3 below, on the same terms and conditions as the Selling Investors;

(c)   to execute and deliver all related documentation and take such other action in support of the Sale of the Company as shall reasonably be requested by the

Company or the Selling Investors in order to carry out the terms and provision of this <u>Section 3</u>, including without limitation executing and delivering instruments of conveyance and transfer, and any purchase agreement, merger agreement, indemnity agreement, escrow agreement, consent, waiver, governmental filing, share certificates duly endorsed for transfer (free and clear of impermissible liens, claims and encumbrances) and any similar or related documents;

(d)   not to deposit, and to cause their Affiliates not to deposit, except as provided in this Agreement, any Shares of the Company owned by such party or Affiliate in a voting trust or subject any Shares to any arrangement or agreement with respect to the voting of such Shares, unless specifically requested to do so by the acquirer in connection with the Sale of the Company;

(e)   to refrain from exercising any dissenters' rights or rights of appraisal under applicable law at any time with respect to such Sale of the Company; and

(f)   if the consideration to be paid in exchange for the Shares pursuant to this <u>Section 3</u> includes any securities and due receipt thereof by any Stockholder would require under applicable law (x) the registration or qualification of such securities or of any person as a broker or dealer or agent with respect to such securities or (y) the provision to any Stockholder of any information other than such information as a prudent issuer would generally furnish in an offering made solely to "accredited investors" as defined in Regulation D promulgated under the Securities Act of 1933, as amended, the Company may cause to be paid to any such Stockholder in lieu thereof, against surrender of the Shares which would have otherwise been sold by such Stockholder, an amount in cash equal to the fair value (as determined in good faith by the Company) of the securities which such Stockholder would otherwise receive as of the date of the issuance of such securities in exchange for the Shares.

3.3   <u>Exceptions</u>. Notwithstanding the forgoing, a Stockholder will not be required to comply with <u>Section 3.2</u> above in connection with any proposed Sale of the Company (the "**Proposed Sale**") unless:

(a)   any representations and warranties to be made by such Stockholder in connection with the Proposed Sale are limited to representations and warranties related to authority, ownership and the ability to convey title to such Shares, including but not limited to representations and warranties that (i) the Stockholder holds all right, title and interest in and to the Shares such Stockholder purports to hold, free and clear of all liens and encumbrances, (ii) the obligations of the Stockholder in connection with the transaction have been duly authorized, if applicable, (iii) the documents to be entered into by the Stockholder have been duly executed by the Stockholder and delivered to the acquirer and are enforceable against the Stockholder in accordance with their respective terms and (iv) neither the execution and delivery of documents to be entered into in connection with the transaction, nor the performance of the Stockholder's obligations thereunder, will cause a breach or violation of the terms of any agreement, law or judgment, order or decree of any court or governmental agency;

(b)   the Stockholder shall not be liable for the inaccuracy of any representation or warranty made by any other Person in connection with the Proposed Sale, other than the Company;

(c)   the liability for indemnification, if any, of such Stockholder in the Proposed Sale and for the inaccuracy of any representations and warranties made by the

Company in connection with such Proposed Sale, is several and not joint with any other Person, and is pro rata in proportion to the amount of consideration paid to such Stockholder in connection with such Proposed Sale (in accordance with the provisions of the Restated Certificate);

(d)   liability shall be limited to such Stockholder's pro rata share (determined in proportion to proceeds received by such Stockholder in connection with such Proposed Sale in accordance with the provisions of the Restated Certificate) of a negotiated aggregate indemnification amount that applies equally to all Stockholders but that in no event exceeds the amount of consideration actually paid to such Stockholder in connection with such Proposed Sale, except with respect to claims related to fraud by such Stockholder, the liability for which need not be limited as to such Stockholder;

(e)   upon the consummation of the Proposed Sale, (i) each holder of each series of the Company's Preferred Stock and each holder of Common Stock will receive the same form of consideration for their shares of Common Stock and Preferred Stock, (ii) each holder of a series of Preferred Stock will receive the same amount of consideration per share of such series of Preferred Stock, (iii) each holder of Common Stock will receive the same amount of consideration per share of Common Stock, and (iv) unless the holders of at least a majority of the Preferred Stock elect otherwise by written notice given to the Company at least ten (10) days prior to the effective date of any such Proposed Sale, the aggregate consideration receivable by all holders of the Preferred Stock and Common Stock shall be allocated among the holders of Preferred Stock and Common Stock on the basis of the relative liquidation preferences to which the holders of each respective series of Preferred Stock and the holders of Common Stock are entitled in a Deemed Liquidation Event (assuming for this purpose that the Proposed Sale is a Deemed Liquidation Event) in accordance with the Company's Certificate of Incorporation in effect immediately prior to the Proposed Sale; and

(f)   subject to clause (e) above, requiring the same form of consideration to be received by the holders of the Company's Common and Preferred Stock, if any holders of any capital stock of the Company are given an option as to the form and amount of consideration to be received as a result of the Proposed Sale, all holders of such capital stock will be given the same option.

3.4   Restrictions on Sales of Control of the Company. No Stockholder shall be a party to any Stock Sale unless all holders of Preferred Stock are allowed to participate in such transaction and the consideration received pursuant to such transaction is allocated among the parties thereto in the manner specified in the Company's Certificate of Incorporation in effect immediately prior to the Stock Sale (as if such transaction were a Deemed Liquidation Event), unless the holders of at least a majority of the Preferred Stock elect otherwise by written notice given to the Company at least ten (10) days prior to the effective date of any such transaction or series of related transactions.

4.   Remedies.

4.1   Covenants of the Company. The Company agrees to use its best efforts, within the requirements of applicable law, to ensure that the rights granted under this Agreement are effective and that the parties enjoy the benefits of this Agreement. Such actions include, without limitation, the use of the Company's best efforts to cause the nomination and election of the directors as provided in this Agreement.

4.2   <u>Irrevocable Proxy</u>. Each party to this Agreement hereby constitutes and appoints the President and Treasurer of the Company, and, if applicable, a designee of the Selling Investors, and each of them, with full power of substitution, as the proxies of the party with respect to the matters set forth herein, including without limitation, election of persons as members of the Board in accordance with <u>Section 1</u> hereto, votes to increase authorized shares pursuant to <u>Section 2</u> hereof and votes regarding any Sale of the Company pursuant to <u>Section 3</u> hereof, and hereby authorizes each of them to represent and to vote, if and only if the party (i) fails to vote or (ii) attempts to vote (whether by proxy, in person or by written consent), in a manner which is inconsistent with the terms of this Agreement, all of such party's Shares in favor of the election of persons as members of the Board determined pursuant to and in accordance with the terms and provisions of this Agreement or the increase of authorized shares or approval of any Sale of the Company pursuant to and in accordance with the terms and provisions of <u>Section 2</u> and <u>Section 3</u>, respectively, of this Agreement. The proxy granted pursuant to the immediately preceding sentence is given in consideration of the agreements and covenants of the Company and the parties in connection with the transactions contemplated by this Agreement and, as such, is coupled with an interest and shall be irrevocable unless and until this Agreement terminates or expires pursuant to <u>Section 5</u> hereof. Each party hereto hereby revokes any and all previous proxies with respect to the Shares and shall not hereafter, unless and until this Agreement terminates or expires pursuant to <u>Section 5</u> hereof, purport to grant any other proxy or power of attorney with respect to any of the Shares, deposit any of the Shares into a voting trust or enter into any agreement (other than this Agreement), arrangement or understanding with any person, directly or indirectly, to vote, grant any proxy or give instructions with respect to the voting of any of the Shares, in each case, with respect to any of the matters set forth herein.

4.3   <u>Specific Enforcement</u>. Each party acknowledges and agrees that each party hereto will be irreparably damaged in the event any of the provisions of this Agreement are not performed by the parties in accordance with their specific terms or are otherwise breached. Accordingly, it is agreed that each of the Company and the Stockholders shall be entitled to an injunction to prevent breaches of this Agreement, and to specific enforcement of this Agreement and its terms and provisions in any action instituted in any court of the United States or any state having subject matter jurisdiction.

4.4   <u>Remedies Cumulative</u>. All remedies, either under this Agreement or by law or otherwise afforded to any party, shall be cumulative and not alternative.

5.   <u>Term</u>. This Agreement shall be effective as of the date hereof and shall continue in effect until and shall terminate upon the earliest to occur of (a) the consummation of the Company's first underwritten public offering of its Common Stock (other than a registration statement relating either to the sale of securities to employees of the Company pursuant to its stock option, stock purchase or similar plan or an SEC Rule 145 transaction); (b) the consummation of a Sale of the Company and distribution of proceeds to or escrow for the benefit of the Stockholders in accordance with the Restated Certificate, provided that the provisions of <u>Sections 3 and 4</u> hereof will continue after the closing of any Sale of the Company to the extent necessary to enforce the provisions of <u>Section 3</u> with respect to such Sale of the Company; (c) ten (10) years from the date of this Agreement; and (d) termination of this Agreement in accordance with <u>Section 6.8</u> below.

6. Miscellaneous.

    6.1   Additional Parties.

    (a)   Notwithstanding anything to the contrary contained herein, if the Company issues additional shares of Series B Preferred Stock after the date hereof, as a condition to the issuance of such shares the Company shall require that any purchaser of any shares of Series B Preferred Stock become a party to this Agreement by executing and delivering (i) the Adoption Agreement attached to this Agreement as Exhibit A, or (ii) a counterpart signature page hereto agreeing to be bound by and subject to the terms of this Agreement as an Investor and Stockholder hereunder. In either event, each such person thereafter shall be deemed an Investor and Stockholder for all purposes under this Agreement.

    (b)   In the event that after the date of this Agreement, the Company enters into an agreement with any Person to issue shares of capital stock to such Person (other than to a purchaser of Series B Preferred Stock described in Section 6.1(a) above), following which such Person shall hold Shares constituting one percent (1%) or more of the Company's then outstanding capital stock (treating for this purpose all shares of Common Stock issuable upon exercise of or conversion of outstanding options, warrants or convertible securities, as if exercised and/or converted or exchanged), then, the Company shall cause such Person, as a condition precedent to entering into such agreement, to become a party to this Agreement by executing an Adoption Agreement in the form attached hereto as Exhibit A, agreeing to be bound by and subject to the terms of this Agreement as a Key Holder and a Stockholder and thereafter such person shall be deemed a Key Holder Stockholder for all purposes under this Agreement. Any Person who is a Key Holder Stockholder under this definition and who, at any time after the date of this Agreement, no longer holds Shares constituting one percent (1%) or more of the Company's then outstanding capital stock (as described above) shall cease to be a Key Holder or a Stockholder and may be deleted from this Agreement, subject always to the re-application of this Section 6.1(b) should it again become applicable.

    6.2   Transfers. Each transferee or assignee of any Shares subject to this Agreement shall continue to be subject to the terms hereof, and, as a condition precedent to the Company's recognizing such transfer, each transferee or assignee shall agree in writing to be subject to each of the terms of this Agreement by executing and delivering an Adoption Agreement substantially in the form attached hereto as Exhibit A. Upon the execution and delivery of an Adoption Agreement by any transferee, such transferee shall be deemed to be a party hereto as if such transferee were the transferor and such transferee's signature appeared on the signature pages of this Agreement and shall be deemed to be an Investor and Stockholder, or Key Holder and Stockholder, as applicable. The Company shall not permit the transfer of the Shares subject to this Agreement on its books or issue a new certificate representing any such Shares unless and until such transferee shall have complied with the terms of this Section 6.2. Each certificate representing the Shares subject to this Agreement if issued on or after the date of this Agreement shall be endorsed by the Company with the legend set forth in Section 6.12.

    6.3   Successors and Assigns. The terms of this Agreement shall inure to the benefit of and be binding upon the respective successors and assigns of the parties. Nothing in this Agreement, express or implied, is intended to confer upon any party other than the parties hereto or their respective successors and assigns any rights, remedies, obligations, or liabilities under or by reason of this Agreement, except as expressly provided in this Agreement.

6.4   Governing Law. This Agreement shall be governed by, and construed in accordance with, the laws of the State of Delaware, regardless of the laws that might otherwise govern under applicable principles of conflicts of law.

6.5   Counterparts; Facsimile. This Agreement may be executed and delivered by facsimile signature and in two or more counterparts, each of which shall be deemed an original, but all of which together shall constitute one and the same instrument.

6.6   Titles and Subtitles. The titles and subtitles used in this Agreement are used for convenience only and are not to be considered in construing or interpreting this Agreement.

6.7   Notices. All notices and other communications given or made pursuant to this Agreement shall be in writing and shall be deemed effectively given: (a) upon personal delivery to the party to be notified, (b) when sent by confirmed electronic mail or facsimile if sent during normal business hours of the recipient, and if not so confirmed, then on the next business day, (c) five (5) days after having been sent by registered or certified mail, return receipt requested, postage prepaid, or (d) one (1) business day after the business day of deposit with a nationally recognized overnight courier, specifying next business day delivery, with written verification of receipt. All communications shall be sent to the respective parties at their address as set forth on Schedule A or Schedule B hereto, or to such email address, facsimile number or address as subsequently modified by written notice given in accordance with this Section 6.7.

6.8   Consent Required to Amend, Terminate or Waive. This Agreement may be amended or modified and the observance of any term hereof may be waived (either generally or in a particular instance and either retroactively or prospectively) only by a written instrument executed by (i) the Company and (ii) the holders of a majority of the shares of Common Stock issued or issuable upon conversion of the shares of Preferred Stock held by the Investors (voting as a single class and on an as-converted basis). Notwithstanding the foregoing:

(a)   this Agreement may not be amended or terminated and the observance of any term of this Agreement may not be waived with respect to any Investor or Key Holder without the written consent of such Investor or Key Holder unless such amendment, termination or waiver applies to all Investors or Key Holders, as the case may be, in the same fashion;

(b)   the consent of the Key Holders shall not be required for any amendment or waiver if such amendment or waiver does not apply to the Key Holders;

(c)   any provision hereof may be waived by the waiving party on such party's own behalf, without the consent of any other party;

(d)   for so long as Ocean holds any shares of Series A Preferred Stock, neither Section 1.2(a) nor Section 6.8(d) of this Agreement shall be amended or waived (other than as provided in Section 1.3) without the written consent of Ocean;

(e)   for so long as TransPacific holds any shares of Series A Preferred Stock, neither Section 1.2(b) nor Section 6.8(e) of this Agreement shall be amended or waived (other than as provided in Section 1.3) without the written consent of TransPacific;

(f)   for so long as JTP holds any shares of Series B Preferred Stock, neither Section 1.2(c) nor Section 6.8(f) of this Agreement shall be amended or waived (other than as provided in Section 1.3) without the written consent of JTP; and

(g)   the addition or deletion of parties to this Agreement pursuant to Sections 6.1 or 6.2, above, shall not constitute amendments to this Agreement and therefore are not subject to the approval requirements of this Section 6.8.

The Company shall give prompt written notice of any amendment, termination or waiver hereunder to any party that did not consent in writing thereto. Any amendment, termination or waiver effected in accordance with this Section 6.8 shall be binding on each party and all of such party's successors and permitted assigns, whether or not any such party, successor or assignee entered into or approved such amendment, termination or waiver.

6.9   Delays or Omissions. No delay or omission to exercise any right, power or remedy accruing to any party under this Agreement, upon any breach or default of any other party under this Agreement, shall impair any such right, power or remedy of such non-breaching or non-defaulting party nor shall it be construed to be a waiver of any such breach or default, or an acquiescence therein, or of or in any similar breach or default thereafter occurring; nor shall any waiver of any single breach or default be deemed a waiver of any other breach or default previously or thereafter occurring. Any waiver, permit, consent or approval of any kind or character on the part of any party of any breach or default under this Agreement, or any waiver on the part of any party of any provisions or conditions of this Agreement, must be in writing and shall be effective only to the extent specifically set forth in such writing. All remedies, either under this Agreement or by law or otherwise afforded to any party, shall be cumulative and not alternative.

6.10   Severability. The invalidity or unenforceability of any provision hereof shall in no way affect the validity or enforceability of any other provision.

6.11   Entire Agreement. This Agreement (including the Schedules and Exhibits hereto), the Restated Certificate and the other Transaction Agreements (as defined in the Purchase Agreement) constitute the full and entire understanding and agreement between the parties with respect to the subject matter hereof, and any other written or oral agreement relating to the subject matter hereof existing between the parties are expressly cancelled. Upon the effectiveness of this Agreement, the Prior Agreement shall be deemed amended and restated to read in its entirety as set forth in this Agreement.

6.12   Legend on Share Certificates. Each certificate representing any Shares issued after the date hereof shall be endorsed by the Company with a legend reading substantially as follows:

"THE SHARES EVIDENCED HEREBY ARE SUBJECT TO A VOTING AGREEMENT, AS MAY BE AMENDED FROM TIME TO TIME, (A COPY OF WHICH MAY BE OBTAINED UPON WRITTEN REQUEST FROM THE COMPANY), AND BY ACCEPTING ANY INTEREST IN SUCH SHARES THE PERSON ACCEPTING SUCH INTEREST SHALL BE DEEMED TO AGREE TO AND SHALL BECOME BOUND BY ALL THE PROVISIONS OF THAT VOTING AGREEMENT, INCLUDING CERTAIN RESTRICTIONS ON TRANSFER AND OWNERSHIP SET FORTH THEREIN."

The Company, by its execution of this Agreement, agrees that it will cause the certificates evidencing the Shares issued after the date hereof to bear the legend required by this <u>Section 6.12</u> of this Agreement, and it shall supply, free of charge, a copy of this Agreement to any holder of a certificate evidencing Shares upon written request from such holder to the Company at its principal office. The parties to this Agreement do hereby agree that the failure to cause the certificates evidencing the Shares to bear the legend required by this <u>Section 6.12</u> herein and/or the failure of the Company to supply, free of charge, a copy of this Agreement as provided hereunder shall not affect the validity or enforcement of this Agreement.

    6.13   <u>Stock Splits, Stock Dividends, etc</u>. In the event of any issuance of Shares hereafter to any of the Stockholders (including, without limitation, in connection with any stock split, stock dividend, recapitalization, reorganization, or the like), such Shares shall become subject to this Agreement and shall be endorsed with the legend set forth in <u>Section 6.12</u>.

    6.14   <u>Manner of Voting</u>. The voting of Shares pursuant to this Agreement may be effected in person, by proxy, by written consent or in any other manner permitted by applicable law.

    6.15   <u>Further Assurances</u>. At any time or from time to time after the date hereof, the parties agree to cooperate with each other, and at the request of any other party, to execute and deliver any further instruments or documents and to take all such further action as the other party may reasonably request in order to evidence or effectuate the consummation of the transactions contemplated hereby and to otherwise carry out the intent of the parties hereunder.

    6.16   <u>Dispute Resolution</u>. The parties (a) hereby irrevocably and unconditionally submit to the jurisdiction of the state courts of California and to the jurisdiction of the United States District Court for Central District of California for the purpose of any suit, action or other proceeding arising out of or based upon this Agreement, (b) agree not to commence any suit, action or other proceeding arising out of or based upon this Agreement except in the state courts of California or the United States District Court for the Central District of California, and (c) hereby waive, and agree not to assert, by way of motion, as a defense, or otherwise, in any such suit, action or proceeding, any claim that it is not subject personally to the jurisdiction of the above-named courts, that its property is exempt or immune from attachment or execution, that the suit, action or proceeding is brought in an inconvenient forum, that the venue of the suit, action or proceeding is improper or that this Agreement or the subject matter hereof may not be enforced in or by such court. The prevailing party shall be entitled to reasonable attorneys' fees, costs, and necessary disbursements in addition to any other relief to which such party may be entitled. Each of the parties to this Agreement consents to personal jurisdiction for any equitable action sought in the U.S. District Court for the Central District of California or any court of the State of California having subject matter jurisdiction.

    6.17   <u>Costs of Enforcement</u>. If any party to this Agreement seeks to enforce its rights under this Agreement by legal proceedings, the non-prevailing party shall pay all costs and expenses incurred by the prevailing party, including, without limitation, all reasonable attorneys' fees.

    6.18   <u>Special Waiver</u>. Each party to this Agreement acknowledges that Maynard & Warren, LLP, outside general counsel to the Company, has in the past performed and is now or may in the future represent one or more Investors or their affiliates in matters unrelated to the transactions contemplated by this Agreement (the

"Financing"), including representation of such Investors or their affiliates in matters of a similar nature to the Financing. The applicable rules of professional conduct require that Maynard & Warren inform the parties hereunder of this representation and obtain their consent. Maynard & Warren has served as outside general counsel to the Company and has negotiated the terms of the Financing solely on behalf of the Company. The Company and each Investor hereby (a) acknowledge that they have had an opportunity to ask for and have obtained information relevant to such representation, including disclosure of the reasonably foreseeable adverse consequences of such representation and (b) acknowledge that with respect to the Financing, Maynard & Warren has represented solely the Company, and not any Investor or any shareholder, director or employee of the Company or any Investor.

[Remainder of this page intentionally left blank. Signature Page follows.]

IN WITNESS WHEREOF, the parties have executed this Amended and Restated Voting Agreement as of the date first written above.

COMPANY:

LEARNING, INC.

By:_____

Name: Tracy R. Roman

Title: President and Chief Executive Officer

Address: 913 East California Blvd.
            Pasadena, CA 91106

SIGNATURE PAGE TO AMENDED AND RESTATED VOTING AGREEMENT

IN WITNESS WHEREOF, the parties have executed this Amended and Restated Voting Agreement as of the date first written above.

KEY HOLDERS:

By:_____
Name: Tracy R. Roman

By:_____
Name: Amy E. Turner

INVESTORS:

JOSEPH TECHNOLOGY PARTNERS, L.P.
By: Joseph Technology Ventures, LLC
Its: General Partner

By:_____
Name: Alexander Suh
Title: Managing Director

OCEAN VENTURE PARTNERS, L.P.
By: Ocean Ventures, LLC
Its: General Partner

By:_____
Name: Akinobu Yorihiro
Title: President and Managing Director

TRANSPACIFIC VENTURE PARTNERS, L.P.
By: TransPacific Management, L.L.C.
Its: General Partner

By:_____
Name: Alexandre Sood
Title: Manager

SIGNATURE PAGE TO AMENDED AND RESTATED VOTING AGREEMENT

<u>**EXHIBIT A**</u>

ADOPTION AGREEMENT

This Adoption Agreement ("**Adoption Agreement**") is executed on _____, 20____, by the undersigned (the "**Holder**") pursuant to the terms of that certain Amended and Restated Voting Agreement dated as of July 10, 20____ (the "**Agreement**"), by and among the Company and certain of its Stockholders, as such Agreement may be amended or amended and restated hereafter. Capitalized terms used but not defined in this Adoption Agreement shall have the respective meanings ascribed to such terms in the Agreement. By the execution of this Adoption Agreement, the Holder agrees as follows.

1.1 <u>Acknowledgment</u>. Holder acknowledges that Holder is acquiring certain shares of the capital stock of the Company (the "**Stock**") or options, warrants or other rights to purchase such Stock (the "**Options**"), for one of the following reasons (Check the correct box):

☐ as a transferee of Shares from a party in such party's capacity as an "Investor" bound by the Agreement, and after such transfer, Holder shall be considered an "Investor" and a "Stockholder" for all purposes of the Agreement.

☐ as a transferee of Shares from a party in such party's capacity as a "Key Holder" bound by the Agreement, and after such transfer, Holder shall be considered a "Key Holder" and a "Stockholder" for all purposes of the Agreement.

☐ as a new Investor in accordance with <u>Section 6.1(a)</u> of the Agreement, such that Holder will be an "Investor" and "Stockholder" for all purposes of the Agreement.

☐ in accordance with <u>Section 6.1(b)</u> of the Agreement, as a new party who is not a new Investor, in which case Holder will be a "Key Holder" and "Stockholder" for all purposes of the Agreement.

1.2 <u>Agreement</u>. Holder hereby (a) agrees that the Stock and/or Options, and any other shares of capital stock or securities required by the Agreement to be bound thereby, shall be bound by and subject to the terms of the Agreement and (b) adopts the Agreement with the same force and effect as if Holder were originally a party thereto.

1.3 <u>Notice</u>. Any notice required or permitted by the Agreement shall be given to Holder at the address or facsimile number listed below Holder's signature hereto.

HOLDER:_____

By:_____

Name and Title of Signatory

Address: _____

_____

Facsimile Number: _____

ACCEPTED AND AGREED:

Learning, Inc.

By: _____

Title: _____

SAMPLE INVESTOR RIGHTS AGREEMENT

FIBER OPTIC DEVICES INC.

**AMENDED AND RESTATED
INVESTOR RIGHTS AGREEMENT**

THIS AMENDED AND RESTATED INVESTOR RIGHTS AGREEMENT is made as of February 8, 20_____ by and among Fiber Optic Devices Inc., a California corporation (the "Company"), the holders of the Company's Series One Convertible Preferred Stock (the "Series One Preferred") as listed on Exhibit A (the "Series One Holders"), the holders of the Company's Series Two Convertible Preferred Stock (the "Series Two Preferred") as listed on Exhibit B (the "Series Two Holders") and the purchasers of the Company's Series Three Convertible Preferred Stock (the "Series Three Preferred") as listed on Exhibit C (the "Series Three Investors").

R E C I T A L S

WHEREAS, in connection with the issuance of the Series Two Preferred, the Company, the Series Two Holders and the Series One Holders entered into an Investor Rights Agreement dated as of March 10, [3 years ago], as amended and supplemented (the "Series Two Investor Rights Agreement");

WHEREAS, in order to induce the Series Three Investors to enter into the Series Three Convertible Preferred Stock Purchase Agreement of even date herewith (the "Series Three Purchase Agreement"), the Series Two Holders and the Series One Holders desire to amend and restate the Series Two Investor Rights Agreement and to accept the rights created pursuant hereto in lieu of the rights granted to them under that former agreement and, pursuant to Section 5.1 thereof, the Series Two Holders and Series One Holders holding greater than sixty percent (60%) of the Registrable Securities (as defined pursuant to that agreement) have executed this Agreement so as to amend and restate the Series Two Investor Rights Agreement in its entirety;

WHEREAS, the sale of the Series Three Preferred to the Series Three Investors under the terms of the Series Three Purchase Agreement is conditioned upon the extension of the rights set forth herein, including the registration rights set forth herein, and the Company desires to extend such rights.

NOW THEREFORE, in consideration of the foregoing, the parties agree as follows:

1.   Registration Rights.

1.1   Certain Definitions. As used in this Agreement, the following terms shall have the following respective meanings:

"Affiliate" of any person or entity shall mean any other Person or entity which, directly or indirectly, controls, is controlled by or is under common control with such Person or entity.

"Commission" shall mean the Securities and Exchange Commission of the United States or any other U.S. federal agency at the time administering the Securities Act.

"Investor" shall mean each of the Series Three Investors, Series Two Holders, and Series One Holders (and their transferees as permitted by Section 1.11) holding

Registrable Securities or securities convertible into, exchangeable for, or exercisable for Registrable Securities.

"Initiating Investors" shall mean Investors who in the aggregate hold at least fifty percent (50%) of the Registrable Securities and join in a request referred to in Section 1.2(a).

"Other Investors" shall mean holders of Company securities, other than Investors, proposing to distribute their securities pursuant to a registration referred to in this Agreement.

"Qualified Public Offering" shall mean a firm commitment public offering of the Registrable Securities pursuant to an effective registration statement under the Securities Act, resulting in aggregate gross proceeds to the Company (before the deduction of underwriter's commissions and expenses) of at least $35,000,000 at a per-share price of not less than $5.00 (as adjusted for stock splits, recapitalizations, stock dividends and the like).

"Preferred Stock" shall mean the Series Three Preferred, Series Two Preferred, and Series One Preferred.

"Registrable Securities" means any Common Stock issuable or issued on conversion of the Series Three Preferred, Series Two Preferred or Series One Preferred Stock now held or hereafter acquired by any Investor. Shares of Common Stock shall only be treated as Registrable Securities if they have not been (A) sold to or through a broker or dealer or underwriter in a public distribution or a public securities transaction, or (B) sold in a single transaction exempt from the registration and prospectus delivery requirements of the Securities Act so that all transfer restrictions and restrictive legends with respect thereto are removed upon the consummation of that sale.

The terms "register," "registered," and "registration" refer to a registration effected by preparing and filing a registration statement in compliance with the Securities Act, and the declaration or ordering of the effectiveness of that registration statement.

"Registration Expenses" shall mean all expenses, excluding Selling Expenses (as defined below) except as otherwise stated below, incurred by the Company in complying with Sections 1.2, 1.3 and 1.4 hereof, including, without limitation, all registration, qualification and filing fees, printing expenses, escrow fees, fees and disbursements of counsel for the Company and reasonable fees and disbursements of one counsel for the Investors selected by the Investors and approved by the Company (which consent shall not be unreasonably withheld), Blue Sky fees and expenses and the expense of any special audits incident to or required by any such registration (but excluding the compensation of regular employees of the Company, which shall be paid in any event by the Company).

"Rule 145 Transaction" shall mean a transaction described under Rule 145 as promulgated under the Securities Act, as such Rule may be amended from time to time, or any similar successor rule that may be promulgated by the Commission.

"Securities Act" shall mean the Securities Act of 1933, as amended, and the rules and regulations of the Commission thereunder, or any similar United States federal statute.

"Selling Expenses" shall mean all underwriting discounts, selling commissions and stock transfer taxes applicable to the securities registered by Investors. These expenses shall be borne by Investors.

"Selling Investors" shall mean each Investor who holds Registrable Securities included in a registration statement under the Securities Act pursuant to this Agreement.

1.2 Requested Registrations.

(a) Request for Registration. In case the Company shall receive from Initiating Investors a written request that the Company effect any registration, qualification or compliance with respect to Registrable Securities offered to the public with an anticipated aggregate offering price of not less than $5,000,000 (a "Registration Notice"), the Company will:

(i) promptly give written notice of the proposed registration, qualification or compliance to all other Investors; and

(ii) as soon as practicable, use its best efforts to effect the registration, qualification or compliance (including, without limitation, appropriate qualification under applicable Blue Sky or other state securities laws and appropriate compliance with applicable regulations issued under the Securities Act and any other governmental requirements or regulations) as may be so requested and as would permit or facilitate the sale and distribution of all or such portion of such Registrable Securities as are specified in such request, together with all or such portion of the Registrable Securities of any Investor joining in such request as are specified in a written request received by the Company from any Investor within twenty (20) days after such Investor's receipt of the written notice from the Company. Notwithstanding the foregoing, the Company shall not be obligated to take any action to effect any registration, qualification or compliance pursuant to this Section 1.2:

(A) In any particular jurisdiction in which the Company would be required to execute a general consent to service of process in effecting such registration, qualification or compliance unless the Company is already subject to service in such jurisdiction and except as may be required by the Securities Act;

(B) Prior to the earlier of five years from the date hereof or six (6) months after the Company's first registered public offering;

(C) If the Company delivers notice to the Investors within thirty (30) days of any Registration Notice of the Company's intent to file a registration statement for a registered public offering within ninety (90) days.

(D) During the period starting with the date sixty (60) days prior to the Company's estimated date of filing of, and ending on the date six (6) months immediately following the effective date of, any registration statement pertaining to securities of the Company sold by the Company (other than a registration of securities in a Rule 145 transaction or with respect to an employee benefit plan), provided that the Company is actively employing in good faith all reasonable efforts to cause such registration statement to become effective;

(E) After the Company has effected three registrations pursuant to this Section 1.2, and such registrations have been declared or ordered effective; or

(F) If the Company shall furnish to such Investors a certificate signed by the President of the Company stating that in the good faith judgment of the Board of Directors it would be seriously detrimental to the Company or its shareholders for a registration statement to be filed in the near future, then the Company's obligation to use its best efforts to register, qualify or comply under this Section 1.2 shall be deferred for a period not to exceed ninety (90) days from the date of receipt of written request from the Initiating Investors, provided, however, that the Company shall not utilize this right more than once in any twelve (12) month period.

Subject to the foregoing clauses (A) through (F), the Company shall file a registration statement covering the Registrable Securities so requested to be registered as soon as practicable, after receipt of the request or requests of the Initiating Investors.

(b) <u>Underwriting</u>. In the event that a registration pursuant to this Section 1.2 is for a registered public offering involving an underwriting, the Company shall so advise the Investors as part of the notice given pursuant to Section 1.2(a)(i). In that event, the right of any Investor to registration pursuant to Section 1.2 shall be conditioned upon that Investor's participation in the underwriting arrangements required by this Section 1.2, and the inclusion of that Investor's Registrable Securities in the underwriting to the extent requested shall be limited to the extent provided herein. The Company shall (together with all Investors and Other Investors proposing to distribute their securities through the underwriting) enter into an underwriting agreement in customary form with the managing underwriter selected for the underwriting by the Company, but subject to the reasonable approval of the Investors holding a majority of the Registrable Securities held by all Investors participating in the offering. Notwithstanding any other provision of this Section 1.2, if the managing underwriter advises the Initiating Investors in writing that marketing factors require a limitation of the number of shares to be underwritten, then the Company shall so advise all Investors and Other Investors proposing to distribute their securities through such underwriting, and the number of shares that may be included in the registration and underwriting shall be allocated only to the Investors on a pro rata basis. No Registrable Securities or other securities excluded from the underwriting by reason of the underwriter's marketing limitation shall be included in the registration. No securities held by an Other Investor shall be included in a registration pursuant to this Section 1.2 if such participation would reduce the number of shares includable by the Investors unless the holders of at least sixty percent (60%) of the Registrable Securities consent to such participation. If any Investor or Other Investor disapproves of the terms of the underwriting, that person may elect to withdraw therefrom by written notice to the Company, the managing underwriter and the Initiating Investors. The Registrable Securities and/or other securities so withdrawn shall also be withdrawn from registration and shall not be transferred in a public distribution prior to one hundred eighty (180) days after the effective date of the registration statement relating thereto, or another shorter period of time as the underwriters may require pursuant to Section 1.12.

1.3 <u>Company Registrations</u>.

(a) <u>Notice of Registration</u>. If at any time or from time to time the Company shall determine to register any of its securities, either for its own account or the account of a security holder or holders, other than (X) a registration relating solely to stock option or other employee benefit plans or (Y) a registration relating solely to a Commission Rule 145 transaction, the Company will:

(i)   promptly give to each Investor written notice thereof; and

(ii)   include in such registration (and any related qualification under Blue Sky laws or other compliance), and in any underwriting involved therein, all the Registrable Securities specified in a written request or requests received by the Company from any Investor within twenty (20) days after that Investor's receipt of the written notice from the Company.

(b)   <u>Underwriting</u>. If the registration of which the Company gives notice is for a registered public offering involving an underwriting, the Company shall so advise the Investors as a part of the written notice given pursuant to <u>Section 1.3(a)(i)</u>. In such event the right of any Investor to registration pursuant to this <u>Section 1.3</u> shall be conditioned upon that Investor's participation in the underwriting and the inclusion of Registrable Securities in the underwriting to the extent provided herein. All Investors proposing to distribute their securities through such underwriting shall, together with the Company and Other Investors, enter into an underwriting agreement in customary form with the managing underwriter selected for such underwriting by the Company. Notwithstanding any other provision of this <u>Section 1.3</u>, if the managing underwriter determines that marketing factors require a limitation of the number of shares to be underwritten, the managing underwriter may limit the Registrable Securities and other securities to be included in the registration. The Company shall so advise all Investors and Other Investors, and the number of shares that may be included in the registration and underwriting shall be allocated only to the Company (if the registration has been initiated by the Company); provided, however, that in a registered public offering other than the Company's initial public offering, no less than twenty-five percent (25%) of the number of shares that may be included in the offering shall be allocated among the holders of Registrable Securities; provided, further, that the number of shares of Registrable Securities to be included in such offering shall not be reduced unless all securities held by Other Investors proposing to include securities in such offering pursuant to piggyback registration rights are first entirely excluded from the registration unless the holders of at least sixty percent (60%) of the Registrable Securities consent to such participation. To facilitate the allocation of shares in accordance with the above provisions, the Company may round the number of shares allocated to any Investor or Other Investor to the nearest one hundred (100) shares. If any Investor or Other Investor disapproves of the terms of the underwriting, that person may elect to withdraw therefrom by written notice to the Company and the managing underwriter. Any securities excluded or withdrawn from the underwriting shall be withdrawn from the registration, and shall not be transferred in a public distribution prior to one hundred eighty (180) days after the effective date of the registration statement relating thereto, or another shorter period of time as the underwriters may require pursuant to <u>Section 1.12</u>.

(c)   <u>Right to Terminate Registration</u>. The Company shall have the right to terminate or withdraw any registration initiated by it under this <u>Section 1.3</u> prior to the effectiveness of the registration whether or not any Investor has elected to include Registrable Securities in the registration; provided, however, if the requisite number of Investors elect to use one of their demand registration rights, pursuant to <u>Section 1.2</u> hereof, then the registration shall be governed by <u>Section 1.2</u> and it shall not be terminated by the Company.

1.4   <u>Registrations on Form S-3</u>.

(a)   <u>Request for Registration</u>. If at any time or from time to time any Investor or Investors request that the Company file a registration statement on Form S-3 (or any successor form to Form S-3) for a public offering of shares of the Registrable Securities with a reasonably anticipated aggregate price to the public of at least $1,000,000 and the Company is a registrant entitled to use Form S-3 to register the Registrable Securities for that type of offering, the Company will:

(i)   promptly give written notice of the proposed registration to all other Investors; and

(ii)   use its best efforts to cause those Registrable Securities to be registered for the offering on that form and to cause such Registrable Securities to be qualified in those jurisdictions as the Investor or Investors may reasonably request, together with all or such portion of the Registrable Securities of any Investor joining in such request as are specified in a written request received by the Company from any Investor within twenty (20) days after such Investor's receipt of the written notice from the Company.

The substantive provisions of <u>Section 1.2(b)</u> shall be applicable to each such registration initiated under this <u>Section 1.4</u> involving an underwriting.

(b)   <u>Limitations</u>. Notwithstanding the foregoing, the Company shall not be obligated to take any action pursuant to this <u>Section 1.4</u>:

(i)   in any particular jurisdiction in which the Company would be required to execute a general consent to service of process in effecting a registration, qualification or compliance unless the Company is already subject to service in that jurisdiction and except as may be required by the Securities Act;

(ii)   if the Company, within ten (10) days of the receipt of the request of the Investors requesting registration under this <u>Section 1.4</u>, gives notice of its bona fide intention to effect the filing of a registration statement with the Commission within ninety (90) days of receipt of the request (other than with respect to a registration statement relating to a Rule 145 transaction, an offering solely to employees or any other registration not appropriate for the registration of Registrable Securities);

(iii)   within six (6) months immediately following the effective date of any registration statement pertaining to securities of the Company (other than a registration of securities in a Rule 145 transaction or with respect to a stock option or other employee benefit plan); or

(iv)   if the Company shall furnish to the Investors a certificate signed by the President of the Company stating that in the good faith judgment of the Board of Directors it would be seriously detrimental to the Company or its shareholders for a registration statement to be filed in the near future, then the Company's obligation to use its best efforts to file a registration statement shall be deferred for a period not to exceed ninety (90) days from the receipt of the request to file the registration by the Investor; <u>provided</u>, <u>however</u>, that the Company shall not utilize this right more than once in any twelve (12) month period.

1.5   <u>Limitations on Subsequent Registration Rights</u>. From and after the date hereof, the Company will not, without the prior written consent of Investors holding sixty percent (60%) of the then outstanding Registrable Securities, enter into any agreement with any Investor or prospective Investor of any securities of the Company extending registration rights to such Investor or prospective Investor, unless the extension of such registration rights would be subordinate to the rights of the Investors under this Agreement.

1.6   Expenses of Registration.

(a)   Registration Expenses. The Company shall bear all Registration Expenses incurred in connection with all registrations pursuant to Sections 1.2, 1.3 and 1.4. In the event any Initiating Investors withdraw a Registration Notice for a registered public offering involving an underwriting, abandon a registration statement or, following an effective registration pursuant to Section 1.2 hereof, do not sell Registrable Securities, then all Registration Expenses in respect of such Registration Notice shall be borne, at the Initiating Investors' option, either by the Initiating Investors or by the Company (in which case, if borne by the Company, the withdrawn or abandoned registration shall be deemed to be an effective registration for purposes of Section 1.2(a)(ii)(E) hereof); provided, that, if at the time of such withdrawal, the Initiating Investors have learned of a material adverse change in the condition, business, or prospects of the Company from that known to the Initiating Investors at the time of their request and have withdrawn the request with reasonable promptness following disclosure by the Company of such material adverse change, then all Registration Expenses in respect of such Registration Notice shall be borne by the Company and the withdrawn or abandoned registration shall not be deemed to be an effective registration for purposes of Section 1.2(a)(ii)(E) hereof.

(b)   Selling Expenses. All Selling Expenses relating to securities registered on behalf of the Investors and Other Investors shall be borne by the Investors and Other Investors pro rata on the basis of the number of shares so registered.

1.7   Registration and Qualification. If and whenever the Company is required to use its best efforts to effect the registration of any Registrable Securities under the Securities Act pursuant to this Agreement, the Company will as promptly as is practicable:

(a)   prepare and file with the Commission, as soon as practicable, and use its best efforts to cause to become and remain effective for at least ninety (90) days following its effectiveness, a registration statement under the Securities Act relating to the Registrable Securities to be offered on the form as the Initiating Investors, or if not filed pursuant to Section 1.2 or Section 1.4 hereof, the Company, may determine and for which the Company then qualifies;

(b)   prepare and file with the Commission any amendments (including post-effective amendments) and supplements to the registration statement and the prospectus used in connection therewith as may be necessary to keep the registration statement effective and to comply with the provisions of the Securities Act with respect to the disposition of all Registrable Securities until the earlier of the time that all of the Registrable Securities have been disposed of in accordance with the intended methods of disposition set forth in the registration statement or the expiration of one hundred eighty (180) days after the registration statement becomes effective; provided that this one hundred eighty (180) day period shall be extended in the case of a registration pursuant to Section 1.2 hereof for that number of days that equals the number of days elapsing from (i) the date the written notice contemplated by Section 1.7(f) hereof is given by the

Company to (ii) the date on which the Company delivers to the Selling Investors the supplement or amendment contemplated by Section 1.7(f) hereof;

(c)   furnish to the Selling Investors and to any underwriter of Registrable Securities that number of conformed copies of the registration statement and of each amendment and supplement thereto (in each case including all exhibits), that number of copies of the prospectus included in the registration statement (including each preliminary prospectus and any summary prospectus), those documents incorporated by reference in such registration statement or prospectus, and any other documents, as the Selling Investors or the underwriter may reasonably request in order to facilitate the public offering of the securities;

(d)   make every reasonable effort to obtain the withdrawal of any order suspending the effectiveness of the registration statement at the earliest possible moment;

(e)   if requested by an Initiating Investor, (i) furnish to each Selling Investor an opinion of counsel for the Company addressed to each Selling Investor and dated the date of the closing under the underwriting agreement (if any) (or if the offering is not underwritten, dated the effective date of the registration statement), and (ii) use its best efforts to furnish to each Selling Investor a "comfort" or "special procedures" letter addressed to each Selling Investor and signed by the independent public accountants who have audited the Company's financial statements included in the registration statement, in each case covering substantially the same matters with respect to the registration statement (and the prospectus included therein) as are customarily covered in opinions of issuer's counsel and in accountants' letters delivered to underwriters in underwritten public offerings of securities and any other matters as the Selling Investors may reasonably request and, in the case of the accountants' letter, with respect to events subsequent to the date of such financial statements;

(f)   immediately notify the Selling Investors in writing (i) at any time when a prospectus relating to a registration hereunder is required to be delivered under the Securities Act of the happening of any event as a result of which the prospectus included in the registration statement, as then in effect, includes an untrue statement of a material fact or omits to state any material fact required to be stated therein or necessary to make the statements therein, in light of the circumstances under which they were made, not misleading, and (ii) of any request by the Commission or any other regulatory body or other body having jurisdiction for any amendment of or supplement to any registration statement or other document relating to the offering, and in either case (i) or (ii), at the request of a Selling Investor, immediately prepare and furnish to those Selling Investors a reasonable number of copies of a supplement to or an amendment of the prospectus as may be necessary so that, as thereafter delivered to the Investors of the Registrable Securities, that prospectus shall not include an untrue statement of a material fact or omit to state a material fact required to be stated therein or necessary to make the statements therein, in light of the circumstances under which they are made, not misleading;

(g)   use its best efforts to list all Registrable Securities covered by a registration statement on each securities exchange and inter-dealer quotation system on which a class of common equity securities of the Company is then listed, and to pay all fees and expenses in connection therewith;

(h)   upon the transfer of shares by a Selling Investor in connection with a registration hereunder, furnish unlegended certificates representing ownership of the Registrable Securities being sought in denominations as shall be requested by the Selling Investors or the underwriters;

(i)   keep Investors advised as to the initiation of each registration, qualification and compliance and as to the completion thereof;

(j)   register or qualify the Registrable Securities covered by such registration statement under the securities or Blue Sky laws of such states as the Investors shall reasonably request, maintain any such registration or qualification current until the earlier of the sale of the Registrable Securities so registered or ninety (90) days subsequent to the effective date of the registration statement, and take any and all other actions either necessary or advisable to enable the Investors to consummate the public sale or other disposition of the Registrable Securities in jurisdictions where the Investors desire to effect such sales or other disposition (but the Company shall not be required to take any action that would subject it to the general jurisdiction of the courts of any jurisdiction in which it is not so subject or to qualify as a foreign corporation in any jurisdiction where the Company is not so qualified, unless the Company is already subject to service in such jurisdiction);

(k)   in the event of any underwritten public offering, enter into and perform its obligations under an underwriting agreement, in usual and customary form, with the managing underwriter of such offering;

(l)   provide a transfer agent and registrar for all Registrable Securities registered pursuant hereunder and a CUSIP number for all such Registrable Securities, in each case not later than the effective date of such registration; and

(m)   furnish the Investors, at least five business days before filing a registration statement that registers such Registrable Securities, with a draft registration statement and copies of all such documents proposed to be filed therewith.

1.8   Indemnification.

(a)   By Company. The Company will indemnify each Investor, each of its officers, directors, partners and agents, and each person controlling an Investor within the meaning of Section 15 of the Securities Act, with respect to whom registration, qualification or compliance has been effected pursuant to this Agreement, and each underwriter, if any, and each person who controls any underwriter within the meaning of Section 15 of the Securities Act, against all expenses, claims, losses, damages or liabilities (or actions in respect thereof), including any of the foregoing incurred in settlement of any litigation, commenced or threatened, arising out of or based on any untrue statement (or alleged untrue statement) of a material fact contained in any registration statement, prospectus, offering circular or other document, or any amendment or supplement thereto, incident to any registration, qualification or compliance, or based on any omission (or alleged omission) to state therein a material fact required to be stated therein or necessary to make the statements therein, in light of the circumstances in which they were made, not misleading, or any violation by the Company of the Securities Act or any rule or regulation promulgated under the Securities Act applicable to the Company in connection with a registration, qualification or compliance, and the Company will reimburse each Investor, each of its officers, directors, partners and agents, each person controlling an Investor, each underwriter and each person who controls any underwriter, for any legal and any other expenses reasonably incurred in connection with investigating, preparing or defending any claim, loss, damage, liability or action, provided that the Company will not be liable in any case to the extent that any claim, loss, damage, liability or expense arises out of or is based on any untrue statement or omission or alleged untrue statement or omission, made in reliance upon and in conformity with written information furnished to the Company by an instrument duly executed by an Investor, controlling person or underwriter and stated to be specifically for use therein, and provided further, that the indemnity agreement contained in this Section 1.8(a) shall not apply to amounts paid in settlement of any such claim, loss, damage, liability or expense if such settlement is effected without the consent of the Company, which consent shall not be unreasonably withheld. If the Investors are represented by counsel other than counsel for the Company, the Company will not be obligated under this Section 1.8(a) to reimburse legal fees and expenses of more than one separate counsel for the Investors.

(b) By Investors. Each Selling Investor will indemnify the Company, each of its directors, officers and agents, each underwriter, if any, of the Company's securities covered by such a registration statement, each person who controls the Company or an underwriter within the meaning of Section 15 of the Securities Act, and each other Selling Investor, against all claims, losses, damages and liabilities (or actions in respect thereof) arising out of or based on any untrue statement (or alleged untrue statement) of a material fact contained in a registration statement, prospectus, offering circular or other document, or any omission (or alleged omission) to state therein a material fact required to be stated therein or necessary to make the statements therein not misleading, and will reimburse the Company, the Selling Investors, directors, officers, agents, underwriters or control persons for any legal or any other expenses reasonably incurred in connection with investigating or defending any claim, loss, damage, liability or action, in each case to the extent, but only to the extent, that the untrue statement (or alleged untrue statement) or omission (or alleged omission) is made in the registration statement, prospectus, offering circular or other document in reliance upon and in conformity with written information furnished to the Company by an instrument duly executed by such Selling Investor and stated to be specifically for use therein, provided that the indemnity agreement contained in this Section 1.8(b) shall not apply to amounts paid in settlement of any such claim, loss, damage, liability or action if such settlement is effected without the consent of the Investor, which consent shall not be unreasonably withheld. Notwithstanding the foregoing, the liability of each Selling Investor under this subsection (b) shall be limited in an amount equal to the net proceeds from the shares sold by that Selling Investor, unless such liability arises out of or is based on willful misconduct by the Selling Investor.

(c) Procedure for Indemnification. Each party indemnified under paragraph (a) or (b) of this Section 1.8 (the "Indemnified Party") shall, promptly after receipt of notice of any claim or the commencement of any action against such Indemnified Party in respect of which indemnity may be sought, notify the party required to provide indemnification (the "Indemnifying Party") in writing of the claim or the commencement thereof; provided that the failure of the Indemnified Party to notify the Indemnifying Party shall not relieve the Indemnifying Party from any liability it may have to an Indemnified Party on account of the indemnity agreement contained in paragraph (a) or (b) of this Section 1.8, unless the Indemnifying Party was materially prejudiced by that failure, and in no event shall relieve the Indemnifying Party from any other liability it may have to that Indemnified Party. If any claim or action shall be brought against an Indemnified Party, it shall notify the Indemnifying Party thereof and the Indemnifying Party shall be entitled to participate therein, and, to the extent that it wishes, jointly with any other similarly notified indemnifying party, to assume the defense thereof with counsel reasonably satisfactory to the Indemnified Party. After notice from the Indemnifying Party to the Indemnified Party of its election to assume the defense of any claim or action, the Indemnifying Party shall not be liable (except to the extent the proviso to this sentence is applicable, in which event it will be so liable) to the Indemnified Party under this Section 1.8 for any legal or other expenses subsequently incurred by the Indemnified Party in connection with the defense thereof other than reasonable costs of investigation; provided that each Indemnified Party shall have the right to employ separate counsel to represent it and assume its defense (in which case, the Indemnifying Party shall not represent it) if (i) upon the advice of counsel, the representation of both parties by the same counsel would be inappropriate due to actual or potential differing interests between them, or (ii) in the event the Indemnifying Party has not assumed the defense thereof within ten (10) days of receipt of notice of such claim or commencement of action, and in each case the fees and expenses of one such separate counsel shall be paid by the Indemnifying Party. If any Indemnified Party employs such separate counsel, it will not enter into any settlement agreement not approved by the Indemnifying Party, whose approval is not to be unreasonably withheld. If the Indemnifying Party so assumes the defense thereof, it may not agree to any settlement of any claim or action as the result of which any remedy or relief, other than monetary damages for which the Indemnifying Party shall be responsible hereunder, shall be applied to or against the Indemnified Party, without the prior written consent of the Indemnified Party. In any action hereunder as to which the Indemnifying Party has assumed the defense thereof with counsel reasonably satisfactory to the Indemnified Party, the Indemnified Party shall continue to be entitled to participate in the defense thereof, with counsel of its own choice, but, except as set forth above, the Indemnifying Party shall not be obligated hereunder to reimburse the Indemnified Party for the costs thereof.

If the indemnification provided for in this Section 1.8 shall for any reason be unavailable to an Indemnified Party in respect of any loss, claim, damage or liability, or any action in respect thereof, referred to therein, then each Indemnifying Party shall, in lieu of indemnifying that Indemnified Party, contribute to the amount paid or payable by that Indemnified Party as a result of the loss, claim, damage or liability, or action in respect thereof, in such proportion as shall be appropriate to reflect the relative fault of the Indemnifying Party on the one hand and the Indemnified Party on the other with respect to the statements or omissions that resulted in the loss, claim, damage or liability, or action in respect thereof, as well as any other relevant equitable considerations. The relative fault shall be determined by reference to whether the untrue or alleged untrue statement of a material fact or omission or alleged omission to state a material fact relates to information supplied specifically for use in any registration statement, prospectus, offering circular or other similar document by the Indemnifying Party on the one hand or the Indemnified Party on the other, the intent of the parties and their relative knowledge, access to information and opportunity to correct or prevent such statement or omission, but not by reference to any Indemnified Party's stock ownership in the Company. In no event, however, shall an Investor of Registrable Securities be required to contribute in excess of the amount of the net proceeds received by that Investor in connection with the sale of Registrable Securities in the offering that is the subject of the loss, claim, damage or liability. The amount paid or payable by an Indemnified Party as a result of the loss, claim, damage or liability, or action in respect thereof, referred to above in this paragraph shall be deemed to include, for purposes of this paragraph, any legal or other expenses reasonably incurred by the Indemnified Party in connection with investigating or defending the action or claim. No person guilty of fraudulent misrepresentation (within the meaning of Section 12(f) of the Securities Act) shall be entitled to contribution from any person who was not guilty of a fraudulent misrepresentation.

1.9   <u>Information by Investor</u>. Investors including any Registrable Securities in any registration shall, upon request, furnish to the Company that information regarding each of them as shall be necessary to enable the Company to comply with the provisions hereof in connection with any registration, qualification or compliance referred to in this Agreement.

1.10   <u>Rule 144 Reporting</u>. With a view to making available the benefits of certain rules and regulations of the Commission that may at any time permit the sale of the Restricted Securities to the public without registration, after a public market exists for the Common Stock of the Company, the Company agrees to use its best efforts to:

(a)   make and keep public information available, as those terms are understood and defined in Rule 144 under the Securities Act, at all times after the effective date that the Company becomes subject to the reporting requirements of the Securities Act or the Securities Exchange Act of 1934, as amended (the "<u>Exchange Act</u>");

(b)   file with the Commission in a timely manner all reports and other documents required of the Company under the Securities Act and the Exchange Act (at any time after it has become subject to such reporting requirements); and

(c)   furnish to any Investor forthwith upon request a written statement by the Company as to its compliance with the reporting requirements of Rule 144 (at any time after ninety (90) days after the effective date of the first registration statement filed by the Company for an offering of its securities to the general public), and of the Securities Act and the Exchange Act (at any time after it has become subject to such reporting requirements), a copy of the most recent annual or quarterly report of the Company, and such other reports and documents of the Company and other information in the possession of or reasonably obtainable by the Company as the Investor may reasonably request in availing itself of any rule or regulation of the Commission allowing that Investor to sell any securities without registration.

1.11   <u>Transfer of Registration Rights</u>. The rights to cause the Company to register securities granted Investors under <u>Sections 1.2</u>, <u>1.3</u> and <u>1.4</u> may be assigned in connection with any transfer or assignment of Registrable Securities by an Investor provided that: (a) the transfer may otherwise be effected in accordance with applicable securities laws; (b) unless waived, the transfer is effected in compliance with the restrictions on transfer contained in this Agreement and in any other agreement between the

Company and the Investor; and (c) the assignee or transferee (i) is a partner or retired partner of any Investor which is a partnership, (ii) is an immediate family member of or a trust for the benefit of any individual Investor, (iii) is an Affiliate of the Investor or (iv) receives at least 1,000,000 shares of Registrable Securities or securities convertible into Registrable Securities and agrees in writing to be bound by the terms of this Agreement and assumes all of the obligations of the transferring Investor hereunder. Subject to the terms of Section 1.13, below, no transfer or assignment will divest an Investor or any subsequent owner of those rights and powers with respect to the shares of Registrable Securities still held, unless all Registrable Securities are transferred or assigned.

1.12   "Market Stand-Off" Agreement. Each Investor hereby agrees that, during the period of duration (not to exceed 180 days) specified by the Company's Board of Directors and an underwriter of Common Stock or other securities of the Company, following the date of the first sale to the public pursuant to a registration statement of the Company filed under the Act, or if required by such underwriter, such longer period of time as is necessary to enable such underwriter to issue a research report or make a public appearance that relates to an earnings release or announcement by the Company within 18 days prior to or after the date that is one hundred eighty (180) days after the effective date of the registration statement relating to such offering, but in any event not to exceed one hundred ninety-eight (198) days following the effective date of the registration statement relating to such offering, it shall not, to the extent requested by the Company and such underwriter, directly or indirectly sell, offer to sell, contract to sell (including, without limitation, any short sale), grant any option to purchase or otherwise transfer or dispose of (other than to donees who agree to be similarly bound) any securities of the Company held by it at any time during such period except Common Stock included in such registration; provided, however, that:

(a)   such agreement shall be applicable only to the registration statement of the Company covering Common Stock (or other securities) to be sold on its behalf to the public in the Company's initial underwritten offering;

(b)   all the officers and directors of the Company and all other persons who hold one percent (1%) or more of the outstanding equity securities of the Company enter into similar agreements, and any early release from such agreements applicable to any officer, director or person who holds one percent (1%) or more of the outstanding equity securities of the Company will apply equally to each Investor; and

(c)   such market stand-off time period shall not exceed 180 (or 198, as provided above) days.

(d)   Notwithstanding the foregoing, the obligations described in this Section 1.12 shall not apply to a registration relating solely to employee benefit plans on Form S-8 or similar forms which may be promulgated in the future, or a registration relating solely to a Commission Rule 145 Transaction on Form S-4 or similar forms which may be promulgated in the future.

This Section 1.12 shall be binding on all transferees or assignees of Registrable Securities, whether or not those persons are entitled to registration rights pursuant to Section 1.11, and if requested by the Company, any transferee or assignee shall confirm in writing its agreement to be bound by the provisions hereof.

1.13   Termination of Registration Rights. Except for the provisions of Section 1.12, the registration rights granted in Sections 1.2, 1.3 and 1.4 shall terminate, with respect to each Investor, on the fifth anniversary of a Qualified Public Offering or at such time as all Registrable Securities held by that Investor can be sold pursuant to Rule 144 within a consecutive three (3) month period without compliance with the registration requirements of the Securities Act. The respective indemnities, representations and warranties of the Investors and the Company shall survive a termination of registration rights by reason of this Section 1.13.

2.   Information Rights.

2.1   Financial Information. The Company will provide to each Investor the following information for so long as that Investor holds 3,000,000 or more Registrable Securities or securities convertible into Registrable Securities or some combination of the foregoing (a "Major Investor"):

(a)   as soon as practicable after the end of each fiscal year, and in any event within one hundred twenty (120) days thereafter, a consolidated balance sheet of the Company and its subsidiaries, if any, as of the end of such fiscal year, and consolidated statements of income, stockholders' equity and cash flows of the Company and its subsidiaries, if any, for that year, prepared in accordance with generally accepted accounting principles ("GAAP") and setting forth in each case in comparative form the figures for the previous fiscal year, all in reasonable detail and all audited by a nationally recognized public accounting firm.

(b)   monthly unaudited financial statements of the Company and its subsidiaries within twenty (20) days after the end of each month upon the Investor's request.

(c)   as soon as practicable after the end of each of the first three (3) fiscal quarters and in any event within thirty (30) days thereafter, a consolidated balance sheet of the Company and its subsidiaries, if any, as of the end of the quarter, consolidated statements of income, consolidated statements of changes in financial condition, and a consolidated statement of cash flow of the Company and its subsidiaries for the quarter and for the current fiscal year to date, and setting forth in each case in comparative form the figures for corresponding months in the previous fiscal year, and setting forth in comparative form the budgeted figures for such quarter and for the current fiscal year then reported, prepared in accordance with GAAP (other than for accompanying notes), subject to changes resulting from year-end audit adjustments, all in reasonable detail and signed by the principal financial or accounting officer of the Company.

(d)   an annual operating plan for the next fiscal year of the Company containing revenue projections, profit and loss projections, cash flow projections, and capital expenditures, all on a quarterly basis, as soon as it is available but in any event within thirty (30) days prior to the beginning of such fiscal year.

The financial statements to be delivered in accordance with Section 2.1(a) and Section 2.1(c) above shall be certified by the Chief Executive Officer or Chief Financial Officer of the Company and shall include a reasonable identification of operating highlights.

2.2   Additional Information. The Company will allow each Major Investor to visit and inspect any of the properties of the Company (upon reasonable advance notice) and will deliver or provide to each Major Investor, with reasonable promptness, any information and data, including access to books, records, officers and accountants, with respect to the Company and its subsidiaries as such Major Investor may from time to time reasonably request; provided, however, that the Company shall not be obligated to provide any information that it considers in good faith to be a trade secret or to contain confidential or classified information unless such Major Investor enters into a confidentiality agreement with the Company.

2.3   Confidential Treatment of Information. Each Investor agrees to use its reasonable efforts to maintain the confidentiality of all nonpublic information obtained by it from the Company (so long as such information is not in the public domain); provided, that (a) each Investor may, to the extent required by law, disclose that information in connection with the sale or transfer of any Registrable Securities or securities convertible into Registrable Securities, if the Investor's transferee agrees in writing to be bound by the provisions hereof, and (b) each Investor may disclose that information (i) at the request of any applicable regulatory authority or in connection with an examination of the Company by that authority, (ii) pursuant to subpoena or other court process, (iii) when required to do so in accordance with the provisions of any applicable law, and (iv) to the Company's independent auditors and other professional advisors provided those persons acknowledge and agree to be bound by the Investor's confidentiality obligations hereunder; *provided*, that notwithstanding the foregoing any Investor may provide financial information to its partners or members as required by any partnership agreement or limited liability operating agreement.

2.4   Termination of Covenants. The rights set forth in Sections 2.1 and 2.2 shall terminate and be of no further force or effect upon the date the Company becomes subject to the reporting requirements of Section 13 or 15(d) of the Securities Exchange Act of 1934, as amended.

2.5   Aggregation. For purposes of this Section 2, "Investor" and "Major Investor" shall include any general partners and affiliates of an Investor or Major Investor. For any such aggregated group, the entity in such group owning the greatest number of shares in the Company shall receive the financial information described in Section 2.1 hereof.

3.   Right of First Refusal.

3.1   General. Except for (i) securities issued pursuant to conversion rights applicable to the Company's Convertible Preferred Stock, as that term is defined in the Company's Amended and Restated Articles of Incorporation (as may be amended or restated from time to time) (the "Restated Articles"), (ii) securities issued in a Qualified Public Offering or any public offering, (iii) securities issued pursuant to the Company's acquisition of another corporation, or all or a portion of its assets, by merger, purchase of assets or other corporate reorganization approved by the Board (including a majority of the directors designated by the Preferred Stock), (iv) securities issued in connection with any stock split or stock dividend of the Company, (v) shares of Common Stock issued to employees, officers, or directors of, or contractors, consultants or advisors to, the Company solely for incentive purposes pursuant to stock purchase or stock option plans, stock bonuses or awards, contracts or other arrangements that are approved by the Company's Board of Directors, including, with respect to grants to officers of the Company, the approval of a majority of outside directors, (vi) warrants or other securities issued to financial institutions or lenders in connection with lease lines or loans approved by the Company's Board of Directors (including a majority of the directors designated by the Preferred Stock), (vii) securities issued in connection with joint venture or development agreements unanimously approved by the Company's Board of Directors, and (viii) securities issued pursuant to the Series Three Purchase Agreement, the Company will not, nor will it permit any subsidiary to, authorize or issue any securities of the Company of any class and will not authorize, issue or grant any options, warrants, conversion rights or other rights to purchase or acquire any securities of the Company of any class without offering the Major Investors the right of first refusal described below.

3.2   Right of First Refusal. Subject to Section 3.1, each Major Investor shall have a right of first refusal to purchase an amount of securities of the Company of any class or kind the Company proposes to sell sufficient to maintain such Major Investor's proportionate beneficial ownership interest in the Company, on a fully-diluted basis. If the Company wishes to make any sale of its securities, it shall deliver to the Major Investors written notice of the proposed sale at least ten (10) business days prior to the sale. The notice shall set forth (i) the Company's bona fide intention to offer securities and (ii) the material terms and conditions of the proposed sale (including the number of securities to be offered and the price, if any, for which the Company proposes to offer such securities), and shall constitute an offer to sell such securities to the Major Investors on those terms and conditions. Any Major Investor may accept this offer, all or part, by delivering a written notice of acceptance to the Company within twenty (20) days after receipt of the Company's notice of the proposed sale. Any Major Investor exercising its right of first refusal shall be entitled to participate in the purchase of the securities on a pro rata basis to the extent necessary to maintain that Major Investor's proportionate beneficial ownership interest in the Company on a fully-diluted basis (for purposes of determining the pro rata interest of the Major Investor, each Major Investor shall be treated as owning that number of shares of Common Stock into which any outstanding convertible securities (or convertible securities for which any outstanding options or warrants may be exercised) owned by such Major Investor (or by any affiliate or partner of such Major Investor) may be converted and for which any outstanding options or warrants owned by such Major Investor (or by any affiliate or partner of such Major Investor) may be exercised). If not all of the Major Investors elect to purchase their full pro rata share of the securities, then the Company shall promptly notify in writing the Major Investors who do so elect and shall offer such Major Investors the right to acquire such unsubscribed shares. The Major Investors shall have five (5) days after receipt of such notice to notify the Company of its election to purchase all or a portion of the unsubscribed shares. If the Major Investors fail to exercise in full the rights of first refusal, the Company shall have ninety (90) days thereafter to sell the shares in respect of which the Major Investors' rights were not exercised, at a price and upon general terms and conditions no more favorable to the purchasers thereof than specified in the Company's notice to the Major Investors pursuant to this Section 3.2. If the Company does not enter into an agreement for the sale of the shares within ninety (90) days after the receipt of the Major Investors' written notice of acceptance, the right provided hereunder shall be deemed to be revived and all future shares of stock of the Company of any class shall not be offered unless first re-offered to the Major Investors in accordance with this Section 3. A Major Investor shall be entitled to apportion the right of first refusal hereby granted among itself and its partners and affiliates in any proportions it deems appropriate.

3.3   <u>Expiration of Right of First Refusal</u>. The right of first refusal granted under this Agreement shall terminate immediately prior to the occurrence of a Qualified Public Offering.

4.   <u>Additional Company Covenants</u>. The Company covenants to the Purchasers as follows:

4.1   <u>Key-Employee Insurance</u>. If not already in effect, the Company, within sixty (60) days of the "<u>Closing Date</u>" (as defined in the Series Three Purchase Agreement), shall procure key-man life insurance policies for each of the Company's CEO, Vice President of Engineering and Chief Technology Officer in the amount of $1,000,000, naming the Company as beneficiary.

4.2   <u>Proprietary Information and Invention Assignment Agreement</u>. The Company shall cause all future employees and consultants to sign Proprietary Information and Invention Assignment Agreements in the form attached as <u>Exhibit D</u> hereto or a successor form approved by the Board of Directors.

4.3   <u>Qualified Small Business</u>. The Company will use reasonable efforts to comply with the reporting and recordkeeping requirements of Section 1202 of the Code, any regulations promulgated thereunder and any similar state laws and regulations, and agrees not to repurchase any stock of the Company if such repurchase would cause the Shares not to so qualify as "Qualified Small Business Stock," so long as the Company's Board of Directors determines that it is in the best interests of and not unduly burdensome to the Company to comply with the provisions of Section 1202 of the Code. The Company further covenants to submit to its shareholders and to state and federal taxation authorities such form and filings as may be required to document such compliance, including the California Franchise Tax Board Form 3565, Small Business Stock Questionnaire, with its franchise or income tax return for the current income year.

4.4   <u>Stock Vesting</u>. Unless otherwise unanimously approved by the Board of Directors, all stock options and other stock equivalents issued after the date of this Agreement to employees, directors, consultants and other service providers shall be subject to vesting as follows: (a) twenty-five percent (25%) of such stock shall vest at the end of the first year following the earlier of the date of issuance or such person's services commencement date with the company, and (b) seventy-five percent (75%) of such stock shall vest monthly over the remaining three (3) years. With respect to any shares of stock purchased by any such person, the Company's repurchase option shall provide that upon such person's termination of employment or service with the Company, with or without cause, the Company or its assignee (to the extent permissible under applicable securities laws and other laws) shall have the option to purchase at cost any unvested shares of stock held by such person.

4.5   <u>Assignment of Right of First Refusal</u>. In the event the Company elects not to exercise any right of first refusal or right of first offer the Company may have on a proposed transfer of any of the Company's outstanding capital stock pursuant to the Company's charter documents, by contract or otherwise, the Company shall, to the extent it may do so, assign such right of first refusal or right of first offer to each Purchaser. In the event of such assignment, each Purchaser shall have a right to purchase its pro rata portion of the capital stock proposed to be transferred.

4.6   <u>Reimbursement of Board Expenses</u>. The Company shall reimburse all reasonable out-of-pocket travel-related expenses of the directors in attending meetings of the Board of Directors and any committees thereof.

4.7   <u>No Conversion to Flow-Through Entity</u>. The Company will not convert from a corporation to a partnership, limited liability company or other "flow-through" entity without the consent of any investors that would be adversely affected thereby.

4.8   <u>Indemnification Agreements</u>. The Company shall enter into customary indemnification agreements with its directors, to the extent not already in place, as soon as is practicable after the Closing Date.

4.9   <u>Executives to be Bound by Other Agreements</u>. The Company agrees that, following the Initial Closing, each officer, employee, director or consultant (other than one who primarily holds the Company's Preferred Stock) who, as a result of his or her receipt of an equity incentive grant by the Company, or other acquisition of Common Stock or right to receive Common Stock other than by conversion of Preferred Stock, which together would represent more than Two Million (2,000,000) shares (as adjusted for stock splits, combinations, or other recapitalization events occurring after the Initial Closing), together with the persons specifically named in the Co-Sale Agreement (as defined in the Series Three Purchase Agreement), shall be required, as a condition to receipt of such equity incentive grant or other acquisition to enter into the Co-Sale Agreement as a "Significant Shareholder" (as that term is defined in the Co-Sale Agreement), and the Voting Agreement (as defined in the Series Three Purchase Agreement) as a "Shareholder" (as that term is defined in the Voting Agreement) and to be bound by the terms of those agreements for so long as his or her shareholdings meet the threshold stated above.

4.10   <u>Compliance with Laws</u>. The Company shall use commercially reasonable efforts to comply with all applicable state and federal laws, ordinances and regulations, including without limitation, the Employee Retirement Income Security Act of 1974 and any federal, state and local income, sales, use, franchise, transfer, social security, payroll, employee withholding, or other tax laws, ordinances and regulations.

4.11   <u>Compensation Committee</u>. The Company shall maintain a Compensation Committee of the Board of Directors comprised of at least two (2) non-employee Directors.

4.12   <u>Audit Committee</u>. The Company shall maintain an Audit Committee of the Board of Directors comprised of at least two (2) non-employee Directors.

4.13   <u>SBIC Investors</u>.

(i)   The proceeds from the issuance and sale of the securities purchased by each SBIC Investor (the "Proceeds") pursuant to the Series Three Purchase Agreement shall be used by the Company for its growth, modernization or expansion. So long as any SBIC Investor holds shares of Series Three Preferred, the Company shall provide each SBIC Investor and the Small Business Administration (the "SBA"), at such SBIC Investor's or the SBA's cost and expense, reasonable access to the Company's books and records for the purpose of confirming the use of Proceeds.

(ii)   For a period of one year following the Closing Date the Company shall not change the nature of its business activity if such change would render the Company ineligible as provided in 13 C.F.R. Section 107.720.

(iii)   So long as any SBIC Investor holds any securities of the Company, the Company will at all times comply with the nondiscrimination requirements of 13 C.F.R. Parts 112, 113 and 117.

(iv)   So long as any SBIC Investor holds shares of Series Three Preferred Stock, upon request, the Company promptly (and in any event within thirty (30) days of such request) will furnish to each SBIC Investor, at such SBIC Investor's cost and expense, all information reasonably requested by such SBIC Investor in order for such SBIC Investor to comply with the requirements of 13 C.F.R. Section 107.620 or to prepare and file SBA Form 468 and any other information requested or required by any governmental agency asserting jurisdiction over such SBIC Investor. Any submission of any financial information under this Section shall include a certificate of the Company's President, Chief Executive Officer, Treasurer or Chief Financial Officer.

4.14   Notice of Certain Events. For so long as any shares of Preferred Stock remain outstanding, the Company shall provide notice to each Major Investor promptly upon the occurrence of any of the following: (i) the filing of any action, suit, or legal proceeding initiated against the Company, (ii) any material default of an instrument or contract to which the Company is a party and (iii) any other substantial and material corporate event deemed by the Board of Directors to warrant notification hereunder; provided that, with respect to clauses (i) and (ii) above, the result of such event would result in a material adverse effect upon the assets, condition or affairs of the Company.

4.15   Transactions with Affiliates. The Company shall not, without the approval of the disinterested members of the Board, engage in any loans, leases, contracts or other transactions with any director, officer or key employee of the Company, or any member of any such person's immediate family, including the parents, spouse, children and other relatives of any such person.

4.16   Prompt Payment of Taxes, Etc. The Company will promptly pay and discharge, or cause to be paid and discharged, when due and payable, all lawful taxes, assessments and governmental charges or levies imposed upon the income, profits, property or business of the Company or any subsidiary; provided, however, that any such tax, assessment, charge or levy need not be paid if the validity thereof shall currently be contested in good faith by appropriate proceedings and if the Company shall have set aside on its books adequate reserves with respect thereto; and provided, further, that the Company will pay all such taxes, assessments, charges or levies forthwith upon the commencement of proceedings to foreclose any lien which may have attached as security therefor.

4.17   Termination of Covenants. The rights set forth in this Section 4 shall terminate and be of no further force or effect upon the date the Company becomes subject to the reporting requirements of Section 13 or 15(d) of the Securities Exchange Act of 1934, as amended.

5.   Miscellaneous.

5.1   Waivers and Amendments. With the written consent of the Company and the Investors holding more than sixty percent (60%) of the aggregate Registrable Securities or securities convertible into Registrable Securities, and any combination of the foregoing, the obligations of the Company and the rights of the Investors under this Agreement may be waived (either generally or in a particular instance, either retroactively or prospectively and either for a specified period of time or indefinitely), and with the same consent, the Company, when authorized by resolution of its Board of Directors, may amend this Agreement or enter into a supplementary agreement for the purpose of adding any provisions to this Agreement; provided, however, that any amendment or waiver to a right specific to a party hereto shall require such party's consent, specifically including, without limitation, the information rights and rights of first refusal set forth in Sections 2 and 3 hereof. Neither this Agreement nor any provisions hereof may be changed, waived, discharged or terminated orally, but only by a signed statement in writing. Any amendment, waiver or supplementary agreement effected in accordance with this paragraph shall be binding upon the Company, each Investor and each future Investor. Notwithstanding the foregoing, no consent or approval shall be required to add additional Investors as signatories to this Agreement, provided that such Investors were issued Series Three Preferred pursuant to the Series Three Purchase Agreement.

    5.2   Notices. All notices and other communications required or permitted hereunder shall be in writing (or in the form of a telecopy (confirmed in writing) to be given only during the recipient's normal business hours unless arrangements have otherwise been made to receive a notice by telex or telecopy outside of normal business hours) and shall be mailed by registered or certified mail, postage prepaid, or otherwise delivered by hand, messenger, or telecopy (as provided above) addressed (a) if to an Investor, at the address for that Investor set forth on the exhibits hereto or at any other address as that Investor shall have furnished to the Company in writing, or until an Investor so furnishes an address to the Company, then to and at the address of the last Investor of such securities who has so furnished an address to the Company, or (b) if to the Company, to its principal executive offices and addressed to the attention of the Corporate Secretary, or at any other address as the Company shall have furnished in writing to the Investors.

    5.3   Descriptive Headings. The descriptive headings herein are for convenience only and shall not be deemed to limit or otherwise affect the construction of any provisions hereof.

    5.4   Governing Law. This Agreement shall be governed by and interpreted under the laws of the State of California as applied to agreements among California residents, made and to be performed entirely within the State of California.

    5.5   Counterparts. This Agreement may be executed in one or more counterparts, each of which shall for all purposes be deemed to be an original and all of which shall constitute the same instrument, but only one of which need be produced.

    5.6   Facsimile Signatures. Any signature page delivered by a fax machine or telecopy machine shall be binding to the same extent as an original signature page, with regard to any agreement subject to the terms hereof or any amendment thereto. Any party who delivers such a signature page agrees to later deliver an original counterpart to any party which requires it.

    5.7   Expenses. If any action at law or in equity is necessary to enforce or interpret the terms of this Agreement, the prevailing party shall be entitled to reasonable attorneys' fees, costs and necessary disbursements in addition to any other relief to which such party may be entitled.

5.8   <u>Successors and Assigns</u>. Except as otherwise expressly provided in this Agreement, this Agreement shall benefit and bind the successors, assigns, heirs, executors and administrators of the parties to this Agreement.

5.9   <u>Entire Agreement</u>. This Agreement constitutes the full and entire understanding and agreement between the parties with regard to the subject matter of this Agreement.

5.10   <u>Separability; Severability</u>. Unless expressly provided in this Agreement, the rights of each Investor under this Agreement are several rights, not rights jointly held with any other Investors. Any invalidity, illegality or limitation on the enforceability of this Agreement with respect to any Investor shall not affect the validity, legality or enforceability of this Agreement with respect to the other Investors. If any provision of this Agreement is judicially determined to be invalid, illegal or unenforceable, the validity, legality and enforceability of the remaining provisions shall not be affected or impaired.

5.11   <u>Stock Splits</u>. All references to numbers of shares in this Agreement shall be appropriately adjusted to reflect any stock dividend, split, combination or other recapitalization of shares by the Company occurring after the date of this Agreement.

5.12   <u>Delays or Omissions</u>. It is agreed that no delay or omission to exercise any right, power, or remedy accruing to any Investor, upon any breach, default or noncompliance of the Company under this Agreement shall impair any such right, power, or remedy, nor shall it be construed to be a waiver of any such breach, default or noncompliance, or any acquiescence therein, or of any similar breach, default or noncompliance thereafter occurring. It is further agreed that any waiver, permit, consent, or approval of any kind or character on an Investor's part of any breach, default, or noncompliance under the Agreement, or any waiver on such Investor's part of any provisions or conditions of this Agreement must be in writing and shall be effective only to the extent specifically set forth in such writing. All remedies, either under this Agreement, by law, or otherwise afforded to Investors, shall be cumulative and not alternative.

IN WITNESS WHEREOF, the parties have executed this Agreement as of the date first above written.

COMPANY: **FIBER OPTIC DEVICES INC.**
                            a California corporation

                            By: _____
                                Amnon Yariv
                                President

INVESTORS: **SAND HILL VENTURE PARTNERS, L.P.**
                                By: Sand Hill Venture Management Co., Ltd.
                                Its: General Partner

                                By: _____

                                William Hearst
                                Director

                                MENLO PARK VENTURE PARTNERS VII, L.P.
                                By: Menlo Park Ventures Management VII, LLC
                                Its: General Partner

                                By: _____

                                T. A. Edison
                                Managing Director

                                **MENLO PARK VENTURES PARALLEL VII,
                                FUND, L.P.**
                                By: Menlo Park Ventures Management VII, LLC
                                Its: General Partner

                                By: _____

                                T. A. Edison
                                Managing Director

                                **MENLO PARK VENTURES VII ASSOCIATES
                                FUND, L.P.**
                                By: Menlo Park Ventures Management VII, LLC
                                Its: General Partner

                                By: _____

                                T. A. Edison
                                Managing Director

                                [Additional Signatories omitted in light of space
                                considerations]

AMENDED & RESTATED INVESTOR RIGHTS AGMT SIGNATURE PAGE

SAMPLE RIGHT OF FIRST REFUSAL AND CO-SALE AGREEMENT

FIBER OPTIC DEVICES INC.

**RIGHT OF FIRST REFUSAL
AND
CO-SALE AGREEMENT**

THIS AMENDED AND RESTATED RIGHT OF FIRST REFUSAL AND CO-SALE AGREEMENT (the "Agreement") is made as of February 8, 20____ by and among Fiber Optic Devices Inc., a California corporation (the "Company") and the holders of the Company's Series A Convertible Preferred Stock (the "Series A Preferred") as listed on Exhibit A hereto (the "Series A Investors") and certain holders of the Company's Common Stock (the "Common Stock") as listed on Schedule A hereto.

RECITALS

WHEREAS, the Series A Investors are concurrently herewith purchasing from the Company shares of the Series A Preferred pursuant to a Series A Convertible Preferred Stock Purchase Agreement of even date herewith (the "Series A Purchase Agreement") and entering into an Investor Rights Agreement, also of even date herewith (the "Investor Rights Agreement");

WHEREAS, the sale of the Series A Preferred as contemplated by the Series A Purchase Agreement is conditioned upon the rights set forth herein being extended to each Series A Investor; and

WHEREAS, the Company desires to extend the right of first refusal and co-sale rights set forth herein.

NOW, THEREFORE, the parties agree as follows:

1. Definitions. For purposes of this Agreement, the following terms shall have the following meanings.

1.1 "Common Stock Equivalents" means and includes all shares of the Company's Common Stock issued and outstanding at the relevant time plus (i) all shares of Common Stock that may be issued upon exercise of any options, warrants and other rights of any kind that are then exercisable, and (ii) all shares of Common Stock that may be issued upon conversion or exchange of (A) the Series A Preferred and all other preferred stock and debt securities that may be issued after the date hereof, which are by their terms then convertible into or exchangeable for Common Stock, or (B) any convertible securities issuable upon exercise of options, warrants or other rights that are then exercisable.

1.2 "Investor Stock" means the Common Stock Equivalents currently owned or hereafter acquired by the Series A Investors.

1.3 "Major Investor" means Series A Investors holding an aggregate of 3,000,000 or more shares of Investor Stock (as adjusted for stock splits, combinations or other recapitalization events occurring after the Initial Closing).

1.4   "<u>Preferred Stock</u>" collectively means the Series A Preferred and any subsequent series of preferred stock that is senior to or pari passu with the Series A Preferred.

1.5   "<u>Significant Shareholders</u>" means each present or former officer, employee, director or consultant (other than those who primarily hold the Company's Preferred Stock) who, after the Initial Closing (as defined in the Series A Purchase Agreement), together with any transferees contemplated by <u>Section 4.1</u>, below, owns Common Stock or options or rights to purchase Common Stock of the Company that together would represent more than One Million (1,000,000) shares (as adjusted for stock splits, combinations or other recapitalization events occurring after the Initial Closing). Additional persons shall become Significant Shareholders, and signatories to this Agreement, as required by Section 4.9 of the Investor Rights Agreement. Any person who is a Significant Shareholder under this definition and who, at any time after the date of this Agreement, no longer holds more than One Million (1,000,000) shares (as described above) shall cease to be a Significant Shareholder and may be deleted from this Agreement pursuant to <u>Section 6.12</u> below, subject always to the re-application of that Section 4.9 should it again become applicable. The Significant Shareholders shall be listed on <u>Schedule A</u> hereto.

2.   <u>Restrictions on Transfer; Right of First Refusal.</u>

2.1   <u>General Restriction</u>. Except as otherwise provided in this Agreement, the Significant Shareholders may not sell, transfer, assign, pledge, hypothecate, gift or otherwise dispose of any of the Significant Shareholder Stock, or any right or interest therein (collectively referred to as a "<u>Transfer</u>"), unless the Transfer is conducted in accordance with the terms of this Agreement. Any other purported sale, transfer, hypothecation, or disposition will be null and void.

2.2   <u>Notice of Proposed Transfer</u>. Before any Significant Shareholder may Transfer any of the Significant Shareholder Stock, the Significant Shareholder shall deliver simultaneously to the Company and each of the Major Investors a written notice at least thirty (30) days prior to the closing of such transfer (the "<u>Significant Shareholder Notice</u>") stating (i) the Significant Shareholder's bona fide intention to Transfer that Significant Shareholder Stock, (ii) the bona fide number, class and series of the Significant Shareholder Stock proposed to be transferred, (iii) the name of each proposed purchaser or other transferee, and (iv) the bona fide cash price or other consideration (along with a cash-equivalence for any non-cash consideration) per share for which the Significant Shareholder proposes to transfer the Significant Shareholder Stock (the "<u>Offered Price</u>"). The Significant Shareholder Stock proposed to be sold or otherwise transferred shall hereinafter be referred to as the "Offered Stock."

2.3   <u>Company Right of First Refusal</u>. For a period of fifteen (15) days following receipt of a Significant Shareholder Notice, the Company shall have the right to notify the Significant Shareholder of its intent to purchase all of the Offered Stock subject to such Significant Shareholder Notice at the same price and on substantially equivalent terms and conditions as set forth therein. The Company's purchase right shall be exercised or waived by written notice signed by an officer of the Company (the "<u>Company Notice</u>") and delivered to the Significant Shareholder and each Major Investor. The Company shall effect the purchase of the Offered Stock no more than five (5) business days after delivery of the Company Notice, and at such time the Significant

Shareholder shall deliver to the Company the certificate(s) representing the Offered Stock to be purchased by the Company, each certificate to be properly endorsed for transfer. The Offered Stock so purchased shall thereupon be cancelled and cease to be issued and outstanding shares of the Company's Common Stock.

2.4   Major Investor Right of First Refusal. Should the Company determine not to exercise its opportunity, the Major Investors shall have the opportunity, pro rata in proportion to their ownership of all of the Investor Stock then outstanding, on an as-converted-to-Common Stock basis, to purchase all the securities that are the subject of the Transfer at the same price and substantially equivalent terms as those offered by the offeror. This right shall continue for fifteen (15) days following the date of the Company Notice that it will not exercise its purchase opportunity or that opportunity has expired. The Major Investors shall be responsible for communicating among themselves and informing the transferring Significant Shareholder whether they will be exercising their Right of First Refusal. If all of the Major Investors do not choose to exercise their opportunity to purchase, then the holders who are participating in the purchase may allocate the unallocated portion of the Transfer among themselves, pro rata in proportion to their relative ownership of the Investor Stock, on an as-converted-to-Common Stock basis. If neither the Company nor the Major Investors exercises the Right of First Offer, the selling Significant Shareholder may Transfer the securities to the third party specified in the notice on the terms set forth therein, provided that any such Transfer by a shareholder shall be subject to Section 3 of this Agreement. Subject to Section 2.5 below, the Rights of First Refusal contained in this Agreement supersedes any previous Right of First Refusal the Company may have on transfers by Significant Shareholders, including the Right of First Refusal set forth in certain Stock Purchase and Restriction Agreements by and between the Company and certain persons who may be, from time to time, Significant Shareholders.

2.5   Company Repurchase Right. Notwithstanding anything to the contrary herein, the parties hereto agree that the Company retains the right to repurchase a Significant Shareholder's unvested shares, pursuant to the terms of the Restricted Stock Purchase Agreements that may be in effect from time to time under the terms of the Company's 20____ Stock Incentive Plan, in the event that the Significant Share-holder's employment with the Company terminates.

3.   Rights of Co-Sale.

3.1   Major Investors' Rights. Before any or all of the Significant Shareholder Stock now or hereafter held by the Significant Shareholders may be sold or otherwise transferred (including a transfer by gift or operation of law), each Major Investor shall have a right of co-sale with respect to that Significant Shareholder Stock, all on the terms and conditions set forth in this Section 3 and subject to the Right of First Refusal set forth in Section 2 above.

3.2   Right of Co-Sale.

(a)   Exercise of Right of Co-Sale. Each Major Investor shall then have the right to participate in the Significant Shareholder's sale of the Offered Stock to the proposed purchaser or other transferee pursuant to the specified price and other terms and conditions of the sale as set forth in the Significant Shareholder Notice and in accordance with the price and other terms and conditions of the sale as set forth in this Section 3.2 (the "Right of Co-Sale"). For purposes of the preceding sentence, the participation of a Major Investor shall be deemed to be in accordance with the specified price of any sale if the Offered Price for which the Significant Shareholder Stock is to be sold, on a Common Stock Equivalent basis, is equivalent to the per-share price at which the Investor Stock will also be sold, also on a Common Stock Equivalent basis (that is, the equivalence of price and other terms and conditions shall be determined solely on an as-exercised, as-converted basis with respect to any Common Stock Equivalents that are not Common Stock). To the extent a Major Investor exercises his, her or its Right of Co-Sale, the number of shares of Offered Stock that the Significant Shareholder may sell pursuant to the Significant Shareholder Notice shall be correspondingly reduced. The Right of Co-Sale of each Major Investor shall be subject to the following terms and conditions:

Each Major Investor may sell all or any part of that number of shares of Common Stock owned by that Major Investor (including shares of Common Stock issued or issuable upon the exercise, conversion or exchange of Common Stock Equivalents) that is not in excess of the number obtained by multiplying the aggregate number of shares of Common Stock Equivalents constituting the Offered Stock by a fraction (A) the numerator of which is the number of shares of Investor Stock then held by the Major Investor, and (B) the denominator of which is the total number of Common Stock Equivalents then owned by the selling Significant Shareholder(s) plus the total number such shares of Investor Stock then owned by the Major Investors.

Each Major Investor may effect his, her or its election to participate in the sale subject to this Section 3.2 by delivering to the Company within five (5) days after the expiration of the Right of First Refusal periods identified in Section 2 written election to participate in the sale of the Offered Stock setting forth the number and type of shares that the Major Investor elects to include in the sale, accompanied by one or more certificates or other documentation, properly endorsed for transfer, representing those shares. The Company shall keep the Significant Shareholder informed as to the Major Investors' elections to participate.

If any Major Investor fails to elect to fully participate in the Significant Shareholder's sale pursuant to this Section 3.2, the Company shall promptly give notice of that failure to the Major Investors who did so elect (the "Participants"). This notice may be made by telephone if confirmed in writing within two (2) days. The Participants shall have five (5) business days from the date the notice was given to agree to sell their pro rata share of the unsold portion. For purposes of this paragraph, a Participant's pro rata share shall be the ratio of (x) the number of shares of Investor Stock held by such Participant to (y) the total number of shares of Investor Stock included in the sale by all the Participants.

(b) Delivery of Stock Certificates and Proceeds. Upon the closing of the sale subject to this Section 3.2, the stock certificate(s) or other documentation representing the Investor Stock to be transferred shall be transferred and delivered to the purchaser or transferee pursuant to the terms and conditions specified in the Significant Shareholder Notice, and there shall be promptly thereafter remitted to each Participant that portion of the sale proceeds to which he, she or it is entitled by reason of participating in the sale.

3.3 Offering Significant Shareholder's Right to Transfer. The Significant Shareholder may sell or transfer that portion of the Offered Stock permitted to be sold by the Significant Shareholder, after application of the Right of Co-Sale contained in Section 3.2 hereof, to any person named as the transferee in the Significant Shareholder Notice, at the Offered Price and upon the other terms and conditions set forth in the Significant Shareholder Notice, provided that the sale or other transfer (i) is consummated within sixty (60) days after the date of the Significant Shareholder Notice and (ii) is in accordance with all the terms of this Agreement. If the Offered Stock is sold or transferred in accordance with the terms and conditions of this Agreement, then the transferee(s) of the Offered Stock shall thereafter hold the Offered Stock free of this Agreement. If the Offered Stock is not so sold or otherwise transferred during such sixty (60) day period, then the Significant Shareholder shall not sell or otherwise transfer any of the Offered Stock without complying again in full with the provisions of this Agreement.

3.4   Effect of Prohibited Transfer. In the event a Significant Shareholder should sell any Significant Shareholder Stock in contravention of the co-sale rights of the Major Investors under this Agreement (a "Prohibited Transfer"), the Major Investors, in addition to all other remedies available at law, in equity or hereunder, shall have the put option provided below, and the Significant Shareholder shall be bound by the applicable provisions of that option.

3.5   Put Option. In the event of a Prohibited Transfer, each Major Investor shall have the right to sell to the Significant Shareholder the type and number of shares of Investor Stock equal to the number of shares each Major Investor would have been entitled to transfer to the Major Investor or transferee under Section 3.2 hereof had the Prohibited Transfer been effected pursuant to and in compliance with the terms hereof. This sale shall be made on the following terms and conditions:

(a)   The price per share at which the Investor Stock is to be sold to the Significant Shareholder shall be equal to the price per share (on an as-converted basis) paid by the transferee to the Significant Shareholder in the Prohibited Transfer. The Significant Shareholder shall also reimburse each Major Investor for any and all fees and expenses, including legal fees and expenses, incurred pursuant to the exercise or the attempted exercise of the Major Investor's rights under Section 3.

(b)   Within ninety (90) days after the later of the dates on which the Major Investor (A) receives notice of the Prohibited Transfer or (B) otherwise becomes aware of the Prohibited Transfer, each Major Investor, if exercising the option created hereby, shall deliver to the Significant Shareholder the certificate or certificates representing shares to be sold, each certificate to be properly endorsed for transfer.

(c)   The Significant Shareholder shall, upon receipt of the certificate or certificates for the shares to be sold by a Major Investor pursuant to this Section 3.5, pay the aggregate purchase price therefor and the amount of reimbursable fees and expenses, as specified in Section 3.5(a), in cash or by other means acceptable to the Major Investor.

(d)   Notwithstanding the foregoing, any attempt by a Significant Shareholder to transfer Significant Shareholder Stock in violation of Section 3 hereof shall be void and the Company agrees it will not effect such a transfer nor will it treat any alleged transferee as the holder of such shares without the written consent of a majority in interest of the Major Investors.

4. Exceptions, Termination.
    4.1 Exception for Certain Family Gifts. Notwithstanding anything in this Agreement to the contrary, transfers of Significant Shareholder Stock by gift to the Significant Shareholder's immediate family members or to trusts for the exclusive benefit of such family members, or transfers of Significant Shareholder Stock by will or intestate succession, shall be exempt from the Right of First Refusal and Right of Co-Sale set forth in this Agreement, provided that each transferee or other recipient agrees in writing to hold the Significant Shareholder Stock so transferred subject to all of the provisions of this Agreement so that such transferee is bound by all provisions of this Agreement as if such transferee were a "Significant Shareholder" hereunder and that there shall be no further transfer of such Significant Shareholder Stock except in accordance with the terms of this Agreement. Any transferee or other recipient not so agreeing may not receive any shares of Significant Shareholder Stock. For purposes of this Section 4.1, the term "immediate family" shall mean the spouse, child, grandchild, father, mother, brother or sister of the Significant Shareholder or of the spouse of the Significant Shareholder, the adopted child or adopted grandchild of the Significant Shareholder, or the spouse of any child, adopted child, grandchild or adopted grandchild of the Significant Shareholder.
    4.2 Other Exceptions. Notwithstanding anything in this Agreement to the contrary, the Right of First Refusal and Right of Co-Sale set forth in this Agreement shall not apply to any transfer or series of transfers of shares by a Significant Shareholder (i) that, over the term of this Agreement, amount to no more than five percent (5%) of the Significant Shareholder Stock held by a Significant Shareholder (and as adjusted for stock splits, stock dividends and the like), (ii) pursuant to a reorganization or merger of the Company with or into any other corporation or entity in which the Major Investors' shares in the Company are also purchased or a sale of all or substantially all of the assets of the Company, (iii) pursuant to the winding up and dissolution of the Company, or (iv) in connection with the first sale of the Company's Common Stock pursuant to an effective registration statement under the Securities Act of 1933, as amended, with respect to a firm commitment underwritten public offering in which the Preferred Stock is converted into Common Stock (a "Public Offering").
    4.3 Termination of Rights. The Right of First Refusal and Right of Co-Sale set forth herein shall terminate upon the earlier to occur of (i) ten (10) years from the date of this Agreement, (ii) the closing of a Public Offering, (iii) the date on which this Agreement is terminated by a written agreement to such effect executed by the Company and holders of sixty percent (60%) of the shares of Investor Stock then held by the Investors, or (iv) the date on which the Major Investors own less than twenty percent (20%) of the Common Stock Equivalents (or securities convertible into Common Stock Equivalents) collectively owned by them on the date hereof (as adjusted for stock splits, stock dividends, recapitalizations and the like).
5. Restrictive Legend and Stop-Transfer Orders.
    5.1 Legend. The Significant Shareholders understand and agree that the Company shall cause the legend set forth below, or a legend substantially equivalent thereto, to be placed upon any certificate(s) evidencing ownership of the Significant Shareholder Stock:

THE SHARES REPRESENTED BY THIS CERTIFICATE ARE SUBJECT TO CERTAIN RESTRICTIONS ON TRANSFER SET FORTH IN A RIGHT OF FIRST REFUSAL AND CO-SALE AGREEMENT ENTERED INTO BY THE ORIGINAL HOLDER OF THESE SHARES, THE COMPANY AND CERTAIN OTHER SIGNIFICANT SHAREHOLDERS OF THE COMPANY, A COPY OF WHICH IS ON FILE AT THE PRINCIPAL OFFICE OF THE COMPANY. RIGHTS OF FIRST OFFER ARE BINDING ON TRANSFEREES OF THESE SHARES UNDER SOME CIRCUMSTANCES.

5.2   <u>Stop Transfer Instructions</u>. To insure compliance with the restrictions referred to herein, the Significant Shareholders agree that the Company may issue appropriate "stop transfer" certificates or instructions and that, if the Company transfers its own securities, it may make appropriate notations to the same effect in its records.

6.   <u>Miscellaneous Provisions</u>.

6.1   <u>Notices</u>. All notices and other communications required or permitted hereunder shall be in writing (or in the form of a telecopy (confirmed in writing) to be given only during the recipient's normal business hours unless arrangements have otherwise been made to receive a notice by telex or telecopy outside of normal business hours) and shall be mailed by registered or certified mail, postage prepaid, or otherwise delivered by hand, messenger, or telecopy (as provided above) addressed (a) if to an Investor or Significant Shareholder, at the address for that Investor or Significant Shareholder set forth on the exhibits and schedules hereto or at any other address as that Investor or Significant Shareholder shall have furnished to the Company in writing or (b) if to any other holder of Investor Stock or Significant Shareholder Stock, at the address that holder shall have furnished the Company in writing or, until a holder so furnishes an address to the Company, then to and at the address of the last holder of the Investor Stock or Significant Shareholder Stock who has so furnished an address to the Company or (c) if to the Company, to its principal executive offices and addressed to the attention of the Corporate Secretary, or at any other address as the Company shall have furnished in writing to the Investors.

6.2   <u>Binding on Successors and Assigns</u>. This Agreement, and the rights and obligations of the parties hereunder, shall inure to the benefit of, and be binding upon, their respective successors, assigns and legal representatives.

6.3   <u>Severability</u>. If one or more of the provisions of this Agreement should, for any reason, be held to be invalid, illegal or unenforceable in any respect, such invalidity, illegality or unenforceability shall not affect any other provisions of this Agreement, and such invalid, illegal or unenforceable provision shall be enforced to the extent permissible.

6.4   <u>Amendment</u>. Any amendment, modification or waiver of this Agreement shall be effective only with the written consent of (i) Investors holding more than sixty percent (60%) of the then outstanding Investor Stock, (ii) Significant Shareholders holding a majority of the then outstanding Significant Shareholder Stock, provided, that if such amendment is by its terms adverse to any Significant Stockholder in a manner different than it is to the holders of a majority of the Significant Shareholder Stock consenting to such amendment, then such amendment shall require the written consent of such Significant Shareholder, and (iii) the Company; provided, further, that any person may waive, reduce or release (in whole or in part) any of its rights hereunder without the consent of any other parties hereto. Notwithstanding the foregoing, any amendment or waiver to a right specific to a party hereto shall require such party's consent. Any waiver by a party of its rights hereunder shall be effective only if evidenced by a written instrument executed by a duly authorized representative of such party.

6.5   Governing Law. This Agreement shall be governed by and construed in accordance with the laws of the State of California as applied to agreements among California residents entered into and to be performed entirely within California.

6.6   Obligations of Company. The Company agrees to use its best efforts to enforce and abide by the terms of this Agreement, to inform the Investors of any breach hereof (to the extent the Company has knowledge thereof) and to assist the Investors in the exercise of their rights hereunder.

6.7   Expenses. If any action at law or in equity is necessary to enforce or interpret the terms of this Agreement, the prevailing party shall be entitled to reasonable attorneys' fees, costs and necessary disbursements in addition to any other relief to which such party may be entitled.

6.8   Counterparts. This Agreement may be executed in any number of counterparts, each of which shall be deemed an original and all of which together shall constitute one and the same instrument.

6.9   Facsimile Signatures. Any signature page delivered by a fax machine or telecopy machine shall be binding to the same extent as an original signature page, with regard to any agreement subject to the terms hereof or any amendment thereto. Any party who delivers such a signature page agrees to later deliver an original counterpart to any party which requests it.

6.10   Entire Agreement. This Agreement, together with the exhibits hereto, constitutes the entire understanding and agreement of the parties with respect to the subject matter hereof and supersedes all prior understandings and agreements with respect to such subject matter, except as may specifically be set forth herein.

6.11   Ownership. The Significant Shareholders represent and warrant that each is the sole legal and beneficial owner of those shares of Significant Shareholder Stock he, she, or it currently holds as set forth on Schedule A hereto and that no other person has any interest (other than a community property interest) in such shares.

6.12   Additional Parties. Notwithstanding Section 6.4 above, no consent or approval shall be required to (i) add additional Investors as signatories to this Agreement, provided that such Investors were issued Series A Preferred pursuant to the Series A Purchase Agreement, (ii) update the shares shown and the numbers on the Exhibits or Schedules hereto to reflect the issuance of Series A Preferred or changes in Significant Shareholder holdings, or (iii) add additional Significant Shareholders, or delete then-existing Significant Shareholders, consistent with the provisions of Section 4.9 of the Investor Rights Agreement and Section 1.5, above.

[REMAINDER OF PAGE INTENTIONALLY LEFT BLANK]

IN WITNESS WHEREOF, the parties hereto have executed this Agreement as of the date first written above.

COMPANY: **FIBER OPTIC DEVICES INC.**, a California corporation

                            By: _____
                                 Amnon Yariv
                                 President

INVESTORS:

                            SAND HILL VENTURE PARTNERS, L.P.
                            By: Sand Hill Venture Management Co., Ltd.
                                 Its: General Partner

                            By: _____
                                 William Hearst
                                 Director

                            MENLO PARK VENTURE PARTNERS VII, L.P.
                            By: Menlo Park Ventures Management VII, LLC
                                 Its: General Partner

                            By: _____
                                 T. A. Edison
                                 Managing Director

                            MENLO PARK VENTURES VII ASSOCIATES FUND, L.P.
                            By: Menlo Park Ventures Management VII, LLC
                                 Its: General Partner

                            By: _____
                                 T. A. Edison
                                 Managing Director

"SIGNIFICANT SHAREHOLDERS"

                            _____

                            _____

                            _____

[THE FOLLOWING, CURRENTLY BLANK, ARE SHOWN ON THE SAME PAGE FOR CONVENIENCE]

EXHIBIT A

SERIES A INVESTORS

Name	Investment Amount Share Purchased

SCHEDULE A

Significant Shareholders

Name	Significant Shareholder Stock *

* Includes shares issuable upon exercise of options to purchase Common Stock.

SAMPLE CLOSING DOCUMENT CHECKLIST

	Cellular Components, Inc. (the "Company") Series C Preferred Stock Financing Closing Document Checklist Closing Date: December _____, 2015 ("Closing")			
No.	**Document Name/Action Taken**	**Parties (sig. req'd)**	**Status**	**Current Draft Doc. #**
	Transaction Documents			
1.	Series C Preferred Stock Purchase Agreement (the "Purchase Agreement"): Each of the following must be delivered — [UNDERLINED EXHIBITS ARE NOT SEPARATELY LISTED ON THIS CHECKLIST BUT MUST BE DELIVERED] Exhibit A–Schedule of Purchasers ("Purchasers") Exhibit B – Amended and Restated Articles of Incorporation Exhibit C–Schedule of Exceptions Exhibit D – Form of Amended and Restated Investors' Rights Agreement Exhibit E – Form of Amended and Restated Co-Sale/First Refusal Agreement Exhibit F – Form of Amended and Restated Voting Agreement Exhibit G – Opinion of Company Counsel Exhibit H–Financial Statements Exhibit I–Confidentiality and Invention Assignment Agreement	Company (CEO) and Purchasers	Initial draft delivered	2015-12-14
2.	Amended and Restated Articles of Incorporation	Company (CEO, CFO)	Initial draft delivered, comments incorporated	2015-12-13(1)

No.	Document Name/Action Taken	Parties (sig. req'd)	Status	Current Draft Doc. #
3.	Amended and Restated Investor Rights Agreement	Company (CEO) Purchasers	Initial draft delivered, comments incorporated	2015-12-13(1)
4.	Amended and Restated Co-Sale/ First Refusal Agreement	Company (CFO), major common holders and Purchasers	Initial draft delivered, comments incorporated	2015-12-13(1)
5.	Amended and Restated Voting Agreement	Company (CFO), major common holders and Purchasers	Initial draft delivered, comments incorporated	2015-12-14
	Closing Obligations of Company			
6.	Compliance Certificate of the Company executed by the Chief Executive Officer and Financial Officer and attesting to the matters set forth in Sections 6.2 and 6.3	Company (CEO and CFO)	Initial draft prepared	2015-12-07
7.	Opinion of Legal Counsel for the Company	Company Counsel	To be drafted	
8.	Officer's Certificate in Support of Opinion of Company Counsel	Company (CEO, CFO)	Initial draft prepared	2015-12-07
9.	Good Standing Certificates for the Company issued by the State of California and the Franchise Tax Board of California	Company Counsel to obtain		
10.	Board Resolutions authorizing the Financing, increasing option pool, approving Amended and Restated Articles and accepting resignation of one director.	Company Board	Company Counsel to draft	

No.	Document Name/Action Taken	Parties (sig. req'd)	Status	Current Draft Doc. #
11.	Shareholder Resolutions authorizing the Financing, and the option pool increase, and Amended and Restated Articles of Incorporation, amendment of IRA, Co-Sale and Voting Agreements	Company and Company shareholders	Initial draft provided	2015-12-14
12.	Rights offering shareholder transmittal letter conveying written consent and soliciting accredited investor indications of interest for participation in Second Closing	Company Counsel	Initial draft provided and comments incorporated	2015-12-14
13.	Shareholder Statement of Interest form	Shareholders	Initial draft provided and comments incorporated	2015-12-14
14.	Management Rights Letters, executed in form satisfactory to requesting investors and Investor Counsel	Company (CEO/ CFO)	Investor Counsel to draft	
	Post-Closing Obligations			
15.	Series C Preferred Stock Certificates, update share register	Company (CEO and CFO)	Company Counsel to do	
16.	File 25102(f) notice / Form D with California Department of Corporations / SEC	Company (CFO)	Company Counsel to do	

INDEX